Marketing Scales Handbook

A Compilation of Multi-Item Measures

Volume III

Marketing Scales Handbook

A Compilation of Multi-Item Measures

Volume III

Gordon C. Bruner II   •   Karen E. James   •   Paul J. Hensel

American Marketing Association
Chicago, Illinois USA

Copyright © 2001, American Marketing Association
All rights reserved.

Library of Congress Cataloging-in-Publication Data

Bruner, Gordon C., 1954–
 Marketing scales handbook : a compilation of multi-item measures /
 Gordon C. Bruner, Karen E. James, Paul J. Hensel
  p.   cm
 Includes index.
  1. Marketing research—Statistical methods—Handbooks, manuals,
 etc. 2. Scaling (Social sciences)—Handbook, manuals, etc.
 I. James, Karen E. II. Hensel, Paul J. III. Title.
 HF5415.3.B785   2001
 658.8'3028—dc20   92-18858
                                                       CIP

ISBN: 0-87757-290-9

American Marketing Association
311 S. Wacker Drive, Chicago, Illinois 60606 USA
 Francesca Van Gorp Cooley, Editor
 Elisabeth Nevins, Copy Editor
 Charles Chandler, Editorial Project Assistant

Cover design by Liz Novak

Manufactured in the United States of America

Table of Contents

....

Scale No.	Consumer Behavior-Related Scales	Page No.

Table of Contents

Table of Contents

Scale No.   **Advertising-Related Scales**   **Page No.**

Scale No.   Organizational Behavior-Related Scales   Page No.

Table of Contents

Table of Contents

Table of Contents

Acknowledgments

....

We want to express our appreciation to the many researchers who developed, used, and/or reported the measures on which this book is based. Many authors were contacted by mail, telephone, and e-mail when more information was needed about a scale. Not all got back to us, but the following are among those who responded and enabled us to provide more complete information than otherwise would have been possible. Our gratitude is extended to:

Jennifer L. Aaker
Chris T. Allen
Jonalee Andrews
Barry J. Babin
Richard P. Bagozzi
Julie Baker
Kapil Bawa
Sharon Beatty
Lance A. Bettencourt
James M. Carman
Pratibha A. Dabholkar
Jacqueline Eastman
Gavan J. Fitzsimons
David R. Fortin
Hubert Gatignon
Ronald E. Goldsmith
Linda K. Good
Louisa Ha
Pamela Homer
Barbara E. Kahn
Punam A. Keller
Scott W. Kelly
Robert J. Kent
Susan Knasko
Scott Koslow
Kathleen T. Lacher
Randy Larsen

Walfried M. Lassar
Michael LaTour
France Leclerc
Donald R. Lichtenstein
Ken Lord
Debbie MacInnis
Lawrence J. Marks
Joan Meyers-Levy
David Mick
Sanjay Mishra
Banwari Mittal
Todd Mooradian
David J. Moore
David L. Mothersbaugh
Darrel D. Muehling
Richard G. Netemeyer
Prashanth U. Nyer
Richard L. Oliver
Eric M. Olson
Laura Peracchio
A. Parasuraman
Robert Ping
Bruce Pinkleton
Linda L. Price
Sanjay Putrevu
Brian T. Ratchford
Marsha L. Richins

Acknowledgments

Dennis W. Rook
Edward Rosbergen
Jeffrey K. Sager
Denise Schoenbachler
Subhash Sharma
Lois Smith
Richard Spreng
Marla Stafford

Debu Talukdar
Ron D. Taylor
Carolyn Tripp
Rao Unnava
Joe Urbany
Michel Wedel
Kathy Winsted
Jean-Marc Xuereb

At SIU, we are grateful to Steve Williams and Sara Green, who successively managed the Office of Scale Research. We appreciate the help received from Suzana Rodrigues and Joanne Copeland at LSU-Shreveport. At UNO, thanks go to Dean Timothy Ryan and Dr. Raymond Fisk (Marketing Department Chair) for their continued support. Elisabeth Nevins provided tremendous help toward the end by copy-editing the material. We also want to express our appreciation to the American Marketing Association for its ongoing interest in making this information available to our discipline. In particular at AMA, our thanks are extended to Francesca Van Gorp Cooley and her assistants, who have personally struggled with us to get each volume edited and printed.

Finally, our thanks go out to our respective family members: Lesa, Mark, Jon, Katy, and Trey (from Gordon); to Marc (from Karen); and Victoria, Jeremy, Emilia, and Elijah (from Paul).

May your measures always be valid!

Gordon C. Bruner II
Southern Illinois University–Carbondale

Karen E. James
Louisiana State University–Shreveport

Paul J. Hensel
University of New Orleans

August 2000

Introduction

·····················

The first two volumes of this series were published in 1992 and 1996 and quickly became bestsellers for the American Marketing Association. This third volume covers the scales that were reported in articles published from 1994 to 1997. As with Volume II, this new book should **not** be viewed as a revision of the previously published material, because scales from the first two volumes were not automatically included in this third book. In fact, as we discuss further, the contents of this third volume are predominately new. Unless a scale reported in the first two volumes was used again between 1994 and 1997, it was not included in Volume III, and the first two volumes have hundreds of scales not contained here. Given that, Volume III is properly viewed as *complementing* Volumes I and II rather than superseding them.

In addition to the time period covered, a few other differences between Volume III and the previous volumes should be noted. It was clear rather quickly when working on this new volume that many more scales were being used in our field than could be reviewed in the time available. Several steps were taken to reduce the work involved in examining all of the scales. First, more uses were treated as "see also" than were in the past. As before, some were treated this way because insufficient information was available to enable us to provide a reasonable description of the items used and/or a scale's psychometric quality. More so than in the past, however, we treated some uses for which we had plenty of information as "see also" because there were so many total uses that we did not believe it was necessary to describe every single use in detail. Therefore, this volume introduces *selected* uses for several scales (e.g., Attitude Toward the Ad, Social Desirability Bias, Involvement [Enduring], and Role Ambiguity). We still tried to cite every known usage in the domain reviewed, but only four to six uses were described in detail.

Second, we were forced to make cuts in the domain of journals covered. The six journals from the first volume are still included: *Journal of Advertising, Journal of Advertising Research, Journal of the Academy of Marketing Science, Journal of Consumer Research, Journal of Marketing,* and *Journal of Marketing Research.* Volume II introduced two more: the *Journal of Retailing* and the *Journal of Personal Selling and Sales Management (JPSSM).* Unfortunately, we simply ran out of time to review scales reported in *JPSSM* for this volume. Despite this cut, the sales-related scales appear to be covered quite well due to their abundant use in other journals we reviewed.

As with the first two volumes, only multi-item scales were reviewed. Scales were included only if they had three items or more. Furthermore, a minimum amount of information was required for a scale to be described. The most important information was the scale items and reliability.

Readers are urged to take care in the selection of scales. Naïve scale users would do well to read up on psychometrics to improve their ability to evaluate alternative measures and make a selection. A suggested reading list is provided at the end of the book in which a rich explanation of psychometric issues can be found.

Introduction

This volume is divided into sections, as the previous volumes were. The first group of scales (402 scales) relates to consumer behavior. The second section, the smallest (83 scales), is related to advertising measures. The third section is composed of scales used in something other than consumer research. The majority of the scales come from studies of salespeople, marketing management, or product distributors. For the first time in the series, this is the largest section (456 scales).

We have attempted to describe scales of like constructs that use similar sets of items together. Our rule was that if scales appeared to be measuring the same thing and had approximately half or more items in common, they were written up together. This means that there are many cases in which substantially different scales for the same or similar constructs exist (e.g., #5–#9). This rule was difficult to apply with respect to two scales: the semantic differential versions of Attitude Toward the Product/Brand (#53) and Attitude Toward the Ad (#439, #442, and #445). Although these two have been the most popular constructs to measure in scholarly marketing research using multi-item scales, there has been little agreement on how to measure them; that is, they both have been measured dozens of ways with dozens of items. Several years of working with the hodgepodge of attitude-toward-the-ad scales led to an initial grouping, however. A full explanation of the logic and analysis that led to the grouping has been published. (See the full citation for Bruner 1998 in the "Readings" section.) Unfortunately, similar efforts to unravel the mess of scales purporting to measure attitude toward the product/brand have not been as successful. Therefore, many measures have been written up together because, at least on the surface, they appear to be measuring the same construct in roughly the same way (multiple semantic differentials), even if they do not share items in common.

Finally, the structure of our scale descriptions remains the same as it was in the first two volumes and is described in the following table.

TABLE

Description of Scale Write-Up Format

SCALE NAME: A short, descriptive name of the construct being measured.

SCALE DESCRIPTION: A sentence or two describing the physical structure of the measure(s) and the psychological construct apparently being assessed. The number of items, the number of points on the scale, and its Likert or semantic differential type are typically specified. If significantly different names were used by authors of articles, they are usually noted here.

SCALE ORIGIN: Limited information about the creation of the scale, if known. Most of the scales originated in one article in the domain and were not known to have been used again.

SAMPLES: Brief descriptions of the samples to which the scales have been administered. For those scales with many uses, such as Attitude Toward the Product/Brand, descriptions of the samples used in just a few representative studies are provided.

RELIABILITY: For the most part, reliability is described in terms of internal consistency, most typically with Cronbach's alpha. If known, other issues related to reliability are mentioned as well, such as item–total and test–retest correlations.

VALIDITY: Evidence supporting the scale's validity. Most studies did not report helpful information. Some simply reported factor analyses, which may offer some limited evidence of dimensionality. In rare cases, scale authors assessed convergent or discriminant validity. In some instances, the nomological or face validity of the scales could be commented on even if the scale authors provided little or no other information.

ADMINISTRATION: The manner in which a scale was administered to a sample. In the overwhelming majority of cases, scales were of the paper-and-pencil variety and were part of self-administered questionnaires. In most cases, the interpretation of scale scores are described here as well.

MAJOR FINDINGS: A very brief summary of some findings associated with a scale. Although the information offers the reader an idea of previous research results related to a specific scale, it is not intended to replace a thorough review of the relevant literature.

COMMENTS: This field is not always used, but occasionally, something significant was observed in writing up a scale that we believed should be pointed out to readers. If the psychometric characteristics of a scale were judged to be poor, it was mentioned. Also, when other studies were considered to be potentially relevant to the scale's usage but were not fully described for some reason, they were cited here as "see also."

REFERENCES: Every source cited in the write-up is referenced here using the *Journal of Marketing* style. Titles of the seven primary journals from which scales were taken are abbreviated as follows:

Journal of the Academy of Marketing Science = JAMS
Journal of Advertising = JA
Journal of Advertising Research = JAR
Journal of Consumer Research = JCR
Journal of Marketing = JM
Journal of Marketing Research = JMR
Journal of Retailing = JR

Titles of other cited journals and sources are referenced less frequently and written out in full.

SCALE ITEMS: The scale items used in published research are listed here, as are the directions for administering the scale, if known. Also, in most cases, there is an indication of the graphic scale that was used to record responses to items. If an item is followed by an (r), it means that the numerical response to the item should be reverse coded when calculating scale scores. Other idiosyncrasies may be noted as well. For example, when slightly different versions of the same scale are discussed in the same write-up, an indication is given as to which items were used in particular studies.

Part I

Consumer Behavior-Related Scales

SCALE NAME: Affect (General)

SCALE DESCRIPTION: Three semantic differential items measuring a person's affective response to some stimulus.

SCALE ORIGIN: The scale used by Kim, Allen, and Kardes (1996) was borrowed from Stuart, Shimp, and Engle (1987). It appears the scale was original to the latter.

SAMPLES: Kim, Allen, and Kardes (1996) only used the scale in Experiment 2 of the multiple studies on which they reported. That experiment was based on data collected from **90** people (51% women).

RELIABILITY: An alpha of **.95** was reported for the scale by Kim, Allen, and Kardes (1996).

VALIDITY: No examination of the scale's validity was reported by Kim, Allen, and Kardes (1996).

ADMINISTRATION: The scale was self-administered by subjects in the experiment by Kim, Allen, and Kardes (1996). Higher scores on the scale indicated that respondents had a very positive affective reaction to some specified stimulus to which they were exposed.

MAJOR FINDINGS: Kim, Allen, and Kardes (1996) examined the role of **affective responses** and inferential beliefs as mediators of attitudes formed through classical conditioning. Although affective response was found to be a significant predictor of brand attitude, it explained much less variance than did beliefs about the target attribute.

REFERENCES:
Kim, John, Chris T. Allen, and Frank R. Kardes (1996), "An Investigation of the Mediational Mechanisms Underlying Attitudinal Conditioning," *JMR,* 33 (August), 318–28.
Stuart, Elnora W., Terence A. Shimp, and Randall W. Engle (1987), "Classical Conditioning of Consumer Attitudes: Four Experiments in an Advertising Context," *JCR,* 14 (December), 334–49.

SCALE ITEMS:*

1. Unpleasant   :___:___:___:___:___:___:___: Pleasant
                1   2   3   4   5   6   7

2. Dislike   Like
   very much   :___:___:___:___:___:___:___: very much
                1   2   3   4   5   6   7

3. Left me with a   Left me with a
   bad feeling   :___:___:___:___:___:___:___: good feeling
                1   2   3   4   5   6   7

*The number of points on the response scales used by Kim, Allen, and Kardes (1996) was not specified.

SCALE NAME: Affect (Music)

SCALE DESCRIPTION: A multi-item, semantic differential ratings scale measuring the degree to which a person likes some stimulus and perceives it to be "good." Lord, Lee, and Sauer (1995) and Obermiller (1985) used three-item subsets of this scale.

SCALE ORIGIN: The items were among a group of 93 generated by Holbrook and Huber (1979). The stimuli being examined in their study were jazz recordings, and their purpose was to examine different methods of extracting affective bias from perceptions and attitudes, particularly in the area of consumer aesthetics. Data were collected from 16 subjects responding to bulletin board ads at Columbia University. Each subject expressed a strong interest in jazz and was paid $5 for participating. Eight of the 93 items were found to have high correlations ($-.70 < r > +.70$) with the bad/good item. Scores of nine items (1–9 below) were summed to create a global measure of affective evaluation. An alpha of **.95** was reported for the scale. An indication of the scale's validity was given by the high average intraindividual correlation between scale scores and preference rankings made of the jazz recordings ($r = .80$).

SAMPLES: Dillon, Mulani, and Frederick (1984) reanalyzed the data used by Holbrook and Huber (1979).

The sample used by Lacher and Mizerski (1994) came from undergraduate business students at a large, Southern U.S. university. Usable data were collected from **215** students, of whom 52% were men and who ranged in age from 19 to 36 years.

The sample used by Lord, Lee, and Sauer (1995) was composed of **328** undergraduate marketing students. The students participated in groups of approximately 20 per session and received extra credit in the course. A little more than half (55%) of the sample were men.

The experiment by Obermiller (1985) used 155 undergraduates at the University of Washington. They were randomly grouped and assigned to experimental treatments.

RELIABILITY: Dillon, Mulani, and Frederick (1984) reanalyzed the data used by Holbrook and Huber (1979). Alphas for the fast and slow tempo songs in the study by Lacher and Mizerski (1994) were **.93** and **.91**, respectively (Lacher 1997). An alpha of **.95** was reported for the version of the scale used by Lord, Lee, and Sauer (1995). Obermiller (1985) calculated alphas for 16 short-tone sequences, and they ranged from **.70** to **.85**.

VALIDITY: No examination of scale validity was reported in any of the studies.

ADMINISTRATION: The scale was self-administered, along with other measures, in each study after subjects had been exposed to musical stimuli. Higher scores on the scale suggested that respondents liked a particular musical stimulus (e.g., jazz recording), whereas low scores implied that respondents did not like a stimulus or feel that it was good.

MAJOR FINDINGS: Building on the work of Holbrook and Huber (1979) and using the same data, Dillon, Mulani, and Frederick (1984) illustrated another means of removing distortion in perceptual judgments. The method they proposed involved a two-step, double-centering transformation. In essence, this procedure shifts the means of the observations and the variables to the same value. The authors imply that their method is superior because it does not require that data be ignored nor is it as arbitrary in transforming the data.

Lacher and Mizerski (1994) investigated the effects music creates in a listener and how those reactions influence the intention to purchase the music. Specifically, **affect towards the music** did not have a significant influence on purchase intention, but it did have a moderate effect on the need to reexperience the music, though not as strong as another variable (experiential response, #154).

Lord, Lee, and Sauer (1995) examined the antecedents of attitude toward the ad. Liking of background music (**affect**) in simulated radio commercials was found to have a significant, positive impact on attitude toward the ad in several conditions.

The study by Obermiller (1985) tested two competing models of exposure effects by examining the impact of processing style on affect formation under repetition. The results failed to support either theory strongly. Although the results generally showed a significant association between **affective evaluation** on both the number of exposures and the processing style, the mediating roles of confidence and familiarity suggested a more complex relationship between learning and liking than was expected.

COMMENTS: Because this scale has been used only with music stimuli, some adjustment and retesting may be necessary if it is used with different stimuli.

REFERENCES:

Dillon, William R., Narendra Mulani, and Donald G. Frederick (1984), "Removing Perceptual Distortion in Product Space Analysis," *JMR*, 11 (May), 184–93.

Holbrook, Morris B. and Joel Huber (1979), "Separating Perceptual Dimensions from Affective Overtones: An Application to Consumer Aesthetics," *JCR*, 5 (March), 272–82.

Lacher, Kathleen T. and Richard Mizerski (1994), "An Exploratory Study of the Responses and Relationships Involved in the Evaluation of and in the Intention to Purchase New Rock Music," *JCR*, 21 (September), 366–80.

———— (1997), personal correspondence.

Lord, Kenneth R., Myung-Soo Lee, and Paul L. Sauer (1995), "The Combined Influence Hypothesis: Central and Peripheral Antecedents of Attitude Toward the Ad," *JA*, 24 (Spring), 73–85.

Obermiller, Carl (1985), "Varieties of Mere Exposure: The Effects of Processing Style and Repetition on Affective Response," *JCR*, 12 (June), 17–30.

SCALE ITEMS:

1. Bad   :___:___:___:___:___:___: Good
            1   2   3   4   5   6

2. Distasteful   :___:___:___:___:___:___: Tasty
                 1   2   3   4   5   6

3. Untalented   :___:___:___:___:___:___: Talented
                 1   2   3   4   5   6

4. Tasteless   :___:___:___:___:___:___: Tasteful
                 1   2   3   4   5   6

5. Unimaginative :___:___:___:___:___:___: Imaginative
                  1   2   3   4   5   6

6. Dull   :___:___:___:___:___:___: Exciting
             1   2   3   4   5   6

7. Unpleasant   :___:___:___:___:___:___: Pleasant
                 1   2   3   4   5   6

#2 *Affect (Music)*

8. Forgettable   :___:___:___:___:___:___: Memorable
                            1   2   3   4   5   6

9. Boring   :___:___:___:___:___:___: Interesting
                            1   2   3   4   5   6

10. Unfavorable   :___:___:___:___:___:___: Favorable
                            1   2   3   4   5   6

Dillon, Mulani, and Frederick (1984): 1–9; 6-point
Lacher and Mizerski (1994): 1–9; 6-point
Lord, Lee, and Sauer (1995): 1, 7, 10; 7-point (unclear)
Obermiller (1985): 1, 7, 9; 7-point

SCALE NAME: Affect Intensity

SCALE DESCRIPTION: Forty Likert-type items purported to measure the strength with which a person experiences his or her emotions. The construct was viewed by the scale creator (Larsen 1984) as being stable within an individual and generalizable across specific emotions, such that those who experience strong negative emotions will also experience their positive emotions strongly. It is also viewed as being distinct from *emotionality* and *moodiness*, because these tend to imply the more frequent than average experience of negative emotions, whereas **affect intensity** means that emotions are experienced on a rather "normal" frequency but are intense regardless of their specific content. The measure has been referred to by its creator and other users as "AIM" (Affect Intensity Measure).

SCALE ORIGIN: The scale was constructed by Larsen (1984) in his dissertation and has undergone much testing in several published studies. A total of 342 items originally were generated; through various stages of purification, they were whittled down until "a satisfactory set of forty items remained" (Larsen and Diener 1987, p. 8). Although the factor analysis showed five highly correlated dimensions, second-order factoring indicated that one major factor underlies the set (Larsen 1984). Alphas of .90 to .94 were found across four separate samples, and test-retest stability was around .81. The substantial evidence in support of the scale's validity is reviewed by Larsen and Diener (1987).

SAMPLES: Two studies were reported by Mooradian (1996), both of which gathered data from undergraduates enrolled in a marketing course. Studies 1 and 2 had **78** and **73** respondents, respectively. No respondents from Study 1 were in Study 2.

Moore, Harris, and Chen (1995) conducted two experiments. Data were gathered for the first experiment from 153 undergraduates who were fulfilling a psychology course requirement at a large, Southwestern U.S. university. The sample was 53% women, and ages ranged from 20 to 27 years. Subjects for Experiment 2 were 90 psychology majors. In both cases, the subjects had scores in either the upper or lower quartiles according to the AIM scale and were invited to participate in the experiment several weeks later.

RELIABILITY: Alphas of **.92** and **.91** were reported for the scale by Mooradian (1996) for Studies 1 and 2, respectively. An alpha of **.81** was reported by Moore (1997; Moore, Harris, and Chen 1995).

VALIDITY: None of the studies reported explicitly examining the scale's validity beyond what had been conducted by its creator.

ADMINISTRATION: Each user of the scale appears to have had subjects self-administer the measure several weeks before the actual study was conducted. Higher scores on the scale indicated that respondents responded more strongly (not more frequently) with their emotions to events in their lives compared with those who scored low.

MAJOR FINDINGS: Mooradian (1996) compared extraversion/neuroticism and **affective intensity** for their ability to explain individual differences in specific, transient, affective responses to ads. The findings indicated that **affect intensity** is largely redundant with extraversion and neuroticism in explaining ad-evoked feelings.

The experiment conducted by Moore, Harris, and Chen (1995) investigated the extent to which differences in **affect intensity** influenced responses to emotional ad appeals. After seeing an ad for an organization devoted to the prevention of cruelty to children, those subjects with high **affect intensity** had significantly more positive attitudes toward the organization than did those with low **affect intensity**.

COMMENTS: See also Moore and Harris (1996).

REFERENCES:
Larsen, Randy J. (1984), "Theory and Measurement of Affect Intensity as an Individual Difference Characteristic," *Dissertation Abstracts International,* 85, 2297B (University Microfilms No. 84-22112).

———— and Ed Diener (1987), "Affect Intensity as an Individual Difference Characteristic: A Review," *Journal of Research in Personality,* 21, 1–39.

Mooradian, Todd A. (1996), "Personality and Ad-Evoked Feelings: The Case for Extraversion and Neuroticism," *JAMS,* 24 (Spring), 99–109.

Moore, David J. (1997), personal correspondence.

———— and William D. Harris (1996), "Affect Intensity and the Consumer's Attitude Toward High Impact Emotional Advertising Appeals," *JA,* 25 (Summer), 37–50.

————, ————, and Hong C. Chen (1995), "Affect Intensity: An Individual Difference Response to Advertising Appeals," *JCR,* 22 (September), 154–64.

SCALE ITEMS:*

Directions: The following questions refer to the emotional reactions to typical life events. Please indicate how YOU react to these events by placing a number from the following scale in the blank space preceding each item. Please base your answers on how YOU react, not on how you think others react or how you think a person should react.

Never	Almost Never	Occasionally	Usually	Almost Always	Always
1————	————2————	————3————	————4————	————5————	————6

1. ____ When I accomplish something difficult, I feel delighted or elated.
2. ____ When I feel happy, it is a strong type of exuberance.
3. ____ I enjoy being with other people very much.
4. ____ I feel pretty bad when I tell a lie.
5. ____ When I solve a small personal problem, I feel euphoric.
6. ____ My emotions tend to be more intense than those of most people.
7. ____ My happy moods are so strong that I feel like I'm "in heaven."
8. ____ I get overly enthusiastic.
9. ____ If I complete a task I thought was impossible, I am ecstatic.
10. ____ My heart races at the anticipation of some exciting event.
11. ____ Sad movies deeply touch me.
12. ____ When I'm happy, it's a feeling of being untroubled and content rather than being zestful and aroused. **(r)**
13. ____ When I talk in front of a group for the first time, my voice gets shaky and my heart races.
14. ____ When something good happens, I am usually much more jubilant than others.
15. ____ My friends might say I'm emotional.
16. ____ The memories I like the most are of those times when I felt content and peaceful rather than zestful and enthusiastic. **(r)**
17. ____ The sight of someone who is hurt badly affects me strongly.
18. ____ When I'm feeling well, it's easy for me to go from being in a good mood to being really joyful.
19. ____ "Calm and cool" could easily describe me. **(r)**
20. ____ When I'm happy, I feel like I'm bursting with joy.
21. ____ Seeing a picture of some violent car accident in a newspaper makes me feel sick to my stomach.

22. ____ When I'm happy, I feel very energetic.
23. ____ When I receive an award, I become overjoyed.
24. ____ When I succeed at something, my reaction is calm contentment. **(r)**
25. ____ When I do something wrong I have strong feelings of shame and guilt.
26. ____ I can remain calm even on the most trying days. **(r)**
27. ____ When things are going good, I feel "on top of the world."
28. ____ When I get angry, it's easy for me to still be rational and not overreact. **(r)**
29. ____ When I know I have done something very well, I feel relaxed and content rather than excited and elated. **(r)**
30. ____ When I do feel anxiety, it is normally very strong.
31. ____ My negative moods are mild in intensity. **(r)**
32. ____ When I am excited over something, I want to share my feelings with everyone.
33. ____ When I feel happiness, it is a quiet type of contentment. **(r)**
34. ____ My friends would probably say I'm a tense or "high-strung" person.
35. ____ When I'm happy, I bubble over with energy.
36. ____ When I feel guilty, this emotion is quite strong.
37. ____ I would characterize my happy moods as closer to contentment than to joy. **(r)**
38. ____ When someone compliments me, I get so happy I could "burst."
39. ____ When I am nervous, I get shaky all over.
40. ____ When I am happy, the feeling is more like contentment and inner calm than one of exhilaration and excitement. **(r)**

*The directions and response format shown were used by Larsen and Diener (1987), as well as by Moore (1997; Moore and Harris 1996; Moore, Harris, and Chen 1995). Mooradian (1996) used a five-point *strongly disagree/strongly agree* response format.

SCALE NAME: Affective Response (Evaluation of Service Environment)

SCALE DESCRIPTION: Three one-word items measuring the extent to which a consumer feels that the atmosphere inside a service provider's physical facility is stressful.

SCALE ORIGIN: Although not stated explicitly, it appears that the scale is original to the study by Hui, Dubé, and Chebat (1997).

SAMPLES: The data gathered by Hui, Dubé, and Chebat (1997) were collected from undergraduate business students at a Canadian university. The sample was composed of **116** subjects, with an average age of 24.3 years, and was almost evenly split on gender (59 men).

RELIABILITY: The alpha reported for the scale was **.78** (Hui, Dubé, and Chebat 1997).

VALIDITY: The confirmatory factor analysis conducted by Hui, Dubé, and Chebat (1997) on this scale, as well as two others in their study, provided evidence of the scale's unidimensionality and discriminant validity.

ADMINISTRATION: Subjects completed the scale, along with other parts of a self-administered questionnaire, after they were exposed to one of five experimental treatment groups (Hui, Dubé, and Chebat 1997). Higher scores on the scale indicated that respondents viewed some specified service environment as very stressful.

MAJOR FINDINGS: Hui, Dubé, and Chebat (1997) examined the influence of music on consumers' responses to waiting for services. The findings indicated that though the presence of music had a significant positive effect on **affective response to the service organization,** the valence of the music (pre-categorized as liked/disliked) was not a significant moderator of the music's impact.

REFERENCES:
Hui, Michael K., Laurette Dubé, and Jean-Charles Chebat (1997), "The Impact of Music on Consumers' Reactions to Waiting for Services," *JR,* 73 (1), 87–104.

SCALE ITEMS:*
Using the response scale (below), to what extent do you consider the _____ to be:

Not at all   :___:___:___:___:___:___:___: Very much
           1 2 3 4 5 6 7

1. Stressful
2. Tense
3. Rushed

*The reconstruction of the scale here is based on the brief description provided by Hui, Dube, and Chebat (1997) and may not be exactly the same as the one they used. The phrase they apparently used in the blank was *bank setting.*

SCALE NAME: Affect Response (Negative)

SCALE DESCRIPTION: Various versions of the scale have been used to measure the degree of negative affect a person has toward some specified stimulus. Some of the scales differ in their temporal instructions, whereas others vary the items used. Therefore, the items can be used to measure a respondent's mood state at a particular point in time, or at the other extreme, reference to a year's time may be used as something more like a trait measure of affect. Richins's (1997) version in particular is somewhat different, in that it focuses just on fear rather than on a broader negative affect.

SCALE ORIGIN: The scale used in three of the studies (Dubé and Morgan 1996; Lord, Lee, and Sauer 1994; Mano and Oliver 1993) was developed by Watson, Clark, and Tellegen (1988). The ten negative items and ten positive items constitute the Positive and Negative Affect Schedule (PANAS). Seven versions of the scale, using the same items, were tested in which the time period of interest varied from "right now" to "during the last year." Alphas ranged from .84 to .87 using data from college students. The stability of each of these versions was tested using 101 students and with eight-week intervals. The resulting test-retest correlations ranged from .39 to .71. A factor analysis of the ten positive and ten negative items indicated that the positive items all had high loadings (>.50) on the same factor. Evidence of the scale's validity was also provided. By design, the scales were supposed to be independent (uncorrelated), and the evidence bore this out.

Richins (1997) drew terms from previous measures as well as her own series of studies to develop and refine several emotion-related scales into the CES (Consumption Emotion Set).

SAMPLES: Data were gathered by Dubé and Morgan (1996) from **96** patients who stayed at least two days in a French-Canadian hospital. A little more than half (55%) of the sample were men, and the median age was 46 years. Patients apparently volunteered to participate, and a lottery ($250) was used as an incentive.

Lord, Lee, and Sauer (1994) collected data from undergraduate students in a introductory marketing course. Students received extra credit for their participation, and analysis was based on **324** completed survey forms.

Data were collected by Mano and Oliver (1993) from **118** undergraduate business students attending a Midwestern U.S. university.

Six studies were reported by Richins (1997) as part of the process of developing the CES, only two of which had reliability information. Study 4 was based on data from **448** college students. Two surveys were conducted in Study 5: Survey 1 was completed by **256** college students, and there were **194** student respondents to Survey 2.

RELIABILITY: Alphas of **.92; .89;** and **.87** were reported for the scale by Dubé and Morgan (1996); Lord, Lee, and Sauer (1994); and Mano and Oliver (1993), respectively. As noted previously, reliability was reported by Richins (1997) only for Studies 4 ($\alpha = $ **.82**) and 5 ($\alpha = $ **.74**).

VALIDITY: The validity of the scale was not specifically addressed in any of the studies. However, Richins (1997) expended a great deal of effort in a creative use of MDS (multi-dimensional scaling) to note whether the items that composed each scale she was creating clustered together.

ADMINISTRATION: The scale was part of longer questionnaires self-administered by students in the classroom studies by Lord, Lee, and Sauer (1994) and Mano and Oliver (1993). In the study by Dubé and Morgan (1996), patients filled out the emotion scales at the same time each day with regard to how they felt that day, but on the day of check-out, they were asked to about the overall emotional reaction to their stay. In the studies performed by Richins (1997), particularly Studies 4 and 5, the scale was just part of a larger instrument containing many emotion-related measures to which students responded with regard to recent consumption situations. A high score suggested that a stimulus evoked a very negative affective reaction in someone. In the case of Richins's (1997) subscale, higher scores implied in particular that a person had been very scared by the specified event/stimulus.

MAJOR FINDINGS: Dubé and Morgan (1996) examined how emotional states experienced over time were integrated to form global judgments of consumption emotions and satisfaction. The results indicated that men's first-day positive emotion and women's first-day **negative emotion** were significant predictors of satisfaction with their hospital stay.

The study by Lord, Lee, and Sauer (1994) examined the influence of program context on attitude toward the ad. No findings were reported with regard to **negative affect,** apparently because it was not one of the primary variables in the theory being tested.

Mano and Oliver (1993) examined the dimensionality and causal structure of product evaluation, affect, and satisfaction. Among the many findings involving emotion was that **negative affectivity** was significantly greater for subjects in a high involvement manipulation.

On the basis of a review of previously developed measures of emotion, Richins (1997) conducted six studies with the purpose of producing a set of scales that were particularly suited for assessing consumption experiences. The CES instrument was a result of the studies, one subscale of which measures **fear**. In general, the instrument was more successful in representing the diversity of consumption emotions than were the other instruments tested.

REFERENCES:

Dubé, Laurette and Michael S. Morgan (1996), "Trend Effects and Gender Differences in Retrospective Judgments of Consumption Emotions," *JCR,* 23 (September), 156–62.

Lord, Kenneth R., Myung-Soo Lee, and Paul L. Sauer (1994), "Program Context Antecedents of Attitude toward Radio Commercials," *JAMS,* 22 (1), 3–15.

Mano, Haim and Richard L. Oliver (1993), "Assessing the Dimensionality and Structure of the Consumption Experience: Evaluation, Feeling, and Satisfaction," *JCR,* 20 (December), 451–66.

Richins, Marsha L. (1997), "Measuring Emotions in the Consumption Experience," *JCR,* 24 (September), 127–46.

Watson, David, Lee Anna Clark, and Auke Tellegen (1988), "Development and Validation of Brief Measures of Positive and Negative Affect: The PANAS Scales," *Journal of Personality and Social Psychology,* 54 (6), 1063–70.

SCALE ITEMS:*

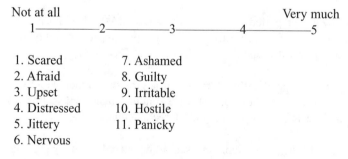

Not at all   Very much
1————————2————————3————————4————————5

1. Scared   7. Ashamed
2. Afraid   8. Guilty
3. Upset   9. Irritable
4. Distressed   10. Hostile
5. Jittery   11. Panicky
6. Nervous

*Richins (1997) used items 1, 2, and 11 with a four-point scale ranging from *not at all* to *strongly*.

SCALE NAME: Affect Response (Negative)

SCALE DESCRIPTION: Four-item, seven-point summated ratings scale measuring the degree to which a person who has just been exposed to some stimulus describes his or her emotional response in negative terms such as sadness and anger. The stimulus used in the study conducted by Price, Arnould, and Tierney (1995) was a river rafting trip.

SCALE ORIGIN: The scale appears to have been used first as a set of items by Price, Arnould, and Tierney (1995). Three of the items were part of a larger scale used by Edell and Burke (1987) to measure affective reactions to ads. (See #306, Vol. I.)

SAMPLES: Very little information was provided by Price, Arnould, and Tierney (1995) regarding their sample. The reader is referred to a previous article (Arnould and Price 1993), which provides only a limited description of the sample. The respondents are described simply as a stratified random sample of people taking multiday river trips with one of three clients' rafting companies. A total of **137** clients filled out posttrip questionnaires, but only 97 of those had completed pretrip surveys.

RELIABILITY: An alpha of **.87** was reported by Price, Arnould, and Tierney (1995).

VALIDITY: No specific examination of the scale's validity was reported by Price, Arnould, and Tierney (1995).

ADMINISTRATION: The scale was self-administered by respondents as part of a larger survey after they had finished a rafting trip (Price, Arnould, and Tierney 1995). Higher scores on the scale suggested that respondents were upset by something about the stimulus to which they were exposed and felt sad and/or angry about it.

MAJOR FINDINGS: Building on the same basic study as used by Arnould and Price (1993), Price, Arnould, and Tierney (1995) examined service encounters that were "extreme" in certain dimensions. Among the findings were that there was no significant relationship between perceived performance of the service provider and **negative affect** and that satisfaction was only slightly influenced by **negative affect**.

REFERENCES:

Arnould, Eric J. and Linda L. Price (1993), "River Magic: Extraordinary Experience and the Extended Service Encounter," *JCR*, 20 (June), 24–45.

Edell, Julie E. and Marian C. Burke (1987), "The Power of Feelings in Understanding Advertising Effects," *JCR*, 14 (December), 421–33.

Price, Linda L., Eric J. Arnould, and Patrick Tierney (1995), "Going to Extremes: Managing Service Encounters and Assessing Provider Performance," *JM*, 59 (April), 83–97.

SCALE ITEMS: *

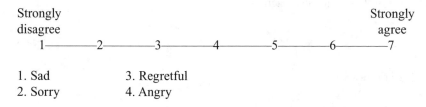

Strongly   Strongly
disagree   agree
 1———2———3———4———5———6———7

1. Sad   3. Regretful
2. Sorry   4. Angry

*The response format was not specifically described by Price, Arnould, and Tierney (1995), but appears to have been something similar to what is shown here.

SCALE NAME: Affect Response (Negative)

SCALE DESCRIPTION: Four negative descriptors of a person's affective reaction to some stimulus. These descriptors are of moderate intensity and, as such, may appear as something less than full-fledged emotions.

SCALE ORIGIN: The scale was developed by Derbaix (1995) for use in his study. Some 50 items related to affective reactions were pretested with 70 consumers who watched ten unfamiliar commercials in their homes. The items in this scale were among the 21 that "emerged" from the pretest (Derbaix 1995, p. 473).

SAMPLES: Data were collected by Derbaix (1995, p. 472) from **228** people who were contacted by "study collaborators." They were instructed not to gather data from students, friends, or extended family members. Participants were paid $15.

RELIABILITY: An alpha of **.64** was reported for the scale (Derbaix 1995).

VALIDITY: No examination of the scale's validity was reported by Derbaix (1995). In a related issue, however, the author reported that a factor analysis was conducted on 21 items (mentioned previously) and two dimensions were found: one positive and one negative. Summated scales were developed using the results of the factor analysis and judgment. Derbaix (195, p. 473) noted that he tried to "avoid the aggregation of emotions with sentiments," with the result that this scale has the less intense level of negative affect descriptors (sentiments), whereas the other items, which loaded on the negative dimension, were more intense descriptors and were used to compose another scale (#8). Thus, it is doubtful that these two scales have discriminant validity because their items loaded on the same dimension.

ADMINISTRATION: The scale was self-administered by respondents along with other measures after they were exposed to a television program and some commercials (Derbaix 1995). High scores on the scale indicated that respondents experienced a negative affective reaction to the specified stimulus.

MAJOR FINDINGS: Derbaix (1995) examined the influence of affective reactions evoked by ads on Aad and Ab. The study is distinguished by methodological factors expected to improve ecological validity. Among the findings was that the moderate negative **affective** reaction scale had significant affects on Aad for both known and unknown brands.

COMMENTS: The low reliability, along with the dubious discriminant validity, suggests that the scale should be used cautiously until further improvements in its psychometric qualities have been made.

REFERENCES:
Derbaix, Christian (1995), "The Impact of Affective Reactions on Attitudes Toward the Advertisement and the Brand: A Step Toward Ecological Validity," *JMR*, 32 (November), 470–79.

SCALE ITEMS:*
Here is a list of affective reactions you have perhaps experienced while seeing the advertisement. Please indicate how much you felt each of these affective reactions.

Not at all :___:___:___:___:___: A lot
          1   2   3   4   5

1. Worried   3. Unpleasant surprise
2. Irritated   4. Bored

*Although the scale stem was provided in the article by Derbaix (1995), the response format was not. Thus, the number of points and the verbal anchors are unknown; the one shown here is merely a possibility.

SCALE NAME: Affect Response (Negative)

SCALE DESCRIPTION: Three one-word negative descriptors of a person's affective reaction to some stimulus. These descriptors suggest strong intensity and, as such, appear to represent emotions rather than less intense sentiments.

SCALE ORIGIN: The scale was developed by Derbaix (1995) for use in his study. Some 50 items related to affective reactions were pretested with 70 consumers who watched ten unfamiliar commercials in their homes. The items in this scale were among the 21 that "emerged" from the pretest (Derbaix 1995, p. 473).

SAMPLES: Data were collected by Derbaix (1995, p. 472) from **228** people who were contacted by "study collaborators." They were instructed not to gather data from students, friends, or extended family members. Participants were paid $15.

RELIABILITY: An alpha of **.75** was reported for the scale (Derbaix 1995).

VALIDITY: No examination of the scale's validity was reported by Derbaix (1995). In a related issue, however, the author reported that a factor analysis was conducted on 21 items (mentioned previously) and two dimensions were found: one positive and one negative. Summated scales were developed using the results of the factor analysis and judgment. Derbaix (1995, p. 473) noted that he tried to "avoid the aggregation of emotions with sentiments," with the result that this scale has the more intense level of negative affect descriptors (emotions), whereas the other items, which loaded on the negative dimension, were less intense descriptors and were used to compose another scale (#7). Thus, it is doubtful that the scales have discriminant validity because their items loaded on the same dimension.

ADMINISTRATION: The scale was self-administered by respondents along with other measures after they were exposed to a television program and some commercials (Derbaix 1995). High scores on the scale indicated that respondents experienced a negative affective reaction to the specified stimulus.

MAJOR FINDINGS: Derbaix (1995) examined the influence of affective reactions evoked by ads on Aad and Ab. The study is distinguished by methodological factors expected to improve ecological validity. Although some significant findings were found with regard to moderate intensity negative affective reactions (#7), no significant findings were reported that involved the strong negative **affective** reaction scale.

REFERENCES:
Derbaix, Christian (1995), "The Impact of Affective Reactions on Attitudes Toward the Advertisement and the Brand: A Step Toward Ecological Validity," *JMR*, 32 (November), 470–79.

SCALE ITEMS:*
Here is a list of affective reactions you have perhaps experienced while seeing the advertisement. Please indicate how much you felt each of these affective reactions.

Not at all　:___:___:___:___:___:　A lot
　　　　　　　1　2　3　4　5

1. Disgust
2. Anger
3. Fear

*Although the scale stem was provided in the article by Derbaix (1995), the response scale was not. Thus, the number of points and the verbal anchors are unknown; the one shown here is merely a possibility.

SCALE NAME: Affective Response (Negative)

SCALE DESCRIPTION: Fifteen five-point descriptors measuring a person's overall negative emotional reaction to some stimulus. The scale is a combination of three subdimensions: anger, fear, and discouragement. A five-item, seven-point scale very similar to the anger subdimension was used by Nyer (1997).

SCALE ORIGIN: Although Murry and Dacin (1996) appear to have selected items from the pool of adjectives offered by Plutchik (1980, p. 170), the scale itself is original to their study. On the basis of some undescribed pretests, they narrowed the set of items that would assess positive and negative emotions down to 25.

Nyer (1997) drew on Shaver and colleagues (1987) and Holbrook and Batra (1987, 1988) for items; those authors in turn had drawn on others to develop their measures.

SAMPLES: Data were collected by Murry and Dacin (1996) in an experiment involving **162** undergraduate students. Students were randomly assigned to eight television-viewing conditions, and the experiment took place in a lounge with two to five subjects at a time.

Nyer (1997) gathered data from **164** students attending a Midwestern U.S. university. Students were mostly nonbusiness majors and were recruited from several locations on campus. As an incentive to participate, subjects were paid $10 and had a chance to win $200. The experiment was run with one student at a time.

RELIABILITY: Murry and Dacin (1996) reported a reliability of **.91** for a linear combination of the items. An alpha of **.94** was reported for the version of the scale used by Nyer (1997).

VALIDITY: No explicit examination of the scale's validity was mentioned by Murry and Dacin (1996). However, a confirmatory factor analysis was conducted on the set of 25 emotion-related terms (Murry 1997). Two subscales were expected to relate to a positive emotional dimension, and three were expected to relate to a negative emotional dimension. Indeed, a second-order negative emotion factor was found to underlie the *anger* (#1–#7), *fear* (#8–#12), and *discouraged* (#13–#15) subscales.

Nyer (1997) indicated that he tested the scale along with others in his study for convergent and discriminant validity. However, beyond noting that the items loaded high on the same dimension in an exploratory factor analysis, no details were provided in support of the measure's validity.

ADMINISTRATION: The scale was self-administered by subjects along with other measures immediately after they were exposed to the treatment stimulus (Murry and Dacin 1996; Nyer 1997). Higher scores on the scale suggested that a stimulus to which respondents were exposed to evoked a very negative (angry, fearful, discouraged) feeling.

MAJOR FINDINGS: Murry and Dacin (1996) studied how emotions elicited by television programs affect viewers' liking for the programs. The results indicated that **negative emotions** had a strong detrimental impact on program liking, but this was moderated by viewers' perceptions of program reality and personal relevance.

The experiment conducted by Nyer (1997) examined the effect of cognitive appraisals on consumption emotions and the latter's effect on word-of-mouth intentions. Among the findings was that a model that included **anger** and sadness, as well as joy/satisfaction, significantly improved the prediction of intended word-of-mouth promotion (positive and negative).

REFERENCES:

Holbrook, Morris B. and Rajeev Batra (1987), "Assessing the Role of Emotions as Mediators of Consumer Responses to Advertising," *JCR*, 14 (December), 404–20.

———— and ———— (1988), "Toward a Standardized Emotional Profile (SEP) Useful in Measuring Responses to the Nonverbal Components of Advertising," in *Nonverbal Communication in Advertising*, Sidney Hecker and David W. Stewart, eds. Lexington, MA: D.C. Heath, 95–109.

Murry, John P., Jr. (1997), personal correspondence.

———— and Peter A. Dacin (1996), "Cognitive Moderators of Negative-Emotion Effects: Implications for Understanding Media Context," *JCR*, 22 (March), 439–47.

Nyer, Prashanth U. (1997), "A Study of the Relationships Between Cognitive Appraisals and Consumption Emotions," *JAMS*, 25 (Fall), 296–304.

Plutchik, Robert (1980), *Emotion: A Psychoevolutionary Synthesis*. New York: Harper and Row Publishers.

Shaver, Phillip, Judith Schwartz, Donald Kirson, and Acry O'Connor (1987), "Emotion Knowledge: Further Exploration of a Prototype Approach," *Journal of Personality and Social Psychology*, 52 (6), 1061–86.

SCALE ITEMS:*

```
Did not feel                    Felt very
   at all      :___:___:___:___:___:  strongly
              1   2   3   4   5
```

1. Annoyed
2. Irritated
3. Resentful
4. Furious
5. Bitter
6. Angry
7. Fed up
8. Afraid
9. Scared
10. Worried
11. Nervous
12. Hopeless
13. Puzzled
14. Discouraged
15. Bewildered
16. Enraged

*Murry and Dacin (1996) used items 1–15 and the response scale shown. Nyer (1997) used items 1, 2, 4, 6, and 16 with a seven-point *not at all/very much* response format.

SCALE NAME: Affective Response (Positive)

SCALE DESCRIPTION: A three-item, Likert-like scale measuring the degree to which a person has experienced positive feelings due to some stimulus. The scale appears to measure the feeling evoked by some stimulus rather than the stimulus itself.

SCALE ORIGIN: Taylor (1995) wanted a measure of "negative affect" for use in her study and, using data from the main study (described subsequently), performed an exploratory factor analysis on eight items. Two affect scales were derived: one she described as *positive* and one described as *negative*.

SAMPLES: Taylor (1995) collected data from **232** undergraduate business students attending a mid-sized university. Some of these subjects (n = 68) were part of a control group, but the rest were broken down into groups of between 24 and 31 for the experimental treatments.

RELIABILITY: An alpha of **.79** was reported for the version of the scale used by Taylor (1995).

VALIDITY: The validity of the scale was not specifically addressed by Taylor (1995). However, as noted previously, she performed an exploratory factor analysis on eight items and found evidence of two dimensions. The four items shown here loaded highest on what she called the *positive affect* factor.

ADMINISTRATION: Subjects in the experiment conducted by Taylor (1995) self-administered the scale, along with other measures, after the experimental manipulation. Higher scores on the scale indicated that respondents were feeling happy as a result of some stimulus to which they were exposed.

MAJOR FINDINGS: The purpose of the experiment by Taylor (1995) was to investigate the effects of a delay, perceived control over a delay, and what fills the time during the delay. Findings related to the measure of **positive affect** were not reported in the article. It appears that the scale was described only because it was a byproduct of the process of developing a measure of negative affect for use as a manipulation check in the analysis.

REFERENCES:
Taylor, Shirley (1994), "Waiting for Service: The Relationship Between Delays and Evaluations of Service," *JM*, 58 (April), 56–69.
——— (1995), "The Effects of Filled Waiting Time and Service Provider Control over the Delay on Evaluations of Service," *JAMS*, 23 (Winter), 38–48.

SCALE ITEMS: *

Not at all :___:___:___:___:___:___:___: Very
           1 2 3   4 5   6 7

1. Good
2. Happy
3. Satisfied

*Taylor (1995) did not describe the type of response scale she used with these items, but the one shown here is what she used for similar measures in previous studies (Taylor 1994).

SCALE NAME: Affective Response (Positive)

SCALE DESCRIPTION: A ten-item, five-point scale measuring the degree of positive affect a person has toward some specified stimulus. As noted subsequently, several versions of the scale were created and tested that vary in their temporal instructions. Therefore, the items can be used to measure a person's mood state at a particular point in time, or at the other extreme, reference to a year's time may be used as something more like a trait measure of affect. A four-item variation of the scale was used by Babin, Boles, and Darden (1995) and was referred to as *interest*. Richins's (1997) version of the scale was composed of three four-point items and was intended to capture the level of excitement a person felt during a consumption experience.

SCALE ORIGIN: The scale was developed by Watson, Clark, and Tellegen (1988). The ten positive items and ten negative items constitute the Positive and Negative Affect Schedule (PANAS). Seven versions of the scale, using the same items, were tested, in which the time period of interest varied from "right now" to "during the last year." Alphas ranged from .86 to .90 using data from college students. The stability of each of these versions was tested using 101 students and with eight-week intervals. The resulting test-retest correlations ranged from .47 to .68. A factor analysis of the ten positive and ten negative items indicated that the positive items all had high loadings (>.50) on the same factor. Evidence of the scale's validity was also provided. By design, the scales were supposed to be independent (uncorrelated), and the evidence bore this out.

Babin, Boles, and Darden (1995) modified a scale developed by Holbrook and Batra (1988). The latter developed a three-item scale to measure *activation*, but the former added the item *interested* and viewed the scale as measuring "the extent to which one's system is energized with respect to allocating attention capacity" to some stimulus (Babin, Boles, and Darden 1995, p. 103).

Richins (1997) drew on terms in previous measures as well as her own series of studies to develop and refine several emotion-related scales into the CES (Consumption Emotion Set).

SAMPLES: The data were gathered by Babin, Boles, and Darden (1995) from **163** undergraduate marketing students who were randomly assigned to one of three experimental conditions.

Data were gathered by Dubé and Morgan (1996) from **96** patients who stayed at least two days in a French-Canadian hospital. A little more than half (55%) of the sample were men, and the median age was 46 years. Patients apparently volunteered to participate, and a lottery ($250) was used as an incentive.

Lord, Lee, and Sauer (1994) collected data from undergraduate students in a introductory marketing course. Students received extra credit for their participation, and analysis was based on **324** completed survey forms.

Data were collected by Mano and Oliver (1993) from **118** undergraduate business students attending a Midwestern U.S. university.

Six studies were reported by Richins (1997) as part of the process of developing the CES, only two of which had reliability information. Study 4 was based on data from **448** college students. Two surveys were conducted in Study 5: Survey 1 was completed by **256** college students, and there were **194** student respondents to Survey 2.

RELIABILITY: Alphas of **.77** (Babin, Boles, and Darden 1995), **.88** (Dubé and Morgan 1996), **.78** (Lord, Lee, and Sauer 1994), and **.90** (Mano and Oliver 1993) have been reported for the scale. As noted previously, reliability was reported by Richins (1997) for only Studies 4 (α = **.88**) and 5 (α = **.89**).

VALIDITY: The validity of the scale was not specifically addressed in any of the studies conducted by Babin, Boles, and Darden (1995); Lord, Lee, and Sauer (1994); or Mano and Oliver (1993). Dubé and Morgan (1996) stated that a factor analysis was conducted on this scale's items, along with those for another (#5), and revealed a two-factor structure. One item (*excited*) loaded on the other factor and was, presumably, dropped from the final version of the scale.

Richins (1997) did not directly examine the validity of her scale either. A great deal of effort was expended, however, in a creative use of MDS (multi-dimensional scaling) to note whether the items that composed each scale clustered together.

ADMINISTRATION: The scale was part of longer questionnaires self-administered by students in class-room studies by Lord, Lee, and Sauer (1994) and Mano and Oliver (1993). Babin, Boles, and Darden (1995) had subjects complete the scale along with other measures after they were exposed to experimental manipu-lation. In the study by Dubé and Morgan (1996), patients filled out the emotion scales at the same time each day with regard to how they felt that day, but on the day of check-out, they completed the scale with respect to the overall emotional reaction to their stay. In the studies performed by Richins (1997), particularly Studies 4 and 5, the scale was just part of a larger instrument containing many emotion-related measures. A high score suggested that a stimulus evoked a very positive affective reaction in the person exposed to it.

MAJOR FINDINGS: The study by Babin, Boles, and Darden (1995) examined salesperson stereotypes and their influence on the sales environment. The findings showed that the three types of car salespeople differed in the **interest** they evoked in consumers, such that the *pushy* salesperson evoked less than the *typical* salesperson.

Dubé and Morgan (1996) examined how emotional states experienced over time were integrated to form global judgments of consumption emotions and satisfaction. The results indicated that men's first-day **positive emotion** and women's first day negative emotion were significant predictors of satisfaction with their hospital stay.

The study by Lord, Lee, and Sauer (1994) examined the influence of program context on attitude toward the ad. No findings were reported with regard to **positive affect**, apparently because it was not one of the primary variables in the theory being tested.

Mano and Oliver (1993) examined the dimensionality and causal structure of product evaluation, affect, and satisfaction. Among the many findings involving emotion was that **positive affectivity** was significantly greater for subjects in a high involvement manipulation.

On the basis of a review of previously developed measures of emotion, Richins (1997) conducted six studies with the purpose of producing a set of scales particularly suited for assessing consumption expe-riences. The CES instrument was a result of the studies, one subscale of which measures the excitement type **positive affect**. In general, the instrument was more successful in representing the diversity of con-sumption emotions than were the other instruments tested.

COMMENTS: See also Kelley and Hoffman (1997).

REFERENCES:
Babin, Barry J., James S. Boles, and William R. Darden (1995), "Salesperson Stereotypes, Consumer Emotions, and Their Impact on Information Processing," *JAMS*, 23 (Spring), 94–105.
Dubé, Laurette and Michael S. Morgan (1996), "Trend Effects and Gender Differences in Retrospective Judgments of Consumption Emotions," *JCR*, 23 (September), 156–62.
Holbrook, Morris B. and Rajeev Batra (1988), "Toward a Standardized Emotional Profile (SEP) Useful in Measuring Responses to the Nonverbal Components of Advertising," in *Nonverbal Communication in Advertising*, Sidney Hecker and David W. Stewart, eds. Lexington, MA: D.C. Heath, 95–109.
Kelley, Scott W. and K. Douglas Hoffman (1997), "An Investigation of Positive Affect, Prosocial Behaviors and Service Quality," *JR*, 73 (3), 407–27.

Lord, Kenneth R., Myung-Soo Lee, and Paul L. Sauer (1994), "Program Context Antecedents of Attitude Toward Radio Commercials," *JAMS*, 22 (1), 3–15.

Mano, Haim and Richard L. Oliver (1993), "Assessing the Dimensionality and Structure of the Consumption Experience: Evaluation, Feeling, and Satisfaction," *JCR*, 20 (December), 451–66.

Richins, Marsha L. (1997), "Measuring Emotions in the Consumption Experience," *JCR*, 24 (September), 127–46.

Watson, David, Lee Anna Clark, and Auke Tellegen (1988), "Development and Validation of Brief Measures of Positive and Negative Affect: The PANAS Scales," *Journal of Personality and Social Psychology*, 54 (6), 1063–70.

SCALE ITEMS:

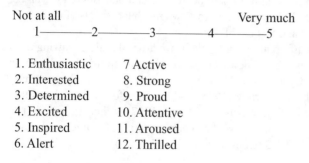

Not at all   Very much
1————2————3————4————5

1. Enthusiastic   7 Active
2. Interested   8. Strong
3. Determined   9. Proud
4. Excited   10. Attentive
5. Inspired   11. Aroused
6. Alert   12. Thrilled

Babin, Boles, and Darden (1995): 2, 4, 7, 11; 7-point
Dubé and Morgan (1996): 1–10; 7-point
Lord, Lee, and Sauer (1994): 1–10; 5-point
Mano and Oliver (1993): 1–10; 5-point
Richins (1997): 1, 4, 12; 4-point

SCALE NAME: Affective Response (Positive)

SCALE DESCRIPTION: Multiple items measuring the degree to which a person who has just been exposed to some stimulus describes his or her emotional response in positive terms such as happy, elated, or pleased. The sample in the study conducted by Price, Arnould, and Tierney (1995) was responding to a river rafting trip it had been on and used a four-item, seven-point scale. The version of the scale used by Oliver, Rust, and Varki (1997) had three five-point items and was responded to by patrons after attending a symphony concert. Richins's (1997) version of the scale was composed of three four-point items and was intended to capture the level of joyful feelings a person felt during a consumption experience.

SCALE ORIGIN: The version of the scale used by Price, Arnould, and Tierney (1995) appears to be original to their study. Although all the items had been used previously by Edell and Burke (1987), the four items used by Price, Arnould, and Tierney (1995) were taken from two much larger sets of items used to measure affective reactions to ads. (See #310 and #311, Vol. I.)

Oliver, Rust, and Varki (1997) described a different origin for their two arousal scales, drawing most directly from the pool of items proposed by Larsen and Diener (1992, p. 31), who in turn had drawn on the work of others. The three items Oliver, Rust, and Varki (1997) used in their second study were relatively similar to those used by Price, Arnould, and Tierney (1995) and are therefore reported together here. (See #15 for the version of the scale used by Oliver, Rust, and Varki [1997] in their first study.)

Richins (1997) drew on terms in previous measures as well as her own series of studies to develop and refine several emotion-related scales into the CES (Consumption Emotion Set).

SAMPLES: Every little information was provided by Price, Arnould, and Tierney (1995) regarding their sample. The reader is referred to a previous article (Arnould and Price 1993) that provides only a limited description of the sample. The respondents are described simply as a stratified random sample of people taking multiday river trips with one of three clients' rafting companies. It appears that a total of 137 clients filled out posttrip questionnaires, but only 97 of those had completed pretrip surveys.

Oliver, Rust, and Varki (1997) reported on the use of the scale in the second of two studies that involved patronage rather than product consumption. The second study examined single-ticket purchasers at a symphony concert in a large city. Patrons were approached as they arrived but did not receive and complete the questionnaire until the concert was over. Usable surveys were received from **104** people. The modal respondent was a single woman between the ages of 20 and 30 years.

Six studies were reported by Richins (1997) as part of the process of developing the CES, only two of which had reliability information. Study 4 was based on data from **448** college students. Two surveys were conducted in Study 5: Survey 1 was completed by **256** college students, and there were **194** student respondents to Survey 2.

RELIABILITY: Alphas of **.84** and **.82** were reported by Oliver, Rust, and Varki (1997) and Price, Arnould, and Tierney (1995), respectively. As noted previously, reliability was reported by Richins (1997) only for Studies 4 ($\alpha = .91$) and 5 ($\alpha = .88$).

VALIDITY: No specific examination of the scale's validity was reported by either Price, Arnould, and Tierney (1995) or Oliver, Rust, and Varki (1997). However, the latter conducted two rounds of factor analysis. The first analysis involved 24 emotion items taken from the sources noted. Those items loading highest on the first factor (high positive affect) were subsequently examined in a second factor analysis. Common to both of their studies, two dimensions were identified: affect and arousal. However, loadings on the affect factor varied between the two studies and led to the use of rather different sets of items.

Richins (1997) did not directly examine the validity of her scale either. A great deal of effort was expended, however, in a creative use of MDS (multi-dimensional scaling) to note whether the items that composed each scale clustered together.

ADMINISTRATION: The scale was self-administered by respondents as part of a larger survey after they had finished a rafting trip (Price, Arnould, and Tierney 1995). Likewise, respondents in the second study by Oliver, Rust, and Varki (1997) completed the scale along with other measures after leaving the concert. In the studies performed by Richins (1997), particularly Studies 4 and 5, the scale was part of a larger instrument containing many emotion-related measures. Higher scores on the scale suggested that respondents were pleased by something about the stimulus to which they were exposed and felt good about it.

MAJOR FINDINGS: Building on the same basic study as Arnould and Price (1993), Price, Arnould, and Tierney (1995) examined service encounters that were "extreme" in certain dimensions. Contrary to expectations, perceived performance of the service provider did not have a significant impact on satisfaction, though it appeared that its influence was mediated by **positive affect** response.

The purpose of the studies by Oliver, Rust, and Varki (1997) was to establish a behavioral basis for customer *delight* by empirically testing its antecedents and consequences. The findings indicated that positive **affect** was a function of arousal and positive disconfirmation and that **affect** was the only significant driver of delight.

On the basis of a review of previously developed measures of emotion, Richins (1997) conducted six studies with the purpose of producing a set of scales particularly suited for assessing consumption experiences. The CES instrument was a result of the studies, one subscale of which measures the joyful type **positive affect.** In general, the instrument was more successful in representing the diversity of consumption emotions than were the other instruments tested.

REFERENCES:

Arnould, Eric J. and Linda L. Price (1993), "River Magic: Extraordinary Experience and the Extended Service Encounter," *JCR,* 20 (June), 24–45.

Edell, Julie E. and Marian C. Burke (1987), "The Power of Feelings in Understanding Advertising Effects," *JCR,* 14 (December), 421–33.

Larsen, Randy J. and Edward Diener (1992), "Promises and Problems with the Circumplex Model of Emotion," in *Emotion,* Margaret S. Clark, ed. Newbury Park, CA: Sage Publications, 25–59.

Oliver, Richard L., Roland T. Rust, and Sajeev Varki (1997), "Customer Delight: Foundations, Findings, and Managerial Insight," *JR,* 73 (3), 311–36.

Price, Linda L., Eric J. Arnould, and Patrick Tierney (1995), "Going to Extremes: Managing Service Encounters and Assessing Provider Performance," *JM,* 59 (April), 83–97.

Richins, Marsha L. (1997), "Measuring Emotions in the Consumption Experience," *JCR,* 24 (September), 127–46.

SCALE ITEMS:*

During your _____, how frequently did you feel each of the following?

Never	Hardly Ever	Sometimes	Quite Often	Always
1	2	3	4	5

1. Happy
2. Elated
3. Pleased
4. Warm-hearted
5. Stimulated
6. Joyful

*The directions and the response scale are those used by Oliver, Rust, and Varki (1997). Their version of the scale used only items 1, 2, and 5. Price, Arnould, and Tierney (1995) used the first four items and appear to have used a seven-point response scale, but the nature of the directions and the scales anchors are unknown. Richins (1997) used items 1, 3, and 6 with a four-point response scale anchored by *not at all* and *strongly.*

SCALE NAME: Affective Response (Positive)

SCALE DESCRIPTION: Five one-word positive descriptors of a person's affective reaction to some stimulus. These descriptors are moderate in intensity as described subsequently.

SCALE ORIGIN: The scale was developed by Derbaix (1995) for use in his study. Some 50 items related to affective reactions were pretested with 70 consumers who watched ten unfamiliar commercials in their homes. The items in this scale were among the 21 that "emerged" from the pretest (Derbaix 1995, p. 473).

SAMPLES: Data were collected by Derbaix (1995, p. 472) from **228** people who were contacted by "study collaborators." The collaborators were instructed not to gather data from students, friends, or extended family members. Participants were paid $15.

RELIABILITY: An alpha of **.78** was reported for the scale (Derbaix 1995).

VALIDITY: No examination of the scale's validity was reported by Derbaix (1995). In a related issue, however, the author reports that a factor analysis was conducted on 21 items (mentioned previously), and two dimensions were found: one positive and one negative. Summated scales were developed using the results of the factor analysis and judgment. Derbaix (1995, p. 473) said that he tried to "avoid the aggregation of emotions with sentiments," with the result that this scale had the less-intense level of positive affect descriptors (sentiments), whereas the other items that loaded on the positive dimension were more intense descriptors and were used to compose another scale (#14). Therefore, it is doubtful that the scales have discriminant validity, because their items loaded on the same dimension.

ADMINISTRATION: The scale was self-administered by respondents, along with other measures, after they were exposed to a television program and some commercials (Derbaix 1995). High scores on the scale indicated that respondents experienced a positive affective reaction to the specified stimulus.

MAJOR FINDINGS: Derbaix (1995) examined the influence of affective reactions evoked by ads on Aad and Ab. The study was distinguished by methodological factors that were expected to improve ecological validity. Among the findings was that the moderate positive **affective** reaction scale had significant impacts on Aad for both known and unknown brands.

REFERENCES:
Derbaix, Christian (1995), "The Impact of Affective Reactions on Attitudes Toward the Advertisement and the Brand: A Step Toward Ecological Validity," *JMR*, 32 (November), 470–79.

SCALE ITEMS:*
Here is a list of affective reactions you have perhaps experienced while seeing the advertisement. Please indicate how much you felt each of these affective reactions.

Not at all　:___:___:___:___:___:　A lot
　　　　　　　 1　 2　 3　 4　 5

1. Interested　　　4. Inquiring
2. Moved　　　　　5. Confident
3. Captivated

*Although the scale stem was provided in the article by Derbaix (1995), the response scale was not. Thus, the number of points and the verbal anchors are unknown, and those shown here are merely a possibility.

SCALE NAME: Affective Response (Positive)

SCALE DESCRIPTION: Five one-word positive descriptors of a person's affective reaction to some stimulus. These descriptors suggest strong intensity and, as such, appear to represent emotions rather than less-intense sentiments.

SCALE ORIGIN: The scale was developed by Derbaix (1995) for use in his study. Some 50 items related to affective reactions were pretested with 70 consumers who watched ten unfamiliar commercials in their homes. The items in this scale were among the 21 that "emerged" from the pretest (Derbaix 1995, p. 473).

SAMPLES: Data were collected by Derbaix (1995, p. 472) from **228** people who were contacted by "study collaborators." The collaborators were instructed not to gather data from students, friends, or extended family members. Participants were paid $15.

RELIABILITY: An alpha of **.89** was reported for the scale (Derbaix 1995).

VALIDITY: No examination of the scale's validity was reported by Derbaix (1995). In a related issue, however, the author reports that a factor analysis was conducted on 21 items (mentioned previously), and two dimensions were found: one positive and one negative. Summated scales were developed using the results of the factor analysis and judgment. Derbaix (1995, p. 473) said that he tried to "avoid the aggregation of emotions with sentiments," with the result that this scale has the more intense level of positive affect descriptors (emotions), whereas the other items that loaded on the positive dimension were less-intense descriptors and were used to compose another scale (#13). Therefore, it is doubtful that the scales have discriminant validity, because their items loaded on the same dimension.

ADMINISTRATION: The scale was self-administered by respondents, along with other measures, after they were exposed to a television program and some commercials (Derbaix 1995). High scores on the scale indicated that respondents experienced a positive affective reaction to the specified stimulus.

MAJOR FINDINGS: Derbaix (1995) examined the influence of affective reactions evoked by ads on A_{ad} and A_b. The study was distinguished by methodological factors that were expected to improve ecological validity. Among the findings was that, for known brands, the strong positive **affective** reaction scale had a significant impact on A_{ad} but not on A_b.

REFERENCES:
Derbaix, Christian (1995), "The Impact of Affective Reactions on Attitudes Toward the Advertisement and the Brand: A Step Toward Ecological Validity," *JMR*, 32 (November), 470–79.

SCALE ITEMS:*
Here is a list of affective reactions you have perhaps experienced while seeing the advertisement. Please indicate how much you felt each of these affective reactions.

Not at all :___:___:___:___:___: A lot
           1   2   3   4   5

1. Delighted   4. Satisfied
2. Enthusiastic   5. Amused
3. Appealed

*Although the scale stem was provided in the article by Derbaix (1995), the response scale was not. Thus, the number of points and the verbal anchors are unknown, and those shown here are merely a possibility.

SCALE NAME: Affective Response (Positive)

SCALE DESCRIPTION: Multiple five-point descriptors measuring a person's overall positive emotional reaction to some stimulus. Murry and Dacin (1996) used ten items, and Oliver, Rust, and Varki (1997) used six.

SCALE ORIGIN: Although Murry and Dacin (1996) appear to have selected items from the pool of adjectives offered by Plutchik (1980, p. 170), the scale itself is original to their study. On the basis of some undescribed pretests, they narrowed the set of items to 25 that would assess positive and negative emotions.

Oliver, Rust, and Varki (1997) described a different origin for their two arousal scales, drawing most directly from the pool of items proposed by Larsen and Diener (1992, p. 31), who had in turn drawn on the work of others. The six items Oliver, Rust, and Varki (1997) used in their first study were relatively similar to the set used by Murry and Dacin (1996) and are, thus, reported together here. (See #12 for the version of the scale used by Oliver, Rust, and Varki [1997] in their second study.)

SAMPLES: Data were collected by Murry and Dacin (1996) in an experiment involving **162** undergraduate students. Students were randomly assigned to eight television viewing conditions, and the experiment took place in a lounge with two to five subjects at a time.

Oliver, Rust, and Varki (1997) reported on the use of two different arousal scales in the two studies they conducted. The sample of the first study was composed of visitors to a recreational wildlife theme park who were approached as they entered the park but completed the form after exiting. Valid data were received from **90** patrons. The typical respondent was a married woman between the ages of 25 and 34 years.

RELIABILITY: Murry and Dacin (1996) reported a reliability of **.97** for a linear combination of the items. An alpha of **.895** was reported for the version of the scale used by Oliver, Rust, and Varki (1997) in their first study.

VALIDITY: No explicit examination of the scale's validity was mentioned by Murry and Dacin (1996). However, a confirmatory factor analysis was conducted on the set of 25 emotion-related terms. Two subscales were expected to relate to a positive emotional dimension, and three were expected to relate to a negative emotional dimension. Indeed, a second-order positive emotion factor was found to underlie the *happiness* (#1–#6) and *contented* (#7–#10) subscales.

Similarly, Oliver, Rust, and Varki (1997) conducted two rounds of factor analysis. The first analysis involved 24 emotion items taken from the sources noted previously. Those items loading highest on the first factor (high positive affect) were subsequently examined in a second factor analysis. Common to both of their studies, two dimensions were identified: affect and arousal. However, loadings on the affect factor varied between the two studies and led to the use of rather different sets of items.

ADMINISTRATION: The scale was self-administered by subjects, along with other measures, immediately after they were exposed to the treatment stimulus (Murry and Dacin 1996). Likewise, respondents in the first study by Oliver, Rust, and Varki (1997) completed the scale along with other measures after leaving the park. High scores on the scale suggested that a stimulus to which respondents had been exposed evoked a very positive (happy and contented) feeling.

MAJOR FINDINGS: Murry and Dacin (1996) studied how emotions elicited by television programs affect viewers' liking for the programs. Not surprising, the results indicated that **positive emotions** had a significant and direct impact on program liking.

The purpose of the studies by Oliver, Rust, and Varki (1997) was to establish a behavioral basis for customer *delight* by empirically testing its antecedents and consequences. The findings indicated that positive **affect** was a function of arousal and positive disconfirmation and **affect** was the primary driver of delight.

REFERENCES:

Larsen, Randy J. and Edward Diener (1992), "Promises and Problems with the Circumplex Model of Emotion," in *Emotion*, Margaret S. Clark, ed. Newbury Park, CA: Sage Publications, 25–59.

Murry, John P., Jr., and Peter A. Dacin (1996), "Cognitive Moderators of Negative-Emotion Effects: Implications for Understanding Media Context," *JCR*, 22 (March), 439–47.

Oliver, Richard L., Roland T. Rust, and Sajeev Varki (1997), "Customer Delight: Foundations, Findings, and Managerial Insight," *JR*, 73 (3), 311–36.

Plutchik, Robert (1980), *Emotion: A Psychoevolutionary Synthesis*. New York: Harper and Row Publishers.

SCALE ITEMS:*

```
Did not feel                    Felt very
   at all      :___:___:___:___:___: strongly
               1   2   3   4   5
```

1. Delighted
2. Happy
3. Cheerful
4. Pleased
5. Friendly
6. Eager
7. Cooperative
8. Tolerant
9. Attentive
10. Patient
11. Contented
12. Excited
13. Enthused

*The response scale used by Murry and Dacin (1996) had the following endpoints: *did not feel at all* and *felt very strongly*. The anchors used by Oliver, Rust, and Varki (1997) were *never* and *always*.

SCALE NAME: Affective Response to Waiting

SCALE DESCRIPTION: Three one-word items measuring the extent to which a consumer feels that the wait he or she has experienced in a service encounter has been frustrating.

SCALE ORIGIN: Although not stated explicitly, it appears that the scale is original to the study by Hui, Dubé, and Chebat (1997).

SAMPLES: The data gathered by Hui, Dubé, and Chebat (1997) were collected from undergraduate business students at a Canadian university. The sample was composed of **116** subjects, with an average age of 24.3 years, and was almost evenly split on gender (59 men).

RELIABILITY: The alpha reported for the scale was **.83** (Hui, Dubé, and Chebat 1997).

VALIDITY: The confirmatory factor analysis conducted by Hui, Dubé, and Chebat (1997) on this scale, as well as two others in their study, provided evidence of the scale's unidimensionality and discriminant validity.

ADMINISTRATION: Subjects completed the scale, along with other parts of a self-administered questionnaire, after they were exposed to one of five experimental treatment groups (Hui, Dubé, and Chebat 1997). Higher scores on the scale indicated that respondents felt that a specified wait they experienced was very frustrating.

MAJOR FINDINGS: Hui, Dubé, and Chebat (1997) examined the influence of music on consumers' responses to waiting for services. The findings indicated that **affective response to a wait** is a significant mediator between the presence of music and service evaluation and that positively valenced music (precategorized as liked/disliked) produced a stronger effect on **affective response** than did negatively valenced music.

REFERENCES:
Hui, Michael K., Laurette Dubé, and Jean-Charles Chebat (1997), "The Impact of Music on Consumers' Reactions to Waiting for Services," *JR,* 73 (1), 87–104.

SCALE ITEMS:*
Directions: Using the response scale (below), how do you feel about the wait in line you experienced in the _____ ?

Not at all   :___:___:___:___:___:___:___: Very much
            1   2   3   4   5   6   7

1. Frustrated
2. Irritated
3. Dissatisfied

*The reconstruction of the scale here is based on the brief description provided by Hui, Dubé, and Chebat (1997) and may not be exactly the same as the one they used. The phrase they apparently used in the blank was *bank setting.*

SCALE NAME: Air Pollution (Social Norms)

SCALE DESCRIPTION: Four seven-point Likert-type statements measuring the extent to which a consumer is concerned about air pollution, with an emphasis on the role played by electrical power plants.

SCALE ORIGIN: The scale is original to Osterhus (1997). His purpose with the scale was to operationalize a *social norm* construct in the context of energy conservation.

SAMPLES: The sample for the study by Osterhus (1997) came from rural, urban, and suburban neighborhoods of a Midwestern U.S. area. Subjects were recruited through random-digit dialing and then were sent a paper questionnaire. Nonrespondents were mailed another questionnaire. Ultimately, **1128** usable responses were received.

RELIABILITY: An alpha of **.67** was reported for the scale by Osterhus (1997).

VALIDITY: Confirmatory factor analysis was used by Osterhus (1997) to help purify the scales. Although details of the quality of this **social norm** scale were not specified, support for the scale's convergent and discriminant validities was implied.

ADMINISTRATION: The scale was self-administered by respondents, along with other measures, in a mail survey format (Osterhus 1997). Higher scores on the scale suggested that respondents were very concerned about air pollution.

MAJOR FINDINGS: Osterhus (1997) investigated how and when prosocial positions influence consumer choice. Among the findings, social norms were found to have a significant, positive influence on **conservation** attitude.

REFERENCES:
Osterhus, Thomas L. (1997), "Pro-Social Consumer Influence Strategies: When and How Do They Work?" *JM*, 61 (October), 16–29.

SCALE ITEMS:

Disagree :___:___:___:___:___:___:___: Agree
            1   2   3   4   5   6   7

1. Much more fuss is being made about air pollution than is really justified. **(r)**

2. Natural resources must be preserved even if people must do without some products.

3. We're very concerned about the environmental effects of air pollution caused by electricity-generating plants.

4. Pollution doesn't really affect my life. **(r)**

SCALE NAME: Alienation (Consumer)

SCALE DESCRIPTION: A seven-item, six-point, Likert-type scale measuring the degree to which a consumer has negative beliefs about and is alienated from business in general.

SCALE ORIGIN: The scale is original to Singh (1990), but he notes that he drew on the work of Allison (1978). The latter developed a 35-item measure of consumer alienation. Although the two scales have some similar items and measure the same construct, they are not the same scale nor is one a subset of the other.

SAMPLES: Data were collected from four samples by Singh (1988, 1990). Four slightly different survey instruments were used that varied in the dissatisfying experience to which they referred. One thousand households were sent a questionnaire for each of the four service categories studied: car repairs, grocery stores, medical care, and banking. Response rates were estimated to be higher than 50% for each category, given that only approximately 30% of the random samples had dissatisfying experiences worthy of reporting on a questionnaire.

Ultimately, usable data ranged from **116** respondents in the repair service sample to **125** in the medical care sample. Detailed demographic information for each of the four samples is provided in the article. The profiles of the four samples varied somewhat because the instrument itself indicated that the questionnaire was to be completed by the person in the household who dealt most with the specified service category. For example, men mostly filled out the questionnaire regarding auto repair (67%), whereas women generally filled out the one pertaining to grocery shopping (73%).

RELIABILITY: An alpha of **.80** was reported by Singh (1990) for the car repair version of the scale.

VALIDITY: The items in this scale were analyzed using common factor analysis. The results were interpreted as showing evidence of unidimensionality, with the main factor explaining **47%** of the total variance.

ADMINISTRATION: The scale was administered in a mail survey instrument along with many other scales and measures. Those consumers with high scores on the scale have indicated that they believed businesses in general do not care about consumers, whereas those with low scores were likely to have more positive beliefs about business.

MAJOR FINDINGS: In a detailed study of consumer complaint behavior, Singh (1990) concluded that there were four consumer clusters with distinct response styles: passives, voicers, irates, and activists. Profiles were developed for each cluster. **Alienation** was found to discriminate significantly among the clusters, such that activists and irates were more likely to be **alienated** from the marketplace than were voicers and passives.

Building on the previous studies, Singh and Wilkes (1996) proposed a model of consumer complaint responses and tested a portion of it. Among their findings was that **alienation** had a significant positive relationship with attitude toward complaining for two of the three service categories.

COMMENTS: As noted previously, four transactions were examined in the study by Singh (1990). However, only the items relating to car repair were reported. To the extent that researchers wish to use the scale to study complaints in a nonrepair context, one of the other three versions of the scale might be more appropriate.

REFERENCES:

Allison, Neil K. (1978), "A Psychometric Development of a Test for Consumer Alienation from the Marketplace," *JMR*, 15 (November), 565–75.

Singh, Jagdip (1988), "Consumer Complaint Intentions and Behaviors: Definitional and Taxonomical Issues," *JM*, 52 (January), 93–107.

——— (1990), "A Typology of Consumer Dissatisfaction Response Styles," *JR*, 66 (Spring), 57–97.

——— and Robert E. Wilkes (1996), "When Consumers Complain: A Path Analysis of the Key Antecedents of Consumer Compliant Response Estimates," *JAMS*, 24 (Fall), 350–65.

SCALE ITEMS:

Strongly disagree	Moderately disagree	Slightly disagree	Slightly agree	Moderately agree	Strongly agree
1	2	3	4	5	6

1. Most companies care nothing at all about the consumer.

2. Shopping is usually an unpleasant experience.

3. Consumers are unable to determine what products will be sold in the stores.

4. In general, companies are plain dishonest in their dealings with the consumer.

5. Business firms stand behind their products and guarantees. **(r)**

6. The consumer is usually the least important consideration to most companies.

7. As soon as they make a sale, most businesses forget about the buyer.

SCALE NAME: Amused

SCALE DESCRIPTION: A three-item, six-point summated ratings scale measuring the degree to which a person describes feeling a sense of amusement on exposure to some stimulus (e.g., music). Phrasing of the scale was such that it measured respondents' emotional reaction to a stimulus rather than the attitude toward the stimulus itself.

SCALE ORIGIN: Lacher and Mizerski (1994) indicated that the scale was taken from Asmus (1985). Each of the three items were in the *humor* factor Asmus (1985) identified in his development of a multidimensional instrument for measuring affective responses to music. Although not explicitly stated in the article, two items from Asmus's activity scale were dropped by Lacher and Mizerski (1994, p. 374) during their pretesting (using 219 undergraduate students) of the scale when those items did not remain constant over the two songs tested and the two extraction methods used. Alphas for the fast and slow tempo songs in the pretest were **.87** and **.71**, respectively (Lacher 1997).

SAMPLES: The sample used by Lacher and Mizerski (1994) came from undergraduate business students at a large, Southern U.S. university. Usable data were collected from **215** students, 52% of whom were men and who ranged in age from 19 to 36 years.

RELIABILITY: Lacher and Mizerski (1994) did not report the alpha for the scale used in the main study, but on the basis of the pretest results, it appears it would have been acceptable.

VALIDITY: No examination of scale validity was reported by Lacher and Mizerski (1994) beyond what could be construed from the factor analyses in the study's pretest (noted previously).

ADMINISTRATION: The scale was self-administered along with other measures in the study by Lacher and Mizerski (1994). Students heard two songs played twice. The second time the songs were played, the students filled out this scale along with other measures. Higher scores on the scale indicated that respondents perceived that a particular song evoked a humorous feeling in them.

MAJOR FINDINGS: Lacher and Mizerski (1994) investigated the responses music evoked in listeners and how those reactions affected the intention to purchase the music. Among the findings was that a feeling of being **amused** did not have a significant influence on any of the other responses to the music being examined.

COMMENTS: Although there is nothing in the items themselves to keep them from being applied to other stimuli, it should be noted that this scale specifically was developed and tested for measuring emotional reactions to music.

REFERENCES:

Asmus, Edward P. (1985), "The Development of a Multidimensional Instrument for the Measurement of Affective Responses to Music," *Psychology of Music*, 13 (1), 19–30.

Lacher, Kathleen T. (1997), personal correspondence.

———— and Richard Mizerski (1994), "An Exploratory Study of the Responses and Relationships Involved in the Evaluation of, and in the Intention to Purchase New Rock Music," *JCR*, 21 (September), 366–80.

SCALE ITEMS:*
DIRECTIONS: Rate each item below in terms of its appropriateness in describing the feelings and emotions you had in response to the music.

Strongly   Strongly
disagree :___:___:___:___:___:___: agree
      1 2 3 4 5 6

1. Humorous
2. Comical
3. Amusing

*The actual directions for filling out the scale were not provided in the article but likely were similar to this.

#20 Anger

SCALE NAME: Anger

SCALE DESCRIPTION: Multiple items purported to capture a person's frustration and irritation with some stimulus. In the studies by Taylor (1994; Taylor and Claxton 1994), a seven-point, seven-item scale was used. As a result of the studies by Richins (1997), a four-point, three-item scale was developed.

SCALE ORIGIN: Although the items used by Taylor (1994; Taylor and Claxton 1994) could have come from several sources, most notably Edell and Burke (1987), the scale as a whole does not appear to be a modification of any one previously used scale. The process used to gather a sample of items and then refine them suggests that the scale should be considered original.

Likewise, Richins (1997) drew on terms from previous measures as well as her own series of studies to develop and refine several emotion-related scales into the CES (Consumption Emotion Set).

SAMPLES: Six studies were reported by Richins (1997) as part of the process of developing the CES, only two of which had reliability information. Study 4 was based on data from **448** college students. Two surveys were conducted in Study 5: Survey 1 was completed by **256** college students, and there were **194** student respondents to Survey 2.

The settings for the data collection used in the studies by Taylor (1994; Taylor and Claxton 1994) were airline boarding lounges and inside the planes themselves. Each passenger approached was given two questionnaires; one was completed while waiting to board the plane, and the other was filled out toward the end of their flight. (Flight attendants made announcements when it was time to complete the second questionnaire and collected them after passengers filled them out.)

Taylor (1994) focused on data from passengers on 18 delayed flights. A total of **210** usable survey forms were returned.

Data for Taylor and Claxton (1994) were obtained from passengers of 17 delayed and 19 nondelayed flights out of a large Western North American city. From the delayed flights, 249 of the first questionnaire and 192 of the second questionnaire were completed. For nondelayed flights, 260 of the first questionnaire and 210 of the second questionnaire were completed.

RELIABILITY: As noted, reliability was reported by Richins (1997) only for Studies 4 (α = .91) and 5 (α = .87). Alphas of .92 and .90 were reported for the versions of the scale used by Taylor (1994) and Taylor and Claxton (1994), respectively.

VALIDITY: Richins (1997) did not directly examine the validity of the scale. A great deal of effort was expended, however, in a creative use of MDS (multi-dimensional scaling) to note whether the items that composed each scale clustered together.

No examination of the scale's validity was reported by Taylor and Claxton (1994). Some idea of the scale's dimensionality can be gleaned from the principal component factor analysis that was conducted on the items that composed this scale and the items for two other mood-related scales. The seven items in the **anger** scale all loaded on the same factor and had low loadings on the other two factors presented.

Likewise, Taylor (1994) described the results of factor analysis of the four items she used and four items that composed another scale (#24). Two dimensions were clear and accounted for 69% of the variance.

ADMINISTRATION: In the studies performed by Richins (1997), particularly Studies 4 and 5, the scale was just part of a larger instrument containing many emotion-related measures. As used by Taylor (1994; Taylor and Claxton 1994), the scale was apparently included as part of the first of the two questionnaires passengers were asked to complete. A high score on the scale suggested that a person was very irritated.

MAJOR FINDINGS: On the basis of a review of previously developed measures of emotion, Richins (1997) conducted six studies with the purpose of producing a set of scales that were particularly suited for assessing consumption experiences. The CES instrument was a result of the studies, one subscale of which measures **anger**. In general, the instrument was more successful in representing the diversity of consumption emotions than were the other instruments tested.

Taylor (1994) tested a model of the influence of flight delay duration on affective and evaluative reactions to the delay. Among the significant findings was that the longer the delay, the more a consumer feels annoyed and **angry**.

Taylor and Claxton (1994) investigated the degree to which a flight delay can change the relative importance of service criteria in terms of their impact on performance judgments in a compensatory evaluation model. The findings confirmed that the delayed passengers were significantly more **angry** than those passengers whose flights were not delayed.

REFERENCES:

Edell, Julie E. and Marian C. Burke (1987), "The Power of Feelings in Understanding Advertising Effects," *JCR*, 14 (December), 421–33.

Richins, Marsha L. (1997), "Measuring Emotions in the Consumption Experience," *JCR*, 24 (September), 127–46.

Taylor, Shirley (1994), "Waiting for Service: The Relationship Between Delays and Evaluations of Service," *JM*, 58 (April), 56–69.

———— and John D. Claxton (1994), "Delays and the Dynamics of Service Evaluations," *JAMS*, 22 (Summer), 254–64.

SCALE ITEMS:*

Not at all :___:___:___:___:___:___:___: Very
          1   2   3   4   5   6   7

1. Bored
2. Annoyed
3. Powerless
4. Angry
5. Irritated
6. Helpless
7. Frustrated

*Taylor (1994) used items 2, 4, 5, and 7. Taylor and Claxton (1994) used all seven items. Richins (1997) used items 4, 5, and 7 with a four-point scale ranging from *not at all* to *strongly*.

SCALE NAME: Anticipated Interaction with Salesperson

SCALE DESCRIPTION: Four seven-point Likert-type items that measure the degree to which a customer expects to contact a specific salesperson with whom he or she has interacted with in the past to conduct business.

SCALE ORIGIN: The scale appears to be original to Ramsey and Sohi (1997), though they drew inspiration from another measure of the construct by Crosby, Evans, and Cowles (1990).

SAMPLES: Data were gathered by Ramsey and Sohi (1997) through a mail survey of 500 new car buyers. The list of people who had bought cars in the previous six months came from a car dealership. Usable survey forms were returned by **173** respondents, the majority of whom were men (70%). Most of the group (60%) had at least some college education, the median household income was $46,000, 72% were married, and the average age was 42 years.

RELIABILITY: An alpha of **.97** was reported for the scale by Ramsey and Sohi (1997).

VALIDITY: After the exploratory factor analysis, Ramsey and Sohi (1997) used confirmatory factor analysis to provide evidence of unidimensionality and discriminant validity.

ADMINISTRATION: The scale was self-administered by respondents as part of a larger mail survey instrument (Ramsey and Sohi 1997). Higher scores on the scale indicated that respondents considered it very likely that they would contact some specific salesperson again to do business.

MAJOR FINDINGS: Ramsey and Sohi (1997) developed and tested a model of the impact of salesperson listening behavior on customer trust, satisfaction, and **anticipated interaction** with the salesperson. Customer perception of salesperson listening behavior was found to have a significant positive impact on **anticipated interaction**.

REFERENCES:

Crosby, Lawrence A., Kenneth R. Evans, and Deborah Cowles (1990), "Relationship Quality in Services Selling: An Interpersonal Influence Perspective," *JM*, 54 (July), 68–81.

Ramsey, Rosemary P. and Ravipreet S. Sohi (1997), "Listening to Your Customers: The Impact of Perceived Salesperson Listening Behavior on Relationship Outcomes," *JAMS*, 25 (Spring), 127–37.

SCALE ITEMS:

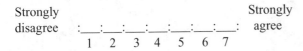

Strongly
disagree :___:___:___:___:___:___:___: Strongly agree
　　　　　1　2　3　4　5　6　7

1. It is probable that I will contact this salesperson again.

2. I am willing to discuss business with this salesperson again.

3. I plan to continue doing business with this salesperson.

4. I will purchase from this salesperson again.

SCALE NAME: Anticipated Negative Consequences

SCALE DESCRIPTION: Three five-point Likert-type statements purported to measure the extent to which a respondent thinks that a person who has received an injury using a product realized that such an unfortunate outcome was a possible consequence of using the product.

SCALE ORIGIN: The scale was apparently constructed by Griffin, Babin, and Attaway (1996) for use in their study.

SAMPLES: Students collected data for the study by Griffin, Babin, and Attaway (1996) for course credit. They were assigned to distribute questionnaires in various parts of a midsized Midwestern U.S. city. In some cases, the instruments were picked up by students, whereas in others, they were mailed back. Of the 420 survey instruments dropped off, **262** were returned. No other information about the sample was provided, except that it was considered to be representative of the area from which it was drawn and only adults (older than 18 years of age) were selected to respond.

RELIABILITY: Griffin, Babin, and Attaway (1996) reported an alpha of **.76** for the scale.

VALIDITY: Because of concerns about the level of correlation between this measure and another (#57), Griffin, Babin, and Attaway (1996) checked the discriminant validity between the two. The evidence provided support for their discriminant validity.

ADMINISTRATION: The scale was self-administered by respondents as part of a larger survey instrument (Griffin, Babin, and Attaway 1996). Higher scores on the scale indicated that respondents believed that someone else they had heard or read about probably anticipated a negative consequence was possible as the result of using a product.

MAJOR FINDINGS: Griffin, Babin, and Attaway (1996) explored the attribution of blame toward marketers when negative consequences resulted from use their products. Among the findings was that the greater the **anticipated negative consequences** of using a product, the more likely a person was to place the blame on the consumer rather than on the marketer.

REFERENCES:
Griffin, Mitch, Barry J. Babin, and Jill Attaway (1996), "Anticipation of Injurious Consumption Outcomes and Its Impact on Consumer Attributions of Blame," *JAMS*, 24 (Fall), 314–27.

SCALE ITEMS:

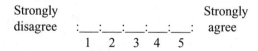

Strongly disagree :___:___:___:___:___: Strongly agree
 1 2 3 4 5

1. The victim should have known that an injury might occur.

2. The victim recognized the danger of using this product.

3. When using the product, the victim could not have known an injury was possible. **(r)**

SCALE NAME: Anxiety State

SCALE DESCRIPTION: Three seven-point items in a semantic differential format intended to capture the state (as opposed to trait) of anxiety a person is feeling a some point in time.

SCALE ORIGIN: Although Pham (1996) may have received inspiration from previous work, the scale appears to be original to his study.

SAMPLES: Data were gathered by Pham (1996) from undergraduate students for his three experiments. The scale only was used, however, in Experiment 3, which involved **57** students.

RELIABILITY: An alpha of **.89** was reported for the scale (Pham 1996).

VALIDITY: No examination of the scale's validity was reported by Pham (1996). It was stated, however, that a factor analysis of the items in this scale, as well as two others (#203 and #237), yielded a three-factor solution in which the items loaded on one factor.

ADMINISTRATION: The scale was part of a larger self-administered questionnaire that subjects filled out after being exposed to ads in the experimental treatments (Pham 1996). Higher scores on the scale indicated that respondents were experiencing high levels of the state of anxiety.

MAJOR FINDINGS: Pham (1996) proposed that two types of processes underlie arousal effects on persuasion: the "selection" and the "representation" effects. **Anxiety** (state) appeared to increase the relative impact of product claims up to a point, after which their influence decreased.

REFERENCES:
Pham, Michel Tuan (1996), "Cue Representation and Selection Effects of Arousal on Persuasion," *JCR*, 22 (March), 373–87.

SCALE ITEMS:
I am:

1. Relaxed   :___:___:___:___:___:___:___: Tense
                 1   2   3   4   5   6   7

2. Calm   :___:___:___:___:___:___:___: Anxious
                 1   2   3   4   5   6   7

3. Confident   :___:___:___:___:___:___:___: Nervous
                 1   2   3   4   5   6   7

SCALE NAME: Anxious

SCALE DESCRIPTION: A seven-point summated scale purported to measure a person's level of uncertainty and uneasiness due to some stimulus. In the studies by Taylor (1994; Taylor and Claxton 1994), the stimulus was an airline flight.

SCALE ORIGIN: Although the authors (Taylor and Claxton 1994) took items from several sources, the scale as a whole does not appear to be a modification of any one previously used scale. The process used to gather the sample of items and then refine them suggests that the scale should be considered original.

SAMPLES: The settings for the data collection used by the two studies (Taylor 1994; Taylor and Claxton 1994) were airline boarding lounges and inside the planes themselves. Each passenger approached was given two questionnaires; one was completed while waiting to board the plane, and the other was filled out toward the end of their flight. (Flight attendants made announcements when it was time to complete the second questionnaire and collected them after passengers filled them out.)

Taylor (1994) focused on data from passengers on 18 delayed flights. A total of **210** usable survey forms were returned.

Data for Taylor and Claxton (1994) were obtained from passengers of 17 delayed and 19 nondelayed flights out of a large Western North American city. From the delayed flights, 249 of the first questionnaire and 192 of the second questionnaire were completed. For nondelayed flights, 260 of the first questionnaire and 210 of the second questionnaire were completed.

RELIABILITY: Alphas of **.73** and **.57** were reported for the slightly different versions of the scale used by Taylor (1994) and Taylor and Claxton (1994), respectively.

VALIDITY: No examination of the scale's validity was reported by Taylor and Claxton (1994). Some idea of the scale's dimensionality can be gleaned from the principal component analysis that was conducted on the items that composed this scale and the items for two other mood-related scales. The three items in the **anxious** scale all loaded on the same factor and had low loadings on the other two factors presented.

Likewise, Taylor (1994) described the results of factor analysis of the four items she used and four items that composed another scale (#20). Two dimensions were clear and accounted for 69% of the variance.

ADMINISTRATION: The scale was apparently included as part of the first of the two questionnaires passengers were asked to complete (Taylor 1994; Taylor and Claxton 1994). A high score on the scale suggested that a person was very upset about something.

MAJOR FINDINGS: Both studies examined various effects of flight delays. In particular, Taylor (1994) tested a model of the influence of delay duration on affective and evaluative reactions to the delay. Among the significant findings was that the longer the delay, the more a consumer feels **anxious** and uneasy.

Taylor and Claxton (1994) investigated the degree to which a flight delay can change the relative importance of service criteria in terms of their impact on performance judgments in a compensatory evaluation model. The findings did not indicate that the delayed passengers were significantly more **anxious** than those passengers whose flights were not delayed. However, the authors admitted that the scale's low reliability could have contributed to this unexpected finding.

#24 *Anxious*

COMMENTS: Depending on which items are used, this scale may have a problem with internal consistency. Further testing is necessary to determine if some items should not be used (e.g., #2).

REFERENCES:
Taylor, Shirley (1994), "Waiting for Service: The Relationship Between Delays and Evaluations of Service," *JM*, 58 (April), 56–69.

———— and John D. Claxton (1994), "Delays and the Dynamics of Service Evaluations," *JAMS*, 22 (Summer), 254–64.

SCALE ITEMS:*

Not at all :___:___:___:___:___:___:___: Very
       1   2   3   4   5   6   7

1. Anxious
2. Excited
3. Uneasy
4. Unsettled
5. Uncertain

*Taylor (1994) used items 1, 3, 4, and 5. Taylor and Claxton (1994) used items 1–3.

SCALE NAME: Arousal

SCALE DESCRIPTION: Five unipolar items with a seven-point response format purported to measure a person's perceived state of psychological and physiological activation. The scale is theorized to vary from sleep at one extreme to frenzied excitement at the other. Two versions were used by Broach, Page, and Wilson (1995): one to measure arousal before the experimental manipulation (*prior arousal*) and one to measure the effect of the treatment (*program arousal*).

SCALE ORIGIN: Broach, Page, and Wilson (1995) stated that the items for the scale were selected from Averill's (1975) semantic atlas of emotional words. However, use of the terms as a set in a summated format appears to be original to their own study. The scale was pretested with approximately 25 undergraduate students. The alphas for the version used with four different programs ranged from .91 to .98.

SAMPLES: Data were gathered by Broach, Page, and Wilson (1995) from students enrolled in undergraduate marketing or communications classes at a major Midwestern U.S. university. A set of 20 students evenly split on gender were placed in each of four treatment conditions, for a total of **80** subjects. Students received a nominal financial compensation for their participation, and the 11 subjects who guessed the study's purpose were replaced.

RELIABILITY: Alphas ranging from **.92** to **.96** (*prior arousal*) and **.93** to **.98** (*program arousal*) were reported for the scale (Broach, Page, and Wilson 1995).

VALIDITY: No examination of the scale's validity was reported by Broach, Page, and Wilson (1995).

ADMINISTRATION: The *prior arousal* version of the scale was completed by subjects before they were exposed to a 10-minute program and four 30-second commercials. Following that, subjects filled out the *program arousal* version of the scale (Broach, Page, and Wilson 1995). Higher scores on the scale indicated that subjects felt very energized at that moment.

MAJOR FINDINGS: The purpose of the experiment conducted by Broach, Page, and Wilson (1995) was to examine the impact of television programs on viewers' perceptions of ads. Among the findings was that a set of emotionally neutral commercials was perceived to be significantly more pleasant by those subjects who had just viewed high **arousal**, pleasant programs than by those who had seen high **arousal**, unpleasant programs.

REFERENCES:
Averill, James R. (1975), "A Semantic Atlas of Emotional Concepts," *JSAS Catalogue of Selected Documents in Psychology*, 330.
Broach, V. Carter, Jr., Thomas J. Page Jr., and R. Dale Wilson (1995), "Television Programming and Its Influence on Viewers' Perceptions of Commercials: The Role of Program Arousal and Pleasantness," *JA*, 24 (Winter), 45–54.

SCALE ITEMS:
Scale stem for version measuring *prior arousal*: "Presently, I feel..."
Scale stem for version measuring *program arousal*: "Did the TV program as a whole make you feel..."

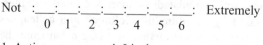

Not :___:___:___:___:___:___:___: Extremely
    0 1 2 3 4 5 6

1. Active   4. Lively
2. Excited   5. Activated
3. Stimulated

SCALE NAME: Arousal

SCALE DESCRIPTION: A six-item, seven-point semantic differential summated ratings scale measuring a person's arousal-related emotional reaction to some environmental stimulus.

SCALE ORIGIN: This scale is taken from Mehrabian and Russell's (1974) work. On the basis of previous work by others as well as their own research, they proposed that there are three factors that compose all emotional reactions to environmental stimuli. They referred to the three factors as pleasure, **arousal**, and dominance. A series of studies was used to develop measures of each factor. A study of the "final" set of items used 214 University of California undergraduates, each of whom used the scales to evaluate a different subset of six situations. (The analysis was based, therefore, on 1284 observations.) A principal components factor analysis with oblique rotation was used, and the expected three factors emerged. Pleasure, **arousal**, and dominance explained 27%, 23%, and 14% of the available evidence, respectively. Scores on the pleasure scale had correlations of −.07 and .03 with **arousal** and dominance, respectively. Dominance had a correlation of .18 with **arousal**.

SAMPLES: Donovan and colleagues (1994) gathered data from **30** female shoppers in each of two discount department stores. The stores were located near each other in a low- to middle-class socioeconomic neighborhood. Shoppers were approached at random on entering the store and asked if they would agree to participate. Only shoppers who were between 18 and 35 years of age were included to reduce the heterogeneity of the sample.

Holbrook and colleagues (1984) used **60** MBA students with a mean age of 25.6 years.

The number of "judges" used by Olney, Holbrook, and Batra (1991) was not stated. It appears, however, that it was a small group (e.g., 20) composed of MBA students.

Simpson, Horton, and Brown (1996) gathered data from **169** students from two neighboring Southern U.S. universities. The sample was evenly split on gender, with most respondents being European American (77.3%) and between 18 and 25 years of age (80%).

RELIABILITY:
.77 (Donovan et al. 1994)
.89 (Holbrook et al. 1984)
.97 (Olney, Holbrook, and Batra 1991)
.96 (Simpson, Horton, and Brown 1996)

VALIDITY: No specific examination of the scale's validity was reported in the articles. However, a principal components factor analysis performed by Donovan and colleagues (1994) indicated that all six of the arousal-related items loaded highest on the same dimension and low on one related to pleasure.

ADMINISTRATION: Donovan and colleagues (1994) had respondents complete the scale along with other measures after they had shopped in a store. The scale was self-administered along with several other measures in the middle of individual experimental sessions. Olney, Holbrook, and Batra (1991) and Simpson, Horton, and Brown (1996) used the scale after respondents had been exposed to ads. Lower scores on the scale suggested that respondents were stimulated by some specified stimulus, whereas higher scores implied that they were unaroused by the stimulus. Holbrook and colleagues (1984) noted that scores were normalized for each individual by subtracting the scale mean from the response to each item and then summing the corrected numeric responses.

MAJOR FINDINGS: The purpose of the study by Donovan and colleagues (1994) was to understand the emotions experienced while shopping and their affect on shopping behavior. The findings indicated that **arousal** was negatively associated with unplanned spending.

The study by Holbrook and colleagues (1984) examined the role played by emotions, performance, and personality in the enjoyment of games. In general, it was found that emotions depend on personality–game congruity, perceived complexity, and prior performance. Specifically, the **arousal** expressed while playing a video game was most significantly predicted by the perceived complexity of the game.

Olney, Holbrook, and Batra (1991) tested a hierarchical model of advertising effects on viewing time. Among the findings was that **arousal** appeared to be strongly related to ad viewing time.

The effect of male nudity in advertising was examined by Simpson, Horton, and Brown (1996). Not surprising, the results showed that women were more **aroused** by the male models than were male respondents, regardless of the level of dress. However, the level of dress associated with the most **arousal** for the female respondents was in the "suggestive" (no shirt) ad rather than the one with full nudity.

COMMENTS: As noted, this scale was developed along with two other scales, dominance and pleasure. Although scored separately, they are typically used together in a study.

See also Havlena and Holbrook (1986), Menon and Kahn (1995), and Mitchell, Kahn, and Knasko (1995).

REFERENCES:

Donovan, Robert J., John R. Rossiter, Gilian Marcoolyn, and Andrew Nesdale (1994), "Store Atmosphere and Purchasing Behavior," *JR*, 70 (3), 283–94.

Havlena, William J. and Morris B. Holbrook (1986), "The Varieties of Consumption Experience: Comparing Two Typologies of Emotion in Consumer Behavior," *JCR*, 13 (December), 394–404.

Holbrook, Morris B., Robert W. Chestnut, Terence A. Oliva, and Eric A. Greenleaf (1984), "Play as a Consumption Experience: The Roles of Emotions, Performance, and Personality in the Enjoyment of Games," *JCR*, 11 (September), 728–39.

Mehrabian, Albert and James A. Russell (1974), *An Approach to Environmental Psychology*. Cambridge, MA: The MIT Press.

Menon, Satya and Barbara E. Kahn (1995), "The Impact of Context on Variety Seeking in Product Choices," *JCR*, 22 (December), 285–95.

Mitchell, Deborah, Barbara E. Kahn, and Susan C. Knasko (1995), "There's Something in the Air: Effects of Congruent or Incongruent Ambient Odor on Consumer Decision Making," *JCR*, 22 (September), 229–38.

Olney, Thomas J., Morris B. Holbrook, and Rajeev Batra (1991), "Consumer Responses to Advertising: The Effects of Ad Content, Emotions, and Attitude Toward the Ad on Viewing Time," *JCR*, 17 (March), 440–53.

Simpson, Penny M., Steve Horton, and Gene Brown (1996), "Male Nudity in Advertisements: A Modified Replication and Extension of Gender and Product Effects," *JAMS*, 24 (Summer), 257–62.

SCALE ITEMS:*

Directions: Rate your emotions according to the way the _____ made you feel.

Stimulated :___:___:___:___:___:___:___: Relaxed
　　　　　　 7　6　5　4　3　2　1

Excited :___:___:___:___:___:___:___: Calm
　　　　　 7　6　5　4　3　2　1

#26 *Arousal*

Frenzied :___:___:___:___:___:___:___: Sluggish
              7 6 5 4 3 2 1

Jittery :___:___:___:___:___:___:___: Dull
              7 6 5 4 3 2 1

Wide-awake :___:___:___:___:___:___:___: Sleepy
              7 6 5 4 3 2 1

Aroused :___:___:___:___:___:___:___: Unaroused
              7 6 5 4 3 2 1

*This is a possible scale stem that can be used with the items.

SCALE NAME: Arousal

SCALE DESCRIPTION: Four six-point descriptors of a person's arousal-related emotional reaction to an environmental stimulus.

SCALE ORIGIN: This scale is based on Mehrabian and Russell's (1974) work but has been modified in a couple of ways. Mehrabian and Russell's (1974) scale had six bipolar adjectives (see #26), whereas this scale by Babin and Darden (1995) used three of their positive descriptors and one of their negative descriptors. The latter also used a six-point "felt" response scale, as noted subsequently.

SAMPLES: Data were gathered by Babin and Darden (1995) by intercepting shoppers as they left one of ten top stores in a major Southeastern U.S. regional mall. Respondents were interviewed one at a time, and a small incentive was provided for their participation. The sample was considered to be representative of the mall's shoppers. The analysis appears to have been based on data from **118** shoppers.

RELIABILITY: An alpha of **.86** was reported for the scale (Babin and Darden 1995). The construct reliability was .87, and variance extracted was .63.

VALIDITY: The results of a confirmatory factor analysis supported the measurement model in the study (Babin and Darden 1995). This provides some limited evidence of the scale's unidimensionality, as well as its convergent and discriminant validities.

ADMINISTRATION: The scale apparently was administered to respondents by interviewers along with many other items in a questionnaire (Babin and Darden 1995). Higher scores on the scale suggested that respondents were strongly aroused by some specified stimulus.

MAJOR FINDINGS: The purpose of the study by Babin and Darden (1995) was to examine the role of self-regulation as a moderator of relationships between shopping emotions and shopping experience evaluations. Among the findings was that **arousal** had significant positive impacts on resource expenditures and on utilitarian and hedonic shopping values.

REFERENCES:

Babin, Barry J. and William R. Darden (1995), "Consumer Self-Regulation in a Retail Environment," *JR*, 71 (1), 47–70.

Mehrabian, Albert and James A. Russell (1974), *An Approach to Environmental Psychology*. Cambridge, MA: The MIT Press.

SCALE ITEMS:*

Directions: Thinking back on how you felt while shopping in this store, please use the following scale to describe how you felt.

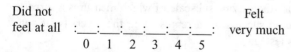

Did not
feel at all :___:___:___:___:___:___: Felt very much
          0   1   2   3   4   5

1. Aroused
2. Stimulated
3. Excited
4. Sleepy **(r)**

*Although the actual scale stem was not provided in the article, this reconstruction is based on the description that was given.

SCALE NAME: Arousal

SCALE DESCRIPTION: A three-item scale measuring a respondent's surprise-related emotional reaction to some specified stimulus. A five-point version was used by Mano and Oliver (1993), whereas Richins (1997) employed a slightly different four-point version.

SCALE ORIGIN: Although drawn in general from the work of Watson, Clark, and Tellegen (1988), the items used by Mano and Oliver (1993) appear to have been used first as a summated scale by Mano (1991). With 224 college students, the scale was reported to have an alpha of .72. A factor analysis did *not* find that the three items loaded on the same factor, though a cluster analysis grouped them together along with a couple of *elation*-related items.

Richins (1997) drew on terms in previous measures as well as her own series of studies to develop and refine several emotion-related scales into the CES (Consumption Emotion Set).

SAMPLES: Data were collected by Mano and Oliver (1993) from **118** undergraduate business students attending a Midwestern U.S. university.

Six studies were reported by Richins (1997) as part of the process of developing the CES, only one of which had reliability information for this scale. Two surveys were conducted in that study: Survey 1 was completed by **256** college students, and there were **194** student respondents to Survey 2.

RELIABILITY: Alphas of **.60** and **.81** were reported for the scale by Mano and Oliver (1993) and Richins (1997), respectively.

VALIDITY: The validity of the scale was not specifically addressed by Mano and Oliver (1993). Richins (1997) did not directly examine the validity of her scale either. A great deal of effort was expended, however, in a creative use of MDS (multi-dimensional scaling) to note whether the items that composed each scale clustered together.

ADMINISTRATION: The scale was part of a longer questionnaire self-administered by students in a classroom (Mano and Oliver 1993). In the studies performed by Richins (1997), particularly Studies 4 and 5, the scale was just part of a larger instrument that contained many emotion-related measures. A high score suggested that the respondent was feeling surprised by some stimulus.

MAJOR FINDINGS: Mano and Oliver (1993) examined the dimensionality and causal structure of product evaluation, affect, and satisfaction. Among the many findings involving the **arousal** emotion was that it was significantly greater for subjects in a high-involvement manipulation.

On the basis of a review of previously developed measures of emotion, Richins (1997) conducted six studies with the purpose of producing a set of scales particularly suited for assessing consumption experiences. The CES instrument was a result of the studies, one subscale of which measures a surprise type of **arousal.** In general, the instrument was more successful in representing the diversity of consumption emotions than were the other instruments tested.

COMMENTS: See also Oliver, Rust, and Varki (1997) for a two-item version of the scale.

REFERENCES:
Mano, Haim (1991), "The Structure and Intensity of Emotional Experiences: Method and Context Convergence," *Multivariate Behavioral Research*, 26 (3), 389–411.
——— and Richard L. Oliver (1993), "Assessing the Dimensionality and Structure of the Consumption Experience: Evaluation, Feeling, and Satisfaction," *JCR*, 20 (December), 451–66.

Oliver, Richard L., Roland T. Rust, and Sajeev Varki (1997), "Customer Delight: Foundations, Findings, and Managerial Insight," *JR*, 73 (3), 311–36.

Richins, Marsha L. (1997), "Measuring Emotions in the Consumption Experience," *JCR*, 24 (September), 127–46.

Watson, David, Lee Anna Clark, and Auke Tellegen (1988), "Development and Validation of Brief Measures of Positive and Negative Affect: The PANAS Scales," *Journal of Personality and Social Psychology*, 54 (6), 1063–70.

SCALE ITEMS:*

Not at all   Very much

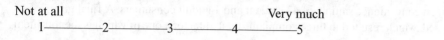

1. Aroused
2. Astonished
3. Surprised
4. Amazed

*The response scale shown is that used by Mano and Oliver (1993). They used the first three items. In contrast, Richins (1997) used items 2, 3, and 4 with a four-point response scale anchored by *not at all* and *strongly*.

SCALE NAME: Attitude Toward Complaining (Personal Norms)

SCALE DESCRIPTION: A multi-item, Likert-type scale measuring a consumer's personal belief that consumers should complain after a dissatisfying transaction has occurred. Richins (1983) used a four-item, five-point scale, and Singh (1990; Singh and Wilkes 1996) used a five-item, six-point scale. Although the two scales are not exactly the same, they have two items in common and appear to measure the same construct.

SCALE ORIGIN: The origin of the scale used by Richins (1983) is provided in Richins (1982), which shares the same database. Thirty-one items were generated on the basis of depth interviews with 16 consumers and tested using a convenience sample of 43 student and 14 adult consumers. A final group of 15 items was factor analyzed, which resulted in three complaint-related factors, one of which is the four-item scale discussed here.

Singh (1990; Singh and Wilkes 1996) modified Richins's version of the scale: Three items were added and two were dropped. Two of the three items added by Singh were slight modifications of items used in the ten-item measure described by Day (1984).

SAMPLES: The sample used by Richins (1982, 1983) was composed of respondents from one of three groups: 400 questionnaires were mailed to a random sample of residents of a Western standard metropolitan statistical area, 212 were mailed to members of a consumer protection group residing in the same area, and 198 were sent to people who had registered a complaint with either the government or a private consumer protection group in the past year. After this mailing and a reminder postcard, **356** usable forms were returned for analysis.

Data were collected from four samples by Singh (1988, 1990; Singh and Wilkes 1996). Four slightly different survey instruments were used that varied in the dissatisfying experience to which they referred. One thousand households were sent a questionnaire for each of the four service categories studied: car repairs, grocery stores, medical care, and banking. Response rates were estimated to be greater than 50% for each category, given that only approximately 30% of the random samples had dissatisfying experiences worthy of reporting on a questionnaire. Ultimately, usable data ranged from **116** respondents in the repair service sample to **125** in the medical care sample. Detailed demographic information for each of the four samples was provided in the article. The profiles of the four samples varied somewhat because the instrument itself indicated that the questionnaire was to be completed by the person in the household who dealt most with the specified service category. For example, men mostly filled out the questionnaire regarding auto repair (67%), whereas women generally filled out the one pertaining to grocery shopping (73%).

RELIABILITY: Alphas of **.62** and **.67** were reported by Richins (1983) and Singh (1990), respectively. The following alphas were reported by Singh and Wilkes (1996): **.73** (car repair), **.81** (medical care), and **.77** (banking services).

VALIDITY: Information regarding the unidimensionality of the scale used by Richins (1983) was provided in Richins (1982), as described above in the "Scale Origin" section.

Singh (1990) factor analyzed eight items: five from his version of this scale and three items from the Societal Benefits version of the scale. A two-factor structure with negligible cross-loadings resulted.

ADMINISTRATION: The scale was self-administered in mail surveys along with several other measures. Lower scores on the scale suggested that respondents perceived complaining to be an acceptable and justified behavior, whereas higher scores implied that respondents thought it was inappropriate to complain.

MAJOR FINDINGS: The study by Richins (1983) reported on the construction of consumer assertiveness and aggressiveness scales. Furthermore, the findings indicated that consumers can be divided into four categories depending on the strategies they use to interact with marketers and their representatives: consumers high on both traits, low on both traits, and low on one trait and high on the other. Those consumers who perceived **complaining to be the most acceptable** were also the most aggressive, whereas those who thought it was **the least appropriate** were low on aggressiveness and assertiveness.

In a detailed study of consumer complaint behavior, Singh (1990) concluded that there were four consumer clusters with distinct response styles: passives, voicers, irates, and activists. Profiles were developed for each cluster. Activists were described as being the group with the most positive **attitude about complaining due to personal norms**, whereas the passives had the least positive attitude.

Building on the previous studies, Singh and Wilkes (1996) proposed a model of consumer complaint responses and tested a portion of it. Among their findings was that prior complaining experience had a significant positive relationship with **attitude toward complaining**, regardless of the service category involved.

REFERENCES:

Day, Ralph L. (1984), "Modeling Choices Among Alternative Responses to Dissatisfaction," in *Advances in Consumer Research*, Vol. 11, Tom Kinnear, ed. Provo, UT: Association for Consumer Research, 496–99.

Richins, Marsha L. (1982), "An Investigation of Consumers' Attitudes Toward Complaining," in *Advances in Consumer Research*, Vol. 9, Andrew Mitchell, ed. Ann Arbor, MI: Association for Consumer Research, 502–506.

———— (1983), "An Analysis of Consumer Interaction Styles in the Marketplace," *JCR*, 10 (June), 73–82.

Singh, Jagdip (1988), "Consumer Complaint Intentions and Behaviors: Definitional and Taxonomical Issues," *JM*, 52 (January), 93–107.

———— (1990), "A Typology of Consumer Dissatisfaction Response Styles," *JR*, 66 (Spring), 57–97.

———— and Robert E. Wilkes (1996), "When Consumers Complain: A Path Analysis of the Key Antecedents of Consumer Compliant Response Estimates," *JAMS*, 24 (Fall), 350–65.

SCALE ITEMS:*

Strongly agree	Agree	Neutral	Disagree	Strongly disagree
1—————	—2—————	—3—————	—4—————	—5

1. Most people don't make enough complaints to businesses about unsatisfactory products.

2. I feel a sense of accomplishment when I have managed to get a complaint to a store taken care of satisfactorily.

3. People are bound to end up with unsatisfactory products once in a while so they shouldn't complain {about them}. **(r)**

4. It bothers me quite a bit if I don't complain about an unsatisfactory product {when I know I should}.

5. It sometimes feels good to get my dissatisfaction and frustration with the product off my chest by complaining.

6. I often complain when I'm dissatisfied with business or products because I feel it is my duty to do so.

7. I don't like people who complain to stores because usually their complaints are unreasonable. **(r)**

*Richins (1982, 1983) used items 1, 2, and the long versions of 3 and 4. Singh (1990; Singh and Wilkes 1996) used a six-point scale with items 5, 6, 7, and the short versions of 3 and 4.

SCALE NAME: Attitude Toward Cosmetic Pharmaceuticals

SCALE DESCRIPTION: Four five-point Likert-type statements that measure the attitude a physician has about the development of cosmetic pharmaceuticals, with a special emphasis on the value the products have for his or her patients.

SCALE ORIGIN: Although the source of the scale is not explicitly stated by Petroshius, Titus, and Hatch (1995), it appears to be original to their study.

SAMPLES: Data were gathered by Petroshius, Titus, and Hatch (1995) by conducting a survey of physicians in the Midwestern United States. The questionnaires were delivered by pharmaceutical representatives to 250 physicians during their normal visits. Respondents could either mail in the completed forms or have the reps pick them up later. Usable forms were received from **143** physicians (73% men) who varied in age, experience, and type of practice. The largest specialty represented in the sample was dermatology (52%), which was purposeful given the objectives of the study.

RELIABILITY: An alpha of **.76** was reported for the scale by Petroshius, Titus, and Hatch (1995).

VALIDITY: No examination of the scale's validity was reported by Petroshius, Titus, and Hatch (1995).

ADMINISTRATION: The scale was self-administered by the physicians along with the other measures in the questionnaire (Petroshius, Titus, and Hatch 1995). Higher scores on the scale indicated that the responding physicians had very positive attitudes about the development of cosmetic pharmaceutical products.

MAJOR FINDINGS: Petroshius, Titus, and Hatch (1995) studied physician attitudes toward the advertising of prescription drugs, particularly cosmetic pharmaceuticals, and the effect of these attitudes on other attitudes and behaviors. The findings indicated that one of the most influential effects on a physician's responsiveness to patients' requests for specific medication was the physician's **attitude toward cosmetic pharmaceuticals**.

REFERENCES:

Petroshius, Susan M., Philip A. Titus, and Kathryn J. Hatch (1995), "Physician Attitudes Toward Pharmaceutical Drug Advertising," *JAR*, 35 (November/December), 41–51.

SCALE ITEMS:

Strongly   Strongly
disagree   :___:___:___:___:___: agree

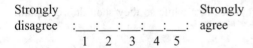
         1   2   3   4   5

1. I'm glad to see that pharmaceutical companies are developing more products associated with cosmetic conditions (e.g., aging skin, hair loss).

2. In general, the new cosmetic pharmaceutical products are worthwhile for my patients.

3. I don't believe that cosmetic problems are very important health issues. **(r)**

4. I believe that the current cosmetic pharmaceutical products are valuable and necessary for my patients.

SCALE NAME: Attitude Toward Coupon Use

SCALE DESCRIPTION: Three five-point rating scales purporting to capture a consumer's attitude toward the use of coupons for grocery products.

SCALE ORIGIN: The source of the scale is not specified by Mittal (1994), but it appears to be original to his study.

SAMPLES: Mittal (1994) gathered data from female members of six voluntary organizations, as well as from mall intercepts. A total of **184** provided complete survey questionnaires. Most of the respondents were white (85%), married (71%), and were at least 35 years of age (63%). Although it did not mirror the U.S. population, the sample included a wide variety of demographic categories.

RELIABILITY: The construct reliability (LISREL) was reported to be **.91** (Mittal 1994).

VALIDITY: The validity of the scale was not specifically addressed by Mittal (1994), except to say that the tests that were conducted provided support for discriminant validity.

ADMINISTRATION: The scale was part of a larger self-administered mail survey instrument (Mittal 1994). Higher scores on the scale indicated that respondents had more positive attitudes toward the use of coupons in supermarkets.

MAJOR FINDINGS: The study by Mittal (1994) proposed that demographics are poor predictors of coupon usage; instead he illustrated the value of three layers of mediating variables. Not surprisingly, one of the strongest effects involved **coupon use attitudes**, such that it had a positive relationship with the perceived economic benefits of using coupons.

REFERENCES:
Mittal, Banwari (1994), "An Integrated Framework for Relating Diverse Consumer Characteristics to Supermarket Coupon Redemption," *JMR*, 31 (November), 533–44.

SCALE ITEMS:

1. Overall, do you like or dislike using coupons?

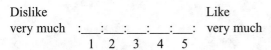

Dislike   Like
very much   :___:___:___:___:___: very much
               1   2   3   4   5

2. Personally for me, using coupons for supermarket products is or would be:

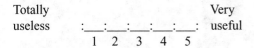

Totally   Very
useless   :___:___:___:___:___: useful
               1   2   3   4   5

3. Taking everything into account, do you consider using coupons for supermarket shopping foolish or wise?

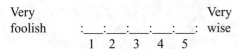

Very   Very
foolish   :___:___:___:___:___: wise
              1   2   3   4   5

SCALE NAME: Attitude Toward Drug Use

SCALE DESCRIPTION: Five five-point semantic differentials measuring a person's feelings about using drugs.

SCALE ORIGIN: Schoenbachler and Whittler (1996) did not specify the source of the scale, but it is likely to have been original to their study.

SAMPLES: Data were collected by Schoenbachler and Whittler (1996) from a sample of **371** seventh- and eight-grade students from a metropolitan middle school. No other information was provided about the sample.

RELIABILITY: An alpha of **.96** was reported for the scale (Schoenbachler and Whittler 1996).

VALIDITY: No examination of the scale's validity was reported by Schoenbachler and Whittler (1996).

ADMINISTRATION: The subjects completed the scale as part of a larger instrument they filled out after being exposed to an experimental stimulus (Schoenbachler and Whittler 1996). As calculated by those authors, lower scores on the scale suggested that respondents had more positive attitudes toward drug usage.

MAJOR FINDINGS: The purpose of the experiment by Schoenbachler and Whittler (1996) was to examine threat appeal advertising using the *ordered protection model*. As hypothesized, a social threat appeared to produce a significantly worse **attitude toward using drugs** than a physical threat.

REFERENCES:
Schoenbachler, Denise D. (1997), personal correspondence.
—— and Tommy E. Whittler (1996), "Adolescent Processing of Social and Physical Threat Communications," *JA*, 25 (Winter), 37–54.

SCALE ITEMS:*
DIRECTIONS: Recently, several experts have said the war on drugs should focus on drug use prevention.

"For me, using drugs would be..."

| Extremely pleasant | :___:___:___:___:___: | Extremely unpleasant |
| 1 2 3 4 5 | | |

| Extremely good | :___:___:___:___:___: | Extremely bad |
| 1 2 3 4 5 | | |

| Extremely valuable | :___:___:___:___:___: | Extremely worthless |
| 1 2 3 4 5 | | |

| Extremely favorable | :___:___:___:___:___: | Extremely unfavorable |
| 1 2 3 4 5 | | |

| Extremely acceptable | :___:___:___:___:___: | Extremely unacceptable |
| 1 2 3 4 5 | | |

*The scale stem and directions were provided by Schoenbachler (1997).

SCALE NAME: Attitude Toward New Uses for Products

SCALE DESCRIPTION: Four bipolar adjectives to measure a person's attitude toward the appropriateness of a particular established product being used for some (specified) new and different purpose.

SCALE ORIGIN: The scale is apparently original to the study by Wansink (1994). Wansink and Ray (1996) substituted a new item for one of the four used by Wansink (1994).

SAMPLES: Data were gathered for Study 1 by Wansink (1994) from eight parent–teacher associations (PTAs) in the New England area of the United States. A $6 donation was made to the organizations for each of the **293** people who volunteered. A majority of these people were between the ages of 30 and 45 years (77%) and did not work outside the home (52%). In Study 2, **211** parents from PTAs were recruited.

Similarly, Wansink and Ray (1996) collected data from **195** members of PTAs, and $6 was given to the respective organizations for each completion. All of the subjects were women, and the majority (84%) were between the ages of 30 to 45 years and were not employed outside the home (82%).

RELIABILITY: An alpha of **.91** (Study 1) was reported for the scale by Wansink (1994). (No alpha for Study 2 was reported.) Wansink and Ray (1996) reported an alpha of **.92** for their use of the scale.

VALIDITY: No examination of the scale's validity was reported in either study.

ADMINISTRATION: Respondents filled out the scale, along with other measures, as part of larger self-administered questionnaires after they were exposed to experimental stimuli (Wansink 1994; Wansink and Ray 1996). Higher scores on the scale suggested that respondents had a positive attitude toward the specified mature product being used for new purposes.

MAJOR FINDINGS: The two studies reported by Wansink (1994) investigated the effect of advertised product features on substitution-in-use decisions and how those features moderated the impact of comparison ads. Among the findings of the two studies was that when products were similar, distinct attribute claims produced better **attitudes toward new product uses** than common attribute claims.

The experiment conducted by Wansink and Ray (1996) examined how advertising can best influence consumers to use a mature brand in new situations. As hypothesized, ads showing congruent uses of a brand were associated with better **attitudes toward the new uses** than were ads featuring incongruent uses.

REFERENCES:
Wansink, Brian (1994), "Advertising's Impact on Category Substitution," *JMR*, 31 (November), 505–15.
——— and Michael L. Ray (1996), "Advertising Strategies to Increase Usage Frequency," *JM*, 60 (January), 31–46.

SCALE ITEMS:

1. Bad :___:___:___:___:___:___:___: Good
           1   2   3   4   5   6   7

2. Unappealing :___:___:___:___:___:___:___: Appealing
           1   2   3   4   5   6   7

3. Inappropriate :___:___:___:___:___:___: Appropriate
               1   2   3   4   5   6   7

4. Unreasonable :___:___:___:___:___:___: Reasonable
              1   2   3   4   5   6   7

5. Incongruent :___:___:___:___:___:___: Congruent
            1   2   3   4   5   6   7

Wansink (1994): 1–4; 9-point
Wansink and Ray (1996): 1, 2, 4, 5; 7-point

SCALE NAME: Attitude Toward Nicotine Patch

SCALE DESCRIPTION: Six seven-point statements purported to measure a smoker's attitude toward a nicotine patch, particularly as it relates to certain behavioral intentions such as using it and recommending it to others.

SCALE ORIGIN: The source of the scale used by Keller and Block (1996) was not cited, which may indicate that the scale is original to their study.

SAMPLES: Data for the experiment run by Keller and Block (1996) came from **97** smokers who were recruited from a pool of students at a large Eastern U.S. university. They had smoked for an average of 4.2 years, a majority (62%) of them claimed to have suffered from smoking side effects, and most (73%) of them had tried to quit at least once.

RELIABILITY: An alpha of **.90** was reported for the scale (Keller and Block 1996).

VALIDITY: No examination of the scale's validity was reported by Keller and Block (1996).

ADMINISTRATION: The scale was self-administered by students, along with other measures, after they had been exposed to a pamphlet on smoking (Keller and Block 1996). Higher scores on the scale indicated that respondents had a positive attitude toward the nicotine patch, such that they are not only likely to use it themselves, but recommend it to others.

MAJOR FINDINGS: The experiment conducted by Keller and Block (1996) investigated the conditions under which information that stimulates fear is likely to be effective. Among the many findings was that fear arousal did not have a significant direct effect on **attitude toward the nicotine patch**, but instead, it stimulated elaboration on the part of the message that affects attitude.

REFERENCES:
Keller, Punam Anand (1997), personal correspondence.
———— and Lauren Goldberg Block (1996), "Increasing the Persuasiveness of Fear Appeals: The Effect of Arousal and Elaboration," *JCR*, 22 (March), 448–59.

SCALE ITEMS:*
1. How likely are you to follow the recommendations to stop smoking by using the patch?
2. How likely are you to buy the patch?
3. How likely are you to recommend the patch to a friend?
4. How likely are you to discuss the patch with a friend?

Very unlikely :___:___:___:___:___:___:___: Very likely
               1   2   3   4   5   6   7

5. How interested are you in learning more about the patch?

Not interested :___:___:___:___:___:___:___: Very interested
               1   2   3   4   5   6   7

6. Would you like to receive an additional information sheet on the patch?

Definitely no :___:___:___:___:___:___:___: Definitely yes
              1   2   3   4   5   6   7

*The items are described generally in Keller and Block (1996), but the exact phrasing comes from Keller (1997). The first four items use the *unlikely/likely* response scale.

SCALE NAME: Attitude Toward Ordering Option

SCALE DESCRIPTION: A four-item, seven-point semantic differential scale measuring a person's evaluation of a specified method of placing an order. As described subsequently, the setting used by Dabholkar (1994) was ordering at a fast-food restaurant, and two options were compared: touch-screen ordering versus verbally placing the order with an employee.

SCALE ORIGIN: The origin of the scale appears to be Dabholkar (1994). Refinement of the scale occurred with a pretest sample that consisted of 141 undergraduate students. A six-item version of the scale produced alphas of .90 for both the touch-screen and verbal options.

SAMPLES: The final sample used by Dabholkar (1994) was composed of **305** undergraduates attending a large university. The sample was 56.7% women, and the average age was almost 25 years. Data were collected in classrooms, and participation was voluntary.

RELIABILITY: Dabholkar (1994) reported construct reliabilities of **.91** and **.89** for the touch-screen and verbal versions of the scale, respectively.

VALIDITY: The validity of the scale was not explicitly addressed by Dabholkar (1994). However, results of a confirmatory factor analysis indicated that both versions of the scale were unidimensional.

ADMINISTRATION: The scale used by Dabholkar (1994) was only one of several in the questionnaire that was completed by respondents. Higher scores on the scale suggested better attitudes toward the specified method of ordering food.

MAJOR FINDINGS: The purpose of the study by Dabholkar (1994) was to integrate attitudinal and information-processing literatures to better understand the mental comparisons used by consumers to make choices. The results of the study provided strong support for the Expectancy Comparison Model, in which the choice is made by comparing expectancy value components across options before the formation of attitudes toward those options.

REFERENCES:

Dabholkar, Pratibha (1994), "Incorporating Choice into an Attitudinal Framework: Analyzing Models of Mental Comparison Processes," *JCR*, 21 (June), 100–118.

SCALE ITEMS:

DIRECTIONS: In the situation described, how would you describe your feelings toward using the _____ ordering option to order fast food?*

1. Bad   :___:___:___:___:___:___:___: Good
              1   2   3   4   5   6   7

2. Unpleasant   :___:___:___:___:___:___:___: Pleasant
              1   2   3   4   5   6   7

3. Harmful   :___:___:___:___:___:___:___: Beneficial
              1   2   3   4   5   6   7

4. Unfavorable   :___:___:___:___:___:___:___: Favorable
              1   2   3   4   5   6   7

*Either *touch screen* or *verbal* was placed in the blank. The following descriptors may have been used by Dabholkar (1994) instead of numbers (as shown here) on the graphic scales: 1 and 7 = extremely; 2 and 6 = quite; 3 and 5 = slightly; and 4 = neither.

SCALE NAME: Attitude Toward Political Candidates

SCALE DESCRIPTION: Nine seven-point semantic differentials that measure a person's attitude toward a specific political candidate.

SCALE ORIGIN: Pinkleton (1997) stated that he drew on several previous studies that also examined negative political advertising (e.g., Johnson-Cartee and Copeland 1991).

SAMPLES: The sample used by Pinkleton (1997) was primarily composed of communication and business undergraduate students attending a public university in the Southwestern United States. The sample apparently was composed of **165** students, approximately evenly split on gender, and all respondents were of legal voting age.

RELIABILITY: The internal consistency of the scale was examined four times in the study by Pinkleton (1997). Pretest and posttest alphas with the sponsor version of the scale were **.81** and **.90**, respectively. Likewise, the pretest and posttest alphas for the targeted candidate version of the scale were **.83** and **.87**, respectively.

VALIDITY: No specific examination of the scale's validity was reported by Pinkleton (1997).

ADMINISTRATION: Subjects completed the scale in the experiment by Pinkleton (1997) both before and after being exposed to negative, comparative political advertising stimuli. Higher scores on the scale suggested that people had a very positive attitude toward some specific political candidate.

MAJOR FINDINGS: The experiment conducted by Pinkleton (1997) examined the effects of negative, comparative advertising on evaluations of both sponsoring and targeted candidates, as well as on advertising attitudes. Among the findings was that a political ad containing the most negative information was associated with the greatest negative **attitude change toward the candidate**.

REFERENCES:

Johnson-Cartee, Karen S. and Gary A. Copeland (1991), *Negative Political Advertising: Coming of Age.* Hillsdale, NJ: Lawrence Erlbaum Associates.

Pinkleton, Bruce (1997), "The Effects of Negative Comparative Political Advertising on Candidate Evaluations and Advertising Evaluations: An Exploration," *JA*, 26 (Spring), 19–29.

———— (1999), personal correspondence.

SCALE ITEMS:*

DIRECTIONS: Please rate _____ on the following characteristics by circling the appropriate number:

Not
believable   :___:___:___:___:___:___:___: Believable

                  1   2   3   4   5   6   7

Unconcerned   :___:___:___:___:___:___:___: Concerned
                  1   2   3   4   5   6   7

Dishonest	:__:__:__:__:__:__:	Honest
	1 2 3 4 5 6 7	

Unintelligent	:__:__:__:__:__:__:	Intelligent
	1 2 3 4 5 6 7	

Unpersuasive	:__:__:__:__:__:__:	Persuasive
	1 2 3 4 5 6 7	

Insincere	:__:__:__:__:__:__:	Sincere
	1 2 3 4 5 6 7	

Unqualified	:__:__:__:__:__:__:	Qualified
	1 2 3 4 5 6 7	

Bad	:__:__:__:__:__:__:	Good
	1 2 3 4 5 6 7	

Unethical	:__:__:__:__:__:__:	Ethical
	1 2 3 4 5 6 7	

*The scale items and stem were provided by Pinkleton (1999). The candidate's name should be placed in the space.

SCALE NAME: Attitude Toward Store Background Music

SCALE DESCRIPTION: A three-item, seven-point Likert-type scale measuring a shopper's attitude toward the background music played in a store. Although the scale has been described as measuring "the store ambient factor" (Baker, Grewal, and Parasuraman 1994; Baker, Levy, and Grewal 1992), it is clear from an examination of the items that only the music aspect of the retail atmosphere is assessed.

SCALE ORIGIN: The scale used by Baker, Levy, and Grewal (1992) and Baker, Grewal, and Parasuraman (1994) was original to the former study (Baker 1993).

SAMPLES: The data analyzed by Baker, Levy, and Grewal (1992) came from an experiment using **147** undergraduate students. The study used a 2 (store ambient levels) $\times$ 2 (store social levels) between-subjects factorial design with between 35 and 39 subjects per cell.

Data were collected by Baker, Grewal, and Parasuraman (1994) in an experiment involving **297** subjects. The subjects were undergraduate students taking marketing classes at a large university.

RELIABILITY: Alphas of **.91** and **.90** were reported for the scale by Baker, Levy, and Grewal (1992) and Baker, Grewal, and Parasuraman (1994), respectively.

VALIDITY: No examination of the scale's validity was reported in either study. However, a sense of the scale's unidimensionality is provided by Baker, Grewal, and Parasuraman (1994), who state that the results of a principal components factor analysis conducted on items from this scale, as well as two others, supported a three-factor solution.

ADMINISTRATION: The scale was self-administered by subjects as part of larger questionnaires after they were exposed to experimental stimuli (Baker, Grewal, and Parasuraman 1994; Baker, Levy, and Grewal 1992). A high score on the scale indicated that a consumer had a positive opinion about a store's background music, whereas a low score suggested that a shopper considered it unpleasant and inappropriate.

MAJOR FINDINGS: The study by Baker, Levy, and Grewal (1992) examined the effects of two retail atmospheric factors—ambient and social cues—on respondents' pleasure, arousal, and shopping intentions. Measurement of **attitude toward background music** was used only a check on an experimental treatment, and indeed, the results indicated that the manipulation was perceived as intended.

Baker, Grewal, and Parasuraman (1994) investigated how retail store environment affects consumers' attitudes about service and product quality. The results indicated that **attitude toward background music** and social factors significantly influenced store images, but a design factor did not.

COMMENTS: Subjects responded to the scale items after viewing a video of a retail interior. Some slight modification in the wording of items #1 and #2 is necessary if the scale is used with actual shoppers, as noted subsequently.

REFERENCES:
Baker, Julie (1993), personal correspondence.
———, Dhruv Grewal, and A. Parasuraman (1994), "The Influence of Store Environment on Quality Inferences and Store Image," *JAMS*, 22 (4), 328–39.
———, Michael Levy, and Dhruv Grewal (1992), "An Experimental Approach to Making Retail Store Environmental Decisions," *JR*, 68 (Winter), 445–60.

#37 *Attitude Toward Store Background Music*

SCALE ITEMS: *

Strongly   Strongly
disagree   :___:___:___:___:___:___:___: agree
         1   2   3   4   5   6   7

1. The background music (in the video) would make shopping in this store pleasant.

2. (If I shopped at this store,) the background music (that I heard on the video would bother) bothered me. **(r)**

3. The background music was appropriate.

*If the items were used with actual shoppers, the phrases in parentheses would not be necessary.

SCALE NAME: Attitude Toward the Act (Semantic Differential)

SCALE DESCRIPTION: Several bipolar adjectives presumed to measure the subject's overall evaluation of a purchase activity. The various versions of the scale discussed here have between three and five items. They are similar, in that they have at least two items in common with every other version and most share three items in common with at least one other scale usage. Although all users did not describe the number of points on their scales, it is clear that the majority employed seven-point scales.

SCALE ORIGIN: Oliver and Bearden (1985) cited Ajzen and Fishbein (1980) as the source of their scale. Although none of the authors of the other studies was as explicit in describing the origins of their measures, the overlap between their sets of items and those offered in Ajzen and Fishbein (1980, pp. 261, 262, and 267) is too similar to be coincidental. Two of the items that follow (1 and 4) are also among the set of items recommended by Osgood, Suci, and Tannenbaum (1957) for measuring the evaluative dimension of semantic judgment.

SAMPLES: The data used by Allen, Machleit, and Kleine (1992) came from a stratified sample of people with diverse experience with blood donation. Nine hundred questionnaires were mailed, and **361** usable forms were returned. Because all respondents previously had donated blood, limited information was known about them and a comparison with nonrespondents was possible. Respondents were a little older, less likely to be men, and more likely to be heavier donors than nonrespondents were.

Bagozzi (1982) used **136** students, **7** faculty, and **27** staff members chosen from a variety of places and times at a university. A quota sample was used, in that recruitment for each category of respondent was halted when it reached the proportion characteristic of previous blood drives at the university. The sample included both genders.

The sample used by Gardner, Mitchell, and Russo (1985) was composed of **25** male and female volunteers on a university campus, most of whom were students or recent graduates.

Little is known about the sample used by Grossbart, Muehling, and Kangun (1986) beyond that it was composed of **111** undergraduate students randomly assigned to treatment conditions. The groups were described as similar in their product class experience and demographics.

Hastak (1990) used **160** undergraduate student subjects in a four-way (2 $\times$ 2 $\times$ 2 $\times$ 2) factorial design. There were 10 subjects per cell.

Mitchell (1986) used **69** students volunteers recruited from undergraduate business classes, each of whom were paid $4 for their participation. There were either 17 or 18 subjects in each of the four cells of the design.

Mitchell and Olson (1981) used **71** upperclass volunteers of both sexes from an introductory marketing course. Subjects were paid for participation in the study.

All that is known about the sample used by Muehling (1987) is that it was composed of **133** students randomly assigned to one of six treatment conditions.

The experiment conducted by Netemeyer and Bearden (1992) was based on data from a sample of **372** undergraduate students. They were randomly assigned to a 2 (informational influence) $\times$ 2 (normative influence) design. The sample was split approximately in half to test two different models of behavioral intention. Therefore, there were four cells per model tested with each cell having between 46 and 49 subjects.

Oliver and Bearden (1985) used data from **353** members of a bistate consumer panel who responded to two questionnaires and received a four-week supply of diet suppressant capsules between the two questionnaires. Panel members were selected to be representative of urban and suburban households with family incomes greater that $10,000 annually. Subjects were typically white (89%), female (56%), and had at least some education beyond high school (70%).

Raju and Hastak (1983) used **61** undergraduate student volunteers ranging in age from 19 to 23 years. Subjects were randomly assigned to one of three groups and paid $4 each for participating in the study.

Many samples of varying characteristics were used in the studies reported by Shimp and Sharma (1987), but the one in which this **attitude toward the act** scale was used had **145** college students, approximately 60% of whom were men and who had a mean age of 21.5 years.

RELIABILITY: LISREL estimates of scale reliability were **.95** in Bagozzi (1982) and **.86** in Oliver and Bearden (1985). Two models were tested by Netemeyer and Bearden (1992), and the alphas were separately calculated as **.90** and **.89**. The following alphas were reported in the other studies: **.72** (Allen, Machleit, and Kleine 1992); **.97** (Gardner, Mitchell, and Russo 1985); **.95** (Grossbart, Muehling, and Kangun 1986); greater than **.90** (Hastak 1990); **.85** and **.88** (Mitchell 1986); **.85** (Mitchell and Olson 1981); **.90** and **.95** (Muehling 1987); **.87** (Raju and Hastak 1983); and **.92** and **.90** (Shimp and Sharma 1987).

VALIDITY: Bagozzi (1981, 1982) provided some evidence of convergent validity for his six-item version of the scale. Using the same items as Bagozzi (1981, 1982), Allen, Machleit, and Kleine (1992) used LISREL to confirm the scale's unidimensionality. The scale was used by Shimp and Sharma (1987) to provide evidence of their CETSCALE's nomological validity. Beyond that, little or no direct testing of this scale's validity was clearly described in the other articles.

ADMINISTRATION: The following phrases were used in the cited studies to lead into the sets of bipolar adjectives: "Donating blood for me would be (is). . ." Bagozzi (1981, 1982); "Taking (this appetite suppressant) is. . ." (Oliver and Bearden 1985); and "From your perspective, buying foreign-made products is..." (Shimp and Sharma 1987). The typical scenario for administering the scale was as part of a larger questionnaire filled out by subjects after they were exposed to a product in an ad. Higher scores on the scale suggested that respondents had a positive attitude toward some act, such as purchasing a specified product, whereas low scores indicated that they had a bad attitude about it.

MAJOR FINDINGS: The study by Allen, Machleit, and Kleine (1992) examined whether emotions affect behavior through attitudes or instead are better viewed as having a separate and distinct impact. Among the many findings was that emotions can have a direct effect on behavior (e.g., donating blood) that is not captured by attitude (e.g., **attitude toward the act**.)

Using LISREL, Bagozzi (1982) found strong evidence that **attitude toward the act** influences behavioral intention but does not directly influence behavior. The results also indicated that the overall expectancy value judgment directly determines behavioral intentions and **attitude toward the act** but does not directly affect future behavior.

Gardner, Mitchell, and Russo (1985) conceptualized involvement as having two dimensions: intensity (amount of attention) and direction (type of processing strategy). They conducted an experiment that varied the direction component of involvement and noted its effect on **attitude toward the act** of purchasing and using the product. As hypothesized, those in the low involvement condition retained less correct brand knowledge than those in the high involvement condition but expressed more positive attitudes toward buying and using the brand.

The relative effectiveness of various comparative ads and noncomparative ads was examined by Grossbart, Muehling, and Kangun (1986). A confusing array of attitudinal effects were found, depending on the type of comparison made in the ads. **Attitude toward the act** of buying the advertised product was examined only as a covariate and was not found to have a significant effect on the findings.

Hastak (1990) reported on some effects of taking thought measurements immediately after ad exposure. The findings indicated that thought measurements could increase correlations between an expectancy value measure and other postexposure types of measures, such as **attitude toward the act.** The degree of the impact appeared to be affected by the product category and was especially greater for those subjects who were high in message response involvement.

The study by Mitchell (1986) examined the influence of the visual and verbal components of ads on attitudes toward the brand and the ad. It was found that affect-laden ads had a significant effect on both attitudes that was not attributable to product attribute beliefs. This visual manipulation was evaluated as having only a marginal effect on **attitude toward the act** of purchasing and using the product shown in the ad.

In a now classic study, Mitchell and Olson (1981) examined whether product attribute beliefs are the only determinants of brand attitude. Their results suggested that attitude toward the ad has its greatest effect on attitude toward the brand and **attitude toward the act** of purchasing but less of an impact on behavioral intentions. In contrast, **attitude toward the act** was found to be the major influence on behavioral intention, as predicted by Fishbein's theory.

Muehling (1987) tested the effect of five different comparative advertising treatment conditions on **attitude toward the acts** of purchasing the sponsor's brand and the competitor's brand. For each type of comparative advertisement tested, the attitude toward the ad had a significant, positive influence on attitude toward purchasing the sponsor's brand but no significant effect was found for attitude toward purchasing the competitor's brand.

Netemeyer and Bearden (1992) conducted an experiment to compare the causal structure and predictive ability of the models of behavioral intentions by Ajzen and Fishbein (1980) and Miniard and Cohen (1983). Some evidence was found that higher perceptions of information source expertise were associated with better **attitudes toward the act**, and this was especially true with Miniard and Cohen's model.

Oliver and Bearden (1985) examined a extension of the crossover path in Fishbein's behavioral intention model. Both **attitude toward the act** and the subjective norm were found to have a significant impact on behavioral intentions, with the impact of the former being much greater. The authors concluded that a person's attitude toward an act is strengthened the more the person believes that significant others also support it.

Raju and Hastak (1983) studied the influence of coupons on pretrial cognitive structure. Significant intercorrelations were found among **attitude toward the act** of buying the brand, attitude toward the brand, belief structure, and behavioral intentions. The results indicated that the magnitude of a coupon has a significant impact on behavioral intention but little if any effect on belief structure, attitude toward the brand, and attitude toward buying the brand.

The purpose of the studies described by Shimp and Sharma (1987) was to introduce the concept of consumer ethnocentrism and validate a scale for its measurement (CETSCALE). As part of the validation process, **attitude toward the act** of buying foreign-made products was found to be negatively related to consumer ethnocentrism.

COMMENTS: See also Haugtvedt and Wegener (1994) for a variation on the scale as used to measure attitude toward implementation of a new graduation testing procedure and attitude toward building more nuclear power plants.

REFERENCES:
Ajzen, Icek and Martin Fishbein (1980), *Understanding Attitudes and Predicting Social Behavior*. Englewood Cliffs, NJ: Prentice Hall.
Allen, Chris T., Karen A. Machleit, and Susan Schultz Kleine (1992), "A Comparison of Attitudes and Emotions as Predictors of Behavior at Diverse Levels of Behavioral Experience," *JCR*, 18 (March), 493–504.
Bagozzi, Richard P. (1981), "Attitudes, Intentions, and Behavior: A Test of Some Key Hypotheses," *Journal of Personality and Social Psychology*, 41 (4), 607–27.
——— (1982), "A Field Investigation of Causal Relations Among Cognitions, Affect, Intentions, and Behavior," *JMR*, 19 (November), 562–84.
Gardner, Meryl Paula, Andrew A. Mitchell, and J. Edward Russo (1985), "Low Involvement Strategies for Processing Advertisements," *JA*, 14 (2), 44–56.

Grossbart, Sanford, Darrel D. Muehling, and Norman Kangun (1986), "Verbal and Visual References to Competition in Comparative Advertising," *JA*, 15 (1), 10–23.

Hastak, Manoj (1990), "Does Retrospective Thought Measurement Influence Subsequent Measures of Cognitive Structure in an Advertising Context?" *JA*, 19 (3), 3–13.

Haugtvedt, Curtis P. and Duane T. Wegener (1994), "Message Order Effects in Persuasion: An Attitude Strength Perspective," *JCR*, 21 (June), 205–18.

Miniard, Paul W. and Joel B. Cohen (1983), "Modeling Personal and Normative Influences on Behavior," *JCR*, 10 (September), 169–80.

Mitchell, Andrew A. (1986), "The Effect of Verbal and Visual Components of Advertisements on Brand Attitudes and Attitude Toward the Advertisement," *JCR*, 13 (June), 12–24.

————— and Jerry C. Olson (1981), "Are Product Attribute Beliefs the Only Mediator of Advertising Effects on Brand Attitude?" *JMR*, 18 (August), 318–32.

Muehling, Darrel D. (1987), "Comparative Advertising: The Influence of Attitude-Toward-the-Ad on Brand Evaluation," *JA*, 16 (4), 43–49.

Netemeyer, Richard G. and William O. Bearden (1992), "A Comparative Analysis of Two Models of Behavioral Intention," *JAMS*, 20 (Winter), 49–59.

Oliver, Richard L. and William O. Bearden (1985), "Crossover Effects in the Theory of Reasoned Action: A Moderating Influence Attempt," *JCR*, 12 (December), 324–40.

Osgood, Charles E., George J. Suci, and Percy H. Tannenbaum (1957), *The Measurement of Meaning*. Urbana, IL: University of Illinois Press.

Raju, P.S. and Manoj Hastak (1983), "Pre-Trial Cognitive Effects of Cents-Off Coupons," *JA*, 12 (2), 24–33.

Shimp, Terence A. and Subhash Sharma (1987), "Consumer Ethnocentrism: Construction and Validation of the CETSCALE," *JMR*, 24 (August), 280–89.

SCALE ITEMS: *

1. Bad	1———2———3———4———5———6———7						Good
2. Foolish	1———2———3———4———5———6———7						Wise
3. Harmful	1———2———3———4———5———6———7						Beneficial
4. Unpleasant	1———2———3———4———5———6———7						Pleasant
5. Unsafe	1———2———3———4———5———6———7						Safe
6. Punishing	1———2———3———4———5———6———7						Rewarding

*The items used in particular studies are indicated with reference to their numbers above.

Allen, Machleit, and Kleine (1992): 1, 2, 4, 5, 6
Bagozzi (1982): 1, 2, 4, 5, 6
Gardner, Mitchell, and Russo (1985): 1–3
Grossbart, Muehling, and Kangun (1986): 1–3
Hastak (1990): 1–4
Mitchell (1986): 1–3
Mitchell and Olson (1981): 1–3
Muehling (1987): 1–3
Netemeyer and Bearden (1992): 1–3
Oliver and Bearden (1985): 1, 2, 4
Raju and Hastak (1983): 1–4
Shimp and Sharma (1987): 1–3

SCALE NAME: Attitude Toward the Bank

SCALE DESCRIPTION: Three seven-point items measuring the extent to which a consumer expresses a positive attitude and intention regarding a specified bank. The scale was referred to by Hui, Dubé, and Chebat (1997) as *approach behavior toward the organization.*

SCALE ORIGIN: Although not stated explicitly, it appears that the scale is original to the study by Hui, Dubé, and Chebat (1997).

SAMPLES: The data gathered by Hui, Dubé, and Chebat (1997) were collected from undergraduate business students at a Canadian university. The sample was composed of **116** subjects, with an average age of 24.3 years, and was almost evenly split on gender (59 men).

RELIABILITY: The alpha reported for the scale was **.84** (Hui, Dubé, and Chebat 1997).

VALIDITY: The confirmatory factor analysis conducted by Hui, Dubé, and Chebat (1997) on this scale, as well as two others in their study, provided evidence of the scale's unidimensionality and discriminant validity.

ADMINISTRATION: Subjects completed the scale along with other parts of a self-administered questionnaire after they were exposed to one of five experimental treatment groups (Hui, Dubé, and Chebat 1997). Higher scores on the scale indicated that respondents had a very positive attitude and intention regarding a specific bank.

MAJOR FINDINGS: Hui, Dubé, and Chebat (1997) examined the influence of music on consumers' responses to waiting for services. Among the findings was that **attitude and intention toward a bank** was influenced directly by affective responses to the service environment (generally) and the wait in line (specifically).

REFERENCES:
Hui, Michael K., Laurette Dubé, and Jean-Charles Chebat (1997), "The Impact of Music on Consumers' Reactions to Waiting for Services," *JR*, 73 (1), 87–104.

SCALE ITEMS:*
1. I like the bank.

Not at all :___:___:___:___:___:___:___: Very much
                 1   2   3   4   5   6   7

2. I will recommend the bank to my friends.

Certainly   Certainly
no   :___:___:___:___:___:___:___: yes
                1   2   3   4   5   6   7

3. I will stay a customer of the bank.

Very   Very
unlikely :___:___:___:___:___:___:___: likely
                1   2   3   4   5   6   7

SCALE NAME: Attitude Toward the Brand

SCALE DESCRIPTION: Five-item, seven-point Likert-type measure that provides an indication of a consumer's attitude about a specified brand and the act of purchasing the brand.

SCALE ORIGIN: Although not specifically stated as such, the scale appears to be original to the study by Putrevu and Lord (1994).

SAMPLES: Data were gathered by Putrevu and Lord (1994) from students in an introductory undergraduate marketing course taught at a Northeastern U.S. university. Apparently, usable data were collected from **100** students who voluntarily participated for extra credit in the course. Demographic data about the respondents were collected but were not described in the article.

RELIABILITY: Putrevu and Lord (1994) reported an alpha of **.87** for the scale.

VALIDITY: No evidence of the scale's validity was presented in the article by Putrevu and Lord (1994). The unidimensionality of the scale is suspect because two of the items (1 and 2) are measures of a person's attitude toward the act of purchasing the product, which has been treated as distinct from a person's attitude toward the brand itself (e.g., Bagozzi 1982; Mitchell and Olson 1981).

ADMINISTRATION: The scale was administered to students by Putrevu and Lord (1994) along with other measures as part of an in-class experiment. Higher scores on the scale indicated that a consumer had a favorable view of both the specified brand and the act of buying it.

MAJOR FINDINGS: Putrevu and Lord (1994) examined the relative effectiveness of comparative and noncomparative advertising for products characterized by varying degrees of affective and cognitive involvement. The findings indicated that more positive **brand attitudes** were associated with comparative ads for those products that evoked affective and cognitive motivations simultaneously.

REFERENCES:

Bagozzi, Richard P. (1982), "A Field Investigation of Causal Relations Among Cognitions, Affect, Intentions, and Behavior," *JMR*, 19 (November), 562–84.

Mitchell, Andrew A. and Jerry C. Olson (1981), "Are Product Attribute Beliefs the Only Mediator of Advertising Effects on Brand Attitude?" *JMR*, 18 (August), 318–32.

Putrevu, Sanjay and Kenneth R. Lord (1994), "Comparative and Noncomparative Advertising: Attitudinal Effects Under Cognitive and Affective Involvement Conditions," *JA*, 23 (June), 77–90.

SCALE ITEMS:

Disagree :__:__:__:__:__:__:__: Agree
           1 2 3 4 5 6 7

1. The decision to buy *(brand)* is foolish. **(r)**

2. Buying *(brand)* is a good decision.

3. I think *(brand)* is a satisfactory brand.

4. I think *(brand)* has a lot of beneficial characteristics.

5. I have a favorable opinion of *(brand)*.

SCALE NAME: Attitude Toward the Brand

SCALE DESCRIPTION: Five-item, seven-point semantic differential scale purported to measure a consumer's evaluation of a product. Depending on the mix of items used, the scale has some similarity to measures of purchase intention, as well as of product quality.

SCALE ORIGIN: Although not specifically stated in the article, the scale appears to be original to Peracchio and Meyers-Levy (1994). Some modifications were made in later uses of the scale by Meyers-Levy and Peracchio (1995) and Peracchio and Meyers-Levy (1997).

SAMPLES: The scale was used in two experiments conducted by Meyers-Levy and Peracchio (1995). The first used **46** students enrolled in marketing classes, whereas the second had **166** students.

Data in the study by Peracchio and Meyers-Levy (1994) were collected from **493** college students in marketing classes. Subjects were assigned randomly to treatments, and the experiments were run during class time. No other information about the sample was provided.

Peracchio and Meyers-Levy (1997) conducted two experiments in which the scale was used. Subjects were described as being students from marketing classes, with **59** in Experiment 1 and **128** in Experiment 2.

RELIABILITY: Alphas of **.71** (Experiment 1, bicycle), **.91** (Experiment 2, bicycle), and **.92** (Experiment 2, clothing) were reported for the scale by Meyers-Levy and Peracchio (1995). An alpha of **.89** was reported for scale for both jeans and beer by Peracchio and Meyers-Levy (1994). Peracchio and Meyers-Levy (1997) reported alphas of **.85** and **.92** for evaluations of beer and ski products, respectively. No alphas for the scale as used in their second experiment were reported.

VALIDITY: No specific evidence of the scale's validity was provided in any of the studies. In terms of dimensionality, it was stated by Peracchio and Meyers-Levy (1994, p. 196) that for "both the beer and the jeans, the five items loaded on single factors."

ADMINISTRATION: In each of the studies, the self-administered scale was completed by subjects after they were exposed to experimental stimuli. The first study reported by Peracchio and Meyers-Levy (1997) was distinct from the others, however, in that stimuli were presented and responses were recorded on PCs rather than on paper. Higher scores on the scale suggested that respondents had a positive evaluation of some particular product to which they had been exposed.

MAJOR FINDINGS: Meyers-Levy and Peracchio (1995) examined the relative persuasiveness of color versus black-and-white ads. Among the findings was that, when an ad was very demanding to process, better **brand attitudes** were associated with the black-and-white ad than with the color ad.

The study by Peracchio and Meyers-Levy (1994) investigated the effect of cropping objects in print ads on product evaluations. The results indicated that cropping-induced ambiguity can enhance viewer **brand attitudes** if they are motivated to engage in closure of the ambiguous object and if the cropped object is not directly relevant to ad claims.

Two experiments conducted by Peracchio and Meyers-Levy (1997) were used to study how ad execution variables intended to stimulate persuasion can affect the resources required to process an ad in varying motivation conditions. Among the findings was that, in the context of factual ad copy (versus narrative), **brand attitudes** were more favorable when the layout had the picture and the copy separated (versus integrated).

COMMENTS: Despite the limited evidence that suggests the scale is internally consistent and unidimensional, more rigorous testing may show that it is tapping into two or more factors. It is not clear except in some general sense what high scores on this scale mean: It could mean that consumers are willing to purchase the item, it could mean that they believe the product is of high quality, or it could mean they think it represents a good value for the money. These have been considered as separate constructs in prior research, and strong consideration should be given to measuring them with different scales so it is clearer to researchers what a score on the scale means.

REFERENCES:

Meyers-Levy, Joan and Laura A. Peracchio (1995), "Understanding the Effects of Color: How the Correspondence Between Available and Required Resources Affects Attitudes," *JCR*, 22 (September), 121–38.

Peracchio, Laura A. and Joan Meyers-Levy (1994), "How Ambiguous Cropped Objects in Ad Photos Can Affect Product Evaluations," *JCR*, 21 (June), 190–204.

———— and ———— (1997), "Evaluating Persuasion-Enhancing Techniques from a Resource-Matching Perspective," *JCR*, 24 (September), 178–91.

SCALE ITEMS:*

1. I would not purchase this product   :___:___:___:___:___:___:___: I would purchase this product
       1   2   3   4   5   6   7

2. Mediocre   :___:___:___:___:___:___:___: Exceptional product
       1   2   3   4   5   6   7

3. Not at all high quality   :___:___:___:___:___:___:___: Extremely high quality
       1   2   3   4   5   6   7

4. Poor value   :___:___:___:___:___:___:___: Excellent value
       1   2   3   4   5   6   7

5. Poorly made   :___:___:___:___:___:___:___: Well made
       1   2   3   4   5   6   7

6. Boring   :___:___:___:___:___:___:___: Exciting
       1   2   3   4   5   6   7

7. Not a worthwhile product   :___:___:___:___:___:___:___: A worthwhile product
       1   2   3   4   5   6   7

8. Unappealing product   :___:___:___:___:___:___:___: Appealing product
       1   2   3   4   5   6   7

*Peracchio and Meyers-Levy (1994) used items 1–5. Meyers-Levy and Peracchio (1995) used items 4–7 and one similar to 1. Peracchio and Meyers-Levy (1997) used items the same or similar to 3, 4, 5, and 7, as well as an additional item (8). Variations were made in item 5 in each of the studies depending on the product being evaluated (e.g., crafted, designed). See the articles for specific terms.

SCALE NAME: Attitude Toward the Brand (Food)

SCALE DESCRIPTION: Five four-point items measuring the degree to which a person has a positive attitude toward some specific brand of food product. The product examined by Prasad and Smith (1994) was a breakfast cereal aimed at children.

SCALE ORIGIN: Prasad and Smith (1994, p. 346) state that they used a "variation of Rossiter's (1977) summated rating scale." The similarities appear to be that Prasad and Smith (1994) used Rossiter's (1977) response scale (two levels of affirmation and two levels of negation) and developed items intended for use with children. Beyond that, their scales are different.

SAMPLES: The sample used by Prasad and Smith (1994) was composed of second- and third-grade boys recruited from Cub Scout Troops in a Midwestern U.S. town. Their ages ranged from seven to nine years. Usable data were gathered from **95** boys.

RELIABILITY: An alpha of **.87** was reported for the scale by Prasad and Smith (1994).

VALIDITY: To examination of the scale's validity was reported by Prasad and Smith (1994).

ADMINISTRATION: The scale was administered to subjects after they watched one of two programs (violent/nonviolent) that contained the commercial of interest (Prasad and Smith 1994). Higher scores on the scale indicated that viewers had very positive attitudes toward the brand in question.

MAJOR FINDINGS: Prasad and Smith (1994) investigated the effects of violent programs on children's ad attitudes and recall. Among the findings was that **brand attitudes** were significantly worse when the commercial followed a high rather than a low violence program.

COMMENTS: Items (shown as "Scale Items") were stated hypothetically because the test commercial was deliberately selected for a brand with which the children were unlikely to have been familiar; that is, the brand was not advertised or distributed in their region. It should also be kept in mind that this scale was developed and tested with children and breakfast cereal in mind. If modifications are desired so the scale can be used for other food products or with adults, further testing is needed.

REFERENCES:

Prasad, V. Kanti and Lois J. Smith (1994), "Television Commercials in Violent Programming: An Experimental Evaluation of Their Effects on Children," *JAMS*, 22 (4), 340–51.
Rossiter, John R. (1977), "Reliability of a Short Test Measuring Children's Attitudes Toward TV Commercials," *JCR*, 3 (March), 179–84.
Smith, Lois J. (1999), personal correspondence.

SCALE ITEMS:*
1 = NO; 2 = no; 3 = yes; 4 = YES.

1. I would like _____.

2. _____ would not taste good. **(r)**

3. I would like to have _____ for breakfast.

4. I would like to have _____ for a snack.

5. _____ would not be good for me to eat. **(r)**

*Scale items were provided by Smith (1999). The name of the product should be placed in the blank space.

SCALE NAME: Attitude Toward the Brand (Status)

SCALE DESCRIPTION: Three five-point semantic differentials used to measure a consumer's attitude toward a brand with an emphasis on the perceived status aspects of the product.

SCALE ORIGIN: Although Rosenberg, Pieters, and Wedel (1997) cite Batra and Ahtola (1990) and received inspiration from their distinction between hedonic and utilitarian components of brand attitude, it appears that the scale is original to the former because no items were taken from the latter. Even though the scale was apparently intended to capture the hedonic component of brand attitude, the items themselves focus exclusively on a status-factor.

SAMPLES: The experiment conducted by Rosenberg, Pieters, and Wedel (1997) was based on data collected from **115** adult female consumers (20 to 39 years of age). The experiment took place in the headquarters of a market research firm in the Netherlands, and subjects were paid the equivalent of $10 for their effort.

RELIABILITY: An alpha of **.69** was reported for the scale by Rosenberg, Pieters, and Wedel (1997).

VALIDITY: No examination of the scale's validity was reported by Rosenberg, Pieters, and Wedel (1997).

ADMINISTRATION: The scale was appears to have been self-administered by subjects, along with other measures, after they were exposed to experimental stimuli (Rosenberg, Pieters, and Wedel 1997). Higher scores on the scale indicated a better (more positive) brand attitude.

MAJOR FINDINGS: Rosenberg, Pieters, and Wedel (1997, p. 306) propose that consumers vary in their "visual gaze duration patterns." A methodology was presented for measuring the effect of the physical properties of print advertisements on visual attention that takes this variation among consumers into account. Those subjects in a group who paid the most attention to the pictorial portions of the advertisement and little or no attention to the body text produced the highest **brand attitude (status)** scores.

COMMENTS: The internal consistency for the scale is rather low. It might be increased by the addition of a few more items, taking care to keep the measure unidimensional.

REFERENCES:
Batra, Rajeev and Olli T. Ahtola (1990), "Measuring the Hedonic and Utilitarian Sources of Consumer Attitudes," *Marketing Letters*, 2 (April), 159–70.
Rosbergen, Edward, Rik Pieters, and Michel Wedel (1997), "Visual Attention to Advertising: A Segment-Level Analysis," *JCR*, 24 (December), 305–14.

SCALE ITEMS:
To me, _____ is:

Bad   :___:___:___:___: Good
              1   2   3   4   5

No value   Value for
for money   :___:___:___:___: money
              1   2   3   4   5

Low   High
quality   :___:___:___:___: quality
              1   2   3   4   5

SCALE NAME: Attitude Toward the Brand (Unipolar)

SCALE DESCRIPTION: Multi-item summated scale that purports to measure a consumer's overall evaluation of a specified brand/product. Although the uses described here have different sets of items and points on their response scales, they are similar in that they both use unipolar adjectives rather than the more common bipolar adjectives as items. Furthermore, a high degree of commonality exists among the items employed in the different studies.

SCALE ORIGIN: Despite the references provided by LaTour, Snipes, and Bliss (1996) and LaTour and Henthorne (1994), the scales appear to be original to their respective studies and were not borrowed from any other known study. The version used by LaTour and Rotfeld (1997) is a modification of the one used by LaTour, Snipes, and Bliss (1996).

SAMPLES: Data were gathered by LaTour and Henthorne (1994, p. 83) through mall intercept surveys in a "culturally vibrant MSA in the mid-Gulf Coast region." Interviewers were trained and rotated in a random pattern throughout the mall. Of the shoppers approached, 85% participated. To complete the questionnaire, shoppers were taken to a private yet monitored area. Usable survey forms were collected from **199** respondents. The sample was described as having an average age of 34.3 years and an average of 13.8 years of education and as coming from widely different income levels. A little more than half of the respondents were women (53%), 75.7% were white, and 47.5% were married.

LaTour, Snipes, and Bliss (1996), as well as LaTour and Rotfeld (1997), collected data from **305** respondents through the use of a mall intercept survey in a "demographically diverse SMSA in the southeastern United States" (LaTour, Snipes, and Bliss 1996, p. 62). Female shoppers were approached "at random" during all hours of the mall's operation over nine weeks, and those volunteering were assigned randomly to one of two treatments. The majority of the respondents were white (79%) and married (34%). The mean age of respondents was 28 years, and the mean education level was 14 years.

RELIABILITY: Alphas of **.74, .93,** and **.92** were reported for the scale by LaTour and Henthorne (1994), LaTour, Snipes, and Bliss (1996; LaTour 1997), and LaTour and Rotfeld (1997), respectively.

VALIDITY: No evidence of the scale's validity was presented in any of the studies, though LaTour, Snipes, and Bliss (1996) and LaTour and Rotfeld (1997) indicated that factor analyses provided evidence of their scales' unidimensionalities.

ADMINISTRATION: Respondents completed the scale along with other measures in the self-administered questionnaire used by LaTour and Henthorne (1994). Likewise, respondents in LaTour, Snipes, and Bliss's (1996) and LaTour and Rotfeld's (1997) field experiments completed the scale along with other measures after being exposed to treatment stimuli. High scores on the scale indicated that a consumer had a very positive view of the specified brand.

MAJOR FINDINGS: LaTour and Henthorne (1994) investigated the ethical judgments made by consumers regarding sexual appeals in print advertising. The results showed that strong sex-related appeals were not viewed favorably. Specifically, the group that received an ad with a "mild" sexual appeal viewed the brand significantly better than the group that received an ad with a strong, overt sexual appeal.

The field experiment conducted by LaTour, Snipes, and Bliss (1996) examined the perceived ethicality of the use of fear appeals with a potentially sensitive audience. Among the findings was that subjects seeing the ad with the stronger fear appeal had somewhat better **attitudes toward the brand** than subjects who saw the ad with the milder fear appeal, though the difference was not quite significant.

The field experiment conducted by LaTour and Rotfeld (1997) was intended to clarify the distinction between threats and psychological responses to the threats. The results indicated that arousal (energy) had a direct positive impact on attitude toward the ad and purchase intention but only indirectly increased positive **brand attitude**.

REFERENCES:

LaTour, Michael S. (1997), personal correspondence.

——— and Tony L. Henthorne (1994), "Ethical Judgments of Sexual Appeals in Print Advertising," *JA*, 23 (September), 81–90.

——— and Herbert J. Rotfeld (1997), "There Are Threats and (Maybe) Fear-Caused Arousal: Theory and Confusions of Appeals to Fear and Fear Arousal Itself," *JA*, 26 (Fall), 45–59.

———, Robin L. Snipes, and Sara J. Bliss (1996), "Don't Be Afraid to Use Fear Appeals: An Experimental Study," *JAR*, 36 (March/April), 59–67.

SCALE ITEMS:

No, definitely not	:___:___:___:___:___:___:	Yes, definitely
	1 2 3 4 5 6 7	

1. High quality
2. Unsatisfactory **(r)**
3. Appealing
4. Inferior **(r)**
5. Interesting
6. Desirable
7. Good
8. Useful
9. Distinctive

LaTour and Henthorne (1994): 1–4; 7-point
LaTour and Rotfeld (1997): 1, 3, 6–9; 6-point
LaTour, Snipes, and Bliss (1996): 1, 3, 5–8; 6-point

SCALE NAME: Attitude Toward the Brand Name

SCALE DESCRIPTION: Six-item, seven-point semantic differential measuring the degree to which a person views a brand name as being acceptable.

SCALE ORIGIN: No information about the source of the scale was provided by Schmitt, Pan, and Tavassoli (1994), but it appears to be original to their study.

SAMPLES: Data related to use of the scale described here were collected by Schmitt, Pan, and Tavassoli (1994) from **16** native Chinese speakers in China and **26** native English speakers in the United States. This procedure was a pretest rather than the main study.

RELIABILITY: An alpha of **.97** was reported for the scale by Schmitt, Pan, and Tavassoli (1994).

VALIDITY: No examination of scale validity was reported by Schmitt, Pan, and Tavassoli (1994).

ADMINISTRATION: The scale was apparently self-administered along with other measures as part of pretest (Schmitt, Pan, and Tavassoli 1994). Higher scores on the scale suggested that respondents had a positive view of a particular brand name.

MAJOR FINDINGS: Schmitt, Pan, and Tavassoli (1994) investigated the effect of the structural differences between English and Chinese on memory of verbal information. As noted previously, **brand name attitudes** were measured as part of a pretest rather than in the main study. No significant differences were found between Chinese and English stimuli in **brand name attitudes**.

REFERENCES:
Schmitt, Bernd H., Yigang Pan, and Nader T. Tavassoli (1994), "Language and Consumer Memory: The Impact of Linguistic Differences Between Chinese and English," *JCR*, 21 (December), 419–31.

SCALE ITEMS: How acceptable do you think this word is as a brand name?

1. Dislike   :___:___:___:___:___:___:___: Like
                    1   2   3   4   5   6   7

2. Negative   :___:___:___:___:___:___:___: Positive
                    1   2   3   4   5   6   7

3. Bad   :___:___:___:___:___:___:___: Good
                    1   2   3   4   5   6   7

4. Disagreeable   :___:___:___:___:___:___:___: Agreeable
                    1   2   3   4   5   6   7

5. Unpleasant   :___:___:___:___:___:___:___: Pleasant
                    1   2   3   4   5   6   7

6. Not at all   Very
   acceptable   :___:___:___:___:___:___:___: acceptable
                    1   2   3   4   5   6   7

SCALE NAME: Attitude Toward the Business (Originality)

SCALE DESCRIPTION: The three-item, nine-point semantic differential scale measures a person's evaluation of the uniqueness dimension of some specific store or company.

SCALE ORIGIN: Although not stated by Homer (1995), the scale appears to be original to her study.

SAMPLES: The sample for the study by Homer (1995) consisted of **245** business students at a Western U.S. university. Respondents were of both genders, volunteered to participate, and were randomly assigned to one of the treatments in the 2 × 2 factorial design.

RELIABILITY: An alpha of **.91** was reported for the scale (Homer 1995).

VALIDITY: No examination of the scale's validity was reported by Homer (1995), though it was stated that a factor analysis was conducted and the items in this scale loaded on the same dimension.

ADMINISTRATION: The scale was self-administered by subjects, along with other measures, after they were exposed to experimental stimuli (Homer 1995). Higher scores on the scale indicated that respondents viewed a store/company as unique in an exciting (apparently positive) way.

MAJOR FINDINGS: Replicating Kirmani (1990), Homer (1995) studied the effects of ad size on ad-based memory, perceptions, and attitudinal evaluations. The results related to **originality** were not separately described, but in general, it appears that attitude toward the business was better for those who were exposed to the larger yellow pages ads.

REFERENCES:
Homer, Pamela M. (1995), "Ad Size as an Indicator of Perceived Advertising Costs and Effort: The Effects on Memory and Perceptions," *JA*, 24 (Winter), 1–12.
Kirmani, Amna (1990), "The Effect of Perceived Advertising Costs on Brand Perceptions," *JCR*, 17 (September), 160–71.

SCALE ITEMS:
Please express your attitudes toward _____.*

Dull   :___:___:___:___:___:___:___:___: Exciting
        1 2 3 4 5 6 7 8 9

Unoriginal   :___:___:___:___:___:___:___:___: Original
        1 2 3 4 5 6 7 8 9

Not unique   :___:___:___:___:___:___:___:___: Unique
        1 2 3 4 5 6 7 8 9

*The name of the business should be placed in the blank.

SCALE NAME: Attitude Toward the Business (Overall)

SCALE DESCRIPTION: The nine-item, nine-point semantic differential scale measures a person's overall evaluation of some specific store or company.

SCALE ORIGIN: Although not stated by Homer (1995), the scale appears to be original to her study.

SAMPLES: The sample for the study by Homer (1995) consisted of **245** business students at a Western U.S. university. Respondents were of both genders, volunteered to participate, and were randomly assigned to one of the treatments in the 2×2 factorial design.

RELIABILITY: An alpha of **.97** was reported for the scale (Homer 1995).

VALIDITY: No examination of the scale's validity was reported by Homer (1995), though it was stated that a factor analysis was conducted and the items in this scale loaded on the same dimension.

ADMINISTRATION: The scale was self-administered by subjects, along with other measures, after they were exposed to experimental stimuli (Homer 1995). Higher scores on the scale indicated that respondents had a positive attitude about the specified store or company.

MAJOR FINDINGS: Replicating Kirmani (1990), Homer (1995) studied the effects of ad size on ad-based memory, perceptions, and attitudinal evaluations. Among the findings was that **attitude toward the business** was better for those who were exposed to the larger yellow pages ads.

REFERENCES:

Homer, Pamela M. (1995), "Ad Size as an Indicator of Perceived Advertising Costs and Effort: The Effects on Memory and Perceptions," *JA*, 24 (Winter), 1–12.

Kirmani, Amna (1990), "The Effect of Perceived Advertising Costs on Brand Perceptions," *JCR*, 17 (September), 160–71.

SCALE ITEMS: Please express your attitudes toward _____.*

Negative   :___:___:___:___:___:___:___:___: Positive
         1 2 3 4 5 6 7 8 9

Unpleasant   :___:___:___:___:___:___:___:___: Pleasant
         1 2 3 4 5 6 7 8 9

Disagreeable :___:___:___:___:___:___:___:___: Agreeable
         1 2 3 4 5 6 7 8 9

Worthless   :___:___:___:___:___:___:___:___: Valuable
         1 2 3 4 5 6 7 8 9

Bad   :___:___:___:___:___:___:___:___: Good
         1 2 3 4 5 6 7 8 9

Foolish   :___:___:___:___:___:___:___:___: Wise
         1 2 3 4 5 6 7 8 9

Unfavorable :___:___:___:___:___:___:___:___: Favorable
         1 2 3 4 5 6 7 8 9

Dislike a lot :___:___:___:___:___:___:___:___: Like a lot
         1 2 3 4 5 6 7 8 9

Useless   :___:___:___:___:___:___:___:___: Useful
         1 2 3 4 5 6 7 8 9

*The name of the business should be placed in the blank.

SCALE NAME: Attitude Toward the Conservation Activity

SCALE DESCRIPTION: Three seven-point Likert-type statements measuring a consumer's attitude toward an activity designed to save energy. As used by Osterhus (1997), the focal activity was a program offered by an electrical utility company whereby monetary incentives (credits) were offered to consumers for their willingness to have their air conditioner use reduced during times of peak electrical demand.

SCALE ORIGIN: The scale is original to Osterhus (1997). His purpose with the scale was to operationalize an *awareness of consequences* construct in the context of energy conservation.

SAMPLES: The sample for the study by Osterhus (1997) came from rural, urban, and suburban neighborhoods of a Midwestern U.S. area. Subjects were recruited through random-digit dialing and then were sent a paper questionnaire. Nonrespondents were mailed another questionnaire. Ultimately, **1128** usable responses were received.

RELIABILITY: An alpha of **.84** was reported for the scale by Osterhus (1997).

VALIDITY: Confirmatory factor analysis was used by Osterhus (1997) to help purify the scales. Evidence was generally in support of the discriminant and convergent validity of this scale, though there was some concern about its distinctiveness with respect to a measure of the personal obligations to conserve energy (#101).

ADMINISTRATION: The scale was self-administered by respondents along with other measures in a mail survey format (Osterhus 1997). Higher scores on the scale suggested that respondents strongly agreed that the conservation activity had positive consequences on the environment.

MAJOR FINDINGS: Osterhus (1997) investigated how and when prosocial positions are expected to influence consumer choice. Among the findings was that **attitude toward a particular conservation activity** was significantly associated with personal norms regarding conservation of energy.

REFERENCES:
Osterhus, Thomas L. (1997), "Pro-Social Consumer Influence Strategies: When and How Do They Work?" *JM*, 61 (October), 16–29.

SCALE ITEMS:*

Disagree   :___:___:___:___:___:___:___: Agree
             1   2   3   4   5   6   7

1. The _____ helps the environment.

2. The _____ helps preserve clean air.

3. Participating in the _____ will help future generations.

*The name of the focal conservation activity should be placed in the blanks.

SCALE NAME: Attitude Toward the English Language

SCALE DESCRIPTION: A three-item scale measuring the degree to which a person has a positive opinion of English as a language.

SCALE ORIGIN: The scale appears to have been developed by Koslow, Shamdasani, and Touchstone (1994) for their study.

SAMPLES: Data were gathered by Koslow, Shamdasani, and Touchstone (1994) in personal interviews with shoppers at three southern California supermarkets. Bilingual interviewers were used and asked to approach only those shoppers who appeared to be Hispanic. Of the 413 interviews that were begun, **367** yielded enough information to be useful in the analysis. The sample was 56% men, 60.7% were between the ages of 20 and 39 years, and 57.2% indicated that they were bilingual native Spanish speakers.

RELIABILITY: An alpha of **.522** was reported for the scale by Koslow, Shamdasani, and Touchstone (1994).

VALIDITY: The validity of the scale was not specifically addressed in the study (Koslow, Shamdasani, and Touchstone 1994).

ADMINISTRATION: The scale was part of a longer questionnaire administered by trained bilingual interviewers (Koslow, Shamdasani, and Touchstone 1994). The respondents were first greeted and recruited in Spanish and then asked in what language they would prefer the interview to be conducted. As with the rest of the survey instrument, the scale was first developed in English, and the back-translation method used to help refine the quality of the Spanish version. A little more than one-fourth of the respondents chose to have the interview conducted in English, and the remaining portion of the sample chose Spanish. Therefore, the scale items were read to respondents rather than being self-administered. High scores on the scale suggested that respondents had a very positive attitude toward the English language. The scores on each items were *not* standardized before summing, which means that item #2 carries more weight in determining overall scores on the scale than the other two items do (Koslow 1996). Although not typical, its appropriateness could be justified if supported by evidence from a factor analysis.

MAJOR FINDINGS: The study by Koslow, Shamdasani, and Touchstone (1994) examined how consumers in an ethnic subculture respond to the use of their language in advertising. No significant relationship was found between **attitude toward the English language** and affect toward an ad that was varied for different respondent groups in the language used (i.e., Spanish, English, both).

COMMENTS: The internal consistency of the scale is so low as to be considered dangerously close to unreliable. Further developmental work is needed with the scale before it is used again.

REFERENCES:
Koslow, Scott (1996), personal correspondence.
——, Prem N. Shamdasani, and Ellen E. Touchstone (1994), "Exploring Language Effects in Ethnic Advertising: A Socioliguistic Perspective," *JCR*, 20 (March), 575–85.

SCALE ITEMS:

Is the English language:

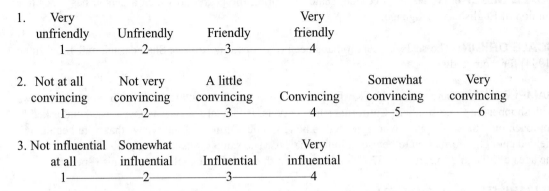

1. Very
    unfriendly   Unfriendly   Friendly   Very
    friendly
    1————————2————————3————————4

2. Not at all   Not very   A little   Somewhat   Very
    convincing   convincing   convincing   Convincing   convincing   convincing
    1————————2————————3————————4————————5————————6

3. Not influential   Somewhat   Very
   at all   influential   Influential   influential
   1————————2————————3————————4

SCALE NAME: Attitude Toward the Object

SCALE DESCRIPTION: A three-item, seven-point semantic differential measuring how much a person likes some specified object. In Lord, Lee, and Sauer (1994), the object was a radio program.

SCALE ORIGIN: No information was provided by Lord, Lee, and Sauer (1994) as to the source of the scale, but it would appear to be original to their study.

SAMPLES: Lord, Lee, and Sauer (1994) collected data from undergraduate students in an introductory marketing course. Students received extra credit for their participation, and analysis was based on **324** completed survey forms.

RELIABILITY: An alpha of **.89** was reported for the scale by Lord, Lee, and Sauer (1994).

VALIDITY: The validity of the scale was not specifically addressed in the study (Lord, Lee, and Sauer 1994).

ADMINISTRATION: The scale was part of a longer questionnaire self-administered by students in a classroom experiment by Lord, Lee, and Sauer (1994). High scores on the scale suggested that respondents had a very positive attitude toward some specified object.

MAJOR FINDINGS: The study by Lord, Lee, and Sauer (1994) examined the influence of program context on attitude toward the ad. It was hypothesized that more positive attitudes toward a program enhanced motivation to process ads in the program. The results supported the hypothesis.

REFERENCES:
Lord, Kenneth R., Myung-Soo Lee, and Paul L. Sauer (1994), "Program Context Antecedents of Attitude Toward Radio Commercials," *JAMS*, 22 (1), 3–15.

SCALE ITEMS:
(Name of Object)

1. Bad $\quad$:___:___:___:___:___:___:___: Good
$\qquad\qquad$ 1 $\quad$ 2 $\quad$ 3 $\quad$ 4 $\quad$ 5 $\quad$ 6 $\quad$ 7

2. Unpleasant $\quad$:___:___:___:___:___:___:___: Pleasant
$\qquad\qquad$ 1 $\quad$ 2 $\quad$ 3 $\quad$ 4 $\quad$ 5 $\quad$ 6 $\quad$ 7

3. Unfavorable $\quad$:___:___:___:___:___:___:___: Favorable
$\qquad\qquad$ 1 $\quad$ 2 $\quad$ 3 $\quad$ 4 $\quad$ 5 $\quad$ 6 $\quad$ 7

SCALE NAME: Attitude Toward the Offer

SCALE DESCRIPTION: A variety of items measuring a person's attitude about a certain product offered at a certain price. As used by Lichtenstein and Bearden (1989), the scale is composed of four bipolar adjectives and one Likert-type item, each of which employs a nine-point response format. Three-item, seven-point versions of the scale have also been used (Biswas and Burton 1993; Inman, Peter, and Raghubir 1997; Lichtenstein, Burton, and Karson 1991), as has a four-item, seven-point version (Bobinski, Cox, and Cox 1996).

SCALE ORIGIN: There is no information to indicate that the primary form of the various versions of the scale originated elsewhere than in the study reported in both Burton and Lichtenstein (1988) and Lichtenstein and Bearden (1989).

SAMPLES: Biswas and Burton (1993) reported on two studies in their article. In the first one, data were collected from 392 undergraduate business students. Little more is said about the sample except that there was a nearly equal portion of each gender and that respondents were randomly assigned to 1 of the 12 treatments. The second sample was composed of **303** nonstudents who were recruited by students in a marketing course. All of those in the sample were older than the age of 18, with a median of 40 years of age. A little more than half were women (56%), and the median household income was $35,000.

Data were collected in an experiment conducted by Bobinski, Cox, and Cox (1996) from student volunteers in management courses at an Eastern U.S. university. Usable responses were received from **129** students. A little more than half of the sample were men (53%), and the mean age was 20.6 years.

Analyses in Burton and Lichtenstein (1988), as well as Lichtenstein and Bearden (1989), were based on the same data collected from 278 undergraduate business students. The students were randomly assigned to 1 of 12 treatment conditions in a $2 \times 2 \times 3$ experimental design. There were between 21 and 28 students per cell.

Inman, Peter, and Raghubir (1997) reported on four studies in their article, only the third of which employed the scale. That study was based on data from **182** undergraduate business students attending a large Midwestern U.S. university.

Lichtenstein, Burton, and Karson (1991) used **830** undergraduate business majors and randomly assigned each of them to 1 of 31 conditions in a 5×6 (plus control group) between-subjects experimental design. There were between 22 to 29 subjects per cell.

RELIABILITY: Alphas of **.86, .92, .92,** and **.95** were reported for the scale as used by Bobinski, Cox, and Cox (1996), Burton and Lichtenstein (1988; Lichtenstein and Bearden 1989), Inman, Peter, and Raghubir (1997), and Lichtenstein, Burton, and Karson (1991), respectively. Biswas and Burton (1993) reported alphas of **.95** and **.94** in their first and second studies, respectively.

VALIDITY: No specific examination of scale validity was reported in any of the studies. However, Biswas and Burton (1993) mention that, though **attitude toward the offer** was highly correlated with a measure of the **perceived value of the offer,** confirmatory factor analysis provided evidence of a two- rather than a one-factor model. Similar evidence was reported by Bobinski, Cox, and Cox (1996).

ADMINISTRATION: In most of the situations, the scale was self-administered by subjects along with several other measures after they were exposed to experimental stimuli. Higher scores on the scale implied that respondents held a positive attitude about some specified deal (price and product), whereas lower scores suggested that respondents had unfavorable attitudes about an offer.

MAJOR FINDINGS: Biswas and Burton (1993) investigated the impact of three different price claims on various perceptions and intentions. Among the many findings was that **attitude toward the offer** was better for larger discount ranges than for smaller ones.

The effect of a retailer's rationale for a price reduction was examined by Bobinski, Cox, and Cox (1996). The results showed that **attitudes toward the offer** were best when a rationale was provided (e.g., volume purchase) along with a reference price (i.e., higher "regular" price).

The study reported by Burton and Lichtenstein (1988; Lichtenstein and Bearden 1989) examined the influence of merchant-supplied reference prices, ad distinctiveness, and ad message consistency on perception of source credibility, value of the deal, and attitude toward the deal. In Burton and Lichtenstein (1988), the findings indicated that both the cognitive and the affective components of attitude toward the ad were significant predictors of **attitude toward the offer** beyond that which could be explained by other components examined. Among many other findings reported in Lichtenstein and Bearden (1989), **attitude toward the offer** was better for plausible-high merchant-supplied prices than for implausible-high merchant-supplied prices.

In general, Inman, Peter, and Raghubir (1997) examined the degree to which consumers use restrictions to evaluate deals. Results of Study 3 indicated that, at a low discount level, unrestricted deals were rated better, but at a greater discount level, deals with quantity and time restrictions were rated higher.

Lichtenstein, Burton, and Karson (1991) studied the way reference price ads were phrased (semantic cues) and consumer's price-related responses. High distinctiveness semantic cues indicate the difference between the advertised price and what is charged by competitors, whereas low consistency cues compare prices charged at other times by the same retailer. Among the many findings was that, for implausibly high external reference prices, semantic cues suggest high distinctiveness produced significantly better **attitudes toward the offer** than low consistency cues.

REFERENCES:

Biswas, Abhijit and Scot Burton (1993), "Consumer Perceptions of Tensile Price Claims in Advertisements: An Assessment of Claim Types Across Different Discount Levels," *JAMS*, 21 (Summer), 217–29.

Bobinski, George S., Jr., Dena Cox, and Anthony Cox (1996), "Retail 'Sale' Advertising, Perceived Retailer Credibility, and Price Rationale," *JR*, 72 (3), 291–306.

Burton, Scot and Donald R. Lichtenstein (1988), "The Effect of Ad Claims and Ad Context on Attitude Toward the Advertisement," *JA*, 17 (1), 3–11.

Inman, J. Jeffrey, Anil C. Peter, and Priya Raghubir (1997), "Framing the Deal: The Role of Restrictions in Accentuating Deal Value," *JCR*, 24 (June), 68–79.

Lichtenstein, Donald R. and William O. Bearden (1989), "Contextual Influences on Perceptions of Merchant-Supplied Reference Prices," *JCR*, 16 (June), 55–66.

———, Scot Burton, and Eric J. Karson (1991), "The Effect of Semantic Cues on Consumer Perceptions of Reference Price Ads," *JCR*, 18 (December), 380–91.

SCALE ITEMS:
My attitude toward this deal is:

1. Unfavorable :___:___:___:___:___:___:___: Favorable

2. Bad :___:___:___:___:___:___:___: Good

3. Harmful :___:___:___:___:___:___:___: Beneficial

4. Unattractive :___:___:___:___:___:___:___: Attractive

5. Poor   :___:___:___:___:___:___: Excellent

6. Very
   disadvantageous   :___:___:___:___:___:___: Very
   advantageous

7. Worthless   :___:___:___:___:___:___: Valuable

8. I like this deal:

   Strongly disagree   :___:___:___:___:___:___: Strongly agree

Biswas and Burton (1993): 1, 2, 5; 7-point
Bobinski, Cox, and Cox (1996): 1*, 2*, 3*, 6; 7-point
Inman, Peter, and Raghubir (1997): 2*, 4*, 7; 7-point
Lichtenstein and Bearden (1989): 1, 2, 3, 4, 8; 9-point
Lichtenstein, Burton, and Karson (1991): 1, 2, 5; 7-point

SCALE NAME: Attitude Toward the Organization

SCALE DESCRIPTION: Three seven-point semantic differentials measuring a person's evaluation of an organization, particularly in terms of what the person thinks its value is to society.

SCALE ORIGIN: The first two items in this scale have been used in many semantic differential measures of attitudes toward objects (e.g., #53). However, there has been no known previous use of this set of items to measure attitude toward an organization. Thus, though it is not explicitly stated as original, the scale seems to have been developed for use in the study by Moore, Harris, and Chen (1995).

SAMPLES: Moore, Harris, and Chen (1995) conducted two experiments, only the first of which employed the **attitude toward the organization** scale. Data were gathered for the first experiment from 153 undergraduates who were fulfilling a psychology course requirement at a large, Southwestern U.S. university. The sample was 53% women, and ages ranged from 20 to 27 years.

RELIABILITY: An alpha of **.96** was reported for the scale by Moore, Harris, and Chen (1995).

VALIDITY: No examination of the scale's validity was reported by Moore, Harris, and Chen (1995).

ADMINISTRATION: The scale was self-administered by subjects, along with other measures, after they were exposed to experimental stimuli (Moore, Harris, and Chen 1995). Higher scores on the scale indicated that respondents held strong positive attitudes toward the organization.

MAJOR FINDINGS: The experiment conducted by Moore, Harris, and Chen (1995) investigated the extent to which differences in affect intensity influenced responses to emotional ad appeals. After seeing an ad for an organization devoted to the prevention of cruelty to children, those subjects with high affect intensity had significantly more positive **attitudes toward the organization** than did those with low affect intensity.

REFERENCES:
Moore, David J., William D. Harris, and Hong C. Chen (1995), "Affect Intensity: An Individual Difference Response to Advertising Appeals," *JCR*, 22 (September), 154–64.

SCALE ITEMS:
The organization is:

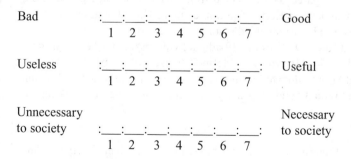

SCALE NAME: Attitude Toward the Product/Brand (Semantic Differential)

SCALE DESCRIPTION: Various bipolar adjectives presumed to measure the subject's overall evaluation of the product or brand. The various versions of the scale are similar, in that they are not specific to any particular product or brand under investigation, though certain adjectives may not be appropriate in some cases. Stafford and Day (1995) made slightly different use of the scale than most others by measuring attitudes toward a *service* rather than a *good*.

SCALE ORIGIN: There is no common origin for these scales, and many of them are unique in that the sets of items of which they are composed have been used as a set in just one or two studies. Some items have been used much more than others, but *good/bad* is by far the most commonly used bipolar adjective. Most of the scales have also used *favorable/unfavorable* and/or *pleasant/unpleasant*. At the other extreme, there are several items (e.g., #22 to #26) that appear to have been used just once.

Taylor, Miracle, and Wilson (1997) developed a Korean version of the scale using the back-translation method.

SELECTED SAMPLES: Gelb and Zinkhan (1986) used **120** employed adult subjects enrolled in graduate or undergraduate business classes on a part-time basis. Ninety-six of the 120 subjects were used in the final analysis.

The study by Keller (1991a) was based on data collected from **103** adults who were either members of a local parent–teacher association (PTA) or employees of a large private university. A majority of the sample was women (89%), half had at least a college degree, and half were older than 40 years of age. For their participation, subjects either received a small fee and participated in a lottery or a contribution was made to their organization. Subjects were assigned randomly to experimental conditions.

MacKenzie, Lutz, and Belch (1986) used the scale in two experiments. In the first experiment, **260** people were recruited from two church organizations. They ranged in age from 18 to 75 years, and 69% were women. The subjects in the second experiment were **225** undergraduate- and master's-level business students who volunteered for the study.

Complete and usable data were received from **999** members of a national mail panel by Peterson, Wilson, and Brown (1992). Respondents averaged 44 years of age, 64% were married, 53% were women, and 27% were college graduates.

Subjects for the experiment conducted by Stafford and Day (1995) were recruited through civic and religious organizations, and volunteers were paid $6. Subjects ranged in age from 21 to over 60 years, had incomes of less than $25,000 to more than $50,000, and a little more than half were women. Usable questionnaires were received from 137 subjects.

Taylor, Miracle, and Wilson (1997) compared data collected from **101** female undergraduate students in the United States and **101** similar students in Korea. The women in the United States were attending a Midwestern university, whereas those in Korea attended a university in Seoul.

Data were collected by Wansink and Ray (1992) from 239 adults living in the northern California area. Analysis seems to have been based on the **219** who were defined as users of the product. Subjects were recruited through PTA groups, and $6 was donated to the respective organization for each volunteer. Most of the subjects (80%) were between 30 and 45 years of age, and most were not working outside the home.

SELECTED RELIABILITIES: Reported internal consistencies ranged from less than .70 (Iyer 1988) to .98 (Holbrook and Batra 1987). Specific reliabilities are provided for the selected studies described in the **Samples** and **Findings** sections:

.91 by Gelb and Zinkhan (1986);
.94 by Keller (1991a);
.92 in both experiments by MacKenzie, Lutz, and Belch (1986);
.80 by Peterson, Wilson, and Brown (1992);
.97 by Stafford and Day (1995);
.96 and .93 for the English and Korean versions of the scale, respectively, by Taylor, Miracle, and Wilson (1997); and
.936 by Wansink and Ray (1992).

VALIDITY: Little if any evidence of scale validity was provided in the majority of the studies. A few studies conducted some testing, however, of unidimensionality (e.g., Anand and Sternthal 1990; MacInnis and Park 1991).

Batra and Stayman (1990) performed confirmatory factor analysis on their ten-item scale and indicated that there were two factors, one more hedonic and the other more utilitarian. However, because use of the two scales separately led to findings not significantly different from those of the combined items, the latter was not discussed any further in their article.

Darley and Smith (1993) conducted several tests to determine if the three multi-item measures they used (**brand attitude**, ad attitude, and ad credibility) were sufficiently representative of their respective latent constructs. Among the findings was that a three-factor model fit the data better than a one-factor model. This provides some evidence of the scale's discriminant validity.

Miller and Marks (1992) performed a factor analysis of nine items expected to measure either attitude toward the ad or **attitude toward the brand.** All the items had loadings of .65 or higher on the expected factors, which was used to support a claim of each scale's discriminant validity.

ADMINISTRATION: Respondents typically complete the scale as part of a longer instrument administered in a survey or experimental context. Subjects are asked to evaluate a specific good or service using some set of bi-polar adjectives and marking the scales appropriately. The overwhelming majority of scales have employed seven-point response alternatives. Scores on the overall scale can be calculated as the sum or the mean of numeric responses to the individual items. Higher scores typically indicate a better attitude toward some specified object.

SELECTED FINDINGS: Gelb and Zinkhan (1986) found that humor is related positively to **brand attitude. Brand attitude** was also found to have significant correlations with purchase intention probability and choice behavior.

Keller (1991a) tested three propositions regarding conditions in which retrieval cues should work. In general, the results indicated that processing goal and retrieval cues influences how cognitive responses are associated with **brand attitudes**.

MacKenzie, Lutz, and Belch (1986) examined four competing models of attitude toward the ad's role as a mediator of ad influence on **brand attitudes** and purchase intentions. The dual mediation hypothesis was found to be the superior model and provided strong evidence of attitude toward the ad's direct effect on **brand attitude**, as well as its indirect effect through brand cognitions.

The primary issue investigated by Peterson, Wilson, and Brown (1992) was the effect advertised claims of customer satisfaction had on consumer attitudes and intentions. The findings indicated that there were no significant differences in **brand attitudes** between those consumers exposed to ads with various claims of customer satisfaction and those exposed to ads with no such claims.

The appropriateness of certain media and message strategies for two broad categories of retail services were tested by Stafford and Day (1995). No statistically significant effect was found for the different ad strategies on **attitude toward the service.**

Taylor, Miracle, and Wilson (1997) compared the effectiveness of commercials different in their information content between U.S. and Korean students. Among the findings was that Koreans had significantly lower **attitudes** than Americans toward **brands** shown in commercials judged to be high in information.

Wansink and Ray (1992) compared different measures of attitudes and consumption to determine the one that best predicted later consumption for those consumers who already were using the brand. On the basis of the results, the authors concluded that **brand attitude** was a weak predictor of consumption. It was a better predictor of the average monthly consumption of light users than of heavy users.

COMMENTS: See also Debevec and Iyer (1986); Health, McCarthy, and Mothersbaugh (1994); Holmes and Crocker (1987); Kamins and Marks (1987); Maheswaran (1994); Nyer (1997); Prakash (1992); Sheffet (1983); Smith and Swinyard (1983); Tripp, Jensen, and Carlson (1994); and Unnava, Burnkrant, and Erevelles (1994). Some variations on the scale can also be found in Batra and Ray (1986a), Batra and Stayman (1990), as well as Stayman and Batra (1991).

As is obvious from the material presented here, a wide variety of bipolar adjectives has been used over the years to measure **brand attitude**. No one set of items has been declared the optimal scale. Definitive studies of the psychometric quality of alternative versions of the measure are certainly needed. In the meantime, it is clear that some items are much more widely used than others, and researchers should consider using a set that has been used before rather than generating yet another unique set with unknown comparability to previous studies of the construct.

REFERENCES:

Aaker, Jennifer L. and Durairaj Maheswaran (1997), "The Effect of Cultural Orientation on Persuasion," *JCR*, 24 (December), 315–28.

Alpert, Frank H. and Michael A. Kamins (1995), "An Empirical Investigation of Consumer Memory, Attitude, and Perceptions Toward Pioneer and Follower Brands," *JM*, 59 (October), 34–45.

Anand, Punam and Brian Sternthal (1990), "Ease of Message Processing as a Moderator of Repetition Effects in Advertising," *JMR*, 27 (August), 345–53.

Babin, Laurie and Alvin C. Burns (1997), "Effects of Print Ad Pictures and Copy Containing Instructions to Imagine on Mental Imagery that Mediates Attitudes," *JA*, 26 (Fall), 33–44.

Batra, Rajeev and Michael L. Ray (1986a), "Situational Effects of Advertising Repetition: The Moderating Influence of Motivation, Ability, and Opportunity to Respond," *JCR*, 12 (March), 432–45.

———— and Michael L. Ray (1986b), "Affective Responses Mediating Acceptance of Advertising," *JCR*, 13 (September), 234–49.

———— and Douglas Stayman (1990), "The Role of Mood in Advertising Effectiveness," *JCR*, 17 (September), 203–14.

Bello, Daniel C., Robert E. Pitts, and Michael J. Etzel (1983), "The Communication Effects of Controversial Sexual Content in Television Programs and Commercials," *JA*, 12 (3), 32–42.

Berger, Ida E. and Andrew A. Mitchell (1989), "The Effect of Advertising on Attitude Accessibility, Attitude Confidence, and the Attitude-Behavior Relationship," *JCR*, 16 (December), 269–79.

Bone, Paula Fitzgerald and Pam Scholder Ellen (1992), "The Generation and Consequences of Communication-Evoked Imagery," *JCR*, 19 (June), 93–104.

Burnkrant, Robert E. and H. Rao Unnava (1995), "Effects of Self-Referencing on Persuasion," *JCR*, 22 (June), 17–26.

Chattopadhyay, Amitava and Kunal Basu (1990), "Humor in Advertising: The Moderating Role of Prior Brand Evaluation," *JMR*, 27 (November), 466–76.

———— and Prakash Nedungadi (1992), "Does Attitude Toward the Ad Endure? The Moderating Effects of Attention and Delay," *JCR*, 19 (June), 26–33.

Cox, Dena Saliagas and Anthony D. Cox (1988), "What Does Familiarity Breed? Complexity as a Moderator of Repetition Effects in Advertisement Evaluations," *JCR*, 15 (June), 111–16.

———— and William B. Locander (1987), "Product Novelty: Does It Moderate the Relationship Between Ad Attitudes and Brand Attitudes," *JA*, 16 (3), 39–44.

Darley, William K. and Robert E. Smith (1993), "Advertising Claim Objectivity: Antecedents and Effects," *JM*, 57 (October), 100–113.

———— and ———— (1995), "Gender Differences in Information Processing Strategies: An Empirical Test of the Selectivity Model in Advertising Response," *JA*, 24 (Spring), 41–56.

Debevec, Kathleen and Easwar Iyer (1986), "The Influence of Spokespersons in Altering a Product's Gender Image: Implications for Advertising Effectiveness," *JA*, 15 (4), 12–20.

Deshpandé, Rohit and Douglas Stayman (1994), "A Tale of Two Cities: Distinctiveness Theory and Advertising Effectiveness," *JMR*, 31 (February), 57–64.

Droge, Cornelia (1989), "Shaping the Route to Attitude Change: Central Versus Peripheral Processing Through Comparative Versus Noncomparative Advertising," *JMR*, 26 (May), 193–204.

Edell, Julie and Kevin Lane Keller (1989), "The Information Processing of Coordinated Media Campaigns," *JMR*, 26 (May), 149–63.

Gardner, Meryl Paula, Andrew A. Mitchell, and J. Edward Russo (1985), "Low Involvement Strategies for Processing Advertisements," *JA*, 14 (2), 4–12, 56.

Gelb, Betsy G. and George M. Zinkhan (1986), "Humor and Advertising Effectiveness After Repeated Exposures to a Radio Commercial," *JA*, 15 (2), 15–20+.

Gill, James D., Sanford Grossbart, and Russell N. Laczniak (1988), "Influence of Involvement, Commitment, and Familiarity on Brand Beliefs and Attitudes of Viewers Exposed to Alternative Advertising Claim Strategies," *JA*, 17 (2), 33–43.

Goodstein, Ronald C. (1993), "Category-Based Applications and Extensions in Advertising: Motivating More Extensive Ad Processing," *JCR*, 20 (June), 87–99.

Gotlieb, Jerry B. and John E. Swan (1990), "An Application of the Elaboration Likelihood Model," *JAMS*, 18 (Summer), 221–28.

Grossbart, Sanford, Darrel D. Muehling, and Norman Kangun (1986), "Verbal and Visual References to Competition in Comparative Advertising," *JA*, 15 (1), 10–23.

Hastak, Manoj (1990), "Does Retrospective Thought Measurement Influence Subsequent Measures of Cognitive Structure in an Advertising Context?" *JA*, 19 (3), 3–13.

———— and Jerry C. Olson (1989), "Assessing the Role of Brand Related Cognitive Responses as Mediators of Communication Effects," *JCR*, 15 (March), 444–56.

Health, Timothy B., Michael S. McCarthy, and David L. Mothersbaugh (1994), "Spokesperson Fame and Vividness Effects in the Context of Issue-Relevant Thinking: The Moderating Role of Competitive Setting," *JCR*, 20 (March), 520–34.

Herr, Paul M., Frank R. Kardes, and John Kim (1991), "Effects of Word-of-Mouth and Product Attribute Information on Persuasion: An Accessibility–Diagnosticity Perspective," *JCR*, 17 (March), 454–62.

Holbrook, Morris B. and Rajeev Batra (1987), "Assessing the Role of Emotions as Mediators of Consumer Responses to Advertising," *JCR*, 14 (December), 404–20.

Holmes, John H. and Kenneth E. Crocker (1987), "Predispositions and the Comparative Effectiveness of Rational, Emotional, and Discrepant Appeals for Both High Involvement and Low Involvement Products," *JAMS*, 15 (Spring), 27–35.

Homer, Pamela M. (1990), "The Mediating Role of Attitude Toward the Ad: Some Additional Evidence," *JMR*, 27 (February), 78–86.

———— and Lynn R. Kahle (1990), "Source Expertise, Time of Source Identification, and Involvement in Persuasion: An Elaborative Processing Perspective," *JA*, 19 (1), 30–39.

Iyer, Easwar S. (1988), "The Influence of Verbal Content and Relative Newness on the Effectiveness of Comparative Advertising," *JA*, 17 (3), 15–21.

Kamins, Micheal A. and Lawrance J. Marks (1987), "Advertising Puffery: The Impact of Using Two-Sided Claims on Product Attitude and Purchase Intention," *JA*, 16 (4), 6–15.

Kardes, Frank R. and Gurumurthy Kalyanaram (1992), "Order-of-Entry Effects on Consumer Memory and Judgment: An Information Integration Perspective," *JMR*, 29 (August), 343–57.

Keller, Kevin Lane (1991a), "Cue Compatibility and Framing in Advertising," *JMR*, 28 (February), 42–57.

——— (1991b), "Memory and Evaluation Effects in Competitive Advertising Environments," *JCR*, 17 (March), 463–76.

Kelleris, James J., Anthony D. Cox, and Dena Cox (1993), "The Effect of Background Music on Ad Processing: A Contingency Explanation," *JM*, 57 (October), 114–25.

Kim, John, Chris T. Allen, and Frank R. Kardes (1996), "An Investigation of the Mediational Mechanisms Underlying Attitudinal Conditioning," *JMR*, 33 (August), 318–28.

Laczniak, Russell N. and Darrel D. Muehling (1993), "The Relationship Between Experimental Manipulations and Tests of Theory in an Advertising Message Involvement Context," *JA*, 22 (September), 59–74.

Leclerc, France (1998), personal correspondence.

——— and John D.C. Little (1997), "Can Advertising Copy Make FSI Coupons More Effective?" *JMR*, 34 (November), 473–84.

Lim, Jeen-Su, William K. Darley, and John O. Summers (1994), "An Assessment of Country of Origin Effects Under Alternative Presentation Formats," *JAMS*, 22 (3), 272–82.

Loken, Barbara and James Ward (1990), "Alternative Approaches to Understanding the Determinants of Typicality," *JCR*, 17 (September), 111–26.

Lord, Kenneth R., Myung-Soo Lee, and Paul L. Sauer (1994), "Program Context Antecedents of Attitude Toward Radio Commercials," *JAMS*, 22 (1), 3–15.

———, ———, and ——— (1995), "The Combined Influence Hypothesis: Central and Peripheral Antecedents of Attitude Toward the Ad," *JA*, 24 (Spring), 73–85.

Machleit, Karen A., Chris T. Allen, and Thomas J. Madden (1993), "The Mature Brand and Brand Interest: An Alternative Consequence of Ad-Evoked Affect," *JM*, 57 (October), 72–82.

MacInnis, Deborah J. and C. Whan Park (1991), "The Differential Role of Characteristics of Music on High- and Low-Involvement Consumers' Processing of Ads," *JCR*, 18 (September), 161–73.

MacKenzie, Scott B. and Richard J. Lutz (1989), "An Empirical Examination of the Structural Antecedents of Attitude Toward the Ad in an Advertising Pretesting Context," *JM*, 53 (April), 48–65.

———, ———, and George E. Belch (1986), "The Role of Attitude Toward the Ad as a Mediator of Advertising Effectiveness: A Test of Competing Explanations," *JMR*, 23 (May), 130–43.

——— and Richard A. Spreng (1992), "How Does Motivation Moderate the Impact of Central and Peripheral Processing on Brand Attitudes and Intentions," *JCR*, 18 (March), 519–29.

Macklin, M. Carole, Norman T. Bruvold, and Carole Lynn Shea (1985), "Is It Always as Simple as 'Keep It Simple'?" *JA*, 14 (4), 28–35.

Maheswaran, Durairaj (1994), "Country of Origin as a Stereotype: Effects of Consumer Expertise and Attribute Strength on Product Evaluations," *JCR*, 21 (September), 354–65.

McQuarrie, Edward F. and David Glen Mick (1992), "On Resonance: A Critical Pluralistic Inquiry into Advertising Rhetoric," *JCR*, 19 (September), 180–97.

Mick, David Glen (1992), "Levels of Subjective Comprehension in Advertising Processing and Their Relations to Ad Perceptions, Attitudes, and Memory," *JCR*, 18 (March), 411–24.

Miller, Darryl W. and Lawrence J. Marks (1992), "Mental Imagery and Sound Effects in Radio Commercials," *JA*, 21 (4), 83–93.

Miniard, Paul W., Sunil Bhatla, Kenneth R. Lord, Peter R. Dickson, and H. Rao Unnava (1991), "Picture-Based Persuasion Processes and the Moderating Role of Involvement," *JCR*, 18 (June), 92–107.

———, ———, and Randall L. Rose (1990), "On the Formation and Relationship of Ad and Brand Attitudes: An Experimental and Causal Analysis," *JMR*, 27 (August), 290–303.

———, Deepak Sirdeshmukh, and Daniel E. Innis (1992), "Peripheral Persuasion and Brand Choice," *JCR*, 19 (September), 226–39.

Mitchell, Andrew A. (1986), "The Effect of Verbal and Visual Components of Advertisements on Brand Attitudes and Attitude Toward the Advertisement," *JCR*, 13 (June), 12–24.

———— and Jerry C. Olson (1981), "Are Product Attribute Beliefs the Only Mediator of Advertising Effects on Brand Attitude?" *JMR*, 18 (August), 318–32.

Mittal, Banwari (1990), "The Relative Roles of Brand Beliefs and Attitude Toward the Ad as Mediators of Brand Attitude: A Second Look," *JMR*, 27 (May), 209–19.

Moore, David J., John C. Mowen, and Richard Reardon (1994), "Multiple Sources in Advertising Appeals: When Product Endorsers Are Paid by the Advertising Sponsor," *JAMS*, 22 (Summer), 234–43.

Muehling, Darrel D., Russell N. Laczniak, and Jeffrey J. Stoltman (1991), "The Moderating Effects of Ad Message Involvement: A Reassessment," *JA*, 20 (June), 29–38.

Munch, James M. and John L. Swasy (1988), "Rhetorical Question, Summarization Frequency, and Argument Strength Effects on Recall," *JCR*, 15 (June), 69–76.

Murry, John P., Jr., John L. Lastovicka, and Surendra N. Singh (1992), "Feeling and Liking Responses to Television Programs: An Examination of Two Explanations for Media-Context Effects," *JCR*, 18 (March), 441–51.

Nyer, Prashanth U. (1997), "A Study of the Relationships Between Cognitive Appraisals and Consumption Emotions," *JAMS*, 25 (Fall), 296–304.

Peterson, Robert A., William R. Wilson, and Steven P. Brown (1992), "Effects of Advertised Customer Satisfaction Claims on Consumer Attitudes and Purchase Intentions," *JAR*, 32 (March/April), 34–40.

Pham, Michel Tuan (1996), "Cue Representation and Selection Effects of Arousal on Persuasion," *JCR*, 22 (March), 373–87.

Prakash, Ved (1992), "Sex Roles and Advertising Preferences," *JAR*, 32 (May/June), 43–52.

Raju, P.S. and Manoj Hastak (1983), "Pre-Trial Cognitive Effects of Cents-Off Coupons," *JA*, 12 (2), 24–33.

Rosbergen, Edward, Rik Pieters, and Michel Wedel (1997), "Visual Attention to Advertising: A Segment-Level Analysis," *JCR*, 24 (December), 305–14.

Rossiter, John R. and Larry Percy (1980), "Attitude Change Through Visual Imagery in Advertising," *JA*, 9 (2), 10–16.

Sanbonmatsu, David and Frank R. Kardes (1988), "The Effects of Physiological Arousal on Information Processing and Persuasion," *JCR*, 15 (December), 379–85.

Sheffet, Mary Jane (1983), "An Experimental Investigation of the Documentation of Advertising Claims," *JA*, 12 (1), 19–29.

Shiv, Baba, Julie A. Edell, and John W. Payne (1997), "Factors Affecting the Impact of Negatively and Positively Framed Ad Messages," *JCR*, 24 (December), 285–94.

Simpson, Penny M., Steve Horton, and Gene Brown (1996), "Male Nudity in Advertisements: A Modified Replication and Extension of Gender and Product Effects," *JAMS*, 24 (Summer), 257–62.

Singh, Surendra N. and Catherine Cole (1993), "The Effects of Length, Content, and Repetition on Television Commercial Effectiveness," *JMR*, 30 (February), 91–104.

Sirgy, M. Joseph, Dhruv Grewal, Tamara F. Mangleburg, Jae-ok Park, Kye-Sung Chon, C.B. Claiborne, J.S. Johar, and Harold Berkman (1997), "Assessing the Predictive Validity of Two Methods of Measuring Self-Image Congruence," *JAMS*, 25 (Summer), 229–41.

Smith, Robert E. (1993), "Integrating Information From Advertising and Trial: Processes and Effects on Consumer Response to Product Information," *JMR*, 30 (May), 204–19.

———— and William R. Swinyard (1983), "Attitude–Behavior Consistency: The Impact of Product Trial Versus Advertising," *JMR*, 20 (August), 257–67.

Stafford, Marla Royne and Ellen Day (1995), "Retail Services Advertising: The Effects of Appeal, Medium, and Service," *JA*, 24 (Spring), 57–71.

Stayman, Douglas M. and Rajeev Batra (1991), "Encoding and Retrieval of Ad Affect in Memory," *JMR*, 28 (May), 232–39.

Stout, Patricia and Benedicta L. Burda (1989), "Zipped Commericals: Are They Effective?" *JA*, 18 (4), 23–32.

Stuart, Elnora W., Terence A. Shimp, and Randall W. Engle (1987), "Classical Conditioning of Consumer Attitudes: Four Experiments in an Advertising Context," *JCR*, 14 (December), 334–49.

Sujan, Mita and James R. Bettman (1989), "The Effects of Brand Positioning Strategies on Consumers' Brand and Category Perceptions: Some Insights from Schema Research," *JMR*, 26 (November), 454–67.

———, ———, and Hans Baumgartner (1993), "Influencing Consumer Judgments Using Autobiographical Memories: A Self-Referencing Perspective," *JMR*, 30 (November), 422–36.

Taylor, Charles R., Gordon E. Miracle, and R. Dale Wilson (1997), "The Impact of Information Level on the Effectiveness of U.S. and Korean Television Commercials," *JA*, 26 (Spring), 1–18.

Tripp, Carolyn, Thomas D. Jensen, and Les Carlson (1994), "The Effects of Multiple Product Endorsements by Celebrities on Consumers' Attitudes and Intentions," *JCR*, 20 (March), 535–47.

Unnava, H. Rao, Robert E. Burnkrant, and Sunil Erevelles (1994), "Effects of Presentation Order and Communication Modality on Recall and Attitude," *JCR*, 21 (September), 481–90.

Wansink, Brian and Michael L. Ray (1992), "Estimating an Advertisement's Impact on One's Consumption of a Brand," *JAR*, 32 (May/June), 9–16.

Ward, James C., Mary Jo Bitner, and John Barnes (1992), "Measuring the Prototypicality and Meaning of Retail Environments," *JR*, 68 (Summer), 194–220.

Whittler, Tommy E. (1991), "The Effects of Actors' Race in Commercial Advertising: Review and Extension," *JA*, 20 (1), 54–60.

——— and Joan DiMeo (1991), "Viewers' Reactions to Racial Cues in Advertising Stimuli," *JAR*, 31 (December), 37–46.

Yi, Youjae (1990a), "Cognitive and Affective Priming Effects of the Context for Print Advertisements," *JA*, 19 (2), 40–48.

——— (1990b), "The Effects of Contextual Priming in Print Advertisements," *JCR*, 17 (September), 215–22.

Zhang, Yong (1996), "Responses to Humorous Advertising: The Moderating Effect of Need for Cognition," *JA*, 25 (Spring), 15–32.

——— and Betsy D. Gelb (1996), "Matching Advertising Appeals to Culture: The Influence of Products' Use Conditions," *JA*, 25 (Fall), 29–46.

Zinkhan, George M., William B. Locander, and James H. Leigh (1986), "Dimensional Relationships of Aided Recall and Recognition," *JA*, 15 (1), 38–46.

SCALE ITEMS: Rate your overall feelings about using the brand:*

1. Good/Bad
2. Like/Dislike
3. Pleasant/Unpleasant
4. High quality/Poor quality
5. Agreeable/Disagreeable
6. Satisfactory/Dissatisfactory
7. Wise/Foolish
8. Beneficial/Harmful
9. Favorable/Unfavorable
10. Distinctive/Common
11. Likable/Unlikable

12. Positive/Negative
13. Buy/Would not buy
14. Attractive/Unattractive
15. Enjoyable/Unenjoyable
16. Useful/Useless
17. Desirable/Undesirable
18. Nice/Awful
19. Important/Unimportant
20. Beneficial/Not beneficial
21. Valuable/Worthless
22. Appetizing/Unappetizing
23. Unique/Not unique
24. Expensive/Inexpensive
25. Needed/Not needed
26. Fond of/Not fond of
27. Superior/Inferior
28. Interesting/Boring
29. Tasteful/Tasteless
30. Appealing/Unappealing
31. For me/Not for me
32. Appropriate/Inappropriate
33. Reasonable/Unreasonable
34. Value for money/No value for money

*Directions could be something similar to this. Scale items used in specific studies are listed next, with an indication of the number of response alternatives, if known. Some authors have used scale anchors that have essentially the same meaning but minor semantic differences, such as *like/not like* instead of *like very much/dislike very much*. For purposes of parsimony, one version is reported, and slight variations are noted with an asterisk (*). Finally, for ease of reporting, the positive anchors (when clear) are listed on the left.

Aaker and Maheswaran (1997): 1*, 9*, 13*, 16*; 9-point
Alpert and Kamins (1995) {overall attitude}: 2*, 9*, 12*; 7-point
Anand and Sternthal (1990): 1, 2, 3, 13, 15; 7-point
Babin and Burns (1997): 1, 14, 17, 28*, 30, 31, 32, 33; 7-point
Batra and Ray (1986b) {first use}: 1, 3, 16, 18, 19; 7-point
Batra and Ray (1986b) {second use}: 3, 16, 18, 19
Batra and Stayman (1990): 1, 2, 3, 4*, 5, 9, 12, 16, 20, 21
Bello, Pitts, and Etzel (1983): 1*, 4*, 7*, 8*, 10*, 16*, 17*; 7-point
Berger and Mitchell (1989): 1, 2*; 7-point
Bone and Ellen (1992): 1, 7, 9, 16
Burnkrant and Unnava (1995): 1, 3, 8, 17, 18, 27; 7-point
Chattopadhyay and Basu (1990): 1, 2, 18*; 9-point
Chattopadhyay and Nedungadi (1992): 1, 2, 18*; 9-point
Cox and Cox (1988): 1, 3, 11; 9-point
Cox and Locander (1987): 1, 3, 11; 9-point
Darley and Smith (1993): 1, 4, 11*
Darley and Smith (1995): 1, 3, 4, 11*
Deshpandé and Stayman (1994): 1, 3, 4*, 12, 16, 21; 7-point

Droge (1989): 1, 3, 5, 6*, 7, 8; 7-point
Edell and Keller (1989): 1*, 2*; 7-point
Gardner, Mitchell, and Russo (1985): 1, 2*, 4
Gelb and Zinkhan (1986): 1, 6*, 9
Gill, Grossbart, and Laczniak (1988): 1*, 2*, 9*, 21*; 7-point
Goodstein (1993): 1, 9, 11; 7-point
Gotlieb and Swan (1990): 1, 6*, 9
Grossbart, Muehling, and Kangun (1986): 1, 9, 12; 7-point
Hastak and Olson (1989; Hastak 1990): 1, 2, 4; 7-point
Health, McCarthy, and Mothersbaugh (1994): 1, 6*, 9; 9-point
Herr, Kardes, and Kim (1991): 1, 9, 17; 11-point
Holbrook and Batra (1987): 1*, 2*, 9*, 12*; 7-point
Homer (1990): 1, 2, 9; 9-point
Homer and Kahle (1990): 1, 6*, 17
Iyer (1988): 1, 8, 16; 7-point
Kardes and Kalyanaram (1992): 1*, 6, 9*; 11-point
Keller (1991a): 1, 3, 4, 5, 8, 11, 16, 18, 19; 7-point
Keller (1991b): 1, 3, 4, 11; 7-point
Kelleris, Cox, and Cox (1993): 1, 2, 11*, 28*, 29; 7-point
Kim, Allen, and Kardes (1996): 1, 2*, 3, 4, 14, 27, 28; 7-point (unclear)
Laczniak and Muehling (1993): 1*, 2*, 4, 9*, 21; 7-point
Leclerc and Little (1997): 1, 6*, 9; 9-point
Lim, Darley, and Summers (1994): 1, 9, 11*; 7-point
Loken and Ward (1990): 1, 4, 6*; 11-point
Lord, Lee, and Sauer (1994, 1995): 1, 3, 9; 7-point
Machleit, Allen, and Madden (1993): 1, 7*, 17; 7-point
MacInnis and Park (1991): 1*, 9, 11*, 30; 7-point
MacKenzie and Lutz (1989): 1, 3, 9; 7-point
MacKenzie, Lutz, and Belch (1986): 1, 7, 9; 7-point
MacKenzie and Spreng (1992): 1, 3, 9; 7-point
Macklin, Bruvold, and Shea (1985): 1, 3, 18, 21, 27, 28; 7-point
Maheswaran (1994): 1, 9, 16*; 9-point
McQuarrie and Mick (1992): 1*, 4*, 21; 7-point
Mick (1992): 1, 3, 21; 9-point
Miller and Marks (1992): 1, 2*, 3, 4, 25; 7-point
Miniard et al. (1991): 2*, 9, 12; 7-point
Miniard, Bhatla, and Rose (1990): 2, 9, 12; 7-point
Miniard, Sirdeshmukh, and Innis (1992) {initial measure}: 9, 12, 30; 11-point
Miniard, Sirdeshmukh, and Innis (1992) {final measure}: 1, 14, 17; 7-point
Mitchell (1986): 1, 2, 3; 7-point
Mitchell and Olson (1981): 1, 2*, 3, 4; 5-point
Mittal (1990): 1, 2, 17; 7-point
Moore, Mowen, and Reardon (1994): 1, 9, 20*; 7-point
Muehling, Laczniak, and Stoltman (1991): 1, 9, 12; 7-point
Munch and Swasy (1988): 1, 3, 12; 7-point
Murry, Lastovicka, and Singh (1992): 1, 3, 7, 8, 9, 11*; 5-point (unclear)
Peterson, Wilson, and Brown (1992): 4, 16*, 17*, 23, 24
Pham (1996) {experiment 1}: 1, 6*, 9; 7-point
Pham (1996) {experiments 2 and 3}: 1, 2, 6*, 9

Raju and Hastak (1983): 1, 2*, 4; 7-point
Rosenberg, Pieters, and Wedel (1997): 1, 4*, 34; 5-point
Rossiter and Percy (1980): 1, 3, 27, 28; 7-point
Sanbonmatsu and Kardes (1988): 1, 6, 9; 9-point
Shiv, Edell, and Payne (1997): 1, 3, 4*, 11*, 30; 7-point
Simpson, Horton, and Brown (1996): 1, 2, 3, 4, 5, 8*, 9, 12, 16, 21; 9-point
Singh and Cole (1993): 2*, 8*, 15, 16, 19, 21, 26; 7-point
Sirgy et al. (1997): 1*, 6*, 9*; 5-point
Smith (1993): 1, 3, 9
Smith and Swinyard (1983): 1, 3, 5, 6; 7-point
Stafford and Day (1995): 1, 9, 12; 7-point
Stout and Burda (1989): 2, 9; 7-point
Stuart, Shimp, and Engle (1987): 1, 2*, 3, 4, 14, 27, 28; 7-point
Sujan and Bettman (1989): 1, 9, 12; 7-point
Sujan, Bettman, and Baumgartner (1993): 1, 3, 9, 12; 9-point
Taylor, Miracle, and Wilson (1997): 3, 8, 9, 12; 7-point
Tripp, Jensen, and Carlson (1994): 1, 2*, 3, 4*; 7-point
Unnava, Burnkrant, and Erevelles (1994): 1*, 14, 17*, 18*; 7-point
Wansink and Ray (1992): 1*, 4*, 11, 22; 7-point
Ward, Bitner, and Barnes (1992): 1, 4, 6*; 11-point
Whittler (1991): 1, 4*, 6*; 15-point
Whittler and DiMeo (1991): 1, 4*, 6*; 15-point
Yi (1990a): 1, 2, 3; 7-point
Yi (1990b): 1, 2, 9; 7-point
Zhang (1996): 1, 11*, 18*; 9-point
Zhang and Gelb (1996): 1, 11*, 18*; 9-point
Zinkhan, Locander, and Leigh (1986): 1, 3, 21; 8-point

SCALE NAME: Attitude Toward the Service Provider

SCALE DESCRIPTION: Three seven-point bipolar adjectives used to measure a respondent's attitude toward a person or organization that renders a service.

SCALE ORIGIN: Stafford (1996; Day and Stafford 1997) cites an attitude-toward-the-brand measure by Yi (1990) as the source of the items. Thus, this scale is basically an Ab scale modified so the scale stem focuses the respondent's attention on the provider of some service rather than on a product.

SAMPLES: Day and Stafford (1997) collected their data from **126** undergraduate students from two universities. A little more than half the sample were men (55%), 16.7 % were married, and the average age was nearly 24 years. No compensation was provided, and participation was voluntary.

The scale was used in two experiments conducted by Stafford (1996). Subjects were recruited from three religious and civic organizations that received an honorarium ($10 in Experiment 1, $5 in Experiment 2) per completed questionnaire. Analysis was based on complete data from **80** and **89** subjects for Experiments 1 and 2, respectively. Both samples had a wide cross-section of age and incomes. The main differences between the groups were that Study 2 had more men than Study 1 (47% versus 38%) and had a greater percentage of older people in higher income categories.

RELIABILITY: An alpha of **.97** was reported for the scale as used in Experiment 1 by Stafford (1996). The alpha for the scale in the study by Day and Stafford (1997; Stafford 1999) was **.94**.

VALIDITY: No examination of the scale's validity was reported.

ADMINISTRATION: In both studies, the scale was part of a self-administered questionnaire completed by subjects after they were exposed to experimental stimuli (Day and Stafford 1997; Stafford 1996). Higher scores on the scale suggested that a person had a very favorable attitude toward a specified service provider.

MAJOR FINDINGS: An experiment was conducted by Day and Stafford (1997) to investigate potential problems service retailers might encounter when using older-age cues in their advertising. **Attitude toward the service** was not found to be significantly affected by older-age cues.

The experiments by Stafford (1996) investigated whether the presence of visual and verbal tangible cues had an impact on ad effectiveness. As hypothesized, print ads with tangible verbal cues were associated with significantly more **attitudes toward the service provider** than were ads with intangible cues.

REFERENCES:
Day, Ellen and Marla Royne Stafford (1997), "Age-Related Cues in Retail Services Advertising: Their Effects on Younger Consumers," *JR*, 73 (2), 211–33.

Stafford, Marla Royne (1996), "Tangibility in Services Advertising: An Investigation of Verbal Versus Visual Cues," *JA*, 25 (Fall), 13–28.

———— (1999), personal correspondence.

Yi, Youjae (1990), "Cognitive and Affective Priming Effects of the Context for Print Advertisements," *JA*, 19 (2), 40–48.

SCALE ITEMS: *

Use the following scales to indicate your feelings about *name of service provider*.

1. Bad   :___:___:___:___:___:___:___: Good
                   1   2   3   4   5   6   7

2. Unfavorable   :___:___:___:___:___:___:___: Favorable
                   1   2   3   4   5   6   7

3. Negative   :___:___:___:___:___:___:___: Positive
                   1   2   3   4   5   6   7

*The phrasing of the scale stem was not specified in the articles. The name of the service provider should be placed in the blank.

SCALE NAME: Attitude Toward the Spanish Language

SCALE DESCRIPTION: A three-item scale measuring the degree to which a person has a positive opinion of Spanish as a language.

SCALE ORIGIN: The scale appears to have been developed by Koslow, Shamdasani, and Touchstone (1994) for their study.

SAMPLES: Data were gathered by Koslow, Shamdasani, and Touchstone (1994) in personal interviews with shoppers at three southern California supermarkets. Bilingual interviewers were used and asked to approach only those shoppers who appeared to be Hispanic. Of the 413 interviews that were begun, **367** yielded enough information to be useful in the analysis. The sample was 56% men, 60.7% were between the ages of 20 and 39 years, and 57.2% indicated that they were bilingual native Spanish speakers.

RELIABILITY: An alpha of **.774** was reported for the scale by Koslow, Shamdasani, and Touchstone (1994).

VALIDITY: The validity of the scale was not specifically addressed in the study (Koslow, Shamdasani, and Touchstone 1994).

ADMINISTRATION: The scale was part of a longer questionnaire administered by trained bilingual interviewers (Koslow, Shamdasani, and Touchstone 1994). The respondents were first greeted and recruited in Spanish and then asked in what language they would prefer the interview be conducted. As with the rest of the survey instrument, the scale was first developed in English, and the back-translation method was used to help refine the quality of the Spanish version. A little more than one-fourth of the respondents chose to have the interview conducted in English, and the remaining portion of the sample chose Spanish. Therefore, the scale items were read to respondents rather than being self-administered.

High scores on the scale suggested that respondents had a very positive attitude toward the Spanish language. The scores on each items were *not* standardized before summing, which means that item #2 carries more weight in determining overall scores on the scale than the other two items (Koslow 1996). Although not typical, its appropriateness could be justified if supported by evidence from a factor analysis.

MAJOR FINDINGS: The study by Koslow, Shamdasani, and Touchstone (1994) examined how consumers in an ethnic subculture respond to the use of their language in advertising. No significant relationship was found between **attitude toward the Spanish language** and affect toward an ad that was varied for different respondent groups in the language used (i.e., Spanish, English, both).

REFERENCES:
Koslow, Scott (1996), personal correspondence.
———, Prem N. Shamdasani, and Ellen E. Touchstone (1994), "Exploring Language Effects in Ethnic Advertising: A Socioliguistic Perspective," *JCR*, 20 (March), 575–85.

SCALE ITEMS:

Is the Spanish language:

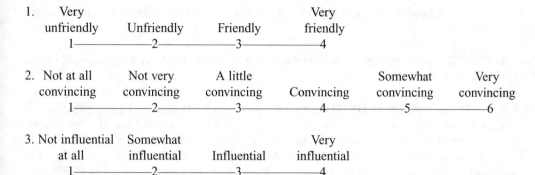

1. Very   Very
    unfriendly   Unfriendly   Friendly   friendly
        1————————2————————3————————4

2. Not at all   Not very   A little   Somewhat   Very
    convincing   convincing   convincing   Convincing   convincing   convincing
        1————————2————————3————————4————————5————————6

3. Not influential   Somewhat   Very
      at all   influential   Influential   influential
        1————————2————————3————————4

SCALE NAME: Attribute Favorability

SCALE DESCRIPTION: A three-item, nine-point semantic differential scale that measures the degree to which a person believes that the terms in which a product and its features have been described are positive and better than the competition's.

SCALE ORIGIN: The scale appears to be original to Maheswaran (1994). Aaker and Maheswaran (1997) used it with few if any changes.

SAMPLES: Aaker and Maheswaran (1997) reported on two experiments they conducted, both of which used the **attribute** scale as a manipulation check. Subjects in both experiments came from the undergraduate management program at Chinese University in Hong Kong and included students of both sexes, but all were of Chinese ethnic origin who were born and raised in Hong Kong. Sample sizes were **136** and **119** for Experiments 1 and 2, respectively. Use of subjects from the Chinese culture was deliberate, because it was known from previous research to be on the extreme pole of collectivism.

Data were gathered by Maheswaran (1994) in Study 1 from **119** students in an undergraduate management program who participated for extra credit. Data were collected in small group sessions, and subjects were randomly assigned to conditions. No effects of gender or involvement were observed. Study 2 collected information from **135** students that were apparently similar to those in Study 1.

RELIABILITY: Alphas for the scale as used in Experiments 1 and 2 by Aaker and Maheswaran (1997) were **.84** and **.83**, respectively. Alphas of **.87** (PCs) and **.81** (stereo systems) were reported for the scale by Maheswaran (1994) in Studies 1 and 2, respectively.

VALIDITY: No information regarding the scale's validity was reported in the articles by Aaker and Maheswaran (1997) or Maheswaran (1994). However, some sense of the scale's validity comes from its use as a manipulation check. (See "Findings" below.)

ADMINISTRATION: The scale was self-administered by subjects in the studies by Aaker and Maheswaran (1997) and Maheswaran (1994), along with other measures, after they were exposed to reading material containing experimental stimuli. Higher scores on the scale indicated that the respondents believed that a product was described favorably in some specified medium.

MAJOR FINDINGS: The generalizability of persuasion effects predicted by dual process models was examined in the context of a non-Western, collectivistic culture by Aaker and Maheswaran (1997). The **attribute favorability** scale was used as a manipulation check and showed that those who received information that was expected to be viewed as positive rated the product significantly better than those in the other treatment, who received a negative product description.

Similarly, Maheswaran (1994) examined the effects of country of origin image, consumer expertise, and attribute strength on product evaluations. **The attribute favorability** scale was used merely as a manipulation check. In Studies 1 and 2, the data clearly supported that those product descriptions the researcher had intended subjects to view as favorable scored better than those descriptions that were manipulated to be viewed as unfavorable.

COMMENTS: The medium used by Maheswaran (1994) was a booklet that subjects read, but it appears that the scale is amenable for use with other media to which the subjects could be exposed (e.g., television, radio, magazine, PC).

REFERENCES:

Aaker, Jennifer L. (1998), personal correspondence.
——— and Durairaj Maheswaran (1997), "The Effect of Cultural Orientation on Persuasion," *JCR*, 24 (December), 315–28.
Maheswaran, Durairaj (1994), "Country of Origin as a Stereotype: Effects of Consumer Expertise and Attribute Strength on Product Evaluations," *JCR*, 21 (September), 354–65.

SCALE ITEMS:*

DIRECTIONS: The product description of the *brand name/model* indicated it as:

Having few positive features	:___:___:___:___:___:___:___:___:	Having many positive features
	-4 -3 -2 -1 0 1 2 3 4	

Having many negative features	:___:___:___:___:___:___:___:___:	Having few negative features
	-4 -3 -2 -1 0 1 2 3 4	

Inferior to competing brands	:___:___:___:___:___:___:___:___:	Superior to competing brands
	-4 -3 -2 -1 0 1 2 3 4	

*These are the items and scale stem used by Aaker and Maheswaran (1997; Aaker 1998). The items used by Maheswaran (1994) appear to have been the same or very similar, except that 1 through 9 were the numerical anchors to the scale.

SCALE NAME: Attribution of Blame

SCALE DESCRIPTION: Four five-point items purported to measure the extent to which responsibility for an accident resulting from the use of a manufacturer's product should be placed on the manufacturer or the user.

SCALE ORIGIN: Griffin, Babin, and Attaway (1996) apparently drew inspiration for the scale (though not the actual structure) from a previous effort to measure causality assignments in an achievement context (Russell 1982).

SAMPLES: Students collected data for the study by Griffin, Babin, and Attaway (1996) for course credit. The students were assigned to distribute questionnaires in various parts of a midsized Midwestern U.S. city. In some cases, the instruments were picked up by students, whereas in others, they were mailed back. Of the 420 survey instruments dropped off, **262** were returned. No other information about the sample was provided except that it was considered to be representative of the area from which it was drawn and only adults (older than 18 years of age) were selected to respond.

RELIABILITY: Griffin, Babin, and Attaway (1996) reported an alpha of **.92** for the scale.

VALIDITY: Because of concerns about the level of correlation between this measure and another (#22), Griffin, Babin, and Attaway (1996) checked the discriminant validity between the two. The evidence provided support for their discriminant validity.

ADMINISTRATION: The scale was self-administered by respondents as part of a larger survey instrument (Griffin, Babin, and Attaway 1996). Higher scores on the scale indicated that respondents believed that the manufacturer was to blame for the accident.

MAJOR FINDINGS: Griffin, Babin, and Attaway (1996) explored the attribution of blame toward marketers when negative consequences result from use of their products. Among the findings was that the greater the anticipated negative consequences of using a product, the more likely a person **attributes blame** to the consumer rather than the marketer.

REFERENCES:
Griffin, Mitch, Barry J. Babin, and Jill Attaway (1996), "Anticipation of Injurious Consumption Outcomes and Its Impact on Consumer Attributions of Blame," *JAMS*, 24 (Fall), 314–27.
Russell, Dan (1982), "The Causal Dimension Scale: A Measure of How Individuals Perceive Causes," *Journal of Personality and Social Psychology*, 42 (June), 1137–45.

SCALE ITEMS:

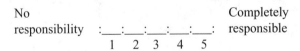

No
responsibility   :___:___:___:___:___: Completely
responsible
           1   2   3   4   5

1. How much do you blame the product's manufacturer?

2. How responsible was the product manufacturer for the accident?

3. How much blame do you place on the victim for the accident? **(r)**

4. How responsible was the victim for he accident? **(r)**

SCALE NAME: Authority

SCALE DESCRIPTION: Eight seven-point Likert-type statements that evaluate the degree to which a person views him- or herself as a leader and desires to have influence over others.

SCALE ORIGIN: The scale is original to the study by Raskin and Terry (1988) and is part of the Narcissistic Personality Inventory (NPI). Of the 40-item NPI, the 8 items shown here loaded highest on the same dimension and were labeled **authority**. The internal consistency of these items as a set was estimated to be .73 (n = 1018). The scale showed little or no relationship with age and gender. Considerable evidence in support of the scale's nomological validity was provided.

SAMPLES: Various samples were collected and used by Netemeyer, Burton, and Lichtenstein (1995) in the process of validating other scales. The **authority** scale was used in one study that consisted of 186 students and 264 "nonstudent adults." It was used in another study with data from 27 football players from a nationally ranked NCAA Division I team.

RELIABILITY: Alphas of **.91** (students) and **.92** (nonstudent adults) were found for the scale by Netemeyer, Burton, and Lichtenstein (1995; Netemeyer 1997).

VALIDITY: Although the validity of the scale was not directly examined by Netemeyer, Burton, and Lichtenstein (1995), the scale was used to help establish the construct validity of four vanity-related scales. **Authority** had significant positive correlations with all of the vanity scales except one, physical concern (#397).

ADMINISTRATION: As noted, the scale was used in two studies, and it appears to have been part of larger questionnaires that were self-administered by respondents (Netemeyer, Burton, and Lichtenstein 1995). Higher scores on the scale indicated that respondents liked to be leaders and use authority.

MAJOR FINDINGS: Netemeyer, Burton, and Lichtenstein (1995) investigated vanity and developed four scales for its measurement. Most of the article discussed the results of the rather extensive validation process. Among the findings was that achievement view vanity (#396) had a strong positive relationship with **authority**.

REFERENCES:
Netemeyer, Richard G. (1997), personal correspondence.
——, Scot Burton, and Donald R. Lichtenstein (1995), "Trait Aspects of Vanity: Measurement and Relevance to Consumer Behavior," *JCR*, 21 (March), 612–26.
Raskin, Robert and Howard Terry (1988), "A Principal-Components Analysis of the Narcissistic Personality Inventory and Further Evidence of its Construct Validity," *Journal of Personality and Social Psychology*, 54 (May), 890–902.

SCALE ITEMS:

Strongly   Strongly
disagree   :___:___:___:___:___:___:___: agree

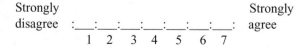

              1   2   3   4   5   6   7

#58 *Authority*

1. I would prefer to be a leader.

2. I see myself as a good leader.

3. I will be a success.

4. People always seem to recognize my authority.

5. I have a natural talent for influencing people.

6. I am assertive.

7. I like to have authority over other people.

8. I am a born leader.

SCALE NAME: Behavioral Intention

SCALE DESCRIPTION: A semantic differential scale measuring the stated inclination of a person to engage in a specified behavior. In most of the studies described, the behavior was a purchase, but the items are general enough to refer to nonpurchase behaviors as well (e.g., likelihood of shopping at a store, paying attention to an ad, using a coupon). One version of the scale used by Machleit, Allen, and Madden (1993) (referred to as *contact intention*) measured a consumer's motivation to try the brand if he or she was in the market for the product. Stafford (1996; Day and Stafford 1997) used the scale to measure *patronage intention*, and Urbany and colleagues (1997) measured *willingness to rent an apartment*. The various versions of the scale differ in the number and set of items employed. However, the uses were similar in that they had multiple items in common. (See the "Scale Items" section.)

SCALE ORIGIN: Little information was provided in most of the studies about the origin of the particular sets of items they used. Because it is unlikely that they would have independently arrived at such similar sets of items, they must have, instead, built on some unspecified source and one another. The books by Fishbein (Ajzen and Fishbein 1980; Fishbein and Ajzen 1975) are possible sources, though only item #1 figures prominently in those books as a way to measure **behavioral intention**.

Taylor, Miracle, and Wilson (1997) developed a Korean version of the scale using the back-translation method.

SELECTED SAMPLES: MacKenzie, Lutz, and Belch (1986) used the scale in two experiments. In the first experiment, **260** people were recruited from two church organizations. They ranged in age from 18 to 75 years, and 69% were women. The subjects in the second experiment were **225** undergraduate- and master's-level business students who volunteered for the study.

The experiment conducted by Netemeyer and Bearden (1992) was based on data from a sample of **372** undergraduate students. They were randomly assigned to a 2 (informational influence) × 2 (normative influence) design. The sample was split approximately in half to test two different models of behavioral intention. Therefore, there were four cells per model tested, with each cell having between 46 and 49 subjects.

Oliver and Bearden (1985) used data from **353** members of a bistate consumer panel who responded to two questionnaires and received a four-week supply of diet suppressant capsules between the two questionnaires. Panel members were selected to be representative of urban and suburban households with family incomes greater than $10,000 annually. Subjects were typically white (89%), female (56%), and had at least some education beyond high school (70%).

The scale was used in two experiments conducted by Stafford (1996). Subjects were recruited from three religious and civic organizations that received an honorarium ($10 in Experiment 1, $5 in Experiment 2) per completed questionnaire. Analysis was based on complete data from **80** and **89** subjects for Experiments 1 and 2, respectively. Both samples had a wide cross-section of age and incomes, with the main difference between the groups being that Experiment 2 had more men than Experiment 1 (47% versus 38%) and had a greater percentage of older people in higher income categories.

Taylor, Miracle, and Wilson (1997) compared data collected from **101** female undergraduate students in the United States and **101** similar students in Korea. The women in the United States were attending a Midwestern university, whereas those in Korea attended a university in Seoul.

SELECTED RELIABILITIES: Reported internal consistencies range from **.84** (Shimp and Sharma 1987) to **.97** (Homer 1995). Specific reliabilities are provided for the selected studies described in the "Samples" and "Findings" sections.

Alphas of **.88** and **.90** were reported by MacKenzie, Lutz, and Belch (1986) for their first and second experiments, respectively. Two models of behavioral intention were tested by Netemeyer and Bearden

(1992), and alphas were separately calculated as **.91** and **.90**. The LISREL estimate of reliability was **.87** as reported by Oliver and Bearden (1985). Stafford (1996) reported an alpha of **.94**. Alphas for the scale as used by Taylor, Miracle, and Wilson (1997) in the United States and Korea were **.98** and **.97**, respectively.

VALIDITY: In none of the studies was the scale's validity fully addressed. Although not specifically examining the validity of **behavioral intention**, Machleit, Allen, and Madden (1993) used confirmatory factor analysis to provide evidence that another measure (brand interest, #139, Vol. II) and two measures of **behavioral intention** (purchase and contact) were not measures of the same construct (discriminant validity). Similarly, a couple of tests generally described by Urbany and colleagues (1997) provided support for a claim of discriminant validity for the scale, but the details relative to this particular scale were not given.

A correlation matrix was provided by MacKenzie and Spreng (1992) between the items in the **behavioral intention** scale and several others that sheds some limited light on the issue of validity. For example, the intercorrelations of the **intention** scale items ranged between .47 and .88, which provides some evidence that the items are measuring the same thing. In contrast, the correlations between the **intention** items and items measuring related but theoretically distinct constructs were much lower.

ADMINISTRATION: Administration was similar in most of the studies, in that the scale was given to subjects as part of a larger questionnaire after they had viewed some test stimulus. In contrast, Oliver and Bearden (1985) included the scale on a questionnaire sent to panel subjects before they received a test stimulus. In the study by Machleit, Allen, and Madden (1993), subjects filled out the measure both before and after being exposed to an ad. A high score on the scale indicated that a person planned on engaging in a certain behavior, whereas a low score suggested that a person was unlikely to do something.

SELECTED FINDINGS: MacKenzie, Lutz, and Belch (1986) examined four competing models of attitude toward the ad's role as a mediator of ad influence on brand attitudes and **purchase intentions**. The dual mediation hypothesis was found to be the superior model and provided evidence that attitude toward the ad does not have a significant direct effect on **behavioral intentions**.

Netemeyer and Bearden (1992) conducted an experiment to compare the causal structure and predictive ability of the models of behavioral intentions by Ajzen and Fishbein (1980) and Miniard and Cohen (1983). The former was much better than the latter at **predicting behavioral intention**.

Oliver and Bearden (1985) examined an extension of the crossover path in the Fishbein behavioral intention model. Both attitude toward the act and the subjective norm were found to have a significant impact on **behavioral intentions**, though the impact of the former was much greater. Furthermore, the results indicated that **behavioral intention** had a significant impact on self-reported behavior.

The experiments by Stafford (1996) investigated whether the presence of visual and verbal tangible cues had an impact on ad effectiveness. As was hypothesized, print ads with tangible verbal cues were associated with significantly more positive behavioral intentions than were ads with intangible cues.

Taylor, Miracle, and Wilson (1997) compared the effectiveness of commercials that differed in their information content between U.S. and Korean students. Among the findings was that Koreans had higher **purchase intentions** than Americans toward products shown in commercials judged to be low in information.

COMMENTS: See also Dabholkar (1994); Dabholkar, Thorpe, and Rentz (1996); Lim, Darley, and Summers (1994); Prakash (1992); Schuhwerk and Lefkoff-Hagius (1995); and Tripp, Jensen, and Carlson (1994).

REFERENCES:

Ajzen, Icek and Martin Fishbein (1980), *Understanding Attitudes and Predicting Social Behavior.* Englewood Cliffs, NJ: Prentice-Hall.

Chattopadhyay, Amitava and Kunal Basu (1990), "Humor in Advertising: The Moderating Role of Prior Brand Evaluation," *JMR*, 27 (November), 466–76.

Dabholkar, Pratibha (1994), "Incorporating Choice into an Attitudinal Framework: Analyzing Models of Mental Comparison Processes," *JCR*, 21 (June), 100–118.

———, Dayle I. Thorpe, and Joseph O. Rentz (1996), "A Measure of Service Quality for Retail Stores: Scale Development and Validation," *JAMS*, 24 (Winter), 3–16.

Day, Ellen and Marla Royne Stafford (1997), "Age-Related Cues in Retail Services Advertising: Their Effects on Younger Consumers," *JR*, 73 (2), 211–33.

Fishbein, Martin and Icek Ajzen (1975), *Belief, Attitude, Intention, and Behavior: An Introduction to Theory and Research*. Reading, MA: Addison-Wesley.

Gill, James D., Sanford Grossbart, and Russell N. Laczniak (1988), "Influence of Involvement, Commitment and Familiarity on Brand Beliefs and Attitudes of Viewers Exposed to Alternative Claim Strategies," *JA*, 17 (2), 33–43.

Gotlieb, Jerry B. and Dan Sarel (1991), "Comparative Advertising Effectiveness: The Role of Involvement and Source Credibility," *JA*, 20 (1), 38–45.

——— and ——— (1992), "The Influence of Type of Advertisement, Price, and Source Credibility on Perceived Quality," *JAMS*, 20 (Summer), 253–60.

Grossbart, Sanford, Darrel D. Muehling, and Norman Kangun (1986), "Verbal and Visual References to Competition in Comparative Advertising," *JA*, 15 (1), 10–23.

Homer, Pamela M. (1995), "Ad Size as an Indicator of Perceived Advertising Costs and Effort: The Effects on Memory and Perceptions," *JA*, 24 (Winter), 1–12.

Lacher, Kathleen T. and Richard Mizerski (1994), "An Exploratory Study of the Responses and Relationships Involved in the Evaluation of, and in the Intention to Purchase New Rock Music," *JCR*, 21 (September), 366–80.

Lim, Jeen-Su, William K. Darley, and John O. Summers (1994), "An Assessment of Country of Origin Effects Under Alternative Presentation Formats," *JAMS*, 22 (3), 272–82.

Machleit, Karen A., Chris T. Allen, and Thomas J. Madden (1993), "The Mature Brand and Brand Interest: An Alternative Consequence of Ad-Evoked Affect," *JM*, 57 (October), 72–82.

MacKenzie, Scott B., Richard J. Lutz, and George E. Belch (1986), "The Role of Attitude Toward the Ad as a Mediator of Advertising Effectiveness: A Test of Competing Explanations," *JMR*, 23 (May), 130–43.

——— and Richard A. Spreng (1992), "How Does Motivation Moderate the Impact of Central and Peripheral Processing on Brand Attitudes and Intentions," *JCR*, 18 (March), 519–29.

Miniard, Paul W. and Joel B. Cohen (1983), "Modeling Personal and Normative Influences on Behavior," *JCR*, 10 (September), 169–80.

Netemeyer, Richard G. and William O. Bearden (1992), "A Comparative Analysis of Two Models of Behavioral Intention," *JAMS*, 20 (Winter), 49–59.

Oliver, Richard L. and William O. Bearden (1985), "Crossover Effects in the Theory of Reasoned Action: A Moderating Influence Attempt," *JCR*, 12 (December) 324–40.

Prakash, Ved (1992), "Sex Roles and Advertising Preferences," *JAR*, 32 (May/June), 43–52.

Schuhwerk, Melody E. and Roxanne Lefkoff-Hagius (1995), "Green or Non-Green? Does Type of Appeal Matter When Advertising a Green Product?" *JA*, 24 (Summer), 45–54.

Shimp, Terence A. and Subhash Sharma (1987), "Consumer Ethnocentrism: Construction and Validation of the CETSCALE," *JMR*, 24 (August), 280–89.

Simpson, Penny M., Steve Horton, and Gene Brown (1996), "Male Nudity in Advertisements: A Modified Replication and Extension of Gender and Product Effects," *JAMS*, 24 (Summer), 257–62.

Singh, Surendra N. and Catherine Cole (1993), "The Effects of Length, Content, and Repetition on Television Commercial Effectiveness," *JMR*, 30 (February), 91–104.

Stafford, Marla Royne (1996), "Tangibility in Services Advertising: An Investigation of Verbal Versus Visual Cues," *JA*, 25 (Fall), 13–28.

——— and Ellen Day (1995), "Retail Services Advertising: The Effects of Appeal, Medium, and Service," *JA*, 24 (Spring), 57–71.

Taylor, Charles R., Gordon E. Miracle, and R. Dale Wilson (1997), "The Impact of Information Level on the Effectiveness of U.S. and Korean Television Commercials," *JA*, 26 (Spring), 1–18.

Tripp, Carolyn, Thomas D. Jensen, and Les Carlson (1994), "The Effects of Multiple Product Endorsements by Celebrities on Consumers' Attitudes and Intentions," *JCR*, 20 (March), 535–47.

Urbany, Joel E., William O. Bearden, Ajit Kaicker, and Melinda Smith-de Borrero (1997), "Transaction Utility Effects When Quality Is Uncertain," *JAMS*, 25 (Winter), 45–55.

Yi, Youjae (1990a), "Cognitive and Affective Priming Effects of the Context for Print Advertisements," *JA*, 19 (2), 40–48.

——— (1990b), "The Effects of Contextual Priming in Print Advertisements," *JCR*, 17 (September), 215–22.

Zhang, Yong (1996), "Responses to Humorous Advertising: The Moderating Effect of Need for Cognition," *JA*, 25 (Spring), 15–32.

SCALE ITEMS: * (sample scale stem)

Rate the probability that you would purchase the product:

1. Unlikely   1———2———3———4———5———6———7   Likely

2. Nonexistent   1———2———3———4———5———6———7   Existent

3. Improbable   1———2———3———4———5———6———7   Probable

4. Impossible   1———2———3———4———5———6———7   Possible

5. Uncertain   1———2———3———4———5———6———7   Certain

6. Definitely   Definitely
   would   would
   not use   1———2———3———4———5———6———7   use

Chattopadhyay and Basu (1990): 1, 3, 4;

Dabholkar (1994): 1, 4, 6; 7-point for first two items, 5-point for last item

Day and Stafford (1997): 1, 3, 4; 7-point

Gill, Grossbart, and Laczniak (1988) 1, 2, 3, 4;

Gotlieb and Sarel (1991, 1992): 1, 3, 4;

Grossbart, Muehling, and Kangun (1986): two uses of 1 and 3; one use of 1, 3, and 5;

Homer (1995): 1, 3, 4; 9-point ("very" used before positive anchors and "not at all" used along with positive descriptors to make negative anchors; e.g., "not at all likely")

Lacher and Mizerski (1994): 1, 3, 4; 6-point

Lim, Darley, and Summers (1994): 1, 3, 4;
Machleit, Allen, and Madden (1993): 1, 3, 4;
MacKenzie, Lutz, and Belch (1986): 1, 3, 4;
MacKenzie and Spreng (1992): 1, 3, 4;
Netemeyer and Bearden (1992): 1, 3, 4;
Oliver and Bearden (1985): 1, 3, 4, 5;
Shimp and Sharma (1987): 1, 3, 5 ("very" used before each adjective);
Simpson, Horton, and Brown (1996): 1, 3, 4; 9-point
Singh and Cole (1993): 1, 3, 4;
Stafford (1996): 1, 3, 4; 7-point
Stafford and Day (1995): 1, 3, 4; 7-point
Taylor, Miracle, and Wilson (1997): 1, 3, 4; 7-point
Tripp, Jensen, and Carlson (1994): 1, 2, 3, 4; 7-point ("very" used before each adjective)
Urbany et al. (1997): 1, 3, 5, 6**; 9-point for the first three items, 11 point for the last item
Yi (1990a, 1990b): 1, 3, 4;
Zhang (1996): 1, 3, 4; 9-point

* In addition to the items, the number of points used in each study on the response scale is provided, if known.
**The actual item used in this study varied somewhat from that shown in the list.

SCALE NAME: Behavioral Intention

SCALE DESCRIPTION: Four seven-point semantic differentials intended to capture the subjective likelihood that someone will return to a place he or she has been (or is) already.

SCALE ORIGIN: Although it shows some resemblance to previously used intentions measures, this scale appears to be different enough to suggest it should be considered original to the work of Oliver, Rust, and Varki (1997).

SAMPLES: Oliver, Rust, and Varki (1997) reported on the use of the scale in two studies that involved patronage rather than product consumption. The sample in the first survey were visitors to a recreational wildlife theme park who were approached as they entered the park but completed the form after exiting. Valid data were received from **90** patrons. The typical respondent was a married woman between the ages of 25 and 34 years. The second study examined single-ticket purchasers at a symphony concert in a large city. Apparently as with the first survey, patrons were approached as they arrived but did not receive and complete the questionnaire until the concert was over. Usable surveys were received from **104** people. The modal respondent was a single woman between the ages of 20 and 30 years.

RELIABILITY: Oliver, Rust, and Varki (1997) reported that the reliabilities were **.89** and **.92** in their first and second studies, respectively.

VALIDITY: No specific examination of the scale's validity was reported in the studies by Oliver, Rust, and Varki (1997).

ADMINISTRATION: The scale was one of many other measures that were self-administered by patrons as they exited a service facility (Oliver, Rust, and Varki 1997). Higher scores on the scale meant that respondents expressed strong intentions to return to the facility in the future.

MAJOR FINDINGS: The purpose of the studies by Oliver, Rust, and Varki (1997) was to establish a behavioral basis for customer *delight* by empirically testing its antecedents and consequences. The findings from both studies indicated that satisfaction was the primary direct antecedent of **intention** to return.

REFERENCES:
Oliver, Richard L., Roland T. Rust, and Sajeev Varki (1997), "Customer Delight: Foundations, Findings, and Managerial Insight," *JR*, 73 (3), 311–36.

SCALE ITEMS:*
In the future, how would you rate your chances of returning to _____?

No chance   :___:___:___:___:___:___:___: Sure to go
                      1   2   3   4   5   6   7

Unlikely   :___:___:___:___:___:___:___: Likely
                      1   2   3   4   5   6   7

Certain to   Certain
not go   :___:___:___:___:___:___:___: to go
                      1   2   3   4   5   6   7

Not   Very
possible   :___:___:___:___:___:___:___: possible
                      1   2   3   4   5   6   7

*The name of the service facility should go in the blank.

SCALE NAME: Behavioral Intention (External Response)

SCALE DESCRIPTION: Three seven-point items measuring the likelihood that a customer of a business who has experienced a problem with its service will complain to others about it and switch to a competitor.

SCALE ORIGIN: The scale is original to Zeithaml, Berry, and Parasuraman (1996). The items composing this scale were part of a 13-item set proposed for measuring a wide range of behavioral intentions appropriate for a service quality context. Factor analysis of the 13 items across four companies showed that there was a considerable amount of similarity in factor structure, particularly as it related to this "external response" dimension.

SAMPLES: Zeithaml, Berry, and Parasuraman (1996) gathered data from mailing lists of current customers generated by four businesses: computer manufacturer, retail chain, automobile insurer, and life insurer. In each case, the names were of end users, except for the computer company, for which it was business customers. A total of 12,470 questionnaires were sent out, and 3,069 were returned.

RELIABILITY: Alphas of **.60, .67, .76,** and **.77** were reported by Zeithaml, Berry, and Parasuraman (1996) for the scale for the computer manufacturer, retail chain, automobile insurer, and life insurer samples, respectively.

VALIDITY: Zeithaml, Berry, and Parasuraman (1996) did not explicitly examine the validity of the scale. However, as noted, they performed oblique factor analyses on the data from the four companies for the 13 items. The three items composing this scale loaded together for each data set.

ADMINISTRATION: The scale was self-administered as part of a much larger mail survey instrument (Zeithaml, Berry, and Parasuraman 1996). Higher scores on the scale indicated that respondents intended to complain to others and switch to a competitor if they experienced a problem with the service they received from a specified business.

MAJOR FINDINGS: Zeithaml, Berry, and Parasuraman (1996) tested a model of the impact of service quality on relevant behaviors. Their results clearly showed that customers who have not reported any service problems have the weakest levels of **external response intentions**.

COMMENTS: Means on this scale ranged from 3.6 for the computer manufacturer's customer sample to 4.3 for the retail chain consumer sample.

REFERENCES:
Zeithaml, Valarie A., Leonard L. Berry, and A. Parasuraman (1996), "The Behavioral Consequences of Service Quality," *JM*, 60 (April), 31–46.

SCALE ITEMS:*
DIRECTIONS: Based on your overall experience with _____'s service, please indicate how likely you are to take the following actions. Circle the number that indicates your likelihood of taking each action.

Not at all   Extremely
likely   :___:___:___:___:___:___:___: likely
         1   2   3   4   5   6   7

1. Switch to a competitor if you are experiencing a problem with _____'s service.

2. Complain to other customers if you experience a problem with _____'s service.

3. Complain to external agencies, such as the Better Business Bureau, if you experience a problem with _____'s service.

*The name of the business should go in the blanks.

#62 *Body Consciousness (Public)*

SCALE NAME: Body Consciousness (Public)

SCALE DESCRIPTION: Six seven-point Likert-type statements that evaluate the degree of concern a person has toward the external appearance of his or her body (e.g., skin, hair, posture). This is in contrast to similar scales that measure a person's excessive concern about physical appearance (#397) or concern for the person's appearance in *clothes* (#82).

SCALE ORIGIN: The scale is original to the study by Miller, Murphy, and Buss (1981). They factor analyzed (n = 1281) fifteen items and called the six items that loaded high on the dimension of interest here *public body consciousness*. Similar factor patterns were found for both male and female college students, and the factor pattern was replicated with two other samples of college students. The stability of the scale was estimated to be .73 on the basis of a sample of 130 undergraduates and a span of two months between administrations. Evidence bearing on the validity of the scale was also provided.

SAMPLES: Various samples were collected and used by Netemeyer, Burton, and Lichtenstein (1995) in the process of validating the scale. The **public body consciousness** scale was used in one study, which was composed of **186** students and **264** "nonstudent adults." It was used in another study with data from **43** professional fashion models.

RELIABILITY: Alphas of **.62** (students), **.80** (nonstudent adults), and **.67** (fashion models) were found by Netemeyer, Burton, and Lichtenstein (1995; Netemeyer 1997).

VALIDITY: Although the validity of the scale was not directly examined by Netemeyer, Burton, and Lichtenstein (1995), it was used to help establish the construct validity of four vanity-related scales. **Public body consciousness** had positive correlations with all of the vanity scales, but their strength and significance depended on the sample.

ADMINISTRATION: As noted, the scale was used in two studies, and it appears to have been part of larger questionnaires that were self-administered by respondents (Netemeyer, Burton, and Lichtenstein 1995). Higher scores on the scale indicated that respondents were preoccupied with the appearance of their bodies.

MAJOR FINDINGS: Netemeyer, Burton, and Lichtenstein (1995) investigated vanity and developed four scales for its measurement. Most of the article discussed the results of the rather extensive validation process. As noted previously, the findings indicated that **public body consciousness** had positive relationships with each of the vanity scales, though only the correlations with physical concern vanity (#397) were strong and significant for each of the samples.

REFERENCES:

Miller, Lynn C., Richard Murphy, and Arnold H. Buss (1981), "Consciousness of Body: Private and Public," *Journal of Personality and Social Psychology*, 41 (August), 397–406.
Netemeyer, Richard G. (1997), personal correspondence.
———, Scot Burton, and Donald R. Lichtenstein (1995), "Trait Aspects of Vanity: Measurement and Relevance to Consumer Behavior," *JCR*, 21 (March), 612–26.

SCALE ITEMS:

Strongly agree :___:___:___:___:___:___: Strongly disagree

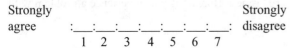

1   2   3   4   5   6   7

1. When with others, I want my hands to be clean and look nice.

2. It's important for me that my skin looks nice ... for example, has no blemishes.

3. I am very aware of my best and worst facial features.

4. I like to make sure that my hair looks right.

5. I think a lot about my body build.

6. I'm concerned about my posture.

SCALE NAME: Brand Beliefs for a Luxury Sedan (Comparative)

SCALE DESCRIPTION: Three seven-point Likert-type items that measure a set of cognitions a person has toward a brand of luxury sedan relative to other domestic luxury sedan brands.

SCALE ORIGIN: The scale was created by Neese and Taylor (1994) for their study.

SAMPLES: Data were collected by Neese and Taylor (1994) using a judgment sample of civic groups' members from across a Southeastern U.S. state. They were expected to be more likely than the population at large to own luxury cars, the product focused on in the study. Indeed, 22.1% of the respondents reported owning one of three brands of luxury sedans. Usable questionnaires were received from **422** respondents. The sample was predominately men, and 41.5% were older than 64 years of age.

RELIABILITY: An alpha of **.83** was reported for the scale by Neese and Taylor (1994).

VALIDITY: No examination of the scale's validity was reported by Neese and Taylor (1994). However, the authors stated in general terms that they used item–total correlations and the results of a factor analyses to purify each of their scales.

ADMINISTRATION: The conditions in which Neese and Taylor (1994) administered the scale were not clearly described. It appears the scale was part of some materials completed by subjects before they were exposed to test stimuli. Higher scores on the scale indicated that respondents believed a specified brand of luxury sedan had several positive characteristics compared with the domestic competition.

MAJOR FINDINGS: Neese and Taylor (1994) examined the ability of comparative advertising to accomplish certain tasks as it interacts with brand information for a high-involvement product. Strong support was found for the hypothesis that comparative ad copy would stimulate significantly more positive **comparative brand beliefs** relative to a noncomparative format.

REFERENCES:
Neese, William T. and Ronald D. Taylor (1994), "Verbal Strategies for Indirect Comparative Advertising," *JAR*, 34 (March/April), 56–69.

SCALE ITEMS:

Strongly   Strongly
disgree   :___:___:___:___:___:___:___: agree

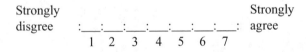

              1   2   3   4   5   6   7

1. This luxury sedan brand is more aerodynamically designed than other domestic luxury sedans.

2. This luxury sedan brand takes less effort to operate than other domestic luxury sedans.

3. This luxury sedan brand is of superior quality to other domestic luxury sedans.

SCALE NAME: Brand Beliefs for a Luxury Sedan (Noncomparative)

SCALE DESCRIPTION: Six seven-point Likert-type items purported to measure a set of noncomparative cognitions a person has toward a brand of luxury sedan.

SCALE ORIGIN: The scale was created by Neese and Taylor (1994) for their study.

SAMPLES: Data were collected by Neese and Taylor (1994) using a judgment sample of civic groups' members from across a Southeastern U.S. state. They were expected to be more likely than the population at large to own luxury cars, the product focused on in the study. Indeed, 22.1% of the respondents reported owning one of three luxury sedans. Usable questionnaires were received from **422** respondents. The sample was predominately men, and 41.5% were older than 64 years of age.

RELIABILITY: An alpha of **.75** was reported for the scale by Neese and Taylor (1994).

VALIDITY: No examination of the scale's validity was reported by Neese and Taylor (1994). However, the authors stated in general terms that they used item–total correlations and the results of a factor analyses to purify each of their scales.

ADMINISTRATION: The conditions in which Neese and Taylor (1994) administered the scale were not clearly described. It appears the scale was part of some materials completed by subjects before they were exposed to test stimuli. Higher scores on the scale indicated that respondents believed a specified brand of luxury sedan had several positive characteristics.

MAJOR FINDINGS: Neese and Taylor (1994) examined the ability of comparative advertising to accomplish certain tasks as it interacts with brand information for a high-involvement product. Strong support was found for the hypothesis that more informative ad copy would stimulate significantly more positive **noncomparative brand beliefs** relative to less informative copy.

REFERENCES:
Neese, William T. and Ronald D. Taylor (1994), "Verbal Strategies for Indirect Comparative Advertising," *JAR*, 34 (March/April), 56–69.

SCALE ITEMS:

Strongly   Strongly
disgree :___:___:___:___:___:___: agree
      1 2 3 4 5 6 7

1. This luxury sedan brand has a 4-CAM, 32-Valve, 250-HP, V8 engine.

2. This luxury sedan brand has an advanced electronic suspension.

3. This luxury sedan brand has full-time all-wheel drive.

4. This luxury sedan brand has an advanced antilock braking system.

5. This luxury sedan brand has both driver- and passenger-side airbags.

6. This luxury sedan brand is full sized.

SCALE NAME: Brand Consciousness

SCALE DESCRIPTION: A three-item, five-point, Likert-type summated ratings scale measuring the degree to which a person expresses a desire to buy "brand-name products." The implication is that the consumer prefers nationally known brands rather than private distributor brands or generic goods.

SCALE ORIGIN: The source of the scale was not stated by Donthu and Gilliland (1996), but it is likely original to their study.

SAMPLES: Donthu and Gilliland (1996) used trained interviewers to call 1000 households in a large city's telephone directory. Interviews were successfully completed with **368** adults of those households. Although some demographic information was employed in the analysis, the data were not reported in such a way that the sample as a whole can be clearly described.

RELIABILITY: An alpha of **.80** was reported for the scale by Donthu and Gilliland (1996).

VALIDITY: No specific examination of the scale's validity was reported by Donthu and Gilliland (1996).

ADMINISTRATION: Donthu and Gilliland (1996) had the scale administered as part of a larger telephone survey. Higher scores on the scale indicated that respondents were very brand conscious in their shopping.

MAJOR FINDINGS: Donthu and Gilliland (1996) profiled infomercial shoppers. Unexpectedly, they were found to be significantly more **brand conscious** than those who had never purchased goods from infomercials.

REFERENCES:
Donthu, Naveen and David Gilliland (1996), "The Infomercial Shopper," *JAR*, 36 (March/April), 69–76.

SCALE ITEMS:

Strongly disagree	Disagree	Neutral	Agree	Strongly agree
1	2	3	4	5

1. I usually purchase brand name products.

2. Store brands are of poor quality. **(r)**

3. All brands are about the same. **(r)**

SCALE NAME: Brand Consciousness

SCALE DESCRIPTION: Four five-point Likert-type items intended to measure a shopping orientation that is characterized by the extent to which a consumer focuses on buying well-known brands.

SCALE ORIGIN: Shim and Gehrt (1996) used a modified version of a scale developed by Sproles and Kendall (1986). The latter created an eight-factor model of what they called *consumer decision-making styles* but what many others in marketing (e.g., Shim and Gehrt 1996) would view as *shopping orientations*. Shim and Gehrt (1996) used four items with the highest factor loadings of the seven items identified by Sproles and Kendall (1986). The latter reported an alpha of .75 for a subscale of the top six items and a .63 for the top three items.

SAMPLES: Shim and Gehrt (1996) collected data from high school students in a Southwestern U.S. state. Twenty-nine principals agreed to participate, and their schools apparently represented many if not all of the counties in the state. Principals were given instructions as to which classes to use (by level) and how many students from each class were needed. Some 1954 usable surveys were returned, with 61.3% from female students and a mean respondent age of 16 years. However, the study focused only on data from **1846** students who were white (56%), Hispanic (32%), or Native American (12%).

RELIABILITY: An alpha of **.72** was reported for the scale by Shim and Gehrt (1996).

VALIDITY: No examination of the scale's validity was reported by Shim and Gehrt (1996).

ADMINISTRATION: Data were gathered in a classroom setting in which students filled out the scale as part of a larger survey instrument (Shim and Gehrt 1996). Higher scores on the scale indicated that respondents were very brand conscious and tended to focus their purchases on higher priced, well-known brands.

MAJOR FINDINGS: The study by Shim and Gehrt (1996) examined differences in shopping orientations among high school students that could be linked to ethnicity. The results showed that white students were significantly less **brand conscious** than Hispanic and Native American students.

REFERENCES:
Shim, Soyeon and Kenneth C. Gehrt (1996), "Hispanic and Native American Adolescents: An Exploratory Study of Their Approach to Shopping," *JR*, 72 (3), 307–24.
Sproles, George B. and Elizabeth L. Kendall (1986), "A Methodology for Profiling Consumers' Decision-Making Styles," *Journal of Consumer Affairs*, 20 (Winter), 267–79.

SCALE ITEMS:

Strongly   Strongly
disagree   :___:___:___:___:___: agree
                 1   2   3   4   5

1. The well-known national brands are best for me.

2. The more expensive brands are usually my choices.

3. The higher the price of a product, the better its quality.

4. Nice department and specialty stores offer me the best products.

SCALE NAME: Brand Differences

SCALE DESCRIPTION: Three seven-point Likert-type items measuring the degree to which a consumer perceives there are differences among some brands being evaluated.

SCALE ORIGIN: The scale used by Van Trijp, Hoyer, and Inman (1996) is original to their study. The authors stated they developed and evaluated eight items in a pretest (n = 86). Their goal was apparently to produce a short scale of involvement with high reliability, and this three-item version was considered to have met those criteria.

SAMPLES: The data gathered by Van Trijp, Hoyer, and Inman (1996) came from 1000 Dutch households that were part of multiweek consumer panel. The number of people providing usable data was not specified nor were their demographic characteristics.

RELIABILITY: An alpha of **.67** was reported by Van Trijp, Hoyer, and Inman (1996) for the scale.

VALIDITY: No examination of the scale's validity was reported by Van Trijp, Hoyer, and Inman (1996).

ADMINISTRATION: Panel members in the study by Van Trijp, Hoyer, and Inman (1996) responded to questionnaires on a PC in their homes connected via modem to a central computer. As coded by these authors, higher scores on the scale indicated that there were small if any perceivable differences between some set of brands.

MAJOR FINDINGS: Van Trijp, Hoyer, and Inman (1996) proposed that brand-switching behavior should be examined by differentiating between intrinsic (e.g., variety seeking) and extrinsic (e.g., brand on sale) motivations. The results indicated that variety seeking was more likely than repeat purchasing behavior when smaller **brand differences** were perceived.

COMMENTS: The range of scores on the scale (Van Trijp, Hoyer, and Inman 1996) was from 3 to 21 with a mean of 10.5 and a standard deviation of 4.1.

The reliability of this scale is low enough that more developmental work is called for before it is used further.

REFERENCES:
Van Trijp, Has C.M., Wayne D. Hoyer, and J. Jeffrey Inman (1996), "Why Switch? Product Category-Level Explanations for True Variety-Seeking Behavior," *JMR*, 33 (August) 281–92.

SCALE ITEMS:

Completely   Completely
disagree   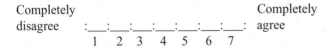   agree

1. Differences among brands are large. **(r)**

2. Differences among brands are hard to judge.

3. The best brand is hard to judge.

SCALE NAME: Brand Equity

SCALE DESCRIPTION: Twelve seven-point Likert-type statements that are purported to measure the perceived value of a brand based on its name and image. The focal brand in the study was Spiegel, a clothing-related catalog.

SCALE ORIGIN: Inspiration for the scale developed by Ha (1996, 1997) came primarily from Aaker's (1991) multidimensional conceptualization of the brand equity construct.

SAMPLES: The sample for the experiment conducted by Ha (1996) was selected from among students enrolled in general education classes at two Midwestern universities in the United States. Students volunteered for the study and received a pen for their participation. A usable sample of **112** responses was collected. The median age of the group was 20 years, nearly half (48%) were majoring in a science-related area, and more than half (64%) were women.

RELIABILITY: An alpha of **.93** was calculated for the scale (Ha 1997).

VALIDITY: No specific information regarding the scale's validity was reported by Ha (1996). In a related matter, the scale has four subdimensions, and though the high alpha suggests that they may all load on a second-order factor, a more rigorous examination of the dimensionality of these items is needed.

ADMINISTRATION: The scale was self-administered by subjects after they were exposed to the experimental stimuli (Ha 1996). Higher scores on the scale indicated that respondents perceived the brand in question to have high value.

MAJOR FINDINGS: Ha (1996) used an experiment to investigate the effect of clutter on advertising effectiveness. Three dimensions of clutter were examined: quantity of ads in a vehicle, competitiveness of the ads, and intrusiveness of those ads. The findings indicated that none of the three dimensions of clutter had a significant impact on **brand equity**.

REFERENCES:
Aaker, David A. (1991), *Managing Brand Equity*. New York: The Free Press.
Ha, Louisa (1997), personal correspondence.
——— (1996), "Advertising Clutter in Consumer Magazines: Dimensions and Effects," *JAR*, 36 (July/August), 76–84.

SCALE ITEMS:*

Completely   Completely
disagree   :___:___:___:___:___:___:___: agree
                 1   2   3   4   5   6   7

1. The image of _____ is the same as the other clothing brands. **(r)**

2. The image of _____ represents what I would like to be.

3. I feel bad using this brand. **(r)**

4. I would rank this brand as my _____ choice if I purchase clothes. **(r)**

5. I won't mind paying a higher price for this brand.

6. If the catalog of this brand is not sent to me free, I am willing to pay to get one.

7. I agree with the claim that _____ products are simple, stylish, and of good value.

8. The quality of the brand is superior to other brands.

9. _____ is most suitable to my needs.

10. _____ is the most popular brand in the category.

11. When I need to buy clothes, I will think of _____ immediately.

12. When asked about brands in clothing, _____ will come to mind immediately.

*The name of the brand should be placed in the blanks, except for #4, where the blank is left for the respondent to write in a ranking. If respondents indicate that the focal brand is their "number one" choice, it is coded as 1 and reverse coded to 7. Similarly, if the focal brand is their "number 2" choice, it is coded as 2 and reverse coded to 6.

SCALE NAME: Brand Familiarity

SCALE DESCRIPTION: Three seven-point bipolar adjectives measuring the degree of awareness a consumer has of some specified product or brand.

SCALE ORIGIN: The scale was apparently used first by Machleit, Allen, and Madden (1993), though no information regarding its psychometric quality was provided.

SAMPLES: Data were collected by Kent and Allen (1994) from **84** students. They met in one of two sessions, and each student received booklets containing the experimental manipulations embedded in sets of print ads. No other information about the subjects was provided.

RELIABILITY: No information about the scale's reliability as it was used in the main study was provided by Kent and Allen (1994), but it was noted that its alpha "exceeded .85" in a pretest (n = 32 students).

VALIDITY: No specific examination was made of the scale's validity by Kent and Allen (1994), but some information bearing on predictive validity is noted subsequently.

ADMINISTRATION: Student subjects completed the scale along with other measures after they were exposed to experimental stimuli (Kent and Allen 1994). Higher scores on the scale indicated that respondents felt they were very familiar with the specified product.

MAJOR FINDINGS: Kent and Allen (1994) investigated the role played by **brand familiarity** in increasing ad memorability. The **brand familiarity** scale was used as a manipulation check. Subjects who received the high familiarity treatment scored a much higher mean on **brand familiarity** than did those in the unfamiliar condition.

REFERENCES:
Kent, Robert J. and Chris T. Allen (1994), "Competitive Interference Effects in Consumer Memory for Advertising: The Role of Brand Familiarity," *JM*, 58 (July), 97–105.
Machleit, Karen A., Chris T. Allen, and Thomas J. Madden (1993), "The Mature Brand and Brand Interest: An Alternative Consequence of Ad-Evoked Affect," *JM*, 57 (October), 72–82.

SCALE ITEMS:
Regarding the product _____, are you:

1. Unfamiliar : ___:___:___:___:___:___:___: Familiar
           1   2   3   4   5   6   7

2. Inexperienced : ___:___:___:___:___:___:___: Experienced
           1   2   3   4   5   6   7

3. Not
   knowledgeable :___:___:___:___:___:___:___: Knowledgeable
           1   2   3   4   5   6   7

SCALE NAME: Brand Loyalty

SCALE DESCRIPTION: A three-item, seven-point, Likert-type scale measuring the degree to which a consumer expresses loyalty to a brand and is unwilling to even try others.

SCALE ORIGIN: Although not stated to be original, the scale seems to have been developed for the study by Putrevu and Lord (1994) rather than being borrowed from any previous research.

SAMPLES: Data were gathered by Putrevu and Lord (1994) from students in an introductory under-graduate marketing course taught at a Northeastern U.S. university. Apparently, usable data were collected from **100** students who voluntarily participated for extra credit in the course. Demographic data about the respondents were collected but were not described in the article.

RELIABILITY: Putrevu and Lord (1994) reported an alpha of **.59** for the scale. This is so low as to be considered evidence of unreliability.

VALIDITY: No evidence of the scale's validity was provided by Putrevu and Lord (1994). However, close scrutiny of the items indicates that more than one factor appears to be represented. The lack of reliability and the appearance of multidimensionality strongly suggest that the scale is not valid and should not be used further until substantial improvement in its psychometric quality is made.

ADMINISTRATION: The scale was administered to students by Putrevu and Lord (1994) along with other measures as part of an in-class experiment. Higher scores on the scale suggested that a consumer had a positive opinion of a brand and is probably loyal in buying it.

MAJOR FINDINGS: Putrevu and Lord (1994) examined the relative effectiveness of comparative and noncomparative advertising for products characterized by varying degrees of affective and cognitive involvement. There was no difference in attitude toward the brand between those who differed in **brand loyalty** when a noncomparative ad was used. When a comparative ad was used, however, those who were low in **brand loyalty** had significantly better brand attitudes.

REFERENCES:
Putrevu, Sanjay and Kenneth R. Lord (1994), "Comparative and Noncomparative Advertising: Attitudinal Effects Under Cognitive and Affective Involvement Conditions," *JA*, 23 (June), 77–90.

SCALE ITEMS:
DIRECTIONS: Use the following scale to indicate the level of agreement you have with each of the statements regarding the brand of *(product name)* you buy most frequently.*

Disagree :___:___:___:___:___:___:___: Agree
           1 2 3 4 5 6 7

1. I always purchase the above brand of *(product)*.

2. I am willing to buy a new brand of *(product)*. **(r)**

3. My overall opinion of the brand of *(product)* I presently use is very good.

*The directions for completing the measure were not provided in the article but likely were similar to this.

SCALE NAME: Brand Loyalty

SCALE DESCRIPTION: Three five-point Likert-type items that purport to capture a consumer's preference for a few brands of grocery products and his or her expressed tendency to limit purchases to just those brands. This scale measures a sort of generalized brand loyalty or loyalty proneness regardless of product category rather than determining the degree of loyalty a consumer has toward a particular brand.

SCALE ORIGIN: The source of the scale was not specified by Mittal (1994).

SAMPLES: Mittal (1994) gathered data from female members of six voluntary organizations as well as from mall intercepts. A total of 184 provided complete survey questionnaires. Most of the respondents were white (85%), married (71%), and at least 35 years of age (63%). Although it does not mirror the U.S. population, the sample included a wide variety of demographic categories.

RELIABILITY: The construct reliability (LISREL) was reported to be **.76** (Mittal 1994).

VALIDITY: The validity of the scale was not specifically addressed by Mittal (1994), except to say that the conducted tests provided support for discriminant validity.

ADMINISTRATION: The scale was part of a larger self-administered mail survey instrument (Mittal 1994). Higher scores on the scale indicated that respondents had a lot of brand loyalty toward certain brands of products carried by supermarkets.

MAJOR FINDINGS: The study by Mittal (1994) proposed that demographics are poor predictors of coupon usage, and instead, he illustrated the value of three layers of mediating variables. Among the findings was that those who were financially well off tended to be more **brand loyal**.

REFERENCES:
Mittal, Banwari (1994), "An Integrated Framework for Relating Diverse Consumer Characteristics to Supermarket Coupon Redemption," *JMR*, 31 (November), 533–44.

SCALE ITEMS:

1. For most supermarket items, I have favorite brands and limit my purchase to them.

2. In most product categories in the supermarket, there are certain brands for which I (and my family) have a definite preference.

3. I and my family will consumer only certain brands, not others.

SCALE NAME: Brand Personality (Competence)

SCALE DESCRIPTION: Nine items and a five-point response format indicating the degree to which a consumer views a brand as having personality-like characteristics typified by the following facets: reliable, intelligent, and successful.

SCALE ORIGIN: The scale was constructed by Aaker (1997) as part of a larger set of 42 items that was proposed for the measurement of five brand personality dimensions. She viewed these measures as distinct from those of product-related attributes, which are more utilitarian in function. In contrast, brand personality is supposed to serve a symbolic or self-expressive function. Before conducting the two studies (described subsequently), two pretests were used to reduce an initial list of items (309) to something more manageable (114).

SAMPLES The two studies conducted by Aaker (1997) gathered data from members of a national mail panel intended to be representative of the U.S. population. The analysis in the first study was based on **631** responses (of 1200 survey forms that were sent) that evaluated subsets of 37 brands. In the second study, **180** responses (of 250 questionnaires that were sent) evaluated 20 brands in ten product categories.

RELIABILITY: An alpha of **.93** was reported for the scale by Aaker (1997) on the basis of data from the first study. With data from a subsample of the first study's respondents (n = 81), the scale's stability (two month test–retest reliability) was estimated to be .76.

VALIDITY: A variety of steps and analyses were taken with data from Studies 1 and 2 that provided support for the stability of the five-factor structure represented in the full set of 42 items.

ADMINISTRATION: In both studies conducted by Aaker (1997), the items composing this scale were part of a larger list intended to measure brand personality dimensions. The items were self-reported in a mail survey format. Higher scores on this scale indicated that respondents viewed a brand as having a "personality" characterized by reliability and successfulness.

MAJOR FINDINGS: The purpose of the studies reported by Aaker (1997) was to propose and test a theoretical framework for the brand personality construct. No findings involving the scale were reported beyond the details related to those issues mentioned previously, except that the brand found to best represent this dimension was *The Wall Street Journal*.

COMMENTS: Using the combined results of Studies 1 and 2, the mean and standard deviation for this scale were reported to be 3.17 and 1.02, respectively.

REFERENCES:
Aaker, Jennifer L. (1997), "Dimensions of Brand Personality," *JMR*, 34 (August), 347–56.

SCALE ITEMS:

Not at all descriptive :___:___:___:___:___: Extremely descriptive
                        1   2   3   4   5

1. Reliable   6. Corporate
2. Hard-working   7. Successful
3. Secure   8. Leader
4. Intelligent   9. Confident
5. Technical

SCALE NAME: Brand Personality (Excitement)

SCALE DESCRIPTION: Eleven items with a five-point response format indicating the degree to which a consumer views a brand as having personality-like characteristics typified by the following facets: daring, spirited, imaginative, and up-to-date.

SCALE ORIGIN: The scale was constructed by Aaker (1997) as part of a larger set of 42 items that were proposed for the measurement of five brand personality dimensions. She viewed these measures as distinct from those of product-related attributes, which are more utilitarian in function. In contrast, brand personality is supposed to serve a symbolic or self-expressive function. Before conducting the two studies (described subsequently), two pretests were used to reduce an initial list of items (309) to something more manageable (114).

SAMPLES: The two studies conducted by Aaker (1997) gathered data from members of a national mail panel intended to be representative of the U.S. population. The analysis in the first study was based on **631** responses (of 1200 survey forms that were sent) that evaluated subsets of 37 brands. In the second study, **180** responses (of 250 questionnaires that were sent) evaluated 20 brands in ten product categories.

RELIABILITY: An alpha of **.95** was reported for the scale by Aaker (1997) on the basis of data from the first study. With data from a subsample of the first study's respondents (n = 81), the scale's stability (two month test–retest reliability) was estimated to be .74.

VALIDITY: A variety of steps and analyses were taken with data from Studies 1 and 2 that provided support for the stability of the five-factor structure represented in the full set of 42 items.

ADMINISTRATION: In both studies conducted by Aaker (1997), the items composing this scale were part of a larger list intended to measure brand personality dimensions. The items were self-reported in a mail survey format. Higher scores on this scale indicated that respondents viewed a brand as having a "personality" characterized by facets such as daring and up-to-date.

MAJOR FINDINGS: The purpose of the studies reported by Aaker (1997) was to propose and test a theoretical framework for the brand personality construct. No findings using the scale were reported beyond the details related to those issues mentioned previously, except that the brand found to best represent this dimension was the MTV channel.

COMMENTS: Using the combined results of Studies 1 and 2, the mean and standard deviation for this scale were reported to be 2.79 and 1.05, respectively.

REFERENCES:
Aaker, Jennifer L. (1997), "Dimensions of Brand Personality," *JMR*, 34 (August), 347–56.

SCALE ITEMS:

Not at all descriptive :___:___:___:___:___: Extremely descriptive
                     1   2   3   4   5

1. Daring
2. Trendy
3. Exciting
4. Spirited
5. Cool
6. Young
7. Imaginative
8. Unique
9. Up-to-date
10. Independent
11. Contemporary

SCALE NAME: Brand Personality (Ruggedness)

SCALE DESCRIPTION: Five items and a five-point response format indicating the degree to which a consumer views a brand as having personality-like characteristics typified by toughness and masculinity.

SCALE ORIGIN: The scale was constructed by Aaker (1997) as part of a larger set of 42 items that was proposed for the measurement of five brand personality dimensions. She viewed these measures as distinct from those of product-related attributes, which are more utilitarian in function. In contrast, brand personality is supposed to serve a symbolic or self-expressive function. Before conducting the two studies (described subsequently), two pretests were used to reduce an initial list of items (309) to something more manageable (114).

SAMPLES: The two studies conducted by Aaker (1997) gathered data from members of a national mail panel intended to be representative of the U.S. population. The analysis in the first study was based on **631** responses (of 1200 survey forms that were sent) that evaluated subsets of 37 brands. In the second study, **180** responses (of 250 questionnaires that were sent) evaluated 20 brands in ten product categories.

RELIABILITY: An alpha of **.90** was reported for the scale by Aaker (1997) on the basis of data from the first study. With data from a subsample of the first study's respondents (n = 81), the scale's stability (two month test–retest reliability) was estimated to be .77.

VALIDITY: A variety of steps and analyses were taken with data from Studies 1 and 2 that provided support for the stability of the five-factor structure represented in the full set of 42 items.

ADMINISTRATION: In both studies conducted by Aaker (1997), the items composing this scale were part of a larger list intended to measure brand personality dimensions. The items were self-reported in a mail survey format. Higher scores on this scale indicated that respondents viewed a brand as having a "personality" characterized by toughness and masculinity.

MAJOR FINDINGS: The purpose of the studies reported by Aaker (1997) was to propose and test a theoretical framework for the brand personality construct. No findings involving the scale were reported beyond the details related to those issues mentioned previously, except that the brand found to best represent this dimension was Nike tennis shoes.

COMMENTS: Using the combined results of Studies 1 and 2, the mean and standard deviation for this scale were reported to be 2.49 and 1.08, respectively.

REFERENCES:
Aaker, Jennifer L. (1997), "Dimensions of Brand Personality," *JMR*, 34 (August), 347–56.

SCALE ITEMS:

Not at all descriptive :___:___:___:___:___: Extremely descriptive
                    1   2   3   4   5

1. Outdoorsy   4. Tough
2. Masculine   5. Rugged
3. Western

SCALE NAME: Brand Personality (Sincerity)

SCALE DESCRIPTION: Eleven items with a five-point response format indicating the degree to which a consumer views a brand as having personality-like characteristics typified by the following facets: down-to-earth, honest, wholesome, and cheerful.

SCALE ORIGIN: The scale was constructed by Aaker (1997) as part of a larger set of 42 items that was proposed for the measurement of five brand personality dimensions. She viewed these measures as distinct from those of product-related attributes, which are more utilitarian in function. In contrast, brand personality is supposed to serve a symbolic or self-expressive function. Before conducting the two studies (described subsequently), two pretests were used to reduce an initial list of items (309) to something more manageable (114).

SAMPLES: The two studies conducted by Aaker (1997) gathered data from members of a national mail panel intended to be representative of the U.S. population. The analysis in the first study was based on **631** responses (of 1200 survey forms that were sent) that evaluated subsets of 37 brands. In the second study, **180** responses (of 250 questionnaires that were sent) evaluated 20 brands in ten product categories.

RELIABILITY: An alpha of **.93** was reported for the scale by Aaker (1997) on the basis of data from the first study. With data from a subsample of the first study's respondents (n = 81), the scale's stability (two month test–retest reliability) was estimated to be .75.

VALIDITY: A variety of steps and analyses were taken with data from Studies 1 and 2 that provided support for the stability of the five-factor structure represented in the full set of 42 items.

ADMINISTRATION: In both studies conducted by Aaker (1997), the items composing this scale were part of a larger list intended to measure brand personality dimensions. The items were self-reported in a mail survey format. Higher scores on this scale indicated that respondents viewed a brand as having a "personality" characterized by facets such as honesty and cheerfulness.

MAJOR FINDINGS: The purpose of the studies reported by Aaker (1997) was to propose and test a theoretical framework for the brand personality construct. No findings using the scale were reported beyond the details related to those issues mentioned previously, except that the brand found to best represent this dimension was Hallmark cards.

COMMENTS: Using the combined results of Studies 1 and 2, the mean and standard deviation for this scale were reported to be 2.72 and .99, respectively.

REFERENCES:
Aaker, Jennifer L. (1997), "Dimensions of Brand Personality," *JMR*, 34 (August), 347–56.

SCALE ITEMS:

Not at all descriptive :___:___:___:___:___: Extremely descriptive
                 1   2   3   4   5

1. Down-to-earth
2. Family-oriented
3. Small-town
4. Honest
5. Sincere
6. Real
7. Wholesome
8. Original
9. Cheerful
10. Sentimental
11. Friendly

SCALE NAME: Brand Personality (Sophistication)

SCALE DESCRIPTION: Six items and a five-point response format indicating the degree to which a consumer views a brand as having personality-like characteristics typified by good looks and charm.

SCALE ORIGIN: The scale was constructed by Aaker (1997) as part of a larger set of 42 items that was proposed for the measurement of five brand personality dimensions. She viewed these measures as distinct from those of product-related attributes, which are more utilitarian in function. In contrast, brand personality is supposed to serve a symbolic or self-expressive function. Before conducting the two studies (described subsequently), two pretests were used to reduce an initial list of items (309) to something more manageable (114).

SAMPLES: The two studies conducted by Aaker (1997) gathered data from members of a national mail panel intended to be representative of the U.S. population. The analysis in the first study was based on **631** responses (of 1200 survey forms that were sent) that evaluated subsets of 37 brands. In the second study, **180** responses (of 250 questionnaires that were sent) evaluated 20 brands in ten product categories.

RELIABILITY: An alpha of **.91** was reported for the scale by Aaker (1997) on the basis of data from the first study. With data from a subsample of the first study's respondents (n = 81), the scale's stability (two month test–retest reliability) was estimated to be .75.

VALIDITY: A variety of steps and analyses were taken with data from Studies 1 and 2 that provided support for the stability of the five-factor structure represented in the full set of 42 items.

ADMINISTRATION: In both studies conducted by Aaker (1997), the items composing this scale were part of a larger list intended to measure brand personality dimensions. The items were self-reported in a mail survey format. Higher scores on this scale indicated that respondents viewed a brand as having a "personality" characterized by good looks and charm.

MAJOR FINDINGS: The purpose of the studies reported by Aaker (1997) was to propose and test a theoretical framework for the brand personality construct. No findings involving the scale were reported beyond the details related to those issues mentioned previously, except that the brand found to best represent this dimension was Guess jeans.

COMMENTS: Using the combined results of Studies 1 and 2, the mean and standard deviation for this scale were reported to be 2.66 and 1.02, respectively.

REFERENCES:
Aaker, Jennifer L. (1997), "Dimensions of Brand Personality," *JMR*, 34 (August), 347–56.

SCALE ITEMS:

Not at all descriptive :___:___:___:___:___: Extremely descriptive
                        1   2   3   4   5

1. Upper class   4. Charming
2. Glamorous   5. Feminine
3. Good looking   6. Smooth

SCALE NAME: Brand Preference

SCALE DESCRIPTION: Three five-point Likert-type statements measuring the degree to which a person views a focal brand as preferable to a referent brand.

SCALE ORIGIN: Although not explicitly stated, the scale appears to have been developed by Sirgy and colleagues (1997) for use in Study 4 of the six they conducted.

SAMPLES: Study 4 was based on data collected from eight samples, each corresponding to a different product. Students in college marketing courses were the subjects, and usable data were gathered from **428** students.

RELIABILITY: Alphas ranging from **.72** to **.98** were reported for the scale as used with eight different products (Sirgy et al. 1997).

VALIDITY: No examination of the scale's validity was reported (Sirgy et al. 1997).

ADMINISTRATION: The scale was apparently self-administered by students (Sirgy et al. 1997) as part of a in-class survey. Higher scores on the scale suggested that respondents viewed a focal brand as preferable to a referent brand.

MAJOR FINDINGS: As noted, Sirgy and colleagues (1997) conducted six studies in support of a new method for measuring **self-image congruency** that was more direct than previous measures. In Study 4, the new measure was found to be more predictive of **brand preference** than a traditional measure.

REFERENCES:
Sirgy, M. Joseph, Dhruv Grewal, Tamara F. Mangleburg, Jae-ok Park, Kye-Sung Chon, C.B. Claiborne, J.S. Johar, and Harold Berkman (1997), "Assessing the Predictive Validity of Two Methods of Measuring Self-Image Congruence," *JAMS*, 25 (Summer), 229–41.

SCALE ITEMS:

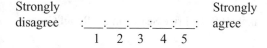

Strongly
disagree   :___:___:___:___: agree
         1   2   3   4   5

Strongly agree

1. I like [focal brand] better than [referent brand].

2. I would use [focal brand] more than I would use [referent brand].

3. I would be inclined to buy a [focal brand] over a [referent brand].

SCALE NAME: Budget Constraints

SCALE DESCRIPTION: Three five-point Likert-type statements measuring the degree to which a consumer perceives having insufficient funds to cover his or her needs.

SCALE ORIGIN: Although Urbany, Dickson, and Kalapurakal (1996) may have drawn inspiration from previous work, the scale appears to be original to their study.

SAMPLES: The data used by Urbany, Dickson, and Kalapurakal (1996) were collected as part of a larger survey by a leading market research firm. Telephone interviews were conducted with the primary grocery shoppers from households selected at random. Respondents were requested to participate in a second stage that would involve a mail survey. The survey yielded **343** usable responses. The average age of respondents was 44.7 years, and they were overwhelmingly women (83%)

RELIABILITY: An alpha of **.87** was reported for the scale by Urbany, Dickson, and Kalapurakal (1996).

VALIDITY: Urbany, Dickson, and Kalapurakal (1996) tested the discriminant validity of the **budget constraints** scale using pairwise confirmatory factor analysis and six other measures. The evidence of three separate tests on each of the six pairs supported a claim of discriminant validity.

ADMINISTRATION: The data analyzed by Urbany, Dickson, and Kalapurakal (1996) were gathered in a mail survey. Higher scores suggested that respondents believed they were having to function under severe budget constraints.

MAJOR FINDINGS: Urbany, Dickson, and Kalapurakal (1996) developed a model of price search for the retail grocery industry that included a relatively complete accounting of economic and noneconomic returns, as well as search costs. The findings showed that perceived **budget constraints** did not account for a significant amount of variance in self-reported price-comparison behavior.

COMMENTS: Urbany, Dickson, and Kalapurakal (1996) reported a mean response of 2.59 on the scale.

REFERENCES:
Urbany, Joel E., Peter R. Dickson, and Rosemary Kalapurakal (1996), "Price Search in the Retail Grocery Market," *JM*, 60 (April), 91–104.

SCALE ITEMS:

Strongly   Strongly
disagree   :___:___:___:___:___: agree
             1   2   3   4   5

1. I frequently have problems making ends meet.

2. My budgeting is always tight.

3. I often have to spend more money than I have available.

SCALE NAME: Calm

SCALE DESCRIPTION: A three-item, six-point summated ratings scale measuring the degree to which a person describes feeling a sense of peace and tranquillity on exposure to some stimulus (e.g., music). Phrasing of the scale was such that it measured a respondent's emotional reaction to a stimulus rather than the attitude toward the stimulus itself.

SCALE ORIGIN: Lacher and Mizerski (1994) indicated that the scale was taken from Asmus (1985). Two of the items came from the *sedative* factor, and one was from the *pastoral* factor Asmus (1985) identified in his development of a multidimensional instrument for measuring affective responses to music. A pretest was conducted by Lacher and Mizerski (1994) using 219 undergraduate students to ensure that the scale items remained constant over the two songs tested and the two extraction methods used. Alphas for the fast and slow tempo songs in the pretest were **.86** and **.89**, respectively (Lacher 1997).

SAMPLES: The sample used by Lacher and Mizerski (1994) were undergraduate business students at a large Southern U.S. university. Usable data were collected from **215** students who were composed of 52% men and who ranged in age from 19 to 36 years.

RELIABILITY: Lacher and Mizerski (1994) did not report the alpha for the scale as used in the main study, but based on the pretest results, it would likely have been acceptable.

VALIDITY: No examination of scale validity was reported by Lacher and Mizerski (1994) beyond what could be construed from the factor analyses in the study's pretest (as noted).

ADMINISTRATION: The scale was self-administered, along with other measures, in the study by Lacher and Mizerski (1994). Students heard two songs played twice and filled out this scale, along with other measures, the second time the songs were played. Higher scores on the scale indicated that respondents perceived that a particular song evoked a feeling of serenity in them.

MAJOR FINDINGS: Lacher and Mizerski (1994) investigated the responses music evokes in a listener and how those reactions affect the intention to purchase the music. Among the findings was that a feeling of **calmness** did not have a significant influence on any of the other responses to the music being examined.

COMMENTS: Although there is nothing in the items themselves to keep them from being applied to other stimuli, it should be kept in mind that this scale has been specifically developed and tested for measuring emotional reactions to music.

REFERENCES:
Asmus, Edward P. (1985), "The Development of a Multidimensional Instrument for the Measurement of Affective Responses to Music," *Psychology of Music*, 13 (1), 19–30.
Lacher, Kathleen T. (1997), personal correspondence.
——— and Richard Mizerski (1994), "An Exploratory Study of the Responses and Relationships Involved in the Evaluation of, and in the Intention to Purchase New Rock Music," *JCR*, 21 (September), 366–80.

#79 *Calm*

SCALE ITEMS:

DIRECTIONS: Rate each item below in terms of its appropriateness in describing the feelings and emotions you had in response to the music.*

Strongly   Strongly
disagree   :___:___:___:___:___:___: agree
            1   2   3   4   5   6

1. Calm

2. Tranquil

3. Relaxing

*The actual directions for filling out the scale were not provided in the article but likely were similar to this.

SCALE NAME: Choice Confusion

SCALE DESCRIPTION: Four five-point Likert-type items intended to measure a shopping orientation characterized by a lack of certainty about where to shop and what to buy due to the great abundance of options. The scale was referred to as *confused by overchoice* by Shim and Gehrt (1996).

SCALE ORIGIN: Shim and Gehrt (1996) used a scale developed by Sproles and Kendall (1986). The latter created an eight-factor model of what they called *consumer decision making styles* but what many others in marketing (e.g., Shim and Gehrt 1996) would view as *shopping orientations*. Sproles and Kendall (1986) reported alphas of .55 for the four-item scale and .51 for the three items that loaded highest on the factor.

SAMPLES: Shim and Gehrt (1996) collected data from high school students in a Southwestern U.S. state. Twenty-nine principals agreed to participate, and their schools apparently represented many, if not all, of the counties in the state. Principals were given instructions as to which classes to use (by level) and how many students from each class were needed. Some 1954 usable surveys were returned, with 61.3% from female students, and the mean age of the respondents was 16 years. However, the study focused only on data from **1846** students who were white (56%), Hispanic (32%), or Native American (12%).

RELIABILITY: An alpha of **.62** was reported for the scale by Shim and Gehrt (1996).

VALIDITY: No examination of the scale's validity was reported by Shim and Gehrt (1996).

ADMINISTRATION: Data were gathered in a classroom setting in which students filled out the scale as part of a larger survey instrument (Shim and Gehrt 1996). Higher scores on the scale indicated that respondents felt very confused in their shopping because of the number of products and stores from which they had to choose.

MAJOR FINDINGS: The study by Shim and Gehrt (1996) examined differences in shopping orientations among high school students that could be linked to ethnicity. The results showed that white students had significantly less **choice confusion** than Hispanics, who in turn had significantly less **choice confusion** than Native American students.

COMMENTS: The internal consistency of the scale is somewhat low, and further development is called for.

REFERENCES:
Shim, Soyeon and Kenneth C. Gehrt (1996), "Hispanic and Native American Adolescents: An Exploratory Study of Their Approach to Shopping," *JR*, 72 (3), 307–24.
Sproles, George B. and Elizabeth L. Kendall (1986), "A Methodology for Profiling Consumers' Decision-Making Styles," *Journal of Consumer Affairs,* 20 (Winter), 267–79.

SCALE ITEMS:

Strongly   Strongly
disagree   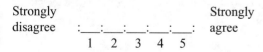 agree

1. There are so many brands to choose from that often I feel confused.

2. Sometimes it's hard to choose which stores to shop.

3. The more I learn about products, the harder it seems to choose the best.

4. All the information I get on different products confuses me.

SCALE NAME: Choice Task Meaningfulness

SCALE DESCRIPTION: Three seven-point semantic differentials measuring the degree to which a person views a choice task as being likable and familiar.

SCALE ORIGIN: Although the source of the scale was not directly addressed by Sen and Johnson (1997), it appears to be original to their studies.

SAMPLES: Sen and Johnson (1997) reported on two studies, the first of which had 36 subjects and the second 96. The former sample was composed of undergraduate students, and the second probably was students as well, though it was not explicitly described as such.

RELIABILITY: The alpha for the scale was reported to be **.81** for the first study (Sen and Johnson 1997). No reliability was reported for the scale as used in the second study.

VALIDITY: No examination of the scale's validity was reported by Sen and Johnson (1997).

ADMINISTRATION: The scale was self-administered by subjects, along with other measures, after they participated in a choice task (Sen and Johnson 1997). Higher scores on the scale indicated greater meaningfulness of a choice task.

MAJOR FINDINGS: Sen and Johnson (1997) investigated why preference for a product might be produced by mere possession of it, even if actual possession does not occur. **Choice task meaningfulness** was found to be a significant positive moderator of a coupon-induced mere possession effect.

REFERENCES:
Sen, Sankar and Eric J. Johnson (1997), "Mere-Possession Effects Without Possession in Consumer Choice," *JCR*, 24 (June), 105–117.

SCALE ITEMS:

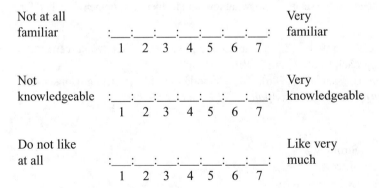

Not at all
familiar   :___:___:___:___:___:___:___: Very familiar
              1   2   3   4   5   6   7

Not
knowledgeable :___:___:___:___:___:___:___: Very knowledgeable
                1   2   3   4   5   6   7

Do not like
at all   :___:___:___:___:___:___:___: Like very much
              1   2   3   4   5   6   7

SCALE NAME: Clothing Concern

SCALE DESCRIPTION: Sixteen seven-point Likert-type statements that evaluate a person's concern about clothes as they affect his or her appearance. The scale measures the degree to which a respondent is willing to invest time, money, and effort into clothes and how they will look.

SCALE ORIGIN: As used by Netemeyer, Burton, and Lichtenstein (1995), the scale is original to the study by Gurel and Gurel (1979). However, the items come from a larger inventory of items refined by Creekmore (1971, pp. 98–101) from several earlier Master's theses conducted at Michigan State University in the late 1960s. Gurel and Gurel (1979) factor analyzed (n = 500) the 89 items that compose the Creekmore instrument and found that sixteen items loaded high on the first dimension, which they called *concern with personal appearance*. They considered this to be the most central component of clothing interest.

SAMPLES: Various samples were collected and used by Netemeyer, Burton, and Lichtenstein (1995) in the process of validating some other scales. The **clothing concern** scale was used in one study composed of 186 students and 264 "nonstudent adults." It was used in another study with data from 27 football players from a nationally ranked NCAA Division I team. Finally, it was used in a study that was based on data collected from 43 professional fashion models.

RELIABILITY: An alpha of **.89** was found for both the student and nonstudent adult samples by Netemeyer, Burton, and Lichtenstein (1995; Netemeyer 1997), and **.84** was found for the fashion model sample.

VALIDITY: Although the validity of the scale was not directly examined by Netemeyer, Burton, and Lichtenstein (1995), it was used to help establish the construct validity of four vanity-related scales. **Clothing concern** had significant positive correlations with all of the vanity scales, with the possible exception of physical view (#398).

ADMINISTRATION: As noted, the scale was used in three studies. It appears to have been part of larger questionnaires that were self-administered by respondents (Netemeyer, Burton, and Lichtenstein 1995). Higher scores on the scale indicated that respondents were preoccupied with clothes as they related to their personal appearance.

MAJOR FINDINGS: Netemeyer, Burton, and Lichtenstein (1995) investigated vanity and developed four scales for its measurement. Most of the article discussed the results of the rather extensive validation process. As noted, the findings indicated that **clothing concern** had positive relationships with each of the vanity scales, though the correlation with physical view vanity (#398) was not significant in two of the samples (nonstudent adults and models). The highest correlation for all of the samples was with physical concern vanity (#397).

REFERENCES:
Creekmore, A.M. (1971), *Methods of Measuring Clothing Variables*. Michigan Agricultural Experiment Station Project No. 783, Michigan State University.
Gurel, Lois M. and Lee Gurel (1979), "Clothing Interest: Conceptualization and Measurement," *Home Economics Research Journal*, 7 (May), 274–82.
Netemeyer, Richard G. (1997), personal correspondence.
———, Scot Burton, and Donald R. Lichtenstein (1995), "Trait Aspects of Vanity: Measurement and Relevance to Consumer Behavior," *JCR*, 21 (March), 612–26.

SCALE ITEMS:

Strongly   Strongly
disagree   :__:__:__:__:__:__:__: agree
        1   2   3   4   5   6   7

1. I carefully coordinate the accessories that I wear with each outfit.

2. I pay a lot of attention to pleasing color combinations.

3. I keep my shoes clean and neat.

4. I spend more time than others coordinating the colors in my clothes.

5. I see that my out-of-season clothing is cleaned and stored.

6. I am more concerned about the care of my clothing than my friends are about theirs.

7. The way I look in my clothes is important to me.

8. I look over the clothing in my wardrobe before each season so that I know what I have.

9. I have something to wear for any occasion that occurs.

10. I carefully plan each purchase so that I know what I need when I get to the store.

11. I wear clothes that have buttons or snaps missing. **(r)**

12. I wear a raincoat or carry an umbrella to protect my clothes in rainy weather.

13. I plan for and prepare clothes to wear several days in advance.

14. I consider the fabric texture with the line of the garment when choosing my clothes.

15. I have a long-term idea for purchasing more expensive items of clothing such as coats or suits.

16. It bothers me when my shirt tail keeps coming out.

SCALE NAME: Clothing Style Preference

SCALE DESCRIPTION: Three seven-point Likert-type statements measuring the degree to which a person views some set of clothes to be preferable to wear in a certain context. The context examined by Sirgy and colleagues (1997) was work.

SCALE ORIGIN: Although not explicitly stated, the scale appears to have been developed by Sirgy and colleagues (1997) for use in Study 2 of the six they conducted.

SAMPLES: Study 2 was based on data gathered from a mail survey of **229** female faculty and staff employed at two universities in the Southeastern United States.

RELIABILITY: Alphas of **.83, .77,** and **.73** were reported for the scale as used with reference to outfits described as classic, feminine, and dramatic, respectively (Sirgy et al. 1997).

VALIDITY: No examination of the scale's validity was reported (Sirgy et al. 1997).

ADMINISTRATION: The scale was self-administered by respondents as part of a mail survey (Sirgy et al. 1997). The scale was apparently filled out three times, once after each viewing of pictures of women wearing three different outfits. Higher scores on the scale suggested that respondents viewed a clothing outfit as the sort they would choose to wear in a particular context.

MAJOR FINDINGS: As noted, Sirgy and colleagues (1997) conducted six studies in support of a new method for measuring **self-image congruency** that was more direct than previous measures. In Study 2, the new measure was found to be more predictive of **clothing style preference** than a traditional measure.

REFERENCES:
Sirgy, M. Joseph, Dhruv Grewal, Tamara F. Mangleburg, Jae-ok Park, Kye-Sung Chon, C.B. Claiborne, J.S. Johar, and Harold Berkman (1997), "Assessing the Predictive Validity of Two Methods of Measuring Self-Image Congruence," *JAMS*, 25 (Summer), 229–41.

SCALE ITEMS:*

Strongly   Strongly
disagree   :___:___:___:___:___:___:___: agree
                 1   2   3   4   5   6   7

1. I usually wear an outfit like this to _____.

2. I would prefer to buy an outfit like this for _____.

3. Which of the outfits would you choose for _____?

*The context being examined (e.g., work, leisure, dancing, hiking) should be described in the blanks. For item #3, if the respondent chose the focal outfit, the response was coded as a 7, whereas if they chose another outfit, it was coded as a 1.

SCALE NAME: Collectivism (Coworkers)

SCALE DESCRIPTION: Three seven-point Likert-type items purported to measure the degree to which a person subordinates individual goals to those of the group, coworkers and classmates in particular. The group (rather than the individual) is viewed as the basic unit of survival.

SCALE ORIGIN: The scale was originally developed by Hui (1988, p. 18), who viewed the construct as a personality characteristic such that a person's "identity is derived from the social system rather than from individual attributes." Eight different collectivisms were conceptualized, and subscales were developed for each. However, the reliability of two dimensions was so low that they were dropped. The alphas for the 11-item version of the **coworker/classmates** subscale were .58 and .52 in two studies using pooled data from Chinese and Americans.

Sharma, Shimp, and Shin (1995) collected data with just five of the eleven items but further reduced the final scale to just three on the basis of the results of an exploratory factor analysis.

SAMPLES: Data were gathered from Korean consumers by Sharma, Shimp, and Shin (1995) using two sampling methods. Questionnaires were mailed to 1500 names taken from a economically diverse mailing list company's database. Usable surveys forms were returned by **125** people. The second method involved distributing 700 questionnaires to students at several schools in Seoul and in a southern Korean city. Completed questionnaires were received from **542** people. The samples were not significantly different in their demographic variables or response to dependent variables, so the authors chose to combine them for the analysis. The combined sample was 57% men, there was an average education level of slightly more than 13 years, and the mean age was 42 years.

RELIABILITY: Sharma, Shimp, and Shin (1995) performed confirmatory factor analysis (CFA) on this scale, as well as on others in the study. A reliability coefficient of **.39** for the **collectivism (coworker)** scale was reported on the basis of a holdout sample (n = 333).

VALIDITY: Sharma, Shimp, and Shin (1995) made a general claim of discriminant and convergent validity for all of their scales on the basis of the results of a CFA.

ADMINISTRATION: The scale was self-administered by respondents, along with other measures, in the questionnaire used by Sharma, Shimp, and Shin (1995). The scale also appears to have undergone a rather thorough translation process along with the entire survey instrument. Higher scores on the scale indicated that respondents placed the group before the individual.

MAJOR FINDINGS: The study by Sharma, Shimp, and Shin (1995) identified antecedents of ethnocentricity, as well as the influence of ethnocentricity on attitudes toward imported products. The results supported the hypothesis that people with collectivistic goals would have greater ethnocentric tendencies than those with individualistic goals.

COMMENTS: Despite the authors' general claim of discriminant and convergent validity for their scales, consideration of all of the evidence indicates that the **collectivism (coworker)** scale has inadequate psychometric quality. The longer version of the scale by Hui (1988) already had a very low alpha, so it is no surprise that reducing it to three items made it even lower. A glance at the following items also suggests that the items might not represent the same semantic domain. Improvement in the scale is called for if it is to be used again.

REFERENCES:

Hui, C. Harry (1988), "Measurement of Individual-Collectivism," *Journal of Research in Personality*, 22, 17–36.

Sharma, Subhash, Terence A. Shimp, and Jeongshin Shin (1995), "Consumer Ethnocentrism: A Test of Antecedents and Moderators," *JAMS*, 23 (Winter), 26–37.

SCALE ITEMS:

DIRECTIONS: Please respond to the following statements by circling a number from 1 to 7 according to these directions:

1 = Strongly disagree
2 = Moderately disagree
3 = Slightly disagree
4 = Neither agree nor disagree
5 = Slightly agree
6 = Moderately agree
7 = Strongly agree

1. One needs to return a favor if a colleague lends a helping hand.

2. There is everything to gain and nothing to lose for classmates to group themselves for study and discussion.

3. Classmates' assistance is indispensable to getting a good grade at school.

SCALE NAME: Collectivism (Parents)

SCALE DESCRIPTION: Three seven-point Likert-type items purported to measure the degree to which a person subordinates individual goals to those of his or her parents.

SCALE ORIGIN: The scale was originally developed by Hui (1988, p. 18), who viewed the construct as a personality characteristic such that a person's "identity is derived from the social system rather than from individual attributes." Eight different collectivisms were conceptualized, and subscales were developed for each. However, the reliability of two dimensions was so low that they were dropped. The alphas for the 16-item version of the **parent** subscale were .76 and .66 in two studies that used pooled data from Chinese and American respondents.

Sharma, Shimp, and Shin (1995) collected data with just 6 of the 16 items but further reduced the final scale to 3 on the basis of the results of an exploratory factor analysis.

SAMPLES: Data were gathered from Korean consumers by Sharma, Shimp, and Shin (1995) using two sampling methods. Questionnaires were mailed to 1500 names taken from a economically diverse mailing list company's database. Usable surveys forms were returned by **125** people. The second method involved distributing 700 questionnaires to students at several schools in Seoul and in a southern Korean city. Completed questionnaires were received from **542** people. The samples were not significantly different in their demographic variables or response to dependent variables, so the authors chose to combine them for the analysis. The combined sample was 57% men, there was an average education level of slightly more than 13 years, and the mean age was 42 years.

RELIABILITY: Sharma, Shimp, and Shin (1995) performed confirmatory factor analysis (CFA) on this scale, as well as on others in the study. A reliability coefficient of **.56** for the **collectivism (parents)** scale was reported on the basis of a holdout sample (n = 333).

VALIDITY: Sharma, Shimp, and Shin (1995) made a general claim of discriminant and convergent validity for all of their scales on the basis of the results of a CFA.

ADMINISTRATION: The scale was self-administered by respondents, along with other measures, in the questionnaire used by Sharma, Shimp, and Shin (1995). The scale also appears to have undergone a rather thorough translation process along with the entire survey instrument. Higher scores on the scale indicated that respondents believed it was proper for grown-up children to depend on their parent's advice and follow their lead rather than strike out in a new direction.

MAJOR FINDINGS: The study by Sharma, Shimp, and Shin (1995) identified antecedents of ethnocentricity as well as the influence of ethnocentricity on attitudes toward imported products. The results supported the hypothesis that people with **collectivistic** goals would have greater ethnocentric tendencies than those with individualistic goals.

COMMENTS: Despite the authors' general claim of discriminant and convergent validity for their scales, consideration of all of the evidence indicates that the **collectivism (parents)** scale has low psychometric quality. Improvement in the scale is called for if it is to be used again.

REFERENCES:
Hui, C. Harry (1988), "Measurement of Individual-Collectivism," *Journal of Research in Personality*, 22, 17–36.
Sharma, Subhash, Terence A. Shimp, and Jeongshin Shin (1995), "Consumer Ethnocentrism: A Test of Antecedents and Moderators," *JAMS*, 23 (Winter), 26–37.

SCALE ITEMS:

DIRECTIONS: Please respond to the following statements by circling a number from 1 to 7 according to these directions:

1 = Strongly disagree
2 = Moderately disagree
3 = Slightly disagree
4 = Neither agree nor disagree
5 = Slightly agree
6 = Moderately agree
7 = Strongly agree

1. Young people should take into consideration their parents' advice when making education/career plans.

2. Success and failure in my academic work and career are closely tied to the nurture provided by my parents.

3. I practice the religion of my parents.

SCALE NAME: Commitment (Organizational)

SCALE DESCRIPTION: Fourteen seven-point Likert-type items measuring a consumer's identification with and loyalty to a specified organization. The organization studied by Kelley and Davis (1994) was a health club.

SCALE ORIGIN: Kelley and Davis (1994) slightly modified the commitment scale developed by Porter and his associates (Mowday, Steers, and Porter 1979; Porter et al. 1974). The scale was tested on 2563 employees working in a variety of jobs in nine different organizations, but not all tests were performed on all employees. A great deal of information is provided regarding the scale's reliability and validity (Mowday, Steers, and Porter 1979). In general, the scale showed evidence of high internal consistency (average alphas of .90); reasonable test–retest correlations; and adequate convergent, discriminant, and predictive validities.

    Because the original scale was developed for the assessment of employee commitment to an organization, the changes made by Kelley and Davis (1994) were to adjust the measure for the retail service organization of which a consumer could be a member.

SAMPLES: Data were collected by Kelley and Davis (1994) from members of a health club located in a midsized community in the Southeastern United States. The authors stated that the health club was viewed as the market leader in the area and offered a wide range of services and amenities. Surveys were passed out to members as they came and went from the club on 12 consecutive days. Completed questionnaires were received from **296** individuals. The typical respondent was 36.7 years old, male (65%), had been a member of the club for three years, and worked out an average of three days a week.

RELIABILITY: An alpha of **.86** was reported for the scale by Kelley and Davis (1994). One item was eliminated because of its low item–total correlation.

VALIDITY: The validity of the scale was not specifically examined by Kelley and Davis (1994).

ADMINISTRATION: The scale was completed, along with other scales and measures, in a self-administered survey (Kelley and Davis 1994). Higher scores on the scale suggested that respondents had high involvement in the specified organization of which they are members, whereas low scores indicated that they had little loyalty or commitment.

MAJOR FINDINGS: Kelley and Davis (1994) proposed and tested a model of the antecedents to service recovery expectations. It was found that service quality and customer **organizational commitment** had direct effects on customer service recovery expectations.

COMMENTS: See Scale #527, for use of the original form of this scale in an organizational context.

REFERENCES:
Kelley, Scott W. and Mark A. Davis (1994), "Antecedents to Customer Expectations for Service Recovery," *JAMS*, 22 (Winter), 52–61.

Mowday, Richard T., Richard M. Steers, and Lyman W. Porter (1979), "The Measurement of Organizational Commitment," *Journal of Vocational Behavior*, 14 (April), 224–47.

Porter, Lyman W., Richard M. Steers, Richard T. Mowday, and Paul V. Boulian (1974), "Organizational Commitment, Job Satisfaction, and Turnover Among Psychiatric Technicians," *Journal of Applied Psychology*, 59 (October), 603–609.

SCALE ITEMS:*
DIRECTIONS: Listed below are a series of statements representing possible feelings that members might have about _____. With respect to your own feelings about your _____ please indicate the degree of your agreement or disagreement with each statement by placing a check mark (×) on the line to the right of each statement.

```
Strongly                          Strongly
disagree   :___:___:___:___:___:___:___:   agree
            1   2   3   4   5   6   7
```

1. I am willing to put in a great deal of effort beyond that normally expected in order to help this _____ provide service to me.

2. I talk up this _____ to my friends as a great _____.

3. I feel very little loyalty to this _____. **(r)**

4. I would accept almost any type of service from this _____ and still come back.

5. I find that my values and this _____'s values are very similar.

6. I am proud to tell others that I am a member of this _____.

7. I could just as well be using a different _____ as long as the type of service was similar. **(r)**

8. This _____ really inspires me to help provide service in any way I can.

9. It would take very little change in my present circumstances to cause me to use another _____. **(r)**

10. I am extremely glad that I chose this _____ over others I was considering.

11. There is not too much to be gained by sticking with this _____ indefinitely. **(r)**

12. Often, I find it difficult to agree with this _____'s policies on important matters relating to its members. **(r)**

13. For me this is the best of all possible _____ for which to be a member.

14. Deciding to be a member of this _____ was a definite mistake on my part. **(r)**

*The name of the type of business being studied should be placed in the blanks. As noted, Kelley and Davis (1994) modified the scale to be used with health clubs. The scale appears to be amenable for use with other retail services, with some minor editing.

SCALE NAME: Commitment (Store)

SCALE DESCRIPTION: Three seven-point Likert-type items measuring a customer's sense of obligation to continue shopping at a store and help it succeed. Commitment is defined as being a broader construct than loyalty, such that it "should produce a variety of beneficial behaviors, including but not limited to loyalty" (Bettencourt 1997, p. 388).

SCALE ORIGIN: Although the author received some inspiration from previous measures of commitment (e.g., #86 Kelley and Davis 1994), the scale is original to the work of Bettencourt (1997).

SAMPLES: In the study reported by Bettencourt (1997), data were collected by students of a marketing class. They were instructed to have five surveys completed by people who were regular shoppers for their households. After a verification process, **215** questionnaires remained for data analysis. A majority (70%) of the sample was older than 30 years of age, were women (73%), and had completed at least some college (85%).

RELIABILITY: Bettencourt (1997) reported an alpha of **.79** for the scale.

VALIDITY: The validity of the scale was not explicitly examined in Bettencourt's (1997) study, though evidence of dimensionality was reported. A confirmatory factor analysis (CFA) was performed with items from this scale and two others, which provided support for the three-factor conceptualization. Unfortunately, though a separate measure of loyalty was used in the study (#228), it was not included in this CFA. Thus, critical evidence supporting a claim of discriminant validity between the two measures is lacking.

ADMINISTRATION: The scale was self-administered as part of a much larger survey instrument (Bettencourt 1997). Higher scores on the scale indicated that respondents were very committed to the specified store.

MAJOR FINDINGS: A model of customer voluntary performance was developed and tested by Bettencourt (1997) in the context of grocery store shopping. The findings indicated that customer **commitment** had a significant positive relationship with loyalty.

COMMENTS: The scale mean was 4.63 (Bettencourt 1997). With minor adjustments in phrasing, this scale appears amenable for use with businesses other than grocery stores.

REFERENCES:
Bettencourt, Lance A. (1997), "Customer Voluntary Performance: Customers as Partners in Service Delivery," *JR*, 73 (3), 383–406.
Kelley, Scott W. and Mark A. Davis (1994), "Antecedents to Customer Expectations for Service Recovery," *JAMS*, 22 (Winter), 52–61.

SCALE ITEMS:

Strongly   Strongly
disagree   :___:___:___:___:___:___:___: agree
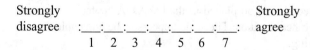
          1   2   3   4   5   6   7

1. I am very committed to this grocery store.

2. I intend to continue shopping at this store over the next few years.

3. I would expend effort on behalf of this store to help it succeed.

SCALE NAME: Comparison Shopping (Check Prices)

SCALE DESCRIPTION: Three seven-point items that measure the degree to which a consumer describes his or her tendency to check price tags of grocery items before making the decision to buy.

SCALE ORIGIN: Although not clear from the article by Putrevu and Ratchford (1997), some of the work on the scales was conducted previously in a dissertation by Putrevu (1992).

SAMPLES: Data were gathered by Putrevu and Ratchford (1997) using a mail survey sent to a random sample of grocery shoppers in a standard metropolitan statistical area in the Northeastern United States. A total of **500** responses was used in the main analysis, and demographics of the final sample were similar to those of the population of interest.

RELIABILITY: An alpha of **.85** was reported for the scale (Putrevu and Ratchford 1997).

VALIDITY: Although the authors stated in general that the scales showed evidence of convergent, discriminant, and content validity, no details of the analyses were provided (Putrevu and Ratchford 1997).

ADMINISTRATION: The scale was part of a larger mail questionnaire (Putrevu and Ratchford 1997). Higher scores on the scale suggested that a consumer frequently checked the prices on grocery products before making purchases.

MAJOR FINDINGS: Putrevu and Ratchford (1997) examined a dynamic model of consumer search behavior that includes human capital. In general, the results indicated that self-reported search for information about buying groceries was associated with perceptions of the costs and benefits of search, as was predicted by the model.

COMMENTS: As presented in the article by Putrevu and Ratchford (1997), this scale was part of a larger measure called "Search." That measure was the mean of the scores from nine scales related to search behavior for grocery product information.

REFERENCES:
Putrevu, Sanjay (1992), "A Theory of Search and Its Empirical Investigation," doctoral dissertation, State University of New York at Buffalo.
——— and Brian T. Ratchford (1997), "A Model of Search Behavior with an Application to Grocery Shopping," *JR*, 73 (4), 463–86.

SCALE ITEMS:

Never   :___:___:___:___:___:___: Always
        1   2   3   4   5   6   7

1. I read price tags of the grocery products that I buy.

2. I check the prices of the grocery products that I purchase.

3. Before buying a product, I check the price.

SCALE NAME: Comparison Shopping (Initial)

SCALE DESCRIPTION: Three five-point Likert-type statements measuring the degree to which a consumer reports having shopped around in the past at different grocery stores to determine which would be the best place to shop regularly. The scale was referred to as *investment search* by Urbany, Dickson, and Kalapurakal (1996).

SCALE ORIGIN: Although Urbany, Dickson, and Kalapurakal (1996) may have drawn inspiration from previous work, the scale appears to be original to their study. A pretest was used to refine the scale before use in the main study.

SAMPLES: The data used by Urbany, Dickson, and Kalapurakal (1996) were collected as part of a larger survey by a leading market research firm. Telephone interviews were conducted with the primary grocery shoppers from households selected at random. Respondents were requested to participate in a second stage that would involve a mail survey. The survey yielded **343** usable responses. The average age of the respondents was 44.7 years, and they were overwhelmingly women (83%).

RELIABILITY: An alpha of **.82** was reported for the scale by Urbany, Dickson, and Kalapurakal (1996).

VALIDITY: Urbany, Dickson, and Kalapurakal (1996) tested the discriminant validity of the **comparison shopper** scale using pairwise confirmatory factor analysis and six other measures. The evidence of three separate tests on each of the six pairs supported a claim of discriminant validity.

ADMINISTRATION: The data analyzed by Urbany, Dickson, and Kalapurakal (1996) were gathered in a mail survey. Higher scores suggested that respondents engaged in comparison shopping, at least initially, to decide where to do most of their grocery shopping.

MAJOR FINDINGS: Urbany, Dickson, and Kalapurakal (1996) developed a model of price search for the retail grocery industry that included a relatively complete accounting of economic and noneconomic returns, as well as search costs. Unexpectedly, the findings showed that an initial **comparison shopping** effort had a significant positive association with continued comparison shopping.

COMMENTS: Urbany, Dickson, and Kalapurakal (1996) reported a mean response of 3.14 on the scale.

REFERENCES:
Urbany, Joel E., Peter R. Dickson, and Rosemary Kalapurakal (1996), "Price Search in the Retail Grocery Market," *JM*, 60 (April), 91–104.

SCALE ITEMS:

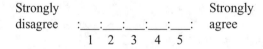

```
Strongly                          Strongly
disagree    :___:___:___:___:___:  agree
              1   2   3   4   5
```

1. I shopped back and forth between several different stores before choosing where I now do most of my grocery shopping.

2. I compared the prices of different stores before finally deciding where to do most of my grocery shopping.

3. I made an extra effort in the beginning to learn about different stores so as to simplify the grocery shopping I do now.

SCALE NAME: Comparison Shopping (Multiple Stores)

SCALE DESCRIPTION: Three seven-point items that measure the degree to which a consumer describes his or her tendency to shop at more than one supermarket to take advantage of the best deals each has to offer.

SCALE ORIGIN: Although not clear from the article by Putrevu and Ratchford (1997), some of the work on the scales was conducted previously in a dissertation by Putrevu (1992).

SAMPLES: Data were gathered by Putrevu and Ratchford (1997) using a mail survey to a random sample of grocery shoppers in a standard metropolitan statistical area in the Northeastern United States. A total of **500** responses was used in the main analysis, and demographics of the final sample were similar to those of the population of interest.

RELIABILITY: An alpha of **.89** was reported for the scale (Putrevu and Ratchford 1997).

VALIDITY: Although the authors stated in general that the scales showed evidence of convergent, discriminant, and content validity, no details of the analyses were provided (Putrevu and Ratchford 1997).

ADMINISTRATION: The scale was part of a larger mail questionnaire (Putrevu and Ratchford 1997). Higher scores on the scale suggested that a consumer frequently shopped at more than one grocery store to get the best buys.

MAJOR FINDINGS: Putrevu and Ratchford (1997) examined a dynamic model of consumer search behavior that includes human capital. In general, the results indicated that self-reported search for information about buying groceries was associated with perceptions of the costs and benefits of search, as was predicted by the model.

COMMENTS: As presented in the article by Putrevu and Ratchford (1997), this scale was part of a larger measure called "Search." That measure was the mean of the scores from nine scales related to search behavior for grocery product information.

REFERENCES:
Putrevu, Sanjay (1992), "A Theory of Search and Its Empirical Investigation," doctoral dissertation, State University of New York at Buffalo.
——— and Brian T. Ratchford (1997), "A Model of Search Behavior with an Application to Grocery Shopping," *JR*, 73 (4), 463–86.

SCALE ITEMS:

Never   :___:___:___:___:___:___:___: Always
       1 2 3 4 5 6 7

1. I shop at more than one supermarket.

2. I visit only one supermarket to complete my weekly grocery purchases. **(r)**

3. To get the best buys, I shop at two or three different supermarkets.

SCALE NAME: Comparison Shopping (Product Attributes)

SCALE DESCRIPTION: Four seven-point items that measure the degree to which a consumer describes his or her tendency to compare brands before buying, with an emphasis on ingredients rather than price.

SCALE ORIGIN: Although not clear from the article by Putrevu and Ratchford (1997), some of the work on the scales was conducted previously in a dissertation by Putrevu (1992).

SAMPLES: Data were gathered by Putrevu and Ratchford (1997) using a mail survey to a random sample of grocery shoppers in a standard metropolitan statistical area in the Northeastern United States. A total of **500** responses was used in the main analysis, and demographics of the final sample were similar to those of the population of interest.

RELIABILITY: An alpha of **.87** was reported for the scale (Putrevu and Ratchford 1997).

VALIDITY: Although the authors stated in general that the scales showed evidence of convergent, discriminant, and content validity, no details of the analyses were provided (Putrevu and Ratchford 1997).

ADMINISTRATION: The scale was part of a larger mail questionnaire (Putrevu and Ratchford 1997). Higher scores on the scale suggested that a consumer frequently compared brands using nonprice criteria.

MAJOR FINDINGS: Putrevu and Ratchford (1997) examined a dynamic model of consumer search behavior that includes human capital. In general, the results indicated that self-reported search for information about buying groceries was associated with perceptions of the costs and benefits of search, as was predicted by the model.

COMMENTS: As presented in the article by Putrevu and Ratchford (1997), this scale was part of a larger measure called "Search." That measure was the mean of the scores from nine scales related to search behavior for grocery product information.

REFERENCES:
Putrevu, Sanjay (1992), "A Theory of Search and Its Empirical Investigation," doctoral dissertation, State University of New York at Buffalo.
——— and Brian T. Ratchford (1997), "A Model of Search Behavior with an Application to Grocery Shopping," *JR*, 73 (4), 463–86.

SCALE ITEMS:

Never   :___:___:___:___:___:___:___: Always
            1   2   3   4   5   6   7

1. I check the calories, fat, and other nutritional information on packages before deciding to buy a specific brand.

2. I compare brands on factors other than price.

3. I compare brands on factors like calories, fat, nutritional value, etc.

4. I compare the ingredients of different brands.

SCALE NAME: Comparison Shopping (Routine)

SCALE DESCRIPTION: Three items that measure the frequency with which a consumer engages in comparative shopping for grocery products. The scale was referred to as *compare* by Urbany, Dickson, and Kalapurakal (1996).

SCALE ORIGIN: Although Urbany, Dickson, and Kalapurakal (1996) may have drawn inspiration from previous work, the scale appears to be original to their study.

SAMPLES: The data used by Urbany, Dickson, and Kalapurakal (1996) were collected as part of a larger survey by a leading market research firm. Telephone interviews were conducted with the primary grocery shoppers from households selected at random. Respondents were requested to participate in a second stage that would involve a mail survey. Usable responses were obtained from **343** respondents who responded to both surveys. The average age of the respondents was 44.7 years, and they were overwhelmingly women (83%).

RELIABILITY: An alpha of **.81** was reported for the scale by Urbany, Dickson, and Kalapurakal (1996).

VALIDITY: No examination of the scale's validity was reported by Urbany, Dickson, and Kalapurakal (1996) beyond noting that the variance extracted was .61.

ADMINISTRATION: Data for one of the scale items came from the first stage of data collection (described previously), whereas the other two items were part of the mail survey in the second stage (Urbany, Dickson, and Kalapurakal 1996). Higher scores suggested that respondents frequently (e.g., weekly) engaged in comparison grocery shopping. Because of the differences in points on the response scales, item scores were standardized before computing scale scores.

MAJOR FINDINGS: Urbany, Dickson, and Kalapurakal (1996) developed a model of price search for the retail grocery industry that included a relatively complete accounting of economic and noneconomic returns, as well as search costs. Unexpectedly, the findings showed that an initial comparison shopping effort has a significant positive association **with routine comparison shopping**.

REFERENCES:
Urbany, Joel E., Peter R. Dickson, and Rosemary Kalapurakal (1996), "Price Search in the Retail Grocery Market," *JM*, 60 (April), 91–104.

SCALE ITEMS:

Strongly   Strongly
disagree   :__:__:__:__: agree

          1 2 3 4 5

1. I compare the prices of different stores.

2. I often compare the prices of fruit and vegetables at two or more grocery stores.

3. How often do you compare the specific prices of grocery stores?

  Weekly   Monthly   Less often   Never
    1————————2————————3————————4

SCALE NAME: Comparison Shopping (Unit Prices)

SCALE DESCRIPTION: Four seven-point items that measure the degree to which a consumer describes his or her tendency to compare unit prices of products when grocery shopping.

SCALE ORIGIN: Although not clear from the article by Putrevu and Ratchford (1997), some of the work on the scales was conducted previously in a dissertation by Putrevu (1992).

SAMPLES: Data were gathered by Putrevu and Ratchford (1997) using a mail survey to a random sample of grocery shoppers in a standard metropolitan statistical area in the Northeastern United States. A total of **500** responses was used in the main analysis, and demographics of the final sample were similar to those of the population of interest.

RELIABILITY: An alpha of **.91** was reported for the scale (Putrevu and Ratchford 1997).

VALIDITY: Although the authors stated in general that the scales showed evidence of convergent, discriminant, and content validity, no details of the analyses were provided (Putrevu and Ratchford 1997).

ADMINISTRATION: The scale was part of a larger mail questionnaire (Putrevu and Ratchford 1997). Higher scores on the scale suggested that a consumer frequently used unit prices to compare and evaluate products when shopping.

MAJOR FINDINGS: Putrevu and Ratchford (1997) examined a dynamic model of consumer search behavior that includes human capital. In general, the results indicated that self-reported search for information about buying groceries was associated with perceptions of the costs and benefits of search, as was predicted by the model.

COMMENTS: As presented in the article by Putrevu and Ratchford (1997), this scale was part of a larger measure called "Search." That measure was the mean of the scores from nine scales related to search behavior for grocery product information.

REFERENCES:
Putrevu, Sanjay (1992), "A Theory of Search and Its Empirical Investigation," doctoral dissertation, State University of New York at Buffalo.
———— and Brian T. Ratchford (1997), "A Model of Search Behavior with an Application to Grocery Shopping," *JR*, 73 (4), 463–86.

SCALE ITEMS:

Never   :___:___:___:___:___:___:___: Always
       1   2   3   4   5   6   7

1. I compare unit prices across different package sizes.

2. I compare unit prices across brands.

3. I check unit prices of products I buy.

4. Before buying a product, I check the unit price.

SCALE NAME: Complaint Intentions (Private)

SCALE DESCRIPTION: A three-item, six-point summated ratings scale measuring the likelihood that a consumer would express his or her dissatisfaction after a purchase to parties not involved in the exchange, such as friends and relatives, so those parties also will not use that service again.

SCALE ORIGIN: Although Singh (1988, 1990) drew on information previously documented by Day (1984), the scale was original. Along with other scales developed in the study, the items were modified on the basis of data collected in a pretest of faculty and staff.

SAMPLES: Data were collected from four samples by Singh (1988, 1990). Four slightly different survey instruments, which varied in the dissatisfying experience to which they referred, were used. One thousand households were sent a questionnaire for each of the four service categories studied: car repairs, grocery stores, medical care, and banking. Response rates were estimated to be greater than 50% for each category, given that only around 30% of the random samples had dissatisfying experiences worthy of reporting on a questionnaire. Ultimately, usable data ranged from **116** respondents in the repair service sample to **125** in the medical care sample.

Detailed demographic information for each of the four samples is provided in the article. However, it is difficult to summarize the four profiles because they varied somewhat. This variation was most likely due to the instrument itself, which indicated that the questionnaire was to be completed by the person in the household who dealt most with the specified service category. For example, men mostly filled out the questionnaire regarding auto repair (67%), whereas women generally filled out the one pertaining to grocery shopping (73%).

RELIABILITY: An alpha of **.77** was reported by Singh (1990) for the car repair version of the scale.

VALIDITY: Using data from the car repair sample, the items in this scale, along with those for two other related complaint intentions scales (voice and third party), were analyzed using exploratory factor analysis (Singh 1988, 1990). A three-factor structure was obtained and examined using confirmatory factor analysis (CFA) for the other three data sets. Results of the CFA provided further support for the three-factor structure and discriminant validity. See Singh (1988) for more validation information.

ADMINISTRATION: The scale was administered by Singh (1988, 1990) in a mail survey instrument, along with many other scales and measures. Higher scores on the scale indicated that respondents were very likely to express their complaints to friends and relatives after a dissatisfying experience occurred, whereas those with low scores were not as likely to say anything.

MAJOR FINDINGS: In a detailed study of consumer complaint behavior, Singh (1990) concluded that there were four consumer clusters with distinct response styles: passives, voicers, irates, and activists. Profiles were developed for each cluster. There was significant variation among the four clusters in their **intentions to complain privately.** Specifically, approximately twice as many irates said they would complain privately compared with passives and voicers.

COMMENTS: As noted, four transactions were examined in the study by Singh (1988, 1990). However, only the items relating to car repair were reported. To the extent that a researcher wished to use the scale to study complaints in a nonrepair context, one of the other three versions of the scale might be more appropriate.

See also Singh and Wilkes (1996) for further analysis of a portion of the same database used by Singh (1988, 1990).

#94 *Complaint Intentions (Private)*

REFERENCES:

Day, Ralph L. (1984), "Modeling Choices Among Alternative Responses to Dissatisfaction," in *Advances in Consumer Research*, Vol. 11, Tom Kinnear, ed. Provo, UT: Association of Consumer Research, 496–99.

Singh, Jagdip (1988), "Consumer Complaint Intentions and Behaviors: Definitional and Taxonomical Issues," *JM*, 52 (January), 93–107.

——— (1990), "A Typology of Consumer Dissatisfaction Response Styles," *JR*, 66 (Spring), 57–97.

——— and Robert E. Wilkes (1996), "When Consumers Complain: A Path Analysis of the Key Antecedents of Consumer Compliant Response Estimates," *JAMS*, 24 (Fall), 350–65.

SCALE ITEMS:

Very unlikely :___:___:___:___:___:___: Very likely
     1   2   3   4   5   6

How likely is it that you would:

1. Decide not to use the repair shop again?

2. Speak to your friends and relatives about your bad experience?

3. Convince your friends and relatives not to use that repair shop?

SCALE NAME: Complaint Intentions (Third Party)

SCALE DESCRIPTION: A four-item, six-point summated ratings scale measuring the likelihood that a consumer would express his or her dissatisfaction after a purchase to parties who were not involved in the exchange but who could bring some pressure to bear on the offending marketer. Such third parties could be consumer organizations, the media, or lawyers.

SCALE ORIGIN: Although Singh (1988, 1990) drew on information previously documented by Day (1984), the scale was original. Along with other scales developed in the study, the items were modified on the basis of data collected in a pretest of faculty and staff.

SAMPLES: Data were collected from four samples by Singh (1988, 1990). Four slightly different survey instruments, which varied in the dissatisfying experience to which they referred, were used. One thousand households were sent a questionnaire for each of the four service categories studied: car repairs, grocery stores, medical care, and banking. Response rates were estimated to be greater than 50% for each category, given that only approximately 30% of the random samples had dissatisfying experiences worthy of reporting on a questionnaire. Ultimately, usable data ranged from **116** respondents in the repair service sample to **125** in the medical care sample.

Detailed demographic information for each of the four samples is provided in the article. However, it is difficult to summarize the four profiles because they varied somewhat. This variation was most likely due to the instrument itself, which indicated that the questionnaire was to be completed by the person in the household who dealt most with the specified service category. For example, men mostly filled out the questionnaire regarding auto repair (67%), whereas women generally filled out the one pertaining to grocery shopping (73%).

RELIABILITY: An alpha of **.84** was reported by Singh (1990) for the car repair version of the scale.

VALIDITY: Using data from the car repair sample, the items in this scale, along with those for two other related complaint intentions scales (voice and private), were analyzed using exploratory factor analysis (Singh 1988, 1990). A three-factor structure was obtained and examined using confirmatory factor analysis (CFA) for the other three data sets. Results of the CFA provided further support for the three-factor structure and discriminant validity. See Singh (1988) for more validation information.

ADMINISTRATION: The scale was administered by Singh (1988, 1990) in a mail survey instrument, along with many other scales and measures. Higher scores on the scale indicated that respondents were very likely to express their complaints after a dissatisfying experience to third parties not involved in the exchange to seek some remedy, whereas those with low scores were not likely to approach those parties.

MAJOR FINDINGS: In a detailed study of consumer complaint behavior, Singh (1990) concluded that there were four consumer clusters with distinct response styles: passives, voicers, irates, and activists. Profiles were developed for each cluster. **Intention to complain to third parties** was the least likely type of complaining that would occur for each of the clusters, but there was still some significant variation among the groups. Specifically, a greater percentage of actives, more than three times as great as passives and voicers, was likely to complain this way.

COMMENTS: As noted, four transactions were examined in the study by Singh (1988, 1990). However, only the items relating to the car repair were reported. To the extent that a researcher wished to use the scale to study complaints in a nonrepair context, one of the other three versions of the scale might be more appropriate.

See also Singh and Wilkes (1996) for further analysis of a portion of the same database used by Singh (1988, 1990).

REFERENCES:

Day, Ralph L. (1984), "Modeling Choices Among Alternative Responses to Dissatisfaction," in *Advances in Consumer Research*, Vol. 11, Tom Kinnear, ed. Provo, UT: Association for Consumer Research, 496–99.

Singh, Jagdip (1988), "Consumer Complaint Intentions and Behaviors: Definitional and Taxonomical Issues," *JM*, 52 (January), 93–107.

——— (1990), "A Typology of Consumer Dissatisfaction Response Styles," *JR*, 66 (Spring), 57–97.

——— and Robert E. Wilkes (1996), "When Consumers Complain: A Path Analysis of the Key Antecedents of Consumer Compliant Response Estimates," *JAMS*, 24 (Fall), 350–65.

SCALE ITEMS:

Very unlikely :___:___:___:___:___:___: Very likely
            1   2   3   4   5   6

How likely is it that you would:

1. Complain to a consumer agency and ask them to make the repair shop take care of your problem?

2. Write a letter to a local newspaper about your bad experience?

3. Report to a consumer agency so that they can warn other consumers?

4. Take some legal action against the repair shop/manufacturer?

SCALE NAME: Complaint Intentions (Voice)

SCALE DESCRIPTION: A three-item, six-point summated ratings scale measuring the likelihood that a consumer would aim complaints at those marketers (e.g., salespersons, managers) involved in the offending transaction.

SCALE ORIGIN: Although Singh (1988, 1990) drew on information previously documented by Day (1984), the scales are original. Along with other scales developed in the study, the items were modified on the basis of data collected in a pretest of faculty and staff.

SAMPLES: Data were collected from four samples by Singh (1988, 1990). Four slightly different survey instruments, which varied in the dissatisfying experience to which they referred, were used. One thousand households were sent a questionnaire for each of the four service categories studied: car repairs, grocery stores, medical care, and banking. Response rates were estimated to be greater than 50% for each category, given that only approximately 30% of the random samples had dissatisfying experiences worthy of reporting on a questionnaire. Ultimately, usable data ranged from **116** respondents in the repair service sample to **125** in the medical care sample.

Detailed demographic information for each of the four samples is provided in the article. However, it is difficult to summarize the four profiles because they varied somewhat. This variation was most likely due to the instrument itself, which indicated that the questionnaire was to be completed by the person in the household who dealt most with the specified service category. For example, men mostly filled out the questionnaire regarding auto repair (67%), whereas women generally filled out the one pertaining to grocery shopping (73%).

RELIABILITY: An alpha of **.75** was reported by Singh (1990) for the car repair version of the scale.

VALIDITY: Using data from the car repair sample, the items in this scale, along with those for two other related complaint intentions scales (private and third party), were analyzed using exploratory factor analysis (Singh 1988, 1990). A three-factor structure was obtained and examined using confirmatory factor analysis (CFA) for the other three data sets. Results of the CFA provided further support for the three-factor structure and discriminant validity. See Singh (1988) for more validation information.

ADMINISTRATION: The scale was administered by Singh (1988, 1990) in a mail survey instrument along with many other scales and measures. Higher scores on the scale indicated that respondents were very likely to complain to service providers if a dissatisfying experience occurred, whereas those with low scores were more likely to do nothing.

MAJOR FINDINGS: In a detailed study of consumer complaint behavior, Singh (1990) concluded that there were four consumer clusters with distinct response styles: passives, voicers, irates, and activists. Profiles were developed for each cluster. There was significant variation among the four clusters in their **intentions to voice complaints.** Specifically, twice as many voicers said they would voice their complaints compared with passives.

COMMENTS: As noted, four transactions were examined in the study by Singh (1988, 1990). However, only the items relating to the car repair were reported. To the extent that a researcher wished to use the scale to study complaints in a nonrepair context, one of the other three versions of the scale might be more appropriate.

See also Singh and Wilkes (1996) for further analysis of a portion of the same database used by Singh (1988, 1990).

REFERENCES:

Day, Ralph L. (1984), "Modeling Choices Among Alternative Responses to Dissatisfaction," in *Advances in Consumer Research*, Vol. 11, Tom Kinnear, ed. Provo, UT: Association for Consumer Research, 496–99.

Singh, Jagdip (1988), "Consumer Complaint Intentions and Behaviors: Definitional and Taxonomical Issues," *JM*, 52 (January), 93–107.

―――― (1990), "A Typology of Consumer Dissatisfaction Response Styles," *JR*, 66 (Spring), 57–97.

―――― and Robert E. Wilkes (1996), "When Consumers Complain: A Path Analysis of the Key Antecedents of Consumer Compliant Response Estimates," *JAMS*, 24 (Fall), 350–65.

SCALE ITEMS:

Very unlikely :___:___:___:___:___:___: Very likely
        1   2   3   4   5   6

How likely is it that you would:

1. Forget the incident and do nothing? **(r)**

2. Definitely complain to the store manager on your next trip?

3. Go back or call the repair shop immediately and ask them to take care of the problem?

SCALE NAME: Complaint Likelihood (Direct)

SCALE DESCRIPTION: Three seven-point statements measuring the lack of motivation a consumer expresses having to complain to a store or return a product when it is unsatisfactory. The measure is direct in the sense that the focus of the potential complaint behavior is the source of the problem (the retailer) versus complaining privately to friends and family (#94) or taking the complaint to a third party (#95). The scale was referred to by Blodgett, Hill, and Tax (1997) as *attitude toward complaining.*

SCALE ORIGIN: Although Blodgett, Hill, and Tax (1997) may have drawn inspiration from previous measures, this scale appears to be original to their study.

SAMPLES: Data were collected by Blodgett, Hill, and Tax (1997) using a quasi-experimental design and subjects from three different locations: a Southern U.S. university, a Midwestern U.S. university, and a Canadian university. Subjects came from local church groups, as well as from the faculty and staff at the universities. Usable responses were received from **265** subjects. Among the demographic information provided for the sample was that a majority were white (86%) and women (61%). There was wide diversity in the sample on other characteristics such as age, occupation, education, and income.

RELIABILITY: An alpha of **.78** was reported for the scale by Blodgett, Hill, and Tax (1997).

VALIDITY: No examination of the scale's validity was reported by Blodgett, Hill, and Tax (1997).

ADMINISTRATION: The scale was administered to subjects, along with other measures, after they had been exposed to experimental stimuli (Blodgett, Hill, and Tax 1997). Higher scores on the scale indicated that respondents were not likely to return products to the store from which they were purchased or complain about it directly to the retailer when the products were unsatisfactory.

MAJOR FINDINGS: The study by Blodgett, Hill, and Tax (1997) examined the effects of various types of *justice* on complainants' negative word of mouth and likelihood of repatronage. The **complaint likelihood** scale was included as a check on confounding effects. Subjects' **complaint likelihoods** were not significantly different across the various levels of justice (distributive, interactional, procedural) and provided support for the internal validity of the experiment.

REFERENCES:
Blodgett, Jeffrey G., Donna J. Hill, and Stephen S. Tax (1997), "The Effects of Distributive, Procedural, and Interactional Justice on Postcomplaint Behavior," *JR*, 73 (2), 185–210.

SCALE ITEMS:

Strongly   Strongly
disagree   :___:___:___:___:___:___:___: agree

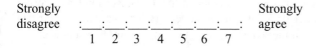

              1   2   3   4   5   6   7

1. I am usually reluctant to complain to a store regardless of how bad a product is.

2. I am less likely to return an unsatisfactory product than are most people I know.

3. If a defective product is inexpensive, I usually keep it rather than ask for a refund or to exchange it.

#SCALE NAME: Compulsive Buying

SCALE DESCRIPTION: A measure of the degree to which a consumer makes an excessive amount of purchases, according to his or her disposable income, as a means of dealing with undesirable mood states. Compulsive buyers are thought to engage in purchasing behavior to alleviate negative feelings. Some improvement in mood may follow buying episodes, but it is temporary and the behavior "becomes very difficult to stop and ultimately results in harmful consequences" (O'Guinn and Faber 1989, p. 155).

SCALE ORIGIN: The scale was constructed and tested by Faber and O'Guinn (1992). The scale built on previous work by the authors, as well as by others (Faber and O'Guinn 1989; Faber, O'Guinn, and Krych 1987). The version used by Babin, Darden, and Griffin (1994) was based on that earlier work rather than on the "final" version of the scale and therefore is a little different.

SAMPLES: In the study by Babin, Darden, and Griffin (1994), data were gathered from a sample of adults living in a large Midwestern U.S. community. Students were trained to conduct interviews and then allowed to select potential respondents representative of a regional mall's demographic profile. Data were gathered before, during, and after the students accompanied respondents on a shopping trip to the mall. Ultimately, complete information was gathered from **404** respondents. Independent contact with some respondents at random provided no reason to suspect the authenticity of the data.

Two samples were employed by Faber and O'Guinn (1992). One was of **388** completed responses (out of 808 questionnaires sent) from people who had written an organization that aided compulsive buyers. A second group was used for comparison purposes and was intended to represent the general population. Eight hundred questionnaires were mailed to people in three Illinois areas: Chicago, Springfield, and Bloomington-Normal. Three mailings produced a total of **292** completed survey forms.

RELIABILITY: An alpha of **.76** was reported for the five-item version of the scale used by Babin, Darden, and Griffin (1994). The full seven-item version of the scale was reported by Faber and O'Guinn (1992) as having an alpha of **.95**.

VALIDITY: Faber and O'Guinn (1992) provided data in support of the scale's face, criterion, and external validities. In addition, their factor analysis indicated that the items were unidimensional.

ADMINISTRATION: The compulsive buying scale was self-administered by shoppers in the study by Babin, Darden, and Griffin (1994). In the studies by Faber and O'Guinn (1992), the scale was self-administered, along with other measures, in a mail survey format.

Faber and O'Guinn (1992) calculated scale scores using weights on the items. Respondents scoring two standard deviations from the mean were labeled as compulsive buyers. Babin, Darden, and Griffin (1994) calculated scores on the five-item version of the scale they used by simply summing scores on the items (Babin 2000).

MAJOR FINDINGS: Babin, Darden, and Griffin (1994) reported a series of studies in which two scales were constructed and refined that measured two dimensions of personal shopping values: hedonic and utilitarian. In the process of establishing the scales' nomological validities, correlations with other variables to which they were expected to relate were measured. Shopping value (hedonic) (#369) was found to have a moderate but significant correlation with **compulsive buying**, whereas shopping value (utilitarian) (# 370) did not have a significant correlation with it.

Faber and O'Guinn (1992) reported on the development and testing of a scale to identify **compulsive buyers**. Among the results was that the scale was able to correctly classify 88% of the subjects.

COMMENTS: As constructed and used by Faber and O'Guinn (1992), the scale items are weighted to produce the scale score. However, Faber (2000) has indicated that the scale has been used successfully by others without weighting (e.g., Babin, Darden, and Griffin 1994).

See also Faber and colleagues (1995).

REFERENCES:

Babin, Barry J. (2000), personal correspondence.

———, William R. Darden, and Mitch Griffin (1994), "Work and/or Fun: Measuring Hedonic and Utilitarian Shopping Value," *JCR*, 20 (March), 644–56.

Faber, Ronald J. (2000), personal correspondence.

———, Gary A. Christenson, Martine de Zwaan, and James Mitchell (1995), "Two Forms of Compulsive Consumption: Comorbidity of Compulsive Buying and Binge Eating," *JCR*, 22 (December), 296–304.

——— and Thomas C. O'Guinn (1989), "Classifying Compulsive Consumers: Advances in the Development of a Diagnostic Tool," in *Advances in Consumer Research*, Vol. 16, Thomas K. Srull, ed. Provo, UT: Association for Consumer Research, 738–44.

——— and ——— (1992), "A Clinical Screener for Compulsive Buying," *JCR*, 19 (December), 459–69.

———, ———, and Raymond Krych (1987), "Compulsive Consumption," in *Advances in Consumer Research*, Vol. 14, Melanie Wallendorf and Paul Anderson, eds. Provo, UT: Association for Consumer Research, 132–35.

SCALE ITEMS:*

Please indicate how often you have done each of the following things:

1. Felt others would be horrified if they knew of my spending habits.

2. Bought things even though I couldn't afford them.

3. Wrote a check when I knew I didn't have enough money in the bank to cover it.

4. Bought myself something in order to make myself feel better.

5. Felt anxious or nervous on days I didn't go shopping.

6. Made only the minimum payments on my credit cards.

Very often	Often	Sometimes	Rarely	Never
1	2	3	4	5

7. If I have any money left at the end of the pay period, I just have to spend it.

8. Having more money would solve my problems.

9. I have bought something, got home, and didn't know why I had bought it.

Strongly
agree   :___:___:___:___:___: Strongly disagree
          1   2   3   4   5

*The version used by Faber and O'Guinn (1992) used the first six items with a frequency response scale such as the one following item 6; for item 7 they used a Likert-type scale. Babin, Darden, and Griffin (1994) used Likert-type versions of items similar to 1, 5, and 6 and added items 8 and 9.

SCALE NAME: Confidence (Task)

SCALE DESCRIPTION: Three seven-point semantic differentials measuring the degree to which a person feels certain about actions he or she has taken. As used by Urbany and colleagues (1997), the action was the rating of quality respondents made in the studies described.

SCALE ORIGIN: There is no information to indicate that the scale is anything other than original to the studies by Urbany and colleagues (1997).

SAMPLES: Urbany and colleagues (1997) reported on two studies, both of which used data collected from undergraduates attending a major state university. Apparently, complete data were gathered from **200** students in Study 1 and **393** students in Study 2.

RELIABILITY: Alphas of **.93** and **.94** were reported for the scale by Urbany and colleagues (1997).

VALIDITY: No examination of the scale's validity was reported by Urbany and colleagues (1997).

ADMINISTRATION: Students self-administered the scale, along with other measures, after they were exposed to experimental stimuli and after quality ratings of experimental stimuli were made (Urbany et al. 1997). Higher scores on the scale suggested that respondents were very sure about the actions they had taken (or responses given) in some activity in which they had engaged.

MAJOR FINDINGS: The experiments conducted by Urbany and colleagues (1997) examined the role of transaction utility in determining choice when product quality was uncertain. Measurement of the **confidence** respondents had in their ratings of quality was used as a manipulation check. As was expected, the quality assurance manipulation successfully increased respondent **confidence** in the judgments of product quality.

REFERENCES:
Urbany, Joel E., William O. Bearden, Ajit Kaicker, and Melinda Smith-de Borrero (1997), "Transaction Utility Effects When Quality Is Uncertain," *JAMS*, 25 (Winter), 45–55.

SCALE ITEMS:*
DIRECTIONS: Please indicate the level of confidence you have in the ratings of quality you gave.

Uncertain   :___:___:___:___:___:___: Certain
                 1   2   3   4   5   6   7

Not sure   :___:___:___:___:___:___: Sure
                 1   2   3   4   5   6   7

Not confident   :___:___:___:___:___:___: Confident
                 1   2   3   4   5   6   7

*The scale stem used by Urbany and colleagues (1977) was not described but may have been similar to this.

SCALE NAME: Conformity Motivation (Consumption)

SCALE DESCRIPTION: A seven-item, seven-point Likert-type scale purported to measure the degree to which a consumer is concerned about adhering to group norms regarding what products/brands to buy. The scale was referred to by Kahle (1995b) as *role-relaxed consumer*.

SCALE ORIGIN: Although the construct was discussed by Kahle (1995a), it was in a follow-up article (Kahle 1995b) that the scale was apparently presented for the first time.

SAMPLES: Data were collected by Kahle (1995b) from members of a Market Facts mail panel. The quota sample was balanced to reflect the gender, age, income, education, and population distribution of the United States. A 63% response rate was experienced (**633** usable questionnaires returned) from the 1000 questionnaires mailed.

RELIABILITY: An alpha of **.76** was reported for the scale by Kahle (1995b).

VALIDITY: No examination of the scale's validity was reported by Kahle (1995b).

ADMINISTRATION: The scale items were embedded in a larger set of questions in a mail survey instrument (Kahle 199b). Scores could range from 7 to 49. Low scores were interpreted to mean the respondents were highly susceptible to social influence on their consumption, whereas high scores suggested that respondents were not motivated to conform to group norms (role relaxed).

MAJOR FINDINGS: The purpose of the study by Kahle (1995b) was to present a measure of the role-relaxed consumer (**conformity motivation**) and note its relationship with some values such consumers might hold. Among the findings reported was that the less consumers were **motivated by conformity** to group norms (role relaxed), the more they valued self-respect and equality.

COMMENTS: Kahle (1995b) reported a mean score of 21.96 and a standard deviation of 7.5 for the scale.

REFERENCES:
Kahle, Lynn R. (1995a), "Observations: Role-Relaxed Consumers: A Trend of the Nineties," *JAR*, 35 (2), 37–47.
——— (1995b), "Observations: Role-Relaxed Consumers: Empirical Evidence," *JAR*, 35 (May/June), 59–62.

SCALE ITEMS:
DIRECTIONS: People have differing opinions when it comes to shopping for and buying products. We'd like your opinion about the statements listed below. If you *agree* strongly with a statement, you may mark a one (1) or two (2). If you *disagree* strongly, you may mark a six (6) or a seven (7). You can mark any number from one to seven to tell us how you feel.

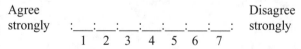

Agree   Disagree
strongly   :___:___:___:___:___:___:___: strongly
                1   2   3   4   5   6   7

1. How elegant and attractive a product is is as important as how well it works.

2. It is important that others think well of how I dress and look.

3. When I am uncertain how to act in a social situation, I try to do what others are doing.

4. My friends and I tend to buy the same brands.

5. If I were to buy something expensive, I would worry about what others would think of me.

6. I buy brands that will make me look good in front of my friends.

7. When I buy the same things my friends buy, I feel closer to them.

SCALE NAME: Conservation (Energy)

SCALE DESCRIPTION: Three seven-point Likert-type statements measuring the extent to which a consumer feels a personal obligation to conserve natural resources, with an emphasis on energy resources.

SCALE ORIGIN: The scale is original to Osterhus (1997). His purpose with the scale was to operationalize a *personal norm* construct in the context of energy conservation.

SAMPLES: The sample for the study by Osterhus (1997) came from rural, urban, and suburban neighborhoods of a Midwestern U.S. area. Subjects were recruited through random-digit telephone dialing and then were sent a paper questionnaire. Nonrespondents were mailed another questionnaire. Ultimately, **1128** usable responses were received.

RELIABILITY: An alpha of **.75** was reported for the scale by Osterhus (1997).

VALIDITY: Confirmatory factor analysis was used by Osterhus (1997) to help purify the scales. Evidence was generally in support of the discriminant and convergent validity of this scale, though there was some concern about its distinctiveness with respect to a measure of the consequences of the electric company's conservation program (#48).

ADMINISTRATION: The scale was self-administered by respondents, along with other measures, in a mail survey format (Osterhus 1997). Higher scores on the scale suggested that respondents felt strongly that they should save energy.

MAJOR FINDINGS: Osterhus (1997) investigated how and when prosocial positions are expected to influence consumer choice. Among the findings, social norms were found to have a significant positive influence on **conservation** attitudes.

REFERENCES:
Osterhus, Thomas L. (1997), "Pro-Social Consumer Influence Strategies: When and How Do They Work?" *JM*, 61 (October), 16–29.

SCALE ITEMS:

Disagree   :___:___:___:___:___:___:___: Agree
                1   2   3   4   5   6   7

1. I feel an obligation to save energy where possible.

2. I should do what I can to conserve natural resources.

3. I feel I must do something to help future generations.

SCALE NAME: Contribution to Purchase Decision (Initiation Stage)

SCALE DESCRIPTION: A four-item, six-point summated rating scale purported to measure the relative influence a consumer perceives to have had on the first stage of the decision process for a recent purchase compared with the total contribution made by the other members of the family living in the home. The scale was apparently used twice by Beatty and Talpade (1994): once for the sample (teens) to evaluate relative contributions in a decision regarding a durable product for *teenager* use and another time related to a durable product for *family* use.

SCALE ORIGIN: The scale was constructed by Beatty and Talpade (1994) for their study. Preliminary to the main study, 36 students filled out 26 items related to three stages of the decision process: **initiation**, search, and decision. Traditional techniques were used to purify the scale and resulted in 16 items being used in the main study (4 for the **initiation stage** and 6 each for the other two stages).

SAMPLES: Beatty and Talpade (1994) gathered data for their main study from **382** students attending a freshman-orientation session at a Southeastern U.S. university. The sample was almost exactly split between men and women, and 68% were 18 years of age. More than half (64%) had worked outside the home in the last six months. Most of the students (91%) lived with both parents, and nearly half (47%) were from dual-income households.

RELIABILITY: Alphas of **.95** and **.92** were reported for the family and teenager versions of the scale (Beatty and Talpade 1994).

VALIDITY: The validity of the scale was not directly assessed by Beatty and Talpade (1994). However, an exploratory factor analysis of the items in this scale and two others led to the elimination of more items. A two-factor model was produced and found to have adequate fit when subsequently tested with confirmatory factor analysis.

ADMINISTRATION: The scale was self-administered by students as part of a larger survey instrument (Beatty and Talpade 1994). High scores on the scale suggested that the teens viewed themselves as having made significantly large contributions to the initial stage of the decision process for some recent purchase, whereas low scores indicated they perceived themselves as having had little or no influence on that stage.

MAJOR FINDINGS: The study by Beatty and Talpade (1994) built on previous research of adolescent influence on family decision making. Among the results was that teenager influence was significantly higher for the **initiation stage** of the decision process than at the search or decision stages for both family and teen purchases.

REFERENCES:
Beatty, Sharon E. and Salil Talpade (1994), "Adolescent Influence in Family Decision Making: A Replication with Extension," *JCR*, 21 (September), 332–41.

SCALE ITEMS:*
DIRECTIONS: Using the response scale below, please indicate for each of the four statements the relative contribution you made in a recent purchase versus the total contribution made by all of the other family members living at home.

#102 *Contribution to Purchase Decision (Initiation Stage)*

| I did not | | | Equal | | | The entire |
| contribute at all | | | contribution | | | contribution was mine |

0————1————2————3————4————5————6

1. Bringing up the idea to buy the product.

2. Getting people to realize that this product was needed.

3. Realizing that this product would be useful to have.

4. Getting others to start thinking about buying the product.

*The actual directions were not provided but are recreated here on the basis of the description provided in the article.

SCALE NAME: Contribution to Purchase Decision (Search/Decision Stage)

SCALE DESCRIPTION: A five-item, six-point summated rating scale purported to measure the relative influence a consumer perceives to have had on the search or decision stages for a recent purchase compared with the total contribution made by the other members of the family living in the home. The scale was apparently used twice by Beatty and Talpade (1994): once for the sample (teens) to evaluate relative contributions in a decision regarding a durable product for *teenager* use and another time related to a durable product for *family* use.

SCALE ORIGIN: The scale was constructed by Beatty and Talpade (1994) for their study. Preliminary to the main study, 36 students filled out 26 items related to three stages of the decision process: initiation, **search**, and **decision**. Traditional techniques were used to purify the scale and resulted in 16 items being used in the main study (4 for the initiation stage and 6 each for the other two stages).

SAMPLES: Beatty and Talpade (1994) gathered data for their main study from **382** students attending a freshman-orientation session at a Southeastern U.S. university. The sample was almost exactly split between men and women, and 68% were 18 years of age. More than half (64%) had worked outside the home in the last six months. Most of the students (91%) lived with both parents, and nearly half (47%) were from dual-income households.

RELIABILITY: Alphas of **.94** and **.95** were reported for the family and teenager versions of the scale (Beatty and Talpade 1994).

VALIDITY: The validity of the scale was not directly assessed by Beatty and Talpade (1994). However, an exploratory factor analysis of the items in the three scales mentioned previously led to the elimination of more items. A two-factor model was produced with one of the factors as a combination of the **search** and **decision stage** scales. Subsequent testing with confirmatory factor analysis provided support for the two-factor model.

ADMINISTRATION: The scale was self-administered by students as part of a larger survey instrument (Beatty and Talpade 1994). High scores on the scale suggested that the teens viewed themselves as having made significantly large contributions on the search/decision stage of the decision process for some recent purchase, whereas low scores indicated they perceived themselves as having had little or no influence on that stage.

MAJOR FINDINGS: The study by Beatty and Talpade (1994) built on previous research of adolescent influence on family decision making. Among the results was that teenager influence was significantly higher for the initiation stage of the decision process than at the **search/decision stage** for both family and teen purchases.

REFERENCES:
Beatty, Sharon E. and Salil Talpade (1994), "Adolescent Influence in Family Decision Making: A Replication with Extension," *JCR*, 21 (September), 332–41.

SCALE ITEMS:*
DIRECTIONS: Using the response scale below, please indicate for each of the four statements the relative contribution you made in a recent purchase versus the total contribution made by all of the other family members living at home.

#103 *Contribution to Purchase Decision (Search/Decision Stage)*

I did not			Equal			The entire
contribute at all			contribution			contribution was mine

0————————1————————2————————3————————4————————5————————6

1. Visiting the store(s) to look for different brands/models of the product.

2. Examining different brands/models at the store.

3. Picking up the product from the store.

4. Deciding on the brand/model that was finally purchased.

5. Deciding on which store to actually buy the product from.

*The actual directions were not provided but are recreated here on the basis of the description provided in the article.

SCALE NAME: Cooperation

SCALE DESCRIPTION: Seven seven-point Likert-type items measuring a customer's discretionary actions that contribute to service quality delivery. These actions facilitate successful interaction with service employees and may have implications for other customers as well (Bettencourt 1997, p. 386).

SCALE ORIGIN: Although the author received some inspiration from previous measures of similar constructs (e.g., Kelly, Skinner, and Donnelly 1992), the scale is original to the work of Bettencourt (1997).

SAMPLES: In the study reported by Bettencourt (1997), data were collected by students of a marketing class. They were instructed to have five surveys completed by people who were regular shoppers for their households. After a verification process, **215** questionnaires remained for data analysis. A majority (70%) of the sample was older than 30 years of age, were women (73%), and had completed at least some college (85%).

RELIABILITY: Bettencourt (1997) reported an alpha of **.69** for the scale.

VALIDITY: The validity of the scale was not explicitly examined, though evidence of dimensionality was reported. Bettencourt (1997) performed a confirmatory factor analysis with items from this scale and two others that provided support for the three-factor conceptualization.

ADMINISTRATION: The scale was self-administered as part of a much larger survey instrument (Bettencourt 1997). Higher scores on the scale meant that respondents engaged in behaviors that indicated a lot of cooperation with a store and its employees.

MAJOR FINDINGS: A model of customer voluntary performance was developed and tested by Bettencourt (1997) in the context of grocery store shopping. The findings indicated that a store's perceived support for customers had a significant positive relationship with their **cooperation**.

COMMENTS: The reliability of this scale is low enough to be considered only marginally acceptable. Refinement appears to be called for before it is used further.

REFERENCES:
Bettencourt, Lance A. (1997), "Customer Voluntary Performance: Customers as Partners in Service Delivery," *JR*, 73 (3), 383–406.
Kelley, Scott W., Steven J. Skinner, and James H. Donnelly Jr. (1992), "Organizational Socialization of Service Customers," *Journal of Business Research*, 25 (November), 197–214.

SCALE ITEMS:

Strongly   Strongly
disagree   :___:___:___:___:___:___:___: agree
                 1   2   3   4   5   6   7

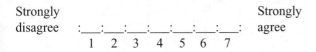

1. I try to keep this store clean (e.g., not leaving plastic bags on produce displays, leaving shelf displays neat).

2. The employees of this store get my full cooperation.

3. I carefully observe the rules and policies of this store.

4. I go out of my way to treat this store's personnel with kindness and respect.

5. When I leave this store, I place my shopping cart in a designated spot, instead of next to my car.

6. I do things to make the cashier's job easier (e.g., bag my own groceries, place UPC labels on conveyor facing cashier).

7. If I am writing a check, I fill out the basic information before getting to the front of the check-out line.

SCALE NAME: Cosmetics Use

SCALE DESCRIPTION: Three seven-point Likert-type statements that evaluate the use and importance that makeup plays in a consumer's everyday life.

SCALE ORIGIN: Although not explicitly stated by Netemeyer, Burton, and Lichtenstein (1995), the scale is original to their study (Netemeyer 1997).

SAMPLES: Various samples were collected and used by Netemeyer, Burton, and Lichtenstein (1995) in the process of validating some other scales. The **cosmetics use** scale was used in one study composed of 186 students and 264 "nonstudent adults." It was also used in a study based on data collected from 43 professional fashion models.

RELIABILITY: Alphas of **.82** (students), **.84** (nonstudent adults), and **.68** (fashion models) were found for the scale (Netemeyer 1997; Netemeyer, Burton, and Lichtenstein 1995).

VALIDITY: The validity of the scale was not examined by Netemeyer, Burton, and Lichtenstein (1995).

ADMINISTRATION: As noted, the scale was used with three samples, and in each case, it appears to have been part of larger questionnaires that were self-administered by respondents (Netemeyer, Burton, and Lichtenstein 1995). Higher scores on the scale indicated that cosmetics were important enough to respondents for them to be used routinely (every day).

MAJOR FINDINGS: Netemeyer, Burton, and Lichtenstein (1995) investigated vanity and developed four scales for its measurement. Most of the article discussed the results of the rather extensive validation process. Although the findings varied somewhat among studies, **cosmetics use** tended to have low or insignificant correlations with all of the vanity scales except physical concern vanity (#397).

REFERENCES:
Netemeyer, Richard G. (1997), personal correspondence.
———, Scot Burton, and Donald R. Lichtenstein (1995), "Trait Aspects of Vanity: Measurement and Relevance to Consumer Behavior," *JCR*, 21 (March), 612–26.

SCALE ITEMS:

Strongly   Strongly
disagree   :___:___:___:___:___:___: agree
            1   2   3   4   5   6   7

1. I put on cosmetics routinely each morning.

2. I only wear cosmetics on special occasions. **(r)**

3. The use of cosmetics is important to me.

SCALE NAME: Country-of-Origin Image (People)

SCALE DESCRIPTION: A ten-point summated scale used to measure a person's attitude toward the people of another country in which a product has been produced. The final version of the scale used in the analysis of German products had five items, whereas the version used for Korean products had six. This scale was referred to as "General Country Attribute" (the people facet) by Parameswaran and Pisharodi (1994).

SCALE ORIGIN: Parameswaran and Pisharodi (1994) cite several previous studies with which the lead author was involved as sources of the items used in the scale (e.g., Yaprak and Parameswaran 1986). However, the extent of adaptation indicates that, though items may have been borrowed from previous studies, this version of the scale was developed in this study. Further information about this study and the testing of this scale can be found in Pisharodi and Parameswaran (1992).

SAMPLES: Parameswaran and Pisharodi (1994) gathered data in a Midwestern metropolitan area of the United States that was viewed as having a heterogeneous mixture of ethnic groups. Membership lists of several ethnic group associations were obtained, and surveys were hand-delivered to a systematic sample. Of the 1025 questionnaires distributed, **678** usable forms were returned. No other descriptive information about the sample was provided.

RELIABILITY: The final five-item version of the scale used for German products had a standardized alpha of **.872**, and the six-item Korean version had an alpha of **.858**.

VALIDITY: Parameswaran and Pisharodi (1994) used confirmatory factor analysis in an iterative process of progressive respecification to finalize the several multi-item scales used in their study. The versions of the country-of-origin image (people) scale used for German and Korean products began with 12 items, but ill-fitting items were weeded out or developed into a separate scale. Although detailed information was not provided for each scale, the authors stated that the final adjusted measurement model satisfied the unidimensionality criterion. Information bearing on convergent and discriminant validity may have been available from the analysis but was not discussed in the article.

ADMINISTRATION: The questionnaire used by Parameswaran and Pisharodi (1994) had the respondents evaluate cars and blenders from both Germany and Korea. Higher scores on this scale suggested that consumers from one country had a favorable attitude toward the people from another country in which a product originates.

MAJOR FINDINGS: The purpose of the research by Parameswaran and Pisharodi (1994) was to improve the definition and measurement of scales used in the study of country-of-origin effects. Their findings indicated that country-of-origin image was best measured with two scales rather than one: One scale (shown subsequently) provided a noncomparative evaluation of the people in the other country, whereas the other scale involved comparisons between the two cultures.

COMMENTS: See also a modification of the scale by Netemeyer, Durvasula, and Lichtenstein (1991).

REFERENCES:
Netemeyer, Richard G., Srinvas Durvasula and Donald R. Lichtenstein (1991), "A Cross-National Assessment of the Reliability and Validity of the CETSCALE," *JMR*, 28 (August), 320–27.
Parameswaran, Ravi and R. Mohan Pisharodi (1994), "Facets of Country of Origin Image: An Empirical Assessment," *JA*, 23 (March), 43–56.

Pisharodi, R. Mohan and Ravi Parameswaran (1992), "Confirmatory Factor Analysis of a Country-of-Origin Scale: Initial Results," in *Advances in Consumer Research*, Vol. 19, John F. Sherry Jr. and Brian Sternthal, eds. Provo, UT: Association for Consumer Research, 706–14.

Yaprak, Attila and Ravi Parameswaran (1986), "Strategy Formulation in Multinational Marketing: A Deductive, Paradigm-Integrating Approach," in *Advances in International Marketing*, Vol. 1, S. Tamer Cavusgil, ed. Greenwich, CT: JAI Press, 21–45.

SCALE ITEMS:*

Using the statements below, indicate the extent to which each is appropriate to describe the people of *(the country name)*.

```
Not at all                                        Most
appropriate :___:___:___:___:___:___:___:___:___:___: appropriate
              1    2    3    4    5    6    7    8    9   10
```

1. Friendly and likable

2. Artistic and creative

3. Well-educated

4. Hard working

5. Achieving high standards

6. Raised standard of living

7. Technical skills

*Items 3, 4, and 5-7 composed the final version of the scale for German products; items 1–3 and 5-7 composed the Korean version. Also, the instructions for filling out the scale were not provided in the article but appear to have been similar to what is shown here.

SCALE NAME: Country-of-Origin Image (Similarity)

SCALE DESCRIPTION: A three-item, ten-point summated scale used to measure a person's perception of the similarity between his or her own country and the one in which a product has been produced. This scale was referred to as "General Country Attribute" (the interaction facet) by Parameswaran and Pisharodi (1994).

SCALE ORIGIN: Parameswaran and Pisharodi (1994) cite several previous studies with which the lead author was involved as sources of the items used in the scale (e.g., Yaprak and Parameswaran 1986). However, the extent of adaptation indicates that, though items may have been borrowed from previous studies, this version of the scale was developed in this study. Further information about this study and the testing of this scale can be found in Pisharodi and Parameswaran (1992).

SAMPLES: Parameswaran and Pisharodi (1994) gathered data in a Midwestern metropolitan area of the United States that was viewed as having a heterogeneous mixture of ethnic groups. Membership lists of several ethnic group associations were obtained, and surveys were hand-delivered to a systematic sample. Of the 1025 questionnaires distributed, **678** usable forms were returned. No other descriptive information about the sample was provided.

RELIABILITY: The final three-item version of the scale used for German products had a standardized alpha of **.849**, and the Korean version had an alpha of **.675**.

VALIDITY: Parameswaran and Pisharodi (1994) used confirmatory factor analysis in an iterative process of progressive respecification to finalize the several multi-item scales used in their study. The version of the country-of-origin image (similarity) scale used for German and Korean products began with 12 items, but ill-fitting items were weeded out or developed into a separate scale. Although detailed information was not provided for each scale, the authors stated that the final adjusted measurement model satisfied the unidimensionality criterion. Information bearing on convergent and discriminant validity may have been available from the analysis but was not discussed in the article.

ADMINISTRATION: The questionnaire used by Parameswaran and Pisharodi (1994) had the respondents evaluate cars and blenders from both Germany and Korea. Higher scores on this scale suggested that consumers from one country viewed another country in which a product originated as similar in several ways to their own.

MAJOR FINDINGS: The purpose of the research by Parameswaran and Pisharodi (1994) was to improve the definition and measurement of scales used in the study of country-of-origin effects. Their findings indicated that country-of-origin image was best measured with two scales rather than one: one scale (shown subsequently) involved comparisons between the two cultures, whereas the other provided a noncomparative evaluation of the people in the other country.

REFERENCES:
Parameswaran, Ravi and R. Mohan Pisharodi (1994), "Facets of Country of Origin Image: An Empirical Assessment," *JA*, 23 (March), 43–56.
Pisharodi, R. Mohan and Ravi Parameswaran (1992), "Confirmatory Factor Analysis of a Country-of-Origin Scale: Initial Results," in *Advances in Consumer Research*, Vol. 19, John F. Sherry Jr. and Brian Sternthal, eds. Provo, UT: Association for Consumer Research, 706–14.

Yaprak, Attila and Ravi Parameswaran (1986), "Strategy Formulation in Multinational Marketing: A Deductive, Paradigm-Integrating Approach," in *Advances in International Marketing*, Vol. 1, S. Tamer Cavusgil, ed. Greenwich, CT: JAI Press, 21–45.

SCALE ITEMS:*
DIRECTIONS: Using the statements below, indicate the extent to which each is appropriate to describe the people of *(the country name)*.

Not at all   Most
appropriate : 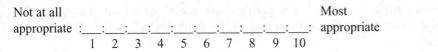 appropriate

1. Similar political views

2. Economically similar

3. Culturally similar

*The directions for filling out the scale were not provided in the article but appear to have been similar to this.

SCALE NAME: Country-of-Origin Product Image (Cars)

SCALE DESCRIPTION: A four-item, ten-point summated scale used to measure a person's evaluation of some aspects of a particular car made in a particular country. This scale was referred to as "Specific Product Attributes" (cars) by Parameswaran and Pisharodi (1994).

SCALE ORIGIN: The items composing the initial version of this scale are similar to those reported in an article by Parameswaran and Yaprak (1986). Parameswaran and Pisharodi (1994) indicate that their survey instrument used ten items for this scale, but the purification process left the final version with only four. Further information about this study and the testing of this scale can be found in Pisharodi and Parameswaran (1992).

SAMPLES: Parameswaran and Pisharodi (1994) gathered data in a Midwestern metropolitan area of the United States that was viewed as having a heterogeneous mixture of ethnic groups. Membership lists of several ethnic group associations were obtained, and surveys were hand-delivered to a systematic sample. Of the 1025 questionnaires distributed, **678** usable forms were returned. No other descriptive information about the sample was provided.

RELIABILITY: The final version of the scale used for German cars had a standardized alpha of **.819**, and the Korean version had an alpha of **.849**.

VALIDITY: Parameswaran and Pisharodi (1994) used confirmatory factor analysis in an iterative process of progressive respecification to finalize the several multi-item scales used in their study. The version of the country-of-origin product image (cars) scale used for German and Korean products began with 10 items, but ill-fitting items were weeded out. Although detailed information was not provided for each scale, the authors stated that the final adjusted measurement model satisfied the unidimensionality criterion. Information bearing on convergent and discriminant validity may have been available from the analysis but was not discussed in the article.

ADMINISTRATION: The questionnaire used by Parameswaran and Pisharodi (1994) had the respondents evaluate cars from both Germany and Korea. Higher scores on this scale suggested that consumers from one country viewed a particular car made in another country as having several specific positive characteristics. The specific brands and models of cars the survey recipients were asked to evaluate were the German **Volkswagen** *Jetta* and the Korean **Hyundai** *Stellar*.

MAJOR FINDINGS: The purpose of the research by Parameswaran and Pisharodi (1994) was to improve the definition and measurement of scales used in the study of country-of-origin effects. Their findings indicated that specific product attributes, originally theorized to be a single construct, were best measured using two scales. One of those scales involved cars' desirable attributes (shown subsequently), and the other related to cars' negative attributes. Unfortunately, only one of the original ten items was negative, so a multiple-item scale of the undesirable attributes could not be constructed.

REFERENCES:

Parameswaran, Ravi and R. Mohan Pisharodi (1994), "Facets of Country of Origin Image: An Empirical Assessment," *JA*, 23 (March), 43–56.

———— and Attila Yaprak (1986), "A Cross-National Comparison of Consumer Research Measures," *Journal of International Business Studies*, 18 (Spring), 35–49.

Pisharodi, R. Mohan and Ravi Parameswaran (1992), "Confirmatory Factor Analysis of a Country-of-Origin Scale: Initial Results," in *Advances in Consumer Research*, Vol. 19, John F. Sherry Jr. and Brian Sternthal, eds. Provo, UT: Association for Consumer Research, 706–14.

SCALE ITEMS:*

DIRECTIONS: Using the statements below, indicate the extent to which each is appropriate to describe a *(the name of the car)* made in *(the country name)*.

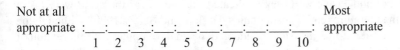

Not at all
appropriate :___:___:___:___:___:___:___:___:___: appropriate
         1   2   3   4   5   6   7   8   9   10

Most

1. Workmanship good

2. Handles well

3. Little maintenance

4. Made to last

*The directions for filling out the scale were not provided in the article but appear to have been similar to this.

SCALE NAME: Country-of-Origin Product Image (Desirable Attributes)

SCALE DESCRIPTION: A multi-item, ten-point summated scale used to measure a person's evaluation of some positive aspects of products made in another country. The final versions of the scale used in the analysis of German and Korean products had three items, but only two of them were the same. This scale was referred to as "General Product Attributes" (positive attributes relating to product image) by Parameswaran and Pisharodi (1994).

SCALE ORIGIN: Parameswaran and Pisharodi (1994) indicated that items for the scale were taken from among the many cited in the literature (e.g., Papadopoulos, Heslop, and Beracs 1990). Although the items themselves may have been used before, the extent of adaptation and development of this version of the scale was original to this study. Further information about this study and the testing of this scale can be found in Pisharodi and Parameswaran (1992).

SAMPLES: Parameswaran and Pisharodi (1994) gathered data in a Midwestern metropolitan area of the United States that was viewed as having a heterogeneous mixture of ethnic groups. Membership lists of several ethnic group associations were obtained, and surveys were hand-delivered to a systematic sample. Of the 1025 questionnaires distributed, **678** usable forms were returned. No other descriptive information about the sample was provided.

RELIABILITY: The final version of the scale used for German products had a standardized alpha of **.796**, and the Korean version had an alpha of **.788**.

VALIDITY: Parameswaran and Pisharodi (1994) used confirmatory factor analysis in an iterative process of progressive respecification to finalize the several multi-item scales used in their study. The version of the country-of-origin product image (desirable attributes) scale used for German and Korean products began with 18 items, but ill-fitting items were weeded out or developed into a separate scale. Although detailed information was not provided for each scale, the authors stated that the final adjusted measurement model satisfied the unidimensionality criterion. Information bearing on convergent and discriminant validity may have been available from the analysis but was not discussed in the article.

ADMINISTRATION: The questionnaire used by Parameswaran and Pisharodi (1994) had respondents evaluate cars and blenders from both Germany and Korea. Higher scores on this scale suggested that consumers from one country viewed products made in another country as having several specific positive characteristics.

MAJOR FINDINGS: The purpose of the research by Parameswaran and Pisharodi (1994) was to improve the definition and measurement of scales used in the study of country-of-origin effects. Their findings indicated that general product attributes, originally theorized to be a single construct, were best measured using three scales. One of those scales involved the products' desirable product attributes (shown subsequently), whereas the other two related to the products' negative attributes and distributional/advertising issues.

REFERENCES:

Papadopoulos, Nicolas, Louis A. Heslop, and Gary J. Beracs (1990), "National Stereotypes and Product Evaluations in a Socialist Country," *International Marketing Review*, 7 (Spring), 32–47.

Parameswaran, Ravi and R. Mohan Pisharodi (1994), "Facets of Country of Origin Image: An Empirical Assessment," *JA*, 23 (March), 43–56.

Pisharodi, R. Mohan and Ravi Parameswaran (1992), "Confirmatory Factor Analysis of a Country-of-Origin Scale: Initial Results," in *Advances in Consumer Research*, Vol. 19, John F. Sherry Jr. and Brian Sternthal, eds. Provo, UT: Association for Consumer Research, 706–14.

SCALE ITEMS:*
DIRECTIONS: Using the statements below, indicate the extent to which each is appropriate to describe products made in *(the country name)*.

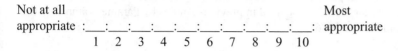

Not at all   Most
appropriate :___:___:___:___:___:___:___:___:___: appropriate
         1   2   3   4   5   6   7   8   9   10

1. Long lasting

2. Prestigious products

3. Good value

4. High technology

*Items 1–3 were in the version of the scale used to evaluate German products, and the Korean version used items 1, 2, and 4. Also, the directions for filling out the scale were not provided in the article but appear to have been similar to this.

SCALE NAME: Country-of-Origin Product Image (Desirable Blender Attributes)

SCALE DESCRIPTION: An eight-item, ten-point summated scale used to measure a person's evaluation of some positive aspects of a particular brand of blender made in a specified country. This scale was referred to as "Specific Product Attributes" (positive blender attributes) by Parameswaran and Pisharodi (1994).

SCALE ORIGIN: Although the scale appears to be original to the study by Parameswaran and Pisharodi (1994), several of the items are very similar to those used in previous studies by Parameswaran for other products (e.g., Parameswaran and Yaprak 1986).

SAMPLES: Parameswaran and Pisharodi (1994) gathered data in a Midwestern metropolitan area of the United States that was viewed as having a heterogeneous mixture of ethnic groups. Membership lists of several ethnic group associations were obtained, and surveys were hand-delivered to a systematic sample. Of the 1025 questionnaires distributed, **678** usable forms were returned. No other descriptive information about the sample was provided.

RELIABILITY: The final version of the scale used for German blenders had a standardized alpha of **.943**, and the Korean version had an alpha of **.924**.

VALIDITY: Parameswaran and Pisharodi (1994) used confirmatory factor analysis in an iterative process of progressive respecification to finalize the several multi-item scales used in their study. The version of the country-of-origin product image (desirable blender attributes) scale used for German and Korean products began with 11 items, which were eventually divided between two scales. Although detailed information was not provided for each scale, the authors stated that the final adjusted measurement model satisfied the unidimensionality criterion. Information bearing on convergent and discriminant validity may have been available from the analysis but was not discussed in the article.

ADMINISTRATION: The questionnaire used by Parameswaran and Pisharodi (1994) had the respondents evaluate blenders from both Germany and Korea. Higher scores on this scale suggested that consumers from one country viewed a particular brand of blender made in another country as having several specific positive characteristics. The specific brands of blenders the survey recipients were asked to evaluate were the German ***Krups*** and the Korean ***Goldstar***.

MAJOR FINDINGS: The purpose of the research by Parameswaran and Pisharodi (1994) was to improve the definition and measurement of scales used in the study of country-of-origin effects. Their findings indicated that specific product attributes, originally theorized to be a single construct, were best measured using two scales. One of those scales involved blenders' desirable attributes (shown subsequently), and the other related to their negative attributes.

REFERENCES:

Parameswaran, Ravi and R. Mohan Pisharodi (1994), "Facets of Country of Origin Image: An Empirical Assessment," *JA*, 23 (March), 43–56.

——— and Attila Yaprak (1986), "A Cross-National Comparison of Consumer Research Measures," *Journal of International Business Studies*, 18 (Spring), 35–49.

SCALE ITEMS:*

DIRECTIONS: Using the statements below, indicate the extent to which each is appropriate to describe a *(the name of the blender)* made in *(the country name)*.

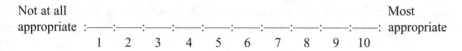

```
Not at all                                              Most
appropriate :——:——:——:——:——:——:——:——:——:——: appropriate
             1   2   3   4   5   6   7   8   9   10
```

1. High quality

2. Very good workmanship

3. Exterior design attractive

4. Compact

5. Versatile

6. Operate very quietly

7. Good value for the money

8. Overall excellent

*The directions for filling out the scale were not provided in the article but appear to have been similar to this.

SCALE NAME: Country-of-Origin Product Image (Distribution/Advertising)

SCALE DESCRIPTION: A multi-item, ten-point summated scale used to measure a person's evaluation of some distribution- and advertising-related aspects of products made in another country. The final version of the scale used in the analysis of German products had four items, whereas the version used for Korean products had three. This scale was referred to as "General Product Attributes" (promotional/distributional image) by Parameswaran and Pisharodi (1994).

SCALE ORIGIN: The items composing the initial version of this scale are similar to those reported in an article by Parameswaran and Yaprak (1986). Parameswaran and Pisharodi (1994) indicate that their survey instrument used eighteen items for this scale, but the purification process left the final version with only five. Further information about this study and the testing of this scale can be found in Pisharodi and Parameswaran (1992).

SAMPLES: Parameswaran and Pisharodi (1994) gathered data in a Midwestern metropolitan area of the United States that was viewed as having a heterogeneous mixture of ethnic groups. Membership lists of several ethnic group associations were obtained, and surveys were hand-delivered to a systematic sample. Of the 1025 questionnaires distributed, **678** usable forms were returned. No other descriptive information about the sample was provided.

RELIABILITY: The final version of the scale used for German products had a standardized alpha of **.735**, and the Korean version had an alpha of **.59**. The latter is rather low and should be improved before extensive use is made of the scale.

VALIDITY: Parameswaran and Pisharodi (1994) used confirmatory factor analysis in an iterative process of progressive respecification to finalize the several multi-item scales used in their study. The version of the country-of-origin product image (distribution/advertising) scale used for German and Korean products began with 18 items, but ill-fitting items were weeded out or developed into a separate scale. Although detailed information was not provided for each scale, the authors stated that the final adjusted measurement model satisfied the unidimensionality criterion. Information bearing on convergent and discriminant validity may have been available from the analysis but was not discussed in the article.

ADMINISTRATION: The questionnaire used by Parameswaran and Pisharodi (1994) had the respondents evaluate cars and blenders from both Germany and Korea. Higher scores on this scale suggested that consumers from one country viewed products made in another country as being widely distributed and advertised.

MAJOR FINDINGS: The purpose of the research by Parameswaran and Pisharodi (1994) was to improve the definition and measurement of scales used in the study of country-of-origin effects. Their findings indicated that general product attributes, originally theorized to be a single construct, were best measured using three scales. One of those scales involved the extent of the products' availability and promotion (shown subsequently), whereas the other two related to positive and negative product attributes.

REFERENCES:
Parameswaran, Ravi and R. Mohan Pisharodi (1994), "Facets of Country of Origin Image: An Empirical Assessment," *JA*, 23 (March), 43–56.
——— and Attila Yaprak (1986), "A Cross-National Comparison of Consumer Research Measures," *Journal of International Business Studies*, 18 (Spring), 35–49.

Pisharodi, R. Mohan and Ravi Parameswaran (1992), "Confirmatory Factor Analysis of a Country-of-Origin Scale: Initial Results," in *Advances in Consumer Research*, Vol. 19, John F. Sherry Jr. and Brian Sternthal, eds. Provo, UT: Association for Consumer Research, 706–14.

SCALE ITEMS:*

DIRECTIONS: Using the statements below, indicate the extent to which each is appropriate to describe products made in *(the country name)*.

Not at all   Most

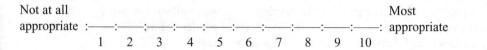

appropriate :——:——:——:——:——:——:——:——:——:——: appropriate

           1   2   3   4   5   6   7   8   9   10

1. Sold in many countries

2. Intensely advertised

3. Easily available

4. Advertising informative

*All of the items were in the version of the scale used to evaluate German products, but the Korean version did not have item 4. Also, the directions for filling out the scale were not provided in the article but appear to have been similar to this.

#112 *Country-of-Origin Product Image (General)*

SCALE NAME: Country-of-Origin Product Image (General)

SCALE DESCRIPTION: A three-item, nine-point Likert-type scale that measures the degree to which a person has a positive attitude about some specified product from some particular country.

SCALE ORIGIN: The scale appears to be original to Maheswaran (1994).

SAMPLES: Data were gathered by Maheswaran (1994) in Study 1 from **119** students in an undergraduate management program who participated for extra credit. Data were collected in small group sessions, and subjects were randomly assigned to conditions. No effects of gender or involvement were observed. Studies 2 and 3 collected information from **135** and **60** students, respectively.

RELIABILITY: Alphas of **.90** (PCs), **.90** (stereo systems), and **.81** (keyboard and modem) were reported for the scale by Maheswaran (1994) in Studies 1, 2, and 3, respectively.

VALIDITY: No information regarding the scale's validity was reported in the article by Maheswaran (1994). However, some sense of the scale's validity comes from its use as a manipulation check. (See the "Findings" section.)

ADMINISTRATION: The scale was self-administered by subjects in the studies by Maheswaran (1994), along with other measures, after they read a booklet that contained experimental stimuli. Higher scores on the scale indicated that the respondents had positive images toward the specified product from the specified country of origin.

MAJOR FINDINGS: Maheswaran (1994) examined the effects of country-of-origin image, consumer expertise, and attribute strength on product evaluations. The **country-of-origin product image** scale was used merely as a manipulation check. In each of the three studies, the data clearly indicated that those countries the researcher had intended subjects to view as the favorable country of origin scored better than those countries that were manipulated to be viewed as unfavorable.

REFERENCES:
Maheswaran, Durairaj (1994), "Country of Origin as a Stereotype: Effects of Consumer Expertise and Attribute Strength on Product Evaluations," *JCR*, 21 (September), 354–65.

SCALE ITEMS:*

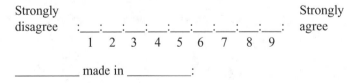

Strongly
disagree   :___:___:___:___:___:___:___:___:___: Strongly agree
            1   2   3   4   5   6   7   8   9

_____ made in _____:

1. Are of high quality.

2. Are technologically superior.

3. Have a good reputation.

*The name of the generic product (e.g., PCs) should go in the first blank, and the name of the country of origin (e.g., Japan) should be placed in the second blank.

SCALE NAME: Country-of-Origin Product Image (Undesirable Attributes)

SCALE DESCRIPTION: A five-item, ten-point summated scale used to measure a person's evaluation of some undesirable aspects of products made in another country. This scale was referred to as "General Product Attribute" (negative) by Parameswaran and Pisharodi (1994).

SCALE ORIGIN: The items composing the initial version of this scale are similar to those reported in an article by Parameswaran and Yaprak (1986). Parameswaran and Pisharodi (1994) indicate that their survey instrument used eighteen items for this scale, but the purification process left the final version with only five. Further information about this study and the testing of this scale can be found in Pisharodi and Parameswaran (1992).

SAMPLES: Parameswaran and Pisharodi (1994) gathered data in a Midwestern metropolitan area of the United States that was viewed as having a heterogeneous mixture of ethnic groups. Membership lists of several ethnic group associations were obtained, and surveys were hand-delivered to a systematic sample. Of the 1025 questionnaires distributed, **678** usable forms were returned. No other descriptive information about the sample was provided.

RELIABILITY: The final five-item version of the scale used for German products had a standardized alpha of **.75**, and the Korean version had an alpha of **.73**.

VALIDITY: Parameswaran and Pisharodi (1994) used confirmatory factor analysis in an iterative process of progressive respecification to finalize the several multi-item scales used in their study. The version of the country-of-origin product image (undesirable attributes) scale used for German and Korean products began with 18 items, but ill-fitting items were weeded out or developed into a separate scale. Although detailed information was not provided for each scale, the authors stated that the final adjusted measurement model satisfied the unidimensionality criterion. Information bearing on convergent and discriminant validity may have been available from the analysis but was not discussed in the article.

ADMINISTRATION: The questionnaire used by Parameswaran and Pisharodi (1994) had the respondents evaluate cars and blenders from both Germany and Korea. Higher scores on this scale suggested that consumers from one country viewed products made in another country as characterized by several negative attributes.

MAJOR FINDINGS: The purpose of the research by Parameswaran and Pisharodi (1994) was to improve the definition and measurement of scales used in the study of country-of-origin effects. Their findings indicated that general product attributes, originally theorized to be a single construct, were best measured using three scales. One of those scales involved the products' undesirable features (shown subsequently), and the other two related to positive attributes.

REFERENCES:

Parameswaran, Ravi and R. Mohan Pisharodi (1994), "Facets of Country of Origin Image: An Empirical Assessment," *JA*, 23 (March), 43–56.

——— and Attila Yaprak (1986), "A Cross-National Comparison of Consumer Research Measures," *Journal of International Business Studies*, 18 (Spring), 35–49.

Pisharodi, R. Mohan and Ravi Parameswaran (1992), "Confirmatory Factor Analysis of a Country-of-Origin Scale: Initial Results," in *Advances in Consumer Research*, Vol. 19, John F. Sherry Jr. and Brian Sternthal, eds. Provo, UT: Association for Consumer Research, 706–14.

#113 *Country-of-Origin Product Image (Undesirable Attributes)*

SCALE ITEMS:*

DIRECTIONS: Using the statements below, indicate the extent to which each is appropriate to describe products made in *(the country name)*.

Not at all
appropriate : __ : __ : __ : __ : __ : __ : __ : __ : __ : __ : appropriate
           1   2   3   4   5   6   7   8   9   10   Most

1. Imitations

2. Not attractive

3. Frequent repairs

4. Difficult to service

5. Cheaply put together

*The directions for filling out the scale were not provided in the article but appear to have been similar to this.

SCALE NAME: Country-of-Origin Product Image (Undesirable Blender Attributes)

SCALE DESCRIPTION: A three-item, ten-point summated scale used to measure a person's evaluation of some negative aspects of a particular brand of blender made in a specified country. This scale was referred to as "Specific Product Attributes" (negative blender attributes) by Parameswaran and Pisharodi (1994).

SCALE ORIGIN: The scale is original to Parameswaran and Pisharodi (1994). The items were developed on the basis of discussions with appliance retailers. The survey used eleven items, but the purification process left the final version of this scale with three.

SAMPLES: Parameswaran and Pisharodi (1994) gathered data in a Midwestern metropolitan area of the United States that was viewed as having a heterogeneous mixture of ethnic groups. Membership lists of several ethnic group associations were obtained, and surveys were hand-delivered to a systematic sample. Of the 1025 questionnaires distributed, **678** usable forms were returned. No other descriptive information about the sample was provided.

RELIABILITY: The final version of the scale used for German blenders had a standardized alpha of **.609**, and the Korean version had an alpha of **.586**. These low values suggest that the scale is not internally consistent. Further developmental work is called for, and caution should be exercised in using it until its psychometric quality has been improved.

VALIDITY: Parameswaran and Pisharodi (1994) used confirmatory factor analysis in an iterative process of progressive respecification to finalize the several multi-item scales used in their study. The version of the country-of-origin product image (undesirable blender attributes) scale used for German and Korean products began with 11 items, which were eventually divided between two scales. Although detailed information was not provided for each scale, the authors stated that the final adjusted measurement model satisfied the unidimensionality criterion. Information bearing on convergent and discriminant validity may have been available from the analysis but was not discussed in the article.

ADMINISTRATION: The questionnaire used by Parameswaran and Pisharodi (1994) had the respondents evaluate blenders from both Germany and Korea. Higher scores on this scale suggested that consumers from one country viewed a particular brand of blender made in another country as having several negative characteristics. The specific brands of blenders the survey recipients were asked to evaluate were the German *Krups* and the Korean *Goldstar*.

MAJOR FINDINGS: The purpose of the research by Parameswaran and Pisharodi (1994) was to improve the definition and measurement of scales used in the study of country-of-origin effects. Their findings indicated that specific product attributes, originally theorized to be a single construct, were best measured using two scales. One of those scales involved blenders' undesirable attributes (shown subsequently), whereas the other related to their positive attributes.

REFERENCES:
Parameswaran, Ravi and R. Mohan Pisharodi (1994), "Facets of Country of Origin Image: An Empirical Assessment," *JA*, 23 (March), 43–56.

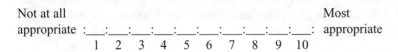

#114 *Country-of-Origin Product Image (Undesirable Blender Attributes)*

SCALE ITEMS:*

DIRECTIONS: Using the statements below, indicate the extent to which each is appropriate to describe a *(the name of the blender)* made in *(the country name)*.

Not at all appropriate :___:___:___:___:___:___:___:___:___:___: Most appropriate
          1   2   3   4   5   6   7   8   9   10

1. Difficult to find spares

2. Not durable

3. Not safe

*The directions for filling out the scale were not provided in the article but appear to have been similar to this.

SCALE NAME: Coupon Use (Economic Benefits)

SCALE DESCRIPTION: A three-item, five-point Likert-type scale purporting to capture a consumer's attitude toward the financial benefits of using coupons.

SCALE ORIGIN: The source of the scale is not specified by Mittal (1994), but it appears to be original to his study.

SAMPLES: Mittal (1994) gathered data from female members of six voluntary organizations, as well as from mall intercepts. A total of 184 respondents provided complete survey questionnaires. Most of the respondents were white (85%), married (71%), and at least 35 years of age (63%). Although it does not mirror the U.S. population, the sample included a wide variety of demographic categories.

RELIABILITY: The construct reliability (LISREL) was reported to be **.79** (Mittal 1994).

VALIDITY: The validity of the scale was not specifically addressed by Mittal (1994), except to note that the tests that were conducted provided support for discriminant validity.

ADMINISTRATION: The scale was part of a larger self-administered mail survey instrument (Mittal 1994). Higher scores on the scale indicated that respondents had highly positive attitudes toward the economic benefits of using coupons.

MAJOR FINDINGS: The study by Mittal (1994) proposed that demographics are poor predictors of coupon usage. Instead, he illustrated the value of three layers of mediating variables. Among the findings was that comparison shoppers had much better attitudes toward the **economic benefits of coupon use** than did noncomparison shoppers.

REFERENCES:
Mittal, Banwari (1994), "An Integrated Framework for Relating Diverse Consumer Characteristics to Supermarket Coupon Redemption," *JMR*, 31 (November), 533–44.

SCALE ITEMS:

Strongly   Strongly
disagree   :___:___:___:___:___: agree

               1   2   3   4   5

1. Coupons can save you a lot of money.

2. The money one can save by using coupons does not amount to much. **(r)**

3. I believe that one helps one's family financially by using coupons.

SCALE NAME: Coupon Use (Others)

SCALE DESCRIPTION: Three five-point, Likert-type items measuring a person's sense of whether others use coupons when they shop. The scale was called *interpersonal influence* by Tat and Bejou (1994)

SCALE ORIGIN: Although not stated explicitly, the scale appears to be original to Tat and Bejou (1994).

SAMPLES: The data were gathered by Tat and Bejou (1994) using a telephone survey in Memphis, Tenn. The telephone number prefixes were deliberately chosen for black neighborhoods to ensure black respondents composed a substantial portion of the sample. Interviews were conducted with **326** individuals who identified themselves as doing the majority of the shopping for their household. Ultimately, 37.2% of the respondents were black. Forty-one percent of the total sample were married, 39% came from households with four or more members, 33% were between the ages of 25 and 34 years, 45% had at least some college-level education, and 41% had incomes greater than $30,000. A detailed breakdown of demographic information by race is provided in the article.

RELIABILITY: An alpha of **.60** was reported for the scale by Tat and Bejou (1994). Alphas of .63 and .65 were reported for blacks and whites, respectively. The internal consistency of the scale is rather low, and caution should be exercised in its use.

VALIDITY: Tat and Bejou (1994) did not directly test the validity of the scale. However, they performed a couple of factor analyses on a total set of 24 items to purify the scales they developed. Factor loadings for both black and white respondents appeared to be reasonable (>.60).

ADMINISTRATION: The scale was administered by telephone interviewers to respondents as part of a larger instrument (Tat and Bejou 1994). Higher scores on the scale suggested that respondents believed the people around them (friends, relatives, and neighbors) used coupons when they shopped.

MAJOR FINDINGS: The purpose of the study by Tat and Bejou (1994) was to compare the differences between blacks and whites on motives for using coupons. Whites agreed significantly more than blacks that **others around them used coupons** when they shopped.

REFERENCES:
Tat, Peter K. and David Bejou (1994), "Examining Black Consumer Motives for Coupon Usage," *JAR*, 34 (March/April), 29–35.

SCALE ITEMS:

Strongly   Strongly
disagree   :___:___:___:___:___: agree
               1   2   3   4   5

1. My friends do not use coupons when they shop. **(r)**

2. My neighbors do not use coupons when they shop. **(r)**

3. My relatives do not use coupons when they shop.

SCALE NAME: Coupon Use (Time Costs)

SCALE DESCRIPTION: A three-item, five-point Likert-type scale purporting to capture a consumer's attitude toward the time involved in using coupons.

SCALE ORIGIN: The source of the scale is not specified by Mittal (1994), but it appears to be original to his study.

SAMPLES: Mittal (1994) gathered data from female members of six voluntary organizations, as well as from mall intercepts. A total of 184 respondents provided complete survey questionnaires. Most of the respondents were white (85%), married (71%), and at least 35 years of age (63%). Although it does not mirror the U.S. population, the sample included a wide variety of demographic categories.

RELIABILITY: The construct reliability (LISREL) was reported to be **.81** (Mittal 1994).

VALIDITY: The validity of the scale was not specifically addressed by Mittal (1994), except to note that this scale and one other (coupon use enjoyment) were highly correlated and did not show the same evidence of discriminant validity as the other measures used in the study.

ADMINISTRATION: The scale was part of a larger self-administered mail survey instrument (Mittal 1994). Higher scores on the scale indicated that respondents believed that the use of coupons was very time consuming.

MAJOR FINDINGS: The study by Mittal (1994) proposed that demographics are poor predictors of coupon usage. Instead, he illustrated the value of three layers of mediating variables. As noted (see the "Validity" section), this scale had such a strong correlation with another scale that the author combined them into one measure (*enjoyment versus hassle*). Among the findings was that comparison shoppers had much better enjoyment versus hassle in using coupons than did noncomparison shoppers.

REFERENCES:
Mittal, Banwari (1994), "An Integrated Framework for Relating Diverse Consumer Characteristics to Supermarket Coupon Redemption," *JMR*, 31 (November), 533–44.

SCALE ITEMS:

Strongly   Strongly
disagree   :___:___:___:___:___: agree
              1   2   3   4   5

1. It is very time consuming to use coupons for supermarket items.

2. One can save a lot of time if one does not get into the habit of using coupons.

3. It doesn't really take much time to take advantage of coupons on a regular basis. **(r)**

SCALE NAME: Coupon Use Limitations

SCALE DESCRIPTION: Three five-point Likert-type items measuring a person's attitude about barriers to the use of coupons. The scale was called *perceived institutional barriers* by Tat and Bejou (1994)

SCALE ORIGIN: Although not stated explicitly, the scale appears to be original to Tat and Bejou (1994).

SAMPLES: The data were gathered by Tat and Bejou (1994) using a telephone survey in Memphis, Tenn. The telephone number prefixes were deliberately chosen for black neighborhoods to ensure that black respondents composed a substantial portion of the sample. Interviews were conducted with **326** individuals who identified themselves as doing the majority of the shopping for their household. Ultimately, 37.2% of the respondents were black. Forty-one percent of the total sample were married, 39% came from households with four or more members, 33% were between the ages of 25 and 34 years, 45% had at least some college-level education, and 41% had incomes greater than $30,000. A detailed breakdown of demographic information by race is provided in the article.

RELIABILITY: An alpha of **.55** was reported for the scale by Tat and Bejou (1994). Alphas of .57 and .56 were reported for blacks and whites, respectively. This internal consistency is too low to be used as is. Further development and testing is called for.

VALIDITY: Tat and Bejou (1994) did not directly test the validity of the scale. However, they performed a couple of factor analyses on a total set of 24 items to purify the scales they developed. Factor loadings for the overall sample were respectable, but the loading of item 2 was rather low for blacks (.43) compared with whites (.68).

ADMINISTRATION: The scale was administered by telephone interviewers to respondents as part of a larger instrument (Tat and Bejou 1994). Higher scores on the scale suggested that respondents believed that there were barriers to the use of coupons.

MAJOR FINDINGS: The purpose of the study by Tat and Bejou (1994) was to compare the differences between blacks and whites on motives for using coupons. Attitudes regarding **coupon use limitations** did not differ significantly on the basis of race.

REFERENCES:
Tat, Peter K. and David Bejou (1994), "Examining Black Consumer Motives for Coupon Usage," *JAR*, 34 (March/April), 29–35.

SCALE ITEMS:

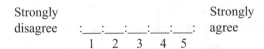

Strongly disagree :___:___:___:___:___: Strongly agree
         1 2 3 4 5

1. Coupons are only good for higher-priced brands.

2. The store where I shop often does not accept coupons.

3. Coupons are good only for larger packages.

SCALE NAME: Cultural Openness

SCALE DESCRIPTION: Seven seven-point Likert-type items purported to measure the degree to which a person is interested in the values and artifacts of other countries as well as desiring to interact with people from those nations.

SCALE ORIGIN: The scale is original to the study by Sharma, Shimp, and Shin (1995).

SAMPLES: Data were gathered from Korean consumers by Sharma, Shimp, and Shin (1995) using two sampling methods. Questionnaires were mailed to 1500 names taken from a economically diverse mailing list company's database. Usable surveys forms were returned by **125** people. The second method involved distributing 700 questionnaires to students at several schools in Seoul and in a southern Korean city. Completed questionnaires were received from **542** people. The samples were not significantly different in their demographic variables or response to dependent variables, so the authors chose to combine them for the analysis. The combined sample was 57% men, there was an average education level of slightly more than 13 years, and the mean age was 42 years.

RELIABILITY: Sharma, Shimp, and Shin (1995) performed confirmatory factor analysis (CFA) on this scale, as well as on others in the study. A reliability coefficient of **.74** for the **cultural openness** scale was reported on the basis of a holdout sample (n = 333).

VALIDITY: Sharma, Shimp, and Shin (1995) made a general claim of discriminant and convergent validity for all of their scales on the basis of results of a CFA.

ADMINISTRATION: The scale was self-administered by respondents, along with other measures, in the questionnaire used by Sharma, Shimp, and Shin (1995). The scale also appears to have undergone a rather thorough translation process along with the entire survey instrument. Higher scores on the scale indicated that respondents were interested in learning more about other cultures and interacting with people from other countries.

MAJOR FINDINGS: The study by Sharma, Shimp, and Shin (1995) identified antecedents of ethnocentricity, as well as the influence of ethnocentricity on attitudes toward imported products. The results indicated that consumers who had high **cultural openness** were less ethnocentric.

COMMENTS: The mean score on the scale was reported to be 35.47.

REFERENCES:
Sharma, Subhash, Terence A. Shimp, and Jeongshin Shin (1995), "Consumer Ethnocentrism: A Test of Antecedents and Moderators," *JAMS*, 23 (Winter), 26–37.

SCALE ITEMS:
DIRECTIONS: Please respond to the following statements by circling a number from 1 to 7 according to these directions:

1 = Strongly disagree
2 = Moderately disagree
3 = Slightly disagree
4 = Neither agree nor disagree

5 = Slightly agree
6 = Moderately agree
7 = Strongly agree

#119 *Cultural Openness*

1. I would like to have opportunities to meet people from other countries.

2. I am very interested in trying food from different countries.

3. We should have a respect for traditions, cultures, and ways of life of other nations.

4. I would like to learn more about other countries.

5. I have a strong desire for overseas travel.

6. I would like to know more about foreign cultures and customs.

7. I have a strong desire to meet and interact with people from foreign countries.

SCALE NAME: Dangerous

SCALE DESCRIPTION: Four five-point Likert-type statements purported to measure the extent to which a consumer considers some specified product class or brand hazardous to use. The product class examined by Griffin, Babin, and Attaway (1996) was power lawn tools.

SCALE ORIGIN: Griffin, Babin, and Attaway (1996, p. 321) stated that the items that composed this scale "were developed and refined" for their study.

SAMPLES: Students collected data for the study by Griffin, Babin, and Attaway (1996) for course credit. They were assigned to distribute questionnaires in various parts of a midsized Midwestern U.S. city. In some cases, the instruments were picked up by students, whereas in others they were mailed back. Of the 420 survey instruments dropped off, **262** were returned. No other information about the sample was provided, except that it was considered representative of the area from which it was drawn and only adults (older than 18 years of age) were selected to respond.

RELIABILITY: Griffin, Babin, and Attaway (1996) reported an alpha of **.80** for the scale.

VALIDITY: No evidence of the scale's validity was provided by Griffin, Babin, and Attaway (1996).

ADMINISTRATION: The scale was self-administered by respondents as part of a larger survey instrument (Griffin, Babin, and Attaway 1996). Higher scores on the scale indicated that respondents strongly believed that the product was dangerous.

MAJOR FINDINGS: Griffin, Babin, and Attaway (1996) explored the attribution of blame toward marketers when negative consequences resulted from the use of their products. Among the findings was that the greater the perceived **danger** of using the product, the less likely a person was to attribute blame to the manufacturer rather than the user.

REFERENCES:
Griffin, Mitch, Barry J. Babin, and Jill Attaway (1996), "Anticipation of Injurious Consumption Outcomes and Its Impact on Consumer Attributions of Blame," *JAMS*, 24 (Fall), 314–27.

SCALE ITEMS:

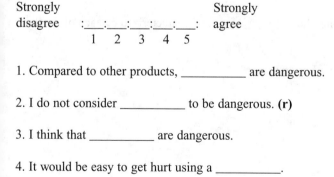

Strongly disagree :___:___:___:___:___: Strongly agree
         1 2 3 4 5

1. Compared to other products, _____ are dangerous.

2. I do not consider _____ to be dangerous. **(r)**

3. I think that _____ are dangerous.

4. It would be easy to get hurt using a _____.

SCALE NAME: Dangerous

SCALE DESCRIPTION: Three seven-point items measuring the extent to which a respondent describes some stimulus as unsafe and scary. The stimulus used by Block and Keller (1995) was a pamphlet about sexually transmitted diseases and how to avoid them. Thus, the scale was measuring the perceived severity of the diseases described.

SCALE ORIGIN: Block and Keller (1995) appear to have derived their scale from a measure used by Meyerowitz and Chaiken (1987). Although not exactly the same, the two are similar in that the latter had two items (*dangerous* and *frightening*) and was referred to as *perceived severity*.

SAMPLES: The scale was employed in both experiments conducted by Block and Keller (1995). **Ninety-four** undergraduate students completed the first experiment, and the second experiment was based on data from **115** undergraduate and graduate students.

RELIABILITY: An alpha of **.83** was reported for the scale for Experiments 1 and 2 (Block and Keller 1995).

VALIDITY: No examination of the scale's validity was reported by Block and Keller (1995), though they did state that a factor analysis indicated the items loaded on one factor.

ADMINISTRATION: The scale was completed by subjects after they were exposed to some health-related information (Block and Keller 1995). High scores on the scale indicated that respondents considered a specified stimulus to be very dangerous, if not life-threatening.

MAJOR FINDINGS: The purpose of the study by Block and Keller (1995) was to examine the relationships among level of efficacy, depth of processing, and framing effects. The perception of **danger** was measured to ensure that the attitude was not confounding experimental treatments; indeed, the findings showed that subjects in the three conditions did not differ significantly in that regard.

REFERENCES:

Block, Lauren G. and Punam Anand Keller (1995), "When to Accentuate the Negative: The Effects of Perceived Efficacy and Message Framing on Intentions to Perform a Health-Related Behavior," *JMR*, 32 (May), 192–203.

Meyerowitz, Beth E. and Shelly Chaiken (1987), "The Effect of Message Framing on Breast Self-Examination Attitudes, Intentions, and Behavior," *Journal of Personality and Social Psychology*, 52 (3), 500–510.

SCALE ITEMS:*

DIRECTIONS: Describe how much you think the _____ can be characterized by each of the three terms below.

Not at all   :___:___:___:___:___:___:___: Very much so
           1 2 3 4 5 6 7

1. Frightening

2. Dangerous

3. Severe

*The actual scale item (directions) and response scale were not provided in the article but would appear to be similar to what is shown here. The blank would be filled with the stimulus to which respondents are to react.

SCALE NAME: Deal Opportunities (Grocery)

SCALE DESCRIPTION: The scale is composed of eight seven-point items and measures the degree to which a consumer perceives that he or she has opportunities to take advantage of grocery store deals, with an emphasis on the use of coupons.

SCALE ORIGIN: Although not clear from the article by Putrevu and Ratchford (1997), some of the work on the scales was conducted previously in a dissertation by Putrevu (1992).

SAMPLES: Data were gathered by Putrevu and Ratchford (1997) using a mail survey to a random sample of grocery shoppers in an standard metropolitan statistical area in the Northeastern United States. A total of **500** responses were used in the main analysis, and demographics of the final sample were similar to those of the population of interest.

RELIABILITY: An alpha of **.72** was reported for the scale (Putrevu and Ratchford 1997).

VALIDITY: Although the authors stated in general that the scales showed evidence of convergent, discriminant, and content validity, no details of the analyses were provided (Putrevu and Ratchford 1997).

ADMINISTRATION: The scale was part of a larger mail questionnaire (Putrevu and Ratchford 1997). Higher scores on the scale suggested that consumers felt that they had many opportunities to take advantage of grocery specials, with an emphasis on taking coupons that could be used.

MAJOR FINDINGS: Putrevu and Ratchford (1997) examined a dynamic model of consumer search behavior that included human capital. The results indicated that the greater the perceived **opportunities for deals**, the greater the amount of external search was.

COMMENTS: A close examination of the items composing this scale suggest that they do not have high face validity. Further purification and improvement appears to be needed.

REFERENCES:
Putrevu, Sanjay (1992), "A Theory of Search and Its Empirical Investigation," unpublished doctoral dissertation, State University of New York at Buffalo.
_____ and Brian T. Ratchford (1997), "A Model of Search Behavior with an Application to Grocery Shopping," *JR*, 73 (4), 463–86.

SCALE ITEMS:

Never   :___:___:___:___:___:___:___: Always
               1   2   3   4   5   6   7

1. Coupons are available for most of the brands of grocery products that I buy.

2. Most supermarkets I go to provide their own store coupons.

3. I get coupons for grocery products in the mail.

4. I can find coupons for the products I buy.

5. I buy the *Sunday* edition of the _____.*

6. I buy the *Monday* edition of the _____.*

7. The products that I buy are on sale/special.

8. When I go grocery shopping, I can find some of the products that I usually buy on special/sale.

*The name of the primary newspaper for the area was used here.

SCALE NAME: Deal Proneness

SCALE DESCRIPTION: Three items purported to measure the extent of sensitivity a consumer has to sales-promotion activity at a shopping center. Two of the items were answered using a five-point Likert-type scale. The response format for the third item was apparently open-ended, and answers of four or more were collapsed into one category, which thus yielded a five-point scale (0 to 4).

SCALE ORIGIN: The scale appears to be original to Roy (1994), though one item (3) was taken from Westbrook and Black (1985).

SAMPLES: The data gathered by Roy (1994) came from usable responses from **710** shoppers at a large southern California mall. Interviews were conducted over period of six days and at varying times of the day.

RELIABILITY: A composite reliability of **.72** was reported for the scale by Roy (1994).

VALIDITY: No examination of the scale's validity was reported by Roy (1994).

ADMINISTRATION: The scale was part of a much larger questionnaire apparently administered by a trained interviewer. Higher scores on the scale appeared to suggest that a shopper was very interested in sales and finding bargains.

MAJOR FINDINGS: The study by Roy (1994) examined some relationships between mall shopping frequency and other variables, such as demographics and shopping motivation. The results of the study provided support for the hypothesis that there is a significant negative relationship between **deal proneness** and mall visit frequency.

REFERENCES:
Roy, Abhik (1994), "Correlates of Mall Visit Frequency," *JR*, 70 (2), 139–61.
Westbrook, Robert A. and William C. Black (1985), "A Motivation-Based Shopper Typology," *JR*, 61 (Spring), 78–103.

SCALE ITEMS:

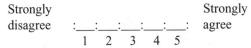

Strongly
disagree   :___:___:___:___:___: Strongly agree
          1   2   3   4   5

1. I wait until there is an advertised sale before going to shop at a mall.

2. I hunt around until I find a real bargain..

3. What is the number of trips made to the mall in the last three months primarily because a sale or promotion was being offered by some store(s) in the mall?*

*The exact phrasing of this item was not provided in the article but would appear to have been something like this. As noted, this item also appeared to be open-ended, and responses were later coded to represent between 0 and 4 (four or more) trips.

SCALE NAME: Deal Proneness (In-Store Promotions)

SCALE DESCRIPTION: Three seven-point items that measure the degree to which a consumer describes his or her tendency to search for several types of in-store promotions when shopping for grocery products. The scale was called *looking for in-store promotions* by Putrevu and Ratchford (1997).

SCALE ORIGIN: Although not clear from the article by Putrevu and Ratchford (1997), some of the work on the scales was conducted previously in a dissertation by Putrevu (1992).

SAMPLES: Data were gathered by Putrevu and Ratchford (1997) using a mail survey to a random sample of grocery shoppers in a standard metropolitan statistical area in the Northeastern United States. A total of **500** responses were used in the main analysis, and demographics of the final sample were similar to those of the population of interest.

RELIABILITY: An alpha of **.68** was reported for the scale (Putrevu and Ratchford 1997). The internal consistency of the scale is low and should be improved before it is used again.

VALIDITY: Although the authors stated in general that the scales showed evidence of convergent, discriminant, and content validity, no details of the analyses were provided (Putrevu and Ratchford 1997).

ADMINISTRATION: The scale was part of a larger mail questionnaire (Putrevu and Ratchford 1997). Higher scores on the scale suggested that a consumer frequently looked for deals and specials when grocery shopping.

MAJOR FINDINGS: Putrevu and Ratchford (1997) examined a dynamic model of consumer search behavior that included human capital. In general, the results indicated that self-reported search for information about buying groceries is associated with perceptions of the costs and benefits of search, as predicted by the model.

COMMENTS: As presented in the article by Putrevu and Ratchford (1997), this scale was part of a larger measure called "Search." That measure was the mean of the scores from nine scales related to grocery product information search behavior.

REFERENCES:
Putrevu, Sanjay (1992), "A Theory of Search and Its Empirical Investigation," doctoral dissertation, State University of New York at Buffalo.
———— and Brian T. Ratchford (1997), "A Model of Search Behavior with an Application to Grocery Shopping," *JR*, 73 (4), 463–86.

SCALE ITEMS:

Never   :___:___:___:___:___:___:___: Always
        1   2   3   4   5   6   7

1. I look for special deals inside the store before buying grocery products.

2. I look for unadvertised specials offered by supermarkets.

3. I look for special displays in supermarkets.

SCALE NAME: Decision Action-Control Orientation

SCALE DESCRIPTION: The scale is purported to measure a person's disposition and/or capacity toward transforming intentions into behavior-related decisions. The measure is composed of 20 forced choice items, with one alternative in each of the 20 items that reflects a "state" orientation and another alternative that reflects an "action" orientation. A state orientation is a mode of control similar to wishful thinking, in which a behavior is desired but little action is taken to make it happen. In contrast, with an action orientation, a person engages in tasks that bring about the desired behavior. Finally, half of the items (1–10) assess cognitive manifestations of action and state orientations, and the other half (11–20) assess behavioral manifestations.

SCALE ORIGIN: The scale was constructed by Kuhl (1985). In a study of 115 unspecified subjects, an alpha of .79 was found for the scale. Theoretically expected correlations were found between the scale and test anxiety, extroversion, self-consciousness, achievement motivation, future orientation, and cognitive complexity. The author concluded that the moderate to low size of these correlations suggested that a considerable amount of variance in action control could not be attributable to these personality variables.

SAMPLES: Data were gathered by Babin and Darden (1995) by intercepting shoppers as they left one of the ten top stores in a major Southeastern U.S. regional mall. Respondents were interviewed one at a time, and a small incentive was provided for their participation. The sample was considered to be representative of the mall's shoppers. The analysis appears to have been based on data from **118** shoppers.

The data for the study by Bagozzi, Baumgartner, and Yi (1992) were collected in two questionnaires, administered a week apart to female staff members of a major university. **One hundred forty-nine** women completed both questionnaires and provided complete information. To encourage subjects to participate in the study, a lottery with several cash prizes was used.

RELIABILITY: An alpha of **.71** was reported for the scale (Babin and Darden 1995). An alpha of **.61** was reported for the scale by Bagozzi, Baumgartner, and Yi (1992). Realizing that this was low, the authors also calculated alphas using polychoric correlations, which are more appropriate for the 20 dichotomous measures that compose the scale. With this alteration, a more respectable value of .75 was found.

VALIDITY: No examination of the scale's validity was reported by Babin and Darden (1995). Using a separate sample of 56 undergraduate students, the discriminant validity of the scale was examined by Bagozzi, Baumgartner, and Yi (1992). After examining the pattern of correlations, the authors concluded that there was some theoretical overlap of action control with several personality-related variables but that there was enough variance left unexplained to indicate that action control was a distinct construct.

ADMINISTRATION: The scale was apparently administered to respondents by interviewers along with many other items in a questionnaire (Babin and Darden 1995). The scale was administered by Bagozzi, Baumgartner, and Yi (1992) in the first questionnaire of two that were sent by campus mail to staff members of a university. Scores were calculated by summing the action-oriented response alternatives selected by respondents. Higher scores on the scale suggested that respondents had an action orientation, whereas those with low scores were classified as state oriented.

MAJOR FINDINGS: The purpose of the study by Babin and Darden (1995) was to examine the role of self-regulation as a moderator of relationships between shopping emotions and shopping experience evaluations. Among the findings was that dominance (#138) had a significant negative impact on resource expenditures for only those shoppers with a **state orientation**.

Bagozzi, Baumgartner, and Yi (1992) investigated the role played by **decision action control** in moderating relationships in the theory of reasoned action. This was studied in the context of coupon usage. They found that normative considerations were more important for those with a **state orientation**, whereas attitudinal considerations were more important for **action-oriented** people.

COMMENTS: The scale mean in the study by Babin and Darden (1995) was 9.6 (s = 3.2), and the median score was 10.

REFERENCES:
Babin, Barry J. and William R. Darden (1995), "Consumer Self-Regulation in a Retail Environment," *JR*, 71 (1), 47–70.
Bagozzi, Richard P., Hans Baumgartner, and Youjae Yi (1992), "State Versus Action Orientation and the Theory of Reasoned Action: An Application to Coupon Usage," *JCR*, 18 (March), 505–18.
Kuhl, Julius (1985), "Volitional Mediators of Cognition-Behavior Consistency: Self-Regulatory Processes and Action Versus State Orientation," in *Action Control: From Cognition to Behavior*, Julius Kuhl and Jeurgen Beckmann, eds. Berlin: Springer-Verlag, 101–28.

SCALE ITEMS:
DIRECTIONS: Consider each situation described below and the response options. Select the response alternative that would complete the sentence as it best describes you.

1. If I had to work at home,
   _____ I would often have problems getting started.
   _____ I would usually start immediately.*

2. When I want to see someone again,
   _____ I try to set a date for the visit right away.*
   _____ I plan to do it someday.

3. When I have a lot of important things to take care of,
   _____ I often don't know where to start.
   _____ It is easy for me to make a plan and then stick to it.*

4. When I have two things I would like to do and can do only one,
   _____ I decide between them rather quickly.*
   _____ I wouldn't know right away which was most important to me.

5. When I have to do something that is unpleasant,
   _____ I'd rather do it right away.*
   _____ I avoid doing it until it's absolutely necessary.

6. When I really want to finish an extensive assignment in an afternoon,
   _____ it often happens that something distracts me.
   _____ I can really concentrate on the assignment.*

7. When I have to complete a difficult assignment,
   _____ I can concentrate on the individual parts of the assignment.*
   _____ I can easily lose my concentration on the assignment.

8. When I fear that I'll lose interest during a tedious assignment,
   _____ I complete the unpleasant things first.
   _____ I start with the easier parts first.*

9. When it's absolutely necessary that I perform an unpleasant duty,
   _____ I finish it as soon as possible.*
   _____ it takes a while before I start on it.

10. When I've planned to do something unfamiliar in the following week,
    _____ it can happen that I change my plans at the last moment.
    _____ I stick with what I've planned.*

11. When I know that something has to be done soon,
    _____ I often think about how nice it would be if I were already finished with it.
    _____ I just think about how I can finish it the fastest.*

12. When I'm sitting at home and feel like doing something,
    _____ I decide on one thing relatively fast and don't think much about other possibilities.*
    _____ I like to consider several possibilities before I decide on something.

13. When I don't have anything special to do and am bored,
    _____ I sometimes contemplate what I can do.
    _____ it usually occurs to me soon what I can do.*

14. When I have a hard time getting started on a difficult problem,
    _____ the problem seems huge to me.
    _____ I think about how I can get through the problem in a fairly pleasant way.*

15. When I have to solve a difficult problem,
    _____ I think about a lot of different things before I really start on the problem.
    _____ I think about which way would be best to try first.*

16. When I'm trying to solve a difficult problem and there are two solutions that seem equally good to me,
    _____ I make a spontaneous decision for one of the two without thinking much about it.*
    _____ I try to figure out whether or not one of the two solutions is really better than the other.

17. When I have to study for a test,
    _____ I think a lot about where I should start.
    _____ I don't think about it too much, I just start with what I think is most important.*

18. When I've made a plan to learn how to master something difficult,
    _____ I first try it out before I think about other possibilities.*
    _____ before I start, I first consider whether or not there's a better plan.

19. When I'm faced with the problem of what to do with an hour of free time,
    _____ sometimes I think about it for a long time.
    _____ I come up with something appropriate relatively soon.*

20. When I've planned to buy just one piece of clothing but then see several things that I like,
    _____ I think a lot about which piece I should buy.
    _____ I usually don't think about it very long and decide relatively soon.*

*Action-oriented items are indicated by an asterisk and are coded as 1; the other item in each pair indicates a state orientation and is coded as 0.

SCALE NAME: Decision-Maker Role (Major Products for Family)

SCALE DESCRIPTION: Three phrases (product categories) and a seven-point response format that gauge the relative role played by a child (versus the parents) in decisions to purchase products that are "major" (relatively high-priced) and for use by the family (not just for the child).

SCALE ORIGIN: The scale is original to the study by Kim and Lee (1997).

SAMPLES: Data were collected by Kim and Lee (1997) with the cooperation of two high schools in an Eastern Canadian metropolitan area. Questionnaires were passed out to students who filled out their version in class. Students were supposed to take two complementary questionnaires home for their parents to complete. Of the 400 questionnaires that were passed out, usable data from **107** family triads were received.

RELIABILITY: Alphas of **.78** (fathers), **.86** (mothers), and **.78** (children) were reported for the scale by Kim and Lee (1997).

VALIDITY: Because the purpose of the study by Kim and Lee (1997) was to develop and validate measures, much analysis was discussed in the article pertaining to those activities. Briefly, using a traditional purification process as well as confirmatory factor analysis and Multitrait-Multimethod data analysis, support was shown for the scale's convergent and discriminant validity.

ADMINISTRATION: As noted previously (see "Samples"), data for the children's version of the scale came from questionnaires self-administered by teenagers during class time at high school. The parents' versions were taken home by the teenagers, filled out by the parents, and then either mailed to the researchers or brought by the students back to school (Kim and Lee (1997). Higher scores on the scale suggested that the focal children made the purchase decision for the listed products (described by the researchers as "major") almost entirely by themselves.

MAJOR FINDINGS: Kim and Lee (1997) set out to develop "triadic" measures of children's relative influence in four categories of purchase decisions: minor products for child, minor products for family, major products for child, and **major products for family**. This approach, along with confirmatory factor analysis and multiple-influence, multiple-rater data analysis, provided support for the validity of the measures.

COMMENTS: The authors admit that use of an initial set of 20 items to represent the four decision-making categories led to incongruent factor patterns for the three groups (mother, father, and children). Because one of the goals of their study was to develop measures with the same items for the three groups, an effort was made to eliminate items, such that similar factor patterns resulted. The elimination of 9 of the items and the movement of some items from one category to another could indicate some misspecification. Furthermore, there are other potential dimensions on which systematic variation in children's influence could be found beyond those used to develop this scale (e.g., public/private consumption, durable/nondurable).

REFERENCES:
Kim, Chankon and Hanjoon Lee (1997), "Development of Family Triadic Measures for Children's Purchase Influence," *JMR*, 34 (August), 307–21.

SCALE ITEMS:
Scale stem in children's version of questionnaire:

Between you and your parents, who decides what to buy for the following products:

#126 *Decision-Maker Role (Major Projects for Family)*

Scale anchors in children's version of questionnaire:

1 = My parents entirely
4 = My parents and I jointly
7 = Myself entirely

Scale stem in parents' version of questionnaire:

Between you (you and your spouse) and your child who brought this questionnaire, who decides what to buy for the following products:

Scale anchors in parents' version of questionnaire:

1 = My spouse and I entirely
4 = We and our child jointly
7 = Our child entirely

Scale items for parents' and children's versions of scale:

1. A family car

2. A house for the family

3. A television set for the family

SCALE NAME: Decision-Maker Role (Minor Products for Child)

SCALE DESCRIPTION: Three phrases (product categories) and a seven-point response format that gauge the relative role played by a child (versus the parents) in decisions to purchase products that are "minor" (relatively low-priced) and primarily for use by the child (versus for the family).

SCALE ORIGIN: The scale is original to the study by Kim and Lee (1997).

SAMPLES: Data were collected by Kim and Lee (1997) with the cooperation of two high schools in an Eastern Canadian metropolitan area. Questionnaires were passed out to students who filled out their version in class. Students were supposed to take two complementary questionnaires home for their parents to complete. Of the 400 questionnaires that were passed out, usable data from **107** family triads were received.

RELIABILITY: Alphas of **.80** (fathers), **.67** (mothers), and **.79** (children) were reported for the scale by Kim and Lee (1997).

VALIDITY: Because the purpose of the study by Kim and Lee (1997) was to develop and validate measures, much analysis was discussed in the article pertaining to those activities. Briefly, using a traditional purification process as well as confirmatory factor analysis and Multitrait-Multimethod data analysis, support was shown for the scale's convergent and discriminant validity.

ADMINISTRATION: As noted previously (see "Samples"), data for the children's version of the scale came from questionnaires self-administered by teenagers during class time at high school. The parents' versions were taken home by the teenagers, filled out by the parents, and then either mailed to the researchers or brought by the students back to school (Kim and Lee (1997). Higher scores on the scale suggested that the focal children made the purchase decision for the listed products (described by the researchers as "minor") almost entirely by themselves.

MAJOR FINDINGS: Kim and Lee (1997) set out to develop "triadic" measures of children's relative influence in four categories of purchase decisions: **minor products for child**, minor products for family, major products for child, and major products for family. This approach, along with confirmatory factor analysis and multiple-influence, multiple-rater data analysis, provided support for the validity of the measures.

COMMENTS: The authors admit that use of an initial set of 20 items to represent the four decision-making categories led to incongruent factor patterns for the three groups (mother, father, and children). Because one of the goals of their study was to develop measures with the same items for the three groups, an effort was made to eliminate items, such that similar factor patterns resulted. The elimination of 9 of the items and the movement of some items from one category to another could indicate some misspecification. Furthermore, there are other potential dimensions on which systematic variation in children's influence could be found beyond those used to develop this scale (e.g., public/private consumption, durable/nondurable).

REFERENCES:
Kim, Chankon and Hanjoon Lee (1997), "Development of Family Triadic Measures for Children's Purchase Influence," *JMR*, 34 (August), 307–21.

SCALE ITEMS:
Scale stem in children's version of questionnaire:

Between you and your parents, who decides what to buy for the following products:

#127 *Decision-Maker Role (Minor Products for Child)*

Scale anchors in children's version of questionnaire:

1 = My parents entirely
4 = My parents and I jointly
7 = Myself entirely

Scale stem in parents' version of questionnaire:

Between you (you and your spouse) and your child who brought this questionnaire, who decides what to buy for the following products:

Scale anchors in parents' version of questionnaire:

1 = My spouse and I entirely
4 = We and our child jointly
7 = Our child entirely

Scale items for parents' and children's versions of scale:

1. Clothes for the child

2. Records for the child

3. Shoes for the child

SCALE NAME: Decision-Maker Role (Minor Products for Family)

SCALE DESCRIPTION: Three phrases (product categories) and a seven-point response format that gauges the relative role played by a child (versus the parents) in decisions to purchase products that are "minor" (relatively low-priced) and for use by the family (not just for the child).

SCALE ORIGIN: The scale is original to the study by Kim and Lee (1997).

SAMPLES: Data were collected by Kim and Lee (1997) with the cooperation of two high schools in an Eastern Canadian metropolitan area. Questionnaires were passed out to students who filled out their version in class. Students were supposed to take two complementary questionnaires home for their parents to complete. Of the 400 questionnaires that were passed out, usable data from **107** family triads were received.

RELIABILITY: Alphas of **.79** (fathers), **.79** (mothers), and **.76** (children) were reported for the scale by Kim and Lee (1997).

VALIDITY: Because the purpose of the study by Kim and Lee (1997) was to develop and validate measures, much analysis was discussed in the article pertaining to those activities. Briefly, using a traditional purification process as well as confirmatory factor analysis and Multitrait-Multimethod data analysis, support was shown for the scale's convergent and discriminant validity.

ADMINISTRATION: As noted previously (see "Samples"), data for the children's version of the scale came from questionnaires self-administered by teenagers during class time at high school. The parents' versions were taken home by the teenagers, filled out by the parents, and then either mailed to the researchers or brought by the students back to school (Kim and Lee 1997). Higher scores on the scale suggested that the focal children made the purchase decision for the listed products (described by the researchers as "minor") almost entirely by themselves.

MAJOR FINDINGS: Kim and Lee (1997) set out to develop "triadic" measures of children's relative influence in four categories of purchase decisions: minor products for child, **minor products for family**, major products for child, and major products for family. This approach, along with confirmatory factor analysis and multiple-influence, multiple-rater data analysis, provided support for the validity of the measures.

COMMENTS: The authors admit that use of an initial set of 20 items to represent the four decision-making categories led to incongruent factor patterns for the three groups (mother, father, and children). Because one of the goals of their study was to develop measures with the same items for the three groups, an effort was made to eliminate items, such that similar factor patterns resulted. The elimination of 9 of the items and the movement of some items from one category to another could indicate some misspecification. Furthermore, there are other potential dimensions on which systematic variation in children's influence could be found beyond those used to develop this scale (e.g., public/private consumption, durable/nondurable).

REFERENCES:
Kim, Chankon and Hanjoon Lee (1997), "Development of Family Triadic Measures for Children's Purchase Influence," *JMR*, 34 (August), 307–21.

#128 *Decision-Maker Role (Minor Products for Family)*

SCALE ITEMS:

Scale stem in children's version of questionnaire:

Between you and your parents, who decides what to buy for the following products:

Scale anchors in children's version of questionnaire:

1 = My parents entirely
4 = My parents and I jointly
7 = Myself entirely

Scale stem in parents' version of questionnaire:

Between you (you and your spouse) and your child who brought this questionnaire, who decides what to buy for the following products:

Scale anchors in parents' version of questionnaire:

1 = My spouse and I entirely
4 = We and our child jointly
7 = Our child entirely

Scale items for parents' and children's versions of scale:

1. Toothpaste for the family

2. Shampoo for the family

3. Ketchup for the family

SCALE NAME: Decision-Making Style

SCALE DESCRIPTION: Twenty seven-point Likert-type statements that are purported to assess a person's natural disposition to use either a rational or an intuitive decision-making style (DMS). A rational DMS involves thoughtfully attending to information, whereas an intuitive DMS amounts to relying on general feelings or simple heuristic rules as the basis for a decision.

SCALE ORIGIN: The scale is original to Buck and Daniels (1985).

SAMPLES: Meyers-Levy and Peracchio (1996) gathered data for their experiment from **229** undergraduates taking marketing courses. A majority (63%) of the sample were men.

RELIABILITY: An alpha of **.84** was reported by Meyers-Levy and Peracchio (1996) for the scale.

VALIDITY: No examination of the scale's validity was reported by Meyers-Levy and Peracchio (1996).

ADMINISTRATION: Subjects responded to the scale, along with other measures, after they were exposed to the treatment stimulus (Meyers-Levy and Peracchio 1996). Higher scores on the scale appeared to indicate that respondents had a rational DMS, whereas lower scores suggested the respondents had an intuitive DMS.

MAJOR FINDINGS: Meyers-Levy and Peracchio (1996) examined how variation in the level of self-referencing affects persuasion and what factors moderate the effects. Among the many findings was that respondents with a **rational decision-making style** who read ads that used second-person wording evaluated products significantly better than those who read ads that used third-person wording.

REFERENCES:

Buck, Jacqueline N. and M. Harry Daniels (1985), *Assessment of Career Decision-Making Manual*. Los Angeles: Western Psychological Services.

Meyers-Levy, Joan and Laura A. Peracchio (1996), "Moderators of the Impact of Self-Reference on Persuasion," *JCR*, 22 (March), 408–23.

SCALE ITEMS:

DIRECTIONS: This exercise is to determine the style you use when making daily decisions. Answers to questions should reflect the way in which you typically make your decisions. There are no right or wrong answers, we only ask that you provide honest and accurate answers. Please circle the number of your choice. Answers nearer 1 indicate that you strongly disagree with the statement. Answers nearer 7 indicate that you strongly agree with the statement.

Strongly
disagree   :__:__:__:__:__:__:__: agree
       1 2 3 4 5 6 7

1. I am very systematic when I go about making a decision.

2. I make decisions pretty creatively, following my own inner instincts. **(r)**

3. I usually make my decisions based on how things are for me right now rather than how they'll be in the future. **(r)**

4. I rarely make a decision without gathering all the information I can find.

5. I often make a decision which is right for me without knowing why I made the decision. **(r)**

6. When I make a decision, I consider its consequences in relation to decisions I will have to make later on.

7. Even on important decisions I make up my mind pretty quickly. **(r)**

8. When I make a decision I trust my inner feelings and reactions. **(r)**

9. When I need to make a decision I take my time to think through it carefully.

10. I often decide on something without checking it out and getting the facts. **(r)**

11. I put off many decisions because thinking about them makes me uneasy.

12. When a decision is coming up, I look far enough ahead so I'll have enough time to plan and think it through before I have to act.

13. I don't really think about the decision: it's in the back of my mind for a while, then suddenly it will hit me and I know what I will do. **(r)**

14. Before I do anything, I have a carefully worked out plan.

15. In coming to a decision about something, I usually use my imagination or fantasies to see how I would feel if I did it. **(r)**

16. I don't have a rational reason for most decisions I make. **(r)**

17. I don't make decisions hastily because I want to be sure I make the right decisions.

18. A decision is right for me if it is emotionally satisfying. **(r)**

19. Often I see each of my decisions as stages in my progress toward a definite goal.

20. I like to learn as much as I can about possible consequences of a decision before I make it.

SCALE NAME: Delay Duration

SCALE DESCRIPTION: A three-item scale purported to measure the length of time a person perceives a delay to have lasted. The response scale used by Taylor (1994) was somewhat open-ended and was measured in hours.

SCALE ORIGIN: The scale is original to Taylor (1994).

SAMPLES: The settings for the data collection used by Taylor (1994) were an airline boarding lounge and inside the planes themselves. Each passenger approached was given two questionnaires; one was completed while waiting to board the plane, and the other was filled out toward the end of the flight. (Flight attendants made announcements when it was time to complete the second questionnaire and collected them after passengers filled them out.) Data from passengers on 18 delayed flights were collected, and **210** usable survey forms were returned.

RELIABILITY: An alpha of **.85** was reported for the scale used by Taylor (1994).

VALIDITY: No examination of the scale's validity was reported by Taylor (1994).

ADMINISTRATION: The scale was included as part of the first of the two questionnaires passengers were asked to complete (Taylor 1994). As noted (see "Samples"), the first survey instrument was given to the respondents, and they were asked to complete it while waiting to board their flights. It should also be noted that item 1, actual delay duration, was not on the survey instrument but was measured by the interviewers. Scale scores were calculated as the average of three things: the actual delay (1), the perceived delay (3), and the difference between the actual delay and the expected delay (1 minus 2). A high score on the scale suggested that respondents perceived that they had been waiting an unexpectedly long time for something to occur.

MAJOR FINDINGS: Taylor (1994) tested a model of the influence of delay duration on affective and evaluative reactions to an airline flight delay. Among the significant findings was that the longer the perceived **delay,** the more respondents felt annoyed and anxious.

REFERENCES:
Taylor, Shirley (1994), "Waiting for Service: The Relationship Between Delays and Evaluations of Service," *JM*, 58 (April), 56–69.

SCALE ITEMS:*

1. Actual length of delay: ___ hours

2. If you expected a delay, how long did you think it would be? ___ hours

3. How long did the delay seem to be? ___ hours

*Item 1 was recorded by the interviewers and not asked of the respondents. Also, the respondents either were asked to estimate in terms of hours or their answers were rounded to hours.

SCALE NAME: Disconfirmation (Museum Services)

SCALE DESCRIPTION: A four-item, five-point summated rating scale measuring the degree to which a consumer's expectations regarding a museum and its services have been met.

SCALE ORIGIN: Although modeled after measures of disconfirmation similar to those by Oliver and Swan (1989), this measure is original to Bhattacharya, Rao, and Glynn (1995).

SAMPLES: Bhattacharya, Rao, and Glynn (1995) gathered data from members of an art museum in a major city in the Southeastern United States. Questionnaires were mailed to a proportionate stratified random sample of the various membership categories. Two free guest passes were included with the questionnaires as a token of appreciation and incentive to respond. A 30% response rate produced **306** completed survey forms. Although not representative of the population at large, the authors considered the sample to be similar to those reported of art consumers. Respondents were approximately 52 years of age, predominately white (96%), and mostly women (66%).

RELIABILITY: An alpha of **.65** was reported for the scale by Bhattacharya, Rao, and Glynn (1995). This suggests that the scale had lower internal consistency than is desirable, and further work is called for to improve and test its psychometric qualities.

VALIDITY: No evidence of the scale's validity was reported by Bhattacharya, Rao, and Glynn (1995).

ADMINISTRATION: The scale was self-administered by respondents as part of a larger mail survey questionnaire (Bhattacharya, Rao, and Glynn 1995). High scores on the scale indicated that respondents believed the museum had lived up to their expectations.

MAJOR FINDINGS: Bhattacharya, Rao, and Glynn (1995) used social identity theory to develop and test a conceptual framework for the identification a person feels toward an organization of which he or she is a member. The findings showed that there was a significant positive relationship between **disconfirmation** and identification. This means that the more a person's expectations are met by an organization, the greater his or her identification with that organization.

REFERENCES:

Bhattacharya, C.B., Hayagreeva Rao, and Mary Ann Glynn (1995), "Understanding the Bond of Identification: An Investigation of Its Correlates Among Art Museum Members," *JM*, 59 (October), 46–57.

Oliver, Richard L. and John E. Swan (1989), "Consumer Perceptions of Interpersonal Equity and Satisfaction in Transactions," *JM*, 53 (April), 21–35.

SCALE ITEMS:*

DIRECTIONS: Using the following response scale, please indicate the extent to which your expectations of each of the four museum dimensions listed below have been met.

Much worse   Much better
than expected   :___:___:___:___: than expected
                  1   2   3   4   5

1. The permanent art collection

2. The traveling exhibitions

3. Special events

4. The gift shop

*The directions were not supplied in the article by Bhattacharya, Rao, and Glynn (1995) but would appear to have been similar to those constructed here.

SCALE NAME: Discount Age Segmentation Cue

SCALE DESCRIPTION: A three-item, five-point Likert-type measure of the degree to which a consumer believes that a discount is to be used only by those of a specified age group (senior citizens). The scale was referred to by Tepper (1994) as *age segmentation cue manipulation check.*

SCALE ORIGIN: The scale is original to Tepper (1994), though the work apparently was conducted in an earlier, uncited dissertation.

SAMPLES: Data for the between-subjects experimental design were gathered by Tepper (1994) through a mail survey. Recipients were identified through a snowball sampling technique that produced a list of 1206 noninstitutionalized people living in two large Southeastern cities in the United States. Of the questionnaires distributed, **784** were returned and usable. Significant differences were found for chronological age across treatment groups. Also, some differences involving age may have existed between respondents and nonrespondents (both chronological age and age group identity). See the article for further details.

RELIABILITY: An alpha of **.76** was reported for the scale by Tepper (1994). The range of alphas for the six treatment groups was .67 to .82.

VALIDITY: Some limited evidence of the scale's validity can be construed from the information provided by Tepper (1994). The scores of two groups of respondents were compared: those who had been told the discount was for senior citizens and those who had been told that it was a "privileged customer discount" offered to "special" customers. Scores for those who had received the age manipulation cue were significantly higher than for those who did not receive it.

ADMINISTRATION: Respondents completed the scale along with other measures in the self-administered mail questionnaire (Tepper 1994). High scores on the scale suggested that respondents believed a discount was for senior citizens only. (The type of discount studied by Tepper [1994] was for "senior citizens" or "special customers," depending on the treatment group.)

MAJOR FINDINGS: Tepper (1994) investigated the influence of various age segmentation cues on discount usage intentions. As noted, the **discount age segmentation cue** was used only as a manipulation check, and no separate findings are reported about it apart from what was mentioned regarding its validity.

REFERENCES:
Tepper, Kelly (1994), "The Role of Labeling Processes in Elderly Consumers' Responses to Age Segmentation Cues," *JCR,* 20 (March), 503–19.

SCALE ITEMS:

Strongly   Strongly
disagree   :__:__:__:__:__: agree
                 1   2   3   4   5

1. Only people over a certain age are eligible for this discount.

2. Young people would never use this discount.

3. These discounts are specifically for senior citizens.

SCALE NAME: Discount Credibility

SCALE DESCRIPTION: A five-item, five-point Likert-type measure of the degree to which a consumer believes that a discount represents a bona fide reduction in the normal price for a product.

SCALE ORIGIN: The scale is original to Tepper (1994), though the work apparently was conducted in an earlier, uncited dissertation.

SAMPLES: Data for the between-subjects experimental design were gathered by Tepper (1994) through a mail survey. Recipients were identified through a snowball sampling technique, which produced a list of 1206 noninstitutionalized people living in two large Southeastern cities in the United States. Of the questionnaires distributed, **784** were returned and usable. Significant differences were found for chronological age across treatment groups. Also, some differences involving age may have existed between respondents and nonrespondents (both chronological age and age group identity). See the article for further details.

RELIABILITY: An alpha of **.91** was reported for the scale by Tepper (1994). The range of alphas for the six treatment groups was .85 to .94.

VALIDITY: No evidence of the scale's validity was reported in the article by Tepper (1994).

ADMINISTRATION: Respondents completed the scale, along with other measures, in the self-administered mail questionnaire (Tepper 1994). High scores on the scale suggested that respondents believed a discount was real and believable. (The type of discount studied by Tepper [1994] was for "senior citizens" or "special customers," depending on the treatment group .)

MAJOR FINDINGS: Tepper (1994) investigated the influence of various age segmentation cues on discount usage intentions. **Discount credibility** was used as a covariate, and results pertaining to it were not elaborated on in the article. It does appear, however, that **discount credibility** was positively related to discount usage intention for all age groups examined and that the relationship grew stronger as the age of the groups increased.

REFERENCES:

Tepper, Kelly (1994), "The Role of Labeling Processes in Elderly Consumers' Responses to Age Segmentation Cues," *JCR*, 20 (March), 503–19.

SCALE ITEMS:

Strongly disagree   :___:___:___:___:___: Strongly agree

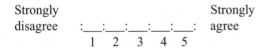

       1   2   3   4   5

1. This offering would be a true discount.

2. This discount is a good deal.

3. I would not be at all leery of this discount program.

4. I would think this was a very credible discount program.

5. Using this discount could result in real savings.

SCALE NAME: Discount Usage (Perceived Self-Devaluation)

SCALE DESCRIPTION: A three-item, five-point Likert-type scale measuring the degree to which a consumer believes that others might not use a discount because of the negative impact it could have on their self-image.

SCALE ORIGIN: The scale is original to Tepper (1994), though the work apparently was conducted in an earlier, uncited dissertation.

SAMPLES: Data for the between-subjects experimental design were gathered by Tepper (1994) through a mail survey. Recipients were identified through a snowball sampling technique, which produced a list of 1206 noninstitutionalized people living in two large Southeastern cities in the United States. Of the questionnaires distributed, **784** were returned and usable. Significant differences were found for chronological age across treatment groups. Also, some differences involving age may have existed between respondents and nonrespondents (both chronological age and age group identity). See the article for further details.

RELIABILITY: An alpha of **.79** was reported for the scale by Tepper (1994). The range of alphas for the six treatment groups was .74 to .81.

VALIDITY: No evidence of the scale's validity was reported in the article by Tepper (1994).

ADMINISTRATION: Respondents completed the scale, along with other measures, in the self-administered mail questionnaire (Tepper 1994). High scores on the scale suggested that respondents believed self-devaluation was associated with use of discounts. (The type of discount studied by Tepper [1994] was for "senior citizens" or "special customers," depending on the treatment group.)

MAJOR FINDINGS: Tepper (1994) investigated the influence of various age segmentation cues on discount usage intentions. The results indicated that two types of responsiveness, **self-devaluation** and perceived stigma, mediate age segmentation cue effects on discount usage intention only for younger elderly respondents.

REFERENCES:
Tepper, Kelly (1994), "The Role of Labeling Processes in Elderly Consumers' Responses to Age Segmentation Cues," *JCR*, 20 (March), 503–19.

SCALE ITEMS:

Strongly   Strongly
disagree   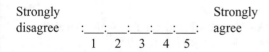   agree

1. Some people may not use this discount to maintain a more positive image of themselves.

2. Some people may not use this discount to preserve a more youthful image of themselves.

3. The first time someone used this discount, it might make them feel bad about themselves.

SCALE NAME: Discount Usage (Perceived Stigma)

SCALE DESCRIPTION A 23-item, five-point Likert-type measure of the degree to which a consumer believes that those who use a discount are devalued and discriminated against by three groups of people: store employees, other customers, and others in the users' shopping party.

SCALE ORIGIN: The scale is original to Tepper (1994), though the work apparently was conducted in an earlier, uncited dissertation.

SAMPLES: Data for the between-subjects experimental design were gathered by Tepper (1994) through a mail survey. Recipients were identified through a snowball sampling technique, which produced a list of 1206 noninstitutionalized people living in two large Southeastern cities in the United States. Of the questionnaires distributed, **784** were returned and usable. Significant differences were found for chronological age across treatment groups. Also, some differences involving age may have existed between respondents and nonrespondents (both chronological age and age group identity). See the article for further details.

RELIABILITY: An alpha of **.94** was reported for the scale by Tepper (1994). The range of alphas for the six treatment groups was .91 to .94.

VALIDITY: No evidence of the scale's validity was reported in the article by Tepper (1994).

ADMINISTRATION: Respondents completed the scale, along with other measures, in the self-administered mail questionnaire (Tepper 1994). High scores on the scale suggested that respondents believed a stigma was associated with use of discounts. (The type of discount studied by Tepper [1994] was for "senior citizens" or "special customers," depending on the treatment group .)

MAJOR FINDINGS: Tepper (1994) investigated the influence of various age segmentation cues on discount usage intentions. The results indicated that two types of responsiveness, self-devaluation and **perceived stigma**, mediate age segmentation cue effects on discount usage intention only for younger elderly respondents.

COMMENTS: The deliberate phrasing of the items, such that they relate to three groups of people (employees, other customers, and others in users' party) and two stigma types (discrimination and devaluation), suggests that this is not a unidimensional scale. Although a high alpha indicates the internal consistency of the scale, this does not mean that the items necessarily measure the same construct (Gerbing and Anderson 1988).

REFERENCES:

Gerbing, David W. and James C. Anderson (1988), "An Updated Paradigm for Scale Development Incorporating Unidimensionality and Its Assessment," *JMR*, 25 (May), 186–92.
Tepper, Kelly (1994), "The Role of Labeling Processes in Elderly Consumers' Responses to Age Segmentation Cues," *JCR*, 20 (March), 503–19.

SCALE ITEMS:

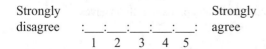

Strongly
disagree   :__:__:__:__: Strongly agree
                1   2   3   4   5

Discrimination

Store Employees

1. Store employees may act less respectful toward the user of this discount.

2. A store employee may become amused when observing a customer taking advantage of this discount.

3. Store employees may become more impatient with the user of this type of discount than with customers taking advantage of other special deals.

4. Store employees may talk down to the person who uses this type of discount.

5. The complaints and comments of the customer using this card may be taken less seriously by store employees than those of other customers.

6. Customers who use this discount may be treated less favorably by store employees than other customers.

7. If a customer reports that an item he is interested in purchasing is missing from the store shelves, the store employee at the register may be less likely to check inventory for customers using this discount.

8. A customer using this discount may receive poorer service than other customers.

Other Customers

1. Other customers may find it humorous that another customer would take advantage of this discount.

2. Other customers may become more impatient with the user of this type of discount than with customers taking advantage of other special deals.

Other in Users' Shopping Party

1. People may act uncomfortable or embarrassed when someone they are shopping with requests this discount.

2. People may tease the person who uses this discount when they are out shopping together.

3. If a person always requests this discount, others may not want to shop with them as often.

Devaluation

Store Employees

1. Store employees typically think that the person who uses this discount is old.

2. If a store employee offered a customer this discount, it might imply that they thought the customer does not possess a youthful appearance.

3. Store employees may think that users of this discount have less money to spend than the average customer.

4. If a customer uses this discount, store employees may view him less favorably.

#135 *Discount Usage (Perceived Stigma)*

Other customers

1. If someone uses this discount, other customers may be less likely to view them as youthful.

2. Other customers may think that more attractive customers would be less likely to use this discount.

3. Other customers may think that users of this discount are not as financially well-off as other customers.

4. Other customers may view the user of this card as a "second-class citizen."

Others in Users' Shopping Party

1. If someone uses this discount, the people they are shopping with will be less likely to view them as youthful.

2. If someone uses this discount, the people they are shopping with will be less likely to view them as youthful.

SCALE NAME: Discount Usage Intention

SCALE DESCRIPTION: A three-item summated measure of a consumer's stated intention to use a specific discount in a particular purchase context.

SCALE ORIGIN: The scale is original to Tepper (1994), though the work apparently was conducted in an earlier, uncited dissertation.

SAMPLES: Data for the between-subjects experimental design were gathered by Tepper (1994) through a mail survey. Recipients were identified through a snowball sampling technique, which produced a list of 1206 noninstitutionalized people living in two large Southeastern cities in the United States. Of the questionnaires distributed, **784** were returned and usable. Significant differences were found for chronological age across treatment groups. Also, some differences involving age may have existed between respondents and nonrespondents (both chronological age and age group identity). See the article for further details.

RELIABILITY: An alpha of **.82** was reported for the scale by Tepper (1994). The range of alphas for the six treatment groups was .78 to .85.

VALIDITY: Some evidence of the scale's predictive validity came from noting the relationship between scores on the scale and actual behavior (whether respondents returned a card requesting more information about the discount). Persons who returned the card had substantially greater scores on **discount usage intention** than did those who did not return the cards.

ADMINISTRATION: Respondents completed the scale, along with other measures, in the self-administered mail questionnaire (Tepper 1994). The scale was scored such that those with high numbers were interpreted as showing less inclination to use the discount in question than those with lower scores. Because item 1 has more response points than items 2 and 3, the scale should not be summated until after the item scores are standardized or put on the same scale. No information regarding this adjustment was provided in the article. (The type of discount studied by Tepper [1994] was for "senior citizens" or "special customers," depending on the treatment group.)

MAJOR FINDINGS: Tepper (1994) investigated the influence of various age segmentation cues on **discount usage intentions**. The results indicated that two types of responsiveness, self devaluation and perceived stigma, mediate age segmentation cue effects on **discount usage intention** only for younger elderly respondents.

REFERENCES:
Tepper, Kelly (1994), "The Role of Labeling Processes in Elderly Consumers' Responses to Age Segmentation Cues," *JCR*, 20 (March), 503–19.

SCALE ITEMS:
(Respondents were asked to indicate their intention to use a 10% discount on a $10 purchase.)

1. What is the probability that you would use this discount? (Place an X in one of the blank spaces.)

Virtually certain (99 chances in 100)   _____
Almost sure (9 chances in 10)   _____
Very probably (8 chances in 10)   _____
Probably (7 chances in 10)   _____

#136 *Discount Usage Intention*

Good possibility (6 chances in 10)   _____
Fairly good possibility (5 chances in 10)   _____
Fair possibility (4 chances in 10)   _____
Some possibility (3 chances in 10)   _____
Very slight possibility (2 chances in 10)   _____
Almost no chance (1 chance in 10)   _____
No chance (0 chance in 10)   _____

2. How interested would you be in using this discount?

| Extremely | | | | Not at all |
| interested | | | | interested |

1————————2————————3————————4————————5

3. How likely is it that you would use this discount?

| Extremely | | | | Not at all |
| likely | | | | likely |

1————————2————————3————————4————————5

SCALE NAME: Discount Usage Social Visibility

SCALE DESCRIPTION: A five-item, five-point Likert-type measure of the degree to which a consumer believes that usage of a discount in a store would be observed by others. The scale was referred to by Tepper (1994) as *social visibility manipulation check.*

SCALE ORIGIN: The scale is original to Tepper (1994), though the work apparently was conducted in an earlier, uncited dissertation.

SAMPLES: Data for the between-subjects experimental design were gathered by Tepper (1994) through a mail survey. Recipients were identified through a snowball sampling technique, which produced a list of 1206 noninstitutionalized people living in two large Southeastern cities in the United States. Of the questionnaires distributed, **784** were returned and usable. Significant differences were found for chronological age across treatment groups. Also, some differences involving age may have existed between respondents and nonrespondents (both chronological age and age group identity). See the article for further details.

RELIABILITY: An alpha of **.76** was reported for the scale by Tepper (1994). The range of alphas for the six treatment groups was .71 to .78.

VALIDITY: Some limited evidence of the scale's validity can be construed from the information provided by Tepper (1994). The scores of two groups of respondents were compared: In one treatment, the discount was described such that its usage would be socially visible, whereas in the other treatment, it was described as a discrete action. Scores for those who received the high social visibility cue were significantly greater than for those who received the low social visibility cue.

ADMINISTRATION: Respondents completed the scale, along with other measures, in the self-administered mail questionnaire (Tepper 1994). High scores on the scale suggested respondents believed that others in the store would notice that the specified discount was being used. (The type of discount studied by Tepper [1994] was for "senior citizens" or "special customers," depending on the treatment group.)

MAJOR FINDINGS: Tepper (1994) investigated the influence of various age segmentation cues on discount usage intentions. As noted, the **discount usage social visibility** scale was merely used as a manipulation check, and no separate findings were reported about it apart from what was mentioned regarding its validity.

REFERENCES:
Tepper, Kelly (1994), "The Role of Labeling Processes in Elderly Consumers' Responses to Age Segmentation Cues," *JCR*, 20 (March), 503–19.

SCALE ITEMS:

Strongly   Strongly
disagree   agree

1————————2————————3————————4————————5

1. Store employees at the register will be aware of the reason the customer is receiving a discount.

2. Other customers will be aware that the user is receiving a discount.

3. Other customers may observe the user taking advantage of the discount.

4. Other customers would hear the user requesting the discount.

5. Store personnel would be aware the customer is using the discount.

SCALE NAME: Dominance

SCALE DESCRIPTION: Four six-point descriptors of a person's dominance-related emotional reaction to an environmental stimulus.

SCALE ORIGIN: This scale is based in spirit on Mehrabian and Russell's (1974) work but has been modified so much as to be considered original to Babin and Darden (1995). Mehrabian and Russell's (1974) scale had six bipolar adjectives (see #90, Vol. II), whereas this one by Babin and Darden (1995) used only one of their positive descriptors and then supplied three other original positive descriptors. The latter also used a six-point "felt" response scale, as noted subsequently.

SAMPLES: Data were gathered by Babin and Darden (1995) by intercepting shoppers as they left one of the ten top stores in a major Southeastern U.S. regional mall. Respondents were interviewed one at a time, and a small incentive was provided for their participation. The sample was considered representative of the mall's shoppers. The analysis appears to have been based on data from **118** shoppers.

RELIABILITY: An alpha of **.82** was reported for the scale (Babin and Darden 1995). The construct reliability was .84, and variance extracted was .57.

VALIDITY: The results of a confirmatory factor analysis supported the measurement model in the study (Babin and Darden 1995). This provides some limited evidence of the scale's unidimensionality, as well as its convergent and discriminant validities.

ADMINISTRATION: The scale was apparently administered to respondents by interviewers, along with many other items, in a questionnaire (Babin and Darden 1995). Higher scores on the scale suggested that respondents experienced strong feelings of control (dominance) on exposure to some specified stimulus.

MAJOR FINDINGS: The purpose of the study by Babin and Darden (1995) was to examine the role of self-regulation as a moderator of relationships between shopping emotions and shopping experience evaluations. Among the findings was that **dominance** had a significant negative impact on resource expenditures only for those shoppers with a state orientation (#125).

REFERENCES:
Babin, Barry J. and William R. Darden (1995), "Consumer Self-Regulation in a Retail Environment," *JR*, 71 (1), 47–70.
Mehrabian, Albert and James A. Russell (1974), *An Approach to Environmental Psychology*. Cambridge, MA: The MIT Press.

SCALE ITEMS:* Thinking back on how you felt while shopping in this store, please use the following scale to describe how you felt.

Did not   Felt
feel at all   :___:___:___:___:___:___: very much
          1 2 3 4 5 6

1. In control

2. Powerful

3. Bold

4. Free

*Although the actual scale stem was not provided in the article, this reconstruction is based on the description that was given.

SCALE NAME: Dominant Language (Spanish)

SCALE DESCRIPTION: A five-item scale measuring the degree to which Spanish is the predominant language used by a person.

SCALE ORIGIN: The scale appears to have been developed by Koslow, Shamdasani, and Touchstone (1994) for their study.

SAMPLES: Data were gathered by Koslow, Shamdasani, and Touchstone (1994) in personal interviews with shoppers at three southern California supermarkets. Bilingual interviewers were used and asked to approach only those shoppers who appeared to be Hispanic. Of the 413 interviews that were begun, **367** yielded enough information to be useful in the analysis. The sample was 56% men, 60.7% were between the ages of 20 and 39 years, and 57.2% indicated that they were bilingual native Spanish speakers.

RELIABILITY: An alpha of **.91** was reported for the scale by Koslow, Shamdasani, and Touchstone (1994).

VALIDITY: The validity of the scale was not specifically addressed in the study (Koslow, Shamdasani, and Touchstone 1994). However, one piece of evidence of the scale's validity is that there was a correlation of .62 between scores on the scale and the language in which the respondent chose to have the interview conducted.

ADMINISTRATION: The scale was part of a longer questionnaire administered by trained bilingual interviewers (Koslow, Shamdasani, and Touchstone 1994). The respondents were first greeted and recruited in Spanish and then asked in what language they would prefer the interview be conducted. As with the rest of the survey instrument, the scale was first developed in English, and the back-translation method was used to help refine the quality of the Spanish version. A little over one-fourth of the respondents chose to have the interview conducted in English; the remaining portion of the sample chose Spanish. Therefore, the scale items were read to respondents rather than being self-administered. High scores on the scale suggested that Spanish was used predominantly or exclusively in the respondent's life. The scores on individual items were not standardized before summing, which means some items carried more weight in determining overall scores on the scale than the other items (Koslow 1996). Although not typical, its appropriateness could be justified if supported by evidence from a factor analysis.

MAJOR FINDINGS: The study by Koslow, Shamdasani, and Touchstone (1994) examined how consumers in an ethnic subculture respond to the use of their language in advertising. No significant relationship was found between **Spanish language dominance** in a person's life and affect toward an ad that was varied for different respondent groups in the language used (Spanish, English, both).

COMMENTS: Although this measure was developed and used with Spanish in mind, it appears to be easily adapted to other languages. Further testing would be prudent, however.

REFERENCES:
Koslow, Scott (1996), personal correspondence.
———, Prem N. Shamdasani, and Ellen E. Touchstone (1994), "Exploring Language Effects in Ethnic Advertising: A Socioliguistic Perspective," *JCR*, 20 (March), 575–85.

#139 *Dominant Language (Spanish)*

SCALE ITEMS:

1. Which language do you use at work (*or* school *if they don't work*)?
   a. English
   b. Both
   c. Spanish

2. Which language do you usually use at home?
   a. English
   b. Both
   c. Spanish

3. Do you watch Spanish TV?

Never   Sometimes   Usually   Always
  1————————2————————3————————4

4. Do you speak a second language?
   a. Yes
   b. No

5. What is your native language?
   a. English
   b. Spanish

SCALE NAME: Economic Threat (Domestic)

SCALE DESCRIPTION: Three seven-point Likert-type items purported to measure the degree to which a person believes the security of the domestic economy in his or her country is threatened by foreign competitors.

SCALE ORIGIN: The scale is original to the study by Sharma, Shimp, and Shin (1995).

SAMPLES: Data were gathered from Korean consumers by Sharma, Shimp, and Shin (1995) using two sampling methods. Questionnaires were mailed to 1500 names taken from an economically diverse mailing list company's database. Usable surveys forms were returned by **125** people. The second method involved distributing 700 questionnaires to students at several schools in Seoul and in a southern Korean city. Completed questionnaires were received from **542** people. The samples were not significantly different in their demographic variables or response to dependent variables, so the authors chose to combine them for the analysis. The combined sample was 57% men, there was an average education level of slightly more than 13 years, and the mean age was 42 years.

RELIABILITY: Sharma, Shimp, and Shin (1995) performed confirmatory factor analysis (CFA) on this scale, as well as on others in the study. A reliability coefficient of **.53** for the **economic threat (domestic)** scale was reported on the basis of a holdout sample (n = 333).

VALIDITY: Sharma, Shimp, and Shin (1995) made a general claim of discriminant and convergent validity for all of their scales on the basis of the results of a CFA.

ADMINISTRATION: The scale was self-administered by respondents, along with other measures, in the questionnaire used by Sharma, Shimp, and Shin (1995). The scale also appears to have undergone a rather thorough translation process, along with the entire survey instrument. Higher scores on the scale indicated that respondents perceived foreign competition as threatening their country's economy.

MAJOR FINDINGS: The study by Sharma, Shimp, and Shin (1995) identified antecedents of ethnocentricity, as well as the influence of ethnocentricity on attitudes toward imported products. The results indicated that ethnocentric consumers are more supportive of importing if the products are seen as less threatening to their country's economy.

REFERENCES:
Sharma, Subhash, Terence A. Shimp, and Jeongshin Shin (1995), "Consumer Ethnocentrism: A Test of Antecedents and Moderators," *JAMS*, 23 (Winter), 26–37.

SCALE ITEMS:
DIRECTIONS: Please respond to the following statements by circling a number from 1 to 7 according to these directions:

1 = Strongly disagree   5 = Slightly agree
2 = Moderately disagree   6 = Moderately agree
3 = Slightly disagree   7 = Strongly agree
4 = Neither agree nor disagree

1. The present recession is due to an excessive amount of competitors.

2. Economic problems are mainly due to excessive foreign competitors.

3. The local economy has suffered the impact of foreign competitors.

SCALE NAME: Economic Threat (Personal)

SCALE DESCRIPTION: Three seven-point Likert-type items purported to measure the degree to which a person believes the security of his or her livelihood or that of a friend is threatened by foreign competitors.

SCALE ORIGIN: The scale is original to the study by Sharma, Shimp, and Shin (1995).

SAMPLES: Data were gathered from Korean consumers by Sharma, Shimp, and Shin (1995) using two sampling methods. Questionnaires were mailed to 1500 names taken from an economically diverse mailing list company's database. Usable surveys forms were returned by **125** people. The second method involved distributing 700 questionnaires to students at several schools in Seoul and in a southern Korean city. Completed questionnaires were received from **542** people. The samples were not significantly different in their demographic variables or response to dependent variables, so the authors chose to combine them for the analysis. The combined sample was 57% men, there was an average education level of slightly over 13 years, and the mean age was 42 years.

RELIABILITY: Sharma, Shimp, and Shin (1995) performed confirmatory factor analysis (CFA) on this scale, as well as on others in the study. A reliability coefficient of **.67** for the **economic threat (personal)** scale was reported on the basis of a holdout sample (n = 333).

VALIDITY: Sharma, Shimp, and Shin (1995) made a general claim of discriminant and convergent validity for all of their scales on the basis of the results of a CFA.

ADMINISTRATION: The scale was self-administered by respondents, along with other measures, in the questionnaire used by Sharma, Shimp, and Shin (1995). The scale also appears to have undergone a rather thorough translation process, along with the entire survey instrument. Higher scores on the scale indicated that respondents perceived foreign competition as threatening to their job security.

MAJOR FINDINGS: The study by Sharma, Shimp, and Shin (1995) identified antecedents of ethnocentricity, as well as the influence of ethnocentricity on attitudes toward imported products. The results indicated that ethnocentric consumers are more supportive of importing if the products are less threatening to their own job security.

REFERENCES:
Sharma, Subhash, Terence A. Shimp, and Jeongshin Shin (1995), "Consumer Ethnocentrism: A Test of Antecedents and Moderators," *JAMS*, 23 (Winter), 26–37.

SCALE ITEMS:
DIRECTIONS: Please respond to the following statements by circling a number from 1 to 7 according to these directions:

1 = Strongly disagree
2 = Moderately disagree
3 = Slightly disagree
4 = Neither agree nor disagree
5 = Slightly agree
6 = Moderately agree
7 = Strongly agree

1. Security of my job/business is heavily influenced by foreign competitors.

2. I have a family member/close friend whose job/business is threatened by foreign competitors.

3. Foreign competitors are hurting my job/business.

SCALE NAME: Emotion (Empathy)

SCALE DESCRIPTION: Three seven-point unipolar items measuring a person's emotional reaction to some stimulus that focuses on those feelings related to strong concern for an individual or situation. It is not intended to measure empathy per se.

SCALE ORIGIN: Although the items have been used in various emotional-related measures, no known use of these items as a set has been made previously. Therefore, though it is not explicitly stated to be original, the scale seems to have been developed for use in the study by Moore, Harris, and Chen (1995).

SAMPLES: Moore, Harris, and Chen (1995) conducted two experiments, only the first of which employed the **empathetic emotion** scale. Data were gathered for the first experiment from **153** undergraduates who were fulfilling a psychology course requirement at a large Southwestern U.S. university. The sample was 53% women, and ages ranged from 20 to 27 years.

RELIABILITY: An alpha of **.90** was reported for the scale by Moore, Harris, and Chen (1995).

VALIDITY: No examination of the scale's validity was reported by Moore, Harris, and Chen (1995).

ADMINISTRATION: The scale was self-administered by subjects, along with other measures, after they were exposed to experimental stimuli (Moore, Harris, and Chen 1995). Higher scores on the scale indicated that respondents experienced a strong emotional feeling of caring and concern toward some object.

MAJOR FINDINGS: The experiment conducted by Moore, Harris, and Chen (1995) investigated the extent to which differences in affect intensity influenced responses to emotional ad appeals. After seeing an ad for an organization devoted to the prevention of cruelty to children, those subjects with high affect intensity had a significantly stronger **empathetic emotional** reaction than did those with low affect intensity.

COMMENTS: Moore, Harris, and Chen (1995) combined this scale's items with those from a scale intended to measure a negative emotional reaction (#143). They did this for two reasons: first, a factor analysis showed that the items were loading on the same factor with high internal consistency (a = .90), and second, there were no appreciable differences in the results when the scales were treated as one instead of two. However, the position taken here is that the face validity of the two sets of items as a whole is suspect, and it is prudent to treat them separately until further testing supports their union.

REFERENCES:
Moore, David J. (1997), personal correspondence.
———, William D. Harris, and Hong C. Chen (1995), "Affect Intensity: An Individual Difference Response to Advertising Appeals," *JCR*, 22 (September), 154–64.

SCALE ITEMS:*
While exposed to the advertisement, how strongly did you feel _____?

Not at all :___:___:___:___:___:___:___: Very
       1   2   3   4   5   6   7

1. Concerned

2. Compassionate

3. Sympathetic

*The anchors for the scale were specified by Moore (1997).

SCALE NAME: Emotion (Negative)

SCALE DESCRIPTION: Five seven-point unipolar items measuring a person's emotional reaction to some stimulus with an emphasis on several "negative" feelings.

SCALE ORIGIN: Although the items have been used in various emotional-related measures, no known use of these items as a set has been made previously. Therefore, though it is not explicitly stated to be original, the scale seems to have been developed for use in the study by Moore, Harris, and Chen (1995).

SAMPLES: Moore, Harris, and Chen (1995) conducted two experiments, only the first of which employed the **negative emotion** scale. Data were gathered for the first experiment from **153** undergraduates who were fulfilling a psychology course requirement at a large Southwestern U.S. university. The sample was 53% women, and ages ranged from 20 to 27 years.

RELIABILITY: An alpha of **.89** was reported for the scale by Moore, Harris, and Chen (1995).

VALIDITY: No examination of the scale's validity was reported by Moore, Harris, and Chen (1995).

ADMINISTRATION: The scale was self-administered by subjects, along with other measures, after they were exposed to experimental stimuli (Moore, Harris, and Chen 1995). Higher scores on the scale indicated that respondents experienced a strong negative emotional reaction toward some object.

MAJOR FINDINGS: The experiment conducted by Moore, Harris, and Chen (1995) investigated the extent to which differences in affect intensity influenced responses to emotional ad appeals. After seeing an ad for an organization devoted to the prevention of cruelty to children, those subjects with high affect intensity had a significantly stronger sense of **negative emotions** than did those with low affect intensity.

COMMENTS: Moore, Harris, and Chen (1995) combined this scale's items with those from a scale intended to measure an empathetic emotional reaction (#142). They did this for two reasons: first, a factor analysis showed the items were loading on the same factor with high internal consistency (a = .90), and second, there were no appreciable differences in the results when the scales were treated as one instead of two. The position taken here is that the face validity of the two sets of items as a whole is suspect, and it is prudent to treat them separately until further testing supports their union. Even the items that compose this scale (shown subsequently) have not typically been used together but rather have been part of several different emotion scales.

REFERENCES:
Moore, David J. (1997), personal correspondence.
———, William D. Harris, and Hong C. Chen (1995), "Affect Intensity: An Individual Difference Response to Advertising Appeals," *JCR*, 22 (September), 154–64.

SCALE ITEMS:* While exposed to the advertisement, how strongly did you feel _____?

Not at all :___:___:___:___:___:___:___: Very
          1   2   3   4   5   6   7

1. Alarmed   4. Worried
2. Angry   5. Sad
3. Frightened

*The anchors for the scale were specified by Moore (1997).

SCALE NAME: Emotion (Positive)

SCALE DESCRIPTION: Six seven-point unipolar items measuring a person's emotional reaction to some stimulus with an emphasis on several "positive" feelings.

SCALE ORIGIN: Although the items have been used in various emotional-related measures, no known use of these items as a set has been made previously. Therefore, though it is not explicitly stated to be original, the scale seems to have been developed for use in the study by Moore, Harris, and Chen (1995).

SAMPLES: Moore, Harris, and Chen (1995) conducted two experiments, only the second of which employed the **positive emotion** scale. Data were gathered for the second experiment from **90** undergraduates who were invited to participate in the study on the basis of their scores (upper and lower quartiles) on another scale (#143) completed three weeks prior. Analysis was probably based on data from fewer than the 90 students, but it is not clear how many.

RELIABILITY: The scale was used by Moore, Harris, and Chen (1995) with six different ads that pretested as being either "emotional" or "nonemotional" (three ads each). The alphas were **.83,** .75, and **.90** for the emotional ads compared with **.89, .93,** and .88 for the nonemotional ads.

VALIDITY: No examination of the scale's validity was reported by Moore, Harris, and Chen (1995).

ADMINISTRATION: The scale was self-administered by subjects, along with other measures, after they were exposed to experimental stimuli (Moore, Harris, and Chen 1995). Higher scores on the scale indicated that respondents experienced a strong positive emotional reaction toward some object.

MAJOR FINDINGS: The experiment conducted by Moore, Harris, and Chen (1995) investigated the extent to which differences in affect intensity influenced responses to emotional ad appeals. Those subjects with high affect intensity had significantly stronger **positive emotional** reactions than did those with low affect intensity after exposure to emotional ads but no significant difference when exposed to nonemotional ads.

REFERENCES:
Moore, David J. (1997), personal correspondence.
———, William D. Harris, and Hong C. Chen (1995), "Affect Intensity: An Individual Difference Response to Advertising Appeals," *JCR*, 22 (September), 154–64.

SCALE ITEMS:* While exposed to the advertisement, how strongly did you feel _____?

Not at all :___:___:___:___:___:___:___: Very
        1   2   3   4   5   6   7

1. Joyous
2. Warm
3. Sentimental
4. Empathetic
5. Amused
6. Compassionate

*The anchors for the scale were specified by Moore (1997).

SCALE NAME: Energy Problems (Attribution of Responsibility)

SCALE DESCRIPTION: Three seven-point Likert-type statements measuring the extent to which a consumer attributes the cause for the country's energy problems to overconsumption and lack of conservation by others.

SCALE ORIGIN: The scale is original to Osterhus (1997). His purpose with the scale was to operationalize a *responsibility attribution* construct in the context of energy conservation.

SAMPLES: The sample for the study by Osterhus (1997) came from rural, urban, and suburban neighborhoods of a Midwestern U.S. area. Subjects were recruited through random-digit dialing and then were sent a paper questionnaire. Nonrespondents were mailed another questionnaire. Ultimately, **1128** usable responses were received.

RELIABILITY: An alpha of **.76** was reported for the scale by Osterhus (1997).

VALIDITY: Confirmatory factor analysis was used by Osterhus (1997) to help purify the scales. Although details of the quality of this **responsibility attribution** scale were not specified, support for the scale's convergent and discriminant validities was implied.

ADMINISTRATION: The scale was self-administered by respondents, along with other measures, in a mail survey format (Osterhus 1997). Higher scores on the scale suggested that respondents blamed the overconsumption of others for the country's energy problems.

MAJOR FINDINGS: Osterhus (1997) investigated how and when prosocial positions are expected to influence consumer choice. Contrary to expectations, **attribution of responsibility** was not found to have a significant impact on personal norms regarding conservation of energy.

REFERENCES:
Osterhus, Thomas L. (1997), "Pro-Social Consumer Influence Strategies: When and How Do They Work?" *JM*, 61 (October), 16–29.

SCALE ITEMS:

Disagree   :___:___:___:___:___:___:___: Agree
             1   2   3   4   5   6   7

1. Overconsumption by individuals has contributed to this country's energy problems.

2. More conservation of energy by individual households would greatly alleviate the energy problem.

3. Overconsumption by individual households has contributed to the country's energy problem.

SCALE NAME: Entitlement

SCALE DESCRIPTION: Six seven-point Likert-type statements that evaluate a person's belief that "the world" owes him or her something.

SCALE ORIGIN: The scale is original to the study by Raskin and Terry (1988) and is part of the Narcissistic Personality Inventory (NPI). Of the 40-item NPI, the 6 items shown here loaded highest on the same dimension and were labeled **entitlement**. The internal consistency of these items as a set was estimated to be .50 (n = 1018). The scale showed little or no relationship with age and gender. Evidence in support of the scale's nomological validity was provided.

SAMPLES: Various samples were collected and used by Netemeyer, Burton, and Lichtenstein (1995) in the process of validating some other scales. The **entitlement** scale was used in one study composed of 186 students and 264 "nonstudent adults." It was used in another study using data from 27 football players from a nationally ranked NCAA Division I team.

RELIABILITY: Alphas of **.80** (students) and **.78** (nonstudent adults) were found for the scale by Netemeyer, Burton, and Lichtenstein (1995; Netemeyer 1997).

VALIDITY: Although the validity of the scale was not directly examined by Netemeyer, Burton, and Lichtenstein (1995), the scale was used to help establish the construct validity of four vanity-related scales. **Entitlement** had significant positive correlations with all of the vanity scales.

ADMINISTRATION: As noted, the scale was used in two studies, and it appears to have been part of larger questionnaires that were self-administered by respondents (Netemeyer, Burton, and Lichtenstein 1995). Higher scores on the scale indicated that respondents believed they are entitled to things from the world.

MAJOR FINDINGS: Netemeyer, Burton, and Lichtenstein (1995) investigated vanity and developed four scales for its measurement. Most of the article discussed the results of the rather extensive validation process. As noted previously, the findings indicated that **entitlement** had positive relationships with each of the vanity scales; the highest correlation for all of the samples was with achievement concern (#395).

REFERENCES:
Netemeyer, Richard G. (1997), personal correspondence.
———, Scot Burton, and Donald R. Lichtenstein (1995), "Trait Aspects of Vanity: Measurement and Relevance to Consumer Behavior," *JCR*, 21 (March), 612–26.
Raskin, Robert and Howard Terry (1988), "A Principal-Components Analysis of the Narcissistic Personality Inventory and Further Evidence of its Construct Validity," *Journal of Personality and Social Psychology*, 54 (May), 890–902.

SCALE ITEMS:

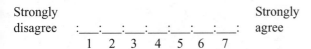

Strongly   Strongly
disagree :___:___:___:___:___:___: agree
           1   2   3   4   5   6   7

#146 *Entitlement*

1. I will never be satisfied until I get all that I deserve.

2. I expect a great deal from other people.

3. I want to amount to something in the eyes of the world.

4. I have a strong will to power.

5. I insist on getting the respect that is due me.

6. If I ruled the world it would be a much better place.

SCALE NAME: Environmental Paradigm

SCALE DESCRIPTION: Twelve four-point Likert-type items purported to measure a person's world-view as it pertains to the environment and people's relationship to it. Response to most of the items appears to hinge on whether humans should adapt to the environment or if it is appropriate to use the environment as humankind desires. The scale was referred to as the *new environmental paradigm* by its creators (Dunlap and Van Liere 1978) because this view was perceived as contrasting with the more dominant paradigm of the time, which was not particularly proenvironment.

SCALE ORIGIN: The scale was constructed by Dunlap and Van Liere (1978). Alphas of .81 (general public) and .76 (environmentalists) were reported. The scale was unidimensional and showed modest evidence of validity.

SAMPLES: Data were collected as part of a larger advertising study from undergraduate students in business and communication (Schuhwerk and Lefkoff-Hagius 1995). Analysis was based on completed questionnaires from **71** students. More than half of the sample were women (56%), and the average age of the respondents was 22 years.

RELIABILITY: Schuhwerk and Lefkoff-Hagius (1995) reported an alpha of **.83** for the scale.

VALIDITY: Although Schuhwerk and Lefkoff-Hagius (1995) did not report explicit validation efforts, they did compare scores on this scale with one they created measuring a related construct (see #202). The correlation of the two scales was .65 and suggests a degree of convergent validity.

ADMINISTRATION: Subjects filled out the scale, along with other measures, after they were exposed to experimental stimuli (Schuhwerk and Lefkoff-Hagius 1995). Higher scores on the scale suggested that respondents had a worldview that stressed environmental quality.

MAJOR FINDINGS: Schuhwerk and Lefkoff-Hagius (1995) examined how consumers respond to ads that vary in their prominence of "green" appeals. The **environmental paradigm** scale was not used in the main analysis and appears to have merely been used in the development of an environmental involvement scale (#202).

REFERENCES:
Dunlap, Riley E. and Kent D. Van Liere (1978), "The 'New Environmental Paradigm,'" *The Journal of Environmental Education*, 9 (Summer), 10–19.
Schuhwerk, Melody E. and Roxanne Lefkoff-Hagius (1995), "Green or Non-Green? Does Type of Appeal Matter When Advertising a Green Product?" *JA*, 24 (Summer), 45–54.

SCALE ITEMS:*

Strongly disagree	Mildly disagree	Mildly agree	Strongly agree
1	2	3	4

1. We are approaching the limit of the number of people the earth can support.

2. The balance of nature is very delicate and easily upset.

3. Humans have the right to modify the natural environment to suit their needs.

4. Mankind was created to rule over the rest of nature.

5. When humans interfere with nature it often produces disastrous consequences.

6. Plants and animals exist primarily to be used by humans.

7. To maintain a healthy economy we will have to develop a "steady state" economy where industrial growth is controlled.

8. Humans must live in harmony with nature in order to survive.

9. The earth is like a spaceship with only limited room and resources.

10. Humans need not adapt to the natural environment because they can remake it to suit their needs.

11. There are limits to growth beyond which our industrialized society cannot expand.

12. Mankind is severely abusing the environment.

*The response format used by Schuhwerk and Lefkoff-Hagius (1995) was not described. This four-point format was used by Dunlap and Van Liere (1978).

SCALE NAME: Ethical Perspective (Idealism)

SCALE DESCRIPTION: Ten five-point Likert-type items purported to measure the degree to which a person's moral philosophy is based on an understanding of the inherent propriety of an action, regardless of its consequences. In particular, the items focus on the assumption that desirable results can be obtained if the "right" action is taken.

SCALE ORIGIN: The scale used by Treise and colleagues (1994) was a slightly modified version of the EPQ (Ethics Perception Questionnaire) scale constructed originally by Forsyth (1980). The changes were limited to rewording some of the statements when it was found that pretest subjects did not understand the phrasing accurately.

The article by Forsyth (1980) provided information that showed the scale had high internal consistency and reasonable stability over time and that it demonstrated convergent, discriminant, and predictive validity.

SAMPLES: Data were gathered by Treise and colleagues (1994) through mall intercept surveys in a Southeastern U.S. city. Interviewers were asked to approach a wide variety of people. Those who volunteered to participate completed the survey in private and were paid $2. Usable survey forms were collected from **292** individuals. A little more than half of the sample were women female (55%), and 57% were described as having a Euro-American ethnicity. Half of the respondents were between the ages of 22 and 40 years, and 74% had more than a high school level of education.

RELIABILITY: An alpha of **.82** was reported for the scale by Treise and colleagues (1994).

VALIDITY: The validity of the scale was not examined by Treise and colleagues (1994). It is worth noting, however, that the scale based on the other dimension of the EPQ (*relativism*) was uncorrelated with this scale (*idealism*). This provides some initial evidence of the scale's discriminant validity.

ADMINISTRATION: The scale was completed by respondents, along with other measures, in a paper-and-pencil format (Treise et al. 1994). Lower scores on the scale suggested that respondents had an idealistic ethical perspective and judged actions in terms of their intrinsic morality, regardless of the context.

MAJOR FINDINGS: The research by Treise and colleagues (1994) studied the influence a person's moral ideology has on perception of several familiar advertising controversies. Among the findings were that those high in **idealism** were more likely to object to cartoon/product tie-ins, gum and candy ads aimed at kids, cigarette ads aimed at inner city minorities, and ads portraying women as contented homemakers.

COMMENTS: A median score of 28 was reported for the scale by Treise and colleagues (1994).

REFERENCES:
Forsyth, Donelson R. (1980), "A Taxonomy of Ethical Ideologies," *Journal of Personality and Social Psychology*, 39 (1), 175–84.
Treise, Debbie, Michael F. Weigold, Jenneane Conna, and Heather Garrison (1994), "Ethics in Advertising: Ideological Correlates of Consumer Perceptions," *JA*, 23 (September), 59–69.

#148 *Ethical Perspective (Idealism)*

SCALE ITEMS:*

Strongly   Strongly
agree   :___:___:___:___:___: disagree
                   1   2   3   4   5

1. A person should make certain that their actions never intentionally harm another even to a small degree.

2. Risks to another should never be tolerated, irrespective of how small the risks might be.

3. The existence of potential harm to others is always wrong, irrespective of the benefits to be gained.

4. One should never psychologically or physically harm another person.

5. One should not perform an action which might in any way threaten the dignity and welfare of another individual.

6. If an action could harm an innocent other, then it should not be done.

7. Deciding whether or not to perform an act by balancing the positive consequences of the act against the negative consequences of the act is immoral.

8. The dignity and welfare of people should be the most important concern of any society.

9. It is never necessary to sacrifice the welfare of others.

10. Moral actions are those which closely match ideals of the most "perfect" action.

*These items are from Forsyth's (1980) version of the scale. The modified items used by Treise and colleagues (1994) were not reported.

SCALE NAME: Ethical Perspective (Relativism)

SCALE DESCRIPTION: Ten five-point Likert-type items purported to measure the degree to which a person's moral philosophy assumes that the propriety of actions should be judged on the basis of the context of time, culture, and place rather than some set of universal moral rules.

SCALE ORIGIN: The scale used by Treise and colleagues (1994) was a slightly modified version of the EPQ (Ethics Perception Questionnaire) scale constructed originally by Forsyth (1980). The changes were limited to rewording some of the statements when it was found that pretest subjects did not understand the phrasing accurately.

   The article by Forsyth (1980) provided information that showed the scale had high internal consistency and reasonable stability over time and that it demonstrated convergent, discriminant, and predictive validity.

SAMPLES: Data were gather by Treise and colleagues (1994) through mall intercept surveys in a Southeastern U.S. city. Interviewers were asked to approach a wide variety of people. Those who volunteered to participate completed the survey in private and were paid $2. Usable survey forms were collected from **292** individuals. A little more than half of the sample were women (55%), and 57% were described as having a Euro-American ethnicity. Half of the respondents were between the ages of 22 and 40 years, and 74% had more than a high school level of education.

RELIABILITY: An alpha of **.82** was reported for the scale by Treise and colleagues (1994).

VALIDITY: The validity of the scale was not examined by Treise and colleagues (1994). It is worth noting, however, that the scale based on the other dimension of the EPQ (*idealism*) was uncorrelated with this scale (*relativism*). This provides some initial evidence of the scale's discriminant validity.

ADMINISTRATION: The scale was completed by respondents, along with other measures, in a paper-and-pencil format (Treise et al. 1994). Lower scores on the scale suggested that respondents viewed ethics from a relativistic point of view and thought the "proper" ethics depended on the person and situation.

MAJOR FINDINGS: The research by Treise and colleagues (1994) studied the influence a person's moral ideology has on perception of several familiar advertising controversies. Among the findings were that those low in **relativism** were more likely to object to cartoon/product tie-ins, gum and candy ads aimed at kids, and ads aimed at inner city minorities for such products as cigarettes, liquor, and lotteries.

COMMENTS: A median score of 22 was reported for the scale by Treise and colleagues (1994).

REFERENCES:
Forsyth, Donelson R. (1980), "A Taxonomy of Ethical Ideologies," *Journal of Personality and Social Psychology*, 39 (1), 175–84.
Treise, Debbie, Michael F. Weigold, Jenneane Conna, and Heather Garrison (1994), "Ethics in Advertising: Ideological Correlates of Consumer Perceptions," *JA*, 23 (September), 59–69.

SCALE ITEMS:*

Strongly   Strongly
agree   :___:___:___:___:___: disagree
            1   2   3   4   5

#149 *Ethical Perspective (Relativism)*

1. There are no ethical principles that are so important that they should be part of any code of ethics.

2. What is ethical varies from one situation and society to another.

3. Moral standards should be seen as being individualistic; what one person considers to be moral may be judged to be immoral by another person.

4. Different types of moralities cannot be compared as to "rightness."

5. Questions of what is ethical for everyone can never be resolved since what is moral or immoral is up to the individual.

6. Moral standards are simply *personal* rules which indicate how a person should behave, and are not to be applied in making judgments of others.

7. Ethical considerations in interpersonal relations are so complex that individuals should be allowed to formulate their own individual codes.

8. Rigidly codifying an ethical position that prevents certain types of actions could stand in the way of better human relations and adjustment.

9. No rule concerning lying can be formulated; whether a lie is permissible or not permissible totally depends upon the situation.

10. Whether a lie is judged to be moral or immoral depends upon the circumstances surrounding the actions.

*These items are from Forsyth's (1980) version of the scale. The modified items used by Treise and colleagues (1994) were not reported.

SCALE NAME: Ethicality (Moral Equity/Relativism Dimension)

SCALE DESCRIPTION: A six-item, seven-point semantic differential that measures the degree to which a person's evaluation of the propriety of some stimulus is based on lessons learned early in life from such institutions as the family and religion, as well as what the person considers socially acceptable.

SCALE ORIGIN: The items in this scale were developed and tested by Reidenbach and Robin (1988, 1990). Along with two more items, these constructed the Multidimensional Ethics Scale (MES). The items shown here were thought to represent two of the MES's three dimensions: *moral equity* and *relativism*. Sometimes these two dimensions are measured together in one simple summated scale (LaTour and Henthorne 1994; LaTour, Snipes, and Bliss 1996), whereas at other times, they are measured separately (Reidenbach and Robin 1990; Smith and Cooper-Martin 1997) (see "Validity").

SAMPLES: Data were gathered by LaTour and Henthorne (1994, p. 83) through mall intercept surveys in a "culturally vibrant MSA in the mid-Gulf Coast region." Interviewers were trained and rotated in a random pattern throughout the mall. Of the shoppers approached, 85% participated. To complete the questionnaire, shoppers were taken to a private yet monitored area. Usable survey forms were collected from **199** individuals. The sample was described as having an average age of 34.3 years and an average of 13.8 years of education and as coming from widely different income levels. A little more than half of the respondents were women (53%), 75.7% were white, and 47.5% were married.

LaTour, Snipes, and Bliss (1996, p. 62) conducted a field experiment using **305** respondents captured through mall intercepts in a "demographically diverse SMSA in the southeastern United States." Given the nature of the study, the sample and the interviewers were all women. The majority of the respondents were white (79%) and married (60%). The mean age of the respondents was 28 years, and the mean education level was 14 years.

Two studies were reported by Smith and Cooper-Martin (1997). In both cases, respondents were approached while they waited for something (to catch a train or see a historic site). Study 1 was based on completed data received from **522** nonstudent adults. The sample was 52% women and 79% white, 38 to 47 was the median age category, and the median education level was a college degree. Study 2 was based on completed surveys from **322** people. The sample was 41% women and 78% white, 38 to 47 was the median age category, and the median education level was a college degree.

RELIABILITY: Alphas of **.92** and **.90** were found for the scale as used by LaTour and Henthorne (1994) and LaTour, Snipes, and Bliss (1996; LaTour 1997), respectively. Smith and Cooper-Martin (1997) measured the subscales of the MES separately in the two studies they conducted and reported the following alpha estimates of reliability for the items: *moral equity* (**.93**, **.91**) and *relativism* (**.70**, **.69**).

VALIDITY: Some evidence of the unidimensionality of the six items comes from the exploratory factor analysis, in which they loaded high ($\geq.78$) on one factor and low ($\leq.38$) on another factor that represented the *contractualism* dimension of ethicality (LaTour and Henthorne 1994). It should be noted that items 1–4 were expected to represent the *moral equity* dimension of ethicality, whereas items 5 and 6 were thought to measure *relativism*. The factor analyses have tended to show, however, that the items load together (LaTour, Snipes, and Bliss 1996).

Smith and Cooper-Martin (1997) provided some evidence that they claim supports the construct validity of the MES, but no evidence was reported that supported the discriminant validity of the subscales.

ADMINISTRATION: In each study, respondents completed the scale, along with other measures, in self-administered questionnaires. Those who scored high on the scale were viewed as evaluating some stimulus positively because of their moral philosophies, which are strongly influenced by traditional morality and social acceptability.

MAJOR FINDINGS: LaTour and Henthorne (1994) investigated the ethical judgments made by consumers regarding sexual appeals in print advertising. The results showed that strong sex-related appeals were not viewed favorably. Specifically, the group that received an ad with a "mild" sexual appeal viewed it as being significantly more **ethical** than the group that received an ad with a strong, overt sexual appeal.

The field experiment conducted by LaTour, Snipes, and Bliss (1996) examined the perceived ethicality of the use of fear appeals with a potentially sensitive audience. Among the findings was that subjects seeing an ad with a strong fear appeal did not consider them significantly different in terms of **ethicality** than did subjects who saw the ad with a milder fear appeal.

The purpose of the studies by Smith and Cooper-Martin (1997) was to examine the conditions in which criticism of target marketing was likely to arise. Among the findings was that targeting of products viewed as more harmful and targeting any products specifically to "vulnerable" groups of consumers are viewed as significantly less **ethical** than alternative strategies.

COMMENTS: See also LaFleur, Reidenbach, Robin, and Forrest (1996) for a use of the scale with advertising professionals.

REFERENCES:

LaFleur, Elizabeth K., R. Eric Reidenbach, Donald P. Robin, and P.J. Forrest (1996), "An Exploration of Rule Configuration Effects on the Ethical Decision Processes of Advertising Professionals," *JAMS*, 24 (1), 66–76.

LaTour, Michael S. (1997), personal correspondence.

———— and Tony L. Henthorne (1994), "Ethical Judgments of Sexual Appeals in Print Advertising," *JA*, 23 (September), 81–90.

————, Robin L. Snipes, and Sara J. Bliss (1996), "Don't Be Afraid to Use Fear Appeals: An Experimental Study," *JAR*, 36 (March/April), 59–67.

Reidenbach, R. Eric and Donald P. Robin (1988), "Some Initial Steps Toward Improving the Measurement of Ethical Evaluations of Marketing Activities," *Journal of Business Ethics*, 7 (July), 871–79.

———— and ———— (1990), "Toward the Development of a Multidimensional Scale for Improving Evaluations of Business Ethics," *Journal of Business Ethics*, 9 (August), 639–53.

Smith, N. Craig and Elizabeth Cooper-Martin (1997), "Ethics and Target Marketing: The Role of Product Harm and Consumer Vulnerability," *JM*, 61 (July), 1–20.

SCALE ITEMS:

1. Unjust   :___:___:___:___:___:___:___: Just
                1   2   3   4   5   6   7

2. Unacceptable   Acceptable
   to my family   :___:___:___:___:___:___:___: to my family
                   1   2   3   4   5   6   7

3. Unfair   :___:___:___:___:___:___:___: Fair
                1   2   3   4   5   6   7

4. Not morally   Morally
   right   :__:__:__:__:__:__:__: right
                      1   2   3   4   5   6   7

5. Culturally   Culturally
   unacceptable   :__:__:__:__:__:__:__: acceptable
                      1   2   3   4   5   6   7

6. Traditionally   Traditionally
   unacceptable   :__:__:__:__:__:__:__: acceptable
                      1   2   3   4   5   6   7

SCALE NAME: Ethnic Identification

SCALE DESCRIPTION: Four five-point Likert-type statements that measure the strength of a person's desire to be associated with a particular subculture. The subculture studied by Donthu and Cherian (1994) was Hispanics in the United States.

SCALE ORIGIN: Although Donthu and Cherian (1994) drew on several previous measures, this scale as a whole is original to their study.

SAMPLES: Donthu and Cherian (1994) mailed survey instruments in both Spanish and English to 1000 people with Hispanic surnames from a database of a major marketing research agency. The questionnaires were refined through a back-translation technique and pretested by bilingual students and a convenience sample.

Envelopes were addressed to the "adult of the household." Just those who identified themselves as Hispanic were included in the final sample. Of the questionnaires returned, **240** (160 men) were considered useful. The average respondent was approximately 30 years of age, had a household income of between $20,000 and $29,000, and had "some schooling."

RELIABILITY: An alpha of **.79** was reported for the scale (Donthu and Cherian 1994).

VALIDITY: No specific examination of scale validity was reported by Donthu and Cherian (1994).

ADMINISTRATION: The scale was self-administered, along with other measures, in a mail survey instrument (Donthu and Cherian 1994). Higher scores on the scale indicated that respondents had a strong identification with a specified ethnic group.

MAJOR FINDINGS: Donthu and Cherian (1994) investigated the impact that strength of ethnic group **identification** had on various aspects of shopping behavior. Among the findings was that those with strong **identification** with the Hispanic culture considered it significantly more important to find Hispanic vendors than did those who had weaker **identification**.

COMMENTS: Donthu and Cherian (1994) used a mean split to separate respondents on the basis of their strength of **identification** with the Hispanic subculture. The group with strong **identification** had a mean of 2.96 (n = 106) on the scale, compared with a mean of 2.26 (n = 134) for those in the group who expressed weaker **identification**.

REFERENCES:
Donthu, Naveen and Joseph Cherian (1994), "Impact of Strength of Ethnic Identification on Hispanic Shopping Behavior," *JR*, 70 (4), 383–93.

SCALE ITEMS:*

1. How strongly do you identify with the *Hispanic* culture?

Not at all   :___:___:___:___:___: A lot
                     1   2   3   4   5

2. How important is it to assimilate with the dominant *Anglo* culture? **(r)**

Not at all   :___:___:___:___:___: A lot
                     1   2   3   4   5

3. How important is it to maintain identity with your *Hispanic* culture?

Not at all :___:___:___:___:___: A lot
            1   2   3   4   5

4. How often do you speak *Spanish*?

Never :___:___:___:___:___: All the time
        1   2   3   4   5

*This scale is reconstructed on the basis of the description in the article by Donthu and Cherian (1994). The italicized terms in these statements could be replaced by other terms if a different ethnic group was being studied.

SCALE NAME: Ethnocentrism (CETSCALE)

SCALE DESCRIPTION: A seventeen-item, seven-point Likert-type summated ratings scale measuring a respondent's attitude toward the appropriateness of purchasing American-made products versus those manufactured in other countries. The scale was called CETSCALE (consumers' ethnocentric tendencies) by its originators (Shimp and Sharma 1987). A revised version of the scale was used by Herche (1992).

SCALE ORIGIN: The scale is original to the studies reported by Shimp and Sharma (1987). Development of the scale passed through several stages and employed many different samples. The information provided here is primarily based on the final seventeen-item version of the scale rather than the larger preliminary sets.

Four separate samples were used to assess the psychometric properties of the CETSCALE. One sample used names and addresses obtained from a list broker. One thousand questionnaires were mailed to each of three deliberately chosen cities: Detroit, Denver, and Los Angeles. The response rate was just less than one-third for each area. At the same time, 950 questionnaires were sent to former panel members in the Carolinas. The response rate was nearly 60%. The total sample size in this "four-areas study" was **1535**. The "Carolinas study" was composed of a group of **417** people who were a part of the "four-areas study." Data for the former study were collected two years prior to the latter. A smaller, ten-item version of the scale was tested in a national consumer goods study. A total of more than **2000** completed responses were received. A fourth study examined data from **145** college students. Although they had varying proportions, each of the samples, except for the student group, had respondents representing most age and income groups.

SAMPLES: Data were collected by Herche (1992) in nationwide mail survey of 1000 car and 1000 PC owners. Eight hundred six people returned questionnaires, but only **520** were complete enough to be used in the analysis. Of these, 320 were from car buyers and 200 were from PC buyers. Most regions of the country and many occupational groups were represented in both of the samples. In addition, a majority of each sample were college graduates and were men, earned more than $35,000 a year, and were married. The mean age of respondents in both samples was in the low to middle 40s. The sample compositions were different, in that the car group had many more retirees and the PC group seemed to have more professionals. The PC group also seemed to be better educated and have greater incomes.

Netemeyer, Durvasula, and Lichtenstein (1991) used undergraduate students studying business in four different countries. The sample consisted of **76** subjects from two universities in Japan, **70** subjects from a college in France, **73** subjects from a college in Germany, and **71** subjects from a major state university in the United States.

Data were gathered from Korean consumers by Sharma, Shimp, and Shin (1995) using two sampling methods. Questionnaires were mailed to 1500 names taken from a economically diverse mailing list company's database. Usable survey forms were returned by **125** people. The second method involved distributing 700 questionnaires to students at several schools in Seoul and in a southern Korean city. Completed questionnaires were received from **542** people. The samples were not significantly different in their demographic variables or response to dependent variables, so the authors chose to combine them for the analysis. The combined sample was 57% men and had an average education level of slightly more than 13 years and a mean age of 42 years.

RELIABILITY: The alpha for the revised version of the scale used by Herche (1992) was **.93**. Netemeyer, Durvasula, and Lichtenstein (1991) reported alphas of **.91**, **.92**, **.94**, and **.95** for the Japanese, French, German, and American samples, respectively. Alphas of between **.94** and **.96** were found for the scale in the four samples used by Shimp and Sharma (1987). Test–retest reliability was estimated with the student sample only. With a five-week interval between administrations, a correlation of .77 was reported.

Sharma, Shimp, and Shin (1995) performed confirmatory factor analysis (CFA) on this scale, as well as on others in the study. A reliability coefficient of **.91** was reported for the CETSCALE on the basis of a holdout sample (n = 333).

VALIDITY: Although bearing somewhat on the scale's predictive validity, the study by Herche (1992) did not directly assess the scale's construct validity. However, the revised version of the scale he used was cited in an previous paper (Herche 1990) as a superior measure to the original CETSCALE. In that earlier paper, Herche argued that the absence of negatively stated items in the scale made it vulnerable to response bias. He developed a version of the scale with seven of the original items stated in the opposite direction, which were reverse coded during summation. The evidence indicated that the revised version of the scale explained substantially more variance than the original and had a better factor structure. He later recanted his recommendations (Herche and Engelland 1994, 1996) by providing evidence that there may be a significant threat to a scale's unidimensionality when both reversed- and standard-polarity items are included.

Using the original version of the scale and CFA, Netemeyer, Durvasula, and Lichtenstein (1991) found evidence that it was unidimensional and had adequate discriminant validity. Moderate support was also found for the scale's nomological validity.

Convergent, discriminant, and nomological validity were addressed by Shimp and Sharma (1987) and provided evidence of the scale's quality. Some of the specific evidence is discussed under "Major findings." Sharma, Shimp, and Shin (1995) made a general claim of discriminant and convergent validity for all of their scales on the basis of the results of a CFA.

ADMINISTRATION: The version of the scale used by Herche (1992) was part of a larger mail survey instrument. Netemeyer, Durvasula, and Lichtenstein (1991) administered the scale as part of a larger questionnaire during class time. The survey instrument went through a series of translations, back-translations, pretests, and retranslations to ensure that the four different language versions were as similar in meaning as possible. The scale was self-administered in the studies conducted by Shimp and Sharma (1987; Sharma, Shimp, and Shin 1995), along with other measures, as part of a larger survey instrument.

Scores on the scale can range from 17 to 119. Higher scores implied that respondents strongly believed in buying American-made products, whereas lower scores suggested that respondents did not think buying domestically produced goods was particularly important.

MAJOR FINDINGS: The predictive validity of the revised version of the CETSCALE was explored by Herche (1992). It was found that the CETSCALE is better than demographic variables in understanding import buying behavior. However, the findings also suggested that the predictive validity of the scale could be product-specific. Specifically, there was a much higher negative correlation between **ethnocentrism** and ownership of goods perceived as being foreign-made for cars than for PCs.

Netemeyer, Durvasula, and Lichtenstein (1991) examined the psychometric properties of the **CETSCALE** using homogeneous samples from four countries that actively trade with one another. The scale was found to be translatable and showed strong evidence of internal consistency and unidimensionality, as well as some evidence of discriminant and nomological validities.

The purpose of the study by Shimp and Sharma (1987) was to describe the construction and validation of the CETSCALE. In one or more samples, **ethnocentrism** was found to have a significant positive correlation with the following variables: patriotism, politicoeconomic conservatism, dogmatism, domestic car ownership, intent to purchase a domestic car, and country-of-origin importance. **Ethnocentrism** had a significant negative correlation with attitude toward foreign-made products.

The study by Sharma, Shimp, and Shin (1995) identified antecedents of **ethnocentricity**, as well as the influence of **ethnocentricity** on the attitude toward imported products. The results supported the hypothesis that people with collectivistic goals would have greater **ethnocentristic** tendencies than those with individualistic goals.

REFERENCES:

Herche, Joel (1990), "The Measurement of Consumer Ethnocentrism: Revisiting the CETSCALE," in *Proceedings of the Thirteenth Annual Conference of the Academy of Marketing Science*, B.J. Dunlap, ed. Cullowhee, NC., Western Carolina University, 371–75.

———— (1992), "A Note on the Predictive Validity of the CETSCALE," *JAMS*, 20 (Summer), 261–64.

———— and Brian Engelland (1994), "Reversed-Polarity Items, Attribution Effects and Scale Dimensionality," *Office of Scale Research Technical Report #9401*, Marketing Department, Southern Illinois University.

———— and ———— (1996), "Reversed-Polarity Items and Scale Unidimensionality," *JAMS*, 24 (Fall), 366–74.

Netemeyer, Richard G., Srinvas Durvasula, and Donald R. Lichtenstein (1991), "A Cross-National Assessment of the Reliability and Validity of the CETSCALE," *JMR*, 28 (August), 320–27.

Sharma, Subhash, Terence A. Shimp, and Jeongshin Shin (1995), "Consumer Ethnocentrism: A Test of Antecedents and Moderators," *JAMS*, 23 (Winter), 26–37.

Shimp, Terence A. and Subhash Sharma (1987), "Consumer Ethnocentrism: Construction and Validation of the CETSCALE," *JMR*, 24 (August), 280–89.

SCALE ITEMS:*

DIRECTIONS: Please respond to the following statements by circling a number from 1 to 7 according to these directions:

1 = Strongly disagree
2 = Moderately disagree
3 = Slightly disagree
4 = Neither agree nor disagree
5 = Slightly agree
6 = Moderately agree
7 = Strongly agree

1. American people should always buy American-made products instead of imports.

2. Only those products that are unavailable in the U.S. should be imported.

3. Buy American-made products. Keep America working.

4. American products first, last, and foremost.

5. Purchasing foreign-made products is un-American.

6. It is not right to purchase foreign products, because it puts Americans out of jobs.

7. A real American should always buy American-made products.

8. We should purchase products manufactured in America instead of letting other countries get rich off us.

9. It is always best to purchase American products.

10. There should be very little trading or purchasing of goods from other countries unless out of necessity.

11. Americans should not buy foreign products, because this hurts American business and causes unemployment.

12. Curbs should be put on all imports.

13. It may cost me in the long run but I prefer to support American products.

14. Foreigners should not be allowed to put their products on our markets.

15. Foreign products should be taxed heavily to reduce their entry into the U.S.

16. We should buy from foreign countries only those products that we cannot obtain within our own country.

17. American consumers who purchase products made in other countries are responsible for putting their fellow Americans out of work.

*The seven items altered by Herche (1990, 1992) were 1, 5, 7, 9, 12, 14, and 17. The alterations in each case essentially amounted to the addition of the word "not" in the sentence. The ten items used in the national consumer goods study by Shimp and Sharma (1987) were 2, 4–8, 11, 13, 16, and 17.

SCALE NAME: Exhibitionism

SCALE DESCRIPTION: Seven seven-point Likert-type statements that evaluate a person's willingness to do whatever it takes to be the center of attention.

SCALE ORIGIN: The scale is original to the study by Raskin and Terry (1988) and is part of the Narcissistic Personality Inventory (NPI). Of the 40-item NPI, the seven items shown here loaded highest on the same dimension and were labeled **exhibitionism**. The internal consistency of these items as a set was estimated to be .63 (n = 1018). The scale showed little or no relationship with age and gender. Considerable evidence in support of the scale's nomological validity was provided.

SAMPLES: Various samples were collected and used by Netemeyer, Burton, and Lichtenstein (1995) in the process of validating other scales. The **exhibitionism** scale was used in one study composed of 186 students and 264 "nonstudent adults." It was used in another study with data from 27 football players from a nationally ranked NCAA Division I team.

RELIABILITY: Alphas of **.84** (students) and **.86** (nonstudent adults) were found for the scale by Netemeyer, Burton, and Lichtenstein (1995; Netemeyer 1997).

VALIDITY: Although the validity of the scale was not directly examined by Netemeyer, Burton, and Lichtenstein (1995), the scale was used to help establish the construct validity of four vanity-related scales. **Exhibitionism** had significant positive correlations with all of the vanity scales, with the possible exception of physical concern (#397), depending on the sample.

ADMINISTRATION: As noted, the scale was used in two studies, and it appears to have been part of larger questionnaires that were self-administered by respondents (Netemeyer, Burton, and Lichtenstein 1995). Higher scores on the scale indicated that respondents craved attention and were willing to do what it takes to attract it.

MAJOR FINDINGS: Netemeyer, Burton, and Lichtenstein (1995) investigated vanity and developed four scales for its measurement. Most of the article discussed the results of the rather extensive validation process. Among the findings was that **exhibitionism** had positive relationships with each of the vanity scales, with the strongest relationships being with physical view (#398) and achievement concern (#395).

REFERENCES:
Netemeyer, Richard G. (1997), personal correspondence.
———, Scot Burton, and Donald R. Lichtenstein (1995), "Trait Aspects of Vanity: Measurement and Relevance to Consumer Behavior," *JCR*, 21 (March), 612–26.
Raskin, Robert and Howard Terry (1988), "A Principal-Components Analysis of the Narcissistic Personality Inventory and Further Evidence of its Construct Validity," *Journal of Personality and Social Psychology*, 54 (May), 890–902.

SCALE ITEMS:

Strongly disagree : __ : __ : __ : __ : __ : __ : Strongly agree
1 2 3 4 5 6 7

1. I am apt to show off if I get the chance.

2. Modesty doesn't become me.

3. I get upset when people don't notice how I look when I go out in public.

4. I like to be the center of attention.

5. I would do almost anything on a dare.

6. I really like to be the center of attention.

7. I like to start new fads and fashions.

SCALE NAME: Experiential Response to Music

SCALE DESCRIPTION: A five-item, six-point Likert-type scale measuring the degree to which a person reports being absorbed by a song or feels carried off or lost in the experience.

SCALE ORIGIN: The multi-item version of this scale appears to be original to Mizerski and colleagues (1988), who built on an item developed by Swanson (1978) for measuring involvement in various activities. Mizerski and colleagues (1988) used the scale with four different songs, and the alphas ranged from .90 to .93. The study also provided evidence for the convergent and discriminant validity of the scale.

SAMPLES: The sample used by Lacher and Mizerski (1994) came from undergraduate business students at a large Southern U.S. university. Usable data were collected from **215** students, who were composed of 52% men and ranged in age from 19 to 36 years.

RELIABILITY: Alphas for the fast- and slow-tempo songs in the study by Lacher and Mizerski (1994) were **.85** and **.92**, respectively (Lacher 1997).

VALIDITY: No examination of scale validity was reported by Lacher and Mizerski (1994) beyond that noted for the study's pretest.

ADMINISTRATION: The scale was self-administered, along with other measures, in the study by Lacher and Mizerski (1994). Students heard a song twice, and the second time it was played, they filled out this scale along with other measures. Higher scores on the scale indicated that respondents perceived that a particular song had absorbed them so much that they felt carried away by the music.

MAJOR FINDINGS: Lacher and Mizerski (1994) investigated the responses music evokes in a listener and how those reactions affect the intention to purchase the music. Among the findings was that the **experiential response** had a greater direct effect on the need to reexperience the music (#239) than did affect toward the music (#2).

REFERENCES:

Lacher, Kathleen T. (1997), personal correspondence.

———— and Richard Mizerski (1994), "An Exploratory Study of the Responses and Relationships Involved in the Evaluation of and in the Intention to Purchase New Rock Music," *JCR*, 21 (September), 366–80.

Mizerski, Richard, Marya J. Pucely, Pamela Perrewe, and Lori Baldwin (1988), "An Experimental Evaluation of Music Involvement Measures and Their Relationship with Consumer Purchasing Behavior," *Popular Music & Society*, 12 (Fall), 79–96.

Swanson, Guy E. (1978), "Travels Through Innerspace: Family Structure and Openness to Absorbing Experiences," *American Journal of Sociology*, 83 (4), 890–919.

SCALE ITEMS:

Strongly   Strongly
disagree   :___:___:___:___:___: agree
             1   2   3   4   5   6

1. I felt "carried off" by the music.

2. I felt as if I were part of the song.

3. I felt deeply about the song.

4. I will feel the experience of this song for a while.

5. I "got into" the song.

SCALE NAME: Exploitativeness

SCALE DESCRIPTION: Five seven-point Likert-type statements that evaluate a person's stated ability to manipulate and deceive others.

SCALE ORIGIN: The scale is original to the study by Raskin and Terry (1988) and is part of the Narcissistic Personality Inventory (NPI). Of the 40-item NPI, the five items shown here loaded highest on the same dimension and were labeled **exploitativeness**. The internal consistency of these items as a set was estimated to be .63 (n = 1018). The scale showed little or no relationship with age and gender. Evidence in support of the scale's nomological validity was provided.

SAMPLES: Various samples were collected and used by Netemeyer, Burton, and Lichtenstein (1995) in the process of validating other scales. The **exploitativeness** scale was used in one study composed of 186 students and 264 "nonstudent adults." It was used in another study with data from 27 football players from a nationally ranked NCAA Division I team.

RELIABILITY: Alphas of **.87** (students) and **.85** (nonstudent adults) were found for the scale by Netemeyer, Burton, and Lichtenstein (1995; Netemeyer 1997).

VALIDITY: Although the validity of the scale was not directly examined by Netemeyer, Burton, and Lichtenstein (1995), the scale was used to help establish the construct validity of four vanity-related scales. **Exploitativeness** had significant positive correlations with all of the vanity scales, with the exception of physical concern (#397), though it depended on the sample.

ADMINISTRATION: As noted, the scale was used in two studies, and it appears to have been part of larger questionnaires that were self-administered by respondents (Netemeyer, Burton, and Lichtenstein 1995). Higher scores on the scale indicated that respondents believed they have the ability to manipulate and deceive others.

MAJOR FINDINGS: Netemeyer, Burton, and Lichtenstein (1995) investigated vanity and developed four scales for its measurement. Most of the article discussed the results of the rather extensive validation process. As noted previously, the findings indicated that **exploitativeness** had positive relationships with each of the vanity scales, with the possible exception of the physical concern scale (#397) because correlations were different for the football players compared with the other samples.

REFERENCES:
Netemeyer, Richard G. (1997), personal correspondence.
———, Scot Burton, and Donald R. Lichtenstein (1995), "Trait Aspects of Vanity: Measurement and Relevance to Consumer Behavior," *JCR*, 21 (March), 612–26.
Raskin, Robert and Howard Terry (1988), "A Principal-Components Analysis of the Narcissistic Personality Inventory and Further Evidence of its Construct Validity," *Journal of Personality and Social Psychology*, 54 (May), 890–902.

SCALE ITEMS:

Strongly   Strongly
disgree   :___:___:___:___:___:___:___: agree
      1   2   3   4   5   6   7

#155 *Exploitativeness*

1. I can read people like a book.

2. I can make anybody believe anything I want them to.

3. I find it easy to manipulate people.

4. I can usually talk my way out of anything.

5. Everybody likes to hear my stories.

SCALE NAME: Exploratory Consumer Tendencies

SCALE DESCRIPTION: Multiple Likert-type items measuring the degree to which a person expresses preference for consumer-related situations that call for greater exploratory consumer behavior and that produce stimulation from the person's environment. The scale was referred to as *optimum stimulation level* (OSL) by Menon and Kahn (1995), though it would appear that OSL is a more general personality trait that is one determinant of (rather than being equivalent to) the consumer behaviors referred to in this scale. Following Baumgartner and Steenkamp (1996), Van Trijp, Hoyer, and Inman (1996) referred to their measure as *exploratory acquisition of products* and viewed it as measuring the consumer's need for variety.

SCALE ORIGIN: The scale used by Menon and Kahn (1995) is a 30-item subset of 39 items developed by Raju (1980). An initial pool of 90 items related to exploratory behavior and lifestyle were compiled and tested for low social desirability bias and high item–total correlations. Thirty-nine items were found to meet the criteria and were tested with two separate samples. Menon and Kahn (1995) used those items that Raju's (1980) findings indicated had the highest correlations with arousal-seeking tendency (Mehrabian and Russell 1974, pp. 218, 219) and were not specific to any product category (Kahn 1997).

Van Trijp, Hoyer, and Inman (1996) used a six-item version of a scale validated by Baumgartner and Steenkamp (1996), which in turn was mostly composed of items taken from Raju (1980). Van Trijp, Hoyer, and Inman (1996) indicate that, using Baumgartner and Steenkamp's (1996) own data, the six-item scale had an extremely high correlation (r = .96) with the ten-item version.

SAMPLES: Menon and Kahn (1995) conducted two experiments, but the **exploratory tendency** scale appears to have been used just in the first one. Complete data were collected from **54** undergraduate students attending a university in the Northeastern United States. Students participated in the study as a requirement in a marketing course.

The data gathered by Van Trijp, Hoyer, and Inman (1996) came from 1000 Dutch households that were part of multiweek consumer panel. The number of people providing usable data was not specified nor were their demographic characteristics.

RELIABILITY: Alphas of **.88** and **.79** were reported by Menon and Kahn (1995) and Van Trijp, Hoyer, and Inman (1996), respectively, for their different versions of the scale.

VALIDITY: No examination of the scale's validity was reported by either by Menon and Kahn (1995) or Van Trijp, Hoyer, and Inman (1996).

ADMINISTRATION: Subjects completed the scale, along with other measures, on the fourth and last day of the experiment (Menon and Kahn 1995). Panel members in the study by Van Trijp, Hoyer, and Inman (1996) responded to questionnaires on a PC in their homes, connected by modem to a central computer. Higher scores on the scale indicated that respondents had a tendency to choose consumption-related activities and situations that call for more variety rather than sticking with the tried and true.

MAJOR FINDINGS: The purpose of the study by Menon and Kahn (1995) was to determine if increasing the variety in the choice context could decrease the amount of variety seeking in product choices and, thereby, improve brand loyalty even for those with high **exploratory tendencies**. The data confirmed this hypothesis.

Van Trijp, Hoyer, and Inman (1996) proposed that brand-switching behavior should be examined by differentiating between intrinsic (e.g., variety-seeking) and extrinsic (e.g., brand on sale) motivations.

The results indicated that variety switchers had a higher need for **exploratory** behavior than repeat purchasers did.

COMMENTS: Although the scale has high internal consistency, it almost certainly does not have unidimensionality. This conclusion is based on comments by Raju (1980) that his judgment and the results of a factor analysis led to the breaking up of the large set of items into seven different scales. Testing is called for to determine the dimensionality of this set of 30 items (a subset of Raju's 39 items). If it is not unidimensional, it would be inappropriate to use it as a summated rating scale (Gerbing and Anderson 1988).

The range of scores on the six-item version of the scale (Van Trijp, Hoyer, and Inman 1996) was from 6 to 29, with a mean of 17.7 and a standard deviation of 3.9.

REFERENCES:

Baumgartner, Hans and Jan-Benedict E.M. Steenkamp (1996), "Exploratory Consumer Buying Behavior: Conceptualization and Measurement," *International Journal of Research in Marketing*, 13 (2), 121–37.

Gerbing, David W. and James C. Anderson (1988), "An Updated Paradigm for Scale Development Incorporating Uni-dimensionality and Its Assessment," *JMR*, 25 (May), 186–92.

Kahn, Barbara E. (1997), personal correspondence.

Mehrabian, Albert and James A. Russell (1974), *An Approach to Environmental Psychology*. Cambridge, MA: The MIT Press.

Menon, Satya and Barbara E. Kahn (1995), "The Impact of Context on Variety Seeking in Product Choices," *JCR*, 22 (December), 285–95.

Raju, P. S. (1980), "Optimum Stimulation Level: Its Relationship to Personality, Demographics, and Exploratory Behavior," *JCR*, 7 (December), 272–82.

Van Trijp, Has C.M., Wayne D. Hoyer, and J. Jeffrey Inman (1996), "Why Switch? Product Category-Level Explanations for True Variety-Seeking Behavior," *JMR*, 33 (August), 281–92.

SCALE ITEMS:
DIRECTIONS: Please rate how much you agree or disagree with each of the following statements on the 9-point scale shown here. Note that '+4' implies very strong agreement, '–4' implies very strong disagreement, and '0' implies 'neither agree nor disagree.'

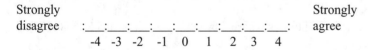

Strongly
disagree   :___:___:___:___:___:___:___:___: Strongly
         -4 -3 -2 -1 0 1 2 3 4   agree

1. Even though certain food products are available in a number of different flavors, I always tend to buy the same flavor. **(r)**

2. When I eat out, I like to try the most unusual items the restaurant serves, even if I am not sure I would like them.

3. I like to shop around and look at displays.

4. I like to browse through mail-order catalogs even when I don't plan to buy anything.

5. When I see a new or different brand on the shelf, I pick it up just to see what it is like.

6. I often read the information on the packages of products just out of curiosity.

7. I am the kind of person who would try any new product once.

8. A new store or restaurant is not something I would be eager to find out about. **(r)**

9. When I go to a restaurant, I feel it is safer to order dishes I am familiar with. **(r)**

10. I am very cautious in trying new/different products.

11. Even for an important date or dinner, I wouldn't be wary of trying a new or unfamiliar restaurant.

12. I generally read even my junk mail just to know what it is about.

13. I enjoy sampling different brands of commonplace products for the sake of comparison.

14. I would rather stick with a brand I usually buy than try something I am not very sure of. **(r)**

15. I usually throw away mail advertisements without reading them. **(r)**

16. If I like a brand, I rarely switch from it just to try something different. **(r)**

17. I often read advertisements just out of curiosity.

18. I would prefer to keep using old appliances and gadgets even if it means having to get them fixed, rather than buy new ones every few years. **(r)**

19. I would rather wait for others to try a new store or restaurant than try it myself. **(r)**

20. I get bored with buying the same brands even if they are good.

21. When I see a new brand somewhat different from the usual, I investigate it.

22. I never buy something I don't know about at the risk of making a mistake. **(r)**

23. I would get tired of flying the same airline every time.

24. If I buy appliances, I will buy only well-established brands. **(r)**

25. Investigating new brands of grocery and other similar products is generally a waste of time. **(r)**

26. I rarely read advertisements that just seem to contain a lot of information. **(r)**

27. A lot of times I feel the urge to buy something really different from the brands I usually buy.

28. I enjoy taking chances in buying unfamiliar brands just to get some variety in my purchases.

29. If I did a lot of flying, I would probably like to try all the different airlines, instead of flying just one most of the time.

30. I enjoy exploring several different alternatives or brands while shopping.

Menon and Kahn (1995): 1–30; 9-point
Van Trijp, Hoyer, and Inman (1996): 1, 9, 10, 14, 16, 28; 5-point

SCALE NAME: External Search (Friends Advice)

SCALE DESCRIPTION: Three seven-point items that measure the degree to which a consumer describes his or her tendency to discuss grocery shopping with friends and seek their advice.

SCALE ORIGIN: Although not clear from the article by Putrevu and Ratchford (1997), some of the work on the scales was conducted previously in a dissertation by Putrevu (1992).

SAMPLES: Data were gathered by Putrevu and Ratchford (1997) using a mail survey to a random sample of grocery shoppers in a standard metropolitan statistical area in the Northeastern United States. A total of **500** responses were used in the main analysis, and demographics of the final sample were similar to those of the population of interest.

RELIABILITY: An alpha of **.79** was reported for the scale (Putrevu and Ratchford 1997).

VALIDITY: Although the authors stated in general that the scales showed evidence of convergent, discriminant, and content validity, no details of the analyses were provided (Putrevu and Ratchford 1997).

ADMINISTRATION: The scale was part of a larger mail questionnaire (Putrevu and Ratchford 1997). Higher scores on the scale suggested that a consumer frequently talked about grocery shopping with friends and was interested in their suggestions.

MAJOR FINDINGS: Putrevu and Ratchford (1997) examined a dynamic model of consumer search behavior that includes human capital. In general, the results indicated that self-reported search for information about buying groceries is associated with perceptions of the costs and benefits of search, as predicted by the model.

COMMENTS: As presented in the article by Putrevu and Ratchford (1997), this scale was part of a larger measure called "Search." That measure was the mean of the scores from nine scales related to search behavior for grocery product information .

REFERENCES:
Putrevu, Sanjay (1992), "A Theory of Search and Its Empirical Investigation," doctoral dissertation, State University of New York at Buffalo.
———— and Brian T. Ratchford (1997), "A Model of Search Behavior with an Application to Grocery Shopping," *JR*, 73 (4), 463–86.

SCALE ITEMS:

Never   :___:___:___:___:___:___:___: Always
       1   2   3   4   5   6   7

1. My friends tell me if there is a sale/special at a supermarket.

2. I discuss grocery shopping with my friends.

3. I seek out the advice of my friends regarding which supermarkets to buy grocery products.

SCALE NAME: Exuberance

SCALE DESCRIPTION: A three-item, six-point summated ratings scale measuring the degree to which a person describes him- or herself as being thrilled and exhilarated by some stimulus (e.g., music). Phrasing of the scale was such that it measured the respondent's emotional reaction to a stimulus rather than attitude toward the stimulus itself.

SCALE ORIGIN: Lacher and Mizerski (1994) indicated that the scale was taken from Asmus (1985). Each of the three items here were in the *activity* factor Asmus (1985) identified in his development of a multidimensional instrument for measuring affective responses to music. Although not explicitly stated, one item from Asmus's activity scale, *determined*, was apparently dropped by Lacher and Mizerski (1994, p. 374) during their pretesting (219 undergraduate students) of the scale when it did not remain constant over the two songs tested and the two extraction methods used. Alphas for the fast- and slow-tempo songs in the pretest were **.81** and **.78**, respectively (Lacher 1997).

SAMPLES: The sample used by Lacher and Mizerski (1994) came from undergraduate business students at a large Southern U.S. university. Usable data were collected from **215** students, who were composed of 52% men and ranged in age from 19 to 36 years.

RELIABILITY: Lacher and Mizerski (1994) did not report the alphas for the scale as used in the main study, but on the basis of the pretest results, it appears it would have been acceptable.

VALIDITY: No examination of scale validity was reported by Lacher and Mizerski (1994) beyond what could be construed from the factor analyses in the study's pretest (noted previously).

ADMINISTRATION: The scale was self-administered, along with other measures in the study, by Lacher and Mizerski (1994). Students heard two songs played twice, and the second time the songs were played, they filled out this scale along with other measures. Higher scores on the scale indicated that respondents perceived that a particular song evoked a feeling of energy and excitement in them.

MAJOR FINDINGS: Lacher and Mizerski (1994) investigated the responses music evokes in a listener and how those reactions affect the intention to purchase the music. Among the findings was that a feeling of **exuberance** had a moderate positive effect on affect toward the music to which the respondent was listening.

COMMENTS: Although there is nothing in the items themselves to keep them from being applied to other stimuli, it should be kept in mind that this scale has been specifically developed and tested for measuring emotional reactions to music.

REFERENCES:

Asmus, Edward P. (1985), "The Development of a Multidimensional Instrument for the Measurement of Affective Responses to Music," *Psychology of Music*, 13 (1), 19–30.

Lacher, Kathleen T. (1997), personal correspondence.

————— and Richard Mizerski (1994), "An Exploratory Study of the Responses and Relationships Involved in the Evaluation of, and in the Intention to Purchase New Rock Music," *JCR*, 21 (September), 366–80.

#158 *Exuberance*

SCALE ITEMS:*

DIRECTIONS: Rate each item below in terms of its appropriateness in describing the feelings and emotions you had in response to the music.

Strongly   Strongly
disagree   :___:___:___:___:___:___: agree
                    1   2   3   4   5   6

1. Vigorous

2. Vibrant

3. Exuberant

*The actual directions for filling out the scale were not provided in the article but were likely to have been similiar to this.

SCALE NAME: Familiarity of Purchase Situation

SCALE DESCRIPTION: Three nine-point items measuring the degree to which a consumer reports being familiar with a particular buying situation.

SCALE ORIGIN: No information about the scale's source was provided by Shapiro, MacInnis, and Heckler (1997), but it is probably original to their study. The scale was used in a pretest ($\alpha = .93$, n = 18) as well as in the main study.

SAMPLES: The experiment conducted by Shapiro, MacInnis, and Heckler (1997) was based on data gathered from **152** undergraduate marketing students. Class credit was given for students' participation, subjects were randomly assigned to treatment groups, and there were between three and ten subjects per session.

RELIABILITY: An alpha of **.80** was reported for the scale in the main study by Shapiro, MacInnis, and Heckler (1997).

VALIDITY: No examination of the scale's validity was reported by Shapiro, MacInnis, and Heckler (1997).

ADMINISTRATION: The scale was self-administered by subjects, along with other measures, after they were exposed to experimental stimuli in the study by Shapiro, MacInnis, and Heckler (1997). Higher scores on the scale suggested that respondents were very familiar with the specified product buying context.

MAJOR FINDINGS: Shapiro, MacInnis, and Heckler (1997) examined the extent to which incidental exposure to an advertised product would increase the probability of the product being included in a person's consideration set. **Purchase situation familiarity** was included as a manipulation check. The familiar conditions had higher mean scale scores than those conditions that were supposed to be relatively unfamiliar.

COMMENTS: Although the internal consistency was quite acceptable according to the evidence provided by Shapiro, MacInnis, and Heckler (1997), the dimensionality of the scale is of concern. Note in the subsequent items that item 1 asks about what a respondent thinks is familiar to others, whereas items 2 and 3 refer to what is familiar to the respondent. This apparent lack of unidimensionality might not have been a problem when used as a manipulation check, but it should be addressed if the scale is considered for use as a primary measure in a study.

REFERENCES:
Shapiro, Stewart, Deborah J. MacInnis, and Susan E. Heckler (1997), "The Effects of Incidental Ad Exposure on the Formation of Consideration Sets," *JCR*, 24 (June), 94–104.

SCALE ITEMS:

1. How familiar do you think people in general are with purchasing products for this situation?

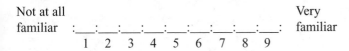

Not at all   Very
familiar :___:___:___:___:___:___:___:___: familiar
       1 2 3 4 5 6 7 8 9

2. How familiar are you with purchasing products for this circumstance?

Not at all   Very
familiar   :___:___:___:___:___:___:___:___:___: familiar
            1   2   3   4   5   6   7   8   9

3. How frequently have you seen or heard of products that have been bought for this particular circumstance?

Not at all   Very
frequently :___:___:___:___:___:___:___:___:___: frequently
            1   2   3   4   5   6   7   8   9

SCALE NAME: Family Meal Importance

SCALE DESCRIPTION: Five seven-point items that measure the degree to which a consumer believes that having home-cooked meals for the family is important.

SCALE ORIGIN: Although not clear from the article by Putrevu and Ratchford (1997), some of the work on the scales was conducted previously in a dissertation by Putrevu (1992).

SAMPLES: Data were gathered by Putrevu and Ratchford (1997) using a mail survey to a random sample of grocery shoppers in a standard metropolitan statistical area in the Northeastern United States. A total of **500** responses were used in the main analysis, and demographics of the final sample were similar to those of the population of interest.

RELIABILITY: An alpha of **.79** was reported for the scale (Putrevu and Ratchford 1997).

VALIDITY: Although the authors stated in general that the scales showed evidence of convergent, discriminant, and content validity, no details of the analyses were provided (Putrevu and Ratchford 1997).

ADMINISTRATION: The scale was part of a larger mail questionnaire (Putrevu and Ratchford 1997). Higher scores on the scale suggested that consumers felt it was very important to have home-cooked meals for their families.

MAJOR FINDINGS: Putrevu and Ratchford (1997) examined a dynamic model of consumer search behavior that includes human capital. The results indicated that the greater the **importance of home-cooked meals** (and the purchase of grocery products that goes along with it), the greater the amount of grocery-related external search.

REFERENCES:
Putrevu, Sanjay (1992), "A Theory of Search and Its Empirical Investigation," doctoral dissertation, State University of New York at Buffalo.
——— and Brian T. Ratchford (1997), "A Model of Search Behavior with an Application to Grocery Shopping," *JR*, 73 (4), 463–86.

SCALE ITEMS:

Doesn't describe   Describes me
me at all   :__:__:__:__:__:__:__: very well
                 1   2   3   4   5   6   7

1. Grocery purchases are very important to me.

2. I prefer to eat out rather than cook at home. **(r)**

3. Eating the evening meal at home is very important to me.

4. For me, it is important to have the right products to prepare the family meal.

5. I prefer eating out to home-cooked meals. **(r)**

SCALE NAME: Family Resources (Intangible)

SCALE DESCRIPTION: Five five-point items measuring the perceived adequacy of the level of intangible support a person recalls being provided by his or her family while growing up.

SCALE ORIGIN: Rindfleisch, Burroughs, and Denton (1997) indicated that they were guided in selecting items for the scale by examining family sociology literature, particularly Cherlin (1992) and McLanahan and Booth (1989).

SAMPLES: Rindfleisch, Burroughs, and Denton (1997) initially collected data for their study by mailing questionnaires to households in a medium-sized, Midwestern U.S. city and focusing on younger adults (20 to 32 years of age) but avoiding zip codes likely to have high student populations. Because that approach produced only a small number of people from disrupted families (31 of 135 respondents), two ads were placed in separate Sunday issues of the city's major newspaper. The ads requested 20- to 30-year-old persons from divorced (first ad) or intact (second ad) families to participate. After calling a telephone number, subjects were mailed a survey form and $5 for their effort. In total, these efforts produced **261** respondents, 165 from intact families and 96 from disrupted families.

RELIABILITY: An alpha of **.92** was reported for the scale (Rindfleisch, Burroughs, and Denton 1997). When the items from this scale and #162 were combined, the alpha was reported to be .90.

VALIDITY: Although factor analysis is not a strong test of validity, the results of that by Rindfleisch, Burroughs, and Denton (1997) showed that the five items composing this scale loaded on a different dimension than three other family resource items (see #162). However, in another factor analysis in which the items from the two family resource scales were examined along with items from a family stressor scale (#163), all of the resource items loaded together. This may be why the authors reported their findings with the eight resource items combined into one scale. The authors bolstered their claim of the combined scale's validity somewhat by showing that respondents from disrupted families scored significantly lower than those from intact families.

ADMINISTRATION: The scale was self-administered as part of a larger mail survey questionnaire (Rindfleisch, Burroughs, and Denton 1997). Higher scores on the scale indicated that respondents viewed the quantity and quality of the intangible support provided to them by their family when growing up as being very good.

MAJOR FINDINGS: Rindfleisch, Burroughs, and Denton (1997) examined how alternative family structures affected materialistic attitudes and compulsive consumption. The results indicated that **family resources** partially mediated the effect of family structure on compulsive buying.

REFERENCES:
Cherlin, Andrew (1992), *Marriage, Divorce, Remarriage*. Cambridge, MA: Harvard University Press.
McLanahan, Sara S. and Karen Booth (1989), "Mother-Only Families: Problems, Prospects and Politics," *Journal of Marriage and the Family*, 51 (August), 557–80.
Rindfleisch, Aric, James E. Burroughs, and Frank Denton (1997), "Family Structure, Materialism, and Compulsive Consumption," *JCR*, 23 (March), 312–25.

SCALE ITEMS:
My evaluation of the total support (quantity and quality) provided by my family while I was growing up breaks down as follows:

Inadequate   Exceptional
support   :___:___:___:___:___: support
                 1   2   3   4   5

1. Time and attention

2. Discipline

3. Life skills and instruction

4. Emotional support and love

5. Role modeling and guidance

SCALE NAME: Family Resources (Tangible)

SCALE DESCRIPTION: Three five-point items measuring the perceived adequacy of the level of tangible support a person recalls being provided by his or her family while growing up.

SCALE ORIGIN: Rindfleisch, Burroughs, and Denton (1997) indicated that they were guided in selecting items for the scale by examining family sociology literature, particularly Cherlin (1992) and McLanahan and Booth (1989).

SAMPLES: Rindfleisch, Burroughs, and Denton (1997) initially collected data for their study by mailing questionnaires to households in a medium-sized, Midwestern U.S. city and focusing on younger adults (20 to 32 years of age) but avoiding zip codes likely to have high student populations. Because that approach produced only a small number of people from disrupted families (31 of 135 respondents), two ads were placed in separate Sunday issues of the city's major newspaper. The ads requested 20- to 30-year-old persons from divorced (first ad) or intact (second ad) families to participate. After calling a telephone number, subjects were mailed a survey form and $5 for their effort. In total, these efforts produced **261** respondents, 165 from intact families and 96 from disrupted families.

RELIABILITY: An alpha of **.81** was reported for the scale (Rindfleisch, Burroughs, and Denton 1997). When the items from this scale and #161 were combined, the alpha was reported to be .90.

VALIDITY: Although factor analysis is not a strong test of validity, the results of that by Rindfleisch, Burroughs, and Denton (1997) showed that the three items composing this scale loaded on a different dimension than five other family resource items (see #161). However, in another factor analysis in which the items from the two family resource scales were examined along with items from a family stressor scale (#163), all of the resource items loaded together. This may be why the authors reported their findings with the eight resource items combined into one scale. The authors bolstered their claim of the combined scale's validity somewhat by showing that respondents from disrupted families scored significantly lower than those from intact families.

ADMINISTRATION: The scale was self-administered as part of a larger mail survey questionnaire (Rindfleisch, Burroughs, and Denton 1997). Higher scores on the scale indicated that respondents viewed the quantity and quality of the tangible support provided to them by their family when growing up as being very good.

MAJOR FINDINGS: Rindfleisch, Burroughs, and Denton (1997) examined how alternative family structures affected materialistic attitudes and compulsive consumption. The results indicated that **family resources** partially mediated the effect of family structure on compulsive buying.

REFERENCES:
Cherlin, Andrew (1992), *Marriage, Divorce, Remarriage*. Cambridge, MA: Harvard University Press.
McLanahan, Sara S. and Karen Booth (1989), "Mother-Only Families: Problems, Prospects and Politics," *Journal of Marriage and the Family*, 51 (August), 557–80.
Rindfleisch, Aric, James E. Burroughs, and Frank Denton (1997), "Family Structure, Materialism, and Compulsive Consumption," *JCR*, 23 (March), 312–25.

SCALE ITEMS:

My evaluation of the total support (quantity and quality) provided by my family while I was growing up breaks down as follows:

Inadequate   Exceptional

support   :___:___:___:___:___: support

                1 2 3 4 5

1. Spending money

2. Food

3. Clothing

SCALE NAME: Family Stressors

SCALE DESCRIPTION: Ten five-point items measuring the perceived impact a person recalls of a variety of events that potentially disrupted the stability and peace of the family and home while growing up.

SCALE ORIGIN: Rindfleisch, Burroughs, and Denton (1997) indicated that they adapted their scale from the Life Experiences Survey by Sarason, Johnson, and Siegel (1978). However, a examination of the Life Experiences Survey indicates that none of its 57 items was used in the Family Stressors scale. Although there are some similarities between the two scales, it may be most precise to describe the Family Stressors scale as original to Rindfleisch, Burroughs, and Denton (1997), though they received considerable inspiration from the Life Experiences Survey .

SAMPLES: Rindfleisch, Burroughs, and Denton (1997) initially collected data for their study by mailing questionnaires to households in a medium-sized, Midwestern U.S. city and focusing on younger adults (20 to 32 years of age) but avoiding zip codes likely to have high student populations. Because that approach produced only a small number of people from disrupted families (31 of 135 respondents), two ads were placed in separate Sunday issues of the city's major newspaper. The ads requested 20- to 30-year-old persons from divorced (first ad) or intact (second ad) families to participate. After calling a telephone number, subjects were mailed a survey form and $5 for their effort. In total, these efforts produced **261** respondents, 165 from intact families and 96 from disrupted families.

RELIABILITY: An alpha of **.76** was reported for the scale (Rindfleisch, Burroughs, and Denton 1997).

VALIDITY: Although factor analysis is not a strong test of validity, the results from one were used by Rindfleisch, Burroughs, and Denton (1997) as evidence of discriminant validity. Items from the two family resource scales (#161 and #162) were examined along with items from this scale. All of the resource items loaded together, and all but one (3) of the stressor items loaded together. The authors bolstered their claim of the scale's validity by showing that respondents from disrupted families reported significantly more stress than did those from intact families.

ADMINISTRATION: The scale was self-administered as part of a larger mail survey questionnaire (Rindfleisch, Burroughs, and Denton 1997). Higher scores on the scale indicated that respondents viewed the quantity and quality of the potentially disruptive events in their early life to have had very positive impacts on them.

MAJOR FINDINGS: Rindfleisch, Burroughs, and Denton (1997) examined how alternative family structures affected materialistic attitudes and compulsive consumption. The results indicated that **family stressors** partially mediated the effect of family structure on compulsive buying.

COMMENTS: The low (but acceptable) internal consistency and the results of the factor analysis raise some concern about the scale's unidimensionality. This should be examined more rigorously if the scale is used again.

REFERENCES:
Rindfleisch, Aric, James E. Burroughs, and Frank Denton (1997), "Family Structure, Materialism, and Compulsive Consumption," *JCR*, 23 (March), 312–25.
Sarason, Irwin G., James H. Johnson, and Judith M. Siegel (1978), "Assessing the Impact of Life Changes: Development of the Life Experiences Survey," *Journal of Consulting and Clinical Psychology*, 46 (October), 932–46.

SCALE ITEMS:

DIRECTIONS: Considering up through your 18th birthday, please circle the overall extent to which each of the following events impacted your life (positively or negatively) around the time(s) they occurred. Use "No Impact" if the event made no difference or never occurred.

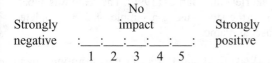

```
                    No
Strongly          impact          Strongly
negative    :___:___:___:___:___:   positive
             1   2   3   4   5
```

1. Move(s) to a different home or place of residence.

2. Difficulties with school or work.

3. A major, abrupt change in your family's financial status.

4. Frequent or lengthy periods in which one or both parents were temporarily absent.

5. Difficulties establishing and/or maintaining social relationships with peers.

6. The loss (other than death) or separation from family members or loved ones.

7. Encounters with juvenile authorities or police.

8. Physical abuse by parents or other family members.

9. Arguments between parents or other family members (including self).

10. Changes in the membership or composition of your family unit other than the divorce of your parents (e.g., remarriage of your parents(s), birth of your child, etc.).

SCALE NAME: Fanaticism

SCALE DESCRIPTION: Three seven-point Likert-type items measuring the degree to which a person indicates being a fan of some form of entertainment, particularly a sports team.

SCALE ORIGIN: The scale seems to be original to Wakefield and Barnes (1996). The scale was apparently pretested and refined, along with other measures in the study, using a sample of 308 completed responses from sports fans attending a minor-league baseball game.

SAMPLES: Data were collected in the main study by Wakefield and Barnes (1996) from those who attended one of two minor-league baseball games in a city different from the one used in the pretest. Final analysis was based on usable data from **250** respondents who appeared to live in the area and would hypothetically have been exposed to the promotional information under study.

RELIABILITY: An alpha of **.93** was reported for the scale (Wakefield and Barnes 1996).

VALIDITY: Although specific evaluation of the scale's validity was not discussed by Wakefield and Barnes (1996), they noted that they used confirmatory factor analysis and that no changes were deemed necessary for this scale.

ADMINISTRATION: The scale was part of a larger survey instrument self-administered by people who attended a baseball game (Wakefield and Barnes 1996). Higher scores on the scale suggested that respondents considered themselves loyal fans of some person, group, or object.

MAJOR FINDINGS: Wakefield and Barnes (1996) tested a model of sales promotion for entertainment services. Among their conclusions was that **loyal fans** perceive greater value from an entertainment service compared with other consumers and are not as interested in sales promotions that entice them with regard to the service.

COMMENTS: The scale scores were reported to have a mean of 5.36 and a standard deviation of 1.53 (Wakefield and Barnes 1996).

Wakefield and Barnes (1996) examined loyalty to a baseball team, but the scale appears amenable for use with other types of entertainment, such as television shows (e.g., *Star Trek*), celebrities (e.g., Elvis), or artists (e.g., Picasso). Some adjustment will be necessary in item 2, however, possibly by dropping the opening phrase.

REFERENCES:
Wakefield, Kirk L. and James H. Barnes (1996), "Retailing Hedonic Consumption: A Model of Sales Promotion of a Leisure Service," *JR*, 72 (4), 409–427.

SCALE ITEMS:*

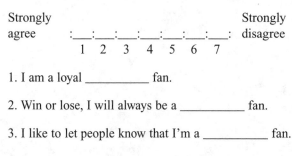

Strongly
agree   :___:___:___:___:___:___:___: Strongly disagree
        1   2   3   4   5   6   7

1. I am a loyal _____ fan.

2. Win or lose, I will always be a _____ fan.

3. I like to let people know that I'm a _____ fan.

*The name of the person, group, or object under study should be placed in the blanks.

SCALE NAME: Fashion Consciousness

SCALE DESCRIPTION: Four five-point Likert-type items intended to measure a shopping orientation that is characterized by the extent to which a consumer focuses on having up-to-date styles, especially as it pertains to clothing.

SCALE ORIGIN: Shim and Gehrt (1996) used a modified version of a scale developed by Sproles and Kendall (1986). The latter created an eight-factor model of what they called *consumer decision making styles* but that many others in marketing (e.g., Shim and Gehrt 1996) would view as *shopping orientations*. Shim and Gehrt (1996) used the four items with the highest factor loadings of the five items identified by Sproles and Kendall (1986). The latter reported an alpha of .74 for the five-item scale and .76 for the three items that loaded highest on the factor.

SAMPLES: Shim and Gehrt (1996) collected data from high school students in a Southwestern U.S. state. Twenty-nine principals agreed to participate, and their schools apparently represented many if not all counties in the state. Principals were given instructions as to which classes to use (by level) and how many students from each class were needed. Some 1954 usable surveys were returned from a sample that was 61.3% girls and had a mean age of 16 years. However, the study focused only on data from **1846** students who were white (56%), Hispanic (32%), or Native American (12%).

RELIABILITY: An alpha of **.70** was reported for the scale by Shim and Gehrt (1996).

VALIDITY: No examination of the scale's validity was reported by Shim and Gehrt (1996).

ADMINISTRATION: Data were gathered in a classroom setting where students filled out the scale as part of a larger survey instrument (Shim and Gehrt 1996). Higher scores on the scale indicated that respondents were very fashion conscious and very interested in having clothing of the latest styles.

MAJOR FINDINGS: The study by Shim and Gehrt (1996) examined differences in shopping orientations among high school students that could be linked to ethnicity. The results showed that white students were significantly less **fashion conscious** than Hispanics but significantly more **fashion conscious** than Native American students.

REFERENCES:
Shim, Soyeon and Kenneth C. Gehrt (1996), "Hispanic and Native American Adolescents: An Exploratory Study of Their Approach to Shopping," *JR*, 72 (3), 307–24.
Sproles, George B. and Elizabeth L. Kendall (1986), "A Methodology for Profiling Consumers' Decision-Making Styles," *Journal of Consumer Affairs*, 20 (Winter), 267–79.

SCALE ITEMS:

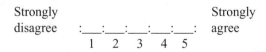

Strongly disagree :___:___:___:___:___: Strongly agree
    1   2   3   4   5

1. I usually have one or more outfits of the newest style.

2. I keep my wardrobe up-to-date with the changing fashions.

3. Fashionable, attractive styling is very important to me.

4. To get variety, I shop different stores and choose different brands.

#166 *Fear*

SCALE NAME: Fear

SCALE DESCRIPTION: Five seven-point items measuring the extent to which a person reports being scared and having related feelings of discomfort upon exposure to some stimulus.

SCALE ORIGIN: Block and Keller (1995) cite Gleicher and Petty (1992) as having a scale similar to theirs. Although the scales may be "similar," they are not the same because the latter used six items and only half of these items were included in the former.

SAMPLES: The scale was employed in both experiments conducted by Block and Keller (1995). **Ninety-four** undergraduate students completed the first experiment, and the second experiment was based on data from **115** undergraduate and graduate students.

RELIABILITY: Alphas of **.87** and **.89** were reported for the scale as used in Experiments 1 and 2, respectively (Block and Keller 1995).

VALIDITY: No examination of the scale's validity was reported by Block and Keller (1995), though they did state that a factor analysis indicated the items loaded on one factor.

ADMINISTRATION: The scale was completed by subjects after they were exposed to some health-related information (Block and Keller 1995). High scores on the scale indicated that respondents felt scared as they were exposed to some specified stimulus.

MAJOR FINDINGS: The purpose of the study by Block and Keller (1995) was to examine the relationships among level of efficacy, depth of processing, and framing effects. **Fear** was measured merely to ensure that the emotional reaction was not confounding experimental treatments, and indeed, the findings showed that subjects in the three conditions did not differ significantly in their **fear**.

REFERENCES:

Block, Lauren G. and Punam Anand Keller (1995), "When to Accentuate the Negative: The Effects of Perceived Efficacy and Message Framing on Intentions to Perform a Health-Related Behavior," *JMR*, 32 (May), 192–203.

Gleicher, Faith and Richard E. Petty (1992), "Expectations of Reassurance Influence the Nature of Fear-Stimulated Attitude Change," *Journal of Experimental Social Psychology*, 28 (January), 86–100.

SCALE ITEMS:

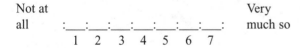

Not at
all   :___:___:___:___:___:___:___: Very
much so
          1   2   3   4   5   6   7

1. Fearful

2. Nervous

3. Scared

4. Nauseated

5. Uncomfortable

SCALE NAME: Financial Health

SCALE DESCRIPTION: Three five-point Likert-type items that purport to capture a person's attitude toward his or her own financial well-being.

SCALE ORIGIN: The source of the scale was not specified by Mittal (1994).

SAMPLES: Mittal (1994) gathered data from female members of six voluntary organizations, as well as from mall intercepts. A total of 184 people provided complete survey questionnaires. Most of the respondents were white (85%), married (71%), and at least 35 years of age (63%). Although it does not mirror the U.S. population, the sample included a wide variety of demographic categories.

RELIABILITY: The construct reliability (LISREL) was reported to be **.71** (Mittal 1994).

VALIDITY: The validity of the scale was not specifically addressed by Mittal (1994), except to note the tests that were conducted provided support for discriminant validity.

ADMINISTRATION: The scale was part of a larger self-administered mail survey instrument (Mittal 1994). Higher scores on the scale indicated that respondents considered themselves well-off financially.

MAJOR FINDINGS: The study by Mittal (1994) proposed that demographics are poor predictors of coupon usage, and instead, he illustrated the value of three layers of mediating variables. Among the findings was that those who were **financially healthy** also tended to be more brand loyal.

REFERENCES:
Mittal, Banwari (1994), "An Integrated Framework for Relating Diverse Consumer Characteristics to Supermarket Coupon Redemption," *JMR*, 31 (November), 533–44.

SCALE ITEMS:

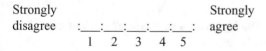

Strongly disagree :___:___:___:___:___: Strongly agree
　　　　　　　1　2　3　4　5

1. I consider myself financially well off.

2. I am generally on a tight budget. **(r)**

3. An unexpected expense of $1000 would put us in financial hardship. **(r)**

SCALE NAME: Flattery

SCALE DESCRIPTION: Three seven point semantic differentials measuring how a person thinks another person feels about him or her. Because Howard, Gengler, and Jain (1995) administered this scale after subjects had received a compliment-like manipulation (name remembering), the scale was viewed as capturing a sort of flattery construct. However, in another context, the scale might be used to measure what a person thinks another person's attitude is toward him or her, with an emphasis more on general affect rather than something specific such as flattery.

SCALE ORIGIN: The scale was constructed by Howard, Gengler, and Jain (1995, p. 204) and described as having received "extensive pretesting."

SAMPLES: The scale appears to have been used only in the second of three experiments reported by Howard, Gengler, and Jain (1995). That experiment had **31** subjects (college students) who were randomly assigned to three experimental conditions.

RELIABILITY: An alpha of **.91** was reported for the scale by Howard, Gengler, and Jain (1995).

VALIDITY: No examination of the scale's validity was reported by Howard, Gengler, and Jain (1995).

ADMINISTRATION: Subjects completed the scale, along with other measures, after they were exposed to the experimental treatment (Howard, Gengler, and Jain 1995). Higher scores on the scale indicated that subjects felt that another person had made them feel valued.

MAJOR FINDINGS: The purpose of the experiments conducted by Howard, Gengler, and Jain (1995) was to examine the effect of remembering someone's name on compliance with a purchase request. The findings indicated that those students whose names a professor "remembered" perceived greater **flattery** than those whose names the professor acted as if he could not recall.

COMMENTS: Although Howard, Gengler, and Jain (1995) used the scale with reference to a professor, it appears to be amenable for use with salespeople and others, though some retesting should be conducted to ensure its unidimensionality and reliability.

REFERENCES:
Howard, Daniel J., Charles Gengler, and Ambuj Jain (1995), "What's in a Name? A Complimentary Means of Persuasion," *JCR*, 22 (September), 200–211.

SCALE ITEMS:
My professor:

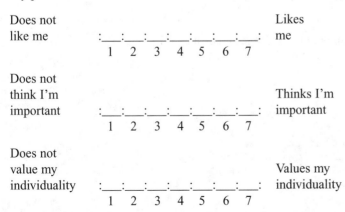

SCALE NAME: Frustration

SCALE DESCRIPTION: A four-item Likert-type scale measuring the degree to which a person has experienced feeling uneasy and angry because of some stimulus. Taylor (1995) referred to the measure as *negative affect*.

SCALE ORIGIN: Taylor (1995) wanted a measure of "negative affect" for use in her study and, using data from the main study (described subsequently), performed an exploratory factor analysis on eight items. Two affect scales were derived: one she described as *positive* and one described as *negative*. Although the origin of the items was not stated, Taylor had used these items before (Taylor 1994); however, the items were split between two scales at that time: #20 and #24.

SAMPLES: Taylor (1995) collected data from **232** undergraduate business students attending a mid-sized U.S. university. Some of these subjects (n = 68) were part of a control group, but the rest were broken down into groups of between 24 and 31 subjects for the experimental treatments.

RELIABILITY: An alpha of **.65** was reported for the version of the scale used by Taylor (1995), which was admitted to be lower than desirable. As noted, Taylor's (1994) own previous research suggested that these items belong to two different constructs: one having to do with a feeling of uncertainty (items 1 and 4) and one that has more to do with a feeling of anger (items 2 and 3).

VALIDITY: The validity of the scale was not specifically addressed by Taylor (1995). However, as noted previously, she performed an exploratory factor analysis on eight items and found evidence of two dimensions. The four items shown here loaded highest on what she called the *negative affect* factor.

ADMINISTRATION: Subjects in the experiment conducted by Taylor (1995) self-administered the scale, along with other measures, after the experimental manipulation. Higher scores on the scale indicated that respondents were uneasy and frustrated by some stimulus to which they had been exposed.

MAJOR FINDINGS: The purpose of the experiment by Taylor (1995) was to investigate the effects of a delay, perceived control over a delay, and what fills the time during the delay. **Frustration** was used as a manipulation check and was not found to differ significantly between subjects in the experimental treatments or between delayed and nondelayed subjects

REFERENCES:
Taylor, Shirley (1994), "Waiting for Service: The Relationship Between Delays and Evaluations of Service," *JM*, 58 (April), 56–69.
———— (1995), "The Effects of Filled Waiting Time and Service Provider Control over the Delay on Evaluations of Service," *JAMS*, 23 (Winter), 38–48.

SCALE ITEMS:*

Not at all :___:___:___:___:___:___:___: Very
       1   2   3   4   5   6   7

1. Uneasy   3. Angry

2. Frustrated   4. Uncertain

*Taylor (1995) did not describe the type of response scale she used with these items, but the one shown here is similar to what she used for similar measures in previous studies (Taylor 1994).

SCALE NAME: Glamorous

SCALE DESCRIPTION: A seven-item, seven-point scale measuring the extent to which one person (target) is viewed by another person (respondent) as attractive and cool.

SCALE ORIGIN: The scale is apparently original to Pechmann and Ratneshwar (1994).

SAMPLES: Data were gathered by Pechmann and Ratneshwar (1994) from **304** seventh-grade students from four middle schools in southern California. There were slightly more girls (58%) than boys. Schools were deliberately selected to ensure that they adequately represented the California student population on factors that might be related to smoking (gender, socioeconomic status, and race). Therefore, only 44% were white, and the remaining respondents identified with other groups.

RELIABILITY: An alpha of **.88** was reported for the scale (Pechmann and Ratneshwar 1994).

VALIDITY: No specific examination of the scale's validity was reported by Pechmann and Ratneshwar (1994). However, 13 items used to evaluate the target (Student A) were submitted to a factor analysis, and it was concluded that the seven items composing this scale loaded together.

ADMINISTRATION: The scale was administered on a PC, along with other questionnaire items, after subjects were exposed to stimulus ads in a mock magazine (Pechmann and Ratneshwar 1994). Higher scores on the scale suggested that respondents viewed someone as attractive and cool.

MAJOR FINDINGS: Pechmann and Ratneshwar (1994) examined the impact of smoking and anti-smoking ads on nonsmoking youth's evaluative judgments of a peer who smokes. The results indicated that those who viewed antismoking ads (versus unrelated ones) rated a peer who smoked as significantly less **glamorous** than another (control) peer.

REFERENCES:

Pechmann, Cornelia and S. Ratneshwar (1994), "The Effects of Antismoking and Cigarette Advertising on Young Adolescents' Perceptions of Peers Who Smoke," *JCR*, 21 (September), 236–51.

SCALE ITEMS:

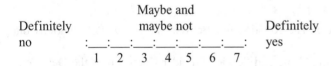

```
                   Maybe and
Definitely          maybe not              Definitely
no        :___:___:___:___:___:___:       yes
            1   2   3   4   5   6   7
```

1. Good-looking

2. Attractive

3. Exciting

4. Adventurous

5. Popular

6. Has friends

7. Cool

SCALE NAME: Grandiosity

SCALE DESCRIPTION: Ten seven-point Likert-type statements that evaluate the extent of a person's exaggerated sense of self-esteem and superiority over others.

SCALE ORIGIN: The scale was constructed and tested by Robbins and Patton (1985). In terms of reliability, an alpha of .76 (n = 453) and a test–retest stability of .80 (n = 133) were found. Some evidence was provided regarding the unidimensionality of the scale, yet half of the items had loadings below .50. Evidence supporting a claim for concurrent validity was also provided.

SAMPLES: Various samples were collected and used by Netemeyer, Burton, and Lichtenstein (1995) though the **grandiosity** scale was used only in Study 1. It had two groups: 145 students from a major U.S. university and 277 "nonstudent adults."

RELIABILITY: Alphas of **.80** (students) and **.86** (nonstudent adults) were found for the scale by Netemeyer, Burton, and Lichtenstein (1995; Netemeyer 1997).

VALIDITY: Although the validity of the scale was not directly examined by Netemeyer, Burton, and Lichtenstein (1995), the scale was used to help establish the construct validity of four vanity-related scales. As noted (see "Findings"), **grandiosity** had significant positive correlations with each of the vanity scales.

ADMINISTRATION: The scale was used in Study 1 as part of a larger questionnaire that was self-administered by respondents (Netemeyer, Burton, and Lichtenstein 1995). Higher scores on the scale indicated that respondents had an overblown sense of self-esteem and felt superior to others.

MAJOR FINDINGS: Netemeyer, Burton, and Lichtenstein (1995) investigated vanity and developed four scales for its measurement. Most of the article discussed the results of the rather extensive validation process. **Grandiosity** had significant positive correlations with all of the vanity scales; the highest correlation was with achievement concern vanity (#395).

REFERENCES:
Netemeyer, Richard G. (1997), personal correspondence.
———, Scot Burton, and Donald R. Lichtenstein (1995), "Trait Aspects of Vanity: Measurement and Relevance to Consumer Behavior," *JCR*, 21 (March), 612–26.
Robbins, Steven B. and Michael J. Patton (1985), "Self-Psychology and Career Development: Construction of the Superiority and Goal Instability Scales," *Journal of Counseling Psychology*, 32 (April), 221–31.

SCALE ITEMS:

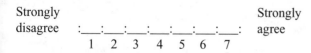

Strongly disagree :___:___:___:___:___:___:___: Strongly agree
1   2   3   4   5   6   7

1. My friends follow my lead.

2. I deserve favors from others.

3. I'm witty and charming with others.

4. My looks are one of the things that attract others to me.

5. I could show up my friends if I wanted to.

6. Running the show means a lot to me.

7. Being admired by others helps me feel fantastic.

8. Achieving out of the ordinary accomplishments would make me feel complete.

9. I catch myself wanting to be a hero.

10. I know that I have more natural talents than most.

SCALE NAME: Grocery Market Knowledge

SCALE DESCRIPTION: Three open-ended items that measure the amount of time (in years) that a consumer has lived in an area and has been the primary grocery shopper for his or her household.

SCALE ORIGIN: Although not clear from the article by Putrevu and Ratchford (1997), some of the work on the scales was conducted previously in a dissertation by Putrevu (1992).

SAMPLES: Data were gathered by Putrevu and Ratchford (1997) using a mail survey to a random sample of grocery shoppers in a standard metropolitan statistical area in the northeastern United States. A total of **500** responses were used in the main analysis, and demographics of the final sample were similar to those of the population of interest.

RELIABILITY: An alpha of **.81** was reported for the scale (Putrevu and Ratchford 1997).

VALIDITY: Although the authors stated in general that the scales showed evidence of convergent, discriminant, and content validity, no details of the analyses were provided (Putrevu and Ratchford 1997).

ADMINISTRATION: The scale was part of a larger mail questionnaire (Putrevu and Ratchford 1997). Higher scores on the scale indicated that consumers had greater experience with the grocery market in their area.

MAJOR FINDINGS: Putrevu and Ratchford (1997) examined a dynamic model of consumer search behavior that includes human capital. The results indicated that the greater the grocery **market knowledge**, the greater was the amount of external search.

REFERENCES:
Putrevu, Sanjay (1992), "A Theory of Search and Its Empirical Investigation," doctoral dissertation, State University of New York at Buffalo.
———— and Brian T. Ratchford (1997), "A Model of Search Behavior with an Application to Grocery Shopping," *JR*, 73 (4), 463–86.

SCALE ITEMS:*

1. Approximately, how many *years* have you been the major grocery shopper for your household?

2. Approximately, how many *years* have you lived in your present neighborhood?

3. Approximately, how many *years* have you lived in the Buffalo area?

*Although not described in the article by Putrevu and Ratchford (1997), it is likely that respondents were asked to write the number of years in a blank next to each question.

SCALE NAME: Grocery Market Knowledge (Price)

SCALE DESCRIPTION: Three five-point Likert-type statements measuring the degree to which a consumer reports having considerable knowledge about the grocery stores in the local shopping area, particularly as it relates to their relative price levels. The scale was called *human capital* by Urbany, Dickson, and Kalapurakal (1996).

SCALE ORIGIN: Although Urbany, Dickson, and Kalapurakal (1996) may have drawn inspiration from previous work, the scale appears to be original to their study.

SAMPLES: The data used by Urbany, Dickson, and Kalapurakal (1996) were collected as part of a larger survey by a leading market research firm. Telephone interviews were conducted with the primary grocery shoppers from households selected at random. Respondents were requested to participate in a second stage that would involve a mail survey. The survey yielded **343** usable responses. The average age of respondents was 44.7 years, and they were overwhelmingly women (83%).

RELIABILITY: An alpha of **.88** was reported for the scale by Urbany, Dickson, and Kalapurakal (1996).

VALIDITY: Urbany, Dickson, and Kalapurakal (1996) tested the discriminant validity of the **grocery market knowledge** scale using pairwise confirmatory factor analysis and six other measures. The evidence of three separate tests on each of the six pairs supported a claim of discriminant validity.

ADMINISTRATION: The data analyzed by Urbany, Dickson, and Kalapurakal (1996) were gathered in a mail survey. Higher scores suggested that respondents were very knowledgeable about the pricing levels of the grocery stores in their shopping areas.

MAJOR FINDINGS: Urbany, Dickson, and Kalapurakal (1996) developed a model of price search for the retail grocery industry that included a relatively complete accounting of economic and noneconomic returns, as well as search costs. The findings showed that pricing-related **grocery market knowledge** accounted for a significant amount of variance in self-reported search behavior.

COMMENTS: Urbany, Dickson, and Kalapurakal (1996) reported a mean response of 3.29 on the scale.

REFERENCES:
Urbany, Joel E., Peter R. Dickson, and Rosemary Kalapurakal (1996), "Price Search in the Retail Grocery Market," *JM*, 60 (April), 91–104.

SCALE ITEMS:

Strongly   Strongly
disagree   :___:___:___:___:___: agree
            1   2   3   4   5

1. I know a lot about _____'s grocery stores.*

2. I know which stores have the best prices.

3. I know which stores have the best price specials.

*The name of the city/town should be placed in the blank.

SCALE NAME: Grocery Market Knowledge (Specialty Departments)

SCALE DESCRIPTION: Three five-point Likert-type statements measuring the degree to which a consumer reports having considerable knowledge about the grocery stores in the local shopping area as it relates to the relative quality of their specialty departments (bakery, deli, and meat).

SCALE ORIGIN: Although Urbany, Dickson, and Kalapurakal (1996) may have drawn inspiration from previous work, the scale appears to be original to their study.

SAMPLES: The data used by Urbany, Dickson, and Kalapurakal (1996) were collected as part of a larger survey by a leading market research firm. Telephone interviews were conducted with the primary grocery shoppers from households selected at random. Respondents were requested to participate in a second stage that would involve a mail survey. The survey yielded **343** usable responses. The average age of respondents was 44.7 years, and they were overwhelmingly women (83%).

RELIABILITY: An alpha of **.88** was reported for the scale by Urbany, Dickson, and Kalapurakal (1996).

VALIDITY: Urbany, Dickson, and Kalapurakal (1996) tested the discriminant validity of the **grocery market knowledge** scale using pairwise confirmatory factor analysis and six other measures. The evidence of three separate tests on each of the six pairs supported a claim of discriminant validity.

ADMINISTRATION: The data analyzed by Urbany, Dickson, and Kalapurakal (1996) were gathered in a mail survey. Higher scores suggested that respondents were very knowledgeable about the relative quality of the specialty departments in the grocery stores of their shopping areas.

MAJOR FINDINGS: Urbany, Dickson, and Kalapurakal (1996) developed a model of price search for the retail grocery industry that included a relatively complete accounting of economic and noneconomic returns, as well as search costs. The findings showed that **grocery market knowledge** as it related to specialty departments did not account for a significant amount of variance in self-reported search behavior.

COMMENTS: Urbany, Dickson, and Kalapurakal (1996) reported a mean response of 3.63 on the scale.

REFERENCES:
Urbany, Joel E., Peter R. Dickson, and Rosemary Kalapurakal (1996), "Price Search in the Retail Grocery Market," *JM*, 60 (April), 91–104.

SCALE ITEMS:

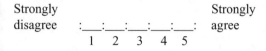

Strongly disagree :___:___:___:___:___: Strongly agree
          1   2   3   4   5

1. I know which grocery stores have the best bakery.

2. I know which grocery stores have the best meat department.

3. I know which grocery stores have the best deli.

SCALE NAME: Helplessness

SCALE DESCRIPTION: Three seven-point descriptors relating to the lack of control and feeling of impotence a consumer experiences after exposure to some stimulus. In the study by Babin, Boles, and Darden (1995), the stimulus being evaluated was a car salesperson as described in the experiment.

SCALE ORIGIN: The scale was developed by Holbrook and Batra (1988). Items were drawn from an exhaustive review of similar scales, and then the authors used their judgment to pick a few items to represent each of 29 emotional dimensions. Twelve judges were used to evaluate 72 commercials, and the alpha for the dimension represented by **helplessness** was reported to be .72.

SAMPLES: The data were gathered by Babin, Boles, and Darden (1995) from **163** undergraduate marketing students who were randomly assigned to one of three experimental conditions.

RELIABILITY: An alpha of **.73** was reported for the scale by Babin, Boles, and Darden (1995).

VALIDITY: No examination of the scale's validity was reported by Babin, Boles, and Darden (1995).

ADMINISTRATION: Babin, Boles, and Darden (1995) had subjects complete the scale, along with other measures, after they were exposed to experimental manipulation. A high score suggested that respondents had a feeling of powerlessness after exposure to some stimulus.

MAJOR FINDINGS: The study by Babin, Boles, and Darden (1995) examined salesperson stereotypes and their influence on the sales environment. The findings showed that the three types of car salespeople differed in the **helplessness** they evoked in consumers, such that *pushy* and *typical* salespeople were about the same, but *atypical* salespeople were associated with much less helplessness.

REFERENCES:

Babin, Barry J., James S. Boles, and William R. Darden (1995), "Salesperson Stereotypes, Consumer Emotions, and Their Impact on Information Processing," *JAMS*, 23 (Spring), 94–105.

Holbrook, Morris B. and Rajeev Batra (1988), "Toward a Standardized Emotional Profile (SEP) Useful in Measuring Responses to the Nonverbal Components of Advertising," in *Nonverbal Communication in Advertising*, Sidney Hecker and David W. Stewart, eds. Lexington, MA: D.C. Heath, 95–109.

SCALE ITEMS:

I felt:

Not at all :___:___:___:___:___:___:___: Very
       1   2   3   4   5   6   7

1. Helpless

2. Powerless

3. Dominated

SCALE NAME: Heroic

SCALE DESCRIPTION: A three-item, six-point summated ratings scale measuring the degree to which a person describes feeling a sense of victory and/or patriotism on exposure to some stimulus (e.g., music). Phrasing of the scale was such that it measured a respondent's emotional reaction to a stimulus rather than attitude toward the stimulus itself.

SCALE ORIGIN: Lacher and Mizerski (1994) indicated that the scale was taken from Asmus (1985). Indeed, each of the three items here were in the *potency* factor Asmus (1985) identified in his development of a multidimensional instrument for measuring affective responses to music. Two items from Asmus's activity scale were dropped by Lacher and Mizerski (1994, p. 374) during their pretesting (219 undergraduate students) of the scale when they did not remain constant over the two songs tested and the two extraction methods used. Alphas for the fast- and slow-tempo songs in the pretest were **.74** and **.73**, respectively (Lacher 1997).

SAMPLES: The sample used by Lacher and Mizerski (1994) came from undergraduate business students at a large Southern U.S. university. Usable data were collected from **215** students, who were composed of 52% men and ranged in age from 19 to 36 years.

RELIABILITY: Lacher and Mizerski (1994) did not report the alpha for the scale as used in the main study.

VALIDITY: No examination of scale validity was reported by Lacher and Mizerski (1994) beyond what could be construed from the factor analyses in the study's pretest (noted previously).

ADMINISTRATION: The scale was self-administered, along with other measures, in the study by Lacher and Mizerski (1994). Students heard two songs played twice, and the second time the songs were played, they filled out this scale along with other measures. Higher scores on the scale indicated that respondents perceived that a particular song evoked a feeling of heroism, victory, and/or patriotism in them.

MAJOR FINDINGS: Lacher and Mizerski (1994) investigated the responses music evokes in a listener and how those reactions affect the intention to purchase the music. Among the findings was that a feeling of **heroism** had a small but significant positive influence on the experiential response toward the music being heard (#154).

COMMENTS: Although there is nothing in the items themselves to keep them from being applied to other stimuli, it should be kept in mind that this scale has been specifically developed and tested for measuring emotional reactions to music.

REFERENCES:
Asmus, Edward P. (1985), "The Development of a Multidimensional Instrument for the Measurement of Affective Responses to Music," *Psychology of Music*, 13 (1), 19–30.
Lacher, Kathleen T. (1997), personal correspondence.
———— and Richard Mizerski (1994), "An Exploratory Study of the Responses and Relationships Involved in the Evaluation of, and in the Intention to Purchase New Rock Music," *JCR*, 21 (September), 366–80.

#176 *Heroic*

SCALE ITEMS:*

DIRECTIONS: Rate each item below in terms of its appropriateness in describing the feelings and emotions you had in response to the music.

Strongly   Strongly
disgree   :__:__:__:__:__:__: agree
                 1   2   3   4   5   6

1. Heroic

2. Victorious

3. Patriotic

*The actual directions for filling out the scale were not provided in the article but were likely to have been similar to this.

SCALE NAME: Homemaker Pride

SCALE DESCRIPTION: Three five-point Likert-type items that appear to measure the value a person places on being a homemaker. The scale measures not only whether the respondent is a homemaker, but also the importance of that role in general.

SCALE ORIGIN: The source of the scale was not specified by Mittal (1994).

SAMPLES: Mittal (1994) gathered data from female members of six voluntary organizations, as well as from mall intercepts. A total of 184 people provided complete survey questionnaires. Most of the respondents were white (85%), married (71%), and at least 35 years of age (63%). Although it did not mirror the U.S. population, the sample included a wide variety of demographic categories.

RELIABILITY: The construct reliability (LISREL) was reported to be **.76 (**Mittal 1994).

VALIDITY: The validity of the scale was not specifically addressed by Mittal (1994), except to note that the tests that were conducted provided support for discriminant validity.

ADMINISTRATION: The scale was part of a larger self-administered mail survey instrument (Mittal 1994). Higher scores on the scale indicated that respondents considered themselves homemakers and that it was a role of which they were proud.

MAJOR FINDINGS: The study by Mittal (1994) proposed that demographics are poor predictors of coupon usage, and instead, he illustrated the value of three layers of mediating variables. Among the findings was that those who expressed **high pride in being homemakers** were very price conscious.

REFERENCES:
Mittal, Banwari (1994), "An Integrated Framework for Relating Diverse Consumer Characteristics to Supermarket Coupon Redemption," *JMR*, 31 (November), 533–44.

SCALE ITEMS:

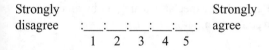

Strongly   Strongly
disagree :___:___:___:___:___: agree
    1 2 3 4 5

1. I take pride in being a homemaker.

2. There are more important things in life than simply being a homemaker. **(r)**

3. Homemaking is just something one does, nothing to feel great about. **(r)**

SCALE NAME: Identification with Organization

SCALE DESCRIPTION: A six-item, five-point Likert-type scale measuring the degree to which a person views him- or herself as psychologically intertwined with the fate of some specified organization. The organization of interest in the study by Bhattacharya, Rao, and Glynn (1995) was an art museum.

SCALE ORIGIN: The scale used by Bhattacharya, Rao, and Glynn (1995) is a slight adaptation of the measure developed by Mael (1988). Reasonably high internal consistency has been found for the scale in a variety of studies: an alpha of .81 was found for the scale in Mael's (1988) original study using employed business and psychology students; .83 was reported by Ashforth (1990) with a sample of managers; and .87 was reported by Mael and Ashforth (1992) based on alumni from an all-men's college.

SAMPLES: Bhattacharya, Rao, and Glynn (1995) gathered data from members of an art museum in a major city of the southeastern United States. Questionnaires were mailed to a proportionate stratified random sample of the various membership categories. Two free guest passes were included with the questionnaires as a token of appreciation and incentive to respond. A 30% response rate produced **306** completed survey forms. Although not representative of the population at large, the authors considered the sample to be similar to those reported of arts consumers. Respondents were approximately 52 years of age, predominately white (96%), and mostly women (66%).

RELIABILITY: An alpha of **.87** was reported for the scale by Bhattacharya, Rao, and Glynn (1995).

VALIDITY: No evidence of the scale's validity was reported by Bhattacharya, Rao, and Glynn (1995).

ADMINISTRATION: The scale was self-administered by respondents as part of a larger mail survey questionnaire (Bhattacharya, Rao, and Glynn 1995). Scale scores were calculated such that high scores indicated that respondents expressed very weak if any identification with the organization, whereas low scores suggested they identified strongly with it.

MAJOR FINDINGS: Bhattacharya, Rao, and Glynn (1995) used social identity theory to develop and test a conceptual framework for the identification a person feels toward an organization of which he or she is a member. The findings showed that there was a significant positive relationship between disconfirmation and **identification**. This means that the more a person's expectations are met by an organization, the greater is his or her **identification with that organization**.

REFERENCES:

Ashforth, Blake E. (1990), "Petty Tyranny in Organizations: A Preliminary Examination of Antecedents and Consequences," working paper, Concordia University.

Bhattacharya, C.B., Hayagreeva Rao, and Mary Ann Glynn (1995), "Understanding the Bond of Identification: An Investigation of Its Correlates Among Art Museum Members," *JM*, 59 (October), 46–57.

Mael, Fred (1988), "Organizational Identification: Construct Redefinition and a Field Application with Organizational Alumni," doctoral dissertation, Wayne State University.

——— and Blake E. Ashforth (1992), "Alumni and Their Alma Mater: A Partial Test of the Reformulated Model of Organizational Identification," *Journal of Organizational Behavior*, 13, 103–23.

SCALE ITEMS:*

Strongly   Strongly
agree   :___:___:___:___:___: disagree
           1   2   3   4   5

1. When someone criticizes the _____, it feels like a personal insult.

2. I am very interested in what others think about the _____.

3. When I talk about the _____, I usually say *we* rather than *they*.

4. The _____'s successes are my successes.

5. When someone praises the _____, it feels like a personal compliment.

6. If a story in the media criticizes the _____, I would feel embarrassed.

*The name of the organization should be placed in the blanks.

SCALE NAME: Imagery Quantity

SCALE DESCRIPTION: Three seven-point Likert-type items purported to measure the number of images that come to mind while processing a stimulus.

SCALE ORIGIN: Although inspiration for the scale came from the work of Ellen and Bone (1991), the items are distinct enough to consider this scale original to Babin and Burns (1997).

SAMPLES: Babin and Burns (1997) gathered data for their experiment in a classroom setting from **186** undergraduate business students. The sample was almost evenly split on gender (52% men).

RELIABILITY: A composite reliability of **.75** was reported by Babin and Burns (1997).

VALIDITY: Babin and Burns (1997) found support for the unidimensionality of the scale, as well as for its discriminant validity.

ADMINISTRATION: The scale was self-administered by students in the experiment, along with other measures, after they were exposed to mock ads (Babin and Burns 1997). A high score on the scale indicated that a person had experienced a lot of images after being exposed to some stimulus.

MAJOR FINDINGS: The experiment conducted by Babin and Burns (1997) examined the mediating role of evoked imagery in attitudinal responses. The research indicated that the use of concrete pictures did not significantly affect the **quantity** or elaboration of evoked imagery in comparison with a less concrete picture or no picture.

REFERENCES:
Babin, Laurie and Alvin C. Burns (1997), "Effects of Print Ad Pictures and Copy Containing Instructions to Imagine on Mental Imagery That Mediates Attitudes," *JA*, 26 (Fall), 33–44.
Ellen, Pam Scholder and Paula Fitzgerald Bone (1991), "Measuring Communication-Evoked Imagery Processing," in *Advances in Consumer Research*, Vol. 18, Rebecca H. Holman and Michael R. Soloman, eds. Provo, UT: Association of Consumer Research, 806–12.

SCALE ITEMS:

Strongly disagree :___:___:___:___:___:___:___: Strongly agree
        1 2 3 4 5 6 7

1. I really only experienced one image. **(r)**

2. I imagined a number of things.

3. Many images came to mind.

SCALE NAME: Imaginal Response to Music

SCALE DESCRIPTION: A three-item, six-point Likert-type scale measuring the degree to which a person indicates that a song has evoked images and triggered memories.

SCALE ORIGIN: The scale is original to Lacher and Mizerski (1994), but the items were adapted from Yingling (1962) and Hargreaves (1982). In a pretest, this scale and two others being developed were administered to a sample of 117 undergraduate students. The procedure was that students heard a song twice, and the second time it was played, they filled out the scales. This was repeated for a second song. Alphas of .60 and .71 were reported for the songs. The data were also subjected to confirmatory factor analysis, which supported a three-factor solution.

SAMPLES: The sample used by Lacher and Mizerski (1994) came from undergraduate business students at a large Southern U.S. university. Usable data were collected from **215** students, 52% of whom were men and who ranged in age from 19 to 36 years.

RELIABILITY: Lacher and Mizerski (1994) did not report any information about the scale's reliability beyond what was noted regarding the pretest.

VALIDITY: No examination of scale validity was reported by Lacher and Mizerski (1994) beyond that noted for the study's pretest.

ADMINISTRATION: The scale was self-administered, along with other measures, in the study by Lacher and Mizerski (1994), and the procedure was similar to that described for the pretest. Higher scores on the scale indicated that respondents perceived that a particular song evoked images and triggered memories.

MAJOR FINDINGS: Lacher and Mizerski (1994) investigated the responses music evokes in a listener and how those reactions affect the intention to purchase the music. Specifically, the **imaginal response to music** had a direct effect on the experiential response (#154), being absorbed or swept away by the listening experience.

COMMENTS: As noted from the alpha levels reported previously, the scale varies in its internal consistency depending on the song. It is not clear why this is true. However, for some songs, the reliability may be so low as to be considered unacceptable. Therefore, further testing and improvement in the scale appears to be needed.

REFERENCES:

Hargreaves, David J. (1982), "Preference and Prejudice in Music: A Psychological Approach," *Popular Music & Society*, 8 (3-4), 13–18.

Lacher, Kathleen T. and Richard Mizerski (1994), "An Exploratory Study of the Responses and Relationships Involved in the Evaluation of, and in the Intention to Purchase New Rock Music," *JCR*, 21 (September), 366–80.

Yingling, Robert W. (1962), "Classification of Reaction Patterns in Listening to Music," *Journal of Research in Music Education*, 10 (Fall), 105–20.

#180 *Imaginal Response to Music*

SCALE ITEMS:

Strongly
disagree   :___:___:___:___:___:___: agree
          1   2   3   4   5   6

1. The song created a picture in my mind.

2. The song made me remember something.

3. The song prompted images in my mind.

SCALE NAME: Imaginary Audience

SCALE DESCRIPTION: Eleven brief scenarios with three response alternatives. The directions and scenarios ask the respondent to imagine being in various situations in which they must choose between participating in a socially awkward or unacceptable activity and refusing to participate. Most of the scenarios have something to do with taking drugs.

SCALE ORIGIN: Schoenbachler and Whittler (1996) adapted a scale originally developed by Elkind and Bowen (1979). That scale had 12 scenarios that respondents would read and respond to by indicating whether they would be willing to participate in the described activity. Half of the items in Elkind and Bowen's (1979) scale were created to be measures of the *transient self-conscious*, and the other half, adapted from Simmons, Rosenberg, and Rosenberg (1973), were to measure the *abiding self-conscious*. Of the eleven items used by Schoenbachler and Whittler (1996), four are slightly modified versions of transient self-conscious items from Elkind and Bowen (1979), and the remaining seven were constructed by the authors to have drug-related content.

SAMPLES: Data were collected by Schoenbachler and Whittler (1996) from a sample of **371** seventh- and eighth-grade students from a metropolitan middle school. No other information was provided about the sample.

RELIABILITY: An alpha of **.62** was reported for the scale (Schoenbachler and Whittler 1996).

VALIDITY: No examination of the scale's validity was reported by Schoenbachler and Whittler (1996).

ADMINISTRATION: The subjects completed the scale as part of a larger instrument they filled out after they were exposed to an experimental stimulus (Schoenbachler and Whittler 1996). As calculated by the authors, the response alternative reflecting willingness to participate was scored as 0, indifference to participate was scored as 1, and unwillingness to participate was scored as 2. Lower scores on the scale appeared to suggest that respondents were more willing to participate in the socially awkward activity.

MAJOR FINDINGS: The purpose of the experiment by Schoenbachler and Whittler (1996) was to examine threat appeal advertising using the *ordered protection model*. Despite expectations, a social threat did not produce a significantly greater **imaginary audience** coping response compared with a physical threat. The authors speculated that this may have been due to the poor quality of the scale.

COMMENTS: Because of the low internal consistency of the scale, its unidimensionality and validity are suspect. Further work is called for to test and improve the scale's psychometric quality.

REFERENCES:
Elkind, David and Robert Bowen (1979), "Imaginary Audience Behavior in Children and Adolescents," *Developmental Psychology*, 15 (1), 38–44.
Schoenbachler, Denise D. (1997), personal correspondence.
——— and Tommy E. Whittler (1996), "Adolescent Processing of Social and Physical Threat Communications," *JA*, 25 (Winter), 37–54.
Simmons, Robert G., Florence Rosenberg, and Morris Rosenberg (1973), "Disturbance in the Self-Image at Adolescence," *American Sociological Review*, 38 (October), 553–68.

SCALE ITEMS:*

DIRECTIONS: Please read the following stories carefully and assume that the events actually happened to you. Place a check next to the answer that best described what you would do or feel in the real situation.

1. You have looked forward to the most exciting party of the year. You arrive after an hour's drive from home. Just as you walk in, a group of your friends approach you and offer you crack. You refuse, and they tell you that everyone at the party is high. Would you stay or go home?

_____ Go home.[2]

_____ Stay, even though I'd feel uncomfortable.[1]

_____ Stay, because being the only person not high wouldn't bother me.[0]

2. It is Friday afternoon and you have just had your hair cut in preparation for the wedding of a relative that weekend. The barber or hairdresser did a terrible job and your hair looks awful. To make it worse, that night is the most important football game of the season and you really want to see it, but there is no way you can keep your head covered without people asking questions. Would you stay home or go to the game anyway?

_____ Go to the game and not worry about my hair.[0]

_____ Go to the game and sit where people won't notice me very much.[1]

_____ Stay home.[2]

3. You have been invited to a party where the most popular kids in school will be. When you arrive at the party, you light up a joint and offer it to the person next to you. He gives you a dirty look and says, "We don't do drugs." Would you:

_____ Finish the joint and have a good time?[0]

_____ Leave the party?[2]

_____ Put the joint out and hope no one else noticed?[1]

4. You are sitting in class and have discovered that your jeans have a small but noticeable split along the side seam. Your teacher has offered extra credit toward his/her grade to anyone who can write the correct answer to a question on the board. Would you get up in front of the class and go to the blackboard, or would you remain seated?

_____ Go to the blackboard as though nothing had happened.[0]

_____ Go to the blackboard and try to hide the split.[1]

_____ Remain seated.[2]

5. You just moved to a new town and started going to a new school. At your old school, everyone met before basketball games and got high before going in to watch the game. You ask a few people you've

met if they want to get high with you before the game. All of them say no, so you get high by your-self and go to the game. While you're at the game, would you wonder what the other kids were think-ing about you?

_____ I wouldn't think about it.[0]

_____ I would wonder about that a lot.[2]

_____ I would wonder about that a little.[1]

6. You have looked forward to the most exciting dress up party of the year. Just as the party is begin-ning, you notice a grease spot on your trousers or skirt. (There is no way to borrow clothes from any-one.) Would you stay or go home?

_____ Go home.[2]

_____ Stay, even though I'd feel uncomfortable.[1]

_____ Stay, because the grease spot wouldn't bother me.[0]

7. You go to a party with your two best friends. After you've been there a while, a kid you don't know invites your two friends to go outside and get high. You didn't realize your friends used drugs, and you've never tried them before. Your friends turn to you and ask if you want to go too. Would you go with them?

_____ I'd go, but wouldn't get high.[1]

_____ I wouldn't go with them.[0]

_____ I'd go and get high with them.[2]

8. Suppose you went to a party where you thought everyone would be high, but when you got there you were the only person who'd done drugs. You'd like to stay and have fun with your friends, but it's very noticeable that you're high. Would you stay or go home?

_____ Go home.[2]

_____ Stay and have fun joking about being high.[0]

_____ Stay, but try to act like you're not high.[1]

9. Your class is supposed to have their picture taken, but you fell the day before and scraped your face. You'd like to be in the picture, but your cheek is red and swollen. Would you have your picture taken anyway or stay out of the picture?

_____ Get your picture taken even though you'd be embarrassed.[1]

_____ Stay out of the picture.[2]

_____ Get your picture taken and not worry about it.[0]

10. You have a date with the best looking guy/girl in school. On the way to the movies, he/she offers you a hit of LSD. You've never tried LSD before, and refuse it. Would you worry that he/she wouldn't ask you out again?

_____ I wouldn't worry about it.[0]

_____ I would wonder about that a little.[1]

_____ I would wonder about that a lot.[2]

11. Some of your friends have recently formed a Champions Against Drugs group in your school. They want you to join too, but they don't realize you get high sometimes. You decide to join the group. Would you:

_____ Continue getting high but try to hide it?[1]

_____ Stop getting high?[2]

_____ Continue getting high and tell your friends you do?[0]

*The numbers at the end of the alternative responses indicate the codes to use in scoring the scale. The directions, scale items, and codes were provided by Schoenbachler (1997).

SCALE NAME: Impulse Buying

SCALE DESCRIPTION: Nine five-point Likert-type items that measure "a consumer's tendency to buy spontaneously, unreflectively, immediately, and kinetically" (Rook and Fisher 1995, p. 306). The construct is viewed as a consumer trait that may produce frequent motivations to buy, even though they are not always acted on.

SCALE ORIGIN: Although previous work had been done on the scale (Rook and Gardner 1993; Rook and Hoch 1985), the most extensive testing was conducted by Rook and Fisher (1995). In that study, 35 items were generated on the basis of a review of literature and pretested on 281 undergraduate business students. The purification process across the pretest and Study 1 samples resulted in a final nine-item scale. As described further here, evidence in support of the measure's convergent and discriminant validity was found (Rook 1997).

SAMPLES: Rook and Fisher (1995) gathered data for their studies from two very different samples. Study 1 was based on data from **212** undergraduate business students, whereas Study 2 used data gathered from **99** completed mall intercept interviews. All of the interviews in the latter sample were conducted on one day just outside a music store. The sample was almost evenly split on gender (51% females) and was rather young (69% were younger than 21 years of age).

RELIABILITY: Alphas of **.88** and **.82** were reported for the scale in Studies 1 and 2, respectively (Rook and Fisher 1995).

VALIDITY: Confirmatory factor analysis was used in both Studies 1 and 2 to provide evidence that the nine-item measure was an acceptable model (Rook and Fisher 1995). The statistics in both studies supported an unidimensional scale. From information not reported in the article (Rook 1997), it is clear that the scale showed evidence of its validity. Specifically, strong positive correlations were found between it and overall impulsiveness, as well as with projections of impulsive purchase decisions on hypothetical consumers. Relatively weak correlations were found between the scale and other measures (sensation seeking, disinhibition seeking, boredom proneness, and future time orientation).

ADMINISTRATION: In both studies by Rook and Fisher (1995), the scale was self-administered by respondents as part of a larger instrument. Higher scores on the scale indicated that respondents thought that they frequently made impulse purchases.

MAJOR FINDINGS: Rook and Fisher (1995) examined the impact of normative evaluations on the impulse buying trait and buying behaviors. As hypothesized, normative evaluations were found to moderate the link between trait (as measured by the scale) and behavioral aspects of **impulse buying**.

COMMENTS: Rook and Fisher (1995) reported scale means of 25.1 and 21.5 in Studies 1 and 2, respectively.

REFERENCES:
Rook, Dennis W. (1997), personal correspondence.
———— and Robert J. Fisher (1995), "Normative Influences on Impulsive Buying Behavior," *JCR*, 22 (December), 305–13.
———— and Meryl Paula Gardner (1993), "In the Mood: Impulse Buying's Affective Antecedents," *Research in Consumer Behavior*, Vol. 6, Janeen Arnold Costa and Russell W. Belk, eds. Greenwich, CT: JAI Press, 1–28.
———— and Stephen J. Hoch (1985), "Consuming Impulses," in *Advances in Consumer Research*, Vol. 12, Morris B. Holbrook and Elizabeth J. Hirschman, eds. Provo, UT: Association for Consumer Research, 23–27.

SCALE ITEMS:

Strongly   Strongly
disagree   :___:___:___:___:___: agree
                    1   2   3   4   5

1. I often buy things spontaneously.

2. "Just do it" describes the way I buy things.

3. I often buy things without thinking.

4. "I see it, I buy it" describes me.

5. "Buy now, think about it later" describes me.

6. Sometimes I feel like buying things on the spur of the moment.

7. I buy things according to how I feel at the moment.

8. I carefully plan most of my purchases. **(r)**

9. Sometimes I am a bit reckless about what I buy.

SCALE NAME: Impulse Buying

SCALE DESCRIPTION: A four-item, five-point Likert-type summated ratings scale measuring the degree to which a person not only indicates that he or she engages in unplanned consumer choice, but likes to purchase that way.

SCALE ORIGIN: The source of the scale was not stated by Donthu and Gilliland (1996), but it is likely original to their study.

SAMPLES: Donthu and Gilliland (1996) used trained interviewers to call 1000 households in a large city telephone directory. Interviews were successfully completed with adults in **368** of those households. Although some demographic information was employed in the analysis, the data were not reported in such a way that the sample as a whole can be clearly described.

RELIABILITY: An alpha of **.87** was reported for the scale by Donthu and Gilliland (1996).

VALIDITY: No specific examination of the scale's validity was reported by Donthu and Gilliland (1996).

ADMINISTRATION: Donthu and Gilliland (1996) had the scale administered as part of a larger telephone survey. Higher scores on the scale indicated that respondents engaged in impulse buying and liked doing so.

MAJOR FINDINGS: Donthu and Gilliland (1996) profiled infomercial shoppers and found that they admitted significantly greater **buying impulsiveness** than those who had never purchased goods from infomercials.

REFERENCES:
Donthu, Naveen and David Gilliland (1996), "The Infomercial Shopper," *JAR*, 36 (March/April), 69–76.

SCALE ITEMS:

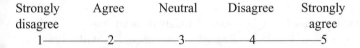

Strongly disagree	Agree	Neutral	Disagree	Strongly agree
1	2	3	4	5

1. I often make unplanned purchases.

2. I like to purchase things on a whim.

3. I think twice before committing myself. **(r)**

4. I always stick to my shopping list. **(r)**

SCALE NAME: Impulse Buying

SCALE DESCRIPTION: The scale is intended to measure the extent to which a consumer is likely to make unplanned, immediate, and unreflective purchases.

SCALE ORIGIN: The scale used by Mick (1996) was developed by Martin, Weun, and Beatty (1993). Several rounds of testing whittled a group of 65 potential items down to an 8-item, two-factor structure with an alpha of .86. Several tests of this version of the scale provided support for a claim of convergent validity. However, the scale's lack of unidimensionality led to some redevelopment effort, such that Weun, Jones, and Beatty (1997) subsequently presented another version. Evidence was provided in support of the scale's unidimensionality, as well as its discriminant and convergent validities. The alphas for this version of the scale were reported to range between .80 to .85.

SAMPLES: Data were collected by Mick (1996) only in the second of two studies he reported. Students taking a marketing research course were asked to distribute the surveys following firm guidelines. This approach produced **172** usable questionnaires. With this sample, the average age was 40 years, and a little more than half (55%) were women.

RELIABILITY: An alpha of **.82** was reported for the scale by Mick (1996).

VALIDITY: No examination of the scale's validity was described by Mick (1996).

ADMINISTRATION: The scale was self-administered by respondents as part of a larger survey instrument (Mick 1996). Higher scores on the scale indicated that respondents engaged in a high level of impulse buying and enjoyed it.

MAJOR FINDINGS: The effect of social desirability bias on the nomological network surrounding the materialism construct was examined by Mick (1996). He found in the second of his two studies that **impulse buying** had a low but significant negative correlation with the component of social desirability referred to as "impression management."

REFERENCES:

Martin, Wendy K., Seungoog Weun, and Sharon Beatty (1993), "Validation of an Impulse Tendency Scale," paper presented at the Association of Consumer Research conference, Nashville, TN.

Mick, David Glen (1996), "Are Studies of Dark Side Variables Confounded by Socially Desirable Responding? The Case of Materialism," *JCR*, 23 (September), 106–19.

Weun, Seungoog, Michael A. Jones, and Sharon E. Beatty (1997), "A Parsimonious Scale to Measure Impulse Buying Tendency," *Proceedings of the American Marketing Association Educators' Summer Conference*. Chicago, IL: American Marketing Association, 306–307.

SCALE ITEMS:*

DIRECTIONS: Please indicate the degree to which the following statements describe your behavior when you are shopping at a mall. Think about the last few times you have been shopping in a mall. Please respond to each question by circling the number from 1 to 7 that most closely corresponds to your position.

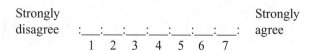

Strongly
disagree :___:___:___:___:___:___:___: Strongly agree
      1 2 3 4 5 6 7

1. Even when I see something I really like, I do not buy it unless it is a planned purchase. **(r)**

2. When I go shopping, I buy things I had not intended to purchase.

3. I avoid buying things that are not on my shopping list. **(r)**

4. It is fun to buy spontaneously.

5. I do not buy until I can make sure I am getting a real bargain. **(r)**

6. When I see something new that really interests me, I buy it right away just to see what it is like.

7. I buy some things without hesitation if I like them when I first see them.

8. When I see something new I really want, I purchase it immediately, even if I had not planned to buy it.

9. I am a person who makes unplanned purchases.

10. When I see something that really interests me, I buy it without considering the consequences.

Martin, Weun, and Beatty (1993): 1–8
Mick (1996): 1–8
Weun, Jones, and Beatty (1997): 2, 4, 5, 9, 10

*These directions were provided in one of the stages of testing conducted by Martin, Weun, and Beatty (1993).

SCALE NAME: Impulse Buying

SCALE DESCRIPTION: Four five-point Likert-type items intended to measure a shopping orientation that is characterized by a lack of planning and care. There is also a sense expressed in the scale that the consumer regrets not being more careful.

SCALE ORIGIN: Shim and Gehrt (1996) used a scale developed by Sproles and Kendall (1986). The latter created an eight-factor model of what they called *consumer decision making styles* but that many others in marketing (e.g., Shim and Gehrt 1996) would view as *shopping orientations*. Shim and Gehrt (1996) used the four items with the highest factor loadings of the five items identified by Sproles and Kendall (1986). The latter reported an alpha of .48 for the five-item scale and a .41 for the three items loading highest on the factor.

SAMPLES: Shim and Gehrt (1996) collected data from high school students in a Southwestern U.S. state. Twenty-nine principals agreed to participate, and their schools apparently represented many if not all counties in the state. Principals were given instructions as to which classes to use (by level) and how many students from each class were needed. Some 1954 usable surveys were returned by students who were 61.3% girls and had a mean age of 16 years. However, the study focused only on data from **1846** students who were white (56%), Hispanic (32%), or Native American (12%).

RELIABILITY: An alpha of **.45** was reported for the scale by Shim and Gehrt (1996).

VALIDITY: No examination of the scale's validity was reported by Shim and Gehrt (1996).

ADMINISTRATION: Data were gathered in a classroom setting in which students filled out the scale as part of a larger survey instrument (Shim and Gehrt 1996). Higher scores on the scale indicated that respondents were very impulsive in their shopping.

MAJOR FINDINGS: The study by Shim and Gehrt (1996) examined differences in shopping orientations among high school students that could be linked to ethnicity. The results showed that white students expressed significantly less **impulsive buying** tendencies than Hispanics and Native Americans, with the latter expressing the most **impulsivity**.

COMMENTS: The internal consistency of the scale is unacceptably low, and it should not be used again until further development and testing can substantially improve its psychometric quality.

REFERENCES:

Shim, Soyeon and Kenneth C. Gehrt (1996), "Hispanic and Native American Adolescents: An Exploratory Study of Their Approach to Shopping," *JR*, 72 (3), 307–24.

Sproles, George B. and Elizabeth L. Kendall (1986), "A Methodology for Profiling Consumers' Decision-Making Styles," *Journal of Consumer Affairs*, 20 (Winter), 267–79.

SCALE ITEMS:

Strongly disagree :___:___:___:___:___: Strongly agree
             1   2   3   4   5

1. I should plan my shopping more carefully than I do.

2. I am impulsive when purchasing.

3. Often I make careless purchases I later wish I had not.

4. I take the time to shop carefully for best buys. **(r)**

SCALE NAME: Impulse Buying (Music)

SCALE DESCRIPTION: Three five-point Likert-type items that measure the degree of specificity with which a consumer planned a purchase of some music (album) before entering a store.

SCALE ORIGIN: The source of the scale was not specified by Rook and Fisher (1995), though it is rather clear that it is original to their work.

SAMPLES: Rook and Fisher (1995) gathered data for their studies from two very different samples, though the scale was only used in Study 2. In it, data were gathered from **99** completed mall intercept interviews. All of the interviews were conducted on one day just outside a music store. The sample was almost evenly split on gender (51% females) and was rather young (69% were younger than 21 years of age).

RELIABILITY: An alpha of **.93** was reported for the scale by Rook and Fisher (1995).

VALIDITY: No examination of the scale's validity was reported by Rook and Fisher (1995). However, the correlation between the scale and two others that measured aspects of impulse buying were provided. The correlations were low ($\leq$.21) but significant. (See "Major Findings.")

ADMINISTRATION: The scale was self-administered by respondents as part of a larger instrument. Higher scores on the scale indicated that respondents impulsively purchased a piece of recorded music. A 0 was assigned by Rook and Fisher (1995) if no purchases were made.

MAJOR FINDINGS: Rook and Fisher (1995) examined the impact of normative evaluations on the impulse buying trait and buying behaviors. When respondents were divided into three groups on the basis of their evaluations of the appropriateness of impulse buying for an individual in a scenario, only those in the group that was most favorable toward the character engaging in impulse buying had a significant positive correlation ($r = .58$) between their own **impulse buying of music** and their predisposition toward impulse buying in general (#182).

COMMENTS: Rook and Fisher (1995) reported a scale mean of 1.8. Furthermore, this scale should be used for each recording a person has purchased. That is, during a single shopping trip, one recording purchase might be well planned, whereas another might be quite impulsive.

REFERENCES:
Rook, Dennis W. (1997), personal correspondence.
———— and Robert J. Fisher (1995), "Normative Influences on Impulsive Buying Behavior," *JCR*, 22 (December), 305–13.

SCALE ITEMS:*
DIRECTIONS: Let's take a look at only the musical recordings you bought here today. Think about how much each of the following statements applies to each of your purchases, and circle the number closest to how you feel.

Strongly   Strongly
disagree   :___:___:___:___:___: agree
            1   2   3   4   5

1. When I got to the store, I knew I wanted to buy something in this general <u>music category</u>, e.g., rock, rap, hip hop, country, etc.

2. I planned to buy something by this particular <u>artist or group</u>.

3. I planned on buying this <u>exact</u> CD/album/tape.

*The items and directions shown here were only briefly described in the article by Rook and Fisher (1995) but were explicitly provided in personal correspondence (Rook 1997).

SCALE NAME: Innovativeness

SCALE DESCRIPTION: A three-item, five-point Likert-type summated ratings scale measuring the degree to which a person expresses a desire to take chances and try new things.

SCALE ORIGIN: The source of the scale was not stated by Donthu and Gilliland (1996), but it is likely original to their study.

SAMPLES: Donthu and Gilliland (1996) used trained interviewers to call 1000 households in a large city telephone directory. Interviews were successfully completed with adults in **368** of those households. Although some demographic information was employed in the analysis, the data were not reported in such a way that the sample as a whole can be clearly described.

RELIABILITY: An alpha of **.70** was reported for the scale by Donthu and Gilliland (1996).

VALIDITY: No specific examination of the scale's validity was reported by Donthu and Gilliland (1996).

ADMINISTRATION: Donthu and Gilliland (1996) had the scale administered as part of a larger telephone survey. Higher scores on the scale indicated that respondents were very innovative.

MAJOR FINDINGS: Donthu and Gilliland (1996) profiled infomercial shoppers and found that they were significantly more **innovative** than those who had never purchased goods from infomercials.

REFERENCES:
Donthu, Naveen and David Gilliland (1996), "The Infomercial Shopper," *JAR*, 36 (March/April), 69–76.

SCALE ITEMS:

Strongly disagree	Agree	Neutral	Disagree	Strongly agree
1	2	3	4	5

1. I like to take chances.

2. I like to experiment with new ways of doing things.

3. New products are usually gimmicks. **(r)**

SCALE NAME: Innovativeness (Domain Specific)

SCALE DESCRIPTION: A six-item, five-point Likert-type scale measuring the tendency to learn about and adopt innovations (new products) within a specific domain of interest. The scale is intended to be distinct from a generalized personality trait at one extreme and a highly specific, single product purchase at the other extreme.

SCALE ORIGIN: The scale was constructed by Goldsmith and Hofacker (1991). Their desire was to develop a short, flexible measure of consumer innovativeness modeled after King and Summers's (1970) measure of opinion leadership.

SAMPLES: Flynn, Goldsmith, and Eastman (1996) reported on five studies, but only one (Study 3) employed the **innovativeness** scale. Data for that study came from **391** undergraduate students at a large university. Questionnaires were completed in class. The respondents ranged in age from 18 to 64 years (median = 21). The sample was 72% women and 83% white.

Six different studies were described in the article by Goldsmith and Hofacker (1991) as being used to examine various aspects of the scale's reliability and validity. Study 1 was composed of **309** complete questionnaires from 151 men and 157 women who had a mean age of 21.6 years. The data were collected by 31 college students in a marketing research class who were each asked to conduct personal interviews with five men and five women. In Study 2, 28 marketing research students were asked to have five men and five women self-administer the scale. This resulted in **275** usable questionnaires from 146 men and 129 women who had a mean age of 21.5 years. Study 3 was based on **97** completed questionnaires collected by two male interviewers. This all-female sample had a mean age of 22.1. A mall intercept approach was used in Study 4 to collect data. Highly trained interviewers gathered usable information from **462** adults. The sample had the following characteristics: 44% had at least a college degree, 48.7% were under 30 years of age, 40% were married, 64.1% were white, and a little more than half (51.3%) were women. In Study 5, the scale's stability was assessed by administering a questionnaire to **75** students in a marketing research class. Fifteen weeks later, **70** of the same students filled out the scale again. Finally, Study 6 was composed of completed questionnaires from **306** respondents. The data from 152 men and 154 women were collected by students in two marketing research classes; the subjects had a mean age of 21.3 years.

RELIABILITY: An alpha of **.83** was estimated for the scale in Study 3 (fashion) by Flynn, Goldsmith, and Eastman (1996; Goldsmith 1997). Because they used multiple studies, as described, several examinations of the scale's internal consistency were reported by Goldsmith and Hofacker (1991). The following alphas were calculated: **.83** (Study 2, records); **.82** (Study 3, records); **.79** (Study 4, fashion); **.81** (Study 4, electronics); **.88** (Study 5, records, n = 75); **.90** (Study 4, records, n = 70); and **.85, .83,** and **.83** for records, fashion, and scent, respectively, in Study 6. The stability of the scale as measured in Study 5 was .86.

VALIDITY: The validity of the scale was not directly examined by Flynn, Goldsmith, and Eastman (1996). However, because it was part of an effort to examine the nomological validity of two other scales (#243 and #245), some sense of its own nomological validity can be gained. For example, high positive correlations were found between **innovativeness** and opinion leadership, product involvement, and product knowledge. No relationship was found between **innovativeness** and opinion seeking.

Validity of the scale was examined in detail by Goldsmith and Hofacker (1991). Data from Study 2 were subjected to both exploratory and confirmatory factor analysis with similar results: The items loaded on the same factor and were unidimensional. Also in Study 2, a pattern of significant positive correlations with seven criterion measures provided evidence of the scale's criterion validity. Studies 3, 4, and 5 had results very similar to Study 2's, in that the evidence supported the notion that the scale was unidimensional and had criterion validity. In addition, Study 5 provided evidence of discriminant validity, in that the scale was not significantly correlated with yea-saying or social desirability bias. Study 6 measured innovativeness in three product categories (music, fashion, and scent). Using a multitrait, multimethod approach, the authors concluded that there was strong evidence of convergent and discriminant validity.

ADMINISTRATION: In the study by Flynn, Goldsmith, and Eastman (1996), the scale was part of a larger survey instrument self-administered by students in class. As noted previously, the six studies conducted by Goldsmith and Hofacker (1991) involved two main types of administration; in most, the scale was administered as part of a personal interview, whereas in the other studies, it was included in a self-administered questionnaire. Higher scores on the scale indicated that consumers not only had knowledge and interest about new products in a specified category, but also perceived themselves as among the first to purchase those new items.

MAJOR FINDINGS: Flynn, Goldsmith, and Eastman (1996) reported on the development and testing of opinion leadership and opinion-seeking scales (#243 and #245). **Innovativeness** was included along with several other measures merely to help establish the nomological validity of the two opinion-related scales. As noted, **innovativeness** had a high positive association with opinion leadership but no significant relationship with opinion seeking.

The purpose of the studies by Goldsmith and Hofacker (1991) was to provide evidence of the **innovativeness** scale's psychometric quality. This appears to have been accomplished. They further showed that, though the items are Likert-type statements, they seem to be amenable for use in several product categories. Among the interesting findings not described thus far here were that, for both records and fashion, high correlations were found between innovativeness and opinion leadership. Also, though record **innovativeness** was not related to **innovativeness** for fashion or scent, the latter two were significantly associated.

COMMENTS: The authors claim that the scale is most appropriate for studying product in categories that are purchased rather frequently. Products that are bought less often might not be measured as well with this scale because there are fewer attitudes and behaviors for consumers to draw on in making their responses.

For other uses of the scale, see Goldsmith and Flynn (1992) and Flynn and Goldsmith (1993). German and French versions can be found in Goldsmith, d'Hauteville, and Flynn (1998).

REFERENCES:
Flynn, Leisa R. and Ronald E. Goldsmith (1993), "Identifying Innovators in Consumer Service Markets," *The Service Industries Journal*, 13 (July), 97–109.
———, ———, and Jacqueline K. Eastman (1996), "Opinion Leaders and Opinion Seekers: Two New Measurement Scales," *JAMS*, 24 (Spring), 137–47.
Goldsmith, Ronald E. (1997), personal correspondence.
———, Francois d'Hauteville, and Leisa R. Flynn (1998), "Theory and Measurement of Consumer Innovativeness," *European Journal of Marketing*, 32 (3/4), 340–53.
——— and Leisa Reinecke Flynn (1992), "Identifying Innovators in Consumer Markets," *European Journal of Marketing*, 26 (12), 42–55.
——— and Charles F. Hofacker (1991), "Measuring Consumer Innovativeness," *JAMS*, 19 (Summer), 209–21.
King, Charles W. and John O. Summers (1970), "Overlap of Opinion Leadership Across Consumer Product Categories," *JMR*, 7 (February), 43–50.

SCALE ITEMS:*

Strongly   Strongly
disagree   :___:___:___:___:___: agree
            1   2   3   4   5

1. In general, I am among the last in my circle of friends to buy a new _____ when it appears. **(r)**

2. If I heard that a new _____ was available in the store, I would not be interested enough to buy it. **(r)**

3. Compared to my friends I own few _____. **(r)**

4. In general, I am the last in my circle of friends to know the latest _____. **(r)**

5. I will buy a new _____, even if I haven't heard it yet.

6. I know the names of new _____ before other people do.

SCALE NAME: Intellectual Environment

SCALE DESCRIPTION: Five phrases purported to measure a person's (e.g., a former student's) evaluation of several aspects of his or her college education experience.

SCALE ORIGIN: The scale was apparently developed for use in the study reported by Halstead, Hartman, and Schmidt (1994).

SAMPLES: Analysis by Halstead, Hartman, and Schmidt (1994) was based on data collected from **475** alumni of a major university in the Eastern United States. The data were collected as part of a larger school assessment program. Questionnaires were mailed to the population (1223) of former students who had graduated within the previous four years. There was a 38.8% response rate. Calls to 28 former students who had not sent back a survey form indicated that there was no significant nonresponse bias. The sample was 52% women, with an average age of 24 years. The average income reported was $33,000, and 39 states, as well as several foreign countries, were represented.

RELIABILITY: Cronbach's alpha for the scale was reported to be **.70** (Halstead, Hartman, and Schmidt 1994).

VALIDITY: Confirmatory factor analysis supported the unidimensionality of the scale (Halstead, Hartman, and Schmidt 1994). There was also some limited evidence provided of the scale's convergent and discriminant validity.

ADMINISTRATION: The scale was part of a larger mail survey instrument (Hartman, and Schmidt 1994). High scores on the scale indicated that respondents had a very positive view of the intellectual environment they experienced at the university from which they graduated.

MAJOR FINDINGS: Halstead, Hartman, and Schmidt (1994) investigated a model that proposed that alumni satisfaction with their college education is a function of the intellectual environment they experienced and the preparation they received for employment. The findings indicated that there was a significant direct effect of intellectual environment on satisfaction.

REFERENCES:
Halstead, Diane, David Hartman, and Sandra L. Schmidt (1994), "Multisource Effects on the Satisfaction Formation Process," *JAMS*, 22 (2), 114–29.

SCALE ITEMS:
DIRECTIONS: According to your experience, please assess the strengths and weaknesses of the following aspects of the school:

Very weak   :___:___:___:___:___: Very strong
                1   2   3   4   5

1. Teaching ability of the faculty.

2. Intellectual capacity of the student body.

3. Student organizations.

4. Interaction between faculty and students.

5. Interaction between administration and students.

SCALE NAME: Intention to Use Credit Card

SCALE DESCRIPTION: Six five-point statements measuring a person's perceived likelihood of using a specified credit card. The scale also appears to capture the level of involvement the person wants to have with the image or cause linked with the card and its sponsoring organization. The organization studied by Sirgy and colleagues (1997) was the Sierra Club, and the cause was environmentalism.

SCALE ORIGIN: Although not explicitly stated, the scale appears to have been developed by Sirgy and colleagues (1997) for use in Study 5 of the six they conducted.

SAMPLES: Study 5 was based on data collected from junior and senior business majors through in-class surveys. Usable data were gathered from **320** students.

RELIABILITY: An alpha of **.77** was reported for the scale by Sirgy and colleagues (1997).

VALIDITY: No examination of the scale's validity was reported (Sirgy et al. 1997).

ADMINISTRATION: The scale was apparently self-administered by students (Sirgy et al. 1997) as part of a in-class survey. Higher scores on the scale suggested that respondents viewed some specified credit card, its image, and its sponsoring organization positively enough to want to use it.

MAJOR FINDINGS: As noted, Sirgy and colleagues (1997) conducted six studies in support of a new method for measuring **self-image congruency** that was more direct than previous measures. In Study 5, the new measure was found to be more predictive of **intention to use a credit card** with a similar image than a traditional measure was.

COMMENTS: As noted, the scale explicitly referred to a image type (environmental), as well as a sponsoring organization (Sierra Club). It appears to be amenable for use with different images and different organizations, though further testing and adjustment would be necessary.

REFERENCES:
Sirgy, M. Joseph, Dhruv Grewal, Tamara F. Mangleburg, Jae-ok Park, Kye-Sung Chon, C.B. Claiborne, J.S. Johar, and Harold Berkman (1997), "Assessing the Predictive Validity of Two Methods of Measuring Self-Image Congruence," *JAMS*, 25 (Summer), 229–41.

SCALE ITEMS:*

Unlikely :___:___:___:___:___: Likely
        1 2 3 4 5

1. What is the likelihood you will see the benefit of a credit card that makes a statement about you, like the _____ card?

2. What is the likelihood that you will recommend that your friends use an [environmental] credit card like the _____ card.

3. What is the likelihood that you will feel you have made a contribution after using an [environmental] credit card like the _____ card?

4. What is the likelihood that you will use a credit card like the _____ card?

5. What is the likelihood that you will look for more information on [environmental] credit cards?

6. What is the likelihood that you will compare the benefits of several [environmental] credit cards?

*The name of the credit card company and/or sponsoring organization should be placed in the blanks.

SCALE NAME: Interpersonal Influence Susceptibility

SCALE DESCRIPTION: The Likert-type scale measures the degree to which a person expresses the tendency to seek information about products by observing others' behavior and asking for their opinions. Bearden, Netemeyer, and Teel (1989, p. 473) referred to the scale as *consumer susceptibility to interpersonal influence* (CSII) and defined it as a consumer's "willingness to conform to the expectations of others regarding the purchase decision." They measured it using two scales with a total of twelve items in a seven-point response format. In contrast, Boush, Friestad, and Rose's (1994) version had just three items and a five-point response scale. Day and Stafford's (1997) version used all twelve items in one scale and apparently had a seven-point response format.

SCALE ORIGIN: This measure was constructed by Bearden, Netemeyer, and Teel (1989). A series of studies were conducted by the authors to determine the reliability and validity of the scale, only a portion of which are discussed here. On the basis of a review of previous research, 166 items were generated that were suspected to measure one of the three hypothesized dimensions of interpersonal influence susceptibility: *informational, normative,* and *value expressiveness.* After ambiguous and essentially identical items were dropped, the content validity of the remaining items was evaluated by five judges. Then, the remaining items were rated again by four more judges for their clarity in representing one of the dimensions of the construct. Some other aspects of the analysis are described subsequently.

Boush, Friestad, and Rose (1994) performed a pretest on items borrowed from Bearden, Netemeyer, and Teel (1989). Two items were taken from the *informational* version of the CSII (Vol. 1, #121), and one item was taken from the *normative* version (see Vol. 1, #135). Some changes in wording were also made.

Day and Stafford (1997) chose to combined the items from the two dimensions (*informational* and *normative*) of the original set of measures used by Bearden, Netemeyer, and Teel (1989). The former also modified the wording of items in some cases to make them more amenable to the retail context.

SAMPLES: Sixty-two items were initially administered by Bearden, Netemeyer, and Teel (1989) to a convenience sample of **220** adult consumers. Fifteen items were reevaluated by a convenience sample of **141** undergraduate students.

Data were gathered by Boush, Friestad, and Rose (1994) from students at two middle schools (grades 6–8) in a medium-sized city in the Pacific Northwest of the United States. A survey instrument was administered to students during the first and last weeks of the school year. Analysis was generally based on information received from the **426** students who completed the questionnaire during both of its administrations.

Day and Stafford (1997) collected their data from **126** undergraduate students from two universities. A little more than half the sample were men (55%), 16.7 % were married, and the average age was nearly 24 years. No compensation was provided, and participation was voluntary.

RELIABILITY: Bearden, Netemeyer, and Teel (1989) reported alphas for the eight-item normative dimension as.**87** and .**88** in the first and second administrations, respectively. The alphas for the four-item informational dimension were .**83** and .**82** in the first and second administrations, respectively. LISREL estimates of reliability were very similar. Thirty-five students from the second administration participated in a test of the scales' three-week stabilities (test–retest reliability). Correlations of .75 and .79 were reported between the scores for the informational and normative dimensions, respectively.

Alphas of .**62** and .**67** were reported for the scale for its first and second administrations, respectively, by Boush, Friestad, and Rose (1994). The version of the scale used by Day and Stafford (1997) was reported to have an alpha of .**87**.

VALIDITY: Although there was initial effort by Bearden, Netemeyer, and Teel (1989) to develop separate scales to measure the three hypothesized dimensions of the construct (consumer susceptibility to interpersonal influence), there was strong evidence of discriminant and convergent validity for the informational dimension but not for the utilitarian and value expressive dimensions. Their items were combined to form one scale. Confirmatory factor analysis indicated a stable two-factor correlated structure (the normative and informational factors). Some further analyses that provided evidence of construct validity are discussed under "Major Findings."

The validity of the scale was not specifically addressed in the study by Boush, Friestad, and Rose (1994). However, the authors performed a principal components analysis of the combined items of this scale with those of another scale (#315). They reported that the results "yielded a simple structure solution" (Boush, Friestad, and Rose 1994, p. 170).

ADMINISTRATION: The scale was self-administered in each of the studies reported by Bearden, Netemeyer, and Teel (1989). The scale used by Boush, Friestad, and Rose (1994) was part of a longer questionnaire self-administered by students in groups of 25 to 30 during the period with which they began each school day. Day and Stafford (1997) had participants self-administer the scale as part of a larger questionnaire after they were exposed to an experimental stimulus. Higher scores on the scale indicated that respondents were very likely to seek information from others about products by observing their behavior and/or asking them directly.

MAJOR FINDINGS: The purpose of the study by Bearden, Netemeyer, and Teel (1989) was to develop scales for measuring the dimensions of **consumer susceptibility to interpersonal influence**. A series of studies provided support for a two-factor model. Among the many findings were that the normative factor positively correlated much more strongly with a measure of attention to social comparison information than with the informational factor, the normative factor had a significantly stronger positive correlation than the informational factor with a measure of compliance motivation, and both factors had similar negative correlations with a measure of self-esteem.

The study by Boush, Friestad, and Rose (1994) explored adolescents' skepticism toward advertising and their beliefs about the persuasive tactics used by advertisers. The findings indicated that **interpersonal influence susceptibility** had a significant and negative relationship with disbelief of advertising claims.

An experiment was conducted by Day and Stafford (1997) to investigate potential problems service retailers could encounter when using older-age cues in their advertising. Specifically, one of the findings was that **interpersonal influence susceptibility** moderated the patronage intention of young adults when they are accompanied by other young adults.

COMMENTS: There is evidence that the full set of 12 items developed by Bearden, Netemeyer, and Teel (1989) is multidimensional. Yet the studies by Boush, Friestad, and Rose (1994) and Day and Stafford (1997) combined items from both dimensions. Further testing appears to be called for to determine what is most appropriate.

Furthermore, as acknowledged by Boush, Friestad, and Rose (1994, p. 173), the internal consistency of their version of the scale is low enough to warrant caution in using it again, particularly with nonadolescents respondents.

REFERENCES:

Bearden, William O., Richard G. Netemeyer, and Jesse E. Teel (1989), "Measurement of Consumer Susceptibility to Interpersonal Influence," *JCR*, 15 (March), 473–81.

Boush, David M., Marian Friestad, and Gregory M. Rose (1994), "Adolescent Skepticism Toward TV Advertising and Knowledge of Advertiser Tactics," *JCR*, 21 (June), 165–75.

Day, Ellen and Marla Royne Stafford (1997), "Age-Related Cues in Retail Services Advertising: Their Effects on Younger Consumers," *JR*, 73 (2), 211–33.

#191 *Interpersonal Influence Susceptibility*

SCALE ITEMS:*

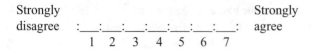

Strongly disagree :___:___:___:___:___:___:___: agree
                    1 2 3 4 5 6 7

1. I rarely purchase the latest fashion styles until I am sure my friends approve of them.

2. It is important that others like the products and brands I buy.

3. When buying products, I generally purchase those brands that I think others will approve of.

4. If other people can see me using a product, I often purchase the brand they expect me to buy.

5. I like to know what brands and products make good impressions on others.

6. I achieve a sense of belonging by purchasing the same products and brands that others purchase.

7. If I want to be like someone, I often try to buy the same brands that they buy.

8. I often identify with other people by purchasing the same products and brands they purchase.

9. To make sure I buy the right product or brand, I often observe what others are buying and using.

10. If I have little experience with a product, I often ask my friends about the product.

11. I often consult other people to help choose the best alternative available from a product class.

12. I frequently gather information from friends or family about a product before I buy.

*Items 1–8 and 9–12 constitute the normative and informational dimensions, respectively, as used by Bearden, Netemeyer, and Teel (1989). Boush, Friestad, and Rose (1994) used a five-point response format with items similar to 3, 9, and 10. Day and Stafford (1997) used all twelve items but with slightly modified wording such that references to products and brands were changed to stores or service firms.

SCALE NAME: Intolerance for Ambiguity

SCALE DESCRIPTION: Sixteen Likert-type statements purported to measure an individual's tendency to interpret situations that cannot be adequately categorized (ambiguous), because of a lack of sufficient cues, as sources of threat.

SCALE ORIGIN: The scale used by Richardson, Jain, and Dick (1996) was created by Budner (1962). The latter reported on tests of the measure with 17 different samples. Although a substantial amount of data are offered in support of the measure's validity, its reliability ranged from .39 to .62 for the different samples. Budner (1962) realized this was a problem but gave several explanations for it, the most important of which was that the measure was attempting to tap into multiple constructs and thus should be expected to have a lower reliability.

SAMPLES: Richardson, Jain, and Dick (1996) gathered data from shoppers intercepted randomly in a shopping mall of a large Northeastern U.S. metropolitan area. The survey instrument was given to the shoppers, who were asked to complete it within a week and mail it to a local university. Responding qualified them for a cash giveaway. The analysis was based on data from **582** respondents.

RELIABILITY: An alpha of **.56** was reported for the scale by Richardson, Jain, and Dick (1996).

VALIDITY: Richardson, Jain, and Dick (1996) did not examine the validity of the scale or at least did not explicitly discuss it in the article.

ADMINISTRATION: The scale was self-administered by respondents as part of a larger survey instrument (Richardson, Jain, and Dick 1996). Higher scores on the scale indicated that respondents had a greater intolerance of ambiguity.

MAJOR FINDINGS: The study by Richardson, Jain, and Dick (1996) built a framework for viewing consumer proneness for private brands. Among the findings was that greater **intolerance of ambiguity** produces a greater tendency to rely on extrinsic cues when judging product quality and less favorable value-for-money perceptions.

COMMENTS: There is no doubt that the scale lacks sufficient internal consistency. This is probably because the set of items taps into multiple constructs. Therefore, more work is called for before this measure is used further.

REFERENCES:
Budner, Stanley (1962), "Intolerance of Ambiguity as a Personality Variable," *Journal of Personality*, 30 (March), 29–50.
Richardson, Paul S., Arun K. Jain, and Alan Dick (1996), "Household Store Brand Proneness: A Framework," *JR*, 72 (2), 159–85.

SCALE ITEMS:*

1. An expert who doesn't come up with a definite answer probably doesn't know too much.

2. There is really no such thing as a problem that can't be solved.

3. A good job is one where what is to be done and how it is to be done are always clear.

4. In the long run it is possible to get more done by tackling small, simple problems rather than large and complicated ones.

5. What we are used to is always preferable to what is unfamiliar.

6. A person who leads an even, regular life in which few surprises or unexpected happenings arise, really has a lot to be grateful for.

7. I like parties where I know most of the people more than ones where all or most of the people are complete strangers.

8. The sooner we all acquire similar values and ideals the better.

9. I would like to live in a foreign country for a while. **(r)**

10. People who fit their lives to a schedule probably miss most of the joy of living. **(r)**

11. It is more fun to tackle a complicated problem than to solve a simple one. **(r)**

12. Often the most interesting and stimulating people are those who don't mind being different and original. **(r)**

13. People who insist upon a yes or no answer just don't know how complicated things really are. **(r)**

14. Many of our most important decisions are based upon insufficient information. **(r)**

15. Teachers or supervisors who hand out vague assignments give a chance for one to show initiative and originality. **(r)**

16. A good teacher is one who makes you wonder about your way of looking at things. **(r)**

*The response scale used by Richardson, Jain, and Dick (1996) was not described. The response scale used by Budner (1962) is as follows:

Strong disagreement = 1
Moderate disagreement = 2
Slight disagreement = 3
Slight agreement = 5
Moderate agreement = 6
Strong agreement = 7

Apparently, the numerical anchors were not shown on the instrument; respondents simply chose among six categories with varying verbal descriptions. The 4 was reserved for use by those who did not respond to a statement.

SCALE NAME: Involvement (Cents-Off Offers)

SCALE DESCRIPTION: A seven-item, seven-point Likert-type scale measuring a consumer's propensity to buy brands that have price-off offers regardless of the amount of money involved. This measures a general tendency rather than the likelihood that the behavior occurs for any particular product category. The authors of the scale called it *cents-off proneness* (Lichtenstein, Burton, and Netemeyer 1997; Lichtenstein, Netemeyer, and Burton 1995).

SCALE ORIGIN: The scale is original to the studies by Lichtenstein, Netemeyer, and Burton (1995), though some of the items are similar to ones developed previously by the same authors for other measures (e.g., Lichtenstein, Netemeyer, and Burton 1990). In an effort to develop several deal-proneness measures, 91 items were generated and tested with 341 nonstudent adults. Using factor analysis and other tests, seven items were deleted, which left 84 to be used in the two studies reported in Lichtenstein, Netemeyer, and Burton (1995). Lichtenstein, Burton, and Netemeyer (1997) presented 49 of the items for the measurement of eight different deal-proneness types.

SAMPLES: The sample employed by Lichtenstein, Netemeyer, and Burton (1995) in their first study came from shoppers in one of two grocery stores in the Midwestern United States. (This is also the sample used by Lichtenstein, Burton, and Netemeyer 1997.) Shoppers were approached and asked if they would participate in the survey. If so, they were given the instrument and asked to fill it out later and mail it back. Completed questionnaires were received from **582** shoppers. A majority of the sample were women (75.9%), and more than half (58.6%) were married. The median household income was $35,000 to $49,000, and the median age was 35 to 44 years of age. The survey in Study 2 was distributed similarly to that in Study 1. Usable forms were received back from **402** people, most of whom were women (77.9%) and married (67.3%). The median income and age were the same as in the first study.

RELIABILITY: An alpha of **.90** was reported for the scale by Lichtenstein, Netemeyer, and Burton (1995; Lichtenstein, Burton, and Netemeyer 1997) for both studies.

VALIDITY: Confirmatory factor analyses were used in both studies by Lichtenstein, Netemeyer, and Burton (1995; Lichtenstein, Burton, and Netemeyer 1997). A variety of data was produced in support of the scale's unidimensionality and discriminant validity.

ADMINISTRATION: In the studies by Lichtenstein, Netemeyer, and Burton (1995; Lichtenstein, Burton, and Netemeyer 1997), the scale was part of a survey instrument self-administered by shoppers after they left the grocery store. Higher scores on the scale indicated that consumers were very interested in price-off deals.

MAJOR FINDINGS: The purpose of the study by Lichtenstein, Burton, and Netemeyer (1997) was to determine if there were consumer segments that had a tendency to be "deal prone" in general. Among the findings was that, in both the two- and three-cluster analyses of shoppers, there was a generalized deal-proneness group that had significantly higher mean scores on the **cents-off involvement** scale compared with clusters of shoppers who were less deal prone.

Although the first study in Lichtenstein, Netemeyer, and Burton (1995) shares the same sample as that described previously, its purpose, as well as that for Study 2, was to compare competing models of deal proneness that varied on the level of specificity. In neither study did **involvement with cents-off offers** have a significant relationship with any of the many marketplace behaviors that were studied.

#193 *Involvement (Cents-Off Offers)*

COMMENTS: Lichtenstein, Netemeyer, and Burton (1995) reported means on the scale of 25.08 and 25.18 for Studies 1 and 2, respectively.

REFERENCES:

Lichtenstein, Donald R., Scot Burton, and Richard G. Netemeyer (1997), "An Examination of Deal Proneness Across Sales Promotion Types: A Consumer Segmentation Perspective," *JR*, 73 (2), 283–97.

———, Richard G. Netemeyer, and Scot Burton (1990), "Distinguishing Coupon Proneness from Value Consciousness: An Acquisition-Transaction Utility Theory Perspective," *JM*, 54 (July), 54–67.

———, ———, and ——— (1995), "Assessing the Domain Specificity of Deal Proneness: A Field Study," *JCR*, 22 (December), 314–26.

SCALE ITEMS:

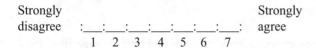

Strongly
disagree   :___:___:___:___:___:___:___: Strongly agree
        1 2 3 4 5 6 7

1. Buying products with cents-off deals makes me feel good.

2. I am more likely to buy a brand if it has a cents-off deal on the label.

3. I enjoy buying products with cents-off deals, regardless of the amount I save by doing so.

4. Compared to most people, I would say I have a positive attitude toward cents-off deals.

5. Beyond the money I save, buying products with cents-off deals gives me a sense of joy.

6. Cents-off deals can save a shopper a lot of money.

7. Compared to most people, I am more likely to buy products with cents-off deals.

SCALE NAME: Involvement (Contests/Sweepstakes)

SCALE DESCRIPTION: A six-item, seven-point Likert-type scale measuring a consumer's enjoyment of contests/sweepstakes and tendency to buy products associated with such games. This measures a general tendency rather than the likelihood that the behavior occurs for any particular product category. Lichtenstein, Netemeyer, and Burton (1995; Lichtenstein, Burton, and Netemeyer 1997) referred the scale as *contest/sweepstakes proneness*.

SCALE ORIGIN: The scale is original to the studies by Lichtenstein, Netemeyer, and Burton (1995), though some of the items are similar to ones developed previously by the same authors for other measures (e.g., Lichtenstein, Netemeyer, and Burton 1990). In an effort to develop several deal-proneness measures, 91 items were generated and tested with 341 nonstudent adults. Using factor analysis and other tests, seven items were deleted, which left 84 to be used in the two studies reported in Lichtenstein, Netemeyer, and Burton (1995). Lichtenstein, Burton, and Netemeyer (1997) presented 49 of the items for the measurement of eight different deal-proneness types.

SAMPLES: The sample employed by Lichtenstein, Netemeyer, and Burton (1995) in their first study came from shoppers in one of two grocery stores in the Midwestern United States. (This is also the sample used by Lichtenstein, Burton, and Netemeyer 1997.) Shoppers were approached and asked if they would participate in the survey. If so, they were given the instrument and asked to fill it out later and mail it back. Completed questionnaires were received from **582** shoppers. A majority of the sample were women (75.9%), and more than half (58.6%) were married. The median household income was $35,000 to $49,000, and the median age was 35 to 44 years of age. The survey in Study 2 was distributed similarly to that in Study 1. Usable forms were received back from **402** people, most of whom were women (77.9%) and married (67.3%). The median income and age were the same as in the first study.

RELIABILITY: Alphas of **.90** and **.91** were reported for the scale by Lichtenstein, Netemeyer, and Burton (1995) for Studies 1 (Lichtenstein, Burton, and Netemeyer 1997) and 2, respectively.

VALIDITY: Confirmatory factor analyses were used in both studies by Lichtenstein, Netemeyer, and Burton (1995; Lichtenstein, Burton, and Netemeyer 1997), and it was concluded that the scale was unidimensional and showed evidence of discriminant validity.

ADMINISTRATION: In the studies by Lichtenstein, Netemeyer, and Burton (1995; Lichtenstein, Burton, and Netemeyer 1997), the scale was part of a survey instrument self-administered by shoppers after they left the grocery store. Higher scores on the scale indicated that consumers were very interested in contests/sweepstakes and enjoyed purchasing products associated with them.

MAJOR FINDINGS: The purpose of the study by Lichtenstein, Burton, and Netemeyer (1997) was to determine if there were consumer segments that had a tendency to be "deal prone" in general. Among the findings was that, in both the two- and three-cluster analyses of shoppers, there was a generalized deal-proneness group that had significantly higher mean scores on the **contests/sweepstakes involvement** scale compared with clusters of shoppers who were less deal prone.

Although the first study in Lichtenstein, Netemeyer, and Burton (1995) shares the same sample as that described previously, its purpose, as well as that for Study 2, was to compare competing models of deal proneness that varied on the level of specificity. Among the findings was that **involvement with contests/sweepstakes** had a stronger relationship (positive) than any of the other deal-proneness measures with the frequency of entering **contests/sweepstakes**.

#194 *Involvement (Contests/Sweepstakes)*

COMMENTS: Lichtenstein, Netemeyer, and Burton (1995) reported means on the scale of 12.94 and 10.73 for Studies 1 and 2, respectively.

REFERENCES:

Lichtenstein, Donald R., Scot Burton, and Richard G. Netemeyer (1997), "An Examination of Deal Proneness Across Sales Promotion Types: A Consumer Segmentation Perspective," *JR*, 73 (2), 283–97.

———, Richard G. Netemeyer, and Scot Burton (1990), "Distinguishing Coupon Proneness from Value Consciousness: An Acquisition-Transaction Utility Theory Perspective," *JM*, 54 (July), 54–67.

———, ———, and ——— (1995), "Assessing the Domain Specificity of Deal Proneness: A Field Study," *JCR*, 22 (December), 314–26.

SCALE ITEMS:

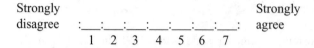

Strongly
disagree   :___:___:___:___:___:___:___: Strongly agree
        1   2   3   4   5   6   7

1. I enjoy entering manufacturers' contests.

2. When I buy a brand that is connected to a contest or sweepstake, I feel that it is a good deal.

3. I have favorite brands, but if possible, I buy the brand that is connected with a contest or sweepstakes.

4. I feel compelled to respond to contest or sweepstakes offers.

5. Manufacturers' contests and sweepstakes are fun to enter, even if I know I'll never win.

6. If I am indifferent between two brands, I would purchase the one that has a contest or sweepstakes associated with it.

SCALE NAME: Involvement (Coupons)

SCALE DESCRIPTION: A multi-item, seven-point Likert-type scale measuring the degree to which a consumer reports using coupons and enjoying it. A five-item version was used by Lichtenstein, Ridgway, and Netemeyer (1993), Lichtenstein, Netemeyer, and Burton (1995), and Lichtenstein, Burton, and Netemeyer (1997). In these studies, the scale was referred to as *coupon proneness*.

SCALE ORIGIN: The scale is original to Lichtenstein, Netemeyer, and Burton (1990). Five marketing academicians judged the appropriateness of 33 items generated to represent the construct. Twenty-five items remained after this procedure. On the basis of a second round of five additional judges assessing the face validity of the items, all items were retained. The items were then interspersed throughout a questionnaire given to 263 undergraduate and graduate business students. The eight items composing the final version of the scale were those that had corrected item–total correlations equal to or greater than .40. Confirmatory factor analysis (CFA) provided evidence that the items were unidimensional and had discriminant validity. The construct reliability was calculated to be .88.

SAMPLES: Biwa, Srinivasan, and Srivastava (1997) collected data for their study from grocery shoppers in a Southwestern U.S. city. Shoppers from two stores of a major grocery chain were approached while standing in the checkout line. Completed survey forms were received from **345** shoppers. The sample was mostly women (78%) who were, on average, 39 years of age, worked 37 hours per week, and came from households of 2.8 people.

The data for the main study by Lichtenstein, Netemeyer, and Burton (1990) came from a convenience sample of **350** nonstudent adults from a medium-size standard metropolitan statistical area. The majority of the sample were women (57%) and married (69%). College graduates composed 40% of the sample. The median age of respondents was between 35 and 44 years of age, and household income was between $30,000 and $39,999.

The sample employed by Lichtenstein, Netemeyer, and Burton (1995) in their first study came from shoppers in one of two grocery stores in the Midwestern United States. (This is also the sample used by Lichtenstein, Burton, and Netemeyer 1997.) Shoppers were approached and asked if they would participate in the survey. If so, they were given the instrument and asked to fill it out later and mail it back. Completed questionnaires were received from **582** shoppers. A majority of the sample were women (75.9%), and more than half (58.6%) were married. The median household income was $35,000 to $49,000, and the median age was 35 to 44 years of age. The survey in Study 2 was distributed similarly to Study 1. Usable forms were received back from **402** people, most of whom were women (77.9%) and married (67.3%). The median income and age were the same as in the first study.

Lichtenstein, Ridgway, and Netemeyer (1993) used the same database described for the first study by Lichtenstein, Netemeyer, and Burton (1995).

RELIABILITY: The internal consistency of the scale was calculated by Lichtenstein, Netemeyer, and Burton (1990) to be **.88**, and item–total correlations were greater than .40. Alphas of **.88** and **.86** were reported for the scale by Lichtenstein, Netemeyer, and Burton (1995) for Studies 1 (Lichtenstein, Burton, and Netemeyer 1997) and 2, respectively. An alpha of **.84** was calculated for the scale as used by Biwa, Srinivasan, and Srivastava (1997; Biwa 1998).

VALIDITY: Confirmatory factor analyses were used in each of the studies by Lichtenstein and colleagues (Lichtenstein, Burton, and Netemeyer 1997; Lichtenstein, Netemeyer, and Burton 1990; Lichtenstein, Ridgway, and Netemeyer 1993; Lichtenstein, Netemeyer and Burton 1995), and the evidence indicated that the scale was unidimensional and showed evidence of discriminant validity. Lichtenstein, Ridgway, and Netemeyer (1993) stated that, after using CFA, items with low standardized factor loadings were dropped. This is likely the reason that fewer items composed the scale in the latter studies compared with the first.

ADMINISTRATION: Lichtenstein, Netemeyer, and Burton (1990) did not describe the manner in which the scale was administered to the subjects in their study. However, it was clear that the scale was just one of many measures that composed the survey instrument. In the studies reported by Biwa, Srinivasan, and Srivastava (1997), Lichtenstein, Burton, and Netemeyer (1997), Lichtenstein, Netemeyer, and Burton (1995), and Lichtenstein, Ridgway, and Netemeyer (1993), the scale was part of larger survey instruments self-administered by shoppers after they left the grocery store. Higher scores on the scale indicated that respondents used and enjoyed coupons a lot, whereas low scores suggested they had little or no involvement with coupons.

MAJOR FINDINGS: Biwa, Srinivasan, and Srivastava (1997) proposed a model of coupon redemption that considers the joint effects of coupon attractiveness and **coupon involvement** but does not require their explicit measurement. The results showed that the model using redemption intentions data outperformed an approach that included more traditional, explicit measures, including **coupon involvement**.

The purpose of the study by Lichtenstein, Burton, and Netemeyer (1997) was to determine if there were consumer segments that had a tendency to be "deal prone" in general. Among the findings was that, in both the two- and three-cluster analyses of shoppers, there was a generalized deal-proneness group that had significantly higher mean scores on the **coupon involvement** scale compared with clusters of shoppers who were less deal prone.

The study by Lichtenstein, Netemeyer, and Burton (1990) examined the effect of both value consciousness and **coupon involvement** on coupon redemption behavior. One of the major findings was that value consciousness explained a significant amount of variance in redemption behavior after accounting for **coupon involvement**.

The purpose of the two studies reported by Lichtenstein, Netemeyer, and Burton (1995) was to compare competing models of deal proneness that varied on the level of specificity. **Coupon involvement** was the most positive predictor of quantity and dollar amount of coupon coupons redeemed of several deal-proneness variables tested. Lichtenstein, Ridgway, and Netemeyer (1993) identified and measured seven related but distinct price perception constructs. The dependent variable that **coupon involvement** predicted most strongly was coupon redemption frequency (self-reported).

COMMENTS: Lichtenstein, Netemeyer, and Burton (1995) reported means on the scale of 19.26 and 19.18 for Studies 1 and 2, respectively.

REFERENCES:
Biwa, Kapil (1998), personal correspondence.

———, Srini S. Srinivasan, and Rajendra K. Srivastava (1997), "Coupon Attractiveness and Coupon Proneness: A Framework for Modeling Coupon Redemption," *JMR*, 34 (November), 517–25.

Lichtenstein, Donald R., Scot Burton, and Richard G. Netemeyer (1997), "An Examination of Deal Proneness Across Sales Promotion Types: A Consumer Segmentation Perspective," *JR*, 73 (2), 283–97.

———, Richard G. Netemeyer, and Scot Burton (1990), "Distinguishing Coupon Proneness from Value Consciousness: An Acquisition-Transaction Utility Theory Perspective," *JM*, 54 (July), 54–67.

———, ———, and ——— (1995), "Assessing the Domain Specificity of Deal Proneness: A Field Study," *JCR*, 22 (December), 314–26.

———, Nancy M. Ridgway, and Richard G. Netemeyer (1993), "Price Perceptions and Consumer Shopping Behavior: A Field Study," *JMR*, 30 (May), 234–45.

SCALE ITEMS:*

Strongly ... Strongly
disagree :___:___:___:___:___:___:___: agree
⠀⠀⠀⠀⠀⠀ 1⠀ 2⠀ 3⠀ 4⠀ 5⠀ 6⠀ 7

1. Redeeming coupons makes me feel good.

2. I enjoy clipping coupons out of the newspapers.

3. When I use coupons, I feel that I am getting a good deal.

4. I enjoy using coupons, regardless of the amount I save by doing so.

5. I have favorite brands, but most of the time I buy the brand I have a coupon for.

6. I am more likely to buy brands for which I have a coupon.

7. Coupons have caused me to buy products I normally would not buy.

8. Beyond the money I save, redeeming coupons gives me a sense of joy.

*All of these items were used by Lichtenstein, Netemeyer, and Burton (1990), but only items 1–4 and 8 were used by Lichtenstein, Burton, and Netemeyer (1997), Lichtenstein, Ridgway, and Netemeyer (1993), and Lichtenstein, Netemeyer, and Burton (1995). Biwa, Srinivasan, and Srivastava (1997) were not explicit about which items they used, but it would appear that they used the original version of the scale.

SCALE NAME: Involvement (Coupons)

SCALE DESCRIPTION: Eight five-point Likert-type items measuring a person's interest in the collection and use of coupons. The scale was called *attitudes toward couponing* by Tat and Bejou (1994).

SCALE ORIGIN: Although not stated explicitly, the scale appears to be original to Tat and Bejou (1994).

SAMPLES: The data were gathered by Tat and Bejou (1994) using a telephone survey in Memphis, Tenn. The telephone number prefixes were deliberately chosen for black neighborhoods to ensure blacks composed a substantial portion of the sample. Interviews were conducted with **326** individuals who identified themselves as doing the majority of the shopping for their household. Ultimately, 37.2% of the respondents were black. Forty-one percent of the total sample were married, 39% came from households with four or more members, 33% were between the ages of 25 and 34 years, 45% had at least some college level education, and 41% had incomes over $30,000. Consult the article for a detailed breakdown of demographic information by race.

RELIABILITY: An alpha of **.88** was reported for the scale by Tat and Bejou (1994). Alphas of .85 and .87 were reported for blacks and whites, respectively.

VALIDITY: Tat and Bejou (1994) did not directly test the validity of the scale. However, they performed a couple of factor analyses on a total set of 24 items to purify the scales they developed. Factor loadings for both black and white respondents appeared to be reasonable (>.60).

ADMINISTRATION: The scale was administered by telephone interviewers to respondents as part of a larger instrument (Tat and Bejou 1994). Higher scores on the scale suggested that respondents had a strong involvement with the collection and use of coupons.

MAJOR FINDINGS: The purpose of the study by Tat and Bejou (1994) was to compare the differences between blacks and whites on motives for using coupons. **Involvement with coupons** did not differ significantly on the basis of race.

REFERENCES:

Tat, Peter K. and David Bejou (1994), "Examining Black Consumer Motives for Coupon Usage," *JAR*, 34 (March/April), 29–35.

SCALE ITEMS:

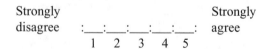

Strongly disagree :___:___:___:___:___: Strongly agree
           1   2   3   4   5

1. I enjoy collecting coupons.

2. Collecting coupons is too troublesome. **(r)**

3. I feel good about using coupons to save money.

4. Collecting coupons is a good use of time.

5. Time spent on collecting coupons is not worth the money saved. **(r)**

6. Using coupons makes shopping more enjoyable.

7. I am too busy to collect coupons. **(r)**

8. I would use more coupons if I could find them.

SCALE NAME: Involvement (Coupons)

SCALE DESCRIPTION: A four-item, five-point Likert-type scale purporting to capture the gratification a consumer derives from collecting and redeeming coupons.

SCALE ORIGIN: The source of the scale is not specified by Mittal (1994), but it appears to be original to his study.

SAMPLES: Mittal (1994) gathered data from female members of six voluntary organizations, as well as from mall intercepts. A total of 184 people provided complete survey questionnaires. Most of the respondents were white (85%), married (71%), and at least 35 years of age (63%). Although it does not mirror the U.S. population, the sample included a wide variety of demographic categories.

RELIABILITY: The construct reliability (LISREL) was reported to be **.91** (Mittal 1994).

VALIDITY: The validity of the scale was not specifically addressed by Mittal (1994), except to note that this scale and one other (time costs of coupon use) were highly correlated and did not show the same evidence of discriminant validity as did the other measures used in the study.

ADMINISTRATION: The scale was part of a larger self-administered mail survey instrument (Mittal 1994). Higher scores on the scale indicated that respondents enjoyed the collection and use of coupons very much.

MAJOR FINDINGS: The study by Mittal (1994) proposed that demographics are poor predictors of coupon usage, and instead, he illustrated the value of three layers of mediating variables. As noted ("Validity"), this scale had such a strong correlation with another scale that the author combined them into one measure (*enjoyment versus hassle*). Among the findings was that comparison shoppers had much better enjoyment versus hassle in using coupons than did noncomparison shoppers.

REFERENCES:
Mittal, Banwari (1994), "An Integrated Framework for Relating Diverse Consumer Characteristics to Supermarket Coupon Redemption," *JMR*, 31 (November), 533–44.

SCALE ITEMS:

Strongly   Strongly
disagree   :___:___:___:___:___: agree
     1   2   3   4   5

1. I quite enjoy clipping, organizing, and using coupons.

2. Clipping, organizing, and using coupons is no fun. **(r)**

3. Clipping, organizing, and using coupons has become a habit with me that I have come to like.

4. It is a hassle to cut out, maintain, and redeem coupons. **(r)**

SCALE NAME: Involvement (Coupons)

SCALE DESCRIPTION: Six seven-point items that measure the degree to which a consumer describes him- or herself as engaging in behavior related to the collection and use of grocery coupons.

SCALE ORIGIN: Although not clear from the article by Putrevu and Ratchford (1997), some of the work on the scales was conducted previously in a dissertation by Putrevu (1992).

SAMPLES: Data were gathered by Putrevu and Ratchford (1997) using a mail survey to a random sample of grocery shoppers in a standard metropolitan statistical area in the Northeastern United States. A total of **500** responses were used in the main analysis, and demographics of the final sample were similar to those of the population of interest.

RELIABILITY: An alpha of **.92** was reported for the scale (Putrevu and Ratchford 1997).

VALIDITY: Although the authors stated in general that the scales showed evidence of convergent, discriminant, and content validity, no details of the analyses were provided (Putrevu and Ratchford 1997).

ADMINISTRATION: The scale was part of a larger mail questionnaire (Putrevu and Ratchford 1997). Higher scores on the scale suggested that a consumer frequently collected and used grocery store coupons.

MAJOR FINDINGS: Putrevu and Ratchford (1997) examined a dynamic model of consumer search behavior that includes human capital. In general, the results indicated that self-reported search for information about buying groceries is associated with perceptions of the costs and benefits of search, as predicted by the model.

COMMENTS: As presented in the article by Putrevu and Ratchford (1997), this scale was part of a larger measure called "Search." That measure was the mean of the scores from nine scales related to search behavior for grocery product information.

REFERENCES:
Putrevu, Sanjay (1992), "A Theory of Search and Its Empirical Investigation," doctoral dissertation, State University of New York at Buffalo.
———— and Brian T. Ratchford (1997), "A Model of Search Behavior with an Application to Grocery Shopping," *JR*, 73 (4), 463–86.

SCALE ITEMS:

Never   :___:___:___:___:___:___:___: Always
　　　　　1　　2　　3　　4　　5　　6　　7

1. I cut out coupons for grocery products.

2. I use cents-off coupons for grocery products.

3. I look for products for which I have a coupon.

4. Before buying a product, I check to see if I have a coupon for it.

5. I collect coupons for grocery products.

6. When I receive or clip a coupon, I save it for future use.

SCALE NAME: Involvement (Ego)

SCALE DESCRIPTION: Seven seven-point Likert-type items purported to measure the importance a class of products has for a person's values and egos. The category studied by Neese and Taylor (1994) was luxury sedans.

SCALE ORIGIN: Neese and Taylor (1994) appear to have been inspired by a scale developed by Lastovicka and Gardner (1979). (See Vol. II, #153). Although the items in the two scales are conceptually similar, there are enough phrasing differences to make them distinct measures of the same construct.

SAMPLES: Data were collected by Neese and Taylor (1994) using a judgment sample of civic groups members from across a Southeastern U.S. state. They were expected to be more likely than the population at large to own luxury cars, the product focused on in the study. Indeed, 22.1% of the respondents reported owning one of three luxury sedans. Usable questionnaires were received from **422** respondents. The sample was predominately men, and 41.5% were older than 64 years of age.

RELIABILITY: An alpha of **.90** was reported for the scale by Neese and Taylor (1994).

VALIDITY: No examination of the scale's validity was reported by Neese and Taylor (1994). However, using item–total correlations and results of a factor analysis, items were eliminated from the scale.

ADMINISTRATION: The conditions in which Neese and Taylor (1994) administered the scale were not clearly described. It appears the scale was part of some materials completed by subjects before they were exposed to test stimuli. Higher scores on the scale indicated that the ownership of a product (such as luxury sedans) was very important to the egos of respondents.

MAJOR FINDINGS: Neese and Taylor (1994) examined the ability of comparative advertising to accomplish certain tasks as it interacts with brand information for a high-involvement product. **Ego involvement** in the product (luxury sedans) was found to have no significant relationship with any of the dependent variables, except the brand beliefs related to comparisons.

COMMENTS: The scale was used by Neese and Taylor to measure involvement with luxury sedans, but it appears to be amenable for use with other product categories. An additional change that could make the scale more general is to use a different first word in item 6, such as "using" or "owning."

REFERENCES:

Lastovicka, John L. and David M. Gardner (1970), *Attitude Research Plays for High Stakes*, John C. Maloney and Bernard Silverman, eds. Chicago: American Marketing Association.

Neese, William T. and Ronald D. Taylor (1994), "Verbal Strategies for Indirect Comparative Advertising," *JAR*, 34 (March/April), 56–69.

SCALE ITEMS:*

Strongly   Strongly
disagree   :___:___:___:___:___:___:___: agree
                 1   2   3   4   5   6   7

1. Others view me favorably because I own a _____.

2. I use a _____ to express the real me.

3. _____ are very important to me personally.

4. I can protect my ego by owning a _____.

5. A _____ is important to my value system.

6. Driving a _____ is the way to behave.

7. _____ help determine what others think of me.

*The name of the product category should be placed in the blanks.

SCALE NAME: Involvement (End-of-Aisle Displays)

SCALE DESCRIPTION: A seven-item, seven-point Likert-type scale measuring a consumer's attitude toward end-of-aisle displays and stated tendency to buy products displayed on them. This measures a general tendency rather than the likelihood that the behavior occurs for any particular product category. Lichtenstein, Burton, and Netemeyer (1997) and Lichtenstein, Netemeyer, and Burton (1995) referred to the scale as *end-of-aisle-display proneness.*

SCALE ORIGIN: The scale is original to the studies by Lichtenstein, Netemeyer, and Burton (1995), though some of the items are similar to ones developed previously by the same authors for other measures (e.g., Lichtenstein, Netemeyer, and Burton 1990). In an effort to develop several deal-proneness measures, 91 items were generated and tested with 341 nonstudent adults. Using factor analysis and other tests, seven items were deleted, which left 84 to be used in the two studies reported in Lichtenstein, Netemeyer, and Burton (1995). Lichtenstein, Burton, and Netemeyer (1997) presented 49 of the items for the measurement of eight different deal-proneness types.

SAMPLES: The sample employed by Lichtenstein, Netemeyer, and Burton (1995) in their first study came from shoppers in one of two grocery stores in the Midwestern United States. (This is also the sample used by Lichtenstein, Burton, and Netemeyer 1997.) Shoppers were approached and asked if they would participate in the survey. If so, they were given the instrument and asked to fill it out later and mail it back. Completed questionnaires were received from **582** shoppers. A majority of the sample were women (75.9%), and more than half (58.6%) were married. The median household income was $35,000 to $49,000, and the median age was 35 to 44 years of age. The survey in Study 2 was distributed similarly to that in Study 1. Usable forms were received back from **402** people, most of whom were women (77.9%) and married (67.3%). The median income and age were the same as in the first study.

RELIABILITY: Alphas of **.89** and **.90** were reported for the scale by Lichtenstein, Netemeyer, and Burton (1995) for Studies 1 (Lichtenstein, Burton, and Netemeyer 1997) and 2, respectively.

VALIDITY: Confirmatory factor analyses were used in both studies by Lichtenstein, Netemeyer, and Burton (1995; Lichtenstein, Burton, and Netemeyer 1997), and it was concluded that the scale was unidimensional and showed evidence of discriminant validity.

ADMINISTRATION: In the studies by Lichtenstein, Netemeyer, and Burton (1995; Lichtenstein, Burton, and Netemeyer 1997), the scale was part of a survey instrument self-administered by shoppers after they left the grocery store. Higher scores on the scale indicated that consumers had positive attitudes toward end-of-aisle displays and were likely to purchase items displayed in them.

MAJOR FINDINGS: The purpose of the study by Lichtenstein, Burton, and Netemeyer (1997) was to determine if there were consumer segments that had a tendency to be "deal prone" in general. Among the findings was that, in both the two- and three-cluster analyses of shoppers, there was a generalized deal-proneness group that had significantly higher mean scores on the **displays involvement** scale compared with clusters of shoppers who were less deal prone.

Although the first study in Lichtenstein, Netemeyer, and Burton (1995) shares the same sample as that described previously, its purpose, as well as that for Study 2, was to compare competing models of deal proneness that varied on the level of specificity. Among the findings was that **involvement with displays** had a stronger relationship (negative) than any of the other deal-proneness measures with the tendency to prepare a shopping list for visits to the grocery store.

COMMENTS: Lichtenstein, Netemeyer, and Burton (1995) reported means on the scale of 18.93 and 18.55 for Studies 1 and 2, respectively.

REFERENCES:

Lichtenstein, Donald R., Scot Burton, and Richard G. Netemeyer (1997), "An Examination of Deal Proneness Across Sales Promotion Types: A Consumer Segmentation Perspective," *JR*, 73 (2), 283–97.

———, Richard G. Netemeyer, and Scot Burton (1990), "Distinguishing Coupon Proneness from Value Consciousness: An Acquisition-Transaction Utility Theory Perspective," *JM*, 54 (July), 54–67.

———, ———, and ——— (1995), "Assessing the Domain Specificity of Deal Proneness: A Field Study," *JCR*, 22 (December), 314–26.

SCALE ITEMS:

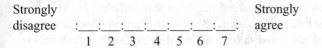

Strongly
disagree   :___:___:___:___:___:___:___: agree
       1   2   3   4   5   6   7

1. You usually save money when you buy a product from an end-of-aisle display.

2. I am more likely to buy brands that are displayed at the end of the aisle.

3. End-of-aisle displays have influenced me to buy brands I normally would not buy.

4. Beyond the money I save, buying from end-of-aisle displays gives me a sense of joy.

5. I believe that one can save a lot of money buying from end-of-aisle displays.

6. The prices of products displayed at the ends of aisles are usually good.

7. Compared to most people, I am more likely to buy brands on end-of-aisle displays.

SCALE NAME: Involvement (Enduring)

SCALE DESCRIPTION: A twenty-item, seven-point semantic differential scale measuring the enduring and intrinsic (rather than situational) relevance of an object to a person. The scale is easily customized to measure involvement with a product category, a particular brand, an ad for a particular brand, or a particular purchase decision. The scale was referred to as Personal Involvement Inventory (PII) by the originator (Zaichkowsky 1985). Abbreviated versions of the scale have been used by Lichtenstein and colleagues (Lichtenstein, Bloch, and Black 1988; Lichtenstein, Netemeyer, and Burton 1990), Lord, Lee, and Sauer (1994), Maheswaran and Meyers-Levy (1990), Mick (1992), Mittal (1990), and Singh and Cole (1993).

For a greatly modified version of the scale, see Steenkamp and Wedel (1991), where store involvement was measured in Holland. Also see McQuarrie and Munson (1987) for another modified version of the scale (RPII). Finally, Neese and Taylor (1994) used only positive anchors to make two Likert-type scales for the study of luxury sedans.

SCALE ORIGIN: Although previous research was reviewed and may have provided ideas for scale items, the scale as a unit was generated and tested first by Zaichkowsky (1985). Construction of the scale used four data sets of 286 undergraduate psychology students, two data sets with 49 MBA students, and two data sets with 57 clerical and administrative staff members. The stability of the measure was checked over two subject groups for four products and produced test–retest correlations from .88 to .93. Internal consistency was calculated with the same data as ranging from .95 to .97 (Cronbach's alpha). Content validity was demonstrated by the scale through the use of expert judges at two points: first, by reducing the list of word pairs to those most appropriate for measuring the construct, and second, by successful classification of open-ended statements from subjects. Criterion validity was examined by demonstrating the similarity between subjects' average involvement levels with four products and the expected degree of involvement based on previous studies. Construct validity was checked for three products by noting the association between subjects' scale scores and their statements of behavior expected to reflect involvement. For each of the three products, there was a positive relationship between scale scores and responses to statements.

The scale used by Maheswaran and Meyers-Levy (1990) may not have been directly derived from the Zaichkowsky measure and is very short but is similar enough to be viewed here as measuring the same thing.

SELECTED SAMPLES: Houston and Walker (1996) administered this scale to a sample of **203** female college students ranging in age from 19 to 47 years. On the basis of their scores, 40 respondents were selected and placed into either a high- or low-scoring group. This smaller sample is the one on which the analysis was based.

Lichtenstein, Bloch, and Black (1988) mailed questionnaires to 1800 participants in a regional running event. Analysis was based on the **452** persons who responded within five weeks. Compared with the area's general population, the respondents were more likely to be younger, male, and with higher education and income.

Lord, Lee, and Sauer (1994) collected data from undergraduate students in a introductory marketing course. Students received extra credit for their participation, and analysis was based on **324** competed survey forms.

The study conducted by Maheswaran and Meyers-Levy (1990) used a sample of **98** undergraduate students who received extra course credit for participating. The data were gathered from small groups of students (5 to 7 at a time) and then analyzed as a 2 × 2 factorial design.

The experiment conducted by Mick (1992) was based on data collected from **161** (53% female) undergraduates attending a large U.S. university. Students received extra credit for their participation and were also eligible for the drawing of a new CD player.

SELECTED RELIABILITIES: Reported internal consistencies have ranged from **.80** (Lord, Lee, and Sauer 1994) to **.98** (Houston and Walker 1996; Mishra, Umesh, and Stem 1993). Specific reliabilities are

provided here for the selected studies described in the "Selected Samples" and "Major Findings" sections:
.98 by Houston and Walker (1996);
.93 by Lichtenstein, Bloch, and Black (1988);
.80 by Lord, Lee, and Sauer 1994;
.89 by Maheswaran and Meyers-Levy (1990); and
.96 by Mick (1992).

VALIDITY: No test of validity was reported by most of the studies. A factor analysis of the 20-item scale performed by Mick (1992) produced a two-factor solution. Only the 16 items loading strongly on the first factor were retained for calculating scale scores.

Houston and Walker (1996) were concerned about the dimensionality of the scale and tested it further using confirmatory factor analysis. Although evidence was found for two factors, the test for discriminant validity they applied was not met, which led them to treat the two dimensions as one for purposes of the scale.

ADMINISTRATION: The scale was used by both Celsi and Olson (1988) and Houston and Walker (1996) as a screening instrument before their main studies. Lichtenstein, Bloch, and Black (1988) administered it in a mail survey along with many other measures. Lord, Lee, and Sauer (1994), Gotlieb and Sarel (1991), Laczniak and Muehling (1993), Maheswaran and Meyers-Levy (1990), Miller and Marks (1992), and Singh and Cole (1993) had subjects complete the scale, along with other measures, after they were exposed to some stimulus. In the study by Mick (1992), the scale was self-administered by subjects in a phase four weeks prior to the exposure to experimental stimuli. Little was said by Gotlieb and Swan (1990) about the setting in which they administered the scale.

Scores were calculated by summing numerical responses to items and reverse coding when necessary. Lower scores suggested that a person had little involvement with the object. Higher scores implied that people were very interested and personally involved with the object. The objects examined in the studies were playing tennis (Celsi and Olson 1988), VCRs (Gotlieb and Sarel 1991), legal services (Gotlieb and Swan 1990), sending greeting cards (Houston and Walker 1996), 35mm cameras (Laczniak and Muehling 1993), running shoes (Lichtenstein, Bloch, and Black 1988), regularly purchased grocery products (Lichtenstein, Netemeyer, and Burton 1990), diagnostic blood tests (Maheswaran and Meyers-Levy 1990), lawnmowers and tires (Miller and Marks 1992), and hotels (Stafford 1996).

SELECTED FINDINGS: The study by Houston and Walker (1996) used a cognitive mapping methodology to explore the goal structures that are activated by consumers' feelings of self-reliance (**involvement**) with a product. Despite expectations, there were no significant differences in the complexity of the decision maps associated with the groups that varied in their **enduring involvement**.

Lichtenstein, Bloch, and Black (1988) examined the cognitive trade-offs consumers make between price and product quality. The findings indicated that there was an positive relationship between product **involvement** and price–quality inferences, as well as price acceptability level, but an inverse correlation with price consciousness.

The study by Lord, Lee, and Sauer (1994) examined the influence of program context on attitude toward the ad. It was hypothesized that more personal **involvement** in a program would enhance motivation to process ads in the program. The results supported the hypothesis.

Maheswaran and Meyers-Levy (1990) examined the persuasiveness of different ways to frame a message and the role played by issue **involvement**. A manipulation check was made among the treatments and indicated that significantly different levels of **involvement** had been induced in the subjects.

The experiment by Mick (1992) studied the levels of subjective comprehension in terms of its effect on various attitudes and memory. **Involvement** was measured merely to provide evidence that the product chosen for study (CD players) was associated with high **involvement** for the study group.

COMMENTS: Zaichkowsky (1985) admitted that a smaller number of items composing the scale might be almost as reliable as the 20-item version but warned against haphazardly reducing the number of items. She also pointed out that, though the scale could be used for various purposes, her work mainly focused on demonstrating its quality regarding product involvement. More research was called for to verify its quality for other objects, such as ads and purchase decisions.

See also Haugtvedt and Wegener (1994), Machleit, Allen, and Madden (1993), Mano and Oliver (1993), Murry, Lastovicka, and Singh (1992), and Spreng, MacKenzie, and Olshavsky (1996) for other uses of the scale.

REFERENCES:
Allen, Chris T. (1994), personal correspondence.
Celsi, Richard L. and Jerry C. Olson (1988), "The Role of Involvement in Attention and Comprehension Processes," *JCR*, 15 (September), 210–24.
Gotlieb, Jerry B. and Dan Sarel (1991), "Comparative Advertising Effectiveness: The Role of Involvement and Source Credibility," *JA*, 20 (1), 38–45.
——— and John E. Swan (1990), "An Application of the Elaboration Likelihood Model," *JAMS*, 18 (Summer), 221–28.
Haugtvedt, Curtis P. and Duane T. Wegener (1994), "Message Order Effects in Persuasion: An Attitude Strength Perspective," *JCR*, 21 (June), 205–18.
Houston, Mark B. and Beth A. Walker (1996), "Self-Relevance and Purchase Goals: Mapping a Consumer Decision," *JAMS*, 24 (Summer), 232–45.
Laczniak, Russell N. and Darrel D. Muehling (1993), "The Relationship Between Experimental Manipulations and Tests of Theory in an Advertising Message Involvement Context," *JA*, 22 (September), 59–74.
Lichtenstein, Donald R., Peter H. Bloch, and William C. Black (1988), "Correlates of Price Acceptability," *JCR*, 15 (September), 243–52.
———, Richard D. Netemeyer, and Scot Burton (1990), "Distinguishing Coupon Proneness from Value Consciousness: An Acquisition-Transaction Utility Theory Perspective," *JM*, 54 (July), 54–67.
Lord, Kenneth R., Myung-Soo Lee, and Paul L. Sauer (1994), "Program Context Antecedents of Attitude Toward Radio Commercials," *JAMS*, 22 (1), 3–15.
Maheswaran, Durairja and Joan Meyers-Levy (1990), "The Influence of Message Framing and Issue Involvement," *JMR*, 27 (August), 361–67.
Machleit, Karen A., Chris T. Allen, and Thomas J. Madden (1993), "The Mature Brand and Brand Interest: An Alternative Consequence of Ad-Evoked Affect," *JM*, 57 (October), 72–82.
Mano, Haim and Richard L. Oliver (1993), "Assessing the Dimensionality and Structure of the Consumption Experience: Evaluation, Feeling, and Satisfaction," *JCR*, 20 (December), 451–66.
Marks, Lawrence J. (1994), personal correspondence.
McQuarrie, Edward F. and J. Michael Munson (1987), "The Zaichkowsky Personal Inventory: Modification and Extension," in *Advances in Consumer Research*, Vol. 14, Melanie Wallendorf and Paul Anderson, eds. Provo, UT: Association for Consumer Research, 36–40.
Mick, David Glen (1992), "Levels of Subjective Comprehension in Advertising Processing and Their Relations to Ad Perceptions, Attitudes, and Memory," *JCR*, 18 (March), 411–24.
Miller, Darryl W. and Lawrence J. Marks (1992), "Mental Imagery and Sound Effects in Radio Commercials," *JA*, 21 (4), 83–93.
Mishra, Sanjay (1994), personal correspondence.
———, U.N. Umesh, and Donald E. Stem Jr. (1993), "Antecedents of the Attraction Effect: An Information-Processing Approach," *JMR*, 30 (August), 331–49.
Mittal, Banwari (1990), "The Relative Roles of Brand Beliefs and Attitude Toward the Ad as Mediators of Brand Attitude: A Second Look," *JMR*, 27 (May), 209–19.

Muehling, Darrel D. (1994), personal correspondence.

Murry, John P., Jr., John L. Lastovicka, and Surendra N. Singh (1992), "Feeling and Liking Responses to Television Programs: An Examination of Two Explanations for Media-Context Effects," *JCR*, 18 (March), 441–51.

Neese, William T. and Ronald D. Taylor (1994), "Verbal Strategies for Indirect Comparative Advertising," *JAR*, 34 (March/April), 56–69.

Singh, Surendra N. and Catherine Cole (1993), "The Effects of Length, Content, and Repetition on Television Commercial Effectiveness," *JMR*, 30 (February), 91–104.

Spreng, Richard A., Scott B. MacKenzie, and Richard W. Olshavsky (1996), "A Reexamination of the Determinants of Consumer Satisfaction," *JM*, 60 (July), 15–32.

Stafford, Marla Royne (1996), "Tangibility in Services Advertising: An Investigation of Verbal Versus Visual Cues," *JA*, 25 (Fall), 13–28.

Steenkamp, Jan-Benedict E.M. and Michel Wedel (1991), "Segmenting Retail Markets on Store Image Using a Consumer-Based Methodology," *JR*, 67 (Fall), 300–320.

Zaichkowsky, Judith L. (1985), "Measuring the Involvement Construct," *JCR*, 12 (December), 341–52.

SCALE ITEMS:* (Name of object)

1. Important :___:___:___:___:___:___:___: Unimportant **(r)**
2. Of no concern :___:___:___:___:___:___:___: Of concern to me
3. Irrelevant :___:___:___:___:___:___:___: Relevant
4. Means a lot to me :___:___:___:___:___:___:___: Means nothing to me **(r)**
5. Useless :___:___:___:___:___:___:___: Useful
6. Valuable :___:___:___:___:___:___:___: Worthless **(r)**
7. Trivial :___:___:___:___:___:___:___: Fundamental
8. Beneficial :___:___:___:___:___:___:___: Not beneficial **(r)**
9. Matters to me :___:___:___:___:___:___:___: Doesn't matter **(r)**
10. Uninterested :___:___:___:___:___:___:___: Interested
11. Significant :___:___:___:___:___:___:___: Insignificant **(r)**
12. Vital :___:___:___:___:___:___:___: Superfluous **(r)**
13. Boring :___:___:___:___:___:___:___: Interesting
14. Unexciting :___:___:___:___:___:___:___: Exciting
15. Appealing :___:___:___:___:___:___:___: Unappealing **(r)**
16. Mundane :___:___:___:___:___:___:___: Fascinating
17. Essential :___:___:___:___:___:___:___: Nonessential **(r)**
18. Undesirable :___:___:___:___:___:___:___: Desirable
19. Wanted :___:___:___:___:___:___:___: Unwanted **(r)**
20. Not needed :___:___:___:___:___:___:___: Needed
21. Not involved :___:___:___:___:___:___:___: Highly involved

Houston and Walker (1996): 1–20
Lichtenstein, Bloch, and Black (1988): 1–6, 8, 17, and 20
Lichtenstein, Netemeyer, and Burton (1990): 1–4, 6, 8, 9, 13–15, and 17
Lord, Lee, and Sauer (1994): 1–3, 8, and 12
Maheswaran and Joan Meyers-Levy (1990): short phrases based on 3, 10, and 21.
Mick (1992): 1–6, 8–11, 13–16, 18, and 19
Miller and Marks (1992; Marks 1994): 1–20
Stafford (1996): 1–20
Zaichkowsky (1985): 1–20

*Items are numerically coded from 1 (left) to 7 (right). When known, the items used by particular authors are listed.

SCALE NAME: Involvement (Environment)

SCALE DESCRIPTION: Four seven-point Likert-type items that appear to measure a person's concern for the environment and willingness to work toward its protection.

SCALE ORIGIN: The scale is original to Schuhwerk and Lefkoff-Hagius (1995). Some developmental effort was conducted prior to the work described in the 1995 article, but no details were provided.

SAMPLES: Data were collected as part of a larger advertising study from undergraduate students in business and communication (Schuhwerk and Lefkoff-Hagius 1995). Analysis was based on completed questionnaires from **71** students. More than half the sample were women (56%), and the average age of the respondents was 22 years.

RELIABILITY: Schuhwerk and Lefkoff-Hagius (1995) reported an alpha of **.90** for the scale.

VALIDITY: Although Schuhwerk and Lefkoff-Hagius (1995) did not report explicit validation efforts, they compared scores on the **environmental involvement** scale with those on a related measure, the New Environment Paradigm (#147). The correlation of the two scales was .65, which suggests a degree convergent validity.

ADMINISTRATION: Subjects filled out the scale, along with other measures, after they were exposed to experimental stimuli (Schuhwerk and Lefkoff-Hagius 1995). Higher scores on the scale suggested that respondents were very involved with and concerned about the quality of the environment.

MAJOR FINDINGS: Schuhwerk and Lefkoff-Hagius (1995) examined how consumers responded to ads that vary in their prominence of "green" appeals. There was no difference in purchase intention or attitude toward the ad for those with **high environmental involvement**, but there was for those with low **involvement**.

REFERENCES:
Schuhwerk, Melody E. and Roxanne Lefkoff-Hagius (1995), "Green or Non-Green? Does Type of Appeal Matter When Advertising a Green Product?" *JA*, 24 (Summer), 45–54.

SCALE ITEMS:

Strongly   Strongly
disagree   :___:___:___:___:___:___:___: agree
              1   2   3   4   5   6   7

1. I am concerned about the environment.

2. The condition of the environment affects the quality of my life.

3. I am willing to make sacrifices to protect the environment.

4. My actions impact on the environment.

SCALE NAME: Involvement (Experimental Task)

SCALE DESCRIPTION: Four semantic differential items measuring the degree to which a subject, who has just taken part in an experiment, indicates being seriously concerned with the activities requested of him or her. As written, the items focus on tasks related to looking at ads and evaluating products.

SCALE ORIGIN: Pham (1996) did not describe the source of his scale, but it is likely original to his study.

SAMPLES: Data were gathered by Pham (1996) for his three experiments from undergraduate students. The scale was used, however, just in Experiment 3, which involved **57** students.

RELIABILITY: An alpha of **.76** was reported for the scale used by Pham (1996).

VALIDITY: No examination of the scale's validity was reported by (Pham 1996). He stated, however, that a factor analysis of the items in this scale, as well as two others (#23 and #237), yielded a three-factor solution in which the items shown subsequently loaded on one factor.

ADMINISTRATION: The scale was self-administered by subjects as part of a questionnaire after they were exposed to experimental stimuli (Pham 1996). High scores on the scale indicated that subjects had strong involvement in the experimental tasks they just engaged in.

MAJOR FINDINGS: Pham (1996) proposed that two types of processes underlie arousal effects on persuasion: the "selection" and the "representation" effects. **Involvement with the experimental task** was included in the study as a possible confounding effect. The results indicated that trait anxiety was not significantly associated with **task involvement**, as was expected.

REFERENCES:
Pham, Michel Tuan (1996), "Cue Representation and Selection Effects of Arousal on Persuasion," *JCR*, 22 (March), 373–87.

SCALE ITEMS:*

1. I *was/wasn't* very motivated to reach an accurate evaluation of the _____.

2. I *did/did not* put much effort into the evaluation of the products.

3. It was *important/unimportant* to read the ads carefully.

4. I am *confident/not sure* that I evaluated the products thoroughly.

*The type and number of points on the response scale were not described in the article; thus, the physical layout of the sacle is not clear. The blank in item 1 should be filled with the generic term for what subjects are asked to evaluate.

SCALE NAME: Involvement (Premiums)

SCALE DESCRIPTION: A six-item, seven-point Likert-type scale measuring a consumer's fondness for purchasing products that have another item with them for free. This measures a general tendency rather than the likelihood that the behavior occurs for any particular product category. Lichtenstein, Burton, and Netemeyer (1997) and Lichtenstein, Netemeyer, and Burton (1995) referred the scale as *free-gift-with-purchase proneness*.

SCALE ORIGIN: The scale is original to the studies by Lichtenstein, Netemeyer, and Burton (1995), though some of the items are similar to ones developed previously by the same authors for other measures (e.g., Lichtenstein, Netemeyer, and Burton 1990). In an effort to develop several deal-proneness measures, 91 items were generated and tested with 341 nonstudent adults. Using factor analysis and other tests, seven items were deleted, which left 84 to be used in the two studies described here. Lichtenstein, Burton, and Netemeyer (1997) presented 49 of the items for the measurement of eight different deal-proneness types.

SAMPLES: The sample employed by Lichtenstein, Netemeyer, and Burton (1995) in their first study came from shoppers in one of two grocery stores in the Midwestern United States. (This is also the sample used in Lichtenstein, Burton, and Netemeyer 1997.) Shoppers were approached and asked if they would participate in the survey. If so, they were given the instrument and asked to fill it out later and mail it back. Completed questionnaires were received from **582** shoppers. A majority of the sample were women (75.9%), and more than half (58.6%) were married. The median household income was $35,000 to $49,000, and the median age was 35 to 44 years of age. The survey in Study 2 was distributed similarly to that in Study 1. Usable forms were received back from **402** people, most of whom were women (77.9%) and married (67.3%). The median income and age were the same as in the first study.

RELIABILITY: An alpha of **.91** was reported for the scale by Lichtenstein, Netemeyer, and Burton (1995; Lichtenstein, Burton, and Netemeyer 1997) for both Studies 1 and 2.

VALIDITY: Confirmatory factor analyses were used in the studies by Lichtenstein, Netemeyer, and Burton (1995; Lichtenstein, Burton, and Netemeyer 1997), and it was concluded that the scale was unidimensional and showed evidence of discriminant validity.

ADMINISTRATION: In the studies by Lichtenstein, Netemeyer, and Burton (1995; Lichtenstein, Burton, and Netemeyer 1997), the scale was part of a survey instrument self-administered by shoppers after they left the grocery store. Higher scores on the scale indicated that consumers were very interested in and enjoyed buying products that came with "free gifts."

MAJOR FINDINGS: The purpose of the study by Lichtenstein, Burton, and Netemeyer (1997) was to determine if there were consumer segments that had a tendency to be "deal prone" in general. Among the findings was that, in both the two- and three-cluster analyses of shoppers, there was a generalized deal-proneness group that had significantly higher mean scores on the **premium involvement** scale compared with clusters of shoppers who were less deal prone.

Although the first study in Lichtenstein, Netemeyer, and Burton (1995) shares the same sample as that described previously, its purpose, as well as that for Study 2, was to compare competing models of deal proneness that varied on the level of specificity. Although **involvement with premiums** was found to have a few significant relationships with some marketplace behaviors in Study 1, none of these relationships was found (with significance) in Study 2.

COMMENTS: Lichtenstein, Netemeyer, and Burton (1995) reported means on the scale of 17.74 and 15.93 for Studies 1 and 2, respectively.

REFERENCES:

Lichtenstein, Donald R., Scot Burton, and Richard G. Netemeyer (1997), "An Examination of Deal Proneness Across Sales Promotion Types: A Consumer Segmentation Perspective," *JR*, 73 (2), 283–97.

———, Richard G. Netemeyer, and Scot Burton (1990), "Distinguishing Coupon Proneness from Value Consciousness: An Acquisition-Transaction Utility Theory Perspective," *JM*, 54 (July), 54–67.

———, ———, and ——— (1995), "Assessing the Domain Specificity of Deal Proneness: A Field Study," *JCR*, 22 (December), 314–26.

SCALE ITEMS:

Strongly   Strongly
disagree   :___:___:___:___:___:___:___: agree

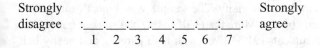

1. I enjoy buying products that come with a free gift.

2. I enjoy buying a brand that comes with a free gift, regardless of the value of the free gift.

3. I have favorite brands, but when I encounter a free gift offer, I am more likely to buy the brand that comes with the free gift.

4. Seeing a brand that comes with a free gift has influenced me to buy brands I normally would not buy.

5. Beyond the money I save, buying a brand that comes with a free gift gives me a sense of joy.

6. Compared to most people, I am more likely to buy brands that come with free gifts.

SCALE NAME: Involvement (Product Class)

SCALE DESCRIPTION: A four-item, five-point Likert-type rating scale measuring a person's interest in some specified category of products. The scale was apparently used twice by Beatty and Talpade (1994): once for the sample (teens) to evaluate relative contributions in a decision regarding a durable product for *teenager* use and another time related to a durable product for *family* use. A three-item version of the scale was used by Flynn, Goldsmith, and Eastman (1996).

SCALE ORIGIN: The four-item scale is original to Beatty and Talpade (1994), though three of the items were adapted from a scale reported by Mittal and Lee (1988, 1989), and another item was adapted from a scale by Bloch (1981). The three-item scale used by Flynn, Goldsmith, and Eastman (1996) was apparently based on the version reported by Mittal and Lee (1989).

SAMPLES: Beatty and Talpade (1994) gathered data for their main study from **382** students attending a freshman-orientation session at a Southeastern U.S. university. The sample was almost exactly split between men and women, and 68% were 18 years of age. More than half (64%) had worked outside the home in the previous six months. Most of the students (91%) lived with both parents, and nearly half (47%) were from dual-income households.

Flynn, Goldsmith, and Eastman (1996) reported on five studies, but only one (3) employed the **involvement** scale. Data for that study came from **391** undergraduate students at a large university. Questionnaires were completed in class. The respondents ranged in age from 18 to 64 years (median = 21). The sample was 72% women and 83% white.

RELIABILITY: Alphas of **.74** and **.80** were reported for the family and teenager applications of the scale, respectively (Beatty and Talpade 1994). An alpha of **.93** was estimated for the scale in study 3 (fashion) by Flynn, Goldsmith, and Eastman (1996; Goldsmith 1997).

VALIDITY: The validity of the scale was not directly assessed by Beatty and Talpade (1994) or Flynn, Goldsmith, and Eastman (1996). However, because it was part of an effort in the latter study to examine the nomological validity of two other scales (#243 and #245), some sense of its own nomological validity can be gained. For example, high positive correlations were found between **involvement** and opinion leadership, innovativeness, and product knowledge. No relationship was found between **involvement** and opinion seeking.

ADMINISTRATION: The scale was self-administered by students as part of a larger survey instrument (Beatty and Talpade 1994; Flynn, Goldsmith, and Eastman 1996). High scores on the scale suggested that respondents viewed some particular product category as being very important to them.

MAJOR FINDINGS: The study by Beatty and Talpade (1994) built on previous research of adolescent influence on family decision making. Among the results was that the greater teenagers' perceived **product involvement** with a product class, the higher their perceived influence on the initiation and search/decision stages for both family and teen purchases was.

Flynn, Goldsmith, and Eastman (1996) reported on the development and testing of opinion leadership and opinion-seeking scales (#243 and #245). **Involvement** was included along with several other measures merely to help establish the nomological validity of the two opinion-related scales. As noted, **involvement** had a high positive association with opinion leadership but no significant relationship with opinion seeking.

REFERENCES:

Beatty, Sharon E. and Salil Talpade (1994), "Adolescent Influence in Family Decision Making: A Replication with Extension," *JCR*, 21 (September), 332–41.

Bloch, Peter E. (1981), "An Exploration into the Scaling of Consumers' Involvement with a Product Class," in *Advances in Consumer Research*, Vol. 8, Kent B. Monroe, ed. Ann Arbor, MI: Association for Consumer Research, 61–65.

Flynn, Leisa R., Ronald E. Goldsmith, and Jacqueline K. Eastman (1996), "Opinion Leaders and Opinion Seekers: Two New Measurement Scales," *JAMS*, 24 (Spring), 137–47.

Goldsmith, Ronald E. (1997), personal correspondence.

Mittal, Banwari and Myung-Soo Lee (1988), "Separating Brand-Choice Involvement from Product Involvement via Consumer Involvement Profiles," in *Advances in Consumer Research*, Vol. 15, Michael J. Houston, ed. Provo, UT: Association for Consumer Research, 43–46.

———— and ———— (1989), "A Causal Model of Consumer Involvement," *Journal of Economic Psychology*, 10, 363–89.

SCALE ITEMS: *

Strongly disagree	Disagree	Neutral	Agree	Strongly agree
1	2	3	4	5

1. In general I have a strong interest in this product category.

2. This product category is very important to me.

3. This product category matters a lot to me.

4. I get bored when other people talk to me about this product category. **(r)**

*This is the version of the scale used by Beatty and Talpade (1994). Flynn, Goldsmith, and Eastman (1996) used items 1–3 with some slight differences in wording.

SCALE NAME: Involvement (Product Class)

SCALE DESCRIPTION: Three seven-point Likert-type items measuring the degree of interest a consumer expresses having in a specified product category.

SCALE ORIGIN: The scale used by Van Trijp, Hoyer, and Inman (1996) is original to their study. The authors stated that a review of literature produced 14 items that were evaluated in a pretest (n = 86). Their goal was apparently to produce a short scale of involvement with high reliability, and this three-item version was considered to have met that criterion.

SAMPLES: The data gathered by Van Trijp, Hoyer, and Inman (1996) came from 1000 Dutch households that were part of multiweek consumer panel. The number of people providing usable data was not specified, nor were their demographic characteristics.

RELIABILITY: An alpha of **.69** was reported by Van Trijp, Hoyer, and Inman (1996) for the scale.

VALIDITY: No examination of the scale's validity was reported by Van Trijp, Hoyer, and Inman (1996).

ADMINISTRATION: Panel members in the study by Van Trijp, Hoyer, and Inman (1996) responded to questionnaires on a PC in their homes connected by modem to a central computer. As coded by these authors, higher scores on the scale indicated that a specified product category was of *low* importance to the respondents.

MAJOR FINDINGS: Van Trijp, Hoyer, and Inman (1996) proposed that brand-switching behavior should be examined by differentiating between intrinsic (e.g., variety-seeking) and extrinsic (e.g., brand on sale) motivations. The results indicated that variety seeking was more likely than repeat purchasing behavior when **involvement** was lower.

COMMENTS: The range of scores on the scale (Van Trijp, Hoyer, and Inman 1996) was from 3 to 21 with a mean of 10.5 and a standard deviation of 4.1.

REFERENCES:
Van Trijp, Has C.M., Wayne D. Hoyer, and J. Jeffrey Inman (1996), "Why Switch? Product Category-Level Explanations for True Variety-Seeking Behavior," *JMR*, 33 (August), 281–92.

SCALE ITEMS:

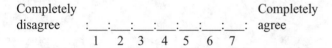

Completely   Completely
disagree   :__:__:__:__:__:__:__: agree
                 1   2   3   4   5   6   7

1. Compared to other products, this product is important to me. **(r)**

2. I'm not interested in this product.

3. When I buy a brand from this product category, I choose very carefully. **(r)**

SCALE NAME: Involvement (Product Class)

SCALE DESCRIPTION: Four seven-point Likert-type items measuring the extent to which a person expresses an interest in a product category and views it as an expression of his or her lifestyle. The category studied by Moorthy, Ratchford, and Talukdar (1997) was cars.

SCALE ORIGIN: The scale was developed by Moorthy, Ratchford, and Talukdar (1997) for use in their study on the basis of previous work conducted by Srinivasan and Ratchford (1991) and Beatty and Smith (1987).

SAMPLES: Moorthy, Ratchford, and Talukdar (1997) gathered data from new car buyers in the Greater Rochester area in northern New York over a six-month period. Surveys were passed out to new car buyers at four dealerships that represented a variety of U.S. and Japanese manufacturers. Shoppers were given two survey forms: one to fill out if they had already bought a car and the other to complete if they were still in the process of buying a car. Fifty-one respondents filled out the "already purchased" form; another 51 completed the "in-process" form initially but bought cars within two months.

RELIABILITY: Alphas of **.81** and **.83** were reported for the scale for the two groups of respondents (Moorthy, Ratchford, and Talukdar 1997).

VALIDITY: No examination of the scale's validity was reported by Moorthy, Ratchford, and Talukdar (1997).

ADMINISTRATION: Questionnaires were passed out by one of the researchers, but the forms were self-administered by respondents later at their convenience and mailed back to the researchers (Moorthy, Ratchford, and Talukdar 1997). Higher scores on the scale indicated that respondents were very involved cognitively and behaviorally with the specific product category.

MAJOR FINDINGS: Moorthy, Ratchford, and Talukdar (1997) presented a comprehensive model for understanding consumer external search activity. The framework stressed the influence of prior brand perceptions on the search process. As expected, the findings showed an inverted-U-shaped relationship between purchase experience and amount of search, though the specific effects of **product involvement** were not discussed.

COMMENTS: Although the scale appears to be amenable for use with product categories other than automobiles, item 4 may need to be modified or dropped in those cases in which it does not make sense. Retesting of the modified scale's psychometric properties will then be needed.

REFERENCES:
Moorthy, Sridhar, Brian T. Ratchford, and Debabrata Talukdar (1997), "Consumer Information Search Revisited: Theory and Empirical Analysis," *JCR*, 23 (March), 263–77.
Srinivasan, Narasimhan and Brian T. Ratchford (1991), "An Empirical Test of a External Search for Automobiles," *JCR*, 18 (September), 233–42.

SCALE ITEMS:*

Strongly disagree :___:___:___:___:___:___:___: Strongly agree
　　　　　　　1　2　3　4　5　6　7

1. I have a strong interest in _____.

2. I value _____ as an important part of my current lifestyle.

3. A lot can be said about a person from the _____ s/he owns.

4. I like to work on _____ myself.

*The name of the product category should be placed in the blanks.

SCALE NAME: Involvement (Product-Related Pleasure)

SCALE DESCRIPTION: Three semantic differentials used to measure the importance of a brand or product category to a consumer, with an emphasis on a hedonic aspect of the product's consumption or usage.

SCALE ORIGIN: The scale used by Rosbergen, Pieters, and Wedel (1997) was developed by Jain and Srinivasan (1990). The latter conducted a study that compared various involvement scales. Although the multidimensional structure of involvement they ultimately endorsed was very similar to that proposed by Laurent and Kapferer (1985), the items came from several studies. On the basis of a factor analysis (oblique rotation) that pooled data from ten products, the items shown here were those that loaded highest on the *pleasantness* dimension.

SAMPLES: The experiment conducted by Rosbergen, Pieters, and Wedel (1997) was based on data collected from **115** adult female consumers (20 to 39 years of age). The experiment took place in the headquarters of a market research firm in the Netherlands, and subjects were paid the equivalent of $10 for their effort.

RELIABILITY: The construct reliability of the scale was reported by Rosbergen, Pieters, and Wedel (1997) to be **.66**.

VALIDITY: No examination of the scale's validity was reported by Rosbergen, Pieters, and Wedel (1997). However, the confirmatory factor analysis they conducted of these items and the others recommended by Jain and Srinivasan (1990) for the measurement of involvement provided some support for the expected five-dimensional structure proposed by Laurent and Kapferer (1985).

ADMINISTRATION: The scale appears to have been self-administered by subjects, along with other measures, after they were exposed to experimental stimuli (Rosbergen, Pieters, and Wedel 1997). Higher scores on the scale indicated greater involvement with the product as it relates to producing pleasure.

MAJOR FINDINGS: Rosbergen, Pieters, and Wedel (1997, p. 306) proposed that consumers vary in their "visual gaze duration patterns." A methodology was presented for measuring the effect of the physical properties of print ads on visual attention that takes this variation among consumers into account. Although the authors concluded that the different dimensions of involvement had varying effects on visual attention factors, the specific results related to the **pleasure** component were not clear.

COMMENTS: The internal consistency for the scale is rather low. It might be increased by the addition of a few more items, making sure to maintain the scale's unidimensionality. Candidates for addition can be found in Jain and Srinivasan's (1990) article, in which nine items other than those listed here loaded on the same factor.

REFERENCES:

Jain, Kapil and Narasimhan Srinivasan (1990), "An Empirical Assessment of Multiple Operationalizations of Involvement," in *Advances in Consumer Research*, Vol. 17, Marvin E. Goldberg, Gerald Gorn, and Richard W. Pollay, eds. Provo, UT: Association for Consumer Research, 594–602.

Laurent, Gilles and Jean-Noel Kapferer (1985), "Measuring Consumer Involvement Profiles," *JMR*, 22 (February), 41–53.

Rosbergen, Edward, Rik Pieters, and Michel Wedel (1997), "Visual Attention to Advertising: A Segment-Level Analysis," *JCR*, 24 (December), 305–14.

SCALE ITEMS:*

Using the following descriptors, please indicate your feelings about _____.

I do not find it
pleasurable   :___:___:___:___:___:___:___: I find it
                 1   2   3   4   5   6   7   pleasurable

Unexciting   :___:___:___:___:___:___:___: Exciting
            1   2   3   4   5   6   7

Not fun   :___:___:___:___:___:___:___: Fun
         1   2   3   4   5   6   7

*The scale stem and the number of points on the response scale were not specified by Rosbergen, Pieters, and Wedel (1997). The stem shown above is a possibility. The name of the product should be placed in the blank.

SCALE NAME: Involvement (Product-Related Relevance)

SCALE DESCRIPTION: Three semantic differentials used to measure the importance of a brand or product category to a consumer, with an emphasis on the extent to which the product is viewed as not just helpful, but necessary to have.

SCALE ORIGIN: The scale used by Rosbergen, Pieters, and Wedel (1997) was developed by Jain and Srinivasan (1990). The latter conducted a study that compared various involvement scales. Although the multidimensional structure of involvement they ultimately endorsed was very similar to that proposed by Laurent and Kapferer (1985), the items came from several other studies. On the basis of a factor analysis (oblique rotation) that pooled data from ten products, the items shown here were those that loaded highest on the *relevance* dimension.

SAMPLES: The experiment conducted by Rosbergen, Pieters, and Wedel (1997) was based on data collected from **115** adult female consumers (20 to 39 years of age). The experiment took place in the headquarters of a market research firm in the Netherlands, and subjects were paid the equivalent of $10 for their effort.

RELIABILITY: The construct reliability of the scale used by Rosbergen, Pieters, and Wedel (1997) was **.76** (Rosbergen 1998).

VALIDITY: No examination of the scale's validity was reported by Rosbergen, Pieters, and Wedel (1997). However, the confirmatory factor analysis they conducted of these items and the others recommended by Jain and Srinivasan (1990) for the measurement of involvement provided some support for the expected five-dimensional structure proposed by Laurent and Kapferer (1985).

ADMINISTRATION: The scale appears to have been self-administered by subjects, along with other measures, after they were exposed to experimental stimuli (Rosbergen, Pieters, and Wedel 1997). Higher scores on the scale indicated consumers' greater involvement with the product, particularly as it relates to how vital they view it to be to them.

MAJOR FINDINGS: Rosbergen, Pieters, and Wedel (1997, p. 306) proposed that consumers vary in their "visual gaze duration patterns." A methodology was presented for measuring the effect of the physical properties of print ads on visual attention that takes this variation among consumers into account. Although the authors concluded that the different dimensions of involvement had varying effects on visual attention factors, the specific results related to the **relevance** component were not clearly discussed.

REFERENCES:

Jain, Kapil and Narasimhan Srinivasan (1990), "An Empirical Assessment of Multiple Operationalizations of Involvement," in *Advances in Consumer Research*, Vol. 17, Marvin E. Goldberg, Gerald Gorn, and Richard W. Pollay, eds. Provo, UT: Association for Consumer Research, 594–602.

Laurent, Gilles and Jean-Noel Kapferer (1985), "Measuring Consumer Involvement Profiles," *JMR*, 22 (February), 41–53.

Rosbergen, Edward (1998), personal correspondence.

———, Rik Pieters, and Michel Wedel (1997), "Visual Attention to Advertising: A Segment-Level Analysis," *JCR*, 24 (December), 305–14.

SCALE ITEMS:*

Using the following descriptors, please describe how important _____ is to you.

Nonessential	:___:___:___:___:___:___:___:	Essential
	1 2 3 4 5 6 7	

Not beneficial	:___:___:___:___:___:___:___:	Beneficial
	1 2 3 4 5 6 7	

Not needed	:___:___:___:___:___:___:___:	Needed
	1 2 3 4 5 6 7	

*The scale stem and the number of points on the response scale were not specified by Rosbergen, Pieters, and Wedel (1997). The stem shown above is a possibility. The name of the product should be placed in the blank.

SCALE NAME: Involvement (Product-Related Risk Importance)

SCALE DESCRIPTION: Three semantic differentials used to measure the importance of a brand or product category to a consumer, with an emphasis on the extent to which the consumer would be personally disturbed about making a bad decision. Perhaps this means that the consumer thinks his or her pride and ego would be damaged by making a poor choice.

SCALE ORIGIN: The scale used by Rosbergen, Pieters, and Wedel (1997) was developed by Jain and Srinivasan (1990). The latter conducted a study that compared various involvement scales. Although the multidimensional structure of involvement they ultimately endorsed was very similar to that proposed by Laurent and Kapferer (1985), the items came from several other studies. On the basis of a factor analysis (oblique rotation) that pooled data from ten products, the items shown here were those that loaded highest on the *risk importance* dimension.

SAMPLES: The experiment conducted by Rosbergen, Pieters, and Wedel (1997) was based on data collected from **115** adult female consumers (20 to 39 years of age). The experiment took place in the headquarters of a market research firm in the Netherlands, and subjects were paid the equivalent of $10 for their effort.

RELIABILITY: The construct reliability of the scale used by Rosbergen, Pieters, and Wedel (1997) was **.83** (Rosbergen 1998).

VALIDITY: No examination of the scale's validity was reported by Rosbergen, Pieters, and Wedel (1997). However, the confirmatory factor analysis they conducted of these items and the others recommended by Jain and Srinivasan (1990) for the measurement of involvement provided some support for the expected five-dimensional structure proposed by Laurent and Kapferer (1985).

ADMINISTRATION: The scale appears to have been self-administered by subjects, along with other measures, after they were exposed to experimental stimuli (Rosbergen, Pieters, and Wedel 1997). Higher scores on the scale indicated consumers' greater involvement with the product, particularly as it relates to the risk of annoying themselves by making a bad decision.

MAJOR FINDINGS: Rosbergen, Pieters, and Wedel (1997, p. 306) proposed that consumers vary in their "visual gaze duration patterns." A methodology was presented for measuring the effect of the physical properties of print ads on visual attention that takes this variation among consumers into account. Although the authors concluded that the different dimensions of involvement had varying effects on visual attention factors, the specific results related to the **risk importance** component were not clearly discussed.

REFERENCES:
Jain, Kapil and Narasimhan Srinivasan (1990), "An Empirical Assessment of Multiple Operationalizations of Involvement," in *Advances in Consumer Research*, Vol. 17, Marvin E. Goldberg, Gerald Gorn, and Richard W. Pollay, eds. Provo, UT: Association for Consumer Research, 594–602.

Laurent, Gilles and Jean-Noel Kapferer (1985), "Measuring Consumer Involvement Profiles," *JMR*, 22 (February), 41–53.

Rosbergen, Edward (1998), personal correspondence.

——, Rik Pieters, and Michel Wedel (1997), "Visual Attention to Advertising: A Segment-Level Analysis," *JCR*, 24 (December), 305–14.

SCALE ITEMS:*

Using the following statements, please describe how difficult it is for you to buy _____.

It is not annoying to make an unsuitable purchase	:__:__:__:__:__:__:	It is really annoying to make an unsuitable purchase
	1 2 3 4 5 6 7	

A poor choice would not be upsetting	:__:__:__:__:__:__:	A poor choice would be upsetting
	1 2 3 4 5 6 7	

Little to lose by choosing poorly	:__:__:__:__:__:__:	A lot to lose by choosing poorly
	1 2 3 4 5 6 7	

*The scale stem and the number of points on the response scale were not specified by Rosbergen, Pieters, and Wedel (1997). The stem shown above is a possibility. The name of the product should be placed in the blank.

SCALE NAME: Involvement (Product-Related Risk Probability)

SCALE DESCRIPTION: Three semantic differentials used to measure the importance of a brand or product category to a consumer, with an emphasis on the extent to which the consumer is confident the right purchase decision is being made.

SCALE ORIGIN: The scale used by Rosbergen, Pieters, and Wedel (1997) was developed by Jain and Srinivasan (1990). The latter conducted a study that compared various involvement scales. Although the multidimensional structure of involvement they ultimately endorsed was very similar to that proposed by Laurent and Kapferer (1985), the items came from several other studies. On the basis of a factor analysis (oblique rotation) that pooled data from ten products, the items shown here were those that loaded highest on the *risk probability* dimension.

SAMPLES: The experiment conducted by Rosbergen, Pieters, and Wedel (1997) was based on data collected from 115 adult female consumers (20 to 39 years of age). The experiment took place in the headquarters of a market research firm in the Netherlands, and subjects were paid the equivalent of $10 for their effort.

RELIABILITY: The construct reliability of the scale used by Rosbergen, Pieters, and Wedel (1997) was .72 (Rosbergen 1998).

VALIDITY: No examination of the scale's validity was reported by Rosbergen, Pieters, and Wedel (1997). However, the confirmatory factor analysis they conducted of these items and the others recommended by Jain and Srinivasan (1990) for the measurement of involvement provided some support for the expected five-dimensional structure proposed by Laurent and Kapferer (1985).

ADMINISTRATION: The scale appears to have been self-administered by subjects, along with other measures, after they were exposed to experimental stimuli (Rosbergen, Pieters, and Wedel 1997). Higher scores on the scale indicated consumers' greater involvement with the product, particularly as it relates to the certainty they have in the correctness of the purchase decision.

MAJOR FINDINGS: Rosbergen, Pieters, and Wedel (1997, p. 306) proposed that consumers vary in their "visual gaze duration patterns." A methodology was presented for measuring the effect of the physical properties of print ads on visual attention that takes this variation among consumers into account. Although the authors concluded that the different dimensions of involvement had varying effects on visual attention factors, the specific results related to the **risk probability** component were not clearly discussed.

REFERENCES:

Jain, Kapil and Narasimhan Srinivasan (1990), "An Empirical Assessment of Multiple Operationalizations of Involvement," in *Advances in Consumer Research*, Vol. 17, Marvin E. Goldberg, Gerald Gorn, and Richard W. Pollay, eds. Provo, UT: Association for Consumer Research, 594–602.

Laurent, Gilles and Jean-Noel Kapferer (1985), "Measuring Consumer Involvement Profiles," *JMR*, 22 (February), 41–53.

Rosbergen, Edward (1998), personal correspondence.

———, Rik Pieters, and Michel Wedel (1997), "Visual Attention to Advertising: A Segment-Level Analysis," *JCR*, 24 (December), 305–14.

SCALE ITEMS:*

Using the following statements, please describe how difficult it is for you to buy _____.

In purchasing it,

I am uncertain of my choice	:___:___:___:___:___:___:	I am certain of my choice
	1 2 3 4 5 6 7	

I never know if I am making the right purchase	:___:___:___:___:___:___:	I know for sure I am making the right purchase
	1 2 3 4 5 6 7	

I feel a bit at a loss in choosing it	:___:___:___:___:___:___:	I don't feel at a loss in choosing it
	1 2 3 4 5 6 7	

*The scale stem and the number of points on the response scale were not specified by Rosbergen, Pieters, and Wedel (1997). The stem shown above is a possibility. The name of the product should be placed in the blank.

SCALE NAME: Involvement (Product-Related Sign)

SCALE DESCRIPTION: Three semantic differentials used to measure the importance of a brand or product category to a consumer, with an emphasis on the extent to which the product is viewed as expressing something about the user to others.

SCALE ORIGIN: The scale used by Rosbergen, Pieters, and Wedel (1997) was developed by Jain and Srinivasan (1990). The latter conducted a study that compared various involvement scales. Although the multidimensional structure of involvement they ultimately endorsed was very similar to that proposed by Laurent and Kapferer (1985), the items came from several other studies. On the basis of a factor analysis (oblique rotation) that pooled data from ten products, the items shown here were those that loaded highest on the *sign* dimension.

SAMPLES: The experiment conducted by Rosbergen, Pieters, and Wedel (1997) was based on data collected from **115** adult female consumers (20 to 39 years of age). The experiment took place in the headquarters of a market research firm in the Netherlands, and subjects were paid the equivalent of $10 for their effort.

RELIABILITY: The construct reliability of the scale was reported by Rosbergen, Pieters, and Wedel (1997) to be **.87**.

VALIDITY: No examination of the scale's validity was reported by Rosbergen, Pieters, and Wedel (1997). However, the confirmatory factor analysis they conducted of these items and the others recommended by Jain and Srinivasan (1990) for the measurement of involvement provided some support for the expected five-dimensional structure proposed by Laurent and Kapferer (1985).

ADMINISTRATION: The scale appears to have been self-administered by subjects, along with other measures, after they were exposed to experimental stimuli (Rosbergen, Pieters, and Wedel 1997). Higher scores on the scale indicated greater involvement with the product as it relates to its ability to be a sign to others.

MAJOR FINDINGS: Rosbergen, Pieters, and Wedel (1997, p. 306) proposed that consumers vary in their "visual gaze duration patterns." A methodology was presented for measuring the effect of the physical properties of print ads on visual attention that takes this variation among consumers into account. Although the authors concluded that the different dimensions of involvement had varying effects on visual attention factors, the specific results related to the **sign** component were not clear.

REFERENCES:

Jain, Kapil and Narasimhan Srinivasan (1990), "An Empirical Assessment of Multiple Operationalizations of Involvement," in *Advances in Consumer Research*, Vol. 17, Marvin E. Goldberg, Gerald Gorn, and Richard W. Pollay, Provo, UT: Association for Consumer Research, 594–602.

Laurent, Gilles and Jean-Noel Kapferer (1985), "Measuring Consumer Involvement Profiles," *JMR*, 22 (February), 41–53.

Rosbergen, Edward, Rik Pieters, and Michel Wedel (1997), "Visual Attention to Advertising: A Segment-Level Analysis," *JCR*, 24 (December), 305–14.

SCALE ITEMS:*

Using the following statements, please indicate how you think about _____.

Doesn't tell others about me	:___:___:___:___:___:___:___:	Tells others about me
	1 2 3 4 5 6 7	

Others won't use to judge me	:___:___:___:___:___:___:___:	Others use to judge me
	1 2 3 4 5 6 7	

Does not portray an image of me to others	:___:___:___:___:___:___:___:	Portrays an image of me to others
	1 2 3 4 5 6 7	

*The scale stem and the number of points on the response scale were not specified by Rosbergen, Pieters, and Wedel (1997). The stem shown above is a possibility. The name of the product should be placed in the blank.

SCALE NAME: Involvement (Rebates)

SCALE DESCRIPTION: A six-item, seven-point Likert-type scale measuring a consumer's enjoyment of cash refund offers and tendency to buy products associated with such offers. This measures a general tendency rather than the likelihood that the behavior occurs for any particular product category. Lichtenstein, Netemeyer, and Burton (1995; Lichtenstein, Burton, and Netemeyer 1997) referred the scale as *rebate/refund proneness*.

SCALE ORIGIN: The scale is original to the studies by Lichtenstein, Netemeyer, and Burton (1995), though some of the items are similar to ones developed previously by the same authors for other measures (e.g., Lichtenstein, Netemeyer, and Burton 1990). In an effort to develop several deal-proneness measures, 91 items were generated and tested with 341 nonstudent adults. Using factor analysis and other tests, seven items were deleted, which left 84 to be used in the two studies reported in Lichtenstein, Netemeyer, and Burton (1995). Lichtenstein, Burton, and Netemeyer (1997) presented 49 of the items for the measurement of eight different deal-proneness types.

SAMPLES: The sample employed by Lichtenstein, Netemeyer, and Burton (1995) in their first study came from shoppers in one of two grocery stores in the Midwestern United States. (This is also the sample used by Lichtenstein, Burton, and Netemeyer 1997.) Shoppers were approached and asked if they would participate in the survey. If so, they were given the instrument and asked to fill it out later and mail it back. Completed questionnaires were received from **582** shoppers. A majority of the sample were women (75.9%), and more than half (58.6%) were married. The median household income was $35,000 to $49,000, and the median age was 35 to 44 years of age. The survey in Study 2 was distributed similarly to that in Study 1. Usable forms were received back from **402** people, most of whom were women (77.9%) and married (67.3%). The median income and age were the same as in the first study.

RELIABILITY: Alphas of **.86** and **.83** were reported for the scale by Lichtenstein, Netemeyer, and Burton (1995) for Studies 1 (Lichtenstein, Burton, and Netemeyer 1997) and 2, respectively.

VALIDITY: Confirmatory factor analyses were used in both studies by Lichtenstein, Netemeyer, and Burton (1995; Lichtenstein, Burton, and Netemeyer 1997), and it was concluded that the scale was unidimensional and showed evidence of discriminant validity.

ADMINISTRATION: In the studies by Lichtenstein, Netemeyer, and Burton (1995; Lichtenstein, Burton, and Netemeyer 1997), the scale was part of a survey instrument self-administered by shoppers after they left the grocery store. Higher scores on the scale indicated that consumers were very interested in and enjoyed purchasing products that had refund offers with them.

MAJOR FINDINGS: The purpose of the study by Lichtenstein, Burton, and Netemeyer (1997) was to determine if there were consumer segments that had a tendency to be "deal prone" in general. Among the findings was that, in both the two- and three-cluster analyses of shoppers, there was a generalized deal-proneness group that had significantly higher mean scores on the **rebate involvement** scale compared with clusters of shoppers who were less deal prone.

Although the first study in Lichtenstein, Netemeyer, and Burton (1995) shares the same sample as that described previously, its purpose, as well as that for Study 2, was to compare competing models of deal proneness that varied on the level of specificity. Among the findings was that **involvement with rebates** had a stronger relationship (positive) than any of the other deal-proneness measures with the frequency of acting on rebate offers.

COMMENTS: Lichtenstein, Netemeyer, and Burton (1995) reported means on the scale of 16.15 and 16.10 for Studies 1 and 2, respectively.

REFERENCES:

Lichtenstein, Donald R., Scot Burton, and Richard G. Netemeyer (1997), "An Examination of Deal Proneness Across Sales Promotion Types: A Consumer Segmentation Perspective," *JR*, 73 (2), 283–97.

——, Richard G. Netemeyer, and Scot Burton (1990), "Distinguishing Coupon Proneness from Value Consciousness: An Acquisition-Transaction Utility Theory Perspective," *JM*, 54 (July), 54–67.

——, ——, and —— (1995), "Assessing the Domain Specificity of Deal Proneness: A Field Study," *JCR*, 22 (December), 314–26.

SCALE ITEMS:

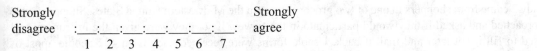

Strongly disagree : __:__:__:__:__:__:__: Strongly agree
   1   2   3   4   5   6   7

1. Receiving cash rebates makes me feel good.

2. I enjoy buying brands that offer cash rebates, regardless of the amount of money I save by doing so.

3. By the time you pay postage, mail-in cash rebates are <u>not</u> worth the hassle. **(r)**

4. I have favorite brands, but if possible, I buy the brand that offers a cash rebate.

5. Beyond the money I save, buying products that offer a rebate gives me a sense of joy.

6. I'm usually <u>not</u> motivated to respond to rebate offers. **(r)**

SCALE NAME: Involvement (Sales Promotion Deals)

SCALE DESCRIPTION: An eight-item, seven-point Likert-type scale measuring a consumer's enjoyment of sales promotion deals and tendency to buy products associated with such offers. This measures a general tendency rather than the likelihood that the behavior occurs for any particular product category. Lichtenstein, Netemeyer, and Burton (1995) referred to the scale as *general deal proneness*.

SCALE ORIGIN: The scale is original to the studies by Lichtenstein, Netemeyer, and Burton (1995), though some of the items are similar to ones developed previously by the same authors for other measures (e.g., Lichtenstein, Netemeyer, and Burton 1990). In an effort to develop a deal-proneness measure not specific to any particular type of deal, 43 items were generated and purified to a final set of eight by using a pretest sample.

SAMPLES: The scale was not used in Study 1 of Lichtenstein, Netemeyer, and Burton (1995). Data for Study 2 came from shoppers in one of two grocery stores in the Midwestern United States. Shoppers were approached and asked if they would participate in the survey. If so, they were given the instrument and asked to fill it out later and mail it back. Usable forms were received back from **402** people, most of whom were women (77.9%) and married (67.3%).

RELIABILITY: Alphas of **.90** and **.91** were reported for the scale by Lichtenstein, Netemeyer, and Burton (1995) for a pretest and Study 2, respectively.

VALIDITY: Confirmatory factor analysis was used by Lichtenstein, Netemeyer, and Burton (1995) to conclude that the scale was unidimensional and showed evidence of discriminant validity. Some evidence of the scale's predictive validity was also indicated because the scale had significant positive associations with most of the marketplace behaviors examined in the study.

ADMINISTRATION: In the study by Lichtenstein, Netemeyer, and Burton (1995), the scale was part of a survey instrument self-administered by shoppers after they left the grocery store. Higher scores on the scale indicated that consumers were very interested in sales promotion deals and enjoyed purchasing products associated with them.

MAJOR FINDINGS: The purpose of the two studies reported by Lichtenstein, Netemeyer, and Burton (1995) was to compare competing models of deal proneness that varied on the level of specificity. Among the findings was that, though **involvement with deals** had strong relationships (positive) with most of the marketplace behaviors that were examined, the "full model" that included eight domain-specific deal measures explained significantly more variance.

COMMENTS: Lichtenstein, Netemeyer, and Burton (1995) reported means on the scale of 32.66 and 36.06 for the pretest and Study 2, respectively.

REFERENCES:

Lichtenstein, Donald R., Richard G. Netemeyer, and Scot Burton (1990), "Distinguishing Coupon Proneness from Value Consciousness: An Acquisition- Transaction Utility Theory Perspective," *JM*, 54 (July), 54–67.

———, ———, and ——— (1995), "Assessing the Domain Specificity of Deal Proneness: A Field Study," *JCR*, 22 (December), 314–26.

SCALE ITEMS:

Strongly   Strongly
disagree   :___:___:___:___:___:___:___: agree
                1   2   3   4   5   6   7

1. I enjoy buying a brand that is "on deal."

2. Beyond the money I save, buying brands on deal makes me happy.

3. Compared to other people, I am very likely to purchase brands that come with promotional offers.

4. Receiving a promotional deal with a product purchase makes me feel like I am a good shopper.

5. I'm usually <u>not</u> motivated to respond to promotional deals on products. **(r)**

6. When I purchase a brand that is offering a special promotion, I feel that it is a good buy.

7. I feel like a successful shopper when I purchase products that offer special promotions.

8. I love special promotional offers for products.

SCALE NAME: Involvement (Sales)

SCALE DESCRIPTION: A six-item, seven-point Likert-type scale measuring a consumer's tendency to buy the brands that are on sale. This measures a general tendency rather than the likelihood that the behavior occurs for any particular product category. Lichtenstein and colleagues (Lichtenstein, Burton, and Netemeyer 1997; Lichtenstein, Netemeyer, and Burton 1995; Lichtenstein, Ridgway, and Netemeyer 1993) referred to the scale as *sale proneness*.

SCALE ORIGIN: The scale is original to Lichtenstein, Ridgway, and Netemeyer (1993). Eight items in Lichtenstein, Netemeyer, and Burton's (1990) coupon proneness scale were modified, and more were generated specifically for this study. A total of 18 items were tested along with many others in a pretest. The sample was composed of 341 nonstudent adult consumers who had the grocery-shopping responsibility for their households. Factor analysis and coefficient alpha were used to eliminate weaker items. The 16 items remaining for this scale were reported to have an alpha of .90. These items were used in the main study, though the next round of analysis eliminated 10 of them. Of the remaining 6 items in the final version of the scale, 3 were very similar to items used by Lichtenstein, Netemeyer, and Burton (1990).

SAMPLES: The sample employed by Lichtenstein, Burton, and Netemeyer (1997) and the first study in Lichtenstein, Netemeyer, and Burton (1995) was the same as used by Lichtenstein, Ridgway, and Netemeyer (1993). The survey in Study 2 was distributed similarly to that in Study 1. Usable forms were received back from **402** people, most of whom were women (77.9%) and married (67.3%). The median income and age were the same as in the first study.

Lichtenstein, Ridgway, and Netemeyer (1993) collected data from shoppers who had received questionnaires in one of two grocery stores in a Western standard metropolitan statistical area (Boulder, Colo.). One thousand questionnaires were handed out at the stores, and **582** usable ones were returned by mail. A majority of the sample were women (75.9%) and married (58.6%). The median annual income range was $35,000 to $49,999, and the median age range was 35 to 44 years.

RELIABILITY: The main study by Lichtenstein, Ridgway, and Netemeyer (1993; Lichtenstein, Burton, and Netemeyer 1997; Study 1 by Lichtenstein, Netemeyer, and Burton 1995) showed an alpha for the scale of **.88**. An alpha of **.86** was reported for the scale by Lichtenstein, Netemeyer, and Burton (1995) in Study 2.

VALIDITY: Confirmatory factor analyses were used in the studies by Lichtenstein and colleagues (Lichtenstein, Burton, and Netemeyer 1997; Lichtenstein, Netemeyer, and Burton 1995; Lichtenstein, Ridgway, and Netemeyer 1993), and it was concluded that the scale was unidimensional and showed evidence of discriminant validity.

ADMINISTRATION: In the studies by Lichtenstein and colleagues (Lichtenstein, Burton, and Netemeyer 1997; Lichtenstein, Netemeyer, and Burton 1995; Lichtenstein, Ridgway, and Netemeyer 1993), the scale was part of a survey instrument self-administered by shoppers after they left the grocery store. Higher scores on the scale indicated that consumers were very interested in sales and liked to buy the brands that were on sale, whereas lower scores suggested that they were more likely to be motivated by something like brand loyalty rather than price.

MAJOR FINDINGS: The purpose of the study by Lichtenstein, Burton, and Netemeyer (1997) was to determine if there were consumer segments that had a tendency to be "deal prone" in general. Among the findings was that, in both the two- and three-cluster analyses of shoppers, there was a generalized deal-proneness group that had significantly higher mean scores on the **sale involvement** scale compared with clusters of shoppers who were less deal prone.

Although the first study in Lichtenstein, Netemeyer, and Burton (1995) shares the same sample as that described previously, its purpose, as well as that for Study 2, was to compare competing models of deal proneness that varied on the level of specificity. **Involvement with sales** was the strongest predictor of in-store sale item purchases, except for contest/sweepstakes involvement (#194).

Lichtenstein, Ridgway, and Netemeyer (1993) identified and measured seven related but distinct price perception constructs. The dependent variable that **sale involvement** predicted most strongly was actual number of items purchased in a grocery store that were on sale.

COMMENTS: Lichtenstein, Netemeyer, and Burton (1995) reported means on the scale of 23.56 and 24.54 for Studies 1 and 2, respectively.

REFERENCES:

Lichtenstein, Donald R., Scot Burton, and Richard G. Netemeyer (1997), "An Examination of Deal Proneness Across Sales Promotion Types: A Consumer Segmentation Perspective," *JR*, 73 (2), 283–97.

———, Richard G. Netemeyer, and Scot Burton (1990), "Distinguishing Coupon Proneness from Value Consciousness: An Acquisition-Transaction Utility Theory Perspective," *JM*, 54 (July), 54–67.

———, ———, and ——— (1995), "Assessing the Domain Specificity of Deal Proneness: A Field Study," *JCR*, 22 (December), 314–26.

———, Nancy M. Ridgway, and Richard G. Netemeyer (1993), "Price Perceptions and Consumer Shopping Behavior: A Field Study," *JMR*, 30 (May), 234–45.

SCALE ITEMS:

Strongly   Strongly
disagree   :__:__:__:__:__:__:__: agree
          1 2 3 4 5 6 7

1. If a product is on sale, that can be a reason for me to buy it.

2. When I buy a brand that's on sale, I feel that I am getting a good deal.

3. I have favorite brands, but most of the time I buy the brand that's on sale.

4. One should try to buy the brand that's on sale.

5. I am more likely to buy brands that are on sale.

6. Compared to most people, I am more likely to buy brands that are on special.

SCALE NAME: Involvement (Situational)

SCALE DESCRIPTION: A multi-item, seven-point semantic differential scale measuring the temporary (rather than enduring and/or intrinsic) relevance of an object to a person. Whereas enduring involvement is ongoing and probably related to a product class, situational involvement is a passing motivation because it is related to a certain situation. The scale is easily customized to measure involvement with a product category, a particular brand, an ad for a particular brand, or a particular purchase decision.

SCALE ORIGIN: The items for the scale come from the Personal Involvement Inventory (PII) by Zaichkowsky (1985). However, that scale was constructed to assess enduring involvement. In contrast, Houston and Walker (1996) and Lichtenstein, Netemeyer, and Burton (1990) have used a subset of the PII items and specifically modified instructions to measure a distinct but related construct: situational involvement.

SAMPLES: Houston and Walker (1996) administered this scale to a sample of **203** female college students ranging in age from 19 to 47 years. On the basis of their scores, 40 respondents were selected and placed into either a high- or low-scoring group. This smaller sample is the one on which the analysis was based.

The data for the main study by Lichtenstein, Netemeyer, and Burton (1990) came from a convenience sample of **350** nonstudent adults from a medium-sized standard metropolitan statistical area. The majority of the sample were women (57%) and married (69%). College graduates composed 40% of the sample. The median age of respondents was between 35 and 44 years, and household income was between $30,000 and $39,999.

RELIABILITY: An alpha of **.99** was reported for the scale by Houston and Walker (1996). Lichtenstein, Netemeyer, and Burton (1990) reported the reliability (LISREL estimate) of their version of the scale to be **.96.**

VALIDITY: Houston and Walker (1996) examined the discriminant validity of the scale with the larger version of the scale (#201). They concluded that the two were related but distinct constructs. They also stated that the items composing the situational involvement scale loaded on a single factor in principle components analysis.

Although the scale may have been used to help validate another scale or two developed in the study, no explicit test of the situational involvement scale's validity was reported by Lichtenstein, Netemeyer, and Burton (1990).

ADMINISTRATION: Lichtenstein, Netemeyer, and Burton (1990) did not describe the manner in which the scale was administered to the subjects in their study. However, it was clear that the scale was just one of many measures that composed the survey instrument. Likewise, Houston and Walker (1996) did not say much about the context in which their version of the scale was administered. Higher scores indicated that a specified situation was very relevant to respondents.

MAJOR FINDINGS: The study by Houston and Walker (1996) used a cognitive mapping methodology to explore the goal structures that are activated by consumers' feelings of self-reliance (**involvement**) with a product. Despite expectations, there were no significant differences in the complexity of the decision maps associated with the groups that varied in their **situational involvement**.

The study by Lichtenstein, Netemeyer, and Burton (1990) examined the effect of both value consciousness and coupon involvement on coupon redemption behavior. One of the major findings was that value consciousness had a much lower positive relationship with **situational involvement** (grocery products) than did coupon involvement.

REFERENCES:

Houston, Mark B. and Beth A. Walker (1996), "Self-Relevance and Purchase Goals: Mapping a Consumer Decision," *JAMS*, 24 (Summer), 232–45.

Lichtenstein, Donald R., Richard G. Netemeyer, and Scot Burton (1990), "Distinguishing Coupon Proneness from Value Consciousness: An Acquisition-Transaction Utility Theory Perspective," *JM*, 54 (July), 54–67.

Zaichkowsky, Judith L. (1985), "Measuring the Involvement Construct," *JCR*, 12 (December), 341–52.

SCALE ITEMS:*

1. Unimportant   :__:__:__:__:__:__: Important
               1 2 3 4 5 6 7

2. Of no concern   :__:__:__:__:__:__: Of concern to me
               1 2 3 4 5 6 7

3. Irrelevant   :__:__:__:__:__:__: Relevant
               1 2 3 4 5 6 7

4. Means nothing to me   :__:__:__:__:__:__: Means a lot to me
               1 2 3 4 5 6 7

5. Worthless   :__:__:__:__:__:__: Valuable
               1 2 3 4 5 6 7

6. Not beneficial   :__:__:__:__:__:__: Beneficial
               1 2 3 4 5 6 7

7. Doesn't matter   :__:__:__:__:__:__: Matters to me
               1 2 3 4 5 6 7

8. Boring   :__:__:__:__:__:__: Interesting
               1 2 3 4 5 6 7

9. Unexciting   :__:__:__:__:__:__: Exciting
               1 2 3 4 5 6 7

10. Unappealing   :__:__:__:__:__:__: Appealing
               1 2 3 4 5 6 7

11. Nonessential   :__:__:__:__:__:__: Essential
               1 2 3 4 5 6 7

12. Insignificant   :__:__:__:__:__:__: Significant to me
               1 2 3 4 5 6 7

*The directions shown here are those as used by Lichtenstein, Netemeyer, and Burton (1990) but would obviously need to change on the basis of the object toward which situational involvement is being measured. Houston and Walker (1996) used items 1–4, 7, and 12, whereas Lichtenstein, Netemeyer, and Burton (1990) used items 1–11.

SCALE NAME: Involvement (Televised Soccer Game)

SCALE DESCRIPTION: Eight seven-point items, seven of which are of the Likert-type format. The scale seems to measure a person's overall interest in soccer but most particularly gauges the degree to which a person was involved in watching a particular game on television.

SCALE ORIGIN: The scale is original to the study by Tavassoli, Shultz, and Fitzsimons (1995). The authors explained that the scale "was developed to capture both the enduring antecedents of program involvement ... and its consequences ... or subjective felt state of program involvement" (Tavassoli, Shultz, and Fitzsimons 1995, p. 66).

SAMPLES: Data were gathered for the experiment by Tavassoli, Shultz, and Fitzsimons (1995) from **86** college students who were randomly assigned to one of the two treatments. Although participation was required (to reach those with widely varying levels of involvement), subjects were paid $5 and given the chance to win $200.

RELIABILITY: An alpha of **.94** was reported for the scale by Tavassoli, Shultz, and Fitzsimons (1995).

VALIDITY: Both exploratory and confirmatory factor analyses provided evidence of the items' unidimensionality. A posttest conducted by Tavassoli, Shultz, and Fitzsimons (1995) showed the soccer involvement scale to be highly correlated ($r = .71$) with a similar measure, Zaichkowsky's (1985) personal involvement inventory (#201). This provides a sense of the scale's convergent validity.

ADMINISTRATION: The scale was apparently self-administered by students in the experiment conducted by Tavassoli, Shultz, and Fitzsimons (1995), along with other measures, after they were exposed to experimental stimuli (watching a soccer game along with commercials and other material). Scale scores were not calculated as the simple sum of numerical responses to the scale items, though there is nothing to preclude that it be done that way. Instead, standardized factor loadings from the confirmatory factor analysis were used to weight the responses to the eight items. Higher scores meant that respondents exhibited strong involvement with a soccer program to which they had been exposed.

MAJOR FINDINGS: Tavassoli, Shultz, and Fitzsimons (1995) investigated the effect of program involvement on information processing. Among the findings was that advertising effectiveness is highest under moderate compared with high or low levels of program **involvement**.

COMMENTS: The authors appeared to realize that the face validity of the scale was suspect because the items were tapping into multiple dimensions (see "Scale Origin"). Furthermore, item 7 measures involvement in the study, not in soccer per se. Although that might have correlated well with the other items in the context in which it was used in the experiment conducted by Tavassoli, Shultz, and Fitzsimons (1995), it would be risky to assume it would do so in studies that did not so totally focus on soccer and nothing else. For example, if a researcher was examining the degree of involvement a subject had in watching soccer and other programming as part of a study of television watching habits, item 7, as well as several other items, would need to be changed or eliminated.

REFERENCES:
Tavassoli, Nader T., Clifford J. Shultz II, and Gavan J. Fitzsimons (1995), "Program Involvement: Are Moderate Levels Best for Ad memory and Attitude Toward the Ad?" *JAR*, 35 (September/October), 61–72.
Zaichkowsky, Judith L. (1985), "Measuring the Involvement Construct," *JCR*, 12 (December), 341–52.

SCALE ITEMS:

Strongly   Strongly
disagree   :___:___:___:___:___:___:___: agree
            1   2   3   4   5   6   7

1. I am a soccer fan.

2. I will watch many World Cup ___ games on TV.*

3. I can play soccer well.

4. I think watching the game was exciting.

5. I enjoyed watching the game.

6. At times I really "got into" the game.

7. So far, I regret having participated in this study. (r)

8. How many World Cup ___ games did you see on TV?*

None   :___:___:___:___:___:___:___: Six or more
          1   2   3   4   5   6   7

*In item 2, the year of an upcoming World Cup should be placed in the blank, whereas the year of a recent World Cup should go in the blank in item 8.

SCALE NAME: Involvement (Two-for-One Deals)

SCALE DESCRIPTION: A six-item, seven-point Likert-type scale measuring a consumer's inclination to buy brands that have "two-for-one" offers regardless of the amount of money being saved. This measures a general tendency rather than the likelihood that the behavior occurs for any particular product category. Lichtenstein, Netemeyer, and Burton (1995; Lichtenstein, Burton, and Netemeyer 1997) referred to the scale as *buy one-get one free proneness*.

SCALE ORIGIN: The scale is original to the studies by Lichtenstein, Netemeyer, and Burton (1995), though some of the items are similar to ones developed previously by the same authors for other measures (e.g., Lichtenstein, Netemeyer, and Burton 1990). In an effort to develop several deal proneness measures, 91 items were generated and tested with 341 nonstudent adults. Using factor analysis and other tests, seven items were deleted, which left 84 to be used in the two studies reported by Lichtenstein, Netemeyer, and Burton (1995). Lichtenstein, Burton, and Netemeyer (1997) presented 49 of the items for the measurement of eight different deal-proneness types.

SAMPLES: The sample employed by Lichtenstein, Netemeyer, and Burton (1995) in their first study came from shoppers in one of two grocery stores in the Midwestern United States. (This is also the sample used in Lichtenstein, Burton, and Netemeyer 1997.) Shoppers were approached and asked if they would participate in the survey. If so, they were given the instrument and asked to fill it out later and mail it back. Completed questionnaires were received from **582** shoppers. A majority of the sample were women (75.9%), and more than half (58.6%) were married. The median household income was $35,000 to $49,000, and the median age was 35 to 44 years of age. The survey in Study 2 was distributed similarly to that in Study 1. Usable forms were received back from **402** people, most of whom were women (77.9%) and married (67.3%). The median income and age were the same as in the first study.

RELIABILITY: Alphas of **.86** and **.84** were reported for the scale by Lichtenstein, Netemeyer, and Burton (1995) for Studies 1 (Lichtenstein, Burton, and Netemeyer 1997) and 2, respectively.

VALIDITY: Confirmatory factor analyses were used in both studies by Lichtenstein, Netemeyer, and Burton (1995; Lichtenstein, Burton, and Netemeyer 1997). A variety of data were produced in support of the scale's unidimensionality and discriminant validity.

ADMINISTRATION: In the studies by Lichtenstein, Netemeyer, and Burton (1995; Lichtenstein, Burton, and Netemeyer 1997), the scale was part of a survey instrument self-administered by shoppers after they left the grocery store. Higher scores on the scale indicated that consumers were very interested in "two-for-one" offers and found enjoyment in buying products that way.

MAJOR FINDINGS: The purpose of the study by Lichtenstein, Burton, and Netemeyer (1997) was to determine if there were consumer segments that had a tendency to be "deal prone" in general. Among the findings was that, in both the two- and three-cluster analyses of shoppers, there was a generalized deal-proneness group that had significantly higher mean scores on the **two-for-one involvement** scale compared with clusters of shoppers who were less deal prone.

Although the first study in Lichtenstein, Netemeyer, and Burton (1995) shares the same sample as that described previously, its purpose, as well as that for Study 2, was to compare competing models of deal proneness that varied on the level of specificity. In neither study did **involvement with "two-for-one" offers** have many significant relationships with the marketplace behaviors that were studied. In Study 1, it only had a significant relationship (negative) with the quantity of coupons redeemed, and in Study 2, it only had a significant relationship (negative) with the dollar value of coupons redeemed.

COMMENTS: Lichtenstein, Netemeyer, and Burton (1995) reported means on the scale of 28.96 and 30.05 for Studies 1 and 2, respectively.

REFERENCES:

Lichtenstein, Donald R., Scot Burton, and Richard G. Netemeyer (1997), "An Examination of Deal Proneness Across Sales Promotion Types: A Consumer Segmentation Perspective," *JR*, 73 (2), 283–97.

———, Richard G. Netemeyer, and Scot Burton (1990), "Distinguishing Coupon Proneness from Value Consciousness: An Acquisition-Transaction Utility Theory Perspective," *JM*, 54 (July), 54–67.

———, ———, and ——— (1995), "Assessing the Domain Specificity of Deal Proneness: A Field Study," *JCR*, 22 (December), 314–26.

SCALE ITEMS:

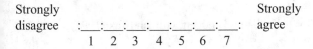

Strongly disagree :___:___:___:___:___:___:___: Strongly agree
             1   2   3   4   5   6   7

1. I enjoy buying a brand that offers a "buy-one-get-one-free" deal.

2. When I buy a product on a "buy-one-get-one-free" offer, I feel that I am getting a good deal.

3. I enjoy buying a product that offers a "2 for 1" deal, regardless of the amount I save by doing so.

4. I have favorite brands, but if I see a "2 for 1" offer, I am more likely to buy that brand.

5. When I take advantage of a "buy-one-get-one-free" offer, I feel good.

6. I don't believe that "2 for 1" deals save you much money. **(r)**

SCALE NAME: Justice (Distributive)

SCALE DESCRIPTION: Four seven-point statements measuring the perceived fairness of the tangible outcome of a dispute or disagreement between at least two parties (e.g., retail manager and customer).

SCALE ORIGIN: Although Blodgett, Hill, and Tax (1997) may have drawn inspiration from previous measures, this scale appears to be original to their study.

SAMPLES: Data were collected by Blodgett, Hill, and Tax (1997) using a quasi-experimental design and subjects from three different locations: a Midsouth U.S. university, a Midwestern U.S. university, and a Canadian university. Subjects came from local church groups and faculty and staff at the universities. Usable responses were received from **265** subjects. Among the demographic information provided for the sample was that a majority were white (86%) and women (61%). There was wide diversity in the sample on other characteristics such as age, occupation, education, and income.

RELIABILITY: An alpha of **.92** was reported for the scale by Blodgett, Hill, and Tax (1997).

VALIDITY: Blodgett, Hill, and Tax (1997) provided some limited evidence of the scale's convergent and discriminant validity. Scores on the scale varied significantly and predictably across the levels of the distributive justice manipulation but not on the manipulation of the other forms of justice (interactional and procedural).

ADMINISTRATION: The scale was administered to subjects, along with other measures, after they had been exposed to experimental stimuli (Blodgett, Hill, and Tax 1997). Higher scores on the scale indicated that respondents thought the tangible outcome of a dispute (e.g., discount, refund, exchange) between a manager and a customer was very fair.

MAJOR FINDINGS: The study by Blodgett, Hill, and Tax (1997) examined the effects of various types of *justice* on complainants' negative word of mouth and likelihood of repatronage. Among the findings was that two types of justice (**distributive** and interactional) were positively associated with negative word-of-mouth intentions, whereas a third type (procedural) had no significant relationship with it.

COMMENTS: The phrasing of the items in this scale is unique because the items were developed for an experiment in which subjects were asked to *imagine* being the consumer in a scenario they were presented. With some adjustment and retesting, the items appear to be amenable for use in situations in which the respondents have actually visited the store themselves.

REFERENCES:
Blodgett, Jeffrey G., Donna J. Hill, and Stephen S. Tax (1997), "The Effects of Distributive, Procedural, and Interactional Justice on Postcomplaint Behavior," *JR*, 73 (2), 185–210.

SCALE ITEMS:

1. Compared to what you expected, the "discount" offered was:

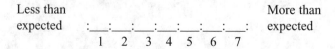

Less than   More than
expected   :___:___:___:___:___:___:___: expected
                    1   2   3   4   5   6   7

2. Taking everything into consideration, the manager's offer was quite fair.

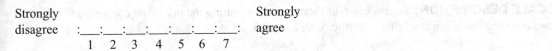

Strongly   Strongly
disagree   :___:___:___:___:___:___:___: agree
            1   2   3   4   5   6   7

3. The customer did not get what was deserved (i.e., regarding a refund or exchange). **(r)**

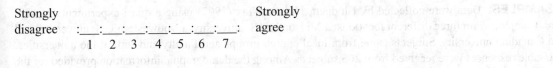

Strongly   Strongly
disagree   :___:___:___:___:___:___:___: agree
            1   2   3   4   5   6   7

4. Given the circumstances, I feel that the retailer offered adequate compensation.

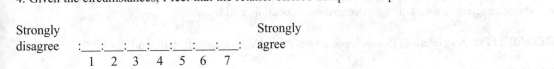

Strongly   Strongly
disagree   :___:___:___:___:___:___:___: agree
            1   2   3   4   5   6   7

SCALE NAME: Justice (Interactional)

SCALE DESCRIPTION: Four seven-point statements measuring the perceived courtesy and respect a customer is given when resolving a conflict with a retailer.

SCALE ORIGIN: Although Blodgett, Hill, and Tax (1997) may have drawn inspiration from previous measures, this scale appears to be original to their study.

SAMPLES: Data were collected by Blodgett, Hill, and Tax (1997) using a quasi-experimental design and subjects from three different locations: a Midsouth U.S. university, a Midwestern U.S. university, and a Canadian university. Subjects came from local church groups and faculty and staff at the universities. Usable responses were received from **265** subjects. Among the demographic information provided for the sample was that a majority were white (86%) and women (61%). There was wide diversity in the sample on other characteristics such as age, occupation, education, and income.

RELIABILITY: An alpha of **.95** was reported for the scale by Blodgett, Hill, and Tax (1997).

VALIDITY: Blodgett, Hill, and Tax (1997) provided some limited evidence of the scale's convergent validity. Scores on the scale varied significantly and predictably across the levels of the interactional justice manipulation. However, there was some confounding with the manipulation of the other forms of justice (interactional and distributive), which raises some doubts about its discriminant validity.

ADMINISTRATION: The scale was administered to subjects, along with other measures, after they had been exposed to experimental stimuli (Blodgett, Hill, and Tax 1997). Higher scores on the scale indicated that respondents thought the manner in which a dispute between a manager/retail employees and a customer was resolved was very polite and respectful.

MAJOR FINDINGS: The study by Blodgett, Hill, and Tax (1997) examined the effects of various types of *justice* on complainants' negative word of mouth and likelihood of repatronage. Among the findings was that two types of justice (distributive and **interactional**) were positively associated with negative word-of-mouth intentions, whereas a third type (procedural) had no significant relationship with it.

COMMENTS: The phrasing of the items in this scale is unique because the items were developed for an experiment in which subjects were asked to *imagine* being the consumer in a scenario they were presented. With some adjustment and retesting, the items appear to be amenable for use in situations in which the respondents have actually visited the store themselves.

REFERENCES:
Blodgett, Jeffrey G., Donna J. Hill, and Stephen S. Tax (1997), "The Effects of Distributive, Procedural, and Interactional Justice on Postcomplaint Behavior," *JR*, 73 (2), 185–210.

SCALE ITEMS:

1. The customer was treated with courtesy and respect.

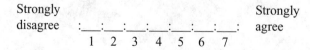

Strongly
disagree :___:___:___:___:___:___:___: Strongly agree
      1 2 3 4 5 6 7

2. The employees seemed to care about the customer.

Strongly   Strongly
disagree   :___:___:___:___:___:___:___: agree
              1   2   3   4   5   6   7

3. The employees listened politely to what the customer had to say.

Strongly   Strongly
disagree   :___:___:___:___:___:___:___: agree
              1   2   3   4   5   6   7

4. I feel that the customer was treated rudely. **(r)**

Strongly   Strongly
disagree   :___:___:___:___:___:___:___: agree
              1   2   3   4   5   6   7

SCALE NAME: Justice (Procedural)

SCALE DESCRIPTION: Three seven-point statements measuring the perceived fairness of the criteria and policies used by a retailer to resolve a dispute with a customer.

SCALE ORIGIN: Although Blodgett, Hill, and Tax (1997) may have drawn inspiration from previous measures, this scale appears to be original to their study.

SAMPLES: Data were collected by Blodgett, Hill, and Tax (1997) using a quasi-experimental design and subjects from three different locations: a Midsouth U.S. university, a Midwestern U.S. university, and a Canadian university. Subjects came from local church groups and faculty and staff at the universities. Usable responses were received from **265** subjects. Among the demographic information provided for the sample was that a majority were white (86%) and women (61%). There was wide diversity in the sample on other characteristics such as age, occupation, education, and income.

RELIABILITY: An alpha of **.85** was reported for the scale by Blodgett, Hill, and Tax (1997).

VALIDITY: Blodgett, Hill, and Tax (1997) provided some limited evidence of the scale's convergent and discriminant validity. Scores on the scale varied significantly and predictably across the levels of the procedural justice manipulation but not on the manipulation of the other forms of justice (interactional and distributive).

ADMINISTRATION: The scale was administered to subjects, along with other measures, after they had been exposed to experimental stimuli (Blodgett, Hill, and Tax 1997). Higher scores on the scale indicated that respondents thought the procedures used to arrive at an outcome of a dispute between a manager and a customer were very fair.

MAJOR FINDINGS: The study by Blodgett, Hill, and Tax (1997) examined the effects of various types of *justice* on complainants' negative word of mouth and likelihood of repatronage. Among the findings was that two types of justice (distributive and interactional) were positively associated with negative word-of-mouth intentions, whereas a third type (**procedural**) had no significant relationship with it.

COMMENTS: The phrasing of the items in this scale is unique because the items were developed for an experiment in which subjects were asked to *imagine* being the consumer in a scenario they were presented. With some adjustment and retesting, the items appear to be amenable for use in situations in which the respondents have actually visited the store themselves.

REFERENCES:
Blodgett, Jeffrey G., Donna J. Hill, and Stephen S. Tax (1997), "The Effects of Distributive, Procedural, and Interactional Justice on Postcomplaint Behavior," *JR*, 73 (2), 185–210.

SCALE ITEMS:

1. The customer's complaint was handled in a very timely manner.

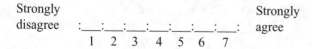

Strongly   Strongly
disagree   :___:___:___:___:___:___:___: agree
              1   2   3   4   5   6   7

2. The customer's complaint was not resolved as quickly as it should have been. **(r)**

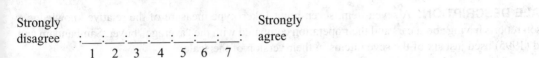

Strongly   Strongly
disagree   :__:__:__:__:__:__: agree
       1 2 3 4 5 6 7

3. The customer had to make too many trips to the store in order to resolve the problem. **(r)**

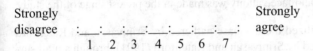

Strongly   Strongly
disagree   :__:__:__:__:__:__: agree
       1 2 3 4 5 6 7

SCALE NAME: Knowledge (Cars)

SCALE DESCRIPTION: A seven-item, seven-point Likert-type measure of the relative knowledge a person reports having about cars and their operation compared with the "average" buyer. Sambandam and Lord (1995) used just six of the seven items in their version of the scale.

SCALE ORIGIN: Although not expressly stated in the article, the scale appears to be have been first used in published research by Srinivasan and Ratchford (1991), which was based on Srinivasan's (1987) dissertation. Some initial assessment of scale reliability and face validity was made in the pretest stage of the study.

SAMPLES: Sambandam and Lord (1995) utilized the database gathered by Srinivasan and Ratchford (1991). A sample of new car buyers was obtained by Srinivasan and Ratchford (1991) through a mail survey of new car registrants in the Buffalo, N.Y., area. More than 3000 people were sent three mailings of the questionnaire, and ultimately, **1401** usable responses were received. No demographic description of the respondents was provided.

RELIABILITY: An alpha of **.87** was reported for the scale by Srinivasan and Ratchford (1991). Sambandam and Lord (1995) found their version of the scale to have a construct reliability of **.93**.

VALIDITY: No discussion of this scale's validity was provided by Sambandam and Lord (1995) or Srinivasan and Ratchford (1991).

ADMINISTRATION: The scale was used, along with other measures, in a mail survey instrument. A lower score on the scale indicated that a consumer reported having a lot of familiarity with cars and their workings compared with other people.

MAJOR FINDINGS: The purpose of the study by Sambandam and Lord (1995) was to examine the influence of consideration-set size on switching behavior in the purchase of cars. Among the findings was that prior experience had a significant positive impact on perceived **knowledge of cars**, which in turn had significant positive effects on satisfaction and media search.

Srinivasan and Ratchford (1991) examined a model of the determinants of external search for new car purchases. As hypothesized, product **knowledge** had a negative effect on perceived risk and positive effects on both evoked-set size and perceived search benefits.

REFERENCES:

Sambandam, Rajan and Kenneth R. Lord (1995), "Switching Behavior in Automobile Markets: A Consideration-Sets Model," *JAMS*, 23 (Winter), 57–65.

Srinivasan, Narasimhan (1987), "A Causal Model of External Search For Information For Durables: A Particular Investigation in the Case of New Automobiles," doctoral dissertation, State University of New York at Buffalo.

———— and Brian T. Ratchford (1991), "An Empirical Test of a External Search for Automobiles," *JCR*, 18 (September), 233–42.

SCALE ITEMS:*

DIRECTIONS: There are no right or wrong answers to the following statements and a large number of people agree and disagree. Kindly indicate your personal opinion by circling any one number for each statement.

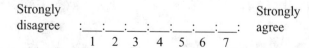

Strongly disagree :___:___:___:___:___:___: Strongly agree
            1 2 3 4 5 6 7

1. Compared to the average person, I know a lot about cars.

2. I like to work on cars myself.

3. I don't understand a lot of my car's workings. **(r)**

4. I know how an internal combustion engine works.

5. My friends consider me an expert on cars.

6. Please rate your knowledge of cars compared to the average buyer by circling one number:

One of the least
knowledgeable   :___:___:___:___:___:___:___: One of the most
knowledgeable
                   1   2   3   4   5   6   7

7. Please circle one of the numbers below to describe your familiarity with cars:

Not at all
familiar   :___:___:___:___:___:___:___: Extremely
familiar
                   1   2   3   4   5   6   7

*Sambandam and Lord (1995) used all of the items except 7.

SCALE NAME: Knowledge (Product Class)

SCALE DESCRIPTION: A three-item, nine-point rating scale purported to measure the extent of knowledge a person reports having about some specified product class. The product category studied by Park, Mothersbaugh, and Feick (1994) was CD players.

SCALE ORIGIN: The scale was apparently developed for use in the study by Park, Mothersbaugh, and Feick (1994).

SAMPLES: Park, Mothersbaugh, and Feick (1994) gathered data from a convenience sample of **156** graduate students attending a Northeastern U.S. university. The students were recruited and paid to participate in a "consumer knowledge study." Respondents filled out the questionnaires in small groups at their own pace. A majority of the sample were men (62%) and an average of 27 years of age.

RELIABILITY: Park, Mothersbaugh, and Feick (1994) reported an alpha of **.91** with item–total correlations ranging from .82 to .83.

VALIDITY: The validity of the scale was not directly examined by Park, Mothersbaugh, and Feick (1994).

ADMINISTRATION: The scale was administered by Park, Mothersbaugh, and Feick (1994) in a larger survey instrument. Higher scores on the scale indicated that respondents reported themselves to be very knowledgeable of the specified product, whereas low scores suggested that respondents considered themselves to have little information about the product class compared with others.

MAJOR FINDINGS: The study by Park, Mothersbaugh, and Feick (1994) investigated the determinants of self-assessed **knowledge** (perceived degree of knowledge about a product class). Product experience was found to be have a significant positive relationship with self-assessed knowledge, as well as with the amount of stored product-class information.

REFERENCES:
Mothersbaugh, David L. (1997), personal correspondence.
Park, C. Whan, David L. Mothersbaugh, and Lawrence Feick (1994), "Consumer Knowledge Assessment," *JCR*, 21 (June), 71–82.

SCALE ITEMS:*

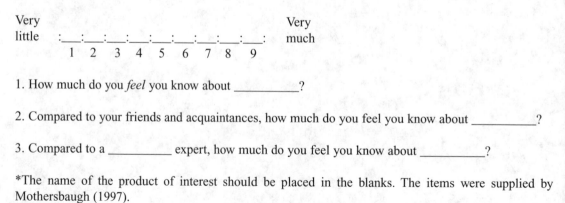

Very little :___:___:___:___:___:___:___:___:___: Very much
        1 2 3 4 5 6 7 8 9

1. How much do you *feel* you know about _____?

2. Compared to your friends and acquaintances, how much do you feel you know about _____?

3. Compared to a _____ expert, how much do you feel you know about _____?

*The name of the product of interest should be placed in the blanks. The items were supplied by Mothersbaugh (1997).

SCALE NAME: Knowledge (Product Class)

SCALE DESCRIPTION: A three-item, five-point summated rating scale purported to measure a person's subjective knowledge about some specified category of products. The scale was apparently used twice by Beatty and Talpade (1994): once for the sample (teens) to evaluate relative contributions in a decision regarding a durable product for *teenager* use and another time related to a durable product for *family* use.

SCALE ORIGIN: Beatty and Talpade (1994) state that the items came from Beatty and Smith (1987). However, the earlier scale had four items, compared with three in this one. Only one item from the previous scale was reported in the article, and it is not one of those listed here.

SAMPLES: Beatty and Talpade (1994) gathered data for their main study from **382** students attending a freshman-orientation session at a Southeastern U.S. university. The sample was almost exactly split between men and women, and 68% were 18 years of age. More than half (64%) had worked outside the home in the past six months. Most of the students (91%) lived with both parents, and nearly half (47%) were from dual-income households.

RELIABILITY: An alpha of **.86** was reported for both the family and teenager "versions" of the scale (Beatty and Talpade 1994).

VALIDITY: The validity of the scale was not directly assessed by Beatty and Talpade (1994).

ADMINISTRATION: The scale was self-administered by students as part of a larger survey instrument (Beatty and Talpade 1994). High scores on the scale suggested that respondents viewed themselves as being very familiar with and knowledgeable of some particular product category as compared with the "average" person.

MAJOR FINDINGS: The study by Beatty and Talpade (1994) built on previous research of adolescent influence on family decision making. Among the results was that a teen's **perceived product knowledge** was not found to significantly affect decision-making processes for durables for family use. Furthermore, though it had an impact on the initiation stage of the decision process, the influence was not significant with respect to the search/decision stage.

REFERENCES:

Beatty, Sharon E. and Scott M. Smith (1987), "External Search Effort: An Investigation Across Several Product Categories," *JCR*, 14 (June), 83–95.

———— and Salil Talpade (1994), "Adolescent Influence in Family Decision Making: A Replication with Extension," *JCR*, 21 (September), 332–41.

SCALE ITEMS:

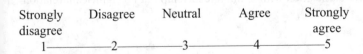

Strongly disagree	Disagree	Neutral	Agree	Strongly agree
1	2	3	4	5

Before purchasing this product:

1. I had a lot of experience with this product.

2. As compared to the average person, I would have said that I was highly knowledgeable about this product category.

3. I would have described myself as being very familiar with this product category.

SCALE NAME: Knowledge (Product Class)

SCALE DESCRIPTION: A seven-point Likert-type rating scale measuring a person's self-reported familiarity and expertise with a particular product category. This is a subjective measure of product knowledge and is considered to be distinct from, though related to, objective knowledge and experience.

SCALE ORIGIN: The three-item scale used by Flynn, Goldsmith, and Eastman (1996) in Study 1 was a preliminary version of a measure of product knowledge made for use with rock music. A six-item version was used in Study 3 by Flynn, Goldsmith, and Eastman (1996). (See also Study 1 by Flynn and Goldsmith 1999.) Eventually, much effort was invested in validating the measure, which led to further changes, and the authors strongly recommended the use of the final version of the scale, as reported in Flynn and Goldsmith (1999).

SAMPLES: Flynn, Goldsmith, and Eastman (1996) reported on five studies, but only two (1 and 3) employed **knowledge** scales. Study 1 consisted of usable data from **219** undergraduate students with ages ranging from 18 to 39 years (mean = 21.2). The sample was almost evenly split on gender and was mostly (82.6%) white. Data for Study 3 came from **391** undergraduates who completed the questionnaires in class. The respondents ranged in age from 18 to 64 years (median = 21). The sample was 72% women and 83% white.

RELIABILITY: The three-item preliminary version of scale used by Flynn, Goldsmith, and Eastman (1996) in Study 1 had an alpha of **.82** (Goldsmith 1997). The alpha for the six-item **knowledge** scale used by Flynn, Goldsmith, and Eastman (1996) in Study 3 was approximately **.93** (Flynn and Goldsmith 1999).

VALIDITY: The validity of the scale was not directly assessed by Flynn, Goldsmith, and Eastman (1996). However, because it was part of an effort to examine the nomological validity of two other scales (#243 and #245), some sense of its own nomological validity can be gained. For example, high positive correlations were found between **knowledge** and opinion leadership, innovativeness, and product involvement. No relationship was found between **knowledge** and opinion seeking.

ADMINISTRATION: The scale was self-administered by students as part of a larger survey instrument (Flynn, Goldsmith, and Eastman 1996). High scores on the scale suggested that respondents viewed themselves as being very knowledgeable about the specified product category.

MAJOR FINDINGS: Flynn, Goldsmith, and Eastman (1996) reported on the development and testing of opinion leadership and opinion-seeking scales (#243 and #245). **Knowledge** was included along with several other measures merely to help establish the nomological validity of the two opinion-related scales. As noted, **knowledge** had a high positive association with opinion leadership but no significant relationship with opinion seeking.

REFERENCES:
Flynn, Leisa R. and Ronald E. Goldsmith (1999), "A Short, Reliable Measure of Subjective Knowledge," *Journal of Business Research*, forthcoming.
———, ——— and Jacqueline K. Eastman (1996), "Opinion Leaders and Opinion Seekers: Two New Measurement Scales," *JAMS*, 24 (Spring), 137–47.
Goldsmith, Ronald E. (1997), personal correspondence.

SCALE ITEMS: *

Strongly
disagree   :___:___:___:___:___:___:___: Strongly agree
        1   2   3   4   5   6   7

1. I feel quite knowledgeable about _____.

2. Among my circle of friends, I'm one of the "experts" on _____.

3. I rarely come across a _____ that I haven't heard of.

4. I know pretty much about _____.

5. I do not feel very knowledgeable about _____. **(r)**

6. Compared to most other people, I know less about _____. **(r)**

7. When it comes to _____, I really don't know a lot. **(r)**

8. I have heard of most of the new _____ that are around.

*Items 1–3 were used by Flynn, Goldsmith, and Eastman (1996) with rock music in Study 1. The items used in their Study 3, with fashion, were apparently 2 and 4–8. The final five-item version of the scale reported by Flynn and Goldsmith (1999) was composed of 2 and 4–7.

SCALE NAME: Love (Romantic)

SCALE DESCRIPTION: Three four-point items intended to capture the level of passion or romance that a person feels during a consumption experience.

SCALE ORIGIN: Richins (1997) drew on terms in previous measures, as well as her own series of studies, to develop and refine several emotion-related scales into the CES (consumption emotion set).

SAMPLES: Six studies were reported by Richins (1997) as part of the process of developing the CES, only two of which had reliability information. Study 4 was based on data from **448** college students. Two surveys were conducted in Study 5: Survey 1 was completed by **256** college students, and there were **194** student respondents to Survey 2.

RELIABILITY: As noted, reliability was reported by Richins (1997) for only Studies 4 and 5, both of which had alphas of **.82**.

VALIDITY: Richins (1997) did not directly examine the validity of the scale. A great deal of effort was expended, however, in a creative use of multidimensional scaling to note whether the items that composed each scale clustered together.

ADMINISTRATION: In the studies performed by Richins (1997), particularly Studies 4 and 5, the scale was just part of a larger instrument that contained many emotion-related measures. A high score on the scale suggested that a person experienced a strong sense of romantic love as a result of some event/stimulus.

MAJOR FINDINGS: On the basis of a review of previously developed measures of emotion, Richins (1997) conducted six studies with the purpose of producing a set of scales particularly suited for assessing consumption experiences. The CES instrument was a result of the studies, one subscale of which measures **romantic love**. In general, the instrument was more successful in representing the diversity of consumption emotions than the other instruments tested.

REFERENCES:
Richins, Marsha L. (1997), "Measuring Emotions in the Consumption Experience," *JCR*, 24 (September), 127–46.

SCALE ITEMS:

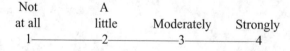

Not at all	A little	Moderately	Strongly
1	2	3	4

1. Sexy

2. Romantic

3. Passionate

SCALE NAME: Love (Tender)

SCALE DESCRIPTION: Three four-point items intended to capture the level of warm-hearted affection a person feels during a consumption experience.

SCALE ORIGIN: Richins (1997) drew on terms in previous measures, as well as her own series of studies, to develop and refine several emotion-related scales into the CES (consumption emotion set).

SAMPLES: Six studies were reported by Richins (1997) as part of the process of developing the CES, only two of which had reliability information. Study 4 was based on data from **448** college students. Two surveys were conducted in Study 5: Survey 1 was completed by **256** college students, and there were **194** student respondents to Survey 2.

RELIABILITY: As noted, reliability was reported by Richins (1997) for only Studies 4 and 5, both of which had alphas of **.86**.

VALIDITY: Richins (1997) did not directly examine the validity of the scale. A great deal of effort was expended, however, in a creative use of multidimensional scaling to note whether the items that composed each scale clustered together.

ADMINISTRATION: In the studies performed by Richins (1997), particularly Studies 4 and 5, the scale was just part of a larger instrument that contained many emotion-related measures. A high score on the scale suggested that a person experienced a strong sense of sentimental love as a result of some event/stimulus.

MAJOR FINDINGS: On the basis of a review of previously developed measures of emotion, Richins (1997) conducted six studies with the purpose of producing a set of scales particularly suited for assessing consumption experiences. The CES instrument was a result of the studies, one subscale of which measures **sentimental love**. In general, the instrument was more successful in representing the diversity of consumption emotions than the other instruments tested.

REFERENCES:
Richins, Marsha L. (1997), "Measuring Emotions in the Consumption Experience," *JCR*, 24 (September), 127–46.

SCALE ITEMS:

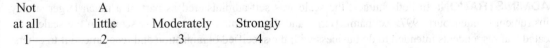

Not   A
at all   little   Moderately   Strongly
1————2————3————4

1. Loving

2. Sentimental

3. Warm-hearted

SCALE NAME: Loyalty (Organizational)

SCALE DESCRIPTION: Seven-point items measuring the likelihood that a customer of a business (service) expects to do business with the organization in the future and engage in positive word-of-mouth communications about it. The version developed by Zeithaml, Berry, and Parasuraman (1996) had five items and used a likelihood response scale. The version used by Bettencourt (1997) had three items in a Likert-type format.

SCALE ORIGIN: The scale is original to Zeithaml, Berry, and Parasuraman (1996). The items composing this scale were part of a 13-item set proposed for measuring a wide range of behavioral intentions appropriate for a service-quality context. Factor analysis of the 13 items across four companies showed that there was a considerable amount of similarity in factor structure, particularly as it related to this "loyalty" dimension.

Bettencourt (1997) modified three of the items used by Zeithaml, Berry, and Parasuraman (1996) to relate more to the grocery shopping experience.

SAMPLES: In the study reported by Bettencourt (1997), data were collected by students in a marketing class. They were instructed to have five surveys completed by people who were regular shoppers for their households. After a verification process, **215** questionnaires remained for data analysis. A majority (70%) of the sample was over 30 years of age, it was predominately women (73%), and most (85%) had completed at least some college.

Zeithaml, Berry, and Parasuraman (1996) gathered data from mailing lists of current customers generated by four businesses: computer manufacturer, retail chain, automobile insurer, and life insurer. The names were of end users in each case, except for the computer company, for which it was business customers. A total of 12,470 questionnaires were sent out, and 3069 were returned.

RELIABILITY: Bettencourt (1997) reported an alpha of **.75** for his version of the scale. Alphas of **.93**, **.94**, **.94**, and **.93** were reported by Zeithaml, Berry, and Parasuraman (1996) for the scale with the computer manufacturer, retail chain, automobile insurer, and life insurer samples, respectively.

VALIDITY: The validity of the scale was not explicitly examined in either study, though evidence of dimensionality was reported. Bettencourt (1997) performed a confirmatory factor analysis with items from his scale and two others, which provided support for the three-factor conceptualization. Likewise, Zeithaml, Berry, and Parasuraman (1996) performed oblique factor analyses on data from the four companies for the 13 items. The five items composing this scale tended to load together for each data set.

ADMINISTRATION: In both studies, the scale was self-administered as part of a much larger survey instrument (Bettencourt 1997; Zeithaml, Berry, and Parasuraman 1996). Higher scores on the scale indicated that respondents intended to do business with the specified organization and recommend it to others.

MAJOR FINDINGS: A model of customer voluntary performance was developed and tested by Bettencourt (1997) in the context of grocery store shopping. The findings indicated that customer commitment had a significant positive relationship with **loyalty**.

Zeithaml, Berry, and Parasuraman (1996) tested a model of the impact of service quality on relevant behaviors. Their results clearly showed that customers who have not reported any service problems have the strongest levels of **loyalty** intentions.

COMMENTS: The scale mean in Bettencourt's (1997) study was 4.85. Means in Zeithaml, Berry, and Parasuraman (1996) were higher, ranging from 4.9 for the retail chain consumer sample to 5.6 for the car insurer client sample.

REFERENCES:

Bettencourt, Lance A. (1997), "Customer Voluntary Performance: Customers as Partners in Service Delivery," *JR*, 73 (3), 383–406.

Zeithaml, Valarie A., Leonard L. Berry, and A. Parasuraman (1996), "The Behavioral Consequences of Service Quality," *JM*, 60 (April), 31–46.

SCALE ITEMS:

Bettencourt (1997):

Strongly   Strongly
disagree   :___:___:___:___:___:___: agree
               1   2   3   4   5   6   7

1. I say positive things about this store to others.

2. I encourage friends and relatives to shop at this store.

3. I make an effort to use this store for all of my grocery shopping needs.

Zeithaml, Berry, and Parasuraman (1996):*

Not at all   Extremely
likely   :___:___:___:___:___:___: likely
             1   2   3   4   5   6   7

1. Say positive things about _____ to other people.

2. Recommend _____ to someone who seeks your advice.

3. Encourage friends and relatives to do business with _____.

4. Consider _____ your first choice to buy _____ services.

5. Do more business with _____ in the next few years.

*The name of the business should be in the blanks. The generic name of the service should be placed in the scond blank of item 4.

SCALE NAME: Loyalty Proneness

SCALE DESCRIPTION: Four five-point Likert-type items intended to measure a shopping orientation that is characterized by loyalty toward brands and stores, with an emphasis on the former. The scale was referred to as *habitual and brand-loyal shopping conscious* by Shim and Gehrt (1996).

SCALE ORIGIN: Shim and Gehrt (1996) used a scale developed by Sproles and Kendall (1986). The latter created an eight-factor model of what they called *consumer decision making styles* but that many others in marketing (e.g., Shim and Gehrt 1996) would view as *shopping orientations*. Sproles and Kendall (1986) reported an alpha of .53 for the four-item scale and a .54 for the three items that loaded highest on the factor.

SAMPLES: Shim and Gehrt (1996) collected data from high school students in a Southwestern U.S. state. Twenty-nine principals agreed to participate, and their schools apparently represented many if not all counties in the state. Principals were given instructions as to which classes to use (by level) and how many students from each class were needed. Some 1954 usable surveys were returned by a sample that was 61.3% girls and had a mean age of 16 years. However, the study focused only on data from **1846** students who were white (56%), Hispanic (32%), or Native American (12%).

RELIABILITY: An alpha of **.63** was reported for the scale by Shim and Gehrt (1996).

VALIDITY: No examination of the scale's validity was reported by Shim and Gehrt (1996).

ADMINISTRATION: Data were gathered in a classroom setting in which students filled out the scale as part of a larger survey instrument (Shim and Gehrt 1996). Higher scores on the scale indicated that respondents were very loyal in their shopping, particularly when it came to the brands they bought.

MAJOR FINDINGS: The study by Shim and Gehrt (1996) examined differences in shopping orientations among high school students that could be linked to ethnicity. The results showed that white students did not express significantly different **loyalty proneness** in their shopping compared with Hispanics, but both groups were significantly more **loyalty prone** than Native American students.

COMMENTS: The internal consistency is somewhat low, possibly because loyalty to both brands and stores was included together in the scale. Further development and testing of the scale is called for if it is to be used again.

REFERENCES:

Shim, Soyeon and Kenneth C. Gehrt (1996), "Hispanic and Native American Adolescents: An Exploratory Study of Their Approach to Shopping," *JR*, 72 (3), 307–24.
Sproles, George B. and Elizabeth L. Kendall (1986), "A Methodology for Profiling Consumers' Decision-Making Styles," *Journal of Consumer Affairs*, 20 (Winter), 267–79.

SCALE ITEMS:

```
Strongly                          Strongly
disagree    ___:___:___:___:___:  agree
             1   2   3   4   5
```

1. I have favorite brands I buy over and over.

2. Once I find a product or brand I like, I stick with it.

3. I go to the same stores each time I shop.

4. I change brands I buy regularly. **(r)**

SCALE NAME: Market Maven

SCALE DESCRIPTION: Six Likert-type statements measuring the degree to which a person has a wide range of knowledge regarding products to buy, places to shop, and other consumption-related activities and influences others by passing on this information.

SCALE ORIGIN: The scale is original to Feick and Price (1987). A set of 40 items was originally generated. This was reduced to 19 items by a group of marketing academicians and practitioners. The reduced set was administered to 265 part-time MBA students at a major Northeastern U.S. university. Because a short scale was needed for a telephone survey, factor analysis, item–total correlations, and Cronbach's alpha were used to reduce the list to the final set of 6 items. This final set had an alpha of .84 and item–total correlations from .51 to .67. Details of the scale's use in the main study are discussed subsequently.

SAMPLES: A survey was conducted by Feick and Price (1987) using random digit dialing of the telephone numbers of people living in one of the 48 contiguous states. A total of 1531 successful interviews were conducted. Although 64% of the sample was women, the authors reported that the other demographic characteristics were similar to those in the 1980 census and the 1984 update. The survey form was the same for all interviewees except that one group (n = 771) was asked some questions about common food and household items, whereas the other (n = 760) was asked about nonprescription drugs, health, and beauty items.

The data used by Urbany, Dickson, and Kalapurakal (1996) were collected as part of a larger survey by a leading market research firm. Telephone interviews were conducted with the primary grocery shoppers from households selected at random. Respondents were requested to participate in a second stage that would involve a mail survey. The survey yielded **343** usable responses. The average age of respondents was 44.7 years, and they were overwhelmingly women (83%).

RELIABILITY: Alphas of **.82** and **.89** were reported for the scale by Feick and Price (1987) and Urbany, Dickson, and Kalapurakal (1996), respectively.

VALIDITY: A factor analysis conducted in a pilot study by Feick and Price (1987), mentioned previously, indicated that the items loaded together. This was noted also in another pilot study. A telephone survey was made of 303 male and female heads of households in a large Northeastern U.S. metropolitan area. Evidence of discriminant validity was provided by the pattern of loadings in the factor analysis. Two factors were produced: the **market maven** items loaded on one factor, and items from a seven-item opinion leadership scale (King and Summers 1970) and a one-item opinion leadership scale loaded on the other factor.

Urbany, Dickson, and Kalapurakal (1996) tested the discriminant validity of the **market maven** scale using pairwise confirmatory factor analysis and six other measures. The evidence of three separate tests supported a claim of discriminant validity.

ADMINISTRATION: The scale was administered by Feick and Price (1987) to interviewees, along with other measures, in a telephone survey. The data analyzed by Urbany, Dickson, and Kalapurakal (1996) were gathered in a mail survey. Scores on the scale can range from 6 to 42. Higher scores suggested that consumers were very likely to have a lot of shopping knowledge and influence others, whereas lower scores implied that they were not market mavens.

MAJOR FINDINGS: Feick and Price (1987) identified and examined a type of consumer they referred to as the "market maven." Support was found for all hypotheses advanced. Those scoring high on the market maven scale were aware of new products earlier, engaged in more information seeking, disseminated information about a variety of products to others, and showed greater market interest and attentiveness. The findings indicated that market mavens were distinct as a group from opinion leaders and early adopters.

Urbany, Dickson, and Kalapurakal (1996) developed a model of price search for the retail grocery industry that included a relatively complete accounting of economic and noneconomic returns, as well as search costs. The findings showed that **market mavenism** accounted for a significant amount of variance in specials-related search beyond that explained by economic costs and returns.

COMMENTS: Urbany, Dickson, and Kalapurakal (1996) reported a mean response of 3.59 on the scale.

REFERENCES:

Feick, Lawrence F. and Linda L. Price (1987), "The Market Maven: A Diffuser of Marketplace Information," *JM*, 51 (January), 83–97.

King, Charles W. and John O. Summers (1970), "Overlap of Opinion Leadership Across Consumer Product Categories," *JMR*, 7 (February), 43–50.

Urbany, Joel E., Peter R. Dickson, and Rosemary Kalapurakal (1996), "Price Search in the Retail Grocery Market," *JM*, 60 (April), 91–104.

SCALE ITEMS:*

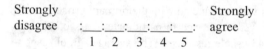

Strongly disagree :___:___:___:___:___: Strongly agree
　　　　　　　　1　2　3　4　5

1. I like introducing new brands and products to my friends.

2. I like helping people by providing them with information about many kinds of products.

3. People ask me for information about products, places to shop, or sales.

4. If someone asked where to get the best buy on several types of products, I could tell him or her where to shop.

5. My friends think of me as a good source of information when it comes to new products or sales.

6. Think about a person who has information about a variety of products and likes to share this information with others. This person knows about new products, sales, stores, and so on, but does not necessarily feel he or she is an expert on one particular product. How well would you say that this description fits you?

7. I know a lot of different products, stores, and sales and I like sharing this information.

*This is the version of the scale used by Feick and Price (1987) with a seven-point response format. With a five-point response scale, Urbany, Dickson, and Kalapurakal (1996) used items 1-5 (with slight variations in wording) and item 7 (rather than 6).

SCALE NAME: Marriage Role Attitude

SCALE DESCRIPTION: Twenty-eight five-point Likert-type items measuring a person's attitude about the proper roles for husbands and wives to play in a marriage.

SCALE ORIGIN: The scale was constructed as part of dissertation research by Jacobson (1950). Through a series of steps, the item pool was reduced from 60 to the final 28. Split-half reliability was calculated to be .91 on the basis of responses from 20 married couples and 20 divorced couples. Test–retest reliability (20 days) was reported to be .79. As evidence bearing on validity, the scale was administered to 10 persons perceived to hold conventional attitudes and 11 persons expected to hold more egalitarian views. The mean score of the traditional group was much lower than that of the egalitarian group.

SAMPLES: Ford, LaTour, and Henthorne (1995) gathered data from married couples in two countries: China and the United States. Demographic data were well described in the study, and only a few characteristics are provided here. The Chinese sample was composed of 100 couples living in Beijing City (63 couples) and surrounding areas. In contrast, the U.S. sample had 102 couples who were surveyed in a mall intercept in a large mid-Atlantic U.S. metro area. Although the samples were similar in terms of mean ages, they varied on the basis of education, income, and occupation.

RELIABILITY: Alphas from .73 to .89 were reported for the scale by Ford, LaTour, and Henthorne (1995).

VALIDITY: No examination of the scale's validity was reported by Ford, LaTour, and Henthorne (1995).

ADMINISTRATION: The scale was apparently self-administered, along with other measures, as part of a larger questionnaire (Ford, LaTour, and Henthorne 1995). The Chinese respondents were explicitly described as filling out the survey instrument by themselves in private. Higher scores on the scale indicated that a person had more egalitarian views of the spousal roles in a marriage.

MAJOR FINDINGS: The purpose of the study by Ford, LaTour, and Henthorne (1995) was to compare differences in decision making across many product categories. Among the many findings was that, as expected, the Chinese couples had much more traditional **marriage role attitudes** than the U.S. couples.

REFERENCES:
Ford, John B., Michael S. LaTour, and Tony L. Henthorne (1995), "Perception of Marital Roles in Purchase Decision Processes: A Cross-Cultural Study," *JAMS*, 23 (Spring), 120–31.
Jacobson, Alver Hilding (1950), "A Study of Conflict in Attitude Toward the Roles of the Husband and the Wife in Marriage," doctoral dissertation, Ohio State University.

SCALE ITEMS:
DIRECTIONS: Please respond to the following questions by marking your choice by each scale.

```
Strongly                      Strongly
disagree    :__:__:__:__:__:  agree
             1   2   3   4   5
```

1. The husband should decide whether or not to have children.

2. The husband should help with the housework. **(r)**

3. The wife should be free to go out nights by herself. **(r)**

4. The wife should take her husband's religion as her own.

5. The wife should take a job if she wants to. **(r)**

6. The husband should help take care of the children. **(r)**

7. If the wife wants children, the husband should agree. **(r)**

8. If the husband insists, the wife should quit a needed job.

9. The husband should help wash dishes. **(r)**

10. If a husband sleeps with another woman, his wife can sleep with another man. **(r)**

11. Wives are too independent these days.

12. If the husband wants children, the wife should agree.

13. The husband should decide how to spend any extra money.

14. Husbands should be more strict with their wives.

15. A married woman should not work outside the home.

16. What a husband does in his spare time is his business.

17. The husband should decide where to live.

18. The woman's place is in the home.

19. The wife should fit her life to her husband's.

20. The wife should mend and sew the family's clothes.

21. The husband's wishes should be first in most things.

22. Marriage is the best career for a woman.

23. The husband should be #1 in the household.

24. Marriage should be a full-time job for the wife.

25. If the husband sleeps with another woman, his wife should put up with it until he comes to his senses.

26. It's okay for a wife to earn as much as her husband. **(r)**

27. A wife should let her husband decide most things.

28. Almost all money matters should be decided by the husband.

SCALE NAME: Materialism (Centrality)

SCALE DESCRIPTION: A seven-item, five-point Likert-type summated ratings scale measuring the degree to which a person believes that buying and owning things are important in his or her life.

SCALE ORIGIN: The scale is original to Richins and Dawson (1990, 1992a). The first paper describes the preliminary work in constructing the scale. Items were generated through open-ended discussions with consumers, noting how materialistic people were described in the literature, and adapting a few items used in prior studies. Using three studies with student samples, the more than 100 original items were condensed to 29 items that represented approximately four factors. The items relating to the centrality factor either loaded on different factors or had low communalities. At least two of the items shown, however, were part of that an asceticism scale tested in the prior studies.

SAMPLES: Various samples were collected and used by Netemeyer, Burton, and Lichtenstein (1995) in the process of validating some other scales. One study using the **materialism** scale was conducted using addresses found in a *Who's Who* directory for one state. Analysis was based on the 267 completed questionnaires that were returned. Yet another study used data collected from 43 professional fashion models.

Four surveys were described in the article by Richins and Dawson (1992a) as being used to refine and test the materialism scale. Little was noted about the samples except that the data were collected in each case through a mail survey. The households were randomly chosen and sent a survey form, followed by a reminder letter and a second copy of the questionnaire two weeks later. Survey 1 was made in a medium-sized Northeastern U.S. city and was composed of **144** people. There were **250** people in the second sample, all of whom lived in a large Western U.S. city. A large Western city was also the site of the third survey, which ultimately had **235** usable questionnaires. Finally, the fourth survey was composed of **86** people from a Northeastern U.S. college town and **119** people from a Northeastern rural area.

The analysis described in Richins (1994) appears to have used two of these samples: the 144 urban and 119 rural respondents.

RELIABILITY: Alphas ranging between .71 and .75 were reported for the scale by Richins and Dawson (1992a). The stability of the scale was estimated using 58 students at an urban university. The test–retest correlation (three-week interval) was .82. An alpha of .81 was found for the scale as used with the fashion model sample by Netemeyer, Burton, and Lichtenstein (1995; Netemeyer 1997).

VALIDITY: Although the validity of the scale was not directly examined by Netemeyer, Burton, and Lichtenstein (1995), it was used to help establish the construct validity of four vanity-related scales. The **materialism** scale had significant positive correlations with two of the vanity scales involving concern for appearance and achievement. (See "Major Findings" for details.)

The validity of the scale was addressed a variety of ways by Richins and Dawson (1992a). For example, the results of an exploratory factor analysis of the seven centrality items, as well as eleven items composing two other components of materialism (success and happiness), showed that the centrality items had their highest loadings ($|\geq.49|$) on the same factor. Some evidence of discriminant validity came from the scale's very low correlation ($r = -.12$) with a measure of social desirability. The rest of the evidence provided generally positive support for nomological validity but was reported just for the overall scale, with items for the three components combined.

ADMINISTRATION: The scale was one of several measures in each of the studies and was self-administered (Netemeyer, Burton, and Lichtenstein 1995; Richins and Dawson 1992a). Higher scores on the scale indicated that respondents had a tendency to believe that the acquisition and possessions of material objects is important in life.

MAJOR FINDINGS: Netemeyer, Burton, and Lichtenstein (1995) investigated vanity and developed four scales for its measurement. Most of the article discussed the results of the rather extensive validation process. As noted, the findings indicated that **materialism** had positive relationships with two vanity scales: physical concern (#397) and achievement concern (#395). Its relationship with physical view vanity (#398) appeared to be insignificant, whereas the relationship with achievement view vanity (#396) varied in significance depending on the sample.

The purpose of the several surveys conducted by Richins and Dawson (1992a) was to construct a new measure of materialism. Except for some basic psychometric qualities, no relationship between the scale and other constructs was made in the article. However, among the most significant of the many findings shown in supplementary material (Richins and Dawson 1992b) was that those high in **material centrality** spent two and one-half times less than those low in **material centrality** on contributions to church/charities.

Richins (1994) studied the possessions that were used to express the material values of their owners. Results were described for the whole materialism instrument rather than being broken down by the subscales (**centrality**, happiness, and success). Among the findings was that the possessions of those who were most materialistic were more socially visible and expensive than those of people who were low in materialism.

COMMENTS: Although reported separately here, Richins and Dawson (1992a) argued for combining scores of the three components of materialism. Much of the article's information is about the overall instrument's psychometric quality. For example, in the same studies as described here, it was reported to have alphas between .80 to .88 and a test–retest reliability of .87.

See also Mick (1996) and Rindfleisch, Burroughs, and Denton (1997).

REFERENCES:

Mick, David Glen (1996), "Are Studies of Dark Side Variables Confounded by Socially Desirable Responding? The Case of Materialism," *JCR*, 23 (September), 106–19.

Netemeyer, Richard G. (1997), personal correspondence.

———, Scot Burton, and Donald R. Lichtenstein (1995), "Trait Aspects of Vanity: Measurement and Relevance to Consumer Behavior," *JCR*, 21 (March), 612–26.

Richins, Marsha L. (1994), "Special Possessions and the Expression of Material Values," *JCR*, 21 (December), 522–33.

——— and Scott Dawson (1990), "A Preliminary Report of Scale Development," in *Advances in Consumer Research*, Vol. 17. Marvin E. Goldberg, Gerald Gorn, and Richard W. Pollay, eds., Provo, UT: Association for Consumer Research, 169–75.

——— and ——— (1992a), "A Consumer Values Orientation for Materialism and Its Measurement: Scale Development and Validation," *JCR*, 19 (December), 303–16.

——— and ——— (1992b), "A Consumer Values Orientation for Materialism and Its Measurement: Scale Development and Validation," unpublished results of hypothesis tests by subscale, available from the authors.

Rindfleisch, Aric, James E. Burroughs, and Frank Denton (1997), "Family Structure, Materialism, and Compulsive Consumption," *JCR*, 23 (March), 312–25.

SCALE ITEMS:

Strongly disagree	Disagree	Neutral	Agree	Strongly agree
1	2	3	4	5

1. I usually buy only the things I need. **(r)**

2. I try to keep my life simple, as far as possessions are concerned. **(r)**

3. The things I own aren't all that important to me. **(r)**

4. I enjoy spending money on things that aren't that practical.

5. Buying things gives me a lot of pleasure.

6. I like a lot of luxury in my life.

7. I put less emphasis on material things than most people I know. **(r)**

SCALE NAME: Materialism (Happiness)

SCALE DESCRIPTION: A five-item, five-point Likert-type summated ratings scale measuring the degree to which a person believes that the number and quality of a person's possessions are necessary to achieve happiness in life.

SCALE ORIGIN: The scale is original to Richins and Dawson (1990, 1992a). The first paper describes the preliminary work in constructing the scale. Items were generated through open-ended discussions with consumers, noting how materialistic people were described in the literature, and adapting a few items used in prior studies. Using three studies with student samples, the more than 100 original items were condensed to 29 items that represented approximately four factors. The factor related to the final scale shown always had the highest reliabilities (.75–.80).

SAMPLES: Four surveys were described in the article by Richins and Dawson (1992a) as being used to refine and test the materialism scale. Little was noted about the samples except that the data were collected in each case through a mail survey. The households were randomly chosen and sent a survey form, followed by a reminder letter and a second copy of the questionnaire two weeks later. Survey 1 was made in a medium-sized Northeastern U.S. city and was composed of **144** people. There were **250** people in the second sample, all of whom lived in a large Western U.S. city. A large Western city was also the site of the third survey, which ultimately had **235** usable questionnaires. Finally, the fourth survey was composed of **86** people from a Northeastern U.S. college town and **119** people from a Northeastern rural area.

The analysis described in Richins (1994) appears to have used two of these samples: the 144 urban and 119 rural respondents.

RELIABILITY: Alphas ranging between .73 and .83 were reported for the scale by Richins and Dawson (1992a). The stability of the scale was estimated using 58 students at an urban university. The test–retest correlation (three-week interval) was .86.

VALIDITY: The validity of the scale was addressed a variety of ways by Richins and Dawson (1992a). For example, the results of an exploratory factor analysis of the five happiness items, as well as thirteen items composing two other components of materialism (centrality and success), showed that the happiness items had their highest loadings ($|\geq.55|$) on the same factor. Some evidence of discriminant validity came from the scale's very low correlation ($r = -.03$) with a measure of social desirability. The rest of the evidence provided generally positive support for nomological validity but was reported just for the overall scale, with items for the three components combined.

ADMINISTRATION: The scale was one of several measures in each of the studies, which were self-administered Richins and Dawson (1992a). Higher scores on the scale indicated that respondents had a tendency to believe that a person's possessions are needed for happiness in life.

MAJOR FINDINGS: The purpose of the several surveys conducted by Richins and Dawson (1992a) was to construct a new measure of materialism. Except for some basic psychometric qualities, no relationship between the scale and other constructs was made in the article. However, among the most significant of the many findings shown in supplementary material (Richins and Dawson 1992b) was that those high in **material happiness** for buying the things they wanted spent less than half as much on contributions to church/charities and gifts/loans to friends/relatives than those low in it.

Richins (1994) studied the possessions that were used to express the material values of their owners. Results were described for the whole materialism instrument rather than being broken down by the subscales (centrality, **happiness**, and success). Among the findings was that the possessions of those who were most materialistic were more socially visible and expensive than those of people who were low in materialism.

COMMENTS: Although reported separately here, Richins and Dawson (1992a) argued for combining the scores of the three components of materialism. Much of the article's information is about the overall instrument's psychometric quality. For example, in the same studies as described here, it was reported to have alphas between .80 to .88 and a test–retest reliability of .87.

See also Mick (1996) and Rindfleisch, Burroughs, and Denton (1997).

REFERENCES:

Mick, David Glen (1996), "Are Studies of Dark Side Variables Confounded by Socially Desirable Responding? The Case of Materialism," *JCR*, 23 (September), 106–19.

Richins, Marsha L. (1994), "Special Possessions and the Expression of Material Values," *JCR*, 21 (December), 522–33.

——— and Scott Dawson (1990), "A Preliminary Report of Scale Development," in *Advances in Consumer Research*, Vol. 17, Marvin E. Goldberg, Gerald Gorn, and Richard W. Pollay, eds., Provo, UT: Association for Consumer Research, 169–75.

——— and ——— (1992a), "A Consumer Values Orientation for Materialism and Its Measurement: Scale Development and Validation," *JCR*, 19 (December), 303–16.

——— and ——— (1992b), "A Consumer Values Orientation for Materialism and Its Measurement: Scale Development and Validation," unpublished results of hypothesis tests by subscale, available from the authors.

Rindfleisch, Aric, James E. Burroughs, and Frank Denton (1997), "Family Structure, Materialism, and Compulsive Consumption," *JCR*, 23 (March), 312–25.

SCALE ITEMS:

Strongly disagree	Disagree	Neutral	Agree	Strongly agree
1————	—2————	——3————	——4————	——5

1. I have all the things I really need to enjoy life. **(r)**

2. My life would be better if I owned certain things I don't have.

3. I wouldn't be any happier if I owned nicer things. **(r)**

4. I'd be happier if I could afford to buy more things.

5. It sometimes bothers me quite a bit that I can't afford to buy all the things I'd like.

SCALE NAME: Materialism (Student)

SCALE DESCRIPTION: A five-item, seven-point Likert-type scale indicating the degree to which a person is oriented toward having money and spending it. Brand and Greenberg (1994) referred to the measure as *consumer-oriented attitude*, and it appears to be particularly suited for student respondents.

SCALE ORIGIN: Brand and Greenberg (1994) did not explicitly state the source of the scale, but it appears to be original to their study.

SAMPLES: The data were gathered by Brand and Greenberg (1994) from students in four Michigan public high schools. Two of the selected schools had been receiving *Channel One*, whereas the other two had not. The schools were matched on a variety of relevant criteria, and only students in tenth-grade history and government classes were surveyed. From the schools receiving the program, **373** students completed the survey (mean age 15.5 years, 52% boys). Completed surveys were collected from **454** students (mean age 15.8 years, 52% boys) who attended schools that did not receive *Channel One*.

RELIABILITY: An alpha of **.52** was reported for the scale by Brand and Greenberg (1994).

VALIDITY: No information regarding the scale's validity was reported by Brand and Greenberg (1994).

ADMINISTRATION: Although not expressly stated, it appears that Brand and Greenberg (1994) administered the scale as part of a larger instrument to students in a classroom setting. Higher scores on the scale indicated that respondents were more oriented to consumption and had materialistic values.

MAJOR FINDINGS: Brand and Greenberg (1994) examined the impact of the advertising in *Channel One* programs on high school students. The broadcast consists of ten-minute programs with two minutes of ads designed for teens. Students attending schools that received the programs expressed significantly greater **materialism** than those attending schools that did not get *Channel One*. However, it should be noted that, with the former group of students, the mean score was near the middle of the scale, which indicates that even they were not expressing a high level of **materialism**.

COMMENTS: Although the scale was prepared with high school students in mind, it appears to be amenable for use with other groups if a change is made in item 4. However, a greater concern is the very low reliability of the scale. This indicates that more developmental work is necessary before the measure is used again with any respondents.

REFERENCES:
Brand, Jeffrey E. and Bradley S. Greenberg (1994), "Commercials in the Classroom: The Impact of *Channel One* Advertising," *JAR*, 34 (January/February), 18–27.

SCALE ITEMS:

Strongly disagree :___:___:___:___:___:___: Strongly agree
  1 2 3 4 5 6 7

1. When I watch commercials, I usually want what is shown.

2. Most people who have a lot of money are happier than most people who have only a little money.

3. Money isn't everything. **(r)**

4. Having a nice car is important, but school is more important. **(r)**

5. I don't care whether my clothes have a designer label on them. **(r)**

SCALE NAME: Materialism (Success)

SCALE DESCRIPTION: A six-item, five-point Likert-type summated ratings scale measuring the degree to which a person believes that the number and quality of a person's possessions are an indicator of his or her success in life.

SCALE ORIGIN: The scale is original to Richins and Dawson (1990, 1992a). The first paper describes the preliminary work in constructing the scale. Items were generated through open-ended discussions with consumers, noting how materialistic people were described in the literature, and adapting a few items used in prior studies. Using three studies with student samples, the more than 100 original items were condensed to 29 items that represented approximately four factors. The factor related to the final scale shown here always had the highest reliabilities (.80–.85).

SAMPLES: Various samples were collected and used by Netemeyer, Burton, and Lichtenstein (1995) in the process of validating some other scales, and the materialism scale was used in all but one of the studies. Study 1 had two groups: 145 students from a major U.S. university and 277 "nonstudent adults." Study 2 did not employ the scale. A third study was conducted using addresses found in a *Who's Who* directory for one state. Analysis was based on the 267 completed questionnaires that were returned. A fourth study focused on 27 football players from a nationally ranked NCAA Division I team. The fifth and final study was based on data collected from 43 professional fashion models.

Four surveys were described in the article by Richins and Dawson (1992a) as being used to refine and test the materialism scale. Little was noted about the samples except that the data were collected in each case through a mail survey. The households were randomly chosen and sent a survey form, followed by a reminder letter and a second copy of the questionnaire two weeks later. Survey 1 was made in a medium-sized Northeastern U.S. city and was composed of **144** people. There were **250** people in the second sample, all of whom were living in a large Western U.S. city. A large Western city was also the site of the third survey, which ultimately had **235** usable questionnaires. Finally, the fourth survey was composed of **86** people from a Northeastern U.S. college town and **119** people from a Northeastern rural area.

The analysis described in Richins (1994) appears to have used two of these samples: the 144 urban and 119 rural respondents.

RELIABILITY: Alphas ranging between .74 and .78 were reported for the scale by Richins and Dawson (1992a). The stability of the scale was estimated using 58 students at an urban university. The test–retest correlation (three-week interval) was .82. Among the alphas for the scale found by Netemeyer, Burton, and Lichtenstein (1995; Netemeyer 1997) were .90 (students), .85 (nonstudents adults), and .76 (fashion models).

VALIDITY: Although the validity of the scale was not directly examined by Netemeyer, Burton, and Lichtenstein (1995), the scale was used to help establish the construct validity of four vanity-related scales. As noted (see "Major Findings"), **materialism** had significant positive correlations with each of the vanity scales.

The validity of the scale was addressed a variety of ways by Richins and Dawson (1992a). For example, the results of an exploratory factor analysis of the six success items, as well as twelve items composing two other components of materialism (centrality and happiness), showed that the success items had their highest loadings ($|\geq .43|$) on the same factor. Some evidence of discriminant validity came from the scale's very low correlation ($r = -.06$) with a measure of social desirability. The rest of the evidence provided generally positive support for nomological validity but was reported just for the overall scale, with items for the three components combined.

ADMINISTRATION: The scale was one of several measures in each of the studies that were self-administered by Netemeyer, Burton, and Lichtenstein (1995) and Richins and Dawson (1992a). Higher scores on the scale indicated that respondents had a tendency to believe that a person's possessions are an important symbol of success in life.

MAJOR FINDINGS: Netemeyer, Burton, and Lichtenstein (1995) investigated vanity and developed four scales for its measurement. Most of the article discussed the results of the rather extensive validation process. **Material success** had significant positive correlations with all of the vanity scales, the highest correlation tending to be with achievement concern vanity (#395).

The purpose of the several surveys conducted by Richins and Dawson (1992a) was to construct a new measure of materialism. Except for some basic psychometric qualities, no relationship between the scale and other constructs was made in the article. However, among the most significant of the many findings shown in supplementary material (Richins and Dawson 1992b) was that those subjects high in **material success** stated that they spent more than twice as much as those low in **material success** on buying the things they wanted but less than half as much on contributions to church/charities.

Richins (1994) studied the possessions that were used to express the material values of their owners. Results were described for the whole materialism instrument rather than being broken down by the subscales (centrality, happiness, and **success**). Among the findings was that the possessions of those who were most materialistic were more socially visible and expensive than those of people who were low in materialism.

COMMENTS: Although reported separately here, Richins and Dawson (1992a) argued for combining scores of the three components of materialism. Much of the article's information is about the overall instrument's psychometric quality. For example, in the same studies as described here, it was reported to have alphas between .80 to .88 and a test–retest reliability of .87.

See also Mick (1996) and Rindfleisch, Burroughs, and Denton (1997).

REFERENCES:

Mick, David Glen (1996), "Are Studies of Dark Side Variables Confounded by Socially Desirable Responding? The Case of Materialism," *JCR*, 23 (September), 106–19.

Netemeyer, Richard G. (1997), personal correspondence.

———, Scot Burton, and Donald R. Lichtenstein (1995), "Trait Aspects of Vanity: Measurement and Relevance to Consumer Behavior," *JCR*, 21 (March), 612–26.

Richins, Marsha L. (1994), "Special Possessions and the Expression of Material Values," *JCR*, 21 (December), 522–33.

——— and Scott Dawson (1990), "A Preliminary Report of Scale Development," in *Advances in Consumer Research*, Vol. 17, Marvin E. Goldberg, Gerald Gorn, and Richard W. Pollay, eds., Provo, UT: Association for Consumer Research, 169–75.

——— and ——— (1992a), "A Consumer Values Orientation for Materialism and Its Measurement: Scale Development and Validation," *JCR*, 19 (December), 303–16.

——— and ——— (1992b), "A Consumer Values Orientation for Materialism and Its Measurement: Scale Development and Validation," unpublished results of hypothesis tests by subscale, available from the authors.

Rindfleisch, Aric, James E. Burroughs, and Frank Denton (1997), "Family Structure, Materialism, and Compulsive Consumption," *JCR*, 23 (March), 312–25.

SCALE ITEMS:

Strongly disagree	Disagree	Neutral	Agree	Strongly agree
1	2	3	4	5

1. I admire people who own expensive homes, cars, and clothes.

2. Some of the most important achievements in life include acquiring material possessions.

3. I don't place much emphasis on the amount of material objects people own as a sign of success. **(r)**

4. The things I own say a lot about how well I'm doing in life.

5. I like to own things that impress people.

6. I don't pay much attention to the material objects other people own. **(r)**

SCALE NAME: Mood

SCALE DESCRIPTION: Three seven-point semantic differentials measuring how a person feels at some particular point in time. Although the scale might be considered a measure of affect in a general sense, it is not technically an attitude because there is no object to which to respond (e.g., ad, product).

SCALE ORIGIN: Howard, Gengler, and Jain (1995) indicated that they modified a scale originally developed by Wood, Saltzberg, and Goldsamt (1990). The latter measure had four items and a very different response format. No information about its psychometric quality was offered except that the four items apparently loaded high on the same dimension when factor analyzed along with six other emotion-related terms.

SAMPLES: The scale appears to have been used just in the second of three experiments reported by Howard, Gengler, and Jain (1995). That experiment had **31** subjects (college students) who were randomly assigned to three experimental conditions.

RELIABILITY: An alpha of **.84** was reported for the scale by Howard, Gengler, and Jain (1995).

VALIDITY: No examination of the scale's validity was reported by Howard, Gengler, and Jain (1995).

ADMINISTRATION: Subjects completed the scale, along with other measures, after they were exposed to the experimental treatment (Howard, Gengler, and Jain 1995). Higher scores on the scale indicated that subjects were in a good mood at that point in time.

MAJOR FINDINGS: The purpose of the experiments conducted by Howard, Gengler, and Jain (1995) was to examine the effect of remembering someone's name on compliance with a purchase request. The findings indicated that those students whose names had been "remembered" by a professor were subsequently in better **moods** than those whose names the professor acted as if he could not recall.

REFERENCES:

Howard, Daniel J., Charles Gengler, and Ambuj Jain (1995), "What's in a Name? A Complimentary Means of Persuasion," *JCR*, 22 (September), 200–211.

Wood, Judith V., Judith A. Saltzberg, and Lloyd A. Goldsamt (1990), "Does Affect Induce Self-Focused Attention," *Journal of Personality and Social Psychology*, 58 (May), 899–908.

SCALE ITEMS:

DIRECTIONS: Place an X in the space that corresponds to how you feel now.

Not
happy :___:___:___:___:___:___:___: Happy
       1   2   3   4   5   6   7

Not
cheerful :___:___:___:___:___:___:___: Cheerful
       1   2   3   4   5   6   7

Not
hopeful :___:___:___:___:___:___:___: Hopeful
       1   2   3   4   5   6   7

SCALE NAME: Mood (Global)

SCALE DESCRIPTION: A multi-item semantic differential measuring a particular state of feeling of transient duration. The scale measures mood at a particular point in time on a simple good/bad continuum rather than attempting to assess various dimensions of mood. Swinyard (1993) used a four-item, seven-point version. Pham (1996) used a three-item version that probably (though was not explicitly stated to) had a seven-point response scale.

SCALE ORIGIN: Although Swinyard (1993) noted that the scale was adapted from a scale developed by Peterson and Sauber (1983), they are different enough to be treated separately here. It appears that both scales measure the same construct, but the items are very different. Pham (1996) did not describe the origin of his scale, but it is strikingly similar to the one used by Swinyard (1993).

SAMPLES: Data were gathered by Pham (1996) for his three experiments from undergraduate students. The scale was utilized, however, just in Experiment 3, which involved **57** students.

Little description was provided about the sample used by Swinyard (1993) in his experiment, except that it was composed of **109** undergraduate business students. Another person besides the class instructor conducted the experiment, and students were monitored to ensure that they worked quietly and independently on their randomly assigned exercises.

RELIABILITY: Alphas of **.94** and **.85** were reported for the versions of the scale used by Pham (1996) and Swinyard (1993), respectively. The latter indicated that data were collected for another item but that it was not used in the final version of the scale because of its unacceptably low item–total correlation.

VALIDITY: No examination of the scale's validity was reported by either author (Pham 1996; Swinyard 1993). Pham (1996) stated, however, that a factor analysis of the items in this scale, as well as two others (#23 and #203), yielded a three-factor solution in which the items shown here loaded on one factor.

ADMINISTRATION: In both studies, the scale was self-administered by subjects as part of a questionnaire after they were exposed to experimental stimuli (Pham 1996; Swinyard 1993). A high score on the scale indicated that a person was in a good mood, whereas a low score suggested that a person was sad, irritable, or upset in some way.

MAJOR FINDINGS: Pham (1996) proposed that two types of processes underlie arousal effects on persuasion: the "selection" and the "representation" effects. **Mood** was included in the study as a possible confounding effect. The results indicated that **mood** had a significant negative association with state anxiety.

Swinyard (1993) investigated the impact of **mood** and other factors on shopping intentions. The **mood** scale was used a manipulation check, which was considered to be successful. Although **mood** was not found to have a significant main effect on shopping intentions, it did appear to play important roles in several interaction effects.

REFERENCES:

Peterson, Robert and Matthew Sauber (1983), "A Mood Scale For Survey Research," in *Proceedings of the American Marketing Association's Educators' Conference*. Chicago: American Marketing Association, 409–14.

Pham, Michel Tuan (1996), "Cue Representation and Selection Effects of Arousal on Persuasion," *JCR*, 22 (March), 373–87.

Swinyard, William R. (1993), "The Effects of Mood, Involvement, and Quality of Store Experience on Shopping Intentions," *JCR*, 20 (September), 271–80.

#237 *Mood (Global)*

SCALE ITEMS:

1. Sad   :__:__:__:__:__:__:__: Happy
                      1   2   3   4   5   6   7

2. Bad mood   :__:__:__:__:__:__:__: Good mood
                      1   2   3   4   5   6   7

3. Irritable   :__:__:__:__:__:__:__: Pleased
                      1   2   3   4   5   6   7

4. Depressed   :__:__:__:__:__:__:__: Cheerful
                      1   2   3   4   5   6   7

Pham (1996): 1*, 2, 3*; 7-point (unclear)
Swinyard (1996): 1–4; 7-point

*One of the anchors was different from that shown.

SCALE NAME: Need for Cognition

SCALE DESCRIPTION: Eighteen Likert-type items that are supposed to measure a person's tendency to engage in and enjoy effortful information processing.

SCALE ORIGIN: The scale was developed by Cacioppo, Petty, and Kao (1984) and was itself a short form of a 34-item version (Cacioppo and Petty 1982). The short version was reported to have a theta coefficient (maximized Cronbach's alpha) of .90 compared with the long version's .91. Also, the two versions of the scale had a correlation of .95. Finally, factor analysis indicated that all items except one had substantial and higher loadings on the first factor than on subsequent factors. It is unclear why the weak item was not suggested for elimination in future use, and because factor loadings were not presented in the article, it is unknown which particular item it is.

SAMPLES: The sample used by Batra and Stayman (1990) was composed of **251** undergraduate business students attending the University of Texas and recruited from student organizations. The organizations, as well as the students, were given $3 apiece for their participation.

Darley and Smith (1993) used the mall intercept method of recruiting respondents. The final number of subjects was not directly specified, but the article noted that thirty subjects were randomly assigned to each treatment of the 3 × 2 factorial design. Therefore, it is assumed that analysis was based on data from approximately 180 subjects. All respondents were 18 years of age or older with only 27% being older than 45. The sample was split almost evenly on gender (51% men) and marital status (56% married).

A similar set of respondents was recruited by Darley and Smith (1995) in a shopping mall. The sample was 52% women and consisted of **120** subjects. A little more than half (59%) were married, and 46% were between 25 and 45 years of age.

Inman, Peter, and Raghubir (1997) reported on four studies in their article, only the second of which employed the **need for cognition** scale. That study was based on data from **73** undergraduate business students attending a large West Coast (U.S.) university.

RELIABILITY: Alphas for scale of **.88** (Batra and Stayman 1990), **.88** (Darley and Smith 1993), **.88** (Darley and Smith 1995), and **.86** (Inman, Peter, and Raghubir 1997) were reported.

VALIDITY: No information regarding the scale's validity was reported in any of the studies.

ADMINISTRATION: Batra and Stayman (1990) administered the scale to subjects at the beginning of an experiment before a mood manipulation stimulus was presented, whereas the subjects in Darley and Smith's (1993) experiment filled out the scale, along with other measures, after they were exposed to the experimental stimulus. Inman, Peter, and Raghubir (1997) had students complete the scale two weeks before the experiment. Higher scores on the scale indicated that respondents engaged in and enjoyed effortful cognitive activities.

MAJOR FINDINGS: Batra and Stayman (1990) investigated the influence of mood on brand attitudes. Although no main effect of **need for cognition** on brand attitude was found, there were several significant interaction effects. Specifically, the attitudinal effect of mood was greater for those with low **need for cognition**. In contrast, the attitudinal effect of argument quality was greater for those with high **need for cognition**.

The objectivity of claims made in advertising, as well as media type (print or radio), were examined by Darley and Smith (1993). **Need for cognition** was examined solely as a covariate. The only dependent measure on which it had an effect was brand beliefs.

Darley and Smith (1995) examined the differences between men and women in information processing of objective/subjective claims for high-/low-risk products. **Need for cognition** was included solely as a covariate and was found to be significantly associated with brand attitude.

In general, Inman, Peter, and Raghubir (1997) examined the degree to which consumers use restrictions to evaluate deals. Results of Study 2 indicated that people with **low need for cognition** were significantly affected by the presence of deal restrictions, whereas those with high **need for cognition** were not.

COMMENTS: Also see Garbarino and Edell (1997), Inman, McAlister, and Hoyer (1990), MacKenzie (1986), Meyers-Levy and Tybout (1989, 1997), O'Guinn and Shrum (1997), Peracchio and Tybout (1996), and Zhang (1996) for other uses of the scale.

REFERENCES:
Batra, Rajeev and Douglas M. Stayman (1990), "The Role of Mood in Advertising Effectiveness," *JCR*, 17 (September), 203–14.
Cacioppo, John T. and Richard E. Petty (1982), "The Need for Cognition," *Journal of Personality and Social Psychology*, 42 (1), 116–31.
———, ———, and Chuan Feng Kao (1984), "The Efficient Assessment of Need for Cognition," *Journal of Personality Assessment*, 48 (3), 306, 307.
Darley, William K. and Robert E. Smith (1993), "Advertising Claim Objectivity: Antecedents and Effects," *JM*, 57 (October), 100–113.
——— and ——— (1995), "Gender Differences in Information Processing Strategies: An Empirical Test of the Selectivity Model in Advertising Response," *JA*, 24 (Spring), 41–56.
Garbarino, Ellen C. and Julie A. Edell (1997), "Cognitive Effort, Affect, and Choice," *JCR*, 24 (September), 147–58.
Inman, J. Jeffrey, Leigh McAlister, and Wayne D. Hoyer (1990), "Promotion Signal: Proxy for a Price Cut?" *JCR*, 17 (June), 74–81.
———, Anil C. Peter, and Priya Raghubir (1997), "Framing the Deal: The Role of Restrictions in Accentuating Deal Value," *JCR*, 24 (June), 68–79.
MacKenzie, Scott B. (1986), "The Role of Attention in Mediating the Effect of Advertising on Attribute Importance," *JCR*, 13 (September), 174–95.
Meyers-Levy, Joan and Alice M. Tybout (1989), "Schema Congruity as a Basis for Product Evaluation," *JCR*, 16 (June), 39–54.
——— and ——— (1997), "Context Effects at Encoding and Judgment in Consumption Settings: The Role of Cognitive Resources," *JCR*, 24 (June), 1–14.
O'Guinn, Thomas C. and L.J. Shrum (1997), "The Role of Television in the Construction of Consumer Reality," *JCR*, 23 (March), 278–94.
Peracchio, Laura A. and Alice M. Tybout (1996), "The Moderating Role of Prior Knowledge in Schema-Based Product Evaluation," *JCR*, 23 (December), 177–92.
Zhang, Yong (1996), "Responses to Humorous Advertising: The Moderating Effect of Need for Cognition," *JA*, 25 (Spring), 15–32.

SCALE ITEMS:*

Strongly   Strongly
disagree   :___:___:___:___:___: agree

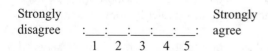

1. I would prefer complex to simple problems.

2. I like to have the responsibility of handling a situation that requires a lot of thinking.

3. Thinking is not my idea of fun. **(r)**

4. I would rather do something that requires little thought than something that is sure to challenge my thinking abilities. **(r)**

5. I try to anticipate and avoid situations where there is a likely chance I will have to think in depth about something. **(r)**

6. I find satisfaction in deliberating hard and for long hours.

7. I only think as hard as I have to. **(r)**

8. I prefer to think about small, daily projects to long-term ones. **(r)**

9. I like tasks that require little thought once I have learned them. **(r)**

10. The idea of relying on thought to make my way to the top appeals to me.

11. I really enjoy a task that involves coming up with new solutions to problems.

12. Learning new ways to think doesn't excite me very much. **(r)**

13. I prefer my life to be filled with puzzles that I must solve.

14. The notion of thinking abstractly is appealing to me.

15. I would prefer a task that is intellectual, difficult, and important to one that is somewhat important but does not require much thought.

16. I feel relief rather than satisfaction after completing a task that required a lot of mental effort. **(r)**

17. It's enough for me that something gets the job done: I don't care how or why it works. **(r)**

18. I usually end up deliberating about issues even when they do not affect me personally.

*The response format used in the reported articles is rarely described, but something common such as that shown would appear to be adequate.

SCALE NAME: Need to Reexperience Music

SCALE DESCRIPTION: A three-item, six-point Likert-type scale measuring the degree to which a person expresses a desire to hear a piece of music again and have temporal control over it. As modeled in the study by Lacher and Mizerski (1994), the construct represented by this measure lies between affect and purchase intention and is distinguished from them.

SCALE ORIGIN: The scale is original to Lacher and Mizerski (1994). In a pretest, this scale and two others being developed were administered to a sample of 117 undergraduate students. The procedure was that students heard a song twice, and the second time it was played, they filled out the scales. This was repeated for a second song. Alphas of .90 and .92 were reported for the songs. The data were also subjected to confirmatory factor analysis, which supported a three-factor solution.

SAMPLES: The sample used by Lacher and Mizerski (1994) came from undergraduate business students at a large Southern U.S. university. Usable data were collected from **215** students, who were composed of 52% men and ranged in age from 19 to 36 years.

RELIABILITY: Lacher and Mizerski (1994) did not report the alpha for the scale as used in the main study, but on the basis of the pretest results, it would likely have been quite high.

VALIDITY: No examination of scale validity was reported by Lacher and Mizerski (1994) beyond that noted for the study's pretest.

ADMINISTRATION: The scale was self-administered, along with other measures, in the study by Lacher and Mizerski (1994), and the procedure was similar to that described for the pretest. Higher scores on the scale indicated that respondents wanted to hear a song again and had control over when and how often that occurs.

MAJOR FINDINGS: Lacher and Mizerski (1994) investigated the responses music evokes in a listener and how those reactions affect the intention to purchase the music. Specifically, **need to reexperience the music** had a strong direct effect on purchase intention.

REFERENCES:

Lacher, Kathleen T. and Richard Mizerski (1994), "An Exploratory Study of the Responses and Relationships Involved in the Evaluation of, and in the Intention to Purchase New Rock Music," *JCR*, 21 (September), 366–80.

SCALE ITEMS:

Strongly   Strongly
disagree   :___:___:___:___:___:___: agree
                   1   2   3   4   5   6

1. I would enjoy listening to this song again.

2. I would like to play this song for my friends.

3. I want to be able to listen to this song whenever I feel like it.

SCALE NAME: Normative Evaluation

SCALE DESCRIPTION: Ten five-point semantic differentials that measure a consumer's judgment of the appropriateness of engaging in some specified act. In the studies by Rook and Fisher (1995), *the act* was making an impulsive purchase in a particular situation. It appears this scale is amenable for use as a measure of *attitude toward the act*, with *the act* depending on the phrasing of the instructions or scale stem.

SCALE ORIGIN: The source of the scale was not specified by Rook and Fisher (1995), though it appears to be original to their work.

SAMPLES: Rook and Fisher (1995) gathered data for their studies from two very different samples. Study 1 was based on data from **212** undergraduate business students, whereas Study 2 used data gathered from **99** completed mall intercept interviews. All of the interviews in the latter sample were conducted on one day just outside a music store. The sample was almost evenly split on gender (51% females) and was rather young (69% less than 21 years of age).

RELIABILITY: The reliability of the scale was measured for Study 1 and for two different versions in Study 2 (Rook and Fisher 1995). Specifically, in Studies 1 ($\alpha = .91$) and 2 ($\alpha = .90$), respondents read a scenario about someone who might make an impulse purchase. In addition, respondents in Study 2 ($\alpha = .82$) were asked to react to the supposition that they themselves had made a impulse purchase in the music store they had just left. As used for the scenario version in Study 2, the scale only had eight items. Items 2 and 4 were removed because of low item–total correlations.

VALIDITY: No examination of the scale's validity was reported by Rook and Fisher (1995).

ADMINISTRATION: In both studies by Rook and Fisher (1995), the scale was self-administered by respondents as part of a larger instrument. Lower scores on the scale indicated that respondents thought that a specified act was appropriate for the defined situation.

MAJOR FINDINGS: Rook and Fisher (1995) examined the impact of **normative evaluations** on the impulse buying trait and buying behaviors. As hypothesized, **normative evaluations** were found to moderate the link between trait (as measured by the scale) and behavioral aspects of impulse buying.

COMMENTS: Rook and Fisher (1995) reported scale means of 30.4 (ten-item), 28.1 (eight-item), and 28.7 (ten-item) in Studies 1 and 2, respectively.

REFERENCES:
Rook, Dennis W. and Robert J. Fisher (1995), "Normative Influences on Impulsive Buying Behavior," *JCR*, 22 (December), 305–13.

SCALE ITEMS:

1. Bad   :___:___:___:___:___: Good
               5   4   3   2   1

2. Crazy   :___:___:___:___:___: Rational
               5   4   3   2   1

3. Wasteful   :___:___:___:___:___: Productive
               5   4   3   2   1

4. Unattractive :___:___:___:___:___: Attractive
               5   4   3   2   1

5. Stupid   :___:___:___:___:___: Smart
               5   4   3   2   1

6. Unacceptable :___:___:___:___:___: Acceptable
               5   4   3   2   1

7. Selfish   :___:___:___:___:___: Generous
               5   4   3   2   1

8. Silly   :___:___:___:___:___: Sober
               5   4   3   2   1

9. Childish   :___:___:___:___:___: Mature
               5   4   3   2   1

10. Wrong   :___:___:___:___:___: Right
               5   4   3   2   1

SCALE NAME: Normativeness of Situation (Sending Card)

SCALE DESCRIPTION: Four seven-point Likert-type statements that attempt to measure the degree to which a behavior is expected of someone and is part of the social norms within which that person operates. The behaviors compared by Houston and Walker (1996) were the sending of different types of greeting cards.

SCALE ORIGIN: Houston and Walker (1996) apparently developed the scale for use in their study.

SAMPLES: Houston and Walker (1996) administered this scale to a sample of **203** female college students ranging in age from 19 to 47 years. On the basis of their scores, 40 respondents were selected and placed into either a high- or low-scoring group. This smaller sample is the one on which the analysis was based.

RELIABILITY: An alpha of **.96** was reported for the scale by Houston and Walker (1996).

VALIDITY: No examination of the scale's validity was described by Houston and Walker (1996).

ADMINISTRATION: Houston and Walker (1996) did not say much about the context in which the scale was administered except that it was filled out by students in the first phase of a two-part study. Most likely, the respondents read about a situation and, on the basis of that, were asked to complete the scale. As used by these authors, lower scores indicated that some specified situation had a higher level of normativeness associated with it.

MAJOR FINDINGS: The study by Houston and Walker (1996) used a cognitive mapping methodology to explore the goal structures that are activated by consumers' feelings of self-reliance with a product. The results showed that sending a wedding card was more **normative** than sending a "thinking-of-you" card.

REFERENCES:
Houston, Mark B. and Beth A. Walker (1996), "Self-Relevance and Purchase Goals: Mapping a Consumer Decision," *JAMS*, 24 (Summer), 232–45.

SCALE ITEMS:

Strongly   Strongly
agree   :___:___:___:___:___:___:___: disagree
                1   2   3   4   5   6   7

1. I feel like I have to send this type of card.

2. A person expects to receive this type of card from me.

3. If I forgot to send this type of card, the person who would have received it will be disappointed.

4. One should send a card in this situation.

SCALE NAME: Nostalgia Proneness

SCALE DESCRIPTION: An eight-item, nine-point Likert-type scale measuring the degree of preference a person has toward objects that were more common in the past. This measure has also been referred to as *attitude toward the past* (ATP) and the *Nostalgia Index*.

SCALE ORIGIN: A 20-item scale was developed and refined by Holbrook (1993), as detailed subsequently.

SAMPLES: Holbrook (1993) reported using the scale in two studies. The sample in the first study was composed of **167** students (57% men) from two introductory marketing classes at a large graduate school of business. Analysis was limited to those who were between the ages of 21 and 34 years and who indicated that they were from the United States.

Data in the second study were collected by, but not from, students in the same classes during a subsequent semester. They were asked to have questionnaires filled out by Americans of at least 18 years of age who were not present or former students of the school. This led to **156** usable survey forms. The sample was 60% women, and ages ranged from 21 to 85 years.

Holbrook and Schindler (1994) gathered data in a form similar to the second study. The data were collected by students who were enrolled introductory marketing management classes at a large graduate school of business. They were supposed to give the questionnaire to two people of at least 18 years of age who differed in age by 30 years or more and who were native English-speaking Americans. The final sample consisted of **237** respondents (53% women) with a media age of 33 years.

RELIABILITY: The construct reliability and alpha for the scale were reported by Holbrook (1993) to be **.78** in Study 1 and **.73** in Study 2. The larger, 20-item version of the scale was reported by Holbrook and Schindler (1994) to have an alpha of **.77**, whereas the 8-item subset had a construct reliability of **.68**. As admitted by the authors, the level of reliability should have been higher and deserves further developmental effort.

VALIDITY: In Study 1, a confirmatory factor analysis was performed on the original version of the scale, and it did not appear to be unidimensional (Holbrook 1993). After eliminating some items, the eight items shown here were found to fit a one-factor model. A confirmatory factor analysis in Study 2 also provided some evidence of the eight items' unidimensionality.

This same process occurred in Holbrook and Schindler (1994). A confirmatory factor analysis supported the single-factor model for the eight-item version of the scale but not for the full twenty-item measure.

ADMINISTRATION: The scale was self-administered in each of the studies as part of a larger survey instrument (Holbrook 1993; Holbrook and Schindler 1994). A high score on the scale suggested that a person had a great longing for things that were more popular in days gone by, whereas a low score indicated that a person preferred things that are relatively recent and new. Holbrook and Schindler (1994) explained that they normalized scores for each respondent separately and then standardized scores across respondents.

MAJOR FINDINGS: The purpose of the study by Holbrook (1993) was to examine the independent influences of age and **nostalgia proneness** on consumer preferences. The evidence led the author to conclude that both variables are connected to nostalgia-related preferences, but age and **nostalgia proneness** represent different constructs, with only trivial variance shared between them.

Similarly, Holbrook and Schindler (1994) proposed that consumers prefer styles popular during certain sensitive periods of their lives. In particular, it was hypothesized that consumers had age-related preference peaks in their tastes of movie stars. An age-related peak preference was found and moderated by **nostalgia proneness**.

REFERENCES:

Holbrook, Morris B. (1993), "Nostalgia and Consumption Preferences: Some Emerging Patterns of Consumer Tastes," *JCR*, 20 (September), 245–56.

———— and Robert M. Schindler (1994), "Age, Sex, and Attitude Toward the Past as Predictors of Consumers' Aesthetic Tastes for Cultural Products," *JMR*, 31 (August), 412–22.

SCALE ITEMS:

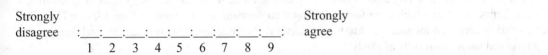

Strongly
disagree   :___:___:___:___:___:___:___:___: Strongly
        1 2 3 4 5 6 7 8 9   agree

1. They don't make 'em like they used to.

2. Things used to be better in the good old days.

3. Products are getting shoddier and shoddier.

4. Technological change will insure a brighter future. **(r)**

5. History involves a steady improvement in human welfare. **(r)**

6. We are experiencing a decline in the quality of life.

7. Steady growth in GNP has brought increased human happiness. **(r)**

8. Modern business constantly builds a better tomorrow. **(r)**

SCALE NAME: Opinion Leadership (Domain Specific)

SCALE DESCRIPTION: Six seven-point Likert-type items that measure a consumer's belief that other consumers approach him or her for information about products to buy and are influenced by the information received. The scale is purposefully constructed to be amenable for adaptation to a variety of product categories but is not a generalized leadership scale. The authors (Flynn, Goldsmith, and Eastman 1996) believe the construct to be monomorphic, such that opinion leadership in technologically advanced cultures tends to focus on one topical area rather than on many (polymorphic).

SCALE ORIGIN: Although opinion leadership had a long history of study and measurement in marketing and sociology, Flynn, Goldsmith, and Eastman (1996) observed that one of the most well-known measures of the construct (Vol. I, #171) lacked content validity and was not unidimensional. Therefore, they conducted a series of five studies to develop and test a better measure. They began by generating a pool of items, some of which were for measuring a cophenomenon: opinion seeking (#245). The items were initially screened for face validity by six doctoral students, revisions were made, and further editing followed using the results of Study 1.

SAMPLES: Five studies with separate samples were conducted by Flynn, Goldsmith, and Eastman (1996). The samples consisted of **224**, **263**, and **391** college students for Studies 1, 2, and 3, respectively. Study 4 was based on data from **99** women attending a professional women's luncheon. Study 5 had two waves because its focus was on test–retest reliability. The first wave had **162** students, and 127 of those students completed the instrument again four weeks later.

RELIABILITY: Flynn, Goldsmith, and Eastman (1996) reported alphas of **.86**, **.78**, **.87**, and **.80** for Studies 1 through 4, respectively. The alphas in Study 5 were **.86** (test 1) and **.91** (test 2). The four-week test–retest measure of stability was .82.

VALIDITY: A considerable amount of information was gathered by Flynn, Goldsmith, and Eastman (1996) in support of the scale's validity, only a portion of which will be provided here. Confirmatory factor analysis of data from Studies 2, 3, and 5 indicated that the scale was unidimensional. Data from Studies 3 and 4 provided evidence of nomological validity.

ADMINISTRATION: In each of the five studies, the scale was part of a larger survey instrument (Flynn, Goldsmith, and Eastman 1996). Higher scores on the scale indicated that respondents believed that others come to them for advice before making a purchase decision for some specified product and that those people are influenced by what they hear.

MAJOR FINDINGS: The purpose of the studies by Flynn, Goldsmith, and Eastman (1996) was to construct and purify **opinion leader** and opinion-seeking scales. Among the findings was that **opinion leadership** was very much related, as expected, to innovativeness, involvement, and perceived knowledge.

COMMENTS: Means for the scale were 22.1, 24.8, 21.6, 20.3, and 20.8 for Studies 2, 3, 4, and 5 and tests 1 and 2, respectively.

REFERENCES:
Flynn, Leisa R., Ronald E. Goldsmith, and Jacqueline K. Eastman (1996), "Opinion Leaders and Opinion Seekers: Two New Measurement Scales," *JAMS*, 24 (Spring), 137–47.

SCALE ITEMS:*

Strongly   Strongly
disagree   :___:___:___:___:___:___:___: agree
                1   2   3   4   5   6   7

1. My opinion on _____ seems not to count with other people. **(r)**

2. When they choose a _____, other people do not turn to me for advice. **(r)**

3. Other people rarely come to me for advice about choosing _____. **(r)**

4. People that I know pick _____ based on what I have told them.

5. I often persuade other people to buy the _____ that I like.

6. I often influence people's opinions about _____.

*The name of the product goes in the blanks. Flynn, Goldsmith, and Eastman (1996) examined CDs and tapes in Studies 1, 2, and 5. Clothing was the focus in Study 3, and environmentally friendly ("green") products were the objects of analysis in Study 5.

SCALE NAME: Opinion Leadership (Domain Specific)

SCALE DESCRIPTION: The scale has been used in various forms to measure a person's tendency to provide information to others. Although it has been referred to as a measure of opinion leadership in all of the studies, an examination of the items suggests that it might be more accurate to think of it in more limited terms (e.g., the degree to which a person provides information to others). Even if a person talks about a topic a lot, it does not necessarily mean that the information is believed and acted on (persuasion). These activities are critical indicators that a person is indeed *leading* the opinions of others, yet they are weak or missing from this scale.

SCALE ORIGIN: The scale was developed by Rogers (1961) and discussed by Rogers and Cartano (1962). The six-item scale was used in a 1957 study of the diffusion of new farm ideas among Ohio farmers. Personal interviews were completed with a statewide, random area sample of 104 farm operators. A split-half reliability of .703 was calculated for the scale. In that study, a crude version of the sociometric technique of measuring opinion leadership produced scores with a correlation of .225 with the scale scores (Rogers 1961; Rogers and Cartano 1962). The validity of the scale was examined in several studies by correlating scale scores with scores from the key informant method, as well as the sociometric technique. Although positive correlations were found, they were not high.

A seven-item version of this scale was used by King and Summers (1970). A series of studies using the modified scale reported alphas ranging from .5 to .87.

Childers (1986) reported an alpha of .66 that was raised to a .68 when one of the seven items was removed from the summated scale. He also found low nomological validity for the scale.

The most thorough examination of the scale's psychometric properties was made by Flynn, Goldsmith, and Eastman (1994). They reported on the testing and modification of the scale in four studies. In brief, they found that the original version of the scale was not unidimensional. Problems seemed to stem from the inclusion of item 5 (see "Scale Items"), and their findings supported its deletion. Despite the scale having acceptable reliability and unidimensionality with the deletion of item 5, the authors raised other questions about the scale and felt it necessarily to construct another one (Flynn, Goldsmith, and Eastman 1996). (See #243).

SAMPLES: Samples were taken by Childers (1986) from the files of a cable television franchise in a large metro area. One sample was of those people who subscribed to cable, whereas another sample was of those who had been contacted but refused to subscribe. Questionnaires were dropped off by an employee of the franchise, but responses were returned by mail. **One hundred seventy-six** questionnaires were returned by the end of the three-week cut-off date.

Davis and Rubin (1983) mailed questionnaires to a sample of two groups in Florida: known adopters of solar energy devices and the general population over the age of 18 years. Analysis was based on 817 usable questionnaires, of which **488** were from solar energy adopters.

Five studies with separate samples were conducted by Flynn, Goldsmith, and Eastman (1996). Only Study 5 used this particular scale (what they referred to as the "revised King and Summers opinion leadership scale"). That study focused on testing the four-week stability of two other measures, and this scale was used just in the first part to help estimate the convergent validity of the new opinion leadership scale being developed (see "Validity"). The sample for the first data collection stage of Study 5 was composed of **162** students in upper division marketing classes at a large Southern U.S. university.

RELIABILITY: The final version of the scale used by Childers (1986) had an alpha of .83. An alpha of .82 was reported by Davis and Rubin (1983), and Flynn, Goldsmith, and Eastman (1996) found an alpha of **.91** for their version of the scale.

VALIDITY: Nomological validity was assessed by Childers (1986), who examined the pattern of correlations between the modified opinion leadership scale and scales measuring other constructs with which it should correlate, according to theory. As expected, the scale had significant though low correlations with several related variables: curiosity about product operation, product usage creativity, perceived risk of adopting cable television, and ownership of technically oriented products. It did not have a significant correlation with risk preferences. Validity was also examined by comparing known groups' scores on the scale for predictable differences. Subscribers to cable television had significantly higher scores than non-subscribers, but no significant difference was found between those who subscribed to premium cable and those who just bought the basic service.

Davis and Rubin (1983) compared scores on their energy-related version of the scale with whether a person had purchased a solar energy device in the past. This produced a highly significant Kendall's tau (.47).

To provide a sense of the convergent validity of their own opinion leadership scale, Flynn, Goldsmith, and Eastman (1996) correlated scores on that scale with those on this scale. In both administrations of Study 5, the correlations were positive and significant, which supported a claim of convergent validity of the new scale. The correlation between this old scale and a measure of perceived knowledge was just as strong, which means that it is primarily emphasizing *information* rather than *persuasion*.

ADMINISTRATION: The scale was self-administered in the studies by respondents in a survey instrument format. Higher scores on the scale indicated that a person reported him- or herself as talking to others a lot about some specified topic/product, whereas lower scores suggested a person had very little of the diffusion aspect of opinion leadership.

MAJOR FINDINGS: The purpose of the study by Childers (1986) was to compare the psychometric properties of the King and Summers (1970) scale with those of a modified version. The main changes were the elimination of an item and the use of a five-point response scale for each item. In most respects, the modified version of the scale was superior to the previous version. The context in which the scale was studied was cable television adoption.

Davis and Rubin (1983) examined a few psychographic variables that might distinguish between energy conscious opinion leader groups. Those with a high amount of **opinion leadership** expressed more energy consciousness, had a higher degree of self-confidence and leadership traits, were more conservative with the use of credit, and had a greater degree of financial optimism.

The purpose of the studies by Flynn, Goldsmith, and Eastman (1996) was to construct and purify **opinion leader** and opinion-seeking scales. As noted, the older **opinion leadership** scale (shown subsequently) was only used in test 1 of Study 5. In addition to the findings reported here related to validity, the results indicated that the scale was not related to the new measure of opinion seeking that was being developed (#245).

COMMENTS: Although not used in the main study reported by Feick and Price (1987), this scale was used in one of their pilot studies to examine the discriminant validity of a one-item generalized opinion leadership scale and a six-item market maven scale.

REFERENCES:

Childers, Terry L. (1986), "Assessment of the Psychometric Properties of an Opinion Leadership Scale," *JMR*, 23 (May), 184–88.

Davis, Duane L. and Ronald S. Rubin (1983), "Identifying the Energy Conscious Consumer: The Case of the Opinion Leader," *JAMS*, 11 (Spring), 169–90.

Feick, Lawrence F. and Linda L. Price (1987), "The Market Maven: A Diffuser of Marketplace Information," *JM*, 51 (January), 83–97.

Flynn, Leisa R., Ronald E. Goldsmith, Jacqueline K. Eastman (1994), "The King and Summers Opinion Leadership Scale: Revision and Refinement," *Journal of Business Research*, 31 (September), 55–64.

——, ——, and —— (1996), "Opinion Leaders and Opinion Seekers: Two New Measurement Scales," *JAMS*, 24 (Spring), 137–47.

King, Charles W. and John O. Summers (1970), "Overlap of Opinion Leadership Across Consumer Product Categories," *JMR*, 7 (February), 43–50.

Rogers, Everett M. (1961), *Characteristics of Innovators and Other Adopter Categories*. Wooster, OH: Ohio Agricultural Experiment Station Research Bulletin #882.

——— and David G. Cartano (1962), "Methods of Measuring Opinion Leadership," *Public Opinion Quarterly*, 26 (Fall), 435–41.

SCALE ITEMS:*

1. In general, do you talk to your friends and neighbors about _____?

Very often   Never

     5————————4————————3————————2————————1

2. When you talk to you friends and neighbors about cable television do you:

Give a great   Give very little
deal of information   information

     5————————4————————3————————2————————1

3. During the past six months, how many people have you told about _____ ?

Told a number   Told
of people   no one

     5————————4————————3————————2————————1

4. Compared with your circle of friends, how likely are you to be asked about _____ ?

Very likely   Not at all
to be asked   likely to be asked

     5————————4————————3————————2————————1

5. If you and your friend were to discuss _____, what part would you be most likely to play? Would you mainly listen to your friends' ideas or would you try to convince them of your ideas?

Convince your friend   Listen to your
 of your idea   friend's ideas

     5————————4————————3————————2————————1

6. In discussions of _____, which of the following happens most often:

You tell your   Your friends tell
friends about _____   you about _____

     5————————4————————3————————2————————1

7. *Overall* in all of your discussions with friends and neighbors are you:

Often used as a   Not used as a
source of advice   source of advice

     5————————4————————3————————2————————1

*The name of the object should go in the blanks. The version shown here is basically what was used by Childers (1986) and Flynn, Goldsmith, and Eastman (1996), except that neither used item 5. The full scale with a dichotomous response format (yes/no) was used by King and Summers (1971) and Davis and Rubin (1983).

SCALE NAME: Opinion Seeking (Domain Specific)

SCALE DESCRIPTION: Six seven-point Likert-type items that measure the propensity for a consumer to seek out the advice of others before making a purchase decision in some specified product category. Although this measure and the construct it is intended to capture were viewed by its developers (Flynn, Goldsmith, and Eastman 1996) as distinct from opinion leadership, they admitted that there could be some relationship. This was believed to be because opinion leaders could certainly seek information from others, but not all opinion seekers would be opinion leaders.

SCALE ORIGIN: Flynn, Goldsmith, and Eastman (1996) observed that opinion seeking was not well documented in the literature and no well-constructed scale was available that could be domain specific. As noted subsequently, they conducted a series of five studies to develop and test such a scale. They began by generating a pool of items, some of which were for measuring a cophenomenon: opinion leadership (#243). They were initially screened for face validity by six doctoral students, revisions were made, and further editing followed using the results of Study 1.

SAMPLES: Five studies with separate samples were conducted by Flynn, Goldsmith, and Eastman (1996). The samples consisted of **224**, **263**, and **391** college students for Studies 1, 2, and 3, respectively. Study 4 was based on data from **99** women attending a professional women's luncheon. Study 5 had two waves because its focus was on test–retest reliability. The first wave had **162** students, and 127 of those students completed the instrument again four weeks later.

RELIABILITY: Flynn, Goldsmith, and Eastman (1996) reported alphas of **.87**, **.88**, **.88**, and **.81** for Studies 1 through 4, respectively. The alphas in Study 5 were **.93** (test 1) and **.92** (test 2). The four-week test–retest measure of stability was .75.

VALIDITY: A considerable amount of information was gathered by Flynn, Goldsmith, and Eastman (1996) in support of the scale's validity, only a portion of which will be provided here. Confirmatory factor analysis of data from Studies 2, 3, and 5 indicated that the scale was unidimensional. Data from Study 4 showed evidence of there being two factors, but the authors had reason to believe it was a methodological artifact related to an item being the first item on the form. Data from Studies 3 and 4 provided evidence of nomological validity.

ADMINISTRATION: In each of the five studies, the scale was part of a larger survey instrument (Flynn, Goldsmith, and Eastman 1996). Higher scores on the scale indicated that respondents solicited the advice of others before making a purchase decision for some specified product.

MAJOR FINDINGS: The purpose of the studies by Flynn, Goldsmith, and Eastman (1996) was to construct and purify opinion leader and **opinion-seeking** scales. Among the findings was that **opinion seeking** was unrelated, as expected, to innovativeness, involvement, and perceived knowledge.

COMMENTS: Means for the scale were 23.6, 24.0, 19.9, 20.5, and 22.3 for Studies 2, 3, 4, and 5 and tests 1 and 2, respectively.

REFERENCES:
Flynn, Leisa R., Ronald E. Goldsmith, and Jacqueline K. Eastman (1996), "Opinion Leaders and Opinion Seekers: Two New Measurement Scales," *JAMS*, 24 (Spring), 137–47.

#245 *Opinion Seeking (Domain Specific)*

SCALE ITEMS:*

Strongly   Strongly
disagree   :___:___:___:___:___:___: agree
            1   2   3   4   5   6   7

1. When I consider buying a _____ I ask other people for advice.

2. I don't need to talk to others before I buy _____. **(r)**

3. I rarely ask other people what _____ to buy. **(r)**

4. I like to get others' opinions before I buy a _____.

5. I feel more comfortable buying a _____ when I have gotten other people's opinions on it.

6. When choosing _____, other people's opinions are not important to me. **(r)**

*The name of the product goes in the blanks. Flynn, Goldsmith, and Eastman (1996) examined CDs and tapes in Studies 1, 2, and 5. Clothing was the focus in Study 3, and environmentally friendly ("green") products were the objects of analysis in Study 5.

SCALE NAME: Optimism

SCALE DESCRIPTION: Three four-point items intended to capture the level of hopeful-type feelings a person felt during a consumption experience.

SCALE ORIGIN: Richins (1997) drew on terms in previous measures, as well as her own series of studies, to develop and refine several emotion-related scales into the CES (Consumption Emotion Set).

SAMPLES: Six studies were reported by Richins (1997) as part of the process of developing the CES, only two of which had reliability information. Study 4 was based on data from **448** college students. Two surveys were conducted in Study 5: Survey 1 was completed by **256** college students, and there were **194** student respondents to Survey 2.

RELIABILITY: As noted, reliability was reported by Richins (1997) only for Studies 4 ($\alpha = .82$) and 5 ($\alpha = .86$).

VALIDITY: Richins (1997) did not directly examine the validity of the scale. A great deal of effort was expended, however, in a creative use of multidimensional scaling to note whether the items that composed each scale clustered together.

ADMINISTRATION: In the studies performed by Richins (1997), particularly Studies 4 and 5, the scale was just part of a larger instrument containing many emotion-related measures. A high score on the scale suggested that a person experienced a strong sense of optimism as a result of some event/stimulus.

MAJOR FINDINGS: On the basis of a review of previously developed measures of emotion, Richins (1997) conducted six studies with the purpose of producing a set of scales particularly suited for assessing consumption experiences. The CES instrument was a result of the studies, one subscale of which measures **optimism**. In general, the instrument was more successful in representing the diversity of consumption emotions than the other instruments tested.

REFERENCES:
Richins, Marsha L. (1997), "Measuring Emotions in the Consumption Experience," *JCR*, 24 (September), 127–46.

SCALE ITEMS:

```
Not            A
at all       little    Moderately    Strongly
  1————————2————————3————————4
```

1. Optimistic

2. Encouraged

3. Hopeful

SCALE NAME: Ordering Option Beliefs (Ease of Use)

SCALE DESCRIPTION: A six-item, seven-point semantic differential scale measuring a person's beliefs regarding the time and effort involved in a specified method of placing an order. As described here, the setting used by Dabholkar (1994) was ordering at a fast-food restaurant, and two options were compared: touch-screen ordering versus verbally placing the order with an employee.

SCALE ORIGIN: The origin of the scale appears to be Dabholkar (1994). Refinement of the scale occurred with a pretest sample that consisted of 141 undergraduate students. The scale produced alphas of .88 (touch-screen ordering) and .80 (verbal ordering).

SAMPLES: The final sample used by Dabholkar (1994) was composed of **305** undergraduates attending a large university. The sample was 56.7% women, and the average age was almost 25 years. Data were collected in classrooms, and participation was voluntary.

RELIABILITY: Dabholkar (1994) reported construct reliabilities of **.92** and **.86** for the touch-screen and verbal versions of the scale, respectively.

VALIDITY: The validity of the scale was not explicitly addressed by Dabholkar (1994). However, results of confirmatory and exploratory factor analyses indicated that both versions of the scale were unidimensional.

ADMINISTRATION: The scale used by Dabholkar (1994) was only one of several in the questionnaire that were completed by respondents. A higher score on the scale indicated that a person believed the specified method of ordering food requires little time and effort.

MAJOR FINDINGS: The purpose of the study by Dabholkar (1994) was to integrate attitudinal and information-processing literatures to better understand the mental comparisons used by consumers to make choices. The results of the study provided strong support for the expectancy comparison model, in which the choice is made by comparing expectancy-value components across options before formation of attitudes toward those options. No results specific to **order options (ease of use)** were described.

REFERENCES:
Dabholkar, Pratibha (1994), "Incorporating Choice into an Attitudinal Framework: Analyzing Models of Mental Comparison Processes," *JCR*, 21 (June), 100–118.

SCALE ITEMS:*
Using a _____ to order fast food . . .

1. Will be
   complicated   :___:___:___:___:___:___:___: Will be
                   1   2   3   4   5   6   7   simple+

2. Will take
   a lot of   Will take
   effort   :___:___:___:___:___:___:___: little
                   1   2   3   4   5   6   7   effort+

3. Will be   Will be
   confusing   :___:___:___:___:___:___:___: clear+
                   1   2   3   4   5   6   7

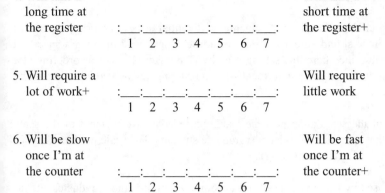

4. Will take a
   long time at
   the register   :___:___:___:___:___:___:___:
                        1   2   3   4   5   6   7

Will take a
short time at
the register+

5. Will require a
   lot of work+   :___:___:___:___:___:___:___:
                        1   2   3   4   5   6   7

Will require
little work

6. Will be slow
   once I'm at
   the counter   :___:___:___:___:___:___:___:
                        1   2   3   4   5   6   7

Will be fast
once I'm at
the counter+

*Either *touch screen* or *verbal* was placed in the blank.

+These particular phrases were not explicitly stated in the article by Dabholkar (1994) and are reconstructions based on the respective semantic opposites that were given.

SCALE NAME: Ordering Option Beliefs (Fun)

SCALE DESCRIPTION: A four-item, seven-point semantic differential scale measuring a person's beliefs regarding the perceived interest and enjoyment that would be experienced in using a specified method of placing an order. As described here, the setting used by Dabholkar (1994) was ordering at a fast-food restaurant, and two options were compared: touch-screen ordering versus verbally placing the order with an employee.

SCALE ORIGIN: The origin of the scale appears to be Dabholkar (1994). Refinement of the scale occurred with a pretest sample that consisted of 141 undergraduate students. The scale produced alphas of .89 (touch-screen ordering) and .81 (verbal ordering).

SAMPLES: The final sample used by Dabholkar (1994) was composed of **305** undergraduates attending a large university. The sample was 56.7% women, and the average age was almost 25 years. Data were collected in classrooms, and participation was voluntary.

RELIABILITY: Dabholkar (1994) reported construct reliabilities of **.90** and **.87** for the touch-screen and verbal versions of the scale, respectively.

VALIDITY: The validity of the scale was not explicitly addressed by Dabholkar (1994). However, results of confirmatory and exploratory factor analyses indicated that both versions of the scale were unidimensional.

ADMINISTRATION: The scale used by Dabholkar (1994) was only one of several in the questionnaire that were completed by respondents. A higher score on the scale indicated that a person believed the specified method of ordering food would be an enjoyable experience.

MAJOR FINDINGS: The purpose of the study by Dabholkar (1994) was to integrate attitudinal and information-processing literatures to better understand the mental comparisons used by consumers to make choices. The results of the study provided strong support for the expectancy comparison model, in which the choice is made by comparing expectancy-value components across options before formation of attitudes toward those options. No results specific to **order options (fun)** were described.

REFERENCES:
Dabholkar, Pratibha (1994), "Incorporating Choice into an Attitudinal Framework: Analyzing Models of Mental Comparison Processes," *JCR*, 21 (June), 100–118.

SCALE ITEMS:*
Using a _____ to order fast food . . .

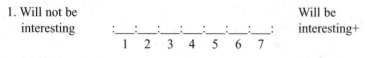

1. Will not be
   interesting   :___:___:___:___:___:___:___: Will be
                     1   2   3   4   5   6   7   interesting+

2. Will not be
   entertaining+   :___:___:___:___:___:___:___: Will be
                     1   2   3   4   5   6   7   entertaining

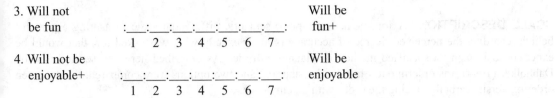

*Either *touch screen* or *verbal* was placed in the blank.

+These particular phrases were not explicitly stated in the article by Dabholkar (1994) and are reconstructions based on the respective semantic opposites that were given.

SCALE NAME: Ordering Option Beliefs (Performance)

SCALE DESCRIPTION: A four-item, seven-point semantic differential scale measuring a person's beliefs regarding the perceived degree of accuracy (getting exactly what was asked for) that would be experienced in using a specified method of placing an order. As described here, the setting used by Dabholkar (1994) was ordering at a fast-food restaurant, and two options were compared: touch-screen ordering versus verbally placing the order with an employee.

SCALE ORIGIN: The origin of the scale appears to be Dabholkar (1994). Refinement of the scale occurred with a pretest sample that consisted of 141 undergraduate students. The scale produced alphas of .81 (touch-screen ordering) and .79 (verbal ordering).

SAMPLES: The final sample used by Dabholkar (1994) was composed of **305** undergraduates attending a large university. The sample was 56.7% women, and the average age was almost 25 years. Data were collected in classrooms, and participation was voluntary.

RELIABILITY: Dabholkar (1994) reported construct reliabilities of **.87** and **.85** for the touch-screen and verbal versions of the scale, respectively.

VALIDITY: The validity of the scale was not explicitly addressed by Dabholkar (1994). However, results of confirmatory and exploratory factor analyses indicated that both versions of the scale were unidimensional.

ADMINISTRATION: The scale used by Dabholkar (1994) was only one of several in the questionnaire that were completed by respondents. A higher score on the scale indicated that a person believed the specified method of ordering food would perform well and produce reliable results.

MAJOR FINDINGS: The purpose of the study by Dabholkar (1994) was to integrate attitudinal and information-processing literatures to better understand the mental comparisons used by consumers to make choices. The results of the study provided strong support for the expectancy comparison model, in which the choice is made by comparing expectancy-value components across options before formation of attitudes toward those options. No results specific to **order options (performance)** were described.

REFERENCES:

Dabholkar, Pratibha (1994), "Incorporating Choice into an Attitudinal Framework: Analyzing Models of Mental Comparison Processes," *JCR*, 21 (June), 100–118.

SCALE ITEMS:* Using a _____ to order fast food . . .

1. Means I will not
   get just what
   I ordered   :___:___:___:___:___:___:___: Means I will
                   1   2   3   4   5   6   7   get just what
                                                      I ordered+

2. Is something
   I don't expect
   to work very
   well   :___:___:___:___:___:___:___: Is something
                   1   2   3   4   5   6   7   I expect to
                                                      work very
                                                      well+

3. Will result
   in errors in
   the order   :___:___:___:___:___:___:___:
                  1   2   3   4   5   6   7

                               Will not result
                               in errors in
                               the order+

4. Will be
   unreliable+   ___:___:___:___:___:___:___:
                  1   2   3   4   5   6   7

                               Will be
                               reliable

*Either *touch screen* or *verbal* was placed in the blank.

+These particular phrases were not explicitly stated in the article by Dabholkar (1994) and are reconstructions based on the respective semantic opposites that were given.

SCALE NAME: Organizational Prestige

SCALE DESCRIPTION: A three-item, five-point Likert-type scale measuring the degree to which a person views an organization of which he or she is a member as having a positive reputation in the community. The organization studied by Bhattacharya, Rao, and Glynn (1995) was an art museum.

SCALE ORIGIN: The scale used by Bhattacharya, Rao, and Glynn (1995) is a subset of the measure developed by Mael (1988; Mael and Ashforth 1992). Of the eight items in the scale, Bhattacharya, Rao, and Glynn (1995) selected just those three they considered to fit the context of a museum. The other items had to do with students, alumni, or faculty of a school.

SAMPLES: Bhattacharya, Rao, and Glynn (1995) gathered data from members of an art museum in a major city of the southeastern United States. Questionnaires were mailed to a proportionate stratified random sample of the various membership categories. Two free guest passes were included with the questionnaires as a token of appreciation and incentive to respond. A 30% response rate produced **306** completed survey forms. Although not representative of the population at large, the authors considered the sample to be similar to those reported for arts consumers. Respondents were approximately 52 years of age, predominately white (96%), and mostly women (66%).

RELIABILITY: An alpha of **.69** was reported for the scale by Bhattacharya, Rao, and Glynn (1995).

VALIDITY: No evidence of the scale's validity was reported by Bhattacharya, Rao, and Glynn (1995).

ADMINISTRATION: The scale was self-administered by respondents as part of a larger mail survey questionnaire (Bhattacharya, Rao, and Glynn 1995). Scale scores were calculated such that high scores indicated that respondents believed that some particular organization of which they were members has a poor reputation in the community.

MAJOR FINDINGS: Bhattacharya, Rao, and Glynn (1995) used social identity theory to develop and test a conceptual framework for the identification a person feels toward an organization of which he or she is a member. The findings showed that there was a significant positive relationship between **organizational prestige** and identification. This means that the more a person views an **organization as having a prestigious reputation** in the community, the greater is his or her identification with that organization.

REFERENCES:

Bhattacharya, C.B., Hayagreeva Rao, and Mary Ann Glynn (1995), "Understanding the Bond of Identification: An Investigation of Its Correlates Among Art Museum Members," *JM*, 59 (October), 46–57.

Mael, Fred (1988), "Organizational Identification: Construct Redefinition and a Field Application with Organizational Alumni," doctoral dissertation, Wayne State University.

————— and Blake E. Ashforth (1992), "Alumni and Their Alma Mater: A Partial Test of the Reformulated Model of Organizational Identification," *Journal of Organizational Behavior*, 13, 103–23.

SCALE ITEMS:*

Strongly   Strongly
agree   :___:___:___:___:___: disagree
                1   2   3   4   5

1. People in my community think highly of membership in the _____.

2. It is considered prestigious in my community to be a member of the _____.

3. The _____ does *not* have an outstanding reputation in my community. **(r)**

*The name of the organization goes in the blanks.

SCALE NAME: Participation

SCALE DESCRIPTION: Seven seven-point Likert-type items measuring the extent to which a customer expresses an active involvement in the running of a store, with emphasis on verbal suggestions and feedback about improving service. This is distinct from the use of the term *participation* as used in some service literature, where it means active involvement in the production of the service.

SCALE ORIGIN: Although it received some inspiration from previous measures of similar constructs, the scale is original to the work of Bettencourt (1997).

SAMPLES: In the study reported by Bettencourt (1997), data were collected by students in a marketing class. They were instructed to have five surveys completed by people who were regular shoppers for their households. After a verification process, **215** questionnaires remained for data analysis. A majority (70%) of the sample was older than 30 years of age, it was predominately women (73%), and most respondents (85%) had completed at least some college.

RELIABILITY: Bettencourt (1997) reported an alpha of **.85** for the scale.

VALIDITY: The validity of the scale was not explicitly examined though evidence of dimensionality was reported. Bettencourt (1997) performed a confirmatory factor analysis (CFA) with items from this scale and two others, which provided support for the three-factor conceptualization.

ADMINISTRATION: The scale was self-administered as part of a much larger survey instrument (Bettencourt 1997). Higher scores on the scale meant that respondents engaged in behaviors that indicated a high level of participation with the improvement of service delivery.

MAJOR FINDINGS: A model of customer voluntary performance was developed and tested by Bettencourt (1997) in the context of grocery store shopping. The findings indicated that customers' commitment to a store has a significant positive relationship with their **participation**.

REFERENCES:
Bettencourt, Lance A. (1997), "Customer Voluntary Performance: Customers as Partners in Service Delivery," *JR*, 73 (3), 383–406.

SCALE ITEMS:

Strongly disagree   Strongly agree

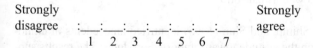

1   2   3   4   5   6   7

1. I let this store know of ways that they can better serve my needs.

2. I make constructive suggestions to this store on how to improve its service.

3. If I have a useful idea on how to improve service, I give it to someone at this store.

4. When I experience a problem at this store, I let someone know so they can improve service.

5. If I notice a problem, I inform an employee of this store even if it does not affect me (e.g., broken glass in an aisle, dairy items past expiration date).

6. If an employee at this store gives me good service, I let them know it.

7. If a price is incorrect to my advantage, I still advise someone at this store.

SCALE NAME: Patriotism/Conservatism

SCALE DESCRIPTION: Eleven seven-point Likert-type items purported to measure the degree to which a person expresses beliefs consistent with a conservative political position and exhibits loyalty to the country. The scale may be best described as measuring something more akin to *pseudopatriotism*, in that several of the items indicate a blind loyalty rather than a love of country based on critical understanding (Levison 1950, p. 107).

SCALE ORIGIN: Sharma, Shimp, and Shin (1995) state that they used a seven-item scale to measure **conservatism** (Ray 1983) and an eight-item scale to measure **patriotism** (Levison 1950). Their analysis indicated that the scales were not empirically distinct though they represented theoretically different constructs. Therefore, some items from both scales were combined, whereas others were deleted, to form a single unidimensional measure.

SAMPLES: Data were gathered from Korean consumers by Sharma, Shimp, and Shin (1995) using two sampling methods. Questionnaires were mailed to 1500 households taken from a economically diverse mailing list company's database. Usable surveys forms were returned by **125** people. The second method involved distributing 700 questionnaires to students at several schools in Seoul and in a southern Korean city. Completed questionnaires were received from **542** people. The samples were not significantly different in their demographic variables or response to dependent variables, so the authors chose to combine them for the analysis. The combined sample was 57% men, there was an average education level of slightly more than 13 years, and the mean age was 42 years.

RELIABILITY: Sharma, Shimp, and Shin (1995) performed confirmatory factor analysis (CFA) on the scale, as well as on others in the study. A reliability coefficient of **.71** for the **patriotism/conservatism** scale was reported on the basis of a holdout sample (n = 333).

VALIDITY: Sharma, Shimp, and Shin (1995) made a general claim of discriminant and convergent validity for all of their scales on the basis of the results of a CFA.

ADMINISTRATION: The scale was self-administered by respondents, along with other measures, in the questionnaire used by Sharma, Shimp, and Shin (1995). The scale also appears to have undergone a rather thorough translation process along with the entire survey instrument. Higher scores on the scale indicated that respondents were conservative as well as patriotic.

MAJOR FINDINGS: The study by Sharma, Shimp, and Shin (1995) identified antecedents of ethnocentricity and the influence of ethnocentricity on the attitude toward imported products. The results supported the hypothesis that people who were **patriotic** and **conservative** had greater ethnocentric tendencies than did those who were liberal and less patriotic.

REFERENCES:

Levinson, Daniel J. (1950), "Politico-Economic Ideology and Group Memberships in Relation to Ethnocentrism," in *The Authoritarian Personality*, T.W. Adorno, Else Frenkel-Brunswik, Daniel J. Levinson, and R. Nevitt Sanford, eds. New York: Harper & Row Publishers, 151-207.

Ray, J.J. (1983), "A Scale to Measure Conservatism of American Public Opinion," *Journal of Social Psychology*, 119 (April), 293–94.

Sharma, Subhash, Terence A. Shimp, and Jeongshin Shin (1995), "Consumer Ethnocentrism: A Test of Antecedents and Moderators," *JAMS*, 23 (Winter), 26–7.

SCALE ITEMS:*
Please respond to the following statements by circling a number from 1 to 7 according to these directions:

1 = Strongly disagree
2 = Moderately disagree
3 = Slightly disagree
4 = Neither agree nor disagree
5 = Slightly agree
6 = Moderately agree
7 = Strongly agree

1. School children should have plenty of discipline.

2. Erotic and obscene literature should be prohibited from public sale.

3. The government should make sure that our armed forces are stronger than those of _____ at all times.

4. People who show disrespect for their country's flag should be punished for it.

5. Patriotism and loyalty are the first and most important requirements of a good citizen.

6. Devoting oneself for one's country is worthwhile.

7. If I were to be born again, I would like to be born as a _____ again.

8. I would not work for a foreign company if the company's work may hurt my country's national interest.

9. We should be willing to fight for our country without questioning whether it is right or wrong.

10. If a person won't fight for his country, he deserves a lot worse than prison or work camp.

11. If my interest conflicts with my country's interest, I will gladly forsake my own interest.

*The first four items were taken from the conservatism scale, and the others were from the patriotism scale. The name of an important national enemy (e.g., North Korea) should be placed in item 3's blank. The term for the people one is studying should go in the blank in 7 (e.g., Korean).

SCALE NAME: Performance (Service Provider)

SCALE DESCRIPTION: An eight-item, seven-point Likert-type summated ratings scale measuring the degree to which a person who has just been involved in a service activity thinks that the person providing the service was effective and performed well. The activity studied by Price, Arnould, and Tierney (1995) was a river rafting trip, and the river guide was the service provider being directly evaluated by the customers.

SCALE ORIGIN: The scale was developed for the research reported by Price, Arnould, and Tierney (1995).

SAMPLES: Very little information was provided by Price, Arnould, and Tierney (1995) regarding their sample. The reader is referred to an earlier article (Arnould and Price 1993), which provides only a limited description of the sample. The respondents are described simply as a stratified random sample of people taking multiday river trips with one of three clients' rafting companies. A total of **137** clients filled out posttrip questionnaires, but only 97 of those had completed pretrip surveys.

RELIABILITY: An alpha of **.91** was reported by Price, Arnould, and Tierney (1995).

VALIDITY: No specific examination of the scale's validity was reported by Price, Arnould, and Tierney (1995). However, 17 items were factor analyzed and found to produce three separate factors. The eight items in this scale composed one of those factors, and their loadings ranged from .43 to .90.

ADMINISTRATION: The scale was self-administered by respondents as part of a larger survey after they finished a rafting trip (Arnould and Price 1993; Price, Arnould, and Tierney 1995). High scores on the scale suggested that respondents considered the service provider to have performed very well.

MAJOR FINDINGS: Building on the same basic study as Arnould and Price (1993), Price, Arnould, and Tierney (1995) found that, contrary to expectations, **performance of the service provider** did not have a significant impact on satisfaction. It did appear, however, that the impact of **performance** was mediated through positive affect response.

COMMENTS: Because of the unique references made in the items, some modification and retesting will be necessary before the scale is used for service encounters other than rafting.

REFERENCES:
Arnould, Eric J. and Linda L. Price (1993), "River Magic: Extraordinary Experience and the Extended Service Encounter," *JCR*, 20 (June), 24–45.
Price, Linda L., Eric J. Arnould, and Patrick Tierney (1995), "Going to Extremes: Managing Service Encounters and Assessing Provider Performance," *JM*, 59 (April), 83–97.

SCALE ITEMS:*

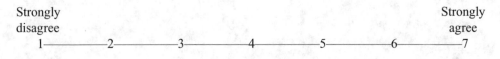

Strongly
disagree

Strongly
agree

1————2————3————4————5————6————7

The service provider:

1. Provided challenges.

2. Made things fun.

3. Created team spirit.

4. Enjoys his/her job.

5. Performed as expected.

6. Made me feel safe.

7. Took care of details.

8. Was a skilled boat handler.

*The response format was not specifically described by Price, Arnould, and Tierney (1995), but it appears it may have been something like what is shown here.

SCALE NAME: Personal Fable Coping Response (Drug Usage)

SCALE DESCRIPTION: Four five-point Likert-type items measuring a person's perception of the probability of the occurrence of negative events related to drug usage. The intent of the measure is to assess the extent of a respondent's sense of immortality in the face of the potential negative consequences of drug usage.

SCALE ORIGIN: Schoenbachler and Whittler (1996) drew inspiration for the scale from Elkind (1967) and Rogers and Mewborn (1976), but the scale itself is original to their study.

SAMPLES: Data were collected by Schoenbachler and Whittler (1996) from a sample of **371** seventh- and eight-grade students from a metropolitan middle school. No other information was provided about the sample.

RELIABILITY: An alpha of **.56** was reported for the scale (Schoenbachler and Whittler 1996).

VALIDITY: No examination of the scale's validity was reported by Schoenbachler and Whittler (1996).

ADMINISTRATION: The subjects completed the scale as part of a larger instrument that they filled out after being exposed to an experimental stimulus (Schoenbachler and Whittler 1996). As calculated by these authors, lower scores indicated that the respondents tended to construct personal fables about their immunity from the harmful effects of drug usage, such that they did not believe bad things would happen to them.

MAJOR FINDINGS: The purpose of the experiment by Schoenbachler and Whittler (1996) was to examine threat appeal advertising using the *ordered protection model.* Despite expectations, a physical threat did not produce a significantly greater **personal fable** coping response compared with a social threat. The authors speculated that this may have been due to the poor quality of the scale.

COMMENTS: Given the very low internal consistency of the scale, it is unlikely to be unidimensional. Further work is called for to test and improve the scale's psychometric quality before it is used again.

REFERENCES:
Elkind, David (1967), "Egocentrism in Adolescence," *Child Development*, 38, 1025–34.
Rogers, Ronald W. and C. Ronald Mewborn (1976), "Fear Appeals and Attitude Change: Effects of a Threat's Noxiousness, Probability of Occurrence, and the Efficacy of Coping Responses," *Journal of Personality and Social Psychology*, 34 (1), 54–61.
Schoenbachler, Denise D. (1997), personal correspondence.
——— and Tommy E. Whittler (1996), "Adolescent Processing of Social and Physical Threat Communications," *JA*, 25 (Winter), 37–54.

SCALE ITEMS:*
Directions: For each of the items below, circle the number that best described your opinion.

Strongly   Strongly
agree   disagree

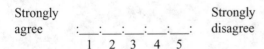

:___:___:___:___:
  1 2 3 4 5

1. Although many people become addicted to drugs, I really don't think I'd become addicted even if I used drugs.

2. If I use drugs a lot, my body will be harmed. **(r)**

3. Even though some people die from using drugs, I am sure that will never happen to me.

4. I am more likely than most of my friends to become addicted to drugs. **(r)**

*The directions and scale items were provided by Schoenbachler (1997).

#255 *Pleasantness*

SCALE NAME: Pleasantness

SCALE DESCRIPTION: Five bipolar adjectives with a seven-point response format purported to measure the feeling a person is experiencing at some point in time or immediately after exposure to some stimulus. Three versions were used by Broach, Page, and Wilson (1995): one to measure how subjects felt before the experimental manipulation (*prior pleasantness*), one to measure the effect of the treatment (*program pleasantness*), and one to measure the feeling evoked by an ad (*commercial pleasantness*).

SCALE ORIGIN: Broach, Page, and Wilson (1995) stated that the items for the scale were selected from Averill's (1975) semantic atlas of emotional words. However, use of the terms as a set in a summated format appears to be original to their own study. The scale was pretested with approximately 25 undergraduate students. The alphas for the version used with four different programs ranged from .85 to .96. Similarly, alphas for *the commercial pleasantness* version of the scale ranged from .90 to .96.

SAMPLES: Data were gathered by Broach, Page, and Wilson (1995) from students enrolled in undergraduate marketing or communications classes at a major Midwestern U.S. university. A set of 20 students evenly split on gender was placed in each of four treatment conditions for a total of **80** subjects. Students received a nominal financial compensation for their participation, and the 11 subjects who guessed the study's purpose were replaced.

RELIABILITY: Alphas ranging from **.86** to **.97** (*prior pleasantness*), **.84** to **.94** (*program pleasantness*), and **.85** to **.97** (*commercial pleasantness*) were reported for the scale (Broach, Page, and Wilson 1995).

VALIDITY: No examination of the scale's validity was reported by Broach, Page, and Wilson (1995).

ADMINISTRATION: The *prior pleasantness* version of the scale was completed by subjects before they were exposed to a 10-minute program and four 30-second commercials. Following the program, they filled out the *program pleasantness* version of the scale and completed the *commercial pleasantness* scale for each of the four commercials (Broach, Page, and Wilson 1995). Higher scores on the scale indicated that subjects felt very positive at that moment.

MAJOR FINDINGS: The purpose of the experiment conducted by Broach, Page, and Wilson (1995) was to examine the impact of television programs on viewers' perceptions of ads. Among the findings was that a set of emotionally neutral commercials were perceived to be significantly more **pleasant** by those subjects who had just viewed high arousal, **pleasant** programs than by those who has seen high arousal, **unpleasant** programs.

REFERENCES:

Averill, James R. (1975), "A Semantic Atlas of Emotional Concepts," *JSAS Catalogue of Selected Documents in Psychology*, 330.

Broach, V. Carter, Jr., Thomas J. Page Jr., and R. Dale Wilson (1995), "Television Programming and Its Influence on Viewers' Perceptions of Commercials: The Role of Program Arousal and Pleasantness," *JA*, 24 (Winter), 45–54.

SCALE ITEMS:

Scale stem for version measuring *prior pleasantness*: "At this time I feel . . ."

Scale stem for version measuring *program pleasantness*: "Did the program as a whole make you feel . . ."

Scale stem for version measuring *commercial pleasantness*: "Did the commercial as a whole make you feel . . ."

1. Negative   :__:__:__:__:__:__: Positive
              -3   -2   -1   0   1   2   3

2. Bad   :__:__:__:__:__:__: Good
              -3   -2   -1   0   1   2   3

3. Awful   :__:__:__:__:__:__: Nice
              -3   -2   -1   0   1   2   3

4. Sad   :__:__:__:__:__:__: Happy
              -3   -2   -1   0   1   2   3

5. Unpleasant   :__:__:__:__:__:__: Pleasant
              -3   -2   -1   0   1   2   3

SCALE NAME: Pleasure

SCALE DESCRIPTION: A multi-item, summated ratings scale measuring a respondent's **pleasure**-related emotional reaction to an environmental stimulus. Holbrook and colleagues (1984) and Donovan and colleagues (1994) used a six-item, semantic differential version of the scale. Hui and Tse (1996) used four of the semantic differentials. Four of the positive anchors were used by themselves in a different version of the scale by Dawson, Bloch, and Ridgway (1990). Mano and Oliver (1993) used four positive items and a five-point response scale.

SCALE ORIGIN: This scale is taken from the work of Mehrabian and Russell (1974). On the basis of previous work by others as well as their own research, they proposed that there are three factors that compose all emotional reactions to environmental stimuli. They referred to the three factors as **pleasure**, arousal, and dominance. A series of studies was used to develop measures of each factor. A study of the "final" set of items used 214 University of California undergraduates, each of whom used the scales to evaluate a different subset of six situations. (The analysis was based, therefore, on 1284 observations.) A principal components factor analysis with oblique rotation was used, and the expected three factors emerged. **Pleasure**, arousal, and dominance explained 27%, 23%, and 14% of the available evidence, respectively. Scores on the **pleasure** scale had correlations of −.07 and .03 with arousal and dominance, respectively.

The set of items used by Mano and Oliver (1993) appears to have been used first as a summated scale by Mano (1991). With 224 college students, the scale was reported to have an alpha of .82. A factor analysis indicated that three of the four items had strong loadings on the same factor, and a cluster analysis grouped all four items together.

SELECTED SAMPLES: Bateson and Hui (1992) conducted two separate studies, one described as a laboratory experiment and the other a field quasi-experiment. The subjects were recruited from the streets of a southern England coastal town and randomly assigned to either a slide or a video setting. Complete data were received from **119** persons (60 with slides and 59 videos). In the second study, passengers in a major train station in London were asked to fill out a questionnaire regarding their experience at the train ticket office. Usable surveys were received back from **92** people.

The sample collected by Dawson, Bloch, and Ridgway (1990) came from a large arts and crafts market in a major West Coast city. Shoppers were approached over four summer days by trained survey administrators and asked to participate. Those who participated were paid $1. The analysis was based on data from **278** respondents. The only significant difference noted between the sample and that of the surrounding standard metropolitan statistical area (SMSA) was that the former contained more women.

Donovan and colleagues (1994) gathered data from 30 female shoppers in each of two discount department stores. The stores were located near each other in a low- to middle-class socioeconomic neighborhood. Shoppers were approached at random on entering the store and asked if they would agree to participate. Only shoppers who were in the 18- to 35-year-old age range were included to reduce the heterogeneity of the sample.

Simpson, Horton, and Brown (1996) gathered data from **169** students from two neighboring Southern U.S. universities. The sample was evenly split on gender, and most respondents were European American (77.3%) and between 18 and 25 years of age (80%).

SELECTED RELIABILITIES: Specific reliabilities are provided for the selected studies described in the "Samples" and "Major Findings" sections:
.86 (Bateson and Hui 1992);
.72 (Dawson, Bloch, and Ridgway 1990);
.88 (Donovan et al. 1994); and
.96 (Simpson, Horton, and Brown 1996).

VALIDITY: Some idea of the scale's convergent validity can be taken from correlations between it and another scale used to measure the same construct (Bateson and Hui 1992, p. 278). In three different situations, the correlations were .65 or higher, which provides evidence that the two measures were tapping into the same construct.

Dawson, Bloch, and Ridgway (1990) performed an exploratory factor analysis on the items composing this scale, as well as three other items composing an arousal scale. Although the items loaded highest on their respective factors, one item (happy) had split loadings.

A principal components factor analysis performed by Donovan and colleagues (1994) indicated that all six of the **pleasure**-related items loaded highest on the same dimension and low on one related to arousal.

ADMINISTRATION: The scale was self-administered by subjects, along with other measures, after they were exposed to experimental stimuli in the studies conducted by Bateson and Hui (1992) and Hui and Tse (1996). The scale was self-administered as part of a larger survey instrument in the field study conducted by Dawson, Bloch, and Ridgway (1990). Donovan and colleagues (1994) had respondents complete the scale, along with other measures, after shopping in a store. Simpson, Horton, and Brown (1996) used the scale with respondents after they had been exposed to ads. Higher scores on the scale suggested that respondents were happy with some specified stimulus, whereas lower scores implied that they were displeased with the stimulus.

SELECTED FINDINGS: Bateson and Hui (1992) investigated the ecological validity of slide and video presentations in controlled (laboratory) settings. The illustration of ecological validity made use of most of the same variables as used in the study by Hui and Bateson (1991) and produced similar findings. In particular, perceived crowding and control both seemed to have been significant effects on **pleasure**.

Dawson, Bloch, and Ridgway (1990) investigated the role played by shopping motives in shaping the emotions triggered during a retail shopping experience. The clearest finding involving the construct measured by this scale was that the **pleasure** experienced by shoppers at the market had a significant positive relationship with their product-related shopping motives and, to a lesser extent, their experience-related motives.

The purpose of the study by Donovan and colleagues (1994) was to understand the emotions experienced while shopping and their effect on shopping behavior. The authors concluded that **pleasure** was positively associated with time spent in the store, as well as with unplanned spending.

The effect of male nudity in advertising was examined by Simpson, Horton, and Brown (1996). Not surprisingly, the results showed that women reacted more favorably to the male models than did men, regardless of the level of dress. However, the level of dress associated with the most **pleasure** from the female respondents was in the "suggestive" (no shirt) ad rather than the one with full nudity.

COMMENTS: As noted, this scale was originally developed along with two other scales, arousal and dominance. Although scored separately, they are typically used together in a study.

See also Havlena and Holbrook (1986), Hui and Bateson (1991), Menon and Kahn (1995), Mitchell, Kahn, and Knasko (1995), and Nyer (1997).

REFERENCES:

Bateson, John E.G. and Michael K. Hui (1992), "The Ecological Validity of Photographic Slides and Videotapes in Simulating the Service Setting," *JCR*, 19 (September), 271–81.

Dawson, Scott, Peter H. Bloch, and Nancy M. Ridgway (1990), "Shopping Motives, Emotional States, and Retail Outcomes," *JR*, 66 (Winter), 408–27.

Donovan, Robert J., John R. Rossiter, Gilian Marcoolyn, and Andrew Nesdale (1994), "Store Atmosphere and Purchasing Behavior," *JR*, 70 (3), 283–94.

Havlena, William J. and Morris B. Holbrook (1986), "The Varieties of Consumption Experience: Comparing Two Typologies of Emotion in Consumer Behavior," *JCR*, 13 (December), 394–404.

Holbrook, Morris B., Robert W. Chestnut, Terence A. Oliva, and Eric A. Greenleaf (1984), "Play as a Consumption Experience: The Roles of Emotions, Performance, and Personality in the Enjoyment of Games," *JCR*, 11(September), 728–39.

Hui, Michael K. and John E.G. Bateson (1991), "Perceived Control and the Effects of Crowding and Consumer Choice on the Service Experience," *JCR*, 18 (September), 174–84.

——— and David K. Tse (1996), "What to Tell Consumers in Waits of Different Lengths: An Integrative Model of Service Evaluation," *JM*, 60 (April), 81–90.

Mano, Haim (1991), "The Structure and Intensity of Emotional Experiences: Method and Context Convergence," *Multivariate Behavioral Research*, 26 (3), 389–411.

——— and Richard L. Oliver (1993), "Assessing the Dimensionality and Structure of the Consumption Experience: Evaluation, Feeling, and Satisfaction," *JCR*, 20 (December), 451–66.

Mehrabian, Albert and James A. Russell (1974), *An Approach to Environmental Psychology*. Cambridge, MA: The MIT Press.

Menon, Satya and Barbara E. Kahn (1995), "The Impact of Context on Variety Seeking in Product Choices," *JCR*, 22 (December), 285–95.

Mitchell, Deborah, Barbara E. Kahn, and Susan C. Knasko (1995), "There's Something in the Air: Effects of Congruent or Incongruent Ambient Odor on Consumer Decision Making," *JCR*, 22 (September), 229–38.

Nyer, Prashanth U. (1997), "A Study of the Relationships Between Cognitive Appraisals and Consumption Emotions," *JAMS*, 25 (Fall), 296–304.

Olney, Thomas J., Morris B. Holbrook, and Rajeev Batra (1991), "Consumer Responses to Advertising: The Effects of Ad Content, Emotions, and Attitude Toward the Ad on Viewing Time," *JCR*, 17 (March), 440–53.

Simpson, Penny M., Steve Horton, and Gene Brown (1996), "Male Nudity in Advertisements: A Modified Replication and Extension of Gender and Product Effects," *JAMS*, 24 (Summer), 257–62.

SCALE ITEMS:*

Rate your emotions according to the way the _____ made you feel.

1. Happy   ___:___:___:___:___:___:___   Unhappy
               7   6   5   4   3   2   1

2. Pleased   ___:___:___:___:___:___:___   Annoyed
               7   6   5   4   3   2   1

3. Satisfied   ___:___:___:___:___:___:___   Unsatisfied
               7   6   5   4   3   2   1

4. Contented   ___:___:___:___:___:___:___   Melancholic
               7   6   5   4   3   2   1

5. Hopeful   ___:___:___:___:___:___:___   Despairing
               7   6   5   4   3   2   1

6. Relaxed   ___:___:___:___:___:___:___   Bored
               7   6   5   4   3   2   1

*This is a possible scale stem that can be used with the items. The items and format shown were used by Holbrook and colleagues (1984), Donovan and colleagues (1994), Olney, Holbrook, and Batra (1991), and Simpson, Horton, and Brown (1996). Hui and Tse (1996) used items 1–3 and 6. The version used by Dawson, Bloch, and Ridgway (1990) used just the positive anchors of items 1, 3, 4, and 6 and a five-point response scale ranging from "does not describe at all" to "describes a great deal." Likewise, Mano and Oliver (1993) used just the positive anchors for items 1–3 and the item "in a good mood." The actual items used by Bateson and Hui (1992) were not explicitly described.

SCALE NAME: Pleasure

SCALE DESCRIPTION: Four six-point descriptors of a person's pleasure-related emotional reaction to an environmental stimulus.

SCALE ORIGIN: This scale is based on the work of Mehrabian and Russell (1974) but has been modified in several ways. Mehrabian and Russell's (1974) scale had six bipolar adjectives (see #256), whereas this one by Babin and Darden (1995) used two of their positive descriptors and one of their negative descriptors, and another negative descriptor was new (*disgusted*). The latter also used a six-point "felt" response scale, as noted subsequently.

SAMPLES: Data were gathered by Babin and Darden (1995) by intercepting shoppers as they left one of the ten top stores in a major Southeastern U.S. regional mall. Respondents were interviewed one at a time, and a small incentive was provided for their participation. The sample was considered to be representative of the mall's shoppers. The analysis appears to have been based on data from **118** shoppers.

RELIABILITY: An alpha of **.91** was reported for the scale (Babin and Darden 1995). The construct reliability was .90, and variance extracted was .69.

VALIDITY: The results of a confirmatory factor analysis supported the measurement model in the study (Babin and Darden 1995). This provides some limited evidence of the scale's unidimensionality, as well as its convergent and discriminant validities.

ADMINISTRATION: The scale was apparently administered to respondents by interviewers, along with many other items, in a questionnaire (Babin and Darden 1995). Higher scores on the scale suggested that respondents experienced a strong feeling of happiness (pleasure) on exposure to some specified stimulus.

MAJOR FINDINGS: The purpose of the study by Babin and Darden (1995) was to examine the role of self-regulation as a moderator of relationships between shopping emotions and shopping experience evaluations. Among the findings was that **pleasure** had significant positive impacts on resource expenditures and utilitarian shopping value.

REFERENCES:

Babin, Barry J. and William R. Darden (1995), "Consumer Self-Regulation in a Retail Environment," *JR*, 71 (1), 47–70.

Mehrabian, Albert and James A. Russell (1974), *An Approach to Environmental Psychology*. Cambridge, MA: The MIT Press.

SCALE ITEMS:*

Thinking back on how you felt while shopping in this store, please use the following scale to describe how you felt.

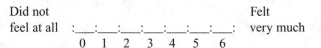

Did not   Felt
feel at all   :__:__:__:__:__:__: very much
           0   1   2   3   4   5   6

1. Happy

2. Satisfied

3. Disgusted **(r)**

4. Annoyed **(r)**

*Although the actual scale stem was not provided in the article, this reconstruction is based on the description that was given.

SCALE NAME: Prepurchase Planning (Grocery Shopping)

SCALE DESCRIPTION: Five seven-point items that measure the degree to which a consumer develops clear purchase intentions before visiting the grocery store.

SCALE ORIGIN: Although it was not clear from the article by Putrevu and Ratchford (1997), some of the work on the scales was conducted earlier in a dissertation by Putrevu (1992).

SAMPLES: Data were gathered by Putrevu and Ratchford (1997) using a mail survey to a random sample of grocery shoppers in a standard metropolitan statistical area (SMSA) in the northeastern United States. A total of **500** responses was used in the main analysis, and demographics of the final sample were similar to those of the population of interest.

RELIABILITY: An alpha of **.72** was reported for the scale (Putrevu and Ratchford 1997).

VALIDITY: Although the authors stated in general that the scales showed evidence of convergent, discriminant, and content validity, no details of the analyses were provided (Putrevu and Ratchford 1997).

ADMINISTRATION: The scale was part of a larger mail questionnaire (Putrevu and Ratchford 1997). Higher scores on the scale suggested that a consumer was very organized and developed shopping plans before going to the grocery store.

MAJOR FINDINGS: Putrevu and Ratchford (1997) examined a dynamic model of consumer search behavior that includes human capital. The results showed that there was a strong positive relationship between **prepurchase planning** and external search activity.

REFERENCES:
Putrevu, Sanjay (1992), "A Theory of Search and Its Empirical Investigation," doctoral dissertation, State University of New York at Buffalo.
———— and Brian T. Ratchford (1997), "A Model of Search Behavior with an Application to Grocery Shopping," *JR*, 73 (4), 463–86.

SCALE ITEMS:

Never :___:___:___:___:___:___:___: Always
      1   2   3   4   5   6   7

1. I prepare a shopping list before going grocery shopping.

2. I pre-sort my coupons before going grocery shopping.

3. I know what products I am going to buy before going to the supermarket.

4. I am a well organized grocery shopper.

5. Before going to the supermarket, I plan my purchases based on the specials available that week.

SCALE NAME: Pressures to be Thin

SCALE DESCRIPTION: Eleven seven-point Likert-type statements that measure the extent to which a person believes that society pressures people to be good looking. The scale seems to be especially focused on women being pressured by the media to have thin-looking figures.

SCALE ORIGIN: Although not explicitly stated by Netemeyer, Burton, and Lichtenstein (1995), the scale is original to their study (Netemeyer 1997).

SAMPLES: Various samples were collected and used by Netemeyer, Burton, and Lichtenstein (1995) in the process of validating some other scales. The thinness scale was only used in a study based on data collected from **43** professional fashion models.

RELIABILITY: An alpha of **.86** was found for the scale (Netemeyer 1997; Netemeyer, Burton, and Lichtenstein 1995).

VALIDITY: The validity of the scale was not examined by Netemeyer, Burton, and Lichtenstein (1995).

ADMINISTRATION: The scale appears to have been part of a larger questionnaire that was self-administered by respondents (Netemeyer, Burton, and Lichtenstein 1995). Higher scores on the scale indicated that respondents strongly believed that women in American culture are pressured to have thin bodies.

MAJOR FINDINGS: Netemeyer, Burton, and Lichtenstein (1995) investigated vanity and developed four scales for its measurement. Most of the article discussed the results of the rather extensive validation process. Correlations between **pressures to be thin** and each of the vanity scales were insignificant.

REFERENCES:
Netemeyer, Richard G. (1997), personal correspondence.
———, Scot Burton, and Donald R. Lichtenstein (1995), "Trait Aspects of Vanity: Measurement and Relevance to Consumer Behavior," *JCR*, 21 (March), 612–26.

SCALE ITEMS:

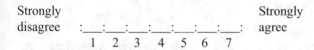

Strongly disagree :___:___:___:___:___:___:___: Strongly agree
 1 2 3 4 5 6 7

1. Today's society places pressure on women to maintain a thin body.

2. Thin women receive greater social rewards than women who are not thin.

3. There are no cultural pressures for a woman to be thin. **(r)**

4. There is definitely a cultural expectation for women to be thin.

5. The media (e.g., advertisements, TV shows, magazines) favors women with thin bodies.

6. Many people feel pressured to try to look like the people portrayed in fashion advertisements and magazines.

7. Society places pressure on people to be physically attractive.

8. Good-looking people receive greater social rewards than people who are not good-looking.

9. There is definitely a cultural expectation for people to be physically attractive.

10. The media (e.g. advertisements, TV shows, magazines) favors people who are good looking.

11. There are no cultural pressures for people to be physically appealing. **(r)**

SCALE NAME: Price Consciousness

SCALE DESCRIPTION: Three five-point Likert-type items that are intended to measure a shopping orientation characterized by a consumer's focus on buying products that are low priced, on sale, or at least good values for the money.

SCALE ORIGIN: Shim and Gehrt (1996) used a modified version of a scale developed by Sproles and Kendall (1986). The latter created an eight-factor model of what they called *consumer decision making styles* but what many others in marketing (e.g., Shim and Gehrt 1996) would view as *shopping orientations*. Shim and Gehrt (1996) used the three items identified by Sproles and Kendall (1986) and added a fourth item to improve reliability. The latter reported an alpha of .48 for their three-item scale.

SAMPLES: Shim and Gehrt (1996) collected data from high school students in a Southwestern U.S. state. Twenty-nine principals agreed to participate, and their schools apparently represented many if not all counties in the state. Principals were given instructions as to which classes to use (by level) and how many students from each class were needed. Some 1954 usable surveys were returned from a sample that was 61.3% girls and that had a mean age of 16 years. However, the study focused only on data from **1846** students who were white (56%), Hispanic (32%), or Native American (12%).

RELIABILITY: An alpha of **.68** was reported for the scale by Shim and Gehrt (1996).

VALIDITY: No examination of the scale's validity was reported by Shim and Gehrt (1996).

ADMINISTRATION: Data were gathered in a classroom setting in which students filled out the scale as part of a larger survey instrument (Shim and Gehrt 1996). Higher scores on the scale indicated that respondents were very price sensitive and attracted to low prices.

MAJOR FINDINGS: The study by Shim and Gehrt (1996) examined differences in shopping orientations among high school students that could be linked to ethnicity. The results showed that white students were significantly more **price conscious** than Hispanic students, who were in turn significantly more **price conscious** than Native American students.

REFERENCES:
Shim, Soyeon and Kenneth C. Gehrt (1996), "Hispanic and Native American Adolescents: An Exploratory Study of Their Approach to Shopping," *JR*, 72 (3), 307–24.
Sproles, George B. and Elizabeth L. Kendall (1986), "A Methodology for Profiling Consumers' Decision-Making Styles," *Journal of Consumer Affairs*, 20 (Winter), 267–79.

SCALE ITEMS:*

Strongly   Strongly
disagree   :__:__:__:__:__: agree
                1   2   3   4   5

1. I buy as much as possible at sale prices.

2. The lower price products are usually my choice.

3. I look carefully to find the best value for the money.

*Sproles and Kendall (1986) used an unidentified fourth item.

SCALE NAME: Price Dispersion (Grocery Stores)

SCALE DESCRIPTION: Five five-point Likert-type statements measuring the degree to which a consumer believes that prices charged by the different grocery stores in the local area (city, town) vary considerably.

SCALE ORIGIN: Although Urbany, Dickson, and Kalapurakal (1996) may have drawn inspiration from previous work, the scale appears to be original to their study.

SAMPLES: The data used by Urbany, Dickson, and Kalapurakal (1996) were collected as part of a larger survey by a leading market research firm. Telephone interviews were conducted with the primary grocery shoppers from households selected at random. Respondents were requested to participate in a second stage that would involve a mail survey. The survey yielded **343** usable responses. The average age of respondents was 44.7 years, and they were overwhelmingly women (83%).

RELIABILITY: An alpha of **.82** was reported for the scale by Urbany, Dickson, and Kalapurakal (1996).

VALIDITY: Urbany, Dickson, and Kalapurakal (1996) tested the discriminant validity of the **price dispersion** scale using pairwise confirmatory factor analysis and six other measures. The evidence of three separate tests on each of the six pairs supported a claim of discriminant validity.

ADMINISTRATION: The data analyzed by Urbany, Dickson, and Kalapurakal (1996) were gathered in a mail survey. Higher scores suggested that respondents believed there was a great deal of price dispersion among the grocery stores in their shopping area.

MAJOR FINDINGS: Urbany, Dickson, and Kalapurakal (1996) developed a model of price search for the retail grocery industry that included a relatively complete accounting of economic and noneconomic returns, as well as search costs. The findings showed that perceived **price dispersion** accounted for a significant amount of variance in self-reported price comparison behavior.

COMMENTS: Urbany, Dickson, and Kalapurakal (1996) reported a mean response of 3.37 on the scale.

REFERENCES:
Urbany, Joel E., Peter R. Dickson, and Rosemary Kalapurakal (1996), "Price Search in the Retail Grocery Market," *JM*, 60 (April), 91–104.

SCALE ITEMS:*

Strongly   Strongly
disagree   :___:___:___:___:___: agree
                 1   2   3   4   5

1. A cart full of the same groceries bought from each of my local grocery stores will cost about the same. **(r)**

2. Prices of individual items may vary between stores, but overall, there isn't much difference in the prices between _____ grocery stores. **(r)**

3. Some grocery stores in _____ have a lot lower prices than others.

4. The price of meats and produce varies a lot between _____ grocery stores.

5. The price of individual items often varies a lot between stores.

*The name of the city should be placed in the blanks.

SCALE NAME: Price Dispersion (Grocery Stores/Products)

SCALE DESCRIPTION: Thirteen seven-point Likert-type items that measure the degree to which a consumer believes that prices for different brands of the same product vary a lot within grocery stores as well as across stores.

SCALE ORIGIN: Although not clear from the article by Putrevu and Ratchford (1997), some of the work on the scales was conducted earlier in a dissertation by Putrevu (1992).

SAMPLES: Data were gathered by Putrevu and Ratchford (1997) using a mail survey to a random sample of grocery shoppers in a standard metropolitan statistical area (SMSA) in the Northeastern United States. A total of **500** responses were used in the main analysis, and demographics of the final sample were similar to those of the population of interest.

RELIABILITY: An alpha of **.73** was reported for the scale (Putrevu and Ratchford 1997).

VALIDITY: Although the authors stated in general that the scales showed evidence of convergent, discriminant, and content validity, no details of the analyses were provided (Putrevu and Ratchford 1997).

ADMINISTRATION: The scale was part of a larger mail questionnaire (Putrevu and Ratchford 1997). Higher scores on the scale suggested that consumers believed that prices vary a lot from brand to brand and store to store.

MAJOR FINDINGS: Putrevu and Ratchford (1997) examined a dynamic model of consumer search behavior that includes human capital. The results indicated that the greater the perceived **price dispersion**, the greater was the amount of external search.

COMMENTS:

The relatively low internal consistency for this large of a scale suggests that the set may not be unidimensional. Indeed, an examination of the items themselves indicates that there appear to be two factors: one that deals with dispersion across brands and one that focuses on dispersion across stores. The dimensionality of this scale should be carefully examined before further use is made of the scale.

REFERENCES:
Putrevu, Sanjay (1992), "A Theory of Search and Its Empirical Investigation," doctoral dissertation, State University of New York at Buffalo.
———— and Brian T. Ratchford (1997), "A Model of Search Behavior with an Application to Grocery Shopping," *JR*, 73 (4), 463–86.

SCALE ITEMS:

Strongly   Strongly
disagree   :___:___:___:___:___:___: agree
                1   2   3   4   5   6   7

1. There is not much difference between different brands. **(r)**

2. All brands of grocery products are alike except for small differences. **(r)**

3. In my opinion, there are several important differences among various brands of products.

4. There is a large price difference between the different brands of grocery products.

5. All brands of grocery products cost about the same. **(r)**

6. The prices of different brands vary a lot.

7. The prices of the different brands change frequently.

8. The prices of different brands rarely change. **(r)**

9. One can save a lot by buying groceries at 2 or 3 supermarkets.

10. No supermarket offers the lowest prices on all grocery products.

11. One can get a better buy of grocery products by shopping at more than one supermarket.

12. Some supermarkets are better for some products while others are better for other products.

13. To get the best selection of grocery products one needs to shop at more than one supermarket.

#263 *Price Perception*

SCALE NAME: Price Perception

SCALE DESCRIPTION: Four open-ended questions measuring a consumer's perceptions of various aspects of a product's price. See "Scale Origin" for more detail.

SCALE ORIGIN: Folkes and Wheat (1995) created a scale that was intended to capture three aspects of price perception: expected price, fair price, and reservation price. Expected price is supposed to get at what consumers think they *will* have to pay for a product, whereas fair price taps into what price consumers think *should* be charged for a product. Reservation price refers to the *most* a consumer is willing to spend on a product.

SAMPLES: Two experiments were conducted by Folkes and Wheat (1995). Data were collected for Experiment 1 from **34** undergraduate business students. In Experiment 2, data were gathered from **45** undergraduate business students different from those in the first experiment.

RELIABILITY: Folkes and Wheat (1995) reported alphas of **.92** and **.91** for the scale in Experiments 1 and 2, respectively.

VALIDITY: No examination of the scale's validity was reported by Folkes and Wheat (1995).

ADMINISTRATION: Subjects in the experiments by Folkes and Wheat (1995) were asked to imagine that they wanted to buy a certain product. Information about the product was presented to them and was followed by a questionnaire. The questions composing this scale were among those on the questionnaire. It would appear that the answers to the four questions were averaged, and higher amounts indicated that respondents believed the product to have a higher price.

MAJOR FINDINGS: The purpose of the experiments conducted by Folkes and Wheat (1995) was to investigate how different types of promotions affected consumer **price perceptions**. Among the findings was that rebates lowered **price perceptions** significantly less than either coupons or sales.

COMMENTS: It is not at all clear that this scale is unidimensional because the questions were designed to tap into different aspects of product pricing. Future usage should be conducted with this concern in mind.

REFERENCES:
Folkes, Valerie and Rita D. Wheat (1995), "Consumers' Price Perceptions of Promoted Products," *JR*, 71 (3), 317–28.

SCALE ITEMS:

1. Asssuming that you wished to purchase this product, what do you think would be the most you would pay for this product? _____

2. What would you consider a fair price for the product? _____

3. What do you think would be a reasonable price for the product? _____

4. What would you expect to have to pay for it? _____

SCALE NAME: Price Consciousness

SCALE DESCRIPTION: The scale is composed of various, Likert-type items measuring the degree to which a consumer focuses on sales and trying to get the "best price."

SCALE ORIGIN: The items that follow and/or the inspiration for them came from an early, classic study of psychographics by Wells and Tigert (1971). One thousand questionnaires were mailed to home-maker members of the Market Facts mail panel. In addition to gathering demographic, product use, and media data, the survey contained 300 statements that have served as the basis for the construction of many lifestyle-related scales ever since. Although the four items for this scale are reported in that article, they were not analyzed as a multi-item scale. The purpose of the article was to explain how psychographics could improve on mere demographic descriptions of target audiences and product users. No psychometric information was reported.

One of the first uses of the items as a multi-item scale was by Darden and Perreault (1976). Analysis was based on self-administered questionnaires completed by 278 suburban housewives randomly selected in Athens, Ga. A split-half reliability of .70 was reported for the scale. Price consciousness did *not* significantly differentiate between the outshopping groups.

SAMPLES: The survey form used by Barak and Stern (1985/1986) was personally distributed to and collected from an age-quota sample of women living in the greater New York metropolitan area. The study focused on the **567** responding women who categorized themselves as either "young" or "middle-aged" and stated an age in years between 25 and 69.

Two mailing lists were used to collect data in Dickerson and Gentry's (1983) study. One was a list of *Psychology Today* subscribers, and the other was a list of members in computer clubs. The former was used to reach nonadopters of computers, whereas the latter was used to reach PC adopters. Analysis was based on a total of **639** questionnaires. Results from a second mailing to nonrespondents indicated that their demographic makeup was not significantly different from respondents'. Compared with 1980 census data, the sample was younger and more up upscale than the general population.

Donthu and Gilliland (1996) used trained interviewers to call 1000 households in a large city telephone directory. Interviews were successfully completed with adults in **368** of those households. Although some demographic information was employed in the analysis, the data were not reported in such a way that the sample as a whole can be clearly described.

Mittal (1994) gathered data from female members of six voluntary organizations, as well as from mall intercepts. A total of 184 people provided complete survey questionnaires. Most of the respondents were white (85%), married (71%), and at least 35 years of age (63%). Although it did not mirror the U.S. population, the sample included a wide variety of demographic categories.

The data were gathered by Tat and Bejou (1994) using a telephone survey in Memphis, Tenn. The telephone number prefixes were deliberately chosen for black neighborhoods to ensure blacks composed a substantial portion of the sample . Interviews were conducted with **326** individuals who identified themselves as doing the majority of the shopping for their household. Ultimately, 37.2% of the respondents were black. Forty-one percent of the total sample were married, 39% came from households with four or more members, 33% were between the ages of 25 and 34 years, 45% had at least some college level education, and 41% had incomes greater than $30,000. Consult the article for a detailed breakdown of demographic information by race.

RELIABILITY: An alpha of **.67** was reported by Dickerson and Gentry (1983). Barak and Stern (1985/1986) say only that the scale's alpha was above **.5**. The version of the scale used by Donthu and Gilliland (1996) was reported to have an alpha of **.72**. The construct reliability (LISREL) for the version of the scale used by Mittal (1994) was reported to be **.69**.

An alpha of **.65** was reported for the scale used by Tat and Bejou (1994). Alphas of .67 and .66 were reported for blacks and whites, respectively. The internal consistency of the scale is somewhat low, and care should be exercised in its use.

VALIDITY: The validity of the scale was not specifically addressed by Mittal (1994) except to note that the tests that were conducted provided support for discriminant validity. Tat and Bejou (1994) did not directly test the validity of the scale. However, they performed a couple of factor analyses on a total set of 24 items to purify the scales they developed. Factor loadings for the overall sample were respectable, but the loading of item 5 was rather low for blacks (.40) compared with whites (.74).

ADMINISTRATION: In each study, the scale was part of a larger self-administered survey instrument. Higher scores on the scale suggested that respondents were very sensitive about prices and that it affected how they shop.

MAJOR FINDINGS: **Price consciousness** was found to discriminate significantly between the female baby-boomer and preboomer generations (Barak and Stern 1985/1986). In contrast, Dickerson and Gentry (1983) failed to find significant evidence that **price consciousness** discriminated between adopters and nonadopters of home computers.

Donthu and Gilliland (1996) profiled infomercial shoppers and found that they were significantly more **price conscious** than those who had never purchased goods from infomercials.

The study by Mittal (1994) proposed that demographics are poor predictors of coupon usage, and instead, he illustrated the value of three layers of mediating variables. Among the findings was that those who were financially well-off tended to be less **price conscious**, whereas those who expressed high pride in being homemakers were very **price conscious**.

The purpose of the study by Tat and Bejou (1994) was to compare the differences between blacks and whites on motives for using coupons. The results suggested that blacks are more **price conscious** than whites.

COMMENTS: It is noteworthy that this scale, in its variety of forms, consistently displays low reliability. A possible reason for this is that three slightly different subconstructs are being measured, such as comparison shopping, inspection of prices of products at the store, and watching ads for sales. Some attention should be given to this issue, along with some redevelopmental effort, if the scale is to be used again.

See also Arora (1985), Burnett and Bush (1986), Heslop, Moran, and Cousineau (1981), Korgaonkar (1984), and Schnaars and Schiffman (1984) for other uses or variations on the measure.

REFERENCES:
Arora, Raj (1985), "Involvement: Its Measurement for Retail Store Research," *JAMS*, 13 (Spring), 229–41.
Barak, Benny and Barbara Stern (1985/1986), "Women's Age in Advertising: An Examination of Two Consumer Age Profiles," *JAR,* 25 (December/January), 38–47.
Burnett, John J. and Alan J. Bush (1986), "Profiling the Yuppies," *JAR*, 26 (April/May), 27–35.
Darden, William R. and William D. Perreault Jr. (1976), "Identifying Interurban Shoppers: Multiproduct Purchase Patterns and Segmentation Profiles," *JMR*, 13 (February), 51–60.
Dickerson, Mary D. and James W. Gentry (1983), "Characteristics of Adopters and Non-Adopters of Home Computers," *JCR*, 10 (September), 225–35.
Donthu, Naveen and David Gilliland (1996), "The Infomercial Shopper," *JAR*, 36 (March/April), 69–76.
Heslop, Louise A., Lori Moran, and Amy Cousineau (1981), "Consciousness in Energy Conservation Behavior: An Exploratory Study," *JCR*, 8 (December), 299–305.

Korgaonkar, Pradeep K. (1984), "Consumer Shopping Orientations, Non-Store Retailers, and Consumers' Patronage Intentions: A Multivariate Investigation," *JAMS*, 12 (Winter), 11–22.

Mittal, Banwari (1994), "An Integrated Framework for Relating Diverse Consumer Characteristics to Supermarket Coupon Redemption," *JMR*, 31 (November), 533–44.

Tat, Peter K. and David Bejou (1994), "Examining Black Consumer Motives for Coupon Usage," *JAR*, 34 (March/April), 29–35.

Wells, William D. and Douglas Tigert (1971), "Activities, Interests, and Opinions," *JAR*, 11 (August), 27–35.

SCALE ITEMS:

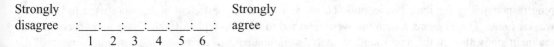

Strongly
disagree   :___:___:___:___:___:___: Strongly agree
              1   2   3   4   5   6

1. I shop a lot for "specials."

2. I find myself checking the prices in the grocery store even for small items.

3. I usually watch the advertisements for announcements of sales.

4. A person can save a lot of money by shopping around for bargains.

5. I check the prices even for inexpensive items.

6. I pay attention to sales and specials.

7. Clothing, furniture, appliances, ... whatever I buy, I shop around to get the best prices.

8. I usually purchase the cheapest item.

9. I usually purchase items on sale only.

Barak and Stern (1985/1986): 1, 2, 3, 4; 6-point
Dickerson and Gentry (1983): 1, 2, 3, 4; 6-point
Donthu and Gilliland (1996): 2*, 4, 8, 9; 5-point
Mittal (1994): 1, 2, 7; 5-point
Tat and Bejou (1994): 1, 5, 6; 5-point

*The statement in this article is similar to the one shown but with slightly different phrasing.

SCALE NAME: Price-Prestige Relationship

SCALE DESCRIPTION: A nine-item, seven-point Likert-type scale measuring a consumer's belief that buying the most expensive brands is a positive experience for him or her and that it impresses others. Lichtenstein, Ridgway, and Netemeyer (1993) referred to the scale as *prestige sensitivity*, whereas Netemeyer, Burton, and Lichtenstein (1995) called it *price-based prestige sensitivity* and only used six of the nine items.

SCALE ORIGIN: The scale is original to Lichtenstein, Ridgway, and Netemeyer (1993). Most of the items were generated specifically for this study. A total of 19 items was tested, along with many others in a pretest. The sample was composed of 341 nonstudent adult consumers who had the grocery shopping responsibility for their households. Factor analysis and coefficient alpha were used to eliminate weaker items. The 11 items remaining were reported to have an alpha of .89. These items were used in the main study, though the next round of analysis eliminated 2 of them, leaving the final version of the scale with 9 items.

SAMPLES: Lichtenstein, Ridgway, and Netemeyer (1993) collected data from shoppers who had received questionnaires in one of two grocery stores in a western standard metropolitan statistical area (Boulder, Colo.). One thousand questionnaires were handed out at the stores, and **582** usable ones were returned by mail. A majority of the sample were women (75.9%) and married (58.6%). The median annual income range was $35,000 to $49,999, and the median age was range was 35 to 44 years.

Various samples were collected and used by Netemeyer, Burton, and Lichtenstein (1995) in the process of validating some other scales. The **price-prestige** scale was used in only one of the studies, which used addresses found in a *Who's Who* directory for one state. Analysis was based on the **267** completed questionnaires that were returned.

RELIABILITY: The main study by Lichtenstein, Ridgway, and Netemeyer (1993) showed an alpha for the scale of **.87**. The smaller version of the scale used by Netemeyer, Burton, and Lichtenstein (1995) had an alpha of **.85** (Netemeyer 1997).

VALIDITY: Confirmatory factor analysis was used by Lichtenstein, Ridgway, and Netemeyer (1993) to conclude that the scale was unidimensional and showed evidence of discriminant validity.

Although the validity of the scale was not directly examined by Netemeyer, Burton, and Lichtenstein (1995), it was used to help establish the construct validity of four vanity-related scales. Price-prestige had positive correlations with all of the vanity scales, though only three were significant.

ADMINISTRATION: In the study by Lichtenstein, Ridgway, and Netemeyer (1993), the scale was part of a survey instrument self-administered by shoppers after leaving the grocery store. Netemeyer, Burton, and Lichtenstein (1995) incorporated the scale into a larger mail survey instrument. A higher score on the scale indicated that a consumer generally believed that purchasing high-priced brands led to greater enjoyment and better impressions, whereas a lower score suggested that the respondent did not think there is any such general association between price and prestige.

MAJOR FINDINGS: Lichtenstein, Ridgway, and Netemeyer (1993) identified and measured seven related but distinct price perception constructs. **Prestige sensitivity** was a significant predictor of coupon redemption frequency (self-reported). Specifically, there was a slightly negative relationship between the two variables.

Netemeyer, Burton, and Lichtenstein (1995) investigated vanity and developed four scales for its measurement. Most of the article discussed the results of the rather extensive validation process. As noted, the findings indicated that the **price-prestige relationship** had positive relationships with each of the vanity scales, though only three were significant. The strongest relationship was with physical concern vanity (#397).

REFERENCES:

Lichtenstein, Donald R., Nancy M. Ridgway, and Richard G. Netemeyer (1993), "Price Perceptions and Consumer Shopping Behavior: A Field Study," *JMR*, 30 (May), 234–45.

Netemeyer, Richard G. (1997), personal correspondence.

———, Scot Burton, and Donald R. Lichtenstein (1995), "Trait Aspects of Vanity: Measurement and Relevance to Consumer Behavior," *JCR*, 21 (March), 612–26.

SCALE ITEMS:*

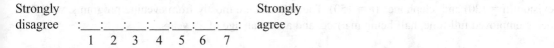

Strongly disagree : ___ : ___ : ___ : ___ : ___ : ___ : ___ : agree Strongly

        1   2   3   4   5   6   7

1. People notice when you buy the most expensive brand of a product.

2. Buying a high priced brand makes me feel good about myself.

3. Buying the most expensive brand of a product makes me feel classy.

4. I enjoy the prestige of buying a high priced brand.

5. It says something to people when you buy the high priced version of a product.

6. Your friends will think you are cheap if you consistently buy the lowest priced version of a product.

7. I have purchased the most expensive brand of a product just because I knew other people would notice.

8. I think others make judgments about me by the kinds of products and brands I buy.

9. Even for a relatively inexpensive product, I think that buying a costly brand is impressive.

*Netemeyer, Burton, and Lichtenstein (1995) used items 1, 3, 4, 5, 7, and 9, whereas Lichtenstein, Ridgway, and Netemeyer (1993) used all of the items.

SCALE NAME: Product Evaluation

SCALE DESCRIPTION: A five-item, seven-point semantic differential measure of several quality-related aspects of a product. The scale probably makes the most sense if used with regard to products made in another country.

SCALE ORIGIN: Although Lim, Darley, and Summers (1994) indicate that the scale was modeled after product assessment measures used in previous country-of-origin studies, the scale as a whole would appear to be original to their research.

SAMPLES: Two types of subjects (business undergraduates and MBAs) and two products (cordless telephones and color televisions) were used by Lim, Darley, and Summers (1994). The undergraduate subjects (n = 138) were tested just with the televisions, whereas separate MBA samples were used for television (n = 120) and telephones (n = 150). The MBAs were mostly from evening programs, with 70% being employed full-time, half being married, and a median age of 29 years.

RELIABILITY: The scale was reported to have alphas of **.79, .76,** and **.77** for the undergraduate/television, MBA/television, and MBA/telephone samples, respectively (Lim, Darley, and Summers 1994)

VALIDITY: No examination of scale validity was reported by Lim, Darley, and Summers (1994).

ADMINISTRATION: The setting for the study was not explicitly stated by Lim, Darley, and Summers (1994), but it would appear to have been a series of classroom experiments. The scale was just one part of a larger questionnaire that was completed by respondents. Higher scores on the scale meant that a product was evaluated more favorably.

MAJOR FINDINGS: The purpose of the experiment by Lim, Darley, and Summers (1994) was to compare the relative impact of several presentation formats on country-of-origin effects. Among the many findings was that the single-cue format produced substantially larger differences in **product evaluation** than the multi-cue formats. Specifically, regardless of which sample or product was involved, the products from Japan were rated more positively than those identified as being made in Mexico, especially when that was all that was known about the products (single-cue format).

REFERENCES:
Lim, Jeen-Su, William K. Darley, and John O. Summers (1994), "An Assessment of Country of Origin Effects Under Alternative Presentation Formats," *JAMS*, 22 (3), 272–82.

SCALE ITEMS:

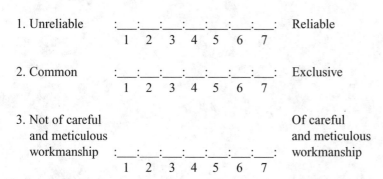

1. Unreliable   :__:__:__:__:__:__: Reliable
        1   2   3   4   5   6   7

2. Common   :__:__:__:__:__:__: Exclusive
        1   2   3   4   5   6   7

3. Not of careful   Of careful
   and meticulous   and meticulous
   workmanship   :__:__:__:__:__:__: workmanship
               1   2   3   4   5   6   7

4. Technically
   backward   :___:___:___:___:___:___: Technically
                  1   2   3   4   5   6   7   advanced

5. Poor
   serviceability   :___:___:___:___:___:___: Good
                  1   2   3   4   5   6   7   serviceability

SCALE NAME: Product Evaluation

SCALE DESCRIPTION: Four seven-point statements that assess the degree to which a person makes a favorable assessment of a product, such that it is viewed as being important to use and would be recommended to others.

SCALE ORIGIN: The source of the scale was not explicitly stated by Meyers-Levy and Peracchio (1996), but it is apparently original to their study.

SAMPLES: Meyers-Levy and Peracchio (1996) gathered data for their experiment from **229** undergraduates taking marketing courses. A majority (63%) of the sample were men.

RELIABILITY: Alphas of **.82** and **.79** were reported by Meyers-Levy and Peracchio (1996) for the insurance and dating service versions of the scale, respectively.

VALIDITY: No examination of the scale's validity was reported by Meyers-Levy and Peracchio (1996).

ADMINISTRATION: Subjects responded to the scale, along with other measures, after they were exposed to the treatment stimulus (Meyers-Levy and Peracchio 1996). Higher scores on the scale appeared to indicate that respondents viewed the product favorably, such that they are likely to buy the product and would recommend it to others.

MAJOR FINDINGS: Meyers-Levy and Peracchio (1996) examined how variation in the level of self-referencing affects persuasion and what factors moderate the effects. Among the many findings was that respondents with a rational decision-making style (#129) who read ads with a second-person wording **evaluated products** significantly better than those who read ads with a third-person wording.

REFERENCES:
Meyers-Levy, Joan and Laura A. Peracchio (1996), "Moderators of the Impact of Self-Reference on Persuasion," *JCR*, 22 (March), 408–23.
Peracchio, Laura A. (1997), personal correspondence.

SCALE ITEMS:*

Not at all   :__:__:__:__:__:__:__: Extremely
              1   2   3   4   5   6   7

Car insurance version

1. How important do you feel it is for drivers to have comprehensive auto insurance?

2. To what extent would you be likely to advise a friend to buy full coverage auto insurance?

3. Assuming you were in the market for auto insurance, how likely is it that you would consider buying insurance from the advertised company?

4. To what extent do you feel it is advisable for people to choose a quality insurance company such as the one featured in the ad?

Dating service version

1. How important do you feel it is to be selective in choosing a dating service?

2. To what extent would you be likely to advise a friend to choose a dating service carefully?

3. Assuming you were thinking about using a dating service, how likely is it that you would consider using the advertised dating service?

4. To what extent do you feel it is advisable for people to choose a quality dating service such as the one featured in the ad?

*Descriptions of the items were provided in the article by Meyers-Levy and Peracchio (1996), but the exact phrasing came from Peracchio (1997).

SCALE NAME: Product Evaluation (Beverage)

SCALE DESCRIPTION: Seven seven-point semantic differentials measuring the degree to which a person expresses a positive opinion of a drink product. The scale can be used before or after a person has tasted the product. If used before drinking a beverage, then the respondent must *imagine* what it would taste like on the basis of the stimuli provided (verbal descriptions, graphics, etc.).

SCALE ORIGIN: Some similarities can be found between this scale and others used to evaluate food products, but there are enough differences to conclude that this one is original to the study reported by Meyers-Levy and Tybout (1997).

SAMPLES: Data were gathered by Meyers-Levy and Tybout (1997) for their first experiment from **81** students (men and women) at a West Coast U.S. university. Experiment 2 was composed of **77** female undergraduates attending a Midwestern U.S. university. In both experiments, subjects were paid $5 for their participation.

RELIABILITY: Alphas of **.85** and **.95** were reported by Meyers-Levy and Tybout (1997) for the scale when used as a pretaste and posttaste measure, respectively, in Experiment 1. Likewise, alphas of **.86** and **.96** were reported for the scale when used as a pretaste and posttaste measure, respectively, in Experiment 2.

VALIDITY: No examination of the scale's validity was reported by Meyers-Levy and Tybout (1997). They stated, however, that a factor analysis indicated that the seven items tapped into a single dimension.

ADMINISTRATION: The scale was administered twice in each experiment by Meyers-Levy and Tybout (1997). It was first completed by subjects after they were exposed to treatment material (product description). Then, they filled out the scale again after actually tasting the beverage. Higher scores on the scale indicated that respondents considered the drink they tasted to be desirable and satisfying.

MAJOR FINDINGS: Meyers-Levy and Tybout (1997) built on a model of context effects (e.g., Martin, Seta, and Crelia 1990) that operates when consumers form opinions about new products. Among the findings in their two experiments was that subjects low in need for cognition gave moderately positive **evaluations** (posttaste) to the beverage despite the treatment conditions. However, **evaluations** made by subjects high in need for cognition indicated context effects that varied depending on the resources required for product categorization.

REFERENCES:
Martin, Leonard L., John J. Seta, and Rick A. Crelia (1990), "Assimilation and Contrast as a Function of People's Willingness and Ability to Expend Effort in Forming an Impression," *Journal of Personality and Social Psychology*, 59 (July), 27–37.
Meyers-Levy, Joan (1998), personal correspondence.
——— and Alice M. Tybout (1989), "Schema Congruity as a Basis for Product Evaluation," *JCR*, 16 (June), 39–54.

SCALE ITEMS:*

1. Unappealing   :__:__:__:__:__:__:__: Very appealing
                     1   2   3   4   5   6   7

2. A product I
    would not try   :__:__:__:__:__:__:__: A product I
                        1   2   3   4   5   6   7   would try

3. Likely to
    taste bad   :__:__:__:__:__:__:__: Likely to
                     1   2   3   4   5   6   7   taste good

4. Unlikely to be
    satisfying   :__:__:__:__:__:__:__: Likely to be
                     1   2   3   4   5   6   7   satisfying

5. Undesirable   :__:__:__:__:__:__:__: Desirable
                   1   2   3   4   5   6   7

6. Unlikely to be
    refreshing   :__:__:__:__:__:__:__: Likely to be
                     1   2   3   4   5   6   7   refreshing

7. Unlikely to be
    of high quality   :__:__:__:__:__:__:__: Likely to be
                        1   2   3   4   5   6   7   of high quality

*These items were generally described in Meyers-Levy and Tybout (1997) and clarified by Myers-Levy (1998).

SCALE NAME: Product Evaluation (Camera)

SCALE DESCRIPTION: Ten nine-point semantic differentials measuring how a person evaluates a camera. It appears that this scale is similar to many typical brand attitude measures (e.g., 53), except that several of the items here are specific to cameras rather than being broad enough to apply to other product categories.

SCALE ORIGIN: Although not explicitly stated, the scale used by Malaviya, Kisielius, and Sternthal (1996) appears to be original to their study.

SAMPLES: An experiment was conducted by Malaviya, Kisielius, and Sternthal (1996) using **168** undergraduate students in an introductory business course. Students were given class credit for their participation, but the actual experiment appears to have been conducted in small groups outside of normal class time.

RELIABILITY: An alpha of **.84** was reported for the scale (Malaviya, Kisielius, and Sternthal 1996).

VALIDITY: No examination of the scale's validity was reported by Malaviya, Kisielius, and Sternthal (1996). However, they stated that factor analysis indicated that the items loaded on a single dimension, which suggests the scale is unidimensional.

ADMINISTRATION: The scale was administered by Malaviya, Kisielius, and Sternthal (1996) to subjects in an experiment after they had been exposed to a version of an ad. Higher scores on the scale indicated that respondents had a positive view of the camera (or to the information about the camera as communicated in an ad) to which they have been exposed.

MAJOR FINDINGS: Malaviya, Kisielius, and Sternthal (1996) studied how the type of elaboration received by an ad influences **brand evaluations**. Among their findings was that, when ads for competing brands were present, **evaluation** of the target brand was significantly better when ad graphics were consistent with ad copy than when they were not. In contrast, when no ads for competing products were present, the ads with pictures supposedly taken by the camera were **evaluated** better than those ads with graphics directly related to the camera attributes mentioned in the copy.

REFERENCES:
Malaviya, Prashant, Jolita Kisielius, and Brian Sternthal (1996), "The Effect of Type of Elaboration on Advertisement Processing and Judgment," *JMR*, 33 (November), 410–21.

SCALE ITEMS:

Bad   :___:___:___:___:___:___:___:___: Good
                 1   2   3   4   5   6   7   8   9

Dislike   :___:___:___:___:___:___:___:___: Like
                 1   2   3   4   5   6   7   8   9

Not
convenient   :___:___:___:___:___:___:___:___: Convenient
                 1   2   3   4   5   6   7   8   9

Not
superior   :___:___:___:___:___:___:___:___: Superior
                        1   2   3   4   5   6   7   8   9

Few unique   Many unique
features   :___:___:___:___:___:___:___:___: features
                        1   2   3   4   5   6   7   8   9

Difficult
to use   :___:___:___:___:___:___:___:___: Easy to use
                        1   2   3   4   5   6   7   8   9

Poor   Good
lens quality   :___:___:___:___:___:___:___:___: lens quality
                        1   2   3   4   5   6   7   8   9

Will not produce   Will produce
good pictures   :___:___:___:___:___:___:___:___: good pictures
                        1   2   3   4   5   6   7   8   9

Low performance   High performance
product   :___:___:___:___:___:___:___:___: product
                        1   2   3   4   5   6   7   8   9

Lacks important   Offers important
benefits   :___:___:___:___:___:___:___:___: benefits
                        1   2   3   4   5   6   7   8   9

SCALE NAME: Product Evaluation (Food)

SCALE DESCRIPTION: Seven seven-point items measuring the degree to which a person not only makes a positive evaluation of a food item, but has an interest in buying it and recommending it to a friend. The scale has an obvious application *after* a person has tasted a food item. If used before tasting or without actually tasting something, then the respondent is having to *imagine* what it would taste like on the basis of the stimuli provided (verbal descriptions, graphics, etc.).

SCALE ORIGIN: The scale was apparently developed for the study conducted by Peracchio and Tybout (1996).

SAMPLES: Peracchio and Tybout (1996) collected data for their experiment from **94** master's-level college students. A little more than half of the sample were men (52%). The incentive to participate was entering subjects in a lottery for a weekend package at a local hotel.

RELIABILITY: Alphas of **.92** and **.95** were reported by Peracchio and Tybout (1996) for the scale when used as pretaste and posttaste measures, respectively.

VALIDITY: No examination of the scale's validity was reported by Peracchio and Tybout (1996).

ADMINISTRATION: The scale was administered twice in the experiment by Peracchio and Tybout (1996). It was first completed by subjects after they were exposed to treatment material (product description). Then, they filled out the scale again after actually tasting the item (cake). Higher scores on the scale indicated that respondents considered the food item they tasted (read about, saw) to be desirable enough to buy and recommend to others.

MAJOR FINDINGS: Peracchio and Tybout (1996) examined the moderating role of prior knowledge in schema-based product evaluation. Men were expected to lack elaborate knowledge and be guided by congruity-base effect. As hypothesized, men **evaluated** a "high calorie dessert" (moderate incongruity) better than a "spicy dessert."

REFERENCES:
Peracchio, Laura A. (1997), personal correspondence.
——— and Alice M. Tybout (1996), "The Moderating Role of Prior Knowledge in Schema-Based Product Evaluation," *JCR*, 23 (December), 177–92.

SCALE ITEMS:*

Not at all :___:___:___:___:___:___:___: Extremely
            1   2   3   4   5   6   7

1. Appealing

2. Tasty

3. Desirable

4. High quality

5. Appetizing

6. I would not be likely to use this product/I would be likely to purchase this product.

7. I would not be likely to recommend this product to a friend/ I would be likely to recommend this product to a friend.

*The items were generally described in Peracchio and Tybout (1996) and clarified by Peracchio (1997). The first five items used the response scale shown; the last two items were apparently responded to in an agree/disagree manner.

SCALE NAME: Product Evaluation (Food)

SCALE DESCRIPTION: Five seven-point semantic differentials measuring the likelihood that a food product has certain characteristics. The characteristics focus on taste, healthiness, and freshness. The scale can be used before or after a person has tasted the product. If used as a pretaste measure, then the respondent must *imagine* what it would taste like on the basis of the stimuli provided (verbal descriptions, graphics, etc.). The measure was referred to as *feature judgments* by Meyers-Levy and Tybout (1997).

SCALE ORIGIN: The scale appears to be original to the study reported by Meyers-Levy and Tybout (1997).

SAMPLES: Meyers-Levy and Tybout (1997) reported on two experiments, only the second of which used this scale. It was composed of **77** female undergraduates attending a Midwestern U.S. university. In both experiments, subjects were paid $5 for their participation.

RELIABILITY: Alphas of **.43** and **.73** were reported by Meyers-Levy and Tybout (1997) for the scale when used as a pretaste and posttaste measure, respectively.

VALIDITY: No examination of the scale's validity was reported by Meyers-Levy and Tybout (1997). They stated, however, that a factor analysis indicated that the five items did not load on an overall affective evaluative scale but broke out into two other dimensions: one appearing to tap into healthiness (items 1 and 2) and the other tapping into freshness (items 3, 4, and 5). Because the hypotheses only dealt with the distinction between the overall affective evaluation and the product feature judgments, it was decided to combine the five items into one measure despite their bidimensional structure.

ADMINISTRATION: The scale was administered twice in the second experiment conducted by Meyers-Levy and Tybout (1997). It was first completed by subjects after they were exposed to treatment material (product description). Then, they filled out the scale again after actually tasting the product. Higher scores on the scale indicated that respondents considered the product they tasted to have certain characteristics (e.g., freshness).

MAJOR FINDINGS: Meyers-Levy and Tybout (1997) built on a model of context effects (e.g., Martin, Seta, and Crelia 1990) that operates when consumers form opinions about new products. The results of Experiment 2 suggested that there was a two-way interaction effect between favorableness of contextual data and resources required for categorization. Product **evaluations** (posttaste) were higher for the negative context compared with the positive context when product categorization required few resources. In contrast, **evaluations** were lower for the negative context compared with the positive context when product categorization required many resources.

COMMENTS: This scale is particularly unstable as a pretaste measure but requires redevelopment even as a posttaste measure because the data indicate that it is not unidimensional. In addition, some thought should be given to dropping item 3 because it would make the measure more generalizable to a variety of foods and beverages.

REFERENCES:
Martin, Leonard L., John J. Seta, and Rick A. Crelia (1990), "Assimilation and Contrast as a Function of People's Willingness and Ability to Expend Effort in Forming an Impression," *Journal of Personality and Social Psychology*, 59 (July), 27–37.
Meyers-Levy, Joan (1998), personal correspondence.

——— and Alice M. Tybout (1989), "Schema Congruity as a Basis for Product Evaluation," *JCR*, 16 (June), 39–54.

SCALE ITEMS:*

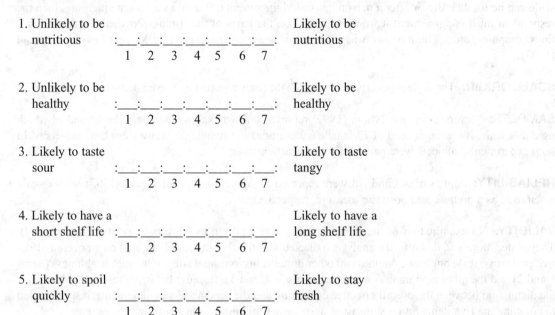

1. Unlikely to be nutritious :___:___:___:___:___:___:___: Likely to be nutritious
   1   2   3   4   5   6   7

2. Unlikely to be healthy :___:___:___:___:___:___:___: Likely to be healthy
   1   2   3   4   5   6   7

3. Likely to taste sour :___:___:___:___:___:___:___: Likely to taste tangy
   1   2   3   4   5   6   7

4. Likely to have a short shelf life :___:___:___:___:___:___:___: Likely to have a long shelf life
   1   2   3   4   5   6   7

5. Likely to spoil quickly :___:___:___:___:___:___:___: Likely to stay fresh
   1   2   3   4   5   6   7

*These items were generally described in Meyers-Levy and Tybout (1997) and clarified by Myers-Levy (1998).

SCALE NAME: Product Experience

SCALE DESCRIPTION: A three-item rating scale purported to measure the extent to which a person reports having owned and used some specified product. The product category studied by Park, Mothersbaugh, and Feick (1994) was CD players.

SCALE ORIGIN: The scale was apparently developed for use in the study by Park, Mothersbaugh, and Feick (1994).

SAMPLES: Park, Mothersbaugh, and Feick (1994) gathered data from a convenience sample of **156** graduate students attending a Northeastern U.S. university. The students were recruited and paid to participate in a "consumer knowledge study." Respondents filled out the questionnaires in small groups at their own pace. A majority of the sample were men (62%) and were an average of 27 years of age.

RELIABILITY: Park, Mothersbaugh, and Feick (1994) reported an alpha of **.87**, with item–total correlations ranging from .61 to .83.

VALIDITY: The validity of the scale was not directly examined by Park, Mothersbaugh, and Feick (1994).

ADMINISTRATION: The scale was administered by Park, Mothersbaugh, and Feick (1994) in a larger survey instrument. Higher scores on the scale indicated that respondents reported themselves to be very experienced with the specified product, whereas low scores suggested that respondents had not owned and/or used such a product. Because two of the items had nine-point response scales and one item was a dichotomous measure, a simple summation of the raw scores is not likely to be appropriate. The authors did not describe how the scale scores were calculated, but standardization of the items' scores before summation is a strong possibility.

MAJOR FINDINGS: The study by Park, Mothersbaugh, and Feick (1994) investigated the determinants of self-assessed knowledge (perceived degree of knowledge about a product class). **Product experience** was found to be have a significant positive relationship with self-assessed knowledge, as well as with the amount of stored product-class information.

REFERENCES:
Mothersbaugh, David L. (1997), personal correspondence.
Park, C. Whan, David L. Mothersbaugh, and Lawrence Feick (1994), "Consumer Knowledge Assessment," *JCR*, 21 (June), 71–82.

SCALE ITEMS:*

1. How often do you use a _____?

Never   :___:___:___:___:___:___:___:___:___: Every day
        1   2   3   4   5   6   7   8   9

2. Do you currently own a _____? No ___ Yes ___

3. Overall, how much time have you spent searching for _____ information?

Very
little   :___:___:___:___:___:___:___:___:___: much
      1   2   3   4   5   6   7   8   9

Very much (header): Very much

*The name of the product of interest should be placed in the blanks. The items were supplied by Mothersbaugh (1997).

SCALE NAME: Product Experience

SCALE DESCRIPTION: Four five-point Likert-type statements purported to measure the extent to which a person reports having a lot of experience with a product and knowledge of how to use it.

SCALE ORIGIN: The source of the scale was not identified by Griffin, Babin, and Attaway (1996) and may very well have been developed by them for use in their study.

SAMPLES: Students collected data for the study by Griffin, Babin, and Attaway (1996) for course credit. They were assigned to distribute questionnaires in various parts of a midsized Midwestern U.S. city. In some cases, the instruments were picked up by students, whereas in others, they were mailed back. Of the 420 survey instruments dropped off, **262** were returned. No other information about the sample was provided, except that it was considered to be representative of the area from which it was drawn and only adults (older than 18 years of age) were selected to respond.

RELIABILITY: Griffin, Babin, and Attaway (1996) reported an alpha of **.86** for the scale.

VALIDITY: No examination of the scale's validity was reported by Griffin, Babin, and Attaway (1996).

ADMINISTRATION: The scale was self-administered by respondents as part of a larger survey instrument (Griffin, Babin, and Attaway 1996). Higher scores on the scale indicated that respondents believed that they had a great deal of experience in using some product described in a case.

MAJOR FINDINGS: Griffin, Babin, and Attaway (1996) explored the attribution of blame toward marketers when negative consequences result from use their products. Despite expectations, no significant relationship was found between **product experience** and the extent to which a person attributes blame for a product injury to the marketer.

REFERENCES:
Griffin, Mitch, Barry J. Babin, and Jill Attaway (1996), "Anticipation of Injurious Consumption Outcomes and Its Impact on Consumer Attributions of Blame," *JAMS*, 24 (Fall), 314–27.

SCALE ITEMS:

```
Strongly                         Strongly
disagree    :__:__:__:__:__:     agree
              1   2   3   4   5
```

1. I have a great deal of skill in using the product described.

2. I use the product in the case frequently.

3. I have experience using the product in the case.

4. I know how to operate the product described in the case.

SCALE NAME: Program Liking

SCALE DESCRIPTION: Six seven-point Likert-type statements measuring a person's liking of a television program.

SCALE ORIGIN: The scale used by Murry and Dacin (1996) is the same as the one used by Murry, Lastovicka, and Singh (1992). Although it is not certain, the scale appears to have been developed as part of that previous study.

SAMPLES: Data were collected by Murry and Dacin (1996) in an experiment involving **162** undergraduate students. Students were randomly assigned to eight television viewing conditions, and the experiment took place in a lounge with 2 to 5 subjects at a time.

RELIABILITY: Murry and Dacin (1996) reported an alpha of **.93** for the scale.

VALIDITY: No explicit examination of the scale's validity was mentioned by Murry and Dacin (1996). However, a confirmatory factor analysis was conducted on a set of fifteen items thought to deal with three different but related constructs. Indeed, the six items composing the **program liking** scale loaded high on the same dimension.

ADMINISTRATION: The scale was self-administered by subjects, along with other measures, immediately after they were exposed to the treatment stimulus (Murry and Dacin 1996). High scores on the scale suggested that respondents liked a particular television program very much.

MAJOR FINDINGS: Murry and Dacin (1996) studied how emotions elicited by television programs affect viewers' liking for the programs. Not surprisingly, the results indicated that positive emotions have a significant and direct impact on **program liking**.

REFERENCES:
Murry, John P., Jr., and Peter A. Dacin (1996), "Cognitive Moderators of Negative-Emotion Effects: Implications for Understanding Media Context," *JCR*, 22 (March), 439–47.
———, John L. Lastovicka, and Surendra N. Singh (1992), "Feeling and Liking Responses to Television Programs: An Examination of Two Explanations for Media Context Effects," *JCR*, 18 (March), 441–51.

SCALE ITEMS:

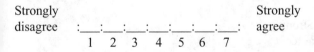

Strongly disagree :__:__:__:__:__:__:__: Strongly agree
 1 2 3 4 5 6 7

1. If I knew this program was going to be on television I would look forward to watching it.

2. I liked watching this program.

3. I would never watch a rerun of this program on television. **(r)**

4. I am glad I had a chance to see this program.

5. There is something about this program that appeals to me.

6. I disliked watching this program more than I do most other TV programs. **(r)**

SCALE NAME: Program Reality

SCALE DESCRIPTION: Five seven-point Likert-type statements measuring the extent to which a viewer of a television program felt that it was an actual account of some events rather than just a fictitious dramatization.

SCALE ORIGIN: The scale used by Murry and Dacin (1996) was developed for use in their experiment.

SAMPLES: Data were collected by Murry and Dacin (1996) in an experiment involving **162** undergraduate students. Students were randomly assigned to eight television viewing conditions, and the experiment took place in a lounge with 2 to 5 subjects at a time.

RELIABILITY: Murry and Dacin (1996) reported an alpha of **.91** for the scale.

VALIDITY: No explicit examination of the scale's validity was mentioned by Murry and Dacin (1996). However, a confirmatory factor analysis was conducted on a set of fifteen items thought to deal with three different but related constructs. Indeed, the five items composing the program reality scale loaded high on the same dimension.

ADMINISTRATION: The scale was self-administered by subjects, along with other measures, immediately after they were exposed to the treatment stimulus (Murry and Dacin 1996). High scores on the scale suggested that respondents thought a program they had seen was real life rather than just a dramatization.

MAJOR FINDINGS: Murry and Dacin (1996) studied how emotions elicited by television programs affect viewers' liking for the programs. The results indicated that negative emotions had a strong detrimental impact on program liking, but this was moderated by viewers' perceptions of **program reality** and personal relevance.

REFERENCES:
Murry, John P., Jr., and Peter A. Dacin (1996), "Cognitive Moderators of Negative-Emotion Effects: Implications for Understanding Media Context," *JCR*, 22 (March), 439–47.

SCALE ITEMS:

Strongly   Strongly
disagree   :__:__:__:__:__:__:__: agree
        1 2 3 4 5 6 7

1. Even though I knew this was only a television program, I felt as if it was real life.

2. While watching this program, I found myself believing that it was real.

3. I found it hard to remember that the program was only a dramatization.

4. I found myself forgetting that I was only watching a television program.

5. I was always aware that the program was only a dramatization. **(r)**

SCALE NAME: Program Relevance

SCALE DESCRIPTION: Four seven-point Likert-type statements measuring the extent to which a viewer of a television program felt that it was applicable to him or her on a personal level.

SCALE ORIGIN: The scale used by Murry and Dacin (1996) was developed for use in their experiment.

SAMPLES: Data were collected by Murry and Dacin (1996) in an experiment involving **162** undergraduate students. Students were randomly assigned to eight television viewing conditions, and the experiment took place in a lounge with 2 to 5 subjects at a time.

RELIABILITY: Murry and Dacin (1996) reported an alpha of **.73** for the scale.

VALIDITY: No explicit examination of the scale's validity was mentioned by Murry and Dacin (1996). However, a confirmatory factor analysis was conducted on a set of fifteen items thought to deal with three different but related constructs. Indeed, the four items composing the **program relevance** scale loaded on the same dimension.

ADMINISTRATION: The scale was self-administered by subjects, along with other measures, immediately after they were exposed to the treatment stimulus (Murry and Dacin 1996). High scores on the scale suggested that respondents thought a program they had seen was quite germane to them personally.

MAJOR FINDINGS: Murry and Dacin (1996) studied how emotions elicited by television programs affect viewers' liking for the programs. The results indicated that negative emotions had a strong detrimental impact on program liking, but this was moderated by viewers' perceptions of program reality and **personal relevance**.

REFERENCES:
Murry, John P., Jr., and Peter A. Dacin (1996), "Cognitive Moderators of Negative-Emotion Effects: Implications for Understanding Media Context," *JCR*, 22 (March), 439–47.

SCALE ITEMS:

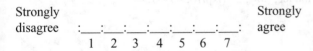

Strongly disagree :___:___:___:___:___:___:___: Strongly agree
        1   2   3   4   5   6   7

1. During the program I kept relating experiences in the story to experiences in my own life.

2. I recently experienced the same emotions as those experienced by the characters in the program.

3. People who are close to me have had a similar experience to those shown in the program.

4. While watching the program I imagined something similar happening to me or somebody I cared about.

SCALE NAME: Provision of Extras (Service Provider)

SCALE DESCRIPTION: A three-item, seven-point Likert-type summated ratings scale measuring the degree to which a person who has just been involved in a service activity thinks that the one providing the service went beyond what was expected and gave something extra. The activity studied by Price, Arnould, and Tierney (1995) was a river-rafting trip, and the river guide was the service provider being evaluated by the customers.

SCALE ORIGIN: The scale was developed for the research reported by Price, Arnould, and Tierney (1995).

SAMPLES: Very little information was provided by Price, Arnould, and Tierney (1995) regarding their sample. The reader is referred to an earlier article (Arnould and Price 1993), which provides only a limited description of the sample. The respondents are described simply as a stratified random sample of people taking multiday river trips with one of three clients' rafting companies. A total of **137** clients filled out posttrip questionnaires, but only 97 of those completed pretrip surveys.

RELIABILITY: An alpha of **.86** was reported by Price, Arnould, and Tierney (1995).

VALIDITY: No specific examination of the scale's validity was reported by Price, Arnould, and Tierney (1995). However, 17 items were factor analyzed and found to produce three separate factors. The three items in this scale composed one of those factors, and their loadings ranged from .59 to .90.

ADMINISTRATION: The scale was self-administered by respondents as part of a larger survey after they had finished a rafting trip (Arnould and Price 1993; Price, Arnould, and Tierney 1995). High scores on the scale suggested that respondents considered the person who performed the service to have done more than was expected and provided something extra to them.

MAJOR FINDINGS: Building on the same basic study as Arnould and Price (1993), Price, Arnould, and Tierney (1995) found that **providing extras** had a significant positive impact on perceived performance of the service provider.

REFERENCES:

Arnould, Eric J. and Linda L. Price (1993), "River Magic: Extraordinary Experience and the Extended Service Encounter," *JCR*, 20 (June), 24–45.

Price, Linda L., Eric J. Arnould, and Patrick Tierney (1995), "Going to Extremes: Managing Service Encounters and Assessing Provider Performance," *JM*, 59 (April), 83–97.

SCALE ITEMS:*

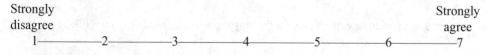

Strongly disagree
1———2———3———4———5———6———7
Strongly agree

The service provider:

1. Gave me something extra.

2. Went out of his/her way.

3. Paid me special attention.

*The response format was not specifically described by Price, Arnould, and Tierney (1995), but it appears it may have been something similar to what is shown here.

SCALE NAME: Purchase Intention

SCALE DESCRIPTION: A three-item, seven-point Likert-type measure of the degree to which a consumer intends to buy (or at least will try to buy) a specified brand in the future.

SCALE ORIGIN: Putrevu and Lord (1994) did not indicate the source of the scale. Although there is some conceptual similarity between this and other measures of the construct, the specific items appear to be distinct. Thus, it is likely that this scale is original.

SAMPLES: Data were gathered by Putrevu and Lord (1994) from students in an introductory undergraduate marketing course taught at a Northeastern U.S. university. Apparently, usable data were collected from **100** students who voluntarily participated for extra credit in the course. Demographic data about the respondents were collected but were not described in the article.

RELIABILITY: Putrevu and Lord (1994) reported an alpha of **.91** for the scale.

VALIDITY: No evidence of the scale's validity was presented in the article by Putrevu and Lord (1994).

ADMINISTRATION: The scale was administered to students by Putrevu and Lord (1994), along with other measures, as part of an in-class experiment. Higher scores on the scale meant that a consumer was expressing a high likelihood of trying, if not buying, some specified product.

MAJOR FINDINGS: Putrevu and Lord (1994) examined the relative effectiveness of comparative and noncomparative advertising for products characterized by varying degrees of affective and cognitive involvement. The findings indicated that the highest levels of **purchase intention** were associated with the treatment using attribute-oriented ads for products with high cognitive but low affective involvement. There was no significant difference between the impact of comparative and noncomparative ads on **purchase intention**, possibly because there was just a single presentation of the ad.

REFERENCES:
Putrevu, Sanjay and Kenneth R. Lord (1994), "Comparative and Noncomparative Advertising: Attitudinal Effects Under Cognitive and Affective Involvement Conditions," *JA*, 23 (June), 77–90.

SCALE ITEMS:

Disagree   :___:___:___:___:___:___:___: Agree
                 1   2   3   4   5   6   7

1. It is very likely that I will buy *(brand)*.

2. I will purchase *(brand)* the next time I need a *(product)*.

3. I will definitely try *(brand)*.

SCALE NAME: Purchase Intention

SCALE DESCRIPTION: The scale is typically characterized by multiple items used to measure the inclination of a consumer to buy a specified product. The various versions of the scale discussed here have between two and four items. Most of the studies appear to have used seven-point response scales, with the exception of Okechuku and Wang (1988), who used a nine-point format. The uses of the scale are similar in that they have at least one item in common with every other version, and all share two items with two of the other three versions.

SCALE ORIGIN: The source of this scale is a study of the physical attractiveness of models in advertisements (Baker and Churchill 1977). Consistent with the tripartite theory of attitudes, scales were developed to measure the cognitive, affective, and conative components of a person's evaluation of an ad. Item–total correlations indicated that the three items expected to capture the conative component (1, 2, and 3) were homogeneous. It should be noted that though the scale was developed to measure the conative dimension of a person's attitude toward an ad, the statements instead measure the conative dimension of attitude toward the brand. This scale, therefore, does not measure behavioral intention toward an ad but could be used with a product described in an ad.

SAMPLES: Kilbourne (1986) used a convenience sample of **49** men and **52** women residing in several communities around a large metropolitan area. The median age was 30 years, the median income was $20,700, and 79% were either college graduates or attending college. The sample used by Kilbourne, Painton and Ridley (1985) was composed of **238** male and **186** female undergraduate students from a Southwestern U.S. university. The students were recruited from marketing, management, or psychology classes but were not required to participate in the experiment.

Data were collected by Neese and Taylor (1994) using a judgment sample of civic groups members from across a Southeastern U.S. state. They were expected to be more likely than the population at large to own luxury cars, the product focused on in the study. Indeed, 22.1% of the respondents reported owning one of three luxury sedans. Usable questionnaires were received from **422** respondents. The sample was predominately men, and 41.5% were older than 64 years of age.

Okechuku and Wang (1988) used subjects recruited at shopping malls and other public places in Detroit and surrounding suburbs in Michigan and in Windsor, London; Sarnia, Toronto; and Hamilton, Ontario. Sample sizes for clothing ads were 27, 27, and 26 for three Chinese ads and 29, 30, and 26 for three North American ads. For shoes, the sample sizes were 26, 26, and 30 for three Chinese ads and 25, 24, and 26 for three North American ads.

The study by Perrien, Dussart, and Paul (1985) was based on **186** questionnaires returned by advertising industry professionals who were members of the Montreal Advertising Club. This represented a 26% response rate. Because French was the official language of the club, the questionnaires were in French. The authors admitted that what little was known about the representativeness of their sample indicated that it was different from the population, at least in terms of the proportions of different professional groups. However, their results indicated that the respondents' professional categories did not affect the evaluation of ads.

RELIABILITY: Alphas of **.73**, **.91**, **.81**, and **.81** were reported by Kilbourne (1986), Kilbourne, Painton and Ridley (1985), Neese and Taylor (1994), and Perrien, Dussart, and Paul (1985), respectively. Okechuku and Wang (1988) reported two alphas: **.82** and **.77** for clothing and shoe ads, respectively. The item-total correlations reported in their study also provide some evidence of scale item homogeneity.

VALIDITY: No examination of the scale's validity was reported by Neese and Taylor (1994), though the authors stated in general terms that they used item–total correlations and the results of a factor analyses to purify each of their scales.

The item-total correlations reported by Okechuku and Wang (1988) indicated that the items composing this scale had much higher correlations with scores on this scale than with correlations with total scores on two other scales (cognitive and affective dimensions of attitude). This provides some evidence of convergent and discriminate validities, though at the item rather than the scale level.

As some evidence of content validity, Perrien, Dussart and Paul (1985) used items taken from the literature and tested them with 15 marketing experts. All were unanimous in connecting the expected items with the proper dimensions of attitude (affective, cognitive, and conative).

ADMINISTRATION: In the studies by Kilbourne (1986) and Okechuku and Wang (1988), the questionnaires were administered to respondents in various field settings after they had read some test ads. The student subjects in the study by Kilbourne, Painton, and Ridley (1985) completed the experiment and the questionnaire in groups. Administration of this scale in Perrien, Dussart and Paul's (1985) study was in a mail survey instrument, and scale items were randomized with those for two other scales. The conditions under which Neese and Taylor (1994) administered the scale were not clearly described. High scores on the scale indicated that respondents were expressing a strong inclination to purchase the specified product, whereas low scores suggested that they did not plan on buying the product.

MAJOR FINDINGS: Kilbourne (1986) found **purchase intentions** were significantly higher for those who had viewed an ad for the product in which the female model in the ad was portrayed as a professional than for those who viewed an ad in which she was portrayed as a housewife. Kilbourne, Painton and Ridley (1985) found significantly higher **purchase intentions** toward Scotch whiskey when the print ad contained a sexual embed than when it did not. A significant difference was not found for another product (a brand of cigarettes) that was also tested.

Neese and Taylor (1994) examined the ability of comparative advertising to accomplish certain tasks as it interacts with brand information for a high-involvement product. No significant support was found for the hypotheses **involving purchase intentions**.

Okechuku and Wang (1988) compared North American subjects' attitudes toward ads from China and North America. They found a significant difference in **purchase intentions** for two different product categories, such that respondents (North Americans) expressed a greater likelihood of purchasing products presented in ads prepared by North Americans than those in ads by Chinese advertisers.

Perrien, Dussart and Paul (1985) examined subjects in the advertising trade and their perceptions of advertising effectiveness. Their findings indicated that the more factual information contained in an ad, the more positively advertisers evaluated it. Specifically, advertisers thought that consumers' **purchase intentions** would be higher for products advertised with much factual content. This finding was not affected by the amount of perceived risk associated with the product or respondents' professional category in the advertising industry.

COMMENTS: Several users of this scale referred to it as a semantic differential. However, it is not described as such here because it does not use a series of bipolar adjectives but is instead composed of a series of different statements responded to on a scale with the same verbal anchors.

REFERENCES:

Baker, Michael J. and Gilbert A. Churchill Jr. (1977), "The Impact of Physically Attractive Models on Advertising Evaluations," *JMR*, 14 (November), 538–55.

Kilbourne, William E. (1986), "An Exploratory Study of Sex Role Stereotyping on Attitudes Toward Magazine Advertisements," *JAMS*, 14 (4), 43–46.

———, Scott Painton, and Danny Ridley (1985), "The Effect of Sexual Embedding on Responses to Magazine Advertisements," *JA*, 14 (2), 48–56.

Neese, William T. and Ronald D. Taylor (1994), "Verbal Strategies for Indirect Comparative Advertising," *JAR*, 34 (March/April), 56–69.

Okechuku, Chike and Gongrong Wang (1988), "The Effectiveness of Chinese Print Advertisements in North America," *JAR*, 28 (October/November), 25–34.

Perrien, Jean, Christian Dussart and Francoise Paul (1985), "Advertisers and the Factual Content of Advertising," *JA*, 14 (1), 30–35, 53.

SCALE ITEMS:*

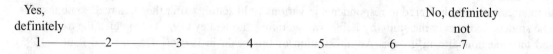

Yes, definitely

No, definitely not

1————2————3————4————5————6————7

1. Would you like to try this product?

2. Would you buy this product if you happened to see it in a store?

3. Would you actively seek out this product in a store in order to purchase it?

*This is the version of the scale reported by Baker and Churchill (1977). Kilbourne, Painton, and Ridley (1985), Kilbourne (1986), and Neese and Taylor (1994) used phrases based on these items. Okechuku and Wang (1988) appear to have used short phrases based on these items. Perrien, Dussart, and Paul (1985) used items that referred to an ad the respondents had been exposed to and then asked questions similar to these items. Their scale also incorporated one bipolar adjective (influential/not influential) that was included to measure the perceived power of the ad to affect purchase behavior.

SCALE NAME: Purchase Intention (Service)

SCALE DESCRIPTION: Three seven-point Likert-type statements purported to measure the likelihood that a consumer will choose a particular service provider the next time the service is needed.

SCALE ORIGIN: Although not explicitly stated by Taylor and Baker (1994), the scale appears to be original to their study.

SAMPLES: Taylor and Baker (1994) analyzed data from **426** completed questionnaires. The data were collected through personal interviews by trained personnel using a convenience sample. Respondents were selected through mall intercepts in seven cities across the United States.

RELIABILITY: An alpha of **.94** was reported for the scale by Taylor and Baker (1994).

VALIDITY: Limited scrutiny of the scale's convergent and discriminant validities was made by Taylor and Baker (1994) based on observed patterns in a correlation matrix. They did not choose to make any comments about this particular scale, though it is clear that the three items composing the scale correlated much higher with one another than they did with items measuring two other related constructs in the study.

ADMINISTRATION: The circumstances surrounding administration were not described in detail by Taylor and Baker (1994), but it appears that the scale was part of a larger questionnaire administered to respondents by trained interviewers. Higher scores on the scale indicated that respondents were very much inclined to purchase a service from the specified provider the next time the service was needed.

MAJOR FINDINGS: Taylor and Baker (1994) studied the role played by service quality and satisfaction in the development of **purchase intentions**. For three of the four industries examined, models of decision making that included the interaction of satisfaction and quality provided a better understanding of **intentions** than did models that merely included main effects.

REFERENCES:
Taylor, Steven A. and Thomas L. Baker (1994), "An Assessment of the Relationship Between Service Quality and Customer Satisfaction in the Formation of Consumers' Purchase Intentions," *JR*, 70 (2), 163–78.

SCALE ITEMS:*

```
Strongly                              Strongly
disagree   :___:___:___:___:___:___:___:   agree
            1   2   3   4   5   6   7
```

1. The next time I need the service of a _____, I will choose _____.

2. If I had needed the services of a _____ during the past year, I would have selected _____.

3. In the next year, if I need the services of a _____ I will select _____.

* The generic name of the service (e.g., airline) should be placed in the first blank of each statement, and the specific name of the service provider (e.g., American Airlines) should go in the second blank.

SCALE NAME: Purchase Involvement (Affective)

SCALE DESCRIPTION: A three-item, seven-point semantic differential rating scale measuring the degree to which a consumer views a purchase decision as being influenced by his or her feelings, versus cognitive thought processes, because of such things as ego gratification, social acceptance, or hedonic motivation.

SCALE ORIGIN: The scale was constructed for the studies reported by Ratchford (1987). The sample for the final study was composed of the 1792 adult members of the Market Facts mail panel who provided responses to the questionnaire. The scale had an alpha of .64.

SAMPLES: Data were gathered by Putrevu and Lord (1994) from students in an introductory undergraduate marketing course taught at a Northeastern U.S. university. Apparently, usable data were collected from **100** students who voluntarily participated for extra credit in the course. Demographic data about the respondents were collected but were not described in the article.

RELIABILITY: Putrevu and Lord (1994) reported an alpha of **.72** for the scale.

VALIDITY: Evidence of the scale's unidimensionality comes from a factor analysis performed by Putrevu and Lord (1994). The analysis included the five items that composed the **purchase involvement (cognitive)** scale, as well as the three items in this scale. The Varimax rotation produced good simple structure. Scale scores for the four products selected to represent the quadrants of the FCB Grid (see "Major Findings") placed them in the correct cells, though not as well as hoped. This provides some limited evidence of the scales' predictive validity.

ADMINISTRATION: The scale was administered to students by Putrevu and Lord (1994), along with other measures, as part of an in-class experiment. Higher scores on the scale suggested that when a consumer buys the specified product, the decision is heavily determined by his or her feelings rather than thinking.

MAJOR FINDINGS: Putrevu and Lord (1994) examined the relative effectiveness of comparative and noncomparative advertising for products characterized by varying degrees of affective and cognitive involvement. The study used four products to represent the four cells of the FCB Grid that prior testing and experience indicated should vary (high/low) in cognitive and affective involvement. The **affective involvement** scale was used as a manipulation check to show that the four products could be correctly placed in the grid's quadrants. Beer and antiperspirants were confirmed to have the highest **affective involvement**, whereas cold remedies and shampoo had the lowest.

REFERENCES:
Putrevu, Sanjay and Kenneth R. Lord (1994), "Comparative and Noncomparative Advertising: Attitudinal Effects Under Cognitive and Affective Involvement Conditions," *JA*, 23 (June), 77–90.
Ratchford, Brian T. (1987), "New Insights About the FCB Grid," *JAR*, 27 (4), 24–38.

SCALE ITEMS:

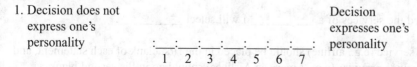

1. Decision does not express one's personality : __:__:__:__:__:__:__: Decision expresses one's personality
1   2   3   4   5   6   7

2. Decision is based
   on little feeling   :___:___:___:___:___:___:___: Decision is based on
                        1   2   3   4   5   6   7   a lot of feeling

3. Decision is not based
   on looks, taste, touch,
   smell or sounds   :___:___:___:___:___:___:___: Decision is based
                        1   2   3   4   5   6   7   on looks, taste, touch,
                                              smell or sounds

SCALE NAME: Purchase Involvement (Cognitive)

SCALE DESCRIPTION: Five seven-point semantic differentials intended to measure the degree to which a consumer's involvement with a purchase is related to *thinking* (utilitarian motives) rather than *feeling* (affective motives).

SCALE ORIGIN: The items in this measure were first used by Ratchford (1987) in two separate scales: one measuring involvement with a purchase decision and another intended to capture the degree to which a decision is made on the basis of thinking rather than feeling. Putrevu and Lord (1994) indicate that they combined the items from these two scales on the basis of the work of Kim and Lord (1991). The latter demonstrated that there was greater validity and strategic value if the thinking scale was combined with the purchase involvement scale. (The three separate scales referred to here can be found in Vol. 1, #34 Attitude Toward the Purchase [Feeling Dimension], #35 Attitude Toward the Purchase [Thinking Dimension], and #142 Involvement [Purchase Decision].)

SAMPLES: Data were gathered by Putrevu and Lord (1994) from students in an introductory under- graduate marketing course taught at a Northeastern U.S. university. Apparently, usable data were col- lected from **100** students who voluntarily participated for extra credit in the course. Demographic data about the respondents were collected but were not described in the article.

RELIABILITY: Putrevu and Lord (1994) reported an alpha of **.74** for the scale.

VALIDITY: Evidence of the scale's unidimensionality comes from a factor analysis performed by Putrevu and Lord (1994). The analysis included the three items that composed the **purchase involvement (affective)** scale, as well as the five items in this scale. The Varimax rotation produced good simple struc- ture. Scale scores for the four products selected to represent the quadrants of the FCB Grid (see "Major Findings") placed them in the correct cells, though not as well as hoped. This provides some limited evi- dence of the scales' predictive validity.

ADMINISTRATION: The scale was administered to students by Putrevu and Lord (1994), along with other measures, as part of an in-class experiment. Higher scores on the scale suggested that when a con- sumer buys the specified product, the decision is cognitively involving and driven by utilitarian motives.

MAJOR FINDINGS: Putrevu and Lord (1994) examined the relative effectiveness of comparative and noncomparative advertising for products characterized by varying degrees of affective and cognitive involvement. The study used four products to represent the four cells of the FCB Grid that prior testing and experience indicated should vary (high/low) in cognitive and affective involvement. The **cognitive involvement** scale was used as a manipulation check to show that the four products could be correctly placed in the grid's quadrants. Cold remedies and antiperspirants were confirmed to have the highest **cog- nitive involvement**, whereas shampoo and beer had the lowest.

REFERENCES:

Kim, Chung K. and Kenneth R. Lord (1991), "A New FCB Grid and Its Strategic Implications for Advertising," in *Proceedings of the Annual Conference of the Administrative Sciences Association of Canada (Marketing)*, Tony Schellink, ed. Niagara Falls, Ontario: Administrative Sciences Association of Canada, 51–60.

Putrevu, Sanjay and Kenneth R. Lord (1994), "Comparative and Noncomparative Advertising: Attitudinal Effects Under Cognitive and Affective Involvement Conditions," *JA*, 23 (June), 77–90.

Ratchford, Brian T. (1987), "New Insights About the FCB Grid," *JAR*, 27 (4), 24–38.

SCALE ITEMS:

1. Unimportant decision :___:___:___:___:___:___:___: Very important decision
   1 2 3 4 5 6 7

2. Decision requires
   little thought :___:___:___:___:___:___:___:
   1 2 3 4 5 6 7
   Decision requires
   a lot of thought

3. Little to lose if
   you choose the
   wrong brand :___:___:___:___:___:___:___:
   1 2 3 4 5 6 7
   A lot to lose if
   you choose the
   wrong brand

4. Decision is not mainly
   logical or objective :___:___:___:___:___:___:___:
   1 2 3 4 5 6 7
   Decision is mainly
   logical or objective

5. Decision is not
   based mainly on the
   functional facts :___:___:___:___:___:___:___:
   1 2 3 4 5 6 7
   Decision is based
   mainly on the
   functional facts

SCALE NAME: Quality (Apartment)

SCALE DESCRIPTION: Six seven-point items measuring the degree to which an apartment featured in an ad is viewed as being of high quality.

SCALE ORIGIN: There is no information to indicate that the scale is anything other than original to the studies by Urbany and colleagues (1997).

SAMPLES: Urbany and colleagues (1997) reported on two studies, both of which utilized data collected from undergraduates attending a major state university. Apparently, complete data were gathered from **200** students in Study 1 and **393** students in Study 2.

RELIABILITY: The construct reliability of the scale for Study 2 was reported to be **.90** (Urbany et al. 1997).

VALIDITY: A couple of tests generally described by Urbany and colleagues (1997) provided support for a claim of discriminant validity for the scale. The details relative to this particular scale were not given.

ADMINISTRATION: Students self-administered the scale, along with other measures, after they were exposed to experimental stimuli (Urbany et al. 1997). Higher scores on the scale suggested that respondents viewed an apartment featured in an ad to be of high quality.

MAJOR FINDINGS: The experiments conducted by Urbany and colleagues (1997) examined the role of transaction utility in determining choice when product quality is uncertain. As hypothesized, transaction utility was a more significant predictor of purchase intention as **product quality** became more certain.

REFERENCES:

Urbany, Joel E., William O. Bearden, Ajit Kaicker, and Melinda Smith-de Borrero (1997), "Transaction Utility Effects When Quality Is Uncertain," *JAMS*, 25 (Winter), 45–55.

SCALE ITEMS:*

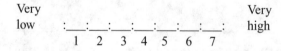

Very low : __ : __ : __ : __ : __ : __ : __ : Very high

      1 2 3 4 5 6 7

1. How would you rate the likely quality of the maintenance service for this advertised apartment?

2. What quality level of carpeting would you expect in this advertised apartment?

3. What quality level of building construction would you expect in this advertised apartment?

4. What quality level of appliances would you expect in this advertised apartment?

5. The quality of this apartment appears to be ...

6. The apartment featured in the advertisement appears to be of ...

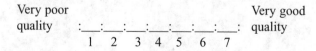

Very poor quality : __ : __ : __ : __ : __ : __ : __ : Very good quality

      1 2 3 4 5 6 7

*Items 1–5 use the *low/high* response scale, whereas item 6 has a different response scale (as shown).

SCALE NAME: Quality Consciousness

SCALE DESCRIPTION: Four five-point Likert-type items that are intended to measure a shopping orientation characterized by the extent to which a consumer is focused on buying products perceived to be of the highest quality.

SCALE ORIGIN: Shim and Gehrt (1996) used a modified version of a scale developed by Sproles and Kendall (1986). The latter created an eight-factor model of what they called *consumer decision making styles* but that many others in marketing (e.g., Shim and Gehrt 1996) would view as *shopping orientations*. Shim and Gehrt (1996) used the four items with the highest factor loadings of the eight items identified by Sproles and Kendall (1986). The latter reported an alpha of .74 for a subscale of the top seven items and a .69 for the top three items.

SAMPLES: Shim and Gehrt (1996) collected data from high school students in a southwestern U.S. state. Twenty-nine principals agreed to participate, and their schools apparently represented many if not all counties in the state. Principals were given instructions as to which classes to use (by level) and how many students from each class were needed. Some 1954 usable surveys were returned from a sample that was 61.3% girls and had a mean age of 16 years. However, the study focused only on data from **1846** students who were white (56%), Hispanic (32%), or Native American (12%).

RELIABILITY: An alpha of **.73** was reported for the scale by Shim and Gehrt (1996).

VALIDITY: No examination of the scale's validity was reported by Shim and Gehrt (1996).

ADMINISTRATION: Data were gathered in a classroom setting in which students filled out the scale as part of a larger survey instrument (Shim and Gehrt 1996). Higher scores on the scale indicated that respondents were highly motivated to shop for the best brands.

MAJOR FINDINGS: The study by Shim and Gehrt (1996) examined differences in shopping orientations among high school students that could be linked to ethnicity. The results showed that white students were significantly more **quality conscious** than Hispanic students, who were in turn significantly more **quality conscious** than Native American students.

REFERENCES:
Shim, Soyeon and Kenneth C. Gehrt (1996), "Hispanic and Native American Adolescents: An Exploratory Study of Their Approach to Shopping," *JR*, 72 (3), 307–24.
Sproles, George B. and Elizabeth L. Kendall (1986), "A Methodology for Profiling Consumers' Decision-Making Styles," *Journal of Consumer Affairs*, 20 (Winter), 267–79.

SCALE ITEMS:

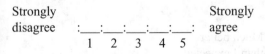

Strongly
disagree   :___:___:___:___:___: agree
         1   2   3   4   5

1. Getting very good quality is very important to me.

2. When it comes to purchasing products, I try to get the very best or perfect choice.

3. In general, I usually try to buy the best overall quality.

4. I make special effort to choose the very best quality products.

SCALE NAME: Quality of Service Environment (Stadium)

SCALE DESCRIPTION: Three seven-point semantic differentials measuring the degree to which a person evaluates the tangible aspects of a sports stadium to be of high quality.

SCALE ORIGIN: The scale seems to be original to Wakefield and Barnes (1996). The scale was apparently pretested and refined, along with other measures in the study, using a sample of 308 completed responses from sports fans attending a minor league baseball game.

SAMPLES: Data were collected in the main study by Wakefield and Barnes (1996) from those who attended one of two minor league baseball games in a city different from the one used in the pretest. Final analysis was based on usable data from **250** respondents who appeared to live in the area and would hypothetically have been exposed to the promotional information under study.

RELIABILITY: An alpha of **.84** was reported for the scale (Wakefield and Barnes 1996).

VALIDITY: Although specific evaluation of the scale's validity was not discussed by Wakefield and Barnes (1996), they noted that they used confirmatory factor analysis and no changes were deemed necessary for this scale.

ADMINISTRATION: The scale was part of a larger survey instrument self-administered by people who attended a baseball game (Wakefield and Barnes 1996). Higher scores on the scale suggested that respondents viewed the specified tangible characteristics of a particular stadium to be of high quality.

MAJOR FINDINGS: Wakefield and Barnes (1996) tested a model of sales promotion for entertainment services. Among their conclusions was that consumers who considered the tangible aspects of the stadium to be of high **quality** also viewed the service to be a better value for the cost.

COMMENTS: The scale scores were reported to have a mean of 5.9 and a standard deviation of .91 (Wakefield and Barnes 1996).

REFERENCES:
Wakefield, Kirk L. and James H. Barnes (1996), "Retailing Hedonic Consumption: A Model of Sales Promotion of a Leisure Service," *JR*, 72 (4), 409–27.

SCALE ITEMS:
Overall, the quality of this stadium's parking, architecture, decor, seating, layout, and scoreboards is:

1. Terrible :___:___:___:___:___:___:___: Great
                  1 2 3 4 5 6 7

2. Much worse   Much better
   than I expected :___:___:___:___:___:___:___: than I expected
                  1 2 3 4 5 6 7

3. Not at all what   Just what
   it should be :___:___:___:___:___:___:___: it should be
                1 2 3 4 5 6 7

SCALE NAME: Rage

SCALE DESCRIPTION: A three-item, six-point summated ratings scale measuring the degree to which a person describes feeling a sense of anger and possibly hatred on exposure to some stimulus (e.g., music). Phrasing of the scale was such that it measured the respondent's emotional reaction to a stimulus rather than the attitude toward the stimulus itself.

SCALE ORIGIN: Lacher and Mizerski (1994) indicated that the scale was taken from Asmus (1985). Indeed, each of the three items here were in the *evil* factor Asmus (1985) identified in his development of a multidimensional instrument for measuring affective responses to music. Although not explicitly stated in the article, two items from Asmus's activity scale were dropped by Lacher and Mizerski (1994, p. 374) during their pretesting (219 undergraduate students) of the scale when they did not remain constant over the two songs tested and the two extraction methods used. Alphas for the fast- and slow-tempo songs in the pretest were **.86** and **.85**, respectively (Lacher 1997).

SAMPLES: The sample used by Lacher and Mizerski (1994) came from undergraduate business students at a large Southern U.S. university. Usable data were collected from **215** students who were 52% men and ranged in age from 19 to 36 years.

RELIABILITY: Lacher and Mizerski (1994) did not report the alpha for the scale as used in the main study, but on the basis of the pretest results, it appears it would have been acceptable.

VALIDITY: No examination of scale validity was reported by Lacher and Mizerski (1994) beyond what could be construed from the factor analyses in the study's pretest.

ADMINISTRATION: The scale was self-administered, along with other measures, in the study by Lacher and Mizerski (1994). Students heard two songs played twice, and the second time the songs were played, they filled out this scale along with other measures. Higher scores on the scale indicated that respondents perceived that a particular song evoked a feeling of anger in them.

MAJOR FINDINGS: Lacher and Mizerski (1994) investigated the responses music evokes in a listener and how those reactions affect the intention to purchase the music. Among the findings was that a feeling of **rage** had a moderate negative effect on affect toward the music being heard.

COMMENTS: Although there is nothing in the items themselves to keep them from being applied to other stimuli, it should be kept in mind that this scale was specifically developed and tested for measuring emotional reactions to music.

REFERENCES:

Asmus, Edward P. (1985), "The Development of a Multidimensional Instrument for the Measurement of Affective Responses to Music," *Psychology of Music*, 13 (1), 19–30.
Lacher, Kathleen T. (1997), personal correspondence.
——— and Richard Mizerski (1994), "An Exploratory Study of the Responses and Relationships Involved in the Evaluation of, and in the Intention to Purchase New Rock Music," *JCR*, 21 (September), 366–80.

#286 *Rage*

SCALE ITEMS:*

Directions: Rate each item below in terms of its appropriateness in describing the feelings and emotions you had in response to the music.

Strongly
disagree   :__:__:__:__:__:__: Strongly
             1 2 3 4 5 6   agree

1. Hate

2. Anger

3. Rage

*The actual directions for filling out the scale were not provided in the article but were likely to have been similar to this.

SCALE NAME: Repatronage Intentions

SCALE DESCRIPTION: Three seven-point statements measuring the likelihood that a person would shop again at a store where some negative event has occurred.

SCALE ORIGIN: Although Blodgett, Hill, and Tax (1997) may have drawn inspiration from previous measures (e.g., Singh 1988), this scale appears to be original to their study.

SAMPLES: Data were collected by Blodgett, Hill, and Tax (1997) using a quasi-experimental design and subjects from three different locations: a Midsouth U.S. university, a Midwestern U.S. university, and a Canadian university. Subjects came from local church groups, as well as faculty and staff at the universities. Usable responses were received from **265** subjects. Among the demographic information provided for the sample was that a majority were white (86%) and women (61%). There was wide diversity in the sample on other characteristics such as age, occupation, education, and income.

RELIABILITY: An alpha of **.91** was reported for the scale by Blodgett, Hill, and Tax (1997).

VALIDITY: No specific examination of the scale's validity was reported by Blodgett, Hill, and Tax (1997).

ADMINISTRATION: The scale was administered to subjects, along with other measures, after they had been exposed to experimental stimuli (Blodgett, Hill, and Tax 1997). Higher scores on the scale indicated that respondents were expressing a strong intention to shop at some specified store again.

MAJOR FINDINGS: The study by Blodgett, Hill, and Tax (1997) examined the effects of various types of *justice* on complainants' negative word of mouth and likelihood of repatronage. In general, it was found that two types of justice (distributive and interactional) were positively associated with **repatronage intentions**, whereas a third type (procedural) had no significant relationship with it.

COMMENTS: The phrasing of the items in this scale is unique because the items were developed for an experiment in which subjects were asked to *imagine* being the consumer in a scenario with which they were presented. With some adjustment and retesting, the items appear to be amenable for use in situations in which the respondents have actually visited the store.

REFERENCES:
Blodgett, Jeffrey G., Donna J. Hill, and Stephen S. Tax (1997), "The Effects of Distributive, Procedural, and Interactional Justice on Postcomplaint Behavior," *JR,* 73 (2), 185–210.
Singh, Jagdip (1988), "Consumer Complaint Intentions and Behaviors: Definitional and Taxonomical Issues," *JM,* 52 (January), 93–107.

SCALE ITEMS:

1. What is the likelihood that you would shop at this retail store in the future?

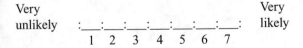

Very
unlikely   :___:___:___:___:___:___:___: Very
        1 2 3 4 5 6 7   likely

2. If this situation had happened to me I would never shop at this store again. **(r)**

Strongly   Strongly
disagree   :___:___:___:___:___:___:___: agree
           1   2   3   4   5   6   7

3. If this had happened to me I would still shop at this store in the future.

Strongly   Strongly
disagree   :___:___:___:___:___:___:___: agree
           1   2   3   4   5   6   7

SCALE NAME: Resource Expenditures

SCALE DESCRIPTION: Five items measuring the relative level of resources spent by a shopper in a store during a recent visit. Three of the items were Likert-type in nature, whereas the two other items were open-ended, and ratio-level data were apparently expected from respondents.

SCALE ORIGIN: This scale is original to the study by Babin and Darden (1995).

SAMPLES: Data were gathered by Babin and Darden (1995) by intercepting shoppers as they left one of the ten top stores in a major Southeastern U.S. regional mall. Respondents were interviewed one at a time, and a small incentive was provided for their participation. The sample was considered to be representative of the mall's shoppers. The analysis appears to have been based on data from **118** shoppers.

RELIABILITY: An alpha of **.73** was reported for the scale (Babin and Darden 1995). The construct reliability was .73, and variance extracted was .36.

VALIDITY: The results of a confirmatory factor analysis supported the measurement model in the study (Babin and Darden 1995). This provides some limited evidence of the scale's unidimensionality, as well as its convergent and discriminant validities.

ADMINISTRATION: The scale was apparently administered to respondents by interviewers along with many other items in a questionnaire (Babin and Darden 1995). Higher scores on the scale suggested that respondents spent a lot of time, money, and energy during a recent visit to a retail store. The authors noted that the scale scores were calculated after normalizing scores on individual items to put them on a common metric.

MAJOR FINDINGS: The purpose of the study by Babin and Darden (1995) was to examine the role of self-regulation as a moderator of relationships between shopping emotions and shopping experience evaluations. Among the findings was that higher **resource expenditures** had a significant positive impact on hedonic shopping value but a negative impact on utilitarian shopping value.

REFERENCES:
Babin, Barry J. and William R. Darden (1995), "Consumer Self-Regulation in a Retail Environment," *JR*, 71 (1), 47–70.

SCALE ITEMS:

```
Strongly                          Strongly
disagree   :___:___:___:___:___:  agree
              1   2   3   4   5
```

1. I talked to several clerks while shopping.

2. I spent more time than I expected to in this store.

3. While shopping, I spent more money than I expected.

4. Please estimate the number of minutes you spent shopping in the store. _____

5. Please indicate the amount of money you spent on items in the store. _____

*The first three items are to be responded to using the Likert scale. The number of points on the response scale was not specified in the article by Babin and Darden (1995). The actual phrasing of the two open-ended items was not provided in the article.

SCALE NAME: Response Difficulty

SCALE DESCRIPTION: Three seven-point items measuring the perceived cognitive effort involved in answering a question. The scale was referred to as the *effort index* by Menon, Raghubir, and Schwarz (1995).

SCALE ORIGIN: Although not explicitly stated, the scale appears to have been developed by Menon, Raghubir, and Schwarz (1995) for use in their study.

SAMPLES: Data were gathered by Menon, Raghubir, and Schwarz (1995) from **177** undergraduate business students taking a marketing course. Students received course credit for their participation.

RELIABILITY: Alphas of **.80** and **.83** were reported by Menon, Raghubir, and Schwarz (1995) for the scale as used with regard to a question about regular and irregular behaviors, respectively (see "Major Findings").

VALIDITY: No examination of the scale's validity was discussed by Menon, Raghubir, and Schwarz (1995).

ADMINISTRATION: The scale was self-administered by subjects in the experiment in response to questions about the frequency of engaging in certain behaviors (Menon, Raghubir, and Schwarz 1995). Higher scores on the scale indicated that respondents considered it to have been very difficult to answer the questions because of the thought that was required.

MAJOR FINDINGS: Menon, Raghubir, and Schwarz (1995) investigated the context of respondents formulating frequency judgments about their past behavior. As anticipated, subjects considered the **response difficulty** to be greater for questions about irregular behaviors (those engaged in infrequently) than for those about regular ones.

REFERENCES:
Menon, Geeta, Priya Raghubir, and Norbert Schwarz (1995), "Behavioral Frequency Judgments: An Accessibility-Diagnosticity Framework," *JCR*, 22 (September), 212–28.

SCALE ITEMS:*
How difficult was it for you to answer the question?

Very little :___:___:___:___:___:___:___: A lot
            1 2 3 4 5 6 7

1. Effort

2. Time

3. Thought

*The exact structure of the scale was not described in the article by Menon, Raghubir, and Schwarz (1995), but it is recreated here on the basis of the information that was provided.

SCALE NAME: Responsiveness to Patient Requests (Medication)

SCALE DESCRIPTION: Three five-point Likert-type statements that measure the attitude a physician has about writing prescriptions for medications that have been specifically requested by patients.

SCALE ORIGIN: Although the source of the scale is not explicitly stated by Petroshius, Titus, and Hatch (1995), it appears to be original to their study.

SAMPLES: Data were gathered by Petroshius, Titus, and Hatch (1995) by conducting a survey of physicians in the Midwestern United States. The questionnaires were delivered by pharmaceutical representatives to 250 physicians during their normal visits. Respondents could either mail in the completed forms or have the reps pick them up later. Usable forms were received from **143** physicians (73% men) who varied on age, experience, and type of practice. The largest specialty represented in the sample was dermatology (52%), which was purposeful given the objectives of the study.

RELIABILITY: An alpha of **.79** was reported for the scale by Petroshius, Titus, and Hatch (1995).

VALIDITY: No examination of the scale's validity was reported by Petroshius, Titus, and Hatch (1995).

ADMINISTRATION: The scale was self-administered by the physicians, along with the other measures, in the questionnaire (Petroshius, Titus, and Hatch 1995). Higher scores on the scale indicated that the responding physicians had very positive attitudes about writing prescriptions for medications that have been requested by patients.

MAJOR FINDINGS: Petroshius, Titus, and Hatch (1995) studied physician attitudes toward the advertising of prescription drugs, particularly cosmetic pharmaceuticals, and the effect of these attitudes on other attitudes and behaviors. The findings indicated that the most influential effect on a physician's **responsiveness to patients' requests** for specific medications was the physician's attitude toward the advertising of cosmetic pharmaceuticals to consumers.

REFERENCES:
Petroshius, Susan M., Philip A. Titus, and Kathryn J. Hatch (1995), "Physician Attitudes Toward Pharmaceutical Drug Advertising," *JAR*, 35 (November/December), 41–51.

SCALE ITEMS:

Strongly   Strongly
disagree   :___:___:___:___:___: agree
              1   2   3   4   5

1. If a patient asks for a specific appropriate medication, I am happy to write a prescription for that product.

2. My patients get better results if they are on medication that they requested.

3. I am frustrated by requests from my patients for medication they've read about in advertisements and would not write the prescription they're asking for. **(r)**

SCALE NAME: Risk (Financial)

SCALE DESCRIPTION: The scale is purported to measure the perceived degree of financial risk associated with a specified product. Financial risk has to do with the uncertainty and monetary loss a person thinks could be incurred if a product does not function at some expected level. Shimp and Bearden (1982) used a three-item, nine-point version of the scale, whereas the version used by Grewel, Gotlieb, and Marmorstein (1994) had three items and a seven-point response format.

SCALE ORIGIN: The scale was apparently origin to the study by Shimp and Bearden (1982).

SAMPLES: Data from three student samples and two nonstudent samples were employed in this study by Shimp and Bearden (1982). A multiscreen television experiment randomly assigned 12 students to each of 18 treatments (n = **216**); the first plastic-tire experiment randomly assigned 11 students to each of 18 treatments (n = **198**); and the second plastic-tire experiment randomly assigned from 10 to 13 students to each of 12 treatments (n = **145**). The nonstudent subjects were contacted using a statewide panel. There were 13 to 20 respondents for each of the 18 treatments in the plastic tire experiment (n = **297**) and the jogging device experiment (n = **293**). The respondents were mostly white, above average in age, and economically upscale.

Grewel, Gotlieb, and Marmorstein (1994) used an in-class experiment to gather data from students enrolled in business classes at a large urban university. Analysis was conducted on data from **131** subjects. No other information was provided about the subjects, except that all but one had used a VCR (the product category tested) in the past year.

RELIABILITY: The following alphas were reported by Shimp and Bearden (1982) for the five separate samples in the order described previously: **.86, .79, .81, .75**, and **.72**. A test–retest correlation of **.57** was calculated using 44 students and a three-week interval.

An alpha of **.77** was reported for the version of the scale used by Grewel, Gotlieb, and Marmorstein (1994).

VALIDITY: The validity of the scale was not specifically examined in the study by Shimp and Bearden (1982). Using confirmatory factor analysis and related tests, Grewel, Gotlieb, and Marmorstein (1994) determined that the scale was not only unidimensional, but that it had discriminant validity with another scale being used: risk (performance) (see #292).

ADMINISTRATION: In the classroom experiments conducted by Shimp and Bearden (1982) and Grewel, Gotlieb, and Marmorstein (1994), the scale was given to students along with other materials and measures. The panel subjects contacted by Shimp and Bearden (1982) were asked to complete the scale, along with other measures, in the packet of materials mailed to them. Higher scores on the scale indicated that respondents associated a lot of financial risk with a product, whereas lower scores suggested that they perceived a product to involve little financial risk.

MAJOR FINDINGS: A series of experiments was designed by Shimp and Bearden (1982) to examine the influence of certain extrinsic cues (warranty quality, warranty reputation, and price) on the risk perceived with innovative product concepts. In contrast to what was expected, only with warranty quality was there significant evidence that the extrinsic cues could reduce perceptions of **financial risk**.

Grewel, Gotlieb, and Marmorstein (1994) used prospect theory to investigate an inconsistency in the literature between price and perceived risk. The results showed that the effect of price on the **financial risk** associated with the purchase of a new brand is greater when an ad is framed positively than when it is framed negatively.

COMMENTS: As noted subsequently, an item was dropped from the scale when it was administered to the two nonstudent samples to help reduce the length of the questionnaire.

REFERENCES:

Grewel, Dhruv, Jerry Gotlieb, and Howard Marmorstein (1994), "The Moderating Effects of Message Framing and Source Credibility on the Price–Perceived Risk Relationship," *JCR*, 21 (June), 145–53.

Shimp, A. Terence and William O. Bearden (1982), "Warranty and Other Extrinsic Cue Effects on Consumers' Risk Perceptions," *JCR*, 9 (June), 38–46.

SCALE ITEMS:*

Considering the sizable investment associated with the purchase of a _____, how risky would you say purchasing the _____ would be?

Not risky
at all   :___:___:___:___:___:___:___:___: Very
              1   2   3   4   5   6   7   8   9   risky

1. Given the expense involved with purchasing _____ today, how much risk would you say would be involved with purchasing the new _____? **(r)**

Substantial
risk   :___:___:___:___:___:___:___:___: Very little
              1   2   3   4   5   6   7   8   9   risk

2. How risky do you feel it would be for you to purchase this new _____? **(r)**

Very
risky   :___:___:___:___:___:___:___:___: Not risky
              1   2   3   4   5   6   7   8   9   at all

3. I think that the purchase of the _____ would lead to financial risk for me because of the possibility of such things as higher maintenance and/or repair costs.

Improbable :___:___:___:___:___:___:___:___: Probable
              1   2   3   4   5   6   7   8   9

*The name of the product should be placed in the blanks. Shimp and Bearden (1982) used items 1–3 for their nonstudents samples and items 1 and 2 for their student samples. Grewel, Gotlieb, and Marmorstein (1994) used item 4 and items similar to 1 and 2.

SCALE NAME: Risk (Performance)

SCALE DESCRIPTION: The scale is purported to measure the perceived degree of performance risk associated with a specified product. Performance risk has to do with the uncertainty and consequence of a product not functioning at some expected level. Shimp and Bearden (1982) used a four-item, nine-point version of the scale, whereas the version used by Grewel, Gotlieb, and Marmorstein (1994) had three items and a seven-point response format.

SCALE ORIGIN: The scale was apparently original to the study by Shimp and Bearden (1982).

SAMPLES: Data from three student samples and two nonstudent samples were employed in this study by Shimp and Bearden (1982). A multiscreen television experiment randomly assigned 12 students to each of 18 treatments (n = **216**); the first plastic-tire experiment randomly assigned 11 students to each of 18 treatments (n = **198**); and the second plastic-tire experiment randomly assigned from 10 to 13 students to each of 12 treatments (n = **145**). The nonstudent subjects were contacted using a statewide panel. There were 13 to 20 respondents for each of the 18 treatments in the plastic tire experiment (n = **297**) and the jogging device experiment (n = **293**). The respondents were mostly white, above average in age, and economically upscale.

Grewel, Gotlieb, and Marmorstein (1994) used an in-class experiment to gather data from students enrolled in business classes at a large urban university. Analysis was conducted on data from **131** subjects. No other information was provided about the subjects except that all but one had used a VCR (the product category tested) in the past year.

RELIABILITY: The following alphas were reported by Shimp and Bearden (1982) for the five separate samples in the order described previously: **.84**, **.77**, **.73**, **.84**, and **.85**. A test–retest correlation of **.74** was calculated using 44 students and a three-week interval.

An alpha of **.90** was reported for the version of the scale used by Grewel, Gotlieb, and Marmorstein (1994).

VALIDITY: The validity of the scale was not specifically examined in the study by Shimp and Bearden (1982). Using confirmatory factor analysis and related tests, Grewel, Gotlieb, and Marmorstein (1994) determined that the scale was not only unidimensional, but that it had discriminant validity with another scale being used: risk (financial) (see #291).

ADMINISTRATION: In the classroom experiments conducted by Shimp and Bearden (1982) and Grewel, Gotlieb, and Marmorstein (1994), the scale was given to students along with other materials and measures. The panel subjects contacted by Shimp and Bearden (1982) were asked to complete the scale, along with other measures, in the packet of materials mailed to them. Higher scores on the scale indicated that respondents associated a lot of performance risk with a product, whereas lower scores suggested that they perceived a product would not function as expected.

MAJOR FINDINGS: A series of experiments was designed by Shimp and Bearden (1982) to examine the influence of certain extrinsic cues (warranty quality, warranty reputation, and price) on the risk perceived with innovative product concepts. In contrast to what was expected, none of the experiments provided significant evidence that the extrinsic cues could reduce perceptions of **performance risk**.

Grewel, Gotlieb, and Marmorstein (1994) used prospect theory to investigate an inconsistency in the literature between price and perceived **performance risk**. The results showed that the effect of price on the **performance risk** associated with the purchase of a new brand is greater when an ad is framed negatively than when it is framed positively.

COMMENTS: As noted subsequently, an item was dropped by Shimp and Bearden (1982) from the scale when it was administered to the two nonstudent samples to help reduce the length of the questionnaire.

REFERENCES:

Grewel, Dhruv, Jerry Gotlieb, and Howard Marmorstein (1994), "The Moderating Effects of Message Framing and Source Credibility on the Price–Perceived Risk Relationship," *JCR*, 21 (June), 145–53.

Shimp, A. Terence and William O. Bearden (1982), "Warranty and Other Extrinsic Cue Effects on Consumers' Risk Perceptions," *JCR*, 9 (June), 38–46.

SCALE ITEMS:*

1. How sure are you about the _____'s ability to perform satisfactorily? **(r)**

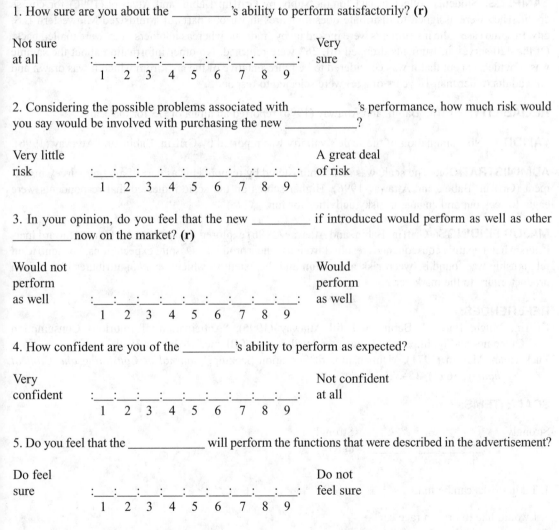

Not sure   Very
at all   :___:___:___:___:___:___:___:___: sure
              1 2 3 4 5 6 7 8 9

2. Considering the possible problems associated with _____'s performance, how much risk would you say would be involved with purchasing the new _____?

Very little   A great deal
risk   :___:___:___:___:___:___:___:___: of risk
              1 2 3 4 5 6 7 8 9

3. In your opinion, do you feel that the new _____ if introduced would perform as well as other _____ now on the market? **(r)**

Would not
perform   Would
as well   :___:___:___:___:___:___:___:___: perform
              1 2 3 4 5 6 7 8 9 as well

4. How confident are you of the _____'s ability to perform as expected?

Very
confident   :___:___:___:___:___:___:___:___: Not confident
              1 2 3 4 5 6 7 8 9 at all

5. Do you feel that the _____ will perform the functions that were described in the advertisement?

Do feel   Do not
sure   :___:___:___:___:___:___:___:___: feel sure
              1 2 3 4 5 6 7 8 9

*The name of the product should be placed in the blanks. Shimp and Bearden (1982) used items 1–4 for their nonstudents samples and items 1–3 for their student samples. Grewel, Gotlieb, and Marmorstein (1994) used items 4, 5, and an item similar to 1 (*certain* was used instead of *sure*).

SCALE NAME: Risk Attraction

SCALE DESCRIPTION: Five five-point Likert-type statements purported to measure the extent to which a person is willing to seek out and engage in risky activities.

SCALE ORIGIN: Griffin, Babin, and Attaway (1996) indicated that the items for the scale came from a subscale of an early version of the sensation-seeking scale (Zuckerman 1971). However, though the items are conceptually similar to some listed in that article, only one item (5) is very similar in wording. Thus, it is not clear whether this scale is a modification of items from Zuckerman (1971) or was borrowed relatively intact from some other (unknown) source.

SAMPLES: Students collected data for the study by Griffin, Babin, and Attaway (1996) for course credit. They were assigned to distribute questionnaires in various parts of a midsized Midwestern U.S. city. In some cases, the instruments were picked up by students, whereas in others, they were mailed back. Of the 420 survey instruments dropped off, **262** were returned. No other information about the sample was provided, except that it was considered to be representative of the area from which it was drawn and only adults (older than 18 years of age) were selected to respond.

RELIABILITY: Griffin, Babin, and Attaway (1996) reported an alpha of **.75** for the scale.

VALIDITY: No examination of the scale's validity was reported by Griffin, Babin, and Attaway (1996).

ADMINISTRATION: The scale was self-administered by respondents as part of a larger survey instrument (Griffin, Babin, and Attaway 1996). Higher scores on the scale indicated that respondents were eager to seek out and engage in risky activities for fun.

MAJOR FINDINGS: Griffin, Babin, and Attaway (1996) explored the attribution of blame toward marketers when negative consequences resulted from use their products. Despite expectations, no significant relationship was found between **risk attraction** and the extent to which a person attributes blame for a product injury to the marketer.

REFERENCES:

Griffin, Mitch, Barry J. Babin, and Jill Attaway (1996), "Anticipation of Injurious Consumption Outcomes and Its Impact on Consumer Attributions of Blame," *JAMS*, 24 (Fall), 314–27.

Zuckerman, Marvin (1971), "Dimensions of Sensation Seeking," *Journal of Consulting and Clinical Psychology*, 36 (1), 35–52.

SCALE ITEMS:

```
Strongly                         Strongly
disagree    :___:___:___:___:___:   agree
             1   2   3   4   5
```

1. Taking risks can be fun.

2. I would like to drive a race car.

3. I sometimes do things I know are dangerous just for fun.

4. I have considered skydiving as a hobby.

5. I prefer friends who are unpredictable.

SCALE NAME: Risk Aversion

SCALE DESCRIPTION: A three-item, five-point Likert-type summated ratings scale measuring the degree to which a person expresses a desire to avoid taking risks.

SCALE ORIGIN: The source of the scale was not stated by Donthu and Gilliland (1996), but it is likely to be original to their study.

SAMPLES: Donthu and Gilliland (1996) used trained interviewers to call 1000 households in a large city telephone directory. Interviews were successfully completed with adults in **368** of those households. Although some demographic information was employed in the analysis, the data were not reported in such a way that the sample as a whole can be clearly described.

RELIABILITY: An alpha of .78 was reported for the scale by Donthu and Gilliland (1996).

VALIDITY: No specific examination of the scale's validity was reported by Donthu and Gilliland (1996).

ADMINISTRATION: Donthu and Gilliland (1996) had the scale administered as part of a larger telephone survey. Higher scores on the scale indicated that respondents were very risk averse.

MAJOR FINDINGS: Donthu and Gilliland (1996) profiled infomercial shoppers and found that they had significantly less **risk aversion** than those who had never purchased goods from infomercials.

REFERENCES:
Donthu, Naveen and David Gilliland (1996), "The Infomercial Shopper," *JAR*, 36 (March/April), 69–76.

SCALE ITEMS:

Strongly disagree	Disagree	Neutral	Agree	Strongly agree
1	2	3	4	5

1. I would rather be safe than sorry.

2. I want to be sure before I purchase anything.

3. I avoid risky things.

#295 *Risk Aversion*

SCALE NAME: Risk Aversion

SCALE DESCRIPTION: Four seven-point Likert-type items measuring the extent to which a person expresses a concern about making a wrong decision when selecting among various alternatives in a specified product category. The category studied by Moorthy, Ratchford, and Talukdar (1997) was cars.

SCALE ORIGIN: The scale was developed by Moorthy, Ratchford, and Talukdar (1997) for use in their study and based on previous work conducted by Srinivasan and Ratchford (1991).

SAMPLES: Moorthy, Ratchford, and Talukdar (1997) gathered data from new car buyers in the greater Rochester area in northern New York state over a six month period. Surveys were passed out to new car buyers at four dealerships that represented a variety of American and Japanese manufacturers. Shoppers were given two survey forms: one to fill out if they had already bought a car and the other to complete if they were still in the process of buying a car. Fifty-one respondents filled out the "already purchased" form; another 51 completed the "in process" form initially but bought cars within two months.

RELIABILITY: Alphas of **.79** and **.74** were reported for the scale for the two groups of respondents (Moorthy, Ratchford, and Talukdar 1997).

VALIDITY: No examination of the scale's validity was reported by Moorthy, Ratchford, and Talukdar (1997).

ADMINISTRATION: Questionnaires were passed out by one of the researchers, but the forms were self-administered by respondents at their convenience and mailed back to the researchers (Moorthy, Ratchford, and Talukdar 1997). Higher scores on the scale indicated that respondents were very concerned about making a poor decision in a specified product category, particularly as it related to potential financial and performance losses they might suffer.

MAJOR FINDINGS: Moorthy, Ratchford, and Talukdar (1997) presented a comprehensive model for understanding consumer external search activity. The framework stressed the influence of prior brand perceptions on the search process. As expected, the findings showed an inverted U-shaped relationship between purchase experience and amount of search, though the specific effects of **risk aversion** were not discussed.

COMMENTS: Two types of risk losses are explicitly measured in the scale: financial and performance. The other types (e.g., social, time, personal) are not explicitly included but might be captured to some extent in item 1.

REFERENCES:

Moorthy, Sridhar, Brian T. Ratchford, and Debabrata Talukdar (1997), "Consumer Information Search Revisited: Theory and Empirical Analysis," *JCR*, 23 (March), 263–77.
Srinivasan, Narasimhan and Brian T. Ratchford (1991), "An Empirical Test of a External Search for Automobiles," *JCR*, 18 (September), 233–42.

SCALE ITEMS:*

Strongly   Strongly
disagree :___:___:___:___:___:___: agree
          1 2 3 4 5 6 7

1. When I buy a _____, it is a big deal if I buy the wrong model by mistake.

2. When I buy a _____, it is a big deal if I do not pay the best price available in the market.

3. I feel very concerned about a potential financial loss from making a poor choice for my new _____

4. I feel very concerned about a potential performance loss from making a poor choice for my new _____.

*The name of the product category should be placed in the blanks.

SCALE NAME: Sadness

SCALE DESCRIPTION: In both versions described here, the scale is composed of three items measuring the degree to which a person describes feeling a sense of depression on exposure to some stimulus (e.g., music). Phrasing of the scale was such that it measures a respondent's emotional reaction to a stimulus rather than the attitude toward the stimulus itself. The version of the scale used by Lacher and Mizerski (1994) used a six-point response format, whereas Richins's (1997) version used four point.

SCALE ORIGIN: Lacher and Mizerski (1994) indicated that the scale was taken from Asmus (1985). Indeed, each of their three items were in the *evil* factor Asmus (1985) identified in his development of a multidimensional instrument for measuring affective responses to music. Although not explicitly stated in the article, two items from Asmus's activity scale were dropped by Lacher and Mizerski (1994, p. 374) during their pretesting (219 undergraduate students) of the scale when they did not remain constant over the two songs tested and the two extraction methods used. Alphas for the fast- and slow-tempo songs in the pretest were **.82** and **.87**, respectively (Lacher 1997).

Richins (1997) began with many emotion-related terms taken from a variety of previous studies and then refined them in a series of studies of her own, which resulted in the development of the CES (Consumption Emotion Set).

SAMPLES: The sample used by Lacher and Mizerski (1994) came from undergraduate business students at a large Southern U.S. university. Usable data were collected from **215** students, 52% of whom were men and who ranged in age from 19 to 36 years.

Six studies were reported by Richins (1997) as part of the process of developing the CES, only two of which had reliability information. Study 4 was based on data from **448** college students. Two surveys were conducted in Study 5: Survey 1 was completed by **256** college students, and there were **194** student respondents to Survey 2.

RELIABILITY: Lacher and Mizerski (1994) did not report the alpha for the scale as used in the main study, but on the basis of the pretest results, it appears it would have been acceptable. As noted, reliability was reported by Richins (1997) only for Studies 4 (α = **.83**) and 5 (α = **.72**).

VALIDITY: No examination of scale validity was reported by Lacher and Mizerski (1994) beyond what could be construed from the factor analyses in the study's pretest. Richins (1997) did not directly examine the validity of the scale either. However, a great deal of effort was expended in a creative use of multidimensional scaling to note whether the items that composed each scale in the CES clustered together in a reasonable fashion.

ADMINISTRATION: The scale was self-administered, along with other measures, in the study by Lacher and Mizerski (1994). Students heard two songs played twice, and the second time the songs were played, they filled out the scale along with other measures. In the studies performed by Richins (1997), particularly Studies 4 and 5, the scale was part of a larger instrument containing many emotion-related measures. Higher scores on the scale indicated that respondents perceived that a particular stimulus or experience evoked a feeling of sadness in them.

MAJOR FINDINGS: Lacher and Mizerski (1994) investigated the responses music evokes in a listener and how those reactions affect the intention to purchase the music. Among the findings was that a feeling of **sadness** did not have a significant influence on any of the other responses to music being examined.

#296 *Sadness*

On the basis of a review of previously developed measures of emotion, Richins (1997) conducted six studies with the purpose of producing a set of scales that were particularly suited for assessing consumption experiences. The CES instrument was a result of the studies, one subscale of which measures **sadness**. In general, the instrument was more successful in representing the diversity of consumption emotions than the other instruments tested.

COMMENTS: Although there is nothing apparent in the items themselves to keep them from being applied to other stimuli or experiences, it should be kept in mind that the version of the scale by Lacher and Mizerski (1994) was specifically developed and tested for measuring emotional reactions to music, whereas the version by Richins (1997) was developed for consumption experiences in general.

REFERENCES:

Asmus, Edward P. (1985), "The Development of a Multidimensional Instrument for the Measurement of Affective Responses to Music," *Psychology of Music*, 13 (1), 19–30.

Lacher, Kathleen T. (1997), personal correspondence.

——— and Richard Mizerski (1994), "An Exploratory Study of the Responses and Relationships Involved in the Evaluation of, and in the Intention to Purchase New Rock Music," *JCR*, 21 (September), 366–80.

Richins, Marsha L. (1997), "Measuring Emotions in the Consumption Experience," *JCR*, 24 (September), 127–46.

SCALE ITEMS:*

Strongly disagree   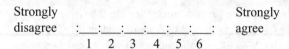   Strongly agree

1. Sad

2. Blue

3. Depressed

4. Miserable

*Items 1–3 were used by Lacher and Mizerski (1994) in the Likert format shown. Richins (1997) used items 1, 3, and 4 with a four-point scale ranging from *not at all* to *strongly*.

SCALE NAME: Sadness

SCALE DESCRIPTION: Five seven-point descriptors measuring the degree to which a person reports feeling an upsetting, unhappy emotional reaction to some stimulus.

SCALE ORIGIN: Nyer (1997) drew on Shaver and colleagues (1987) and Holbrook and Batra (1987, 1988) for items. These latter in turn had drawn on others to develop their measures.

SAMPLES: Nyer (1997) gathered data from **164** students attending a Midwestern U.S. university. Students were mostly nonbusiness majors and were recruited from several locations on campus. As an incentive to participate, subjects were paid $10 and had a chance to win $200. The experiment was run with one student at a time.

RELIABILITY: An alpha of **.91** was reported for the version of the scale used by Nyer (1997).

VALIDITY: Nyer (1997) indicates that he tested the scale, along with others in his study, for convergent and discriminant validity. However, beyond noting that the items loaded high on the same dimension in an exploratory factor analysis, no details were provided in support of this scale's validity.

ADMINISTRATION: The scale was self-administered by subjects, along with other measures, immediately after they were exposed to the treatment stimulus (Nyer 1997). High scores on the scale suggested that a stimulus to which respondents were exposed to evoked a very sad-type feeling.

MAJOR FINDINGS: The experiment conducted by Nyer (1997) examined the effect of cognitive appraisals on consumption emotions and the latter's effect on word-of-mouth intentions. Among the findings was that a model including anger and **sadness** in addition to joy/satisfaction significantly improved the prediction of intended word-of-mouth promotion (positive and negative).

REFERENCES:
Holbrook, Morris B. and Rajeev Batra (1987), "Assessing the Role of Emotions as Mediators of Consumer Responses to Advertising," *JCR*, 14 (December), 404–20.
———— and ———— (1988), "Toward a Standardized Emotional Profile (SEP) Useful in Measuring Responses to the Nonverbal Components of Advertising," in *Nonverbal Communication in Advertising*, Sidney Hecker and David W. Stewart, eds. Lexington, MA: D.C. Heath, 95–109.
Nyer, Prashanth U. (1997), "A Study of the Relationships Between Cognitive Appraisals and Consumption Emotions," *JAMS*, 25 (Fall), 296–304.
Shaver, Phillip, Judith Schwartz, Donald Kirson, and Acry O'Connor (1987), "Emotion Knowledge: Further Exploration of a Prototype Approach," *Journal of Personality and Social Psychology*, 52 (6), 1061–86.

SCALE ITEMS:

Not at all :___:___:___:___:___:___:___: Very much
            1   2   3   4   5   6   7

1. Gloomy

2. Distressed

3. Sorrowful

4. Sad

5. Dejected

SCALE NAME: Salesperson Listening (Evaluating)

SCALE DESCRIPTION: Five seven-point Likert-type items that measure the degree to which a customer perceives a salesperson was listening to him or her, trying to understand his or her needs, and asking for more information when necessary.

SCALE ORIGIN: The scale was constructed by Ramsey and Sohi (1997) along with two others (#299 and #300). To generate items, 80 students were asked to indicate behaviors they thought indicated salespersons were listening to them. Those behaviors listed at least twice by the group were part of the initial set tested. Scales were then purified using exploratory factor analysis.

SAMPLES: Data were gathered by Ramsey and Sohi (1997) through a mail survey of 500 new car buyers. The list of people who had bought cars in the previous six months came from a car dealership. Usable survey forms were returned by **173** respondents, the majority of whom were men (70%). Most of the group (60%) had at least some college education, the median household income was $46,000, 72% were married, and the average age was 42 years.

RELIABILITY: An alpha of **.64** was reported for the scale by Ramsey and Sohi (1997).

VALIDITY: After the exploratory factor analysis , Ramsey and Sohi (1997) used confirmatory factor analysis to provide evidence of unidimensionality and discriminant validity.

ADMINISTRATION: The scale was self-administered by respondents as part of a larger mail survey instrument (Ramsey and Sohi 1997). Higher scores on the scale indicated that respondents thought a specific salesperson during a particular sales encounter listened intently to what they were saying and tactfully asked questions for clarification.

MAJOR FINDINGS: Ramsey and Sohi (1997) developed and tested a model of the impact of salesperson listening behavior on customer trust, satisfaction, and anticipated future interaction with the salesperson. Salesperson listening behavior was found to have three main components, one of which was labeled **evaluating**. Customer perception of salesperson listening behavior was found to have significant positive impacts on customer trust and anticipation of future interaction with the salesperson.

COMMENTS: The internal consistency of the scale is low enough that caution should be exercised in its use.

REFERENCES:
Ramsey, Rosemary P. and Ravipreet S. Sohi (1997), "Listening to Your Customers: The Impact of Perceived Salesperson Listening Behavior on Relationship Outcomes," *JAMS*, 25 (Spring), 127–37.

SCALE ITEMS: *
Please indicate the degree to which you agree or disagree with each of the following statements regarding your interaction with the salesperson.

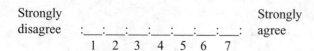

Strongly   Strongly
disagree   :__:__:__:__:__:__:__: agree
          1   2   3   4   5   6   7

1. Asked for more details.

2. Paraphrased my questions.

3. Didn't interrupt me.

4. Changed subject too frequently. **(r)**

5. Tried hard to understand what I was saying.

*The directions were not provided by Ramsey and Sohi (1997) but may have been similar to what is shown here.

SCALE NAME: Salesperson Listening (Responding)

SCALE DESCRIPTION: Four seven-point Likert-type items that measure the degree to which a customer perceives a salesperson was truly listening to him or her based on the responses the salesperson made.

SCALE ORIGIN: The scale was constructed by Ramsey and Sohi (1997) along with two others (#298 and #300). To generate items, 80 students were asked to indicate behaviors they thought indicated salespersons were listening to them. Those behaviors listed at least twice by the group were part of the initial set tested. Scales were then purified using exploratory factor analysis.

SAMPLES: Data were gathered by Ramsey and Sohi (1997) through a mail survey of 500 new car buyers. The list of people who had bought cars in the previous six months came from a car dealership. Usable survey forms were returned by **173** respondents, the majority of whom were men (70%). Most of the group (60%) had at least some college education, the median household income was $46,000, 72% were married, and the average age was 42 years.

RELIABILITY: An alpha of **.91** was reported for the scale by Ramsey and Sohi (1997).

VALIDITY: After the exploratory factor analysis, Ramsey and Sohi (1997) used confirmatory factor analysis to provide evidence of unidimensionality and discriminant validity.

ADMINISTRATION: The scale was self-administered by respondents as part of a larger mail survey instrument (Ramsey and Sohi 1997). Higher scores on the scale indicated that respondents thought a specific salesperson during a particular sales encounter was listening carefully given the comments and questions he or she made.

MAJOR FINDINGS: Ramsey and Sohi (1997) developed and tested a model of the impact of salesperson listening behavior on customer trust, satisfaction, and anticipated future interaction with the salesperson. Salesperson listening behavior was found to have three main components, one of which was labeled **responding**. Customer perception of salesperson listening behavior was found to have significant positive impacts on customer trust and anticipation of future interaction with the salesperson.

REFERENCES:
Ramsey, Rosemary P. and Ravipreet S. Sohi (1997), "Listening to Your Customers: The Impact of Perceived Salesperson Listening Behavior on Relationship Outcomes," *JAMS*, 25 (Spring), 127–37.

SCALE ITEMS: *
Please indicate the degree to which you agree or disagree with each of the following statements regarding your interaction with the salesperson.

Strongly   Strongly
disagree   :___:___:___:___:___:___:___: agree
       1   2   3   4   5   6   7

1. Used full sentences instead of saying yes and no.

2. Offered relevant information to the questions I asked.

3. Showed eagerness in his or her responses.

4. Answered at appropriate times.

*The directions were not provided by Ramsey and Sohi (1997) but may have been similar to what is shown here.

SCALE NAME: Salesperson Listening (Sensing)

SCALE DESCRIPTION: Four seven-point Likert-type items that measure the degree to which a customer perceives a salesperson was paying close attention to verbal and nonverbal cues he or she was sending during the sales encounter.

SCALE ORIGIN: The scale was constructed by Ramsey and Sohi (1997) along with two others (#298 and #299). To generate items, 80 students were asked to indicate behaviors they thought indicated salespersons were listening to them. Those behaviors listed at least twice by the group were part of the initial set tested. Scales were then purified using exploratory factor analysis.

SAMPLES: Data were gathered by Ramsey and Sohi (1997) through a mail survey of 500 new car buyers. The list of people who had bought cars in the previous six months came from a car dealership. Usable survey forms were returned by **173** respondents, the majority of whom were men (70%). Most of the group (60%) had at least some college education, the median household income was $46,000, 72% were married, and the average age was 42 years.

RELIABILITY: An alpha of **.80** was reported for the scale by Ramsey and Sohi (1997).

VALIDITY: After the exploratory factor analysis, Ramsey and Sohi (1997) used confirmatory factor analysis to test evidence of unidimensionality and discriminant validity.

ADMINISTRATION: The scale was self-administered by respondents as part of a larger mail survey instrument (Ramsey and Sohi 1997). Higher scores on the scale indicated that respondents thought a specific salesperson during a particular sales encounter was paying close attention to what they were saying and doing.

MAJOR FINDINGS: Ramsey and Sohi (1997) developed and tested a model of the impact of salesperson listening behavior on customer trust, satisfaction, and anticipated future interaction with the salesperson. Salesperson listening behavior was found to have three main components, one of which was labeled **sensing**. Customer perception of salesperson listening behavior was found to have significant positive impacts on customer trust and anticipation of future interaction with the salesperson.

REFERENCES:
Ramsey, Rosemary P. and Ravipreet S. Sohi (1997), "Listening to Your Customers: The Impact of Perceived Salesperson Listening Behavior on Relationship Outcomes," *JAMS*, 25 (Spring), 127–37.

SCALE ITEMS:*
Please indicate the degree to which you agree or disagree with each of the following statements regarding your interaction with the salesperson.

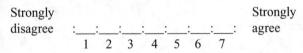

```
Strongly                          Strongly
disagree    :__:__:__:__:__:__:__:  agree
            1   2   3   4   5   6   7
```

1. Focused only on me.

2. Kept firm eye contact.

3. Nonverbal gestures suggested he or she was listening to me.

4. Seemed bored. **(r)**

*The directions were not provided by Ramsey and Sohi (1997) but may have been similar to what is shown here.

SCALE NAME: Salesperson Typicality Manipulation

SCALE DESCRIPTION: Four Likert-type items measuring how typical and common a respondent perceives a salesperson to be on the basis of a depiction to which he or she has been exposed. In the study by Babin, Boles, and Darden (1995), a car salesperson was being evaluated on the basis of a written scenario.

SCALE ORIGIN: The source of the scale was not indicated by Babin, Boles, and Darden (1995), but it would appear to be original to their study.

SAMPLES: The data were gathered by Babin, Boles, and Darden (1995) from **163** undergraduate marketing students who were randomly assigned to one of three experimental conditions.

RELIABILITY: An alpha of **.96** was reported for the scale by Babin, Boles, and Darden (1995).

VALIDITY: No examination of the scale's validity was reported by Babin, Boles, and Darden (1995).

ADMINISTRATION: Babin, Boles, and Darden (1995) had subjects complete the scale, along with other measures, after exposure to experimental manipulation. A high score suggested that respondents believed the salesperson to which they were exposed in some form was illustrative and representative of many other real salespersons.

MAJOR FINDINGS: The study by Babin, Boles, and Darden (1995) examined salesperson stereotypes and their influence on the sales environment. The findings showed that the descriptions of three types of car salespersons differed in their **typicality**, such that the depiction intended to be considered *typical* had the highest score on **typicality**, followed by *pushy* with slightly less **typicality**. The *atypical* salesperson was associated with much less **typicality**.

REFERENCES:
Babin, Barry J., James S. Boles, and William R. Darden (1995), "Salesperson Stereotypes, Consumer Emotions, and Their Impact on Information Processing," *JAMS*, 23 (Spring), 94–105.

SCALE ITEMS:*

Strongly						Strongly
disagree	:__:	:__:	:__:	:__:	:__:	agree
	1	2	3	4	5	

1. The salesperson described is typical of most car salespeople.

2. If asked to describe a typical car salesperson, I would describe him/her a lot like the one in the story.

3. The salesperson described fit my stereotype of a car salesman.

4. Salespersons like the one described are very common.

*The format of the response scale with its number of points and anchors was not provided in the article by Babin, Boles, and Darden (1995) but would likely have been much like this.

SCALE NAME: Satisfaction (General)

SCALE DESCRIPTION: Four seven-point semantic differentials that measure a person's level of satisfaction with some person, place, or thing.

SCALE ORIGIN: Although the items composing the scale have been used in various previous measures, these items as a set are not known to have been used previously. Thus, it is likely that the scale is original to Spreng and Mackroy (1996).

SAMPLES: Data were collected by Spreng and Mackroy (1996) for their study from undergraduate students who were given extra credit for participating. Usable responses were received from **273** students.

RELIABILITY: The construct reliability for the scale was **.93** (Spreng 1998; Spreng and Mackroy 1996).

VALIDITY: Evidence from a confirmatory factor analysis provided evidence of the scale's discriminant validity (Spreng and Mackroy 1996).

ADMINISTRATION: Students completed the scale in the study by Spreng and Mackroy (1996), along with other measures, immediately after their meeting with an advisor (the "service provider" in this case). High scores on the scale suggested that respondents were very satisfied with the service they received from the specified organization.

MAJOR FINDINGS: The study by Spreng and Mackroy (1996) examined the distinction between service quality and **satisfaction**. The results indicated that they were distinct constructs and had different antecedents.

COMMENTS: Two of the items composing the scale (3 and 4) do not appear to have adjective pairs that are polar opposites. This compromises the assumption that the midpoint of a scale is meant to be used when respondents associate the object with neither pole of the adjective pair (Dawes and Smith 1985, p. 534; Osgood, Suci, and Tannenbaum 1957, pp. 29, 83). What effect this could have on interpretation of scale scores is unknown.

REFERENCES:
Dawes, Robyn M. and Tom L. Smith (1985), "Attitude and Opinion Measurement," in *Handbook of Social Psychology,* 3rd ed., Vol. 1, Gardner Lindzey and Elliot Aronson, eds. New York: Random House, 509–66.

Osgood, Charles E., George J. Suci, and Percy H. Tannenbaum (1957), *The Measurement of Meaning.* Urbana, IL: University of Illinois Press.

Spreng, Richard A. (1998), personal correspondence.

———— and Robert D. Mackroy (1996), "An Empirical Examination of a Model of Perceived Service Quality and Satisfaction," *JR,* 72 (2), 201–14.

SCALE ITEMS:
DIRECTIONS: Overall, how do you feel about the _____ services you received?*

Very
dissatisfied :___:___:___:___:___:___:___: Very satisfied
       1   2   3   4   5   6   7

Terrible :___:___:___:___:___:___:___: Delighted
       1   2   3   4   5   6   7

#302 *Satisfaction (General)*

Very
dissatisfied   :___:___:___:___:___:___:___: Not at all
                   1   2   3   4   5   6   7   dissatisfied

Not at all
satisfied   :___:___:___:___:___:___:___: Very
                   1   2   3   4   5   6   7   satisfied

*The generic name of the service provider can be placed in the blank. Spreng and Mackroy (1996) used the word *advisor* because they were studying evaluations of academic advisors by college students.

SCALE NAME: Satisfaction (Generalized)

SCALE DESCRIPTION: A multi-item, seven-point semantic differential summated ratings scale measuring a consumer's degree of satisfaction with some stimulus. The scale has been used with regard to insurance agents, the service policy, and the insurance agency (Crosby and Stephens 1987); shopping (Eroglu and Machleit 1990); and a camcorder (Spreng, MacKenzie, and Olshavsky 1996).

SCALE ORIGIN: On the basis of the statements (or lack thereof) made by the scale users, the origin of the scale is unknown. Because none of the uses described here is exactly the same, it is quite possible they are all original to the studies in which they were used, though they have enough in common to suggest there might have been some common origin.

SAMPLES: The sample was selected from a nationally representative consumer panel and screened for ownership of life insurance. The first wave of the survey was based on **2311** returned and usable questionnaires. The sample was slightly better educated and more upscale than the population at large, but the authors considered the differences to be minor and unrelated to the studied relationships. A year later, **983** respondents to the first wave of the survey (or from a holdout sample) responded to the second wave. Comparison of main sample and holdout sample data did not indicate any bias due to wave 1 premeasurement.

Subjects used by Eroglu and Machleit (1990) were recruited from professional, nonprofit, and church organizations. The sample was composed of **112** adults and had the following characteristics: 58% were women, 70% were married, and 63% were between the ages of 20 and 49 years.

Spreng, MacKenzie, and Olshavsky (1996), conducted an experiment with data gathered from **207** subjects who were recruited from a local church. The church received not only a monetary contribution for each person who volunteered, but also a camcorder used in the study. More than half (56%) of the subjects were women, and the median age was 31 to 35 years. Almost half (49%) had a college degree.

RELIABILITY: Crosby and Stephens (1987) reported the alphas for the scales in both waves to be greater than **.96**. The scale was completed for five slides that represented different levels of retail density in the study by Eroglu and Machleit (1990). Alphas of **.94**, **.91**, **.90**, **.93**, and **.87** were reported for the slides from the least to the most dense retail conditions. No alpha was reported by Spreng, MacKenzie, and Olshavsky (1996), but average variance extracted was indicated to be .85.

VALIDITY: Crosby and Stephens (1987) provided some evidence of their scale's predictive validity by comparing the satisfaction level of four known groups that varied on their policy status. The four groups were those who paid the premium and stayed with the same company, those for whom the policy was still in force but who had not paid the next year's premium yet, those who switched to a different company, and those whose policy lapsed and who had not replaced it with another. The means for each of those groups in wave 1 on the overall satisfaction scale were 5.94, 5.29, 4.99, and 4.79, respectively, which shows that the scale gave an accurate indication of the policy owners' actual behavior.

Neither Eroglu and Machleit (1990) nor Spreng, MacKenzie, and Olshavsky (1996) addressed the validity of their scales. The latter used confirmatory factor analysis to develop their measurement model, which suggests that at least a test of the scale's unidimensionality was made though the results were unreported.

ADMINISTRATION: The scales were self-administered by Crosby and Stephens (1987) as part of a larger mail questionnaire. In the Eroglu and Machleit (1990) study, the scale was filled out by subjects after they viewed each of five experimental slides. Similarly, Spreng, MacKenzie, and Olshavsky (1996) had subjects respond to the scale, along with other measures, after they had been exposed to treatment manipulations. Higher scores indicated greater satisfaction with the object, whereas low scores implied the respondents were not pleased.

MAJOR FINDINGS: The purpose of the study was to compare two proposed models of buyers' satisfaction with life insurance: the relationship generalization model (RGM) and the rational evaluation model (REM). The RGM assumes that consumers generalize positive feelings about the provider to the core service, whereas the REM views consumers as most concerned about core service quality with the relationship merely adding value to it. In general, the results supported the REM over the RGM. This means that, though the agent's performance affects satisfaction, it is balanced against the perceived performance of the core service.

Eroglu and Machleit (1990) examined some of the determinants and outcomes of retail crowding. In conditions of low retail density (crowding), there were positive relationships between time pressure and **shopping satisfaction**. In contrast, in conditions of high retail density, there were negative relationships with **satisfaction**.

An experiment was conducted by Spreng, MacKenzie, and Olshavsky (1996) to test a new model of the satisfaction process that builds on the disconfirmation paradigm. Among their results was that expectations congruency and desires congruency mediate the effects of expectations, desires, and performance on overall **satisfaction**.

REFERENCES:

Crosby, Lawrence A. and Nancy Stephens (1987), "Effects of Relationship Marketing on Satisfaction, Retention, and Prices in the Life Insurance Industry," *JMR*, 24 (November), 404–11.

Eroglu, Segin A. and Karen A. Machleit (1990), "An Empirical Study of Retail Crowding: Antecedents and Consequences," *JR*, 66 (Summer), 201–21.

Spreng, Richard A., Scott B. MacKenzie, and Richard W. Olshavsky (1996), "A Reexamination of the Determinants of Consumer Satisfaction," *JM*, 60 (July), 15–32.

SCALE ITEMS:*

1. Satisfied   :___:___:___:___:___:___:___: Dissatisfied
              7   6   5   4   3   2   1

2. Pleased   :___:___:___:___:___:___:___: Displeased
             7   6   5   4   3   2   1

3. Favorable   :___:___:___:___:___:___:___: Unfavorable
             7   6   5   4   3   2   1

4. Pleasant   :___:___:___:___:___:___:___: Unpleasant
             7   6   5   4   3   2   1

5. I like it
   very much   :___:___:___:___:___:___:___: I didn't like it at all
             7   6   5   4   3   2   1

6. Contented   :___:___:___:___:___:___:___: Frustrated
             7   6   5   4   3   2   1

7. Delighted   :___:___:___:___:___:___:___: Terrible
             7   6   5   4   3   2   1

Crosby and Stephens (1987): 1, 2, 3; 7-point
Eroglu and Machleit (1990): 1*, 2, 4, 5; 7-point
Spreng, MacKenzie, and Olshavsky (1996): 1*, 2*, 6, 7

*Indicates some slight difference in the anchors compared with what is shown.

SCALE NAME: Satisfaction (Generalized)

SCALE DESCRIPTION: In its fullest form, the scale is composed of twelve Likert-type items and measures a consumer's degree of satisfaction with a product he or she has recently purchased. Most of its uses have been in reference to the purchase of cars, but Mano and Oliver (1993) appear to have adapted it so as to be general enough to apply to whatever product a respondent was thinking about.

SCALE ORIGIN: The scale was originally generated and used by Westbrook and Oliver (1981) to measure consumer satisfaction with cars and calculators. Four other satisfaction measures were used as well, and their results were compared in a multitrait, multimethod matrix. Convenience samples of students from two different universities were used (n = **68** + **107**). In terms of internal consistency, the alphas were **.93** and **.96** as measured for cars in the two samples. For both samples, the scale showed strong evidence of construct validity by converging with like constructs and discriminating among unlike constructs. Compared with the other measures of satisfaction, this Likert version produced the greatest dispersion of individual scores while maintaining a symmetrical distribution.

SAMPLES: Data were collected by Mano and Oliver (1993) from **118** undergraduate business students attending a Midwestern U.S. university.

Two samples were used in the study by Oliver (1993), but only one examined **satisfaction with cars**. The sample is the same as the one described in Westbrook and Oliver (1991). The data for the study came from a judgmental area sample. Convenience samples were taken at four shopping centers in a large Northeastern U.S. city and were limited to persons who had purchased a new or used car in the past year. Complete and usable questionnaires were obtained from **125** respondents. A majority (74%) of the sample were men. The average respondent had an income in the $25,000 to $40,000 range and was 33 years of age.

Oliver, Rust, and Varki (1997) reported on the use of the scale in two studies that involved patronage rather than product consumption. The sample in of the first survey was visitors to a recreational wildlife theme park who were approached as they entered but completed the form after exiting the park. Valid data were received from **90** patrons. The typical respondent was a married woman between the ages of 25 and 34 years. The second study examined single-ticket purchasers at a symphony concert in a large city. Apparently as with the first survey, patrons were approached as they arrived but did not receive and complete the questionnaire until the concert was over. Usable surveys were received from **104** people. The modal respondent was a single woman between the ages of 20 and 30 years.

Findings in Oliver and Swan (1989) were based on **184** completed questionnaires from people who had bought new cars within six months prior to the survey. The average respondent was male (67%) and college educated (32%), had an income between $20,000 and $29,999, was 43 years of age, had owned 7.8 cars in his lifetime, and had purchased his latest car 4.5 months previous.

RELIABILITY: Alphas of **.95, .98,** and **.94** were reported for the scale by Mano and Oliver (1993), Oliver (1993), and Westbrook and Oliver (1991), respectively. Oliver, Rust, and Varki (1997) reported that the reliabilities were **.89** and **.87** in their first and second studies, respectively.

VALIDITY: No specific examination of scale validity was reported in any of the studies. However, Mano and Oliver (1993) performed a factor analysis that provided evidence that the scale was unidimensional.

ADMINISTRATION: The name of the product may be put in the blanks to focus the respondent's attention on a specific product (e.g., a car). Alternatively, a phrase such as *the product* can be used if, similar to Mano and Oliver (1993), respondents have been asked to think of a recently purchased product and the wording of the items needs to be more general to allow for the differences that will occur.

The scale was one of many other measures that were self-administered (Mano and Oliver 1993; Oliver 1993; Oliver, Rust, and Varki 1997; Oliver and Swan 1989). Higher scores on the scale suggested that respondents were very satisfied with their cars, whereas low scores implied that customers were not pleased with their cars.

MAJOR FINDINGS: Mano and Oliver (1993) examined the dimensionality and causal structure of product evaluation, affect, and satisfaction. As hypothesized, **satisfaction** was found to have a significant positive relationship with pleasantness, a significant negative relationship with unpleasantness, and no significant relationship with arousal and quietness.

The separate roles of positive and negative affect, attribute performance, and disconfirmation were examined by Oliver (1993) for their impact on satisfaction. Disconfirmation was found to have direct and very significant influence on **satisfaction**.

The purpose of the studies by Oliver, Rust, and Varki (1997) was to establish a behavioral basis for customer *delight* by empirically testing its antecedents and consequences. The findings from both studies indicated that **satisfaction** and delight are related but structurally distinct constructs.

The general purpose of Oliver and Swan's (1989) study was to examine customer perceptions of satisfaction in the context of new car purchases. The results indicated that **car satisfaction** was positively influenced by satisfaction with the dealer and with car disconfirmation but negatively influenced by complaint frequency.

REFERENCES:

Mano, Haim and Richard L. Oliver (1993), "Assessing the Dimensionality and Structure of the Consumption Experience: Evaluation, Feeling, and Satisfaction," *JCR*, 20 (December), 451–66.

Oliver, Richard L. (1993), "Cognitive, Affective, and Attribute Bases of the Satisfaction Response," *JCR*, 20 (December), 418–30.

———, Roland T. Rust, and Sajeev Varki (1997), "Customer Delight: Foundations, Findings, and Managerial Insight," *JR*, 73 (3), 311–36.

——— and John E. Swan (1989), "Equity and Disconfirmation Perceptions as Influences on Merchant and Product Satisfaction," *JCR*, 16 (December), 372–83.

Westbrook, Robert A. and Richard L. Oliver (1981), "Developing Better Measures of Consumer Satisfaction: Some Preliminary Results," in *Advances in Consumer Research*, Vol. 8, Kent B. Monroe, ed. Ann Arbor, MI: Association for Consumer Research, 94–99.

——— and ——— (1991), "The Dimensionality of Consumption Emotion Patterns and Consumer Satisfaction," *JCR*, 18 (June), 84–91.

SCALE ITEMS:*

Strongly disagree			Neither			Strongly agree
1————	—2————	——3————	—4————	—5————	—6————	—7

1. This is one of the best _____ I could have bought.

2. This _____ is exactly what I need.

3. This _____ hasn't worked out as well as I thought it would. **(r)**

4. I am satisfied with my decision to buy this _____.

5. Sometimes I have mixed feelings about keeping it. **(r)**

6. My choice to buy this _____ was a wise one.

7. If I could do it over again, I'd buy a different make/model. **(r)**

8. I have truly enjoyed this _____.

9. I feel bad about my decision to buy this _____. **(r)**

10. I am <u>not</u> happy that I bought this _____. **(r)**

11. Owning this _____ has been a good experience.

12. I'm sure it was the right thing to buy this _____.

*Mano and Oliver (1993), Oliver (1993), and Westbrook and Oliver (1981) used five-point scales, whereas Oliver and Swan (1989) used a seven-point format. Oliver, Rust, and Varki (1997) only used ten of these items (unspecified) and a five-point response scale.

SCALE NAME: Satisfaction (Global)

SCALE DESCRIPTION: Three seven-point Likert-type statements and one seven-point bipolar adjective. The scale is purported to measure the degree to which a consumer is pleased overall with the services performed by some specified company with which he or she apparently had experience.

SCALE ORIGIN: Although not explicitly stated by Taylor and Baker (1994), the scale appears to be original to their study.

SAMPLES: Taylor and Baker (1994) analyzed data from **426** completed questionnaires. The data were collected through personal interviews by trained personnel using a convenience sample. Respondents were selected through mall intercepts in seven cities across the United States.

RELIABILITY: An alpha of **.94** was reported for the scale by Taylor and Baker (1994).

VALIDITY: Limited scrutiny of the scale's convergent and discriminant validities was made by Taylor and Baker (1994) based on observed patterns in a correlation matrix. It appears from these correlations that the items in this scale and those in a related one (#343) do not have adequate discriminant validity.

ADMINISTRATION: The circumstances surrounding administration were not described in detail by Taylor and Baker (1994), but it appears that the scale was part of a larger questionnaire administered to respondents by trained interviewers. Higher scores on the scale indicated that respondents were very satisfied with the service from the specified provider.

MAJOR FINDINGS: Taylor and Baker (1994) studied the role played by service quality and **satisfaction** in the development of purchase intentions. For three of the four industries examined, models of decision making that included the interaction of **satisfaction** and quality provided a better understanding of intentions than did models that merely included main effects.

REFERENCES:
Taylor, Steven A. and Thomas L. Baker (1994), "An Assessment of the Relationship Between Service Quality and Customer Satisfaction in the Formation of Consumers' Purchase Intentions," *JR*, 70 (2), 163–78.

SCALE ITEMS:*

Strongly   Strongly
disagree   :___:___:___:___:___:___:___: agree
                 1   2   3   4   5   6   7

1. If I needed _____ services, I believe that I would be satisfied with _____ services.

2. Overall, in purchasing _____ services, I believe that I would be pleased with _____ services.

3. I believe that purchasing services from _____ is usually a satisfying experience.

4. My feelings toward _____ services can best be characterized as

Very   Very
dissatisfied   :___:___:___:___:___:___:___: satisfied
                     1   2   3   4   5   6   7

*The generic name of the service (e.g., airline) should be placed in the first blank of items 1 and 2, and the specific name of the provider (e.g., American Airlines) should go in the second blank. For items 3 and 4, the name of the service provider should be placed in the blank.

SCALE NAME: Satisfaction (with Activity)

SCALE DESCRIPTION: A six-item, seven-point Likert-type summated ratings scale measuring the degree to which a person who has just been involved in an activity, such as a river rafting trip, thinks that it was a good experience and worth the price.

SCALE ORIGIN: The scale was developed for the research reported by Fisher and Price (1991; Price 1994).

SAMPLES: Very little information was provided by Arnould and Price (1993; Price, Arnould, and Tierney 1995) regarding their sample. The respondents were described simply as a stratified random sample of people taking multiday river trips with one of three clients' rafting companies. A total of **137** clients filled out posttrip questionnaires, but only 97 of those had completed pretrip surveys.

RELIABILITY: Alphas of **.90** and **.93** were reported by Arnould and Price (1993) and Price, Arnould, and Tierney (1995).

VALIDITY: No specific examination of the scale's validity was reported by Arnould and Price (1993) or Price, Arnould, and Tierney (1995).

ADMINISTRATION: The scale was self-administered by respondents as part of a larger survey after they had finished a rafting trip (Arnould and Price 1993; Price, Arnould, and Tierney 1995). High scores on the scale suggested that respondents experienced something quite satisfying, whereas low scores implied that they did not have a good experience.

MAJOR FINDINGS: Arnould and Price (1993) explored the impact of several experiential variables on satisfaction with an extraordinary hedonic experience. There were strong positive correlations between overall **satisfaction** with the river rafting trip and several other variables: the feeling that the experience had produced a communion with others, communion with nature, and personal growth.

Building on the same basic study as Arnould and Price (1993), Price, Arnould, and Tierney (1995) found that, contrary to expectations, performance of the service provider did not have a significant impact on **satisfaction**. It did appear, however, that the impact of performance was mediated through positive affect response.

COMMENTS: See also MacInnis and Price (1990) for another use of the scale.

REFERENCES:

Arnould, Eric J. and Linda L. Price (1993), "River Magic: Extraordinary Experience and the Extended Service Encounter," *JCR*, 20 (June), 24–45.

Fisher, Robert J. and Linda L. Price (1991), "The Relationship Between International Travel Motivations and Cultural Receptivity," *Journal of Leisure Research*, 23 (3), 193–208.

MacInnis, Deborah J. and Linda L. Price (1990), "An Exploratory Study of the Effect of Imagery Processing and Consumer Experience on Expectations and Satisfaction," in *Advances in Consumer Research*, Vol. 17, Marvin E. Goldberg, Gerald Gorn, and Richard W. Pollay, eds. Provo, UT: Association for Consumer Research, 41–47.

Price, Linda L. (1994), personal correspondence.

———, Eric J. Arnould, and Patrick Tierney (1995), "Going to Extremes: Managing Service Encounters and Assessing Provider Performance," *JM*, 59 (April), 83–97.

#306 *Satisfaction (with Activity)*

SCALE ITEMS:

Strongly   Strongly
agree   disagree

1————2————3————4————5————6————7

This _____:

1. had many unique or special moments.

2. had special meaning to me.

3. was as good as I expected.

4. was satisfying to me.

5. stands out as one of my best experiences.

6. was worth the price I paid for it.

SCALE NAME: Satisfaction (with Health Club)

SCALE DESCRIPTION: Eleven seven-point Likert-type items measuring the level of satisfaction a consumer has with a health club, with a particular focus on its equipment and employees.

SCALE ORIGIN: The measure appears to be original to Kelley and Davis (1994). The items were pretested on 95 undergraduate students with health club experience, and items with low item–total correlations (<.25) were eliminated.

SAMPLES: Data were collected by Kelley and Davis (1994) from members of a health club located in a midsized community in the southeastern United States. The authors stated that the health club was viewed as the market leader in the area and offered a wide range of services and amenities. Surveys were passed out to members as they came and went from the club on 12 consecutive days. Completed questionnaires were received from **296** individuals. The typical respondent was 36.7 years of age and male (65%), had been a member of the club for three years, and worked out an average of three days a week.

RELIABILITY: An alpha of **.95** was reported for the scale by Kelley and Davis (1994).

VALIDITY: The validity of the scale was not specifically examined by Kelley and Davis (1994).

ADMINISTRATION: The scale was completed, along with other scales and measures, in a self-administered survey (Kelley and Davis 1994). Higher scores on the scale suggested that respondents were very satisfied with the services, facilities, and employees of some specified health club.

MAJOR FINDINGS: Kelley and Davis (1994) proposed and tested a model of the antecedents to service recovery expectations. Higher levels of perceived service quality were associated with greater customer **satisfaction**.

REFERENCES:
Kelley, Scott W. and Mark A. Davis (1994), "Antecedents to Customer Expectations for Service Recovery," *JAMS*, 22 (Winter), 52–61.

SCALE ITEMS:
Directions: The following questions require you to think about and rate your level of satisfaction or dissatisfaction with various aspects of your health club. Please place a check mark (√) on the line that best represents your level of satisfaction or dissatisfaction with each of the following items. How would you rate your satisfaction or dissatisfaction with regard to:

Very   Very
dissatisfied :___:___:___:___:___:___:___: satisfied

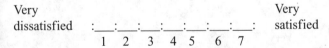

     1 2 3 4 5 6 7

1. The workout/fitness equipment available.

2. The appearance of employees.

3. The ability of employees.

4. The performance of workout/fitness equipment.

5. The willingness of employees to provide service.

6. The promptness of employees.

7. The courtesy of employees.

8. The knowledge of employees.

9. The attention provided me by this health club.

10. The degree to which this health club cares about me.

11. This health club's ability to correct service problems.

SCALE NAME: Satisfaction (with Hospital)

SCALE DESCRIPTION: Four seven-point items measuring the degree to which a patient expresses satisfaction with his or her recent stay in a hospital. The scale is intended to be an overall measure of satisfaction rather than a measure of any particular aspect of a hospital.

SCALE ORIGIN: The source of the scale was not identified by Dubé and Morgan (1996), but it appears to be original to their study.

SAMPLES: Data were gathered by Dubé and Morgan (1996) from **96** patients who stayed at least two days in a French-Canadian hospital. A little more than half (55%) of the sample were men, and the median age was 46 years. Patients apparently volunteered to participate, and a lottery ($250) was used as an incentive.

RELIABILITY: An alpha of **.98** was reported for the scale by Dubé and Morgan (1996).

VALIDITY: The validity of the scale was not specifically addressed by Dubé and Morgan (1996).

ADMINISTRATION: The scale was self-administered by patients as they were checking out from the hospital after their stay (Dubé and Morgan 1996). Higher scores suggested that patients were very satisfied with the hospital during their stay.

MAJOR FINDINGS: Dubé and Morgan (1996) examined how emotional states experienced over time are integrated to form global judgments of consumption emotions and satisfaction. The results indicated that men's first-day positive emotions and women's first-day negative emotions were significant predictors of **satisfaction** with their hospital stay.

REFERENCES:
Dubé, Laurette and Michael S. Morgan (1996), "Trend Effects and Gender Differences in Retrospective Judgments of Consumption Emotions," *JCR*, 23 (September), 156–62.

SCALE ITEMS:*

Very
dissatisfied   :___:___:___:___:___:___:___: satisfied
          1   2   3   4   5   6   7

1. The quality of the services in general.

2. The logistics of service delivery.

3. Employees' attitudes.

4. The general atmosphere of the hospital.

*The exact phrases were not given by Dubé and Morgan (1996) but are recreated here on the basis of the brief descriptions provided in the article.

SCALE NAME: Satisfaction (with Salesperson)

SCALE DESCRIPTION: Three seven-point Likert-type items that measure the degree to which a customer is satisfied with the interaction he or she has had with a particular salesperson.

SCALE ORIGIN: Ramsey and Sohi (1997) cited Lagace, Dahlstrom, and Gassenheimer (1991), who in turn cited Crosby, Evans, and Cowles (1990), as the source of the scale. A comparison of the scales indicates little if any similarity, which suggests that it may be best to describe the scale used by Ramsey and Sohi (1997) as original to their study.

SAMPLES: Data were gathered by Ramsey and Sohi (1997) through a mail survey of 500 new car buyers. The list came from a car dealership's records of people who had bought cars in the previous six months. Usable survey forms were returned by **173** respondents, the majority of whom were men (70%). Most of the group (60%) had at least some college education, the median household income was $46,000, 72% were married, and the average age was 42 years.

RELIABILITY: An alpha of **.93** was reported for the scale by Ramsey and Sohi (1997).

VALIDITY: After the exploratory factor analysis, Ramsey and Sohi (1997) used confirmatory factor analysis to provide evidence of unidimensionality and discriminant validity.

ADMINISTRATION: The scale was self-administered by respondents as part of a larger mail survey instrument (Ramsey and Sohi 1997). Higher scores on the scale indicated that respondents were very satisfied with the experience of interacting with some specific salesperson.

MAJOR FINDINGS: Ramsey and Sohi (1997) developed and tested a model of the impact of salesperson listening behavior on customer trust, **satisfaction**, and anticipated future interaction with the salesperson. Customer perception of salesperson listening behavior was not found to have a significant direct impact on **satisfaction**, though it had an indirect effect through trust.

REFERENCES:
Crosby, Lawrence A., Kenneth R. Evans, and Deborah Cowles (1990), "Relationship Quality in Services Selling: An Interpersonal Influence Perspective," *JM*, 54 (July), 68–81.
Lagace, Rosemary R., Robert Dahlstrom, and Julie B. Gassenheimer (1991), "The Relevance of Ethical Salesperson Behavior on Relationship Quality: The Pharmaceutical Industry," *Journal of Personal Selling & Sales Management*, 11 (Fall), 39–47.
Ramsey, Rosemary P. and Ravipreet S. Sohi (1997), "Listening to Your Customers: The Impact of Perceived Salesperson Listening Behavior on Relationship Outcomes," *JAMS*, 25 (Spring), 127–37.

SCALE ITEMS:

Strongly   Strongly
disagree   :__:__:__:__:__:__:__: agree
          1   2   3   4   5   6   7

1. The amount of contact I have had with this salesperson was adequate.

2. I am satisfied with the level of service this salesperson has provided.

3. In general, I am pretty satisfied with my dealings with this salesperson.

SCALE NAME: Satisfaction (with Server)

SCALE DESCRIPTION: Five seven-point semantic differentials that measure a customer's satisfaction with the interaction that occurred between him or her and an employee (server) of a service provider. In the study by Winsted (1997), respondents were asked to think of a recent encounter with a waiter or waitress in a restaurant.

SCALE ORIGIN: Winsted (1997) built upon a three-item scale used by Crosby, Evans, and Cowles (1990).

SAMPLES: Winsted (1997) had two data collections phases, the second of which included the satisfaction scale. There were two samples, one American and the other Japanese. The American sample was composed of **200** qualified respondents, and the Japanese sample had **176**. College students with means ages in their early 20s constituted the samples in both cases. Only the American sample was involved in the production of the scale shown here.

RELIABILITY: An alpha of **.96** was reported for the scale by Winsted (1997). Item–total correlations ranged between .83 and .92.

VALIDITY: No examination of the scale's validity was reported by Winsted (1997) beyond noting that it was unidimensional.

ADMINISTRATION: The scale was administered to students as part of a much larger paper-and-pencil questionnaire (Winsted 1997). Higher scores on the scale indicated that consumers were very satisfied with a particular server with whom they interacted recently.

MAJOR FINDINGS: Winsted (1997) examined behaviors that consumers in two countries (United States and Japan) used to evaluate service encounters and studied potential differences in the relevant encounter dimensions between the two cultures. The dimensions identified for the United States explained more than three-quarters of the variance in encounter **satisfaction**, whereas the dimensions identified for Japan were able to explain less than half of the variance.

REFERENCES:

Crosby, Lawrence A., Kenneth R. Evans, and Deborah Cowles (1990), "Relationship Quality in Services Selling: An Interpersonal Influence Perspective," *JM*, 54 (July), 68–81.

Winsted, Kathryn Frazer (1997), "The Service Experience in Two Cultures: A Behavioral Perspective," *JR*, 73 (3), 337–60.

——— (1999), personal correspondence.

SCALE ITEMS:*

Directions: Please answer the following questions by circling the number that best represents your evaluation of your interaction with the server.

1. As a result of my interaction with the server, I was:

Very
dissatisfied :__:__:__:__:__:__: Very satisfied

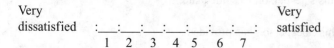

1 2 3 4 5 6 7

2. My feelings about the server's interaction with me were that I was:

Very   Very
displeased   :___:___:___:___:___:___:___: pleased
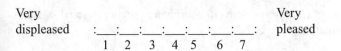
                 1   2   3   4   5   6   7

3. My impression of the interaction of the server with me was:

Very   Very
unfavorable   :___:___:___:___:___:___:___: favorable
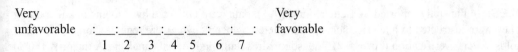
                 1   2   3   4   5   6   7

4. My encounter with the server was:

Worse than   Better than
I expected   :___:___:___:___:___:___:___: I expected
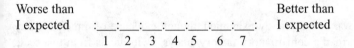
                 1   2   3   4   5   6   7

5. My feelings about being served by this server again would be:

Very   Very
unhappy   :___:___:___:___:___:___:___: happy
              1   2   3   4   5   6   7

*The scale stem and items were provided by Winsted (1999).

#311 *Satisfaction (with Store)*

SCALE NAME: Satisfaction (with Store)

SCALE DESCRIPTION: Three seven-point Likert-type items measuring a customer's global satisfaction with the shopping experience at a particular store.

SCALE ORIGIN: The scale used by Bettencourt (1997) is original to his study but bears some similarity to items used in a study by Bitner and Hubbert (1994).

SAMPLES: In the study reported by Bettencourt (1997), data were collected by students in a marketing class. They were instructed to have five surveys completed by people who were regular shoppers for their households. After a verification process, **215** questionnaires remained for data analysis. A majority (70%) of the sample was over 30 years of age, female (73%), and had completed at least some college (85%).

RELIABILITY: Bettencourt (1997) reported an alpha of **.91** for the scale.

VALIDITY: The validity of the scale was not explicitly examined, though evidence of dimensionality was reported. Bettencourt (1997) performed a confirmatory factory analysis with items from this scale and two others, which provided support for the three-factor conceptualization.

ADMINISTRATION: The scale was self-administered as part of a much larger survey instrument (Bettencourt 1997). Higher scores on the scale suggested that respondents were very satisfied with their shopping experiences at the specified stores.

MAJOR FINDINGS: A model of customer voluntary performance was developed and tested by Bettencourt (1997) in the context of grocery store shopping. The findings indicated that customers' overall **satisfaction** with their shopping experiences at a store had a significant positive relationship with their perception of the store's support for customers.

COMMENTS: Grocery stores were studied by Bettencourt (1997), but it would appear that a little modification to item 1 would allow the scale to be used with other types of stores.

REFERENCES:

Bettencourt, Lance A. (1997), "Customer Voluntary Performance: Customers as Partners in Service Delivery," *JR*, 73 (3), 383–406.

Bitner, Mary Jo and Amy R. Hubbert (1994), "Encounter Satisfaction Versus Overall Satisfaction Versus Quality," in *Service Quality: New Directions in Theory and Practice*, Roland T. Rust and Richard L. Oliver, eds. Thousand Oaks, CA: Sage Publications, 72–94.

SCALE ITEMS:

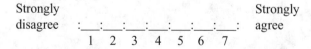

Strongly disagree :___:___:___:___:___:___:___: Strongly agree

       1 2 3 4 5 6 7

1. Compared to other stores, I am very satisfied with this grocery store.

2. Based on all my experience with this store, I am very satisfied.

3. My shopping experiences at this store have always been pleasant.

SCALE NAME: Satisfaction (with University Selection)

SCALE DESCRIPTION: Three five-point Likert-type statements that are intended to measure a person's (e.g., former student's) evaluation of the decision made several years previous regarding a university to attend.

SCALE ORIGIN: Although the scale does not appear to have been used previously as a whole, it has similarities to at least two previous scales (Boulding et al. 1993; Mano and Oliver 1993).

SAMPLES: Analysis by Halstead, Hartman, and Schmidt (1994) was based on data collected from **475** alumni of a major university in the eastern United States. The data were collected as part of a larger school assessment program. Questionnaires were mailed to the population (1223) of former students who had graduated within the previous four years. There was a 38.8% response rate. Calls to 28 former students who had not sent back a survey form indicated that there was no significant nonresponse bias. The sample was 52% women with an average age of 24 years. The average income reported was $33,000, and 39 states and several foreign countries were represented.

RELIABILITY: Cronbach's alpha for the scale was reported to be **.87** (Halstead, Hartman, and Schmidt 1994).

VALIDITY: Confirmatory factor analysis supported the unidimensionality of the scale (Halstead, Hartman, and Schmidt 1994). There was also some evidence provided of the scale's convergent and discriminant validity.

ADMINISTRATION: The scale was part of a larger mail survey instrument (Hartman, and Schmidt 1994). High scores on the scale indicated that respondents expressed a great deal of satisfaction with their choice of a university to attend.

MAJOR FINDINGS: Halstead, Hartman, and Schmidt (1994) investigated a model that proposes that alumni satisfaction with their college education is a function of the intellectual environment they experienced and the preparation they received for employment. The findings indicated that there was a significant direct effect of intellectual environment on satisfaction. Employment preparation only had an indirect effect on satisfaction through the mediation of disconfirmation.

REFERENCES:

Boulding, William, Ajay Kalra, Richard Staelin, and Valarie A. Zeithaml (1993), "A Dynamic Process Model of Service Quality: From Expectations to Behavioral Intentions," *JMR*, 30 (February), 7–27.

Halstead, Diane, David Hartman, and Sandra L. Schmidt (1994), "Multisource Effects on the Satisfaction Formation Process," *JAMS*, 22 (2), 114–29.

Mano, Haim and Richard L. Oliver (1993), "Assessing the Dimensionality and Structure of the Consumption Experience: Evaluation, Feeling, and Satisfaction," *JCR*, 20 (December), 451–66.

SCALE ITEMS:

Strongly   Strongly
disagree   :___:___:___:___:___: agree
        1   2   3   4   5

1. My choice to attend the school was a wise one.

2. If I had to do it again, I would attend the school.

3. I would recommend the school to students interested in a business career.

SCALE NAME: Self-Actualization

SCALE DESCRIPTION: Fifteen Likert-type statements purported to measure the degree to which a person has achieved or is in the process of maximizing his or her full potential. Self-actualization is meant in the sense proposed by Maslow (1970). Traits such as time competence (living in the present rather than the past), inner directedness, and self-esteem are especially stressed in the scale.

SCALE ORIGIN: The scale was developed by Jones and Crandall (1986). The authors primarily used items from a widely accepted measure of self-actualization, the Personal Orientation Inventory (Shostrom 1964, 1975), with the goal of producing a much shorter but valid measure of the construct. In support of the measure, it had significant positive correlations with other measures of self-actualization, and there was a significant difference in scores by people independently identified as being either high or low in self-actualization. Yet the scale had some less supportive characteristics as well. The alpha was only .65, and factor analysis revealed a five-factor structure. Finally, the scale had a significant positive correlation with a well-accepted measure of social desirability bias (#375).

SAMPLES: Data were collected by Mick (1996) in the second of two studies on which he reported. Students taking a marketing research course were asked to distribute the surveys following firm guidelines. This approach produced **172** usable questionnaires. With this sample, the average age was 40 years, and with a little more than half (55%) were women.

RELIABILITY: An alpha of **.66** was reported for the scale by Mick (1996).

VALIDITY: No examination of the scale's validity was described by Mick (1996).

ADMINISTRATION: The scale was self-administered by respondents as part of a larger survey instrument (Mick 1996). Higher scores on the scale indicated that respondents were self-actualizing and believed they were achieving their full potential.

MAJOR FINDINGS: The effect of social desirability bias on the nomological network surrounding the materialism construct was examined by Mick (1996). He found in the second of his two studies that **self-actualization** had a significant positive correlation with the component of social desirability referred to as self-deception.

REFERENCES:

Jones, Alvin and Rick Crandall (1986), "Validation of a Short Index of Self-Actualization," *Personality and Social Psychology*, 12 (March), 63–73.

Maslow, Abraham (1970), *Motivation and Personality*, 2d ed. New York: Harper and Row.

Mick, David Glen (1996), "Are Studies of Dark Side Variables Confounded by Socially Desirable Responding? The Case of Materialism," *JCR*, 23 (September), 106–19.

Shostrom, Everett L. (1964), "A Test for the Measurement of Self-Actualization," *Educational and Psychological Measurement*, 24 (Summer), 207–18.

——— (1975), *Personal Orientation Dimensions*. San Diego, CA: Edits/Educational and Industrial Testing Service.

SCALE ITEMS:*

Disagree   :__:__:__:__: Agree
           1 2 3 4

1. I do not feel ashamed of any of my emotions.

2. I feel I must do what others expect me to do. **(r)**

3. I believe that people are essentially good and can be trusted.

4. I feel free to be angry at those I love.

5. It is always necessary that others approve of what I do. **(r)**

6. I don't accept my own weaknesses. **(r)**

7. I can like people without having to approve of them.

8. I fear failure. **(r)**

9. I avoid attempts to analyze and simplify complex domains. **(r)**

10. It is better to be yourself than to be popular.

11. I have no mission in life to which I feel especially dedicated. **(r)**

12. I can express my feelings even when they may result in undesirable consequences.

13. I do not feel responsible to help anybody. **(r)**

14. I am bothered by fears of being inadequate. **(r)**

15. I am loved because I give love.

*Jones and Crandall (1986) used a four-point Likert-type response scale. Mick (1996) appears to have used something longer, most likely a seven-point scale.

SCALE NAME: Self-Esteem

SCALE DESCRIPTION: A ten-item Likert-type scale measuring the degree to which a person approves of him- or herself. It does not necessarily imply that a person scoring high on the scale considers him- or herself to be perfect or superior to others. A four-point agree/disagree response scale was used by the originator (Rosenberg 1965), and a five-point scale was used by Richins (1991). A four-point scale with various "like me" anchors was used by Richins and Dawson (1992; Richins 1994). The nature of the response scales used by Bearden and Rose (1990), Mick (1996), and Park, Mothersbaugh, and Feick (1994) were not reported.

SCALE ORIGIN: The scale was constructed by Rosenberg (1965) for use in a study of high school students. It was developed with at least four practical and theoretical considerations strongly in mind: that it be easy to administer, that it be completed quickly, that it be unidimensional, and that it have face validity. The Guttman scale of reproducibility was reported as .92, and its scalability was .72. The book provides considerable data that bears on the validity of the scale.

SAMPLES: The article by Bearden and Rose (1990) reported the use of several studies and samples. The only study in which the self-esteem scale was used involved data collected from **85** undergraduate business students. They were urged to volunteer for the study with the chance of winning a random drawing as an incentive.

Data were collected by Mick (1996) in his first study from **266** respondents contacted through a quota-convenience sample. Students taking a marketing research course were asked to distribute the surveys following firm guidelines. The sample was split evenly (50.8% female) on gender, and the mean age was 43.2 years. A similar approach was used in Study 2 and produced **172** usable questionnaires. With this sample, the average age was 40 years, and a little more than half (55%) were women.
Park, Mothersbaugh, and Feick (1994) gathered data from a convenience sample of **156** graduate students attending a Northeastern U.S. university. The students were recruited and paid to participate in a "consumer knowledge study." Respondents filled out the questionnaires in small groups at their own pace. A majority of the sample were men (62%) and were an average of 27 years of age.

The scale was used in all but the first of four studies reported by Richins (1991). Study 2 was composed of **80** female college students, Study 3 had **73** female students enrolled in a beginning marketing course, and Study 4 was composed of **125** female undergraduate students apparently recruited from a principles of marketing class.

Studies with four samples were described in the article by Richins and Dawson (1992), but the self-esteem scale was used in just Survey 3. Little was said about the sample except that the data came from a mail survey of people in a large Western U.S. city. The households were randomly chosen and sent a survey form, followed by a reminder letter, and a second copy of the questionnaire two weeks later. The response rate was 31.3%, resulting in **235** usable questionnaires.

RELIABILITY: Alphas of **.80** and **.81** were reported for the scale by Bearden and Rose (1990) and Richins and Dawson (1992), respectively. Mick (1996) reported alphas of **.87** and **.80** for his Studies 1 and 2, respectively. Alphas of **.86** and **.87** were reported by Richins (1991) for the scale as used in Studies 2 and 3, respectively, but the alpha for the scale's use in Study 4 was not reported. Park, Mothersbaugh, and Feick (1994) reported an alpha of **.86**, with item–total correlations ranging from .48 to .66.

VALIDITY: The validity of the scale was not directly examined by Bearden and Rose (1990), Mick (1996), Park, Mothersbaugh, and Feick (1994), or Richins (1991; Richins and Dawson 1992). However, some idea of its nomological validity can be found in the findings discussed here.

ADMINISTRATION: The scale was administered by Bearden and Rose (1990), Mick (1996), Park, Mothersbaugh, and Feick (1994), and Richins and Dawson (1992) in larger survey instruments. Richins (1991) used the scale in her Study 2 as part of a survey; in Studies 3 and 4 it was used as part of an experiment. Higher scores on the scale indicated that respondents were quite contented with themselves, whereas low scores suggested that respondents lacked respect for themselves.

MAJOR FINDINGS: Bearden and Rose (1990) conducted a series of studies to investigate the reliability and validity of a measure of attention to social comparison information (ATSCI) and the extent to which this construct is a moderator of interpersonal influence. **Self-esteem** was only measured in one study and was little discussed. However, it was reported that **self-esteem** was found, as expected, to have a significant inverse relationship with ATSCI.

The effect of social desirability bias on the nomological network surrounding the materialism construct was examined by Mick (1996). He found in his two studies that **self-esteem** has a significant positive correlation with social desirability bias, most particularly with a component referred to as self-deception.

The study by Park, Mothersbaugh, and Feick (1994) investigated the determinants of self-assessed knowledge (perceived degree of knowledge about a product class). Although it was hypothesized that **self-esteem** would be positively related to self-assessed knowledge, the results did not support the existence of a significant relationship.

Richins (1991) conducted four studies in an effort to better understand how advertising can lead to dissatisfaction with the self. **Self-esteem** was mainly used in the analyses as a covariate related to self-ratings of attractiveness. Therefore, there were no separate results from the studies involving **self-esteem**.

The purpose of the several surveys conducted by Richins and Dawson (1992) was to construct a new measure of materialism. To examine the scale's nomological validity, it was proposed that materialists would be less satisfied with their lives than others. Part of testing that hypothesis came from the association between materialism and **self-esteem**. A significant though very low negative correlation between the two constructs was found ($r = -.12$), which suggests that more materialistic people are somewhat more likely to have less **self-esteem** than others have.

REFERENCES:

Bearden, William O. and Randall L. Rose (1990), "Attention to Social Comparison Information: An Individual Difference Factor Affecting Consumer Conformity," *JCR*, 16 (March), 461–71.

Mick, David Glen (1996), "Are Studies of Dark Side Variables Confounded by Socially Desirable Responding? The Case of Materialism," *JCR*, 23 (September), 106–19.

Park, C. Whan, David L. Mothersbaugh, and Lawrence Feick (1994), "Consumer Knowledge Assessment," *JCR*, 21 (June), 71–82.

Richins, Marsha L. (1991), "Social Comparison and the Idealized Images of Advertising," *JCR*, 18 (June), 71–83.

———— (1994), personal correspondence.

———— and Scott Dawson (1992), "A Consumer Values Orientation for Materialism and Its Measurement: Scale Development and Validation," *JCR*, 19 (December), 303–16.

Rosenberg, Morris (1965), *Society and the Adolescent Self-Image*. Princeton, NJ: Princeton University Press.

#314 *Self-Esteem*

SCALE ITEMS:*

Strongly agree	Agree	Disagree	Strongly disagree
1————	—2————	—3————	—4

1. On the whole, I am satisfied with myself. **(r)**

2. At times I think I am no good at all.

3. I feel that I have a number of good qualities. **(r)**

4. I am able to do things as well as most other people. **(r)**

5. I feel I do not have much to be proud of.

6. I certainly feel useless at times.

7. I feel that I am a person of worth, at least on a equal plane with others. **(r)**

8. I wish I could have more respect for myself.

9. All in all, I am inclined to feel that I am a failure.

10. I take a positive attitude toward myself. **(r)**

*The four-point response scale was used by Rosenberg (1965), and a five-point scale was used by Richins (1991), but it is not known how many points were on the scales as used by Bearden and Rose (1990), Mick (1996), or Park, Mothersbaugh, and Feick (1994). The anchors used by Richins and Dawson (1992) were as follows: 0 = *not at all like me*, 1 = *a little like me*, 2 = *somewhat like me*, and 3 = *a lot like me* (Richins 1994).

SCALE NAME: Self-Esteem

SCALE DESCRIPTION: A three-item, five-point Likert-type scale measuring the extent to which a person has a positive view of him- or herself, as well as of the future.

SCALE ORIGIN: Boush, Friestad, and Rose (1994) stated that the items they used were adapted from the scale by Rosenberg (1965) (#314). A comparison of the items indicates that, though some inspiration may have come from the Rosenberg scale, no items are held in common. Therefore, it is probably more accurate to think of this scale as original to Boush, Friestad, and Rose (1994).

SAMPLES: Data were gathered by Boush, Friestad, and Rose (1994) from students at two middle schools (grades 6–8) in a medium-sized city in the Pacific Northwest of the United States. A survey instrument was administered to students during the first and last weeks of the school year. Analysis was generally based on information received from the **426** students who completed the questionnaire during both of its administrations.

RELIABILITY: Alphas of **.59** and **.73** were reported for the scale for its first and second administrations, respectively (Boush, Friestad, and Rose 1994).

VALIDITY: The validity of the scale was not specifically addressed in the study by Boush, Friestad, and Rose (1994). However, the authors performed a principal components analysis of the combined items of this scale with those of another scale (#191). They reported that the results "yielded a simple structure solution" (Boush, Friestad, and Rose 1994, p. 170).

ADMINISTRATION: The scale was part of a longer questionnaire self-administered by students in groups of 25–30 during the period with which they began each school day (Boush, Friestad, and Rose 1994). High scores on the scale suggested that respondents had high self-esteem, whereas low scores indicated that they had poor self-images and were pessimistic about the future.

MAJOR FINDINGS: The study by Boush, Friestad, and Rose (1994) explored adolescents' skepticism toward advertising and their beliefs about the persuasive tactics used by advertisers. The findings indicated that **self-esteem** had a significant and positive relationship with mistrust of advertiser motives and advertising claims.

COMMENTS: As acknowledged by the authors (Boush, Friestad, and Rose 1994, p. 173), the internal consistency of the scale is low enough to warrant caution in using it again, particularly with nonadolescent respondents.

REFERENCES:
Boush, David M., Marian Friestad, and Gregory M. Rose (1994), "Adolescent Skepticism Toward TV Advertising and Knowledge of Advertiser Tactics," *JCR*, 21 (June), 165–75.
Rosenberg, Morris (1965), *Society and the Adolescent Self-Image*. Princeton, NJ: Princeton University Press.

SCALE ITEMS:

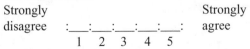

Strongly disagree :___:___:___:___:___: Strongly agree
      1   2   3   4   5

1. I feel good about myself as a person.

2. I can do many things well.

3. I am looking forward to the future.

#316 *Self-Esteem (Appearance)*

SCALE NAME: Self-Esteem (Appearance)

SCALE DESCRIPTION: Six five-point items measuring the level of satisfaction a person has with his or her looks at some point in time. As noted, the scale was intended to be part of a *state* measure of self-esteem rather than a *trait* measure, and this aspect is explicitly communicated in a couple of the scale items, as well as in the directions.

SCALE ORIGIN: The scale was constructed by Heatherton and Polivy (1991). They set out to develop a state measure of self-esteem as opposed to the many trait measures that were available. Considerable testing of the instrument occurred in five studies. As intended, factor analysis supported development of a subscale for the appearance dimension of self-esteem. The studies provided evidence of the subscale's psychometric quality, though its internal consistency was not reported. Men of a variety of ages, though all were undergraduate students, had mean scores of 21 on the appearance subscale, compared with 19 to 21 for women (Heatherton and Polivy 1991, p. 899).

SAMPLES: Martin and Gentry (1997) gathered data for their experiment from **268** girls in the public school system of a city in the Midwestern United States. The girls were in the fourth, sixth, or eighth grade and were vying for two prizes of $50 each for their participation.

RELIABILITY: An alpha of **.94** was reported for the scale by Martin and Gentry (1997).

VALIDITY: No direct examination of the scale's validity was reported by Martin and Gentry (1997).

ADMINISTRATION: Subjects responded to the scale, along with other measures in the questionnaire, after their teachers read each item to them (Martin and Gentry 1997). Higher scores on the scale suggested that respondents were very pleased with their appearance at the time they are responding.

MAJOR FINDINGS: Martin and Gentry (1997) conducted an experiment to determine if young girls compare their physical attractiveness with that of ad models, which then affects their self-perceptions depending on their motive for comparison. The results provided only tentative support for the notion that lack of changes in **appearance self-esteem** occur when motivated to discount the beauty of the ad models.

COMMENTS: Despite the high reliability reported by Martin and Gentry (1997), item 2 seems particularly out of place. Indeed, its factor loading as reported by Heatherton and Polivy (1991) was very low on the appearance dimension, and it apparently cross-loaded on another dimension. Therefore, some adjustment in the scale may be justified to improve its content validity.

REFERENCES:

Heatherton, Todd F. and Janet Polivy (1991), "Development and Validation of a Scale for Measuring State Self-Esteem," *Journal of Personality and Social Psychology*, 60 (6), 895–910.
Martin, Mary C. and James W. Gentry (1997), "Stuck in the Model Trap: The Effects of Beautiful Models in Ads on Female Pre-Adolescents and Adolescents," *JA*, 26 (Summer), 19–33.

SCALE ITEMS:*

Directions: This is a questionnaire designed to measure what you are thinking at this moment. There is, of course, no right answer for any statement. The best answer is what you feel is true of yourself at this moment. Be sure to answer all of the items, even if you are not certain of the best answer. Again, answer these questions as they are true for you RIGHT NOW.

Not at all	A little bit	Somewhat	Very much	Extremely
1————————	—2————————	—3————————	—4————————	—5

1. I feel satisfied with the way my body looks right now.

2. I feel that others respect and admire me.

3. I am dissatisfied with my weight. **(r)**

4. I feel good about myself.

5. I am pleased with my appearance right now.

6. I feel unattractive. **(r)**

*These are the directions used by Heatherton and Polivy (1991).

SCALE NAME: Self-Image Congruence

SCALE DESCRIPTION: The scale is composed of Likert-type statements measuring the degree to which a consumer views some specified behavior to be consistent with his or her self-image in some specified situation. The similarity between a consumer's self-concept and the image held of the product/behavior is the focus of the measure. Two versions of the scale used three items and five-point response formats, whereas another version used five items and a seven-point response scale.

SCALE ORIGIN: Sirgy and colleagues (1997) noted that there were problems with previous approaches to measuring product-/self-image congruity and tested another approach in six studies. This new method of measurement assumes that "self-image congruence is a holistic, gestalt-like perception" (Sirgy et al. 1997, p. 232), compared with traditional techniques that measured the construct less directly through discrepancy scores between product-image and self-concept. However, the new approach did not so much develop a new scale generalizable to a variety of situations but rather an *approach* that could be used to produce scales for different situations. Thus, even though the article covered six studies, only three studies using somewhat similar versions of the scale are described here.

SAMPLES: Generally similar versions of the scale were used in Studies 1, 2, and 3 of the six described by Sirgy and colleagues (1997). Study 1 was composed of **270** shoppers approached in a mall intercept survey. As an incentive, respondents were given a t-shirt for participating. Study 2 was based on data gathered by a mail survey from **229** female faculty and staff employed at two universities in the Southeastern United States. Data for Study 3 were collected from tourists who had visited Norfolk, Va., during a certain period and participated in pleasure travel activities there. Usable responses were received from **152** people.

RELIABILITY: An alpha of **.83** was reported for the scale used in Study 1 (Sirgy et al. 1997). The alphas for the version of the scale used in Study 2 were **.90** (classic outfit) and **.91** (feminine and dramatic outfits). The alpha for the version for the scale used in Study 3 was **.87**.

VALIDITY: Unexpectedly, in Study 1, there was no correlation between scores on the scale and those derived from a more traditional method (Sirgy et al. 1997). Although this meant that no evidence of convergent validity was produced, there was evidence of the scale's predictive validity, as discussed in the "Major Findings" section.

In contrast, more care was devoted to developing the traditional measure in Studies 2 and 3. In those cases, significant though moderate correlations between the traditional measures and the new measures were found. This provided some limited evidence of the new scale's convergent validity.

ADMINISTRATION: Although not completely clear, the scale was apparently read by interviewers in Study 1 to respondents, along with the rest of the brief questionnaire (Sirgy et al. 1997). In Studies 2 and 3, the scale was self-administered by respondents as part of mail surveys. Higher scores on the scale suggested that respondents viewed a product/behavior to be consistent with their own self-concept for the specified situation.

MAJOR FINDINGS: As noted, Sirgy and colleagues (1997) conducted six studies in support of a new method for measuring **self-image congruency** that was more direct than previous measures. In Studies 1, 2, and 3, the new measures were found to be more predictive (preference, satisfaction) than the traditional measures.

REFERENCES:
Sirgy, M. Joseph, Dhruv Grewal, Tamara F. Mangleburg, Jae-ok Park, Kye-Sung Chon, C.B. Claiborne, J.S. Johar, and Harold Berkman (1997), "Assessing the Predictive Validity of Two Methods of Measuring Self-Image Congruence," *JAMS*, 25 (Summer), 229–41.

SCALE ITEMS:*
Directions: Take a moment to think about _____. Think about the kind of person who typically uses _____. Imagine this person in your mind and then describe this person using one or more personal adjectives such as stylish, classy, masculine, sexy, old, athletic, or whatever personal adjectives you can use to describe the typical user of _____. Once you've done this, indicate your agreement or disagreement to the following statements.

Strongly   Strongly
disagree   :___:___:___:___:___: agree
              1   2   3   4   5

1. _____ is consistent with how I see myself.

2. _____ reflects who I am.

3. People similar to me wear _____ .

4. _____ is very much like me.

5. _____ is a mirror image of me.

*The name of the product/brand/context should be described in the blanks. The scale used in Study 1 used items 1, 2, and 3 in a five-point response format and referred to wearing Reebok shoes in a casual context. Items 4 and 5 and items similar to 1, 2, and 3 were used in Study 2 with seven-point response scales and referred to the appropriateness of wearing three different outfits in a work context. The items used in Study 3 were similar to 2, 3, and 4, used a five point response format, and referred to typical visitors to a tourist destination. The actual phrases used in the three studies were somewhat different; an effort has been made here to show the key phrases on which they are based and from which modification could be made for other contexts. See the article for the exact phrasing.

SCALE NAME: Self-Image Congruence (College Major)

SCALE DESCRIPTION: Six five-point Likert-type statements measuring the degree to which a student views the image of those who major in a field as consistent with his or her self-image.

SCALE ORIGIN: Sirgy and colleagues (1997) noted that there were problems with previous approaches to measuring product-/self-image congruity and tested another approach in six studies. This new method of measurement assumes that "self-image congruence is a holistic, gestalt-like perception" (Sirgy et al. 1997, p. 232) compared with traditional techniques that measured the construct less directly through discrepancy scores between product-image and self-concept. However, the new approach did not so much develop a new scale generalizable to a variety of situations but rather an *approach* that could be used to produce scales for different situations. Thus, even though the article covered six studies, only the sixth study using one version of the scale is described here.

SAMPLES: Study 6 was based on data collected from students enrolled in a mass section of a basic marketing course. Complete data were gathered from **252** students, only 52 of whom were marketing majors.

RELIABILITY: An alpha of **.85** was reported for the scale used in Study 6 (Sirgy et al. 1997).

VALIDITY: A significant correlation between the traditional measure and the new measure was found (Sirgy et al. 1997), which provided some limited evidence of the new scale's convergent validity. Also, evidence of the scale's predictive validity was found, as discussed in the "Major Findings" section.

ADMINISTRATION: Although not completely clear, the scale was apparently self-administered by students (Sirgy et al. 1997). Higher scores on the scale suggested that respondents viewed students majoring in a specified field as consistent with their own self-concepts.

MAJOR FINDINGS: As noted, Sirgy and colleagues (1997) conducted six studies in support of a new method for measuring **self-image congruency** that was more direct than previous measures. In Study 6, the new measure was found to be more predictive of a student's major than a traditional measure.

REFERENCES:

Sirgy, M. Joseph, Dhruv Grewal, Tamara F. Mangleburg, Jae-ok Park, Kye-Sung Chon, C.B. Claiborne, J.S. Johar, and Harold Berkman (1997), "Assessing the Predictive Validity of Two Methods of Measuring Self-Image Congruence," *JAMS*, 25 (Summer), 229–41.

SCALE ITEMS:*

Directions: Take a moment to think about _____. Think about the kind of person who typically majors in _____. Imagine this person in your mind and then describe this person using one or more personal adjectives such as stylish, classy, masculine, sexy, old, athletic, or whatever personal adjectives you can use to describe the typical major in _____. Once you've done this, indicate your agreement or disagreement to the following statements.

Strongly
disagree :___:___:___:___:___:

Strongly
agree

     1   2   3   4   5

1. I am very much like the typical _____ major.

2. I can identify with _____ students.

3. I am not at all like any of the _____ students I know. **(r)**

4. The image of the typical _____ student is very dissimilar from the kind of person I am. **(r)**

5. I feel my personal profile is similar to a _____ major.

6. I do not have anything in common with a _____ major. **(r)**

*The name of the field/discipline should be placed in the blanks.

SCALE NAME: Self-Image Congruence (Focal Versus Referent Brand)

SCALE DESCRIPTION: Four five-point Likert-type statements measuring the degree to which a consumer views the use of some focal brand as more consistent with his or her self-image than some referent brand. The similarity between a consumer's self-concept and the image held of the focal brand is the focus of the scale.

SCALE ORIGIN: Sirgy and colleagues (1997) noted that there were problems with previous approaches to measuring product-/self-image congruity and tested another approach in six studies. This new method of measurement assumes that "self-image congruence is a holistic, gestalt-like perception" (Sirgy et al. 1997, p. 232) compared with traditional techniques that measured the construct less directly through discrepancy scores between product-image and self-concept. However, the new approach did not so much develop a new scale generalizable to a variety of situations but rather an *approach* that could be used to produce scales for different situations. Thus, even though the article covered six studies, only the fourth study using one version of the scale is described here.

SAMPLES: Study 4 was based on data collected from eight samples, each corresponding to a different product. Students in college marketing courses were the subjects, and usable data were gathered from **428** students.

RELIABILITY: An alpha of **.82** was reported for the scale used in Study 4 (Sirgy et al. 1997).

VALIDITY: A significant though moderate correlation between the traditional measure and the new measure was found (Sirgy et al. 1997). This provided some limited evidence of the new scale's convergent validity. Also, evidence of the scale's predictive validity was found, as discussed in the "Major Findings" section.

ADMINISTRATION: The scale was apparently self-administered by students (Sirgy et al. 1997) as part of a in-class survey. Higher scores on the scale suggested that respondents viewed a focal brand as much more consistent with their individual self-concepts than some referent brand.

MAJOR FINDINGS: As noted, Sirgy and colleagues (1997) conducted six studies in support of a new method for measuring **self-image congruency** that was more direct than previous measures. In Study 4, as in the other studies, the new measure was found to be more predictive of brand preference than a traditional measure.

REFERENCES:
Sirgy, M. Joseph, Dhruv Grewal, Tamara F. Mangleburg, Jae-ok Park, Kye-Sung Chon, C.B. Claiborne, J.S. Johar, and Harold Berkman (1997), "Assessing the Predictive Validity of Two Methods of Measuring Self-Image Conguence," *JAMS*, 25 (Summer), 229–41.

SCALE ITEMS:
Directions: Take a moment to think about _____. Think about the kind of person who typically uses _____. Imagine this person in your mind and then describe this person using one or more personal adjectives such as stylish, classy, masculine, sexy, old, athletic, or whatever personal adjectives you can use to describe the typical user of _____. Once you've done this, indicate your agreement or disagreement to the following statements.

Strongly
disagree   :___:___:___:___:___: agree
      1   2   3   4   5

1. People who [use focal brand] are much more like me than people who [use referent brand].

2. I can identify with those people who prefer a [focal brand] over a [referent brand].

3. I am very much like the typical person who prefers to [use focal brand] rather than a [referent brand].

4. The image of the [user of focal brand] is highly consistent with how I see myself.

SCALE NAME: Self-Sufficiency

SCALE DESCRIPTION: Six seven-point Likert-type statements that evaluate the degree to which a person views him- or herself as being very responsible and independent.

SCALE ORIGIN: The scale is original to the study by Raskin and Terry (1988) and is part of the narcissistic personality inventory (NPI). Of the 40-item NPI, the six items shown here loaded highest on the same dimension and were labeled **self-sufficiency**. The internal consistency of these items as a set was estimated to be .50 (n = 1018). The scale showed little or no relationship with age and gender. Evidence in support of the scale's nomological validity was provided.

SAMPLES: Various samples were collected and used by Netemeyer, Burton, and Lichtenstein (1995) in the process of validating some other scales. The **self-sufficiency** scale was used in one study composed of 186 students and 264 "nonstudent adults." It was used in another study with data from 27 football players from a nationally ranked NCAA Division I team.

RELIABILITY: Alphas of **.77** (students) and **.80** (nonstudent adults) were found for the scale (Netemeyer 1997; Netemeyer, Burton, and Lichtenstein 1995).

VALIDITY: Although the validity of the scale was not directly examined by Netemeyer, Burton, and Lichtenstein (1995), the scale was used to help establish the construct validity of four vanity-related scales. **Self-sufficiency** had significant positive correlations with all of the vanity scales with the possible exception of one, physical concern (#397), depending on the sample.

ADMINISTRATION: As noted, the scale was used in two studies, and it appears to have been part of larger questionnaires that were self-administered by respondents (Netemeyer, Burton, and Lichtenstein 1995). Higher scores on the scale indicated that respondents viewed themselves as being very self-sufficient.

MAJOR FINDINGS: Netemeyer, Burton, and Lichtenstein (1995) investigated vanity and developed four scales for its measurement. Most of the article discussed the results of the rather extensive validation process. Among the findings was that achievement view vanity (#396) had the strongest positive relationship with **self-sufficiency** among students and nonstudent adults, but with football players achievement concern (#395) had the highest correlation with **self-sufficiency**.

REFERENCES:

Netemeyer, Richard G. (1997), personal correspondence.
———, Scot Burton, and Donald R. Lichtenstein (1995), "Trait Aspects of Vanity: Measurement and Relevance to Consumer Behavior," *JCR*, 21 (March), 612–26.
Raskin, Robert and Howard Terry (1988), "A Principal-Components Analysis of the Narcissistic Personality Inventory and Further Evidence of its Construct Validity," *Journal of Personality and Social Psychology*, 54 (May), 890–902.

SCALE ITEMS:

Strongly   Strongly
disagree   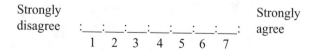   agree

               1   2   3   4   5   6   7

1. I rarely depend on anyone else to get things done.

2. I like to take responsibility for making decisions.

3. I am more capable than other people.

4. I can live my life in any way I want to.

5. I always know what I am doing.

6. I am going to be a great person.

SCALE NAME: Selling Orientation/Customer Orientation (Customer's Perception of Specific Salesperson)

SCALE DESCRIPTION: Twenty-four items in six subscales that use a nine-point response format to measure the degree to which a consumer perceives that a particular car salesperson engaged in behaviors that reflected sincere concern for the customer's needs rather than just trying to make a sale.

SCALE ORIGIN: The scale was originally constructed and tested by Saxe and Weitz (1982) for use with salespeople. The version of the scale by Goff and colleagues (1997) is a modification of that earlier scale, such that customers evaluate salespeople rather than salespeople evaluating themselves. Although similar in perspective to versions by Michaels and Day (1985, Vol. 1, #375) and Brown, Widing, and Coulter (1991, #322), it is different enough to be viewed as a distinct version. For a full review of the original scale and uses of it in industrial marketing contexts see the Customer Orientation (SOCO) scale (#564).

SAMPLES: Goff and colleagues (1997) collected data through a mail survey sent to 2000 people who had purchased new cars within the previous three months. The sample was designed to be nationally stratified from a list of new vehicle registrations. Usable responses were received from 522 people. The respondents were mostly men (60%) and averaged 45 years of age, and a little more than two-thirds were married.

RELIABILITY: As discussed subsequently, Goff and colleagues (1997) used factor analyses to produce three scales for each of the two parts of the SOCO instrument. The alphas for the three customer-orientation subscales (CO1, CO2, CO3) were .82, 59, and .52, respectively. The alphas for the three selling-orientation subscales (SO1, SO2, SO3) were .84, .74, .64, respectively. When the subscales were used as multiple indicators of their respective constructs, the reliabilities (LISREL) were reported to be .91 for customer orientation and .86 for selling orientation.

VALIDITY: Wanting to have multiple indicators of customer orientation and selling orientation, Goff and colleagues (1997) used maximum likelihood factor analysis with oblique rotation to guide the development of subscales. Unfortunately, no analysis was reported that compared the alternative models of SOCO (one primary dimension versus two).

ADMINISTRATION: The instrument was supposed to be self-administered in the study by Goff and colleagues (1997) by the person in the household most involved in the purchase of the car. In their study, a high score on the customer-orientation scale implied that buyers viewed the salesperson with whom they had worked as caring about them. In contrast, a high score on the selling-orientation scale suggested that buyers thought their salesperson was only interested in making a sale.

MAJOR FINDINGS: Goff and colleagues (1997) examined the effect of salesperson behaviors on customer satisfaction with the salesperson, the dealer, the product, and the manufacturer. The results indicated that the use of a **customer orientation** directly influenced customer satisfaction with the salesperson in a positive way, whereas use of a **selling orientation** had a direct negative impact.

COMMENTS: The SOCO scale does not appear to be unidimensional, and strong consideration should be given to measuring it as two or more subscales, as in the study by Goff and colleagues (1997). However, there is also concern that two of the subscales (CO2 and CO3) are not reliable. Further development and testing is needed.

REFERENCES:

Brown, Gene, Robert E. Widing II, and Ronald L. Coulter (1991), "Customer Evaluations of Retail Salespeople Utilizing the SOCO Scale: A Replication, Extension, and Application," *JAMS*, 19 (Fall), 347–51.

Goff, Brent G., James S. Boles, Danny N. Bellenger, and Carrie Stojack (1997), "The Influence of Salesperson Selling Behaviors on Customer Satisfaction with Products," *JR*, 73 (2), 171–83.

Michaels, Ronald E. and Ralph L. Day (1985), "Measuring Customer Orientation of Salespeople: A Replication with Industrial Buyers," *JMR*, 22 (November), 443–46.

Saxe, Robert and Barton A. Weitz (1982), "The SOCO Scale: A Measure of the Customer Orientation of Salespeople," *JMR*, 19 (August), 343–51.

SCALE ITEMS:

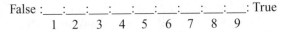

False :___:___:___:___:___:___:___:___:___: True
         1   2   3   4   5   6   7   8   9

Customer Orientation Subscale 1 (CO1)

1. Answered my questions about vehicles as honestly as possible.
2. Provided all the information I asked for.
3. Made me feel comfortable.
4. Had my best interest in mind.
5. Gave an accurate representation of what the vehicle would do for me.

Customer Orientation Subscale 2 (CO2)

6. Tried to figure out what my needs were.
7. Tried to get me to discuss what I needed in a vehicle.
8. Took a problem solving approach in selling to me.
9. Disagreed with me in order to help me make a better decision.

Customer Orientation Subscale 3 (CO3)

10. Was customer-oriented.
11. Tried to influence me through information rather than by pressure.

Salesperson Orientation Subscale 1 (SO1)

1. Purposely prolonged the transaction to wear me down.
2. Involved other salespeople in the process to wear me down.
3. Was always looking for ways to apply pressure to make me buy.
4. Treated me as an opponent.

Salesperson Orientation Subscale 2 (SO2)

5. Applied selling pressure even though s/he knew the vehicle was not right for me.
6. Tried to convince me to buy more vehicle than I needed.
7. Spent more time trying to persuade me than trying to discover my vehicle needs.
8. Made recommendations based on what s/he thought they could sell.
9. Talked first and listened to my needs later.

Salesperson Orientation Subscale 3 (SO3)

10. Agreed with me only to please me.
11. Implied that things were beyond his/her control when they really were not.
12. Stretched the truth in representations about vehicles.
13. Tried to make the vehicle sound as good as possible.

SCALE NAME: Selling Orientation/Customer Orientation (Customer's Perception of Salespeople in General)

SCALE DESCRIPTION: A twenty-four-item, six-point summated ratings scale that measures the degree to which a consumer perceives that salespeople engage in behaviors aimed at increasing long-term customer satisfaction rather than have low concern for customer's needs. The scale could be viewed as a measure of consumers' *attitudes toward salespeople in general*, but the emphasis is certainly on whether salespeople are focused most on making sales or on satisfying customer needs.

SCALE ORIGIN: The scale was originally constructed and tested by Saxe and Weitz (1982) for use with salespeople. The version of the scale by Brown, Widing, and Coulter (1991) is a modification of that earlier scale, such that consumers evaluate salespeople rather than salespeople evaluating themselves. Although somewhat similar to Michaels and Day's (1985, Vol. 1, #375) version in perspective, the differences are that Brown, Widing, and Coulter's (1991) scale is intended for an evaluation of retail salespeople (not industrial salespeople) and was developed independently. For a full review of the original scale and uses of it in industrial marketing contexts, see the Customer Orientation (SOCO) scale (#564).

SAMPLES: The sample analyzed by Brown, Widing, and Coulter (1991) was composed of **348** consumers drawn from a mid-sized Midwestern U.S. city. Four hundred telephone numbers were called, and three follow-up attempts were made, resulting in an 87% response rate. No demographic characteristics of the sample were provided.

RELIABILITY: An alpha of **.81** was reported by Brown, Widing, and Coulter (1991). Mean interitem correlation was .15, and mean item–total correlation was .33.

VALIDITY: Although validity was not directly assessed, some limited evidence was provided by the factor analysis performed by Brown, Widing, and Coulter (1991). The scale is clearly bidimensional; two clear factors were found, one relating to the customer orientation and the other to the selling orientation. The former explained 41% of the variance and had factor loadings between .35 and .67. The second factor explained 34% of the variance and had loadings ranging between .31 and .69.

ADMINISTRATION: The scale was administered to respondents in telephone interviews (Brown, Widing, and Coulter 1991). A high score on the scale suggested that a consumer viewed most salespeople as having a customer orientation, whereas a low score meant that the respondent thought most salespeople are just interested in the sale itself, not the customer's satisfaction.

MAJOR FINDINGS: The purpose of the study by Brown, Widing, and Coulter (1991) was to determine if the SOCO scale (**customer orientation**) could be successfully modified so that consumers could evaluate salespeople. Little substantive detail is provided by the authors about the scale beyond what was reported regarding its psychometric qualities.

COMMENTS: Mean total scores on the scale were reported to be 83 (Brown, Widing, and Coulter 1991, p. 349). The standard deviation was 13, and skewness was −.27.

Because the scale is not unidimensional, some serious thought should be given to measuring the two different orientations separately. Two separate scales would likely be of higher reliability and validity than the present combined version and could explain more variance.

See also Kelley and Hoffman (1997).

REFERENCES:

Brown, Gene, Robert E. Widing II, and Ronald L. Coulter (1991), "Customer Evaluations of Retail Salespeople Utilizing the SOCO Scale: A Replication, Extension, and Application," *JAMS*, 19 (Fall), 347–51.

Kelley, Scott W. and K. Douglas Hoffman (1997), "An Investigation of Positive Affect, Prosocial Behaviors and Service Quality," *JR*, 73 (3), 407–27.

Michaels, Ronald E. and Ralph L. Day (1985), "Measuring Customer Orientation of Salespeople: A Replication with Industrial Buyers," *JMR*, 22 (November), 443–46.

Saxe, Robert and Barton A. Weitz (1982), "The SOCO Scale: A Measure of the Customer Orientation of Salespeople," *JMR*, 19 (August), 343–51.

SCALE ITEMS:*

Directions used in telephone interviews: I'm going to read you some statements regarding retail salespeople behaviors and would like you to tell me if you think the statement is true for:

1. No retail salespeople.
2. Some salespeople.
3. Somewhat less than half of salespeople.
4. Somewhat more than half of salespeople.
5. A lot of salespeople.
6. All salespeople.

1. Salespersons try to help me achieve my goals.

2. Salespersons try to achieve their goals by satisfying customers.

3. A good salesperson has to have a customer's best interest in mind.

4. Salespersons try to get me to discuss my needs with them.

5. Salespersons try to influence a customer with information rather than pressure.

6. Salespersons offer the product of theirs that is best suited to the customer's problem.

7. Salespersons try to find out what kind of product would be most helpful to a customer.

8. Salespersons answer a customer's questions about the product as correctly as they can.

9. Salespersons try to bring a customer with a problem together with a product that helps solve that problem.

10. Salespersons are willing to disagree with a customer in order to help him make a better decision.

11. Salespersons try to give customers an accurate expectation of what the product will do for them.

12. Salespersons try to figure out what a customer's needs are.

13. Salespersons try to sell customers all they can convince him to buy, if customers think it is more than a wise customer would buy. **(r)**

14. Salespersons try to sell as much as they can rather than to satisfy a customer. **(r)**

15. Salespersons keep alert for weaknesses in a customer's personality so they can use them to put pressure on customers to buy. **(r)**

16. If a salesperson is not sure a product is right for a customer, he will still apply pressure to get him to buy. **(r)**

17. Salespersons decide what products to offer on the basis of what they can convince customers to buy, not on the basis of what will satisfy them in the long run. **(r)**

18. Salespersons paint too rosy a picture of their products, to make them sound as good as possible. **(r)**

19. Salespersons spend more time trying to persuade a customer to buy than they do trying to discover customer needs. **(r)**

20. Salespersons stretch the truth in describing a product to a customer. **(r)**

21. Salespersons pretend to agree with customers to please them. **(r)**

22. Salespersons imply to a customer that something is beyond their control when it is not. **(r)**

23. Salespersons begin the sales talk for a product before exploring a customer's needs with him. **(r)**

24. Salespersons treat customers as rivals. **(r)**

*The first twelve items measure the customer orientation, whereas the last twelve measure the selling orientation. Consideration should be given to intermixing the items on a survey instrument.

SCALE NAME: Sensation Seeking

SCALE DESCRIPTION: Forty items intended to capture a person's need for varied and novel sensa-tions as well as his or her willingness to take the risks necessary to achieve those sensations. This is a measure of a personality *trait* rather than a situation-specific *state*. As used by Steenkamp and Baumgartner (1992), the measure was composed of 40 items using a five-point Likert-type response scale. In contrast, Schoenbachler and Whittler (1996) used the original form of the scale that has 40 *pairs* of items between which the respondent is asked to choose.

SCALE ORIGIN: The scale used by Steenkamp and Baumgartner (1992) was adapted from a scale constructed by Zuckerman (1979). The latter has been working on sensation-seeking measures since the early 1960s, and Form V is the name of the version adapted by Steenkamp and Baumgartner (1992). That version was composed of 40 forced-choice pairs of items. Steenkamp and Baumgartner (1992) used 19 of the negative statements and 21 of the positive statements in a Likert-type format. Form V has four subscales: thrill and adventure seeking, experience seeking, disinhibition, and boredom susceptibility.

Much information about the psychometric qualities of Form V can be found in Zuckerman (1979, Ch. 4). Briefly, the scale was found to be quite stable, with a test–retest score of .94. Analyzed separately for both sexes and for two cultures (British and U.S.), internal consistency was greater than .80 for each of the four samples. Factor loadings and internal consistencies of the subscales were generally best for thrill and adventure seeking and worst for boredom susceptibility.

SAMPLES: Data were collected by Schoenbachler and Whittler (1996) from a sample of **371** seventh- and eighth-grade students from a metropolitan middle school. No other information was provided about the sample.

The sample used by Steenkamp and Baumgartner (1992) was composed of **223** volunteers from undergraduate marketing courses at a university. A lottery with cash prizes was used to help motivate stu-dents to participate.

RELIABILITY: An alpha of **.86** was reported for the total scale by Schoenbachler and Whittler (1996). A reliability of **.806** was reported for the total scale by Steenkamp and Baumgartner (1992). Reliabilities of .79, .50, .72, and .50 were found for the thrill seeking, experience seeking, disinhibition, and boredom susceptibility subscales, respectively.

VALIDITY: Steenkamp and Baumgartner (1992) concluded that principal components factor analysis did not provide strong evidence of a unidimensional or four-dimensional structure. Scores on the scale had correlations of between .43 and .60 with three other measures of optimum stimulation level, which provides some evidence of convergent validity. A confirmatory factor analysis of all four scales also pro-vided some evidence of convergent validity because the sensation-seeking scale loaded significantly on the underlying construct, though not nearly as well as a couple of the other scales.

ADMINISTRATION: The scale was administered by Steenkamp and Baumgartner (1992) as part of a larger questionnaire composed primarily of four scales that measured optimum stimulation level in vari-ous ways. The questionnaire was handed out to students in class, and they were asked to bring the com-pleted form back at the next class period. Subjects in the study by Schoenbachler and Whittler (1996) completed the scale as part of a larger instrument they filled out after they were exposed to an experi-mental stimulus. Higher scores on the scale indicated that respondents desired thrills and adventures, whereas low scores indicated a tendency to seek safe and familiar sensations.

MAJOR FINDINGS: The purpose of the experiment by Schoenbachler and Whittler (1996) was to examine threat appeal advertising using the *ordered protection model.* As expected, low **sensation seekers** made more support arguments, and high **sensation seekers** produced more counter arguments.

Steenkamp and Baumgartner (1992) studied the role of optimum stimulation level in exploratory consumer behavior. A weighted composite of the **sensation-seeking** scale and three other well-known measures was used to examine people's desire for stimulation. Beyond the information provided concerning reliability and validity, the article did not discuss the findings from any one scale, but they can be obtained from the authors.

REFERENCES:

Schoenbachler , Denise D. and Tommy E. Whittler (1996), "Adolescent Processing of Social and Physical Threat Communications," *JA*, 25 (Winter), 37–54.

Steenkamp, Jan-Benedict E. M. and Hans Baumgartner (1992), "The Role of Optimum Stimulation Level in Exploratory Consumer Behavior," *JCR*, 19 (December), 434–48.

Zuckerman, Marvin (1979), *Sensation Seeking: Beyond the Optimum Level of Arousal.* Hillsdale, NJ: Lawrence Erlbaum Associates.

SCALE ITEMS:

1. A. I like "wild" uninhibited parties.*
   B. I prefer quiet parties with good conversation.◆
2. A. There are some movies I enjoy seeing a second or even a third time.
   B. I can't stand watching a movie that I've seen before.* ◆
3. A. I often wish I could be a mountain climber.*
   B. I can't understand people who risk their necks climbing mountains. ◆
4. A. I dislike all body odors. ◆
   B. I like some of the earthy body smells.*
5. A. I get bored seeing the same old faces.*
   B. I like the comfortable familiarity of everyday friends. ◆
6. A. I like to explore a strange city or section of town by myself, even if it means getting lost.* ◆
   B. I prefer a guide when I am in a place I don't know well.
7. A. I dislike people who do or say things just to shock or upset others. ◆
   B. When you can predict almost everything a person will do and say he or she must be a bore.*
8. A. I usually don't enjoy a movie or play where I can predict what will happen in advance.* ◆
   B. I don't mind watching a movie or play where I can predict what will happen in advance.
9. A. I have tried marijuana or would like to.* ◆
   B. I would never smoke marijuana.
10. A. I would not like to try any drug which might product strange and dangerous effects on me. ◆
    B. I would like to try some of the new drugs that product hallucinations.*
11. A. A sensible person avoids activities that are dangerous. ◆
    B. I sometimes like to do things that are a little frightening.*
12. A. I dislike "swingers." ◆
    B. I enjoy the company of real "swingers."*
13. A. I find that stimulants make me uncomfortable.
    B. I often like to get high (drinking liquor or smoking marijuana).* ◆
14. A. I like to try new foods that I have never tasted before.* ◆
    B. I order the dishes with which I am familiar, so as to avoid disappointment and unpleasantness.
15. A. I enjoy looking at home movies or travel slides.
    B. Looking at someone's home movies or travel slides bores me tremendously.* ◆

16. A. I would like to take up the sport of water-skiing.* ◆
    B. I would not like to take up water-skiing.
17. A. I would like to try surf-board riding.* ◆
    B. I would not like to try surf-board riding.
18. A. I would like to take off on a trip with no pre-planned or definite routes, or timetable.*
    B. When I go on a trip I like to plan my route and timetable fairly carefully. ◆
19. A. I prefer the "down-to-earth" kinds of people as friends. ◆
    B. I would like to make friends in some of the "far-out" groups like artists or "hippies."*
20. A. I would not like to learn to fly an airplane.
    B. I would like to learn to fly an airplane.* ◆
21. A. I prefer the surface of the water to the depths. ◆
    B. I would like to go scuba diving.*
22. A. I would like to meet some persons who are homosexual (men or women).* ◆
    B. I stay away from anyone I suspect of being "queer."
23. A. I would like to try parachute jumping.* ◆
    B. I would never want to try jumping out of a plane with or without a parachute.
24. A. I prefer friends who are excitingly unpredictable.* ◆
    B. I prefer friends who are reliable and predictable.
25. A. I am not interested in experience for its own sake.
    B. I like to have new and exciting experiences and sensations even if they are a little frightening, unconventional or illegal.* ◆
26. A. The essence of good art is in its clarity, symmetry of form and harmony of colors. ◆
    B. I often find beauty in the "clashing" colors and irregular forms of modern painting.*
27. A. I enjoy spending time in the familiar surroundings of home. ◆
    B. I get very restless if I have to stay around home for any length of time.*
28. A. I like to dive off the high board.* ◆
    B. I don't like the feeling I get standing on the high board (or I don't go near it at all).
29. A. I like to date members of the opposite sex who are physically exciting.*
    B. I like to date members of the opposite sex who share my values. ◆
30. A. Heavy drinking usually ruins a party because some people get loud and boisterous.
    B. Keeping the drinks full is the key to a good party.* ◆
31. A. The worst social sin is to be rude.
    B. The worst social sin is to be a bore.* ◆
32. A. A person should have considerable sexual experience before marriage.* ◆
    B. It's better if two married persons begin their sexual experience with each other.
33. A. Even if I had the money I would not care to associate with flighty persons like those in the "jet set." ◆
    B. I could conceive of myself seeking pleasure around the world with the "jet set."*
34. A. I like people who are sharp and witty even if they do sometimes insult others.*
    B. I dislike people who have their fun at the expense of hurting the feelings of others. ◆
35. A. There is altogether too much portrayal of sex in movies.
    B. I enjoy watching many of the "sexy" scenes in movies.* ◆
36. A. I feel best after taking a couple of drinks.* ◆
    B. Something is wrong with people who need liquor to feel good.
37. A. People should dress according to some standards of taste, neatness, and style.
    B. People should dress in individual ways even if the effects are sometimes strange.* ◆
38. A. Sailing long distances in small sailing crafts is foolhardy. ◆
    B. I would like to sail a long distance in a small but seaworthy sailing craft.*

39. A. I have no patience with dull or boring persons.* ◆
    B. I find something interesting in almost every person I talk with.
40. A. Skiing fast down a high mountain slope is a good way to end up on crutches.
    B. I think I would enjoy the sensations of skiing very fast down a high mountain slope.* ◆

*These are the items in each pair that indicate greater sensation seeking.
◆These are the items used by Steenkamp and Baumgartner (1992). When they are not the same as those marked by the asterisk, they must be reversed coded during the scoring process.

SCALE NAME: Server Encounter Behavior (Authenticity)

SCALE DESCRIPTION: Three seven-point Likert-type items that measure a customer's view of the interaction that occurred between him or her and an employee (server) of a service provider as it pertains to the degree to which the server was viewed as being sincere. In the study by Winsted (1997), respondents were asked to think of a recent encounter with a waiter or waitress in a restaurant.

SCALE ORIGIN: The scale is original to Winsted (1997).

SAMPLES: Winsted (1997) had two data collections phases, the second of which included the satisfaction scale. There were two samples, one American and the other Japanese. The American sample was composed of **200** qualified respondents, and the Japanese sample had **176**. College students with means ages in their early 20s constituted the samples in both cases.

RELIABILITY: An alpha of **.85** was reported for the scale by Winsted (1997).

VALIDITY: No examination of the scale's validity was reported by Winsted (1997) beyond noting that it was unidimensional.

ADMINISTRATION: The scale was administered to students as part of a much larger paper-and-pencil questionnaire (Winsted 1997). Higher scores on the scale indicated that consumers strongly agreed that a specific server they encountered recently appeared to be sincere.

MAJOR FINDINGS: Winsted (1997) examined behaviors that consumers in two countries (United States and Japan) used to evaluate service encounters and studied potential differences in the relevant encounter dimensions between the two cultures. Among the many findings was that **server authenticity** had a significant positive association with satisfaction (with the server).

COMMENTS: A Japanese version of the questionnaire was developed; however, the factor analysis did not lead to the development of a authenticity scale for that sample. See Winsted (1997) for details.

REFERENCES:
Winsted, Kathryn Frazer (1997), "The Service Experience in Two Cultures: A Behavioral Perspective," *JR*, 73 (3), 337–60.
——— (1999), personal correspondence.

SCALE ITEMS:*
Directions: Indicate your level of agreement with each of the following statements by circling a number from 1 to 7.

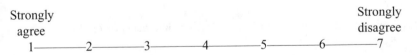

Strongly agree

Strongly disagree

1————2————3————4————5————6————7

The server:

1. seemed phony or fake. **(r)**

2. said things that made it seem true thoughts were not being expressed. **(r)**

3. had a fake smile. **(r)**

*The scale stem and items were provided by Winsted (1999).

SCALE NAME: Server Encounter Behavior (Civility)

SCALE DESCRIPTION: Twelve seven-point Likert-type items that measure a customer's view of the interaction that occurred between him or her and an employee (server) of a service provider as it pertains to the degree to which the server was viewed as being polite and helpful. In the study by Winsted (1997), respondents were asked to think of a recent encounter with a waiter or waitress in a restaurant.

SCALE ORIGIN: The scale is original to Winsted (1997).

SAMPLES: Winsted (1997) had two data collections phases, the second of which included the satisfaction scale. There were two samples, one American and the other Japanese. The American sample was composed of **200** qualified respondents, and the Japanese sample had **176**. College students with means ages in their early 20s constituted the samples in both cases. Only the American sample was involved in the production of the scale shown here.

RELIABILITY: An alpha of **.95** was reported for the scale by Winsted (1997).

VALIDITY: No examination of the scale's validity was reported by Winsted (1997) beyond noting that it was unidimensional. However, one item (6) split loaded and was included in another scale as well (#329).

ADMINISTRATION: The scale was administered to students as part of a much larger paper-and-pencil questionnaire (Winsted 1997). Higher scores on the scale indicated that consumers strongly agreed that a specific server they encountered recently appeared to be polite.

MAJOR FINDINGS: Winsted (1997) examined behaviors that consumers in two countries (United States and Japan) used to evaluate service encounters and studied potential differences in the relevant encounter dimensions between the two cultures. Among the many findings was that **server civility** had a significant positive association with customer satisfaction (with the server).

COMMENTS: A Japanese version of the questionnaire was also used, and the factor analysis led to the development of a somewhat different civility scale for the Japanese sample than the one presented here, which was developed with data from the U.S. sample. See Winsted (1997) for details.

REFERENCES:
Winsted, Kathryn Frazer (1997), "The Service Experience in Two Cultures: A Behavioral Perspective," *JR*, 73 (3), 337–60.
———— (1999), personal correspondence.

SCALE ITEMS:*
Directions: Indicate your level of agreement with each of the following statements by circling a number from 1 to 7.

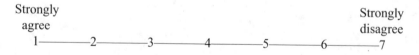

Strongly
agree
1————2————3————4————5————6————7

Strongly
disagree

The server:

1. was annoyed with me. **(r)**

2. acted arrogant. **(r)**

3. had a bad attitude. **(r)**

4. glared at me. **(r)**

5. ignored me. **(r)**

6. did not provide complete service. **(r)**

7. provided incorrect service. **(r)**

8. used facial expressions that suggested lack of genuineness. **(r)**

9. ordered me. **(r)**

10. acted rude to me. **(r)**

11. rushed me. **(r)**

12. was standing around when he or she could have been helping me. **(r)**

*The scale stem and items were provided by Winsted (1999).

SCALE NAME: Server Encounter Behavior (Congeniality)

SCALE DESCRIPTION: Nine seven-point Likert-type items that measure a customer's view of the interaction that occurred between him or her and an employee (server) of a service provider as it pertains to the degree to which the server was warm and friendly. In the study by Winsted (1997), respondents were asked to think of a recent encounter with a waiter or waitress in a restaurant.

SCALE ORIGIN: The scale is original to Winsted (1997).

SAMPLES: Winsted (1997) had two data collections phases, the second of which included the satisfaction scale. There were two samples, one American and the other Japanese. The American sample was composed of **200** qualified respondents, and the Japanese sample had **176**. College students with means ages in their early 20s constituted the samples in both cases. Only the U.S. sample was involved in the production of the scale shown here.

RELIABILITY: An alpha of **.96** was reported for the scale by Winsted (1997).

VALIDITY: No examination of the scale's validity was reported by Winsted (1997) beyond noting that it was unidimensional.

ADMINISTRATION: The scale was administered to students as part of a much larger paper-and-pencil questionnaire (Winsted 1997). Higher scores on the scale indicated that consumers strongly agreed that it was pleasant to interact with a specific server they encountered recently.

MAJOR FINDINGS: Winsted (1997) examined behaviors that consumers in two countries (United States and Japan) used to evaluate service encounters and studied potential differences in the relevant encounter dimensions between the two cultures. Among the many findings was that **server congeniality** had a strong positive association with customer satisfaction (with the server).

COMMENTS: A Japanese version of the questionnaire was developed; however, the factor analysis did not lead to the development of a congeniality scale for that sample. See Winsted (1997) for details.

REFERENCES:
Winsted, Kathryn Frazer (1997), "The Service Experience in Two Cultures: A Behavioral Perspective," *JR*, 73 (3), 337–60.
——— (1999), personal correspondence.

SCALE ITEMS:*
Directions: Indicate your level of agreement with each of the following statements by circling a number from 1 to 7.

Strongly
disagree

Strongly
agree

1————2————3————4————5————6————7

The server:

1. was very enthusiastic.

2. was friendly.

3. seemed happy and cheerful.

4. acted in a personal way.

5. was very pleasant.

6. used facial expressions which made him or her seem very sincere.

7. smiled a lot.

8. did not smile at me. **(r)**

9. was very warm.

*The scale stem and items were provided by Winsted (1999).

SCALE NAME: Server Encounter Behavior (Conversation)

SCALE DESCRIPTION: Five seven-point Likert-type items that measure a customer's view of the interaction that occurred between him or her and an employee (server) of a service provider as it pertains to the degree to which the server engaged in banter and was personable in the conversation. In the study by Winsted (1997), respondents were asked to think of a recent encounter with a waiter or waitress in a restaurant.

SCALE ORIGIN: The scale is original to Winsted (1997).

SAMPLES: Winsted (1997) had two data collections phases, the second of which included the satisfaction scale. There were two samples, one American and the other Japanese. The American sample was composed of **200** qualified respondents, and the Japanese sample had **176**. College students with means ages in their early 20s constituted the samples in both cases. Only the U.S. sample was involved in the production of the scale shown here.

RELIABILITY: An alpha of **.85** was reported for the scale by Winsted (1997).

VALIDITY: No examination of the scale's validity was reported by Winsted (1997) beyond noting that it was unidimensional.

ADMINISTRATION: The scale was administered to students as part of a much larger paper-and-pencil questionnaire (Winsted 1997). Higher scores on the scale indicated that consumers strongly agreed that a specific server they encountered recently was talkative (in a positive way).

MAJOR FINDINGS: Winsted (1997) examined behaviors that consumers in two countries (United States and Japan) used to evaluate service encounters and studied potential differences in the relevant encounter dimensions between the two cultures. Among the many findings was that **server conversation** had a significant positive association with customer satisfaction (with the server).

COMMENTS: A Japanese version of the questionnaire was also used, and the factor analysis led to the development of a somewhat different conversation scale for the Japanese sample than the one presented here, which was developed with data from the U.S. sample. See Winsted (1997) for details.

REFERENCES:
Winsted, Kathryn Frazer (1997), "The Service Experience in Two Cultures: A Behavioral Perspective," *JR*, 73 (3), 337–60.
——— (1999), personal correspondence.

SCALE ITEMS:*
Directions: Indicate your level of agreement with each of the following statements by circling a number from 1 to 7.

Strongly
disagree

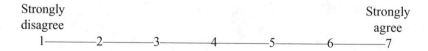

Strongly
agree

The server:

1. talked with me.

2. joked around.

3. shared some of his or her personal experiences with me.

4. expressed his or her personal opinions.

5. engaged in small talk.

*The scale stem and items were provided by Winsted (1999).

SCALE NAME: Server Encounter Behavior (Personalization)

SCALE DESCRIPTION: Three seven-point Likert-type items that measure a customer's view of the interaction that occurred between him or her and an employee (server) of a service provider as it pertains to the degree to which the server used the customer's name when speaking to him or her. In the study by Winsted (1997), respondents were asked to think of a recent encounter with a waiter or waitress in a restaurant.

SCALE ORIGIN: The scale is original to Winsted (1997).

SAMPLES: Winsted (1997) had two data collections phases, the second of which included the satisfaction scale. There were two samples, one American and the other Japanese. The American sample was composed of **200** qualified respondents, and the Japanese sample had **176**. College students with means ages in their early 20s constituted the samples in both cases. Only the U.S. sample was involved in the production of the scale shown here.

RELIABILITY: An alpha of **.94** was reported for the scale by Winsted (1997).

VALIDITY: No examination of the scale's validity was reported by Winsted (1997) beyond noting that it was unidimensional.

ADMINISTRATION: The scale was administered to students as part of a much larger paper-and-pencil questionnaire (Winsted 1997). Higher scores on the scale indicated that consumers strongly agreed that a specific server they encountered recently used their names during the interaction.

MAJOR FINDINGS: Winsted (1997) examined behaviors that consumers in two countries (United States and Japan) used to evaluate service encounters and studied potential differences in the relevant encounter dimensions between the two cultures. Among the many findings was that **server personalization** had a significant positive association with customer satisfaction (with the server).

COMMENTS: A Japanese version of the questionnaire was developed; however, the factor analysis led to the development of a broader personalization scale than the one presented here. See Winsted (1997) for details.

REFERENCES:
Winsted, Kathryn Frazer (1997), "The Service Experience in Two Cultures: A Behavioral Perspective," *JR*, 73 (3), 337–60.
——— (1999), personal correspondence.

SCALE ITEMS:*
Directions: Indicate your level of agreement with each of the following statements by circling a number from 1 to 7.

Strongly   Strongly
disagree   agree
1———2———3———4———5———6———7

The server:

1. asked me for my name.

2. used my name when addressing me.

3. called me by my first name.

*The scale stem and items were provided by Winsted (1999).

SCALE NAME: Server Encounter Behavior (Responsiveness)

SCALE DESCRIPTION: Nine seven-point Likert-type items that measure a customer's view of the interaction that occurred between him or her and an employee (server) of a service provider as it pertains to the degree to which the server was alert and attentive. In the study by Winsted (1997), respondents were asked to think of a recent encounter with a waiter or waitress in a restaurant. This scale was called *Delivery* by Winsted (1997).

SCALE ORIGIN: The scale is original to Winsted (1997).

SAMPLES: Winsted (1997) had two data collections phases, the second of which included the satisfaction scale. There were two samples, one American and the other Japanese. The American sample was composed of **200** qualified respondents, and the Japanese sample had **176**. College students with means ages in their early 20s constituted the samples in both cases. Only the U.S. sample was involved in the production of the scale shown here.

RELIABILITY: An alpha of **.95** was reported for the scale by Winsted (1997).

VALIDITY: No examination of the scale's validity was reported by Winsted (1997) beyond noting that it was unidimensional. However, one item (5) split loaded and was included in another scale as well (#325).

ADMINISTRATION: The scale was administered to students as part of a much larger paper-and-pencil questionnaire (Winsted 1997). Higher scores on the scale indicated that consumers strongly agreed that a specific server they encountered recently provided fast, responsive service.

MAJOR FINDINGS: Winsted (1997) examined behaviors that consumers in two countries (United States and Japan) used to evaluate service encounters and studied potential differences in the relevant encounter dimensions between the two cultures. Among the many findings was that **server responsiveness** had the strongest relationship (positive) with customer satisfaction (with the server) of any of the dimensions examined.

COMMENTS: A Japanese version of the questionnaire was developed; however, the factor analysis did not lead to the development of a responsiveness scale for that sample. See Winsted (1997) for details.

REFERENCES:
Winsted, Kathryn Frazer (1997), "The Service Experience in Two Cultures: A Behavioral Perspective," *JR*, 73 (3), 337–60.
——— (1999), personal correspondence.

SCALE ITEMS:*
Directions: Indicate your level of agreement with each of the following statements by circling a number from 1 to 7.

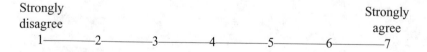

Strongly disagree   Strongly agree

1———2———3———4———5———6———7

The server:

1. anticipated my needs.

2. was very attentive.

3. was very available when needed.

4. checked back on me to see how I was doing.

5. did not provide complete service. **(r)**

6. quickly attended to me.

7. responded to my needs quickly.

8. quickly served me.

9. The timing of the services provided by the server was oriented to my needs.

*The scale stem and items were provided by Winsted (1999).

SCALE NAME: Service Evaluation (Airline Cabin Condition)

SCALE DESCRIPTION: A six-item, seven-point summated scale purported to measure the level of quality an airline passenger perceives there to be for the inside of the plane in which he or she flew, with emphasis on the seat area.

SCALE ORIGIN: The authors (Taylor and Claxton 1994) adapted items from existing airline evaluation forms; thus, the scale as a whole does not appear to be a modification of any one previously used scale. The process used to gather a sample of items and then refine them suggests that the scale should be considered original.

SAMPLES: The settings for the data collection used by Taylor and Claxton (1994) were airline boarding lounges and inside the planes themselves. Each passenger approached was given two questionnaires. One was completed while the respondent was waiting to board the plane, and the other was filled out toward the end of the flight. (Flight attendants made announcements when it was time to complete the second questionnaire and collected them after passengers filled them out.) Data were obtained from passengers of 17 delayed and 19 nondelayed flights out of a large Western U.S. city. Of the delayed flights, 249 of the first questionnaire and 192 of the second questionnaire were completed. For nondelayed flights, 260 of the first questionnaire and 210 of the second questionnaire were completed.

RELIABILITY: Taylor and Claxton (1994) reported an alpha of **.87** for the scale.

VALIDITY: No examination of the scale's validity was reported by Taylor and Claxton (1994). Some idea of the scale's dimensionality can be gleaned from the principal component analysis that was conducted on 16 service attribute items. The three items composing this factor loaded highest on the same factor and had generally low loadings on the other factors.

ADMINISTRATION: The scale was apparently included as part of the second of the two questionnaires passengers were asked to complete (Taylor and Claxton 1994). As noted, the second survey instrument was given to the respondents before they boarded but was not supposed to be completed until toward the end of the flight when flight attendants indicated respondents should complete it. A high score on the scale suggested that a passenger considered the quality of the seating area and cabin to be very good.

MAJOR FINDINGS: Taylor and Claxton (1994) investigated the degree to which a flight delay can change the relative importance of service criteria in terms of their impact on performance judgments in a compensatory evaluation model. The findings did not indicate that nondelayed passengers rated the **cabin** quality significantly differently than did those passengers whose flights were delayed, nor was the **cabin condition** a significant predictor of overall flight service evaluation for either passenger group.

REFERENCES:
Taylor, Shirley and John D. Claxton (1994), "Delays and the Dynamics of Service Evaluations," *JAMS*, 22 (Summer), 254–64.

SCALE ITEMS:

Very bad   :___:___:___:___:___:___:___: Very good
            1   2   3   4   5   6   7

1. Cleanliness of cabin.

2. Condition of cabin.

3. Amount of leg room.

4. Amount of elbow room.

5. Seat cushion comfort.

6. Overall seat comfort.

SCALE NAME: Service Evaluation (Airline Check-In)

SCALE DESCRIPTION: A four-item, seven-point summated scale purported to measure the level of quality an airline passenger perceives there to be with the check-in process.

SCALE ORIGIN: The authors (Taylor and Claxton 1994) adapted items from existing airline evaluation forms; thus, the scale as a whole does not appear to be a modification of any one previously used scale. The process used to gather a sample of items and then refine them suggests that the scale should be considered original.

SAMPLES: The settings for the data collection used by Taylor and Claxton (1994) were airline boarding lounges and inside the planes themselves. Each passenger approached was given two questionnaires. One was completed while the respondent was waiting to board the plane, and the other was filled out toward the end of the flight. (Flight attendants made announcements when it was time to complete the second questionnaire and collected them after passengers filled them out.) Data were obtained from passengers of 17 delayed and 19 nondelayed flights out of a large Western U.S. city. Of the delayed flights, 249 of the first questionnaire and 192 of the second questionnaire were completed. For nondelayed flights, 260 of the first questionnaire and 210 of the second questionnaire were completed.

RELIABILITY: Taylor and Claxton (1994) reported an alpha of **.78** for the scale.

VALIDITY: No examination of the scale's validity was reported by Taylor and Claxton (1994). Some idea of the scale's dimensionality can be gleaned from the principal component analysis that was conducted on 16 service attribute items. The four items composing this factor loaded highest on the same factor. However, item 4 did not load as high on the factor as the other items and had split-loadings with two other factors.

ADMINISTRATION: The scale was apparently included as part of the second of the two questionnaires passengers were asked to complete (Taylor and Claxton 1994). As noted, the second survey instrument was given to the respondents before they boarded but was not supposed to be completed until toward the end of the flight when flight attendants indicated that respondents should complete it. A high score on the scale suggested that a passenger considered the quality of the check-in process to be very good.

MAJOR FINDINGS: Taylor and Claxton (1994) investigated the degree to which a flight delay can change the relative importance of service criteria in terms of their impact on performance judgments in a compensatory evaluation model. The findings indicated that the nondelayed passengers rated the **check-in** aspect of service evaluation significantly higher than did those passengers whose flights were delayed.

REFERENCES:
Taylor, Shirley and John D. Claxton (1994), "Delays and the Dynamics of Service Evaluations," *JAMS*, 22 (Summer), 254–64.

SCALE ITEMS:

Very bad   :___:___:___:___:___:___:___: Very good
           1   2   3   4   5   6   7

1. Bag check speed.

2. Check-in agent friendliness.

3. Check-in agent helpfulness.

4. Boarding procedure.

SCALE NAME: Service Evaluation (Airline Meal)

SCALE DESCRIPTION: A three-item, seven-point summated scale purported to measure the level of quality an airline passenger perceives there to be for the meal served during a flight.

SCALE ORIGIN: The authors (Taylor and Claxton 1994) adapted items from existing airline evaluation forms; thus, the scale as a whole does not appear to be a modification of any one previously used scale. The process used to gather a sample of items and then refine them suggests that the scale should be considered original.

SAMPLES: The settings for the data collection used by Taylor and Claxton (1994) were airline boarding lounges and inside the planes themselves. Each passenger approached was given two questionnaires. One was completed while the respondent was waiting to board the plane, and the other was filled out toward the end of the flight. (Flight attendants made announcements when it was time to complete the second questionnaire and collected them after passengers filled them out.) Data were obtained from passengers of 17 delayed and 19 nondelayed flights out of a large Western U.S. city. Of the delayed flights, 249 of the first questionnaire and 192 of the second questionnaire were completed. For nondelayed flights, 260 of the first questionnaire and 210 of the second questionnaire were completed.

RELIABILITY: Taylor and Claxton (1994) reported an alpha of **.89** for the scale.

VALIDITY: No examination of the scale's validity was reported by Taylor and Claxton (1994). Some idea of the scale's dimensionality can be gleaned from the principal component analysis that was conducted on 16 service attribute items. The three items composing this factor loaded highest on the same factor and had very low loadings on the other factors.

ADMINISTRATION: The scale was apparently included as part of the second of the two questionnaires passengers were asked to complete (Taylor and Claxton 1994). As noted, the second survey instrument was given to the respondents before they boarded but was not supposed to be completed until toward the end of the flight when flight attendants indicated respondents should complete it. A high score on the scale suggested that a passenger considered the quality of the meal to be very good.

MAJOR FINDINGS: Taylor and Claxton (1994) investigated the degree to which a flight delay can change the relative importance of service criteria in terms of their impact on performance judgments in a compensatory evaluation model. The findings did not indicate that nondelayed passengers rated the **meal** quality significantly differently than did those passengers whose flights were delayed. However, **meal** quality was found to be a significant predictor of overall flight service evaluation for both passenger groups.

REFERENCES:

Taylor, Shirley and John D. Claxton (1994), "Delays and the Dynamics of Service Evaluations," *JAMS*, 22 (Summer), 254–64.

SCALE ITEMS:

Very bad   :___:___:___:___:___:___:___: Very good
       1 2 3 4 5 6 7

1. Meal selection.

2. Meal appearance.

3. Meal enjoyment.

SCALE NAME: Service Evaluation (General Airline Flight)

SCALE DESCRIPTION: A five-item, seven-point scale that measures various aspects of an airline flight experience so as to provide a sense of the perceived overall quality of the service.

SCALE ORIGIN: The scale is original to Taylor (1994).

SAMPLES: The setting for the data collection used by Taylor (1994) was an airline boarding lounge and inside the planes themselves. Each passenger approached was given two questionnaires. One was completed while the respondent was waiting to board the plane, and the other was filled out toward the end of their flight. (Flight attendants made announcements when it was time to complete the second questionnaire and collected them after passengers filled them out.) Data from passengers on 18 delayed flights were collected, and **210** usable survey forms were returned.

RELIABILITY: An alpha of **.79** was reported for the scale by Taylor (1994).

VALIDITY: No examination of the scale's validity was reported by Taylor (1994).

ADMINISTRATION: The scale was included as part of the first of the two questionnaires passengers were asked to complete (Taylor 1994). As noted, the second survey instrument was given to the respondents before they boarded but was not to be completed until toward the end of the flight when flight attendants indicated respondents should complete it. A high score on the scale suggested that respondents perceived the flight they were experiencing to be of very good quality.

MAJOR FINDINGS: Taylor (1994) tested a model of the influence of delay duration on affective and evaluative reactions to airline flight delay. The only two significant direct effects on **overall service evaluation** were anger and punctuality.

REFERENCES:
Taylor, Shirley (1994), "Waiting for Service: The Relationship Between Delays and Evaluations of Service," *JM*, 58 (April), 56–69.

SCALE ITEMS:*
Directions: Evaluate each attribute of the flight listed below using the following scale:

Very bad   :___:___:___:___:___:___:___: Very good
                1   2   3   4   5   6   7

1. Check-in.

2. Flight attendants.

3. Meal.

4. Cabin conditions.

5. Considering all aspects of today's plane trip, how would you rate your overall impression?

*This scale has been reconstructed on the basis of information provided in the article and may not be exactly as used by Taylor (1994).

SCALE NAME: Service Quality

SCALE DESCRIPTION: A five-item, seven-point Likert-type scale purported to measure the quality of service provided by a retail store, particularly the aspect relating to the interaction between employees and customers.

SCALE ORIGIN: The scale as a whole is probably original to Baker, Grewal, and Parasuraman (1994), though they say they drew on previous work by others. The scale items are most similar to some items in the SERVQUAL scales by Parasuraman, Berry, and Zeithaml (1991), particularly the *responsiveness* and *empathy* dimensions.

SAMPLES: Data were collected by Baker, Grewal, and Parasuraman (1994) in an experiment involving **297** subjects. The subjects were undergraduate students taking marketing classes at a large university.

RELIABILITY: An alpha of **.84** was reported for the scale by Baker, Grewal, and Parasuraman (1994).

VALIDITY: The validity of the scale was not specifically addressed by Baker, Grewal, and Parasuraman (1994). A sense of its unidimensionality can be gleaned, however, from the results of the principal components factor analysis that was conducted on items from this scale as well as two others. The five items in this scale loaded highest on the same factor ($\geq.66$) and had low loadings on the other two factors ($\leq.36$).

ADMINISTRATION: After subjects watched video tapes, they were asked to complete a self-administered questionnaire that contained this scale, among others (Baker, Grewal, and Parasuraman 1994). High scores on the scale suggested that a person believed a store has high quality of service, especially as it relates to the attention and helpfulness provided by the employees.

MAJOR FINDINGS: Baker, Grewal, and Parasuraman (1994) investigated how retail store environment affects consumers' attitudes about service and product quality. The results indicated that consumers perceived higher **service quality** in a store that appeared to have a "prestige image environment" versus one that had a "discount image" for both ambient and social dimensions.

REFERENCES:

Baker, Julie, Dhruv Grewal, and A. Parasuraman (1994), "The Influence of Store Environment on Quality Inferences and Store Image," *JAMS*, 22 (4), 328–39.

Parasuraman, A., Leonard L. Berry, and Valarie A. Zeithaml (1991), "Refinement and Reassessment of the SERVQUAL Scale," *JR*, 67 (Winter), 420–50.

SCALE ITEMS:

Strongly disagree :__:__:__:__:__:__: Strongly agree
        1   2   3   4   5   6   7

1. Customers could expect to be treated well in this store.

2. Employees of this store could be expected to give customers personal attention.

3. This store's employees would be willing to help customers.

4. This store would offer high-quality service.

5. Employees of this store would not be too busy to respond to customers' requests promptly.

SCALE NAME: Service Quality (Assurance)

SCALE DESCRIPTION: A four-item, seven-point Likert-type scale measuring the degree to which a person thinks the knowledge and courtesy of a service company's employees instill trust and confidence in customers. As described here, the scale relates to the assurance dimension of the SERVQUAL instrument (Parasuraman, Berry, and Zeithaml 1991; Parasuraman, Zeithaml, and Berry 1988) but is not equivalent to it. Each dimension of the SERVQUAL measure is composed of the summated differences between expectation items and perceptual items, not just perceptual items as the scale described here is. Taylor (1995) only used perceptual items.

SCALE ORIGIN: The scale is a part of the larger SERVQUAL instrument described by Parasuraman, Berry, and Zeithaml (1991), which measures five separate dimensions of service quality. That version of the instrument is a revision of a previous version described in detail by Parasuraman, Zeithaml, and Berry (1988), and considerable information is provided in that article about the scale's conceptualization, development, and validation. As far as the assurance dimension is concerned, the revised version kept only one item intact from the previous version and changed the other three items.

SAMPLES: A questionnaire was sent by Parasuraman, Berry, and Zeithaml (1991) to randomly chosen customers of five nationally known companies: one telephone company, two banks, and two insurance companies. A reminder postcard was sent two weeks after the initial mailing. The number of usable questionnaires ranged from 290 to 487 for the five companies. The total completed returns were **1936**, which was a 21% overall response rate. Managers in the companies reviewed the demographic profiles of the respondents and considered them representative of their customer populations.

Taylor (1995) collected data from **232** undergraduate business students attending a midsized university. Some of these subjects (n = 68) were part of a control group, but the rest were broken down into groups of between 24 and 31 for the experimental treatments.

RELIABILITY: The alphas reported by Parasuraman, Berry, and Zeithaml (1991) for the five companies ranged from **.87** to **.91**. These alphas relate to the summated differences between expectation items and perceptual items. The alpha for just the perceptual items was **.92** using the combined sample (Parasuraman 1993). An alpha of **.81** was reported for the version of the scale used by Taylor (1995).

VALIDITY: Parasuraman, Berry, and Zeithaml (1991) reported the results of several factor analyses using oblique rotations. With regard to the perceptual version of the scale using the combined samples, all of the items had their highest loadings on the same factor. However, items from another dimension (responsiveness) also loaded highest on this factor. Therefore, the two scales do not appear to have discriminate validity relative to each other.

ADMINISTRATION: The scale was administered to customers in a mail-survey format by Parasuraman, Berry, and Zeithaml (1991). Subjects in the experiment conducted by Taylor (1995) self-administered the scale, along with other measures, after the experimental manipulation. Higher scores on the perceptual version of the scale indicated that respondents thought employees of a specific service firm were very knowledgeable and courteous, which helped customers feel more confident about their transactions.

MAJOR FINDINGS: Parasuraman, Berry, and Zeithaml (1991) conducted a study to refine their SERVQUAL scales and examine the revised scales in five different customer samples. They also compared their results with those of others who had used the scales. When respondents were asked to divide 100 points among the five service quality dimensions on the basis of importance, the results were the same for each of the five samples: the **assurance** dimension was always was the third most important dimension.

The purpose of the experiment by Taylor (1995) was to investigate the effects of a delay, perceived control over a delay, and what fills the time during the delay. Among the many findings was that evaluation of the **assurance** aspect of service quality was lower for those who felt the service provider (career counselor) had a high degree of control over the delay that was experienced.

COMMENTS: Although this scale can be used by itself, it was designed to be used along with its companion expectation version. For example, the expectation version of item 1 would be something like the following: "The behavior of employees of excellent _____ companies will instill confidence in customers." Researchers are encouraged to measure all of the dimensions to fully capture the domain of service quality.

For further discussion of theoretical and psychometric properties of the SERVQUAL instrument, see Parasuraman, Zeithaml, and Berry (1994), Cronin and Taylor (1994), and Teas (1994).

See also Fischer, Gainer, and Bristor (1997), Kelley and Hoffman (1997), and Teas (1993).

REFERENCES:

Cronin, J. Joseph, Jr. and Steven A. Taylor (1994), "SERVPERF Versus SERVQUAL: Reconciling Performance-Based and Perceptions-Minus-Expectations Measurement of Service Quality," *JM*, 58 (January), 124–31.

Fischer, Eileen, Brenda Gainer, and Julia Bristor (1997), "The Sex of the Service Provider: Does It Influence Perceptions of Service Quality," *JR*, 73 (3), 361–82.

Kelley, Scott W. and K. Douglas Hoffman (1997), "An Investigation of Positive Affect, Prosocial Behaviors and Service Quality," *JR*, 73 (3), 407–27.

Parasuraman, A. (1993), personal correspondence.

———, Leonard L. Berry, and Valarie A. Zeithaml (1991), "Refinement and Reassessment of the SERVQUAL Scale," *JR*, 67 (Winter), 420–50.

———, Valarie A. Zeithaml, and Leonard L. Berry (1988), "SERVQUAL: A Multiple-Item Scale for Measuring Customer Perceptions of Service Quality," *JR*, 64 (Spring), 12–40.

———, ———, and ——— (1994), "Reassessment of Expectations as a Comparison Standard in Measuring Service Quality: Implications for Further Research," *JM*, 58 (January), 111–24.

Taylor, Shirley (1995), "The Effects of Filled Waiting Time and Service Provider Control over the Delay on Evaluations of Service," *JAMS*, 23 (Winter), 38–48.

Teas, R. Kenneth (1993), "Expectations, Performance Evaluation, and Consumers' Perceptions of Quality," *JM*, 57 (October), 18–34.

——— (1994), "Expectations as a Comparison Standard in Measuring Service Quality: An Assessment of a Reassessment," *JM*, 58 (January), 132–39.

SCALE ITEMS:

Directions: The following set of statement relate to your feelings about _____'s service. For each statement, please show the extent to which you believe _____ has the feature described by the statement. Circling a "1" means that you strongly disagree that _____ has that feature, and circling a "7" means that you strongly agree. You may circle any of the numbers in the middle that show how strong your feelings are. There are no right or wrong answers—all we are interested in is a number that best shows your perceptions about _____'s service.

Strongly
disagree :__:__:__:__:__:__: Strongly agree
        1 2 3 4 5 6 7

1. The behavior of employees of _____ instills confidence in customers.

2. You feel safe in your transactions with _____.

3. Employees of _____ are consistently courteous with you.

4. Employees of _____ have the knowledge to answer your questions.

*The name of the specific service firm studied should be placed in the blanks. Taylor (1995) slightly modified these items for use with a specific counselor at a university career counseling service.

SCALE NAME: Service Quality (Assurance)

SCALE DESCRIPTION: Four items and a simple summated nine-point response format that measure the level of assurance a person has in a company, particularly the confidence he or she has in the employees, compared with the desired level (the performance level the company can and should deliver).

SCALE ORIGIN: The scale is a part of the larger SERVQUAL instrument described by Parasuraman, Zeithaml, and Berry (1994b) and Zeithaml, Berry, and Parasuraman (1996) that measures five separate dimensions of service quality. Considerable information is provided by the former about the instrument's conceptualization, development, validation, and diagnostic value. This version of the instrument is a modification of earlier forms (e.g., Parasuraman, Zeithaml, and Berry 1988, 1994a), in that it is intended to be a direct measure of service superiority rather than just capture perceptions or require multiple measures to assess expectations and perceptions. The instrument was refined through two stages of pretesting.

SAMPLES: Data were gathered by Parasuraman, Zeithaml, and Berry (1994b) from subjects obtained from lists of customers provided by four companies: a computer manufacturer, a retail chain, an auto insurer, and a life insurer. A total of 4156 questionnaires were mailed out using this scale's format, and **1135** were received back. (Two other formats were tested as well.)

Zeithaml, Berry, and Parasuraman (1996) gathered data from mailing lists of current customers generated by four businesses: a computer manufacturer, a retail chain, an automobile insurer, and a life insurer. The names were of end users in each case, except for the computer company, for which it was business customers. A total of 12,470 questionnaires were sent out, and **3069** were returned.

RELIABILITY: The alphas reported by Parasuraman, Zeithaml, Berry (1994b) for the four companies ranged from **.86** to **.94**. The values reported by Zeithaml, Berry, and Parasuraman (1996; Parasuraman 1997) ranged from .82 to .91.

VALIDITY: Parasuraman, Zeithaml, Berry (1994b) reported the results of a factor analysis using an oblique rotation. The items composing this scale did not load on the same dimension and might be part of a larger factor that includes items related to *responsiveness* and *empathy*. Further analysis using LISREL provided some support for the five-dimensional structure of the SERVQUAL instrument, though the three-factor model could not be ruled out. Several checks of the scale's validity were made that provided some limited evidence of predictive, convergent, and discriminant validity.

No specific examination of the scale's validity was reported by Zeithaml, Berry, and Parasuraman (1996).

ADMINISTRATION: The scale was administered to customers in a mail survey format (Parasuraman, Zeithaml, and Berry 1994b; Zeithaml, Berry, and Parasuraman 1996). Higher scores on the scale indicated that respondents had a great deal of assurance in the service provided by a specific firm compared with the level of service they think can and should be delivered by such a company.

MAJOR FINDINGS: Parasuraman, Zeithaml, and Berry (1994b) conducted a study to refine their SERVQUAL scales and examine the revised scales in three different formats with four different customer groups. The scale shown here is part of a "one-column format," meaning that one scale for each of the five service quality dimensions was used to measure service superiority directly. Although the one-column format had reasonable psychometric characteristics, its diagnostic value was not considered to be as high as that of the two- and three-column formats, which provided indications of customers' service adequacy in addition to service superiority.

Zeithaml, Berry, and Parasuraman (1996) tested a model of the impact of service quality on relevant behaviors. In general, their results showed that there is a significant positive relationship between perceived service quality and favorable behavioral intentions. A weighted-average performance score was calculated across the SERVQUAL dimensions; no results were reported in this study for the **assurance** dimension by itself.

COMMENTS: Although this scale can be used by itself, it was designed to be used along with its companion measures of the other service quality dimensions. Furthermore, as noted previously, this scale represents the simplest format that Parasuraman, Zeithaml, and Berry (1994b) offered. Refer to their article for details regarding the more complex but potentially more useful versions (two- and three-column formats).

REFERENCES:

Parasuraman, A. (1997), personal correspondence.
———, Valarie A. Zeithaml, and Leonard L. Berry (1988), "SERVQUAL: A Multiple-Item Scale for Measuring Customer Perceptions of Service Quality," *JR*, 64 (Spring), 12–40.
———, ———, and ——— (1994a), "Reassessment of Expectations as a Comparison Standard in Measuring Service Quality: Implications for Further Research," *JM*, 58 (January), 111–24.
———, ———, and ——— (1994b), "Alternative Scales for Measuring Service Quality: A Comparative Assessment Based on Psychometric and Diagnostic Criteria," *JR*, 70 (3), 201–30.
Zeithaml, Valarie A., Leonard L. Berry, and A. Parasuraman (1996), "The Behavioral Consequences of Service Quality," *JM*, 60 (April), 31–46.

SCALE ITEMS:*

Directions: Please think about the quality of service _____ offers compared to your *desired service level*—the level of performance you believe a _____ *can and should deliver* (i.e., the level of service you desire). For each of the following statements, circle the number that indicates how _____'s service compares with your desired service level.

_____'s service performance is:

Lower than my desired service level	The same as my desired service level	Higher than my desired service level	No opinion
:__:__:__:__:__:__:__:__:			
1 2 3 4 5 6 7 8 9			N

1. Employees who instill confidence in customers.

2. Making customers feel safe in their transactions.

3. Employees who are consistently courteous.

4. Employees who have the knowledge to answer customer questions.

*These directions were used by Parasuraman, Zeithaml, and Berry (1994b). Those used by Zeithaml, Berry, and Parasuraman (1996) were slightly different, as was the layout of the scale. Minor changes were made in the items to reflect the different contexts. The blanks should contain the name of the specific service provider being evaluated, except for the second of the four blanks, which should have the general name for the type of service (e.g., auto insurance company) being evaluated.

SCALE NAME: Service Quality (Convenience)

SCALE DESCRIPTION: A three-item, seven-point Likert-type scale measuring the degree to which a person thinks the facility providing some service is convenient to use in terms of location and hours of operation. As used by Andaleeb and Basu (1994), the scale relates to the service received from a car repair establishment.

SCALE ORIGIN: Although drawing inspiration from the SERVQUAL scales by Parasuraman, Zeithaml, and Berry (1988), Andaleeb and Basu (1994) performed their own developmental work and produced a related but unique measure.

SAMPLES: Andaleeb and Basu (1994) gathered their data from a mail survey. Telephone directories of two large cities in the northeastern United States were used to find names and addresses. Questionnaires were apparently directed at a member of the household who owned a car and had experienced automobile repair/service. Of the 550 surveys distributed, **133** were usable.

RELIABILITY: An alpha of **.76** was reported for the scale (Andaleeb and Basu 1994).

VALIDITY: Andaleeb and Basu (1994) provided the results of a factor analysis conducted on 27 items related to service quality. The items on this scale loaded high on the same dimension and lower on the others. In addition, the authors provided a correlation matrix between this scale and four others. Because the correlations in every case were lower than the alphas, it was construed as evidence of discriminant validity. However, the significance and level of the correlations could just as easily have been interpreted as evidence of convergent validity. Thus, strong evidence of the scale's construct validity remains to be provided.

ADMINISTRATION: As noted, the scale was part of a larger mail survey instrument (Andaleeb and Basu 1994). Higher scores on the scale indicated that respondents viewed the service they received from a specified business to have been easy to use.

MAJOR FINDINGS: The purpose of the study by Andaleeb and Basu (1994) was to examine the relationship between a customer's satisfaction with a car repair facility and five dimensions of service quality. Among the many findings was that a higher level of perceived **convenience** is related to greater customer satisfaction with the service performed.

REFERENCES:

Andaleeb, Syed Saad and Amiya K. Basu (1994), "Technical Complexity and Consumer Knowledge as Moderators of Service Quality Evaluation in the Automobile Service Industry," *JR*, 70 (4), 367–81.

Parasuraman, A., Valarie A. Zeithaml, and Leonard L. Berry (1988), "SERVQUAL: A Multiple-Item Scale for Measuring Customer Perceptions of Service Quality," *JR*, 64 (Spring), 12–40.

SCALE ITEMS:

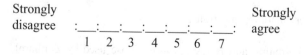

Strongly disagree :___:___:___:___:___:___:___: Strongly agree
        1 2 3 4 5 6 7

1. It was convenient to have my car serviced by this facility.

2. The facility is in an easily accessible location.

3. The facility had convenient hours.

SCALE NAME: Service Quality (Empathy)

SCALE DESCRIPTION: A five-item, seven-point Likert-type scale measuring the degree to which a person thinks a service company's employees give attention to customers and understand their needs. As described here, the scale relates to the empathy dimension of the SERVQUAL instrument (Parasuraman, Berry, and Zeithaml 1991; Parasuraman, Zeithaml, and Berry 1988) but is not equivalent to it. Each dimension of the SERVQUAL measure is composed of the summated differences between expectation items and perceptual items, not just perceptual items as the scale described here is. Carman (1990) used a couple of variations on the scale and described one as a personal attention factor and the other as a courtesy factor. Taylor (1995) only used perceptual items.

SCALE ORIGIN: The scale is a part of the larger SERVQUAL instrument described by Parasuraman, Zeithaml, and Berry (1988; Parasuraman, Berry, and Zeithaml 1991) that measures five separate dimensions of service quality. Considerable information is provided in those articles about the scale's conceptualization, development, and validation.

The version of the scale discussed by Parasuraman, Zeithaml, and Berry (1988) is the one followed to a great extent by Carman (1990). In Parasuraman, Berry, and Zeithaml's 1991 article, some suggestions for changes to the scale were made. As far as the empathy dimension is concerned, the revised version modified all of the items by making them positive rather than negative in wording. Items 6 and 7 were developed by Carman (1990) for use in his tire store study. Taylor (1995) slightly modified the items (specified under "Scale Items") for use with a specific counselor at a university career counseling service.

SAMPLES: Carman (1990) adjusted and tested the SERVQUAL instrument in four different service settings. However, one set of items assessed an empathy factor in a business school placement center (n = 82). Another set of items was used to assess a courtesy factor in a tire store setting (n = 74). Very little description of the samples was provided.

A questionnaire was sent by Parasuraman, Berry, and Zeithaml (1991) to randomly chosen customers of five nationally known companies: one telephone company, two banks, and two insurance companies. A reminder postcard was sent two weeks after the initial mailing. The number of usable questionnaires ranged from 290 to 487 for the five companies. The total completed returns were **1936**, which was a 21% overall response rate. Managers in the companies reviewed the demographic profiles of the respondents and considered them representative of their customer populations.

Taylor (1995) collected data from **232** undergraduate business students attending a midsized university. Some of these subjects (n = 68) were part of a control group, but the rest were broken down into groups of between 24 and 31 for the experimental treatments.

RELIABILITY: Alphas of **.82** and **.84** were reported by Carman (1990) for the use of the scale in the placement center and tire store settings, respectively. The alphas reported by Parasuraman, Berry, and Zeithaml (1991) for the five companies ranged from .85 to .89. These alphas relate to the summated differences between expectation items and perceptual items. The alpha for just the perceptual items was **.90** using the combined sample (Parasuraman 1993). An alpha of **.84** was reported for the version of the scale used by Taylor (1995).

VALIDITY: Carman (1990) factor analyzed the SERVQUAL data from each setting. Only items with loadings greater than .30 on the same factor in at least one setting were used to compose scales (Carman 1994). However, the sets of items used to compose the summated scales for each of the settings were ultimately different based on several factors. These variable results led him to conclude that there were problems with construct validity.

Parasuraman, Berry, and Zeithaml (1991) reported the results of several factor analyses using oblique rotations. With regard to the perceptual version of the scale using the combined samples, all of the items had their highest loadings on the same factor.

ADMINISTRATION: The SERVQUAL instrument was self-administered by respondents after they received service in the study by Carman (1990). The scale was administered to customers in a mail survey format by Parasuraman, Berry, and Zeithaml (1991). Subjects in the experiment conducted by Taylor (1995) self-administered the scale, along with other measures, after the experimental manipulation. Higher scores on the perceptual version of the scale indicated that respondents thought that employees of a service firm were very attentive and understanding of customer needs.

MAJOR FINDINGS: The purpose of Carman's (1990) studies was to test the SERVQUAL instrument in a variety of service settings. Some modifications in wording were always found to be necessary. An **empathy**-related dimension was found in both the placement center and tire store settings; however, as noted , their item compositions were not identical. In fact, Carman (1990) called the set of items in the tire study a courtesy factor and the items in the placement center study a personal attention factor.

Parasuraman, Berry, and Zeithaml (1991) conducted a study to refine their SERVQUAL scales and examine the revised scales in five different customer samples. They also compared their results with those of others who had used the scales. When respondents were asked to divide 100 points among the five service quality dimensions on the basis of their importance, the result was the same for each of the five samples: the **empathy** dimension was always was the next to least most important dimension.

The purpose of the experiment by Taylor (1995) was to investigate the effects of a delay, perceived control over a delay, and what fills the time during the delay. There were few significant findings involving evaluation of the **empathy** aspect of service quality. For example, the evaluation of empathy was approximately the same despite what subjects thought about the service provider's (career counselor) degree of control over the delay that was experienced and what filled the time during the delay.

COMMENTS: Although this scale can be used by itself, it was designed to be used along with its companion expectation version. For example, the expectation version of item 1 would be something like the following: "Excellent companies will give customers individual attention." The authors also encourage researchers to measure all of the dimensions to fully capture the domain of service quality.

For further discussion of theoretical and psychometric properties of the SERVQUAL instrument, see Parasuraman, Zeithaml, and Berry (1994), Cronin and Taylor (1994), and Teas (1994).

See also Fischer, Gainer, and Bristor (1997), Finn and Kayandé (1997), Kelley and Hoffman (1997), and Teas (1993).

REFERENCES:

Carman, James M. (1990), "Consumer Perceptions of Service Quality: An Assessment of the SERVQUAL Dimensions," *JR*, 66 (Spring), 33–55.

———— (1994), personal correspondence.

Cronin, J. Joseph, Jr. and Steven A. Taylor (1994), "SERVPERF Versus SERVQUAL: Reconciling Performance-Based and Perceptions-Minus-Expectations Measurement of Service Quality," *JM*, 58 (January), 124–31.

Finn, Adam and Ujwal Kayandé (1997), "Reliability Assessment and Optimization of Marketing Measurement," *JMR*, 34 (May), 262–75.

Fischer, Eileen, Brenda Gainer, and Julia Bristor (1997), "The Sex of the Service Provider: Does it Influence Perceptions of Service Quality," *JR*, 73 (3), 361–82.

Kelley, Scott W. and K. Douglas Hoffman (1997), "An Investigation of Positive Affect, Prosocial Behaviors and Service Quality," Journal of Retailing, 73 (3), 407–27.

Parasuraman, A. (1993), personal correspondence.

———, Leonard L. Berry, and Valarie A. Zeithaml (1991), "Refinement and Reassessment of the SERVQUAL Scale," *JR*, 67 (Winter), 420–50.

———, Valarie A. Zeithaml, and Leonard L. Berry (1988), "SERVQUAL: A Multiple-Item Scale for Measuring Customer Perceptions of Service Quality," *JR*, 64 (Spring), 12–40.

———, ———, and ——— (1994), "Reassessment of Expectations as a Comparison Standard in Measuring Service Quality: Implications for Further Research," *JM*, 58 (January), 111–24.

Taylor, Shirley (1995), "The Effects of Filled Waiting Time and Service Provider Control over the Delay on Evaluations of Service," *JAMS*, 23 (Winter), 38–48.

Teas, R. Kenneth (1993), "Expectations, Performance Evaluation, and Consumers' Perceptions of Quality," *JM*, 57 (October), 18–34.

——— (1994), "Expectations as a Comparison Standard in Measuring Service Quality: An Assessment of a Reassessment," *JM*, 58 (January), 132–39.

SCALE ITEMS:

Directions: The following set of statement relate to your feelings about _____'s service. For each statement, please show the extent to which you believe _____ has the feature described by the statement. Circling a "1" means that you strongly disagree that _____ has that feature, and circling a "7" means that you strongly agree. You may circle any of the numbers in the middle that show how strong your feelings are. There are no right or wrong answers—all we are interested in is a number that best shows your perceptions about _____'s service.

Strongly   Strongly
disagree   :___:___:___:___:___:___:___: agree
            1   2   3   4   5   6   7

1. _____ does not give you individual attention. **(r)**
2. Employees of _____ do not give you personal attention. **(r)**
3. Employees of _____ do not know what your needs are. **(r)**
4. _____ does not have your best interests at heart. **(r)**
5. _____ does not have operating hours convenient to all their customers. **(r)**
6. My dealings here are very pleasant.
7. The employees of this store know what they are doing.
8. Employees of _____ are too busy to respond to customer requests promptly. **(r)**
9. Employees of _____ are polite.
10. _____ gives you individual attention.
11. _____ has operating hours convenient to all of its customers.
12. _____ has employees who give you personal attention.
13. _____ has your best interests at heart.
14. Employees of _____ understand your specific needs.

*The name of the specific service company being studied should be placed in the blanks. Items 1–5 were the form used by Parasuraman, Zeithaml, and Berry (1988), whereas the revised items (10–14) were recommended in their 1991 article. Statements similar to 2–4 and 8 were used in the placement center study conducted by Carman (1990, 1994). In the tire store study, he used items 2–4, 6, 7, and 9. Taylor (1995) used items similar to 10–14 and adapted them for reference to a specific counselor at a university career counseling office.

#SCALE NAME: Service Quality (Empathy)

SCALE DESCRIPTION: Four items and a simple summated nine-point response format measure the level of caring and attention a person thinks a company exhibits toward its customers, particularly through its employees, compared with the desired level (the performance level the company can and should deliver).

SCALE ORIGIN: The scale is a part of the larger SERVQUAL instrument described by Parasuraman, Zeithaml, and Berry (1994b) and Zeithaml, Berry, and Parasuraman (1996) that measures five separate dimensions of service quality. Considerable information is provided by the former about the instrument's conceptualization, development, validation, and diagnostic value. This version of the instrument is a modification of earlier forms (e.g., Parasuraman, Zeithaml, and Berry 1988, 1994a), in that it is intended to be a direct measure of service superiority rather than just capture perceptions or require multiple measures to assess expectations and perceptions. The instrument was refined through two stages of pretesting.

SAMPLES: Data were gathered by Parasuraman, Zeithaml, and Berry (1994b) from subjects obtained from of customers provided by four companies: a computer manufacturer, a retail chain, an auto insurer, and a life insurer. A total of 4156 questionnaires were mailed out using this scale's format, and **1135** were received back. (Two other formats were tested as well.)

Zeithaml, Berry, and Parasuraman (1996) gathered data from mailing lists of current customers generated by four businesses: a computer manufacturer, a retail chain, an automobile insurer, and a life insurer. The names were of end users in each case, except for the computer company, for which it was business customers. A total of 12,470 questionnaires were sent out, and **3069** were returned.

RELIABILITY: The alphas reported by Parasuraman, Zeithaml, Berry (1994b) for the four companies ranged from .90 to .94. The values reported by Zeithaml, Berry, and Parasuraman (1996; Parasuraman 1997) ranged from .86 to .94.

VALIDITY: Parasuraman, Zeithaml, Berry (1994b) reported the results of a factor analysis using an oblique rotation. The items composing this scale did not load on the same dimension and might be part of a larger factor that includes items related to *responsiveness* and *assurance*. Further analysis using LIS-REL provided some support for the five-dimensional structure of the SERVQUAL instrument, though the three-factor model could not be ruled out. Several checks of the scale's validity were made that provided some limited evidence of predictive, convergent, and discriminant validity.

No specific examination of the scale's validity was reported by Zeithaml, Berry, and Parasuraman (1996).

ADMINISTRATION: The scale was administered to customers in a mail survey format by Parasuraman, Zeithaml, and Berry (1994b) and Zeithaml, Berry, and Parasuraman (1996). Higher scores on the scale indicated that respondents thought the employees of a specific firm were as understanding and caring of customers, if not more so, than the level they think can and should be delivered by such a company.

MAJOR FINDINGS: Parasuraman, Zeithaml, and Berry (1994b) conducted a study to refine their SERVQUAL scales and examine the revised scales in three different formats with four different customer groups. The scale shown here is part of a "one-column format," meaning that one scale for each of the five service quality dimensions was used to measure service superiority directly. Although the one-column format had reasonable psychometric characteristics, its diagnostic value was not considered to be as high as that of the two- and three-column formats, which provided indications of customers' service adequacy in addition to service superiority.

Zeithaml, Berry, and Parasuraman (1996) tested a model of the impact of service quality on relevant behaviors. In general, their results showed that there is a significant positive relationship between perceived service quality and favorable behavioral intentions. A weighted-average performance score was calculated across the SERVQUAL dimensions; no results were reported in this study for the **empathy** dimension by itself.

COMMENTS: Although this scale can be used by itself, it was designed to be used along with its companion measures of the other service quality dimensions. Furthermore, as noted previously, this scale represents the simplest format that Parasuraman, Zeithaml, and Berry (1994b) offered. Refer to their article for details regarding the more complex but potentially more useful versions (two- and three-column formats).

REFERENCES:

Parasuraman, A. (1997), personal correspondence.
———, Valarie A. Zeithaml, and Leonard L. Berry (1988), "SERVQUAL: A Multiple-Item Scale for Measuring Customer Perceptions of Service Quality," *JR*, 64 (Spring), 12–40.
———, ———, and ——— (1994a), "Reassessment of Expectations as a Comparison Standard in Measuring Service Quality: Implications for Further Research," *JM*, 58 (January), 111–24.
———, ———, and ——— (1994b), "Alternative Scales for Measuring Service Quality: A Comparative Assessment Based on Psychometric and Diagnostic Criteria," *JR*, 70 (3), 201–30.
Zeithaml, Valarie A., Leonard L. Berry, and A. Parasuraman (1996), "The Behavioral Consequences of Service Quality," *JM*, 60 (April), 31–46.

SCALE ITEMS:*

Directions: Please think about the quality of service _____ offers compared to your *desired service level*—the level of performance you believe a _____ *can and should deliver* (i.e., the level of service you desire). For each of the following statements, circle the number that indicates how _____'s service compares with your desired service level.

_____'s service performance is:

	The same as	
Lower	my desired	Higher
than my desired	service level	than my desired No
service level :___:___:___:___:___:___:___:___:		service level opinion
1 2 3 4 5 6 7 8 9		N

1. Giving customers individual attention.

2. Employees who deal with customers in a caring fashion.

3. Having the customer's best interest at heart.

4. Employees who understand the needs of their customers.

*These directions were used by Parasuraman, Zeithaml, and Berry (1994b). Those used by Zeithaml, Berry, and Parasuraman (1996) were slightly different, as was the layout of the scale. Minor changes were made in the items to reflect the different contexts. The blanks should contain the name of the specific service provider being evaluated, except for the second of the four blanks, which should have the general name for the type of service (e.g., auto insurance company) being evaluated.

SCALE NAME: Service Quality (Empathy)

SCALE DESCRIPTION: An eight-item, seven-point Likert-type scale measuring the degree to which a person thinks the personnel who performed a particular service exhibited understanding and concern about the work to be conducted. As used by Andaleeb and Basu (1994), the scale relates to the quality of service received from a car repair establishment.

SCALE ORIGIN: Although drawing inspiration and some phrases from the SERVQUAL scales by Parasuraman, Zeithaml, and Berry (1988), Andaleeb and Basu (1994) performed their own developmental work and produced a related but unique measure.

SAMPLES: Andaleeb and Basu (1994) gathered their data from a mail survey. Telephone directories of two large cities in the northeastern United States were used to find names and addresses. Questionnaires were apparently directed at a member of the household who owned a car and had experienced automobile repair/service. Of the 550 surveys distributed, **133** were usable.

RELIABILITY: An alpha of **.95** was reported for the scale (Andaleeb and Basu 1994).

VALIDITY: Andaleeb and Basu (1994) provided the results of a factor analysis conducted on 27 items related to service quality. The items on this scale loaded high on the same dimension and lower on the others. In addition, the authors provided a correlation matrix between this scale and four others. Because the correlations in every case were lower than the alphas, it was construed as evidence of discriminant validity. However, the significance and level of the correlations could just as easily have been interpreted as evidence of convergent validity. Thus, strong evidence of the scale's construct validity remains to be provided.

ADMINISTRATION: As noted, the scale was part of a larger mail survey instrument (Andaleeb and Basu 1994). Higher scores on the scale indicated that respondents believed the employees with whom they interacted (or who provided the service) showed a positive degree of attention and courtesy to them as customers.

MAJOR FINDINGS: The purpose of the study by Andaleeb and Basu (1994) was to examine the relationship between a customer's satisfaction with a car repair facility and five dimensions of service quality. Among the many findings was that a higher level of perceived **empathy** is related to greater customer satisfaction with the service performed.

REFERENCES:

Andaleeb, Syed Saad and Amiya K. Basu (1994), "Technical Complexity and Consumer Knowledge as Moderators of Service Quality Evaluation in the Automobile Service Industry," *JR*, 70 (4), 367–81.
Parasuraman, A., Valarie A. Zeithaml, and Leonard L. Berry (1988), "SERVQUAL: A Multiple-Item Scale for Measuring Customer Perceptions of Service Quality," *JR*, 64 (Spring), 12–40.

SCALE ITEMS:

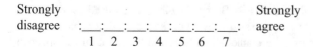

Strongly disagree :___:___:___:___:___:___:___: Strongly agree
               1   2   3   4   5   6   7

1. The service personnel listened to my problem.

2. The service personnel did not pay enough attention to me. **(r)**

3. The facility understood what I wanted.

4. The service personnel explained the work to be performed.

5. The service personnel were respectful.

6. The service personnel were polite.

7. The service personnel were helpful.

8. The service personnel were friendly.

SCALE NAME: Service Quality (Employees)

SCALE DESCRIPTION: Ten five-point items measuring the quality of service perceived to be provided by a particular organization as it pertains to employee-related activities and interactions.

SCALE ORIGIN: The scale used by Hartline and Ferrell (1996) was adapted from the SERVQUAL instrument (e.g., Parasuraman, Zeithaml, and Berry 1988). They used just those items that assessed employee-related aspects of service quality, mainly from the empathy, assurance, and responsiveness components.

SAMPLES: Hartline and Ferrell (1996) gathered data from hotel managers, employees, and customers representing three chains and 279 different hotel units. Only the customers received the **service quality** scale, and **1351** usable responses were returned. Although the response rate was low (5.1%), there was no apparent nonresponse bias according to time-trend analysis. No other demographic information about the sample was provided.

RELIABILITY: An alpha of **.97** was reported for the scale by Hartline and Ferrell (1996).

VALIDITY: The validity of the scale was not addressed by Hartline and Ferrell (1996).

ADMINISTRATION: The scale was part of a larger instrument that was self-administered by hotel guests (Hartline and Ferrell 1996). Higher scores on the scale indicated that customers believed that the quality of service provided by the employees of a specified organization is much better than expected.

MAJOR FINDINGS: The purpose of the study by Hartline and Ferrell (1996) was to develop a model of service employee management and simultaneously examine the manager–employee, employee–role, and employee–customer interfaces. Among the findings was that employee self-efficacy and job satisfaction had significant positive relationships with customers' perceived **service quality**.

REFERENCES:
Hartline, Michael D. and O.C. Ferrell (1996), "The Management of Customer-Contact Service Employees: An Empirical Investigation," *JM*, 60 (October), 52–70.
Parasuraman, A., Valarie A. Zeithaml, and Leonard L. Berry (1988), "SERVQUAL: A Multiple-Item Scale for Measuring Customer Perceptions of Service Quality," *JR*, 64 (Spring), 12–40.

SCALE ITEMS:

Much worse than		Much better than
I expected	:___:___:___:___:___:	I expected
	1 2 3 4 5	

Please rate the quality of service you received in each of the following areas:

1. Receiving prompt service from our employees.

2. Never being too busy to respond to your requests.

3. Employee behaviors that instill confidence in you.

4. The safety you feel in transactions with our employees.

5. The courteousness of our employees.

6. The ability of our employees to answer your questions.

7. The individual attention you received from us.

8. The personal attention you received from our employees.

9. Having your best interests at heart.

10. The ability of our employees to understand your specific needs.

SCALE NAME: Service Quality (Fairness)

SCALE DESCRIPTION: A seven-item, seven-point Likert-type scale measuring the degree to which a person thinks the service provided by a business was fair. As used by Andaleeb and Basu (1994), the scale relates to the quality of service received from a car repair establishment.

SCALE ORIGIN: Although drawing inspiration from the SERVQUAL scales by Parasuraman, Zeithaml, and Berry (1988), Andaleeb and Basu (1994) performed their own developmental work and produced a related but unique measure.

SAMPLES: Andaleeb and Basu (1994) gathered their data from a mail survey. Telephone directories of two large cities in the Northeastern United States were used to find names and addresses. Questionnaires were apparently directed at a member of the household who owned a car and had experienced automobile repair and service. Of the 550 surveys distributed, **133** were usable.

RELIABILITY: An alpha of **.93** was reported for the scale (Andaleeb and Basu 1994).

VALIDITY: Andaleeb and Basu (1994) provided the results of a factor analysis conducted on 27 items related to service quality. The items on this scale loaded very high on the same dimension and low on the others. In addition, the authors provided a correlation matrix between this scale and four others. Because the correlations in every case were lower than the alphas, it was construed as evidence of discriminant validity. However, the significance and level of the correlations could just as easily have been interpreted as evidence of convergent validity. Thus, strong evidence of the scale's construct validity remains to be provided.

ADMINISTRATION: As noted, the scale was part of a larger mail survey instrument (Andaleeb and Basu 1994). Higher scores on the scale indicated that respondents viewed the service they received at a specified business to have been fair.

MAJOR FINDINGS: The purpose of the study by Andaleeb and Basu (1994) was to examine the relationship between a customer's satisfaction with a car repair facility and five dimensions of service quality. Among the many findings was that a higher level of perceived **fairness** is related to greater customer satisfaction with the service performed.

REFERENCES:

Andaleeb, Syed Saad and Amiya K. Basu (1994), "Technical Complexity and Consumer Knowledge as Moderators of Service Quality Evaluation in the Automobile Service Industry," *JR*, 70 (4), 367–81.
Parasuraman, A., Valarie A. Zeithaml, and Leonard L. Berry (1988), "SERVQUAL: A Multiple-Item Scale for Measuring Customer Perceptions of Service Quality," *JR*, 64 (Spring), 12–40.

SCALE ITEMS:

Strongly disagree :___:___:___:___:___:___:___: Strongly agree
          1   2   3   4   5   6   7

1. The facility I went to charged a fair price.

2. I felt I was taken advantage of by this facility. **(r)**

3. The price I paid for labor was fair.

4. The price I paid for parts was fair.

5. I left knowing I was fairly treated.

6. The service personnel were honest.

7. The facility had my best interest in mind.

SCALE NAME: Service Quality (Global)

SCALE DESCRIPTION: Two seven-point Likert-type statements and one bipolar adjective. The scale is purported to measure the degree to which a consumer believes the quality of service provided by some specified company is excellent.

SCALE ORIGIN: Although not explicitly stated by Taylor and Baker (1994), the scale appears to be original to their study.

SAMPLES: Taylor and Baker (1994) analyzed data from **426** completed questionnaires. The data were collected through personal interviews by trained personnel using a convenience sample. Respondents were selected through mall intercepts in seven cities across the United States.

RELIABILITY: An alpha of **.88** was reported for the scale by Taylor and Baker (1994).

VALIDITY: Limited scrutiny of the scale's convergent and discriminant validities was made by Taylor and Baker (1994) on the basis of observed patterns in a correlation matrix. It appears from these correlations that the items in this scale and those in a related one (#305) do not have adequate discriminant validity.

ADMINISTRATION: The circumstances surrounding administration were not described in detail by Taylor and Baker (1994), but it appears that the scale was part of a larger questionnaire administered to respondents by trained interviewers. Higher scores on the scale indicated that respondents viewed the quality of service from the specified provider as being very good.

MAJOR FINDINGS: Taylor and Baker (1994) studied the role played by service **quality** and satisfaction in the development of purchase intentions. For three of the four industries examined, models of decision making that included the interaction of satisfaction and **quality** provided a better understanding of intentions than did models that merely included main effects.

REFERENCES:
Taylor, Steven A. and Thomas L. Baker (1994), "An Assessment of the Relationship Between Service Quality and Customer Satisfaction in the Formation of Consumers' Purchase Intentions," *JR*, 70 (2), 163–78.

SCALE ITEMS:*

Strongly
disagree   :___:___:___:___:___:___:___: Strongly agree
        1   2   3   4   5   6   7

1. I believe that the general quality of _____ services is low. **(r)**

2. Overall, I consider _____ services to be excellent.

3. The quality of _____ services is generally

Poor   :___:___:___:___:___:___:___: Excellent
        1   2   3   4   5   6   7

* The specific name of the provider (e.g., American Airlines) should be placed in the blank.

SCALE NAME: Service Quality (Global)

SCALE DESCRIPTION: Three seven-point semantic differentials that measure how positively a consumer evaluates the quality of service provided by some specified organization.

SCALE ORIGIN: Although the items composing the scale have been used in various other measures, these items as a set are not known to have been used previously. Thus, it is likely that the scale is original to Spreng and Mackroy (1996).

SAMPLES: Data were collected by Spreng and Mackroy (1996) for their study from undergraduate students who were given extra credit for participating. Usable responses were received from **273** students.

RELIABILITY: The construct reliability for the scale was **.97** (Spreng 1998; Spreng and Mackroy 1996).

VALIDITY: Evidence from a confirmatory factor analysis provided evidence of the scale's discriminant validity (Spreng and Mackroy 1996).

ADMINISTRATION: Students completed the scale in the study by Spreng and Mackroy (1996), along with other measures, immediately after their meeting with an advisor (the "service provider" in this case). Higher scores on the scale suggested that respondents considered the service provided by the specified organization to be of high quality.

MAJOR FINDINGS: The study by Spreng and Mackroy (1996) examined the distinction between **service quality** and satisfaction. The results indicated that they were distinct constructs and had different antecedents.

REFERENCES:
Spreng, Richard A. (1998), personal correspondence.
——— and Robert D. Mackroy (1996), "An Empirical Examination of a Model of Perceived Service Quality and Satisfaction," *JR*, 72 (2), 201–14.

SCALE ITEMS:
Directions: Overall, what is the level of service quality you receive from _____?*

| Extremely poor | :___:___:___:___:___:___:___: | Extremely good |
| | 1   2   3   4   5   6   7 | |

| Awful | :___:___:___:___:___:___:___: | Excellent |
| | 1   2   3   4   5   6   7 | |

| Very low | :___:___:___:___:___:___:___: | Very high |
| | 1   2   3   4   5   6   7 | |

*The generic name of the service provider can be placed in the blank. Spreng and Mackroy (1996) used the term *advising services* because they were studying evaluations of the assistance received from academic advisors by college students.

SCALE NAME: Service Quality (Health Club)

SCALE DESCRIPTION: Thirty seven-point Likert-type items purported to measure the perceived level of service quality provided by a particular health club.

SCALE ORIGIN: Kelley and Davis (1994) used the perception items of the SERVQUAL instrument (Parasuraman, Berry, and Zeithaml 1993) as a basis for their scale. They selected those items from SERVQUAL that they thought were pertinent to the health club setting and/or modified others to make them fit the context. The items were pretested on 95 undergraduate students with health club experience. Items found to have low item–total correlations (<.25) were eliminated.

SAMPLES: Data were collected by Kelley and Davis (1994) from members of a health club located in a midsized community in the southeastern United States. The authors stated that the health club was viewed as the market leader in the area and offered a wide range of services and amenities. Surveys were passed out to members as they came to and went from the club on 12 consecutive days. Completed questionnaires were received from **296** individuals. The typical respondent was 36.7 years of age, male (65%), had been a member of the club for three years, and worked out an average of three days a week.

RELIABILITY: An alpha of **.96** was reported for the scale by Kelley and Davis (1994).

VALIDITY: The validity of the scale was not specifically examined by Kelley and Davis (1994).

ADMINISTRATION: The scale was completed, along with other scales and measures, in a self-administered survey (Kelley & Davis 1994). Higher scores on the scale suggested that respondents viewed the quality of service they received from some specified health club as being excellent.

MAJOR FINDINGS: Kelley and Davis (1994) proposed and tested a model of the antecedents to service recovery expectations. It was found that **service quality** and customer organizational commitment had direct effects on customer service recovery expectations.

REFERENCES:
Kelley, Scott W. and Mark A. Davis (1994), "Antecedents to Customer Expectations for Service Recovery," *JAMS*, 22 (Winter), 52–61.
Parasuraman, A., Leonard L. Berry, and Valarie A. Zeithaml (1993), "Research Note: More on Improving Service Quality Measurement," *JR*, 69 (Spring), 140–47.

SCALE ITEMS:
Directions: The following questions require you to think about and rate the quality of your health club. Please place a check mark (√) on the line that best represents how you rate the quality of your health club for each of the following items.

How would you rate the quality of your health club with regard to:

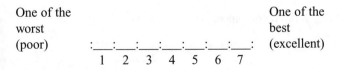

1. The facilities available.

2. The personnel/instructors.

3. The workout equipment available.

4. The other members.

5. Record keeping.

6. The dependability of the employees.

7. The willingness of employees to provide service

8. The promptness of the service provided.

9. The ability of employees in explaining the facilities.

10. Assuring you that problems will be resolved when they arise.

11. Its reputation in the local community.

12. The credibility of its employees.

13. The convenience of location.

14 The politeness of personnel.

15. The level of your physical safety.

16. The confidentiality of your dealings with the health club.

17. The skill of personnel.

18. The amount of information available.

19. The friendliness of personnel.

20. The appearance of personnel.

21. How well they understand your fitness needs.

22. The individual attention you receive.

23. How often personnel recognize you by name.

24. Its accessibility.

25. The convenience of operating hours.

26. The accessibility of training equipment.

27. The ability of employees in explaining the workout equipment.

28. The knowledge of personnel.

29. Billing accuracy.

30. The accessibility of locker room facilities.

SCALE NAME: Service Quality (Personal Interaction of Retailer)

SCALE DESCRIPTION: Nine five-point Likert-type items measuring a customer's sense that the competence of a retailer's employees inspires confidence and that they are helpful.

SCALE ORIGIN: Dabholkar, Thorpe, and Rentz (1996) conducted three qualitative studies to gain insight into factors important to retail customers in evaluating service quality. They drew on several dimensions of the SERVQUAL instrument (Parasuraman, Berry, and Zeithaml 1991) for the basis of their own scale. The measure taps into the degree to which retail employees are viewed as *inspiring confidence* and as being *courteous/helpful*. Subscales of these dimensions were tested as well.

SAMPLES: To test their proposed structure of retail service quality, Dabholkar, Thorpe, and Rentz (1996) conducted two surveys. Data for the first survey came from **227** customers of seven stores in two department store chains located in the southeastern United States. Every fifth customer who entered the store was handed a questionnaire, provided he or she had previously shopped at the store. Respondents self-administered the survey in a quiet area in the store. Study 2 was conducted for purposes of cross-validation and was based on data from **149** customers. Conditions were very similar to the previous study except that data were gathered from just two of the stores in one chain included in Study 1.

RELIABILITY: A construct reliability of **.90** was reported for the scale in the first study by Dabholkar, Thorpe, and Rentz (1996; Dabholkar 1997).

VALIDITY: A general sense of the scale's convergent validity comes from the items' reported high loading on the appropriate factors in both studies by Dabholkar, Thorpe, and Rentz (1996). The authors also stated that there was evidence attesting to the scale's discriminant validity. Support for the scale's predictive validity came from its high positive correlation with two other measures: *intention to shop at the store* (.58) and *intention to recommend the store* (.59).

ADMINISTRATION: The scale was self-administered by respondents as part of a larger questionnaire on entering the store but before shopping (Dabholkar, Thorpe, and Rentz 1996). Higher scores on the scale indicated that customers viewed a store's employees as quite courteous and helpful to the point of instilling confidence in customers.

MAJOR FINDINGS: The purpose of the studies reported by Dabholkar, Thorpe, and Rentz (1996) was to construct and validate retail service quality scales. In doing so, the authors found evidence in support of a hierarchical factor structure, such that there are five dimensions of retail service quality, three of which can be further broken down into two subdimensions. In particular, the **personal interaction** dimension of retail service quality was found to be composed of *inspiring confidence* and *courteous/helpful* subdimensions.

COMMENTS: The *inspiring confidence* and *courteous/helpful* subscales were reported to have reliabilities of .84 (alpha) and .89 (construct).

REFERENCES:
Dabholkar, Pratibha (1997), personal correspondence.
———, Dayle I. Thorpe, and Joseph O. Rentz (1996), "A Measure of Service Quality for Retail Stores: Scale Development and Validation," *JAMS*, 24 (Winter), 3–16.
Parasuraman, A., Leonard L. Berry, and Valarie A. Zeithaml (1991), "Refinement and Reassessment of the SERVQUAL Scale," *JR*, 67 (Winter), 420–50.

#346 *Service Quality (Personal Interaction of Retailer)*

SCALE ITEMS:*

Strongly   Strongly
disagree   :___:___:___:___:___: agree
               1   2   3   4   5

1. Employees in this store have the knowledge to answer customers' questions.

2. The behavior of employees in this store instills confidence in customers.

3. Customers feel safe in their transactions with this store.

4. Employees in this store give prompt service to customers.

5. Employees in this store tell customers exactly when services will be performed.

6. Employees in this store are never too busy to respond to customer's requests.

7. This store gives customers individual attention.

8. Employees in this store are consistently courteous with customers.

9. Employees of this store treat customers courteously on the telephone.

*The *inspiring confidence* subscale is composed of items 1–3, whereas the *courteous/helpful* subscale is composed of items 4–9.

SCALE NAME: Service Quality (Personalization)

SCALE DESCRIPTION: Four five-point Likert-type statements intended to capture the extent to which a customer of some organization perceives that its employees relate to customers as people in face-to-face interactions during the service encounter.

SCALE ORIGIN: The scale is original to Mittal and Lassar (1996). A modified item from the assurance dimension of SERVQUAL (by Parasuraman, Zeithaml, and Berry 1994) was used in the scale, but the other items are original.

SAMPLES: Data were collected by Mittal and Lassar (1996) from two U.S. cities for two service-related businesses. Respondents were recruited from three sources: shopping malls, mailbox drop, and parent–teacher associations and other fund raiser groups. Complete survey forms were received from **233** people, 110 relating to car repair services and 123 relating to health clinic services.

RELIABILITY: Mittal and Lassar (1996) reported alphas of **.91** and **.92** for the scale as used with the health clinic and car repair services, respectively.

VALIDITY: Mittal and Lassar (1996) wrote eight new items they thought related to the personalization construct and mixed them with the items that composed the reliability and responsiveness components of SERVQUAL (#351 and #354). Three expert judges were asked to select those items most related to the personalization construct as it was defined. The six items that emerged from the judges were reduced further to four by examination of their item–total correlations from a pilot study. Evidence pertaining to the scale's criterion validity from the main study was also presented. Finally, a factor analysis indicated that the scale was unidimensional. However, this must have been an analysis of the items by themselves, because the authors also stated that when all sixteen of the items composing their modified SERVQUAL (which they referred to as SERVQUAL-P) were factor analyzed, the items in the personalization component loaded with items from other components.

ADMINISTRATION: The scale was self-administered by respondents as part of a larger questionnaire (Mittal and Lassar 1996). Higher scores on the scale suggested that respondents viewed some specific service organization as having employees who are warm and personal in their interactions with customers.

MAJOR FINDINGS: The purpose of the study by Mittal and Lassar (1996) was to show the importance of the **personalization** aspect of service quality when measuring customer satisfaction and patronage behavior. The authors modified the SERVQUAL instrument (Parasuraman, Zeithaml, and Berry 1994) most particularly by adding the **personalization** component. Among the findings was that **personalization** was a significant predictor of five different criterion variables included in the study, and the influence of **personalization** was greater for health clinic services (where there was more personal interaction) than for car repair services (where there was less).

REFERENCES:

Mittal, Banwari and Walfried M. Lassar (1996), "The Role of Personalization in Service Encounters," *JR*, 72 (1), 95–109.

Parasuraman, A., Valarie A. Zeithaml, and Leonard L. Berry (1994), "Alternative Scales for Measuring Service Quality: A Comparative Assessment Based on Psychometric and Diagnostic Criteria," *JR*, 70 (3), 201–30.

#347 *Service Quality (Personalization)*

SCALE ITEMS:*

1 = Strongly disagree
2 = Disagree
3 = Feel neutral
4 = Somewhat agree
5 = Strongly agree

1. Everyone at _____ is polite and courteous.

2. The _____ employees display personal warmth in their behavior.

3. All the persons working at _____ are friendly and pleasant.

4. The _____ employees take the time to know you personally.

*The name of the business or service organization should be placed in the blanks.

SCALE NAME: Service Quality (Physical Aspects of Retailer)

SCALE DESCRIPTION: Six five-point Likert-type items measuring the visual appeal of a retail facility to a consumer, as well as the perceived convenience of its layout. None of the sentences explicitly mentions the outside of the store, though some sense of its appearance may come from item 2.

SCALE ORIGIN: Dabholkar, Thorpe, and Rentz (1996) conducted three qualitative studies to gain insight into factors important to retail customers in evaluating service quality. They drew on the tangibles dimension (#358) of the SERVQUAL instrument (Parasuraman, Berry, and Zeithaml 1991) for the basis of their own scale. However, it not only taps into the *appearance* of the store, but also the *convenience of layout*. Subscales of these dimensions were tested as well.

SAMPLES: To test their proposed structure of retail service quality, Dabholkar, Thorpe, and Rentz (1996) conducted two surveys. Data for the first survey came from **227** customers of seven stores in two department store chains located in the southeastern United States. Every fifth customer who entered the store was handed a questionnaire, provided he or she had previously shopped at the store. Respondents self-administered the survey in a quiet area in the store. Study 2 was conducted for purposes of cross-validation and was based on data from **149** customers. Conditions were very similar to the previous study except that data were gathered from just two of the stores in one chain included in Study 1.

RELIABILITY: A construct reliability of **.85** was reported for the scale in the first study by Dabholkar, Thorpe, and Rentz (1996; Dabholkar 1997).

VALIDITY: A general sense of the scale's convergent validity comes from the items' reported high loadings highly on the appropriate factors in both studies by Dabholkar, Thorpe, and Rentz (1996). The authors also stated that there was evidence attesting to the scale's discriminant validity. Support for the scale's predictive validity came from its high positive correlation with two other measures: *intention to shop at the store* (.55) and *intention to recommend the store* (.64).

ADMINISTRATION: The scale was self-administered by respondents as part of a larger questionnaire on entering the store but before shopping (Dabholkar, Thorpe, and Rentz 1996). Higher scores on the scale indicated that customers viewed a store to be quite attractive and laid out conveniently.

MAJOR FINDINGS: The purpose of the studies reported by Dabholkar, Thorpe, and Rentz (1996) was to construct and validate retail service quality scales. In doing so, the authors found evidence in support of a hierarchical factor structure, such that there are five dimensions of retail service quality, three of which can be further broken down into two subdimensions. In particular, the **physical aspects** dimension of retail service quality was found to be composed of *appearance* and *convenience* subdimensions.

COMMENTS: The *appearance* and *convenience* subscales were reported to have reliabilities of .81 (construct) and .89 (alpha).

REFERENCES:

Dabholkar, Pratibha (1997), personal correspondence.
———, Dayle I. Thorpe, and Joseph O. Rentz (1996), "A Measure of Service Quality for Retail Stores: Scale Development and Validation," *JAMS*, 24 (Winter), 3–16.
Parasuraman, A., Leonard L. Berry, and Valarie A. Zeithaml (1991), "Refinement and Reassessment of the SERVQUAL Scale," *JR*, 67 (Winter), 420–50.

#348 *Service Quality (Physical Aspects of Retailer)*

SCALE ITEMS:*

Strongly   Strongly
disagree   :___:___:___:___:___: agree
                 1   2   3   4   5

1. This store has modern-looking equipment and fixtures.

2. The physical facilities at this store are visually appealing.

3. Materials associated with this store's service (such as shopping bags, catalogs, or statements) are visually appealing.

4. This store has clean, attractive, and convenient public areas (restrooms, fitting rooms).

5. The store layout at this store makes it easy for customers to find what they need.

6. The store layout at this store makes it easy for customers to move around in the store.

*The *appearance* subscale is composed of items 1–3, whereas the convenience *subscale* is composed of items 4–6.

SCALE NAME: Service Quality (Reliability of Retailer)

SCALE DESCRIPTION: Five five-point Likert-type items measuring the perception that the retailer is keeping any promises made and that it performs its functions well so that customers can get in and out efficiently.

SCALE ORIGIN: Dabholkar, Thorpe, and Rentz (1996) conducted three qualitative studies to gain insight into factors important to retail customers in evaluating service quality. They drew heavily on the reliability dimension (#350) of the SERVQUAL instrument (Parasuraman, Berry, and Zeithaml 1991) for the basis of their own scale. The measure taps into the *promises* made by the store, but also whether it is *doing it right*. Subscales of these dimensions were tested as well.

SAMPLES: To test their proposed structure of retail service quality, Dabholkar, Thorpe, and Rentz (1996) conducted two surveys. Data for the first survey came from **227** customers of seven stores in two department store chains located in the southeastern United States. Every fifth customer who entered the store was handed a questionnaire, provided he or she had previously shopped at the store. Respondents self-administered the survey in a quiet area in the store. Study 2 was conducted for purposes of cross-validation and was based on data from **149** customers. Conditions were very similar to the previous study except that data were gathered from just two of the stores in one chain included in Study 1.

RELIABILITY: A construct reliability of **.90** was reported for the scale in the first study by Dabholkar, Thorpe, and Rentz (1996; Dabholkar 1997).

VALIDITY: A general sense of the scale's convergent validity comes from the items' reported high loading on the appropriate factors in both studies by Dabholkar, Thorpe, and Rentz (1996). The authors also stated that there was evidence attesting to the scale's discriminant validity. Support for the scale's predictive validity came from its positive correlations with two other measures: *intention to shop at the store* (.44) and *intention to recommend the store* (.54).

ADMINISTRATION: The scale was self-administered by respondents as part of a larger questionnaire on entering the store but before shopping (Dabholkar, Thorpe, and Rentz 1996). Higher scores on the scale indicated that customers viewed a store as very reliable.

MAJOR FINDINGS: The purpose of the studies reported by Dabholkar, Thorpe, and Rentz (1996) was to construct and validate retail service quality scales. In doing so, the authors found evidence in support of a hierarchical factor structure such that there are five dimensions of retail service quality, three of which can be further broken down into two subdimensions. In particular, the **reliability** dimension of retail service quality was found to be composed of *promises* and *doing it right* subdimensions.

COMMENTS: The *promises* and *doing it right* subscales were reported to have Cronbach's alpha reliabilities of .83 and .86, respectively.

REFERENCES:
Dabholkar, Pratibha (1997), personal correspondence.
————, Dayle I. Thorpe, and Joseph O. Rentz (1996), "A Measure of Service Quality for Retail Stores: Scale Development and Validation," *JAMS*, 24 (Winter), 3–16.
Parasuraman, A., Leonard L. Berry, and Valarie A. Zeithaml (1991), "Refinement and Reassessment of the SERVQUAL Scale," *JR*, 67 (Winter), 420–50.

#349 *Service Quality (Reliability of Retailer)*

SCALE ITEMS:*

Strongly   Strongly
disagree   :___:___:___:___:___: agree
              1   2   3   4   5

1. When this store promises to do something by a certain time, it will do so.

2. This store provides its services at the time it promises to do so.

3. This store provides the service right the first time.

4. This store has merchandise available when the customers want it.

5. This store insists on error-free sales transactions and records.

*The *promises* subscale is composed of items 1 and 2, whereas the *doing it right* subscale is composed of items 3–5.

SCALE NAME: Service Quality (Reliability)

SCALE DESCRIPTION: A Likert-type scale measuring the degree to which a person thinks a service company is responsible and can be depended on to do what it promises. As described here, the scale relates to the reliability dimension of the SERVQUAL instrument (Parasuraman, Berry, and Zeithaml 1991; Parasuraman, Zeithaml, and Berry 1988) but is not equivalent to it. Each dimension of the SERVQUAL measure is composed of the summated differences between expectation items and perceptual items, not just perceptual items as the scale described here is. Carman (1990) used several variations on the scale, as described subsequently. Taylor (1995) only used perceptual items.

SCALE ORIGIN: The scale is a part of the larger SERVQUAL instrument described by Parasuraman, Zeithaml, and Berry (1988; Parasuraman, Berry, and Zeithaml 1991) that measures five separate dimensions of service quality. Considerable information is provided in those articles about the scale's conceptualization, development, and validation.

The version of the scale discussed by Parasuraman, Zeithaml, and Berry (1988) was followed to a great extent by Carman (1990). In Parasuraman, Berry, and Zeithaml's 1991 article, some suggestions for changes to the scale were made. As far as the reliability dimension is concerned, only two items were kept intact from the original version, and the other three items were changed. Item 6 is original to Carman (1990). Taylor (1995) slightly modified the items (specified under "Scale Items") for use with a specific counselor at a university career counseling service.

SAMPLES: Carman (1990) adjusted and tested the SERVQUAL instrument in four different service settings: a dental school patient clinic (n = 612), a business school placement center (n = 82), a tire store (n = 74), and an acute care hospital (n = 720). The scale used in the hospital setting warranted treatment as a different scale and is, therefore, written up separately.

A questionnaire was sent by Parasuraman, Berry, and Zeithaml (1991) to randomly chosen customers of five nationally known companies: one telephone company, two banks, and two insurance companies. A reminder postcard was sent two weeks after the initial mailing. The number of usable questionnaires ranged from 290 to 487 for the five companies. The total completed returns were **1936**, which was a 21% overall response rate. Managers in the companies reviewed the demographic profiles of the respondents and considered them representative of their customer populations.

Taylor (1995) collected data from **232** undergraduate business students attending a midsized university. Some of these subjects (n = 68) were part of a control group, but the rest were broken down into groups of between 24 and 31 for the experimental treatments.

RELIABILITY: The following alphas were reported by Carman (1990) for the scale: **.51** (tire store), **.52** (placement center), and **.79** (dental clinic). The alphas reported by Parasuraman, Berry, and Zeithaml (1991) for the five companies ranged from .88 to .92. These alphas relate to the summated differences between expectation items and perceptual items. The alpha for just the perceptual items was **.92** using the combined sample (Parasuraman 1993). An alpha of **.86** was reported for the version of the scale used by Taylor (1995).

VALIDITY: Carman (1990) factor analyzed the SERVQUAL data from each setting. Only items with loadings greater than .30 on the same factor in at least one setting were used to compose scales (Carman 1994). However, the sets of items used to compose the summated scales for each of the three settings were ultimately different based on several factors. These variable results led Carman (1990) to conclude that the scale had problems with construct validity.

Parasuraman, Berry, and Zeithaml (1991) reported the results of several factor analyses using oblique rotations. With regard to the perceptual version of the scale using the combined samples, all of the items except for 2 had their highest loadings on the same factor. The item was apparently left in the scale because its loading was greater than .50 in factor analysis of the expectation scores.

ADMINISTRATION: The SERVQUAL instrument was self-administered by respondents after they received service in the study by Carman (1990). The scale was administered to customers in a mail survey format by Parasuraman, Berry, and Zeithaml (1991). Subjects in the experiment conducted by Taylor (1995) self-administered the scale, along with other measures, after the experimental manipulation. Higher scores on the perception version of the scale indicated that respondents thought that a specific service firm can be depended on to do what it says it will do.

MAJOR FINDINGS: The purpose of Carman's (1990) studies was to test the SERVQUAL instrument in a variety of service settings. Some modifications in wording were always found to be necessary. Furthermore, testing of the data indicated that, though a **reliability**-related dimension was found across settings, the items loading on that dimension were not stable.

Parasuraman, Berry, and Zeithaml (1991) conducted a study to refine their SERVQUAL scales and examine the revised scales in five different customer samples. They also compared their results with those of others who had used the scales. When respondents were asked to divide 100 points among the five service quality dimensions on the basis of importance, the result was the same for each of the five samples: the **reliability** dimension was by far the most important.

The purpose of the experiment by Taylor (1995) was to investigate the effects of a delay, perceived control over a delay, and what fills the time during the delay. Among the many findings was that evaluation of the **reliability** aspect of service quality was lower for those whose waiting time was not filled than for those whose delay was filled.

COMMENTS: Although this scale can be used by itself, it was designed to be used along with its companion expectation version. For example, the expectation version of item 1 would be something like the following: "When excellent _____ companies promise to do something by a certain time, they will do so." The authors also encouraged researchers to measure all of the dimensions to fully capture the domain of service quality.

For further discussion of theoretical and psychometric properties of the SERVQUAL instrument, see Parasuraman, Zeithaml, and Berry (1994), Cronin and Taylor (1994), and Teas (1994).

See also Fischer, Gainer, and Bristor (1997), Kelley and Hoffman (1997), and Teas (1993).

REFERENCES:

Carman, James M. (1990), "Consumer Perceptions of Service Quality: An Assessment of the SERVQUAL Dimensions," *JR*, 66 (Spring), 33–55.

——— (1994), personal correspondence.

Cronin, J. Joseph, Jr. and Steven A. Taylor (1994), "SERVPERF Versus SERVQUAL: Reconciling Performance-Based and Perceptions-Minus-Expectations Measurement of Service Quality," *JM*, 58 (January), 124–31.

Fischer, Eileen, Brenda Gainer, and Julia Bristor (1997), "The Sex of the Service Provider: Does it Influence Perceptions of Service Quality," *JR*, 73 (3), 361–82.

Kelley, Scott W. and K. Douglas Hoffman (1997), "An Investigation of Positive Affect, Prosocial Behaviors and Service Quality," *JR*, 73 (3), 407–27.

Parasuraman, A. (1993), personal correspondence.

———, Leonard L. Berry, and Valarie A. Zeithaml (1991), "Refinement and Reassessment of the SERVQUAL Scale," *JR*, 67 (Winter), 420–50.

———, Valarie A. Zeithaml, and Leonard L. Berry (1988), "SERVQUAL: A Multiple-Item Scale for Measuring Customer Perceptions of Service Quality," *JR*, 64 (Spring), 12–40.

———, ———, and ——— (1994), "Reassessment of Expectations as a Comparison Standard in Measuring Service Quality: Implications for Further Research," *JM*, 58 (January), 111–24.

Taylor, Shirley (1995), "The Effects of Filled Waiting Time and Service Provider Control over the Delay on Evaluations of Service," *JAMS*, 23 (Winter), 38–48.

Teas, R. Kenneth (1993), "Expectations, Performance Evaluation, and Consumers' Perceptions of Quality," *JM*, 57 (October), 18–34.

——— (1994), "Expectations as a Comparison Standard in Measuring Service Quality: An Assessment of a Reassessment," *JM*, 58 (January), 132–39.

SCALE ITEMS:*

Directions: The following set of statement relate to your feelings about _____'s service. For each statement, please show the extent to which you believe _____ has the feature described by the statement. Circling a "1" means that you strongly disagree that _____ has that feature, and circling a "7" means that you strongly agree. You may circle any of the numbers in the middle that show how strong your feelings are. There are no right or wrong answers—all we are interested in is a number that best shows your perceptions about _____'s service.

Strongly   Strongly
Disagree   :___:___:___:___:___:___:___: agree
              1   2   3   4   5   6   7

1. When _____ promises to do something by a certain time, it does so.

2. When you have problems, _____ is sympathetic and reassuring.

3. _____ is dependable.

4. _____ provides its services at the time it promises to do so.

5. _____ keeps its records accurately.

6. It is easy to make an appointment there.

7. When you have a problem, _____ shows a sincere interest in solving it.

8. _____ performs the service right the first time.

9. _____ insists on error-free records.

*The name of the specific service firm studied should be placed in the blanks. Items 1–5 were the form used by Parasuraman, Zeithaml, and Berry (1988), whereas items 1, 4, and 7–9 were recommended in Parasuraman, Berry, and Zeithaml's 1991 article. Although not completely clear, it appears that statements similar to the following items were used in the three studies conducted by Carman (1990, 1994): 1, 3, and 5 (tire store); 3, 4, and 5 (placement center); and 1, 4, and 6 (dental clinic). Taylor (1995) used items similar to 1, 4, 7, 8, and 9 and adapted them for reference to a specific counselor at a university career counseling office.

SCALE NAME: Service Quality (Reliability)

SCALE DESCRIPTION: Multiple statements that measure how dependable a person thinks a company is in providing a service. The version by Parasuraman, Zeithaml, and Berry (1994b) goes a bit further and measures perceptions of reliability *compared with the desired service level* (the performance level the company can and should deliver).

SCALE ORIGIN: The scale is a part of the larger SERVQUAL instruments described by Parasuraman, Zeithaml, and Berry (1994b) and Zeithaml, Berry, and Parasuraman (1996) that measured five separate dimensions of service quality. Considerable information is provided in the former about the instrument's conceptualization, development, validation, and diagnostic value. This version of the instrument is a modification of earlier forms (e.g., Parasuraman, Zeithaml, and Berry 1988, 1994a), in that it is intended to be a direct measure of service superiority rather than just capture perceptions or require multiple measures to assess expectations and perceptions. The instrument was refined through two stages of pretesting.

On the basis of their particular task, Mittal and Lassar (1996, p. 106) examined the five items used by Parasuraman, Zeithaml, and Berry (1994b) and determined that only the first three items should be retained to "improve its generality and internal consistency." They also added an item (6) similar to one Parasuraman, Zeithaml, and Berry (1994b) used in measuring the assurance dimension of SERVQUAL (#336), arguing that it belonged more with the **reliability** dimension.

SAMPLES: Data were collected by Mittal and Lassar (1996) from two U.S. cities for two service-related businesses. Respondents were recruited from three sources: shopping malls, mailbox drop, and parent–teacher associations and other fund raiser groups. Complete survey forms were received from **233** people, 110 relating to car repair services and 123 relating to health clinic services.

The data gathered by Parasuraman, Zeithaml, and Berry (1994b) came from people contacted through lists of customers provided by four companies: a computer manufacturer, a retail chain, an auto insurer, and a life insurer. A total of 4156 questionnaires were mailed out using this scale's format, and **1135** were received back. (Two other formats were tested as well.)

Zeithaml, Berry, and Parasuraman (1996) gathered data from mailing lists of current customers generated by four businesses: a computer manufacturer, a retail chain, an automobile insurer, and a life insurer. The names were of end users in each case, except for the computer company, for which it was business customers. A total of 12,470 questionnaires were sent out, and **3069** were returned.

RELIABILITY: The alphas reported by Parasuraman, Zeithaml, Berry (1994b) for the four companies ranged from **.91** to **.95.** The values reported by Zeithaml, Berry, and Parasuraman (1996; Parasuraman 1997) ranged from **.88** to **.95.** Finally, alphas of **.91** (health care), **.88** (car repair), and **.89** (combined) were calculated by Mittal and Lassar (1996; Lassar 1998).

VALIDITY: Parasuraman, Zeithaml, Berry (1994b) reported the results of a factor analysis using an oblique rotation. The items all loaded on the same dimension, though one item (3) had a higher loading on the assurance dimension of service quality. Several checks of the scale's validity were made that provided some limited evidence of predictive, convergent, and discriminant validity.

On the basis of confirmatory factor analysis, Mittal and Lassar (1996) appeared to suggest that the results supported a claim of discriminant validity. No specific examination of the scale's validity was reported by Zeithaml, Berry, and Parasuraman (1996).

ADMINISTRATION: The scale was administered to customers in a mail survey format (Mittal and Lassar 1996; Parasuraman, Zeithaml, and Berry 1994b; Zeithaml, Berry, and Parasuraman 1996).

Higher scores on the scale indicated that respondents thought the service they experienced from a specific firm was as high if not higher than the level of service they think can and should be delivered by such a company.

MAJOR FINDINGS: The purpose of the study by Mittal and Lassar (1996) was to show the importance of the personalization aspect of service quality when measuring customer satisfaction and patronage behavior. The authors modified the SERVQUAL instrument (Parasuraman, Zeithaml, and Berry 1994b) most particularly by adding the personalization component. Their findings seemed to show that, using the modified SERVQUAL, the **reliability** dimension had the strongest relationship with perceptions of the quality of work performed for both contexts examined (health care and car repair).

Parasuraman, Zeithaml, and Berry (1994b) conducted a study to refine their SERVQUAL scales and examine the revised scales in three different formats with four different customer groups. The scale shown here is part of a "one-column format," meaning that one scale for each of the five service quality dimensions was used to measure service superiority directly. Although the one-column format had reasonable psychometric characteristics, its diagnostic value was not considered to be as high as that of the two- and three-column formats, which provided indications of customers' service adequacy in addition to service superiority.

Zeithaml, Berry, and Parasuraman (1996) tested a model of the impact of service quality on relevant behaviors. In general, their results showed that there is a significant positive relationship between perceived service quality and favorable behavioral intentions. A weighted-average performance score was calculated across the SERVQUAL dimensions; no results were reported in this study for the **reliability** dimension by itself.

COMMENTS: Although this scale can be used by itself, it was designed to be used along with its companion measures of the other service quality dimensions. Furthermore, as noted previously, this scale represents the simplest format that Parasuraman, Zeithaml, and Berry (1994b) offered. Refer to their article for details regarding the more complex but potentially more useful versions (two- and three-column formats).

REFERENCES:

Lassar, Walfried M. (1998), personal correspondence.

Mittal, Banwari and Walfried M. Lassar (1996), "The Role of Personalization in Service Encounters," *JR*, 72 (1), 95–109.

Parasuraman, A. (1997), personal correspondence.

———, Valarie A. Zeithaml, and Leonard L. Berry (1988), "SERVQUAL: A Multiple-Item Scale for Measuring Customer Perceptions of Service Quality," *JR*, 64 (Spring), 12–40.

———, ———, and ———(1994a), "Reassessment of Expectations as a Comparison Standard in Measuring Service Quality: Implications for Further Research," *JM*, 58 (January), 111–24.

———, ———, and ——— (1994b), "Alternative Scales for Measuring Service Quality: A Comparative Assessment Based on Psychometric and Diagnostic Criteria," *JR*, 70 (3), 201–30.

Zeithaml, Valarie A., Leonard L. Berry, and A. Parasuraman (1996), "The Behavioral Consequences of Service Quality," *JM*, 60 (April), 31–46.

SCALE ITEMS:*

Directions: Please think about the quality of service _____ offers compared to your *desired service level*—the level of performance you believe a _____ *can and should deliver* (i.e., the level of service you desire). For each of the following statements, circle the number that indicates how _____'s service compares with your desired service level.

#351 *Service Quality (Reliability)*

_____'s service performance is:

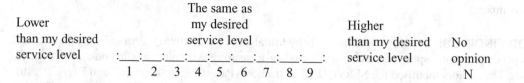

	The same as	
Lower	my desired	Higher
than my desired	service level	than my desired	No
service level	:__:__:__:__:__:__:__:__:	service level	opinion
	1 2 3 4 5 6 7 8 9		N

1. Providing service as promised.

2. Dependability in handling customer service problems.

3. Performing services right the first time.

4. Providing services at the promised time.

5. Keeping customers informed about when services will be performed.

6. All _____'s employees are well-trained and knowledgeable.

*These directions and items 1–5 were used by Parasuraman, Zeithaml, and Berry (1994b). Zeithaml, Berry, and Parasuraman (1996) also used items similar to the first five, but the layout of the scale and the directions were different. Mittal and Lassar (1996) used items 1–3 and 6 in a typical five-point agree/disagree format response. The blanks in the directions should contain the name of the specific service provider being evaluated, except for the second, which should have the general name for the type of service (e.g., auto insurance company) being evaluated. The blank in item 6 should contain the name of the specific service provider being evaluated.

SCALE NAME: Service Quality (Reliability)

SCALE DESCRIPTION: A four-item, seven-point Likert-type scale measuring the degree to which a person thinks the service received was performed properly. As used by Andaleeb and Basu (1994), the scale relates to the quality of service received from a car repair establishment.

SCALE ORIGIN: Although drawing inspiration from the SERVQUAL scales by Parasuraman, Zeithaml, and Berry (1988), Andaleeb and Basu (1994) performed their own developmental work and produced a related but unique measure.

SAMPLES: Andaleeb and Basu (1994) gathered their data from a mail survey. Telephone directories of two large cities in the northeastern United States were used to find names and addresses. Questionnaires were apparently directed at a member of the household who owned a car and had experienced automobile repair/service. Of the 550 surveys distributed, **133** were usable.

RELIABILITY: An alpha of **.93** was reported for the scale (Andaleeb and Basu 1994).

VALIDITY: Andaleeb and Basu (1994) provided the results of a factor analysis conducted on 27 items related to service quality. The items on this scale loaded high on the same dimension and lower on the others. In addition, the authors provided a correlation matrix between this scale and four others. Because the correlations in every case were lower than the alphas, it was construed as evidence of discriminant validity. However, the significance and level of the correlations could just as easily have been interpreted as evidence of convergent validity. Thus, strong evidence of the scale's construct validity remains to be provided.

ADMINISTRATION: As noted, the scale was part of a larger mail survey instrument (Andaleeb and Basu 1994). Higher scores on the scale indicated that respondents viewed the service they received from a specified business to have been conducted in a competent manner.

MAJOR FINDINGS: The purpose of the study by Andaleeb and Basu (1994) was to examine the relationship between a customer's satisfaction with a car repair facility and five dimensions of service quality. Among the many findings was that a higher level of perceived **reliability** is related to greater customer satisfaction with the service performed.

REFERENCES:

Andaleeb, Syed Saad and Amiya K. Basu (1994), "Technical Complexity and Consumer Knowledge as Moderators of Service Quality Evaluation in the Automobile Service Industry," *JR*, 70 (4), 367–81.
Parasuraman, A., Valarie A. Zeithaml, and Leonard L. Berry (1988), "SERVQUAL: A Multiple-Item Scale for Measuring Customer Perceptions of Service Quality," *JR*, 64 (Spring), 12–40.

SCALE ITEMS:

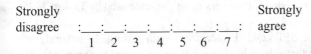

Strongly disagree :___:___:___:___:___:___:___: Strongly agree
  1 2 3 4 5 6 7

1. The facility did the work that was promised.

2. The service personnel were well trained.

3. I felt the service was done correctly on the first visit.

4. The service personnel were competent.

SCALE NAME: Service Quality (Responsiveness)

SCALE DESCRIPTION: A Likert-type scale measuring the degree to which a person thinks a service company's employees are helpful and responsive to customer needs. As described here, the scale relates to the responsiveness dimension of the SERVQUAL instrument (Parasuraman, Berry, and Zeithaml 1991; Parasuraman, Zeithaml, and Berry 1988) but is not equivalent to it. Each dimension of the SERVQUAL measure is composed of the summated differences between expectation items and perceptual items, not just perceptual items as the scale described here is. Carman (1990) used several variations on the scale, as described subsequently. Taylor (1995) only used perceptual items.

SCALE ORIGIN: The scale is a part of the larger SERVQUAL instrument described by Parasuraman, Zeithaml, and Berry (1988; Parasuraman, Berry, and Zeithaml 1991) that measures five separate dimensions of service quality. Considerable information is provided in those articles about the scale's conceptualization, development, and validation.

The version of the scale discussed by Parasuraman, Zeithaml, and Berry (1988) is the one followed to a great extent by Carman (1990). In Parasuraman, Berry, and Zeithaml's 1991 article, some suggestions for changes to the scale were made. As far as the responsiveness dimension is concerned, the revised version modified all of the items by making them positive rather than negative in wording. Items 5 and 6 are original to Carman (1990). Taylor (1995) slightly modified the items (specified under "Scale Items") for use with a specific counselor at a university career counseling service.

SAMPLES: Carman (1990) adjusted and tested the SERVQUAL instrument in four different service settings: a dental school patient clinic (n = 612), a business school placement center (n = 82), a tire store (n = 74), and an acute care hospital (n = 720). The scale used in the hospital setting warranted treatment as a different scale and is, therefore, written up separately.

A questionnaire was sent by Parasuraman, Berry, and Zeithaml (1991) to randomly chosen customers of five nationally known companies: one telephone company, two banks, and two insurance companies. A reminder postcard was sent two weeks after the initial mailing. The number of usable questionnaires ranged from 290 to 487 for the five companies. The total completed returns were **1936**, which was a 21% overall response rate. Managers in the companies reviewed the demographic profiles of the respondents and considered them representative of their customer populations.

Taylor (1995) collected data from **232** undergraduate business students attending a midsized university. Some of these subjects (n = 68) were part of a control group, but the rest were broken down into groups of between 24 and 31 for the experimental treatments.

RELIABILITY: The following alphas were reported by Carman (1990) for the scale: **.64** (tire store), **.75** (placement center), and **.55** (dental clinic). The alphas reported by Parasuraman, Berry, and Zeithaml (1991) for the five companies ranged from .88 to .93. These alphas relate to the summated differences between expectation items and perceptual items. The alpha for just the perceptual items was **.94** using the combined sample (Parasuraman 1993). An alpha of **.80** was reported for the version of the scale used by Taylor (1995).

VALIDITY: Carman (1990) factor analyzed the SERVQUAL data from each setting. In general, only items with loadings greater than .30 on the same factor in at least one setting were used to compose scales (Carman 1994). However, the sets of items used to compose the summated scales for each of the three settings were ultimately different based on several factors. These variable results led Carman (1990) to conclude that the scale had problems with construct validity.

Parasuraman, Berry, and Zeithaml (1991) reported the results of several factor analyses using oblique rotations. With regard to the perceptual version of the scale using the combined samples, the items did *not* load on a single factor. As it is, the perceptual version of the scale is not unidimensional.

The five items were apparently left as a group because their loadings were all greater than .50 in a factor analysis of the expectation scores.

ADMINISTRATION: The instrument was self-administered by respondents after they received service in the study by Carman (1990). The scale was administered to customers in a mail survey format by Parasuraman, Berry, and Zeithaml (1991). Subjects in the experiment conducted by Taylor (1995) self-administered the scale, along with other measures, after the experimental manipulation. Higher scores on the perceptual version of the scale indicated that respondents thought that employees of a specific service firm are very responsive to customer requests.

MAJOR FINDINGS: The purpose of Carman's (1990) studies was to test the SERVQUAL instrument in a variety of service settings. Some modifications in wording were always found to be necessary. Furthermore, testing of the data indicated that, though a **responsiveness**-related dimension was found across settings, the items loading on that dimension were not stable.

Parasuraman, Berry, and Zeithaml (1991) conducted a study to refine their SERVQUAL scales and examine the revised scales in five different customer samples. They also compared their results with those of others who had used the scales. When respondents were asked to divide 100 points among the five service quality dimensions on the basis of importance, the result was the same for each of the five samples: the **responsiveness** dimension was always was the second most important dimension.

The purpose of the experiment by Taylor (1995) was to investigate the effects of a delay, perceived control over a delay, and what fills the time during the delay. Among the many findings was that evaluation of the **responsiveness** aspect of service quality was lower for those who felt the service provider (career counselor) had a high degree of control over the delay that was experienced.

COMMENTS: Although this scale can be used by itself, it was designed to be used along with its companion perceptual version. For example, the perceptual version of item 1 would be something like the following: "Employees of excellent _____ companies will tell customers exactly when services will be performed." The developers also encouraged researchers to measure all of the dimensions to fully capture the domain of service quality.

For further discussion of theoretical and psychometric properties of the SERVQUAL instrument, see Parasuraman, Zeithaml, and Berry (1994), Cronin and Taylor (1994), and Teas (1994).

See also Fischer, Gainer, and Bristor (1997), Finn and Kayandé (1997), Kelley and Hoffman (1997), and Teas (1993).

REFERENCES:

Carman, James M. (1990), "Consumer Perceptions of Service Quality: An Assessment of the SERVQUAL Dimensions," *JR*, 66 (Spring), 33–55.

———— (1994), personal correspondence.

Cronin, J. Joseph, Jr. and Steven A. Taylor (1994), "SERVPERF Versus SERVQUAL: Reconciling Performance-Based and Perceptions-Minus-Expectations Measurement of Service Quality," *JM*, 58 (January), 124–31.

Finn, Adam and Ujwal Kayandé (1997), "Reliability Assessment and Optimization of Marketing Measurement," *JMR*, 34 (May), 262–75.

Fischer, Eileen, Brenda Gainer, and Julia Bristor (1997), "The Sex of the Service Provider: Does it Influence Perceptions of Service Quality," *JR*, 73 (3), 361–82.

Kelley, Scott W. and K. Douglas Hoffman (1997), "An Investigation of Positive Affect, Prosocial Behaviors and Service Quality," *JR*, 73 (3), 407–27.

Parasuraman, A. (1993), personal correspondence.

————, Leonard L. Berry, and Valarie A. Zeithaml (1991), "Refinement and Reassessment of the SERVQUAL Scale," *JR*, 67 (Winter), 420–50.

————, Valarie A. Zeithaml, and Leonard L. Berry (1988), "SERVQUAL: A Multiple-Item Scale for Measuring Customer Perceptions of Service Quality," *JR*, 64 (Spring), 12–40.

————, ————, and ———— (1994), "Reassessment of Expectations as a Comparison Standard in Measuring Service Quality: Implications for Further Research," *JM*, 58 (January), 111–24.

Taylor, Shirley (1995), "The Effects of Filled Waiting Time and Service Provider Control over the Delay on Evaluations of Service," *JAMS*, 23 (Winter), 38–48.

Teas, R. Kenneth (1993), "Expectations, Performance Evaluation, and Consumers' Perceptions of Quality," *JM*, 57 (October), 18–34.

———— (1994), "Expectations as a Comparison Standard in Measuring Service Quality: An Assessment of a Reassessment," *JM*, 58 (January), 132–39.

SCALE ITEMS:

Directions: The following set of statement relate to your feelings about _____'s service. For each statement, please show the extent to which you believe _____ has the feature described by the statement. Circling a "1" means that you strongly disagree that _____ has that feature, and circling a "7" means that you strongly agree. You may circle any of the numbers in the middle that show how strong your feelings are. There are no right or wrong answers—all we are interested in is a number that best shows your perceptions about _____'s service.

Strongly   Strongly
Disagree   :___:___:___:___:___:___:___: agree
                1   2   3   4   5   6   7

1. _____ does not tell customers exactly when services will be performed. **(r)**

2. You do not receive prompt service from _____. **(r)**

3. Employees of _____ are not always willing to help customers. **(r)**

4. Employees of _____ are too busy to respond to customer requests promptly. **(r)**

5. The manual provided by the placement office is informative.

6. There is an adequate choice of interviews at the placement office.

7. Employees of _____ tell you exactly when services will be performed.

8. Employees of _____ give you prompt service.

9. Employees of _____ are always willing to help you.

10. Employees of _____ are never too busy to respond to your requests.

*The name of the specific service firm studied should be placed in the blanks. Items 1–4 were the form used by Parasuraman, Zeithaml, and Berry (1988), whereas the revised version of those items (7–10) were recommended in Parasuraman, Berry, and Zeithaml's 1991 article. Although not completely clear, it appears that statements similar to the following items were used in the three studies conducted by Carman (1990, 1994): 1 and 2 (tire store); 1, 2, 5, and 6 (placement center); and 2 and 4 (dental clinic). Taylor (1995) used items similar to 7–10 and adapted them for reference to a specific counselor at a university career counseling office.

SCALE NAME: Service Quality (Responsiveness)

SCALE DESCRIPTION: Multiple statements that measure how responsive a person thinks a company is in providing timely service to customers. The version by Parasuraman, Zeithaml, and Berry (1994b) goes a bit further and measures perceptions of **responsiveness** *compared with the desired service level* (the performance level the company can and should deliver).

SCALE ORIGIN: The scale is a part of the larger SERVQUAL instrument described by Parasuraman, Zeithaml, and Berry (1994b) and Zeithaml, Berry, and Parasuraman (1996) that measures five separate dimensions of service quality. Considerable information is provided by the former about the instrument's conceptualization, development, validation, and diagnostic value. This version of the instrument is a modification of earlier forms (e.g., Parasuraman, Zeithaml, and Berry 1988, 1994a), in that it is intended to be a direct measure of service superiority rather than just capture perceptions or require multiple measures to measure expectations and perceptions. The instrument was refined through two stages of pretesting.

On the basis of their particular task, Mittal and Lassar (1996) examined the three items used by Parasuraman, Zeithaml, and Berry (1994b) and determined that they should be retained. They also added an item (4) similar to one Parasuraman, Zeithaml, and Berry (1994b) used in measuring the empathy dimension of SERVQUAL (#339), arguing that it could be assimilated into the **responsiveness** dimension as the empathy dimension was to be dropped from their version of the SERVQUAL instrument.

SAMPLES: The data collected by Mittal and Lassar (1996) came from two U.S. cities for two service-related businesses. Respondents were recruited from three sources: shopping malls, mailbox drop, and parent–teacher associations and other fund raiser groups. Complete survey forms were received from **233** people, 110 relating to car repair services and 123 relating to health clinic services.

Data were gathered by Parasuraman, Zeithaml, and Berry (1994b) from subjects obtained from lists of customers provided by four companies: a computer manufacturer, a retail chain, an auto insurer, and a life insurer. A total of 4156 questionnaires were mailed out using this scale's format, and **1135** were received back. (Two other formats were tested as well.)

Zeithaml, Berry, and Parasuraman (1996) gathered data from mailing lists of current customers generated by four businesses: a computer manufacturer, a retail chain, an automobile insurer, and a life insurer. The names were of end users in each case, except for the computer company, for which it was business customers. A total of 12,470 questionnaires were sent out, and **3069** were returned.

RELIABILITY: The alphas reported by Parasuraman, Zeithaml, Berry (1994b) for the four companies ranged from .83 to .91. The values reported by Zeithaml, Berry, and Parasuraman (1996; Parasuraman 1997) ranged from .86 to .96. Finally, alphas of .91 (health care), .92 (car repair), and .92 (combined) were calculated by Mittal and Lassar (1996; Lassar 1998).

VALIDITY: Parasuraman, Zeithaml, Berry (1994b) reported the results of a factor analysis using an oblique rotation. The items composing this scale did not load on the same dimension and might be part of a larger factor that includes items related to *assurance* and *empathy*. Further analysis using LISREL provided some support for the five-dimensional structure of the SERVQUAL instrument, though the three-factor model could not be ruled out. Several checks of the scale's validity were made that provided some limited evidence of predictive, convergent, and discriminant validity.

The exploratory and confirmatory factor analyses conducted by Mittal and Lassar (1996) appeared to bring the discriminant validity of their version of the scale into question. No specific examination of the scale's validity was reported by Zeithaml, Berry, and Parasuraman (1996).

ADMINISTRATION: The scale was administered to customers in a mail survey format (Mittal and Lassar 1996; Parasuraman, Zeithaml, and Berry 1994b; Zeithaml, Berry, and Parasuraman 1996). Higher scores on the scale indicated that respondents thought the service they experienced from a specific firm was as responsive if not more so than the level of service they think can and should be delivered by such a company.

MAJOR FINDINGS: The purpose of the study by Mittal and Lassar (1996) was to show the importance of the personalization aspect of service quality when measuring customer satisfaction and patronage behavior. The authors modified the SERVQUAL instrument (Parasuraman, Zeithaml, and Berry 1994b) most particularly by adding the personalization component. Their findings seemed to show that, using the modified SERVQUAL, the **responsiveness** dimension was a significant predictor of several satisfaction-related variables, especially a simple overall measure of service quality. However, these significant relationships were only found in the car repair context; no significant relationships were found for the **responsiveness** dimension in the health care context.

Parasuraman, Zeithaml, and Berry (1994b) conducted a study to refine their SERVQUAL scales and examine the revised scales in three different formats with four different customer groups. The scale shown here is part of a "one-column format," meaning that one scale for each of the five service quality dimensions was used to measure service superiority directly. Although the one-column format had reasonable psychometric characteristics, its diagnostic value was not considered to be as high as that of the two- and three-column formats, which provided indications of customers' service adequacy in addition to service superiority.

Zeithaml, Berry, and Parasuraman (1996) tested a model of the impact of service quality on relevant behaviors. In general, their results showed that there is a significant positive relationship between perceived service quality and favorable behavioral intentions. A weighted-average performance score was calculated across the SERVQUAL dimensions; no results were reported in this study for the **responsiveness** dimension by itself.

COMMENTS: Although this scale can be used by itself, it was designed to be used along with its companion measures of the other service quality dimensions. Furthermore, as noted previously, this scale represents the simplest format that Parasuraman, Zeithaml, and Berry (1994b) offered. Refer to their article for details regarding the more complex but potentially more useful versions (two- and three-column formats).

REFERENCES:

Lassar, Walfried M. (1998), personal correspondence.

Mittal, Banwari and Walfried M. Lassar (1996), "The Role of Personalization in Service Encounters," *JR*, 72 (1), 95–109.

Parasuraman, A. (1997), personal correspondence.

———, Valarie A. Zeithaml, and Leonard L. Berry (1988), "SERVQUAL: A Multiple-Item Scale for Measuring Customer Perceptions of Service Quality," *JR*, 64 (Spring), 12–40.

———, ———, and ——— (1994a), "Reassessment of Expectations as a Comparison Standard in Measuring Service Quality: Implications for Further Research," *JM*, 58 (January), 111–24.

———, ———, and ——— (1994b), "Alternative Scales for Measuring Service Quality: A Comparative Assessment Based on Psychometric and Diagnostic Criteria," *JR*, 70 (3), 201–30.

Zeithaml, Valarie A., Leonard L. Berry, and A. Parasuraman (1996), "The Behavioral Consequences of Service Quality," *JM*, 60 (April), 31–46.

SCALE ITEMS:*

Directions: Please think about the quality of service _____ offers compared to your *desired service level*—the level of performance you believe a _____ *can and should deliver* (i.e., the level of service you desire). For each of the following statements, circle the number that indicates how _____'s service compares with your desired service level.

_____'s service performance is:

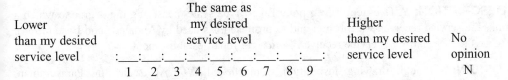

	The same as my desired service level		
Lower than my desired service level	:___:___:___:___:___:___:___:___:	Higher than my desired service level	No opinion
	1 2 3 4 5 6 7 8 9		N

1. Prompt service to customers.

2. Willingness to help customers.

3. Readiness to respond to customer needs.

4. _____ gives customers individual attention.

*These directions and items 1–3 were used by Parasuraman, Zeithaml, and Berry (1994b). Zeithaml, Berry, and Parasuraman (1996) also used items similar to the first three, but the layout of the scale and the directions were different. Mittal and Lassar (1996) used items 1–4 in a typical five-point agree/disagree format response. The blanks in the directions should contain the name of the specific service provider being evaluated, except for the second, which should have the general name for the type of service (e.g., auto insurance company) being evaluated. The blank in item 4 should contain the name of the specific service provider being evaluated.

SCALE NAME: Service Quality (Responsiveness)

SCALE DESCRIPTION: A five-item, seven-point Likert-type scale measuring the degree to which a person thinks the service received was prompt and as promised. As used by Andaleeb and Basu (1994), the scale relates to the quality of service received from a car repair establishment.

SCALE ORIGIN: Although drawing inspiration from the SERVQUAL scales by Parasuraman, Zeithaml, and Berry (1988), Andaleeb and Basu (1994) performed their own developmental work and produced a related but unique measure.

SAMPLES: Andaleeb and Basu (1994) gathered their data from a mail survey. Telephone directories of two large cities in the northeastern United States were used to find names and addresses. Questionnaires were apparently directed at a member of the household who owned a car and had experienced automobile repair/service. Of the 550 surveys distributed, **133** were usable.

RELIABILITY: An alpha of **.90** was reported for the scale (Andaleeb and Basu 1994).

VALIDITY: Andaleeb and Basu (1994) provided the results of a factor analysis conducted on 27 items related to service quality. The items on this scale loaded high on the same dimension and lower on the others. In addition, the authors provided a correlation matrix between this scale and four others. Because the correlations in every case were lower than the alphas, it was construed as evidence of discriminant validity. However, the significance and level of the correlations could just as easily have been interpreted as evidence of convergent validity. Thus, strong evidence of the scale's construct validity remains to be provided.

ADMINISTRATION: As noted, the scale was part of a larger mail survey instrument (Andaleeb and Basu 1994). Higher scores on the scale indicated that respondents viewed the service they received from a specified business to have been conducted in a timely manner.

MAJOR FINDINGS: The purpose of the study by Andaleeb and Basu (1994) was to examine the relationship between a customer's satisfaction with a car repair facility and five dimensions of service quality. Among the many findings was that a higher level of perceived **responsiveness** is related to greater customer satisfaction with the service performed.

REFERENCES:

Andaleeb, Syed Saad and Amiya K. Basu (1994), "Technical Complexity and Consumer Knowledge as Moderators of Service Quality Evaluation in the Automobile Service Industry," *JR*, 70 (4), 367–81.
Parasuraman, A., Valarie A. Zeithaml, and Leonard L. Berry (1988), "SERVQUAL: A Multiple-Item Scale for Measuring Customer Perceptions of Service Quality," *JR*, 64 (Spring), 12–40.

SCALE ITEMS:

Strongly
disagree
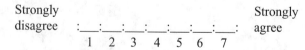
Strongly
agree

1. The service was completed in a timely manner.

2. The facility had my appointment scheduled promptly.

3. The facility scheduled my appointment near the date I desired.

4. Upon arrival, I was quickly waited on.

5. My car was ready when promised.

SCALE NAME: Service Quality (Retailer Policy)

SCALE DESCRIPTION: Five five-point Likert-type items measuring a customer's perception of a store's policies as they relate to several issues that make it more advantageous for people to shop there, such as carrying high-quality products, having convenient parking and hours, and taking credit cards.

SCALE ORIGIN: Dabholkar, Thorpe, and Rentz (1996) conducted three qualitative studies to gain insight into factors important to retail customers in evaluating service quality. They drew general inspiration from the SERVQUAL instrument (Parasuraman, Berry, and Zeithaml 1991), but this dimension and scale are completely new.

SAMPLES: To test their proposed structure of retail service quality, Dabholkar, Thorpe, and Rentz (1996) conducted two surveys. Data for the first survey came from **227** customers of seven stores in two department store chains located in the southeastern United States. Every fifth customer who entered the store was handed a questionnaire, provided he or she had previously shopped at the store. Respondents self-administered the survey in a quiet area in the store. Study 2 was conducted for purposes of cross-validation and was based on data from **149** customers. Conditions were very similar to the previous study except that data were gathered from just two of the stores in one chain included in Study 1.

RELIABILITY: A construct reliability of **.92** was reported for the scale in the first study by Dabholkar, Thorpe, and Rentz (1996; Dabholkar 1997).

VALIDITY: A general sense of the scale's convergent validity comes from the items' reported high loading on the appropriate factors in both studies by Dabholkar, Thorpe, and Rentz (1996). The authors also stated that there was evidence attesting to the scale's discriminant validity. Support for the scale's predictive validity came from its high positive correlation with two other measures: *intention to shop at the store* (.63) and *intention to recommend the store* (.66).

ADMINISTRATION: The scale was self-administered by respondents as part of a larger questionnaire on entering the store but before shopping (Dabholkar, Thorpe, and Rentz 1996). Higher scores on the scale indicated that customers viewed a store as having policies that make it very desirable and convenient for shoppers.

MAJOR FINDINGS: The purpose of the studies reported by Dabholkar, Thorpe, and Rentz (1996) was to construct and validate retail service quality scales. In doing so, the authors found evidence in support of a hierarchical factor structure, such that there are five dimensions of retail service quality, three of which can be further broken down into two subdimensions. **Policy** was found to be one of the primary dimensions of retail service quality, but no subdimensions were proposed or in evidence.

REFERENCES:
Dabholkar, Pratibha (1997), personal correspondence.
———, Dayle I. Thorpe, and Joseph O. Rentz (1996), "A Measure of Service Quality for Retail Stores: Scale Development and Validation," *JAMS*, 24 (Winter), 3–16.
Parasuraman, A., Leonard L. Berry, and Valarie A. Zeithaml (1991), "Refinement and Reassessment of the SERVQUAL Scale," *JR*, 67 (Winter), 420–50.

#356 *Service Quality (Retailer Policy)*

SCALE ITEMS:

Strongly   Strongly
disagree   :___:___:___:___:___: agree
             1   2   3   4   5

1. This store offers high quality merchandise.

2. This store provides plenty of free parking for customers.

3. This store has operating hours convenient to all of their customers.

4. This store accepts most major credit cards.

5. This store offers its own credit card.

SCALE NAME: Service Quality (Retailer Problem Solving)

SCALE DESCRIPTION: Three five-point Likert-type items measuring a customer's perception of a store's commitment to handling customer problems (complaints, returns, exchanges) in a timely manner.

SCALE ORIGIN: Dabholkar, Thorpe, and Rentz (1996) conducted three qualitative studies to gain insight into factors important to retail customers in evaluating service quality. They drew general inspiration from the SERVQUAL instrument (Parasuraman, Berry, and Zeithaml 1991), but this dimension and scale are completely new.

SAMPLES: To test their proposed structure of retail service quality, Dabholkar, Thorpe, and Rentz (1996) conducted two surveys. Data for the first survey came from **227** customers of seven stores in two department store chains located in the southeastern United States. Every fifth customer who entered the store was handed a questionnaire, provided he or she had previously shopped at the store. Respondents self-administered the survey in a quiet area in the store. Study 2 was conducted for purposes of cross-validation and was based on data from **149** customers. Conditions were very similar to the previous study except that data were gathered from just two of the stores in one chain included in Study 1.

RELIABILITY: An alpha of **.87** was reported for the scale in the first study by Dabholkar, Thorpe, and Rentz (1996; Dabholkar 1997).

VALIDITY: A general sense of the scale's convergent validity comes from the items' reported high loading on the appropriate factors in both studies by Dabholkar, Thorpe, and Rentz (1996). The authors also stated that there was evidence attesting to the scale's discriminant validity. Support for the scale's predictive validity came from its high positive correlation with two other measures: *intention to shop at the store* (.66) and *intention to recommend the store* (.64).

ADMINISTRATION: The scale was self-administered by respondents as part of a larger questionnaire on entering the store but before shopping (Dabholkar, Thorpe, and Rentz 1996). Higher scores on the scale indicated that customers viewed a store as very interested in solving customers' problems.

MAJOR FINDINGS: The purpose of the studies reported by Dabholkar, Thorpe, and Rentz (1996) was to construct and validate retail service quality scales. In doing so, the authors found evidence in support of a hierarchical factor structure, such that there are five dimensions of retail service quality, three of which can be further broken down into two subdimensions. **Problem solving** was found to be one of the primary dimensions of retail service quality, but no subdimensions were proposed or in evidence.

REFERENCES:
Dabholkar, Pratibha (1997), personal correspondence.
———, Dayle I. Thorpe, and Joseph O. Rentz (1996), "A Measure of Service Quality for Retail Stores: Scale Development and Validation," *JAMS*, 24 (Winter), 3–16.
Parasuraman, A., Leonard L. Berry, and Valarie A. Zeithaml (1991), "Refinement and Reassessment of the SERVQUAL Scale," *JR*, 67 (Winter), 420–50.

SCALE ITEMS:

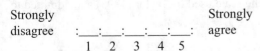

Strongly disagree :___:___:___:___:___: Strongly agree
　　　　　　　　1　　2　　3　　4　　5

1. This store willingly handles returns and exchanges.

2. When a customer has a problem, this store shows a sincere interest in solving it.

3. Employees of this store are able to handle customer complaints directly and immediately.

SCALE NAME: Service Quality (Tangibles)

SCALE DESCRIPTION: A four-item, seven-point Likert-type scale measuring the degree to which a person thinks the material and human aspects of a service company are visually appealing. As described here, the scale relates to the tangibles dimension of the SERVQUAL instrument (Parasuraman, Berry, and Zeithaml 1991; Parasuraman, Zeithaml, and Berry 1988) but is not equivalent to it. Each dimension of the SERVQUAL measure is composed of the summated differences between expectation items and perceptual items, not just perceptual items as the scale described here is. Carman (1990) used several variations on the scale, as described subsequently. Taylor (1995) only used perceptual items.

SCALE ORIGIN: The scale is a part of the larger SERVQUAL instrument described by Parasuraman, Zeithaml, and Berry (1988; Parasuraman, Berry, and Zeithaml 1991) that measures five separate dimensions of service quality. Considerable information is provided in those articles about the scale's conceptualization, development, and validation.

The version of the scale discussed by Parasuraman, Zeithaml, and Berry (1988) was followed to a great extent by Carman (1990). In Parasuraman, Berry, and Zeithaml's 1991 article, some suggestions for changes to the scale were made. As far as the tangibles dimension is concerned, the revised version replaced one item with another item and made slight modifications in wording of two other items. Taylor (1995) slightly modified the items (specified under "Scale Items") for use with a specific counselor at a university career counseling service.

SAMPLES: Carman (1990) adjusted and tested the SERVQUAL instrument in four different service settings: a dental school patient clinic (n = 612), a business school placement center (n = 82), a tire store (n = 74), and an acute care hospital (n = 720). The scale used in the hospital setting warranted treatment as a different scale and is, therefore, written up separately.

A questionnaire was sent by Parasuraman, Berry, and Zeithaml (1991) to randomly chosen customers of five nationally known companies: one telephone company, two banks, and two insurance companies. A reminder postcard was sent two weeks after the initial mailing. The number of usable questionnaires ranged from 290 to 487 for the five companies. The total completed returns were **1936**, which was a 21% overall response rate. Managers in the companies reviewed the demographic profiles of the respondents and considered them representative of their customer populations.

Taylor (1995) collected data from **232** undergraduate business students attending a midsized university. Some of these subjects (n = 68) were part of a control group, but the rest were broken down into groups of between 24 and 31 for the experimental treatments.

RELIABILITY: The following alphas were reported by Carman (1990) for the scale: **.70** (tire store), **.79** (placement center), and **.78** (dental clinic). The alphas reported by Parasuraman, Berry, and Zeithaml (1991) for the five companies ranged from .80 for one of the insurance companies to .86 for one of the banks. These alphas relate to the summated differences between expectation items and perceptual items. The alpha for just the perceptual items was **.86** using the combined sample (Parasuraman 1993). An alpha of **.68** was reported for the version of the scale used by Taylor (1995) and admitted to be lower than desirable.

VALIDITY: Carman (1990) factor analyzed the SERVQUAL data from each setting. Only items with loadings greater than .30 on the same factor in at least one setting were used to compose scales (Carman 1994). However, the sets of items used to compose the summated scales for each of the three settings were ultimately different based on several factors. These variable results led Carman (1990) to conclude that the scale had problems with construct validity.

Parasuraman, Berry, and Zeithaml (1991) reported the results of several factor analyses using oblique rotations. With regard to the perceptual version of the scale using the combined samples, items 1 and 2 had high loadings on one factor, whereas items 3 and 4 were split between that factor and another. The four items were apparently left in the scale because their loadings were all greater than .50 in a factor analysis of the expectation scores.

ADMINISTRATION: The SERVQUAL instrument was self-administered by respondents after they received service in the study by Carman (1990). The scale was administered to customers in a mail survey format by Parasuraman, Berry, and Zeithaml (1991). Subjects in the experiment conducted by Taylor (1995) self-administered the scale, along with other measures, after the experimental manipulation. Higher scores on the perceptual version of the scale indicated that respondents thought that a specific service firm has attractive-looking material assets associated with it.

MAJOR FINDINGS: The purpose of Carman's (1990) studies was to test the SERVQUAL instrument in a variety of service settings. Some modifications in wording were always found to be necessary. Furthermore, testing of the data indicated that, though a **tangibles**-related dimension was found across settings, the items loading on that dimension were not stable.

Parasuraman, Berry, and Zeithaml (1991) conducted a study to refine their SERVQUAL scales and examine the revised scales in five different customer samples. They also compared their results with those of others who had used the scales. With regard to **tangible aspects of service quality**, the authors found that the gap scores were splitting into two subdimensions: one relating to employees/communication materials and the other related to facilities/equipment. The split seemed to be due to differences in the structure of perceptions and not expectations.

The purpose of the experiment by Taylor (1995) was to investigate the effects of a delay, perceived control over a delay, and what fills the time during the delay. Among the many findings was that evaluation of the **tangibles** aspect of service quality was lower for those whose waiting time was not filled than for those whose delay was filled.

COMMENTS: Although this scale can be used by itself, it was designed to be used along with its companion expectation version. For example, the expectation version of item 1 would be something like the following: "Excellent _____ companies will have up-to-date equipment." The authors also encouraged researchers to measure all of the dimensions to fully capture the domain of service quality.

For further discussion of theoretical and psychometric properties of the SERVQUAL instrument, see Parasuraman, Zeithaml, and Berry (1994), Cronin and Taylor (1994), and Teas (1994).

See also Fischer, Gainer, and Bristor (1997), Finn and Kayandé (1997), Kelley and Hoffman (1997), and Teas (1993).

REFERENCES:
Carman, James M. (1990), "Consumer Perceptions of Service Quality: An Assessment of the SERVQUAL Dimensions," *JR*, 66 (Spring), 33–55.
——— (1994), personal correspondence.
Cronin, J. Joseph, Jr. and Steven A. Taylor (1994), "SERVPERF Versus SERVQUAL: Reconciling Performance-Based and Perceptions-Minus-Expectations Measurement of Service Quality," *JM*, 58 (January), 124–31.
Finn, Adam and Ujwal Kayandé (1997), "Reliability Assessment and Optimization of Marketing Measurement," *JMR*, 34 (May), 262–75.
Fischer, Eileen, Brenda Gainer, and Julia Bristor (1997), "The Sex of the Service Provider: Does it Influence Perceptions of Service Quality," *JR*, 73 (3), 361–82.
Kelley, Scott W. and K. Douglas Hoffman (1997), "An Investigation of Positive Affect, Prosocial Behaviors and Service Quality," *JR*, 73 (3), 407–27.

Parasuraman, A. (1993), personal correspondence.

———, Leonard L. Berry, and Valarie A. Zeithaml (1991), "Refinement and Reassessment of the SERVQUAL Scale," *JR*, 67 (Winter), 420–50.

———, Valarie A. Zeithaml, and Leonard L. Berry (1988), "SERVQUAL: A Multiple-Item Scale for Measuring Customer Perceptions of Service Quality," *JR*, 64 (Spring), 12–40.

———, ———, and ——— (1994a), "Reassessment of Expectations as a Comparison Standard in Measuring Service Quality: Implications for Further Research," *JM*, 58 (January), 111–24.

Taylor, Shirley (1995), "The Effects of Filled Waiting Time and Service Provider Control over the Delay on Evaluations of Service," *JAMS*, 23 (Winter), 38–48.

Teas, R. Kenneth (1993), "Expectations, Performance Evaluation, and Consumers' Perceptions of Quality," *JM*, 57 (October), 18–34.

——— (1994), "Expectations as a Comparison Standard in Measuring Service Quality: An Assessment of a Reassessment," *JM*, 58 (January), 132–39.

SCALE ITEMS:

Directions: The following set of statement relate to your feelings about _____'s service. For each statement, please show the extent to which you believe _____ has the feature described by the statement. Circling a "1" means that you strongly disagree that _____ has that feature, and circling a "7" means that you strongly agree. You may circle any of the numbers in the middle that show how strong your feelings are. There are no right or wrong answers—all we are interested in is a number that best shows your perceptions about _____'s service.

Strongly   Strongly
disagree   :___:___:___:___:___:___:___: agree
             1 2 3 4 5 6 7

1. _____ has up-to-date equipment.

2. _____'s physical facilities are visually appealing.

3. _____'s employees are well dressed and appear neat.

4. The appearance of the physical facilities of _____ is in keeping with the type of services provided.

5. _____ does not give you individual attention. **(r)**

6. Employees of _____ do not give you personal attention. **(r)**

7. _____ has modern-looking equipment.

8. _____ employees are neat-appearing.

9. Materials associated with the service (such as pamphlets or statements) are visually appealing at _____.

*The name of the specific service firm studied should be placed in the blanks. Items 1–4 were the form used by Parasuraman, Zeithaml, and Berry (1988), whereas items 2, and 7–9 were used in Parasuraman, Berry, and Zeithaml's 1991 article. Although not completely clear, it appears that statements similar to the following items were used in the three studies conducted by Carman (1990): 2–4 (tire store and placement center) and 2, 3, 5, and 6 (dental clinic). Taylor (1995) used items similar to 2, 7–9 and adapted them for reference to a specific counselor at a university career counseling office.

SCALE NAME: Service Quality (Tangibles)

SCALE DESCRIPTION: Multiple statements that measure how dependable a customer of a company views the quality of some of its most visible attributes. The version by Parasuraman, Zeithaml, and Berry (1994b) goes a bit further and measures perceptions of **tangible** assets *compared with the desired service level* (the performance level the company can and should deliver).

SCALE ORIGIN: The scale is a part of the larger SERVQUAL instrument described by Parasuraman, Zeithaml, and Berry (1994b) and Zeithaml, Berry, and Parasuraman (1996) that measures five separate dimensions of service quality. Considerable information is provided by the former about the instrument's conceptualization, development, validation, and diagnostic value. This version of the instrument is a modification of earlier forms (e.g., Parasuraman, Zeithaml, and Berry 1988, 1994a), in that it is intended to be a direct measure of service superiority rather than just capture perceptions or require multiple measures to assess expectations and perceptions. The instrument was refined through two stages of pretesting.

On the basis of their particular task, Mittal and Lassar (1996) examined the five items used by Parasuraman, Zeithaml, and Berry (1994b), determined that item 5 was "extraneous," and deleted from their version of the scale.

SAMPLES: The data collected by Mittal and Lassar (1996) came from two U.S. cities for two service-related businesses. Respondents were recruited from three sources: shopping malls, mailbox drop, and parent–teacher associations and other fund raiser groups. Complete survey forms were received from **233** people, 110 relating to car repair services and 123 relating to health clinic services.

Data were gathered by Parasuraman, Zeithaml, and Berry (1994b) from subjects obtained from lists of customers provided by four companies: a computer manufacturer, a retail chain, an auto insurer, and a life insurer. A total of 4156 questionnaires were mailed out using this scale's format, and **1135** were received back. (Two other formats were tested as well.)

Zeithaml, Berry, and Parasuraman (1996) gathered data from mailing lists of current customers generated by four businesses: a computer manufacturer, a retail chain, an automobile insurer, and a life insurer. The names were of end users in each case, except for the computer company, for which it was business customers. A total of 12,470 questionnaires were sent out, and **3069** were returned.

RELIABILITY: The alphas reported by Parasuraman, Zeithaml, Berry (1994b) for the four companies ranged from .83 to .91. The values reported by Zeithaml, Berry, and Parasuraman (1996; Parasuraman 1997) ranged from .80 to .89. Finally, alphas of **.85** (health care), **.84** (car repair), and **.85** (combined) were calculated by Mittal and Lassar (1996; Lassar 1998).

VALIDITY: Parasuraman, Zeithaml, Berry (1994b) reported the results of a factor analysis using an oblique rotation. All of the items loaded high on the same dimension except one (4). Several checks of the scale's validity were made that provided some limited evidence of predictive, convergent, and discriminant validity.

On the basis of confirmatory factor analysis, Mittal and Lassar (1996) indicated that the results supported a claim of discriminant validity. No specific examination of the scale's validity was reported by Zeithaml, Berry, and Parasuraman (1996).

ADMINISTRATION: The scale was administered to customers in a mail survey format (Mittal and Lassar 1996; Parasuraman, Zeithaml, and Berry 1994b; Zeithaml, Berry, and Parasuraman 1996). Higher scores on the scale indicated that respondents thought the tangible aspects of a specific firm with which they had experience are as high if not higher than the quality they think can and should be delivered by such a company.

MAJOR FINDINGS: The purpose of the study by Mittal and Lassar (1996) was to show the importance of the personalization aspect of service quality when measuring customer satisfaction and patronage behavior. The authors modified the SERVQUAL instrument (Parasuraman, Zeithaml, and Berry 1994b) most particularly by adding the personalization component. Their findings seemed to show that, using the modified SERVQUAL, the **tangibles** dimension did not have a consistent or strong impact on several satisfaction indicators.

Parasuraman, Zeithaml, and Berry (1994b) conducted a study to refine their SERVQUAL scales and examine the revised scales in three different formats with four different customer groups. The scale shown here is part of a "one-column format," meaning that one scale for each of the five service quality dimensions was used to measure service superiority directly. Although the one-column format had reasonable psychometric characteristics, its diagnostic value was not considered to be as high as that of the two- and three-column formats, which provided indications of customers' service adequacy in addition to service superiority.

Zeithaml, Berry, and Parasuraman (1996) tested a model of the impact of service quality on relevant behaviors. In general, their results showed that there is a significant positive relationship between perceived service quality and favorable behavioral intentions. A weighted-average performance score was calculated across the SERVQUAL dimensions; no results were reported in this study for the **tangibles** dimension by itself.

COMMENTS: Although this scale can be used by itself, it was designed to be used along with its companion measures of the other service quality dimensions. Furthermore, as noted previously, this scale represents the simplest format that Parasuraman, Zeithaml, and Berry (1994b) offered. Refer to their article for details regarding the more complex but potentially more useful versions (two- and three-column formats).

REFERENCES:

Lassar, Walfried M. (1998), personal correspondence.

Mittal, Banwari and Walfried M. Lassar (1996), "The Role of Personalization in Service Encounters," *JR*, 72 (1), 95–109.

Parasuraman, A. (1997), personal correspondence.

———, Valarie A. Zeithaml, and Leonard L. Berry (1988), "SERVQUAL: A   Multiple-Item Scale for Measuring Customer Perceptions of Service Quality," *JR*, 64 (Spring), 12–40.

———, ———, and ——— (1994a), "Reassessment of Expectations as a Comparison Standard in Measuring Service Quality: Implications for Further Research," *JM*, 58 (January), 111–24.

———, ———, and ——— (1994b), "Alternative Scales for Measuring Service Quality: A Comparative Assessment Based on Psychometric and Diagnostic Criteria," *JR*, 70 (3), 201–30.

Zeithaml, Valarie A., Leonard L. Berry, and A. Parasuraman (1996), "The Behavioral Consequences of Service Quality," *JM*, 60 (April), 31–46.

SCALE ITEMS:*

Directions: Please think about the quality of service _____ offers compared to your *desired service level*—the level of performance you believe a _____ *can and should deliver* (i.e., the level of service you desire). For each of the following statements, circle the number that indicates how _____'s service compares with your desired service level.

_____'s service performance is:

Lower than my desired service level	The same as my desired service level	Higher than my desired service level	No opinion
:___:___:___:___:___:___:___:___:			
1 2 3 4 5 6 7 8 9			N

1. Modern equipment.

2. Visually appealing facilities.

3. Employees who have neat, professional appearance.

4. Visually appealing materials associated with the service.

5. Convenient business hours.

*These directions and items 1–5 were used by Parasuraman, Zeithaml, and Berry (1994b). Zeithaml, Berry, and Parasuraman (1996) also used items similar to the first five, but the layout of the scale and the directions were different. Mittal and Lassar (1996) used items similar to 1–4 in a typical five-point agree/disagree format response. The blanks in the directions should contain the name of the specific service provider being evaluated, except for the second, which should have the general name for the type of service (e.g., auto insurance company) being evaluated. The blank in the scale stem should contain the name of the specific service provider being evaluated.

SCALE NAME: Service Recovery Expectations (Health Club)

SCALE DESCRIPTION: Eight scenarios with seven-point response scales evaluating the way a consumer perceives a specified health club would resolve potential service problems.

SCALE ORIGIN: Kelley and Davis (1994) created the scale for use in their study. A sample of 60 health club members submitted examples of service failures. These episodes were screened and edited to produce eight service recovery incidents. A new group of 18 judges familiar with health clubs scaled the scenarios, and they were then pretested on 95 undergraduate students with health club experience. No items were deleted because all had reasonable item–total correlations (>.25). Finally, health club managers examined the scale for wording problems.

SAMPLES: Data were collected by Kelley and Davis (1994) from members of a health club located in a midsized community in the southeastern United States. The authors stated that the health club was viewed as the market leader in the area and offered a wide range of services and amenities. Surveys were passed out to members as they came to and went from the club on 12 consecutive days. Completed questionnaires were received from **296** individuals. The typical respondent was 36.7 years of age, male (65%), had been a member of the club for three years, and worked out an average of three days a week.

RELIABILITY: An alpha of **.78** was reported for the scale by Kelley and Davis (1994).

VALIDITY: The validity of the scale was not specifically examined by Kelley and Davis (1994).

ADMINISTRATION: The scale was completed along with other scales and measures in a self-administered survey (Kelley and Davis 1994). Higher scores on the scale suggested that respondents believed the specified health club would provide excellent resolution to a variety of potential service problems.

MAJOR FINDINGS: Kelley and Davis (1994) proposed and tested a model of the antecedents to service recovery expectations. It was found that service quality and customer organizational commitment had direct effects on customer **service recovery expectations.**

REFERENCES:
Kelley, Scott W. and Mark A. Davis (1994), "Antecedents to Customer Expectations for Service Recovery," *JAMS*, 22 (Winter), 52–61.

SCALE ITEMS:
Directions: The following questions are concerned with the way your health club deals with service problems. After reading each incident you will circle the number which reflects how well your health club would deal with the problem (1 = *poor resolution* and 7 = *excellent resolution*). The sample outcomes to the right of each scale are examples only. You may use them as guides for making your ratings (1–7) of how you expect the problem would be handled.

1. You have scheduled an appointment with a fitness consultant at the health club. Upon arriving for your appointment you are told that the fitness consultant you were scheduled to meet with will not be in today.

   7

   6

   5

   4 You are asked to reschedule your appointment with the fitness consultant after the consultant returns.

   3

   2 You are unable to schedule an appointment until several weeks later.

   1

2. You are overcharged for your annual membership fee at the health club. You call the club and notify them of the error.

    7 You receive a full refund within five days along with a personalized letter of apology.
    6
    5 You receive a full refund within two weeks.
    4
    3
    2 You are asked to bring your bill to the club during regular business hours.
    1

3. You regularly participate in the same aerobics class with the same instructor. Your regular instructor suddenly becomes ill and is unable to lead the class.

    7
    6 Another equally qualified aerobics instructor substitutes for your instructor.
    5
    4 Another less qualified employee substitutes for your instructor.
    3
    2 Your class is canceled.
    1

4. Upon arriving at the club for your daily swim, you discover that the pool is closed due to a chemical imbalance.

    7
    6 Arrangements are made for pool use at another facility.
    5 After an apology for the inconvenience, a fitness counselor suggests some alternative activities while the pool is closed.
    4
    3
    2 A club employee states that the pool will be closed indefinitely, but does not know why.
    1

5. You are injured playing basketball or volleyball after slipping on a wet spot in the gym. The wet spot was caused by a leak in the roof.

    7 The leak is fixed the same day and the health club pays for any needed health care.
    6
    5
    4
    3 An employee asks if you are okay. The leak is fixed two weeks later.
    2 An employee suggests that you check the floor for wet spots and wipe them up before playing again.
    1

6. As a new member you are unfamiliar with the workout equipment. You ask an employee to demonstrate the use of the equipment.

7 The employee stops to personally demonstrate the proper way to use the equipment.
6
5
4 The employee indicates that demonstrations are provided at regularly scheduled times and tells you when the next demonstration is scheduled.
3
2 The employee suggests watching other members who use the equipment and ask them questions to learn the appropriate technique.
1

7. You complain to the club management that the facilities are too crowded and that you must consistently wait to use the equipment.

7
6 The manager politely suggests that you workout at a different time when equipment use is less heavy. The manager provides a list of light use hours.
5
4 The manager states that your concerns will be addressed at the next management meeting and that extended club hours is on the agenda.
3
2 The manager states that it is necessary to maintain a large membership to hold the costs of membership down.
1

8. You purchase a workout outfit from the club. The seams rip out after two workouts. You return to the club with the torn outfit.

7 The club provides a full refund or exchange, "no questions asked."
6
5
4
3 The employee asks how long you have had the outfit. A cash refund equivalent to half the original purchase price is offered.
2
1 The employee indicates that exchanges or refunds are not allowed.

SCALE NAME: Shame

SCALE DESCRIPTION: Three four-point items intended to capture a person's negative emotional concern and uneasiness during a consumption experience.

SCALE ORIGIN: Richins (1997) drew on terms in previous measures, as well as her own series of studies, to develop and refine several emotion-related scales into the CES (Consumption Emotion Set).

SAMPLES: Six studies were reported by Richins (1997) as part of the process of developing the CES, only two of which had reliability information. Study 4 was based on data from **448** college students. Two surveys were conducted in Study 5: Survey 1 was completed by **256** college students, and there were **194** student respondents to Survey 2.

RELIABILITY: As noted, reliability was reported by Richins (1997) for only Studies 4 and 5, which had alphas of **.82** and **.85**, respectively.

VALIDITY: Richins (1997) did not directly examine the validity of the scale. A great deal of effort was expended, however, in a creative use of multidimensional scaling to note whether the items that composed each scale clustered together.

ADMINISTRATION: In the studies performed by Richins (1997), particularly Studies 4 and 5, the scale was part of a larger instrument containing many emotion-related measures. A high score on the scale suggested that a person experienced a strong sense of disgrace because of some event or stimulus.

MAJOR FINDINGS: On the basis of a review of previously developed measures of emotion, Richins (1997) conducted six studies with the purpose of producing a set of scales particularly suited for assessing consumption experiences. The CES instrument was a result of the studies, one subscale of which measures **shame**. In general, the instrument was more successful in representing the diversity of consumption emotions than were the other instruments tested.

REFERENCES:
Richins, Marsha L. (1997), "Measuring Emotions in the Consumption Experience," *JCR*, 24 (September), 127–46.

SCALE ITEMS:

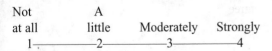

Not at all	A little	Moderately	Strongly
1	2	3	4

1. Embarrassed

2. Ashamed

3. Humiliated

SCALE NAME: Shopping Convenience

SCALE DESCRIPTION: A three-item, five-point Likert-type summated ratings scale measuring the degree to which a person expresses a desire for convenience and simplicity, particularly as it relates to gathering information about products and conducting shopping activity.

SCALE ORIGIN: The source of the scale was not stated by Donthu and Gilliland (1996), but it is likely original to their study.

SAMPLES: Donthu and Gilliland (1996) used trained interviewers to call 1000 households in a large city telephone directory. Interviews were successfully completed with adults in **368** of those households. Although some demographic information was employed in the analysis, the data were not reported in such a way that the sample as a whole can be clearly described.

RELIABILITY: An alpha of **.71** was reported for the scale by Donthu and Gilliland (1996).

VALIDITY: No specific examination of the scale's validity was reported by Donthu and Gilliland (1996).

ADMINISTRATION: Donthu and Gilliland (1996) had the scale administered as part of a larger telephone survey. Higher scores on the scale indicated that respondents were very convenience-oriented in their shopping.

MAJOR FINDINGS: Donthu and Gilliland (1996) profiled infomercial shoppers. Unexpectedly, **convenience** was found to be significantly more important to them than to those who had never purchased goods from infomercials.

COMMENTS: Because of the low level of the scale's alpha and the sense that the items represent different facets of the *convenience* construct, it is quite possible that the scale is not unidimensional. It would be prudent to conduct further testing and development if this scale is to be used again in the future.

REFERENCES:
Donthu, Naveen and David Gilliland (1996), "The Infomercial Shopper," *JAR*, 36 (March/April), 69–76.

SCALE ITEMS:

Strongly disagree	Disagree	Neutral	Agree	Strongly agree
1	2	3	4	5

1. I hate to spend time gathering information on products.

2. I do not like complicated things.

3. It is convenient to shop from home.

SCALE NAME: Shopping Enjoyment

SCALE DESCRIPTION: A three-item, five-point Likert-type summated ratings scale measuring the enjoyment a consumer expresses receiving from the shopping experience. Although not explicitly stated in the scale items, the implication is that this refers to the in-store shopping experience rather than non-store or home-based forms of shopping. The scale was referred to as *emotional lift* by O'Guinn and Faber (1989; Faber and O'Guinn 1992) and *attitude toward shopping* by Donthu and Gilliland (1996).

SCALE ORIGIN: The scale was apparently original to O'Guinn and Faber (1989). The source of the variation used by Donthu and Gilliland (1996) is uncertain but is likely to be original to their study.

SAMPLES: Donthu and Gilliland (1996) used trained interviewers to call 1000 households in a large city telephone directory. Interviews were successfully completed with adults in **368** of those households. Although some demographic information was employed in the analysis, the data were not reported in such a way that the sample as a whole can be clearly described.

Two samples were employed by O'Guinn and Faber (1989). One was of **386** completed responses (out of 808 questionnaires sent) from people who had written an organization that aided compulsive buyers. A second group was used for comparison purposes and was intended to represent the general population. Eight hundred questionnaires were mailed to people in three Illinois areas: Chicago, Springfield, and Bloomington-Normal. Two mailings produced a total of **250** completed survey forms. The database used by Faber and O'Guinn (1992) is basically the same, except that the first sample had more responses (n = 388) and the second survey benefited from a third mailing (n = 292).

RELIABILITY: Alphas of **.89** and **.88** were reported for the scale by O'Guinn and Faber (1989; Faber and O'Guinn 1992) and Donthu and Gilliland (1996), respectively.

VALIDITY: Beyond a factor analysis conducted by O'Guinn and Faber (1992), which indicated that the items loaded together, no specific examination of scale validity was reported.

ADMINISTRATION: The scale was one of several self-administered measures used in mail survey instruments (Faber and O'Guinn 1992; O'Guinn and Faber 1989). Likewise, Donthu and Gilliland (1996) had the scale administered as part of a larger telephone survey. Higher scores on the scale indicated that respondents felt that shopping was an fun activity, whereas lower scores suggested that shopping did not bring them happiness or enjoyment.

MAJOR FINDINGS: Donthu and Gilliland (1996) profiled infomercial shoppers and found that they **enjoyed shopping** (in stores) significantly less than those who had never purchased goods from infomercials.

O'Guinn and Faber (1989) studied compulsive shopping. Their results showed that a sample of compulsive shoppers expressed a significantly greater amount of **shopping enjoyment** than did a general sample of consumers. Although using the same general database, Faber and O'Guinn (1992) reported on the development and testing of a scale to identify compulsive buyers.

REFERENCES:
Donthu, Naveen and David Gilliland (1996), "The Infomercial Shopper," *JAR*, 36 (March/April), 69–76.
Faber, Ronald J. and Thomas C. O'Guinn (1992), "A Clinical Screener for Compulsive Buying," *JCR*, 19 (December), 459–69.
O'Guinn, Thomas C. and Ronald J. Faber (1989), "Compulsive Buying: A Phenomenological Exploration," *JCR*, 16 (September), 147–57.

#363 *Shopping Enjoyment*

SCALE ITEMS:

Strongly   Disagree   Neutral   Agree   Strongly
disagree   agree
1————————2————————3————————4————————5

1. I shop because buying things makes me happy.

2. Shopping is fun.

3. I get a real "high" from shopping.

SCALE NAME: Shopping Enjoyment

SCALE DESCRIPTION: Four five-point Likert-type items intended to measure a shopping orientation that is characterized by the extent to which a consumer views shopping as an enjoyable activity in and of itself. The scale was referred to as *recreational shopping orientation* by Shim and Gehrt (1996).

SCALE ORIGIN: Shim and Gehrt (1996) used a modified version of a scale developed by Sproles and Kendall (1986). The latter created an eight-factor model of what they called *consumer decision making styles* but that many others in marketing (e.g., Shim and Gehrt 1996) would view as *shopping orientations*. Shim and Gehrt (1996) used the four items with the highest factor loadings of the five items identified by Sproles and Kendall (1986). The latter reported an alpha of .76 for the five-item scale and a .71 for the three items that loaded highest on the factor.

SAMPLES: Shim and Gehrt (1996) collected data from high school students in a Southwestern U.S. state. Twenty-nine principals agreed to participate, and their schools apparently represented many if not all counties in the state. Principals were given instructions as to which classes to use (by level) and how many students from each class were needed. Some 1954 usable surveys were returned by a sample that was 61.3% girls and had a mean age of 16 years. However, the study focused only on data from **1846** students who were white (56%), Hispanic (32%), or Native American (12%).

RELIABILITY: An alpha of **.86** was reported for the scale by Shim and Gehrt (1996).

VALIDITY: No examination of the scale's validity was reported by Shim and Gehrt (1996).

ADMINISTRATION: Data were gathered in a classroom setting in which students filled out the scale as part of a larger survey instrument (Shim and Gehrt 1996). Higher scores on the scale indicated that respondents viewed shopping as a very enjoyable activity.

MAJOR FINDINGS: The study by Shim and Gehrt (1996) examined differences in shopping orientations among high school students that could be linked to ethnicity. The results showed that white students expressed significantly less **shopping enjoyment** than Hispanics but significantly more **shopping enjoyment** than Native American students.

REFERENCES:
Shim, Soyeon and Kenneth C. Gehrt (1996), "Hispanic and Native American Adolescents: An Exploratory Study of Their Approach to Shopping," *JR*, 72 (3), 307–24.
Sproles, George B. and Elizabeth L. Kendall (1986), "A Methodology for Profiling Consumers' Decision-Making Styles," *Journal of Consumer Affairs*, 20 (Winter), 267–79.

SCALE ITEMS:

Strongly   Strongly
disagree   :___:___:___:___:___: agree
          1   2   3   4   5

1. Shopping is not a pleasant activity to me. **(r)**

2. Going shopping is one of the enjoyable activities of my life.

3. Shopping the stores wastes my time. **(r)**

4. I enjoy shopping just for the fun of it.

SCALE NAME: Shopping Enjoyment (Grocery)

SCALE DESCRIPTION: Five five-point Likert-type statements measuring the degree to which a consumer believes shopping at a grocery store is a pleasant and likable activity in which to engage.

SCALE ORIGIN: Although Urbany, Dickson, and Kalapurakal (1996) may have drawn inspiration from previous work, the scale appears to be original to their study.

SAMPLES: The data used by Urbany, Dickson, and Kalapurakal (1996) were collected as part of a larger survey by a leading market research firm. Telephone interviews were conducted with the primary grocery shoppers from households selected at random. Respondents were requested to participate in a second stage that would involve a mail survey. The survey yielded **343** usable responses. The average age of respondents was 44.7 years, and they were overwhelmingly women (83%).

RELIABILITY: An alpha of **.93** was reported for the scale by Urbany, Dickson, and Kalapurakal (1996).

VALIDITY: Urbany, Dickson, and Kalapurakal (1996) tested the discriminant validity of the **shopping enjoyment** scale using pairwise confirmatory factor analysis and six other measures. The evidence of three separate tests on each of the six pairs supported a claim of discriminant validity.

ADMINISTRATION: The data analyzed by Urbany, Dickson, and Kalapurakal (1996) were gathered in a mail survey. Higher scores suggested that respondents enjoyed shopping a lot.

MAJOR FINDINGS: Urbany, Dickson, and Kalapurakal (1996) developed a model of price search for the retail grocery industry that included a relatively complete accounting of economic and noneconomic returns, as well as search costs. The findings showed that **shopping enjoyment** did not account for a significant amount of variance in price-related search beyond that explained by economic costs and returns.

COMMENTS: Urbany, Dickson, and Kalapurakal (1996) reported a mean response of 3.34 on the scale.

REFERENCES:
Urbany, Joel E., Peter R. Dickson, and Rosemary Kalapurakal (1996), "Price Search in the Retail Grocery Market," *JM*, 60 (April), 91–104.

SCALE ITEMS:

Strongly
disagree   :___:___:___:___:___: Strongly agree
          1   2   3   4   5

1. I enjoy grocery shopping.

2. Grocery shopping is a chore. **(r)**

3. Grocery shopping is boring. **(r)**

4. Grocery shopping is a pain. **(r)**

5. I view grocery shopping in a positive way.

SCALE NAME: Shopping Enjoyment (Grocery)

SCALE DESCRIPTION: Five seven-point Likert-type items that measure the degree to which a consumer expresses positive feelings about grocery shopping activities.

SCALE ORIGIN: Although some of the items are similar to those in the scales of others, these items as a whole appear to be have been used first in published work by Putrevu and Ratchford (1997).

SAMPLES: Data were gathered by Putrevu and Ratchford (1997) using a mail survey to a random sample of grocery shoppers in a standard metropolitan statistical area in the northeastern United States. A total of **500** responses were used in the main analysis, and demographics of the final sample were similar to those of the population of interest.

RELIABILITY: An alpha of **.91** was reported for the scale (Putrevu and Ratchford 1997).

VALIDITY: Although the authors stated in general that the scales showed evidence of convergent, discriminant, and content validity, no details of the analyses were provided (Putrevu and Ratchford 1997).

ADMINISTRATION: The scale was part of a larger mail questionnaire (Putrevu and Ratchford 1997). Higher scores on the scale suggested that consumers experienced a lot of pleasure from grocery shopping.

MAJOR FINDINGS: Putrevu and Ratchford (1997) examined a dynamic model of consumer search behavior that includes human capital. The results indicated that the greater the **enjoyment of shopping**, the greater was the amount of external search.

REFERENCES:
Putrevu, Sanjay and Brian T. Ratchford (1997), "A Model of Search Behavior with an Application to Grocery Shopping," *JR*, 73 (4), 463–86.

SCALE ITEMS:

Strongly   Strongly
disagree   :___:___:___:___:___:___:___: agree
              1   2   3   4   5   6   7

1. I like grocery shopping.

2. I look forward to my weekly grocery shopping trip.

3. Grocery shopping is fun.

4. I hate grocery shopping. **(r)**

5. Grocery shopping is boring. **(r)**

SCALE NAME: Shopping Orientation (Acquisition)

SCALE DESCRIPTION: Three items purported to measure "the goal-directness of a functional economic shopper" when the goal is the purchase of a good or service (Roy 1994, p. 146). Two of the items were answered using a five-point Likert-type scale. The response format for the third item was not specified. Roy (1994) referred to the scale as *functional economic motivation.*

SCALE ORIGIN: Two items (1 and 2) were taken from two different dimensions of shopping motivation as measured by Westbrook and Black (1985).

SAMPLES: The data gathered by Roy (1994) came from usable responses from **710** shoppers at a large Southern California mall. Interviews were conducted over period of six days and at varying times of the day.

RELIABILITY: A composite reliability of **.62** was reported for the scale by Roy (1994).

VALIDITY: No examination of the scale's validity was reported by Roy (1994).

ADMINISTRATION: The scale was part of a much larger questionnaire apparently administered by a trained interviewer. Higher scores on the scale appeared to suggest that a shopper focused on getting what is needed in the least time possible.

MAJOR FINDINGS: The study by Roy (1994) examined some relationships between mall shopping frequency and other variables, such as demographics and shopping motivation. The results of the study provided support for the hypothesis that there is a significant negative relationship between **acquisition shopping orientation** and mall visit frequency.

COMMENTS: The reliability of the scale is low enough to indicate that it has poor internal consistency and that the items are probably not measuring the same dimension. Item 3 seems especially different from the other two. The scale deserves further improvement and testing before it is used again for hypothesis testing.

REFERENCES:
Roy, Abhik (1994), "Correlates of Mall Visit Frequency," *JR*, 70 (2), 139–61.
Westbrook, Robert A. and William C. Black (1985), "A Motivation-Based Shopper Typology," *JR*, 61 (Spring), 78–103.

SCALE ITEMS:*

Strongly   Strongly
disagree   :___:___:___:___:___: agree
              1   2   3   4   5

1. Shopping for a brand new item to replace and old one.

2. Finding exactly what I want in the least amount of time.

3. The amount spent on a typical trip to the mall.

*The scale stem and directions were not provided but would have likely been something such as *"For each of the statements below, please indicate the degree to which they characterize your reasons for shopping at the mall."* As noted, the response format for item 3 was not specified and might have been open-ended.

SCALE NAME: Shopping Orientation (Recreation)

SCALE DESCRIPTION: Three five-point Likert-type items purported to measure a consumer's need for affiliation when shopping and enjoyment of the sensory stimulation received from the experience. The author (Roy 1994, p. 147) also thought the scale tapped a little into the shopper's need for power and authority (item 2).

SCALE ORIGIN: The items were used first by Westbrook and Black (1985) as part of three different dimensions of shopping motivation.

SAMPLES: The data gathered by Roy (1994) came from usable responses from **710** shoppers at a large Southern California mall. Interviews were conducted over period of six days and at varying times of the day.

RELIABILITY: A composite reliability of **.58** was reported for the scale by Roy (1994).

VALIDITY: No examination of the scale's validity was reported by Roy (1994).

ADMINISTRATION: The scale was part of a much larger questionnaire apparently administered by a trained interviewer. Higher scores on the scale indicated that a shopper liked to shop for reasons related to recreation and personalizing.

MAJOR FINDINGS: The study by Roy (1994) examined some relationships between mall shopping frequency and other variables, such as demographics and shopping motivation. The results of the study provided support for the hypothesis that there is a significant positive relationship between **recreational shopping orientation** and mall visit frequency.

COMMENTS: The reliability of the scale is low enough to suggest that the items are not internally consistent and are probably not measuring the same dimension. Item 2 seems especially different from the other two. The scale deserves further improvement and testing before it is used again for hypothesis testing.

REFERENCES:
Roy, Abhik (1994), "Correlates of Mall Visit Frequency," *JR*, 70 (2), 139–61.
Westbrook, Robert A. and William C. Black (1985), "A Motivation-Based Shopper Typology," *JR*, 61 (Spring), 78–103.

SCALE ITEMS:

Strongly   Strongly
disagree   :___:___:___:___:___: agree
      1 2 3 4 5

1. I enjoy talking with salespeople and other shoppers who are interested in the same things as I am.

2. I like having a salesperson bring merchandise out for me to choose from.

3. I enjoy seeing mall exhibits while shopping.

SCALE NAME: Shopping Value (Hedonic)

SCALE DESCRIPTION: An eleven-item, five-point Likert-type measure of the degree to which a consumer views a recent shopping trip as having been an entertaining and emotionally driven activity. The shopping was enjoyed as an end in itself rather than as just a means to an end (obtaining goods and services).

SCALE ORIGIN: The scale is original to Babin, Darden, and Griffin (1994). The study approached the scale development process methodically with a concern about grounding the scales in theory as well as providing evidence of their psychometric quality.

A literature review, personal interviews, and focus group sessions were used to generate 71 items for this scale and a complementary one (#370). Three experts were provided definitions of the constructs and asked to sort the items into one of three groups: **hedonic**, utilitarian, and other. Forty-eight items were agreed on by all three judges. Five more were agreed on by two judges and with further discussion were retained for the next stage of analysis.

Data from a sample of 125 undergraduate students were used to purify the scales. The scales showed evidence of unidimensionality, reliability, and discriminant and convergent validity. Further testing was conducted to continue the validation process with a more diverse sample, as discussed subsequently.

SAMPLES: Data were gathered by Babin and Darden (1995) by intercepting shoppers as they left one of the ten top stores in a major Southeastern U.S. regional mall. Respondents were interviewed one at a time, and a small incentive was provided for their participation. The sample was considered to be representative of the mall's shoppers. The analysis appears to have been based on data from **118** shoppers.

A sample of adults living in a large Midwestern U.S. community provided data for a more rigorous series of psychometric tests (Babin, Darden, and Griffin 1994). Students were trained to conduct interviews and then were allowed to select potential respondents representative of a regional mall's demographic profile. Data were gathered before, during, and after the students accompanied respondents on a shopping trip to the mall. Ultimately, complete information was gathered from **404** respondents. Independent contact with some respondents at random provided no reason to suspect the authenticity of the data.

RELIABILITY: An alpha of **.91** was reported for the scale by Babin and Darden (1995). The construct reliability was .91, and variance extracted was .48. An alpha of **.93** was reported for the scale as used by Babin, Darden, and Griffin (1994), and the item–total correlations ranged from .67 to .80.

VALIDITY: The results of a confirmatory factor analysis supported the measurement model in both studies (Babin and Darden 1995; Babin, Darden, and Griffin 1994). This provided some limited evidence of the scale's unidimensionality, as well as its convergent and discriminant validities. To investigate the scale's nomological validity, the **shopping value (hedonic)** scale was correlated with other scales to which it was theorized to be related (Babin, Darden, and Griffin 1994). In general, the pattern of expectations was confirmed. (An example of this finding is described in the "Major Findings" section.)

ADMINISTRATION: Babin and Darden (1995) apparently had the scale administered to respondents by interviewers, along with many other items in a questionnaire. In the main part of the study by Babin, Darden, and Griffin (1994), data were gathered in several stages over time. Respondents were called three days after the shopping trip (described previously), and interviewers administered a few measures, including the **shopping value (hedonic)** scale.

The scale appears to be scored in such a way that higher values suggested a person considered a recent shopping trip to have been a pleasurable activity.

MAJOR FINDINGS: The purpose of the study by Babin and Darden (1995) was to examine the role of self-regulation as a moderator of relationships between shopping emotions and shopping experience evaluations. Among the findings was that arousal had significant positive impacts on resource expenditures and on both utilitarian and **hedonic shopping values**.

Babin, Darden, and Griffin (1994) reported a series of studies in which two scales were constructed and refined that measured two dimensions of personal shopping values: **hedonic** and utilitarian. In the process of establishing the scales' nomological validity, correlations with other variables they were expected to relate to were measured. For example, both scales were correlated with a measure of compulsive spending tendencies (#98). **Shopping value (hedonic)** was found to have a moderate but significant correlation with compulsive buying, whereas the shopping value (utilitarian) correlation was insignificant.

COMMENTS: Note that this scale was constructed such that subjects respond to the items <u>after</u> a shopping trip and the items refer specifically to that shopping trip. If there is interest in measuring a consumer's shopping orientation as a pattern followed over a longer period of time, a battery of other scales would need to be used (e.g., Vol. 1 #49, #184, #252, #255) or this one would need to be modified and retested.

REFERENCES:

Babin, Barry J. and William R. Darden (1995), "Consumer Self-Regulation in a Retail Environment," *JR*, 71 (1), 47–70.

———, ———, and Mitch Griffin (1994), "Work and/or Fun: Measuring Hedonic and Utilitarian Shopping Value," *JCR*, 20 (March), 644–56.

SCALE ITEMS:

Strongly   Strongly
disagree   :___:___:___:___:___: agree
                1   2   3   4   5

1. This shopping trip was truly a joy.

2. I continued to shop, not because I had to, but because I wanted to.

3. This shopping trip truly felt like an escape.

4. Compared to other things I could have done, the time spent shopping was truly enjoyable.

5. I enjoyed being immersed in exciting new products.

6. I enjoyed this shopping trip for its own sake, not just for the items I may have purchased.

7. I had a good time because I was able to act on the "spur of the moment."

8. During the trip, I felt the excitement of the hunt.

9. While shopping, I was able to forget my problems.

10. While shopping, I felt a sense of adventure.

11. This shopping trip was not a very nice time out. **(r)**

SCALE NAME: Shopping Value (Utilitarian)

SCALE DESCRIPTION: A four-item, five-point Likert-type measure of the degree to which a consumer agrees that a recent shopping trip allowed him or her to accomplish what was wanted (purchase of the items sought). The scale is supposed to tap into the view that shopping is primarily a means to an end (obtaining goods and services) rather than being enjoyed as an end in itself.

SCALE ORIGIN: The scale is original to Babin, Darden, and Griffin (1994). The study approached the scale development process methodically with a concern about grounding the scales in theory as well as providing evidence of their psychometric quality.

A literature review, personal interviews, and focus group sessions were used to generate 71 items for this scale and a complementary one (#369). Three experts were provided definitions of the constructs and asked to sort the items into one of three groups: hedonic, **utilitarian**, and other. Forty-eight items were agreed on by all three judges. Five more were agreed on by two judges and with further discussion were retained for the next stage of analysis.

Data from a sample of 125 undergraduate students were used to purify the scales. The scales showed evidence of unidimensionality, reliability, and discriminant and convergent validity. Further testing was conducted to continue the validation process with a more diverse sample, as discussed subsequently.

SAMPLES: Data were gathered by Babin and Darden (1995) by intercepting shoppers as they left one of the ten top stores in a major Southeastern U.S. regional mall. Respondents were interviewed one at a time, and a small incentive was provided for their participation. The sample was considered to be representative of the mall's shoppers. The analysis appears to have been based on data from **118** shoppers.

A sample of adults living in a large Midwestern U.S. community provided data for a more rigorous series of psychometric tests (Babin, Darden, and Griffin 1994). Students were trained to conduct interviews and then were allowed to select potential respondents representative of a regional mall's demographic profile. Data were gathered before, during, and after the students accompanied respondents on a shopping trip to the mall. Ultimately, complete information was gathered from **404** respondents. Independent contact with some respondents at random provided no reason to suspect the authenticity of the data.

RELIABILITY: An alpha of **.76** was reported for the scale by Babin and Darden (1995). The construct reliability was .76, and variance extracted was .45. An alpha of **.80** was reported for the scale as used by Babin, Darden, and Griffin (1994), and the item–total correlations ranged from .54 to .64.

VALIDITY: The results of a confirmatory factor analysis supported the measurement model in both studies (Babin and Darden 1995; Babin, Darden, and Griffin 1994). This provided some limited evidence of the scale's unidimensionality, as well as its convergent and discriminant validities. To investigate the scale's nomological validity, the **shopping value (utilitarian)** scale was correlated with other scales to which it was theorized to be related. In general, the pattern of expectations was confirmed. (An example of this finding is described in the "Major Findings" section.)

ADMINISTRATION: Babin and Darden (1995) apparently had the scale administered to respondents by interviewers, along with many other items in a questionnaire. In the main part of the study by Babin, Darden, and Griffin (1994), data were gathered in several stages over time. Respondents were called three days after the shopping trip (described previously), and interviewers administered a few measures, including the **shopping value (utilitarian)** scale.

The scale appears to be scored in such a way that higher values suggested a person considered a recent shopping trip to have accomplished what was planned in terms of purchasing products.

MAJOR FINDINGS: The purpose of the study by Babin and Darden (1995) was to examine the role of self-regulation as a moderator of relationships between shopping emotions and shopping experience evaluations. Among the findings was that arousal had significant positive impacts on resource expenditures and on both **utilitarian** and hedonic shopping values.

Babin, Darden, and Griffin (1994) reported a series of studies in which two scales were constructed and refined that measured two dimensions of personal shopping values: hedonic and **utilitarian**. In the process of establishing the scales' nomological validity, correlations with other variables they were expected to relate to were measured. For example, both scales were correlated with a measure of compulsive spending tendencies (#98). **Shopping value (utilitarian)** was not found to have a significant correlation with compulsive buying, whereas the shopping value (hedonic) measure had a modest and significant correlation.

COMMENTS: Note that this scale was constructed such that subjects respond to the items <u>after</u> a shopping trip and the items refer specifically to that shopping trip. If there is interest in measuring a consumer's shopping orientation as a pattern followed over a longer period of time, a battery of other scales would need to be used (e.g., V. I #49, #184, #252, #255) or this one would need to be modified and retested.

REFERENCES:
Babin, Barry J. and William R. Darden (1995), "Consumer Self-Regulation in a Retail Environment," *JR*, 71 (1), 47–70.
———, ———, and Mitch Griffin (1994), "Work and/or Fun: Measuring Hedonic and Utilitarian Shopping Value," *JCR*, 20 (March), 644–56.

SCALE ITEMS:

Strongly   Strongly
disagree   :___:___:___:___:___: agree
           1   2   3   4   5

1. I accomplished just what I wanted to on this shopping trip.

2. I couldn't buy what I really needed. **(r)**

3. While shopping, I found just the item(s) I was looking for.

4. I was disappointed because I had to go to another store(s) to complete my shopping. **(r)**

SCALE NAME: Skepticism

SCALE DESCRIPTION: Three seven-point descriptors relating to the level of doubt and uncertainty a consumer has with the veracity of some stimulus. In the study by Babin, Boles, and Darden (1995), the stimulus being evaluated was a car salesperson as described in text.

SCALE ORIGIN: The scale was developed by Holbrook and Batra (1988). Items were drawn from an exhaustive review of similar scales, and then the authors used their judgment to pick a few items to represent each of 29 emotional dimensions. Twelve judges were used to evaluate 72 commercials, and the alpha for the dimension represented by **skepticism** was reported to be .93.

SAMPLES: The data were gathered by Babin, Boles, and Darden (1995) from **163** undergraduate marketing students who were randomly assigned to one of three experimental conditions.

RELIABILITY: An alpha of **.93** was reported for the scale by Babin, Boles, and Darden (1995).

VALIDITY: No examination of the scale's validity was reported by Babin, Boles, and Darden (1995).

ADMINISTRATION: Babin, Boles, and Darden (1995) had subjects complete the scale, along with other measures, after they were exposed to experimental manipulation. A high score suggested that respondents had a feeling of mistrust and suspicion after they were exposed to some stimulus.

MAJOR FINDINGS: The study by Babin, Boles, and Darden (1995) examined salesperson stereotypes and their influence on the sales environment. The findings showed that the three types of car salespersons differed in the **skepticism** they evoked in consumers, such that the *pushy* and *typical* salespersons evoked approximately the same amount, but the *atypical* salesperson was associated with much less skepticism.

REFERENCES:
Babin, Barry J., James S. Boles, and William R. Darden (1995), "Salesperson Stereotypes, Consumer Emotions, and Their Impact on Information Processing," *JAMS*, 23 (Spring), 94–105.
Holbrook, Morris B. and Rajeev Batra (1988), "Toward a Standardized Emotional Profile (SEP) Useful in Measuring Responses to the Nonverbal Components of Advertising," in *Nonverbal Communication in Advertising*, Sidney Hecker and David W. Stewart, eds. Lexington, MA: D.C. Heath, 95-109.

SCALE ITEMS:

I felt:

Not at all   :___:___:___:___:___:___:___: Very
        1   2   3   4   5   6   7

1. Skeptical

2. Suspicious

3. Distrustful

SCALE NAME: Skin Cancer Knowledge

SCALE DESCRIPTION: Three Likert-type items measuring the extent to which a person describes him- or herself as knowledgeable about skin cancer, even more so than most people.

SCALE ORIGIN: No information about the scale's source was provided by Block and Keller (1995), but it appears to be original to their study.

SAMPLES: The scale was employed in just the second of two experiments conducted by Block and Keller (1995). The analysis seems to have been based on data from **115** undergraduate and graduate students. Students were compensated ($5) for their participation.

RELIABILITY: An alpha of **.86** was reported for the scale (Block and Keller 1995).

VALIDITY: No examination of the scale's validity was reported by Block and Keller (1995).

ADMINISTRATION: The scale was completed by subjects after they were exposed to some health-related information (Block and Keller 1995). High scores on the scale indicated that respondents considered themselves to be very knowledgeable about skin cancer, possibly more so than most people.

MAJOR FINDINGS: The purpose of the study by Block and Keller (1995) was to examine the relationships among level of efficacy, depth of processing, and framing effects. **Skin cancer knowledge** was measured merely to ensure that the attitude was not confounding experimental treatments, and indeed, the findings showed that subjects in the three conditions did not differ significantly in that regard.

REFERENCES:
Block, Lauren G. and Punam Anand Keller (1995), "When to Accentuate the Negative: The Effects of Perceived Efficacy and Message Framing on Intentions to Perform a Health-Related Behavior," *JMR*, 32 (May), 192–203.

SCALE ITEMS:*

Strongly disagree :___:___:___:___:___:___: Strongly agree
     1   2   3   4   5   6   7

1. I know a lot about skin cancer.

2. I know more about skin cancer than most people.

3. I know a lot about cancer in general.

*The actual response scale and number of points were not specified in the article but would appear to have been similar to what is shown here.

SCALE NAME: Skin Lotion Beliefs

SCALE DESCRIPTION: Five nine-point items that measure a person's beliefs about a skin lotion. In particular, the scale appears to measure the extent to which a person believes that a specific brand of skin lotion has certain benefits compared with other brands.

SCALE ORIGIN: Although not explicitly stated by Muthukrishnan (1995), the scale seems to be original to his study.

SAMPLES: Several experiments were conducted by Muthukrishnan (1995), but the scale appears to have been used in just Experiments 1 and 4. Experiment 1 recruited female volunteers from introductory marketing and psychology classes who were given extra credit for their participation. The scale was used in only one experimental condition, which had approximately 44 subjects. The sample in Experiment 4 was composed of 28 female undergraduates who were randomly assigned to two treatment groups.

RELIABILITY: An alpha of **.69** (Experiment 4) was reported for the scale by Muthukrishnan (1995). (No alpha was reported for the scale as used in Experiment 1).

VALIDITY: No examination of the scale's validity was reported by Muthukrishnan (1995).

ADMINISTRATION: Subjects completed the items in the scale after they were exposed to experimental stimuli (Muthukrishnan 1995). Higher scores on the scale indicated that respondents believed a particular brand of skin lotion had some specified benefits relative to other brands.

MAJOR FINDINGS: The general purpose of the five experiments reported by Muthukrishnan (1995) was to examine the role of decision ambiguity in judgments that consumers make about a currently used brand versus a new, superior competitor. Among those who chose a particular brand of skin lotion, those who thought it was the best brand on the basis of the available information had more extreme **beliefs** than those who thought there was a brand with better benefits (but that was not available for choice).

REFERENCES:
Muthukrishnan, A.V. (1995), "Decision Ambiguity and Incumbent Brand Advantage," *JCR*, 22 (June), 98–109.

SCALE ITEMS:

Least
likely
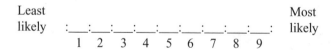

1. Promotes healthy skin texture

2. Restores lost moisture

3. Softens skin

4. Firms and conditions skin

5. Cleanses skin

SCALE NAME: Smartness

SCALE DESCRIPTION: A three-item, seven-point scale measuring the extent to which one person (target) is viewed by another person (respondent) as intelligent and healthy-looking. The scale was referred to as *common sense* by Pechmann and Ratneshwar (1994).

SCALE ORIGIN: The scale is apparently original to Pechmann and Ratneshwar (1994).

SAMPLES: Data were gathered by Pechmann and Ratneshwar (1994) from **304** seventh-grader students from four middle schools in Southern California. There were slightly more girls (58%) than boys. Schools were deliberately selected to ensure that they adequately represented the California student population on factors that might be related to smoking (gender, socioeconomic status, and race). Therefore, only 44% were white, and the remaining respondents identified with other groups.

RELIABILITY: An alpha of **.87** was reported for the scale (Pechmann and Ratneshwar 1994).

VALIDITY: No specific examination of the scale's validity was reported by Pechmann and Ratneshwar (1994). However, 13 items used to evaluate the target (Student A) were submitted to a factor analysis, and it was concluded that the three items composing this scale loaded together.

ADMINISTRATION: The scale was administered on a PC, along with other questionnaire items, after subjects were exposed to stimulus ads in a mock magazine (Pechmann and Ratneshwar 1994). Higher scores on the scale suggested that respondents viewed someone as intelligent and healthy.

MAJOR FINDINGS: Pechmann and Ratneshwar (1994) examined the impact of smoking and anti-smoking ads on nonsmoking youth's evaluative judgments of a peer who smokes. The results indicated that those who watched antismoking ads (versus unrelated ones) rated a peer who smoked as significantly less **smart** than another (control) peer.

REFERENCES:
Pechmann, Cornelia and S. Ratneshwar (1994), "The Effects of Antismoking and Cigarette Advertising on Young Adolescents' Perceptions of Peers Who Smoke," *JCR*, 21 (September), 236–51.

SCALE ITEMS:

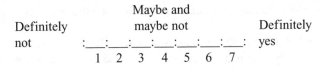

	Maybe and	
Definitely	maybe not	Definitely
not	:___:___:___:___:___:___:	yes
	1　2　3　4　5　6　7	

1. Intelligent

2. Smart

3. Healthy

SCALE NAME: Social Desirability Bias (Marlowe-Crowne)

SCALE DESCRIPTION: A summated ratings scale purporting to measure the degree to which people describe themselves in socially acceptable terms to gain the approval of others. The original version of the scale has 33 items and uses a true/false response format. However, abbreviated versions have typically been used in marketing research, and Likert-type response scales have been applied in a couple of cases.

SCALE ORIGIN: The scale was developed by Crowne and Marlowe (1960) by generating items related to behaviors that are culturally sanctioned but unlikely to occur. Two sets of ten faculty and graduate student judges helped narrow an original inventory of 50 items down to the final set of 33. An internal consistency of .88 (K-R 20) was calculated for the scale using a sample of 10 male and 29 female undergraduates in an abnormal psychology class at Ohio State University. Their mean age was 24.4 years, with a range of 19 to 46 years. Thirty-one of these same people completed the instrument a month later, and a test–retest correlation of .89 was calculated. Scores of those 31 students plus 81 others in a course on exceptional children were found to have a correlation of .35 ($p < .01$) with scores on the Edward's Social Desirability Scale. Considerable work was performed on correlating scale scores with Minnesota Multiphasic Personality Inventory (MMPI) variables. The authors interpreted the findings as being "more in accord with a definition of social desirability" than the Edwards scale (Crowne and Marlowe 1960, p. 354).

Examinations of abbreviated versions of the scale can be found in Ballard, Crino, and Rubenfeld (1988), Fraboni and Cooper (1989), Reynolds (1982), and Strahan and Gerbasi (1972).

SELECTED SAMPLES: The same data set was reported on in two articles by Carlson and Grossbart (1988; Grossbart, Carlson, and Walsh 1991). The survey instrument was distributed to mothers of students at three elementary schools of an unidentified U.S. city. The schools were chosen on a convenience basis but appeared to represent a variety of socioeconomic areas of the city. An $1 contribution to the parent–teacher organization for each completed questionnaire returned by the children was offered. Analysis was based on **451** completed questionnaires. Ninety-three percent of the responding mothers indicated that they were the primary person in the child's socialization.

The scale was used by Mick (1996) in the first of two studies he conducted. Data were collected in the first study from **266** respondents contacted through a quota-convenience sample. Students taking a marketing research course were asked to distribute the surveys following firm guidelines. The sample was split evenly (50.8% female) on gender, and the mean age was 43.2 years.

The study by Moore, Bearden, and Teel (1985) was based on complete responses received over three time periods from **198** members of the University of South Carolina Consumer Panel. Comparison of the known characteristics of the respondents and the total 360 members of the panel did not indicate any significant response bias.

Various samples were collected and used by Netemeyer, Burton, and Lichtenstein (1995), though the **social desirability bias** scale was used only in Study 1. It had two groups: 145 students from a major American university and 277 "nonstudent adults."

Studies with four samples were described in the article by Richins and Dawson (1992), but the social desirability scale was used in just Survey 1. Little was said about the sample except that the data came from a mail survey of people in a medium-sized Northeastern U.S. city. The households were randomly chosen and sent a survey form, followed by a reminder letter, and a second copy of the questionnaire two weeks later. The response rate was 36%, resulting in **144** usable questionnaires.

SELECTED RELIABILITIES: Many of the studies did not provide any information regarding the reliability of the scale. Reliabilities are provided for the studies described in the "Selected Samples" and "Selected Findings" sections:

.71 by Grossbart, Carlson, and Walsh (1991);
.80 (K-R 20) by Mick (1996);
.83 (K-R 20) by Moore, Bearden, and Teel (1985);
.72 and **.77** for the student and nonstudent samples, respectively, by Netemeyer, Burton, and Lichtenstein (1995; Netemeyer 1997); and
.70 by Richins and Dawson (1992; Richins 1994).

VALIDITY: Grossbart, Carlson, and Walsh (1991) reported a beta of .50 for the modified version of the scale they used. Some evidence of the ten-item version's convergent validity was provided by Goldsmith and Hofacker (1991), who reported a significant positive correlation between the social desirability scale and a lie scale (Eysenck 1958).

No specific examination of the scale's validity was conducted in the other studies. However, as described in the findings, the scale has been typically used to provide evidence of other scales' discriminant validity.

ADMINISTRATION: The scale was self-administered in all of the studies along with other scales. Scores on the original version of the scale ranged between 0 and 33. The higher the score on the scale, the more it appeared that a person tends to respond to questions in a manner he or she deems socially desirable, whereas a low score implied that the respondent is less likely to answer questions that way.

SELECTED FINDINGS: Carlson and Grossbart (1988; Grossbart, Carlson, and Walsh 1991) investigated the relationship between general parental socialization styles and children's consumer socialization. **Social desirability bias** was not specifically focused on in the study but was merely included as a covariate. It was found to be positively related to the shopping with child scale and negatively related to the materialism scale.

The effect of **social desirability bias** on the nomological network surrounding the materialism construct was examined by Mick (1996). He found in his two studies that self-esteem had a significant positive correlation with **social desirability bias**, most particularly with a component referred to as self-deception.

The influence of labeling ("helpful people like yourself") and dependency ("depend upon individual contributions") on potential donor attitudes was examined by Moore, Bearden, and Teel (1985). The **social desirability** scale did not have significant correlations with any of the covariate or dependent measures used in the study.

Netemeyer, Burton, and Lichtenstein (1995) investigated vanity and developed four scales for its measurement. Most of the article discussed the results of the rather extensive validation process. Although the correlations between **social desirability bias** and the vanity scales tended to be low or insignificant, significant negative correlations were found between it and achievement concern vanity (#395).

The purpose of the several surveys conducted by Richins and Dawson (1992) was to construct a new measure of materialism. To examine the scale's discriminant validity, the association between materialism and **social desirability** was tested. Near-zero correlations were found between the two constructs, as well as between **social desirability** and the materialism subscales (success, centrality, and happiness).

COMMENTS: This scale is typically used when constructing scales for measuring particular constructs, not by itself. If the correlation between scores on the social desirability scale and another measure is high, it suggests the latter is measuring respondents' desire to answer in socially acceptable ways. If the correlation is low, it is evidence that the scale is relatively free of social desirability bias. Some caution in its use may be called for because it may not be unidimensional, as indicated by its low beta coefficient (Grossbart, Carlson, and Walsh 1991). Further validation is needed.

See other uses of the scale by Bagozzi and Warshaw (1990); Childers, Houston, and Heckler (1985); Friedman and Churchill (1987); Putrevu and Lord (1994); Raju (1980); Richins (1983); Saxe and Weitz (1982); Unger and Kerman (1983); and Westbrook (1980, 1987).

REFERENCES:

Bagozzi, Richard P. (1994), personal correspondence.

——— and Paul R. Warshaw (1990), "Trying to Consume," *JCR*, 17 (September), 127–40.

Ballard, Rebecca, Michael D. Crino, and Stephen Rubenfeld (1988), "Social Desirability Response Bias and the Marlowe-Crowne Social Desirability Scale," *Psychological Reports*, 63 (August), 227–37.

Carlson, Les and Sanford Grossbart (1988), "Parental Style and Consumer Socialization of Children," *JCR*, 15 (June), 77–94.

Childers, Terry L., Michael J. Houston, and Susan E. Heckler (1985), "Measurement of Individual Differences in Visual Versus Verbal Information Processing," *JCR*, 12 (September), 125–34.

Crowne, Douglas P. and David Marlowe (1960), "A New Scale of Social Desirability Independent of Psychopathology," *Journal of Consulting Psychology*, 24 (August), 349–54.

Eysenck, Hans J. (1958), "A Short Questionnaire for the Measurement of Two Dimensions of Personality," *Journal of Applied Psychology*, 42, 14-17.

Fisher, Robert J. (1993), "Social Desirability Bias and the Validity of Indirect Questioning," *JCR*, 20 (September), 303–15.

Fraboni, Maryann and Douglas Cooper (1989), "Further Validation of Three Short Forms of the Marlowe-Crowne Scale of Social Desirability," *Psychological Reports*, 65 (2), 595–600.

Friedman, Margaret L. and Gilbert A. Churchill Jr. (1987), "Using Consumer Perceptions and a Contingency Approach to Improve Health Care Delivery," *JCR*, 13 (March), 492–510.

Goldsmith, Ronald E. and Charles F. Hofacker (1991), "Measuring Consumer Innovativeness," *JAMS*, 19 (Summer), 209–21.

Grossbart, Sanford, Les Carlson, and Ann Walsh (1991), "Consumer Socialization and Frequency of Shopping with Children," *JAMS*, 19 (Summer), 155–63.

Mick, David Glen (1996), "Are Studies of Dark Side Variables Confounded by Socially Desirable Responding? The Case of Materialism," *JCR*, 23 (September), 106–19.

Moore, Ellen M., William O. Bearden, and Jesse E. Teel (1985), "Use of Labeling and Assertions of Dependency in Appeals for Consumer Support," *JCR*, 12 (June), 90–96.

Netemeyer, Richard G. (1997), personal correspondence.

———, Scot Burton, and Donald R. Lichtenstein (1995), "Trait Aspects of Vanity: Measurement and Relevance to Consumer Behavior," *JCR*, 21 (March), 612–26.

Putrevu, Sanjay and Kenneth R. Lord (1994), "Comparative and Noncomparative Advertising: Attitudinal Effects Under Cognitive and Affective Involvement Conditions," *JA*, 23 (June), 77–90.

Raju, P. S. (1980), "Optimum Stimulation Level: Its Relationship to Personality, Demographics, and Exploratory Behavior," *JCR*, 7 (December), 272–82.

Reynolds, William M. (1982), "Development of Reliable and Valid Short Forms of the Marlowe-Crowne Social Desirability Scale," *Journal of Clinical Psychology*, 38 (January), 119–25.

Richins, Marsha L. (1983), "An Analysis of Consumer Interaction Styles in the Marketplace," *JCR*, 10 (June), 73–82.

——— (1994), personal correspondence.

——— and Scott Dawson (1992), "A Consumer Values Orientation for Materialism and Its Measurement: Scale Development and Validation," *JCR*, 19 (December), 303–16.

Saxe, Robert and Barton A. Weitz (1982), "The SOCO Scale: A Measure of the Customer Orientation of Salespeople," *JMR*, 19 (August), 343–51.

Strahan, Robert and Kathleen Carrese Gerbasi (1972), "Short, Homogeneous Versions of the Marlowe-Crowne Social Desirability Scale," *Journal of Clinical Psychology*, 28 (April), 191–93.

Unger, Lynette S. and Jerome B. Kernan (1983), "On the Meaning of Leisure: An Investigation of Some Determinants of the Subjective Experience," *JCR*, 9 (March), 381–91.

Westbrook, Robert A. (1980), "Intrapersonal Affective Influences on Consumer Satisfaction with Products," *JCR*, 7 (June), 49–54.

——— (1987), "Product/Consumption-Based Affective Responses and Postpurchase Processes," *JMR*, 24 (August), 258–70.

SCALE ITEMS:*

1. Before voting I thoroughly investigate the qualifications of all the candidates. (T)
2. I never hesitate to go out of my way to help someone in trouble. (T)
3. It is sometimes hard for me to go on with my work if I am not encouraged.   (F)
4. I have never intensely disliked anyone. (T)
5. On occasion I have had doubts about my ability to succeed in life. (F)
6. I sometimes feel resentful when I don't get my way. (F)
7. I am always careful about my manner of dress. (T)
8. My table manners at home are as good as when I eat out in a restaurant. (T)
9. If I could get into a movie without paying and be sure I was not seen I would probably do it. (F)
10. On a few occasions, I have given up doing something because I thought too little of my ability. (F)
11. I like gossip at times. (F)
12. There have been times when I felt like rebelling against people in authority even though I knew they were right. (F)
13. No matter who I'm talking to, I'm always a good listener. (T)
14. I can remember "playing sick" to get out of something. (F)
15. There have been occasions when I took advantage of someone. (F)
16. I'm always willing to admit it when I've made a mistake. (T)
17. I always try to practice what I preach. (T)
18. I don't find it particularly difficult to get along with loud-mouthed, obnoxious people. (T)
19. I sometimes try to get even rather than forgive and forget. (F)
20. When I don't know something I don't at all mind admitting it. (T)
21. I am always courteous, even to people who are disagreeable. (T)
22. At times I have really insisted on having things my way. (F)
23. There have been occasions when I felt like smashing things. (F)
24. I would never think of letting someone else be punished for my wrong-doings. (T)
25. I never resent being asked to return a favor. (T)
26. I have never been irked when people expressed ideas very different from my own. (T)
27. I never make a long trip without checking the safety of my car. (T)
28. There have been times when I was quite jealous of the good fortune of others. (F)
29. I have almost never felt the urge to tell someone off. (T)
30. I am sometimes irritated by people who ask favors of me. (F)
31. I have never felt that I was punished without cause. (T)
32. I sometimes think when people have a misfortune they only got what they deserved. (F)
33. I have never deliberately said something that hurt someone's feelings. (T)

* Respondents should receive a point each time they answer in a socially desirable manner. Social desirability is indicated if respondents answer as indicated at the end of each item . For example, if a respondent answers "true" to item 1, that is considered to be answering in a socially desirable manner.

Carlson and Grossbart (1988; Grossbart, Carlson, and Walsh 1991): 1–19; T/F
Fisher (1993): 3, 6, 10, 12, 13, 15, 16, 19, 21, 26, 28, 30, and 33; T/F
Goldsmith and Hofacker (1991): 11, 15–17, 19, 22, 23, 25, 26, and 33; T/F
Mick (1996): 1–33; T/F
Netemeyer, Burton, and Lichtenstein (1995): 11, 15–17, 19, 22, 23, 25, 26, and 33; 7-point
Richins and Dawson (1992): 6–8, 12, 16, 19, 21, 26, 30, and 33; 5-point

SCALE NAME: Status Concern

SCALE DESCRIPTION: Ten seven-point Likert-type statements that evaluate the degree to which a person values ambition and social status as appropriate life goals.

SCALE ORIGIN: The scale is original to the study by Kaufman (1957). He mentioned that the reliability (split-half) was .78 but that the evidence indicated the scale was not "strictly unidimensional."

SAMPLES: Various samples were collected and used by Netemeyer, Burton, and Lichtenstein (1995) in the process of validating some other scales. The **status concern** scale was used in one study composed of 186 students and 264 "nonstudent adults." Another study was conducted using addresses found in a *Who's Who* directory for one state. Analysis was based on the 267 completed questionnaires that were returned. Yet another study focused on 27 football players from a nationally ranked NCAA Division I team.

RELIABILITY: An alpha of **.85** was found for scale in both samples of the first study (Netemeyer 1997; Netemeyer, Burton, and Lichtenstein 1995).

VALIDITY: Although the validity of the scale was not directly examined by Netemeyer, Burton, and Lichtenstein (1995), it was used to help establish the construct validity of four vanity-related scales. **Status concern** had positive correlations with all of the vanity scales, but their strength and significance depended on the sample.

ADMINISTRATION: As noted, the scale was used in three studies, and it appears to have been part of larger questionnaires that were self-administered by respondents (Netemeyer, Burton, and Lichtenstein 1995). Higher scores on the scale indicated that respondents were very sensitive toward the roles ambition and status play in achieving success.

MAJOR FINDINGS: Netemeyer, Burton, and Lichtenstein (1995) investigated vanity and developed four scales for its measurement. Most of the article discussed the results of the rather extensive validation process. As noted, the findings indicated that **status concern** had positive relationships with each of the vanity scales. The strongest relationship across all samples appeared to be with achievement concern vanity (#395).

REFERENCES:
Kaufman, Walter C. (1957), "Status, Authoritarianism, and Anti-Semitism," *The American Journal of Sociology*, 62 (January), 379–82.
Netemeyer, Richard G. (1997), personal correspondence.
———, Scot Burton, and Donald R. Lichtenstein (1995), "Trait Aspects of Vanity: Measurement and Relevance to Consumer Behavior," *JCR*, 21 (March), 612–26.

SCALE ITEMS:

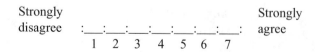

Strongly disagree :___:___:___:___:___:___:___: Strongly agree
            1   2   3   4   5   6   7

1. The extent of a man's ambition to better himself is a pretty good indication of his character.

2. In order to merit the respect of others, a person should show the desire to better himself.

3. One of the things you should consider in choosing friends is whether they can help you make your way in the world.

4. Ambition is the most important factor in determining success in life.

5. One should always try to live in a highly respectable area, even though it entails sacrifices.

6. Before joining any civic or political association, it is usually important to find out whether it has the backing of people who have achieved a respected social position.

7. Possession of proper social etiquette is usually the mark of a desirable person.

8. The raising of one's social position is one of the more important goals in life.

9. It is worth considerable effort to assure one's self of a good name with the right kind of people.

10. An ambitious person can almost always achieve his goals.

SCALE NAME: Status Consumption

SCALE DESCRIPTION: Five Likert-type statements measuring the tendency to purchase goods and services for the social prestige they give to their users. The construct has been defined by its authors as "the motivational process by which individuals strive to improve their social standing through the conspicuous consumption of consumer products that confer and symbolize status both for the individual and the surrounding others" (Eastman, Goldsmith, and Flynn 1997, p. 8).

SCALE ORIGIN: The scale used by Flynn, Goldsmith, and Eastman (1996) was developed by Eastman in her doctoral dissertation (Kilsheimer 1993). Many studies have subsequently been performed using the scale, most of which are reported in Eastman, Goldsmith, and Flynn (1997). As reported there, the original version of the scale had fourteen items and was not unidimensional. Subsequent work led to the reduction of the scale to five items.

SAMPLES: Flynn, Goldsmith, and Eastman (1996) reported on five studies, but only one (Study 3) employed the **status consumption** scale. Data for that study came from **391** undergraduate students at a large university. Questionnaires were completed in class. The respondents ranged in age from 18 to 64 years (median = 21). The sample was 72% women and 83% white.

RELIABILITY: The alpha for the fourteen-item version of the scale used by Flynn, Goldsmith, and Eastman (1996) was **.89** (Eastman, Goldsmith, and Flynn 1997). The five-item version has had alphas ranging from .81 to .87 and a stability (six week test–retest) of .78 (Eastman, Goldsmith, and Flynn 1997).

VALIDITY: Although no examination of the scale's validity was reported by Flynn, Goldsmith, and Eastman (1996), quite a bit of work has been conducted and reported elsewhere (e.g., Eastman, Goldsmith, and Flynn 1997). As noted, the fourteen-item version of the scale was multidimensional, and considerable work was conducted to develop and test the five-item version. It has been found to be unidimensional and free from social desirability response bias, and evidence has been collected in support of its criterion and construct validities.

ADMINISTRATION: In the study by Flynn, Goldsmith, and Eastman (1996), the scale was part of a larger survey instrument self-administered by students in class. Higher scores on the scale indicated that respondents tended to buy products because of the perceived status they confer on those who own them.

MAJOR FINDINGS: Flynn, Goldsmith, and Eastman (1996) reported on the development and testing of opinion leadership and opinion-seeking scales. **Status consumption** was included, along with several other measures, merely to help establish the nomological validity of the two opinion-related scales. **Status consumption** had a moderate positive association with opinion leadership and a weak but still significant relationship with opinion seeking.

COMMENTS: Eastman strongly urged the use of the five-item version of the scale (1997). Note also that a Spanish version of that scale has been developed and tested (Eastman et al. 1997).

REFERENCES:
Eastman, Jacqueline K. (1997), personal correspondence.

———, Bill Fredenberger, David Campbell, and Stephen Calvert (1997), "The Relationship Between Status Consumption and Materialism: A Cross-Cultural Comparison of Chinese, Mexican, and American Students," *Journal of Marketing Theory and Practice*, 5 (Winter), 52–66.

————, Ronald E. Goldsmith, and Leisa R. Flynn (1997), "Status Consumption in Consumer Behavior: Scale Development and Validation," working paper.

Flynn, Leisa R., Ronald E. Goldsmith, and Jacqueline K. Eastman (1996), "Opinion Leaders and Opinion Seekers: Two New Measurement Scales," *JAMS*, 24 (Spring), 137–47.

Kilsheimer, Jacqueline C. (1993), "Status Consumption: The Development ad Implications of a Scale Measuring the Motivation to Consume for Status," doctoral dissertation, Florida State University.

SCALE ITEMS:*

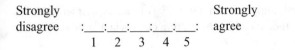

Strongly
disagree   :___:___:___:___:___: agree
        1   2   3   4   5

Strongly agree

1. I am interested in new products with status.

2. I would buy a product just because it has status.

3. I would pay more for a product if it had status.

4. The status of a product is irrelevant to me. **(r)**

5. A product is more valuable to me if has some snob appeal.

*These items represent the version of the scale that has been validated.

#378 *Store Design*

SCALE NAME: Store Design

SCALE DESCRIPTION: A four-item, seven-point Likert-type scale measuring the degree to which a customer holds positive perceptions of a retail store's facilities, particularly with regard to interior design factors such as color scheme and organization of merchandise.

SCALE ORIGIN: The origin of the scale was not stated explicitly by Baker, Grewal, and Parasuraman (1994). It may have been developed for their study, though they drew heavily on Baker (1986).

SAMPLES: Data were collected by Baker, Grewal, and Parasuraman (1994) in an experiment involving **297** subjects. The subjects were undergraduate students taking marketing classes at a large university.

RELIABILITY: An alpha of **.78** was reported for the scale by Baker, Grewal, and Parasuraman (1994).

VALIDITY: The validity of the scale was not specifically addressed by Baker, Grewal, and Parasuraman (1994). However, a sense of the scale's unidimensionality comes from the results of a principal components factor analysis they conducted, which shows that items from this scale as well as two others supported a three-factor solution.

ADMINISTRATION: After subjects watched videotapes, they were asked to complete a self-administered questionnaire that contained this scale, among others (Baker, Grewal, and Parasuraman 1994). High scores on the scale suggested that respondents believed the interior design of a store is pleasant and attractive.

MAJOR FINDINGS: Baker, Grewal, and Parasuraman (1994) investigated how retail store environment affects consumers' attitudes about service and product quality. The results indicated that *ambient* and *social* factors significantly influenced **store images** but a **store design** factor did not.

REFERENCES:
Baker, Julie (1986), "The Role of the Environment in Marketing Services: The Consumer Perspective," in *The Services Challenge: Integrating for Competitive Advantage*, John A. Czepiel et al., eds. Chicago, IL: American Marketing Association, 79–84.
———, Dhruv Grewal, and A. Parasuraman (1994), "The Influence of Store Environment on Quality Inferences and Store Image," *JAMS*, 22 (4), 328–39.

SCALE ITEMS:

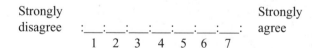

Strongly disagree :__:__:__:__:__:__:__: Strongly agree
          1 2 3 4 5 6 7

1. The color scheme was pleasing.

2. The colors used in the store appeared to be currently fashionable.

3. The physical facilities were attractive.

4. The merchandise in the store appeared organized.

SCALE NAME: Store Image (Pleasantness)

SCALE DESCRIPTION: A four-item, seven-point Likert-type scale measuring the degree to which a customer holds positive perceptions of a retail store, particularly with regard to the pleasantness of shopping there.

SCALE ORIGIN: The scale as a whole is probably original to Baker, Grewal, and Parasuraman (1994), though they say they drew on previous work by others.

SAMPLES: Data were collected by Baker, Grewal, and Parasuraman (1994) in an experiment involving **297** subjects. The subjects were undergraduate students taking marketing classes at a large university.

RELIABILITY: An alpha of **.81** was reported for the scale by Baker, Grewal, and Parasuraman (1994).

VALIDITY: The validity of the scale was not specifically addressed by Baker, Grewal, and Parasuraman (1994). A sense of its unidimensionality can be gleaned, however, from the results of the principal components factor analysis that was conducted on items from this scale as well as two others. The four items in this scale loaded highest on the same factor ($\geq.70$) and had low loadings on the other two factors ($\leq.38$).

ADMINISTRATION: After subjects watched videotapes, they were asked to complete a self-administered questionnaire that contained this scale, among others (Baker, Grewal, and Parasuraman 1994). High scores on the scale suggested that respondents had positive images of some specified store such that they believe it is a pleasant place to shop.

MAJOR FINDINGS: Baker, Grewal, and Parasuraman (1994) investigated how retail store environment affects consumers' attitudes about service and product quality. The results indicated that *ambient* and *social* factors significantly influenced **store images** but a *design* factor did not.

REFERENCES:
Baker, Julie, Dhruv Grewal, and A. Parasuraman (1994), "The Influence of Store Environment on Quality Inferences and Store Image," *JAMS*, 22 (4), 328–39.

SCALE ITEMS:

Strongly   Strongly
disagree   :__:__:__:__:__:__:__: agree
             1   2   3   4   5   6   7

1. This store would be a pleasant place to shop.

2. The store has a pleasant atmosphere.

3. This store is clean.

4. The store is attractive.

SCALE NAME: Store Personnel (Quantity and Quality)

SCALE DESCRIPTION: A four-item, seven-point Likert-type scale measuring a shopper's attitude about the number and quality of the employees working in a store. Although Baker, Levy, and Grewal (1992) and Baker, Grewal, and Parasuraman (1994) described the scale as measuring "the store social factor," it is clear from an examination of the items that only the employee aspect of retail social interaction was assessed.

SCALE ORIGIN: The scale used by Baker, Levy, and Grewal (1992) and Baker, Grewal, and Parasuraman (1994) was original to the former study (Baker 1993).

SAMPLES: The data analyzed by Baker, Levy, and Grewal (1992) came from an experiment using **147** undergraduate students. The study used a 2 (store ambient levels) × 2 (store social levels) between-subjects factorial design with between 35 to 39 subjects per cell.

Data were collected by Baker, Grewal, and Parasuraman (1994) in an experiment involving **297** subjects. The subjects were undergraduate students taking marketing classes at a large university.

RELIABILITY: Alphas of **.86** and **.83** were reported for the scale by Baker, Levy, and Grewal (1992) and Baker, Grewal, and Parasuraman (1994), respectively.

VALIDITY: No examination of the scale's validity was reported in either study. However, a sense of the scale's unidimensionality is provided in Baker, Grewal, and Parasuraman (1994), where it is stated that the results of a principal components factor analysis conducted on items from this scale as well as two others supported a three-factor solution.

ADMINISTRATION: The scale was self-administered by subjects as part of a larger questionnaire after they were exposed to experimental stimuli (Baker, Grewal, and Parasuraman 1994; Baker, Levy, and Grewal 1992). A high score on the scale indicated that a consumer had a positive opinion about the quantity and quality of employees observed in a store, whereas a low score suggested that a shopper considered several aspects of the store's personnel to be inadequate.

MAJOR FINDINGS: The study by Baker, Levy, and Grewal (1992) examined the effects of two retail atmospheric factors, ambient and social cues, on respondents' pleasure, arousal, and shopping intentions. Measurement of attitude about the adequacy of **store personnel** was used only as a check on an experimental treatment, and indeed, the results indicated that the manipulation was perceived as intended.

Baker, Grewal, and Parasuraman (1994) investigated how retail store environment affects consumers' attitudes about service and product quality. The results indicated that attitudes regarding background music and **store personnel** significantly influenced store images, but a design factor did not.

COMMENTS: Some slight modification in the wording of the items might be necessary if the scale is used with actual shoppers rather than subjects simulating a shopping experience as in the experiment described here.

REFERENCES:

Baker, Julie (1993), personal correspondence.

————, Dhruv Grewal, and A. Parasuraman (1994), "The Influence of Store Environment on Quality Inferences and Store Image," *JAMS*, 22 (4), 328–39.

————, Michael Levy, and Dhruv Grewal (1992), "An Experimental Approach to Making Retail Store Environmental Decisions," *JR*, 68 (Winter), 445–60.

SCALE ITEMS:

Strongly   Strongly
disagree   :___:___:___:___:___:___:___: agree
               1   2   3   4   5   6   7

1. There were enough employees in the store to service customers.

2. The employees were dressed and appeared neat.

3. The employees seemed like they would be friendly.

4. The employees seemed like they would be helpful.

SCALE NAME: Superiority

SCALE DESCRIPTION: Five seven-point Likert-type statements that evaluate a person's sense of being special and having very high (and possibly exaggerated) self-esteem.

SCALE ORIGIN: The scale is original to the study by Raskin and Terry (1988) and is part of the narcissistic personality inventory (NPI). Of the 40-item NPI, the five items shown here loaded highest on the same dimension and were labeled **superiority**. The internal consistency of these items as a set was estimated to be .54 (n = 1018). The scale showed little or no relationship with age and gender. Evidence in support of the scale's nomological validity was provided.

SAMPLES: Various samples were collected and used by Netemeyer, Burton, and Lichtenstein (1995) in the process of validating some other scales. The **superiority** scale was used in one study composed of 186 students and 264 "nonstudent adults." It was used in another study with data from 27 football players from a nationally ranked NCAA Division I team.

RELIABILITY: Alphas of **.78** (students) and **.76** (nonstudents adults) were found for the scale (Netemeyer 1997; Netemeyer, Burton, and Lichtenstein 1995).

VALIDITY: Although the validity of the scale was not directly examined by Netemeyer, Burton, and Lichtenstein (1995), the scale was used to help establish the construct validity of four vanity-related scales. **Superiority** had significant positive correlations with all of the vanity scales.

ADMINISTRATION: As noted, the scale was used in two studies, and it appears to have been part of larger questionnaires that were self-administered by respondents (Netemeyer, Burton, and Lichtenstein 1995). Higher scores on the scale indicated that respondents viewed themselves as exceptional individuals.

MAJOR FINDINGS: Netemeyer, Burton, and Lichtenstein (1995) investigated vanity and developed four scales for its measurement. Most of the article discussed the results of the rather extensive validation process. Among the findings was that **superiority** had strong positive relationships with each of the vanity scales, though the strongest relationship appeared to depend on the sample.

REFERENCES:

Netemeyer, Richard G. (1997), personal correspondence.

————, Scot Burton, and Donald R. Lichtenstein (1995), "Trait Aspects of Vanity: Measurement and Relevance to Consumer Behavior," *JCR*, 21 (March), 612–26.

Raskin, Robert and Howard Terry (1988), "A Principal-Components Analysis of the Narcissistic Personality Inventory and Further Evidence of its Construct Validity," *Journal of Personality and Social Psychology*, 54 (May), 890–902.

SCALE ITEMS:

Strongly   Strongly
disagree   :___:___:___:___:___:___:___: agree
                  1   2   3   4   5   6   7

1. I am an extraordinary person.

2. I know that I am good because everybody keeps telling me so.

3. I like to be complimented.

4. I think I am a very special person.

5. I wish somebody would someday write my biography.

SCALE NAME: Supply Control (Electricity)

SCALE DESCRIPTION: Three seven-point Likert-type statements measuring the extent to which a consumer is unwilling to let his or her electrical supplier control the limit of the power that a household receives.

SCALE ORIGIN: The scale is original to Osterhus (1997). His purpose with the scale was to operationalize a *personal cost* construct in the context of energy conservation.

SAMPLES: The sample for the study by Osterhus (1997) came from rural, urban, and suburban neighborhoods of a Midwestern U.S. area. Subjects were recruited with random-digit dialing and then sent a paper questionnaire. Nonrespondents were mailed another questionnaire. Ultimately, **1128** usable responses were received.

RELIABILITY: An alpha of **.78** was reported for the scale by Osterhus (1997).

VALIDITY: Confirmatory factor analysis was used by Osterhus (1997) to help purify the scales. Although details of the quality of the **supply control** scale were not specified, support for the scale's convergent and discriminant validities was implied.

ADMINISTRATION: The scale was self-administered by respondents, along with other measures, in a mail survey format (Osterhus 1997). Higher scores on the scale suggested that respondents were unwilling to give up control over the amount of power that their households receive to their electrical supplier. In the terminology of the study's author, they were not willing to pay the *personal cost* of this electrical conservation activity.

MAJOR FINDINGS: Osterhus (1997) investigated how and when prosocial positions are expected to influence consumer choice. Among the findings was that **supply control** was found to have a significantly negative behavioral impact; that is, higher scores on the **control** scale were associated with lower willingness to allow interruptions of power to air conditioners.

REFERENCES:
Osterhus, Thomas L. (1997), "Pro-Social Consumer Influence Strategies: When and How Do They Work?" *JM*, 61 (October), 16–29.

SCALE ITEMS:

Disagree :___:___:___:___:___:___:___: Agree
         1   2   3   4   5   6   7

1. I couldn't accept any restriction on the amount of electrical power used in my household at any time.

2. Letting the electrical company limit the amount of use of electricity would interfere with the comfort of our home.

3. I wouldn't want to put up with worrying about when the electric company might want me to limit my use of electricity.

SCALE NAME: Support for Customers

SCALE DESCRIPTION: Fourteen seven-point Likert-type items measuring a customer's perception of the degree to which a store values his or her business and cares about his or her well-being.

SCALE ORIGIN: The scale used by Bettencourt (1997) is a modification of the short form of the organizational support measure developed by Eisenberger and colleagues (1986).

SAMPLES: In the study reported by Bettencourt (1997), data were collected by students in a marketing class. They were instructed to have five surveys completed by people who were regular shoppers for their households. After a verification process, **215** questionnaires remained for data analysis. A majority (70%) of the sample was older than 30 years of age, it was predominately women (73%), and most (85%) had completed at least some college.

RELIABILITY: Bettencourt (1997) reported an alpha of **.93** for the scale.

VALIDITY: The validity of the scale was not explicitly examined, though evidence of dimensionality was reported. Bettencourt (1997) performed a confirmatory factor analysis with items from this scale and two others, which provided support for the three-factor conceptualization.

ADMINISTRATION: The scale was self-administered as part of a much larger survey instrument (Bettencourt 1997). Higher scores on the scale suggested that respondents believed a store was concerned about them personally.

MAJOR FINDINGS: A model of customer voluntary performance was developed and tested by Bettencourt (1997) in the context of grocery store shopping. The findings indicated that a store's perceived **support for customers** had a significant positive relationship with the customers' cooperation.

REFERENCES:

Bettencourt, Lance A. (1997), "Customer Voluntary Performance: Customers as Partners in Service Delivery," *JR*, 73 (3), 383–406.

Eisenberger, Robert, Robin Huntington, Steven Hutchinson, and Deborah Sowa (1986), "Perceived Organizational Support," *Journal of Applied Psychology*, 71 (August), 500–507.

SCALE ITEMS:

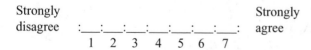

Strongly disagree :___:___:___:___:___:___: Strongly agree
 1 2 3 4 5 6 7

1. This store values my contribution to its well-being.

2. This store strongly considers my needs and wants.

3. This store would ignore any complaint from me. **(r)**

4. Help is available from this store when I have a problem.

5. This store really cares about my well-being.

6. This store cares about my opinions.

7. This store tries to provide the best service possible.

8. I am just another customer to this store. **(r)**

9. This store fails to appreciate any extra effort from me. **(r)**

10. This store disregards my best interests when it makes decisions that affect me. **(r)**

11. This store cares about my general satisfaction.

12. This store is willing to help me when I have a special request.

13. If given the opportunity, this store would take advantage of me. **(r)**

14. This store shows very little concern for me. **(r)**

SCALE NAME: Time Pressure

SCALE DESCRIPTION: Three five-point Likert-type items that appear to measure the lack of time a person perceives there to be available for doing what needs to be done in his or her life.

SCALE ORIGIN: The source of the scale was not specified by Mittal (1994).

SAMPLES: Mittal (1994) gathered data from female members of six voluntary organizations, as well as from mall intercepts. A total of 184 people provided complete survey questionnaires. Most of the respondents were white (85%), married (71%), and at least 35 years of age (63%). Although it does not mirror the U.S. population, the sample included a wide variety of demographic categories.

RELIABILITY: The construct reliability (LISREL) was reported to be **.79** (Mittal 1994).

VALIDITY: The validity of the scale was not specifically addressed by Mittal (1994) except to note that the tests that were conducted provided support for discriminant validity.

ADMINISTRATION: The scale was part of a larger self-administered mail survey instrument (Mittal 1994). Higher scores on the scale indicated that respondents considered themselves to be very busy.

MAJOR FINDINGS: The study by Mittal (1994) proposed that demographics are poor predictors of coupon usage, and instead, he illustrated the value of three layers of mediating variables. Among the findings was that education had the strongest effect on perceived **time pressure**, not quantity of work hours per week, as was expected.

REFERENCES:
Mittal, Banwari (1994), "An Integrated Framework for Relating Diverse Consumer Characteristics to Supermarket Coupon Redemption," *JMR*, 31 (November), 533–44.

SCALE ITEMS:

Strongly disagree :___:___:___:___: Strongly agree
          1   2   3   4   5

1. I am too busy to relax.

2. I am often juggling my time between too many things.

3. "So much to do, so little time;" this saying applies very well to me.

SCALE NAME: Time Pressure (Grocery Shopping)

SCALE DESCRIPTION: Five seven-point items that measure the degree to which a consumer describes his or her grocery shopping as being rushed and hurried because of a lack of time.

SCALE ORIGIN: Although not clear from the article by Putrevu and Ratchford (1997), some of the work on the scales was conducted previously in a dissertation by Putrevu (1992).

SAMPLES: Data were gathered by Putrevu and Ratchford (1997) using a mail survey to a random sample of grocery shoppers in an standard metropolitan statistical area in the Northeastern United States. A total of **500** responses were used in the main analysis, and demographics of the final sample were similar to those of the population of interest.

RELIABILITY: An alpha of **.90** was reported for the scale (Putrevu and Ratchford 1997).

VALIDITY: Although the authors stated in general that the scales showed evidence of convergent, discriminant, and content validity, no details of the analyses were provided (Putrevu and Ratchford 1997).

ADMINISTRATION: The scale was part of a larger mail questionnaire (Putrevu and Ratchford 1997). Higher scores on the scale suggested that a consumer was frequently pressed for time and forced to rush through grocery shopping.

MAJOR FINDINGS: Putrevu and Ratchford (1997) examined a dynamic model of consumer search behavior that includes human capital. It was expected that the higher the felt **time pressure**, the less external search would be conducted, but the results did not confirm this.

REFERENCES:
Putrevu, Sanjay (1992), "A Theory of Search and Its Empirical Investigation," doctoral dissertation, State University of New York at Buffalo.
——— and Brian T. Ratchford (1997), "A Model of Search Behavior with an Application to Grocery Shopping," *JR*, 73 (4), 463–86.

SCALE ITEMS:

Never　:__:__:__:__:__:__:__:　Always
　　　　　1　2　3　4　5　6　7

1. I find myself pressed for time when I go grocery shopping.

2. I am in a hurry when I do my grocery shopping.

3. I have only a limited amount of time in which to finish my grocery shopping.

4. I finish my grocery shopping fast because I have other things to do.

5. I have more than enough time to complete my weekly grocery shopping. **(r)**

SCALE NAME: Transaction Utility

SCALE DESCRIPTION: Four seven-point semantic differentials measuring the degree to which a product is priced substantially higher than what was expected. The product examined by Urbany and colleagues (1997) was an apartment.

SCALE ORIGIN: There is no information to indicate that the scale is anything other than original to the studies by Urbany and colleagues (1997).

SAMPLES: Urbany and colleagues (1997) reported on two studies, both of which used data collected from undergraduates attending a major state university. Apparently, complete data were gathered from **200** students in Study 1 and **393** students in Study 2.

RELIABILITY: The construct reliability of the scale for Study 2 was reported to be **.93** (Urbany et al. 1997).

VALIDITY: A couple of tests generally described by Urbany and colleagues (1997) provided support for a claim of discriminant validity for the scale. The details relative to this particular scale were not given.

ADMINISTRATION: Students self-administered the scale, along with other measures, after they were exposed to experimental stimuli (Urbany et al. 1997). Higher scores on the scale suggested that respondents viewed some specified product and price combination to be so much higher than expected that was viewed as a bad deal or even a "rip-off."

MAJOR FINDINGS: The experiments conducted by Urbany and colleagues (1997) examined the role of transaction utility in determining choice when product quality is uncertain. As hypothesized, **transaction utility** was a more significant predictor of purchase intention as product quality became more certain.

REFERENCES:
Urbany, Joel E., William O. Bearden, Ajit Kaicker, and Melinda Smith-de Borrero (1997), "Transaction Utility Effects When Quality Is Uncertain," *JAMS*, 25 (Winter), 45–55.

SCALE ITEMS:*
Compared to what I expect this apartment normally rents for, the advertised rent of $XXX appears to be . . .

Low   :___:___:___:___:___:___: High
           1   2   3   4   5   6   7

Inexpensive   :___:___:___:___:___:___: Expensive
           1   2   3   4   5   6   7

Reasonable   :___:___:___:___:___:___: Outrageous
           1   2   3   4   5   6   7

Underpriced   :___:___:___:___:___:___: Overpriced
           1   2   3   4   5   6   7

*This is the scale stem used by Urbany and colleagues (1997) relative to an apartment rental decision. With minor wording changes, the scale appears to be amenable for use with other products.

SCALE NAME: Trust in Salesperson

SCALE DESCRIPTION: Four seven-point Likert-type items that measure the degree to which a customer considers a salesperson to have been credible and cordial during their interaction(s).

SCALE ORIGIN: Although Ramsey and Sohi (1997) may have received stimulation for their scale from previous measures of trust (Crosby, Evans, and Cowles 1990; MacDonald, Kessel, and Fuller 1972), their scale appears to be original rather than borrowed or adapted.

SAMPLES: Data were gathered by Ramsey and Sohi (1997) through a mail survey of 500 new car buyers. The list of people who had bought cars in the previous six months came from a car dealership. Usable survey forms were returned by **173** respondents, the majority of whom were men (70%). Most of the group (60%) had at least some college education, the median household income was $46,000, 72% were married, and the average age was 42 years.

RELIABILITY: An alpha of **.90** was reported for the scale by Ramsey and Sohi (1997).

VALIDITY: After the exploratory factor analysis, Ramsey and Sohi (1997) used confirmatory factor analysis to provide evidence of unidimensionality and discriminant validity.

ADMINISTRATION: The scale was self-administered by respondents as part of a larger mail survey instrument (Ramsey and Sohi 1997). Higher scores on the scale indicated that respondents thought a specific salesperson during a particular sales encounter was amiable and quite trustworthy.

MAJOR FINDINGS: Ramsey and Sohi (1997) developed and tested a model of the impact of salesperson listening behavior on customer **trust**, satisfaction, and anticipated future interaction with salesperson. Customer perception of salesperson listening behavior was found to have a significant positive impact on **trust**.

REFERENCES:
Crosby, Lawrence A., Kenneth R. Evans, and Deborah Cowles (1990), "Relationship Quality in Services Selling: An Interpersonal Influence Perspective," *JM*, 54 (July), 68–81.
MacDonald, A.P., Jr., Vicki S. Kessel, and James B. Fuller (1972), "Self-Disclosure and Two Kinds of Trust," *Psychological Reports*, 30 (February/April), 143–48.
Ramsey, Rosemary P. and Ravipreet S. Sohi (1997), "Listening to Your Customers: The Impact of Perceived Salesperson Listening Behavior on Relationship Outcomes," *JAMS*, 25 (Spring), 127–37.

SCALE ITEMS:

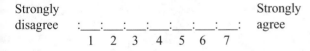

Strongly disagree :___:___:___:___:___:___:___: Strongly agree
       1 2 3 4 5 6 7

1. This salesperson was friendly and approachable.

2. This salesperson was sincere.

3. This salesperson was honest.

4. I felt very little risk was involved when dealing with this salesperson.

SCALE NAME: Trust in Source's Position Toward the Environment

SCALE DESCRIPTION: Seven, seven-point Likert-type statements measuring the extent to which a consumer believes that some specified source can be trusted in the activities in which it engages to help protect the environment. The source in the study by Osterhus (1997) was a utility company.

SCALE ORIGIN: The scale is original to Osterhus (1997). His purpose with the scale was to operationalize a *trust* construct in the context of energy conservation.

SAMPLES: The sample for the study by Osterhus (1997) came from rural, urban, and suburban neighborhoods of a Midwestern U.S. area. Subjects were recruited by random-digit dialing and then sent a paper questionnaire. Nonrespondents were mailed another questionnaire. Ultimately, 1128 usable responses were received. However, the **trust** scale was not part of the first questionnaire and was measured in a follow-up study with the same sample. Seventy-one percent (**798** of 1128) of the original sample participated in the follow-up.

RELIABILITY: Osterhus (1997) reported the reliability for a full seven-item scale, as well as a three-item subscale. The alphas for these scales were reported to be **.86** and **.82**, respectively.

VALIDITY: No examination of the scale's validity was reported by Osterhus (1997).

ADMINISTRATION: The scale was self-administered by respondents in a mail survey format (Osterhus 1997). Higher scores on the scale suggested that respondents trusted that some entity would do what is right to protect the environment.

MAJOR FINDINGS: Osterhus (1997) investigated how and when prosocial positions are expected to influence consumer choice. For a variety of reasons, the hypotheses involving **trust** were difficult to test. However, there was some limited evidence that, for those respondents with rather high **trust** as well as high attribution of responsibility (#145), personal norms regarding conservation of energy (#100) had a significant impact on their behavior.

COMMENTS: Although Osterhus (1997) used the scale with respect to a power plant, most of the items are not that specific. The exception is item 6. It may make sense to eliminate that item, especially because its factor loading (.38) was much worse than that of the rest of the items and lower than is typically deemed acceptable for use in a unidimensional scale.

REFERENCES:
Osterhus, Thomas L. (1997), "Pro-Social Consumer Influence Strategies: When and How Do They Work?" *JM*, 61 (October), 16–29.

SCALE ITEMS:*

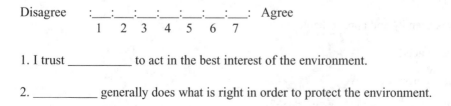

Disagree   :___:___:___:___:___:___:___: Agree
           1   2   3   4   5   6   7

1. I trust _____ to act in the best interest of the environment.

2. _____ generally does what is right in order to protect the environment.

3. I think _____ does all that it can to protect the environment.

4. Currently, _____ is effective in its efforts to help protect the environment.

5. _____ should be doing more to help protect the environment. **(r)**

6. _____ needs to clean up its power plants before it asks me to clean up the environment. **(r)**

7. _____ is not concerned with protecting the environment. **(r)**

*The name of the focal conservation activity should be placed in the blanks. The first three items composed the subscale.

SCALE NAME: Understanding

SCALE DESCRIPTION: A six-item, seven-point Likert-type summated ratings scale measuring the degree to which a person who has just been involved in a service activity thinks that a "connection" was made with the person providing the service. That is, that the provider and client did not just play their separate roles but revealed something about each other, which resulted in a unique experience. The activity studied by Price, Arnould, and Tierney (1995) was a river rafting trip, and the river guide was the service provider being evaluated by the customers.

SCALE ORIGIN: The scale was developed for the research reported by Price, Arnould, and Tierney (1995).

SAMPLES: Very little information was provided by Price, Arnould, and Tierney (1995) regarding their sample. The reader is referred to a previous article (Arnould and Price 1993) that provides only a limited description of the sample. The respondents are described simply as a stratified random sample of people taking multiday river trips with one of three clients' rafting companies. A total of **137** clients filled out posttrip questionnaires, but only 97 of those had completed pretrip surveys.

RELIABILITY: An alpha of **.90** was reported by Price, Arnould, and Tierney (1995).

VALIDITY: No specific examination of the scale's validity was reported by Price, Arnould, and Tierney (1995). However, seventeen items were factor analyzed and found to produce three separate factors. The six items in this scale composed one of those factors, and their loadings ranged from .59 to .87.

ADMINISTRATION: The scale was self-administered by respondents as part of a larger survey after they had finished a rafting trip (Arnould and Price 1993; Price, Arnould, and Tierney 1995). High scores on the scale suggested that respondents considered the service provider to have understood them well and developed a personal "connection" with them.

MAJOR FINDINGS: Building on the same basic study as Arnould and Price (1993), Price, Arnould, and Tierney (1995) found that **understanding** had a significant positive impact on perceived performance of the service provider.

REFERENCES:

Arnould, Eric J. and Linda L. Price (1993), "River Magic: Extraordinary Experience and the Extended Service Encounter," *JCR*, 20 (June), 24–45.

Price, Linda L., Eric J. Arnould, and Patrick Tierney (1995), "Going to Extremes: Managing Service Encounters and Assessing Provider Performance," *JM*, 59 (April), 83–97.

SCALE ITEMS:

Strongly disagree | Strongly agree

1———2———3———4———5———6———7

The service provider:

1. Connected to my life.

2. Revealed something personal.

3. Invited me to reveal myself.

4. Understood me.

5. Seems like own person.

6. Out of the ordinary.

SCALE NAME: Value (Ability to Judge)

SCALE DESCRIPTION: Seven seven-point items that measure the degree to which a consumer expresses having the ability to judge "good deals" across brands and stores, especially when it comes to grocery shopping.

SCALE ORIGIN: Although not clear from the article by Putrevu and Ratchford (1997), some of the work on the scales was conducted previously in a dissertation by Putrevu (1992).

SAMPLES: Data were gathered by Putrevu and Ratchford (1997) using a mail survey to a random sample of grocery shoppers in an standard metropolitan statistical area in the northeastern United States. A total of **500** responses were used in the main analysis, and demographics of the final sample were similar to those of the population of interest.

RELIABILITY: An alpha of **.76** was reported for the scale (Putrevu and Ratchford 1997).

VALIDITY: Although the authors stated in general that the scales showed evidence of convergent, discriminant, and content validity, no details of the analyses were provided (Putrevu and Ratchford 1997).

ADMINISTRATION: The scale was part of a larger mail questionnaire (Putrevu and Ratchford 1997). Higher scores on the scale suggested that consumers thought that they were very capable at judging values across brands and stores.

MAJOR FINDINGS: Putrevu and Ratchford (1997) examined a dynamic model of consumer search behavior that includes human capital. The results indicated that the greater the perceived **ability to judge grocery-related values**, the greater was the amount of grocery-related external search.

REFERENCES:
Putrevu, Sanjay (1992), "A Theory of Search and Its Empirical Investigation," doctoral dissertation, State University of New York at Buffalo.
———— and Brian T. Ratchford (1997), "A Model of Search Behavior with an Application to Grocery Shopping," *JR*, 73 (4), 463–86.

SCALE ITEMS:

Doesn't describe   Describes me
me at all   :___:___:___:___:___:___:___: very well
               1 2 3 4 5 6 7

1. I can easily compare a new brand with existing brands to determine whether it is good or bad.

2. I have a hard time comparing different brands of grocery products. **(r)**

3. I can easily tell if a sale/special price is a good deal.

4. It's hard for me to tell if a sale/special price is a good buy. **(r)**

5. I am quite capable of distinguishing good brands from bad ones.

6. I can tell which supermarket gives me the best value.

7. I have a hard time judging supermarkets on factors like price, quality and selection of products. **(r)**

SCALE NAME: Value (Offer)

SCALE DESCRIPTION: Several seven-point Likert-type statements measuring the perceived value of a deal given a certain product offered at a certain price. The product examined in the study by Urbany, Bearden, and Weilbaker (1988) was televisions, and a three-item scale was employed. In the study by Grewal, Marmorstein, and Sharma (1996), a four-item version of the scale was used to evaluate a shirt advertisement.

SCALE ORIGIN: Grewal, Marmorstein, and Sharma (1996) modified the version of the scale used by Urbany, Bearden, and Weilbaker (1988), who in turn built on previous measures (e.g., Berkowitz and Walton 1980; Della Bitta, Monroe, and McGinnis 1981)

SAMPLES: Two experiments were conducted by Grewal, Marmorstein, and Sharma (1996) with undergraduate student subjects. The first experiment had **146** students, and Experiment 2 had **145** students.

Urbany, Bearden, and Weilbaker (1988) also reported two studies. Both used junior- and senior-level undergraduate business majors, one with **150** students and the other with **168**.

RELIABILITY: Grewal, Marmorstein, and Sharma (1996) reported alphas of **.93** and **.92** for the scale's use in Experiments 1 and 2, respectively. Alphas of **.79** and **.86** were obtained by Urbany, Bearden, and Weilbaker (1988) in the two uses of their scale.

VALIDITY: No examination of the scales' validity was reported in either study.

ADMINISTRATION: The scale was self-administered by subjects in the experiments by Grewal, Marmorstein, and Sharma (1996) after they were exposed to treatment stimuli. In the two studies by Urbany, Bearden, and Weilbaker (1988), students responded to questions posed to them on a PC in a university computer lab. Higher scores on the scale implied that respondents perceived a deal (price and product) to be a very good value, whereas lower scores meant that respondents did not think that the offer was a good buy.

MAJOR FINDINGS: The experiments conducted by Grewal, Marmorstein, and Sharma (1996) investigated the proposition that consumer responses to price-related semantic cues depend on the decision context and the level of processing evoked by the discount size. Their findings showed that, at least when it came to perceived **value of the offer**, consumers' preferences for price information were significantly influenced by the decision context.

Urbany, Bearden, and Weilbaker (1988) studied the effect of price claims on consumer perceptions and price search behavior. Their findings from two experiments indicated that ads with high plausible reference prices for products led to greater perceptions of **value** than did ads with no reference prices provided.

COMMENTS: See also a variation on the scale used by Urbany and colleagues (1997).

REFERENCES:

Berkowitz, Eric N. and John R. Walton (1980), "Contextual Influences on Consumer Price Responses: An Experimental Analysis," *JMR*, 17 (August), 349–58.

Della Bitta, Albert J., Kent B. Monroe, and John M. McGinnis (1981), "Consumer Perceptions of Comparative Price Advertisements," *JMR*, 18 (November), 416–27.

Grewal, Dhruv, Howard Marmorstein, and Arun Sharma (1996), "Communicating Price Information Through Semantic Cues: The Moderating Effects of Situation and Discount Size," *JCR*, 23 (September), 148–55.

Urbany, Joel E., William O. Bearden, Ajit Kaicker, and Melinda Smith-de Borrero (1997), "Transaction Utility Effects When Quality Is Uncertain," *JAMS*, 25 (Winter), 45–55.

———, ———, and Dan C. Weilbaker (1988), "The Effect of Plausible and Exaggerated Reference Prices on Consumer Perceptions and Price Search," *JCR*, 15 (June), 95–110.

SCALE ITEMS:*

Directions: Please evaluate the offer by circling the response on each of the scale below.

```
Strongly                                Strongly
disagree    :___:___:___:___:___:___:___:  agree
            1   2   3   4   5   6   7
```

1. The advertised _____ is an excellent buy for the money.

2. At the sale price, the _____ is not a very good value for the money. (r)

3. The advertised offer represents an extremely fair price.

4. At the sale price, this _____ is probably worth the money.

5. This _____ appears to be a great deal.

*The directions are those used by Grewal, Marmorstein, and Sharma (1996). They used items 3–5 and a positive version of 2. Urbany, Bearden, and Weilbaker (1988) used items 1–3. The name of the product should be placed in the blanks.

SCALE NAME: Value (Offer)

SCALE DESCRIPTION: Four items that measure a consumer's perceived value of a deal given a certain product offered at a certain price. All of the studies employed seven-point response formats except Burton and Lichtenstein (1988; Lichtenstein and Bearden 1989), who used nine-point scales.

SCALE ORIGIN: The bipolar phrases employed in the studies were used originally by Berkowitz and Walton (1980) but not in a summated format. A simple summated scale was apparently not used until the study by Burton and Lichtenstein (1988; Lichtenstein and Bearden 1989).

SAMPLES: Biswas and Burton (1993) reported on two studies in their article. In the first one, data were collected from **392** undergraduate business students. Little more is said about the sample except there was an nearly equal portion of each gender and they were randomly assigned to one of the twelve treatments. The second sample was composed of **303** nonstudents who were recruited by students in a marketing course. All of those in the sample were over the age of 18 with a median age of 40 years. A little more than half were women (56%), and the median household income was $35,000.

Data were collected in an experiment conducted by Bobinski, Cox, and Cox (1996) from student volunteers in management courses at an Eastern U.S. university. Usable responses were received from **129** students. A little more than half of the sample were men (53%), and the mean age was 20.6 years.

Analysis in Burton and Lichtenstein (1988) and Lichtenstein and Bearden (1989) was based on the same data collected from **278** undergraduate business students. The students were randomly assigned to one of twelve treatment conditions in a $2 \times 2 \times 3$ experimental design. There were between 21 and 28 students per cell.

Lichtenstein, Burton, and Karson (1991) used **830** undergraduate business majors and randomly assigned each of them to one of thirty-one conditions in a 5×6 (plus control group) between-subjects experimental design. There were between 22 to 29 subjects per cell.

RELIABILITY: Alphas of **.86**, **.80**, and **.90** were reported for the scales used by Bobinski, Cox, and Cox (1996), Burton and Lichtenstein (1988; Lichtenstein and Bearden 1989), and Lichtenstein, Burton, and Karson (1991), respectively. Biswas and Burton (1993) reported alphas of **.78** and **.85** in their first and second studies, respectively.

VALIDITY: No specific examination of scale validity was reported in any of the studies. However, Biswas and Burton (1993) mentioned that, though *perceived value of the offer* was highly correlated with a measure of the *attitude toward the offer*, confirmatory factor analysis provided evidence of a two- rather than one-factor model. Similar evidence was reported by Bobinski, Cox, and Cox (1996).

ADMINISTRATION: The scale used by Bobinski, Cox, and Cox (1996), Burton and Lichtenstein (1988; Lichtenstein and Bearden 1989), and Lichtenstein, Burton, and Karson (1991) was self-administered by subjects, along with several other measures, in experimental settings. Higher scores on the scale implied that respondents perceived a deal (price and product) to be a very good value, whereas lower scores meant that respondents did not think that the offer was a good buy.

MAJOR FINDINGS: Biswas and Burton (1993) investigated the impact of three different price claims on various perceptions and intentions. Among the many findings was that **perceptions of the offer's value** were better for larger discount ranges than for smaller.

The effect of a retailer's rationale for a price reduction was examined by Bobinski, Cox, and Cox (1996). The results showed that the perceived **value of the offer** was best when a rationale (e.g., volume purchase), as well as a reference price (i.e., higher "regular" price), was provided.

The study reported by Burton and Lichtenstein (1988; Lichtenstein and Bearden 1989) examined the influence of merchant-supplied reference prices, ad distinctiveness, and ad message consistency on perceptions of source credibility, value of the deal, and attitude toward the deal. In Burton and Lichtenstein (1988), the findings indicated that perceptions of the **value of the offer** were strongly related to several measures of attitude toward the ad. Furthermore, a price discount was shown to have a significant effect on attitude toward the ad even after covarying out perceptions regarding the **value of the offer.** Among many other findings reported in Lichtenstein and Bearden (1989), perceived **value of the offer** was greatest when the retailers used distinctive ads that did not offer similar deals frequently. Also, the perceived **value of the offer** was greater for plausible high merchant-supplied prices than for implausible merchant-supplied prices.

Lichtenstein, Burton, and Karson (1991) studied the way reference price ads were phrased (semantic cues) and consumer's price-related responses. High distinctiveness semantic cues indicate the difference between the advertised price and what is charged by competitors, whereas low consistency cues compare prices charged at other times by the same retailer. Among the many findings was that, for implausibly high external reference prices, semantic cues that suggest high distinctiveness produced significantly better perceptions of the **offer's value** than did low consistency cues.

COMMENTS: The specific products examined in the studies were a t-shirt (Bobinski, Cox, and Cox 1996), a desk (Burton and Lichtenstein 1988; Lichtenstein and Bearden 1989), and a calculator (Lichtenstein, Burton, and Karson 1991), but the items in the scale here are general enough that they should be amenable for use in studying many other product categories.

See also a Likert-type version of the scale used by Urbany, Bearden, and Weilbaker (1988).

REFERENCES:

Berkowitz, Eric N. and John R. Walton (1980), "Contextual Influences on Consumer Price Responses: An Experimental Analysis," *JMR*, 17 (August), 349–58.

Biswas, Abhijit and Scot Burton (1993), "Consumer Perceptions of Tensile Price Claims in Advertisements: An Assessment of Claim Types Across Different Discount Levels," *JAMS*, 21 (Summer), 217–29.

Bobinski, George S., Jr., Dena Cox, and Anthony Cox (1996), "Retail 'Sale' Advertising, Perceived Retailer Credibility, and Price Rationale," *JR*, 72 (3), 291–306.

Burton, Scot and Donald R. Lichtenstein (1988), "The Effect of Ad Claims and Ad Context on Attitude Toward the Advertisement," *JA*, 17 (1), 3–11.

Lichtenstein, Donald R. and William O. Bearden (1989), "Contextual Influences on Perceptions of Merchant-Supplied Reference Prices," *JCR*, 16 (June), 55–66.

———, Scot Burton, and Eric J. Karson (1991), "The Effect of Semantic Cues on Consumer Perceptions of Reference Price Ads," *JCR*, 18 (December), 380–91.

Urbany, Joel E., William O. Bearden, and Dan C. Weilbaker (1988), "The Effect of Plausible and Exaggerated Reference Prices on Consumer Perceptions and Price Search," *JCR*, 15 (June), 95–110.

SCALE ITEMS:

1. The _____ is:

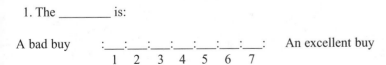

A bad buy   :___:___:___:___:___:___:___: An excellent buy
                1   2   3   4   5   6   7

#392 *Value (Offer)*

2. The prices represent:

		An extremely
No savings at all	:___:___:___:___:___:___:___:	large savings
	1 2 3 4 5 6 7	

3. The price is:

An extremely		An extremely
unfair price	:___:___:___:___:___:___:___:	fair price
	1 2 3 4 5 6 7	

4. The _____ is:

		An extremely
Not a good value	:___:___:___:___:___:___:___:	good value
	1 2 3 4 5 6 7	

SCALE NAME: Value (Offer)

SCALE DESCRIPTION: Three seven-point semantic differentials measuring the degree to which a person considers the normal price charged for a specified form of entertainment to be a good value.

SCALE ORIGIN: Although the scale bears similarity to some other measures of the construct, the source of this particular version appears to be Wakefield and Barnes (1996). The scale was apparently pretested and refined, along with other measures, in the study using a sample of 308 completed responses from sports fans attending a minor league baseball game.

SAMPLES: Data were collected in the main study by Wakefield and Barnes (1996) from those who attended one of two minor league baseball games in a city different from the one used in the pretest. Final analysis was based on usable data from **250** respondents who appeared to live in the area and would hypothetically have been exposed to the promotional information under study.

RELIABILITY: An alpha of **.93** was reported for the scale (Wakefield and Barnes 1996).

VALIDITY: Although specific evaluation of the scale's validity was not discussed by Wakefield and Barnes (1996), they noted that they used confirmatory factor analysis and that no changes were deemed necessary for this scale.

ADMINISTRATION: The scale was part of a larger survey instrument self-administered by people who attended a baseball game (Wakefield and Barnes 1996). Higher scores on the scale suggested that respondents viewed the prices normally charged for a specified form of entertainment service to be a good deal.

MAJOR FINDINGS: Wakefield and Barnes (1996) tested a model of sales promotion for entertainment services. Among their conclusions was that consumers who considered the tangible aspects of a sports stadium to be of high quality also viewed the service to be a better **value** for the cost.

COMMENTS: The scale scores were reported to have a mean of 5.79 and a standard deviation of 1.22 (Wakefield and Barnes 1996).

REFERENCES:
Wakefield, Kirk L. and James H. Barnes (1996), "Retailing Hedonic Consumption: A Model of Sales Promotion of a Leisure Service," *JR*, 72 (4), 409–27.

SCALE ITEMS:

Generally speaking, the regular prices are:

A bad buy   :___:___:___:___:___:___:___: A good buy
                               1 2 3 4 5 6 7

Not worth
the money   :___:___:___:___:___:___:___: Worth the money
                               1 2 3 4 5 6 7

Too high for the quality
of entertainment   :___:___:___:___:___:___:___: Not too high for the quality of entertainment
                               1 2 3 4 5 6 7

SCALE NAME: Value Consciousness

SCALE DESCRIPTION: Three five-point Likert-type statements that measure a consumer's expressed tendency to buy products perceived to be good value for the money.

SCALE ORIGIN: The scale appears to be original to Donthu and Cherian (1994).

SAMPLES: Donthu and Cherian (1994) mailed survey instruments in both Spanish and English to 1000 people with Hispanic surnames from a database from a major marketing research agency. The questionnaires were refined through a back-translation technique and pretested by bilingual students as well as by a convenience sample.

Envelopes were addressed to the "adult of the household." Just those who identified themselves as Hispanic were included in the final sample. Of the questionnaires returned, only **240** (160 men) were considered useful. The average respondent was in his or her 30s, had a household income of between $20,000 to $29,000, and had "some schooling."

RELIABILITY: An alpha of **.81** was reported for the scale (Donthu and Cherian 1994).

VALIDITY: No specific examination of scale validity was reported by Donthu and Cherian (1994).

ADMINISTRATION: The scale was self-administered, along with other measures, in a mail survey instrument (Donthu and Cherian 1994). Higher scores on the scale indicated that respondents were very interested in purchasing those brands perceived as "a good deal."

MAJOR FINDINGS: Donthu and Cherian (1994) investigated the impact that strength of ethnic group identification had on various aspects of shopping behavior. Among the findings was that those with strong identification with the Hispanic culture were less **value conscious** than were those who had weaker identification.

REFERENCES:

Donthu, Naveen and Joseph Cherian (1994), "Impact of Strength of Ethnic Identification on Hispanic Shopping Behavior," *JR*, 70 (4), 383–93.

SCALE ITEMS:

Strongly   Strongly
disagree   :___:___:___:___:___: agree
           1   2   3   4   5

I generally purchase . . .

1. A product for which I have a coupon.

2. The brand which is on sale.

3. The brand on which I get a good deal.

SCALE NAME: Vanity (Achievement Concern)

SCALE DESCRIPTION: Five seven-point Likert-type statements that evaluate a person's excessive concern for personal accomplishments and need for others to acknowledge his or her success.

SCALE ORIGIN: The scale is original to the study by Netemeyer, Burton, and Lichtenstein (1995). The purpose of the study was to examine vanity and develop some scales for its measurement. The study was extremely thorough and well done in constructing and validating the scales. Only some of the most relevant information is reported here.

SAMPLES: Various samples were collected and used by Netemeyer, Burton, and Lichtenstein (1995) in the process of validating the scale. Study 1 had two groups: 145 students from a major U.S. university and 277 "nonstudent adults." Study 2 was composed of 186 different students and 264 "nonstudent adults." A third study was conducted using addresses found in a *Who's Who* directory for one state. Analysis was based on the 267 completed questionnaires that were returned. A fourth study focused on 27 football players from a nationally ranked NCAA Division I team. The fifth and final study was based on data collected from 43 professional fashion models.

RELIABILITY: The following alphas were found for the scale by Netemeyer, Burton, and Lichtenstein (1995): **.80** (Study 1, students), **.86** (Study 1, nonstudents), **.82** (Study 2, students), **.86** (Study 2, nonstudents), **.84** (*Who's Who* members), **.78** (football players), and **.81** (fashion models).

VALIDITY: Several rounds of confirmatory factor analysis by Netemeyer, Burton, and Lichtenstein (1995) helped provide evidence that the scale is unidimensional. A pattern of correlations between the scale and other measures with which it should be related was found. This provided evidence of the scale's convergent and predictive validities. A variety of tests were conducted, and all supported a claim of the scale's discriminant validity Also, low correlations were found between the scale and a measure of social desirability bias, which indicates that the scale is not very susceptible to respondents merely providing socially desirable answers.

ADMINISTRATION: As noted, the scale was used in five studies with seven samples, and in each case, it appears to have been part of a larger questionnaire that was self-administered by respondents (Netemeyer, Burton, and Lichtenstein 1995). Higher scores on the scale indicated that respondents were quite vain in the sense that they expressed extreme concern about their accomplishments.

MAJOR FINDINGS: Netemeyer, Burton, and Lichtenstein (1995) investigated vanity and developed four scales for its measurement. Most of the article discussed the results of the rather extensive validation process. Among the findings was that **achievement concern vanity** had strong positive relationships with grandiosity and narcissism.

COMMENTS: Means on the scale were provided for several groups and ranged from 19.3 for nonstudents (Study 1) to 23.1 for fashion models.

REFERENCES:
Netemeyer, Richard G., Scot Burton, and Donald R. Lichtenstein (1995), "Trait Aspects of Vanity: Measurement and Relevance to Consumer Behavior," *JCR*, 21 (March), 612–26.

#395 *Vanity (Achievement Concern)*

SCALE ITEMS:

Strongly   Strongly
disagree   :___:___:___:___:___:___:___: agree
                    1   2   3   4   5   6   7

1. Professional achievements are an obsession to me.

2. I want others to look up to me because of my accomplishments.

3. I am more concerned with professional success than most people I know.

4. Achieving greater success than my peers is important to me.

5. I want my achievements to be recognized by others.

SCALE NAME: Vanity (Achievement View)

SCALE DESCRIPTION: Five seven-point Likert-type statements that evaluate a person's positive and possibly inflated view of his or her own accomplishments, particularly as it relates to others' opinions of his or her success.

SCALE ORIGIN: The scale is original to the study by Netemeyer, Burton, and Lichtenstein (1995). The purpose of the study was to examine vanity and develop some scales for its measurement. The study was extremely thorough and well done in terms of constructing and validating the scales. Only some of the most relevant information is reported here.

SAMPLES: Various samples were collected and used by Netemeyer, Burton, and Lichtenstein (1995) in the process of validating the scale. Study 1 had two groups: 145 students from a major U.S. university and 277 "nonstudent adults." Study 2 was composed of 186 different students and 264 "nonstudent adults." A third study was conducted using addresses found in a *Who's Who* directory for one state. Analysis was based on the 267 completed questionnaires that were returned. A fourth study focused on 27 football players from a nationally ranked NCAA Division I team. The fifth and final study was based on data collected from 43 professional fashion models.

RELIABILITY: The following alphas were found for the scale by Netemeyer, Burton, and Lichtenstein (1995): **.84** (Study 1, students), **.84** (Study 1, nonstudents), **.89** (Study 2, students), **.88** (Study 2, nonstudents), **.87** (*Who's Who* members), **.80** (football players), and **.77** (fashion models).

VALIDITY: Several rounds of confirmatory factor analysis by Netemeyer, Burton, and Lichtenstein (1995) helped provide evidence that the scale is unidimensional. A pattern of correlations between the scale and other measures with which it should be related was found. This provided evidence of the scale's convergent and predictive validities. A variety of tests were conducted, and all supported a claim of the scale's discriminant validity. Also, low, insignificant correlations were found between the scale and a measure of social desirability bias, which indicates that the scale is apparently not susceptible to respondents merely providing socially desirable answers.

ADMINISTRATION: As noted, the scale was used in five studies with seven samples, and in each case, it appears to have been part of a larger questionnaire that was self-administered by respondents (Netemeyer, Burton, and Lichtenstein 1995). Higher scores on the scale indicated that respondents were quite vain in the sense that they expressed very high opinions of their accomplishments and thought that others consider them successful as well.

MAJOR FINDINGS: Netemeyer, Burton, and Lichtenstein (1995) investigated vanity and developed four scales for its measurement. Most of the article dealt with the results of the rather extensive validation process. Among the findings was that **achievement view vanity** had strong positive relationships with grandiosity and narcissism.

COMMENTS: Means on the scale were provided for several groups and ranged from 21.0 for students (Study 2) to 26.9 for *Who's Who* members.

REFERENCES:
Netemeyer, Richard G., Scot Burton, and Donald R. Lichtenstein (1995), "Trait Aspects of Vanity: Measurement and Relevance to Consumer Behavior," *JCR*, 21 (March), 612–26.

#396 *Vanity (Achievement View)*

SCALE ITEMS:

Strongly   Strongly
disagree   :___:___:___:___:___:___:___: agree
           1   2   3   4   5   6   7

1. In a professional sense, I am a very successful person.

2. My achievements are highly regarded by others.

3. I am an accomplished person.

4. I am a good example of professional success.

5. Others wish they were as successful as me.

SCALE NAME: Vanity (Physical Concern)

SCALE DESCRIPTION: Five seven-point Likert-type statements that evaluate a person's excessive concern for his or her physical appearance.

SCALE ORIGIN: The scale is original to the study by Netemeyer, Burton, and Lichtenstein (1995). The purpose of the study was to examine vanity and develop some scales for its measurement. The study was extremely thorough and well done in constructing and validating the scales. Only some of the most relevant information is reported here.

SAMPLES: Various samples were collected and used by Netemeyer, Burton, and Lichtenstein (1995) in the process of validating the scale. Study 1 had two groups: 145 students from a major U.S. university and 277 "nonstudent adults." Study 2 was composed of 186 different students and 264 "nonstudent adults." A third study was conducted using addresses found in a *Who's Who* directory for one state. Analysis was based on the 267 completed questionnaires that were returned. A fourth study focused on 27 football players from a nationally ranked NCAA Division I team. The fifth and final study was based on data collected from 43 professional fashion models.

RELIABILITY: The following alphas were found for the scale by Netemeyer, Burton, and Lichtenstein (1995): **.86** (Study 1, students), **.85** (Study 1, nonstudents), **.83** (Study 2, students), **.87** (Study 2, nonstudents), **.90** (*Who's Who* members), **.86** (football players), and **.87** (fashion models).

VALIDITY: Several rounds of confirmatory factor analysis by Netemeyer, Burton, and Lichtenstein (1995) helped provide evidence that the scale is unidimensional. A pattern of correlations between the scale and other measures with which it should be related was found. This provided evidence of the scale's convergent and predictive validities. A variety of tests were conducted, and all supported a claim of the scale's discriminant validity Also, low, insignificant correlations were found between the scale and a measure of social desirability bias, which indicates that the scale is apparently not susceptible to respondents merely providing socially desirable answers.

ADMINISTRATION: As noted, the scale was used in five studies with seven samples, and in each case, it appears to have been part of a larger questionnaire that was self-administered by respondents (Netemeyer, Burton, and Lichtenstein 1995). Higher scores on the scale indicated that respondents were quite vain in the sense that they expressed extreme concern about their appearance.

MAJOR FINDINGS: Netemeyer, Burton, and Lichtenstein (1995) investigated vanity and developed four scales for its measurement. Most of the article discussed the results of the rather extensive validation process. Among the findings was that **physical concern vanity** had strong positive relationships with concern for clothing and public body consciousness.

COMMENTS: Means on the scale were provided for several groups and ranged from 21.3 for football players to 25.4 for fashion models.

REFERENCES:
Netemeyer, Richard G., Scot Burton, and Donald R. Lichtenstein (1995), "Trait Aspects of Vanity: Measurement and Relevance to Consumer Behavior," *JCR*, 21 (March), 612–26.

#397 *Vanity (Physical Concern)*

SCALE ITEMS:

Strongly   Strongly
disagree   :___:___:___:___:___:___:___: agree
                    1   2   3   4   5   6   7

1. The way I look is extremely important to me.

2. I am very concerned about my appearance.

3. I would feel embarrassed if I was around people and did not look my best.

4. Looking my best is worth the effort.

5. It is important that I always look good.

SCALE NAME: Vanity (Physical View)

SCALE DESCRIPTION: Six seven-point Likert-type statements that evaluate a person's positive and possibly inflated view of his or her physical appearance, particularly as it relates to others' opinions of his or her appearance.

SCALE ORIGIN: The scale is original to the study by Netemeyer, Burton, and Lichtenstein (1995). The purpose of the study was to examine vanity and develop some scales for its measurement. The study was extremely thorough and well done in terms of constructing and validating the scales. Only some of the most relevant information is reported here.

SAMPLES: Various samples were collected and used by Netemeyer, Burton, and Lichtenstein (1995) in the process of validating the scale. Study 1 had two groups: 145 students from a major U.S. university and 277 "nonstudent adults." Study 2 was composed of 186 different students and 264 "nonstudent adults." A third study was conducted using addresses found in a *Who's Who* directory for one state. Analysis was based on the 267 completed questionnaires that were returned. A fourth study focused on 27 football players from a nationally ranked NCAA Division I team. The fifth and final study was based on data collected from 43 professional fashion models.

RELIABILITY: The following alphas were found for the scale by Netemeyer, Burton, and Lichtenstein (1995): **.88** (Study 1, students), **.90** (Study 1, nonstudents), **.89** (Study 2, students), **.92** (Study 2, nonstudents), **.91** (*Who's Who* members), **.77** (football players), and **.89** (fashion models).

VALIDITY: Several rounds of confirmatory factor analysis by Netemeyer, Burton, and Lichtenstein (1995) helped provide evidence that the scale is unidimensional. A pattern of correlations between the scale and other measures with which it should be related was found. This provided evidence of the scale's convergent and predictive validities. A variety of tests were conducted, and all supported a claim of the scale's discriminant validity. Also, low and/or insignificant correlations were found between the scale and a measure of social desirability bias, which indicates that the scale is apparently not susceptible to respondents merely providing socially desirable answers.

ADMINISTRATION: As noted, the scale was used in five studies with seven samples, and in each case, it appears to have been part of a larger questionnaire that was self-administered by respondents (Netemeyer, Burton, and Lichtenstein 1995). Higher scores on the scale indicated that respondents were quite vain in the sense that they expressed very high opinions of their appearance and thought that others consider them attractive as well.

MAJOR FINDINGS: Netemeyer, Burton, and Lichtenstein (1995) investigated vanity and developed four scales for its measurement. Most of the article dealt with the results of the rather extensive validation process. Among the findings was that **physical view vanity** had strong positive relationships with grandiosity and narcissism.

COMMENTS: Means on the scale were provided for several groups and ranged from 20.6 for students (Study 2) to 26.9 for fashion models.

REFERENCES:
Netemeyer, Richard G., Scot Burton, and Donald R. Lichtenstein (1995), "Trait Aspects of Vanity: Measurement and Relevance to Consumer Behavior," *JCR*, 21 (March), 612–26.

#398 *Vanity (Physical View)*

SCALE ITEMS:

Strongly   Strongly
disagree   :___:___:___:___:___:___:___: agree
           1   2   3   4   5   6   7

1. People notice how attractive I am.

2. My looks are very appealing to others.

3. People are envious of my good looks.

4. I am a very good-looking individual.

5. My body is sexually appealing.

6. I have the type of body that people want to look at.

SCALE NAME: Variety-Seeking Tendency

SCALE DESCRIPTION: A three-item, five-point Likert-type summated ratings scale measuring the degree to which a person expresses a desire to try new and different things.

SCALE ORIGIN: The source of the scale was not stated by Donthu and Gilliland (1996), but it is likely to be original to their study.

SAMPLES: Donthu and Gilliland (1996) used trained interviewers to call 1000 households in a large city telephone directory. Interviews were successfully completed with adults in **368** of those households. Although some demographic information was employed in the analysis, the data were not reported in such a way that the sample as a whole can be clearly described.

RELIABILITY: An alpha of **.87** was reported for the scale by Donthu and Gilliland (1996).

VALIDITY: No specific examination of the scale's validity was reported by Donthu and Gilliland (1996).

ADMINISTRATION: Donthu and Gilliland (1996) had the scale administered as part of a larger telephone survey. Higher scores on the scale indicated that respondents liked a lot of variety in their lives.

MAJOR FINDINGS: Donthu and Gilliland (1996) profiled infomercial shoppers and found that they expressed a significantly greater desire for **variety seeking** than did those who had never purchased goods from infomercials.

REFERENCES:
Donthu, Naveen and David Gilliland (1996), "The Infomercial Shopper," *JAR*, 36 (March/April), 69–76.

SCALE ITEMS:

Strongly disagree	Disagree	Neutral	Agree	Strongly agree
1	2	3	4	5

1. I like to try different things.

2. I like a great deal of variety.

3. I like new and different styles.

#400 *Variety-Seeking Tendency (Entertainment)*

SCALE NAME: Variety-Seeking Tendency (Entertainment)

SCALE DESCRIPTION: Three seven-point Likert-type items measuring the degree to which a person desires to go to new entertainment spots when going out rather than returning to familiar places.

SCALE ORIGIN: The scale used by Wakefield and Barnes (1996), though inspired by the scale developed by Raju (1980), is different enough to be considered original. The scale was pretested and refined using a sample of 308 completed responses from sports fans attending a minor league baseball game.

SAMPLES: Data were collected in the main study by Wakefield and Barnes (1996) from those who attended one of two minor league baseball games in a city different from the one used in the pretest. Final analysis was based on usable data from **250** respondents who appeared to live in the area and would hypothetically have been exposed to the promotional information under study.

RELIABILITY: An alpha of **.77** was reported for the scale (Wakefield and Barnes 1996).

VALIDITY: Although specific evaluation of the scale's validity was not discussed by Wakefield and Barnes (1996), they noted that they used confirmatory factor analysis and that no changes were deemed necessary for this scale.

ADMINISTRATION: The scale was part of a larger survey instrument self-administered by people who attended a baseball game (Wakefield and Barnes 1996). Higher scores on the scale suggested that respondents were very eager to try out new and different places of entertainment rather than sticking with what is known and familiar.

MAJOR FINDINGS: Wakefield and Barnes (1996) tested a model of sales promotion for entertainment services. Among their conclusions was that **variety-seeking** consumers are not likely to repatronize an entertainment service without additional sales promotions enticing them to do so.

COMMENTS: The scale scores were reported to have a mean of 4.12 and a standard deviation of 1.34 (Wakefield and Barnes 1996).

REFERENCES:
Raju, P. S. (1980), "Optimum Stimulation Level: Its Relationship to Personality, Demographics, and Exploratory Behavior," *JCR*, 7 (December), 272–82.
Wakefield, Kirk L. and James H. Barnes (1996), "Retailing Hedonic Consumption: A Model of Sales Promotion of a Leisure Service," *JR*, 72 (4), 409–27.

SCALE ITEMS:

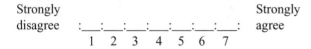

Strongly disagree :___:___:___:___:___:___:___: Strongly agree
          1 2 3 4 5 6 7

1. I enjoy going to different entertainment spots for the sake of comparison.

2. If I have a choice when I go out, I'd rather try someplace new than go to the places I already know.

3. I tend to go to a lot of different entertainment spots, just for the sake of a change of pace.

SCALE NAME: Word-of-Mouth Intentions (Negative)

SCALE DESCRIPTION: Three seven-point statements measuring the likelihood that a person would tell friends and relatives about some negative event that has occurred at a store and advise them not to shop there.

SCALE ORIGIN: Although Blodgett, Hill, and Tax (1997) may have drawn inspiration from previous measures (e.g., Singh 1988), this scale appears to be original to their study.

SAMPLES: Data were collected by Blodgett, Hill, and Tax (1997) using a quasi-experimental design and subjects from three different locations: a Midsouth U.S. university, a Midwestern U.S. university, and a Canadian university. Subjects came from local church groups as well as faculty and staff at the universities. Usable responses were received from **265** subjects. Among the demographic information provided for the sample was that a majority were white (86%) and women (61%). There was wide diversity in the sample on other characteristics such as age, occupation, education, and income.

RELIABILITY: An alpha of **.87** was reported for the scale by Blodgett, Hill, and Tax (1997).

VALIDITY: No specific examination of the scale's validity was reported by Blodgett, Hill, and Tax (1997).

ADMINISTRATION: The scale was administered to subjects, along with other measures, after they had been exposed to experimental stimuli (Blodgett, Hill, and Tax 1997). Higher scores on the scale indicated that respondents were expressing a strong intention to speak with others about not shopping at some specified store.

MAJOR FINDINGS: The study by Blodgett, Hill, and Tax (1997) examined the effects of various types of *justice* on complainants' **negative word of mouth** and likelihood of repatronage. In general, it was found that two types of justice (distributive and interactional) were positively associated with **negative word-of-mouth intentions**, whereas a third type (procedural) had no significant relationship with it.

COMMENTS: The phrasing of the items in this scale is unique because the items were developed for an experiment in which subjects were asked to *imagine* being the consumer in a scenario with which they were presented. With some adjustment and retesting, the items appear to be amenable for use in situations in which the respondents have actually visited the store themselves.

REFERENCES:
Blodgett, Jeffrey G., Donna J. Hill, and Stephen S. Tax (1997), "The Effects of Distributive, Procedural, and Interactional Justice on Postcomplaint Behavior," *JR*, 73 (2), 185–210.
Singh, Jagdip (1988), "Consumer Complaint Intentions and Behaviors: Definitional and Taxonomical Issues," *JM*, 52 (January), 93–107.

SCALE ITEMS:
1. How likely would you be to warn your friends and relatives not to shop at this retail store?

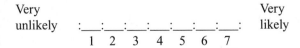

Very
unlikely   :__:__:__:__:__:__:__: Very
likely
           1   2   3   4   5   6   7

#401 *Word-of-Mouth Intentions (Negative)*

2. If this had happened to me I would complain to my friends and relatives about this store.

Very   Very

unlikely   :___:___:___:___:___:___:___: likely

             1   2   3   4   5   6   7

3. If this had happened to me I would make sure to tell my fiends and relatives not to shop at this store.

Strongly   Strongly

disagree   :___:___:___:___:___:___:___: agree

             1   2   3   4   5   6   7

SCALE NAME: Worry

SCALE DESCRIPTION: Three four-point items intended to capture a person's negative emotional concern and uneasiness during a consumption experience.

SCALE ORIGIN: Richins (1997) drew on terms in previous measures, as well as her own series of studies, to develop and refine several emotion-related scales into the CES (Consumption Emotion Set).

SAMPLES: Six studies were reported by Richins (1997) as part of the process of developing the CES, only two of which had reliability information. Study 4 was based on data from **448** college students. Two surveys were conducted in Study 5: Survey 1 was completed by **256** college students, and there were **194** student respondents to Survey 2.

RELIABILITY: As noted, reliability was reported by Richins (1997) only for Studies 4 and 5; in both, the scale had an alpha of **.77**.

VALIDITY: Richins (1997) did not directly examine the validity of the scale. A great deal of effort was expended, however, in a creative use of multidimensional scaling to note whether the items that composed each scale clustered together.

ADMINISTRATION: In the studies performed by Richins (1997), particularly Studies 4 and 5, the scale was just part of a larger instrument containing many emotion-related measures. A high score on the scale suggested that a person was very worried.

MAJOR FINDINGS: On the basis of a review of previously developed measures of emotion, Richins (1997) conducted six studies with the purpose of producing a set of scales particularly suited for assessing consumption experiences. The CES instrument was a result of the studies, one subscale of which measures **worry**. In general, the instrument was more successful in representing the diversity of consumption emotions than were the other instruments tested.

REFERENCES:
Richins, Marsha L. (1997), "Measuring Emotions in the Consumption Experience," *JCR*, 24 (September), 127–46.

SCALE ITEMS:

Not at all — A little — Moderately — Strongly
1————2————3————4

1. Nervous

2. Worried

3. Tense

Part II

Advertising-Related Scales

SCALE NAME: Ad Avoidance (Magazines)

SCALE DESCRIPTION: Three seven-point items measuring the frequency with which a person reports ignoring, flipping past, and eliminating ads in magazines.

SCALE ORIGIN: The scale appears to be original to Speck and Elliot (1997). They imply that the measures used in their main study have undergone a great deal of refinement because they are "based on previous research, input from academic and industry reviewers, and two pretests" (Speck and Elliot 1997, p. 67).

SAMPLES: Data were collected for the main study conducted by Speck and Elliot (1997) from the National Family Opinion's consumer panel. Of the 1500 survey forms mailed out, **946** were returned and usable. See the article for detailed information regarding respondent demographics. The overall panel is balanced to match census distributions, and it also appears that the sample was reasonably well balanced.

RELIABILITY: An alpha of **.66** was reported for the scale (Speck and Elliot 1997).

VALIDITY: No examination of the scale's validity was reported by Speck and Elliot (1997).

ADMINISTRATION: The scale was included as part of a larger mail survey form sent to a portion of a national consumer panel by Speck and Elliot (1997). Higher scores on the scale indicated that. while reading magazines, respondents frequently engaged in activities that can be interpreted as "avoiding" ads.

MAJOR FINDINGS: The study conducted by Speck and Elliot (1997) attempted to identify some predictors of **ad avoidance**. It was highest for television, with magazines being second highest.

COMMENTS: The internal consistency of the scale is low enough to justify caution in its use until its psychometric quality can be improved.

REFERENCES:
Speck, Paul Surgi and Michael T. Elliot (1997), "Predictors of Advertising Avoidance in Print and Broadcast Media," *JA*, 26 (Fall), 61–76.

SCALE ITEMS:
How often do you do each of the following?

Never　:___:___:___:___:___:___:___:　Always
　　　　　　1　　2　　3　　4　　5　　6　　7

1. Rip out or discard advertising inserts before reading a magazine.

2. Flip past large advertising sections in a magazine.

3. Ignore magazine ads.

SCALE NAME: Ad Avoidance (Newspapers)

SCALE DESCRIPTION: Three seven-point items measuring the frequency with which a person reports ignoring ads in newspapers.

SCALE ORIGIN: The scale appears to be original to Speck and Elliot (1997). They imply that the measures used in their main study have undergone a great deal of refinement because they are "based on previous research, input from academic and industry reviewers, and two pretests" (Speck and Elliot 1997, p. 67).

SAMPLES: Data were collected for the main study conducted by Speck and Elliot (1997) from National Family Opinion's consumer panel. Of the 1500 survey forms mailed out, **946** were returned and usable. See the article for detailed information regarding respondent demographics. The overall panel is balanced to match census distributions, and it appears that the sample also was reasonably well balanced.

RELIABILITY: An alpha of **.89** was reported for the scale (Speck and Elliot 1997).

VALIDITY: No examination of the scale's validity was reported by Speck and Elliot (1997).

ADMINISTRATION: The scale was included as part of a larger mail survey form sent to a portion of a national consumer panel by Speck and Elliot (1997). Higher scores on the scale indicated that, while reading newspapers, respondents frequently engaged in activities that can be interpreted as "avoiding" the ads.

MAJOR FINDINGS: The study conducted by Speck and Elliot (1997) attempted to identify some predictors of **ad avoidance**. Among the findings was that **avoidance** was highest for television ads and second highest for magazine ads, with newspaper ads significantly less **avoided** than either.

REFERENCES:

Speck, Paul Surgi and Michael T. Elliot (1997), "Predictors of Advertising Avoidance in Print and Broadcast Media," *JA*, 26 (Fall), 61–76.

SCALE ITEMS:

How often do you do each of the following?

Never   :___:___:___:___:___:___:___: Always
        1   2   3   4   5   6   7

1. Discard advertising inserts before you read a newspaper.

2. Skip over newspaper pages that are mainly advertising.

3. Ignore newspaper ads.

SCALE NAME: Ad Avoidance (Radio)

SCALE DESCRIPTION: Three seven-point items measuring the frequency with which a person reports in some way avoiding (ignoring, "zapping") radio commercials.

SCALE ORIGIN: The scale appears to be original to Speck and Elliot (1997). They imply that the measures used in their main study have undergone a great deal of refinement because they are "based on previous research, input from academic and industry reviewers, and two pretests" (Speck and Elliot 1997, p. 67).

SAMPLES: Data were collected for the main study conducted by Speck and Elliot (1997) from National Family Opinion's consumer panel. Of the 1500 survey forms mailed out, **946** were returned and usable. See the article for detailed information regarding respondent demographics. The overall panel is balanced to match census distributions, and it appears that the sample also was reasonably well balanced.

RELIABILITY: An alpha of **.83** was reported for the scale (Speck and Elliot 1997).

VALIDITY: No examination of the scale's validity was reported by Speck and Elliot (1997).

ADMINISTRATION: The scale was included as part of a larger mail survey form sent to a portion of a national consumer panel by Speck and Elliot (1997). Higher scores on the scale indicated that respondents, while listening to the radio, frequently engaged in activities that can be interpreted as "avoiding" the commercials.

MAJOR FINDINGS: The study conducted by Speck and Elliot (1997) attempted to identify some predictors of **ad avoidance**. Among the findings was that **avoidance** was lowest for radio commercials of the four media examined.

REFERENCES:
Speck, Paul Surgi and Michael T. Elliot (1997), "Predictors of Advertising Avoidance in Print and Broadcast Media," *JA*, 26 (Fall), 61–76.

SCALE ITEMS:
How often do you do each of the following?

Never   :___:___:___:___:___:___:___: Always
            1   2   3   4   5   6   7

1. Switch radio stations during commercials.

2. Skip past radio stations that are in commercial.

3. Tune out radio commercials.

SCALE NAME: Ad Avoidance (Television)

SCALE DESCRIPTION: Three seven-point items measuring the frequency with which a person reports in some way avoiding (ignoring, "zipping," "zapping") television commercials.

SCALE ORIGIN: The scale appears to be original to Speck and Elliot (1997). They imply that the measures used in their main study have undergone a great deal of refinement because they are "based on previous research, input from academic and industry reviewers, and two pretests" (Speck and Elliot 1997, p. 67).

SAMPLES: Data were collected for the main study conducted by Speck and Elliot (1997) from National Family Opinion's consumer panel. Of the 1500 survey forms mailed out, **946** were returned and usable. See the article for detailed information regarding respondent demographics. The overall panel is balanced to match census distributions, and it appears that the sample also was reasonably well balanced.

RELIABILITY: An alpha of **.76** was reported for the scale (Speck and Elliot 1997).

VALIDITY: No examination of the scale's validity was reported by Speck and Elliot (1997).

ADMINISTRATION: The scale was included as part of a larger mail survey form sent to a portion of a national consumer panel by Speck and Elliot (1997). Higher scores on the scale indicated that, while watching television, respondents frequently engaged in activities that can be interpreted as "avoiding" the commercials.

MAJOR FINDINGS: The study conducted by Speck and Elliot (1997) attempted to identify some predictors of **ad avoidance**. Among the findings was that **avoidance** was highest for television ads.

REFERENCES:

Speck, Paul Surgi and Michael T. Elliot (1997), "Predictors of Advertising Avoidance in Print and Broadcast Media," *JA*, 26 (Fall), 61–76.

SCALE ITEMS:

How often do you do each of the following?

Never　　:___:___:___:___:___:___:___:　Always
　　　　　　1　 2　 3　 4　 5　 6　 7

1. Switch TV channel during commercials.

2. Skip past TV channels that are in commercial.

3. Tune out TV commercials.

SCALE NAME: Ad Copy/Ad Picture (Ease of Relating)

SCALE DESCRIPTION: Four seven-point items intended to measure the extent to which a person is able to easily relate the copy in an advertisement to the accompanying picture of the product in the ad.

SCALE ORIGIN: Although not specifically stated in the article, the scale appears to be original to Peracchio and Meyers-Levy (1997).

SAMPLES: The scale was used in a pretest prior to the two experiments conducted by Peracchio and Meyers-Levy (1997). Although not explicitly identified, the **63** subjects were apparently college students.

RELIABILITY: Peracchio and Meyers-Levy (1997) reported alphas of **.70** and **.80** for evaluations of beer and ski products, respectively.

VALIDITY: No specific evidence of the scale's validity was provided by Peracchio and Meyers-Levy (1997).

ADMINISTRATION:: In one of the pretests conducted by Peracchio and Meyers-Levy (1997), the scale was self-administered by subjects after they viewed the ad. Higher scores on the scale suggested that respondents were able to relate the ad copy to the ad picture easily.

MAJOR FINDINGS: Two experiments conducted by Peracchio and Meyers-Levy (1997) were used to study how ad execution variables intended to stimulate persuasion could affect the resources required to process an ad under varying motivation conditions. As noted, the scale was used in a pretest to "examine the degree to which subjects found it resource demanding to cross-reference and thus substantiate the ad copy by examining the ad picture" (Peracchio and Meyers-Levy 1997, p. 182). The results indicated that substantiating ad copy was easier when it and the picture were integrated rather than separated.

REFERENCES:
Peracchio, Laura A. and Joan Meyers-Levy (1997), "Evaluating Persuasion-Enhancing Techniques from a Resource-Matching Perspective," *JCR*, 24 (September), 178–91.

SCALE ITEMS:*

1. To what extent did you refer to the picture as you examined the product's features?

Not at all :___:___:___:___:___:___:___: A lot
$\quad\quad$ 1 $\quad$ 2 $\quad$ 3 $\quad$ 4 $\quad$ 5 $\quad$ 6 $\quad$ 7

2. How easy was it to relate the ad copy to the ad picture?

Easy $\quad$:___:___:___:___:___:___:___: A lot
$\quad\quad$ 1 $\quad$ 2 $\quad$ 3 $\quad$ 4 $\quad$ 5 $\quad$ 6 $\quad$ 7

3. To what extent did the placement of the ad copy facilitate examination of the picture?

Not at all :___:___:___:___:___:___:___: A lot
$\quad\quad$ 1 $\quad$ 2 $\quad$ 3 $\quad$ 4 $\quad$ 5 $\quad$ 6 $\quad$ 7

4. To what extent did you examine the ad picture as the ad copy was reviewed?

Not at all :___:___:___:___:___:___:___: A lot
$\quad\quad$ 1 $\quad$ 2 $\quad$ 3 $\quad$ 4 $\quad$ 5 $\quad$ 6 $\quad$ 7

*The exact phrasing of the items and response scale anchors were not given by Peracchio and Meyers-Levy (1997) and are reconstructed here on the basis of the descriptions provided in the article.

SCALE NAME: Ad Copy/Ad Picture (Relevance)

SCALE DESCRIPTION: Four seven-point items intended to measure the extent to which a picture in an ad is considered relevant to the accompanying ad copy.

SCALE ORIGIN: Although not specifically stated in the article, the scale appears to be original to Peracchio and Meyers-Levy (1997).

SAMPLES: The scale was used in a pretest prior to the two experiments conducted by Peracchio and Meyers-Levy (1997). Although not explicitly identified, the **51** subjects were apparently college students.

RELIABILITY: Peracchio and Meyers-Levy (1997) reported alphas of **.91** and **.92** for evaluations of beer and ski products, respectively.

VALIDITY: No specific evidence of the scale's validity was provided by Peracchio and Meyers-Levy (1997).

ADMINISTRATION: In one of the pretests conducted by Peracchio and Meyers-Levy (1997), the scale was self-administered by subjects after they viewed the ad. Higher scores on the scale suggested that respondents perceived the ad picture as very relevant to its accompanying ad copy.

MAJOR FINDINGS: Two experiments conducted by Peracchio and Meyers-Levy (1997) were used to study how ad execution variables intended to stimulate persuasion can affect the resources required to process an ad under varying motivation conditions. As noted, the scale was used in a pretest to confirm that the ad copy/picture relevance in each of four experimental treatment conditions was similar (equally relevant).

REFERENCES:
Peracchio, Laura A. and Joan Meyers-Levy (1997), "Evaluating Persuasion-Enhancing Techniques from a Resource-Matching Perspective," *JCR*, 24 (September), 178–91.

SCALE ITEMS:*

1. The picture _____ relevant to the ad copy.

Was not :___:___:___:___:___:___:___: Was
          1   2   3   4   5   6   7

2. The copy _____ relevant to the ad picture.

Was not :___:___:___:___:___:___:___: Was
          1   2   3   4   5   6   7

3. The picture and the copy _____ contain the same information.

Did not :___:___:___:___:___:___:___: Did
          1   2   3   4   5   6   7

4. The picture _____ pertinent to the ad copy.

Was not :___:___:___:___:___:___:___: Was
          1   2   3   4   5   6   7

*The exact phrasing of the items and response scale anchors were not given by Peracchio and Meyers-Levy (1997) and are reconstructed here on the basis of the descriptions provided in the article.

SCALE NAME: Ad Credibility

SCALE DESCRIPTION: A four-item, seven-point Likert-type measure that provides an indication of a consumer's attitude about the truthfulness of some specified advertisement.

SCALE ORIGIN: Although not specifically stated as such, the scale appears to be original to the study by Putrevu and Lord (1994).

SAMPLES: Data were gathered by Putrevu and Lord (1994) from students in an introductory under-graduate marketing course taught at a Northeastern U.S. university. Apparently, usable data were collected from **100** students who voluntarily participated for extra credit in the course. Demographic data about the respondents were collected but were not described in the article.

RELIABILITY: Putrevu and Lord (1994) reported an alpha of **.81** for the scale.

VALIDITY: No evidence of the scale's validity was presented in the article by Putrevu and Lord (1994).

ADMINISTRATION: The scale was administered to students by Putrevu and Lord (1994), along with other measures, as part of an in-class experiment. Higher scores on the scale indicated that a consumer considered an ad believable and, in particular, that the claims it made were true.

MAJOR FINDINGS: Putrevu and Lord (1994) examined the relative effectiveness of comparative and noncomparative advertising for products characterized by varying degrees of affective and cognitive involvement. The findings indicated that the **ad credibility** of noncomparative ads was more positive for products low rather than high in affective involvement.

REFERENCES:
Putrevu, Sanjay and Kenneth R. Lord (1994), "Comparative and Noncomparative Advertising: Attitudinal Effects Under Cognitive and Affective Involvement Conditions," *JA*, 23 (June), 77–90.

SCALE ITEMS:

Disagree :___:___:___:___:___:___:___: Agree
        1 2 3 4 5 6 7

1. The claims in the ad are true.

2. I believe the claims in the ad.

3. The ad is sincere.

4. I think the ad is dishonest.

SCALE NAME: Ad Credibility (Claim)

SCALE DESCRIPTION: Three seven-point bipolar adjectives measuring the plausibility of the claims made in an ad for a product.

SCALE ORIGIN: The scale was apparently developed by Kent and Allen (1994).

SAMPLES: Data were collected in the main study by Kent and Allen (1994) from 84 students. However, the scale appears to have been used in just the pretest, which included **32** students.

RELIABILITY: An alpha that exceeded **.85** was reported for the scale used in the pretest by Kent and Allen (1994).

VALIDITY: No specific examination was made of the scale's validity by Kent and Allen (1994).

ADMINISTRATION: Student subjects in a pretest completed the scale along with a couple of other measures after they were exposed to test ads (Kent and Allen 1994). Higher scores on the scale indicated that respondents felt that the brand claims made in the ad were plausible.

MAJOR FINDINGS: Kent and Allen (1994) investigated the role played by brand familiarity in increasing ad memorability. **Ad claim credibility** was measured merely to help preselect ads for the main study, such that those used would be viewed by subjects as making plausible claims.

REFERENCES:
Kent, Robert J. and Chris T. Allen (1994), "Competitive Interference Effects in Consumer Memory for Advertising: The Role of Brand Familiarity," *JM*, 58 (July), 97–105.

SCALE ITEMS:

I felt that the claim that _____ was:*

1. Not plausible   :___:___:___:___:___:___:___: Plausible
                     1   2   3   4   5   6   7

2. Not credible   :___:___:___:___:___:___:___: Credible
                     1   2   3   4   5   6   7

3. Didn't   Did
   make sense   :___:___:___:___:___:___:___: make sense
                      1   2   3   4   5   6   7

*The product name and claim should be inserted here.

SCALE NAME: Ad Medium Effectiveness (Enthusiasm)

SCALE DESCRIPTION: Three items with a five-point response format that appear to measure perceptions about the degree to which an advertising medium is able to express excitement and pass that enthusiasm on to the client and the ad agency. As used by King, Reid, and Morrison (1997), the scale was meant to be completed by respondents knowledgeable with media planing.

SCALE ORIGIN: Some 28 items were developed in pretests and used by King, Reid, and Morrison (1997) in their main survey to measure the relative effectiveness of newspaper advertising for national accounts compared with other media. The items were factor analyzed, and a seven-factor solution was offered. The scale comes from the factor that explains the most variance, which they called *agency/client enthusiasm.*

SAMPLES: Data were gathered by King, Reid, and Morrison (1997) from ad agencies listed in *Advertising Age*'s list of top U.S. agencies, according to 1993 domestic billings. Of the **129** questionnaires returned, 87 different agencies were represented. In brief, approximately 56% of the respondents were women, nearly all (95%) had at least a bachelor's degree, and 55% worked for firms with less than $150 million in billings.

RELIABILITY: An alpha of **.72** was reported for the scale by King, Reid, and Morrison (1997).

VALIDITY: No examination of the scale's validity was reported by King, Reid, and Morrison (1997).

ADMINISTRATION: The scale was self-administered by respondents as part of a larger mail survey instrument (King, Reid, and Morrison 1997). High scores on the scale indicated that respondents believed that the specified medium was effective in creating enthusiasm in clients and ad agencies.

MAJOR FINDINGS: The purpose of the study by King, Reid, and Morrison (1997) was to compare media planners' judgments of the effectiveness of newspaper advertising for national accounts with other media. Of the several measures of effectiveness used, newspapers scored very poorly on the **enthusiasm** issue (.68 out of 5), which suggests that media planners think newspapers are ineffective in their creativity and produce little or no enthusiasm in their clients and ad agencies.

REFERENCES:
King, Karen Whitehill, Leonard N. Reid, and Margaret Morrison (1997), "Large-Agency Media Specialists' Opinions on Newspaper Advertising for National Accounts," *JA*, 26 (Summer), 1–17.

SCALE ITEMS:

Not at all   Extremely
effective   :___:___:___:___:___: effective
           1   2   3   4   5

1. Ability to produce enthusiasm among agency creatives.

2. Ability to deliver creative impact.

3. Ability to produce enthusiasm among clients themselves.

SCALE NAME: Ad Medium Effectiveness (Sales Impact)

SCALE DESCRIPTION: Seven items with a five-point response format that appear to measure perceptions about the ability of an advertising medium to accomplish sales-related goals. As used by King, Reid, and Morrison (1997), the scale was meant to be completed by respondents knowledgeable with media planing.

SCALE ORIGIN: Some 28 items were developed in pretests and used by King, Reid, and Morrison (1997) in their main survey to measure the relative effectiveness of newspaper advertising for national accounts compared with other media. The items were factor analyzed, and a seven-factor solution was offered. The scale comes from the factor that explains the most variance, which they called *client concerns*.

SAMPLES: Data were gathered by King, Reid, and Morrison (1997) from ad agencies listed in *Advertising Age*'s list of top U.S. agencies, according to 1993 domestic billings. Of the **129** questionnaires returned, 87 different agencies were represented. In brief, approximately 56% of the respondents were women, nearly all (95%) had at least a bachelor's degree, and 55% worked for firms with less than $150 million in billings.

RELIABILITY: An alpha of **.84** was reported for the scale by King, Reid, and Morrison (1997).

VALIDITY: No examination of the scale's validity was reported by King, Reid, and Morrison (1997).

ADMINISTRATION: The scale was self-administered by respondents as part of a larger mail survey instrument (King, Reid, and Morrison 1997). High scores on the scale indicated that respondents believed that the specified medium was very effective in achieving several sales-related goals.

MAJOR FINDINGS: The purpose of the study by King, Reid, and Morrison (1997) was to compare media planners' judgments of the effectiveness of newspaper advertising for national accounts with other media. Of the several measures of effectiveness used, newspapers scored best on **sales-related effectiveness**, though the score was not particularly high (3.7 out of 5).

REFERENCES:
King, Karen Whitehill, Leonard N. Reid, and Margaret Morrison (1997), "Large-Agency Media Specialists' Opinions on Newspaper Advertising for National Accounts," *JA*, 26 (Summer), 1–17.

SCALE ITEMS:

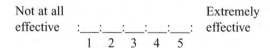

Not at all   Extremely
effective   :___:___:___:___:___: effective
                1   2   3   4   5

1. Ability to immediately impact buyer behavior.

2. Ability to increase sales.

3. Ability to deliver simple sales message.

4. Coordination of timing of promotion with image ads.

5. Ability to increase product trial.

6. Ability to increase market share.

7. Ability to deliver complex sales message.

SCALE NAME: Ad Medium Effectiveness (Sales Representatives)

SCALE DESCRIPTION: Five items with a five-point response format that appear to measure perceptions about the ability of sales representatives of an advertising medium to inform and persuade potential clients of their medium's advertising attractiveness. As used by King, Reid, and Morrison (1997), the scale was meant to be completed by respondents knowledgeable with media planing.

SCALE ORIGIN: Some 28 items were developed in pretests and used by King, Reid, and Morrison (1997) in their main survey to measure the relative effectiveness of newspaper advertising for national accounts compared with other media. The items were factor analyzed, and a seven-factor solution was offered. The scale comes from the factor that explains the most variance, which they called *planning convenience*.

SAMPLES: Data were gathered by King, Reid, and Morrison (1997) from ad agencies listed in *Advertising Age*'s list of top U.S. agencies, according to 1993 domestic billings. Of the **129** questionnaires returned, 87 different agencies were represented. In brief, approximately 56% of the respondents were women, nearly all (95%) had at least a bachelor's degree, and 55% worked for firms with less than $150 million in billings.

RELIABILITY: An alpha of **.82** was reported for the scale by King, Reid, and Morrison (1997).

VALIDITY: No examination of the scale's validity was reported by King, Reid, and Morrison (1997).

ADMINISTRATION: The scale was self-administered by respondents as part of a larger mail survey instrument (King, Reid, and Morrison 1997). High scores on the scale indicated that respondents believed that the specified medium was very effective, in the sense that its sales reps provide information that make it appear attractive compared with other media.

MAJOR FINDINGS: The purpose of the study by King, Reid, and Morrison (1997) was to compare media planners' judgments of the effectiveness of newspaper advertising for national accounts with other media. Of the several measures of effectiveness used, newspapers did not score very well on the **sales representatives** issue (2.75 out of 5), which suggests that media planners think newspaper sales reps are only slightly effective in making the medium compare well against the alternatives.

REFERENCES:
King, Karen Whitehill, Leonard N. Reid, and Margaret Morrison (1997), "Large-Agency Media Specialists' Opinions on Newspaper Advertising for National Accounts," *JA*, 26 (Summer), 1–17.

SCALE ITEMS:

Not at all   Extremely
effective   :___:___:___:___:___: effective
                 1   2   3   4   5

1. Ability to provide audience research.

2. Competence of sales representatives.

3. Ability of reps to sell against other media.

4. Standardization of placement and billing of ads.

5. Willingness to educate agencies and clients about the medium.

SCALE NAME: Ad Medium Effectiveness (Targeting)

SCALE DESCRIPTION: Four items with a five-point response format that measure perceptions about the degree to which an advertising medium is able to target specified audiences efficiently. As used by King, Reid, and Morrison (1997), the scale was meant to be completed by respondents knowledgeable with media planing.

SCALE ORIGIN: Some 28 items were developed in pretests and used by King, Reid, and Morrison (1997) in their main survey to measure the relative effectiveness of newspaper advertising for national accounts compared with other media. The items were factor analyzed, and a seven-factor solution was offered. The scale comes from the factor that explains the most variance, which they called *targeting efficiency*.

SAMPLES: Data were gathered by King, Reid, and Morrison (1997) from ad agencies listed in *Advertising Age*'s list of top U.S. agencies, according to 1993 domestic billings. Of the **129** questionnaires returned, 87 different agencies were represented. In brief, approximately 56% of the respondents were women, nearly all (95%) had at least a bachelor's degree, and 55% worked for firms with less than $150 million in billings.

RELIABILITY: An alpha of **.68** was reported for the scale by King, Reid, and Morrison (1997).

VALIDITY: No examination of the scale's validity was reported by King, Reid, and Morrison (1997).

ADMINISTRATION: The scale was self-administered by respondents as part of a larger mail survey instrument (King, Reid, and Morrison 1997). High scores on the scale indicated that respondents believed that the specified medium was very effective in its ability to target markets efficiently.

MAJOR FINDINGS: The purpose of the study by King, Reid, and Morrison (1997) was to compare media planners' judgments of the effectiveness of newspaper advertising for national accounts with other media. Of the several measures of effectiveness used, newspapers scored only slightly well on the **targeting** issue (2.73 out of 5), which suggests that media planners think newspapers are mediocre in their ability to segment the market and then target particular audiences.

COMMENTS: The reliability of the scale is not very good and might be improved by dropping item 4, which has an extremely low loading on the factor (.37).

REFERENCES:
King, Karen Whitehill, Leonard N. Reid, and Margaret Morrison (1997), "Large-Agency Media Specialists' Opinions on Newspaper Advertising for National Accounts," *JA*, 26 (Summer), 1–17.

SCALE ITEMS:

Not at all   Extremely
effective   :___:___:___:___:___: effective
                 1   2   3   4   5

1. Ability to reach specific audiences efficiently.

2. Ability to reach entire target (total audience potential).

3. Ability to reach 18- to 49-year-olds.

4. Cost per thousand of target efficiently reached.

SCALE NAME: Ad Medium Effectiveness (Versatility)

SCALE DESCRIPTION: Eight items with a five-point response format that appear to measure perceptions about the degree to which an advertising medium offers a variety of benefits, such as opportunity for promotion tie-ins, ability to negotiate ad placement, and quality of reproduction. As used by King, Reid, and Morrison (1997), the scale was meant to be completed by respondents knowledgeable with media planing.

SCALE ORIGIN: Some 28 items were developed in pretests and used by King, Reid, and Morrison (1997) in their main survey to measure the relative effectiveness of newspaper advertising for national accounts compared with other media. The items were factor analyzed, and a seven-factor solution was offered. The scale comes from the factor that explains the most variance, which they called *planning details*.

SAMPLES: Data were gathered by King, Reid, and Morrison (1997) from ad agencies listed in *Advertising Age*'s list of top U.S. agencies, according to 1993 domestic billings. Of the **129** questionnaires returned, 87 different agencies were represented. In brief, approximately 56% of the respondents were women, nearly all (95%) had at least a bachelor's degree, and 55% worked for firms with less than $150 million in billings.

RELIABILITY: An alpha of **.80** was reported for the scale by King, Reid, and Morrison (1997).

VALIDITY: No examination of the scale's validity was reported by King, Reid, and Morrison (1997).

ADMINISTRATION: The scale was self-administered by respondents as part of a larger mail survey instrument (King, Reid, and Morrison 1997). High scores on the scale indicated that respondents believed that the specified medium was very versatile in the variety of advertising opportunities and benefits it offered to its clients.

MAJOR FINDINGS: The purpose of the study by King, Reid, and Morrison (1997) was to compare media planners' judgments of the effectiveness of newspaper advertising for national accounts with other media. Of the several measures of effectiveness used, newspapers did not score very well on the **versatility** issue (2.55 out of 5), which suggests that media planners think newspapers are only slightly versatile in the opportunities and benefits they provide compared with other advertising alternatives.

REFERENCES:
King, Karen Whitehill, Leonard N. Reid, and Margaret Morrison (1997), "Large-Agency Media Specialists' Opinions on Newspaper Advertising for National Accounts," *JA*, 26 (Summer), 1–17.

SCALE ITEMS:

```
Not at all                     Extremely
effective    :__:__:__:__:__:  effective
              1   2   3   4   5
```

1. Opportunities for promotion tie-ins.

2. Willingness to negotiate on rates and ad placement.

3. Value-added opportunities offered.

4. Program or editorial environment in which ad will appear.

5. Ability to build brand's image.

6. Quality reproduction and presentation.

7. Ability to function as a primary medium.

8. Overall contribution to client's marketing programs.

SCALE NAME: Ad Message Involvement

SCALE DESCRIPTION: Four seven-point, Likert-type statements that are purported to measure the degree of a person's motivation to process a specific ad message.

SCALE ORIGIN: The scale used by Ha (1994, 1996, 1997) was based on adapting 4 of the 25 items used by Laczniak and Muehling (1993). The latter had used the items to measure four different ad-related measures.

SAMPLES: The sample for the experiment conducted by Ha (1996) was selected from among students enrolled in general education classes at two Midwestern universities in the United States. Students volunteered for the study and received a pen for their participation. A usable sample of **112** responses was collected. The median age of the group was 20 years, nearly half (48%) were majoring in a science-related area, and more than half (64%) were women.

RELIABILITY: An alpha of **.97** was calculated for the scale (Ha 1997).

VALIDITY: No specific information regarding the scale's validity was reported by Ha (1996).

ADMINISTRATION: The scale was self-administered by subjects after they were exposed to the experimental stimuli (Ha 1996). Higher scores on the scale indicated that respondents were highly motivated to process a specific ad.

MAJOR FINDINGS: Ha (1996) used an experiment to investigate the effect of clutter on advertising effectiveness. Three dimensions of clutter were examined: quantity of ads in a vehicle, competitiveness of the ads, and intrusiveness of those ads. The findings indicated that **advertising message involvement** was not significantly affected by any of the three dimensions of clutter, though it came close to significance for competitiveness of the ads.

REFERENCES:

Ha, Louisa (1994), *Advertising Clutter and Its Impact on Brand Equity,* doctoral dissertation, Michigan State University.
———— (1996), "Advertising Clutter in Consumer Magazines: Dimensions and Effects," *JAR,* 36 (July/August), 76–84.
———— (1997), personal correspondence.
Laczniak, Russell N. and Darrel D. Muehling (1993), "Toward a Better Understanding of the Role of Advertising Message Involvement in Ad Processing," *Psychology and Marketing,* 10 (4), 301–19.

SCALE ITEMS:

Strongly   Strongly
disagree   :___:___:___:___:___:___:___: agree
                 1   2   3   4   5   6   7

1. I paid attention to the content of the ad.

2. I carefully read the content of the ad.

3. When I saw the ad, I concentrated on its contents.

4. I expended effort looking at the content of this ad.

SCALE NAME: Ad Size Manipulation

SCALE DESCRIPTION: The three-item, Likert-type scale measures a subject's perception of the degree to which two ads are of different size.

SCALE ORIGIN: Although not stated by Homer (1995), the scale appears to be original to her study.

SAMPLES: The sample for the study by Homer (1995) consisted of **245** business students at a Western U.S. university. Respondents were of both genders, volunteered to participate, and were randomly assigned to one of the treatments in the 2 × 2 factorial design.

RELIABILITY: Based on pretest analysis (n = 250), an alpha of **.87** was reported for the scale (Homer 1997).

VALIDITY: No examination of the scale's validity was reported by Homer (1995).

ADMINISTRATION: The scale was apparently self-administered by subjects, along with other measures, after they were exposed to experimental stimuli (Homer 1995). Higher scores on the scale indicated that respondents viewed an ad as being larger than other ads around it.

MAJOR FINDINGS: Replicating Kirmani (1990), Homer (1995) studied the effects of **ad size** on ad-based memory, perceptions, and attitudinal evaluations. It was important to ensure that subjects in the different treatments were getting an effective **manipulation of ad size**. The scale indicated that those in the treatments with larger yellow-page ads perceived the ads as larger than those in the conditions in which the ads on a page shared the same dimensions.

REFERENCES:
Homer, Pamela M. (1995), "Ad Size as an Indicator of Perceived Advertising Costs and Effort: The Effects on Memory and Perceptions," *JA*, 24 (Winter), 1–12.
——— (1997), personal correspondence.
Kirmani, Amna (1990), "The Effect of Perceived Advertising Costs on Brand Perceptions," *JCR*, 17 (September), 160–71.

SCALE ITEMS:

Disagree   :___:___:___:___:___: Agree
                1   2   3   4   5

1. The ads were of the same size and shape. **(r)**

2. The ads varied in size.

3. The _____ was larger than the other ads.*

*The names of the target ad under study should be placed in the blank. These statements are recreated on the basis of their brief description in the article.

SCALE NAME: Affective Response to Ad (Fear)

SCALE DESCRIPTION: Four seven-point bipolar adjectives purported to measure the degree to which a person who has just been exposed to an ad has experienced fearfulness.

SCALE ORIGIN: The source of the scale used by Keller and Block (1996) was not cited and thus may indicate that it is original to their study.

SAMPLES: Data for the experiment run by Keller and Block (1996) came from **97** smokers who were recruited from a pool of students at a large eastern U.S. university. They had smoked for an average of 4.2 years, a majority (62%) of whom claimed to have suffered from smoking side effects, and most (73%) had tried to quit at least once.

RELIABILITY: An alpha of **.89** was reported for the scale (Keller and Block 1996).

VALIDITY: No examination of the scale's validity was reported by Keller and Block (1996).

ADMINISTRATION: The scale was self-administered by students, along with other measures, after they had been exposed to a pamphlet on smoking (Keller and Block 1996). Higher scores on the scale indicated that those respondents have had more fear aroused in them by exposure to some stimulus (e.g., ad) than those who have lower scores.

MAJOR FINDINGS: The experiment conducted by Keller and Block (1996) investigated the conditions under which information that stimulates **fear** is likely to be effective. Among the many findings was that, under a condition of objective processing, high **fear** arousal was more persuasive than low **fear** arousal.

REFERENCES:

Keller, Punam Anand and Lauren Goldberg Block (1996), "Increasing the Persuasiveness of Fear Appeals: The Effect of Arousal and Elaboration," *JCR*, 22 (March), 448–59.

SCALE ITEMS:

Very unafraid :___:___:___:___:___:___:___: Very afraid
             1 2 3 4 5 6 7

Relaxed   :___:___:___:___:___:___:___: Tense
             1 2 3 4 5 6 7

Calm   :___:___:___:___:___:___:___: Agitated
             1 2 3 4 5 6 7

Restful   :___:___:___:___:___:___:___: Excited
             1 2 3 4 5 6 7

SCALE NAME: Affective Response to Ad (Negative Feelings)

SCALE DESCRIPTION: Several unipolar items purported to measure the degree of negative feelings a consumer reports experiencing when exposed to a specific advertisement. The scale has been used over time with varying numbers of items. Fourteen- and 20-item versions were used by Edell and Burke (1987), and a 14 item version was used by Burke and Edell (1989). A much smaller but somewhat similar three-item version was employed by Madden, Allen, and Twible (1988). Mooradian (1996) used a five-item scale.

There is an important distinction between this measure and one such as #445. As Mooradian (1996, p. 101) stated in the directions used with his scale, subjects were to describe "reactions to the ad, not to how you would describe the ad." Admittedly, there should be a high correspondence between the two, but they are still theoretically different constructs.

SCALE ORIGIN: Madden, Allen, and Twible (1988) cited Abelson and colleagues (1982), Madden (1982), and Nowlis (1970) as sources of their items. Mooradian's (1996) version of the scale is very similar to one used by Goodstein, Edell, and Moore (1990). Ultimately, most of the items composing the various versions of the scale can be found in the "Reaction Profile for TV Commercials" developed by Wells, Leavitt, and McConville (1971).

SAMPLES: The subjects used by Edell and Burke (1987), as well as by Burke and Edell (1989), were recruited by newspaper ads and announcements on a university campus. Two small samples (**29** and **32**) were used in the former study, and **191** was the size of the latter.

Madden, Allen, and Twible (1988) used **143** students recruited in an undergraduate course. The study was conducted in a language lab with groups of 15 to 20 students.

Two studies were reported by Mooradian (1996), both gathering data from undergraduates enrolled in a marketing course. Studies 1 and 2 had **78** and **73** respondents, respectively. No respondents from Study 1 were in Study 2.

RELIABILITY: Burke and Edell (1989) reported an alpha of **.88**. Alphas of **.96** (n = 29) and **.89** (n = 32) were reported by Edell and Burke (1987). Madden, Allen, and Twible (1988) reported a composite reliability of **.75** for their version of the measure. Alphas of **.81** and **.80** were reported by Mooradian for the versions of the scale used in his Studies 1 and 2, respectively. It should be noted that though Study 2 used a simple summated scale, Study 1 was based on the factor scores of 59 items.

VALIDITY: All of the studies used factor analyses to some degree for purifying the measures, but the validity of the scale has not been thoroughly examined. Madden, Allen, and Twible (1988) found some support for the discriminant validity of their abbreviated version of the measure. Specifically, whereas discriminant validity was found between **negative affective response** and positive affective response (#421), the claim could not be made for **negative affective response** and attitude toward the ad (#445).

ADMINISTRATION: Edell and Burke (1987) and Burke and Edell (1989) brought subjects to a theater to view the stimuli and gather data. Madden, Allen, and Twible (1988) used a language lab in which subjects were isolated from one another and input their responses into computer terminals. Mooradian (1996) exposed students to stimuli and collected data during normal class time. Higher scores on the scale suggested that respondents reported experiencing very strong negative emotional reactions to the ads to which they were exposed.

MAJOR FINDINGS: Edell and Burke (1987) investigated the role of feelings in understanding attitude toward the ad. Among the findings was that feelings generated by the ad (e.g., **negative**) contributed uniquely to predictions of attitude –toward –the ad and brand beyond that provided by measures of an ad's characteristics. Subsequently, in Burke and Edell's (1989) study, the findings indicated that **negative responses** to ads had significant (negative) direct and indirect effects on brand attitudes.

Madden, Allen, and Twible's (1988) findings investigated the distinction between cognitive evaluation and affective reaction in advertising response data. The study was not designed to evoke **negative feelings** and no significant effects were observed.

Mooradian (1996) compared extroversion and neuroticism and affective intensity for their ability to explain individual differences in specific, transient affective responses to ads. The findings indicated that affect intensity is largely redundant to extroversion and neuroticism in explaining **negative responses to ads**.

COMMENTS: Several different constructs appear to be represented by the full set of items . Some of them appear to indicate a disinterested type of feeling (e.g., 1, 6, 8), whereas others reflect a sense of skepticism (e.g., 2, 7, 13). An even more intensely negative feeling is shown in several of the other terms (e.g., 3, 5, 10). Users should select items on the basis of their face validity for the facet of interest and then use factor analysis to evaluate and refine the scale's unidimensionality.

REFERENCES:

Abelson, Robert P., Donald R. Kinder, Mark D. Peters, and Susan T. Fiske (1982), "Affective and Semantic Components in Political Person Perceptions," *Journal of Personality and Social Psychology*, 42 (April), 619–30.

Burke, Marian Chapman and Julie A. Edell (1989), "The Impact of Feelings on Ad-Based Affect and Cognitions," *JMR*, 26 (February), 69–83.

Edell, Julie E. and Marian C. Burke (1987), "The Power of Feelings in Understanding Advertising Effects," *JCR*, 14 (December), 421–33.

Goodstein, Ronald C., Julie A. Edell, and Marian Chapman Moore (1990), "When Are Feelings Generated? Assessing the Presence and Reliability of Feelings Based on Storyboards and Animatics," in *Emotion in Advertising*, Stuart J. Agres, Julie A. Edell, and Tony M. Dubitsky, eds. New York: Quorum Books, 175–93.

Madden, Thomas J. (1982), *Humor in Advertising: Application of a Hierarchy of Effects Paradigm*, doctoral dissertation, University of Massachusetts.

———, Chris T. Allen, and Jacquelyn L. Twible (1988), "Attitude Toward the Ad: An Assessment of Diverse Measurement Indices Under Different Processing Sets," *JMR*, 25 (August), 242–52.

Mooradian, Todd A. (1996), "Personality and Ad-Evoked Feelings: The Case for Extraversion and Neuroticism," *JAMS*, 24 (Spring), 99–109.

Nowlis, Vincent (1970), "Mood, Behavior and Experience," in *Feelings and Emotions*, Magda B. Arnold, ed. New York: Academic Press Inc., 261–77.

Wells, William D., Clark Leavitt, and Maureen McConville (1971), "A Reaction Profile for TV Commercials," *JAR*, 11 (December), 11–17.

SCALE ITEMS:

DIRECTIONS: We would like you to tell us how the ad you just saw made you feel. We are interested in your reactions to the ad, not how you would describe it. Please tell us how much you felt each of these feelings while you were watching this commercial. If you felt the feeling *very strongly* put a 5; *strongly* put a 4; *somewhat strongly* put a 3; *not very strongly* put a 2; *not at all* put a 1.

1. Bored
2. Critical
3. Defiant
4. Depressed

  5. Disgusted
  6. Disinterested
  7. Dubious
  8. Dull
  9. Lonely
10. Offended
11. Regretful
12. Sad
13. Skeptical
14. Suspicious
15. Angry
16. Annoyed
17. Bad
18. Fed-up
19. Insulted
20. Irritated
21. Repulsed

Burke and Edell (1989): 1–14; 5-point
Edell and Burke (1987): 1–20 (Study 1); 1–14 (Study 2); both 5-point
Madden, Allen, and Twible (1988): 19–21; 6-point
Mooradian (1996): 2, 6, 10, 13, 14 (Study 2) 5-point

SCALE NAME: Affective Response to Ad (Uneasy Feelings)

SCALE DESCRIPTION: Six five-point unipolar items purported to measure the degree of worry and tension a consumer reports experiencing when exposed to some specific advertisement. There is an important distinction between this measure and one such as #445. As Mooradian (1996, p. 101) stated in the directions used with his scale, subjects were to describe "reactions to the ad, not to how you would describe the ad." Admittedly, there should be a high correspondence between the two, but they are still theoretically different constructs.

SCALE ORIGIN: The scale used by Mooradian (1996) is a subset of that developed by Goodstein, Edell, and Moore (1990). The latter's version had 15 items and an alpha of .93.

SAMPLES: Two studies were reported by Mooradian (1996), both gathering data from undergraduates enrolled in a marketing course. Studies 1 and 2 had **78** and **73** respondents, respectively. No respondents from Study 1 were in Study 2. It should be noted that whereas Study 2 used a simple summation of the six items shown, Study 1 was based on the factor scores of 59 items.

RELIABILITY: Alphas of **.95** and **.84** were reported by Mooradian (1996) for the versions of the scale used in Studies 1 and 2, respectively.

VALIDITY: A maximum likelihood factor analysis was used by Mooradian (1996) in his first study to examine the factor structure of 59 items. A four-dimensional solution was identified with *uneasiness* being described as one of the factors. The dimensionality of the version of the scale used in his second study was not described.

ADMINISTRATION: Mooradian (1996) exposed students to stimuli and collected data during normal class time. Higher scores on the scale suggested that respondents reported experiencing very strong feelings of uneasiness due to the ads to which they were exposed.

MAJOR FINDINGS: Mooradian (1996) compared extroversion and neuroticism and affective intensity for their ability to explain individual differences in specific, transient affective responses to ads. Except with regard to **uneasy feelings**, the findings indicated that affect intensity is largely redundant to extroversion and neuroticism in explaining ad-evoked responses.

REFERENCES:

Goodstein, Ronald C., Julie A. Edell, and Marian Chapman Moore (1990), "When Are Feelings Generated? Assessing the Presence and Reliability of Feelings Based on Storyboards and Animatics," in *Emotion in Advertising*, Stuart J. Agres, Julie A. Edell, and Tony M. Dubitsky, eds. New York: Quorum Books, 175–93.

Mooradian, Todd A. (1996), "Personality and Ad-Evoked Feelings: The Case for Extraversion and Neuroticism," *JAMS*, 24 (Spring), 99–109.

SCALE ITEMS:*

DIRECTIONS: Using the scale below, please use the following terms to describe your reactions to the ad, not to how you would describe the ad.

Not at all   :___:___:___:___:___: Very strongly
         1   2   3   4   5

1. Anxious   4. Sad
2. Concerned   5. Uneasy
3. Regretful   6. Lonely

*The directions provided here are based on the brief description provided by Mooradian (1996).

SCALE NAME: Affective Response to Ad (Upbeat Feelings)

SCALE DESCRIPTION: Several unipolar items purported to measure the degree of "upbeat" feelings a consumer reports experiencing when exposed to a specific advertisement. The scale has been used with varying numbers of items, mostly single-word descriptors, to measure the positive feelings evoked by an ad. Thirty-two- and 26-item versions were used by Edell and Burke (1987), and a 27-item version was used by Burke and Edell (1989). A much smaller but somewhat similar five-item version was employed by Madden, Allen, and Twible (1988). Mooradian (1996) used a 6-item scale in his study.

There is an important distinction between this measure and one such as #445. As Mooradian (1996, p. 101) stated in the directions used with his scale, subjects were to describe "reactions to the ad, not to how you would describe the ad." Admittedly, there should be a high correspondence between the two, but they are still theoretically different constructs.

SCALE ORIGIN: All or most of the items composing the various versions of the scale can be found in the "Reaction Profile for TV Commercials" developed by Wells, Leavitt, and McConville (1971). Madden, Allen, and Twible (1988) cited Abelson and colleagues (1982), Madden (1982), and Nowlis (1970) as sources of their items.

SAMPLES: The subjects used by Edell and Burke (1987), as well as by Burke and Edell (1989), were recruited by newspaper ads and announcements on a university campus. Two small samples (**29** and **32**) were used in the former study, and **191** was the size of the latter.

Madden, Allen, and Twible (1988) used **143** students recruited in an undergraduate course. The study was conducted in a language lab with groups of 15 to 20 students.

Two studies were reported by Mooradian (1996), both gathering data from undergraduates enrolled in a marketing course. Studies 1 and 2 had **78** and **73** respondents, respectively. No respondents from Study 1 were in Study 2.

RELIABILITY: Burke and Edell (1989) reported an alpha of **.95**. Alphas of **.98** (n = 29) and **.95** (n = 32) were reported by Edell and Burke (1987). Madden, Allen, and Twible (1988) reported a composite reliability of **.89** for their version of the measure. Alphas of **.94** and **.91** were reported by Mooradian for the versions of the scale used in his Studies 1 and 2, respectively. It should be noted that whereas Study 2 used a simple summated scale, Study 1 was based on the factor scores of 59 items.

VALIDITY: The validity of the scale has not been adequately addressed in any of the studies, though Madden, Allen, and Twible (1988) found some support for the discriminant validity of their measure. All of the studies used factor analyses to some degree for purifying the measures.

ADMINISTRATION: Edell and Burke (1987) and Burke and Edell (1989) brought subjects to a theater to view the stimuli and gather data. Madden, Allen, and Twible (1988) used a language lab in which subjects were isolated from one another and input their responses into computer terminals. Mooradian (1996) exposed students to stimuli and collected data during normal class time. Higher scores on the scale suggested that respondents reported experiencing very strong positive emotional reactions to the ads to which they were exposed.

MAJOR FINDINGS: Edell and Burke (1987) investigated the role of feelings in understanding attitude toward the ad. Among the findings was that feelings generated by the ad (e.g., **upbeat**) contributed uniquely to predictions of attitude toward the ad and brand beyond that provided by measures of an ad's characteristics. Subsequent to that, Burke and Edell (1989) reported that ads associated with stronger **upbeat** feelings were evaluated better, as were the brands presented in those advertisements.

Among the things investigated by Madden, Allen, and Twible (1988) was how processing effort might influence cognitive evaluation of and affective reactions to ads that varied in humor.The results indicated that processing a humorous ad that subjects had been told to evaluate resulted in significantly less positive feelings (upbeat) than the same ad in a condition in which subjects listened to an ad without knowing they would later be asked questions about it.

Mooradian (1996) compared extroversion and neuroticism and affective intensity for their ability to explain individual differences in specific, transient affective responses to ads. The findings indicated that affect intensity is largely redundant to extroversion and neuroticism in explaining ad-evoked responses such as **upbeat** feelings.

REFERENCES:

Abelson, Robert P., Donald R. Kinder, Mark D. Peters, and Susan T. Fiske (1982), "Affective and Semantic Components in Political Person Perceptions," *Journal of Personality and Social Psychology*, 42 (April), 619–30.

Burke, Marian Chapman and Julie A. Edell (1989), "The Impact of Feelings on Ad-Based Affect and Cognitions," *JMR*, 26 (February), 69–83.

Edell, Julie E. and Marian C. Burke (1987), "The Power of Feelings in Understanding Advertising Effects," *JCR*, 14 (December), 421–33.

Madden, Thomas J. (1982), *Humor in Advertising: Application of a Hierarchy of Effects Paradigm*, doctoral dissertation, University of Massachusetts.

———, Chris T. Allen, and Jacquelyn L. Twible (1988), "Attitude Toward the Ad: An Assessment of Diverse Measurement Indices Under Different Processing Sets," *JMR*, 25 (August), 242–52.

Mooradian, Todd A. (1996), "Personality and Ad-Evoked Feelings: The Case for Extraversion and Neuroticism," *JAMS*, 24 (Spring), 99–109.

Nowlis, Vincent (1970), "Mood, Behavior and Experience," in *Feelings and Emotions*, Magda B. Arnold, ed. New York: Academic Press Inc., 261–77.

Wells, William D., Clark Leavitt, and Maureen McConville (1971), "A Reaction Profile for TV Commercials," *JAR*, 11 (December), 11–17.

SCALE ITEMS:

DIRECTIONS: We would like you to tell us how the ad you just saw made you feel. We are interested in your reactions to the ad, not how you would describe it. Please tell us how much you felt each of these feelings while you were watching this commercial. If you felt the feeling *very strongly* put a 5; *strongly* put a 4; *somewhat strongly* put a 3; *not very strongly* put a 2; *not at all* put a 1.

1. Active
2. Alive
3. Amused
4. Attentive
5. Attractive
6. Carefree
7. Cheerful
8. Confident
9. Creative
10. Delighted
11. Elated
12. Energetic
13. Happy
14. Humorous

15. Independent
16. Industrious
17. Inspired
18. Interested
19. Joyous
20. Lighthearted
21. Playful
22. Pleased
23. Proud
24. Satisfied
25. Silly
26. Stimulated
27. Strong
28. Adventurous
29. Enthusiastic
30. Excited
31. Exhilarated
32. Good
33. Lively
34. Soothed

Burke and Edell (1989): 1–27; 5-point
Edell and Burke (1987): 1–24, 26–33 (Study 1); 1–24, 26, 27 (Study 2); both 5-point
Madden, Allen, and Twible (1988): 7, 22, 26, 32, 34; 6-point
Mooradian (1996): 3, 6, 7, 13, 21, 25 (Study 2); 5-point

SCALE NAME: Affective Response to Ad (Warm Feelings)

SCALE DESCRIPTION: Several unipolar items purported to measure the degree of "warm" feelings a consumer reports experiencing when exposed to a specific advertisement. The scale has been used with varying numbers of items. A 13-item version was used by Edell and Burke (1987) in their first study. A 12-item version was used by Burke and Edell (1989) and by Edell and Burke (1987) in their second study. Mooradian (1996) used a five-item version.

There is an important distinction between this measure and one such as #445. As Mooradian (1996, p. 101) stated in the directions used with his scale, subjects were to describe "reactions to the ad, not to how you would describe the ad." Admittedly, there should be a high correspondence between the two, but they are still theoretically distinct constructs.

SCALE ORIGIN: The scale was developed by Edell and Burke in a pilot test described in an Appendix to their 1987 article. Sixty people recruited on a college campus viewed 16 television commercials. Afterward, they were asked to write down any feelings the ads evoked. They also were given a checklist of 169 terms to use to describe their affective responses to the ads. Sixty of the checklist items and nine more from the open-ended task were used as the initial feelings inventory, which was subsequently factor analyzed in Study 1. Three feelings factors were produced: upbeat (#421), negative (#419), and **warm**.

SAMPLES: The subjects used by Edell and Burke (1987), as well as by Burke and Edell (1989), were recruited by newspaper ads and announcements on a university campus. Two small samples (**29** and **32**) were used in the former study, and **191** was the size of the latter.

Two studies were reported by Mooradian (1996), both gathering data from undergraduates enrolled in a marketing course. Studies 1 and 2 had **78** and **73** respondents, respectively. No respondents from Study 1 were in Study 2.

RELIABILITY: Burke and Edell (1989) reported an alpha of **.89**. Alphas of **.93** (n = 29) and **.90** (n = 32) were reported by Edell and Burke (1987). Alphas of **.71** and **.91** were reported by Mooradian for the versions of the scale used in his Studies 1 and 2, respectively. It should be noted that whereas Study 2 used a simple summated scale, Study 1 was based on the factor scores of 59 items.

VALIDITY: The validity of the scale has not been adequately addressed in any of the studies, though all of them used factor analyses to some degree to purify the measures.

ADMINISTRATION: Edell and Burke (1987) and Burke and Edell (1989) brought subjects to a theater to view the stimuli and gather data. Mooradian (1996) exposed students to stimuli and collected data during normal class time. Higher scores on the scale suggested that respondents reported experiencing very strong sentimental emotional reactions to the ads to which they were exposed.

MAJOR FINDINGS: Burke and Edell (1989) examined the path taken by feelings that ultimately affect attitude toward the brand. Their results indicated that, though **warm** feelings had both positive and negative effects on brand attitude (via different paths), the net effect is positive. Previous to that study, Edell and Burke (1987) investigated the role of feelings in understanding attitude toward the ad. Among the findings was that feelings generated by the ad (e.g., **warmth**) contributed uniquely to predictions of attitude toward the ad and brand beyond that provided by measures of an ad's characteristics.

Mooradian (1996) compared extroversion and neuroticism and affective intensity for their ability to explain individual differences in specific, transient affective responses to ads. The findings indicated that affect intensity is largely redundant to with extroversion and neuroticism in explaining ad-evoked feelings such as **warmth**.

REFERENCES:

Burke, Marian Chapman and Julie A. Edell (1989), "The Impact of Feelings on Ad-Based Affect and Cognitions," *JMR*, 26 (February), 69–83.

Edell, Julie E. and Marian C. Burke (1987), "The Power of Feelings in Understanding Advertising Effects," *JCR*, 14 (December), 421–33.

Mooradian, Todd A. (1996), "Personality and Ad-Evoked Feelings: The Case for Extraversion and Neuroticism," *JAMS*, 24 (Spring), 99–109.

SCALE ITEMS:

DIRECTIONS: We would like you to tell us how the ad you just saw made you feel. We are interested in your reactions to the ad, not how you would describe it. Please tell us how much you felt each of these feelings while you were watching this commercial. If you felt the feeling *very strongly* put a 5; *strongly* put a 4; *somewhat strongly* put a 3; *not very strongly* put a 2; *not at all* put a 1.

1. Affectionate
2. Calm
3. Concerned
4. Contemplative
5. Emotional
6. Hopeful
7. Kind
8. Moved
9. Peaceful
10. Pensive
11. Sentimental
12. Warmhearted
13. Touched

Burke and Edell (1989): 1–12; 5-point
Edell and Burke (1987): 1–13 (Study 1); 1–12 (Study 2); both 5-point
Mooradian (1996): 1, 6, 7, 9, 12 (Study 2); 5-point

SCALE NAME: Argument Strength

SCALE DESCRIPTION: The scale is purported to measure the perceived quality and validity of the message claims in an advertisement. Although each of the uses cited here used a slightly different version of the scale, all had at least two items in common.

SCALE ORIGIN: Two of the items (1 and 2) were used by Petty, Cacioppo, and Schumann (1983) to measure *argument quality*, but the items were not summated into a scale. Lord, Lee, and Sauer (1995) cited the study by Petty, Cacioppo, and Schumann (1983) as previous work measuring the same construct. Neither of the studies by Whittler (1991; Whittler and DiMeo 1991) nor that by Zhang (1996) specifically referenced Petty, Cacioppo, and Schumann (1983) as the origin of the items that composed their versions of the scale, but it is likely that it was the source of inspiration.

SAMPLES: The sample used by Lord, Lee, and Sauer (1995) was composed of **328** undergraduate marketing students. The students participated in groups of approximately 20 per session and received extra credit in the course. A little more than half (55%) of the sample were men.

Data were gathered by Pham (1996) for his three experiments from undergraduate students. The scale was only used in Experiments 2 and 3, which involved **133** and **57** students, respectively.

Whittler and Dimeo (1991) had total of **160** paid, white volunteers in their sample. The sample was selected from several social and civic organizations in a southern city (YWCA, PTA, women's club). Of the total sample, 73% were women with ages ranging from 17 to 55 years. A majority of the sample (82%) was married, and 60% percent earned more than $39,999 per year. All but one participant obtained a high school diploma, and 58% percent had college degrees.

Whittler (1991) reported two studies. In Study 1, he had a sample of **160** white and **140** black undergraduate students. In Study 2, he had a sample of **160** Southeastern U.S. white adults.

All that is known about the sample used by Zhang (1996) is that data were gathered from **240** students in undergraduate and graduate business courses.

RELIABILITY: Alphas of **.76, .92,** and **.94** were reported for the scale as used by Lord, Lee, and Sauer (1995), Whittler and DiMeo (1991), and Zhang (1996), respectively. Whittler (1991) reported alphas of **.87** in Study 1 and **.92** in Study 2. Alphas ranged from **.90** to **.92** in the four uses made of the scale by Pham (1996).

VALIDITY: No examination of scale's validity was reported in any of the studies.

ADMINISTRATION: In each of the studies, respondents were exposed to a stimulus and then completed the scale along with other measures. Higher scores on the scale indicated that respondents viewed the claims made in the ad as valid.

MAJOR FINDINGS: Lord, Lee, and Sauer (1995) examined the antecedents of attitude –toward –the ad. **Argument strength** was found to have a significant, positive impact on attitude –toward –the ad under several conditions.

Pham (1996) proposed that two types of processes underlie arousal effects on persuasion: the "selection" and the "representation" effects. The **argument strength** scale was mainly used as a manipulation check and, indeed, confirmed that the treatments had successfully manipulated the construct.

Both studies by Whittler (1991, Whittler and DiMeo 1991) examined the effect of actors' race in ads. Whittler and DiMeo's (1991) results indicated that respondents rated the message claims in the white actor condition as **stronger** than those in the black actor condition. Whittler (1991) failed to find support for relationships between an actors' race or a respondent's racial identification and **argument strength**.

The purpose of the experiment conducted by Zhang (1996) was to examine the effects of humor and need for cognition on responses to print ads. **Argument strength** was used merely as a manipulation check, and indeed, the ad with weak arguments was viewed as having less **argument strength** than the ad with strong arguments.

REFERENCES:

Lord, Kenneth R., Myung-Soo Lee, and Paul L. Sauer (1995), "The Combined Influence Hypothesis: Central and Peripheral Antecedents of Attitude Toward the Ad," *JA*, 24 (Spring), 73–85.

Petty, Richard E., John T. Cacioppo, and David Schumann (1983), "Central and Peripheral Routes to Advertising Effectiveness: The Moderating Role of Involvement," *JCR*, 10 (September), 135–46.

Pham, Michel Tuan (1996), "Cue Representation and Selection Effects of Arousal on Persuasion," *JCR*, 22 (March), 373–87.

Whittler, Tommy E. (1991), "The Effects of Actors' Race in Commercial Advertising: Review and Extension," *JA*, (20) 1, 54–60.

————— and Joan DiMeo (1991), "Viewer's Reaction to Racial Cues in Advertising Stimuli," *JAR*, (31) 6, 37–46.

Zhang, Yong (1996), "Responses to Humorous Advertising: The Moderating Effect of Need for Cognition," *JA*, 25 (Spring), 15–32.

SCALE ITEMS:

1. Strong :___:___:___:___:___:___:___: Weak
            7 6 5 4 3 2 1

2. Persuasive :___:___:___:___:___:___:___: Unpersuasive
            7 6 5 4 3 2 1

3. Important :___:___:___:___:___:___:___: Unimportant
            7 6 5 4 3 2 1

4. Believable :___:___:___:___:___:___:___: Unbelievable
            7 6 5 4 3 2 1

5. Informative :___:___:___:___:___:___:___: Uninformative
            7 6 5 4 3 2 1

6. Convincing :___:___:___:___:___:___:___: Not Convincing
            7 6 5 4 3 2 1

7. Good argument :___:___:___:___:___:___:___: Bad argument
            7 6 5 4 3 2 1

Lord, Lee, and Sauer (1995): 1, 2, 4, 5
Pham (1996): 1, 2*, 6
Whittler (1991): 1–4; 15-point
Whittler and DiMeo (1991): 1–4; 15-point
Zhang (1996): 1, 2, 6, 7; 9-point

*One of the anchors was slightly different from the one shown.

SCALE NAME: Arousal (Energy)

SCALE DESCRIPTION: Five four-point items purported to measure the general activation and energy arousal a person is feeling at some point in time.

SCALE ORIGIN: The scale is part of the Activation-DeactivationAdjective Checklist used by Thayer (1978), the reliability and validity of which has "been determined through multiple replications and electrophysiological measures" (Henthorne, LaTour, and Nataraajan 1993, p. 64). It is claimed that this is a more accurate measure of total body arousal than more typical physiological measures (e.g., heart rate, respiration) (Clements, Hafer, and Vermillion 1976).

SAMPLES: Henthorne, LaTour, and Nataraajan (1993) obtained **201** usable responses through the use of mall intercepts. The sample consisted of 88 men and 113 women. The total sample had an average education of 13.7 years. The majority of the sample was white (80 %) and had an average age of 31.5 years.

LaTour, Pitts, and Snook-Luther (1990) had a sample of **202** business students who were taking a introductory management course at a southern U.S. university. The mean age of the sample was 20.98 years.

Data were collected by LaTour and Rotfeld (1997) through mall intercepts in a demographically diverse area in the southeastern United States. Female shoppers were approached "at random" during all hours of the mall's operation over nine weeks, and those volunteering were randomly assigned to one of two treatments. The **305** subjects composing the sample had a wide range of income and education levels, were mostly white (79%), had an average age of 28 years, and one-third (34%) were married.

RELIABILITY: Alphas of **.82**, **.91**, and **.87** have been reported for the scale in the studies by Henthorne, LaTour, and Nataraajan (1993); LaTour, Pitts, and Snook-Luther (1990); and LaTour and Rotfeld (1997), respectively.

VALIDITY: The validity of the scale was not explicitly examined by Henthorne, LaTour, and Nataraajan (1993) or LaTour, Pitts, and Snook-Luther (1990). LaTour and Rotfeld (1997) indicated that they conducted confirmatory factor analysis that supported the unidimensionality of the scale. Although the scale was highly correlated with a companion measure (#425), they viewed the evidence from the confirmatory factor analysis as supporting a claim for its discriminant validity.

ADMINISTRATION: Henthorne, LaTour, and Nataraajan (1993) and LaTour and Rotfeld (1997) collected the data through the use of mall intercepts. The setting for the experiment conducted by LaTour, Pitts, and Snook-Luther (1990) was described as a "laboratory." Respondents in each of these experiments completed the scale as part of a larger questionnaire after they were exposed to treatment stimuli. Higher scores indicated that participants just felt a high level of arousal energy.

MAJOR FINDINGS: Henthorne, LaTour, and Nataraajan (1993) intended to study the theoretical supposition that increasing tension generates **energy** to a certain point and that, beyond that "threshold," increasing tension arouses anxiety, which begins to deplete energy. Their findings indicated that print ad–induced arousal effects fell short of the threshold point. The "appeal with picture" stimulus also fell short of the tension generation threshold, separating the two hypothesized models.

LaTour, Pitts, and Snook-Luther (1990) found that **energy** had a direct and positive effect on ad impressions. The correlation between tension and **energy** was positive. Both energy and calmness increased positive ad impressions, which they expected to happen only if the correlation between energy and tension was large and negative. They found that the correlation was positive.

The field experiment conducted by LaTour and Rotfeld (1997) was intended to clarify the distinction between threats and psychological responses to the threats. The results indicated that **arousal (energy)** had a direct positive impact on attitude toward the ad and purchase intention but only indirectly increased positive brand attitude.

REFERENCES:

Clements, Paul R., Marilyn N. Hafer, and Mary E. Vermillion (1976), "Psychometric Diurnal and Electrophysiological Correlates of Activation," *Journal of Personality and Social Psychology*, 33 (4), 344–87.

Henthorne, Tony L., Michael S. LaTour, and Rajan Nataraajan (1993), "Fear Appeals in Print Advertising: An Analysis of Arousal and Ad Response," *JA*, 22 (2), 59–69.

LaTour, Michael S., Robert E. Pitts, and David C. Snook-Luther (1990), "Female Nudity, Arousal, and Ad Response: An Experimental Investigation," *JA*, (19) 4, 51–62.

——— and Herbert J. Rotfeld (1997), "There Are Threats and (Maybe) Fear-Caused Arousal: Theory and Confusions of Appeals to Fear and Fear Arousal Itself," *JA*, 26 (Fall), 45–59.

Thayer, Robert E. (1978), "Toward a Psychological Theory of Multidimensional Activation (Arousal)," *Motivation and Emotion*, 2 (1), 1–33.

SCALE ITEMS:

Definitely do not feel :___:___:___:___: Definitely feel
　　　　　　　　　　　 0　 1　 2　 3

1. Active
2. Energetic
3. Vigorous
4. Lively
5. Full of Pep

SCALE NAME: Arousal (Tension)

SCALE DESCRIPTION: Five four-point items purported to measure the "high activation" (tension arousal) a person experiences at some point in time.

SCALE ORIGIN: The scale is part of the Activation-Deactivation Adjective Checklist used by Thayer (1978), the reliability and validity of which has "been determined through multiple replications and electrophysiological measures" (Henthorne, LaTour, and Nataraajan 1993, p. 64). It is claimed that this is a more accurate measure of total body arousal than more typical physiological measures (e.g., heart rate, respiration) (Clements, Hafer, and Vermillion 1976).

SAMPLES: Henthorne, LaTour, and Nataraajan (1993) obtained **201** usable responses through the use of mall intercepts. The sample consisted of 88 men and 113 women. The total sample had an average education of 13.7 years. The majority of the sample was white (80 %) and had an average age of 31.5 years.

LaTour, Pitts, and Snook-Luther (1990) had a sample of **202** business students who were taking a introductory management course at a Southern U.S. university. The mean age of the sample was 20.98 years.

Data were collected by LaTour and Rotfeld (1997) through mall intercepts in a demographically diverse area in the Southeastern United States. Female shoppers were approached "at random" during all hours of the mall's operation over nine weeks, and those volunteering were randomly assigned to one of two treatments. The **305** subjects composing the sample had a wide range of income and education levels, were mostly white (79%), had an average age of 28 years, and one-third (34%) were married.

RELIABILITY: Alphas of **.81**, **.84**, and **.89** have been reported for the scale in the studies by Henthorne, LaTour, and Nataraajan (1993), LaTour, Pitts, and Snook-Luther (1990), and LaTour and Rotfeld (1997), respectively.

VALIDITY: The validity of the scale was not explicitly examined by Henthorne, LaTour, and Nataraajan (1993) or LaTour, Pitts, and Snook-Luther (1990). LaTour and Rotfeld (1997) indicated that they conducted confirmatory factor analysis that supported the unidimensionality of the scale. Although the scale was highly correlated with a companion measure (#424), they viewed the evidence from the confirmatory factor analysis as supporting a claim for its discriminant validity.

ADMINISTRATION: Henthorne, LaTour, and Nataraajan (1993) and LaTour and Rotfeld (1997) collected the data through the use of mall intercepts. The setting for the experiment conducted by LaTour, Pitts, and Snook-Luther (1990) was described as a "laboratory." Respondents in each of these experiments completed the scale as part of a larger questionnaire after they were exposed to treatment stimuli. Higher scores indicated that participants had a high level of tension.

MAJOR FINDINGS: Henthorne, LaTour, and Nataraajan (1993) intended to study the theoretical supposition that increasing **tension** generates energy to a certain point and that, beyond that "threshold," increasing **tension** arouses anxiety, which begins to deplete energy. Their findings indicated that print ad–induced arousal effects fell short of the threshold point.

LaTour, Pitts, and Snook-Luther (1990) found that the main effects of a high level of nudity are on arousal, increasing **tension** and fatigue, and decreasing calmness. The seminude condition had almost the opposite effect of high nudity: less **tension**, less fatigue, and more calmness.

The field experiment conducted by LaTour and Rotfeld (1997) was intended to clarify the distinction between threats and psychological responses to the threats. The results indicated that the only direct effect of **arousal (tension)** was to increase arousal (energy).

REFERENCES:

Clements, Paul R., Marilyn N. Hafer, and Mary E. Vermillion (1976), "Psychometric Diurnal and Electrophysiological Correlates of Activation," *Journal of Personality and Social Psychology*, 33 (4), 344–87.

Henthorne, Tony L., Michael S. LaTour, and Rajan Nataraajan (1993), "Fear Appeals in Print Advertising: An Analysis of Arousal and Ad Response," *JA*, 22 (2), 59–69.

LaTour, Michael S., Robert E. Pitts, and David C. Snook-Luther (1990), "Female Nudity, Arousal, and Ad Response: An Experimental Investigation," *JA*, (19) 4, 51–62.

——— and Herbert J. Rotfeld (1997), "There Are Threats and (Maybe) Fear-Caused Arousal: Theory and Confusions of Appeals to Fear and Fear Arousal Itself," *JA*, 26 (Fall), 45–59.

Thayer, Robert E. (1978), "Toward a Psychological Theory of Multidimensional Activation (Arousal)," *Motivation and Emotion*, 2 (1), 1–33.

SCALE ITEMS:

Definitely do not feel :___:___:___:___: Definitely feel
$\quad\quad\quad\quad\quad\quad\quad$ 0 $\quad$ 1 $\quad$ 2 $\quad$ 3

1. Jittery
2. Intense
3. Fearful
4. Clutched-up
5. Tense

SCALE NAME: Attitude Toward Advertising

SCALE DESCRIPTION: A three-item, five-point, Likert-type summated ratings scale measuring the degree to which a person expresses a positive attitude toward advertising in general, particularly in the sense of it being credible and useful.

SCALE ORIGIN: The source of the scale was not stated by Donthu and Gilliland (1996), but it is likely original to their study.

SAMPLES: Donthu and Gilliland (1996) used trained interviewers to call 1000 householdslisted in a large city telephone directory. Interviews were successfully completed with adults in **368** of those households. Although some demographic information was employed in the analysis, the data were not reported in such a way that the sample as a whole can be described clearly.

RELIABILITY: An alpha of **.75** was reported for the scale by Donthu and Gilliland (1996).

VALIDITY: No specific examination of the scale's validity was reported by Donthu and Gilliland (1996).

ADMINISTRATION: Donthu and Gilliland (1996) had the scale administered as part of a larger telephone survey. Higher scores on the scale indicated that respondents had positive attitudes toward advertising in general.

MAJOR FINDINGS: Donthu and Gilliland (1996) profiled infomercial shoppers and found that they expressed significantly more positive **attitudes toward advertising** than those who had never purchased goods from infomercials.

REFERENCES:
Donthu, Naveen and David Gilliland (1996), "The Infomercial Shopper," *JAR*, 36 (March/April), 69–76.

SCALE ITEMS:

Strongly disagree	Disagree	Neutral	Agree	Strongly agree
1	2	3	4	5

1. Advertisements provide useful information.

2. I think that advertisements are often deceptive. **(r)**

3. I usually do not pay attention to advertisements. **(r)**

SCALE NAME: Attitude Toward Advertising of Cosmetic Pharmaceuticals

SCALE DESCRIPTION: Six five-point, Likert-type statements that measure the attitude a physician has regarding the aiming of advertising for cosmetic pharmaceuticals at consumers.

SCALE ORIGIN: Although the source of the scale is not explicitly stated by Petroshius, Titus, and Hatch (1995), it appears original to their study.

SAMPLES: Data were gathered by Petroshius, Titus, and Hatch (1995) by conducting a survey of physicians in the Midwestern United States. The questionnaires were delivered by pharmaceutical representatives to 250 physicians during their normal visits. Respondents could either mail in the completed forms or have the reps pick them up later. Usable forms were received from **143** physicians (73% male) who varied in age, experience, and type of practice. The largest specialty represented in the sample was dermatology (52%), which was purposeful, given the objectives of the study.

RELIABILITY: An alpha of **.88** was reported for the scale by Petroshius, Titus, and Hatch (1995).

VALIDITY: No examination of the scale's validity was reported by Petroshius, Titus, and Hatch (1995).

ADMINISTRATION: The scale was self-administered by the physicians, along with the other measures, in the questionnaire (Petroshius, Titus, and Hatch 1995). Higher scores on the scale indicated that the responding physicians had very positive attitudes about ads for cosmetic pharmaceutical products aimed at consumers.

MAJOR FINDINGS: Petroshius, Titus, and Hatch (1995) studied physician attitudes toward the advertising of prescription drugs, particularly cosmetic pharmaceuticals, and the effect of these attitudes on other attitudes and behaviors. The findings indicated that one of the most influential effects on prescription-writing habits is the physician's **attitude toward the advertising of cosmetic pharmaceuticals** to consumers.

REFERENCES:
Petroshius, Susan M., Philip A. Titus, and Kathryn J. Hatch (1995), "Physician Attitudes Toward Pharmaceutical Drug Advertising," *JAR*, 35 (November/December), 41–51.

SCALE ITEMS:*

Strongly   Strongly
disagree   :___:___:___:___:___: agree
            1   2   3   4   5

1. In general, the new cosmetic pharmaceuticals would be more valuable to my practice if they worked better.

2. I think it is necessary for pharmaceutical companies to educate patients about cosmetic products before the patients go to a physician.

3. The advertisements I've seen which promote cosmetic pharmaceuticals to consumers are too scientific for them to understand.

4. I'd rather the pharmaceutical companies bring up issues such as aging skin and hair loss through advertisements so that I don't have to.

5. I'd like to see more advertising of cosmetic pharmaceutical products by pharmaceutical companies in the future.

6. Current advertising of cosmetic pharmaceutical products is too vague for patients to really be motivated to see a physician.

*Whether items should be reverse-coded was not noted in the article by Petroshius, Titus, and Hatch (1995). Although it is clear that some will need to be reverse-coded, it is not perfectly clear in every case. Future users should base the decision on proper analysis of the data.

SCALE NAME: Attitude Toward Advertising (Overall)

SCALE DESCRIPTION: Three, seven-point bipolar adjectives purported to measure a person's opinion about advertising in general without reference to any of its possible dimensions. Its hypothesized dimensions have been measured using scales #449 and #450.

SCALE ORIGIN: The scales appears to have been developed by Muehling (1987).

SAMPLES: Muehling (1987) collected data from **88** undergraduate students. The data gathered by Andrews, Durvasula, and Netemeyer (1994) came from college students in both Russia and the United States. All were undergraduate students majoring in business or economics and were of similar ages (U.S. mean = 21.45 years, Russian mean = 20.31 years). The Russian sample had a somewhat higher proportion of women (62%) than did the U.S. sample (51%). Complete data were received from **212** students, 148 from a major Midwestern U.S. university and 64 from two major universities in the Republic of Russia.

RELIABILITY: Muehling (1987) reported an alpha of **.97** for the scale. Composite reliabilities of **.94** and **.87** were reported by Andrews, Durvasula, and Netemeyer (1994) for the scale in its English and Russian versions, respectively.

VALIDITY: No evidence of dimensionality or validity was reported by Muehling (1987) for this scale. Andrews, Durvasula, and Netemeyer (1994) conducted a series of thorough confirmatory factor analyses on this scale as well as two others measuring very similar constructs (#449 and #450). The results provided support for the discriminant validity of the three scales in both the English and Russian versions.

ADMINISTRATION: Muehling (1987) used the scale as part of a larger self-administered survey instrument in a college classroom. The scale was used by Andrews, Durvasula, and Netemeyer (1994) as part of a larger self-administered questionnaire. The Russian version was developed by an expert not only fluent in English and Russian, but also familiar with the cultural nuances in word meanings. The back-translation method was used, and independent checks were made by two other bilingual experts.

Higher scores on the scale suggested that the subject had a positive attitude toward advertising in general.

MAJOR FINDINGS: Muehling (1987) investigated the antecedents of attitude toward the ad. He found that attitude toward the institution of advertising and attitude toward the instruments of advertising explained more than 57% of the variance in **attitude toward advertising (overall).**

The purposes of the study by Andrews, Durvasula, and Netemeyer (1994) were to demonstrate procedures for testing the cross-national equivalence of ad-related measures and to conduct an initial comparison. Their findings indicated that Russians had more positive **attitudes toward advertising (overall)** than did Americans.

COMMENTS: In terms of mean scores on the scale, Andrews, Durvasula, and Netemeyer (1994) reported 5.36 and 5.92 for the U.S. and Russians samples, respectively. Muehling (1987) reported a mean score of 5.38 for his sample.

#428 *Attitude Toward Advertising (Overall)*

REFERENCES:

Andrews, J. Craig J., Srinivas Durvasula, and Richard G. Netemeyer (1994), "Testing the Cross-National Applicability of U.S. and Russian Advertising Belief and Attitude Measures," *JA*, 23 (1), 71–82.

Muehling, Darrel D. (1987), "An Investigation of Factors Underlying Attitude-Toward-Advertising-in-General," *JA*, 16 (1), 32–40.

SCALE ITEMS:

1. Bad :___:___:___:___:___:___:___: Good
          1   2   3   4   5   6   7

2. Negative :___:___:___:___:___:___:___: Positive
              1   2   3   4   5   6   7

3. Unfavorable :___:___:___:___:___:___:___: Favorable
                 1   2   3   4   5   6   7

SCALE NAME: Attitude Toward Advertising (Vehicle Specific)

SCALE DESCRIPTION: Four seven-point Likert-type statements that are purported to measure a person's overall evaluation of the advertising in a specific advertising vehicle. The vehicle examined by Ha (1996) was a dummy magazine prepared for a college student audience.

SCALE ORIGIN: The scale is original to Ha (1996, 1997), though inspiration came from previous measures of the same sort of construct.

SAMPLES: The sample for the experiment conducted by Ha (1996) was selected from among students enrolled in general education classes at two Midwestern universities in the United States. Students volunteered for the study and received a pen for their participation. A usable sample of **112** responses was collected. The median age of the group was 20 years, nearly half (48%) were majoring in a science-related area, and more than half (64%) were women.

RELIABILITY: An alpha of **.95** was calculated for the scale (Ha 1997).

VALIDITY: No specific information regarding the scale's validity was reported by Ha (1996).

ADMINISTRATION: The scale was self-administered by subjects after they were exposed to the experimental stimuli (Ha 1996). Higher scores on the scale indicated that respondents held positive attitudes toward the advertising in a specified vehicle.

MAJOR FINDINGS: Ha (1996) used an experiment to investigate the effect of clutter on advertising effectiveness. Three dimensions of clutter were examined: quantity of ads in a vehicle, competitiveness of the ads, and intrusiveness of those ads. The findings indicated that **attitudes toward advertising** were significantly more positive when the quantity and intrusiveness of the ads was low verses high.

REFERENCES:
Ha, Louisa (1996), "Advertising Clutter in Consumer Magazines: Dimensions and Effects," *JAR*, 36 (July/August), 76–84.
———— (1997), personal correspondence.

SCALE ITEMS:

Strongly   Strongly
disagree   :___:___:___:___:___:___: agree
          1   2   3   4   5   6   7

1. Too much space is devoted to advertisements in this issue of _____. **(r)**

2. Advertisements interrupt my reading of this issue of _____. **(r)**

3. There are too many advertisements in this issue of _____. **(r)**

4. I like the advertisements in this issue of _____.

#430 *Attitude Toward Direct Marketing*

SCALE NAME: Attitude Toward Direct Marketing

SCALE DESCRIPTION: A three-item, five-point, Likert-type summated ratings scale measuring a subject's attitude about direct marketing activities being aimed at him or her.

SCALE ORIGIN: The source of the scale was not stated by Donthu and Gilliland (1996), but it is likely original to their study.

SAMPLES: Donthu and Gilliland (1996) used trained interviewers to call 1000 households listed in a large city telephone directory. Interviews were successfully completed with adults in **368** of those households. Although some demographic information was employed in the analysis, the data were not reported in such a way that the sample as a whole can be described clearly.

RELIABILITY: An alpha of **.70** was reported for the scale by Donthu and Gilliland (1996).

VALIDITY: No specific examination of the scale's validity was reported by Donthu and Gilliland (1996).

ADMINISTRATION: Donthu and Gilliland (1996) had the scale administered as part of a larger telephone survey. Higher scores on the scale indicated that respondents had positive attitudes toward direct marketing activities being used to reach them.

MAJOR FINDINGS: Donthu and Gilliland (1996) profiled infomercial shoppers and found that they expressed significantly more positive **attitudes toward direct marketing** than those who had never purchased goods from infomercials.

COMMENTS: The low alpha level, as well a close reading of the items, suggests that the scale probably is tapping into more than one dimension. Further developmental work and validation certainly is called for.

REFERENCES:
Donthu, Naveen and David Gilliland (1996), "The Infomercial Shopper," *JAR*, 36 (March/April), 69–76.

SCALE ITEMS:

Strongly disagree	Disgree	Neutral	Agree	Strongly agree

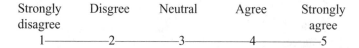

1. Phone solicitations are an invasion of my privacy. **(r)**

2. I enjoy receiving junk mail.

3. I often use catalogues to shop for products.

SCALE NAME: Attitude Toward Pharmaceutical Advertising to Consumers

SCALE DESCRIPTION: Five five-point, Likert-type statements that measure the attitude a physician has regarding the aiming of pharmaceutical advertising at consumers.

SCALE ORIGIN: Although the source of the scale is not explicitly stated by Petroshius, Titus, and Hatch (1995), it appears original to their study.

SAMPLES: Data were gathered by Petroshius, Titus, and Hatch (1995) by conducting a survey of physicians in the Midwestern United States. The questionnaires were delivered by pharmaceutical representatives to 250 physicians during their normal visits. Respondents could either mail in the completed forms or have the reps pick them up later. Usable forms were received from **143** physicians (73% male) who varied in age, experience, and type of practice. The largest specialty represented in the sample was dermatology (52%), which was purposeful, given the objectives of the study.

RELIABILITY: An alpha of .87 was reported for the scale by Petroshius, Titus, and Hatch (1995).

VALIDITY: No examination of the scale's validity was reported by Petroshius, Titus, and Hatch (1995).

ADMINISTRATION: The scale was self-administered by the physicians along with the other measures in the questionnaire (Petroshius, Titus, and Hatch 1995). Higher scores on the scale indicated that the responding physicians had very positive attitudes about pharmaceutical ads being aimed at consumers.

MAJOR FINDINGS: Petroshius, Titus, and Hatch (1995) studied physician attitudes toward the advertising of prescription drugs, particularly cosmetic pharmaceuticals, and the effect of these attitudes on other attitudes and behaviors. The findings indicated that one of the most influential effects on the attention given to pharmaceutical advertisements is the person's **attitude toward the aiming of pharmaceuticals ads at consumers**.

REFERENCES:
Petroshius, Susan M., Philip A. Titus, and Kathryn J. Hatch (1995), "Physician Attitudes Toward Pharmaceutical Drug Advertising," *JAR*, 35 (November/December), 41–51.

SCALE ITEMS:

Strongly   Strongly
disagree   :___:___:___:___:___: agree
             1   2   3   4   5

1. Pharmaceutical advertising directly to consumers provides them with accurate information.

2. I think pharmaceutical companies should not advertise to the general public. **(r)**

3. The advertisements that promote new drugs to my patients are confusing to them. **(r)**

4. Pharmaceutical advertising directed toward consumers makes my patients happier and better informed.

5. I don't like the idea of pharmaceutical companies advertising because health care should not be about making a profit. **(r)**

SCALE NAME: Attitude Toward Pharmaceutical Advertising to Physicians

SCALE DESCRIPTION: Four five-point, Likert-type statements that measure the attitude a person has regarding the aiming of pharmaceutical advertising at physicians.

SCALE ORIGIN: Although the source of the scale is not explicitly stated by Petroshius, Titus, and Hatch (1995), it appears original to their study.

SAMPLES: Data were gathered by Petroshius, Titus, and Hatch (1995) by conducting a survey of physicians in the Midwestern United States. The questionnaires were delivered by pharmaceutical representatives to 250 physicians during their normal visits. Respondents could either mail in the completed forms or have the reps pick them up later. Usable forms were received from **143** physicians (73% male) who varied in age, experience, and type of practice. The largest specialty represented in the sample was dermatology (52%), which was purposeful, given the objectives of the study.

RELIABILITY: An alpha of **.82** was reported for the scale by Petroshius, Titus, and Hatch (1995).

VALIDITY: No examination of the scale's validity was reported by Petroshius, Titus, and Hatch (1995).

ADMINISTRATION: The scale was self-administered by the physicians along with the other measures in the questionnaire (Petroshius, Titus, and Hatch 1995). Higher scores on the scale indicated that the respondents had very positive attitudes about pharmaceutical ads being aimed at physicians.

MAJOR FINDINGS: Petroshius, Titus, and Hatch (1995) studied physician attitudes toward the advertising of prescription drugs, particularly cosmetic pharmaceuticals, and the effect of these attitudes on other attitudes and behaviors. The findings indicated that one of the most influential effects on prescription-writing habits is the physician's **attitude toward the advertising of pharmaceuticals** to them.

REFERENCES:
Petroshius, Susan M., Philip A. Titus, and Kathryn J. Hatch (1995), "Physician Attitudes Toward Pharmaceutical Drug Advertising," *JAR*, 35 (November/December), 41–51.

SCALE ITEMS:

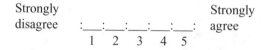

```
Strongly                          Strongly
disagree    :___:___:___:___:___:  agree
              1   2   3   4   5
```

1. Pharmaceutical advertisements give physicians useful information about products.

2. Pharmaceutical advertisements give physicians honest information.

3. Pharmaceutical advertising directed towards physicians is ethical.

4. It is necessary for the FDA to have stricter guidelines concerning the advertisements that pharmaceutical companies place in medical journals. **(r)**

SCALE NAME: Attitude Toward Political Ad (Credibility)

SCALE DESCRIPTION: Three seven-point semantic differentials that measure a person's attitude toward a specific political advertisement to which he or she has been exposed with an emphasis on how fair the ad is viewed to be.

SCALE ORIGIN: Pinkleton (1997) stated that he drew on several previous studies that also examined negative political advertising (e.g., Johnson-Cartee and Copeland 1991).

SAMPLES: The sample used by Pinkleton (1997) was primarily composed of communication and business undergraduate students attending a public university in the southwestern United States. The sample was apparently composed of **165** students andapproximately evenly split on gender, and all respondents were of legal voting age.

RELIABILITY: An alpha of **.73** was reported for the scale (Pinkleton 1997).

VALIDITY: No specific examination of the scale's validity was reported by Pinkleton (1997). However, an exploratory factor analysis was conducted of these items and three others. The results provided some support for the unidimensionality of this scale except that one item (1) loaded high (>.57) on both factors (Pinkleton 1999).

ADMINISTRATION: The scale was included as part of a larger instrument (Pinkleton 1997). Subjects completed the scale after they were exposed to political advertising stimuli. Higher scores on the scale suggested that people viewed a specific political ad they had been exposed to as being very believable and fair.

MAJOR FINDINGS: The experiment conducted by Pinkleton (1997) examined the effects of negative comparative advertising on evaluations of both sponsoring and targeted candidates, as well as on advertising attitudes. Among the findings was that a political ad containing the most negative information also had the worst **credibility**.

REFERENCES:
Johnson-Cartee, Karen S. and Gary A. Copeland (1991), *Negative Political Advertising: Coming of Age*. Hillsdale, NJ: Lawrence Erlbaum Associates.
Pinkleton, Bruce (1997), "The Effects of Negative Comparative Political Advertising on Candidate Evaluations and Advertising Evaluations: An Exploration," *JA*, 26 (Spring), 19–29.
——— (1999), personal correspondence.

SCALE ITEMS:*
DIRECTIONS: Please rate the political advertisement on the following characteristics by circling the appropriate number.

Not
believable :___:___:___:___:___:___:___: Believable
       1 2 3 4 5 6 7

Biased   :___:___:___:___:___:___:___: Unbiased
       1 2 3 4 5 6 7

Unfair   :___:___:___:___:___:___:___: Fair
       1 2 3 4 5 6 7

*The scale items and stem were provided by Pinkleton (1999).

SCALE NAME: Attitude Toward Political Ad (Relevance)

SCALE DESCRIPTION: Three seven-point semantic differentials that measure a person's attitude toward a specific political advertisement to which he or she has been exposed with an emphasis on how interesting and useful the ad is viewed to be.

SCALE ORIGIN: Pinkleton (1997) stated that he drew on several previous studies that also examined negative political advertising (e.g., Johnson-Cartee and Copeland 1991).

SAMPLES: The sample used by Pinkleton (1997) was primarily composed of communication and business undergraduate students attending a public university in the southwestern United States. The sample was apparently composed of **165** students and approximately evenly split on gender, and all respondents were of legal voting age.

RELIABILITY: An alpha of **.71** was reported for the scale (Pinkleton 1997).

VALIDITY: No specific examination of the scale's validity was reported by Pinkleton (1997). However, an exploratory factor analysis was conducted of these items and three others. The results provided some support for the unidimensionality of this scale.

ADMINISTRATION: The scale was included as part of a larger instrument (Pinkleton 1997). Subjects completed the scale after they were exposed to political advertising stimuli. Higher scores on the scale suggested that people viewed a specific political ad they had been exposed to as interesting and useful.

MAJOR FINDINGS: The experiment conducted by Pinkleton (1997) examined the effects of negative comparative advertising on evaluations of both sponsoring and targeted candidates, as well as on advertising attitudes. Among the findings was that the amount of negative information in an ad did not appear to be related to opinions of the ad's **relevance**.

REFERENCES:

Johnson-Cartee, Karen S. and Gary A. Copeland (1991), *Negative Political Advertising: Coming of Age.* Hillsdale, NJ: Lawrence Erlbaum Associates.

Pinkleton, Bruce (1997), "The Effects of Negative Comparative Political Advertising on Candidate Evaluations and Advertising Evaluations: An Exploration," *JA*, 26 (Spring), 19–29.

——— (1999), personal correspondence.

SCALE ITEMS:*

DIRECTIONS: Please rate the political advertisement on the following characteristics by circling the appropriate number.

Uninformative :___:___:___:___:___:___:___: Informative
                  1   2   3   4   5   6   7

Uninteresting :___:___:___:___:___:___:___: Interesting
                  1   2   3   4   5   6   7

Not useful :___:___:___:___:___:___:___: Useful
                  1   2   3   4   5   6   7

*The scale items and stem were provided by Pinkleton (1999).

SCALE NAME: Attitude Toward Public Service Announcements

SCALE DESCRIPTION: Five five-point semantic differentials measuring a person's attitude toward a public service announcement (PSA).

SCALE ORIGIN: Schoenbachler and Whittler (1996) did not specify the source of the scale, but it is likely original to their study.

SAMPLES: Data were collected by Schoenbachler and Whittler (1996) from a sample of **371** seventh- and eight-grade students from a metropolitan middle school. No other information was provided about the sample.

RELIABILITY: An alpha of **.86** was reported for the scale (Schoenbachler and Whittler 1996).

VALIDITY: No examination of the scale's validity was reported by Schoenbachler and Whittler (1996).

ADMINISTRATION: The subjects completed the scale as part of a larger instrument they completed after they were exposed to an experimental stimulus (Schoenbachler and Whittler 1996). As calculated by the authors, lower scores on the scale suggest that respondents have more positive attitudes toward the PSA.

MAJOR FINDINGS: The purpose of the experiment by Schoenbachler and Whittler (1996) was to examine threat appeal advertising using the *ordered protection model*. As hypothesized, a social threat appeared to produce a significantly better **attitude toward the PSA** (antidrug) than a physical threat did.

REFERENCES:
Schoenbachler, Denise D. (1997), personal correspondence.
——— and Tommy E. Whittler (1996), "Adolescent Processing of Social and Physical Threat Communications," *JA*, 25 (Winter), 37–54.

SCALE ITEMS:
DIRECTIONS: We are interested in your opinion of the PSA you looked at. Please circle the number closet to the word that described what you thought about the PSA.*

Do you think the ad about drug use was:

Pleasant　:___:___:___:___:___:　Unpleasant
　　　　　　　1　2　3　4　5

Good　　　:___:___:___:___:___:　Bad
　　　　　　　1　2　3　4　5

Useful　　:___:___:___:___:___:　Useless
　　　　　　　1　2　3　4　5

Valuable　:___:___:___:___:___:　Worthless
　　　　　　　1　2　3　4　5

Beneficial :___:___:___:___:___:　Not beneficial
　　　　　　　1　2　3　4　5

*The scale stem and directions were provided by Schoenbachler (1997).

SCALE NAME: Attitude Toward Sex in Advertising

SCALE DESCRIPTION: A four-item, five point, Likert-type scale measuring a person's evaluation of the use of sex appeals in advertising.

SCALE ORIGIN: Although it is not stated specifically in the article, the scale appears to be original to the study by Treise and colleagues (1994).

SAMPLES: Respondents were recruited by Treise and colleagues (1994) using mall intercepts. The mall was located in the Southeastern United States, and interviewers were told to approach a diverse group of adults. On agreeing to fill out a questionnaire, respondents were allowed to complete the form in private. They were paid $2 for their participation, and analysis was based on responses from **292** people. The sample has a few more women (54.8%) than men (43.5%), and 56.8% identified themselves as "Euro-American." The largest age group was 22 to 30 years of age (29.1%), and 37.7% of the sample indicated they had at least one college degree.

RELIABILITY: An alpha of **.77** was reported for the scale by Treise and colleagues (1994).

VALIDITY: No examination of the scale's validity was reported by Treise and colleagues (1994).

ADMINISTRATION: As noted, the scale was self-administered by respondents along with other measures in a mall intercept setting (Treise et al. 1994). Low scores on the scale appear to have suggested that people had a negative attitude toward the use of sex appeals in advertising.

MAJOR FINDINGS: Consumer perceptions of several controversial advertising practices were examined by Treise and colleagues (1994) as a function of moral ideologies. Although the results indicated that the majority of the respondents were troubled by the use of **sex appeals in advertising**, no significant effect was found between such an attitude and a person's moral philosophy.

REFERENCES:
Treise, Debbie, Michael F. Weigold, Jenneane Conna, and Heather Garrison (1994), "Ethics in Advertising: Ideological Correlates of Consumer Perceptions," *JA*, 23 (September), 59–69.

SCALE ITEMS:

Strongly
agree   :___:___:___:___: Strongly disagree
         1   2   3   4   5

1. Tastefully done, there is nothing wrong with using sexy ads to sell some kinds of products. **(r)**

2. There's too much sex in today's advertising.

3. Nudity in print advertising is not appropriate for general interest magazines.

4. Sexy ads play a role in a teenager's decision to become sexually active.

SCALE NAME: Attitude Toward the Ad

SCALE DESCRIPTION: Seven seven-point items measuring how positive a person's evaluation of some particular advertisement is. Most but not all of the items lean toward cognitive (e.g., informative) rather than affective (e.g., likability) issues.

SCALE ORIGIN: Neese and Taylor (1994, p. 57) cite Holmes and Crocker (1987) as the source of the items for this scale. However, a couple of differences should be noted. First, Holmes and Crocker's scale was composed of bipolar adjectives, whereas Neese and Taylor's scale is more akin to the Likert approach. Second, only six of Holmes and Crocker's ten items were used, and one item (3) came from another source.

SAMPLES: Data were collected by Neese and Taylor (1994) using a judgment sample of civic groups members from across a Southeastern U.S. state. They were expected to be more likely than the population at large to own luxury cars, the product focused on in the study. Indeed, 22.1% of the respondents reported owning one of three luxury sedans. Usable questionnaires were received from **422** respondents. The sample was predominately male, and 41.5% were over 64 years of age.

RELIABILITY: An alpha of **.83** was reported for the scale by Neese and Taylor (1994).

VALIDITY: No examination of the scale's validity was reported by Neese and Taylor (1994). However, the authors stated in general terms that they used item–total correlations and the results of a factor analyses to purify each of their scales.

ADMINISTRATION: The conditions in which Neese and Taylor (1994) administered the scale were not clearly described. It appears that the scale was part of some materials completed by subjects before they were exposed to test stimuli. Higher scores on the scale indicated that respondents had positive thoughts about some specific ad to which they had been exposed.

MAJOR FINDINGS: Neese and Taylor (1994) examined the ability of comparative advertising to accomplish certain tasks as it interacts with brand information for a high involvement product. Only weak support was found for the hypotheses that comparative and informative ad copy would stimulate significantly more positive attitudes toward the ad than noncomparative and less informative formats.

REFERENCES:

Holmes and Crocker (1987), "Predispositions and the Comparative Effectiveness of Rational, Emotional and Discrepant Appeals for Both High Involvement and Low Involvement Products," *JAMS*, 15 (Spring), 27–35.

Neese, William T. and Ronald D. Taylor (1994), "Verbal Strategies for Indirect Comparative Advertising," *JAR*, 34 (March/April), 56–69.

#437 *Attitude Toward the Ad*

SCALE ITEMS:

Strongly   Strongly
disagree   :___:___:___:___:___:___:___: agree
                1   2   3   4   5   6   7

1. Is this ad offensive?

2. Is this ad believable?

3. Is this ad useful?

4. Is this ad informative?

5. Is this ad clear?

6. Is this ad likable?

7. Is this ad convincing?

SCALE NAME: Attitude Toward the Ad

SCALE DESCRIPTION: Three seven-point statements used to measure a person's attitude toward some specific advertisement that he or she has been exposed to with an emphasis on how much the viewer *liked* the ad.

SCALE ORIGIN: The source of the scale was not specified by Kamp and MacInnis (1995), but it appears to be original to their study.

SAMPLES: Kamp and MacInnis (1995) collected their data from **400** consumers who had been recruited by a market research company. The people lived in either the Boston, Mass.; Atlanta, Ga.; Minneapolis, Minn.; or Portland, Ore. metropolitan areas. Respondents were chosen to be representative of the target market for the product being studied (not identified). They were between the ages of 18 and 65 years, with household incomes greater than $20,000, and were mostly women (75%).

RELIABILITY: An alpha of **.90** was reported for the scale by Kamp and MacInnis (1995).

VALIDITY: No examination of the scale's validity was reported by Kamp and MacInnis (1995).

ADMINISTRATION: Respondents completed the scale after being exposed to a test ad (Kamp and MacInnis 1995). A handheld dial was used by respondents, which automatically recorded their responses to this scale and the other measures on the questionnaire. Higher scores on the scale indicated that respondents had very positive attitudes toward the ad to which they were exposed.

MAJOR FINDINGS: Kamp and MacInnis (1995) examined the effect of two emotion-related variables on the nature and intensity of consumers' emotional responses to ads. Among the findings was that **attitude toward the ad** was best when emotional "flow" was dynamic and emotional "integration" was high.

REFERENCES:
Kamp, Edward and Deborah J. MacInnis (1995), "Characteristics of Portrayed Emotions in Commercials: When Does What Is Shown in Ads Affect Viewers?" *JAR*, 35 (November/December), 19–28.
MacInnis, Deborah J. (1999), personal correspondence.

SCALE ITEMS:*

1. Overall, what is your impression of this ad?

Disliked it   Liked it
very much   :___:___:___:___:___:___:___: very much
            1   2   3   4   5   6   7

2. To what degree did you feel positively toward this ad?

Not at all   Very
positive   :___:___:___:___:___:___:___: positive
            1   2   3   4   5   6   7

3. Overall, how well did you like this commercial?

Did not like   Liked it
it at all   :___:___:___:___:___:___:___: very much
            1   2   3   4   5   6   7

*The items and the response format were provided by MacInnis (1999).

SCALE NAME: Attitude Toward the Ad (Affective Component)

SCALE DESCRIPTION: Various bipolar adjectives presumed to measure the subject's evaluation of an advertisement. Most of the scales were part of a pair used together to measure the cognitive and affective components of a person's attitude. Some were developed with the apparent notion that they were general evaluative measures. However, Bruner's (1995, 1998) work suggests that they have more in common with measures of the affective component than they do with general evaluative measures. Work conducted by Petty (Crites, Fabrigar, and Petty 1994; Petty, Wegener, and Fabrigar 1997) supports the notion of separately measuring the affective, cognitive, and general evaluative aspects of attitudes.

SCALE ORIGIN: The source of most of the scales is unclear because most authors did not specify their origin. However, using methods described by Bruner (1995, 1998), approximately half appear to be original, and the remaining were either borrowed or modified from previous research. In a general sense, the basis for these scales can be traced to the work with semantic differentials pioneered by Osgood, Suci, and Tannenbaum (1957). Another source used by several authors, especially those who wanted to measure both the affective and cognitive components of an attitude, is Baker and Churchill (1977).

SELECTED SAMPLES: Laczniak and Muehling's (1993) sample consisted of **280** students from an introductory marketing course. Miller and Marks (1992) used **124** undergraduate marketing students from a large Midwestern university in their sample.

Petroshius and Crocker (1989) used **320** white undergraduate student subjects (160 female). Each subject was assigned randomly to one of sixteen treatment conditions.

The experiment conducted by Rosenberg, Pieters, and Wedel (1997) was based on data collected from **115** adult female consumers (20 to 39 years of age). The experiment took place in the headquarters of a market research firm in the Netherlands, and subjects were paid the equivalent of $10 for their effort.

Zinkhan and Zinkhan (1985) used **160** part-time MBA students randomly split into two groups of 80. Of these students, 134 had full-time jobs, all had bank accounts, and their median income was greater than $25,000 per year.

RELIABILITY: The reported alphas were as follows:
.86 by Burton and Lichtenstein (1988);
.93 (Experiment 1) and **.91** (Experiment 2) by Janiszewski (1988);
.88 by Kilbourne (1986);
.77 by Kilbourne, Painton, and Ridley (1985);
.93 by Laczniak and Muehling (1993);
.88 (clothing advertisements) and **.86** (shoe advertisements) by Okechuku and Wang (1988);
.95 by Olney, Holbrook, and Batra (1991);
.80 by Perrien, Dussart, and Paul (1985);
.75–.87 by Petroshius and Crocker (1989);
.77 by Rosenberg, Pieters, and Wedel (1997);
.92 by Zhang (1996); and
.92 by Zhang and Gelb (1996).

Reliability information was not reported by Zinkhan and Zinkhan (1985).

VALIDITY: Little validity information was provided in most of the studies. Petroshius and Crocker (1989) used factor analysis and noted that the affective and cognitive components in attitude toward the ad constituted 56% of the variance. Janiszewski (1988) reported unidimensionality (Maximum Likelihood Confirmatory analysis) and support for an assumption of independence of errors in measure. Zinkhan and Zinkhan (1985) used factor analysis to reduce the items in the response profile (Schlinger 1979) to four semantic differential scales applicable to print advertisements for financial services.

ADMINISTRATION: In general, paper-and-pencil administration as a part of a longer instrument appears to be the method of choice. Subjects are asked to evaluate a specific advertisement on the basis of the adjective listing and mark the scale appropriately. In some cases (e.g., Petroshius and Crocker 1989), instructions also could be read aloud by the researchers. Laczniak and Muehling (1993) assigned the subjects to one of twelve treatment conditions. Subjects received an ad booklet and were instructed to turn to the inside front cover, read the printed instructions silently, and proceed as directed. After the subjects finished reading, they completed the questionnaires in a pencil-and-paper format. Higher scores on the scale generally implied better (more positive) attitudes toward the ad.

SELECTED FINDINGS: Laczniak and Muehling's (1993) findings indicated that **attitude toward the ad** is significantly related to brand attitudes under low-involvement conditions. The results of a series of regression analyses show different outcomes under different involvement manipulations.

Petroshius and Crocker (1989) found that the physical attractiveness of a spokesperson was significantly related to the subject's affective component of **attitude toward the ad**. None of the other tested sources of variation (sex of communicator, race, product, or sex of subject) was significant as a predictor of the affective component, and no significant interactions were found.

Rosenberg, Pieters, and Wedel (1997, p. 306) proposed that consumers vary in their "visual gaze duration patterns." A methodology that takes this variation among consumers into account was presented for measuring the effect of the physical properties of print advertisements on visual attention.

Zinkhan and Zinkhan (1985) examined the discriminant and predictive validity of four measures of attitude toward the ad: favorable cognitive response, favorable affective response, energy, and familiarity. Subjects' attitudes toward a financial services advertisement were measured using these four scales, which in turn were subjected to discriminant analysis as predictors of subjects' responses to the advertisements. Favorable **cognitive** and **affective** measures both were found to be significant predictors of the behavioral response.

COMMENTS: Although these scales represent a generally recognized method for measuring attitude toward an ad, they have relied heavily on researcher judgement with respect to which specific adjective pairs are appropriate for a given situation. In addition, there has been little rigorous testing of validity. Given this and the available alternatives, future users are urged <u>not</u> to generate yet more items. Instead, it is suggested that they examine the previously published alternatives and select the one that is most appropriate for their study and has shown the most evidence of validity.

Another issue is that there seems to be a lack of concern regarding the precise underlying use of the semantic differential. The semantic differential should be constructed so that the items are anchored by adjectives describing opposites on the semantic continuum. It is arguable whether this requirement is being met in those many cases in which researchers have used bipolar adjectives of the form **X/not X**. Scale items of this form violate the assumption that the midpoint of the scale is meant to be used when the respondent associates the object with neither pole of the adjective pair (Dawes and Smith 1985, p. 534; Osgood, Suci, and Tannenbaum 1957, pp. 29, 83). For example, the midpoint between *interesting* and *boring* would be *neither boring nor interesting*. That is different from the midpoint of a unipolar set such as *interesting/not interesting*. There, the midpoint would be something like *slightly interesting*. The degree to which this violation affects scale scores and interpretation is unknown.

See also Leong, Ang, and Tham (1996).

REFERENCES:

Baker, Michael J. and Gilbert A. Churchill (1977), "The Impact of Physically Attractive Models on Advertising Evaluations," *JMR*, 14 (November), 538–55.

Bruner, Gordon C., II (1995), "The Psychometric Quality of Aad Scales," *Office of Scale Research Technical Report #9501*. Department of Marketing, Southern Illinois University.

———— (1998), "Standardization & Justification: Do Aad Scales Measure Up?" *Journal of Current Issues & Research in Advertising,* 20 (Spring), 1–18.

Burton, Scot and Donald R. Lichtenstein (1988), "The Effect of Ad Claims and Ad Context on Attitude Toward the Advertisement," *JA*, 17 (1), 3–11.

Crites, Stephen L., Jr., Leandre R. Fabrigar, and Richard E. Petty (1994), "Measuring the Affective and Cognitive Properties of Attitudes: Conceptual and Methodological Issues," *Personality and Social Psychology Bulletin*, 20 (December), 619–34.

Dawes, Robyn M. and Tom L. Smith (1985), "Attitude and Opinion Measurement," in *Handbook of Social Psychology*, 3d ed., Vol. 1, Gardner Lindzey and Elliot Aronson, eds. New York: Random House, 509–66.

Janiszewski, Chris (1988), "Preconscious Processing Effects: The Independence of Attitude Formation and Conscious Thought," *JCR*, 15 (September), 199–209.

Kilbourne, William E. (1986), "An Exploratory Study of the Effect of Sex Role Stereotyping on Attitudes Toward Magazine Advertisements," *JAMS*, 14 (Winter), 43–46.

————, Scott Painton, and Danny Ridley (1985), "The Effect of Sexual Embedding on Responses to Magazine Advertisements," *JA*, 14 (2), 48–56.

Laczniak, Russell N. and Darrel D. Muehling (1993), "The Relationship Between Experimental Manipulations and Tests of Theory in an Advertising Message Involvement Context," *JA*, (22) 3, 59–74.

Leong, Siew Meng, Swee Hoon Ang, and Lai Leng Tham (1996), "Increasing Brand Name Recall in Print Advertising Among Asian Consumers," *JA*, 25 (Summer), 65–81.

Okechuku, Chike and Gongrong Wang (1988), "The Effectiveness of Chinese Print Advertisements in North America," *JAR*, 28 (October/November), 25–34.

Olney, Thomas J., Morris B. Holbrook, and Rajeev Batra (1991), "Consumer Responses to Advertising: The Effects of Ad Content, Emotions, and Attitude Toward the Ad on Viewing Time," *JCR*, 17 (March), 440–53.

Osgood, Charles E., George J. Suci, and Percy H. Tannenbaum (1957), *The Measurement of Meaning*. Urbana, IL: University of Illinois Press.

Perrien, Jean, Christian Dussart, and Francoise Paul (1985), "Advertisers and the Factual Content of Advertising," *JA*, 14 (1), 30–35, 53.

Petroshius, Susan M. and Kenneth E. Crocker (1989), "An Empirical Analysis of Spokesperson Characteristics on Advertisement and Product Evaluations," *JAMS*, 17 (Summer), 217–25.

Petty, Richard E., Duane T. Wegener, and Leandre R. Fabrigar (1997), "Attitudes and Attitude Change," *Annual Review of Psychology*, 48, 609–47.

Rosbergen, Edward, Rik Pieters, and Michel Wedel (1997), "Visual Attention to Advertising: A Segment-Level Analysis," *JCR*, 24 (December), 305–14.

Schlinger, Mary Jane (1979), "A Profile of Responses to Commercials," *JAR*, 19 (2), 37–46.

Zhang, Yong (1996), "Responses to Humorous Advertising: The Moderating Effect of Need for Cognition," *JA*, 25 (Spring), 15–32.

———— and Betsy D. Gelb (1996), "Matching Advertising Appeals to Culture: The Influence of Products' Use Conditions," *JA*, 25 (Fall), 29–46.

Zinkhan, George M. and Christian F. Zinkhan (1985), "Response Profiles and Choice Behavior: An Application to Financial Services," *JA*, 14 (3), 39–51, 66.

SCALE ITEMS:

Scale items used in specific studies are listed with an indication of the number of response points if known. Although two studies may have used one or more of the same items, it should not automatically be concluded that the items were exactly the same. Judgment was used to determine when a bipolar adjective was similar to one used before and when it was unique. Slight differences in the bipolar adjectives used, such as *extremely good* versus *good* and *uninteresting* versus *not interesting*, were counted as the same for the purposes of this list.

1. Good/Bad
2. Not irritating/Irritating
3. Interesting/Boring
4. Appealing/Unappealing
5. Impressive/Unimpressive
6. Attractive/Unattractive
7. Eye catching/Not eye catching
8. Pleasant/Unpleasant
9. Likable/Unlikable
10. Soothing/Not soothing
11. Warm hearted/Cold hearted
12. Uplifting/Depressing
13. Affectionate/Not affectionate
14. Dynamic/Dull
15. Refreshing/Depressing
16. Enjoyable/Not enjoyable
17. Worth watching/Not worth watching
18. Beautiful/Ugly
19. Entertaining/Not entertaining
20. Agreeable/Disagreeable

Burton and Lichtenstein (1988): 6, 8, 10, 11, 12, 13; 9-point
Janiszewski (1988): 1, 4, 6, 8, 9; 9-point
Kilbourne (1986): 4, 5, 6; 7-point
Kilbourne, Painton, and Ridley (1985): 4, 5, 6
Laczniak and Muehling (1993): 1, 3, 4, 6, 8, 9, 14, 15, 16; 7-point
Okechuku and Wang (1988): 3, 4, 5, 6, 7
Olney, Holbrook, and Batra (1991): 8, 16, 17, 19
Perrien, Dussart, and Paul (1985): 3, 6, 8, 20; 7-point
Petroshius and Crocker (1989): 3, 4, 5, 6, 7; 7-point
Rosenberg, Pieters, and Wedel (1997): 1, 6, 17; 5-point
Zhang (1996): 2, 3, 8, 9; 9-point
Zhang and Gelb (1996): 2, 3, 8, 9; 9-point
Zinkhan and Zinkhan (1985): 4, 6, 8, 18

SCALE NAME: Attitude Toward the Ad (Claim)

SCALE DESCRIPTION: Five five-point items evaluating the claim portion of an advertisement. The one-word descriptors appear to measure the perceived strength of the ad's arguments.

SCALE ORIGIN: The scale apparently was developed by Derbaix (1995) for use in his study.

SAMPLES: Data were collected by Derbaix (1995, p. 472) from **228** people who were contacted by "study collaborators." They were instructed not to gather data from students, friends, or extended family members. Participants were paid $15.

RELIABILITY: An alpha of **.85** was reported for the scale (Derbaix 1995).

VALIDITY: No examination of the scale's validity was reported by Derbaix (1995).

ADMINISTRATION: The scale was self-administered by respondents, along with other measures, after they were exposed to a television program and some commercials (Derbaix 1995). High scores on the scale indicated that respondents considered an ad to have made some important, convincing arguments.

MAJOR FINDINGS: Derbaix (1995) examined the influence of affective reactions evoked by ads on Aad and Ab. The study is distinguished by its methodological factors, which are expected to improve ecological validity. The findings were not clear regarding the **claim** aspect of **Aad**, but it appears that they showed it was a significant predictor of overall Aad, though not as strong as other variables.

REFERENCES:
Derbaix, Christian (1995), "The Impact of Affective Reactions on Attitudes Toward the Advertisement and the Brand: A Step Toward Ecological Validity," *JMR*, 32 (November), 470–79.

SCALE ITEMS:
Please indicate your opinion about the selling points of the advertisement.

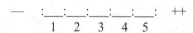

1. Convincing
2. Informative
3. Important
4. Enticing
5. Strong

SCALE NAME: Attitude Toward the Ad (Cognitions)

SCALE DESCRIPTION: The six item, seven-point summative scale appears to measure a subject's attitude toward some specific ad with an emphasis on the beliefs he or she holds about particular attributes the ad may or may not have. These characteristics would be generally considered positive and desirable. The scale was called *the "design" factor* by Homer (1995).

SCALE ORIGIN: Although not stated by Homer (1995), the scale appears to be original to her study.

SAMPLES: The sample for Homer's (1995) study consisted of **245** business students at a Western U.S. university. Respondents were of both genders, volunteered to participate, and were randomly assigned to one of the treatments in the 2 × 2 factorial design.

RELIABILITY: An alpha of **.89** was reported for the scale (Homer 1995).

VALIDITY: No examination of the scale's validity was reported by Homer (1995). It was stated that a factor analysis was conducted and the items in this scale loaded on the same dimension.

ADMINISTRATION: The scale was self-administered by subjects along with other measures after they were exposed to experimental stimuli (Homer 1995). Higher scores on the scale indicated that respondents believed an ad can be described as having a set of positive characteristics.

MAJOR FINDINGS: Replicating Kirmani (1990), Homer (1995) studied the effects of ad size on ad-based memory, perceptions, and attitudinal evaluations. **Attitude Toward the Ad (Cognitions)** was included simply as a covariate, and it was found that larger ads faired better on the measure compared with smaller ads.

REFERENCES:
Homer, Pamela M. (1995), "Ad Size as an Indicator of Perceived Advertising Costs and Effort: The Effects on Memory and Perceptions," *JA*, 24 (Winter), 1–12.
Kirmani, Amna (1990), "The Effect of Perceived Advertising Costs on Brand Perceptions," *JCR*, 17 (September), 160–71.

SCALE ITEMS:
DIRECTIONS: For each of the following characteristics, indicate the extent to which <u>you believe</u> it described the ad for the _____ store.

Not at all   Described the ad
descriptive of the ad   :___:___:___:___:___:___:___: very well
                  1   2   3   4   5   6   7

The ad ...

1. Was believable.

2. Was interesting.

3. Was informative.

4. Was well-designed.

5. Was easy to follow.

6. Was attention getting.

SCALE NAME: Attitude Toward the Ad (Cognitive Component)

SCALE DESCRIPTION: Various bipolar adjectives presumed to measure the cognitive component of a subject's evaluation of an advertisement. Most of the scales were part of a pair used together to measure the cognitive and affective components of a person's attitude. Some were developed with the apparent notion that they were general evaluative measures. However, Bruner's (1995, 1998) work indicated that they had more in common with measures of the *cognitive* component than they did with general evaluative measures. In addition, work conducted by Petty (Crites, Fabrigar, and Petty 1994; Petty, Wegener, and Fabrigar 1997) supports the notion of separately measuring the affective, cognitive, and general evaluative aspects of attitudes.

SCALE ORIGIN: The source of most of the scales is unclear because most authors did not specify their origin. However, using methods described by Bruner (1995, 1998), approximately one-third were borrowed from previously published studies, and the remaining were either original or modified from previous research. In a general sense, the basis for these scales can be traced to the work with semantic differentials pioneered by Osgood, Suci, and Tannenbaum (1957). Another source used by several authors, especially those who wanted to measure both the affective and cognitive components of an attitude, is Baker and Churchill (1977).

SELECTED SAMPLES: Burton and Lichtenstein (1988) used **278** undergraduate business students who were randomly assigned to one of twelve treatment conditions in a 2 × 2 × 3 between-subjects design. It is not clear if the design was balanced or not.

Lord, Lee, and Sauer (1994) collected data from undergraduate students in a introductory marketing course. Students received extra credit for their participation, and analysis was based on **324** competed survey forms.

Okechuku and Wang (1988) used subjects recruited at shopping malls and other public places in Detroit and surrounding suburbs in Michigan and in Windsor, London; Sarnia, Toronto; and Hamilton, Ontario. Sample sizes were 27, 27, and 26 for Chinese ads for three clothing products; 29, 30, and 26 for three North American ads for clothes; 26, 26, and 30 for three Chinese ads for shoes; and 25, 24, and 26 for three North American ads for shoes.

Perrien, Dussart, and Paul (1985) used a sample of **186** members of The Montreal Advertising Club. This represented a 26% response rate. All respondents were French speakers. There was some evidence that the sample was not representative of the population.

RELIABILITY: The reported alphas were as follows:
.73 by Burton and Lichtenstein (1988);
.88 by Donthu (1992);
.65 by Kilbourne (1986);
.57 by Kilbourne, Painton, and Ridley (1985);
.72 by Lord, Lee, and Sauer (1994);
.82 by Miniard, Bhatla, and Rose (1990);
.61 (clothing) and .72 (shoes) by Okechuku and Wang (1988);
.90 by Olney, Holbrook, and Batra (1991);
.78 by Perrien, Dussart, and Paul (1985);
.91 by Peterson, Wilson, and Brown (1992); and
.52 by Petroshius and Crocker (1989).

Reliability information was not reported by Zinkhan and Zinkhan (1985)

VALIDITY: Little validity information was provided in most of the studies. Several used exploratory factor analysis to provide evidence of unidimensionality. Only Burton and Lichtenstein (1988) were more rigorous in their examination of the scale's validity. They subjected their original fifteen items to a confirmatory factor analysis to arrive at six affective and five cognitive items. They also used a separate sample to determine if subjects perceived the affective items as more emotional or "feeling state" descriptive than the cognitive items. The results were highly significant in the expected direction.

ADMINISTRATION: Kilbourne (1986) used a personal interview procedure. In general, however, paper-and-pencil administration as a part of a longer instrument appears to be the method of choice. Subjects are asked to evaluate a specific advertisement on the basis of the adjective listing and mark the scale appropriately. In general, higher scores on the scales were interpreted to mean better (more favorable) attitudes toward the ad.

SELECTED FINDINGS: Burton and Lichtenstein (1988) found that price-oriented **advertising attitudes** were affected by the **cognitive component**, as measured, but not by the affective component. They also found that, after covarying out the effects of the deal in the ads, both affect and cognitions influence attitude toward the deal. They concluded that a two-factor solution to attitude toward the ad is superior to the single component solution.

The study by Lord, Lee, and Sauer (1994) examined the influence of program context on **attitude toward the ad**. Involvement with the ad was significantly related to **ad attitude**, but there was not significant support for the hypothesis that the impact would be greater on one attitude component than another.

Okechuku and Wang (1988) compared North American subjects' **attitudes toward ads** from China and the United States for shoes and clothing. They found no difference in subjects' **cognitive attitudes** toward the ads but did find a significant difference in affective responses.

Perrien, Dussart, and Paul (1985) reported significantly higher **attitudinal scores** as amounts of factual information increased from one to three factual claims, without regard to perceived risk of the product. No differences were found to be dependent on the respondent's professional category (agency, advertiser, media, service).

REFERENCES:

Baker, Michael J. and Gilbert A. Churchill (1977), "The Impact of Physically Attractive Models on Advertising Evaluations," *JMR*, 14 (November), 538–55.

Bruner, Gordon C., II (1995), "The Psychometric Quality of Aad Scales," *Office of Scale Research Technical Report #9501*. Department of Marketing, Southern Illinois University.

——— (1998), "Standardization & Justification: Do Aad Scales Measure Up?" *Journal of Current Issues & Research in Advertising,* 20 (Spring), 1–18.

Burton, Scot and Donald R. Lichtenstein (1988), "The Effect of Ad Claims and Ad Context on Attitude Toward the Advertisement," *JA*, 17 (1), 3–11.

Crites, Stephen L., Jr., Leandre R. Fabrigar, and Richard E. Petty (1994), "Measuring the Affective and Cognitive Properties of Attitudes: Conceptual and Methodological Issues," *Personality and Social Psychology Bulletin*, 20 (December), 619–34.

Donthu, Naveen (1992), "Comparative Advertising Intensity," *JAR*, (32) 6, 53–58.

Kilbourne, William E. (1986), "An Exploratory Study of the Effect of Sex Role Stereotyping on Attitudes Toward Magazine Advertisements," *JAMS*, 14 (Winter), 43–46.

———, Scott Painton, and Danny Ridley (1985), "The Effect of Sexual Embedding on Responses to Magazine Advertisements," *JA*, 14 (2), 48–56.

Lord, Kenneth R., Myung-Soo Lee, and Paul L. Sauer (1994), "Program Context Antecedents of Attitude Toward Radio Commercials," *JAMS*, 22 (1), 3–15.

Miniard, Paul W., Sunil Bhatla, and Randall L. Rose (1990), "On the Formation and Relationship of Ad and Brand Attitudes: An Experimental and Causal Analysis," *JMR,* 27 (August), 290–303.

Okechuku, Chike and Gongrong Wang (1988), "The Effectiveness of Chinese Print Advertisements in North America," *JAR*, 28 (October/November), 25–34.

Olney, Thomas J., Morris B. Holbrook, and Rajeev Batra (1991), "Consumer Responses to Advertising: The Effects of Ad Content, Emotions, and Attitude Toward the Ad on Viewing Time," *JCR,* 17 (March), 440–53.

Osgood, Charles E., George J. Suci, and Percy H. Tannenbaum (1957), *The Measurement of Meaning.* Urbana, IL: University of Illinois Press.

Perrien, Jean, Christian Dussart, and Francoise Paul (1985), "Advertisers and the Factual Content of Advertising," *JA*, 14 (1), 30–35, 53.

Peterson, Robert A., William R. Wilson, and Steven P. Brown (1992), "Effects of Advertised Customer Satisfaction Claims on Consumer Attitudes and Purchase Intention," *JAR*, (32) 2, 34–40.

Petroshius, Susan M. and Kenneth E. Crocker (1989), "An Empirical Analysis of Spokesperson Characteristics on Advertisement and Product Evaluations," *JAMS*, 17 (Summer), 217–25.

Petty, Richard E., Duane T. Wegener, and Leandre R. Fabrigar (1997), "Attitudes and Attitude Change," *Annual Review of Psychology*, 48, 609–47.

Zinkhan, George M. and Christian F. Zinkhan (1985), "Response Profiles and Choice Behavior: An Application to Financial Services," *JA*, 14 (3), 39–51, 66.

SCALE ITEMS:

Scale items used in specific studies are listed with an indication of the number of response points if known. Although two studies may have used one or more of the same items, it should not automatically be concluded that the items were exactly the same. Judgement was used to determine when a bipolar adjective was similar to one used before and when it was unique. Slight differences in the bipolar adjectives used were counted the same for purposes of this list. If every truly different set of bipolar adjectives was listed separately, the list of items would be much longer.

1. Interesting/Boring
2. Trustworthy/Untrustworthy
3. Persuasive/Not at all persuasive
4. Informative/Uninformative
5. Believable/Unbelievable
6. Effective/Not at all effective
7. Appealing/Unappealing
8. Impressive/Unimpressive
9. Attractive/Unattractive
10. Eye catching/Not eye catching
11. Clear/Not clear
12. Convincing/Unconvincing
13. Overall liking/Disliking
14. Clear/Imprecise
15. Complete/Incomplete
16. Well structured/Badly structured
17. Likely/Unlikely
18. Meaningful/Meaningless
19. Valuable/Not valuable
20. Important to me/Not important to me

21. Strong/Weak
22. Helpful/Not helpful
23. Useful/Not useful

Burton and Lichtenstein (1988) (cognitive): 3, 4, 5, 6, 12; 9-point
Donthu (1992): 4, 5, 7, 8, 9, 10, 11, 12, 13, 17; 7-point
Kilbourne (1986) (cognitive): 2,4, 5; 7-point
Kilbourne, Painton, and Ridley (1985) (cognitive): 2, 4, 5
Lord, Lee, and Sauer (1994) (claim): 3, 5, 21
Miniard, Bhatla, and Rose (1990) (claim): 3, 4, 5, 21
Okechuku and Wang (1988) (cognitive): 4, 5, 11; 9-point
Olney, Holbrook, and Batra (1991) (utilitarianism): 4, 20, 22, 23
Perrien, Dussart, and Paul (1985) (cognitive): 4, 14, 15, 16; 7-point
Peterson, Wilson, and Brown (1992): 1, 3, 4, 6, 7; 5-point
Petroshius and Crocker (1989) (cognitive): 4, 5, 11; 7-point
Zinkhan and Zinkhan (1985) (favorable cognition): 12, 18, 19, 20

SCALE NAME: Attitude Toward the Ad (Humor)

SCALE DESCRIPTION: Five nine-point semantic differentials measuring how amusing and funny an ad is perceived to be.

SCALE ORIGIN: Although not explicitly stated, the scale appears to be original to the study by Zhang (1996).

SAMPLES: All that is known about the sample used by Zhang (1996) is that data were gathered from **240** students in undergraduate and graduate business courses.

RELIABILITY: Zhang (1996) reported an alpha of **.91** for the scale.

VALIDITY: No examination of scale's validity was reported by Zhang (1996).

ADMINISTRATION: In each of the studies, respondents were exposed to a booklet containing the experimental stimulus (ad) and then completed the scale along with other measures. Higher scores on the scale indicated that respondents viewed the ad as being very amusing and funny.

MAJOR FINDINGS: The purpose of the experiment conducted by Zhang (1996) was to examine the effects of **humor** and the need for cognition on responses to print ads. Among the findings was that the effect of perceived **humor** in the ads on brand attitude was mediated by overall attitude toward the ad.

REFERENCES:
Zhang, Yong (1996), "Responses to Humorous Advertising: The Moderating Effect of Need for Cognition," *JA*, 25 (Spring), 15–32.

SCALE ITEMS:

1. Not humorous :___:___:___:___:___:___:___:___:___: Humorous
                    –4 –3 –2 –1 0 +1 +2 +3 +4

2. Not funny :___:___:___:___:___:___:___:___:___: Funny
                    –4 –3 –2 –1 0 +1 +2 +3 +4

3. Not playful :___:___:___:___:___:___:___:___:___: Playful
                    –4 –3 –2 –1 0 +1 +2 +3 +4

4. Not amusing :___:___:___:___:___:___:___:___:___: Amusing
                    –4 –3 –2 –1 0 +1 +2 +3 +4

5. Dull :___:___:___:___:___:___:___:___:___: Not dull
                    –4 –3 –2 –1 0 +1 +2 +3 +4

SCALE NAME: Attitude Toward the Ad (Nonclaim)

SCALE DESCRIPTION: Eight five-point items evaluating the executional (nonclaim) portion of an advertisement. The phrases appear to focus on *how* the ad message was presented rather than the strength of its message's arguments.

SCALE ORIGIN: The scale was apparently developed by Derbaix (1995) for use in his study.

SAMPLES: Data were collected by Derbaix (1995, p. 472) from **228** people who were contacted by "study collaborators." They were instructed not to gather data from students, friends, or extended family members. Participants were paid $15.

RELIABILITY: An alpha of **.77** was reported for the scale (Derbaix 1995).

VALIDITY: No examination of the scale's validity was reported by Derbaix (1995).

ADMINISTRATION: The scale was self-administered by respondents, along with other measures, after they were exposed to a television program and some commercials (Derbaix 1995). High scores on the scale indicated that respondents had positive attitudes toward the executional aspects of an ad.

MAJOR FINDINGS: Derbaix (1995) examined the influence of affective reactions evoked by ads on Aad and Ab. The study is distinguished by its methodological factors, which are expected to improve ecological validity. The findings were not clear regarding the **nonclaim** aspect of Aad, but it appears that they showed it was a more significant predictor of overall Aad than the claim portion of Aad (#440).

REFERENCES:
Derbaix, Christian (1995), "The Impact of Affective Reactions on Attitudes Toward the Advertisement and the Brand: A Step Toward Ecological Validity," *JMR*, 32 (November), 470–79.

SCALE ITEMS: Please indicate your opinion about the different components of the advertisement.

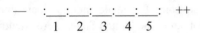

— :___:___:___:___: ++
    1   2   3   4   5

1. The attractiveness of the characters

2. The quality of the music

3. Colors

4. Pace (rhythm)

5. Colors

6. Atmosphere

7. The originality of the pattern

8. The dynamism (vigor) displayed by the advertisement

SCALE NAME: Attitude Toward the Ad (Overall)

SCALE DESCRIPTION: Various bipolar adjectives presumed to measure the subject's evaluation of an advertisement. The scales are similar in that their items are not specific to the advertisements under investigation, though certain adjectives might not be appropriate for every advertisement researchers wish to assess. Seven-point scales seem to be most popular response format, but five- and nine-point scales commonly have been used as well. These scales often are symbolized by **Aad** and appear to be overall evaluations of an ad as opposed to affective or cognitive components of an attitude. Work conducted in recent years both in general psychology (Crites, Fabrigar, and Petty 1994; Petty, Wegener, and Fabrigar 1997) and with advertising (Bruner 1995, 1998) supports the notion of separately measuring the affective, cognitive, and general evaluative aspects of attitudes.

SCALE ORIGIN: The source of most of the scales is unclear because the authors did not specify their origin. However, related investigation suggests that approximately one-third are original, and the remaining are either borrowed or modified from previous research (Bruner 1995, 1998). In a general sense, the basis for these scales can be traced to the work with semantic differentials pioneered by Osgood, Suci, and Tannenbaum (1957). With specific reference to work in marketing, the most common source is Mitchell and Olson (1981). Theirs is a common form of the scale to use when researchers want to measure an overall evaluative response to an ad.

Taylor, Miracle, and Wilson (1997) developed a Korean version of the scale using the back-translation method.

SELECTED SAMPLES: Cox and Cox (1988) used **240** student subjects recruited from MBA classes at a large Southwestern U.S. university. Most subjects worked full time and attended MBA classes on a part-time basis. Ages of subjects ranged from 21 to 62 years, with a median age of 26 years. Forty-five percent of the subjects were women.

Macklin, Bruvold, and Shea (1985) used **127** subjects recruited during a festival at a public elementary magnet school in a large Midwestern U.S. city. Subjects received free tickets to the festival for participation in the study.

Mitchell and Olson (1981) used **71** junior- and senior-level undergraduate students of both sexes who were recruited from an introductory marketing course. Subjects were paid for participation.

Taylor, Miracle, and Wilson (1997) compared data collected from **101** female undergraduate students in the United States and **101** similar students in Korea. The women in the United States were attending a Midwestern university, whereas those in Korea attended a university in Seoul.

Whittler and DiMeo (1991) had a total of **160** paid, white volunteers in their sample. The sample was selected from several social and civic organizations in a southern U.S. city (YWCA, PTA, women's club). Of the total sample, 73% were women, ages ranged from 17 to 55 years, and the majority (82%) were married. More than half (58%) had college degrees, and 60% earned more than $39,999 per year.

SELECTED RELIABILITIES: Reported internal consistencies have ranged from below .69 (Kamins, Marks, and Skinner 1991) to as high as .99 (Holbrook and Batra 1987). Specific reliabilities are provided for the studies described in the "Selected Samples" and "Selected Findings" sections, as follows:

.90 by Cox and Cox (1988);
.85 by Macklin, Bruvold, and Shea (1985);
.87 by Mitchell and Olson (1981);
.95 and **.96** for the English and Korean versions of the scale, respectively, by Taylor, Miracle, and Wilson (1997); and
.84 by Whittler and DiMeo (1991).

VALIDITY: Little validity information was provided in most of the studies. Mitchell and Olson (1981) developed the background for using evaluative belief statements as measures of attitude from Fishbein and Ajzen (1975) and Ahtola (1975) and used only those four items that loaded together out of seven original items in their study. Varimax rotation was used to develop factor structure. Stout and Burda (1989) used a manipulation check to assess the manipulation of brand dominance but not for **Aad**.

Madden, Allen, and Twibble (1988) reported substantive discriminant validity between ad evaluation and a measure of positive affect. They claimed marginal discriminant validity between ad evaluation and a measure of negative affect. Both principle components and confirmatory factor analysis supported the unidimensionality of the scale measure of the ad evaluation construct.

Machleit and Wilson (1988, p. 31) tested their eight-item scale for dimensionality because they acknowledged the possibility that it might tap into both affective and cognitive factors. Their results indicated that there "was not evidence to support discriminant validity between the affective and cognitive dimensions," and they decided to treat the items as a overall measure of **Aad**.

ADMINISTRATION: In general, however, paper-and-pencil administration as a part of a longer instrument appears to be the method of choice. Subjects are asked to evaluate a specific advertisement on the basis of the adjective listing and mark the scale appropriately. In general, higher scores have indicated better attitudes.

SELECTED FINDINGS: Cox and Cox (1988) found that a repeated exposure (two exposures as opposed to one) had a positive and statistically significant effect on the evaluations (**Aad**) of complex advertisements and only a slight and statistically nonsignificant effect on the evaluation of simple ads.

Macklin, Bruvold, and Shea (1985) found that, when the concreteness of verbal messages was held constant, the readability level of the ads made no significant difference on any of the variables examined, including **Aad**. However, the subjects' education and spending on the product category had significant effects on all treatments.

In Mitchell and Olson (1981), **attitude toward ads** was a significant contributor to attitude toward the brand and attitude toward the act of purchasing the brand. The authors concluded that this supports what is now termed the "dual routes" of brand attitude formation.

Taylor, Miracle, and Wilson (1997) compared the effectiveness of commercials that differed in their information content between U.S. and Korean students. Among the findings was that Koreans had significantly lower **attitudes** than Americans toward commercials judged to be high in information.

The results of the study by Whittler and DiMeo (1991) indicated that highly prejudiced whites expressed more favorable evaluations of the ad than less prejudiced whites.

COMMENTS: Although these scales represent a generally recognized method for measuring attitude toward an ad, they have relied heavily on researcher judgement with respect to which specific adjective pairs are appropriate for a given situation. In addition, there has been little rigorous testing of validity. Given this and the available alternatives, future users are urged not to generate more items or unique sets of items. Instead, it is suggested that they examine the previously published alternatives and select the one that is most appropriate for their study and has shown the most evidence of validity.

Another issue is that there seems to be a lack of concern regarding the precise underlying use of the semantic differential. The semantic differential should be constructed so that the items are anchored by adjectives describing opposites on the semantic continuum. It is arguable whether this requirement is being met in those cases in which researchers have used bipolar adjectives of the form **X/not X**. Scale items of this form violate the assumption that the midpoint of the scale is meant to be used when the respondent associates the object with neither pole of the adjective pair (Dawes and Smith 1985, p. 534; Osgood, Suci, and Tannenbaum 1957, pp. 29, 83). For example, the midpoint between *interesting* and *boring* would be *neither boring nor interesting*. That is different from the midpoint of a unipolar set such as *interesting/not interesting*. There, the midpoint would be something like *slightly interesting*. The degree to which this violation affects scale scores and interpretation is unknown.

See also Mooradian (1996); Moore and Harris (1996); and Rubin, Mager, and Friedman (1982). The latter two studies appear to have used many of the same items listed here but not as summated rating scales.

REFERENCES:

Ahtola, Olli T. (1975), "The Vector Model of PREFERENCES: An Alternative to the Fishbein Model," *JMR*, 12 (February), 52–59.

Babin, Laurie and Alvin C. Burns (1997), "Effects of Print Ad Pictures and Copy Containing Instructions to Imagine on Mental Imagery that Mediates Attitudes," *JA*, 26 (Fall), 33–44.

Baumgartner, Hans, Mita Sujan, and Dan Padgett (1997), "Patterns of Affective Reactions to Advertisements: The Integration of Moment-to-Moment Responses into Overall Judgments," *JMR*, 34 (May), 219–32.

Boles, James and Scot Burton (1992), "An Examination of Free Elicitation and Response Scale Measures of Feelings and Judgments Evoked by Television Advertisements," *JAMS*, 20 (Summer), 225–33.

Bruner, Gordon C., II (1995), "The Psychometric Quality of Aad Scales," *Office of Scale Research Technical Report #9501*. Department of Marketing, Southern Illinois University.

———— (1998), "Standardization and Justification: Do Aad Scales Measure Up?" *Journal of Current Issues and Research in Advertising*, 20 (Spring), 1–18.

Bucholz, Laura M. and Robert E. Smith (1991), "The Role of Consumer Involvement in Determining Cognitive Response to Broadcast Advertising," *JA*, 20 (1), 4–17.

Burnkrant, Robert E. and H. Rao Unnava (1995), "Effects of Self-Referencing on Persuasion," *JCR*, 22 (June), 17–26.

Burns, Alvin C., Abhijit Biswas, and Laurie A. Babin (1993), "The Operation of Visual Imagery as a Mediator of Advertising Effects," *JA*, 22 (2), 71–85.

Chattopadhyay, Amitava and Kumal Basu (1990), "Humor in Advertising: The Moderating Role of Prior Brand Evaluation," *JMR*, 27 (November), 466–76.

———— and Prakash Nedungadi (1992), "Does Attitude toward the Ad Endure? The Moderating Effects of Attention and Delay," *JCR*, 19 (June), 26–33.

Cox, Dena S. and Anthony D. Cox (1988), "What Does Familiarity Breed? Complexity as a Moderator of Repetition Effects in Advertisement Evaluation," *JCR*, 15 (June), 111–16.

———— and William B. Locander (1987), "Product Novelty: Does It Moderate the Relationship Between Ad Attitudes and Brand Attitudes?" *JA*, 16 (3), 39–44.

Crites, Stephen L., Jr., Leandre R. Fabrigar, and Richard E. Petty (1994), "Measuring the Affective and Cognitive Properties of Attitudes: Conceptual and Methodological Issues," *Personality and Social Psychology Bulletin*, 20 (December), 619–34.

Darley, William K. and Robert E. Smith (1993), "Advertising Claim Objectivity: Antecedents and Effects," *JM*, 57 (October), 100–13.

———— and ———— (1995), "Gender Differences in Information Processing Strategies: An Empirical Test of the Selectivity Model in Advertising Response," *JA*, 24 (Spring), 41–56.

Dawes, Robyn M. and Tom L. Smith (1985), "Attitude and Opinion Measurement," in *Handbook of Social Psychology*, 3d ed., Vol. 1, Gardner Lindzey and Elliot Aronson, eds. New York: Random House, 509–66.

Day, Ellen and Marla Royne Stafford (1997), "Age-Related Cues in Retail Services Advertising: Their Effects on Younger Consumers," *JR*, 73 (2), 211–33.

Droge, Cornelia (1989), "Shaping the Route to Attitude Change: Central Versus Peripheral Processing Through Comparative Versus Noncomparative Advertising," *JMR*, 26 (May), 193–204.

Fishbein, Martin and Icek Ajzen (1975), *Belief, Attitude, Intention and Behavior: An Introduction to Theory and Research.* Reading, MA: Addison-Wesley.

Gardner, Meryl Paula (1985), "Does Attitude Toward the Ad Affect Brand Attitude Under a Brand Evaluation Set?" *JMR*, 22 (May), 192–98.

Goodstein, Ronald C. (1993), "Category-Based Applications and Extensions in Advertising: Motivating More Extensive Ad Processing," *JCR*, 20 (June), 87–99.

Ha, Louisa (1996), "Advertising Clutter in Consumer Magazines: Dimensions and Effects," *JAR*, 36 (July/August), 76–84.

———— (1997), personal correspondence.

Hastak, Manoj and Jerry C. Olson (1989), "Assessing the Role of Brand Related Cognitive Responses as Mediators of Communications Effects on Cognitive Structure," *JCR*, 15 (March), 444–56.

Hill, Ronald Paul (1988), "An Exploration of the Relationship Between AIDS-Related Anxiety and the Evaluation of Condom Advertisements," *JA*, 17 (Winter), 35–42.

———— (1989), "An Exploration of Voter Responses to Political Advertisements," *JA*, 18 (Winter), 14–22.

Holbrook, Morris B. and Rajeev Batra (1987), "Assessing the Role of Emotions as Mediators of Consumer Responses to Advertising," *JCR*, 14 (December), 404–20.

Homer, Pamela M. (1995), "Ad Size as an Indicator of Perceived Advertising Costs and Effort: The Effects on Memory and Perceptions," *JA*, 24 (Winter), 1–12.

———— and Lynn Kahle (1990), "Source Expertise, Time of Source Identification, and Involvement in Persuasion: An Elaborative Processing Perspective," *JA*, (19) 1, 30–39.

Kahle, Lynn R. and Pamela M. Homer (1985), "Physical Attractiveness of the Celebrity Endorser: A Social Adaption Perspective," *JCR*, 11 (March), 954–61.

Kamins, Michael A. (1990), "An Investigation into the 'Match-Up' Hypothesis in Celebrity Advertising: When Beauty May Be Only Skin Deep," *JA*, 19 (Spring), 4–13.

————, Lawrence J. Marks, and Deborah Skinner (1991), "Television Commercial Evaluation in the Context of Program Induced Mood: Congruency Versus Consistency Effects," *JA*, 20 (Summer), 1–14.

Kellaris, James J., Anthony D. Cox, and Dena Cox (1993), "The Effect of Background Music on Ad Processing: A Contingency Explanation," *JM*, 57 (October), 114–24.

Keller, Kevin Lane (1987), "Memory Factors in Advertising: The Effect of Advertising Retrieval Cues on Brand Evaluations," *JCR*, 14 (December), 316–33.

———— (1991a), "Cue Compatibility and Framing in Advertising," *JMR*, 28 (February), 42–57.

———— (1991b), "Memory and Evaluation Effects in Competitive Advertising Environments," *JCR*, 17 (March), 463–76.

Kirmani, Amna (1997), "Advertising Repetition as a Signal of Quality: If It's Advertised So Much, Something Must Be Wrong," *JA*, 26 (Fall), 77–86.

Lord, Kenneth R., Myung-Soo Lee, and Paul L. Sauer (1994), "Program Context Antecedents of Attitude Toward Radio Commercials," *JAMS*, 22 (1), 3–15.

————, ————, and ———— (1995), "The Combined Influence Hypothesis: Central and Peripheral Antecedents of Attitude Toward the Ad," *JA*, 24, (Spring), 73–85.

Machleit, Karen A., Chris T. Allen, and Thomas J. Madden (1993), "The Mature Brand and Brand Interest: An Alternative Consequence of Ad-Evoked Affect," *JM*, 57 (October), 72–82.

———— and R. Dale Wilson (1988), "Emotional Feelings and Attitude Toward the Advertisement: The Roles of Brand Familiarity and Repetition," *JA*, 17 (3), 27–35.

MacInnis, Deborah J. and C. Whan Park (1991), "The Differential Role of Characteristics of Music on High- and Low-Involvement Consumers' Processing of Ads," *JCR*, 18 (September), 161–73.

———— and Douglas M. Stayman (1993), "Focal and Emotional Integration: Constructs, Measures, and Preliminary Evidence," *JA*, 22 (Winter), 51–65.

MacKenzie, Scott B. and Richard J. Lutz (1989), "An Empirical Examination of the Structural Antecedents of Attitude Toward the Ad in an Advertising Pretesting Context," *JM*, 53 (April), 48–65.

———and Richard A. Spreng (1992), "How Does Motivation Moderate the Impact of Central and Peripheral Processing on Brand Attitudes and Intentions?" *JCR*, 18 (March), 519–29.

Macklin, M. Carole, Norman T. Bruvold, and Carol Lynn Shea (1985), "Is it Always as Simple as 'Keep It Simple!'?" *JA*, 14 (4), 28–35.

Madden, Thomas J., Chris T. Allen, and Jacquelyn L. Twibble (1988), "Attitude Toward the Ad: An Assessment of Diverse Measurement Indices Under Different Processing Sets," *JMR*, 25 (August), 242–52.

McQuarrie, Edward F. and David G. Mick (1992), "On Resonance: A Critical Pluralistic Inquiry into Advertising Rhetoric," *JCR*, 19 (September), 180–97.

Miller, Darryl W. and Lawrence J. Marks (1992), "Mental Imagery and Sound Effects in Radio Commercials," *JA*, (21) 4, 83–93.

Miniard, Paul W., Sunil Bhatla, and Randall L. Rose (1990), "On the Formation and Relationship of Ad and Brand Attitudes: An Experimental and Causal Analysis," *JMR*, 27 (August), 290–303.

Mitchell, Andrew A. (1986), "The Effect of Verbal and Visual Components of Advertisements on Brand Attitudes and Attitude Toward the Advertisement," *JCR*, 13 (June), 12–24.

———and Jerry C. Olson (1981), "Are Product Attribute Beliefs the Only Mediator of Advertising Effects on Brand Attitude?" *JMR*, 18 (August), 318–32.

Mooradian, Todd A. (1996), "Personality and Ad-Evoked Feelings: The Case for Extraversion and Neuroticism," *JAMS*, 24 (Spring), 99–109.

Moore, David J. and William D. Harris (1996), "Affect Intensity and the Consumer's Attitude Toward High Impact Emotional Advertising Appeals," *JA*, 25 (Summer), 37–50.

Muelhing, Darrel D. (1987), "Comparative Advertising: The Influence of Attitude-Toward-the-Ad on Brand Evaluation," *JA*, 16 (4), 43–49.

Murry, John P., Jr., John L. Lastovicka, and Surendra N. Singh (1992), "Feeling and Liking Responses to Television Programs: An Examination of Two Explanations for Media-Context Effects," *JCR*, 18 (March), 441–51.

Osgood, Charles E., George J. Suci, and Percy H. Tannenbaum (1957), *The Measurement of Meaning*. Urbana, IL: University of Illinois Press.

Petty, Richard E., Duane T. Wegener, and Leandre R. Fabrigar (1997), "Attitudes and Attitude Change," *Annual Review of Psychology*, 48, 609–47.

Pham, Michel Tuan (1996), "Cue Representation and Selection Effects of Arousal on Persuasion," *JCR*, 22 (March), 373–87.

Prakash, Ved (1992), "Sex Roles and Advertising Preferences," *JAR*, (32) 3, 43–52.

Rubin, Vicky, Carol Mager, and Hershey H. Friedman (1982), "Company President Versus Spokesperson in Television Commercials," *JAR*, 22 (August/September), 31–33.

Schuhwerk, Melody E. and Roxanne Lefkoff-Hagius (1995), "Green or Non-Green? Does Type of Appeal Matter When Advertising a Green Product?" *JA*, 24 (Summer), 45–54.

Sengupta, Jaideep, Ronald C. Goodstein, and David S. Boninger (1997), "All Cues Are Not Created Equal: Obtaining Attitude Persistence Under Low-Involvement Conditions," *JCR*, 23 (March), 351–61.

Severn, Jessica, George E. Belch, and Michael A. Belch (1990), "The Effects of Sexual and Non-Sexual Advertising Appeals and Information Level on Cognitive Processing and Communication Effectiveness," *JA*, 19 (Spring), 14–22.

Shiv, Baba, Julie A. Edell, and John W. Payne (1997), "Factors Affecting the Impact of Negatively and Positively Framed Ad Messages," *JCR*, 24 (December), 285–94.

Simpson, Penny M., Steve Horton, and Gene Brown (1996), "Male Nudity in Advertisements: A Modified Replication and Extension of Gender and Product Effects," *JAMS*, 24 (Summer), 257–62.

Singh, Surendra N. and Catherine A. Cole (1993), "The Effects of Length, Content, and Repetition on Television Commercial Effectiveness," *JMR*, 30 (February), 91–104.

Smith, Robert E. (1993), "Integrating Information from Advertising and Trial: Processes and Effects on Consumer Response to Product Information," *JMR*, 30 (May), 204–19.

Stafford, Marla Royne (1996), "Tangibility in Services Advertising: An Investigation of Verbal Versus Visual Cues," *JA*, 25 (Fall), 13–28.

———— (1999), personal correspondence.

———— and Ellen Day (1995), "Retail Services Advertising: The Effects of Appeal, Medium, and Service," *JA*, 24 (Spring), 57–71.

Steenkamp, Jan-Benedict E.M. and Hans Baumgartner (1992), "The Role of Optimum Stimulation Level in Exploratory Consumer Behavior," *JCR*, 19 (December), 434–48.

Stout, Patricia A. and Benedicta L. Burda (1989), "Zipped Commercials: Are They Effective?" *JA*, 18 (4), 23–32.

Sujan, Mita, James R. Bettman, and Hans Baumgartner (1993), "Influencing Consumer Judgments Using Autobiographical Memories: A Self-Referencing Perspective," *JMR*, 30 (November), 422–36.

Taylor, Charles R., Gordon E. Miracle, and R. Dale Wilson (1997), "The Impact of Information Level on the Effectiveness of U.S. and Korean Television Commercials," *JA*, 26 (Spring), 1–18.

Tripp, Carolyn, Thomas D. Jensen, and Les Carlson (1994), "The Effects of Multiple Product Endorsements by Celebrities on Consumers' Attitudes and Intentions," *JCR*, 20 (March), 535–47.

Wells, William D. (1964), "EQ, Son of EQ, and the Reaction Profile," *JM*, 28 (October), 45–52.

Whittler, Tommy E. and Joan DiMeo (1991), "Viewer's Reaction to Racial Cues in Advertising Stimuli," *JAR*, (31) 6, 37–46.

Yi, Youjae (1990), "Cognitive and Affective Priming Effects of the Context for Print Advertisements," *JA*, 19 (Summer), 40–48.

———— (1993), "Contextual Priming Effects in Print Advertisements: The Moderating Role of Prior Knowledge," *JA*, (22) 1, 1–10.

SCALE ITEMS:
Rate your beliefs about the ad:*

1. Good	___ ___ ___ ___ ___	Bad
2. Like	___ ___ ___ ___ ___	Dislike
3. Not irritating	___ ___ ___ ___ ___	Irritating
4. Interesting	___ ___ ___ ___ ___	Boring
5. Inoffensive	___ ___ ___ ___ ___	Offensive
6. Persuasive	___ ___ ___ ___ ___	Not at all persuasive
7. Informative	___ ___ ___ ___ ___	Uninformative
8. Believable	___ ___ ___ ___ ___	Unbelievable
9. Effective	___ ___ ___ ___ ___	Not at all effective
10. Appealing	___ ___ ___ ___ ___	Unappealing
11. Attractive	___ ___ ___ ___ ___	Unattractive
12. Favorable	___ ___ ___ ___ ___	Unfavorable
13. Fair	___ ___ ___ ___ ___	Unfair
14. Pleasant	___ ___ ___ ___ ___	Unpleasant
15. Fresh	___ ___ ___ ___ ___	Stale
16. Nice	___ ___ ___ ___ ___	Awful
17. Honest	___ ___ ___ ___ ___	Dishonest
18. Convincing	___ ___ ___ ___ ___	Unconvincing
19. Likable	___ ___ ___ ___ ___	Unlikable

20. Agreeable	___ ___ ___ ___ ___	Disagreeable
21. Tasteful	___ ___ ___ ___ ___	Tasteless
22. Artful	___ ___ ___ ___ ___	Artless
23. Valuable	___ ___ ___ ___ ___	Not valuable
24. Familiar	___ ___ ___ ___ ___	Unfamiliar
25. Positive	___ ___ ___ ___ ___	Negative
26. Dynamic	___ ___ ___ ___ ___	Dull
27. Refreshing	___ ___ ___ ___ ___	Depressing
28. Enjoyable	___ ___ ___ ___ ___	Not enjoyable
29. Useful	___ ___ ___ ___ ___	Useless
30. Entertaining	___ ___ ___ ___ ___	Not entertaining
31. Satisfactory	___ ___ ___ ___ ___	Unsatisfactory
32. Well made	___ ___ ___ ___ ___	Poorly made
33. Fond of	___ ___ ___ ___ ___	Not fond of
34. Not insulting	___ ___ ___ ___ ___	Insulting
35. Original	___ ___ ___ ___ ___	Unoriginal
36. Refined	___ ___ ___ ___ ___	Vulgar
37. Sensitive	___ ___ ___ ___ ___	Insensitive
38. Appropriate	___ ___ ___ ___ ___	Inappropriate

*Directions could be similar to this. Scale items used in specific studies are listed with an indication of the response format, if known. Although two studies may have used one or more of the same items, it should not automatically be concluded that the items were exactly the same. Judgement was used to determine the similarity of adjectives. Slight differences in the bipolar adjectives used, such as *extremely bad* versus *bad* and *uninteresting* versus *interesting*, were counted the same for purposes of this list. If every truly different set of bipolar adjectives was listed separately here, the list of items would be much longer.

Babin and Burns (1997): 1, 4, 12, 14, 16; 7-point
Baumgartner, Sujan, and Padgett (1997): 1, 12, 14, 25; 9-point
Boles and Burton (1992): 1, 2, 12; 7-point*
Bucholz and Smith (1991): 1, 3, 4; 7-point.
Burnkrant and Unnava (1995): 1, 12, 25; 7-point
Burns, Biswas, and Babin (1993): 1, 4, and three unidentified items.
Chattopadhyay and Basu (1990): 3, 4, 14, 19; 9-point
Chattopadhyay and Nedungadi (1992): 1, 4, 14, 19; 9-point
Cox and Cox (1988): 1, 14, 19; 9-point.
Cox and Locander (1987): 1, 14, 19; 9-point.
Darley and Smith (1993): 1, 3, 4*; 7-point
Darley and Smith (1995): 1, 3, 4*, 14; 7-point
Day and Stafford (1997): 1, 2, 12, 25; 7-point
Droge (1989): 1, 3, 4, 5; 7-point
Gardner (1985): 1, 2, 3, 4; 7-point
Goodstein (1993): 1, 12, 19; 7-point
Ha (1996): 2, 4*, 14, 29, 30; 7-point
Hastak and Olson (1989): 1, 2, 14, 16; 7-point
Hill (1988): Global measure: 1, 2, 3, 4, 12; Emotional dimension: 14, 16, 21, 37
Hill (1989): Global measure: 1, 2, 3, 4, 12; Emotional dimension: 14, 16, 21, 37
Holbrook and Batra (1987): 1*, 2*, 12*, 25*; 7-point
Homer (1995): 1, 2, 12, 14, 20, 23, 25, 29, 38; 9-point

Homer and Kahle (1990): 4, 12, 25; 9-point
Kamins (1990): 1, 14, 20, 31; 7-point
Kamins, Marks, and Skinner (1991): 1, 14, 31
Kellaris, Cox, and Cox (1993): 1, 4, 14, 19, 21; 7-point
Keller (1987): 1, 4, 10, 19; 7-point
Keller (1991a): 1, 4, 10, 19; 7-point
Keller (1991b): 1, 2, 4, 10; 7-point
Kirmani (1997): 1, 3, 4, 14; 7-point
Lord, Lee, and Sauer (1994, 1995): 1, 12, 14; 7-point
Machleit and Wilson (1988): 1, 2*, 3, 12, 28*, 32, 33, 34; 7-point
Machleit, Allen, and Madden (1993): 1, 4, 14, 19, 21, 22
MacInnis, and Park (1991): 1, 10, 12, 19; 7-point
MacInnis and Stayman (1993): 1, 2, 10, 25; 7-point
MacKenzie and Lutz (1989): 1, 12, 14; 7-point
MacKenzie and Spreng (1992): 1, 12, 14; 7-point
Macklin, Bruvold, and Shea (1985): 1, 13, 14, 15, 16, 17; 7-point.
Madden, Allen, and Twibble (1988): 1, 4, 14, 19, 21, 22
Miller and Marks (1992): 1, 2, 3, 4
McQuarrie and Mick (1992): 2, 14, 28; 7-point
Miniard, Bhatla, and Rose (1990): 1, 2, 3, 4, 9; 7-point
Mitchell (1986): 1, 2, 3, 4
Mitchell and Olsen (1981): 1, 2, 3, 4
Muehling (1987): 1, 10, 11, 14, 26, 27, 28; 7-point
Murry, Lastovicka, and Singh (1992): 1, 2, 3, 4, 12
Pham (1996): 1, 2, 12, 31
Prakash (1992): 1, 2, 3, 4; 7-point
Schuhwerk and Lefkoff-Hagius (1995): 1, 4, 8, 12, 14, 18; 7-point
Severn, Belch, and Belch (1990): 4, 5, 12, 30, 35; 7-point
Shiv, Edell, and Payne (1997): 1, 10, 19*; 7-point
Simpson, Horton, and Brown (1996): 1, 2, 12, 25; 9-point
Singh and Cole (1993): 1, 4, 7, 8, 14, 18, 19, 21, 22, 24, 30, 34, 36; 7-point
Smith (1993): 1, 12, 14; 7-point
Stafford (1996): 1, 2, 12, 25
Stafford and Day (1995): 1, 2, 3, 4*; 7-point
Steenkamp and Baumgartner (1992): 1, 12, 14, 25; 7-point
Stout and Burda (1989): 2, 12; 7-point
Sujan, Bettman, and Baumgartner (1993): 1, 12, 14, 25; 9-point
Taylor, Miracle, and Wilson (1997): 1, 2, 25, 32; 7-point
Tripp, Jensen, and Carlson (1994): 1, 3*, 4*, 19; 7-point
Whittler and DiMeo (1991): 6, 11, 12; 15-point
Yi (1990): 1, 2, 3, 4; 7-point
Yi (1993): 1, 2, 3, 4; 7-point

SCALE NAME: Attitude Toward the Ad (Unipolar)

SCALE DESCRIPTION: A multi-item summated scale that purports to capture a person's overall evaluation of an ad. Although the uses described vary in both the number of items employed and the points on their response scales, they are alike in that they used a unipolar format rather than the more typical bipolar approach to measure Aad. Furthermore, a high degree of commonality exists among the items employed in the various versions of the scales.

SCALE ORIGIN: Henthorne, LaTour, and Nataraajan (1993) cited LaTour and Pitts (1989) as the source of the items used in their scale; however, only two of their six items actually were taken from that study. LaTour and Henthorne (1994) used two items from the Henthorne, LaTour, and Nataraajan (1993) version of the scale and one item from a measure by LaTour, Pitts, and Snook-Luther (1990). LaTour, Snipes, and Bliss (1996) appear to have drawn on several of these studies, as well as on Madden, Ellen, and Ajzen (1992).

SAMPLES: Henthorne, LaTour, and Nataraajan (1993) obtained **201** usable responses through the use of mall intercept surveys. The sample consisted of 88 men and 113 women. The majority of the respondents were white (80%), had an average age of 31.5 years, and represented a variety of income levels.

Data were gather by LaTour and Henthorne (1994, p. 83) using mall intercept surveys in a "culturally vibrant MSA in the mid-Gulf Coast region." Interviewers were trained and rotated in a random pattern throughout the mall. Of the shoppers approached, 85% participated. To complete the questionnaire, shoppers were taken to a private yet monitored area. Usable survey forms were collected from **199** individuals. The sample was described as having an average age of 34.3 years and an average of 13.8 years of education and coming from widely different income levels. A little more than half of the respondents were women (53%), 75.7% were white, and 47.5% were married.

LaTour, Snipes, and Bliss (1996, p. 62), as well as LaTour and Rotfeld (1997), collected data from **305** respondents through the use of a mall intercept survey in a "demographically diverse SMSA in the southeastern United States." Female shoppers were approached "at random" during all hours of the mall's operation over nine weeks, and those volunteering were randomly assigned to one of two treatments. The majority of the respondents were white (79%) and married (34%). The mean age of respondents was 28 years, and the mean education level was 14 years.

RELIABILITY: Alphas of **.77, .71, .85,** and **.84** were reported for the versions of the scale used by Henthorne, LaTour, and Nataraajan (1993); LaTour and Henthorne (1994); LaTour, Snipes, and Bliss (1996); and LaTour and Rotfeld (1997), respectively.

VALIDITY: No examination of the scale's validity was reported in any of the studies, but Henthorne, LaTour, and Nataraajan (1993), LaTour, Snipes, and Bliss (1996), and LaTour and Rotfeld (1997) indicated that the factor analyses they performed provided evidence of their scales' unidimensionality.

ADMINISTRATION: Respondents in each of the studies completed the scale along with other measures in a self-administered questionnaire in a mall intercept setting (Henthorne, LaTour, and Nataraajan 1993; LaTour and Henthorne 1994; LaTour and Rotfeld 1997; LaTour, Snipes, and Bliss 1996). Those who scored high on the scale were assumed to have positive attitudes toward some specific ad to which they had been exposed, whereas low scores suggested the respondents viewed the ad negatively for some reason (e.g., irritating, offensive, uninformative).

MAJOR FINDINGS: The study by Henthorne, LaTour, and Nataraajan (1993) examined the hypothesis that increasing tension generates energy up to a point, but beyond that, anxiety is aroused, which begins to reduce energy. A model that assumes tension is not high enough to reduce energy found support for a positive path between tension and **Aad**. However, the model that assumed tension was high enough to reduce energy failed to find a significant path between tension and **Aad**, contrary to what was hypothesized.

LaTour and Henthorne (1994) investigated the ethical judgments made by consumers regarding sexual appeals in print advertising. The results showed that strong sex-related appeals were not viewed favorably. Specifically, the group that received an ad with a "mild" sexual appeal viewed it as being significantly more ethical than the group that received an ad with a strong, overt sexual appeal.

The field experiment conducted by LaTour, Snipes, and Bliss (1996) examined the perceived ethicality of the use of fear appeals with a potentially sensitive audience. Among the findings was that subjects viewing the ad with a stronger fear appeal had significantly better **attitudes toward the ad** than subjects who saw the ad with a milder fear appeal.

The field experiment conducted by LaTour and Rotfeld (1997) was intended to clarify the distinction between threats and psychological responses to the threats. The results indicated that arousal (energy) had a direct positive impact on **attitude toward the ad** and purchase intention but only indirectly increased positive brand attitude.

COMMENTS: See uses of related versions of the scale made by LaTour and Pitts (1989) and LaTour, Pitts, and Snook-Luther (1990).

REFERENCES:

Henthorne, Tony L., Michael S. LaTour, and Rajan Nataraajan (1993), "Fear Appeals in Print Advertising: An Analysis of Arousal and Ad Response," *JA*, 22 (2), 59–69.

LaTour, Michael S. and Tony L. Henthorne (1994), "Ethical Judgments of Sexual Appeals in Print Advertising," *JA*, 23 (September), 81–90.

——— and Robert E. Pitts (1989), "Using Fear Appeals in Advertising for AIDS Prevention in the College-Age Population," *Journal of Health Care Marketing*, 9 (September), 5–14.

———, ———, and David C. Snook-Luther (1990), "Female Nudity, Arousal, and Ad Response: An Experimental Investigation," *JA*, 19 (4), 51–62.

——— and Herbert J. Rotfeld (1997), "There are Threats and (Maybe) Fear-Caused Arousal: Theory and Confusions of Appeals to Fear and Fear Arousal Itself, *JA*, 26 (Fall), 45–59.

———, Robin L. Snipes, and Sara J. Bliss (1996), "Don't Be Afraid to Use Fear Appeals: An Experimental Study," *JAR*, 36 (March/April), 59–67.

Madden, Thomas J., Pamela Scholder Ellen, and Icek Ajzen (1992), "A Comparison of the Theory of Planned Behavior and the Theory of Reasoned Action," *Personality and Social Psychology Bulletin*, 18 (1), 3–9.

SCALE ITEMS:

No, definitely not :___:___:___:___:___:___:___: Yes, definitely
                      1   2   3   4   5   6   7

1. Good
2. Interesting
3. Informative
4. Appropriate
5. Easy to understand
6. Objective
7. Irritating
8. Offensive
9. Distinctive

Henthorne, LaTour, and Nataraajan (1993): 1–6; 4-point
LaTour and Henthorne (1994): 1, 3, 7, 8
LaTour and Rotfeld (1997): 1–6; 6-point
LaTour, Snipes, and Bliss (1996): 1, 3, 4, 5, 6, 9; 6-point

SCALE NAME: Attitude Toward the Ad (Uniqueness)

SCALE DESCRIPTION: The four-item, nine-point semantic differential scale measures a subject's evaluation of the *uniqueness* dimension of an advertisement.

SCALE ORIGIN: These items have had only minor usage as part of larger Aad measures (e.g., #445). No known use of these items as a set has been made other than by Homer (1995).

SAMPLES: The sample for the study by Homer (1995) consisted of **245** business students at a Western U.S. university. Respondents were of both genders, volunteered to participate, and were randomly assigned to one of the treatments in the 2 × 2 factorial design.

RELIABILITY: An alpha of **.95** was reported for the scale (Homer 1995).

VALIDITY: No examination of the scale's validity was reported by Homer (1995), though it was stated that a factor analysis was conducted and the items in this scale loaded on the same dimension.

ADMINISTRATION: The scale was self-administered by subjects, along with other measures, after they were exposed to experimental stimuli (Homer 1995). Higher scores on the scale indicated that respondents viewed an ad as quite original and (pleasantly) exciting.

MAJOR FINDINGS: Replicating Kirmani (1990), Homer (1995) studied the effects of ad size on ad-based memory, perceptions, and attitudinal evaluations. **Ad uniqueness** was used in the study as a covariate to account for any nonequivalence across experimental treatments. The ad size manipulation was not found to have a significant effect on respondents' **attitude toward the ads' uniqueness**.

REFERENCES:

Homer, Pamela M. (1995), "Ad Size as an Indicator of Perceived Advertising Costs and Effort: The Effects on Memory and Perceptions," *JA*, 24 (Winter), 1–12.

Kirmani, Amna (1990), "The Effect of Perceived Advertising Costs on Brand Perceptions," *JCR*, 17 (September), 160–71.

SCALE ITEMS:

What are your attitudes toward the **ad** for _____ (not the store).*

Dull   :___:___:___:___:___:___:___:___: Exciting
              1   2   3   4   5   6   7   8   9

Unoriginal   :___:___:___:___:___:___:___:___: Original
              1   2   3   4   5   6   7   8   9

Not unique   :___:___:___:___:___:___:___:___: Unique
              1   2   3   4   5   6   7   8   9

Not entertaining :___:___:___:___:___:___:___:___: Entertaining
                 1   2   3   4   5   6   7   8   9

*The name of the business should be placed in the blank.

SCALE NAME: Attitude Toward the Advertiser (Semantic Differential)

SCALE DESCRIPTION: Various bipolar adjectives designed to capture a consumer's overall evaluation of a specified advertiser.

SCALE ORIGIN: Each of the studies described here uses a slightly different version of the scale, the origin for which is not clear. Only Simpson, Horton, and Brown (1996) indicated a source; they cited MacKenzie and Lutz (1989) and modified their scale by adding one more item.

SAMPLES: MacKenzie and Lutz (1989) used **203** student subjects from a Midwestern U.S. university and **120** MBA and undergraduate student subjects from a major university in southern California.

Little was noted about the sample used by Muehling (1987), except that it was composed of **133** student subjects. Analysis appears to have been based on an even smaller number.

Simpson, Horton, and Brown (1996) gathered data from **169** students from two neighboring southern U.S. universities. The sample was evenly split on gender, with most respondents being European American (77.3%) and between 18 and 25 years of age (80%).

RELIABILITY: Cronbach's alphas of **.96**, **.90**, and **.96** were reported by Muehling (1987), MacKenzie and Lutz (1989), and Simpson, Horton, and Brown (1996), respectively.

VALIDITY: No examination of the scale's validity was reported in any of the studies.

ADMINISTRATION: Although there were variations in the context of administration, the studies were alike in that the scale was completed by respondents after they were exposed to some ad(s) in the context of a larger questionnaire. Higher scores indicated that respondents had very positive attitudes toward the sponsor of the ad to which they has been exposed.

MAJOR FINDINGS: The purpose of the experiment conducted by Muehling (1987) was to investigate the effects of attitude toward the ad in the context of comparative ads. The findings showed that attitude toward the ad had a significant positive influence on **attitude toward the advertiser** in each of five different comparative ad format conditions.

MacKenzie and Lutz (1989) examined the connections among advertiser credibility, **attitude toward the advertiser**, and a detailed casual linkage of various consumer perceptions and attitudes culminating in brand perceptions in a causal model. Among the specific findings was that advertiser credibility had a significant positive effect on **attitude toward the advertiser.**

The effect of male nudity in advertising was examined by Simpson, Horton, and Brown (1996). The results showed that women had better **attitudes toward the advertiser** than did men regardless of the level of dress of the male models in the ads. However, the level of dress associated with the best **attitude toward the advertiser** for the female respondents was the "suggestive" (no shirt) ad rather than full nudity.

REFERENCES:

MacKenzie, Scott B. and Richard J. Lutz (1989), "An Empirical Examination of the Structural Antecedents of Attitude Toward the Ad in an Advertising Pretesting Context," *JM*, 53 (April), 48–65.

Muehling, Darrel D. (1987), "Comparative Advertising: The Influence of Attitude-Toward-the-Brand on Brand Evaluation," *JA*, 16 (4), 43–49.

Simpson, Penny M., Steve Horton, and Gene Brown (1996), "Male Nudity in Advertisements: A Modified Replication and Extension of Gender and Product Effects," *JAMS*, 24 (Summer), 257–62.

#448 *Attitude Toward the Advertiser (Semantic Differential)*

SCALE ITEMS:
Please rate the advertiser of this ad using the following scales.*

1. Good   ___ ___ ___ ___ ___   Bad

2. Pleasant   ___ ___ ___ ___ ___   Unpleasant

3. Favorable   ___ ___ ___ ___ ___   Unfavorable

4. Positive   ___ ___ ___ ___ ___   Negative

5. Reputable   ___ ___ ___ ___ ___   Not reputable

MacKenzie and Lutz (1989): 1, 2, 3; 7-point
Muehling (1987): 1, 3, 4; 7-point
Simpson, Horton, and Brown (1996): 1, 2, 3, 5; 9-point

*The scale stem could be stated similar to this.

SCALE NAME: Attitude Toward the Institution of Advertising

SCALE DESCRIPTION: Various seven-point bipolar adjectives purported to measure a person's opinion about advertising as a social institution as opposed to the methods used by advertisers. The distinction is that even if a person had been exposed to a lot of specific ads that were viewed negatively, he or she might still believe that advertising as a form of communication was valuable.

SCALE ORIGIN: The items come from many studies conducted by Sandage and Leckenby (1980) on students from the years 1960 to 1978. They used the items along with four others to study student attitudes toward advertising. Their experience and testing (exploratory factor analysis) indicated that the four items shown tapped into something distinct from another set of four items (#450). No information about the scale's reliability was provided.

SAMPLES: Muehling (1987) collected data from **88** undergraduate students. The data gathered by Andrews, Durvasula, and Netemeyer (1994) came from college students in both Russia and the United States. All were undergraduate students majoring in business or economics and were of similar ages (U.S. mean = 21.45 years, Russian mean = 20.31 years). The Russian sample had a somewhat higher proportion of women (62%) than did the U.S. sample (51%). Complete data were received from **212** students, 148 from a major Midwestern U.S. university and 64 from two major universities in the Republic of Russia.

RELIABILITY: Muehling (1987) reported an alpha of **.73** for the scale. Composite reliabilities of .79 and .75 were reported by Andrews, Durvasula, and Netemeyer (1994) for the scale in its English and Russian versions, respectively.

VALIDITY: Muehling (1987) subjected the same eight items used by Sandage and Leckenby (1980) to confirmatory factor analysis. The results clearly indicated that the items broke down into the same subsets identified by Sandage and Leckenby (1980).

Andrews, Durvasula, and Netemeyer (1994) conducted a series of thorough confirmatory factor analyses on this scale, as well as two others measuring very similar constructs (#450 and #428). The results provided support for the discriminant validity of the three scales in both the English and Russian versions.

ADMINISTRATION: Muehling (1987) used the scale as part of a larger self-administered survey instrument in a college classroom. The scale was used by Andrews, Durvasula, and Netemeyer (1994) as part of a larger self-administered questionnaire. The Russian version was developed by an expert not only fluent in English and Russian, but also familiar with the cultural nuances in word meanings. The back-translation method was used, and independent checks were made by two other bilingual experts.

Higher scores on the scale suggested that that subject had a positive attitude toward the institution of advertising.

MAJOR FINDINGS: Muehling (1987) investigated the antecedents of attitude toward the ad. He found that **attitude toward the institution of advertising** and attitude toward the instruments of advertising explained more than 57% of the variance in a global measure of advertising attitudes.

The purposes of the study by Andrews, Durvasula, and Netemeyer (1994) were to demonstrate procedures for testing the cross-national equivalence of ad-related measures and to conduct an initial comparison. Their findings indicated that Americans had more positive **attitudes toward the institution of advertising** than did Russians.

#449 *Attitude Toward the Institution of Advertising*

COMMENTS: Andrews, Durvasula, and Netemeyer (1994) state that item #1 (see SCALE ITEMS) was not used because it was part of another similar measure.

In terms of mean scores on the scale, Andrews, Durvasula, and Netemeyer (1994) reported 4.92 and 4.23 for the U.S. and Russian samples, respectively. Muehling (1987) reported a mean score of 5.70 for his sample.

REFERENCES:

Andrews, J. Craig, Srinivas Durvasula, and Richard G. Netemeyer (1994), "Testing the Cross-National Applicability of U.S. and Russian Advertising Belief and Attitude Measures," *JA*, 23 (1), 71–82.

Muehling, Darrel D. (1987), "An Investigation of Factors Underlying Attitude-Toward-Advertising-in-General," *JA*, 16 (1), 32–40.

Sandage, C.H. and John D. Leckenby (1980), "Student Attitudes Toward Advertising: Institution Vs. Instrument," *JA*, 9 (2), 29–32+.

SCALE ITEMS:

1. Bad   __ __ __ __ __ __ __   Good

2. Weak   __ __ __ __ __ __ __   Strong

3. Worthless   __ __ __ __ __ __ __   Valuable

4. Unnecessary   __ __ __ __ __ __ __   Necessary

5. Unimportant   __ __ __ __ __ __ __   Important

Andrews, Durvasula, and Netemeyer (1994): 2–5
Muehling (1987): 1–4
Sandage and Leckenby (1980): 1–4

SCALE NAME: Attitude Toward the Instruments of Advertising

SCALE DESCRIPTION: Various seven-point bipolar adjectives purported to measure a person's opinion about the practices and people characterizing the advertising industry. This is viewed by users of the scale to be different from measuring opinions about advertising as an institution. The distinction is that even if a person had been exposed to a lot of specific ads, tactics, or advertisers that were viewed negatively, he or she might still believe that advertising as a form of communication was valuable.

SCALE ORIGIN: The items come from many studies conducted by Sandage and Leckenby (1980) on students from the years 1960 to 1978. They used the items along with four others to study student attitudes toward advertising. Their experience and testing (exploratory factor analysis) indicated that the four items shown tapped into something distinct from another set of four items (#449). No information about the scale's reliability was provided.

SAMPLES: Muehling (1987) collected data from **88** undergraduate students. The data gathered by Andrews, Durvasula, and Netemeyer (1994) came from college students in both Russia and the United States. All were undergraduate students majoring in business or economics and were of similar ages (U.S. mean = 21.45 years, Russian mean = 20.31 years). The Russian sample had a somewhat higher proportion of women (62%) than did the U.S. sample (51%). Complete data were received from **212** students, 148 from a major Midwestern U.S. university and 64 from two major universities in the Republic of Russia.

RELIABILITY: Muehling (1987) reported an alpha of **.79** for the scale. Composite reliabilities of **.79** and **.72** were reported by Andrews, Durvasula, and Netemeyer (1994) for the scale in its English and Russian versions, respectively.

VALIDITY: Muehling (1987) subjected the same eight items used by Sandage and Leckenby (1980) to confirmatory factor analysis. The results clearly indicated that the items broke down into the same subsets identified by Sandage and Leckenby (1980).

Andrews, Durvasula, and Netemeyer (1994) conducted a series of thorough confirmatory factor analyses on this scale as well as two others measuring very similar constructs (#449 and #428). The results provided support for the discriminant validity of the three scales in both the English and Russian versions.

ADMINISTRATION: Muehling (1987) used the scale as part of a larger self-administered survey instrument in a college classroom. The scale was used by Andrews, Durvasula, and Netemeyer (1994) as part of a larger self-administered questionnaire. The Russian version was developed by an expert not only fluent in English and Russian, but also familiar with the cultural nuances in word meanings. The back-translation method was used, and independent checks were made by two other bilingual experts.

Higher scores on the scale suggested that the subject had a positive attitude toward the instruments used in the advertising industry.

MAJOR FINDINGS: Muehling (1987) investigated the antecedents of attitude toward the ad. He found that attitude toward the institution of advertising and **attitude toward the instruments of advertising** explained more than 57% of the variance in a global measure of advertising attitudes.

The purposes of the study by Andrews, Durvasula, and Netemeyer (1994) were to demonstrate procedures for testing the cross-national equivalence of ad-related measures and to conduct an initial comparison. Contrary to their prediction, their findings did <u>not</u> indicate that Russians had significantly more positive **attitudes toward the instruments of advertising** than did Americans.

#450 *Attitude Toward the Instruments of Advertising*

COMMENTS: Andrews, Durvasula, and Netemeyer (1994) state that item #4 (see SCALE ITEMS) was not used due to item unreliability.

In terms of mean scores on the scale, Andrews, Durvasula, and Netemeyer (1994) reported 4.75 and 4.68 for the U.S. and Russian samples, respectively. Muehling (1987) reported a mean score of 4.32 for his sample.

REFERENCES:

Andrews, J. Craig, Srinivas Durvasula, and Richard G. Netemeyer (1994), "Testing the Cross-National Applicability of U.S. and Russian Advertising Belief and Attitude Measures," *JA*, 23 (1), 71–82.

Muehling, Darrel D. (1987), "An Investigation of Factors Underlying Attitude-Toward-Advertising-in-General," *JA*, 16 (1), 32–40.

Sandage, C.H. and John D. Leckenby (1980), "Student Attitudes Toward Advertising: Institution Vs. Instrument," *JA*, 9 (2), 29–32+.

SCALE ITEMS:

1. Dirty   __ __ __ __ __ __ __   Clean

2. Dishonest   __ __ __ __ __ __ __   Honest

3. Insincere   __ __ __ __ __ __ __   Sincere

4. Dangerous   __ __ __ __ __ __ __   Safe

Andrews, Durvasula, and Netemeyer (1994): 1–3
Muehling (1987): 1–4
Sandage and Leckenby (1980): 1–4

SCALE NAME: Attitude Toward the Television Commercial

SCALE DESCRIPTION: Four four-point items measuring the degree to which a person has a positive attitude toward some specific television commercial to which he or she has been exposed. The commercial examined by Prasad and Smith (1994) was for a breakfast cereal aimed at children.

SCALE ORIGIN: Prasad and Smith (1994, p. 346) stated that they used a "variation of Rossiter's (1977) summated rating scale." The similarities appear to be that Prasad and Smith (1994) used Rossiter's (1977) response scale (two levels of affirmation and two levels of negation) and developed items related to television commercials intended for use with children. Beyond that, their scales are different.

SAMPLES: The sample used by Prasad and Smith (1994) was composed of second- and third-grade boys recruited from Cub Scout Troops in a Midwestern U.S. town. Their ages ranged from seven and nine years. Usable data were gathered from **95** boys.

RELIABILITY: An alpha of **.86** was reported for the scale by Prasad and Smith (1994).

VALIDITY: No examination of the scale's validity was reported by Prasad and Smith (1994).

ADMINISTRATION: The scale was administered to subjects after they watched one of two programs (violent or nonviolent) that contained the commercial of interest (Prasad and Smith 1994). Higher scores on the scale indicated that viewers had very positive attitudes toward the commercial in question.

MAJOR FINDINGS: Prasad and Smith (1994) investigated the effects of violent programs on children's ad attitudes and recall. Among the findings was that **attitudes toward the television commercial** were significantly worse when the commercial followed a high rather than a low violence program.

REFERENCES:
Prasad, V. Kanti and Lois J. Smith (1994), "Television Commercials in Violent Programming: An Experimental Evaluation of Their Effects on Children," *JAMS*, 22 (4), 340–51.
Rossiter, John R. (1977), "Reliability of a Short Test Measuring Children's Attitudes Toward TV Commercials," *JCR*, 3 (March), 179–84.
Smith, Lois J. (1999), personal correspondence.

SCALE ITEMS:*

1 = NO; 2 = no; 3 = yes; 4 = YES

1. I liked the television commercial for _____.

2. The television commercial for _____ was not good. **(r)**

3. The television commercial for _____ was fun to watch.

4. The television commercial for _____ was not very interesting. **(r)**

*Scale items were provided by Smith (1999). The name of the product should be placed in the blank space.

SCALE NAME: Attitude Toward Television Advertising (Disbelief in Ad Claims)

SCALE DESCRIPTION: A five-item, five-point, Likert-type scale measuring the degree of truth a respondent believes there to be in commercials shown on television.

SCALE ORIGIN: Although not perfectly clear, Boush, Friestad, and Rose (1994) began with most, if not all, of the items from a scale originally developed by Rossiter (1977). Several other items were added, the source of which is unknown. After factor analysis of the results (as noted), it became clear that two dimensions were reflected, one tapping into beliefs in ad claims and another indicating distrust of advertiser motives (#456). Given this, only three of the seven items in Rossiter's (1977) scale were part of the scale described here.

SAMPLES: Data were gathered by Boush, Friestad, and Rose (1994) from students at two middle schools (grades 6–8) in a medium-sized city in the Pacific Northwest of the United States. A survey instrument was administered to students during the first and last weeks of the school year. Analysis was generally based on information received from the **426** students who completed the questionnaire during both of its administrations.

RELIABILITY: Alphas of **.57** and **.67** were reported for the scale for its first and second administrations, respectively, by Boush, Friestad, and Rose (1994).

VALIDITY: The validity of the scale was not specifically addressed in the study by Boush, Friestad, and Rose (1994). However, the authors performed a principal components analysis with promax rotation of the combined items of this scale with those of another scale (#456). The two factors that were retained, on the basis of the factor loadings and scree test, led to the development of two scales rather than the one that was originally intended.

ADMINISTRATION: The scale used by Boush, Friestad, and Rose (1994) was part of a longer questionnaire self-administered by students in groups of 25 to 30 during the period with which they began each school day. Although the items were stated in the positive direction, which indicated a positive attitude toward the veracity of television advertising, it is important to note that they were all reversed scored by Boush, Friestad, and Rose (1994) such that higher overall scores meant more negative attitudes (greater skepticism).

MAJOR FINDINGS: The study by Boush, Friestad, and Rose (1994) explored adolescents' skepticism toward advertising and their beliefs about the persuasive tactics used by advertisers. The findings indicated that **disbelief of advertising claims** had a significant negative relationship with interpersonal influence susceptibility but a significant positive relationship with self-esteem.

COMMENTS: As acknowledged by Boush, Friestad, and Rose (1994, p. 173), the internal consistency of the scale is low enough to warrant caution in using it again. Further development and improvement in the scale's psychometric qualities is strongly advised.

REFERENCES:

Boush, David M., Marian Friestad, and Gregory M. Rose (1994), "Adolescent Skepticism Toward TV Advertising and Knowledge of Advertiser Tactics," *JCR*, 21 (June), 165–75.

Rossiter, John R. (1977), "Reliability of a Short Test Measuring Children's Attitudes Toward TV Commercials," *JCR*, 3 (March), 179–84.

SCALE ITEMS:

Strongly   Strongly
disagree   :___:___:___:___:___: agree
           1   2   3   4   5

1. TV commercials tell the truth. **(r)**

2. You can believe what the people in commercials say or do. **(r)**

3. The products advertised on TV are always the best products to buy. **(r)**

4. You can depend on getting the truth from most TV advertising. **(r)**

5. If a TV commercial was not true, it could not be on television. **(r)**

SCALE NAME: Attitude Toward Television Advertising (Frequency and Content)

SCALE DESCRIPTION: A four-item, five-point, Likert-type scale used to measure the degree to which a person believes there are too many commercials on television and that they are not as truthful and informative as they should be.

SCALE ORIGIN: The items in the scale come from three measures developed by Alwitt and Prabhaker (1992). Inspiration for the items they created seems to have come from Bauer and Greyser (1968).

SAMPLES: Alwitt and Prabhaker (1992) mailed a survey to 1200 randomly selected households with listed telephone numbers in the Chicago metropolitan statistical area in March 1990. **Two hundred twenty-eight** usable surveys were returned. Data were collected by Alwitt and Prabhaker (1994) from a Market Facts Household Panel balanced to match national demographic characteristics. Usable questionnaires were received from **794** panel members.

RELIABILITY: An alpha of **.62** was reported for the scale by Alwitt and Prabhaker (1994).

VALIDITY: No examination of scale validity was reported by Alwitt and Prabhaker (1994). However, it was mentioned that a factor analysis was conducted on 27 television-related attitudes. Six factors were produced, and the highest loading items on each factor were used to produce six summated scales.

ADMINISTRATION: The scale was self-administered along with other measures in a mail survey format (Alwitt and Prabhaker 1994). Scores appear to have been calculated such that the lower they were, the more they indicated respondents thought there was too much television advertising, particularly because it is not viewed as truthful and informative as it should be.

MAJOR FINDINGS: The goal of Alwitt and Prabhaker's (1994) study was to examine different reasons people may have unfavorable attitudes about television advertising. Using a nationally representative sample, they found that those who dislike television commercials also believe the **frequency and content of the advertising** are not appropriate.

COMMENTS: Care should be taken with this scale for several reasons. First, its internal consistency is very low, which indicates that the items may not be tapping into the same construct. Even though the authors used factor analysis to conclude that the items were loading on the same factor, it is hard to tell by looking at the items themselves what they all have in common. Items 3 and 4 seem out of place and, in fact, had loadings of less than .50. Second, this observation of a lack of commonness is further supported by noting, as mentioned previously, that in their earlier study (Alwitt and Prabhaker 1992), these items were parts of three different scales. More development and testing is called for before this scale is used further.

REFERENCES:
Alwitt, Linda F. and Paul R. Prabhaker (1992), "Functional and Belief Dimensions of Attitudes to Television Advertising," *JAR*, 32 (5), 30–42.
———— and ———— (1994), "Identifying Who Dislikes Television Advertising: Not By Demographics Alone," *JAR*, 34 (November/December), 17–29.
Bauer, Raymond A. and Stephen A. Greyser (1968), *Advertising in America: The Consumer View.* Boston: Harvard University Press.

SCALE ITEMS:

Strongly   Strongly
  agree   disagree
  1————2————3————4————5

1. Most commercial breaks on TV have too many commercials in a row.

2. There seems to be more advertising on TV now than there used to be.

3. Today's TV ads don't give you as much information as they used to.

4. There is a critical need for more truth in today's TV advertising.

SCALE NAME: Attitude Toward Television Advertising (Helpfulness)

SCALE DESCRIPTION: A five-item, five-point, Likert-type scale that has been used to measure a person's attitude about the helpfulness of television commercials.

SCALE ORIGIN: The items in the scale come from two measures developed by Alwitt and Prabhaker (1992); all but one (4) come from the measure they called *perceptions of the personal and social benefits or costs of TV advertising*. One item in this scale (#2), as well as inspiration for the rest, seems to have come from Bauer and Greyser (1968).

SAMPLES: Alwitt and Prabhaker (1992) mailed a survey to 1200 randomly selected households with listed telephone numbers in the Chicago metropolitan statistical area in March 1990. **Two hundred twenty-eight** usable surveys were returned. Data were collected by Alwitt and Prabhaker (1994) from a Market Facts Household Panel balanced to match national demographic characteristics. Usable questionnaires were received from **794** panel members.

RELIABILITY: An alpha of **.72** was reported for the scale by Alwitt and Prabhaker (1994).

VALIDITY: No examination of scale validity was reported by Alwitt and Prabhaker (1994). However, it was mentioned that a factor analysis was conducted on 27 television-related attitudes. Six factors were produced, and the highest loading items on each factor were used to produce six summated scales.

ADMINISTRATION: The scale was self-administered along with other measures in a mail survey format (Alwitt and Prabhaker 1994). Scores appear to have been calculated such that the higher they were, the more they indicated a respondent's disagreement that television advertising provided helpful information.

MAJOR FINDINGS: The goal of Alwitt and Prabhaker's (1994) study was to examine different reasons people may have unfavorable attitudes about television advertising. Using a nationally representative sample, they found that there was a strong positive association between **attitudes about the helpfulness of television commercials** and liking of television advertising.

REFERENCES:

Alwitt, Linda F. and Paul R. Prabhaker (1992), "Functional and Belief Dimensions of Attitudes to Television Advertising," *JAR*, 32 (5), 30–42.
———— and ———— (1994), "Identifying Who Dislikes Television Advertising: Not By Demographics Alone," *JAR*, 34 (November/December), 17–29.
Bauer, Raymond A. and Stephen A. Greyser (1968), *Advertising in America: The Consumer View*. Boston: Harvard University Press.

SCALE ITEMS:

```
Strongly                    Strongly
  agree                     disagree
   1————2————3————4————5
```

1. TV advertising is a good way to learn about what products and services are available.

2. TV advertising helps raise our standard of living.

3. TV advertisements help me find products that match my personality and interest.

4. TV advertising help me to know which brands have the features I am looking for.

5. A lot of TV advertising is funny or clever.

SCALE NAME: Attitude Toward Television Advertising (Informational Benefits)

SCALE DESCRIPTION: A five-point, Likert-type scale that has been used to measure a person's attitude about the benefits of television commercials in learning about and buying products. A ten-item version of the scale used by Alwitt and Prabhaker (1992) was called *perceptions of the personal and social benefits or costs of TV advertising.* A seven-item version was used by Alwitt and Prabhaker (1994).

SCALE ORIGIN: The items in Alwitt and Prabhaker's (1994) version of the scale come from scales created by Alwitt and Prabhaker (1992). All the items but one (11) came from the scale called *perceptions of the personal and social benefits or costs of TV advertising.* Item 2 and inspiration for the other items produced by Alwitt and Prabhaker (1992) seems to have come from Bauer and Greyser (1968).

SAMPLES: Alwitt and Prabhaker (1992) mailed a survey to 1200 randomly selected households with listed telephone numbers in the Chicago metropolitan statistical area in March 1990. **Two hundred twenty-eight** usable surveys were returned. Data were collected by Alwitt and Prabhaker (1994) from a Market Facts Household Panel balanced to match national demographic characteristics. Usable questionnaires were received from **794** panel members.

RELIABILITY: Alphas of **.86** (1992) and **.74** (1994) were reported by Alwitt and Prabhaker.

VALIDITY: No examination of scale validity was reported in either study by Alwitt and Prabhaker (1992, 1994). However, in Alwitt and Prabhaker (1994), it was mentioned that a factor analysis was conducted on 27 television-related attitudes. Six factors were produced, and the highest loading items on each factor were used to produce six summated scales.

ADMINISTRATION: The scale was self-administered along with other measures in a mail survey format (Alwitt and Prabhaker 1992, 1994). As in Alwitt and Prabhaker (1994), higher scores indicated disagreement that television advertising provided beneficial information.

MAJOR FINDINGS: The goal of Alwitt and Prabhaker's (1992) study was to evaluate why people tend to have unfavorable attitudes about television advertising. After the effects of demographic characteristics and attitudes toward television programs had been removed from the overall liking of television advertising, the multiple regression model indicated that **attitude toward the informational benefits of television advertising** was a significant predictor. Thus, the more respondents perceived that **television advertising had informational benefits**, the more they liked commercials in general. Using a more nationally representative sample, Alwitt and Prabhaker (1994) confirmed this relationship.

REFERENCES:

Alwitt, Linda F. and Paul R. Prabhaker (1992), "Functional and Belief Dimensions of Attitudes to Television Advertising," *JAR*, 32 (5), 30–42.
——— and ——— (1994), "Identifying Who Dislikes Television Advertising: Not By Demographics Alone," *JAR*, 34 (November/December), 17–29.
Bauer, Raymond A. and Stephen A. Greyser (1968), *Advertising in America: The Consumer View.* Boston: Harvard University Press.

SCALE ITEMS:*

Strongly
agree

Strongly
disagree

1———2———3———4———5

#455 *Attitude Toward Television Advertising (Informational Benefits)*

1. TV advertising is a good way to learn about what products and services are available.

2. TV advertising results in better products for the public.

3. In general, TV advertising presents a true picture of the product advertised.

4. You can trust brands advertised on TV more than brands not advertised on TV.

5. TV advertising helps raise our standard of living.

6. TV advertisements help me find products that match my personality and interest.

7. TV advertising helps me to know which brands have the features I am looking for.

8. TV advertising gives me a good idea about products by showing the kinds of people who use them.

9. TV advertising helps me buy the best brand for the price.

10. I am willing to pay more for a product that is advertised on TV.

11. TV advertising mostly tries to create imaginary differences between products that are very similar. (r)

*The first 10 items were used by Alwitt and Prabhaker (1992). Items #2, #3, #4, #8, #9, #10, and #11 were used by Alwitt and Prabhaker (1994).

SCALE NAME: Attitude Toward Television Advertising (Mistrust of Advertiser Motives)

SCALE DESCRIPTION: A six-item, five-point, Likert-type scale measuring the degree of skepticism a person has with commercials shown on television, particularly with the motives of the advertiser.

SCALE ORIGIN: Although not perfectly clear, Boush, Friestad, and Rose (1994) began with most, if not all, of the items from a scale originally developed by Rossiter (1977). Several other items were added, the source of which is unknown. After factor analysis of the results (as noted), it became clear that two dimensions were reflected, one tapping into beliefs in ad claims (#452) and another indicating distrust of advertiser motives. Given this, only two of the seven items in Rossiter's (1977) scale ended up being in the scale described here.

SAMPLES: Data were gathered by Boush, Friestad, and Rose (1994) from students at two middle schools (grades 6–8) in a medium-sized city in the Pacific Northwest of the United States. A survey instrument was administered to students during the first and last weeks of the school year. Analysis was generally based on information received from the **426** students who completed the questionnaire during both of its administrations.

RELIABILITY: Alphas of **.58** and **.73** were reported for the scale for its first and second administrations, respectively, by Boush, Friestad, and Rose (1994).

VALIDITY: The validity of the scale was not specifically addressed in the study by Boush, Friestad, and Rose (1994). However, the authors performed a principal components analysis with promax rotation of the combined items of this scale with those of another scale (#452). The two factors that were retained, on the basis of the factor loadings and scree test, led to the development of two scales rather than the one that was originally intended.

ADMINISTRATION: The scale used by Boush, Friestad, and Rose (1994) was part of a longer questionnaire self-administered by students in groups of 25 to 30 during the period with which they began each school day. Higher scores on the scale indicated a greater degree of mistrust of the motives of television advertisers.

MAJOR FINDINGS: The study by Boush, Friestad, and Rose (1994) explored adolescents' skepticism toward advertising and their beliefs about the persuasive tactics used by advertisers. Among the findings was that **mistrust of television advertisers** had a significant positive relationship with self-esteem.

COMMENTS: As acknowledged by Boush, Friestad, and Rose (1994, p. 173), the internal consistency of the scale is low enough to warrant caution in using it again. Further development and improvement in the scale's psychometric qualities is strongly advised.

REFERENCES:

Boush, David M., Marian Friestad, and Gregory M. Rose (1994), "Adolescent Skepticism Toward TV Advertising and Knowledge of Advertiser Tactics," *JCR*, 21 (June), 165–75.

Rossiter, John R. (1977), "Reliability of a Short Test Measuring Children's Attitudes Toward TV Commercials," *JCR*, 3 (March), 179–84.

SCALE ITEMS:

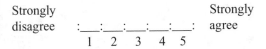

Strongly
disagree   :___:___:___:___:___: Strongly agree
         1   2   3   4   5

#456 *Attitude Toward Television Advertising (Mistrust of Advertiser Motives)*

1. Advertisers care more about getting you to buy things than what is good for you.

2. I often notice tricks that TV advertisers play to get me to buy something.

3. TV commercials try to make people buy things they don't really need.

4. TV commercials are different from TV programs in the way they try to influence you.

5. TV commercials tell only the good things about a product; they don't tell you the bad things.

6. TV commercials are all about the same when it comes to telling the truth.

SCALE NAME: Attitude Toward Television Advertising (Offensive)

SCALE DESCRIPTION: A four-item, five-point, Likert-type scale used to measure the degree to which a person believes that television commercials have gone too far in what they say or show and that they exhibit poor taste.

SCALE ORIGIN: The items in the scale come from two measures developed by Alwitt and Prabhaker (1992). Inspiration for this scale, as well as the others they created, seems to have come from Bauer and Greyser (1968).

SAMPLES: Alwitt and Prabhaker (1992) mailed a survey to 1200 randomly selected households with listed telephone numbers in the Chicago metropolitan statistical area in March 1990. **Two hundred twenty-eight** usable surveys were returned. Data were collected by Alwitt and Prabhaker (1994) from a Market Facts Household Panel balanced to match national demographic characteristics. Usable questionnaires were received from **794** panel members.

RELIABILITY: An alpha of **.68** was reported for the scale by Alwitt and Prabhaker (1994).

VALIDITY: No examination of scale validity was reported by Alwitt and Prabhaker (1994). However, it was mentioned that a factor analysis was conducted on 27 television-related attitudes. Six factors were produced, and the highest loading items on each factor were used to produce six summated scales.

ADMINISTRATION: The scale was self-administered along with other measures in a mail survey format (Alwitt and Prabhaker 1994). Scores appear to have been calculated such that the higher they were, the more they indicated a respondent's disagreement that much of television advertising is in poor taste; that is, high scores suggested that commercials were <u>not</u> offensive.

MAJOR FINDINGS: The goal of Alwitt and Prabhaker's (1994) study was to examine different reasons people may have unfavorable attitudes about television advertising. Using a nationally representative sample, they found that those who disliked television advertising also believed that **commercials were offensive**.

REFERENCES:
Alwitt, Linda F. and Paul R. Prabhaker (1992), "Functional and Belief Dimensions of Attitudes to Television Advertising," *JAR*, 32 (5), 30–42.
——— and ——— (1994), "Identifying Who Dislikes Television Advertising: Not By Demographics Alone," *JAR*, 34 (November/December), 17–29.
Bauer, Raymond A. and Stephen A. Greyser (1968), *Advertising in America: The Consumer View*. Boston: Harvard University Press.

SCALE ITEMS:

Strongly agree
Strongly disagree
1———2———3———4———5

1. There is too much sex in TV advertising.

2. There is too much violence in TV advertising.

3. Most TV commercials are in poor taste.

4. TV ads are more offensive today than they used to be.

SCALE NAME: Attitude Toward Television Advertising (Uninformative)

SCALE DESCRIPTION: A five-item, five-point, Likert-type scale used to measure the degree to which a person believes that television commercials do not provide enough information but instead try to touch the viewers' emotions.

SCALE ORIGIN: The items in the scale come from three measures developed by Alwitt and Prabhaker (1992). Inspiration for the items they created seems to have come from Bauer and Greyser (1968).

SAMPLES: Alwitt and Prabhaker (1992) mailed a survey to 1200 randomly selected households with listed telephone numbers in the Chicago metropolitan statistical area in March 1990. **Two hundred twenty-eight** usable surveys were returned. Data were collected by Alwitt and Prabhaker (1994) from a Market Facts Household Panel balanced to match national demographic characteristics. Usable questionnaires were received from **794** panel members.

RELIABILITY: An alpha of **.61** was reported for the scale by Alwitt and Prabhaker (1994).

VALIDITY: No examination of scale validity was reported by Alwitt and Prabhaker (1994). However, it was mentioned that a factor analysis was conducted on 27 television-related attitudes. Six factors were produced, and the highest loading items on each factor were used to produce six summated scales.

ADMINISTRATION: The scale was self-administered along with other measures in a mail survey format (Alwitt and Prabhaker 1994). Scores appear to have been calculated such that the higher they were, the more they indicated respondents thought that much of television advertising provided helpful information.

MAJOR FINDINGS: The goal of Alwitt and Prabhaker's (1994) study was to examine different reasons people may have unfavorable attitudes about television advertising. Using a nationally representative sample, they found that those who disliked television advertising also believed **commercials were not informative**.

COMMENTS: Care should be taken with this scale for several reasons. Its internal consistency is very low, which indicates that the items may not be tapping into the same construct. Even though the factor analysis referred to by Alwitt and Prabhaker (1994) showed the items loading on the same factor, it is hard to tell by looking at the items themselves what they all have in common. This observation is further supported by noting, as mentioned previously, that in their earlier study (Alwitt and Prabhaker 1992), these items were parts of three different scales. More development and testing is called for before this scale is used further.

REFERENCES:
Alwitt, Linda F. and Paul R. Prabhaker (1992), "Functional and Belief Dimensions of Attitudes to Television Advertising," *JAR*, 32 (5), 30–42.
——— and ——— (1994), "Identifying Who Dislikes Television Advertising: Not By Demographics Alone," *JAR*, 34 (November/December), 17–29.
Bauer, Raymond A. and Stephen A. Greyser (1968), *Advertising in America: The Consumer View.* Boston: Harvard University Press.

SCALE ITEMS:

Strongly
  agree
  1————2————3————4————5

Strongly
  disagree

1. Most TV ads today are not about products themselves, but just create a mood.

2. Today's TV ads tell you more about the people who use a brand than about what the brand does for you.

3. Most TV ads try to work on people's emotions.

4. TV advertising is a main reason our society is so concerned with buying and owning things.

5. TV advertising is upsetting to people because it sets goals for the average person that cannot really be met.

SCALE NAME: Competitive Ad Influence

SCALE DESCRIPTION: Three items that are purported to measure the degree to which a consumer indicates that ads for competing brands are better in some way than the ad for the brand under examination. Viewed in this way, the consumer is expressing a "lack of resistance" to competitors' ads (Ha 1996).

SCALE ORIGIN: The scale is original to the study by Ha (1996, 1997).

SAMPLES: The sample for the experiment conducted by Ha (1996) was selected from among students enrolled in general education classes at two Midwestern universities in the United States. Students volunteered for the study and received a pen for their participation. A usable sample of **112** responses was collected. The median age of the group was 20 years, nearly half (48%) were majoring in a science-related area, and more than half (64%) were women.

RELIABILITY: An alpha of **.91** was calculated for the scale (Ha 1997).

VALIDITY: No specific information regarding the scale's validity was reported by Ha (1996).

ADMINISTRATION: The scale was self-administered by subjects after they were exposed to the experimental stimuli (Ha 1996). Lower scores on the scale indicated that respondents believed that ads for brands in competition with the focal brand were superior in some way.

MAJOR FINDINGS: Ha (1996) used an experiment to investigate the effect of clutter on advertising effectiveness. Three dimensions of clutter were examined: quantity of ads in a vehicle, competitiveness of the ads, and intrusiveness of those ads. The findings indicated that none of the three dimensions had a significant impact on **competitive ad influence**.

REFERENCES:

Ha, Louisa (1996), "Advertising Clutter in Consumer Magazines: Dimensions and Effects," *JAR*, 36 (July/August), 76–84.

——— (1997), personal correspondence.

SCALE ITEMS:*

Strongly   Strongly
agree   :___:___:___:___:___:___:___: disagree
                1   2   3   4   5   6   7

1. The claims in the ads of these other brands are more credible than _____.

2. The ads of these other brands are better in quality than _____.

3. If I were to choose one of the clothing brands (or your best remembered brand's product category) advertised in this issue for purchase, I would choose _____.

*The name of the focal brand should be placed in the blanks in items #1 and #2. The blank in #3 is intended for the respondent to fill in. If the focal brand is named, the item would be coded as 7. If it is not named, it is scored as 1.

SCALE NAME: Credibility

SCALE DESCRIPTION: Three Likert-type items measuring the extent to which a person describes a pamphlet of information as believable. The pamphlet used by Block and Keller (1995) relates to sexually transmitted diseases and how to avoid them.

SCALE ORIGIN: No information about the scale's source was provided by Block and Keller (1995), but it appears original to their study.

SAMPLES: The scale was employed in both experiments conducted by Block and Keller (1995). In the first experiment, **94** undergraduate students completed the scale, and the second experiment was based on data from **115** undergraduate and graduate students.

RELIABILITY: Alphas of **.69** and **.63** were reported for the scale for Experiments 1 and 2, respectively (Block and Keller 1995).

VALIDITY: No examination of the scale's validity was reported by Block and Keller (1995), though they did state that a factor analysis indicated the items loaded on one factor.

ADMINISTRATION: The scale was completed by subjects after they were exposed to some health-related information (Block and Keller 1995). High scores on the scale indicated that respondents considered a specified stimulus to be quite plausible.

MAJOR FINDINGS: The purpose of the study by Block and Keller (1995) was to examine the relationships between level of efficacy, depth of processing, and framing effects. **Credibility** was measured merely to ensure that the attitude was not confounding experimental treatments, and indeed, the findings showed that subjects in the three conditions did not differ significantly in that regard.

REFERENCES:

Block, Lauren G. and Punam Anand Keller (1995), "When to Accentuate the Negative: The Effects of Perceived Efficacy and Message Framing on Intentions to Perform a Health-Related Behavior," *JMR*, 32 (May), 192–203.

SCALE ITEMS:*

Strongly   Strongly
disagree   :___:___:___:___:___:___: agree
        1   2   3   4   5   6   7

1. The information in the pamphlet is credible.

2. I think the information in the pamphlet is exaggerated.

3. I think the information in this pamphlet is unbelievable.

*The actual response scale and number of points were not specified in the article but appear to have been similar to what is shown here.

SCALE NAME: Credibility (Manufacturer)

SCALE DESCRIPTION: Four items intended to measure the credibility of a product's manufacturer and the confidence the manufacturer appears to have in the product being advertised.

SCALE ORIGIN: Although not stated explicitly, the scale appears original to Kirmani's (1997) study.

SAMPLES: Data were collected by Kirmani (1997) from **166** psychology students who were assigned randomly to treatments.

RELIABILITY: An alpha of **.79** was reported for the scale by Kirmani (1997).

VALIDITY: No examination of the scale's validity was reported by Kirmani (1997). As for dimensionality, there is some suggestion that a factor analysis indicated the four items loaded together.

ADMINISTRATION: The scale was apparently self-administered by subjects, along with other measures, after they had been exposed to experimental stimuli (Kirmani 1997). High scores on the scale indicated that the manufacturer had a great deal of credibility with regard to a particular product it makes.

MAJOR FINDINGS: The study by Kirmani (1997) examined the influence of ad repetition on inferences made about brand quality. The findings indicated that perceptions of **manufacturer credibility** mediate the relationship between repetition and perceived brand quality.

REFERENCES:
Kirmani, Amna (1997), "Advertising Repetition as a Signal of Quality: If It's Advertised So Much, Something Must Be Wrong," *JA*, 26 (Fall), 77–86.

SCALE ITEMS:*
The manufacturer of the advertised product is _____.*

Untrustworthy :___:___:___:___:___:___:___: Trustworthy
                1   2   3   4   5   6   7

Incompetent :___:___:___:___:___:___:___: Competent
             1   2   3   4   5   6   7

Dishonest :___:___:___:___:___:___:___: Honest
           1   2   3   4   5   6   7

The manufacturer has _____ in the advertised product.*

Very little
confidence :___:___:___:___:___:___:___: A lot of
            1   2   3   4   5   6   7   confidence

*The actual stems were not provided by Kirmani (1997); these are provided as possibilities based on the information provided.

SCALE NAME: Ease of Ad Claim Substantiation

SCALE DESCRIPTION: A three-item, seven-point summated rating scale purported to measure the effort required by a subject to visually confirm verbal claims made in an advertisement by referring to the product photo in the ad.

SCALE ORIGIN: Although not specifically stated in the article, the scale appears to be original to Meyers-Levy and Peracchio (1995).

SAMPLES: The scale was used in the first of two experiments conducted by Meyers-Levy and Peracchio (1995). The first experiment used **46** students enrolled in marketing classes.

RELIABILITY: An alpha of **.66** was reported for the scale by Meyers-Levy and Peracchio (1995; Peracchio 1997).

VALIDITY: No specific evidence of the scale's validity was provided by Meyers-Levy and Peracchio (1995) beyond that noted in the "Major Findings" section.

ADMINISTRATION: The self-administered scale was completed by subjects after they were exposed to experimental stimuli (Meyers-Levy and Peracchio 1995). Higher scores on the scale suggested that subjects considered the layout of textual and photographic material in an ad to have made it relatively easy to substantiate ad claims.

MAJOR FINDINGS: Meyers-Levy and Peracchio (1995) examined the relative persuasiveness of color versus back-and-white ads. The **substantiation** scale was used merely as a manipulation check. The subjects considered ads that had been deliberately laid out to require "low resource demands" to make it easier to substantiate the claims.

REFERENCES:
Meyers-Levy, Joan and Laura A. Peracchio (1995), "Understanding the Effects of Color: How the Correspondence Between Available and Required Resources Affects Attitudes," *JCR*, 22 (September), 121–38.
Peracchio, Laura A. (1997), personal correspondence.

SCALE ITEMS:

1. I found it _____ to refer to the ad photo when thinking about the product features.

Hard   :___:___:___:___:___:___:___: Easy
              1 2 3 4 5 6 7

2. I readily _____ visually examine the product features discussed in the ad claims.

Could not :___:___:___:___:___:___:___: Could
              1 2 3 4 5 6 7

3. Ad claim placement made it _____ to examine related visual material.

Difficult   :___:___:___:___:___:___:___: Easy
            1 2 3 4 5 6 7

SCALE NAME: Emotional/Rational Appeal

SCALE DESCRIPTION: Four bipolar adjectives purported to measure a person's opinion of the type of execution used in an ad that varies from *emotional* at one extreme to *rational* at the other.

SCALE ORIGIN: Stafford and Day (1995) said they used a modification of a measure from Liu and Stout's (1987) work, but they did not indicate exactly what changes they made. At the very least, Stafford and Day (1995) used the items as a summated scale, whereas Liu and Stout (1987) do not appear to have done so. The latter reported no alpha, and the items were used along with other measures in a pretest to ensure that two commercials varied on the emotional/rational dimension.

SAMPLES: Subjects for the main experiment conducted by Stafford and Day (1995) were recruited through civic and religious organizations, and volunteers were paid $6. Subjects ranged in age from 21 to over 60 years, had incomes of less than $25,000 to more than $50,000, and a little more than half were women. Usable questionnaires were received from **137** subjects.

RELIABILITY: An alpha of **.78** was reported for the scale by Stafford and Day (1995). This check of the scale's reliability was made with a pretest sample rather than with the subjects in the main study. They were described as **40** adults similar to those in the main study.

VALIDITY: No examination of the scale's validity was reported by Stafford and Day (1995).

ADMINISTRATION: Subjects were asked to rate one of the test ads using the scale (Stafford and Day 1995). Higher scores on the scale appeared to mean that respondents viewed an ad as using an emotional appeal as opposed to a rational appeal.

MAJOR FINDINGS: The appropriateness of certain media and message strategies for two broad categories of retail services were tested by Stafford and Day (1995). The **type of appeal** was used as a manipulation check. The results showed that the **rational ad** was associated with more positive attitudes toward the ad than **emotional ads** were for both types of services studied.

REFERENCES:

Liu, Scott S. and Patricia A. Stout (1987), "Effects of Message Modality and Appeal on Advertising Acceptance," *Psychology & Marketing*, 4 (Fall), 167–87.
Stafford, Marla Royne and Ellen Day (1995), "Retail Services Advertising: The Effects of Appeal, Medium, and Service," *JA*, 24 (Spring), 57–71.

SCALE ITEMS:*

1. Tangible   :___:___:___:___:___:___:___: Intangible
                 1   2   3   4   5   6   7

2. Logical   :___:___:___:___:___:___:___: Emotional
                 1   2   3   4   5   6   7

3. Objective   :___:___:___:___:___:___:___: Subjective
                 1   2   3   4   5   6   7

4. Factual   :___:___:___:___:___:___:___: Nonfactual
                 1   2   3   4   5   6   7

*The particulars of the scale used by Stafford and Day (1995) were not described. The information here is taken from Liu and Stout (1987).

SCALE NAME: Emotional Reaction (Strength)

SCALE DESCRIPTION: Eighteen five-point summated rating scales measuring the potency of a person's overall negative emotional response to a stimulus to which he or she has been exposed. The stimulus for response in the study by Schoenbachler and Whittler (1996) was an antidrug-related public service announcement .

SCALE ORIGIN: The items composing this scale are a portion of the Differential Emotions Scale (DES III) by Izard (1979). The eighteen items represent six different "negative" emotions but were combined by Schoenbachler and Whittler (1996) simply to gauge the intensity of negative emotional reaction in general.

SAMPLES: Data were collected by Schoenbachler and Whittler (1996) from a sample of **371** seventh- and eighth-grade students from a metropolitan middle school. No other information was provided about the sample.

RELIABILITY: An alpha of **.92** was reported for the scale (Schoenbachler and Whittler 1996).

VALIDITY: The validity of the scale was not addressed by Schoenbachler and Whittler (1996). Although not stated in the article, a factor analysis appears to have shown that there were six dimensions represented by the eighteen items but that these dimensions were part of one higher order factor (Schoenbachler 1997).

ADMINISTRATION: The subjects completed the scale as part of a larger instrument they filled out after being exposed to an experimental stimulus (Schoenbachler and Whittler 1996). Higher scores on the scale suggested that respondents had experienced more intense negative emotional responses to some stimulus to which they were exposed compared with those respondents with lower scores.

MAJOR FINDINGS: The purpose of the experiment by Schoenbachler and Whittler (1996) was to examine threat appeal advertising using the *ordered protection model*. Despite expectations, higher levels of threat in a communication did not appear to produce correspondingly stronger **emotional responses** in adolescents.

REFERENCES:
Izard, Carroll (1979), "The Differential Emotions Scale for Children (DES-III)," unpublished manuscript, University of Delaware.
Schoenbachler, Denise D. (1997), personal correspondence.
—— and Tommy E. Whittler (1996), "Adolescent Processing of Social and Physical Threat Communications," *JA*, 25 (Winter), 37–54.

SCALE ITEMS:*
DIRECTIONS: Circle one of the numbers nearest the word that best describes how you felt as you looked at the ad about drug use.

Not at all   :__:__:__:__:__: Very much
          1 2 3 4 5

As you looked at the ad, did you...

  1. Feel unhappy, blue, downhearted?

  2. Feel sad and gloomy, almost like crying?

3. Feel discouraged, like you can't make it, nothing is going right?

4. Feel like screaming at somebody or banging on something?

5. Feel angry, irritated, annoyed?

6. Feel so mad you're about to blow up?

7. Feel like something stinks, puts a bad taste in your mouth?

8. Feel disgusted, like something is sickening?

9. Feel like things are so rotten they could make you sick?

10. Feel scared, uneasy, like something might harm you?

11. Feel fearful, like you're in danger, very tense?

12. Feel afraid, shaky, and jittery?

13. Feel ashamed to be seen, like you just want to disappear or get away from people?

14. Feel bashful, embarrassed?

15. Feel shy, like you want to hide?

16. Feel regret, sorry about something you did?

17. Feel like you did something wrong?

18. Feel like you ought to be blamed for something?

*The scale stem, directions, and items were provided by Schoenbachler (1997).

SCALE NAME: Emotional Reaction to Ad (Strength)

SCALE DESCRIPTION: Eight seven-point unipolar terms purported to evaluate the strength of a person's overall emotional reaction to an ad. The scale is apparently intended to measure the *intensity* of an global emotional reaction rather than the particular *type* of emotion experienced.

SCALE ORIGIN: Although Moore and Harris (1996) drew on the literature for their items, the scale as a whole appears to be original to their study.

SAMPLES: Subjects for the experiment conducted by Moore and Harris (1996) were **131** marketing undergraduate students attending a large Midwestern U.S. university. The sample was 52% women, and ages ranged from 19 to 28 years. Participation was apparently voluntary, and students received course credit.

RELIABILITY: Three alphas were reported by Moore and Harris (1996): **.90, .88,** and **.79** for positive emotion, negative emotion, and nonemotional ads, respectively.

VALIDITY: No examination of the scale's validity was reported by Moore and Harris (1996).

ADMINISTRATION: Subjects in the experiment conducted by Moore and Harris (1996) completed the scale, along with other measures, after they were exposed to experimental stimuli (ads). Higher scores on the scale suggested that respondents experienced a strong emotional reaction to some ad to which they were exposed.

MAJOR FINDINGS: Moore and Harris (1996) explored the role of affect intensity in creating emotional responses to advertising. The results indicated that **emotional responses** mediated the influence of affect intensity on attitude toward the ad only for ads with positive emotional appeals.

REFERENCES:
Moore, David J. and William D. Harris (1996), "Affect Intensity and the Consumer's Attitude Toward High Impact Emotional Advertising Appeals," *JA*, 25 (Summer), 37–50.

SCALE ITEMS:
While exposed to the advertisement, how strongly did you feel _____?

Not at all   :___:___:___:___:___:___:___: Very
         1   2   3   4   5   6   7

1. Emotional
2. Happy
3. Joyous
4. Warm
5. Moved
6. Touched
7. Sympathetic
8. Sad

SCALE NAME: Endorser/Product Fit

SCALE DESCRIPTION: Four seven-point, Likert-type statements measuring the degree to which a person perceives there to be a relationship between an endorser and a product, such that the pairing of the two is viewed as a "good fit." This measure was referred to as *relatedness* by Sengupta, Goodstein, and Boninger (1997).

SCALE ORIGIN: Sengupta, Goodstein, and Boninger (1997) may have drawn inspiration from other measures, but the scale appears original to their work. Items 1 and 2 formed the scale as used in a pilot study before their first study, which had an alpha of .93. The authors added two more items when they conducted a pretest before their second study to improve the measure's similarity with two previously measured concepts (relevance and appropriateness).

SAMPLES: Little information was provided by Sengupta, Goodstein, and Boninger (1997) about the sample they used for the pretest except that it came from the same population as that used in their second study (MBA students).

RELIABILITY: An alpha of **.97** was reported for the scale by Sengupta, Goodstein, and Boninger (1997).

VALIDITY: No examination of the scale's validity was reported by Sengupta, Goodstein, and Boninger (1997).

ADMINISTRATION: As noted, the scale was used by Sengupta, Goodstein, and Boninger (1997) in a pretest before their second study. Higher scores on the scale indicated that respondents believed a particular endorser and product pairing were very much related and appropriate.

MAJOR FINDINGS: Sengupta, Goodstein, and Boninger (1997) proposed that different kinds of low-involvement cues lead to varying degrees of attitude persistence. As noted, **endorser/product fit** was measured in a pretest before the second main study as a manipulation check, namely, to confirm that the target population viewed one endorser as being significantly more related to a product than another.

REFERENCES:
Sengupta, Jaideep, Ronald C. Goodstein, and David S. Boninger (1997), "All Cues Are Not Created Equal: Obtaining Attitude Persistence Under Low-Involvement Conditions," *JCR*, 23 (March), 351–61.

SCALE ITEMS:*

Strongly   Strongly
disagree   :___:___:___:___:___:___: agree
       1 2 3 4 5 6 7

1. When I think of _____ as an endorser, _____ is one of the first products I think about.

2. The idea of _____ endorsing _____ represents a very good fit.

3. I think _____ is a relevant endorser for _____.

4. I think _____ is an appropriate endorser for _____.

*The first blank in each item should be filled in with the name of the endorser (e.g., Christie Brinkley), and the second blank should have the name of the product category (e.g., mouthwash).

SCALE NAME: Endorser Status

SCALE DESCRIPTION: Three seven-point items in a semantic differential format intended to capture the degree to which a person views someone who has endorsed a product in an ad as expert and credible.

SCALE ORIGIN: No information about the source of the scale was provided by Pham (1996), but it appears original to his study.

SAMPLES: Data were gathered by Pham (1996) for his three experiments from undergraduate students. Experiments 1, 2, and 3 involved **288**, **133**, and **57** students, respectively.

RELIABILITY: Alphas for the scale ranged from **.83** to **.99** in the three experiments conducted by Pham (1996).

VALIDITY: No examination of the scale's validity was reported by Pham (1996).

ADMINISTRATION: The scale was part of a larger self-administered questionnaire that subjects filled out after they were exposed to ads in the experimental treatments (Pham 1996). Higher scores on the scale indicated that respondents believed that the endorser of a product in an ad to which they were exposed had strong communication status in terms of expertise and credibility.

MAJOR FINDINGS: Pham (1996) proposed that two types of processes underlie arousal effects on persuasion: "selection" and "representation" effects. The **endorser status** scale was mainly used as a manipulation check and, indeed, confirmed that the treatments had successfully manipulated the construct.

REFERENCES:
Pham, Michel Tuan (1996), "Cue Representation and Selection Effects of Arousal on Persuasion," *JCR*, 22 (March), 373–87.

SCALE ITEMS:
The (<u>message source</u>) is:

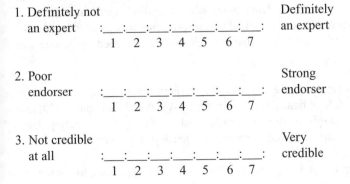

1. Definitely not   Definitely
   an expert   :___:___:___:___:___:___: an expert
            1   2   3   4   5   6   7

2. Poor   Strong
   endorser   :___:___:___:___:___:___: endorser
            1   2   3   4   5   6   7

3. Not credible   Very
   at all   :___:___:___:___:___:___: credible
            1   2   3   4   5   6   7

SCALE NAME: Expertise (Source)

SCALE DESCRIPTION: A multi-item, seven-point semantic differential measuring a consumer's assessment of a specified person's competency and training as a source of information about a particular product. Netemeyer and Bearden (1992) used a five-item scale to measure expertise of a personal source of information (retail employee), and Tripp, Jensen, and Carlson (1994) measured the expertise of celebrity endorsers using a six-item scale.

SCALE ORIGIN: Netemeyer and Bearden (1992) did not indicate the origin of the scale, but Tripp, Jensen, and Carlson (1994) cited McCroskey (1966) as the source of their measure. However, only three items from McCroskey's scale (1966) were incorporated into the version used Tripp, Jensen, and Carlson (1994).

SAMPLES: The experiment conducted by Netemeyer and Bearden (1992) was based on data from a sample of **372** undergraduate students. The students were randomly assigned to a 2 (informational influence) $\times$ 2 (normative influence) design. The sample was split approximately in half in order to test two different models of behavioral intention. Therefore, there were four cells per model tested, with each cell having between 46 and 49 subjects.

Data were gathered by Tripp, Jensen, and Carlson (1994) from a final set of **461** undergraduate students attending one of two universities in a southern U.S. state. This final sample was rather evenly split between men (51.19%) and women (48.81%). They were assigned to 1 of 48 treatment conditions using randomized block procedures.

RELIABILITY: The scale was reported by Netemeyer and Bearden (1992) to have alphas of **.94** and **.91** for the two models of behavioral intention that were tested. An alpha of **.87** was reported for the version of the scale used by Tripp, Jensen, and Carlson (1994).

VALIDITY: No examination of scale validity was reported by either Netemeyer and Bearden (1992) or Tripp, Jensen, and Carlson (1994). The latter indicated that the scale had a beta coefficient of .82, which suggests the scale is unidimensional. However, further testing using confirmatory factor analysis is necessary to better determine the scale's dimensionality.

ADMINISTRATION: In the studies by both Netemeyer and Bearden (1992) and Tripp, Jensen, and Carlson (1994), the scale was self-administered by students, along with several other measures, after an experimental manipulation. Higher scores on the scale implied that respondents perceived the source of the information as an expert, whereas lower scores suggested that respondents believed the source was incompetent.

MAJOR FINDINGS: Netemeyer and Bearden (1992) conducted an experiment to compare the causal structure and predictive ability of the models of behavioral intentions by Ajzen and Fishbein (1980) and Miniard and Cohen (1983). **Expertise** of an information source (audio store employee) was manipulated as part of the experiment. The **expertise** scale was used to provide evidence that a successful manipulation had been made.

Tripp, Jensen, and Carlson (1994) examined the effects of the number of exposures to a celebrity endorser and the number of products he or she endorsed on consumer attitudes and intentions. Among the many findings was that as the number of products endorsed increased, the perceived **expertise** of the endorser decreased.

REFERENCES:

Ajzen, Icek and Martin Fishbein (1980), *Understanding Attitudes and Predicting Social Behavior*. Englewood Cliffs, NJ: Prentice Hall.

McCroskey, James C. (1966), "Scales for the Measurement of Ethos," *Speech Monographs*, 33 (March), 65–72.

Miniard, Paul W. and Joel B. Cohen (1983), "Modeling Personal and Normative Influences on Behavior," *JCR*, 10 (September), 169–80.

Netemeyer, Richard G. and William O. Bearden (1992), "A Comparative Analysis of Two Models of Behavioral Intention," *JAMS*, 20 (Winter), 49–59.

Tripp, Carolyn, Thomas D. Jensen, and Les Carlson (1994), "The Effects of Multiple Product Endorsements by Celebrities on Consumers' Attitudes and Intentions," *JCR*, 20 (March), 535–47.

SCALE ITEMS:*

The (<u>message source</u>) is:

1. Not knowledgeable :__:__:__:__:__:__:__: Knowledgeable
                             1 2 3 4 5 6 7

2. Incompetent :__:__:__:__:__:__:__: Competent
                  1 2 3 4 5 6 7

3. Inexpert :__:__:__:__:__:__:__: Expert
              1 2 3 4 5 6 7

4. Not trained :__:__:__:__:__:__:__: Trained
                1 2 3 4 5 6 7

5. Not experienced :__:__:__:__:__:__:__: Experienced
                    1 2 3 4 5 6 7

6. Unintelligent :__:__:__:__:__:__:__: Intelligent
                 1 2 3 4 5 6 7

7. Uninformed :__:__:__:__:__:__:__: Informed
                1 2 3 4 5 6 7

8. Stupid :__:__:__:__:__:__:__: Bright
           1 2 3 4 5 6 7

*Netemeyer and Bearden (1992) used items 1–5. Tripp, Jensen, and Carlson (1994) used items 2–4 and 6–8.

SCALE NAME: External Search (Advertised Specials)

SCALE DESCRIPTION: Four seven-point items that measure the degree to which a consumer describes him- or herself as checking for advertised specials before grocery shopping with the emphasis of the search being on newspaper ads.

SCALE ORIGIN: Although not clear from the article by Putrevu and Ratchford (1997), some of the work on the scales was conducted earlier in a dissertation by Putrevu (1992).

SAMPLES: Data were gathered by Putrevu and Ratchford (1997) using a mail survey to a random sample of grocery shoppers in a standard metropolitan statistical area in the Northeastern United States. A total of **500** responses were used in the main analysis, and demographics of the final sample were similar to those of the population of interest.

RELIABILITY: An alpha of **.88** was reported for the scale (Putrevu and Ratchford 1997).

VALIDITY: Although the authors stated in general that the scales showed evidence of convergent, discriminant, and content validity, no details of the analyses were provided (Putrevu and Ratchford 1997).

ADMINISTRATION: The scale was part of a larger mail questionnaire (Putrevu and Ratchford 1997). Higher scores on the scale suggested that a consumer frequently looked for advertised specials before going to grocery store.

MAJOR FINDINGS: Putrevu and Ratchford (1997) examined a dynamic model of consumer search behavior that included human capital. In general, the results indicated that self-reported search for information about buying groceries is associated with perceptions of the costs and benefits of search as predicted by the model.

COMMENTS: As presented in the article by Putrevu and Ratchford (1997), this scale was part of a larger measure called "Search." That measure was the mean of the scores from nine scales related to grocery product information search behavior.

REFERENCES:

Putrevu, Sanjay (1992), *A Theory of Search and Its Empirical Investigation*, doctoral dissertation, State University of New York at Buffalo.
———— and Brian T. Ratchford (1997), "A Model of Search Behavior with an Application to Grocery Shopping," *JR*, 73 (4), 463–86.

SCALE ITEMS:

Never :___:___:___:___:___:___:___: Always
       1   2   3   4   5   6   7

1. I look for weekly store inserts in newspapers for grocery items.

2. Before going grocery shopping I check the newspaper for advertisements by various supermarkets.

3. I check the newspaper for advertised specials for grocery products.

4. I shop for advertised specials in supermarkets.

SCALE NAME: External Search (Grocery-Related Articles)

SCALE DESCRIPTION: Three seven-point items that measure the degree to which a consumer reads articles in newspapers and or magazines that evaluate grocery products.

SCALE ORIGIN: Although not clear from the article by Putrevu and Ratchford (1997), some of the work on the scales was conducted earlier in a dissertation by Putrevu (1992).

SAMPLES: Data were gathered by Putrevu and Ratchford (1997) using a mail survey to a random sample of grocery shoppers in a standard metropolitan statistical area in the Northeastern United States. A total of **500** responses were used in the main analysis, and demographics of the final sample were similar to those of the population of interest.

RELIABILITY: An alpha of **.84** was reported for the scale (Putrevu and Ratchford 1997).

VALIDITY: Although the authors stated in general that the scales showed evidence of convergent, discriminant, and content validity, no details of the analyses were provided (Putrevu and Ratchford 1997).

ADMINISTRATION: The scale was part of a larger mail questionnaire (Putrevu and Ratchford 1997). Higher scores on the scale suggested that a consumer frequently read articles about grocery products.

MAJOR FINDINGS: Putrevu and Ratchford (1997) examined a dynamic model of consumer search behavior that includes human capital. In general, the results indicated that self-reported search for information about buying groceries is associated with perceptions of the costs and benefits of search as predicted by the model.

COMMENTS: As presented in the article by Putrevu and Ratchford (1997), this scale was part of a larger measure called "Search." That measure was the mean of the scores from nine scales related to grocery product information search behavior.

REFERENCES:
Putrevu, Sanjay (1992), *A Theory of Search and Its Empirical Investigation*, doctoral dissertation, State University of New York at Buffalo.
——— and Brian T. Ratchford (1997), "A Model of Search Behavior with an Application to Grocery Shopping," *JR*, 73 (4), 463–86.

SCALE ITEMS:

Never :___:___:___:___:___:___:___: Always
       1   2   3   4   5   6   7

1. I read articles in magazines/newspapers about grocery products.

2. I read magazines that evaluate grocery products.

3. I read news features/articles which inform me about the best brands of grocery products.

SCALE NAME: External Search (Quantity)

SCALE DESCRIPTION: Seven information sources responded to on a seven-point scale used to indicate the degree to which a person recalls getting information relevant to some specified purchase. Personal and nonpersonal sources are represented, as are commercial and noncommercial. The purchase studied by Moorthy, Ratchford, and Talukdar (1997) was that of a new car.

SCALE ORIGIN: The scale was developed by Moorthy, Ratchford, and Talukdar (1997) for use in their study. They considered weighting the sources to reflect the effort expended on each but decided that "the consumer's allocation of usage across sources has presumably already taken into account the difficulty of using various sources" (Moorthy, Ratchford, and Talukdar 1997, p. 271).

SAMPLES: Moorthy, Ratchford, and Talukdar (1997) gathered data from new car buyers in the Greater Rochester area in northern New York over a six-month period. Surveys were passed out to new car buyers at four dealerships that represented a variety of U.S. and Japanese manufacturers. Shoppers were given two survey forms: one to fill out if they had already bought a car and the other to complete if they were still in the process of buying a car. Fifty-one respondents filled out the "already purchased" form; another 51 completed the "in-process" form initially but bought cars within two months.

RELIABILITY: Alphas of **.86** and **.82** were reported for the scale for the "in process" and "already purchased" respondents, respectively (Moorthy, Ratchford, and Talukdar 1997).

VALIDITY: No examination of the scale's validity was reported by Moorthy, Ratchford, and Talukdar (1997).

ADMINISTRATION: Questionnaires were passed out by one of the researchers, but the forms were self-administered by respondents at their convenience and mailed back to the researchers (Moorthy, Ratchford, and Talukdar 1997). Higher scores on the scale indicated that respondents had received relevant information regarding a purchase from a large variety of sources.

MAJOR FINDINGS: Moorthy, Ratchford, and Talukdar (1997) presented a comprehensive model for understanding consumer external search activity. The framework stressed the influence of prior brand perceptions on the search process. As expected, the findings showed an inverted U–shaped relationship between purchase experience and **amount of search**.

REFERENCES:
Moorthy, Sridhar, Brian T. Ratchford, and Debabrata Talukdar (1997), "Consumer Information Search Revisited: Theory and Empirical Analysis," *JCR*, 23 (March), 263–77.

SCALE ITEMS:
Did you get any relevant information about _____ from . . .*

Hardly   Quite
anything   :__:__:__:__:__:__:__: a bit
            1   2   3   4   5   6   7

1. Salespersons and dealers?

2. Friends and family?

3. Manufacturers' brochures and pamphlets?

4. TV advertisements?

5. Radio advertisements?

6. Newspaper advertisements?

7. Magazine reports?

*The name of the product category should be placed in the blanks.

SCALE NAME: Imagery Elaboration

SCALE DESCRIPTION: Three seven-point, Likert-type items described as measuring the "activation of stored information in the production of mental images beyond what was provided by the stimulus" to which the subject was exposed (Babin and Burns 1997, p. 37).

SCALE ORIGIN: Although inspiration for the scale came from the work of Ellen and Bone (1991), the items are distinct enough to consider this scale as original to Babin and Burns (1997).

SAMPLES: Babin and Burns (1997) gathered data for their experiment in a classroom setting from **186** undergraduate business students. The sample was almost evenly split on gender (52% male).

RELIABILITY: A composite reliability of **.80** was reported by Babin and Burns (1997).

VALIDITY: Babin and Burns (1997) found support for the unidimensionality of the scale, as well as for its discriminant validity.

ADMINISTRATION: The scale was self-administered by students in the experiment along with other measures after subjects were exposed to mock ads (Babin and Burns 1997). A high score on the scale indicated that a stimulus (e.g., an ad) had stimulated product-related imagery in the subject.

MAJOR FINDINGS: The experiment conducted by Babin and Burns (1997) examined the mediating role of evoked imagery in attitudinal responses. The research indicated that the use of concrete pictures did not significantly affect the quantity or **elaboration** of evoked imagery in comparison with a less concrete picture or no picture.

REFERENCES:

Babin, Laurie and Alvin C. Burns (1997), "Effects of Print Ad Pictures and Copy Containing Instructions to Imagine on Mental Imagery that Mediates Attitudes," *JA*, 26 (Fall), 33–44.

Ellen, Pam Scholder and Paula Fitzgerald Bone (1991), "Measuring Communication-Evoked Imagery Processing," in *Advances in Consumer Research*, Vol. 18, Rebecca H. Holman and Michael R. Soloman, eds. Provo, UT: Association of Consumer Research, 806–12.

SCALE ITEMS:

Strongly   Strongly
disagree   :___:___:___:___:___:___:___: agree
        1   2   3   4   5   6   7

1. I fantasized about the product in the ad.

2. I imagined what it would be like to use the product advertised.

3. I imagined the feel of the product.

SCALE NAME: Involvement (Advertisement)

SCALE DESCRIPTION: The scale appears to measure how much a person reports actively processing an advertisement to which he or she has been exposed. In Lord, Lee, and Sauer (1994, 1995) the ads were mock radio commercials embedded in a recorded radio program, and this measure was referred to as *commercial processing motivation* (CPM; 1994) and later as *response involvement* (1995). The measure is composed of three semantic differentials and one Likert-type item.

SCALE ORIGIN: No information was provided by Lord, Lee, and Sauer (1994, 1995) as to the source of the scale, but it would appear to be original to their study.

SAMPLES: The analyses reported by Lord, Lee, and Sauer in 1994 and 1995 appear to have come from the same database. The data were collected from undergraduate students in a introductory marketing course. Students received extra credit for their participation, and analysis (1995) was based on **328** competed survey forms. (Data for four subjects were discarded for the 1994 study due to incomplete information necessary for the analyses.) The students participated in groups of approximately 20 per session, and a little more than half (55%) of the sample was men.

RELIABILITY: Alphas of **.93** and **.89** were reported for the scale by Lord, Lee, and Sauer in 1994 and 1995, respectively.

VALIDITY: The validity of the scale was not specifically addressed in the study (Lord, Lee, and Sauer 1994, 1995). However, some support for the scale's validity comes from the finding that those who scored higher in the involvement scale also scored higher on a "recognition memory index" created to determine the degree to which respondents could accurately respond to statements made about the ads they heard.

ADMINISTRATION: The scale was part of a longer questionnaire self-administered by students after they were exposed to experimental stimuli (Lord, Lee, and Sauer 1994, 1995). High scores on the scale suggested that respondents were very involved in the ads, whereas low scores suggested they ignored the ads.

MAJOR FINDINGS: Lord, Lee, and Sauer's (1994) study examined the influence of program context on attitude toward the ad. It was found that **involvement with the ad** was significantly related to ad attitude, but there was not significant support for the hypothesis that the impact would be greater on one attitude component than on another.

Similarly, Lord, Lee, and Sauer (1995) examined the antecedents of attitude toward the ad. Among their many findings was that the relationship between argument strength and brand attitude was insignificant for those in **low involvement** groups but significant in **high involvement** groups.

REFERENCES:

Lord, Kenneth R., Myung-Soo Lee, and Paul L. Sauer (1994), "Program Context Antecedents of Attitude Toward Radio Commercials," *JAMS*, 22 (1), 3–15.

———, ———, and ——— (1995), "The Combined Influence Hypothesis: Central and Peripheral Antecedents of Attitude Toward the Ad," *JA*, 24 (Spring), 73–85.

SCALE ITEMS:

While listening to the radio commercials I was:*

1. Very
   uninvolved   __:__:__:__:__:__:__   Very
   involved

         1   2   3   4   5   6   7

2. Concentrating
   very little   __:__:__:__:__:__:__   Concentrating
   very hard

         1   2   3   4   5   6   7

3. Paying very
   little attention   __:__:__:__:__:__:__   Paying a
   lot of attention

         1   2   3   4   5   6   7

4. I carefully considered the advertising claims about the *(product name)*.

   Strongly
   disagree   __:__:__:__:__:__:__   Strongly
   agree

         1   2   3   4   5   6   7

*This is the lead-in phrase used by Lord, Lee, and Sauer (1994). It could be adapted for use with television commercials and possibly print ads.

SCALE NAME: Involvement (Advertisement)

SCALE DESCRIPTION: Eight nine-point semantic differential items that appear to measure the level of interest a person had while reading an advertisement and the importance of the information to him or her.

SCALE ORIGIN: Although the source of the scale was not explicitly stated by Johar (1995), it would appear to be original to her study.

SAMPLES: The scale was used in two experiments conducted by Johar (1995). Data were collected from **65** and **152** college students in Experiments 1 and 2, respectively.

RELIABILITY: Alphas of **.80** and **.88** were reported for the scale as used in Experiments 1 and 2, respectively (Johar 1995).

VALIDITY: No information regarding the scale's validity was reported by Johar (1995).

ADMINISTRATION: Along with the stimuli, instructions, and other questions, this scale was presented to the subjects on a personal computer, and responses were made directly on the machine as well (Johar 1995). High scores on the scale suggested that respondents were very involved in the ads, whereas low scores suggested they considered them irrelevant.

MAJOR FINDINGS: Johar (1995) investigated how the degree of involvement in processing an ad may affect the accuracy of the inferences subjects make. **Involvement** was measured as a manipulation check and indeed showed that the proper treatment group was significantly more **involved** in the ad than the other group.

COMMENTS: Because responses are made to two different scale stems, there is the possibility that two or more dimensions are represented here: one capturing the subject's involvement in the task of reading the ad and another being an evaluation of the personal relevance of the ad's content about a particular product. Before using this scale again, it is suggested that its dimensionality be tested to ensure it is not multidimensional.

REFERENCES:

Johar, Gita Venkataramani (1995), "Consumer Involvement and Deception from Implied Advertising Claims," *JMR*, 32 (August), 267–79.

SCALE ITEMS:

Would you say that while reading the product description you:

1. Were not interested   :___:___:___:___:___:___:___:___: Were very interested
                          -4 -3 -2 -1 0 1 2 3 4

2. Were not absorbed   :___:___:___:___:___:___:___:___: Were very absorbed
                          -4 -3 -2 -1 0 1 2 3 4

3. Skimmed the   Read the
   advertisement quickly :___:___:___:___:___:___:___:___: advertisement thoroughly
                          -4 -3 -2 -1 0 1 2 3 4

Would you say that you found the product description:

4. Unimportant   :___:___:___:___:___:___:___:___: Important
                    −4   −3   −2   −1   0   1   2   3   4

5. Irrelevant   :___:___:___:___:___:___:___:___: Of concern to you
                    −4   −3   −2   −1   0   1   2   3   4

6. Worthless   :___:___:___:___:___:___:___:___: Valuable
                    −4   −3   −2   −1   0   1   2   3   4

7. Boring   :___:___:___:___:___:___:___:___: Interesting
                    −4   −3   −2   −1   0   1   2   3   4

8. Uninvolving   :___:___:___:___:___:___:___:___: Involving
                    −4   −3   −2   −1   0   1   2   3   4

SCALE NAME: Likability (Source)

SCALE DESCRIPTION: A three-item, seven-point semantic differential measuring a consumer's liking of the source of information about a particular product. As used by Tripp, Jensen, and Carlson (1994), the scale specifically measured the likability of a celebrity endorser of a product in an mock magazine ad.

SCALE ORIGIN: Tripp, Jensen, and Carlson (1994) indicated that they created the scale, apparently for use in this study.

SAMPLES: Data were gathered by Tripp, Jensen, and Carlson (1994) from a final set of **461** undergraduates attending one of two universities in a Southern U.S. state. This final sample was rather evenly split between men (51.19%) and women (48.81%). Subjects were assigned to one of 48 treatment conditions using randomized block procedures.

RELIABILITY: An alpha of **.84** was reported for the version of the scale used by Tripp, Jensen, and Carlson (1994).

VALIDITY: No examination of scale validity was reported by Tripp, Jensen, and Carlson (1994). They indicated that the scale had a beta coefficient of .86, which suggests the scale is unidimensional. However, further testing using confirmatory factor analysis is necessary to better determine the scale's dimensionality.

ADMINISTRATION: In the study by Tripp, Jensen, and Carlson (1994), the scale was self-administered by students along with several other measures after an experimental manipulation. Higher scores on the scale implied that respondents perceived the source of the information as likable, whereas lower scores suggested that respondents believed the source was unpleasant.

MAJOR FINDINGS: Tripp, Jensen, and Carlson (1994) examined the effects of the number of exposures to a celebrity endorser and the number of products he or she endorsed on consumer attitudes and intentions. Among the many findings was that as the number of products endorsed increased, the perceived **likability** of the endorser decreased.

REFERENCES:
Tripp, Carolyn, Thomas D. Jensen, and Les Carlson (1994), "The Effects of Multiple Product Endorsements by Celebrities on Consumers' Attitudes and Intentions," *JCR*, 20 (March), 535–47.

SCALE ITEMS:
Did you find the celebrity endorser:

1. Very
   unlikable :___:___:___:___:___:___:___: Very likable
           1 2 3 4 5 6 7

2. Very
   unpleasing :___:___:___:___:___:___:___: Very pleasing
           1 2 3 4 5 6 7

3. Very
   disagreeable :___:___:___:___:___:___:___: Very agreeable
           1 2 3 4 5 6 7

SCALE NAME: Persuasiveness of Brochure

SCALE DESCRIPTION: The various versions of the scale are composed of items measuring the effectiveness of a brochure to change the attitude of a person toward some topic. The specific topics focused on in the scales were health-related. Although there were variations in the versions of the scales reported here, they were similar in that the emphasis in each was on gauging the reader's expressed intention to comply with the behavior suggested in the brochure.

SCALE ORIGIN: Although not explicitly described as such, the scales were apparently developed for use in the experiments by Keller and Block (1997).

SAMPLES: Four experiments were conducted and discussed in the article by Keller and Block (1997). Experiment 1 was based on data from **120** graduate and undergraduate college students, **94** undergraduate smokers composed the sample in Experiment 2, **190** undergraduate students provided data in Experiment 3, and Experiment 4 appeared to be based on data from **63** subjects (not described).

RELIABILITY: Keller and Block (1997) reported alphas of **.80, .78, .84,** and **.82** for the versions of the scale used in Experiments 1 through 4, respectively.

VALIDITY: No examination of the scale's validity was reported by Keller and Block (1997). Furthermore, the only information regarding dimensionality was that the three items composing the version of the scale used in Experiment 4 were described as loading on one factor.

ADMINISTRATION: The scale was apparently self-administered by subjects after they were exposed to varying versions of the brochures in the experiments (Keller and Block 1997). Higher scores on the scale indicated that readers expressed greater inclination to perform the behaviors recommended in the brochure.

MAJOR FINDINGS: Keller and Block (1997) examined the relationship between vividness and persuasion. The results of their four experiments were used to predict when vivid information will be more persuasive than nonvivid information.

REFERENCES:
Keller, Punam Anand (1998), personal correspondence.
——— and Lauren G. Block (1997), "Vividness Effects: A Resource-Matching Perspective," *JCR*, 24 (December), 295–304.

SCALE ITEMS:*

1. I am more likely to do a self-examination now than I was before reading this brochure.

2. I think performing a self-examination is important.

3. Self-examinations are important in the diagnosis of skin cancer.

4. I am more interested in learning about skin cancer and the self-exam now than I was before.

5. How likely are you to call the toll-free number listed in the message?

6. Would you be interested in learning more about the patch?

7. Would you be likely to discuss the patch with a friend?

8. I believe the pamphlet is persuasive.

9. I am likely to follow the recommendations in the brochure.

10. The information in the pamphlet was useless/useful in your decision not to drink and drive.

11. The information presented was not helpful/helpful in reducing the incidence of drinking and driving.

12. The information was not at persuasive/persuasive.

*Items 1–4 were used in Experiment 1, items 5–7 were used in Experiment 2, items 8 and 9 were used in Experiment 3, and the final three items were used in Experiment 4. As can be noted, the focal health issue changed in each case. Based on information from Keller (1998), the response format for items 1–4 was a disagree/agree scale, items 5–9 used very unlikely/very likely anchors, and items 10–12 were semantic differentials. All of them used a seven-point scale.

SCALE NAME: Pharmaceutical Ad Influence on Prescription-Writing Habits

SCALE DESCRIPTION: Three five-point, Likert-type statements that measure the extent to which a physician believes that pharmaceutical advertising has had a positive impact on the prescriptions he or she has subsequently written.

SCALE ORIGIN: Although the source of the scale is not explicitly stated by Petroshius, Titus, and Hatch (1995), it appears original to their study.

SAMPLES: Data were gathered by Petroshius, Titus, and Hatch (1995) by conducting a survey of physicians in the Midwestern United States. The questionnaires were delivered by pharmaceutical representatives to 250 physicians during their normal visits. Respondents could either mail in the completed forms or have the reps pick them up later. Usable forms were received from **143** physicians (73% male) who varied in age, experience, and type of practice. The largest specialty represented in the sample was dermatology (52%), which was purposeful, given the objectives of the study.

RELIABILITY: An alpha of **.89** was reported for the scale by Petroshius, Titus, and Hatch (1995).

VALIDITY: No examination of the scale's validity was reported by Petroshius, Titus, and Hatch (1995).

ADMINISTRATION: The scale was self-administered by the physicians along with the other measures in the questionnaire (Petroshius, Titus, and Hatch 1995). Higher scores on the scale indicated that the responding physicians believed that pharmaceutical ads play a positive role in influencing which prescription they write for a patient.

MAJOR FINDINGS: Petroshius, Titus, and Hatch (1995) studied physician attitudes toward the advertising of prescription drugs, particularly cosmetic pharmaceuticals, and the effect of these attitudes on other attitudes and behaviors. The findings indicated that the most influential effect on **prescription-writing habits** is the physician's attitude toward the advertising of pharmaceuticals to them.

REFERENCES:
Petroshius, Susan M., Philip A. Titus, and Kathryn J. Hatch (1995), "Physician Attitudes Toward Pharmaceutical Drug Advertising," *JAR*, 35 (November/December), 41–51.

SCALE ITEMS:

Strongly   Strongly
disagree   :___:___:___:___:___: agree
           1   2   3   4   5

1. Pharmaceutical ads remind me to write prescriptions for products I like.

2. Pharmaceutical advertisements which are appealing increase my tendency to write prescriptions for the advertised product.

3. The advertisements I see have no impact on what prescriptions I write. **(r)**

SCALE NAME: Resource Demands

SCALE DESCRIPTION: Five seven-point semantic differentials purported to measure the degree to which a stimulus requires a person to devote high cognitive effort to understand it.

SCALE ORIGIN: Although not explicitly described as such, the scale was apparently developed for use in an experiment by Keller and Block (1997).

SAMPLES: Four experiments were conducted and discussed in the article by Keller and Block (1997), but the scale was only described as being used in the fourth experiment. Little is said about its sample except that there were three groups with a total of **63** subjects. Given the nature of the sample in the other three experiments, these subjects were probably college students.

RELIABILITY: Keller and Block (1997) reported an alpha of **.93** for the scale.

VALIDITY: No examination of the scale's validity was reported by Keller and Block (1997), though they did state that all of the items loaded on one factor.

ADMINISTRATION: The scale was apparently self-administered by subjects after they were exposed to the experimental treatment (a pamphlet manipulating the vividness of information). Higher scores on the scale indicated that a stimulus demands a greater allocation of resources to understand.

MAJOR FINDINGS: Keller and Block (1997) examined the relationship between vividness and persuasion. The scale was used as a manipulation check in Experiment 4 to confirm that the more vivid message was also the more **resource demanding**. The results of the experiments were used to predict when vivid information would be more persuasive than nonvivid information.

REFERENCES:
Keller, Punam Anand and Lauren G. Block (1997), "Vividness Effects: A Resource-Matching Perspective," *JCR*, 24 (December), 295–304.

SCALE ITEMS:

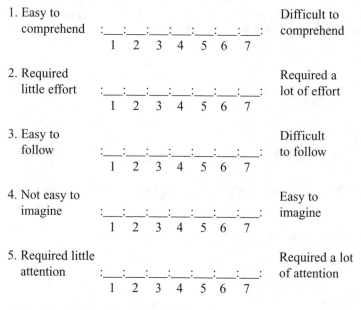

1. Easy to
   comprehend :__:__:__:__:__:__: Difficult to
             1 2 3 4 5 6 7 comprehend

2. Required
   little effort :__:__:__:__:__:__: Required a
             1 2 3 4 5 6 7 lot of effort

3. Easy to
   follow :__:__:__:__:__:__: Difficult
             1 2 3 4 5 6 7 to follow

4. Not easy to
   imagine :__:__:__:__:__:__: Easy to
             1 2 3 4 5 6 7 imagine

5. Required little
   attention :__:__:__:__:__:__: Required a lot
             1 2 3 4 5 6 7 of attention

SCALE NAME: Self-/Brand-Image Congruity

SCALE DESCRIPTION: Three seven-point, Likert-type statements used to measure a person's sense of the fit between the product and him- or herself based on the image presented in a commercial.

SCALE ORIGIN: The source of the scale was not specified by Kamp and MacInnis (1995), but it appears original to their study.

SAMPLES: Kamp and MacInnis (1995) collected their data from **400** consumers who had been recruited by a market research company. The people lived in either the Boston, Mass.; Atlanta, Ga.; Minneapolis, Minn.; or Portland, Or. metropolitan areas. Respondents were chosen as representative of the target market for the product being studied (not identified). They were between the ages of 18 and 65 years, with household incomes greater than $20,000, and were mostly women (75%).

RELIABILITY: An alpha of **.91** was reported for the scale by Kamp and MacInnis (1995).

VALIDITY: No examination of the scale's validity was reported by Kamp and MacInnis (1995).

ADMINISTRATION: Respondents completed the scale after they were exposed to a test ad (Kamp and MacInnis 1995). A handheld dial was used by respondents, which automatically recorded their responses to this scale and the other measures on the questionnaire. Higher scores on the scale indicated that respondents had very positive attitudes toward the appropriateness of a brand for them, given how it was presented in an ad.

MAJOR FINDINGS: Kamp and MacInnis (1995) examined the effect of two emotion-related variables on the nature and intensity of consumers' emotional responses to ads. Among the findings was that **self-/brand-image congruity** was strongest when emotional "flow" was dynamic and emotional "integration" was high.

REFERENCES:

Kamp, Edward and Deborah J. MacInnis (1995), "Characteristics of Portrayed Emotions in Commercials: When Does What Is Shown in Ads Affect Viewers?" *JAR*, 35 (November/December), 19–28.

MacInnis, Deborah J. (1999), personal correspondence.

SCALE ITEMS:*

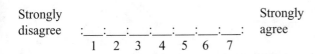

Strongly disagree :___:___:___:___:___:___:___: Strongly agree
         1   2   3   4   5   6   7

1. The commercial made me feel the brand is right for me.

2. The commercial gave me a good feeling about buying _____.

3. The commercial made me feel that using _____ would say something good about me.

*The items and the response format were provided by MacInnis (1999).

SCALE NAME: Self-Referencing

SCALE DESCRIPTION: Five seven-point, Likert-type statements purported to measure the extent to which a person processes information received in an ad by relating it to aspects of his- or herself (own personal experiences).

SCALE ORIGIN: Although not explicitly stated by Burnkrant and Unnava (1995), the scale appears to have been developed for use in their study.

SAMPLES: All that is said about the sample used by Burnkrant and Unnava (1995) is that data were gathered from **61** undergraduate students, who participated in the experiment in exchange for extra course credit.

RELIABILITY: An alpha of **.89** was reported for the scale by Burnkrant and Unnava (1995).

VALIDITY: No information specifically related to the scale's validity was reported by Burnkrant and Unnava (1995), other than that described under the "Major Findings" section.

ADMINISTRATION: The scale was self-administered by students, along with other measures, after they were exposed to experimental stimuli (Burnkrant and Unnava 1995). Higher scores on the scale indicated that an ad to which respondents were exposed caused them to think about their experiences with a specific product.

MAJOR FINDINGS: Burnkrant and Unnava (1995) investigated the influence of **self-referencing** on persuasion. The **self-referencing** scale was used solely as a manipulation check. It was found that those subjects in the high **self-referencing** conditions indeed scored significantly higher on the scale than those in the low **self-referencing** conditions.

REFERENCES:
Burnkrant, Robert E. and H. Rao Unnava (1995), "Effects of Self-Referencing on Persuasion," *JCR*, 22 (June), 17–26.

SCALE ITEMS:*

Strongly   Strongly
disagree   :__:__:__:__:__:__:__: agree
                 1   2   3   4   5   6   7

1. The ad made me think about my experiences with _____.

2. The ad made me think about what it would be like to use the _____.

3. The ad reminded me of my own experiences with _____.

4. I believe the ad was written with me in mind.

5. I believe that the ad related to me personally.

*The exact phrases used by Burnkrant and Unnava (1995) were not explicitly given in the article, but these statements were constructed on the basis of the information provided. Also, the name of the generic product should be placed in the blanks.

SCALE NAME: Source Credibility (General)

SCALE DESCRIPTION: The scale measures the perceived trustworthiness and expertise of the source of a message. It has mostly been used with six items and a seven-point response format, with the exception of Gotlieb and Swan (1990), who used just five items.

SCALE ORIGIN: Gotlieb and Sarel (1991), Gotlieb and Swan (1990), and Grewel, Gotlieb, and Marmorstein (1994) all indicated the scale came from Harmon and Coney (1982). In addition, Harmon and Coney (1982) cited Berlo, Lemert, and Mertz (1969/70) as the source of the items, but only two of the six items come from the final version of the *qualification* dimension of source credibility. The other items come from earlier versions of that dimension or another (*safety*).

SAMPLES: Survey instruments were completed by **148** subjects in the experiment conducted by Gotlieb and Sarel (1991). The subjects were all selected from a pool of upperclass students attending a large urban university and were randomly assigned to treatments in a 2 × 2 × 2 factorial experimental design.

Very little description was provided about the sample used by Gotlieb and Swan (1990). The study was a 2 × 2 × 2 factorial experiment with **126** graduate and undergraduate college students. Fifty-nine percent of the students had visited a lawyer in the last five years.

Grewel, Gotlieb, and Marmorstein (1994) used an in-class experiment to gather data from students enrolled in business classes at a large urban university. Analysis was conducted on data from **131** subjects. No other information was provided about the subjects except that all but one had used a VCR (the product category tested) in the past year.

RELIABILITY: Alphas of **.84**, **.82**, and **.88** were reported for the scale by Gotlieb and Sarel (1991), Gotlieb and Swan (1990), and Grewel, Gotlieb, and Marmorstein (1994), respectively.

VALIDITY: The validity of the scale was not specifically examined in any of the studies. However, in all of them (Gotlieb and Sarel 1991; Gotlieb and Swan 1990; Grewel, Gotlieb, and Marmorstein 1994), the scale was used as a check of a source credibility manipulation. Indeed, the scale confirmed that the manipulations were effective.

ADMINISTRATION: In the classroom experiments conducted by Gotlieb and Sarel (1991), Gotlieb and Swan (1990), and Grewel, Gotlieb, and Marmorstein (1994), the scale was self-administered by students as part of a larger instrument after they had been exposed to test materials. Higher scores on the scale indicated that respondents perceived the source of some message as credible.

MAJOR FINDINGS: In each of the following studies, **source credibility** was a treatment manipulation. Therefore, findings related most directly to the manipulation rather than to scale scores. However, as noted, in each case, the manipulation was successful.

The persuasive effect of **source credibility** in comparative advertising was studied by Gotlieb and Sarel (1991). Their findings showed that a highly **credible source** had a more positive impact on the level of construction-motivated involvement than a low **credibility source**.

Gotlieb and Swan (1990) investigated the influence of price savings on motivation to process a message. The findings indicated that when consumers had product experience and were offered a price savings, a highly credible source had a more positive influence on their attitudes toward the product and the ad than a low credibility source.

Grewel, Gotlieb, and Marmorstein (1994) used prospect theory to investigate an inconsistency in the literature between price and perceived risk. Among the findings was that price had a significant impact on performance risk when **source credibility** was low but not when it was high.

REFERENCES:

Berlo, David K., James B. Lemert, and Robert J. Mertz (1969/70), "Dimensions for Evaluating the Acceptability of Message Sources," *Public Opinion Quarterly*, 33 (4), 563–76.

Gotlieb, Jerry B. and Dan Sarel (1991), "Comparative Advertising Effectiveness: The Role of Involvement and Source Credibility," *JA*, (20) 1, 38–45.

———— and John E. Swan (1990), "An Application of the Elaboration Likelihood Model," *JAMS*, 18 (Summer), 221–28.

Grewel, Dhruv, Jerry Gotlieb, and Howard Marmorstein (1994), "The Moderating Effects of Message Framing and Source Credibility on the Price–Perceived Risk Relationship," *JCR*, 21 (June), 145–53.

Harmon, Robert R. and Kenneth A. Coney (1982), "The Persuasive Effects of Source Credibility in Buy and Lease Situations," *JMR*, 19 (May), 255–60.

SCALE ITEMS:*

The (message source) is:

| Not trustworthy | :___:___:___:___:___:___ | Trustworthy |
| | 1 2 3 4 5 6 7 | |

| Not open-minded | :___:___:___:___:___:___ | Open-minded |
| | 1 2 3 4 5 6 7 | |

| Bad | :___:___:___:___:___:___ | Good |
| | 1 2 3 4 5 6 7 | |

| Not expert | :___:___:___:___:___:___ | Expert |
| | 1 2 3 4 5 6 7 | |

| Not experienced | :___:___:___:___:___:___ | Experienced |
| | 1 2 3 4 5 6 7 | |

| Untrained | :___:___:___:___:___:___ | Trained |
| | 1 2 3 4 5 6 7 | |

*Gotlieb and Sarel (1991) and Grewel, Gotlieb, and Marmorstein (1994) used all six of these items. Gotlieb and Swan (1990) indicated that they only used five items without being specific about which item was dropped or why.

SCALE NAME: Source Credibility (Trustworthiness)

SCALE DESCRIPTION: Various semantic differentials measuring the trustworthiness and sincerity of a source of information. Lichtenstein and Bearden (1989) used a five-item, nine-point scale to measure the credibility of merchant-supplied price information. A five-item, seven-point version of the scale was used by Bobinski, Cox, and Cox (1996) to measure the perceived credibility of a store's ad. Moore, Mowen, and Reardon (1994) used a four-item, seven-point version of the scale to measure the trustworthiness of noncelebrity product endorsers. Tripp, Jensen, and Carlson (1994) measured the credibility of celebrity endorsers using a seven-item, seven-point scale. Ohanian (1990, 1991) also measured the credibility of celebrity endorsers. Although the focus in Ohanian (1990) was on the development of a semantic differential version of the scale, Likert and Staple versions were developed as well, but the exact phrasing of the items was not given in the article.

SCALE ORIGIN: Lichtenstein and Bearden (1989) and Moore, Mowen, and Reardon (1994) did not give any information about the origin of their scales. Although Tripp, Jensen, and Carlson (1994) cited McCroskey (1966) as the source of their measure, they used only one of his six items.

Ohanian (1990, 1991) engaged in considerable developmental work in the construction of her version of the scale, as well as two companion dimensions (*attractiveness* and *expertise*). Although she conducted several exploratory and confirmatory analyses to refine the scales, she cited Bowers and Phillips (1967) and Whitehead (1968) as sources for the items she began with. Ultimately, four of the five items in the final version of her scale were from the trustworthiness factor identified by Whitehead (1968).

SAMPLES: Data were collected in an experiment conducted by Bobinski, Cox, and Cox (1996) from student volunteers in management courses at an Eastern U.S. university. Usable responses were received from **129** students. A little more than half of the sample was men (53%), and the mean age was 20.6 years.

The study by Lichtenstein and Bearden (1989) was based on data collected from **278** undergraduate business students. The students were randomly assigned to one of twelve treatment conditions in a 2 × 2 × 3 experimental design. There were between 21 and 28 students per cell.

Data were collected by Moore, Mowen, and Reardon (1994) for their study from **82** undergraduate students. Participation was one way for the students to receive extra credit in their course. Subjects were randomly assigned to one of four treatments (approximately 20 per cell), but only 4 to 6 students were run at a time in each session.

Ohanian (1990) used two student samples in the exploratory phase of the study. In the confirmatory phase, she used a systematic area-sampling technique. All census tracks in a small Southeastern U.S. city were selected. Interviewers were told to approach a house in an assigned block at random and then approach every other house until the quota for that block was achieved. A total of 360 questionnaires were delivered (180 for each celebrity), and **138** usable questionnaires were collected for Linda Evans and **127** for Tom Selleck. Also, a final test of validity was conducted with 108 undergraduate students.

Ohanian (1991) gathered data from three groups of individuals: one systematically selected from residential neighborhoods (n = 97), a second from the membership of several churches (n = 246), and a third from a student population of graduate and undergraduate students (n = 217). The final sample consisted of data from **542** respondents.

Data were gathered by Tripp, Jensen, and Carlson (1994) from a final set of **461** undergraduates attending one of two universities in a Southern U.S. state. This final sample was rather evenly split between men (51.19%) and women (48.81%). They were assigned to 1 of 48 treatment conditions using randomized block procedures.

RELIABILITY: Alphas of **.91**, **.78**, **.80**, and **.88** were reported for the scales used by Bobinski, Cox, and Cox (1996), Lichtenstein and Bearden (1989), Moore, Mowen, and Reardon (1994), and Tripp, Jensen, and Carlson (1994), respectively. Ohanian (1990) reported construct reliability of **.90** for data related to both celebrity endorsers. Average variance extracted was .63. Specific alpha coefficients were not reported by Ohanian (1991), but she did calculate them for both men and women and for four different celebrity endorser test ads. The alphas were described as being .82 or higher in each case.

VALIDITY: No examination of scale validity was reported by Bobinski, Cox, and Cox (1996), Lichtenstein and Bearden (1989), Moore, Mowen, and Reardon (1994), Ohanian (1991), or Tripp, Jensen, and Carlson (1994). Tripp, Jensen, and Carlson (1994) indicated that the scale had a beta coefficient of .51, which suggests the scale might not be unidimensional. However, further testing using confirmatory factor analysis is necessary to better determine the scale's dimensionality.

Ohanian (1990) tested nomological validity by relating scores on the scale to several self-reported behaviors. The hypothesized pattern was basically confirmed. Convergent and discriminant validity were examined using data from just the Linda Evans test ad and responses from 108 students. The multi-trait–multimethod matrix was used, and the analyses supported a claim of acceptable convergent and discriminant validity for the scale.

ADMINISTRATION: In the studies by Bobinski, Cox, and Cox (1996), Lichtenstein and Bearden (1989), Moore, Mowen, and Reardon (1994), and Tripp, Jensen, and Carlson (1994), the scale was self-administered by students, along with several other measures, in an experimental setting.

Ohanian (1990) provided the self-administered scale along with other measures to college students in two exploratory samples and one of the confirmatory samples referred to in her article. With the sample of adult respondents approached at their homes, the "interviewers" performed delivery and collection functions, but the questionnaires themselves were apparently self-administered.

Ohanian (1991) used trained assistants to monitor each data collection round and read all directions from a prepared script. The source credibility scale was filled out during the second of three phases of data collection.

Higher scores on the scale implied that respondents perceived the source of a message as highly credible, whereas lower scores suggested that respondents believed the source to be untrustworthy.

MAJOR FINDINGS: The effect of a retailer's rationale for a price reduction was examined by Bobinski, Cox, and Cox (1996). The results showed that the perceived **credibility** of the store's ad was best when a volume purchase rationale was provided as well as a reference price (i.e., higher "regular" price).

The study by Lichtenstein and Bearden (1989) examined the influence of merchant-supplied reference prices, ad distinctiveness, and ad message consistency on perception of source credibility, value of the deal, and attitude toward the deal. Among many other findings, perceived **credibility** was higher for plausible high merchant-supplied prices than for implausible high merchant-supplied prices.

The purpose of the study by Moore, Mowen, and Reardon (1994) was to examine the effects of multiple endorsers and perceived payment for endorsement on the response to an ad. It was found that ads with multiple unpaid endorsers had greater **source credibility** than those ads with single unpaid endorsers.

The purpose of the study by Ohanian (1990) was to develop scales to measure celebrity endorsers' perceived **trustworthiness**, expertise, and attractiveness. As noted, the considerable data collected supported a claim of reliability and validity for the scales.

Ohanian (1991) studied the effect of three components of source credibility (expertise, **trustworthiness**, and attractiveness) on purchase intentions. The attractiveness and **trustworthiness** of four different celebrities had no significant impact on purchase intention, but expertise did.

Tripp, Jensen, and Carlson (1994) examined the effects of the number of exposures to a celebrity endorser and the number of products he or she endorsed on consumer attitudes and intentions. Among the many findings was that as the number of products endorsed increased, the **credibility** of the endorser decreased.

REFERENCES:

Bobinski, George S., Jr., Dena Cox, and Anthony Cox (1996), "Retail 'Sale' Advertising, Perceived Retailer Credibility, and Price Rationale," *JR*, 72 (3), 291–306.

Bowers, John W. and William A. Phillips (1967), "A Note on the Generality of Source Credibility Scales," *Speech Monographs*, 34 (August), 185–86.

Lichtenstein, Donald R. and William O. Bearden (1989), "Contextual Influences on Perceptions of Merchant-Supplied Reference Prices," *JCR*, 16 (June), 55–66.

McCroskey, James C. (1966), "Scales for the Measurement of Ethos," *Speech Monographs*, 33 (March), 65–72.

Moore, David J., John C. Mowen, and Richard Reardon (1994), "Multiple Sources in Advertising Appeals: When Product Endorsers Are Paid by the Advertising Sponsor," *JAMS*, 22 (Summer), 234–43.

Ohanian, Roobina (1990), "Construction and Validation of a Scale to Measure Celebrity Endorsers' Perceived Expertise, Trustworthiness, and Attractiveness," *JA*, 19 (3), 39–52.

————— (1991), "The Impact of Celebrity SpokesPersons' Perceived Image on Consumer's Intention to Purchase," *JAR*, 31 (1), 46–54.

Tripp, Carolyn, Thomas D. Jensen, and Les Carlson (1994), "The Effects of Multiple Product Endorsements by Celebrities on Consumers' Attitudes and Intentions," *JCR*, 20 (March), 535–47.

Whitehead, Jack L. (1968), "Factors of Source Credibility," *Quarterly Journal of Speech*, 54 (1), 59–63.

SCALE ITEMS:

The (<u>message source</u>) is:

1. Insincere :___:___:___:___:___:___:___: Sincere
   1　2　3　4　5　6　7

2. Dishonest :___:___:___:___:___:___:___: Honest
   1　2　3　4　5　6　7

3. Not dependable :___:___:___:___:___:___:___: Dependable
   1　2　3　4　5　6　7

4. Not trustworthy :___:___:___:___:___:___:___: Trustworthy
   1　2　3　4　5　6　7

5. Not credible :___:___:___:___:___:___:___: Credible
   1　2　3　4　5　6　7

6. Not biased :___:___:___:___:___:___:___: Biased
   1　2　3　4　5　6　7

7. Not believable :___:___:___:___:___:___:___: Believable
   1　2　3　4　5　6　7

8. Disreputable :___:___:___:___:___:___:___: Reputable
   1　2　3　4　5　6　7

9. Unreliable   :___:___:___:___:___:___:___: Reliable
                     1   2   3   4   5   6   7

10. Untruthful   :___:___:___:___:___:___:___: Truthful
                     1   2   3   4   5   6   7

Bobinski, Cox, and Cox (1996): 1–5*
Lichtenstein and Bearden (1989): 1–5; 9-point
Moore, Mowen, and Reardon (1994): 1, 6, 7, 10
Ohanian (1990, 1991): 1, 2, 3, 4, 9
Tripp, Jensen, and Carlson (1994): 1, 2, 4, 5, 6, 7, 8

*Items used in this study were slight variations of those shown.

SCALE NAME: Visual Imaging

SCALE DESCRIPTION: Four seven-point, Likert-type statements that measure the extent to which an ad stimulated a person to form mental images of what was being described in the ad. It is not clear whether the scale taps more into a person's propensity for visualization or an ad's propensity for stimulating visualization; it appears to lean more toward the latter.

SCALE ORIGIN: The scale used by Unnava, Agarwal, and Haugtvedt (1996) was developed by Unnava and Burnkrant (1991). The earlier study reported an alpha of .89 based on a sample of 107 undergraduate students.

SAMPLES: Unnava, Agarwal, and Haugtvedt (1996) conducted two experiments, only the second of which used the scale. Data in the second experiment were collected from **100** undergraduate students, who received extra credit in their marketing course for participating.

RELIABILITY: An alpha of **.94** was reported for the scale by Unnava, Agarwal, and Haugtvedt (1996).

VALIDITY: No evidence of the scale's validity was reported by Unnava, Agarwal, and Haugtvedt (1996).

ADMINISTRATION: The scale was self-administered by subjects after they were exposed to experimental stimuli (Unnava, Agarwal, and Haugtvedt 1996). Higher scores on the scale appeared to indicate that an ad provoked visual images in the minds of those exposed to it.

MAJOR FINDINGS: Unnava, Agarwal, and Haugtvedt (1996) proposed that message elaboration is impaired when perception and **imaging** compete for the same resources. The findings showed that ad copy provoking high levels of **visual imaging** was remembered better than copy provoking low levels of **imaging** when the ad was presented auditorily. However, the reverse was found to be true when the ad was presented visually.

REFERENCES:
Unnava, H. Rao, Sanjeev Agarwal, and Curtis P. Haugtvedt (1996), "Interactive Effects of Presentation Modality and Message-Generated Imagery on Recall of Advertising Information," *JCR*, 23 (June), 81–88.
———— and Robert E. Burnkrant (1991), "An Imagery-Processing View of the Role of Pictures in Print Advertisements," *JMR*, 28 (May), 226–31.

SCALE ITEMS:

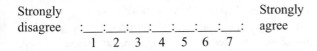

Strongly disagree :___:___:___:___:___:___:___: Strongly agree
      1 2 3 4 5 6 7

1. The ad brought pictures or images to my mind that helped clarify what was said in the ad.

2. As I read the ad, I formed pictures or images about much of what was being discussed in the ad.

3. I found myself thinking of images when I read the ad.

4. It was easy to form images or pictures of what was being said in the ad.

SCALE NAME: Vividness

SCALE DESCRIPTION: The scale is composed of multiple items measuring the degree to which a stimulus is described as being intense and lifelike. A Staple scale was used by Bone and Ellen (1992), but Miller and Marks (1992) and Babin and Burns (1997) used more typical Likert-oriented response formats. (See "Comments" regarding the nature of the construct measured.)

SCALE ORIGIN: The origin of the scale was not specified by Bone and Ellen (1992), but it is clear from Ellen and Bone (1991) that it is original. Vividness was initially measured using eleven items. Exploratory and confirmatory factor analysis led the authors to define the vividness scale with seven items, six of which are indicated here. In two different samples, the seven-item scale was reported to have alphas of .88 (n = 179) and .87 (n = 144). (It appears that the sample referred to as Study 1 in Ellen and Bone [1991] is the same as the one referred to as Study 2 in Bone and Ellen [1992]). Some evidence of the scale's discriminant validity was found, given that it appeared to be related to but distinct from a measure of a person's innate ability to imagine.

The items used by Babin and Burns (1997) came from the original set tested by Ellen and Bone (1991).

SAMPLES: Babin and Burns (1997) gathered data for their experiment in a classroom setting from **186** undergraduate business students. The sample was almost evenly split on gender (52% male).

Two experiments were discussed in the article by Bone and Ellen (1992). The sample for the first experiment was composed of **127** college students, while the second one had **179**. Both experiments were very similar in their collection of data. They took place in an audiovisual lab with students randomly assigned to treatments.

The data gathered by Miller and Marks (1992) came from **124** undergraduate marketing students attending a large Midwestern U.S. university. Volunteers were compensated for their participation with extra credit points.

RELIABILITY: Alphas for the scale were reported by Bone and Ellen (1992) to be **.86** (Study 1) and **.88** (Study 2). The alpha for the scale used by Miller and Marks (1992) was **.90** (Marks 1994). A composite reliability of **.93** was reported by Babin and Burns (1997).

VALIDITY: All of the studies provided some evidence of the scale's unidimensionality. In addition, Babin and Burns (1997) found support for the scale's discriminant validity. Although Babin and Burns (1997) considered the version of the scale they used to have been unidimensional, it is substantially the same as the set Ellen and Bone (1991) concluded to be two factors.

ADMINISTRATION: The scale was self-administered in all of the experiments, along with other measures, after subjects were exposed to mock ads. Subjects were asked to indicate how vivid an image was that they formed while attending to the ads. A high score on the scale indicated that a person experienced an image that was very clear and lifelike, whereas a low score suggested that an image was not conceived well.

MAJOR FINDINGS: The experiment conducted by Babin and Burns (1997) examined the mediating role of evoked imagery in attitudinal responses. The research indicated that elaboration of imagery processing and **vividness** completely mediated the impact of imagery-eliciting strategies on attitude toward the ad.

Bone and Ellen (1992) investigated the influence that imagery had on recall, brand attitudes, and purchase intentions. Two experiments were conducted, and both showed that **vividness** of imagination had a significant positive impact on attitude toward the ad but not on brand attitudes or purchase intentions.

Miller and Marks (1992) investigated the impact of sound effects on processing and reactions to advertisements. For one of the two different products tested, it was found that **imagery vividness** was significantly greater in commercials with sound effects than in those with just a verbal message.

COMMENTS: In the experiments by Bone and Ellen (1992) and Miller and Marks (1992), subjects were not shown any visual stimuli but had to imagine it on the basis of the audio stimuli. Therefore, it may be more appropriate to describe the construct measured as the *vividness of conceiving (rather than perceiving) an image.* Perception implies than the subject is exposed to a stimulus and has the opportunity to attend to it rather than having to create it in the mind.

REFERENCES:

Babin, Laurie and Alvin C. Burns (1997), "Effects of Print Ad Pictures and Copy Containing Instructions to Imagine on Mental Imagery that Mediates Attitudes," *JA*, 26 (Fall), 33–44.

Bone, Paula Fitzgerald and Pam Scholder Ellen (1992), "The Generation and Consequences of Communication-Evoked Imagery," *JCR*, 19 (June), 93–104.

Ellen, Pam Scholder and Paula Fitzgerald Bone (1991), "Measuring Communication-Evoked Imagery Processing," in *Advances in Consumer Research*, Vol. 18, Rebecca H. Holman and Michael R. Soloman, eds. Provo, UT: Association of Consumer Research, 806–12.

Marks, Lawrence J. (1994), personal correspondence.

Miller, Darryl W. and Lawrence J. Marks (1992), "Mental Imagery and Sound Effects in Radio Commercials," *JA*, 21 (4), 83–93.

SCALE ITEMS: *

The imagery which occurred was:

1. Clear
2. Vivid
3. Intense
4. Lifelike
5. Sharp
6. Well-defined
7. Detailed
8. Weak **(r)**
9. Fuzzy **(r)**
10. Vague **(r)**

*A five-point Staple scale was used by Bone and Ellen (1992) to record the responses to items 1–6. Using the same items, Miller and Marks (1992) used a five-point response scale with endpoints labeled "Does not describe at all" and "Describes perfectly." Babin and Burns (1997) used a typical seven-point, Likert-type response format with items 1, 2, and 5–10.

SCALE NAME: Vividness

SCALE DESCRIPTION: Six seven-point semantic differentials purported to measure the degree to which a stimulus has evoked clear and relevant images in the subject.

SCALE ORIGIN: Although not explicitly described as such, the scale was apparently developed for use in an experiment by Keller and Block (1997).

SAMPLES: Four experiments were conducted and discussed in the article by Keller and Block (1997), but the scale was only described as being used in the third. Little is said about its sample except that it was composed of **190** undergraduate students.

RELIABILITY: Keller and Block (1997) reported an alpha of **.89** for the scale.

VALIDITY: No examination of the scale's validity was reported by Keller and Block (1997).

ADMINISTRATION: The scale was apparently self-administered by subjects after they were exposed to the experimental treatment (a brochure manipulating **vividness** of information). Higher scores on the scale indicated greater **vividness**.

MAJOR FINDINGS: Keller and Block (1997) examined the relationship between **vividness** and persuasion. The scale was used as a manipulation check in Experiment 2. The results of the experiments were used to predict when **vivid** information would be more persuasive than nonvivid information.

REFERENCES:
Keller, Punam Anand and Lauren G. Block (1997), "Vividness Effects: A Resource-Matching Perspective," *JCR*, 24 (December), 295–304.

SCALE ITEMS:

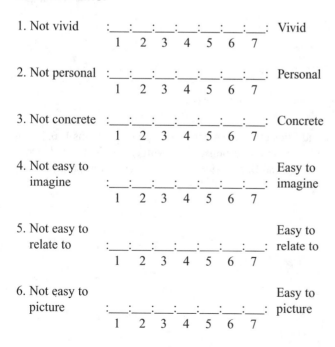

1. Not vivid   :___:___:___:___:___:___:___: Vivid
                 1   2   3   4   5   6   7

2. Not personal :___:___:___:___:___:___:___: Personal
                 1   2   3   4   5   6   7

3. Not concrete :___:___:___:___:___:___:___: Concrete
                 1   2   3   4   5   6   7

4. Not easy to   Easy to
   imagine   :___:___:___:___:___:___:___: imagine
                 1   2   3   4   5   6   7

5. Not easy to   Easy to
   relate to   :___:___:___:___:___:___:___: relate to
                 1   2   3   4   5   6   7

6. Not easy to   Easy to
   picture   :___:___:___:___:___:___:___: picture
                 1   2   3   4   5   6   7

Part III

Organizational Behavior-Related Scales

SCALE NAME: Absence of Bottom-Line Orientation

SCALE DESCRIPTION: Oliver and Anderson (1994) used this four-item, seven-point Likert-type scale to measure the extent to which sales representatives perceive that management does not focus on a salesperson's bottom line when rating sales representative performance.

SCALE ORIGIN: The scale is original to Oliver and Anderson (1994), who pretested the measure in a questionnaire administered to a convenience sample of sales representatives attending trade association functions. The measure was revised on the basis of the pretest and submitted to a factor analysis following administration to the final sample. The authors indicated that some items were dropped, which resulted in the purified measure shown here. The criterion for item exclusion was not indicated, though it was noted by the authors that none of the cross loadings between the six behavior-control/outcome-control measures exceeded the .355 level.

SAMPLES: Oliver and Anderson (1994) surveyed managers and manufacturer's sales representatives employed by independently owned and operated sales agencies serving the electronics industry. Of the 350 randomly selected trade association member firms fitting this designation, 299 expressed interest in participating, and ultimately, **194** usable surveys from management and **347** surveys from manufacturer representatives were returned. The typical respondent was male (92%), a college graduate (64%), approximately 39 years of age, and had an average of 12 years sales experience with 5.5 years in the present job.

RELIABILITY: Oliver and Anderson (1994) reported a coefficient alpha of **.762** for this measure.

VALIDITY: Oliver and Anderson (1994) used the correlation matrix of the independent and classification variables used in the study to provide some evidence of discriminant and convergent validity. Nomological validity was also found to be present.

ADMINISTRATION: Oliver and Anderson (1994) sent managers of the 299 firms indicating interest in the study a packet containing a "manager's survey" and three similar self-administered surveys for salespeople, along with self-addressed, postage-paid reply envelopes. Managers were instructed to distribute one survey each to an "above average rep," a "mid-range rep," and a "below average rep." Each representative was promised confidentiality and the chance to win one of five $100 prizes in a random drawing. The absence of a bottom-line orientation was one of six scales whose scores were combined as formative indicators of the control system employed, which ranged from outcome oriented to behaviorally oriented. It appears that only responses obtained from sales representatives were used in computing this measure. Higher scores on the scale indicated that salespeople perceived management as evaluating their performance on a variety of factors rather than restricting evaluation solely to the bottom line.

MAJOR FINDINGS: Oliver and Anderson (1994) examined how perceptions of the presence of a behavior versus outcome sales control system in the respondents' organizations influenced salespeople's performance outcomes and sales strategies, as well as their affective, cognitive, and behavioral states. The **absence of a bottom-line orientation** was significantly related to a salesperson's sales expertise, extrinsic motivation, motivation to the serve the agency employer, organizational commitment, and acceptance of three factors: authority, cooperation, and performance reviews. A salesperson's ratio of selling to non-selling time, a representative's motivation to work smarter, job satisfaction, participative decision making, infrequent use of objective outcomes, the use of subjective inputs in the evaluation process, the use of pay as a control mechanism, the extent of supervision, and supportive, bureaucratic, and innovative organizational cultures were also significantly related to the **absence of a bottom-line orientation**.

REFERENCES:

Oliver, Richard L. and Erin Anderson (1994), "An Empirical Test of the Consequences of Behavior- and Outcome-Based Sales Control Systems," *JM*, 58 (October), 53–67.

SCALE ITEMS:

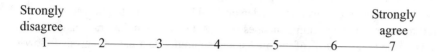

1. When management rates my performance, they take a lot of things into consideration.

2. Management decides who's good by looking strictly at each salesperson's bottom line. **(r)**

3. Only tangible results matter to my manager. **(r)**

4. My manager doesn't care what I do as long as I produce. **(r)**

SCALE NAME: Acceptance (Authority/Direction)

SCALE DESCRIPTION: Oliver and Anderson (1994) used this three-item, seven-point Likert-type scale to measure sales representatives' acceptance of their sales manager's authority, feedback, and instructions.

SCALE ORIGIN: The scale is original to Oliver and Anderson (1994), who pretested the measure in a questionnaire administered to a convenience sample of sales representatives attending trade association functions. The measure was revised on the basis of the pretest.

SAMPLES: Oliver and Anderson (1994) surveyed managers and manufacturer's sales representatives employed by independently owned and operated sales agencies serving the electronics industry. Of the 350 randomly selected trade association member firms fitting this designation, 299 expressed interest in participating, and ultimately, **194** usable surveys from management and **347** surveys from manufacturer representatives were returned. The typical respondent was male (92%), a college graduate (64%), approximately 39 years of age, and had an average of 12 years sales experience with 5.5 years in the present job.

RELIABILITY: Oliver and Anderson (1994) reported a coefficient alpha of **.774** for this measure.

VALIDITY: Oliver and Anderson (1994) used the correlation matrix of the independent and classification variables used in the study to provide some evidence of discriminant and convergent validity. Nomological validity was also found to be present.

ADMINISTRATION: Oliver and Anderson (1994) sent managers of the 299 firms indicating interest in the study a packet containing a "manager's survey" and three similar self-administered surveys for salespeople, along with self-addressed, postage-paid reply envelopes. Managers were instructed to distribute one survey each to an "above average rep," a "mid-range rep," and a "below average rep." Each representative was promised confidentiality and the chance to win one of five $100 prizes in a random drawing. It appears that only responses obtained from sales representatives were used in computing this measure. Higher scores on the scale indicated a greater willingness on the part of the sales representative to accept a sales manager's authority, feedback, and instructions.

MAJOR FINDINGS: Oliver and Anderson (1994) examined how perceptions of the presence of a behavior versus outcome sales control system in the respondents' organizations influenced salespeople's performance outcomes and sales strategies, as well as their affective, cognitive, and behavioral states. Greater **acceptance of authority/direction** was significantly related to the use of a behavior control system.

REFERENCES:
Oliver, Richard L. and Erin Anderson (1994), "An Empirical Test of the Consequences of Behavior- and Outcome-Based Sales Control Systems," *JM*, 58 (October), 53–67.

SCALE ITEMS:

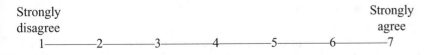

Strongly
disagree
1———2———3———4———5———6———7
Strongly
agree

1. When I'm given advice or instructions, I accept it willingly.

2. I generally accept the authority of management in this firm.

3. I am quite receptive to feedback I receive from superiors.

SCALE NAME: Acceptance (Performance Reviews)

SCALE DESCRIPTION: Oliver and Anderson (1994) used this four-item, seven-point Likert-type scale to measure sales representatives' desire for performance reviews.

SCALE ORIGIN: The scale is original to Oliver and Anderson (1994), who pretested the measure in a questionnaire administered to a convenience sample of sales representatives attending trade association functions. The measure was revised on the basis of the pretest.

SAMPLES: Oliver and Anderson (1994) surveyed managers and manufacturer's sales representatives employed by independently owned and operated sales agencies serving the electronics industry. Of the 350 randomly selected trade association member firms fitting this designation, 299 expressed interest in participating, and ultimately, **194** usable surveys from management and **347** surveys from manufacturer representatives were returned. The typical respondent was male (92%), a college graduate (64%), approximately 39 years of age, and had an average of 12 years sales experience with 5.5 years in the present job.

RELIABILITY: Oliver and Anderson (1994) reported a coefficient alpha of **.807** for this measure.

VALIDITY: Oliver and Anderson (1994) used the correlation matrix of the independent and classification variables used in the study to provide some evidence of discriminant and convergent validity. Nomological validity was also found to be present.

ADMINISTRATION: Oliver and Anderson (1994) sent managers of the 299 firms indicating interest in the study a packet containing a "manager's survey" and three similar self-administered surveys for salespeople, along with self-addressed, postage-paid reply envelopes. Managers were instructed to distribute one survey each to an "above average rep," a "mid-range rep," and a "below average rep." Each representative was promised confidentiality and the chance to win one of five $100 prizes in a random drawing. It appears that only responses obtained from sales representatives were used in computing this measure. Higher scores on the scale indicated a greater desire on the part of the sales representative to receive performance reviews from a sales manager.

MAJOR FINDINGS: Oliver and Anderson (1994) examined how perceptions of the presence of a behavior versus outcome sales control system in the respondents' organizations influenced salespeople's performance outcomes and sales strategies, as well as their affective, cognitive, and behavioral states. Greater **acceptance of performance reviews** was significantly related to the use of a behavior control system.

REFERENCES:

Oliver, Richard L. and Erin Anderson (1994), "An Empirical Test of the Consequences of Behavior- and Outcome-Based Sales Control Systems," *JM*, 58 (October), 53–67.

SCALE ITEMS:

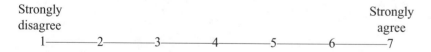

Strongly disagree — Strongly agree
1———2———3———4———5———6———7

1. It is a definite plus to have a thorough review of my performance by management.

2. I like my company to give me frequent, detailed performance feedback.

3. I want to know at all times what management thinks of my performance.

4. I'm the kind of person who needs lots of feedback from my boss.

SCALE NAME: Acceptance (Teamwork/Cooperation)

SCALE DESCRIPTION: Oliver and Anderson (1994) used this five-item, seven-point Likert-type scale to measure sales representatives' attitudes regarding working in teams or demonstrating cooperative behavior toward others.

SCALE ORIGIN: The scale is original to Oliver and Anderson (1994), who pretested the measure in a questionnaire administered to a convenience sample of sales representatives attending trade association functions. The measure was revised on the basis of the pretest.

SAMPLES: Oliver and Anderson (1994) surveyed managers and manufacturer's sales representatives employed by independently owned and operated sales agencies serving the electronics industry. Of the 350 randomly selected trade association member firms fitting this designation, 299 expressed interest in participating, and ultimately, **194** usable surveys from management and **347** surveys from manufacturer representatives were returned. The typical respondent was male (92%), a college graduate (64%), approximately 39 years of age, and had an average of 12 years sales experience with 5.5 years in the present job.

RELIABILITY: Oliver and Anderson (1994) reported a coefficient alpha of **.748** for this measure.

VALIDITY: Oliver and Anderson (1994) used the correlation matrix of the independent and classification variables used in the study to provide some evidence of discriminant and convergent validity. Nomological validity was also found to be present.

ADMINISTRATION: Oliver and Anderson (1994) sent managers of the 299 firms indicating interest in the study a packet containing a "manager's survey" and three similar self-administered surveys for salespeople, along with self-addressed, postage-paid reply envelopes. Managers were instructed to distribute one survey each to an "above average rep," a "mid-range rep," and a "below average rep." Each representative was promised confidentiality and the chance to win one of five $100 prizes in a random drawing. It appears that only responses obtained from sales representatives were used in computing this measure. Higher scores on the scale indicated a greater willingness on the part of the sales representative to engage in teamwork and cooperative behavior.

MAJOR FINDINGS: Oliver and Anderson (1994) examined how perceptions of the presence of a behavior versus outcome sales control system in the respondents' organizations influenced salespeople's performance outcomes and sales strategies, as well as their affective, cognitive, and behavioral states. Greater **acceptance of teamwork/cooperation** was significantly related to the use of a behavior control system.

REFERENCES:
Oliver, Richard L. and Erin Anderson (1994), "An Empirical Test of the Consequences of Behavior- and Outcome-Based Sales Control Systems," *JM*, 58 (October), 53–67.

SCALE ITEMS:

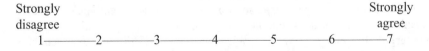

Strongly
disagree

Strongly
agree

1———2———3———4———5———6———7

1. I am known as a team player when performing in groups.

2. I always fulfill my obligations to others I work with.

3. I am willing to do my part for the good of the group.

4. Working with others is a hassle I prefer to avoid. **(r)**

5. Teamwork is something I've always enjoyed doing.

#490 *Account Loss Attributions (External)*

SCALE NAME: Account Loss Attributions (External)

SCALE DESCRIPTION: DeCarlo and Leigh (1996) used this four-item, seven-point Likert-type scale to assess the extent to which a sales manager attributes the cause of a salesperson's poor performance to a lack of ability characterized by poor selling skills, inadequate product knowledge, and a personality inappropriate for developing or maintaining customer relationships.

SCALE ORIGIN: The scale is original to DeCarlo and Leigh (1996).

SAMPLES: DeCarlo and Leigh's (1996) sample consisted of 468 U.S. sales managers, of whom 289 were recruited from a *Fortune* 500 mailing equipment (ME) firm, 103 were recruited from an office equipment (OE) firm, and the final 79 individuals were drawn from a southeast sales and marketing executives (SME) mailing list. Usable responses were obtained from **218** sales managers, of whom 144 (49%) were ME managers, 55 (53.4%) were OE managers, and 19 (25.5%) were SME managers. Post hoc ANOVAS were performed for several firm-level effects to assess the compatibility of the three groups that composed the sample, and no significant differences were found.

RELIABILITY: DeCarlo and Leigh (1996) reported a coefficient alpha of **.54** for the scale.

VALIDITY: The scales used in DeCarlo and Leigh's (1996) study first were factor analyzed; those with multiple-factor solutions were orthogonally rotated, and items with loadings of .30 or lower were eliminated. Confirmatory factor analysis using LISREL 7.16 was used to assess scale dimensionality and discriminant validity; goodness-of-fit indices and t-values associated with individual items were used to identify the final set of scale items representing each construct.

ADMINISTRATION: DeCarlo and Leigh (1996) developed a $2 \times 2 \times 3$ full-factorial, between-group experimentation design in which task attraction, social attraction, and information ambiguity were manipulated to observe the effect on managerial causal attributions and other dependent measures. The questionnaire containing the measure was delivered by mail; nonrespondents were sent a reminder postcard followed by a second questionnaire. A lottery incentive, promises of anonymity, letters of endorsement, and business reply envelopes were also used to enhance response rates. Higher scores on the scale indicated that a sales manager perceived a sales representative as being personally responsible for poor performance, due to a lack of ability characterized by poor selling skills, inadequate product knowledge, and a personality inappropriate for developing or maintaining customer relationships.

MAJOR FINDINGS: DeCarlo and Leigh (1996) examined the relationship between a sales manager's task and social attraction to a salesperson, manager attributions for poor performance, and managerial feedback based on those attributions in an experimental context. Sales managers were more likely to attribute the loss of a major sales account to **external factors**, rather than internal ability or motivation factors, when their social and task attraction to the salesperson was high. Information ambiguity was also found to affect the relationship between causal attributions and cognitive responses, as sales managers agreed more strongly that **external attributions** were the problem when the task difficulty treatment scenario was compared with the personal responsibility treatment scenario.

COMMENTS: The low reliability of this measure suggests that further developmental effort may be required prior to using this scale again.

REFERENCES:
DeCarlo, Thomas E. and Thomas W. Leigh (1996), "Impact of Salesperson Attraction on Sales Managers' Attributions and Feedback," *JM*, 60 (April), 47–66.

SCALE ITEMS:

Strongly   Strongly
disagree   agree
 1————2————3————4————5————6————7

I would probably look to blame the lost major account on...

1. The lack of our product's competitive advantage in this type of market.

2. Our support staff, or service department, provided poor service to this customer.

3. Inadequate support provided to the salesperson to maintain the necessary market/product knowledge.

4. The excessive competitive intensity in this type of market.

SCALE NAME: Account Loss Attributions (Internal Ability)

SCALE DESCRIPTION: DeCarlo and Leigh (1996) used this three-item, seven-point Likert-type scale to assess the extent to which a sales manager attributes the cause of a salesperson's poor performance to a lack of ability characterized by poor selling skills, inadequate product knowledge, and a personality inappropriate for developing or maintaining customer relationships.

SCALE ORIGIN: The scale is original to DeCarlo and Leigh (1996).

SAMPLES: DeCarlo and Leigh's (1996) sample consisted of 468 U.S. sales managers, of whom 289 were recruited from a *Fortune* 500 mailing equipment (ME) firm, 103 were recruited from an office equipment (OE) firm, and the final 79 individuals were drawn from a southeast sales and marketing executives (SME) mailing list (79). Usable responses were obtained from **218** sales managers, of whom 144 (49%) were ME managers, 55 (53.4%) were OE managers, and 19 (25.5%) were SME managers. Post hoc ANOVAS were performed for several firm-level effects to assess the compatibility of the three groups that composed the sample, and no significant differences were found.

RELIABILITY: DeCarlo and Leigh (1996) reported a coefficient alpha of **.73** for the scale.

VALIDITY: The scales used in the DeCarlo and Leigh (1996) study first were factor analyzed; those with multiple-factor solutions were orthogonally rotated, and items with loadings of .30 or lower were eliminated. Confirmatory factor analysis using LISREL 7.16 was used to assess scale dimensionality and discriminant validity; goodness-of-fit indices and t-values associated with individual items were used to identify the final set of scale items representing each construct.

ADMINISTRATION: DeCarlo and Leigh (1996) developed a $2 \times 2 \times 3$ full-factorial, between-group experimentation design in which task attraction, social attraction, and information ambiguity were manipulated to observe the effect on managerial causal attributions and other dependent measures. The questionnaire containing the measure was delivered by mail; nonrespondents were sent a reminder postcard followed by a second questionnaire. A lottery incentive, promises of anonymity, letters of endorsement, and business reply envelopes were also used to enhance response rates. Higher scores on the scale indicated that a sales manager perceived a sales representative as being personally responsible for poor performance, due to a lack of ability characterized by poor selling skills, inadequate product knowledge, and a personality inappropriate for developing or maintaining customer relationships.

MAJOR FINDINGS: DeCarlo and Leigh (1996) examined the relationship between a sales manager's task and social attraction to a salesperson, manager attributions for poor performance, and managerial feedback based on those attributions in an experimental context. Sales managers were more likely to attribute the loss of a major sales account to **internal ability** and motivation factors, rather than external factors, when their social and task attraction to the salesperson was low. Information ambiguity was also found to affect the relationship between causal attributions and cognitive responses, as sales managers agreed more strongly that **internal ability** was the problem and generated more cognitive responses to that effect in the personal responsibility treatment scenario compared with the task difficulty and ambiguous scenarios.

REFERENCES:

DeCarlo, Thomas E. and Thomas W. Leigh (1996), "Impact of Salesperson Attraction on Sales Managers' Attributions and Feedback," *JM*, 60 (April), 47–66.

SCALE ITEMS:

Strongly   Strongly
disagree   agree
  1————2————3————4————5————6————7

I would probably look to blame the lost major account on...

1. Inadequate selling skills for major account presentations.

2. Inadequate product knowledge to sell this type of customer.

3. Not possessing the personality to develop, or keep strong customer relations.

SCALE NAME: Account Loss Attributions (Internal Motivation)

SCALE DESCRIPTION: DeCarlo and Leigh (1996) used this four-item, seven-point Likert-type scale to assess the extent to which a sales manager attributes the cause of a salesperson's poor performance to a lack of motivation and effort on the part of the salesperson.

SCALE ORIGIN: The scale is original to DeCarlo and Leigh (1996).

SAMPLES: DeCarlo and Leigh's (1996) sample consisted of 468 U.S. sales managers, of whom 289 were recruited from a *Fortune* 500 mailing equipment (ME) firm, 103 were recruited from an office equipment (OE) firm, and the final 79 individuals were drawn from a southeast sales and marketing executives (SME) mailing list. Usable responses were obtained from **218** sales managers, of whom 144 (49%) were ME managers, 55 (53.4%) were OE managers, and 19 (25.5%) were SME managers. Post hoc ANOVAS were performed for several firm-level effects to assess the compatibility of the three groups that composed the sample, and no significant differences were found.

RELIABILITY: DeCarlo and Leigh (1996) reported a coefficient alpha of **.83** for the scale.

VALIDITY: The scales used in DeCarlo and Leigh's (1996) study first were factor analyzed; those with multiple-factor solutions were orthogonally rotated, and items with loadings of .30 or lower were eliminated. Confirmatory factor analysis using LISREL 7.16 was used to assess scale dimensionality and discriminant validity; goodness-of-fit indices and t-values associated with individual items were used to identify the final set of scale items representing each construct.

ADMINISTRATION: DeCarlo and Leigh (1996) developed a $2 \times 2 \times 3$ full-factorial, between-group experimentation design in which task attraction, social attraction, and information ambiguity were manipulated to observe the effect on managerial causal attributions and other dependent measures. The questionnaire containing the measure was delivered by mail; nonrespondents were sent a reminder postcard followed by a second questionnaire. A lottery incentive, promises of anonymity, letters of endorsement, and business reply envelopes were also used to enhance response rates. Higher scores on the scale indicated that a sales manager perceived a sales representative as personally responsible for poor performance, due to a lack of motivation and effort on his or her part.

MAJOR FINDINGS: DeCarlo and Leigh (1996) examined the relationship between a sales manager's task and social attraction to a salesperson, manager attributions for poor performance, and managerial feedback based on those attributions in an experimental context. Sales managers were more likely to attribute the loss of a major sales account to **internal motivation** and ability factors, rather than external factors, when their social and task attraction to the salesperson was low. Information ambiguity was also found to affect causal attributions and cognitive responses, as sales managers agreed more strongly that **internal motivation** was the problem and generated more cognitive responses to that effect in the personal responsibility treatment scenario compared with the task difficulty scenarios.

REFERENCES:

DeCarlo, Thomas E. and Thomas W. Leigh (1996), "Impact of Salesperson Attraction on Sales Managers' Attributions and Feedback," *JM*, 60 (April), 47–66.

SCALE ITEMS:

Strongly
disagree

Strongly
agree

1———2———3———4———5———6———7

I would probably look to blame the lost major account on...

1. A lack of sufficient effort.

2. Working less effectively than the average representative.

3. The fact that s/he is an unmotivated individual.

4. This person's usual reluctance to make the required number of sales calls to maintain the types of accounts.

SCALE NAME: Activity Control (Information)

SCALE DESCRIPTION: Challagalla and Shervani (1996) used this five-item, five-point Likert-type summated ratings scale to measure employee perceptions of the degree to which supervisors set sales activity goals, monitored and evaluated performance, and provided feedback related to goal achievement. This measurement assesses those activities undertaken as part of the selling process (call rate, number of demos, reports turned in, customers contacted) rather than the output of those activities (market share, sales volume) or actual selling skills.

SCALE ORIGIN: Challagalla and Shervani (1996) indicated that some of the items used in this measure were adapted from Jaworski and MacInnis's (1989) study. In modifying the measure, Challagalla and Shervani (1996) undertook extensive pretesting and purification procedures in four sequential stages involving both academic experts and industrial salespeople.

SAMPLES: Challagalla and Shervani (1996) surveyed 302 field salespeople employed in the industrial products divisions of two *Fortune* 500 companies. Usable responses were received from **270** salespeople, the majority of whom were college educated men.

RELIABILITY: Challagalla and Shervani (1996) reported a coefficient alpha of **.89** for the scale.

VALIDITY: The nine dimensions of control measured in the study were evaluated by Challagalla and Shervani (1996) using confirmatory factor analysis. This scale demonstrated acceptable levels of convergent and discriminant validity and was found to be unidimensional.

ADMINISTRATION: Challagalla and Shervani (1996) indicated that the scale was self-administered, along with many other measures, in a questionnaire delivered directly to the homes of salespeople. Prior to administration, each salesperson received a note from a senior sales executive in his or her organization alerting him or her to the study. Business reply envelopes, cover letters promising confidentiality, and two follow-up attempts were used to increase response rate. Higher scores on the scale indicated that sales managers were perceived as being highly likely to set selling activity goals, monitor and evaluate salesperson performance, and provide feedback to salespeople related to goal achievement.

MAJOR FINDINGS: Challagalla and Shervani (1996) extended existing conceptual work related to marketing control systems by (1) investigating the effect of information and reinforcement on salesperson job outcomes, (2) separating the global behavior control construct into activity control and capability control, and (3) examining the casual mechanisms by which controls operate. **Activity information** was negatively related to supervisory role ambiguity, which indicated that supervisors who provide goal information and feedback are more likely to convey their expectations effectively to salespeople. However, the provision of **activity information** was shown to reduce customer role ambiguity, which indicated that such information motivates salespeople to better understand customer role expectations. Contrary to expectations, a supervisor's sharing of **activity information** had no direct influence on salesperson performance and was positively, rather than negatively, related to satisfaction with a supervisor.

REFERENCES:

Challagalla, Goutam N. and Tasadduq A. Shervani (1996), "Dimensions and Types of Supervisory Control: Effects on Salesperson Performance and Satisfaction," *JM*, 60 (January), 89–105.

Jaworski, Bernard J. and Deborah J. MacInnis (1989), "Marketing Jobs and Management Controls: Toward a Framework," *JMR*, 26 (November), 406–19.

SCALE ITEMS:

Instructions to respondents:

In answering the following questions, please focus ONLY on *sales activities* (e.g., call rate, number of demos, customers to be contacted, reports to turn in, etc.)

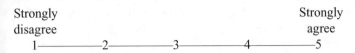

```
Strongly                          Strongly
disagree                          agree
   1————————2————————3————————4————————5
```

1. My manager informs me about the sales activities I am expected to perform.

2. My manager monitors my sales activities.

3. My manager informs me on whether I meet his/her expectations on sales activities.

4. If my manager feels I need to adjust my sales activities, s/he tells me about it.

5. My manager evaluates my sales activities.

SCALE NAME: Activity Control (Punishments)

SCALE DESCRIPTION: Challagalla and Shervani (1996) used this three-item, five-point Likert-type summated ratings scale to measure employee perceptions of the degree to which supervisors punished salespeople who failed to achieve sales activity goals. In this context, sales activities refer to the number of demos, reports turned in, or customers contacted rather than the output of those activities (market share, sales volume) or a person's actual selling skills.

SCALE ORIGIN: Challagalla and Shervani (1996) indicated that some of the items used in this measure were adapted from Podsakoff and colleagues' (1984) study. In modifying the measure, Challagalla and Shervani (1996) undertook extensive pretesting and purification procedures in four sequential stages involving both academic experts and industrial salespeople. Punishment-focused items tying pay and incentives to selling activity goals were deleted after an exploratory factor analysis. Challagalla and Shervani (1996) noted that this action was consistent with pretest feedback, which indicated that the use of pay and incentives to reinforce activity goals was minimal.

SAMPLES: Challagalla and Shervani (1996) surveyed 302 field salespeople employed in the industrial products divisions of two *Fortune* 500 companies. Usable responses were received from **270** salespeople, the majority of whom were college educated men.

RELIABILITY: Challagalla and Shervani (1996) reported a coefficient alpha of **.80** for the scale.

VALIDITY: The nine dimensions of control measured in the study were evaluated by Challagalla and Shervani (1996) using confirmatory factor analysis. This scale demonstrated acceptable levels of convergent and discriminant validity and was found to be unidimensional.

ADMINISTRATION: Challagalla and Shervani (1996) indicated that the scale was self-administered, along with many other measures, in a questionnaire delivered directly to the homes of salespeople. Prior to administration, each salesperson received a note from a senior sales executive in his or her organization alerting him or her to the study. Business reply envelopes, cover letters promising confidentiality, and two follow-up attempts were used to increase response rate. Higher scores on the scale indicated that sales managers were perceived as highly likely to punish salespeople who failed to meet their assigned selling activity goals.

MAJOR FINDINGS: Challagalla and Shervani (1996) extended existing conceptual work related to marketing control systems by (1) investigating the effect of information and reinforcement on salesperson job outcomes, (2) separating the global behavior control construct into activity control and capability control, and (3) examining the casual mechanisms by which controls operate. Contrary to expectations, **activity punishments** were not significantly related to either performance or supervisory role ambiguity and were found to increase, rather than reduce, customer role ambiguity. As expected, **activity punishments** negatively influenced satisfaction with a supervisor.

REFERENCES:

Challagalla, Goutam N. and Tasadduq A. Shervani (1996), "Dimensions and Types of Supervisory Control: Effects on Salesperson Performance and Satisfaction," *JM*, 60 (January), 89–105.

Podsakoff, Philip M., William D. Todor, Richard A. Grover, and Vandra L. Huber (1984), "Situational Moderators of Leader Reward and Punishment Behaviors: Fact or Fiction?" *Organizational Behavior and Human Performance,* 34 (1), 21-63.

SCALE ITEMS:

Instructions to respondents:

In answering the following questions, please focus ONLY on *sales activities* (e.g., call rate, number of demos, customers to be contacted, reports to turn in, etc.)

Strongly disagree — Strongly agree

1————2————3————4————5

1. I would receive an informal warning if my manager is not pleased how I perform sales activities.

2. I would receive a formal reprimand if my supervisor were unhappy with how I perform sales activities.

3. I would be put on probation if my manager is unhappy with how I perform specified sales activities.

SCALE NAME: Activity Control (Rewards)

SCALE DESCRIPTION: Challagalla and Shervani (1996) used this three-item, five-point Likert-type summated ratings scale to measure employee perceptions of the degree to which supervisors rewarded the achievement of sales activity goals, such as number of demos, reports turned in, and customers contacted, rather than the output of those activities (market share, sales volume) or a person's actual selling skills.

SCALE ORIGIN: Challagalla and Shervani (1996) indicated that some of the items used in this measure were adapted from Podsakoff and colleagues' (1984) study. In modifying the measure, Challagalla and Shervani (1996) undertook extensive pretesting and purification procedures in four sequential stages involving both academic experts and industrial salespeople. Reward-focused items tying pay and incentives to selling activity goals were deleted after an exploratory factor analysis. The authors noted that this action was consistent with pretest feedback, which indicated that the use of pay and incentives to reinforce activity goals was minimal.

SAMPLES: Challagalla and Shervani (1996) surveyed 302 field salespeople employed in the industrial products divisions of two *Fortune* 500 companies. Usable responses were received from **270** salespeople, the majority of whom were college educated men.

RELIABILITY: Challagalla and Shervani (1996) reported a coefficient alpha of **.78** for the scale.

VALIDITY: The nine dimensions of control measured in the study were evaluated by Challagalla and Shervani (1996) using confirmatory factor analysis. This scale demonstrated acceptable levels of convergent and discriminant validity and was found to be unidimensional.

ADMINISTRATION: Challagalla and Shervani (1996) indicated that the scale was self-administered, along with many other measures, in a questionnaire delivered directly to the homes of salespeople. Prior to administration, each salesperson received a note from a senior sales executive in his or her organization alerting him or her to the study. Business reply envelopes, cover letters promising confidentiality, and two follow-up attempts were used to increase response rate. Higher scores on the scale indicated that sales managers were perceived as highly likely to reward salespeople who met their assigned selling activity goals.

MAJOR FINDINGS: Challagalla and Shervani (1996) extended existing conceptual work related to marketing control systems by (1) investigating the effect of information and reinforcement on salesperson job outcomes, (2) separating the global behavior control construct into activity control and capability control, and (3) examining the casual mechanisms by which controls operate. **Activity rewards** were negatively related to supervisory role ambiguity, which suggests that rewards motivate salespeople to expend effort in understanding a supervisor's expectations. The negative relationship between **activity rewards** and customer role ambiguity appears to indicate that receiving rewards for performing supervisor-specified activities encourages salespeople to take actions that bring them in closer contact with the customer (such as make more sales call). Contrary to expectations, **activity rewards** had no direct influence on salesperson performance and were positively, rather than negatively, related to satisfaction with a supervisor.

REFERENCES:
Challagalla, Goutam N. and Tasadduq A. Shervani (1996), "Dimensions and Types of Supervisory Control: Effects on Salesperson Performance and Satisfaction," *JM*, 60 (January), 89–105.

Podsakoff, Philip M., William D. Todor, Richard A. Grover, and Vandra L. Huber (1984), "Situational Moderators of Leader Reward and Punishment Behaviors: Fact or Fiction?" *Organizational Behavior and Human Performance,* 34 (1), 21-63.

SCALE ITEMS:

Instructions to respondents:

In answering the following questions, please focus ONLY on *sales activities* (e.g., call rate, number of demos, customers to be contacted, reports to turn in, etc.)

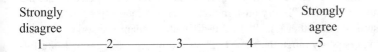

Strongly disagree   Strongly agree

1————2————3————4————5

1. How well I perform specified sales activities would be considered when awarding bonuses/financial rewards.

2. If I perform sales activities well my supervisor would commend me.

3. I would be recognized by my supervisor if s/he were pleased with how well I perform sales activities.

SCALE NAME: Adaptability (Employee)

SCALE DESCRIPTION: Hartline and Ferrell (1996) used this six-item, seven-point Likert-type scale to assess contact employees' ability to adapt to service situations by altering their approach toward customers.

SCALE ORIGIN: Hartline and Ferrell (1996) indicated that the items representing this construct were adapted from Spiro and Weitz's (1990) adaptive selling scale. Six items believed to be redundant were dropped from the measure, and the remaining ten items were rephrased to eliminate the personal-selling orientation of the original statements. Four items, "Every customer requires a unique approach," "I don't change my approach from one customer to another (r)," "I find it difficult to adapt my style to certain customers (r)," and "I treat all customers pretty much the same (r)," were dropped from the measure following a confirmatory factor analysis because of nonsignificant t-values.

SAMPLES: The hotel industry was chosen as the sampling frame for this study. Hartline and Ferrell (1996) sampled the general managers, employees, and customers of 444 hotel units representing three hotel chains, and 236 units returned at least one usable questionnaire from a manager, an employee, and a customer. A total of 1769 usable questionnaires were received from **236** hotel managers, **561** customer contact employees, and **1351** customers.

RELIABILITY: Hartline and Ferrell (1996) reported a coefficient alpha of .77 for this measure.

VALIDITY: Hartline and Ferrell (1996) used confirmatory factor analysis to test the unidimensionality of the measures using separate analyses for managers, employees, and customers. Items with nonsignificant t-values were dropped from the measures. In investigating the discriminant validity of the scales, the authors first averaged the employee and customer responses on the scale and then matched that response with the manager responses to create a single data set in which cases represented hotel units rather than individuals. Hotel units that did not provide at least three responses from employees and customers were dropped, leaving a final sample of 97 matched responses. Confirmatory factor analysis was then used to assess the discriminant validity of the measures.

ADMINISTRATION: Each hotel manager received a survey packet containing instructions, postage-paid reply envelopes, one manager survey, five employee surveys, and forty guest surveys, which were to be self-administered. This measure was included in the employee survey. Hartline and Ferrell (1996) instructed managers to distribute employee surveys to employees in customer contact positions and the guest surveys to guests during check-out. Survey packets were preceded by a letter from the corporate marketing manager endorsing the project and followed by a second wave of materials approximately two months after the first had been distributed. Higher scores on the scale reflected a greater degree of employee adaptability.

MAJOR FINDINGS: Hartline and Ferrell (1996) investigated the management of customer contact service employees and various factors related to service quality using data generated from the customers, contact employees, and managers of hotel units. Hypotheses were tested in the context of structural equation modeling. Contrary to expectations, **employee adaptability** did not have a significant effect on customers' perceptions of service quality, nor did employee self-efficacy have a significant effect on **employee adaptability**. Role ambiguity negatively influenced **employee adaptability**, and contrary to expectations, role conflict had no effect. Behavior-based evaluations increased **employee adaptability**.

REFERENCES:

Hartline, Michael D. and O.C. Ferrell (1996), "The Management of Customer-Contact Service Employees: An Empirical Investigation," *JM*, 60 (October), 52–70.

Spiro, Rosann L. and Barton A. Weitz (1990), "Adaptive Selling: Conceptualization, Measurement, and Nomological Validity," *JMR*, 27 (February), 61–69.

SCALE ITEMS:

Strongly disagree — 1————2————3————4————5————6————7 — Strongly agree

1. When I feel that my approach is not working, I can easily change to another approach.

2. I like to experiment with different approaches.

3. I am very sensitive to the needs of my customers.

4. I vary my approach from situation to situation.

5. I try to understand how one customer differs from another.

6. I feel confident that I can effectively change my approach when necessary.

SCALE NAME: Adaptation (Product)

SCALE DESCRIPTION: Cavusgil and Zou (1994) used this three-item, five-point scale to assess the degree to which an exporter adapted a product and its labeling for a foreign distributor or subsidiary.

SCALE ORIGIN: The scale is original to Cavusgil and Zou (1994), who adopted a parsimonious multiphase research design to operationalize and test measures within their proposed conceptual framework. Preliminary interviews with export marketing managers were used to verify and improve scale items suggested by the literature. Data were collected using the resulting measures and split into two groups. An exploratory factor analysis performed on the analysis subsample using varimax rotation resulted in 17 factors. Only items whose meanings were consistent with the conceptualization of the measure were retained.

SAMPLES: Export marketing managers directly involved with export ventures from 79 firms in 16 industries provided Cavusgil and Zou (1994) with information pertinent to **202** export venture cases. Of the 202 venture cases analyzed, 47.5% were related to consumer goods and 42.6% to industrial goods, but the remainder could not be classified clearly. All respondents were from manufacturing firms with average annual sales in excess of $200 million. The sample was split into analysis and hold-out subsamples, each of which contained **101** export venture cases.

RELIABILITY: Cavusgil and Zou (1994) reported a coefficient alpha of **.559** for this measure.

VALIDITY: Cavusgil and Zou (1994) stated that the content validity of the measure was established during the preliminary interviews. Confirmatory factor analysis performed on the hold-out sample demonstrated patterns of item-to-item correlations and item–factor correlations suggestive of measure unidimensionality.

ADMINISTRATION: Cavusgil and Zou (1994) developed a semistructured instrument that outlined a list of variables and intended scales but contained no specific questions. This allowed the researchers to tailor questions to the specific context of the export venture being discussed or probed during the personal interview. During each in-depth interview, two experienced international marketing researchers independently assigned a score to each of the variables. Scoring was based on the researcher's judgment of the executive's answer to the questions pertinent to the variable, as well as the words used by the executive when expressing an answer. Following the interview, the researchers met to discuss their ratings, resolved differences of opinion, and finalized the scores assigned to each variable. Interrater reliability averaged approximately 80% prior to resolving these differences. Higher scores on the scale indicated that exporters were perceived as making greater adaptations in the product or its labeling.

MAJOR FINDINGS: Cavusgil and Zou (1994) investigated the relationship between marketing strategy and performance in the context of export ventures. **Product adaptation** was one of five factors found to represent the export marketing strategy in an exploratory factor analysis. This structure was confirmed through confirmatory factor analysis with the hold-out sample. Tests of the overall model indicated that the level of **product adaptation** was related strongly and positively to the cultural specificity of the product and a firm's international competence, moderately and positively to product uniqueness and export market competitiveness, and strongly but negatively to the technology orientation of the industry and a firm's experience with the product.

COMMENTS: The low reliability of the measure suggests that further development and refinement may be necessary prior to using this scale again.

REFERENCES:
Cavusgil, S. Tamer and Shaoming Zou (1994), "Marketing Strategy-Performance Relationship: An Investigation of the Empirical Link in Export Market Ventures," *JM*, 58 (January), 1–21.

SCALE ITEMS:

None   Substantial

1——————2——————3——————4——————5

1. Degree of initial product adaptation.

2. Degree of product adaptation subsequent to entry.

3. Extent to which product label is in local language.

SCALE NAME: Adaptation (Promotion)

SCALE DESCRIPTION: Cavusgil and Zou (1994) used this three-item, five-point scale to assess the degree to which an exporter adapted a product's positioning, packaging, and promotional approach to fit the needs of a specific distributor/subsidiary.

SCALE ORIGIN: The scale is original to Cavusgil and Zou (1994), who adopted a parsimonious multiphase research design to operationalize and test measures within their proposed conceptual framework. Preliminary interviews with export marketing managers were used to verify and improve scale items suggested by the literature. Data were collected using the resulting measures and split into two groups. An exploratory factor analysis performed on the analysis subsample using varimax rotation resulted in 17 factors. Only items whose meanings were consistent with the conceptualization of the measure were retained.

SAMPLES: Export marketing managers directly involved with export ventures from 79 firms in 16 industries provided information pertinent to **202** export venture cases. Of the 202 venture cases analyzed, 47.5% were related to consumer goods and 42.6% to industrial goods, but the remainder could not be classified clearly. All respondents were from manufacturing firms with average annual sales in excess of $200 million. The sample was split into analysis and hold-out subsamples, each of which contained **101** export venture cases.

RELIABILITY: Cavusgil and Zou (1994) reported a coefficient alpha of **.857** for this measure.

VALIDITY: Cavusgil and Zou (1994) stated that the content validity of the measure was established during the preliminary interviews. Confirmatory factor analysis performed on the hold-out sample demonstrated patterns of item-to-item correlations and item–factor correlations suggestive of measure unidimensionality.

ADMINISTRATION: Cavusgil and Zou (1994) developed a semistructured instrument that outlined a list of variables and intended scales but contained no specific questions. This allowed the researchers to tailor questions to the specific context of the export venture being discussed or probed during the personal interview. During each in-depth interview, two experienced international marketing researchers independently assigned a score to each of the variables. Scoring was based on the researcher's judgment of the executive's answer to the questions pertinent to the variable, as well as the words used by the executive when expressing an answer. Following the interview, the researchers met to discuss their ratings, resolved differences of opinion, and finalized the scores assigned to each variable. Interrater reliability averaged approximately 80% prior to resolving these differences. Higher scores on the scale indicated that exporters were more willing to adapt the product's positioning, packaging, and promotional approach to fit the needs of a specific distributor/subsidiary.

MAJOR FINDINGS: Cavusgil and Zou (1994) investigated the relationship between marketing strategy and performance in the context of export ventures. **Promotion adaptation** was one of five factors found to represent the export marketing strategy in an exploratory factor analysis. This structure was confirmed by confirmatory factor analysis with the hold-out sample. Tests of the overall model indicated that the level of **promotion adaptation** was related strongly and positively to product uniqueness, a firm's experience with the product, and export market competitiveness; strongly but negatively to the technology orientation of the industry; weakly and positively to a firm's international competence; and weakly but negatively to brand familiarity of export customers.

REFERENCES:
Cavusgil, S. Tamer and Shaoming Zou (1994), "Marketing Strategy-Performance Relationship: An Investigation of the Empirical Link in Export Market Ventures," *JM*, 58 (January), 1–21.

SCALE ITEMS:

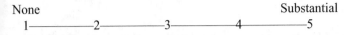

None   Substantial
1————2————3————4————5

1. Degree of adaptation of product positioning strategy

2. Degree of adaptation of packaging.

3. Degree of adaptation of promotional approach.

SCALE NAME: Anticipated Effort (Salesperson)

SCALE DESCRIPTION: Brown, Cron, and Slocum (1997) used this three-item, five-point scale to measure the degree to which salespeople anticipated devoting time and effort to working on a particular promotion relative to other salespeople.

SCALE ORIGIN: There is no information to indicate that the scale is anything other than original to Brown, Cron, and Slocum's (1997) study.

SAMPLES: Sales representatives of a medical supplies distributorship that was participating in a specific promotion were sampled for this study. Brown, Cron, and Slocum (1997) attempted to sample the entire sales force at two points in time. Of the 141-member sales force, **122** returned usable responses to both questionnaires. The average sales goal reported by salespeople for the specific unit on promotion was 3.2 units, though the actual average units sold were 2.5 units. Twenty-five percent of the salespeople met their goal exactly, 52% did not, and 23% exceeded their sales goal.

RELIABILITY: Brown, Cron, and Slocum (1997) reported coefficient alphas of **.92** for the anticipatory territory planning scale and **.94** for the actual territory planning scale.

VALIDITY: No specific examination of the scale's validity was reported by Brown, Cron, and Slocum (1997).

ADMINISTRATION: Brown, Cron, and Slocum (1997) distributed the first questionnaire during a sales meeting in which the focal promotion was introduced and explained. The anticipatory planning scales were included in this questionnaire with other measures. It is not clear how the second questionnaire was distributed, but it also appears to have been self-administered. Salespeople received the second questionnaire, containing the actual planning scales and other measures, following the conclusion of the promotion. Higher scores on the scale indicated that salespeople anticipated devoting more time and effort to working on the promotion compared with other salespeople.

MAJOR FINDINGS: Brown, Cron, and Slocum (1997) investigated the effect of goal-directed positive and negative emotions on salesperson volition, behavior, and performance. **Anticipated effort** was one of three first-order factors that represented the higher-order volition construct in the model tested. Similarly, goal-directed behavior was a higher-order construct represented by actual account territory planning activities and two other constructs. Both positive and negative anticipatory emotions were positively related to a salesperson's anticipated planning of effort and strategies (volition), and volitions were in turn strongly and positively related to goal-directed behavior. Finally, goal-directed behaviors were positively associated with the degree of goal attainment.

REFERENCES:
Brown, Steven P., William L. Cron, and John W. Slocum Jr. (1997), "Effects of Goal-Directed Emotions on Salesperson Volitions, Behavior, and Performance: A Longitudinal Study," *JM*, 61 (January), 39–50.

SCALE ITEMS:

Much less
than average
1————2————3————4————5

Much more
than average

1. Compared to other salespeople, how much time do you anticipate spending on this promotion?

2. Compared to other salespeople, how much intensity of effort do you anticipate putting into this promotion?

3. Compared to other salespeople, how much overall effort do you anticipate putting into this promotion?

SCALE NAME: Attitude Toward Salespeople in General

SCALE DESCRIPTION: Attitude toward salespeople in general was measured using a five-item, seven-point semantic differential scale. Brown (1995) defines this construct as a global evaluative predisposition to respond positively or negatively to salespeople in general.

SCALE ORIGIN: Although the development of the scale appears to be original to Brown (1995), the semantic differential items employed have been used and tested widely in various attitude toward advertising in general studies.

SAMPLES: Brown (1995) administered a pretest questionnaire to assess the reliability and validity of the measures, which was sent to a sample of 100 buyers, of which **39** were returned. Following minor modifications to the questionnaire, the final questionnaire was sent to a regional probability sample of 932 organizational buyers located in 20 Eastern states. Individuals with the job title of "buyer" or "purchasing agent" on the National Association of Purchasing Managers mailing list served as the sampling frame. Usable questionnaires were returned from **379** respondents, for a response rate of 40.67%. Comparisons between early and late respondents suggested that nonresponse bias was not an issue. Of the respondents, 64% worked in manufacturing, 18% in services, 12% in government or nonprofit, and the remaining 6% worked in retail (4%) or agriculture (2%). Sixty-eight percent of respondents were men, with an average age of 40 years and 8.9 years of work experience in purchasing.

RELIABILITY: Brown (1995) calculated a Cronbach's alpha of **.91** for this scale in the final study. No reliability information with respect to the pretest was reported.

VALIDITY: Brown (1995) noted that the purpose of the pretest was to assess the reliability and validity of the measures but provided no specific information related to this measure, other than to report that it performed "adequately" in the pretest. Information pertaining to other measures seemed to imply that discriminant validity was present for the attitude toward advertising in general measure.

ADMINISTRATION: A cover letter, with a self-addressed, stamped reply envelope, accompanied the mailed questionnaire that contained the measures of interest. Respondents were instructed to recall the last sales presentation made by either an insupplier or an outsupplier sales representative. Each respondent was assigned to either the insupplier or the outsupplier condition, but not both, to minimize respondent fatigue. Higher scores on the attitude toward salespeople in general measure indicated a more favorable global evaluation and a predisposition to generally respond to salespeople in a more positive fashion.

MAJOR FINDINGS: Brown (1995) investigated the interrelationships among buyer perceptions of and attitudes toward vendor companies, products, and salespeople, as well as insupplier/outsupplier status (i.e., company currently has or does not have an ongoing relationship with the buyer's firm). The attitude toward the salesperson measure was significantly more favorable for insuppliers. **Attitude toward the salesperson in general** was significantly related to attitude toward salespeople and attitude toward the product for outsuppliers, whereas neither was significantly related to attitude toward the product for insuppliers.

REFERENCES:
Brown, Steven P. (1995), "The Moderating Effects of Insupplier/Outsupplier Status on Organizational Buyer Attitudes," *JAMS*, 23 (3), 170–81.

SCALE ITEMS:

Instructions: We are investigating the effectiveness of interactions between salespeople and organizational buyers. We would like to ask your help in evaluating salespeople who have called on you within the last two weeks. Specifically, we would like to ask you to recall in detail the last sales presentation made to you by a salesperson whose company you currently buy from/do not currently buy from.

The following questions ask for your impressions, evaluations, and thoughts about this salesperson, his or her company, and the products and/or services that the salesperson discussed with you. Your time and help are gratefully appreciated.

Please rate your attitude toward salespeople in general.*

1. Bad   :___:___:___:___:___:___:___: Good
              1   2   3   4   5   6   7

2. Ineffective   :___:___:___:___:___:___:___: Effective
              1   2   3   4   5   6   7

3. Not Useful   :___:___:___:___:___:___:___: Useful
              1   2   3   4   5   6   7

4. Unpleasant   :___:___:___:___:___:___:___: Pleasant
              1   2   3   4   5   6   7

5. Unhelpful   :___:___:___:___:___:___:___: Helpful
              1   2   3   4   5   6   7

*Although no specific additional instructions were indicated by the author, it is probable that the object to be rated was designated in a fashion similar to this.

SCALE NAME: Attitude Toward the Product

SCALE DESCRIPTION: Attitude toward the product was measured using a five-item, seven-point semantic differential scale. Brown (1995) defined this construct as a global evaluative predisposition to respond positively or negatively to a particular product presented by a salesperson.

SCALE ORIGIN: Although the development of the scale appears to be original to Brown (1995), some of the semantic differential items have been previously used in attitude toward the brand consumer studies. This measure is unique because it was developed and tested for use specifically with purchasing agents.

SAMPLES: Brown (1995) administered a pretest questionnaire to assess the reliability and validity of the measures, which was sent to a sample of 100 buyers, of which **39** were returned. Following minor modifications to the questionnaire, the final questionnaire was sent to a regional probability sample of 932 organizational buyers located in 20 Eastern states. Individuals with the job title of "buyer" or "purchasing agent" on the National Association of Purchasing Managers mailing list served as the sampling frame. Usable questionnaires were returned from **379** respondents, for a response rate of 40.67%. Comparisons between early and late respondents suggested that nonresponse bias was not an issue. Of the respondents, 64% worked in manufacturing, 18% in services, 12% in government or nonprofit, and the remaining 6% worked in retail (4%) or agriculture (2%). Sixty-eight percent of respondents were men, with an average age of 40 years and 8.9 years of work experience in purchasing.

RELIABILITY: Brown (1995) calculated a Cronbach's alpha of **.92** for this scale in the final study. No reliability information with respect to the pretest was reported.

VALIDITY: Brown (1995) noted that the purpose of the pretest was to assess the reliability and validity of the measures but provided no specific information related to this measure, other than to report that it performed "adequately" in the pretest. Information pertaining to other measures seemed to imply that discriminant validity was present for the attitude toward the product measure.

ADMINISTRATION: A cover letter, with a self-addressed, stamped reply envelope, accompanied the mail questionnaire that contained the measures of interest. Respondents were instructed to recall the last sales presentation made by either an insupplier or an outsupplier sales representative. Each respondent was assigned to either the insupplier or the outsupplier condition, but not both, to minimize respondent fatigue. Higher scores on the attitude toward the product measure indicated a more favorable global evaluation and a predisposition to respond favorably toward the product presented by the salesperson.

MAJOR FINDINGS: Brown (1995) investigated the interrelationships among buyer perceptions of and attitudes toward vendor companies, products, and salespeople, as well as insupplier/outsupplier status (i.e., company currently has or does not have an ongoing relationship with the buyer's firm). **Attitude toward the product** offered by both insuppliers and outsuppliers was positively related to attitude toward the salesperson, whereas perceived company reputation was significantly related to **product attitudes** for insuppliers only. Product-related cognitions, perceived purchase significance, perceived salesperson experience, and attitude toward salespeople in general were significantly related to **product attitudes** for outsuppliers only. Perceived risk negatively influenced **product attitude** for both insupplier and outsupplier groups.

REFERENCES:
Brown, Steven P. (1995), "The Moderating Effects of Insupplier/Outsupplier Status on Organizational Buyer Attitudes," *JAMS*, 23 (3), 170–81.

#501 *Attitude Toward the Product*

SCALE ITEMS:

Instructions: We are investigating the effectiveness of interactions between salespeople and organizational buyers. We would like to ask your help in evaluating salespeople who have called on you within the last two weeks. Specifically, we would like to ask you to recall in detail the last sales presentation made to you by a salesperson whose company you currently buy from/do not currently buy from.

The following questions ask for your impressions, evaluations, and thoughts about this salesperson, his or her company, and the products and/or services that the salesperson discussed with you. Your time and help are gratefully appreciated.

Please rate your attitude toward the specific salesperson who delivered the presentation you just recalled:*

1. Bad   :____:____:____:____:____:____:____: Good
            1   2   3   4   5   6   7

2. Ineffective :____:____:____:____:____:____:____: Effective
            1   2   3   4   5   6   7

3. Not Useful   :____:____:____:____:____:____:____: Useful
            1   2   3   4   5   6   7

4. Unpleasant   :____:____:____:____:____:____:____: Pleasant
            1   2   3   4   5   6   7

5. Unhelpful   :____:____:____:____:____:____:____: Helpful
            1   2   3   4   5   6   7

*Although no specific additional instructions were indicated by the author, it is probably that the object to be rated was designated in a fashion similar to this.

SCALE NAME: Attitude Toward the Salesperson

SCALE DESCRIPTION: Attitude toward the salesperson was measured using a six-item, seven-point semantic differential scale. Brown (1995) defines this construct as a global evaluative predisposition to respond positively or negatively to a particular salesperson and refers to this measure as "salesperson attitude" in his article.

SCALE ORIGIN: Although the development of the scale appears to be original to Brown (1995), the semantic differential items have been used and tested widely in various attitude toward the ad and attitude toward the brand studies.

SAMPLES: Brown (1995) administered a pretest questionnaire to assess the reliability and validity of the measures, which was sent to a sample of 100 buyers, of which **39** were returned. Following minor modifications to the questionnaire, the final questionnaire was sent to a regional probability sample of 932 organizational buyers located in 20 Eastern states. Individuals with the job title of "buyer" or "purchasing agent" on the National Association of Purchasing Managers mailing list served as the sampling frame. Usable questionnaires were returned from **379** respondents, for a response rate of 40.67%. Comparisons between early and late respondents suggested that nonresponse bias was not an issue. Of the respondents, 64% worked in manufacturing, 18% in services, 12% in government or nonprofit, and the remaining 6% worked in retail (4%) or agriculture (2%). Sixty-eight percent of respondents were men, with an average age of 40 years and 8.9 years of work experience in purchasing.

RELIABILITY: Brown (1995) calculated a Cronbach's alpha of **.95** for this scale in the final study. No reliability information with respect to the pretest was reported.

VALIDITY: Brown (1995) noted that the purpose of the pretest was to assess the reliability and validity of the measures but provided very little information regarding this process. Brown (1995) noted that one measure, salesperson perceptions, did not possess discriminant validity with respect to salesperson attitude and thus was eliminated from the study.

ADMINISTRATION: A cover letter, with a self-addressed, stamped reply envelope, accompanied the mail questionnaire that contained the measures of interest. Respondents were instructed to recall the last sales presentation made by either an insupplier or an outsupplier sales representative. Each respondent was assigned to either the insupplier or the outsupplier condition, but not both, to minimize respondent fatigue. Higher scores on the attitude toward the sales representative measure indicated a more favorable global evaluation and a predisposition to respond to the salesperson in a more positive fashion.

MAJOR FINDINGS: Brown (1995) investigated the interrelationships among buyer perceptions of and attitudes toward vendor companies, products, and salespeople, as well as insupplier/outsupplier status (i.e., company currently has or does not have an ongoing relationship with the buyer's firm). The **attitude toward the salesperson** measure was significantly more favorable for insuppliers. Attitude toward the salesperson in general and perceived salesperson experience were also significantly related to **attitude toward the salesperson**.

REFERENCES:
Brown, Steven P. (1995), "The Moderating Effects of Insupplier/Outsupplier Status on Organizational Buyer Attitudes," *JAMS*, 23 (3), 170–81.

#502 *Attitude Toward the Salesperson*

SCALE ITEMS:

Instructions: We are investigating the effectiveness of interactions between salespeople and organizational buyers. We would like to ask your help in evaluating salespeople who have called on you within the last two weeks. Specifically, we would like to ask you to recall in detail the last sales presentation made to you by a salesperson whose company you currently buy from/do not currently buy from.

The following questions ask for your impressions, evaluations, and thoughts about this salesperson, his or her company, and the products and/or services that the salesperson discussed with you. Your time and help are gratefully appreciated.

Please rate your attitude toward the specific salesperson who delivered the presentation you just recalled:*

1. Bad   :____:____:____:____:____:____:____: Good
              1   2   3   4   5   6   7

2. Ineffective :____:____:____:____:____:____:____: Effective
              1   2   3   4   5   6   7

3. Unpleasant :____:____:____:____:____:____:____: Pleasant
              1   2   3   4   5   6   7

4. Not Useful :____:____:____:____:____:____:____: Useful
              1   2   3   4   5   6   7

5. Unlikable :____:____:____:____:____:____:____: Likable
              1   2   3   4   5   6   7

6. Unhelpful :____:____:____:____:____:____:____: Helpful
              1   2   3   4   5   6   7

*Although no specific additional instructions were indicated by the author, it is probable that the object to be rated was designated in a fashion similar to this.

SCALE NAME: Attraction (Social)

SCALE DESCRIPTION: DeCarlo and Leigh (1996) used this five-item, seven-point Likert-type scale to measure the extent to which a salesperson is perceived to be a friend or social partner. This measure focuses on affective feelings of liking, empathy, and personal friendship.

SCALE ORIGIN: DeCarlo and Leigh (1996) stated that the scale was based on the work of McCroskey and McCain (1974).

SAMPLES: DeCarlo and Leigh's (1996) sample consisted of 468 U.S. sales managers, of whom 289 were recruited from a *Fortune* 500 mailing equipment (ME) firm, 103 were recruited from an office equipment (OE) firm, and the final 79 individuals were drawn from a southeast sales and marketing executives (SME) mailing list. Usable responses were obtained from **218** sales managers, of whom 144 (49%) were ME managers, 55 (53.4%) were OE managers, and 19 (25.5%) were SME managers. Post hoc ANOVAS were performed for several firm-level effects to assess the compatibility of the three groups that composed the sample, and no significant differences were found.

RELIABILITY: DeCarlo and Leigh (1996) reported a coefficient alpha of **.90** for the scale.

VALIDITY: The scales used in DeCarlo and Leigh's (1996) study were first factor analyzed; those with multiple-factor solutions were orthogonally rotated, and items with loadings of .30 or lower were eliminated. Confirmatory factor analysis using LISREL 7.16 was used to assess scale dimensionality and discriminant validity; goodness-of-fit indices and t-values associated with individual items were used to identify the final set of scale items representing each construct.

ADMINISTRATION: DeCarlo and Leigh (1996) developed a $2 \times 2 \times 3$ full-factorial, between-group experimentation design in which task attraction, social attraction, and information ambiguity were manipulated to observe the effect on managerial causal attributions and other dependent measures. The questionnaire containing the measure was delivered by mail, and nonrespondents were sent a reminder postcard followed by a second questionnaire. A lottery incentive, promises of anonymity, letters of endorsement, and business reply envelopes were also used to enhance response rates. Higher scores on the scale indicated that sales managers perceived a sales representative as being a desirable, likable social partner or friend.

MAJOR FINDINGS: DeCarlo and Leigh (1996) examined the relationship between a sales manager's task and social attraction to a salesperson, manager attributions for poor performance, and managerial feedback based on those attributions in an experimental context. **Social attraction** was found to be directly linked to internal ability attributions, internal motivation attributions, and external attributions, in that sales managers were more likely to make external as opposed to internal attributions for the loss of a major account when their **social attraction** to the salesperson was high. **Social attraction** was also related to perceived decision difficulty (cognitive effort) and decision confidence, as sales managers reported having greater decision confidence, as well as less difficulty (effort), when evaluating salespeople who were less **(socially) attractive**. In the absence of mediating causal attributions, sales managers were also less likely to use coercive feedback and more likely to use nonpunitive feedback with salespeople for whom their **social attraction** was high. However, causal attributions were found to mediate the relationship between **social attraction** and the provision of coercive feedback.

REFERENCES:

DeCarlo, Thomas E. and Thomas W. Leigh (1996), "Impact of Salesperson Attraction on Sales Managers' Attributions and Feedback," *JM*, 60 (April), 47–66.

McCroskey, James C. and Thomas A. McCain (1974), "The Measurement of Interpersonal Attraction," *Speech Monographs*, 41 (August), 261–66.

SCALE ITEMS:*

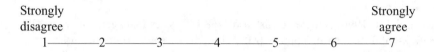

Strongly disagree — Strongly agree

1————2————3————4————5————6————7

1. I think he (she) could be a friend of mine.

2. It would be difficult to meet and talk with this person. **(r)**

3. He (she) just wouldn't fit into my circle of friends. **(r)**

4. I would like to have a friendly chat with this person.

5. We could never establish a personal friendship with each other. **(r)**

*DeCarlo and Leigh (1996) did not specifically indicate that items 2, 3, and 5 should be reversed when listing this measure in their appendix. However, closer examination of the measure suggests that these three items need to be reverse scored to maintain the integrity of the scale.

SCALE NAME: Attraction (Task)

SCALE DESCRIPTION: DeCarlo and Leigh (1996) used this five-item, seven-point Likert-type scale to measure the extent to which a salesperson is perceived to be a desirable work partner by his or her sales manager.

SCALE ORIGIN: DeCarlo and Leigh (1996) stated that the scale was based on the work of McCroskey and McCain (1974).

SAMPLES: DeCarlo and Leigh's (1996) sample consisted of 468 U.S. sales managers, of whom 289 were recruited from a *Fortune* 500 mailing equipment (ME) firm, 103 were recruited from an office equipment (OE) firm, and the final 79 individuals were drawn from a southeast sales and marketing executives (SME) mailing list. Usable responses were obtained from **218** sales managers, of whom 144 (49%) were ME managers, 55 (53.4%) were OE managers, and 19 (25.5%) were SME managers. Post hoc ANOVAS were performed for several firm-level effects to assess the compatibility of the three groups that composed the sample, and no significant differences were found.

RELIABILITY: DeCarlo and Leigh (1996) reported a coefficient alpha of **.92** for the scale.

VALIDITY: The scales used in DeCarlo and Leigh's (1996) study first were factor analyzed; those with multiple-factor solutions were orthogonally rotated, and items with loadings of .30 or lower were eliminated. Confirmatory factor analysis using LISREL 7.16 was used to assess scale dimensionality and discriminant validity; goodness-of-fit indices and t-values associated with individual items were used to identify the final set of scale items representing each construct.

ADMINISTRATION: DeCarlo and Leigh (1996) developed a $2 \times 2 \times 3$ full-factorial, between-group experimentation design in which task attraction, social attraction, and information ambiguity were manipulated to observe the effect on managerial causal attributions and other dependent measures. The questionnaire containing the measure was delivered by mail, and nonrespondents were sent a reminder postcard followed by a second questionnaire. A lottery incentive, promises of anonymity, letters of endorsement, and business reply envelopes were also used to enhance response rates. Higher scores on the scale indicated that sales managers perceived a sales representative as a desirable work partner.

MAJOR FINDINGS: DeCarlo and Leigh (1996) examined the relationship between a sales manager's task and social attraction to a salesperson, manager attributions for poor performance, and managerial feedback based on those attributions in an experimental context. **Task attraction** was found to be directly linked to internal ability attributions, internal motivation attributions, and external attributions, in that sales managers were more likely to make external as opposed to internal attributions for the loss of a major account when their **task attraction** to the salesperson was high. **Task attraction** was also related to external cognitive responses, perceived decision difficulty (cognitive effort), and decision confidence, as sales managers reported having greater decision confidence, as well as less difficulty (effort) and thought, in evaluating salespeople who were less **(task) attractive**. In the absence of mediating causal attributions, sales managers were also less likely to use coercive feedback and more likely to use nonpunitive feedback with salespeople for whom their **task attraction** was high. However, causal attributions were found to mediate the relationship between **task attraction** and the provision of coercive feedback.

#504 *Attraction (Task)*

REFERENCES:

DeCarlo, Thomas E. and Thomas W. Leigh (1996), "Impact of Salesperson Attraction on Sales Managers' Attributions and Feedback," *JM*, 60 (April), 47–66.

McCroskey, James C. and Thomas A. McCain (1974), "The Measurement of Interpersonal Attraction," *Speech Monographs*, 41 (August), 261–66.

SCALE ITEMS:*

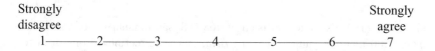

Strongly disagree — Strongly agree

1———2———3———4———5———6———7

1. I have confidence in this salesperson's ability.

2. This person is an effective problem solver.

3. He (she) appears to goof-off when in the field. **(r)**

4. If I wanted to get things done, I could depend on this person.

5. I couldn't get anything accomplished with this person. **(r)**

*DeCarlo and Leigh (1996) did not specifically indicate that items 3 and 5 should be reversed when listing this measure in their appendix. However, closer examination of the measure suggests that they need to be reverse scored to maintain the integrity of the scale.

SCALE NAME: Attractiveness (Supplier)

SCALE DESCRIPTION: Kumar, Scheer, and Steenkamp (1995) used this four-item, seven-point scale to measure dealer perceptions of the extent to which a supplier is capable of providing support and generating store traffic, sales, and profits relative to the next best supplier alternative.

SCALE ORIGIN: Kumar, Scheer, and Steenkamp (1995) adapted the first three items in the scale from Anderson and Narus (1984) and generated the final item on the basis of dealer interviews.

SAMPLES: After deleting duplications among dealerships and dealerships for which no contact person could be identified, Kumar, Scheer, and Steenkamp (1995) sampled the remaining 1640 of the 2100 new car dealers listed on a commercially purchased list for two states in the United States. Also, 1600 new car dealers were randomly selected from a list of 4000 dealers in the entire Netherlands. **Four hundred seventeen** and **289** usable responses were received from U.S. and Dutch dealers, respectively. The data were standardized separately by country to eliminate any culturally idiosyncratic patterns, then pooled for analysis.

RELIABILITY: Kumar, Scheer, and Steenkamp (1995) reported a coefficient alpha of **.87** for the scale.

VALIDITY: Evidence of the convergent validity of the measure was obtained through a confirmatory factor analysis in which all first- and second-order constructs were found to be significant.

ADMINISTRATION: Kumar, Scheer, and Steenkamp (1995) indicated that the questionnaire was originally constructed in English and then translated into Dutch. Back-translation was used to verify the accuracy of the translation. Some minor changes to item and questionnaire phrasing resulted from feedback obtained during face-to-face interviews with Dutch dealership managers. The scale was included with other measures in a self-administered survey delivered by mail to both samples. Cover letters to the U.S. sample were personalized to a specific individual, and a follow-up letter was sent to nonrespondents after four weeks. The lack of personalized cover letters and follow-up with the Dutch sample may have contributed to the lower response rate from this group. Dealers from both countries were asked to report on the automobile suppler (manufacturer or importer) whose product line accounted for the largest share of their firm's sales. Higher scores on the scale indicated that a dealer perceived its supplier as more capable of providing support and generating store traffic, sales, and profits relative to the next best alternative.

MAJOR FINDINGS: Kumar, Scheer, and Steenkamp (1995) investigated how supplier fairness affected the development of long-term relationships between relatively smaller and vulnerable new car dealers and larger and more powerful suppliers. As the **positive outcomes** provided by a supplier (relative to other alternatives) increased, so did the importance of distributive fairness in determining the quality of the relationship. At the same time, the importance of procedural fairness in determining relationship quality was found to decline when the level of **positive outcomes relative to alternatives** increased.

REFERENCES:
Anderson, James C. and James A. Narus (1984), "A Model of the Distributor's Perspective of Distributor-Manufacturer Working Relationships," *JM*, 48 (Fall), 62–74.
Kumar, Nirmalya, Lisa K. Scheer, and Jan-Benedict E.M. Steenkamp (1995a), "The Effects of Supplier Fairness on Vulnerable Resellers," *JMR*, 32 (February), 54–65.

#505 *Attractiveness (Supplier)*

SCALE ITEMS:

Current supplier   Current supplier
  is much less   is much more
    attractive   attractive
    1————2————3————4————5————6————7

How attractive is your current supplier compared to the next best alternative supplier in terms of:

1. Generating sales?

2. Generating profits?

3. Providing support and selling services?

4. Generating customer traffic?

SCALE NAME: Attractiveness (Supplier)

SCALE DESCRIPTION: Four five-point scale items that assess the level of satisfaction that a retailer perceives as existing in the best available alternative relationship with a supplier.

SCALE ORIGIN: Ping (1997) noted that the scale was first published in one of his earlier articles (Ping 1993) and used in subsequent research (Ping 1994). In developing the scale, Ping (1993) generated items on the basis of presurvey interviews with hardware retailers and a review of the relevant literature. The purification process began with nine academicians evaluating how well the items fit the construct; those misclassified by more than one judge were eliminated. The resulting measure was pretested in two different phases. The first pretest sought to clarify possible misinterpretations. Responses from 63 hardware retailers in the second pretest were used to analyze the psychometric properties of the measures using item-to-total correlations, ordered similarity coefficients, and coefficient alpha computations. The final purification of the measure was based on LISREL analysis of data provided by 288 respondents, as reported by Ping (1993). Items were deleted if the internal consistency was improved without detracting from the content validity of the measure. Tests of the discriminant and convergent validity of the measure were also undertaken, and the results were found to be satisfactory.

SAMPLES: Ping (1994, 1997) used a systematic random sampling procedure of U.S. hardware retailers to generate the 600 hardware retailers sampled in the studies reported in both 1994 and 1997. Usable responses were received from **288** and **204** respondents in 1994 and 1997, respectively. The sampling frame in both cases was taken from a hardware retailing trade publication's subscription list.

RELIABILITY: Ping (1994) did not report the specific reliability of the measure, though he noted that all measures in this study demonstrated latent variable reliabilities of .90 or higher. In the 1997 study, Ping reported a coefficient alpha of **.93**.

VALIDITY: Ping (1994, 1997) conducted a confirmatory factor analysis to test the unidimensionality and construct validity of the measure. The measure was judged to be unidimensional, and the average variance extracted demonstrated the scale's convergent and discriminatory validity. Ping (1997) also stated that the measure was content valid.

ADMINISTRATION: The scale was included with other measures as part of a self-administered questionnaire, which was delivered by mail in both of Ping's (1994, 1997) studies. Nonrespondents received multiple postcard reminders. Ping (1997) used a key informant approach, in which key informants represented a single individual, typically a manager, owner, or executive of the hardware store. Higher scores on the scale reflected a greater belief that an alternative relationship would be highly satisfactory.

MAJOR FINDINGS: In the study described in his 1994 article, Ping investigated the moderating role of satisfaction with respect to alternative supplier attractiveness and exit intentions. Using a structural equation analysis technique, Ping (1994) found that the **attractiveness of alternative suppliers** was positively associated with exit intentions for channel customers with lower levels of satisfaction. Higher levels of satisfaction negated this relationship, however, because no significant association **between alternative supplier attractiveness** and exit intentions were found. In his 1997 study, Ping proposed and empirically examined several antecedents to voice, a subject's attempts to change objectionable relationship conditions, in a business-to-business context. The results of his study indicated that the cost of exit was a second-order construct with first-order factor indicators of **alternative supplier attractiveness**, investment in the relationship, and switching costs. Increasing the cost of exit was found to increase the likelihood of voice.

#506 *Attractiveness (Supplier)*

REFERENCES:

Ping, Robert A., Jr. (1993), "The Effects of Satisfaction and Structural Constraints on Retailer Exiting, Voice, Loyalty, Opportunism, and Neglect," *JR*, 69 (Fall), 320–52.

——— (1994), "Does Satisfaction Moderate the Association Between Alternative Attractiveness and Exit Intention in a Marketing Channel?" *JAMS*, 22 (4), 364–71.

——— (1997), "Voice in Business-to-Business Relationships: Cost-of-Exit and Demographic Antecedents," *JR*, 73 (2), 261–81.

SCALE ITEMS:

1. Overall, the <u>alternative</u> wholesaler's policies would benefit my company _____ than/as the <u>current</u> wholesaler's policies. (Circle a letter)

    a. Much more   b. Slightly more   c. As much   d. Slightly less   e. Much less

2. I would be _____ satisfied with the product and service available from the <u>alternative</u> wholesaler than/as the product and service provided by the <u>current</u> wholesaler. (Circle a letter)

    a. Much more   b. Slightly more   c. As much   d. Slightly less   e. Much less

3. In general, I would be _____ satisfied with the <u>alternative</u> wholesaler than/as I am with the <u>current</u> wholesaler. (Circle a letter)

    a. Much more   b. Slightly more   c. As much   d. Slightly less   e. Much less

4. Overall, the <u>alternative</u> wholesaler would be a/an _____ company to do business with than/as the <u>current</u> wholesaler. (Circle a letter)

    a. Much more   b. Slightly more   c. As good as   d. Slightly less   e. Much less

SCALE NAME: Behavioral Intentions to Reciprocate

SCALE DESCRIPTION: Dorsch and Kelley (1994) describe this eight-item, six-point Likert-type scale as measuring purchasing executives' behavioral actions regarding repayment of a gift with respect to making larger orders, being more accessible to the salesperson, or becoming a stronger advocate of the vendor within the company.

SCALE ORIGIN: The scale is original to Dorsch and Kelley (1994), who stated that the measure was developed in accordance with procedures suggested by Churchill (1979) and Nunnally (1978). No other details of the scale development process were provided.

SAMPLES: Dorsch and Kelley (1994) sampled 1197 U.S. purchasing executives representing the ten major standard industrial classification divisions with a single questionnaire mailing. Because of mailing list restrictions, no prior notification, follow-up survey, or reminders were sent. A total of **151** usable questionnaires were received for a response rate of 12.6%. Sample respondents were predominately men (84.8%), located in the Midwest (55.2%), and employed by manufacturing firms (73.5%).

RELIABILITY: Dorsch and Kelley (1994) reported a coefficient alpha of **.95** for this measure.

VALIDITY: No specific examination of the scale's development process or validity was reported by Dorsch and Kelley (1994).

ADMINISTRATION: Dorsch and Kelley (1994) randomly assigned purchasing executives to a 3 (status of relationship) × 2 (cost of gift) × 2 (type of gift) full-factorial, between-subjects research design. On the basis of their cell assignment, respondents were given a hypothetical scenario to read that described their relationship status with a vendor and the nature of the gift provided by that vendor. The scale was part of a self-administered mail survey in which questions related to the measures of interest were answered after respondents had read the scenario. Higher scores on the scale indicated stronger intentions on the part of the purchasing executive to reciprocate the gift with larger orders, greater accessibility, or being a stronger advocate of the vendor to others in the company.

MAJOR FINDINGS: Dorsch and Kelley (1994) investigated the effect of buyer–vendor relationship status (no prior relationship, moderate relationship, or strong relationship), gift type (corporate versus personal), and gift cost (inexpensive versus expensive) on purchasing executives' perceptions of salesperson manipulation, feelings of indebtedness toward the sales representative, and intention to reciprocate vendor gifts. As levels of perceived manipulation on the part of the salesperson increased, purchasing **executives intentions to reciprocate** declined, whereas greater feelings of indebtedness toward the salesperson led to stronger **intentions to reciprocate**. The use of personal gifts resulted in lower **intentions to reciprocate** than did the offer of corporate gifts.

REFERENCES:

Churchill, Gilbert A. (1979), "A Paradigm for Developing Better Measures of Marketing Constructs," *JMR*, 16 (February), 323–32.

Dorsch, Michael J. and Scott W. Kelley (1994), "An Investigation into the Intentions of Purchasing Executives to Reciprocate Vendor Gifts," *JAMS*, 22 (4), 315–27.

Nunnally, Jum C. (1978), *Psychometric Theory*, 2nd ed. New York: McGraw-Hill.

SCALE ITEMS:

Prior to responding to the scale items, respondents read a scenario explaining the specific gift characteristic scenario and percentage of the previous year's business they had hypothetically conducted with the vendor. See Dorsch and Kelley (1994) for details of the experimental manipulation.

Strongly
disagree
1————2————3————4————5————6

Strongly
agree

1. In the future it will be easier for Chris to make an appointment with me.

2. In the future I will be more attentive during Chris's presentations.

3. In the future I will allocate more time for Chris when he calls.

4. In the future, within my organization, I will be a stronger advocate for Chris and his company.

5. In the future I will purchase larger quantities of materials from Chris.

6. In the future I will purchase a larger percentage of total materials from Chris.

7. In the future I will purchase a wider assortment of products from Chris.

8. In the future I will place a long term order with Chris.

SCALE NAME: Brand Positioning (Quality)

SCALE DESCRIPTION: Frazier and Lassar (1996) used this three-item, five-point scale to measure the extent to which a manufacturer attempts to convey to consumers that its brand has superior ability to perform its functions.

SCALE ORIGIN: The scale is original to Frazier and Lassar (1996), who generated items through personal interviews with manufacturers and retailers in the electronics, pet food, and hair care products industries. The authors examined intercorrelations among the items and dropped those that exhibited low correlations.

SAMPLES: Frazier and Lassar (1996) attempted to collect data related to 219 brands of stereo speakers from key informants who represented 209 manufacturing firms. For manufacturers with multiple brands, only those brands produced and marketed by independent divisions were treated as separate observations. A total of **85** usable questionnaires, representing brands marketed by 84 manufacturers, were returned. Of the 85 brands, 58 were home speakers, 22 were automotive speakers, and 5 were specialty speakers.

RELIABILITY: Frazier and Lassar (1996) reported a coefficient alpha of **.86** for this measure.

VALIDITY: Frazier and Lassar (1996) stated that an exploratory factor analysis was used to assess the unidimensionality and discriminant validity of the scale.

ADMINISTRATION: Three versions of the questionnaire were created by Frazier and Lassar (1996), one each for home, car, and specialty speakers. The only difference among questionnaires was the wording used to identify the different speakers. The measure was included in a self-administered mail survey; nonrespondents received a follow-up telephone call and a second mailing. Prior notification and assurances of confidentially were provided in an attempt to increase response rate. Higher scores on the scale indicated that the manufacturer was attempting to convey a quality or prestige image as a means of conveying to consumers the brand's superior ability to perform its functions.

MAJOR FINDINGS: Frazier and Lassar (1996) investigated factors influencing the distribution intensity of brands in the electronics industry. Distribution intensity declined when **brands were positioned on the basis of quality**. However, the inverse relationship between **brand positioning** and distribution intensity was weakened when contractual restrictiveness was high.

REFERENCES:
Frazier, Gary L. and Walfried M. Lassar (1996), "Determinants of Distribution Intensity," *JM*, 60 (October), 39–51.

SCALE ITEMS:

Low end   High end

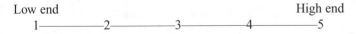

1————————2————————3————————4————————5

How do you position the brand on the following product characteristics?

1. Prestige or image of the brand?

2. Product performance?

3. Overall product quality?

#509 *Brand Sales Volume*

SCALE NAME: Brand Sales Volume

SCALE DESCRIPTION: Frazier and Lassar (1996) used two scales, one with two items and five points and one with one item and seven points, to measure a brand's U.S. sales volume in dollars and units relative to the competition.

SCALE ORIGIN: The scale is original to Frazier and Lassar (1996), who generated items through personal interviews with manufacturers and retailers in the electronics, pet food, and hair care products industries. The authors examined intercorrelations among the items and dropped those that exhibited low correlations.

SAMPLES: Frazier and Lassar (1996) attempted to collect data related to 219 brands of stereo speakers from key informants who represented 209 manufacturing firms. For manufacturers with multiple brands, only brands produced and marketed by independent divisions were treated as separate observations. A total of **85** usable questionnaires, representing brands marketed by 84 manufacturers, were returned. Of the 85 brands, 58 were home speakers, 22 were automotive speakers, and 5 were specialty speakers.

RELIABILITY: Frazier and Lassar (1996) reported a coefficient alpha of **.85** for this measure.

VALIDITY: No specific examination of scale validity was reported by Frazier and Lassar (1996) for this measure.

ADMINISTRATION: Three versions of the questionnaire were created by Frazier and Lassar (1996), one each for home, car, and specialty speakers. The only difference among questionnaires was the wording used to identify the different speakers. The measure was included in a self-administered mail survey; nonrespondents received a follow-up telephone call and a second mailing. Prior notification and assurances of confidentially were provided in an attempt to increase response rate. Higher scores on the scale indicated that the manufacturer rated its brand as having high dollar and unit sales in the United States relative to its competition.

MAJOR FINDINGS: Frazier and Lassar (1996) investigated factors influencing the distribution intensity of brands in the electronics industry. Results indicated that the higher the level of **brand sales** relative to the competition, the greater was the distribution intensity of the brand.

REFERENCES:
Frazier, Gary L. and Walfried M. Lassar (1996), "Determinants of Distribution Intensity," *JM*, 60 (October), 39–51.

SCALE ITEMS:

Low   High

1————2————3————4————5

Relative to your competition, the *sales volume* for your brand in the domestic market:

1. Calculated in *US$* is...

2. Calculated in *US units* is...

Low   High

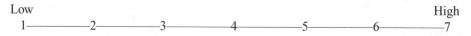

1————2————3————4————5————6————7

3. What was the approximate sales volume (in US$) of your brand in 1991?

SCALE NAME: Capability Control (Information)

SCALE DESCRIPTION: Challagalla and Shervani (1996) used this five-item, five-point Likert-type summated ratings scale to measure employee perceptions of the degree to which supervisors set standards or goals for selling skills, monitored and evaluated selling skills, and provided feedback related to selling skill improvement. This measurement assesses selling skills, such as communication, sales presentation delivery, and negotiation, rather than sales activities (e.g., number of calls, reports, call rate) or sales outcomes (market share or sales volume).

SCALE ORIGIN: Challagalla and Shervani (1996) indicated that some of the items used in this measure were adapted from Jaworski and MacInnis's (1989) study. In modifying the measure, the authors undertook extensive pretesting and purification procedures in four sequential stages involving both academic experts and industrial salespeople.

SAMPLES: Challagalla and Shervani (1996) surveyed 302 field salespeople employed in the industrial products divisions of two *Fortune* 500 companies. Usable responses were received from **270** salespeople, the majority of whom were men and college educated.

RELIABILITY: Challagalla and Shervani (1996) reported a coefficient alpha of **.90** for the scale.

VALIDITY: The nine dimensions of control measured in the study were evaluated by Challagalla and Shervani (1996) using confirmatory factor analysis. This scale demonstrated acceptable levels of convergent and discriminant validity and was found to be unidimensional.

ADMINISTRATION: Challagalla and Shervani (1996) indicated that the scale was self-administered, along with many other measures, in a questionnaire delivered directly to the homes of salespersons. Prior to administration, each salesperson received a note from a senior sales executive in his or her organization alerting him or her to the study. Business reply envelopes, cover letters promising confidentiality, and two follow-up attempts were used to increase response rate. Higher scores on the scale indicated that sales managers were perceived as being highly likely to set standards for selling skills, such as negotiation or sales presentation delivery, and monitor, evaluate, and provide feedback related to a salesperson's skills.

MAJOR FINDINGS: Challagalla and Shervani (1996) extended existing conceptual work related to marketing control systems by (1) investigating the effect of information and reinforcement on salesperson job outcomes, (2) separating the global behavior control construct into activity control and capability control, and (3) examining the casual mechanisms by which controls operate. **Capability information** was negatively related to supervisory role ambiguity, which indicates that supervisors who provide goal information and feedback are more likely to convey their expectations effectively to salespeople. However, the provision of **capability information** was shown to reduce customer role ambiguity, which indicates that such information motivates salespeople to better understand customer role expectations. Contrary to expectations, a supervisor's sharing of **capability information** had no direct influence on salesperson performance. Finally, **capability information** was positively related to satisfaction with a supervisor.

REFERENCES:

Challagalla, Goutam N. and Tasadduq A. Shervani (1996), "Dimensions and Types of Supervisory Control: Effects on Salesperson Performance and Satisfaction," *JM*, 60 (January), 89–105.

Jaworski, Bernard J. and Deborah J. MacInnis (1989), "Marketing Jobs and Management Controls: Toward a Framework," *JMR*, 26 (November), 406–19.

#510 *Capability Control (Information)*

SCALE ITEMS:
Instructions to respondents:
In answering the following questions, please *focus* ONLY on *selling skills/abilities* (e.g., negotiation, communication, presentation, etc.)

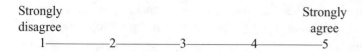

Strongly   Strongly
disagree   agree
   1————————2————————3————————4————————5

1. My manager has standards by which my selling skills are evaluated.

2. My supervisor periodically evaluates the selling skills I use to accomplish a task (e.g., how I negotiate).

3. My manager provides guidance on ways to improve selling skills and abilities.

4. My supervisor evaluates how I make sales presentations and communicate with customers.

5. My manager assists by suggesting why using a particular sales approach may be useful.

SCALE NAME: Capability Control (Punishments)

SCALE DESCRIPTION: Challagalla and Shervani (1996) used this three-item, five-point Likert-type summated ratings scale to measure employee perceptions of the degree to which supervisors administered punishments, such as warnings, reprimands, and probationary status, contingent on the selling skills demonstrated by the salesperson. In this context, selling skills refer to a salesperson's capability in customer communication, sales presentation delivery, and negotiation rather than sales activities (e.g., number of calls, reports, call rate) or sales outcomes (market share or sales volume).

SCALE ORIGIN: Challagalla and Shervani (1996) indicated that some of the items used in this measure were adapted from Podsakoff and colleagues' (1984) study. In modifying the measure, Challagalla and Shervani (1996) undertook extensive pretesting and purification procedures in four sequential stages involving both academic experts and industrial salespeople. Punishment-focused items tying pay and incentives to selling skills were deleted after an exploratory factor analysis. The authors noted that this action was consistent with pretest feedback, which indicated that the use of pay and incentives to reinforce capability goals was minimal.

SAMPLES: Challagalla and Shervani (1996) surveyed 302 field salespeople employed in the industrial products divisions of two *Fortune* 500 companies. Usable responses were received from **270** salespeople, the majority of whom were men and college educated.

RELIABILITY: Challagalla and Shervani (1996) reported a coefficient alpha of **.78** for the scale.

VALIDITY: The nine dimensions of control measured in the study were evaluated by Challagalla and Shervani (1996) using confirmatory factor analysis. This scale demonstrated acceptable levels of convergent and discriminant validity and was found to be unidimensional.

ADMINISTRATION: Challagalla and Shervani (1996) indicated that the scale was self-administered, along with many other measures, in a questionnaire delivered directly to the homes of salespersons. Prior to administration, each salesperson received a note from a senior sales executive in his or her organization alerting him or her to the study. Business reply envelopes, cover letters promising confidentiality, and two follow-up attempts were used to increase response rate. Higher scores on the scale indicated that sales managers were perceived as being more likely to punish salespeople who have inferior selling skills.

MAJOR FINDINGS: Challagalla and Shervani (1996) extended existing conceptual work related to marketing control systems by (1) investigating the effect of information and reinforcement on salesperson job outcomes, (2) separating the global behavior control construct into activity control and capability control, and (3) examining the casual mechanisms by which controls operate. No relationship was found between **capability punishments** and supervisory role ambiguity; however, **capability punishments** lowered customer role ambiguity. The authors speculated that such punishments helped salespeople by focusing their attention on attaining a certain skill proficiency that should enhance their ability to gather information from customers, thus lowering ambiguity. As expected, **capability punishments** were negatively related to both salesperson performance and satisfaction with a supervisor.

REFERENCES:

Challagalla, Goutam N. and Tasadduq A. Shervani (1996), "Dimensions and Types of Supervisory Control: Effects on Salesperson Performance and Satisfaction," *JM*, 60 (January), 89–105.

#511 *Capability Control (Punishments)*

Podsakoff, Philip M., William D. Todor, Richard A. Grover, and Vandra L. Huber (1984), "Situational Moderators of Leader Reward and Punishment Behaviors: Fact or Fiction?" *Organizational Behavior and Human Performance*, 34 (1), 21–63.

SCALE ITEMS:
Instructions to respondents:
In answering the following questions, please *focus* ONLY on *selling skills/abilities* (e.g., negotiation, communication, presentation, etc.)

Strongly disagree — Strongly agree

1————2————3————4————5

1. I would receive an informal warning if my manager is not pleased with my selling abilities.

2. I would receive a formal reprimand if my supervisor is not pleased with my selling skills and abilities.

3. I would be put on probation if my manager is not happy with my selling abilities.

SCALE NAME: Capability Control (Rewards)

SCALE DESCRIPTION: Challagalla and Shervani (1996) used this three-item, five-point Likert-type summated ratings scale to measure employee perceptions of the degree to which supervisors administered rewards contingent on the selling skills demonstrated by the salesperson. In this context, selling skills refer to a salesperson's capability in customer communication, sales presentation delivery, and negotiation rather than sales activities (e.g., number of calls, reports, call rate) or sales outcomes (market share or sales volume).

SCALE ORIGIN: Challagalla and Shervani (1996) indicated that some of the items used in this measure were adapted from Podsakoff and colleagues' (1984) study. In modifying the measure, Challagalla and Shervani (1996) undertook extensive pretesting and purification procedures in four sequential stages involving both academic experts and industrial salespeople. Reward-focused items tying pay and incentives to selling skills were deleted after an exploratory factor analysis. The authors noted that this action was consistent with pretest feedback, which indicated that the use of pay and incentives to reinforce capability goals was minimal.

SAMPLES: Challagalla and Shervani (1996) surveyed 302 field salespeople employed in the industrial products divisions of two *Fortune* 500 companies. Usable responses were received from **270** salespeople, the majority of whom were men and college educated.

RELIABILITY: Challagalla and Shervani (1996) reported a coefficient alpha of **.77** for the scale.

VALIDITY: The nine dimensions of control measured in the study were evaluated by Challagalla and Shervani (1996) using confirmatory factor analysis. This scale demonstrated acceptable levels of convergent and discriminant validity and was found to be unidimensional.

ADMINISTRATION: Challagalla and Shervani (1996) indicated that the scale was self-administered, along with many other measures, in a questionnaire delivered directly to the homes of salespersons. Prior to administration, each salesperson received a note from a senior sales executive in his or her organization alerting him or her to the study. Business reply envelopes, cover letters promising confidentiality, and two follow-up attempts were used to increase response rate. Higher scores on the scale indicated that sales managers were perceived as being more likely to reward salespeople who have superior selling skills.

MAJOR FINDINGS: Challagalla and Shervani (1996) extended existing conceptual work related to marketing control systems by (1) investigating the effect of information and reinforcement on salesperson job outcomes, (2) separating the global behavior control construct into activity control and capability control, and (3) examining the casual mechanisms by which controls operate. **Capability rewards** were negatively related to supervisory role ambiguity, which suggests that rewards motivate salespeople to expend effort in understanding a supervisor's expectations. Contrary to expectations, **capability rewards** had no direct influence on either salesperson performance or customer role ambiguity. Finally, **capability rewards** were positively related to satisfaction with a supervisor.

REFERENCES:

Challagalla, Goutam N. and Tasadduq A. Shervani (1996), "Dimensions and Types of Supervisory Control: Effects on Salesperson Performance and Satisfaction," *JM*, 60 (January), 89–105.

Podsakoff, Philip M., William D. Todor, Richard A. Grover, and Vandra L. Huber (1984), "Situational Moderators of Leader Reward and Punishment Behaviors: Fact or Fiction?" *Organizational Behavior and Human Performance*, 34 (1), 21–63.

#512 *Capability Control (Rewards)*

SCALE ITEMS:
Instructions to respondents:
In answering the following questions, please *focus* ONLY on *selling skills/abilities* (e.g., negotiation, communication, presentation, etc.)

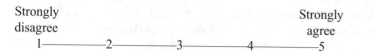

Strongly
disagree

Strongly
agree

1————2————3————4————5

1. Assignment to better territories or accounts depends on how good my selling skills are.

2. I would be commended if I improved my selling skills.

3. Promotion opportunities depend on how good my selling skills and abilities are.

SCALE NAME: Career Success

SCALE DESCRIPTION: Anderson and Robertson (1995) used this five-item, seven-point Likert-type scale to measure the level of broker achievement over time in both absolute and relative terms.

SCALE ORIGIN: Anderson and Robertson (1995) developed the measure used in this study. A detailed construct description was constructed on the basis of a though review of the trade and academic literature. Multiple interviews with brokers, sales managers, and trade association officials were used to generate scale items thought to tap the construct. These items were administered to 208 brokers and factor analyzed to test for unidimensionality. Reliability assessments were also used to purify the measure.

SAMPLES: Anderson and Robertson (1995) mailed questionnaires to the homes of 420 brokers whose names were supplied by cooperating firms; **201** usable responses were obtained. To be evaluated, some hypotheses required the use of archival data regarding the actual sales of house brands made by salespeople. One firm, which provided **150** of the respondents in this study, agreed to supply this information. The authors stated that the respondent demographics closely matched those achieved in a large-scale survey of readers conducted by a nationally distributed trade magazine.

RELIABILITY: Anderson and Robertson (1995) reported a coefficient alpha of **.84** for this measure.

VALIDITY: The convergent validity of the measure was examined by Anderson and Robertson (1995) using the archival and survey data available from the 150-person sample. A strong positive correlation was found between the self-reported career success measure scores and records of recent annual commission income, providing evidence of convergent validity.

ADMINISTRATION: Anderson and Robertson (1995) included the measure as part of a larger self-administered mail questionnaire. A summary of the results was offered in exchange for respondent cooperation. Higher scores on the scale indicated that salespersons viewed their achievements as higher both in absolute and relative terms.

MAJOR FINDINGS: Anderson and Robertson (1995) investigated the relationship between factors thought to influence the sale of house brands by multiline salespeople. Results of the analysis using the full sample indicated that salespeople who are more dependent on the firm and perceive lower mobility risks are more **successful in their careers.** The perception of a customer loyalty hazard also decreases with **career success.** Finally, using the 150-member sample, analysis revealed that salespeople with **successful careers** are more likely to adopt house brands.

REFERENCES:
Anderson, Erin and Thomas S. Robertson (1995), "Inducing Multiline Salespeople to Adopt House Brands," *JM*, 59 (April), 16–31.

SCALE ITEMS:

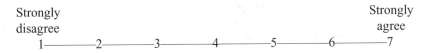

Strongly disagree — 1————2————3————4————5————6————7 — Strongly agree

1. I am one of the most successful brokers I know.

2. I am one of the highest earners in my firm.

3. Other brokers see me as an example of how much money there is to be made in this business.

4. Other brokers consider my career as a broker to be highly successful.

5. I make out all right, but I'm not in the top earnings' category in my firm. **(r)**

SCALE NAME: Centralization

SCALE DESCRIPTION: A five-item, five-point Likert-type scale measuring the extent to which actions and decisions must await approval by superiors in an organization.

SCALE ORIGIN: Menon, Jaworski, and Kohli (1997) reported that the centralization scale used here was developed by Aiken and Hage (1968).

SAMPLES: Using the *Dun and Bradstreet Million Dollar Directory* as the sampling frame, Menon, Jaworski, and Kohli (1997) selected for initial contact every other company name from among the top 1000 companies by sales revenues. Participation from multiple strategic business units (SBU) within an organization was requested. A total of 102 companies agreed to participate, and ultimately, responses representing **222** SBUs were obtained from marketing and nonmarketing executives.

RELIABILITY: Menon, Jaworski, and Kohli (1997) reported a **.88** alpha reliability coefficient.

VALIDITY: No specific examination of scale validity was presented by Menon, Jaworski, and Kohli (1997).

ADMINISTRATION: The 206 marketing and 187 nonmarketing executives identified by participating corporations were directly contacted by Menon, Jaworski, and Kohli (1997). Initial contact was followed by a self-administered mail questionnaire, and a follow-up questionnaire was sent three weeks later to nonrespondents. Most of the marketing (79.6%) and nonmarketing (70%) executives contacted provided data for the study. When both nonmarketing and marketing executives from a single SBU responded, their scores were averaged to provide a single score for the construct. A higher score on the centralization scale indicated that members of the organization lacked decision-making authority.

MAJOR FINDINGS: Menon, Jaworski, and Kohli (1997) investigated the role of organizational factors that affect interdepartmental interactions and the resulting impact on product quality. **Centralization** of decision-making authority was investigated as a potential antecedent of interdepartmental interactions using regression analysis. Results suggested that when decision-making authority was not shared among individuals in the organization, interdepartmental conflict increases and interdepartmental connectedness declines.

REFERENCES:

Aiken, Michael and Jerald Hage (1968), "Organizational Independence and Intra-Organizational Structure," *American Sociological Review*, 33, 912–30.

Menon, Ajay, Bernard J. Jaworski, and Ajay K. Kohli (1997), "Product Quality: Impact of Interdepartmental Interactions," *JAMS*, 25 (3), 187–200.

SCALE ITEMS:

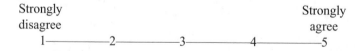

Strongly disagree — Strongly agree

1————2————3————4————5

1. There can be little action taken here until a supervisor approves a decision.

2. A person who wants to make his or her own decision would be quickly discouraged here.

3. Even small matters have to be referred to someone higher up for a final answer.

4. I have to ask my boss before I do almost anything.

5. Any decision I make has to have my boss's approval.

SCALE NAME: Centralization

SCALE DESCRIPTION: Heide and Weiss (1995) used this three-item, seven-point Likert-type scale to measure the extent to which decision-making authority for buying-related activities is concentrated at higher levels of the organization.

SCALE ORIGIN: Heide and Weiss (1995) stated that the specific items used in the scale are based on items originally developed by John and Martin (1984) and McCabe (1987).

SAMPLES: Pretests of the questionnaire were conducted with two different small groups of previous workstation buyers. In the final study, Heide and Weiss (1995) drew a random sample of 900 firms from Installed Technology International's list of firms that had recently purchased workstations. Key informants were identified from this list and contacted by telephone. Of these, 466 agreed to participate in the study and were sent a mail questionnaire. Follow-up telephone calls and a second mailing resulted in **215** usable questionnaires being returned. Industries represented by respondents included computers (31.4%), manufacturing (22.4%), medical (6.2%), services (15.2%), and other (24.8%).

RELIABILITY: Heide and Weiss (1995) reported a coefficient alpha of **.67** for this scale.

VALIDITY: Heide and Weiss (1995) initially evaluated the measure on the basis of item-to-total correlations and exploratory factor analysis. Confirmatory factor analysis was then used to establish unidimensionality. Evidence of discriminant validity was provided by a series of chi-square tests on the respective factor correlations.

ADMINISTRATION: The measure was included in a self-administered mail survey. Heide and Weiss (1995) instructed respondents to answer all questions in the context of their organization's most recent workstation purchase. Higher scores on the centralization scale indicated that the authority for purchasing-related decision making is concentrated at higher organizational levels.

MAJOR FINDINGS: Heide and Weiss (1995) investigated how buyers working in high-technology markets approached decisions in the consideration and choice stages of the purchase process. Specifically, factors influencing whether buyers included new vendors at the consideration stage and whether they ultimately switched to a new vendor at the choice stage were investigated. Heide and Weiss (1995) reported that highly **centralized** buying processes limited the consideration of new vendors and reduced the likelihood that a new vendor would be selected over an existing supplier. However, in those circumstances in which consideration sets were open to new vendors, the **centralization** of buying authority tended to favor the selection of new vendors over existing suppliers at the choice stage.

REFERENCES:
Heide, Jan B. and Allen M. Weiss (1995), "Vendor Consideration and Switching Behavior for Buyers in High-Technology Markets," *JM*, 59 (July), 30–43.
John, George and John Martin (1984), "Effects of Organizational Structure of Marketing Planning on Credibility and Utilization of Plan Output," *JMR*, 21 (May), 170–83.
McCabe, Donald L. (1987), "Buying Group Structure: Constriction at the Top," *JM*, 51 (October), 89–98.

#515 *Centralization*

SCALE ITEMS:

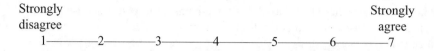

Strongly disagree — Strongly agree

1————2————3————4————5————6————7

1. To a large extent, the outcome of this process was determined by higher-level management.

2. Most aspects of this process were subject to approval by higher-level management (levels above purchasing or eventual product users).

3. Little action could be taken in this process without supervision.

SCALE NAME: Centralization

SCALE DESCRIPTION: The scale assesses the degree to which an organization restricts decision-making authority to higher hierarchical levels in the organization. Kelley, Longfellow, and Malehorn (1996) used an eight-item version of the scale in five- and six-point Likert formats. The version used by Ferrell and Skinner (1988) had five six-point Likert-type items that were phrased to measure the extent to which the employee of one company reports that he or she must seek approval from another company before making decisions.

SCALE ORIGIN: The original version of the scale was by John (1984).

SAMPLES: In Ferrell and Skinner's (1988) study, a self-administered questionnaire was mailed to a sample of 1500 researchers. The frame used was the membership list of the Marketing Research Association. The corporate classification was supplemented by the American Marketing Association membership list. From a single mailing, **550** usable questionnaires were returned. In addition, 52 questionnaires were returned by the post office, resulting in a 37.9% response rate. Thirty-seven percent of the respondents were data subcontractors. More women (86%) than men (14%) represented this type of organization. Respondents employed by research firms were more balanced (54% women and 46% men). Finally, in corporate research departments, 53% of respondents were women, and 47% were men.

In the first sample, Kelley, Longfellow, and Malehorn (1996) surveyed all 122 customer contact personnel employed by a bank located in the Midwest United States; **113** usable responses were obtained, primarily from tellers (88) and customer service representatives (25). A stratified random sample of 381 insurance agents of a large regional insurance company working in a single state was also undertaken. In this second sample, 239 agents representing 75 of the 77 different agencies associated with the company responded, but complete information was obtained from only **185** of these agents.

RELIABILITY: An alpha of **.82** was reported for the scale by Ferrell and Skinner (1988). Kelley, Longfellow, and Malehorn (1996) calculated coefficient alphas of **.727** and **.837** for the measure in Samples 1 and 2, respectively.

VALIDITY: Ferrell and Skinner (1988) assessed the scales using confirmatory factor analysis. Constructs that did not load in excess of .30 were deleted. All items were significant indicators of the construct.

Kelley, Longfellow, and Malehorn (1996) did not specifically discuss the validity of the measures.

ADMINISTRATION: In the study by Ferrell and Skinner (1988), the scale was included in a larger self-administered questionnaire. The scale was apparently scored such that lower scores reflected greater centralization.

In Sample 1 of Kelley, Longfellow, and Malehorn's (1996) study, the measure was included in a questionnaire administered to customer contact bank employees during regularly scheduled weekly meetings held in 15 branch offices. In Sample 2, the scale was included as part of a self-administered questionnaire that was delivered by mail. All responses were converted to z-scores prior to analysis because of the difference in response formats. Higher scores on the scale reflected a higher degree of centralized decision making in the organization.

MAJOR FINDINGS: Three models were examined by Ferrell and Skinner (1988): one for data subcontractors, one for marketing research firms, and one for corporate research departments. The dependent variable was ethical conduct. **Centralization** was found to be related to higher perceived ethical behavior in research firms but was not related significantly to ethical behavior in the other two models.

Kelley, Longfellow, and Malehorn (1996) investigated the antecedents to service employees' use of routine, creative, and deviant discretion in the banking and insurance industries. None of the hypothesized relationships between **centralization** and deviant discretion, creative discretion, or routine discretion was significant. However, contrary to expectations, **centralization** was positively, rather than negatively, related to creative discretion.

COMMENTS: See also John and Martin (1984).

REFERENCES:

Ferrell, O.C., and S.J. Skinner (1988), "Ethical Behavior and Bureaucratic Structure in Marketing Research Organizations," *JMR*, 25 (February), 103–109.

John, George (1984), "An Empirical Investigation of Some Antecedents of Opportunism in a Marketing Channel," *JMR*, 21 (August), 278–89.

——— and J. Martin (1984), "Effects of Organizational Structure of Marketing Planning on Credibility and Utilization of Plan Output," *JMR*, 21 (May), 170–183.

Kelley, Scott W., Timothy Longfellow, and Jack Malehorn (1996), "Organizational Determinants of Service Employees' Exercise of Routine, Creative, and Deviant Discretion," *JR*, 72 (2), 135–57.

SCALE ITEMS:*

Sample 1:

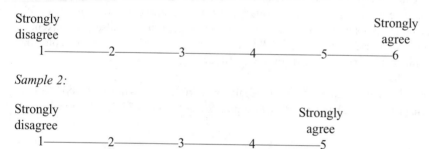

Sample 2:

1. I have the final say in decisions regarding my day-to-day activities. **(r)**

2. Major decisions made by individuals (agents) in this company require the company's approval.

3. In this company, individuals (agents) must refer even quite small matters to someone higher up for the final answer.

4. Dealings in this company are subject to a lot of rules and procedures stating how various aspects of jobs are to be done.

5. Individuals (Agents) of this company have to ask company reps before they do almost anything.

6. Individuals (Agents) of this company can take very little action on the own until the company or its reps approve it.

7. My company makes the major decisions affecting this business and tells its associates (agents) after the fact.

8. Individuals (Agents) of this company are left alone to make day-to-day decisions for themselves. **(r)**

*This is the version of the scale used by Kelley, Longfellow, and Malehorn (1996). Ferrell and Skinner (1988) used items similar to 2–6 and a six-point response format.

SCALE NAME: Centralization (Gasoline Station Decisions)

SCALE DESCRIPTION: Dahlstrom and Nygaard (1995) used this five-point scale to measure the extent to which decision-making authority was concentrated at the refinery or franchiser level for Polish, German, and Norwegian oil and gas retailer respondents. Different combinations of items were used to represent the construct for each country studied.

SCALE ORIGIN: Dahlstrom and Nygaard (1995) adapted the scale from the work of Dwyer and Oh (1987). Item-to-total correlations were examined using a country-by-country analysis of the data; items correlating at .25 or lower were dropped from the measure for a particular country. For the Polish sample, items 1, 2, and 3 were used to represent the construct. Only items 3 and 4 were retained following an analysis of the German data. For the Norwegian sample, items 1, 3, and 5 were used to represent the construct.

SAMPLES: Norwegian, German (formerly East German), and Polish oil and gas retailers were sampled by Dahlstrom and Nygaard (1995). Of the 432 Norwegian service station managers working in the retail network of a single oil refiner who were surveyed, **216** usable responses were obtained. **Forty** of the 44 service station managers in Poland, and **29** of the 50 Leipzig-area dealers in the former East Germany also provided usable data.

RELIABILITY: Dahlstrom and Nygaard (1995) reported coefficient alphas of **.67, .54,** and **.72** for the Polish, German, and Norwegian samples, respectively. However, it should be noted that in the German sample, only two items were used to represent the construct, and thus, the reliability reported is simply the correlation of those items.

VALIDITY: Dahlstrom and Nygaard (1995) did not specifically examine the validity of the measure.

ADMINISTRATION: Dahlstrom and Nygaard (1995) included the scale with other measures as part of a self-administered survey that was delivered by mail to the Norwegian sample. The survey was administered in person by college students to oil and gas retailers in the Polish and German samples. In each case, the questionnaire was translated into the focal language and back-translated into English, typically by university faculty in each country. Higher scores on the scale indicated that the oil and gas retailer perceived having more control over various decisions related to the running of his or her business, whereas lower scores indicated a higher degree of centralized decision making at the refinery or franchiser level.

MAJOR FINDINGS: Dahlstrom and Nygaard (1995) investigated various antecedents to and consequences of interpersonal trust in new and mature market economies using data collected in Norway, Poland, and the former East Germany. **Centralization** was not found to be a significant antecedent to interpersonal trust for any country. In the Polish sample, **centralized decision making**, coupled with uncertainty, raised performance, whereas in the Norwegian sample, the interaction between uncertainty and **centralized decision making** damaged performance. No significant interaction effects between uncertainty and **centralized decision making** were found for the German sample.

REFERENCES:
Dahlstrom, Robert and Arne Nygaard (1995), "An Exploratory Investigation of Interpersonal Trust in New and Mature Market Economies," *JR*, 71 (4), 339–61.
Dwyer, F. Robert and Sejo Oh (1987), "Output Sector Munificence Effects on the Internal Political Economy of Marketing Channels," *JMR*, 24 (3), 347–68.

#517 *Centralization (Gasoline Station Decisions)*

SCALE ITEMS: To what extent do you influence the following decisions?

No influence   Complete control

1————2————3————4————5————6————7

1. Supply of gasoline and mineral oil products.

2. Advertising, sales concepts, and marketing.

3. Opening hours at the station.

4. The number of company products and services sold at the station.

5. Pricing of products sold at the station.

SCALE NAME: Centralization (New Product Decisions)

SCALE DESCRIPTION: Ayers, Dahlstrom, and Skinner (1997) used this five-item, seven-point Likert-type scale to measure the extent to which decision making related to the new product development (NPD) process is concentrated within a few positions.

SCALE ORIGIN: Ayers, Dahlstrom, and Skinner (1997) indicated that the scale was adapted from measures used in the research of Gupta, Raj, and Wilemon (1987) and Spekman and Stern (1979).

SAMPLES: Ayers, Dahlstrom, and Skinner (1997) collected data on 19 NPD projects undertaken by a major U.S. computer manufacturer. Seven project members from each NPD team were selected to participate in the study, five of whom were from R&D, and the remaining two were from marketing. Of the 132 questionnaire booklets distributed, **115** usable surveys were returned.

RELIABILITY: Ayers, Dahlstrom, and Skinner (1997) reported a coefficient alpha of **.75** for the scale.

VALIDITY: An exploratory factor analysis on all items constituting the scales was used to verify the unidimensionality of the measures. No items were dropped on the basis of item-to-total correlations or an analysis of the factor structure. Ayers, Dahlstrom, and Skinner (1997) next subjected the measures to a confirmatory factor analysis to assess their construct validity. Again, no items were deleted on the basis of this analysis. The discriminant validity of the measures was also assessed by confirmatory factory analysis and was found to be acceptable.

ADMINISTRATION: Ayers, Dahlstrom, and Skinner (1997) included the scale with other measures as part of a self-administered questionnaire booklet that was apparently distributed to respondents at their place of employment. A cover letter explaining the study purpose and promises of anonymity accompanied the survey. The questionnaires distributed to R&D and marketing personnel were identical, except that R&D personnel responded to questions about their relationship with marketing and vice versa. Divisional managers designated the project for which responses were sought. Higher scores on the scale indicated that NPD-related decision making was more concentrated within the firm.

MAJOR FINDINGS: Ayers, Dahlstrom, and Skinner (1997) examined the influence of integration among marketing and R&D, managerial controls, and relational norms on new product success. Structural equation modeling was used to test the hypotheses. **Centralization** was found to both enhance the level of integration between marketing and R&D and reduce the level of relational norms. Contrary to expectations, **centralization** increased, rather than decreased, the level of perceived relationship effectiveness between R&D and marketing.

REFERENCES:

Ayers, Doug, Robert Dahlstrom, and Steven J. Skinner (1997), "An Exploratory Investigation of Organizational Antecedents to New Product Success," *JMR*, 34 (February), 107–16.

Gupta, Ashok K., S.P. Raj, and David Wilemon (1987), "Managing the R&D Marketing Interface," *Research Management*, 30 (March/April), 38–43.

Spekman, Robert E. and Louis W. Stern (1979), "Environmental Uncertainty and Buying Group Structure: An Empirical Investigation," *JM*, 43 (Spring), 54–64.

#518 *Centralization (New Product Decisions)*

SCALE ITEMS:
Please indicate your level of agreement with the following.

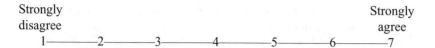

Strongly
disagree

Strongly
agree

1————2————3————4————5————6————7

1. When product-related decisions had to be made for which no rules or procedures existed, I had authority to make the decision. **(r)**

2. When a product-related problem arose, I had to refer the problem to someone higher up in the organization for the answer.

3. When an unusual product-related situation was encountered, I generally went ahead without checking with my supervisor. **(r)**

4. Very few actions were taken without the help of a supervisor.

5. Even small matters had to be referred to someone higher up for a final answer.

SCALE NAME: Centralization (Sales Force)

SCALE DESCRIPTION: Sohi, Smith, and Ford (1996) described this five-item, five-point Likert-type scale as measuring the degree of independence salespeople have with respect to their decision-making authority.

SCALE ORIGIN: Sohi, Smith, and Ford (1996) reported that these items were adapted from the scale used by Hage and Aiken (1969).

SAMPLES: A sample of **30** salespeople from a major Midwestern U.S. corporation were used to pretest the questionnaire. Manufacturing firms in standard industrial classification codes 20–39 were randomly selected from a commercial mailing list, and 1650 salespeople employed by those firms were chosen to serve as the sampling frame. Of the 1542 questionnaires delivered to valid addresses, **230** completed surveys were returned, for a response rate of 14.9%. Respondents were predominately college educated (84%), married (84%), and men (89%) with a median age of 37.5 years and who had held their current sales position an average of 5.8 years. Industries represented included food products, pharmaceuticals, chemical and allied products, rubber and plastic products, electronics and computers, appliances, and audio-visual products. Sohi, Smith, and Ford (1996) reported that nonresponse bias was tested by comparing early and late responders on key variables; no significant differences were found, which suggests that nonresponse bias may not have been a problem.

RELIABILITY: Sohi, Smith, and Ford (1996) reported a coefficient alpha of **.84** for this measure.

VALIDITY: Evidence of discriminant validity was provided by a nested model confirmatory factor analysis that demonstrated that the latent-trait correlations between constructs significantly differed from 1. Sohi, Smith, and Ford (1996) stated that confirmatory factor analysis also provided satisfactory evidence of the unidimensionality of the measure.

ADMINISTRATION: Prior to data collection, the questionnaire was pretested on a small sample of salespeople. Sohi, Smith, and Ford (1996) stated that several items and the questionnaire format were revised on the basis of the pretest results. In the final study, the measure was part of a self-administered mail survey. Cover letters and postage-paid reply envelopes accompanied each questionnaire, and a copy of the survey results was offered as an incentive to participate. Reminder letters were sent three and five weeks after the initial questionnaire mailing. Lower scores on the centralization scale indicated that salespeople enjoyed a greater degree of authority and independence in their decision making.

MAJOR FINDINGS: Sohi, Smith, and Ford (1996) investigated how salespeople's role perceptions, satisfaction, and performance were affected when the sales force is shared across multiple divisions within a company. Results indicated that, as **centralization** increases, the corresponding increase in role ambiguity, which otherwise occurs when a sales force is shared across divisions, declines. Similarly, the negative impact on work satisfaction experienced when sales forces are shared across divisions was lessened when **centralization** increased.

REFERENCES:
Hage, Jerald and Michael Aiken (1969), "Routine Technology, Social Structure and Organizational Goals," *Administrative Science Quarterly*, 14 (September), 366–76.
Sohi, Ravipreet S., Daniel C. Smith, and Neil M. Ford (1996), "How Does Sharing a Sales Force Between Multiple Divisions Affect Salespeople?" *JAMS*, 24 (3), 195–207.

#519 *Centralization (Sales Force)*

SCALE ITEMS:

Strongly   Strongly
disagree   agree
   1————————2————————3————————4————————5

1. To operate effectively, I need greater decision-making authority.

2. Decision-making authority is highly centralized in our organization.

3. In almost every case, I have to obtain my immediate supervisor's approval before taking action.

4. Even small matters related to my job have to be referred to someone else.

5. I am discouraged from making my own decisions.

SCALE NAME: Challenge

SCALE DESCRIPTION: Strutton, Pelton, and Lumpkin (1995) described this three-item, five-point Likert-type scale as a negative indicator of the degree to which safety, stability, and predictability are deemed important to respondents.

SCALE ORIGIN: Strutton, Pelton, and Lumpkin (1995) reported that these items were used and reported as the *security scale* by Hahn (1966).

SAMPLES: Using a sampling frame generated from the telephone directories of two metropolitan statistical areas, Strutton, Pelton, and Lumpkin (1995) first identified a stratified random sample of 1000 organizations likely to have industrial salespeople. A systematic random sampling procedure was then used to identify 450 organizations for telephone contact. Of the 450 individuals contacted, 374 organizational sales managers agreed to allow one company salesperson to be randomly selected to participate in the study. These salespeople returned **322** acceptable questionnaires for an 86% response rate. Seventy-one percent of the sample was 40 years of age or younger, 62% were men, and 76% had incomes of $35,000 or more. All levels of sales experience were adequately represented: 29% of the sample had less than four years experience, 35% has four to ten years experience, and 36% had more than ten years of sales experience.

RELIABILITY: Strutton, Pelton, and Lumpkin (1995) reported a coefficient alpha of **.69** for this measure.

VALIDITY: No specific examination of the scale's validity was reported by Strutton, Pelton, and Lumpkin (1995).

ADMINISTRATION: Strutton, Pelton, and Lumpkin (1995) stated that the scale was part of a self-administered questionnaire that was returned by mail. In addition to answering questions measuring the personality characteristics of challenge, self-determination, and involvement in self and surroundings, respondents described the most stressful job-related situation experienced during the preceding three months. The manner in which they coped with the stressful episode was assessed using Strutton and Lumpkin's (1994) sales-domain-relevant version of the Ways of Coping Checklist. With respect to the challenge measure, the mean values on the summated scale were used to determine the point at which one-third of the sample scored below or above the middle third. Strutton, Pelton, and Lumpkin (1995) then classified 96 salespeople as low-challenge and 132 as high-challenge. Higher scores on the challenge scale indicated a greater likelihood that changes would be perceived as stimulating challenges to growth.

MAJOR FINDINGS: Strutton, Pelton, and Lumpkin (1995) investigated the relationship between how salespeople cope with job stress and the three personality characteristics of challenge, self-determination, and involvement in self and surroundings. Three problem-focused coping tactics, directed problem solving, self-control, and taking responsibility, demonstrated significantly positive associations with the degree to which salespeople valued **challenge**, whereas two emotion-focused coping tactics, seeking social distance and mental distancing, were negatively associated with **challenge**.

REFERENCES:

Hahn, Michael E. (1966), *California Life Goals Evaluation Schedule*. Palo Alto, CA: Western Psychological Services.

Strutton, David, Lou E. Pelton, and James R. Lumpkin (1995), "Personality Characteristics and Salespeople's Choice of Coping Strategies," *JAMS*, 23 (2), 132–40.

#520 *Challenge*

Strutton, David, and James R. Lumpkin (1994), "Problem and Emotion-Focused Coping Dimensions and Sales Presentation Effectiveness," *JAMS*, 22 (1), 28–37.

SCALE ITEMS:

Strongly   Strongly
disagree   agree

1. I easily start in on new tasks.

2. Uncertainty does not bother me.

3. Once in a while, I take a chance on something that isn't sure.

SCALE NAME: Character/Motives (Partner)

SCALE DESCRIPTION: Smith and Barclay (1997) used this five-item, seven-point Likert-type scale to measure partners' perceptions of each other's character and motives. Character refers to the degree to which a person is perceived as being reliable and dependable. Motives refers to the extent to which the partner is perceived as having ulterior motives that guide his or her behavior.

SCALE ORIGIN: Smith and Barclay (1997) indicated that the constructs used in their study were operationalized with a mix of original and adapted scale items generated from the conceptual definition of the constructs, a review of the literature, field interviews, and pretest results. Measures of character and motives were originally conceptualized as separate constructs, but a preliminary analysis indicated that a model in which these dimensions were combined fit the data better. Each of the final items representing this measure passed the extensive preliminary analysis of item reliability and validity described by the authors.

SAMPLES: Smith and Barclay (1997) collected dyadic self-report data in two stages. The sponsor sample was composed of 338 sales representatives working for the Canadian subsidiaries of two multinational companies serving the computer industry. Forty percent of the 338 employees who were randomly selected from employee lists returned completed surveys. Using the names and contact information of relationship partners volunteered by these respondents, the authors then sampled 135 dyadic partners. A total of **103** usable paired responses were obtained.

RELIABILITY: Smith and Barclay (1997) reported coefficient alphas of **.78** for this measure in both the sponsor and the partner model.

VALIDITY: Smith and Barclay (1997) reported extensive testing of the reliability, unidimensionality, and convergent and discriminant validity of the measures used in their study. LISREL and confirmatory factor analysis were used to demonstrate that the scale satisfied each of these standards, though some items from the measures as originally proposed were eliminated in the process.

ADMINISTRATION: Smith and Barclay (1997) included the scale with other measures as part of a self-administered survey that was delivered by internal company mail to sales representatives and by regular U.S. mail to the dyadic partners. E-mail follow-ups were used to increase survey response rate. Half of the sales representatives were instructed to consider a customer situation in the prior six months in which they had had some success with a selling partner, whereas the other half was to told to choose a situation in which they had had little or no success. Participants then responded to questions about the partner, their relationship, and the organization in the context of this situation. Higher scores on the scale indicated greater mutual trust between partners, in that partners perceived each other as reliable, dependable, honest, and not prone to taking action on the basis of ulterior motives.

MAJOR FINDINGS: Smith and Barclay (1997) developed and tested two research models explaining selling partner relationship effectiveness. The first examined four organizational differences from the sponsor's (salesperson's) perspective, and the second examined these same differences from the partner's perspective. In both models, greater perceived differences in the reputations of partner firms, partner job stability, strategic horizons, and goals/control systems led to lower evaluations of the **character and motive** component of mutual perceived trustworthiness.

REFERENCES:
Smith, J. Brock and Donald W. Barclay (1997), "The Effects of Organizational Differences and Trust on the Effectiveness of Selling Partner Relationships," *JM*, 61 (January), 3–21.

#521 *Character/Motives (Partner)*

SCALE ITEMS:*

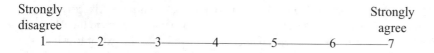

Strongly disagree 1————2————3————4————5————6————7 Strongly agree

1. S/he is not very reliable. **(r)**

2. Sometimes s/he does not follow through on commitments made to me. **(r)**

3. S/he is among the most honest people I know.

4. S/he would use me if it benefited him/her. **(r)**

5. S/he often has ulterior motives. **(r)**

*All of the items in this scale were conceptualized at the individual level and then aggregated to the relationship level by taking the square root of the product of the individual response by the sales representative and partner.

SCALE NAME: Coercion (Supplier's Use)

SCALE DESCRIPTION: Gassenheimer and Ramsey (1994) used this six-item, eight-point scale to measure the level of pressure suppliers applied to dealers in an attempt to control or change important decisions affecting the sale of the supplier's products.

SCALE ORIGIN: The scale is original to Gassenheimer and Ramsey (1994), who generated items on the basis of a review of the literature and in-depth interviews with dealers. Details of the scale purification process were not discussed by Gassenheimer and Ramsey (1994).

SAMPLES: Gassenheimer and Ramsey (1994) sampled key informants of 939 office furniture/systems dealers. The specific person surveyed was identified as being responsible for the evaluation and selection of office furniture/systems suppliers. Of those contacted, **324** key informants returned usable responses.

RELIABILITY: Gassenheimer and Ramsey (1994) calculated separate reliabilities for data pertaining to each of three suppliers evaluated by respondents, as well as an overall reliability for the measure using the pooled data. The alphas for suppliers A, B, and C were **.78, .75,** and **.72,** respectively. A coefficient alpha of **.79** was calculated for the combined data.

VALIDITY: Gassenheimer and Ramsey (1994) did not report an examination of the scale's validity.

ADMINISTRATION: Gassenheimer and Ramsey (1994) included the scale with other measures as part of a self-administered survey that was delivered by mail; nonrespondents received a postcard reminder as well as a second survey mailing. Each dealer was asked to specify its primary (A), secondary (B), and tertiary (C) suppliers and answer questions for each of these suppliers on an individual basis. Higher scores on the scale indicated that a dealer rated a supplier as applying more pressure on it in an attempt to control or change important decisions affecting the sale of the supplier's products.

MAJOR FINDINGS: Gassenheimer and Ramsey (1994) examined the influence of mutual dependence and power–dependence imbalances on primary, secondary, and tertiary supplier–dealer relationships in the office systems/furniture industry. Primary suppliers engaged in greater **coercive influence attempts** by applying significantly higher levels of pressure on dealers than did secondary or tertiary suppliers; similarly, secondary suppliers' **coercive influence attempts** resulted in significantly more pressure than did tertiary suppliers. **Coercive influence attempts** exerted by primary suppliers negatively affected the dealer's satisfaction with that supplier but did not significantly influence satisfaction with secondary and tertiary suppliers.

REFERENCES:
Gassenheimer, Jule B. and Rosemary Ramsey (1994), "The Impact of Dependence on Dealer Satisfaction: A Comparison of Reseller-Supplier Relationships," *JR*, 70 (3), 253–66.

SCALE ITEMS:*
How much pressure did they (your three main suppliers) place on you to change your decisions?

No pressure   Major pressure

0————1————2————3————4————5————6————7

1. Accept new products/lines introduced by the manufacturer.

2. Alter the decision to buy from competing suppliers.

3. Increase your annual minimum volume quotas suggested or requested.

4. Accept unsolicited participation by the manufacturer in selling new accounts.

5. Restrict your implied sales territory for selling the manufacturer's product.

6. Alter the size, investments, and/or appearance of your showroom(s).

*Although Gassenheimer and Ramsey (1994) did not provide the verbatim instructions for this scale, their discussion indicates that they were similar to those listed here.

SCALE NAME: Commitment (Compliance)

SCALE DESCRIPTION: Brown, Lusch, and Nicholson (1995) used this three-item, seven-point Likert-type scale to measure the degree to which a dealer's efforts on behalf of the manufacturer are directly linked to expectations of achieving a favorable response from that manufacturer. Brown, Lusch, and Nicholson (1995) referred to this measure as *"compliance with supplier's wishes"*.

SCALE ORIGIN: Brown, Lusch, and Nicholson (1995) stated the scale was adapted from O'Reilly and Chatman (1986). The measure was refined on the basis of pretest interviews with farm equipment dealers.

SAMPLES: Brown, Lusch, and Nicholson (1995) mailed a questionnaire to 1052 farm equipment dealers located in Iowa, Nebraska, and Kansas. Usable responses were received from a single key informant, typically an owner or manager, for **203** of the dealerships. The sample differed from the population in general in that dealers in this sample reported having significantly higher sales of their primary brand and a significantly smaller workforce.

RELIABILITY: Brown, Lusch, and Nicholson (1995) reported a coefficient alpha of **.67** for this measure.

VALIDITY: The construct validity of the scale was examined using confirmatory factor analysis. Brown, Lusch, and Nicholson (1995) reported that the model achieved an acceptable goodness of fit after two items, "Our private views about the manufacturer are different than those we express publicly" and "In order for our dealership to get rewarded by the manufacturer, it is necessary for us to express the right attitude," were dropped from the measure. However, the reliability coefficient of .674 fell slightly below the .70 standard. A confirmatory factor analysis of all measures used in the study was also undertaken to assess the overall construct validity of the measures. The measurement model's goodness of fit was acceptable, and all construct reliabilities exceeded .70, with the exception of instrumental commitment (.674).

ADMINISTRATION: The scale was included with other measures as part of a self-administered survey that was delivered by mail. Brown, Lusch, and Nicholson (1995) instructed respondents to focus on their relationship with the supplier of the one brand of new farm equipment that accounted for the highest dollar sales in their dealership. Higher scores on the scale indicated that dealer efforts on behalf of the manufacturer and compliance with their wishes were highly dependent on expectations of achieving a favorable response from that manufacturer.

MAJOR FINDINGS: Brown, Lusch, and Nicholson (1995) examined the impact of a supplier's use of various types of power on manufacturer and dealer performance and on the dealer's commitment to the channel relationship. A dealer's **compliance** with supplier wishes was the sole indicator for the instrumental commitment construct used in this study. Structural equation modeling was used to test the study's hypotheses. Results indicated that greater use of mediated power by a manufacturer resulted in greater dealer instrumental commitment, whereas the use of nonmediated power decreased the instrumental commitment of the dealer to the relationship. When manufacturers had more power in the channel relationship, higher levels of instrumental commitment resulted in lower dealer evaluations of manufacturer performance.

REFERENCES:
Brown, James R., Robert F. Lusch, and Carolyn Y. Nicholson (1995), "Power and Relationship Commitment: Their Impact on Marketing Channel Member Performance," *JR*, 71 (4), 363–92.

O'Reilly, Charles, III and Jennifer Chatman (1986), "Organizational Commitment and Psychological Attachment: The Effects of Compliance, Identification, and Internalization on Prosocial Behavior," *Journal of Applied Psychology*, 71 (3), 492–99.

SCALE ITEMS:

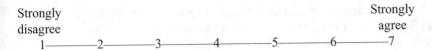

Strongly disagree — Strongly agree
1———2———3———4———5———6———7

1. Unless we are rewarded for it in some way, we see no reason to expend extra effort on behalf of this manufacturer.

2. How hard we work for the manufacturer is directly linked to how much we are rewarded.

3. Bargaining is necessary in order to obtain favorable terms of trade in dealing with this manufacturer.

SCALE NAME: Commitment (Distributor to Relationship with Manufacturer)

SCALE DESCRIPTION: This four-item, seven-point Likert-type scale was used by Andaleeb (1996) to measure respondents' overall willingness to make a greater investment in a relationship and their desire to continue the relationship.

SCALE ORIGIN: Andaleeb (1996) apparently adapted his commitment operationalization from a study conducted by Morgan and Hunt (1994). The reliability of the measure and item-to-total correlations were assessed as part of the purification process and deemed to be acceptable.

SAMPLES: A convenience sample of **72** sales and purchasing managers with considerable negotiation experience participated in a 2 × 2 between-group factorial design experiment. Andaleeb (1996) randomly assigned subjects to treatment conditions.

RELIABILITY: Andaleeb (1996) calculated a coefficient alpha of **.92** for the scale.

VALIDITY: Andaleeb (1996) reported conducting a factor analysis to assess the unidimensionality of the measures used in his study. A single factor with item loadings greater than .8 was extracted for each scale, which suggests that the measures were unidimensional. A confirmatory factor analysis of the measurement model provided some evidence of validity, because the standardized coefficients were significantly different from 0. However, the goodness-of-fit index of .87 was somewhat below the recommended .90 level, though the chi-square and root mean squared residual were found to be satisfactory.

ADMINISTRATION: Andaleeb (1996) provided subjects with information about a contrived manufacturer (supplier)–distributor (buyer) relationship in which the level of trust and dependence on the supplier were manipulated. After reading this information, subjects were instructed to write down their perceptions of the relationship and read a scenario suggesting that an upcoming meeting would consider methods of strengthening the company's growth through cultivation of existing suppliers. Subjects were instructed to indicate whether they thought such ties would be appropriate with the focal supplier. The satisfaction, commitment, dependence, and trust measures were then administered. Higher scores on the scale indicated a stronger willingness on the part of respondents to continue and invest in the manufacturer–distributor relationship.

MAJOR FINDINGS: Andaleeb's (1996) experiment investigated the effect of high and low levels of supplier trust and supplier dependence on satisfaction and commitment for a hypothetical dyadic exchange relationship. After confirming that the trust and dependence manipulation had occurred, Andaleeb (1996) found that both greater trust in and greater dependence on a supplier lead to higher levels of buyer **commitment to the supplier**. However, the level of **commitment** exhibited toward a supplier was found to be much more sensitive to different levels of trust when dependence was low compared with when it was high, thereby indicating the presence of a significant interaction effect between trust and dependence.

REFERENCES:

Andaleeb, Syed Saad (1996), "An Experimental Investigation of Satisfaction and Commitment in Marketing Channels: The Role of Trust and Dependence," *JR*, 72 (1), 77–93.

Morgan, Robert M. and Shelby D. Hunt (1994), "The Commitment-Trust Theory of Relationship Marketing," *JM*, 58 (July), 20–38.

SCALE ITEMS:*

Strongly   Strongly
disagree   agree
1———2———3———4———5———6———7

1. My company should further strength its ties with X.

2. My company should consider committing itself to a longer term involvement with X for its supplies of liqueur.

3. My company's relationship with X should be broken off. **(r)**

4. My company should not switch to a new supplier yet.

*As used by Andaleeb (1996), the company name of the respondent was used at the beginning of each item, and the name of the focal manufacturer was used in items 1, 2, and 3.

SCALE NAME: Commitment (Internalization)

SCALE DESCRIPTION: Brown, Lusch, and Nicholson (1995) used this five-item, seven-point Likert-type scale to measure the degree to which a dealer's attachment or commitment to a manufacturer is due to shared behavior or values between the organizations. Brown, Lusch, and Nicholson (1995) refer to this measure as *dealer's internalization of supplier norms and values.*

SCALE ORIGIN: Brown, Lusch, and Nicholson (1995) stated the scale was adapted from O'Reilly and Chatman (1986). The measure was refined on the basis of pretest interviews with farm equipment dealers.

SAMPLES: Brown, Lusch, and Nicholson (1995) mailed a questionnaire to 1052 farm equipment dealers located in Iowa, Nebraska, and Kansas. Usable responses were received from a single key informant, typically an owner or manager, for **203** of the dealerships. The sample differed from the population in general in that dealers in this sample reported having significantly higher sales of their primary brand and a significantly smaller workforce.

RELIABILITY: Brown, Lusch, and Nicholson (1995) reported a coefficient alpha of **.78** for this measure.

VALIDITY: The construct validity of the scale was examined using confirmatory factor analysis. Brown, Lusch, and Nicholson (1995) reported that the model achieved an acceptable goodness of fit and reliability coefficient. A confirmatory factor analysis of all measures used in the study was also undertaken to assess the overall construct validity of the measures. The measurement model's goodness of fit was acceptable, and all construct reliabilities exceeded .70, with the exception of instrumental commitment (.674).

ADMINISTRATION: The scale was included with other measures as part of a self-administered survey that was delivered by mail. Brown, Lusch, and Nicholson (1995) instructed respondents to focus on their relationship with the supplier of the one brand of new farm equipment that accounted for the highest dollar sales in their dealership. Higher scores on the scale indicated that dealer commitment to the manufacturer was due to greater perceptions of shared values, norms, and behaviors between organizations.

MAJOR FINDINGS: Brown, Lusch, and Nicholson (1995) examined the impact of a supplier's use of various types of power on manufacturer and dealer performance and on the dealer's commitment to the channel relationship. **The internalization aspect of supplier commitment to a manufacturer** was one of two first-order indicators of the normative commitment construct. Structural equation modeling was used to test the study's hypotheses. Results indicated that greater use of mediated power by a manufacturer resulted in greater dealer instrumental commitment and lower dealer normative commitment to the channel relationship. The negative relationship between mediated power and normative commitment was stronger when the dealer had more power in the relationship or power was balanced. Conversely, the use of nonmediated power increased the normative commitment of the dealer to the relationship. The higher the dealer's normative commitment to a manufacturer, the better were the evaluations of manufacturer performance, particularly when dealers had more power in the relationship.

REFERENCES:

Brown, James R., Robert F. Lusch, and Carolyn Y. Nicholson (1995), "Power and Relationship Commitment: Their Impact on Marketing Channel Member Performance," *JR*, 71 (4), 363–92.

O'Reilly, Charles, III and Jennifer Chatman (1986), "Organizational Commitment and Psychological Attachment: The Effects of Compliance, Identification, and Internalization on Prosocial Behavior," *Journal of Applied Psychology*, 71 (3), 492–99.

SCALE ITEMS:

Strongly   Strongly
disagree   agree
1———2———3———4———5———6———7

1. Our attachment to this manufacturer is primarily based on the similarity of our values and those of the manufacturer.

2. The reason we prefer this manufacturer to others is because of what it stands for, its values.

3. During the past year, our dealership's values and those of the manufacturer have become more similar.

4. What this manufacturer stands for is important to our dealership.

5. If the values of this manufacturer were different, our dealership would not be as attached to this manufacturer.

SCALE NAME: Commitment (New Product Success)

SCALE DESCRIPTION: Song and Parry (1997) used this three-item, eleven-point Likert-type scale to measure the degree to which there were people in the firm who were dedicated to the success of the project.

SCALE ORIGIN: The scale was adapted by Song and Parry (1997) from the work of Cooper (1979). Song and Parry (1997) modified scale items on the basis of a review of the literature, pilot studies, and information obtained from 36 in-depth case study interviews conducted with both Japanese and U.S. firms. The items for all scales used by Song and Parry (1997) were evaluated by an academic panel composed of both Japanese and U.S. business and engineering experts; following revisions, the items were judged by a new panel composed of academicians and new product development (NPD) managers. The authors report extensive pretesting of both the Japanese and U.S. versions of the questionnaire.

SAMPLES: Song and Parry (1997) randomly sampled 500 of the 611 firms trading on the Tokyo, Osaka, and Nagoya stock exchanges that had been identified as developing at least four new physical products since 1991. Usable responses pertaining to **788** new product development projects were obtained from 404 Japanese firms. The U.S. sampling frame was taken from companies listed in the *High-Technology Industries Directory*. Of the 643 firms that had introduced a minimum of four new physical products since 1990, 500 firms were randomly sampled (stratified by industry to match the Japanese sample), and 312 U.S. firms provided data on **612** NPD projects, of which 312 were successes and 300 were failures.

RELIABILITY: Song and Parry (1997) reported a coefficient alpha of **.52** for this scale in the Japanese sample and **.65** in the U.S. sample.

VALIDITY: The extensive pretesting and evaluation of the measure with academicians and NPD managers provided strong evidence of the face validity of the measure. The authors did not specifically report any other examination of scale validity.

ADMINISTRATION: The self-administered questionnaire containing the scale was originally developed in English; the Japanese version was prepared using the parallel-translation/double-translation method. Following minor revisions to the questionnaire made on the basis of pretests with bilingual respondents and case study participants, the Japanese sample received a survey packet containing cover letters in both English and Japanese, two Japanese-language questionnaires, and two international postage-paid reply envelopes. Survey packets delivered to U.S. firms were similar, except no Japanese cover letter was included and the surveys were in English. Various incentives, four follow-up letters, and multiple telephone calls and faxes were used to increase the response rate for both samples. Song and Parry (1997) indicated that respondents were asked to answer one questionnaire in the context of a successful new product project introduced after 1991 and one in the context of a new product project that had failed. Higher scores on the scale indicated that individuals existed in the firm who were highly dedicated to the success of the project.

MAJOR FINDINGS: Song and Parry (1997) conceptualized and tested a model of strategic, tactical, and environmental factors thought to influence new product success using data collected from both Japanese and U.S. firms. In both the Japanese and U.S. samples, a high level of **internal commitment** to a project was found to strengthen the relationship between product differentiation and relative product performance. The level of **internal commitment** was also found to be positively related to all five stages of the NPD process.

COMMENTS: The low reliability of the measure indicates that further development and testing may be warranted prior to using this measure again, particularly in Japan.

REFERENCES:

Cooper, Robert G. (1979b), "The Dimensions of Industrial New Product Success and Failure," *JM*, 43 (Summer), 93–103.

Song, X. Michael and Mark E. Parry (1997b), "A Cross-National Comparative Study of New Product Development Processes: Japan and the United States," *JM*, 61 (April), 1–18.

SCALE ITEMS:

Directions: To what extent does each statement listed below correctly describe this selected successful project? Please indicate your degree of agreement or disagreement by circling a number from zero (0) to ten (10) on the scale to the right of each statement. Here: 0 = strongly disagree, 10 = strongly agree, and numbers between 0 and 10 indicate various degrees of agreement or disagreement.

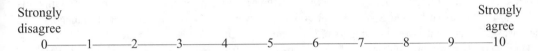

Strongly
disagree

Strongly
agree

0——1——2——3——4——5——6——7——8——9——10

1. This product was strongly supported by senior management throughout the entire development process.

2. A clearly identified individual was an activist in promoting this product's development throughout the product development and the introduction cycle.

3. We were not confident about the commercial success of the product. **(r)**

SCALE NAME: Commitment (Organizational)

SCALE DESCRIPTION: The scale measures an employee's self-reported identification and involvement with a particular organization. It is intended to capture more of the *attitudinal* component of commitment rather than the *behavioral* part and represents something more than passive loyalty (Mowday, Steers, and Porter 1979). The typical format is 15 items and a seven-point Likert-type response scale.

SCALE ORIGIN: The scale was developed by Porter and his colleagues (Mowday, Steers, and Porter 1979; Porter et al. 1974). The article by Mowday, Steers, and Porter (1979) subsumes the earlier study and reports on the testing of the scale with 2563 employees who worked in a variety of jobs in nine different organizations. In general, the scale showed evidence of high internal consistency (average alphas of .90); satisfactory stability (e.g., two month test–retest correlation, r = .72); and acceptable (though far from ideal) convergent, discriminant, and predictive validities. Another version of the scale that only used the nine positive items had alphas ranging from .84 to .90 in samples of three different employee types.

SAMPLES: Good, Page, and Young (1996) collected their data from a major department store with units throughout the Southern United States. Usable responses were received from **383** retail managers. The sample was primarily entry-level managers (73.2%) and women (70%).

Data were gathered by Michaels and colleagues (1988) from two groups. Questionnaires were distributed to full-line salespeople of an industrial building materials manufacturer, and usable questionnaires were returned by **215** salespeople. The second sample was of industrial buyers randomly selected from the National Association of Purchasing Management. Usable surveys were returned by **330** buyers.

Michaels and Dixon (1994) sent questionnaires to two groups: full-line sales representatives of an industrial building materials manufacturer and members of the National Association of Purchasing Management. Usable responses were received from **215** of the sales reps. The sample was geographically dispersed throughout the U.S., 52% were college educated, and almost all were men (99%). The purchasing manager sample was composed of **1005** usable responses. These respondents mainly worked for small- to medium-sized organizations, were mostly men (82%), and 42% were college educated.

The study by Sager (1994) collected data from salespeople who worked for a national manufacturer of branded consumer products. The number of usable responses was apparently **225**. The sample were predominately men (>90%) and college educated (95%) and had an average age of 24 years.

Siguaw, Brown, and Widing (1994) mailed 1644 questionnaires trying to reach salespeople working for companies in the document imaging industry. After two mailings, **278** usable responses were received. The sample were mostly men (81%) and college educated (71.5%) and had an average age of 40.8 years.

RELIABILITY: Good, Page, and Young (1996) reported alphas of **.91** and **.90** for entry- and upper-level retail mangers, respectively. Alphas of **.90** were reported by Michaels and colleagues (1988) for both the salesperson and buyer samples. Michaels and Dixon (1994) reported alphas of **.90** and **.91** for the sales and purchasing samples, respectively. The alpha for the nine-item version of the scale used by Sager (1994) was **.90**. Siguaw, Brown, and Widing (1994) reported an alpha of **.88** for the scale.

VALIDITY: No specific examination of scale validity was discussed in any of the studies. However, the dimensionality of the scale was tested by Sager (1994), who reported that the items loaded on two factors. Nine of the items appeared to measure *affective commitment*, and the remaining six items seemed to relate more to *intention to quit*.

ADMINISTRATION: Each of the studies used the scale as part of a larger self-administered instrument, with return of the questionnaire by mail common to all of the studies. Higher scores on the scale suggested that employee respondents reported high involvement in their organizations, whereas lower scores indicated that they had little loyalty or identification.

MAJOR FINDINGS: The study by Good, Page, and Young (1996) expanded and tested a model of organizational turnover for two levels of management. For both manager groups, it was found that role conflict had a direct negative effect on **organizational commitment**.

The purpose of the study by Michaels and colleagues (1988) was to examine the impact of organizational formalization on several job-related attitudes. Among the significant findings was that higher levels of commitment were related to lower levels of role ambiguity, role conflict, and work alienation for both the salesperson and buyer samples.

Michaels and Dixon (1994) investigated the influence of three potential moderators on role stress–job outcome relationships. Despite expectations, job tenure was not found to be a significant moderator of the relationship between role ambiguity and **organizational commitment** or role conflict and **organizational commitment**. This lack of significance occurred for both samples.

A model of salespeople's job stress was developed and tested by Sager (1994). Job stress was found to have a significant but weak negative impact on **organizational commitment**.

Siguaw, Brown, and Widing (1994) tested a model of the influence of a firm's orientation and that of its salespeople on various job attitudes of the sales force. Among the findings was that the market orientation of the firm had a strong positive effect on a salesperson's **organizational commitment**, whereas role ambiguity and conflict had negative and weaker impacts on it.

REFERENCES:

Good, Linda K., Thomas J. Page Jr., and Clifford E. Young (1996), "Assessing Hierarchical Differences in Job-Related Attitudes and Turnover Among Retail Managers," *JAMS*, 24 (2), 148–56.

Mowday, Richard T., Richard M. Steers, and Lyman W. Porter (1979), "The Measurement of Organizational Commitment," *Journal of Vocational Behavior*, 14 (April), 224–47.

Michaels, Ronald E., William L. Cron, Alan J. Dubinsky, and Eric A. Joachimsthaler (1988), "Influence of Formalization on the Organizational Commitment and Work Alienation of Salespeople and Industrial Buyers," *JMR*, 25 (November), 376–83.

——— and Andrea L. Dixon (1994), "Sellers and Buyers on the Boundary: Potential Moderators of Role Stress-Job Outcome Relationships," *JAMS*, 22 (1), 62–73.

Porter, Lyman, W., Richard M. Steers, Richard T. Mowday, and Paul V. Boulian (1974), "Organizational Commitment, Job Satisfaction, and Turnover Among Psychiatric Technicians," *Journal of Applied Psychology*, 19 (1), 603–609.

Sager, Jeffrey K. (1994b), "A Structural Model Depicting Salespeople's Job Stress," *JAMS*, 22 (1), 74–84.

Siguaw, Judy A., Gene Brown, and Robert E. Widing II (1994), " The Influence of the Market Orientation of the Firm on Sales Force Behavior and Attitudes," *JMR*, 31 (February), 106–16.

SCALE ITEMS:*

Directions: Listed below are a series of statements that represent possible feelings that individuals might have about the company or organization for which they work. With respect to your own feelings about the particular organization for which you are now working please indicate the degree of your agreement or disagreement with each statement by checking one of the seven alternatives below for each statement.

Strongly disagree	Moderately disagree	Slightly disagree	Neither disagree not agree	Slightly agree	Moderately agree	Strongly agree
1	2	3	4	5	6	7

1. I am willing to put in a great deal of effort beyond that normally expected in order to help this organization be successful.

2. I talk up this organization to my friends as a great organization to work for.

3. I feel very little loyalty to this organization. **(r)**

4. I would accept almost any type of job assignment in order to keep working for this organization.

5. I find that my values and the organization's values are very similar.

6. I am proud to tell others that I am part of this organization.

7. I could just as well be working for a different organization as long as the type of work was similar. **(r)**

8. This organization really inspires the very best in me in the way of job performance.

9. It would take very little change in my present circumstances to cause me to leave this organization. **(r)**

10. I am extremely glad that I chose this organization to work for over others I was considering at the time I joined.

11. There's not too much to be gained by sticking with this organization indefinitely. **(r)**

12. Often I find it difficult to agree with this organization's policies on important matters relating to its employees. **(r)**

13. I really care about the fate of this organization.

14. For me this is the best of all possible organizations for which to work.

15. Deciding to work for this organization was a definite mistake on my part. **(r)**

Good, Page, and Young (1996): 1–15; 7-point
Michaels et al. (1988): 1–15; 7-point.
Michaels and Dixon (1994): 1–15; 7-point
Sager (1994): 1, 2, 4–6, 8, 10, 13, 14; 5-point
Siguaw, Brown, and Widing (1994): 1–15; 7-point

*The directions shown are those used with the scale by Mowday, Steers, and Porter (1979).

SCALE NAME: Commitment (Organizational)

SCALE DESCRIPTION: Ganesan and Weitz (1996) used this six-item, seven-point Likert-type scale to measure the affective commitment of a buyer toward an organization. Ganesan and Weitz (1996) referred to this measure as *affective commitment* in their article.

SCALE ORIGIN: Ganesan and Weitz (1996) adapted the scale items from the shortened version of organizational commitment scale originally developed by Mowday, Porter, and Steers (1982).

SAMPLES: Ganesan and Weitz (1996) effectively sampled approximately 1500 retail buyers, divisional merchandise managers, general merchandise managers, and senior merchandise officers whose names appeared on a national list of department, specialty, and discount chain store employees. Usable responses were obtained from **207** respondents.

RELIABILITY: Ganesan and Weitz (1996) reported a coefficient alpha of **.86** for the scale.

VALIDITY: All items that composed the measures used by Ganesan and Weitz (1996) were subjected to a confirmatory factor analysis to assess the unidimensionality of the measures. Of the nine items that composed the shortened organizational commitment scale, only six loaded on the affective commitment construct during the process, and the remaining three items were dropped. Scales demonstrating unidimensionality were then tested for discriminant and convergent validity using LISREL 8.10. The overall model fit was good, demonstrating a goodness-of-fit index of .96, confirmatory fit index of .99, root mean squared error of approximation of .02, and standardized root mean square residual of .06, as well as a nonsignificant chi-square.

ADMINISTRATION: Ganesan and Weitz (1996) included the scale with other measures as part of a self-administered survey that was delivered by mail. Higher scores on the scale indicated that a buyer had a greater affective commitment toward the organization.

MAJOR FINDINGS: Ganesan and Weitz (1996) investigated the impact of various staffing policies on the attitudes and behavior of retail buyers. Buyers' perceptions of promotion opportunities and level of intrinsic motivation significantly influenced their **affective commitment to the organization**. Contrary to predications, neither salary nor incentive compensation was significantly related to a buyer's **affective commitment to the firm**.

REFERENCES:
Ganesan, Shankar and Barton A. Weitz (1996), "The Impact of Staffing Policies on Retail Buyer Job Attitudes and Behaviors," *JR*, 72 (1), 31–56.
Mowday, Richard T., Lyman W. Porter, and Richard M. Steers (1982), *Employee-Organizational Linkages.* New York: Academic Press.

SCALE ITEMS:

Strongly   Strongly
disagree   agree

1————2————3————4————5————6————7

1. I am proud to be part of this organization.

2. I enjoy discussing this organization with people outside it.

3. I really care about the fate of this organization.

4. I am glad that I chose to work for this organization.

5. My values are similar to those of the organization.

6. I am willing to put extra effort beyond expected to make this organization successful.

SCALE NAME: Commitment (Organizational)

SCALE DESCRIPTION: The scale measures the extent to which an employee reports feeling a strong sense of personal identification with an organization and is dedicated to it. The original scale had eight items (Meyer and Allen 1984); as used by Maltz and Kohli (1996) in a marketing context, the scale had six items and a five-point Likert-type format.

SCALE ORIGIN: The scale used by Maltz and Kohli (1996) is a modification of one constructed by Meyer and Allen (1984). Meyer and Allen (1984) viewed organizational commitment as having two components: affective and behavioral. They thought these two components had been confounded in previous studies and developed scales to measure them separately. In two samples, the scale for the affective part (the scale reviewed here) was found to have internal consistency reliability of .88 and .84. The two studies also provided some evidence of the scale's convergent and discriminant validity.

A subsequent study by McGee and Ford (1987) examined the psychometric quality of the two scales. They confirmed that the affective scale had high internal consistency ($\alpha = .88$) and was unidimensional, though one of the original eight items did not exhibit a strong loading on the factor. (This item and another were <u>not</u> used in Maltz and Kohli's [1996] version of the scale reviewed here.)

SAMPLES: The study by Maltz and Kohli (1996) gathered data from middle-level managers working for firms that made high-tech industrial equipment. Through various means, 1061 nonmarketing managers at 270 strategic business units were mailed questionnaires. Usable responses were obtained from **788** managers. The bulk of the respondents were rather evenly spread over three departments: manufacturing, R&D, and finance.

RELIABILITY: An alpha of **.83** was reported for the six-item version of the scale used by Maltz and Kohli (1996).

VALIDITY: No examination of the scale's validity was reported by Maltz and Kohli (1996).

ADMINISTRATION: In the study by Maltz and Kohli (1996), the scale was part of a larger mail survey instrument that was self-administered. Higher scores on the scale were interpreted as meaning that respondents were expressing high levels of the affective type of organizational commitment.

MAJOR FINDINGS: Maltz and Kohli (1996) examined the antecedents and consequences of market intelligence dissemination across functional boundaries. Among the many findings was that the intelligence receiver's **organizational commitment** had a positive influence on dissemination frequency but did not affect trust in the sender of the intelligence.

COMMENTS: The mean and standard deviation for the scale scores in Maltz and Kohli's (1996) study were 3.76 and .80, respectively.

REFERENCES:

Maltz, Elliot and Ajay K. Kohli (1996), "Market Intelligence Dissemination Across Functional Boundaries," *JMR*, 33 (February), 47–61.

McGee, Gail W. and Robert C. Ford (1987), "Two (or More?) Dimensions of Organizational Commitment: Reexamination of the Affective and Continuance Commitment Scales," *Journal of Applied Psychology*, 72 (4), 638–42.

Meyer, John P. and Natalie J. Allen (1984), "Testing the 'Side-Set Theory' of Organizational Commitment: Some Methodological Considerations," *Journal of Applied Psychology*, 69 (3), 372–78.

SCALE ITEMS:

Strongly   Strongly
disagree   agree

1————2————3————4————5

1. I do not feel a strong sense of belonging to the organization. **(r)**

2. I feel emotionally attached to this organization.

3. This organization has a great deal of personal meaning for me.

4. I would be happy to spend the rest of my career with this organization.

5. I enjoy discussing this organization with people outside of it.

6. I really feel this organization's problems are my own.

SCALE NAME: Commitment to Export Venture

SCALE DESCRIPTION: Cavusgil and Zou (1994) used this three-item, five-point scale to assess the extent of planning, resource, and managerial commitment exhibited by an exporter toward a venture with a foreign distributor.

SCALE ORIGIN: The scale is original to Cavusgil and Zou (1994), who adopted a parsimonious multi-phase research design to operationalize and test measures within their proposed conceptual framework. Preliminary interviews with export marketing managers were used to verify and improve scales items suggested by the literature. Data were collected using the resulting measures and split into two groups. An exploratory factor analysis performed on the analysis subsample using varimax rotation resulted in 17 factors. Only items whose meanings were consistent with the conceptualization of the measure were retained.

SAMPLES: Export marketing managers directly involved with export ventures from 79 firms in 16 industries provided Cavusgil and Zou (1994) with information pertinent to **202** export venture cases. Of the 202 venture cases analyzed, 47.5% were related to consumer goods, 42.6% to industrial goods, and the remainder could not be classified clearly. All respondents were from manufacturing firms with average annual sales in excess of $200 million. The sample was split into analysis and hold-out subsamples, each of which contained **101** export venture cases.

RELIABILITY: Cavusgil and Zou (1994) reported a coefficient alpha of **.884** for this measure.

VALIDITY: Cavusgil and Zou (1994) stated that the content validity of the measure was established during the preliminary interviews. Confirmatory factor analysis performed on the hold-out sample demonstrated patterns of item-to-item correlations and item–factor correlations suggestive of measure unidimensionality.

ADMINISTRATION: Cavusgil and Zou (1994) developed a semistructured instrument that outlined a list of variables and intended scales but contained no specific questions. This enabled the researchers to tailor questions to the specific context of the export venture being discussed or probed during the personal interview. During each in-depth interview, two experienced international marketing researchers independently assigned a score to each of the variables. Scoring was based on the researcher's judgment about the executive's answer to the questions pertinent to the variable, as well as the words given by the executive when expressing an answer. Following the interview, the researchers met to discuss their ratings, resolved differences of opinion, and finalized the scores assigned to each variable. Interrater reliability averaged approximately 80% prior to resolving these differences. Higher scores on the scale indicated that exporters were perceived as being more committed toward the venture with the distributor/subsidiary.

MAJOR FINDINGS: Cavusgil and Zou (1994) investigated the relationship between marketing strategy and performance in the context of export ventures. **Commitment to the export venture** was one of three factors found to represent the characteristics of the firm in an exploratory factor analysis. This structure was confirmed through confirmatory factor analysis with the hold-out sample. Tests of the overall model indicated that **commitment to the export venture** was related strongly and positively to the level of support for a foreign distributor/subsidiary and positively but weakly to price competitiveness.

REFERENCES:
Cavusgil, S. Tamer and Shaoming Zou (1994), "Marketing Strategy-Performance Relationship: An Investigation of the Empirical Link in Export Market Ventures," *JM*, 58 (January), 1–21.

SCALE ITEMS:

None   Substantial
  1————2————3————4————5

1. Extent of careful planning for this venture.

2. Extent of management commitment to the venture.

3. Extent of resource commitment to the venture.

SCALE NAME: Commitment to Manufacturer

SCALE DESCRIPTION: Mohr, Fisher, and Nevin (1996) used this three-item, five-point Likert-type scale to assess the degree to which a dealer felt committed to a manufacturer and wanted to continue the relationship.

SCALE ORIGIN: The scale is original to Mohr, Fisher, and Nevin (1996), who followed the procedures for scale development outlined by Churchill (1979). The resulting scale items were pretested and revised in a series of iterative personal interviews with 12 computer dealers.

SAMPLES: Mohr, Fisher, and Nevin (1996) surveyed 557 computer retailer key informants (owners or managers), and **125** usable surveys were returned. The computer retailers selected for study either were affiliated with the microcomputer industry trade association or were one of 53 randomly selected outlets for a major computer franchiser. The average number of workers employed by responding retailers was 22.3, and the average monthly sales volume was $970,000.

RELIABILITY: Mohr, Fisher, and Nevin (1996) reported a coefficient alpha of **.80** for this measure.

VALIDITY: Mohr, Fisher, and Nevin (1996) stated that the measure exhibited acceptable levels of convergent and discriminatory validity based on the results of a confirmatory factor analysis.

ADMINISTRATION: The measure was included by Mohr, Fisher, and Nevin (1996) as part of a self-administered questionnaire that was delivered by mail. Nonrespondents received a reminder letter approximately one month after the initial mailing. Retailers were randomly assigned to answer questions about either their best or their worst relationship with a manufacturer. Higher scores on the scale indicated that retailers were more committed to maintaining a relationship with the manufacturer.

MAJOR FINDINGS: Mohr, Fisher, and Nevin (1996) investigated the relationship between collaborative communication and channel outcomes (satisfaction with the relationship, relationship commitment, relationship coordination) in the context of differing levels of dealer/manufacturer integration (franchise versus company-owned). Hypotheses were tested by hierarchical moderator regression analysis. The results indicated that, with higher levels of manufacturer control, dealers were more satisfied and **committed** to the relationship and reported that their efforts were better coordinated with the manufacturer. However, significant interactions between control and communication demonstrate that higher levels of collaborative communication have stronger, more positive effects on satisfaction, **commitment**, and coordination in low manufacturer control conditions than in situations in which manufacturer control was high, as well as in less integrated relationship conditions (e.g. franchise versus company-owned).

REFERENCES:

Churchill, Gilbert A., Jr. (1979), "A Paradigm for Developing Better Measures of Marketing Constructs," *JMR*, 16 (February), 64–73.

Mohr, Jakki J., Robert J. Fisher, and John R. Nevin (1996), "Collaborative Communication in Interfirm Relationships: Moderating Effects of Integration and Control," *JM*, 60 (July), 103–15.

SCALE ITEMS:

Strongly   Strongly
disagree   agree

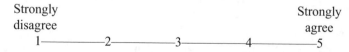

1. We are very committed to carrying this manufacturer's products.

2. We would like to discontinue this manufacturer's product. **(r)**

3. We have a minimal commitment to this manufacturer. **(r)**

SCALE NAME: Commitment to Private Label (Firm)

SCALE DESCRIPTION: Anderson and Robertson (1995) used this nine-item, seven-point Likert-type scale to assess the extent to which brokers perceive their firms as supporting their house brands.

SCALE ORIGIN: Anderson and Robertson (1995) developed the measure used in this study. A detailed construct description was constructed on the basis of a though review of the trade and academic literature. Multiple interviews with brokers, sales managers, and trade association officials were used to generate scale items thought to tap into the construct. These items were administered to 208 brokers and factor analyzed to test for unidimensionality. Reliability assessments were also used to purify the measure. The authors noted that the term "proprietary products" is standard industry terminology and thus appropriate for this measure.

SAMPLES: Anderson and Robertson (1995) mailed questionnaires to the homes of 420 brokers whose names were supplied by cooperating firms; **201** usable responses were obtained. To be evaluated, some hypotheses required the use of archival data regarding the actual sales of house brands made by salespeople. One firm, which provided **150** of the respondents in this study, agreed to supply this information. The authors stated that the respondent demographics closely matched those achieved in a large-scale survey of readers conducted by a nationally distributed trade magazine.

RELIABILITY: Anderson and Robertson (1995) reported a coefficient alpha of **.75** for this measure.

VALIDITY: No specific examination of scale validity was reported by Anderson and Robertson (1995).

ADMINISTRATION: Anderson and Robertson (1995) included the measure as part of a larger self-administered mail questionnaire. A summary of the results was offered in exchange for respondent cooperation. Higher scores on the scale indicated that salespeople perceived higher levels of firm support and backing for house brands.

MAJOR FINDINGS: Anderson and Robertson (1995) investigated the relationship between factors thought to influence the sale of house brands by multiline salespeople. **A firm's commitment to the private label** was not significantly related to the adoption of house products by the sales force.

REFERENCES:
Anderson, Erin and Thomas S. Robertson (1995), "Inducing Multiline Salespeople to Adopt House Brands," *JM*, 59 (April), 16–31.

SCALE ITEMS:

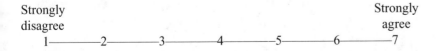

Strongly disagree — Strongly agree
1———2———3———4———5———6———7

1. My firm is going all out to push products that bear the company name.

2. My firm has invested a lot of time and money in proprietary products.

3. My firm is just flirting with proprietary products. **(r)**

4. Proprietary products are not one of the highest priorities in this company. **(r)**

5. This firm is very serious about developing and marketing its own proprietary products.

6. This firm simply hasn't put enough talent and resources behind getting top-performing proprietary products. **(r)**

7. Management makes noise about selling proprietary products, but they haven't put much firepower behind developing them. **(r)**

8. My firm carefully researches and develops its proprietary products before introducing them.

9. My firm's proprietary products' program is rather half-hearted. **(r)**

SCALE NAME: Commitment to Service Quality (Management)

SCALE DESCRIPTION: Hartline and Ferrell (1996) used this six-item, five-point Likert-type scale to assess a manager's affective desire to improve his or her unit's service quality.

SCALE ORIGIN: Hartline and Ferrell (1996) indicated that the items representing this construct were adapted from Mowday, Steers, and Porter's (1979) organizational commitment scale. Items were reworded to reflect a manager's commitment to service quality rather than commitment to the organization. Three items, "I explain to all of my employees the importance of providing high quality services to our customers," "I often discuss quality-related issues with people outside of my organization," and "Providing high quality services to our customers should be the number one priority of my organization," were dropped from the measure following a confirmatory factor analysis because of nonsignificant t-values.

SAMPLES: The hotel industry was chosen as the sampling frame for this study. Hartline and Ferrell (1996) sampled the general managers, employees, and customers of 444 hotel units representing three hotel chains. Of these, 236 different hotel units returned at least one usable questionnaire from a manager, an employee, and a customer. A total of 1769 usable questionnaires were received from **236** hotel managers, **561** customer contact employees, and **1351** customers.

RELIABILITY: Hartline and Ferrell (1996) reported a coefficient alpha of **.87** for this measure.

VALIDITY: Hartline and Ferrell (1996) used confirmatory factor analysis to test the unidimensionality of the measures, using separate analyses for managers, employees, and customers. Items with nonsignificant t-values were dropped from the measures. In investigating the discriminant validity of the scales, the authors first averaged the employee and customer responses on the scale and then matched that response with the manager responses to create a single data set in which cases represented hotel units rather individuals. Hotel units that did not provide at least three responses from employees and customers were dropped, leaving a final sample of 97 matched responses. Confirmatory factor analysis was then used to assess the discriminant validity of the measures.

ADMINISTRATION: Each hotel manager received a survey packet containing instructions, postage-paid reply envelopes, one manager survey, five employee surveys, and forty guest surveys, which were to be self-administered. This measure was included in the manager survey. Hartline and Ferrell (1996) instructed managers to distribute employee surveys to individuals in customer contact positions and the guest surveys during check-out. Survey packets were preceded by a letter from the corporate marketing manager endorsing the project and followed by a second wave of materials approximately two months after the first had been distributed. Higher scores on the scale reflected a higher commitment to service quality on the part of the hotel management.

MAJOR FINDINGS: Hartline and Ferrell (1996) investigated the management of customer-contact service employees and various factors related to service quality using data generated from the customers, contact employees, and managers of hotel units. Hypotheses were tested in the context of structural equation modeling. Increased levels of **management commitment to service quality** resulted in increased management use of empowerment and behavior-based employee evaluations. Although not hypothesized, **management's commitment to service quality** also was found to increase employee job satisfaction.

REFERENCES:
Hartline, Michael D. and O.C. Ferrell (1996), "The Management of Customer-Contact Service Employees: An Empirical Investigation," *JM*, 60 (October), 52–70.

#533 *Commitment to Service Quality (Management)*

Mowday, Richard T., Richard M. Steers, and Lyman W. Porter (1979), "The Measurement of Organizational Commitment," *Journal of Vocational Behavior*, 14 (April), 224–47.

SCALE ITEMS:

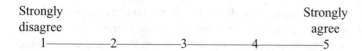

Strongly
disagree
1————2————3————4————5
Strongly
agree

1. I feel strongly about improving the quality of my organization's services.

2. I enjoy discussing quality-related issues with people in my organization.

3. I gain a sense of personal accomplishment in providing quality services to my customers.

4. I am willing to put in a great deal of effort beyond that normally expected in order to help my organization deliver high quality services to our customers.

5. The way I feel about quality is very similar to the way my organization feels about quality.

6. I really care about the quality of my organization's services.

SCALE NAME: Commitment to Supplier

SCALE DESCRIPTION: Kumar, Scheer, and Steenkamp (1995) used this nine-item, seven-point Likert-type scale to measure a firm's affective commitment to and willingness to invest in its partner, as well as expectations of relationship continuity.

SCALE ORIGIN: Kumar, Scheer, and Steenkamp (1995) stated that the items used to measure the affective commitment dimension were based on the construct definition and scales found in organizational research but provided no specific citations. The expectation of continuity dimension was measured using three items previously used by Noordewier, John, and Nevin (1990) and Anderson and Weitz (1989). No indication was given to suggest that the three items measuring willingness to invest are anything other than original to Kumar, Scheer, and Steenkamp's (1995) study.

SAMPLES: Kumar, Scheer, and Steenkamp (1995) mailed surveys to 1640 new car dealers whose names were obtained from a commercial list covering two states; **417** usable responses were returned. No significant differences between early and late respondents was present, which suggests that response bias was not a problem.

RELIABILITY: Kumar, Scheer, and Steenkamp (1995) calculated a coefficient alpha of **.86** for the scale.

VALIDITY: Confirmatory factor analysis was used to assess the validity of the measures. Kumar, Scheer, and Steenkamp (1995) specified affective commitment, willingness to invest, and expectation of continuity as three first-order factors for the second-order factor of commitment. Significant factor loadings on all items were accepted as evidence of convergent validity. Although trust, conflict, and commitment were significantly correlated, as was expected, the intercorrelations were significantly below unity, providing evidence for the discriminant validity of the measure.

ADMINISTRATION: Kumar, Scheer, and Steenkamp (1995) stated that the scale was part of a self-administered mail survey that was accompanied by a personalized cover letter. Dealers who did not respond within four weeks received a reminder letter. Higher scores on the scale indicated that dealers reported stronger affective commitment and willingness to invest in a partner, as well as greater expectations of relationship continuity.

MAJOR FINDINGS: Kumar, Scheer, and Steenkamp (1995) investigated how interdependence asymmetry (the difference between the dealer's dependence on the supplier and the supplier's dependence on the dealer) and total interdependence (the sum of both firms' dependency) affect the development of interfirm trust, **commitment**, and conflict. The results of regression analysis indicated that **commitment** is greater both when total interdependence is higher and when asymmetry interdependence between firms is lower.

REFERENCES:

Anderson, Erin and Barton A. Weitz (1989), "Determinants of Continuity in Conventional Industrial Channel Dyads," *Marketing Science*, 8 (Fall), 310–23.

Kumar, Nirmalya, Lisa K. Scheer, and Jan-Benedict E.M. Steenkamp (1995b), "The Effects of Perceived Interdependence on Dealer Attitudes," *JMR*, 32 (August), 348–56.

Noordewier, Thomas G., George John, and John R. Nevin (1990), "Performance Outcomes of Purchasing Agents in Industrial Buyer-Vendor Relationships," *JM*, 54 (October), 80–93.

#534 *Commitment to Supplier*

SCALE ITEMS:

Strongly   Strongly
disagree   agree
  1————2————3————4————5————6————7

Affective commitment
1. Even if we could, we would not drop the supplier because we like being associated with it.
2. We want to remain a member of the supplier's network because we genuinely enjoy our relationship with it.
3. Our positive feelings towards the supplier are a major reason we continue working with it.

Expectation of continuity
4. We expect our relationship with the supplier to continue for a long time.
5. The renewal of our relationship with the supplier is virtually automatic.
6. It is unlikely our firm will still be doing business with this supplier in two years. **(r)**

Willingness to invest
7. If the supplier requested it, we would be willing to make further investment in supporting the supplier's line.
8. We are willing to put more effort and investment in building our business in the supplier's product.
9. In the future we will work to link our firm with the supplier's in the customer's mind.

SCALE NAME: Communication (Formality)

SCALE DESCRIPTION: Mohr, Fisher, and Nevin (1996) used this four-item, five-point Likert-type scale to assess the degree to which formal mechanisms for communication exist within the dealer–manufacturer relationship.

SCALE ORIGIN: It appears that the scale was original to Anderson, Lodish, and Weitz (1987). Mohr, Fisher, and Nevin (1996) pretested and revised the measure in a series of iterative personal interviews with 12 computer dealers.

SAMPLES: Mohr, Fisher, and Nevin (1996) surveyed 557 computer retailer key informants (owners or managers); **125** usable surveys were returned. The computer retailers selected for study either were affiliated with the microcomputer industry trade association or were one of 53 randomly selected outlets for a major computer franchiser. The average number of workers employed by responding retailers was 22.3, and the average monthly sales volume was $970,000.

RELIABILITY: Mohr, Fisher, and Nevin (1996) reported a coefficient alpha of **.86** for this measure.

VALIDITY: Mohr, Fisher, and Nevin (1996) stated that the measure exhibited acceptable levels of convergent and discriminatory validity according to the results of a confirmatory factor analysis.

ADMINISTRATION: The measure was included by Mohr, Fisher, and Nevin (1996) as part of a self-administered questionnaire that was delivered by mail. Nonrespondents received a reminder letter approximately one month after the initial mailing. Retailers were randomly assigned to answer questions about either their best or their worst relationship with a manufacturer. Higher scores on the scale indicated that communication was more formal, explicit, and detailed as opposed to informal, vague, or loose.

MAJOR FINDINGS: Mohr, Fisher, and Nevin (1996) investigated the relationship between collaborative communication and channel outcomes (satisfaction with the relationship, relationship commitment, relationship coordination) in the context of differing levels of dealer/manufacturer integration (franchise versus company-owned). The **formality of communication** was one of four first-order factors that composed the second-order factor of collaborative communication. Hypotheses were tested by hierarchical moderator regression analysis. The results indicated that, with higher levels of manufacturer control, dealers were more satisfied and committed to the relationship and reported that their efforts were better coordinated with the manufacturer. However, significant interactions between control and communication demonstrate that higher levels of collaborative communication have stronger, more positive effects on satisfaction, commitment, and coordination in low manufacturer control conditions than in situations in which manufacturer control was high.

REFERENCES:
Anderson, Erin, Leonard Lodish, and Barton Weitz (1987), "Resource Allocation Behavior in Conventional Channels," *JMR*, 24 (February), 85–97.
Mohr, Jakki J., Robert J. Fisher, and John R. Nevin (1996), "Collaborative Communication in Interfirm Relationships: Moderating Effects of Integration and Control," *JM*, 60 (July), 103–15.

#535 *Communication (Formality)*

SCALE ITEMS:

Strongly   Strongly
disagree   agree
 1————————2————————3————————4————————5

1. In coordinating our activities with this manufacturer, formal communication channels are followed (i.e., channels are regularized, structured modes versus casual, information, word-of-mouth modes).

2. The terms of our relationship have been written down in detail.

3. The manufacturer's expectations of us are communicated in detail.

4. The terms of our relationship have been explicitly verbalized and discussed.

SCALE NAME: Communication (Information Exchange)

SCALE DESCRIPTION: Li and Dant (1997) described this four-item, five-point Likert-type scale as measuring the extent to which parties in the channel relationship actively exchanged information that could facilitate business activities with each other. Li and Dant (1997) referred to this scale as *communication*.

SCALE ORIGIN: Li and Dant (1997) reported that the items used in this scale were adapted from Heide and John's (1992) measure of information exchange.

SAMPLES: Li and Dant (1997) used a cross-sectional survey approach to sample 2553 office machine dealership key informants (owners/presidents) from the membership list of the National Office Machine Dealers Association. Questionnaires were returned from 573 dealerships; incomplete surveys and those completed by individuals not fitting the key informant status were eliminated from the study. The final sample was composed of **461** distributors, of which 286 were classified as having exclusive dealing (ED) arrangements with the photocopier manufacturer for which they sold the most units, whereas the remaining 175 maintained nonexclusive dealing (NED) arrangements.

RELIABILITY: Li and Dant (1997) reported a reliability coefficient of **.83** for this measure.

VALIDITY: Li and Dant (1997) stated that the five measures used in the study were subjected to confirmatory factor analysis using LISREL. After one of the original five solidarity items, "our relationship with them is best described as a 'cooperative effort'," was dropped, support was found for measure unidimensionality. Convergent and discriminant validity were also found to be satisfactory, providing evidence of construct validity.

ADMINISTRATION: Li and Dant (1997) stated that the scale was part of a self-administered mail questionnaire that was completed by respondents, along with other measures, using a paper-and-pencil format. A cover letter from the National Office Machine Dealers Association endorsing the study accompanied the survey packet. Respondents were instructed to answer their questionnaires in the context of the copier manufacturer for which they sold the most copy machines. On the basis of their response to a question that directly asked whether distributors exclusively sold this focal manufacturer's copiers, respondents were classified as ED or NED. Higher scores on the scale indicated that channel partners freely exchanged information that could prove beneficial to conducting business.

MAJOR FINDINGS: Li and Dant (1997) investigated how exclusive dealing arrangements between manufacturers and dealers affected dealers' perceptions of relationalism, communication, and perceived performance. Results indicate that ED between manufacturers and dealers resulted in a higher level of **communication and information exchange** between channel partners compared with that achieved under NED arrangements.

REFERENCES:
Heide, Jan B. and George John (1992), "Do Norms Matter in Marketing Relationships?," *JM*, 56 (2), 32-44.

Li, Zhan G. and Rajiv P. Dant (1997), "An Exploratory Study of Exclusive Dealing in Channel Relationships," *JAMS*, 25 (3), 201–13.

#536 *Communication (Information Exchange)*

SCALE ITEMS:

Strongly   Strongly
disagree   agree

1————2————3————4————5

1. We keep each other informed about events that affect the other party.

2. We often exchange information informally.

3. We often exchange information beyond what is required by our agreements.

4. We are expected to provide each other with information that may be of help.

SCALE NAME: Communication Bidirectionality (Marketing and Engineering)

SCALE DESCRIPTION: Fisher, Maltz, and Jaworski (1997) used this four-item, five-point Likert-type scale to assess the degree to which communication between marketing and engineering is a two-way process. The scale could easily be adapted to measure the bidirectionality of communication between any two departments.

SCALE ORIGIN: Fisher, Maltz, and Jaworski (1997) indicated that the items developed for this construct were based on the work of Mohr and Nevin (1990). Preliminary scale items were pretested with six marketing managers; those found to be unclear, ambiguous, or not applicable were dropped from the measure. A six-item version of the communication bidirectionality measure was administered in Study 1. Two items, "I always respond to communication from the engineering contact" and "We exchange e-mail frequently," were eliminated on the basis of large modification indices in the confirmatory factor analysis.

SAMPLES: In Study 1, Fisher, Maltz, and Jaworski (1997) sampled 180 marketing managers employed by a *Fortune* 100 firm serving five diverse high-technology markets. The convenience sample was composed of marketing managers attending management training sessions over a three-week period; **89** usable responses were obtained. In Study 2, the authors sampled marketing managers employed by a multinational, business-to-business services firm with 36 business units in six countries outside the United States. A key informant provided a list of 100 firm members employed in a variety of marketing positions that required them to interact with engineering personnel. A total of **72** usable responses were obtained for Study 2.

RELIABILITY: Fisher, Maltz, and Jaworski (1997) reported calculating coefficient alphas for this measure of **.89** in Study 1 and **.88** in Study 2.

VALIDITY: In Study 1, confirmatory factor analyses were conducted in two stages to maintain an acceptable ratio of observations to variables. The first analysis included the original fifteen items that composed the bidirectional communication, information-sharing norms, and relative functional identification (RFI) measures. Fisher, Maltz, and Jaworski (1997) stated that, after two bidirectional communication items and one information sharing norm item were eliminated because of large modification indices, the revised model fit the data acceptably well. Evidence of discriminant validity was provided, in that the correlation between each pair of constructs was significantly different than 1.00.

ADMINISTRATION: The measure was included with other scales in a self-administered questionnaire. For Study 1, a survey packet containing a cover letter, reply envelope, and the survey instrument was distributed to each marketing manager participant of a company-sponsored training session. Fisher, Maltz, and Jaworski (1997) used e-mail and telephone reminders to increase response rates. In Study 2, respondents received the survey packet by mail. Offers of anonymity and shared survey results were provided as incentives to participate. Nonrespondents received a reminder letter followed by a second mail survey packet. In both studies, respondents were instructed to answer questions in the context of their relationship with a single manager in the engineering function with whom they interacted regularly. Higher scores on the measure indicated that respondents perceived a greater a degree of shared communication and feedback with their engineering contact.

MAJOR FINDINGS: Fisher, Maltz, and Jaworski (1997) investigated how RFI, or the strength of marketing managers' psychological connection to their functional area compared with to the firm as a whole, influenced different strategies for improving communication between marketers and engineers. In Study

1, the degree of **bidirectional communication with engineering** was significantly and negatively influenced by psychological distance. Information-sharing norms positively influenced **bidirectional communication**, though this effect was found to be stronger for low-RFI managers than for high-RFI managers. In Study 2, the **bidirectionality of communication with engineering** was found to be positively associated with interdependence, the dynamism of the strategic unit, and the length of the relationship with the engineering contact and negatively associated with psychological distance. Both RFI and information sharing norms had significant effects on the **bidirectionality of communication**. Finally, the effect of both integrated goals and information-sharing norms on **bidirectionality** were found to be stronger for low-RFI managers than for high-RFI managers.

REFERENCES:

Fisher, Robert J., Elliot Maltz, and Bernard J. Jaworski (1997), "Enhancing Communication Between Marketing and Engineering: The Moderating Role of Relative Functional Identification," *JM*, 61 (July), 54–70.

Mohr, Jakki J and John R. Nevin (1990), "Communication Strategies in Marketing Channels: A Theoretical Perspective," *JM*, 54 (October), 36–50.

SCALE ITEMS:

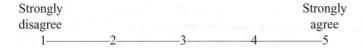

Strongly disagree — Strongly agree
1————2————3————4————5

1. The engineering contact always responds to my communication.

2. We have great dialogues.

3. S/he provides a lot of feedback.

4. There's a lot of two-way communication between me and the engineering contact.

SCALE NAME: Communication Quality

SCALE DESCRIPTION: Mohr and Sohi (1995) used this five-item, five-point semantic differential scale to assess dealers' perceptions of the quality of communication between them and the manufacturer.

SCALE ORIGIN: The scale appears to be original to Mohr and Sohi (1995), though the items were based on the conceptual work of O'Reilly (1982) and Stohl and Redding (1987). The scale was pretested and revised on the basis of a series of personal interviews with 12 computer dealers.

SAMPLES: Mohr and Sohi (1995) sampled members of the Association of Better Computer Dealers, a national industry trade association, and supplemented this list with a random sample of outlets from a major computer franchiser. Of the 557 surveys distributed, **125** usable surveys were returned.

RELIABILITY: Mohr and Sohi (1995) reported a coefficient alpha of **.92** for this measure.

VALIDITY: Mohr and Sohi (1995) stated that a confirmatory factor analysis successfully demonstrated the unidimensionality and convergent and discriminatory validity of the measure.

ADMINISTRATION: The measure was included by Mohr and Sohi (1995) as part of a self-administered questionnaire that was delivered by mail. Nonrespondents received a reminder letter. Each dealer was asked to respond to the questionnaire with respect to a randomly assigned focal manufacturer. Lower scores on the scale indicated that dealers perceived that high-quality communication occurred between they and their manufacturers.

MAJOR FINDINGS: Mohr and Sohi (1995) investigated the relationship between information-sharing norms, quality and satisfaction with communication, and dealers' distortion and withholding of information and the three communication flows of frequency, bidirectionality, and formality. The perceived **quality of communication** was found to be positively associated with a dealer's satisfaction with communication.

REFERENCES:
Mohr, Jakki J. and Ravipreet S. Sohi (1995), "Communication Flows in Distribution Channels: Impact on Assessments of Communication Quality and Satisfaction," *JR*, 71 (4), 393–416.
O'Reilly, Charles (1982), "Variations in Decision Markers' Use of Information Sources: The Impact of Quality and Accessibility of Information," *Academy of Management Journal*, 25 (4), 756–71.
Stohl, Cynthia and W. Charles Redding (1987), "Messages and Message Exchange Processes," in *Handbook of Organizational Communication*, F. Jablin, ed. Newbury Park, CA: Sage Publications, 451–502.

SCALE ITEMS:
To what extent do you feel that your communication with this manufacturer is:

#538 *Communication Quality*

1. Timely   :____:____:____:____:____: Untimely
                   1   2   3   4   5

2. Accurate   :____:____:____:____:____: Inaccurate
                   1   2   3   4   5

3. Adequate :____:____:____:____:____: Inadequate
                   1   2   3   4   5

4. Complete :____:____:____:____:____: Incomplete
                   1   2   3   4   5

5. Credible   :____:____:____:____:____: Not credible
                   1   2   3   4   5

SCALE NAME: Competitive Intensity

SCALE DESCRIPTION: Pelham and Wilson (1996) used a three-item, seven-point scale to measure the degree of hostility in an environment perceived as stemming from competition.

SCALE ORIGIN: Pelham and Wilson (1996) indicated that this scale was taken from Khandwalla's (1977) study.

SAMPLES: A longitudinal database developed by the Center for Entrepreneurship at Eastern Michigan University provided the data for the study. The Center's full panel consists of data provided by the CEOs of 370 Michigan firms, which represents 71% of the firms contacted for initial participation. The data used by Pelham and Wilson (1996) were specific only to those firms providing full information with respect to all measures of interest for both the current and previous years. Of those **68** firms, 32% were classified as wholesalers, 29% as manufacturers, 26% as business services, and 13% as construction. Firm size ranged from 15 to 65 employees, with the average number of employees equaling 23.

RELIABILITY: Pelham and Wilson (1996) reported an alpha of **.69** for this scale.

VALIDITY: Pelham and Wilson (1996) stated that factor loadings and LISREL measurement model squared multiple correlations were taken as evidence of convergent and discriminant validity.

ADMINISTRATION: Pelham and Wilson (1996) did not provide details with respect to how data were collected from panel members by the Center. Higher scores on the scale indicated a greater degree of perceived threat due to a hostile competitive environment.

MAJOR FINDINGS: Pelham and Wilson (1996) investigated the relative impact of market orientation on small business performance compared with that of market structure, firm structure, firm strategy, and relative product quality. Regression analysis was used to test year-to-year differences in most variables, as well as parameters based on independent and lagged variables. In the lagged model, **competitive intensity** during the previous year positively influenced small-firm market orientation, whereas it did not in the short-term.

REFERENCES:
Khandwalla, P.N. (1977), *The Design of Organizations*. New York: Harcourt Brace Jovanovich.
Pelham, Alfred M. and David T. Wilson (1996), "A Longitudinal Study of the Impact of Market Structure, Firm Structure, Strategy, and Market Orientation Culture on Dimensions of Small-Firm Performance," *JAMS*, 24 (1), 27–43.

SCALE ITEMS:*
Directions: Indicate the degree to which the following are threatening to the survival of your firm.

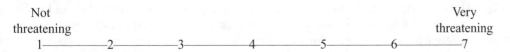

Not threatening						Very threatening
1—————	2—————	3—————	4—————	5—————	6—————	7

1. The business environment.

2. Tough price competition.

3. Competitor's product quality or novelty.

*Verbatim instructions were not provided in the article by Pelham and Wilson (1996) but were likely to have beeen similar to those provided here.

SCALE NAME: Competitive Intensity

SCALE DESCRIPTION: The full six-item, eleven-point Likert-type scale was used by Song and Parry (1997b) to assess the level of interfirm rivalry within the firm's target market for the new product. In a study based on the Japanese data only, Song and Parry (1997a) used a reduced three-item version of the scale.

SCALE ORIGIN: The scale was adapted by Song and Parry (1997a, b) from the work of Cooper (1979). Song and Parry (1997a, b) modified some scale items on the basis of a review of the literature, pilot studies, and information obtained from 36 in-depth case study interviews conducted with both Japanese and U.S. firms. The items for all scales used by Song and Parry (1997a, b) were evaluated by an academic panel composed of both Japanese and U.S. business and engineering experts. Following revisions, the items were judged by a new panel composed of academicians and new product development (NPD) managers. Song and Parry (1997a, b) reported extensive pretesting of both the Japanese and U.S. versions of the questionnaire.

SAMPLES: Song and Parry (1997a, b) randomly sampled 500 of the 611 firms trading on the Tokyo, Osaka, and Nagoya stock exchanges that had been identified as developing at least four new physical products since 1991. Usable responses pertaining to **788** NPD projects were obtained from 404 Japanese firms. The resulting data were randomly split by Song and Parry (1997a) into calibration (n = 394) and validation (n = 394) samples for the purpose of cross-validation. Song and Parry (1997b) said the U.S. sampling frame was from companies listed in the *High-Technology Industries Directory*. Of the 643 firms that had introduced a minimum of four new physical products since 1990, 500 firms were randomly sampled (stratified by industry to match the Japanese sample); 312 U.S. firms provided data on **612** NPD projects, of which 312 were successes and 300 were failures.

RELIABILITY: Song and Parry (1997b) reported a coefficient alpha of **.74** for this scale in the Japanese sample and **.77** in the U.S. sample. Song and Parry (1997a) used a confirmatory factor analysis of the data in the calibration sample to purify the scale. Items loading on multiple constructs or those with low item-to-scale loadings were deleted from the measure. Song and Parry (1997a) reported a coefficient alpha of **.67** for the three-item, purified measure using data from the validation sample.

VALIDITY: The extensive pretesting and evaluation of the measure with academicians and NPD managers provided strong evidence for the face validity of the measure. The authors (1997a, b) did not specifically report any other examination of scale validity.

ADMINISTRATION: The self-administered questionnaire containing the scale was originally developed in English; the Japanese version was prepared using the parallel-translation/double-translation method. Following minor revisions made on the basis of pretests with bilingual respondents and case study participants, the Japanese sample received a survey packet containing cover letters in both English and Japanese, two Japanese-language questionnaires, and two international postage-paid reply envelopes. Survey packets delivered to U.S. firms were similar, except no Japanese cover letter was included and the surveys were in English. Various incentives, four follow-up letters, and multiple telephone calls and faxes were used to increase the response rate with both samples. Song and Parry (1997a, b) indicated that respondents were asked to answer one questionnaire in the context of a successful new product project introduced after 1991 and one in the context of a new product project that had failed. Higher scores on scale indicated greater interfirm rivalry and competitive intensity.

MAJOR FINDINGS: Song and Parry (1997a) conceptualized and tested a model of NPD practices thought to influence the success of new product ventures in Japan. The structural model was estimated with the calibration sample data, and the proposed model and the alternative models were tested using the validation sample. The **competitive intensity** faced by Japanese firms did not significantly influence the relative level of new product success directly. However, **competitive intensity** was found to have a significant and positive effect on the level of competitive and marketing intelligence gathered and a significant negative effect on product competitive advantage.

Song and Parry (1997b) conceptualized and tested a model of strategic, tactical, and environmental factors thought to influence new product success using data collected from both Japanese and U.S. firms. In both the Japanese and U.S. samples, the level of NPD project **competitive intensity** was found to weaken the relationship between product differentiation and relative product performance.

REFERENCES:
Cooper, Robert G. (1979b), "The Dimensions of Industrial New Product Success and Failure," *JM*, 43 (Summer), 93–103.
Song, X. Michael and Mark E. Parry (1997a), "The Determinants of Japanese New Product Successes," *JMR*, 34 (February), 64–76.
———— and ———— (1997b), "A Cross-National Comparative Study of New Product Development Processes: Japan and the United States," *JM*, 61 (April), 1–18.

SCALE ITEMS:*
Directions: To what extent does each statement listed below correctly describe this selected successful project? Please indicate your degree of agreement or disagreement by circling a number from zero (0) to ten (10) on the scale to the right of each statement. Here: 0 = strongly disagree, 10 = strongly agree, and numbers between 0 and 10 indicate various degrees of agreement or disagreement.

Strongly   Strongly
disagree   agree

0———1———2———3———4———5———6———7———8———9———10

1. There was no price competition in this market. **(r)**

2. There were many competitors in this market.

3. There was a strong, dominant competitor—with a large market share—in the market.

4. Potential customers were very loyal to competitor's products.

5. Potential customers were not satisfied with competitor's products. **(r)**

6. New product introductions by competitors were frequent in this market.

*Items 3, 4, and 5 were used by Song and Parry (1997a) in the reduced scale version.

SCALE NAME: Conceptual Utilization Processes

SCALE DESCRIPTION: Moorman (1995) used this nine-item, seven-point Likert-type scale to assess the extent to which organizations valued information and those who provided it and used formal and informal methods of processing information. The focus of this measure is on an organization's commitment to and processing of information rather than the extent to which information is used in making, implementing, or evaluating marketing decisions.

SCALE ORIGIN: The scale is original to Moorman (1995). All measures used by Moorman (1995) were subjected to a purification process following data collection. The author assessed the unidimensionality of the measures in a two-factor confirmatory analysis model using LISREL VII. Items with very weak loadings and those loading on more than one factor were eliminated. The reliability of the measures was assessed by calculating coefficient alphas, and items with low item-to-total correlations were dropped if "doing so did not diminish the measure's coverage of the construct domain" (Moorman 1995, p. 325).

SAMPLES: Moorman (1995) chose to sample the vice presidents of marketing for 300 divisions of firms noted in the 1992 *Advertising Age* list of top 200 advertisers. A total of **92** usable questionnaires were received. No systematic differences were observed between early and late respondents.

RELIABILITY: Moorman (1995) reported a coefficient alpha of **.80** for this scale.

VALIDITY: Moorman (1995) performed a series of two-factor confirmatory analyses using LISREL VII to assess the discriminant validity of the measures used in her study. Chi-square difference tests were performed on constrained versus unconstrained models, and the significantly lower chi-square values observed for all the unconstrained models tested were accepted as evidence of the discriminant validity of the measures.

ADMINISTRATION: The scale was included with other measures in a self-administered questionnaire that was delivered by mail. Moorman's (1995) cover letter explained the survey's purpose and, in an effort to increase response rate, offered to share survey results. Nonrespondents were telephoned after three weeks and sent a second questionnaire two weeks after the telephone reminder. All informants were instructed to answer in the context of the most recent product development project for which their division had been responsible. Focal projects were required to have been on the market for a minimum of 12 months. Higher scores on the scale indicated that an organization valued its information agents and products highly and processed information using formal and informal means.

MAJOR FINDINGS: Moorman (1995) examined the relationship between organizational market information processes, organizational culture, and new product outcomes. Clan-based organizational cultures, which stress participation, teamwork, and cohesiveness, were found to have the strongest positive effect on the **conceptual utilization processes** from among the four types of organizational cultures (adhocracies, markets, hierarchies, clans) tested. Some evidence was found to suggest that **conceptual utilization processes** influenced new product performance ($p > .10$), new product timeliness ($p > .05$), and new product creativity ($p > .05$). This indicates that organizations that value information and formally and informally process information are more likely to introduce a new product that is novel and unique when environmental conditions are favorable to its success, thus enhancing the likelihood that profit, sales, and market share goals will be achieved.

REFERENCES:

Moorman, Christine (1995), "Organizational Market Information Processes: Cultural Antecedents and New Product Outcomes," *JMR*, 32 (August), 318–35.

SCALE ITEMS:

Strongly   Strongly
disagree   agree

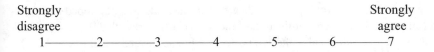

1————2————3————4————5————6————7

During this project, my division had formal or informal processes ...

1. Which summarized information, reducing its complexity.
2. That encouraged decision makers to disagree and to challenge one others opinions.
3. Which encouraged managers to develop predictions regarding the product's success.
4. For organizing information in meaningful ways.
5. For processing information about the product.

During this project, my division ...

6. Valued information as an aid to decision making regarding the project.
7. Viewed new information as disruptive to the project. **(r)**
8. Devalued the role of information providers (e.g., marketing researchers). **(r)**
9. Structured jobs so that information providers played a role in strategy development.

SCALE NAME: Conflict (Interdepartmental)

SCALE DESCRIPTION: A seven-item, five-point Likert-type scale measuring the extent to which tension occurs in interdepartmental interactions and the existence of goal incompatibility between departments.

SCALE ORIGIN: Menon, Jaworski, and Kohli (1997) indicated that the scale was developed and first reported in Jaworski and Kohli (1993). Closer examination of the source article revealed that the sample and data used to develop the scale were identical to those reported in Menon, Jaworski, and Kohli (1997).

SAMPLES: Using the *Dun & Bradstreet Million Dollar Directory* as the sampling frame, Menon, Jaworski, and Kohli (1997) selected for initial contact every other company name from among the top 1000 companies by sales revenues. Participation from multiple strategic business units (SBU) within an organization was requested. A total of 102 companies agreed to participate, and ultimately, responses representing **222** SBUs were obtained from marketing and nonmarketing executives.

RELIABILITY: Menon, Jaworski, and Kohli (1997) reported a **.87** alpha reliability coefficient.

VALIDITY: No specific examination of scale validity was presented by Menon, Jaworski, and Kohli (1997) or Jaworski and Kohli (1993).

ADMINISTRATION: The 206 marketing and 187 nonmarketing executives identified by participating corporations were directly contacted by Menon, Jaworski, and Kohli (1997). Initial contact was followed by a self-administered mail questionnaire, and a follow-up questionnaire was sent three weeks later to nonrespondents. Most (79.6%) of the marketing executives and 70% of the nonmarketing executives contacted provided data for the study. When both nonmarketing and marketing executives from a single SBU responded, their scores were averaged to provide a single score for the construct. A higher score on the interdepartmental conflict scale indicated less goal congruity between departments and interdepartmental interactions characterized by greater levels of tension and distrust.

MAJOR FINDINGS: Menon, Jaworski, and Kohli (1997) investigated the role of organizational factors that affect interdepartmental interactions and the resulting impact on product quality. A key finding suggested that the greater the level of **interdepartmental conflict**, the lower was the level of product quality. The relationship between **interdepartmental conflict** and product quality was found to be robust across various levels of technological and market turbulence. Greater levels of risk aversion among top managers, a high degree of centralized decision making, and more hierarchical levels within the organizational structure led to greater levels of **interdepartmental conflict**, whereas the use of market-focused reward systems resulted in less **interdepartmental conflict**.

REFERENCES:

Jaworski, Bernard and Ajay K. Kohli (1993), "Market Orientation: Antecedents and Consequences," *JM*, 57 (July), 53–70.

Menon, Ajay, Bernard J. Jaworski, and Ajay K. Kohli (1997), "Product Quality: Impact of Interdepartmental Interactions," *JAMS*, 25 (3), 187–200.

SCALE ITEMS:

Strongly   Strongly
disagree   agree
   1————————2————————3————————4————————5

1. Most departments in this business unit get along well with each other. **(r)**

2. When members of several departments get together, tensions frequently run high.

3. People in one department generally dislike interacting with those from other departments.

4. Employees from different departments feel that the goals of their respective departments are in harmony with each other. **(r)**

5. Protecting one's departmental turf is considered to be a way of life this business unit.

6. The objectives pursued by the marketing department are incompatible with those of the manufacturing department.

7. There is little or no interdepartmental conflict in this business unit. **(r)**

#543 Conflict (Supplier)

SCALE NAME: Conflict (Supplier)

SCALE DESCRIPTION: Kumar, Scheer, and Steenkamp (1995) used this scale to measure the level of behavior that impedes, blocks, or frustrates a firm's pursuit of its goals. The measure has two distinct components: perceived conflict and hostility. Perceived conflict taps into the magnitude of present conflict acknowledged by the firm using two seven-point Likert-type items. Hostility assesses the level of a firm's current negative affect toward the partner using four items measured in a five-point format.

SCALE ORIGIN: It appears that Kumar, Scheer, and Steenkamp (1995) adapted the scale items from studies by Frazier, Gill, and Kale (1989) and Brown, Lusch, and Smith (1991).

SAMPLES: Kumar, Scheer, and Steenkamp (1995) mailed surveys to 1640 new car dealers whose names were obtained from a commercial list covering two states; **417** usable responses were returned. No significant differences between early and late respondents was present, which suggests that response bias was not a problem.

RELIABILITY: Kumar, Scheer, and Steenkamp (1995) calculated a coefficient alpha of **.82** for the scale.

VALIDITY: Confirmatory factor analysis was used to assess the validity of the measures. Kumar, Scheer, and Steenkamp (1995) specified perceived conflict and hostility as two first-order factors for the second-order factor of conflict. Significant factor loadings on all items were accepted as evidence of convergent validity. Although trust, conflict, and commitment were significantly correlated, as was expected, the intercorrelations were significantly below unity, providing evidence for the discriminant validity of the measure.

ADMINISTRATION: Kumar, Scheer, and Steenkamp (1995) stated that the scale was part of a self-administered mail survey that was accompanied by a personalized cover letter. Dealers who did not respond in four weeks received a reminder letter. Higher scores on the scale indicated that dealers reported stronger negative feelings toward suppliers and overtly recognized a greater degree of conflict as existing between they and that supplier.

MAJOR FINDINGS: Kumar, Scheer, and Steenkamp (1995) investigated how interdependence asymmetry (the difference between the dealer's dependence on the supplier and the supplier's dependence on the dealer) and total interdependence (the sum of both firms' dependency) affect the development of interfirm trust, commitment, and **conflict**. The results of regression analysis indicated that **conflict** is greater both when total interdependence is lower and when asymmetry interdependence between firms is higher.

REFERENCES:
Brown, James R., Robert F. Lusch, and Laurie P. Smith (1989), "Conflict and Satisfaction in an Industrial Channel of Distribution," *International Journal of Physical Distribution & Logistics Management*, 21 (6), 15–25.
Frazier, Gary L., James D. Gill, and Sudhir H. Kale (1989), "Dealer Dependence Levels and Reciprocal Actions in a Channel of Distribution in a Developing Country," *JM*, 53 (January), 50–69.
Kumar, Nirmalya, Lisa K. Scheer, and Jan-Benedict E.M. Steenkamp (1995b), "The Effects of Perceived Interdependence on Dealer Attitudes," *JMR*, 32 (August), 348–56.

SCALE ITEMS:

Strongly
disagree

Strongly
agree

1————2————3————4————5————6————7

Perceived conflict:

1. A high degree of conflict exists between the supplier and our firm.
2. The supplier and our firm have major disagreements on certain key issues.

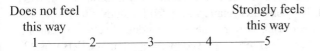

Does not feel
this way

Strongly feels
this way

1————2————3————4————5

Hostility:

When your firm reflects on the relationship with the supplier, does your firm feel:

3. Anger.
4. Frustration.
5. Resentment.
6. Hostility.

SCALE NAME: Conflict (with Manufacturer)

SCALE DESCRIPTION: Mohr, Fisher, and Nevin (1996) used this three-item, five-point Likert-type scale to measure the overall level of disagreement between parties by assessing the frequency and intensity with which the dealer and manufacturer argued about relationship issues.

SCALE ORIGIN: It appears that the scale items used were original to Anderson and Narus (1990). Mohr, Fisher, and Nevin (1996) pretested and revised the measure in a series of iterative personal interviews with 12 computer dealers. One item, "This relationship is marked by a high degree of harmony (r)," was dropped from the measure following a confirmatory factor analysis because of nonsignificant t-values.

SAMPLES: Mohr, Fisher, and Nevin (1996) surveyed 557 computer retailer key informants (owners or managers); **125** usable surveys were returned. The computer retailers selected for study either were affiliated with the microcomputer industry trade association or were one of 53 randomly selected outlets for a major computer franchiser. The average number of workers employed by responding retailers was 22.3, and the average monthly sales volume was $970,000.

RELIABILITY: Mohr, Fisher, and Nevin (1996) reported a coefficient alpha of **.79** for this measure.

VALIDITY: Mohr, Fisher, and Nevin (1996) stated that the measure exhibited acceptable levels of convergent and discriminatory validity according to the results of a confirmatory factor analysis.

ADMINISTRATION: The measure was included by Mohr, Fisher, and Nevin (1996) as part of a self-administered questionnaire that was delivered by mail. Nonrespondents received a reminder letter approximately one month after the initial mailing. Retailers were randomly assigned to answer questions about either their best or their worst relationship with a manufacturer. Higher scores on the scale indicated that retailer and manufacturer activities were more organized and synchronized.

MAJOR FINDINGS: Mohr, Fisher, and Nevin (1996) investigated the relationship between collaborative communication and channel outcomes (satisfaction with the relationship, relationship commitment, relationship coordination) in the context of differing levels of dealer/manufacturer integration (franchise versus company-owned). Hypotheses were tested by hierarchical moderator regression analysis. **Channel conflict** was included as a control variable, and as was expected, a strong negative relationship was found between **channel conflict** and satisfaction with the manufacturer, relationship commitment, and coordination.

REFERENCES:

Anderson, James C. and James Narus (1990), "A Model of Distributor Firm and Manufacturer Firm Working Partnerships," *JM*, 54 (January), 42–58.

Mohr, Jakki J., Robert J. Fisher, and John R. Nevin (1996), "Collaborative Communication in Interfirm Relationships: Moderating Effects of Integration and Control," *JM*, 60 (July), 103–15.

SCALE ITEMS:

Strongly disagree
1————2————3————4————5
Strongly agree

1. We argue frequently with this manufacturer about business issues.

2. Our arguments with this manufacturer are very heated.

3. We disagree with the manufacturer about how we can best achieve our respective goals.

SCALE NAME: Conformity (Need for)

SCALE DESCRIPTION: Kohli and Jaworski (1994) used this four item, five-point Likert-type scale to measure the extent to which a salesperson is concerned about whether his or her behavior conforms to social expectations.

SCALE ORIGIN: Kohli and Jaworski (1994) stated that the scale was adapted from Jackson (1967). One reversed item from the original five-item scale, "I believe in speaking my mind, even if it offends others," was eliminated on the basis of the pretest.

SAMPLES: Because the nature of the study required that salesperson behavior and output be visible to coworkers, thus enabling coworker feedback, Kohli and Jaworski (1994) chose to sample retail auto salespeople. The preliminary set of scale items was first administered to 11 auto salespeople from five dealerships. Their responses enabled scale item and questionnaire revision. The final questionnaire was mailed to 303 salespeople belonging to the nationwide dealership network of a European car manufacturer. A reminder followed by a second questionnaire mailing resulted in usable responses being obtained from **150** salespeople.

RELIABILITY: Kohli and Jaworski (1994) reported a coefficient alpha of **.62** for this measure.

VALIDITY: Kohli and Jaworski (1994) used confirmatory factory analysis to test the unidimensionality of the salesperson need for conformity measure in conjunction with measures of outcome self-feedback, behavioral self-feedback, and experience. Results suggested that the measure was unidimensional. No other specific assessments of validity were discussed by the authors.

ADMINISTRATION: Kohli and Jaworski (1994) stated that the scale was part of a self-administered questionnaire that was delivered by mail. A personally addressed cover letter promising complete confidentiality accompanied the survey, as did a self-addressed reply envelope and ballpoint pen incentive. A reminder was sent one week after the initial mailing, and nonrespondents received a second reminder and questionnaire three weeks after the initial mailing. Lower scores on the scale indicated that a salesperson had a stronger belief in the need to conform to social expectations.

MAJOR FINDINGS: Kohli and Jaworski (1994) investigated how positive output, negative output, positive behavioral, and negative behavioral forms of coworker feedback affected salespeople's output and behavioral role clarity, satisfaction with coworkers, and output and behavioral performance. Salespeople exhibiting a high **need for conformity** to social expectations were hypothesized as being more likely to seek out and pay attention to feedback from coworkers, which would thereby moderate the relationship between coworker feedback and salesperson role clarity. Hierarchical regression analysis failed to support the moderator role of **need for conformity**.

REFERENCES:
Jackson, Douglas N. (1967), *Manual for the Personality Research Forum*. London, Ontario: University of Western Ontario.
Kohli, Ajay K. and Bernard J. Jaworski (1994), "The Influence of Coworker Feedback on Salespeople," *JM*, 58 (October), 82–94.

#545 *Conformity (Need for)*

SCALE ITEMS:

Strongly   Strongly
disagree   agree

1————————2————————3————————4————————5

1. I am very sensitive to what other people think of me.

2. Before making a decision, I often worry whether others will approve of it.

3. My actions are governed by the way people expect me to behave.

4. I can't be bothered trying to find out what others think of me. **(r)**

SCALE NAME: Confrontive Coping

SCALE DESCRIPTION: Strutton and Lumpkin (1994) adapted this four-item, five-point subscale from the Ways of Coping Checklist Scale developed by Folkman and Lazarus (1980, 1985). It attempts to measure the extent to which a salesperson uses confrontational tactics to cope with stressful customer sales presentations. In this study, the original items were screened for applicability to the sales setting. The remaining items were then subjected to factor analysis in a manner similar to that used by Folkman and colleagues (1986), and the subscales were identified in that manner.

SCALE ORIGIN: The items were adapted by Strutton and Lumpkin (1994) for a sales setting from the Ways of Coping Checklist (Folkman and Lazarus 1980, 1985). The original measure contained 43 items developed to measure problem-focused (24 items) and emotion-focused (19 items) tactics for handling stressful situations.

SAMPLES: Strutton and Lumpkin's (1994) sample was a nonprobability sample of **101** nonmanager salespeople from three industries, communications technology (60), textiles (22), and furniture (19), predominantly in the southern United States.

RELIABILITY: Strutton and Lumpkin (1994) reported a Cronbach's alpha of **.69** for this scale.

VALIDITY: No specific validity tests were reported by Strutton and Lumpkin (1994). However, this scale was identified as a separate subscale in Folkman and colleagues' (1986) work.

ADMINISTRATION: Strutton and Lumpkin (1994) asked respondents to describe the most stressful customer-related situation they had encountered during a sales presentation during the previous two months. They were then asked to respond to the items in the scale, along with other scales and demographic questions. Higher scores on the scale indicated that confrontive coping tactics for dealing with stress were used to a greater extent.

MAJOR FINDINGS: Strutton and Lumpkin (1994) found that **confrontive coping** was not significantly related to sales presentation effectiveness in a regression of all subscales on a self-reported measure of presentation effectiveness. The authors reported this as a positive finding and indicated that this strategy would be counterproductive in a sales situation.

REFERENCES:

Folkman, Susan and Richard S. Lazarus (1980), "An Analysis of Coping in a Middle-Aged Community Sample," *Journal of Health and Social Behavior*, 21 (September), 219–39.

———— and ———— (1985), "If It Changes, It Must Be a Process: Study of Emotion and Coping During Three Stages of a College Examination," *Journal of Personality and Social Psychology*, 48 (January), 150–70.

————, ————, Christine Dunkel-Schetter, Anita DeLongis, and Rand J. Gruen (1986), "Dynamics of a Stressful Encounter: Cognitive Appraisal, Coping, and Encounter Outcomes," *Journal of Personality and Social Psychology*, 50 (May), 992–1003.

Strutton, David and James R. Lumpkin (1994), "Problem- and Emotion-Focused Coping Dimensions and Sales Presentation Effectiveness," *JAMS*, 22 (1), 28–37.

#546 *Confrontive Coping*

SCALE ITEMS:

Directions: Indicate the extent to which you used each of the following tactics to cope with a stressful sales presentation experience.

Not used at all :____:____:____:____:____:____: Used a great deal
       1   2   3   4   5

1. Stood my ground and fought for what I wanted.

2. Took a big chance and did something risky.

3. Expressed anger to the person(s) who caused the problem.

4. Did something I did not think would work, but at least I was doing something.

SCALE NAME: Connectedness (Interdepartmental)

SCALE DESCRIPTION: A six-item, five-point Likert-type scale measuring the degree to which formal and informal direct contact occurs among employees of different departments.

SCALE ORIGIN: Menon, Jaworski, and Kohli (1997) indicated that the scale was developed and first reported in Jaworski and Kohli (1993). Closer examination of the source article revealed that the sample and data used to develop the scale were identical to those reported in Menon, Jaworski, and Kohli (1997).

SAMPLES: Using the *Dun & Bradstreet Million Dollar Directory* as the sampling frame, Menon, Jaworski, and Kohli (1997) selected for initial contact every other company name from among the top 1000 companies by sales revenues. Participation from multiple strategic business units (SBU) within an organization was requested. A total of 102 companies agreed to participate, and ultimately, responses representing **222** SBUs were obtained from marketing and nonmarketing executives.

RELIABILITY: Menon, Jaworski, and Kohli (1997) reported a **.80** alpha reliability coefficient. One item with low interitem correlations was eliminated from the original seven-item scale set to yield the final six-item measure shown here.

VALIDITY: No specific examination of scale validity was presented by Menon, Jaworski, and Kohli (1997) or Jaworski and Kohli (1993).

ADMINISTRATION: The 206 marketing and 187 nonmarketing executives identified by participating corporations were directly contacted by Menon, Jaworski, and Kohli (1997). Initial contact was followed by a self-administered mail questionnaire, and a follow-up questionnaire was sent three weeks later to nonrespondents. Most (79.6%) of the marketing executives and 70% of the nonmarketing executives contacted provided data for the study. When both nonmarketing and marketing executives from a single SBU responded, their scores were averaged to provide a single score for the construct. A higher score on the interdepartmental conflict scale indicated less goal congruity between departments and interdepartmental interactions characterized by greater levels of tension and distrust.

MAJOR FINDINGS: Menon, Jaworski, and Kohli (1997) investigated the role of organizational factors affecting interdepartmental interactions and the resulting impact on product quality. A key finding suggested that **interdepartmental connectedness** has a positive impact on the level of product quality and is most important when high technological and market turbulence exist. Greater levels of risk aversion among top managers, greater levels of segregation and compartmentalization of activities within departments, and more hierarchical levels within the organizational structure led to lower levels of **interdepartmental connectedness**, whereas the use of market-focused reward systems appears to increase **interdepartmental connectedness**.

REFERENCES:
Jaworski, Bernard and Ajay K. Kohli (1993), "Market Orientation: Antecedents and Consequences," *JM*, 57 (July), 53–70.
Menon, Ajay, Bernard J. Jaworski, and Ajay K. Kohli (1997), "Product Quality: Impact of Interdepartmental Interactions," *JAMS*, 25 (3), 187–200.

#547 *Connectedness (Interdepartmental)*

SCALE ITEMS:

Strongly   Strongly
disagree   agree

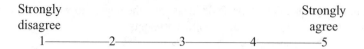

1. In this business unit, it is easy to talk with virtually anyone you need to, regardless of rank or position.

2. There is ample opportunity for informal "hall talk" among individuals from different departments in this business unit.

3. In this business unit, employees from different departments feel comfortable calling each other when the need arises.

4. Managers here discourage employees from discussing work-related matters with those who are not their immediate superiors or subordinates. **(r)**

5. People around here are quite accessible to those in other departments.

6. Junior managers in my department can easily schedule meetings with junior managers in other departments.

SCALE NAME: Contracting Over Roles (Explicit)

SCALE DESCRIPTION: Lusch and Brown (1996) stated that this three-item, seven-point scale was used to assess the extent to which a contract or letter of agreement between a supplier and wholesale distributor explicitly and formally outlined the responsibilities, roles, and performance expectations for each party.

SCALE ORIGIN: Lusch and Brown (1996) indicated that the scale was original to their study. Items were generated following a review of the relevant literature and refined through pretesting.

SAMPLES: A systematic random sample of 3225 firms was drawn by Lusch and Brown (1996) from a mailing list of all U.S. merchant wholesalers and agents/brokers in 16 four-digit standard industrial classification code groups. The sample was further reduced by eliminating firms with more than 20 employees. General managers were identified as the key informants for the remaining firms and were sent a mail questionnaire. Incentives and a follow-up mailing resulted in an initial response rate of 28.8%. However, this study reported usable data specific only to the **454** respondents classified as wholesale distributors and excluded data from agent and broker firms. The authors noted that the average number of suppliers reported by wholesalers in the sample was 45, with the major supplier contributing an average of 49% of the firm's annual volume.

RELIABILITY: Lusch and Brown (1996) reported a composite reliability of **.943** for this scale.

VALIDITY: Lusch and Brown (1996) reported undertaking a thorough review of the practitioner and academic literature, as well as extensive practitioner pretesting, to ensure content validity. Confirmatory factor analysis was used to establish the unidimensionality of the measure. Convergent and discriminant validity were also assessed and found to be satisfactory, which indicates that the measure possessed adequate construct validity.

ADMINISTRATION: The scale was included as part of a self-administered mail survey. A $1 incentive and the promise of shared survey results were offered as participant incentives, and a personalized cover letter accompanied the survey packet. Undeliverable questionnaires were redirected to a replacement firm. A second mailing without a monetary incentive was sent one month later. Lusch and Brown (1996) instructed respondents to answer all questions pertaining to major suppliers in the context of the supplier with which the wholesale distributor did the most business. Higher scores on the measure indicated that the contract between the major supplier and the wholesale distributor was more explicit in defining the expected performance, roles, and responsibilities of each party.

MAJOR FINDINGS: Lusch and Brown (1996) investigated how the type of dependency structure—wholesaler dependent on supplier, supplier dependent on wholesaler, or bilateral dependency—influenced whether a normative or explicit contract was used. The authors also studied whether dependency structure and the type of contract influenced the performance of wholesale distributors. Results indicated that, as supplier dependency on the wholesale distributor increases, the **explicitness of the contract** governing the relationship between the firms increases. Wholesale distributors maintaining a long-term orientation in their relationship with suppliers were found to rely more heavily on **explicit contracts** than did those with short-term orientations. As hypothesized, high bilateral dependency was not associated with **explicit contracts,** and the extent to which **explicit contracts** were used to govern the relationship between firms had no significant bearing on the degree of relational behavior between parties.

#548 *Contracting Over Roles (Explicit)*

REFERENCES:

Lusch, Robert F. and James R. Brown (1996), "Interdependency, Contracting, and Relational Behavior in Marketing Channels," *JM*, 60 (October), 19–38.

SCALE ITEMS:

Completely inaccurate
description
1————2————3————4————5————6————7
Completely accurate
description

1. In dealing with our major supplier, our contract or distribution agreement precisely defines the role of each party.

2. In dealing with our major supplier, our contract or distribution agreement precisely defines the responsibilities of each party.

3. In dealing with our major supplier, our contract or distribution agreement precisely states how each party is to perform.

SCALE NAME: Contracting Over Roles (Normative)

SCALE DESCRIPTION: Lusch and Brown (1996) stated that this three-item, seven-point Likert-type scale was used to assess the extent to which a supplier and wholesale distributor used informal guidelines, rather than explicitly stated formal contracts or letters of agreement, to determine the responsibilities, roles, and performance expectations for each party.

SCALE ORIGIN: Lusch and Brown (1996) indicated that the scale was original to their study. Items were generated following a review of the relevant literature and refined through pretesting.

SAMPLES: A systematic random sample of 3225 firms was drawn by Lusch and Brown (1996) from a mailing list of all U.S. merchant wholesalers and agents/brokers in 16 four-digit standard industrial classification code groups. The sample was further reduced by eliminating firms with more than 20 employees. General managers were identified as the key informants for the remaining firms and were sent a mail questionnaire. Incentives and a follow-up mailing resulted in an initial response rate of 28.8%. However, this study reported usable data specific only to the **454** respondents classified as wholesale distributors and excluded data from agent and broker firms. The authors noted that the average number of suppliers reported by wholesalers in the sample was 45, with the major supplier contributing an average of 49% of the firm's annual volume.

RELIABILITY: Lusch and Brown (1996) reported a composite reliability of **.965** for this scale.

VALIDITY: Lusch and Brown (1996) reported undertaking a thorough review of the practitioner and academic literature, as well as extensive practitioner pretesting, to ensure content validity. Confirmatory factor analysis was used to establish the unidimensionality of the measure. Convergent and discriminant validity were also assessed and found to be satisfactory, which indicates that the measure possessed adequate construct validity.

ADMINISTRATION: The scale was included as part of a self-administered mail survey. A $1 incentive and the promise of shared survey results were offered as participant incentives, and a personalized cover letter accompanied the survey packet. Undeliverable questionnaires were redirected to a replacement firm. A second mailing without a monetary incentive was sent one month later. Lusch and Brown (1996) instructed respondents to answer all questions pertaining to major suppliers in the context of the supplier with which the wholesale distributor did the most business. Because all items in the scale were reversed, higher scores on the measure indicated a greater use of informal guidelines for defining the expected performance, roles, and responsibilities of the major supplier and the wholesale distributor.

MAJOR FINDINGS: Lusch and Brown (1996) investigated how the type of dependency structure—wholesaler dependent on supplier, supplier dependent on wholesaler, or bilateral dependency—influenced whether a normative or explicit contract was used. The authors also studied whether dependency structure and the type of contract influenced the performance of wholesale-distributors. Findings suggested that only in the case of bilateral dependency does high dependency lead to more **normative contracts** between suppliers and wholesale distributors. Relational behavior was positively associated with the use of **normative contracts**, and wholesale distributors who maintained a long-term orientations in their relationships with suppliers were found to rely more heavily on **normative contracts** than did those with short-term orientations. Higher wholesale distributor performance was associated with a greater use of **normative contracts** in governing the relationship between suppliers and wholesale distributors.

#549 *Contracting Over Roles (Normative)*

REFERENCES:

Lusch, Robert F. and James R. Brown (1996), "Interdependency, Contracting, and Relational Behavior in Marketing Channels," *JM,* 60 (October), 19–38.

SCALE ITEMS:

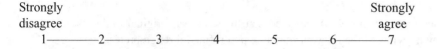

Strongly disagree — Strongly agree

1————2————3————4————5————6————7

1. In dealing with our major supplier, we have a mutual understanding of the role of each party. **(r)**

2. In dealing with our major supplier, we have a mutual understanding of the responsibilities of each party. **(r)**

3. In dealing with our major supplier, we have a mutual understanding of how each party is to perform. **(r)**

SCALE NAME: Control (Interpersonal)

SCALE DESCRIPTION: Pullins, Fine, and Warren (1996) used this ten-item, seven-point Likert-type scale to measure salespersons' perceptions of the degree to which they are able to control situations involving others, including defending their own interests, maintaining group harmony, and developing social relationships.

SCALE ORIGIN: The scale used by Pullins, Fine, and Warren (1996) is one of three subscales in the spheres-of-control battery of items that were developed and refined by Paulhus and Christie (1981) over a two-year period of time.

SAMPLES: Ten regional sales managers and 216 salespeople employed by a national commercial food equipment manufacturer were sampled by Pullins, Fine, and Warren (1996). Regional sales managers did not complete the survey but instead were asked to provide evaluations of salespersons' performance. A total of **194** usable responses were obtained from the sales force, and sales managers provided evaluations for **113** of those sales representatives.

RELIABILITY: Pullins, Fine, and Warren (1996) reported a coefficient alpha of **.70** for this measure.

VALIDITY: No specific examination of the scale's validity was reported by Pullins, Fine, and Warren (1996).

ADMINISTRATION: The scale was included with other measures as part of a self-administered survey that was delivered by mail to members of the sales force. Pullins, Fine, and Warren (1996) included a cover letter with the survey, featuring an endorsement for the project from the company's vice president of sales. Higher scores on the scale indicated that a salesperson rated his or her ability to encourage others to share information about themselves as strong, which thereby suggests that this salesperson was perceived by others as responsive, warm, and a good listener.

MAJOR FINDINGS: Pullins, Fine, and Warren (1996) conducted an exploratory investigation of factors influencing the willingness and ability of salespeople to act as mentors. Regression analysis was used to test hypotheses; tests of ability to mentor were restricted to the 42 salespeople who had actually served as mentors. Salespeople who scored higher with respect to their interpersonal competence, as measured by the **interpersonal control** scale, were neither significantly more willing nor more able to mentor. Sales managers perceived salespeople with more experience and greater job satisfaction as being more likely to choose to mentor; the relationship with interpersonal competence as measured by the **interpersonal control** scale was not significant.

REFERENCES:
Paulhus, Delroy, and R. Christie (1981), "Spheres of Control: An Interactionist Approach to Assessment of Perceived Control," in *Research with the Locus of Control Construct*, Vol. 1, J.H. Lefcourt, ed. New York: Academic Press.
Pullins, Ellen Bolman, Leslie M. Fine, and Wendy L. Warren (1996), "Identifying Peer Mentors in the Sales Force: An Exploratory Investigation of Willingness and Ability," *JAMS*, 24 (2), 125–36.

#550 *Control (Interpersonal)*

SCALE ITEMS:

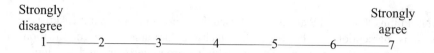

Strongly
disagree
1————2————3————4————5————6————7

Strongly
agree

1. Even when I'm feeling self-confident about most things, I still seem to lack the ability to control social situations. **(r)**

2. I have no trouble making and keeping friends.

3. I'm not good at guiding the course of a conversation with several others. **(r)**

4. I can usually establish a close personal relationship with someone I find attractive.

5. When being interviewed I can usually steer the interviewer toward the topics I want to talk about and away from those I wish to avoid.

6. If I need help in carrying off a plan of mine, it's usually difficult to get others to help. **(r)**

7. If there's someone I want to meet I can usually arrange it.

8. I often find it hard to get my point of view across to others. **(r)**

9. In attempting to smooth over a disagreement I usually make it worse. **(r)**

10. I find it easy to play an important part in most group situations.

SCALE NAME: Control (Wholesaler Over Retailer)

SCALE DESCRIPTION: This 15-item scale was used by Chatterjee, Hyvönen, and Anderson (1995) to measure retailers' perceptions of the overall extent to which a wholesaler actually influences their decisions. Responses for each item were recorded on a 100-point constant sum scale, with the points allocated between the wholesaler and retailer so as to represent the percentage of influence that each has over various retailer business decisions.

SCALE ORIGIN: The scale appears to be original to Chatterjee, Hyvönen, and Anderson (1995), who assessed the unidimensionality of the measure using factor analysis and the reliability of the scale using calculations of coefficient alpha. No items were deleted from the measure.

SAMPLES: Chatterjee, Hyvönen, and Anderson (1995) sampled a cross-section of 305 food and grocery retailers whose names had been submitted by two major wholesalers working in the Finnish market. A total of **236** usable questionnaires were received for an effective response rate of 77.4%. The sample was described as being well distributed across regions of the country, store categories, and store size.

RELIABILITY: Chatterjee, Hyvönen, and Anderson (1995) reported a coefficient alpha of **.85** for this measure.

VALIDITY: Chatterjee, Hyvönen, and Anderson (1995) examined the correlation matrix of the measures used in their study and stated that the low intercorrelations exhibited suggested that the measures offered discriminant validity.

ADMINISTRATION: Although the study was clearly identified to potential respondents as being academic in orientation, the questionnaire was administered in Finnish by members of the Finnish Office of Free Trade to a key informant, typically the top manager or owner of the retail store. The questions were close-ended and had been previously translated and pretested. It is not clear whether the survey was administered at the retailer's place of business or whether retailers came to the Finnish Office of Free Trade. Chatterjee, Hyvönen, and Anderson (1995) indicated that retailers were asked to answer the survey in the context of the focal wholesaler that had provided their name for the study. The relative control of the wholesaler and retailer was interpreted such that 50 points allocated to both the retailer and wholesaler indicated balanced control, 100 points to the wholesaler indicated complete domination of the retailer by the wholesaler, and 100 points to the retailer indicated no wholesaler control whatsoever.

MAJOR FINDINGS: Chatterjee, Hyvönen, and Anderson (1995) investigated purchasing decisions in closed markets with respect to the choice of a concentrated versus balanced sourcing strategy. The **wholesaler's control over the retailer's decisions** was not significantly related to the choice of a concentrated or balanced sourcing strategy.

REFERENCES:
Chatterjee, Sharmila C., Saara Hyvönen, and Erin Anderson (1995), "Concentrated vs. Balanced Sourcing: An Examination of Retailer Purchasing Decisions in Closed Markets," *JR*, 71 (1), 23–46.

#551 *Control (Wholesaler Over Retailer)*

SCALE ITEMS:

Directions: Please indicate the extent to which you consider the wholesaler *actually* influences your decisions concerning your own business in each of the business areas. Please mark out of *100* points.

Retailer   Wholesaler

_____   +   _____   =   100%

1. Product varieties and number of sizes in assortment.

2. Your decisions to add new products.

3. Your decisions to delete new products.

4. Your decisions to realize joint marketing programs in your store.

5. Your decisions concerning store marketing.

6. Your decisions to choose "individual" marketing mix combinations.

7. Pricing decisions of your products.

8. Planning in-store operations.

9. Acquisition of store equipment.

10. Your decisions to participate in joint advertising and campaigns.

11. Purchasing policy of your store and the decisions to purchase from different suppliers.

12. Number of units purchased from industrial suppliers.

13. Number of "campaign" units purchased from this wholesaler.

14. Financial arrangements of your store.

15. Goals, policies, and operations of your store.

SCALE NAME: Control System/Goal Differences (Partner)

SCALE DESCRIPTION: Smith and Barclay (1997) used this five-item, seven-point Likert-type scale to measure the degree of incongruence between partner firms with respect to the procedures used in monitoring, directing, evaluating, and compensating employees, as well as with respect to the organizational goals and tactics that characterized the firm.

SCALE ORIGIN: Smith and Barclay (1997) indicated that the constructs used in their study were operationalized with a mix of original and adapted scale items generated from the conceptual definition of the constructs, a review of the literature, field interviews, and pretest results. Each of the final items representing this measure passed the extensive preliminary analysis of item reliability and validity described by the authors.

SAMPLES: Smith and Barclay (1997) collected dyadic self-report data in two stages. The sponsor sample was composed of 338 sales representatives working for the Canadian subsidiaries of two multinational companies serving the computer industry. Forty percent of the 338 employees who were randomly selected from employee lists returned completed surveys. Using the names and contact information of relationship partners volunteered by these respondents, the authors then sampled the 135 dyadic partners. A total of **103** usable paired responses were obtained.

RELIABILITY: Smith and Barclay (1997) reported coefficient alphas for this measure of **.81** in the sponsor model and **.79** in the partner model.

VALIDITY: Smith and Barclay (1997) reported extensive testing of the reliability, unidimensionality, and convergent and discriminant validity of the measures used in their study. LISREL and confirmatory factor analysis were used to demonstrate that the scale satisfied each of these standards, though some items from the measures as originally proposed were eliminated in the process.

ADMINISTRATION: Smith and Barclay (1997) included the scale with other measures as part of a self-administered survey that was delivered by internal company mail to sales representatives and by regular U.S. mail to the dyadic partners. E-mail follow-ups were used to increase survey response rate. Half of the sales representatives were instructed to consider a customer situation in the prior six months in which they had had some success with a selling partner, whereas the other half were to told to choose a situation in which they had had little or no success. Participants then responded to questions about the partner, their relationship, and the organization in the context of this situation. Higher scores on the scale indicated that greater differences were perceived as existing between the sponsor and partner firm with respect to organizational controls systems and goals.

MAJOR FINDINGS: Smith and Barclay (1997) developed and tested two research models explaining selling partner relationship effectiveness. The first examined four organizational differences from the sponsor's (salesperson's) perspective, and the second examined these same differences from the partner's perspective. In the sponsor model, greater perceived differences in the **control systems and goals of partner firms** led to lower evaluations of the judgment and character/motive components of mutual perceived trustworthiness.

REFERENCES:
Smith, J. Brock and Donald W. Barclay (1997), "The Effects of Organizational Differences and Trust on the Effectiveness of Selling Partner Relationships," *JM*, 61 (January), 3–21.

#552 *Control System/Goal Differences (Partner)*

SCALE ITEMS:*

Strongly   Strongly
disagree   agree

1. Incompatible reward/incentive systems.

2. Procedures for control/influences not at cross purposes. **(r)** **

3. Differences in reward systems get in the way of us working together.

4. Meeting my firm's objectives does not impair this rep's ability to meet his/her own firm's objectives. **(r)** **

5. The goals of our organizations are consistent and compatible. **(r)** **

*All of the items in this scale were conceptualized at the organizational level.

**Smith and Barclay (1997) did not designate these items as reversed. However, this is probably necessary given the nature of the items.

SCALE NAME: Coordination (with Manufacturer)

SCALE DESCRIPTION: Mohr, Fisher, and Nevin (1996) used this three-item, five-point Likert-type scale to assess the degree to which manufacturer and dealer activities were well organized and synchronized.

SCALE ORIGIN: It appears that the scale items used were original to Guiltinan, Rejab, and Rodgers (1980). Mohr, Fisher, and Nevin (1996) pretested and revised the measure in a series of iterative personal interviews with 12 computer dealers.

SAMPLES: Mohr, Fisher, and Nevin (1996) surveyed 557 computer retailer key informants (owners or managers); **125** usable surveys were returned. The computer retailers selected for study either were affiliated with the microcomputer industry trade association or were one of 53 randomly selected outlets for a major computer franchiser. The average number of workers employed by responding retailers was 22.3, and the average monthly sales volume was $970,000.

RELIABILITY: Mohr, Fisher, and Nevin (1996) reported a coefficient alpha of **.75** for this measure.

VALIDITY: Mohr, Fisher, and Nevin (1996) stated that the measure exhibited acceptable levels of convergent and discriminatory validity on the basis of the results of a confirmatory factor analysis.

ADMINISTRATION: The measure was included by Mohr, Fisher, and Nevin (1996) as part of a self-administered questionnaire that was delivered by mail. Nonrespondents received a reminder letter approximately one month after the initial mailing. Retailers were randomly assigned to answer questions about either their best or their worst relationship with a manufacturer. Higher scores on the scale indicated that retailer and manufacturer activities were more organized and synchronized.

MAJOR FINDINGS: Mohr, Fisher, and Nevin (1996) investigated the relationship between collaborative communication and channel outcomes (satisfaction with the relationship, relationship commitment, relationship coordination) in the context of differing levels of dealer/manufacturer integration (franchise versus company-owned). Hypotheses were tested by hierarchical moderator regression analysis. The results indicated that, with higher levels of manufacturer control, dealers were more satisfied and committed to the relationship and reported that their efforts were better **coordinated** with the manufacturer. However, significant interactions between control and communication demonstrated that higher levels of collaborative communication have stronger, more positive effects on satisfaction, commitment, and **coordination** in low manufacturer control conditions than in situations in which manufacturer control was high or in less integrated relationship conditions (e.g., franchise versus company-owned).

REFERENCES:

Guiltinan, Joseph, Ismail Rejab, and William Rodgers (1980), "Factors Influencing Coordination in a Franchise Channel," *JR*, 56 (Fall), 41–58.

Mohr, Jakki J., Robert J. Fisher, and John R. Nevin (1996), "Collaborative Communication in Interfirm Relationships: Moderating Effects of Integration and Control," *JM*, 60 (July), 103–15.

SCALE ITEMS:

Strongly   Strongly
disagree   agree
1————————2————————3————————4————————5

1. Programs at the local level are well-coordinated with the manufacturer's national programs.

2. We feel like we never know what we are supposed to be doing or when we are supposed to be doing it for this manufacturer's products. **(r)**

3. Our activities with this manufacturer are well-coordinated.

SCALE NAME: Coordination Efforts (Behavior-Based)

SCALE DESCRIPTION: Celly and Frazier (1996) used this six-item, seven-point scale to measure the extent to which a supplier's personnel emphasize tasks and activities, such as customer education, that are expected to lead to bottom-line results.

SCALE ORIGIN: The scale is original to Celly and Frazier (1996). Multiple items were developed for the scale using the conceptual definition of the construct, prior research, and information provided during prestudy interviews with suppliers and distributors. Scale items were then purified using item analysis and an exploratory factor analysis.

SAMPLES: Celly and Frazier (1996) effectively sampled 953 distributors randomly selected from Dun's Marketing Services' Direct Access service who had passed a variety of screening processes. The selected distributors serviced one of four industries: machine tools and metalworking machinery, air compressors and packaging equipment, industrial tools, and abrasives and adhesives. **Two hundred seven** usable responses were obtained.

RELIABILITY: Celly and Frazier (1996) reported a coefficient alpha of **.88** for the scale.

VALIDITY: The 14 items comprising the outcome- and behavior-based coordination scales were subjected to a factor analysis by Celly and Frazier (1996) to assess the unidimensionality of the measures. Items loading on multiple factors were dropped from the scale. The discriminant validity of all of the measures used in the study was found to be satisfactory according to the results of a principal components factors analysis with orthogonal rotation.

ADMINISTRATION: Celly and Frazier (1996) included the scale with other measures as part of a self-administered survey that was delivered by mail. Prenotification and reminders, incentives, and a second survey mailing to nonrespondents were used to enhance response rates. Higher scores on the scale indicated that distributors perceived their supplier's personnel as being more likely to emphasize tasks and activities that contributed to outcomes such as sales, market share, and other bottom-line results.

MAJOR FINDINGS: Celly and Frazier (1996) investigated suppliers' use of outcome- and behavior-based coordinator efforts with their distributors. Chow tests comparing information provided by exclusive dealers with that provided by nonexclusive dealers confirmed the appropriateness of analyzing the data jointly. The use of **behavior-based coordination efforts** was positively related to the distributor value added but negatively related to both supplier resource constraints and distributors' perceptions of supplier replaceability. Both environmental uncertainty and supplier familiarity demonstrated strong, positive effects on **behavior-based supplier coordination efforts**.

REFERENCES:
Celly, Kirti Sawhney and Gary L. Frazier (1996), "Outcome-Based and Behavior-Based Coordination Efforts in Channel Relationships," *JMR,* 33 (May), 200–210.

SCALE ITEMS:
Directions: Please consider all your personal interactions, both formal and informal, with this supplier's sales and marketing personnel (e.g., sales representatives, sales managers, marketing managers) during the last year. Include both phone and face-to-face contacts regarding business issues. During such interactions in the past year, indicate below the extent to which the supplier's personnel focused on or emphasized each of the following areas of your business.

#554 *Coordination Efforts (Behavior-Based)*

Very little
emphasis

A great deal
of emphasis

1————2————3————4————5————6————7

1. Individual product line sales.

2. Sales relative to targets.

3. Distributor product and applications knowledge.

4. Selling techniques used by distributor sales reps.

5. Distributor participation in promotional programs.

6. Distributor customer education and support activities.

SCALE NAME: Coordination Efforts (Outcome-Based)

SCALE DESCRIPTION: Celly and Frazier (1996) used this five-item, seven-point scale to measure the extent to which a supplier's personnel emphasize bottom-line results, such as sales growth, in their personal communications with the distributor's personnel.

SCALE ORIGIN: The scale is original to Celly and Frazier (1996). Multiple items were developed for the scale using the conceptual definition of the construct, prior research, and information provided during prestudy interviews with suppliers and distributors. Scale items were then purified using item analysis and an exploratory factor analysis.

SAMPLES: Celly and Frazier (1996) effectively sampled 953 distributors randomly selected from Dun's Marketing Services' Direct Access service who had passed a variety of screening processes. The selected distributors serviced one of four industries: machine tools and metalworking machinery, air compressors and packaging equipment, industrial tools, and abrasives and adhesives. **Two hundred seven** usable responses were obtained.

RELIABILITY: Celly and Frazier (1996) reported a coefficient alpha of **.87** for the scale.

VALIDITY: The 14 items composing the outcome- and behavior-based coordination scales were subjected to a factor analysis by Celly and Frazier (1996) to assess the unidimensionality of the measures. Items loading on multiple factors were dropped from the scale. The discriminant validity of all of the measures used in the study was found to be satisfactory according to the results of a principal components factors analysis with orthogonal rotation.

ADMINISTRATION: Celly and Frazier (1996) included the scale with other measures as part of a self-administered survey that was delivered by mail. Prenotification and reminders, incentives, and a second survey mailing to nonrespondents were used to enhance response rates. Higher scores on the scale indicated that distributors perceived their supplier's personnel as being more likely to emphasize bottom-line results during personal communications.

MAJOR FINDINGS: Celly and Frazier (1996) investigated suppliers' use of outcome- and behavior-based coordinator efforts with their distributors. Chow tests comparing information provided by exclusive dealers with that provided by nonexclusive dealers confirmed the appropriateness of analyzing the data jointly. The use of **outcome-based coordination efforts** was positively related to a distributor's experience with the supplier's product but negatively related to both supplier resource constraints and distributors' perceptions of supplier replaceability. Contrary to expectations, environmental uncertainty was positively, rather than negatively, related to **outcome-based supplier coordination efforts**.

REFERENCES:
Celly, Kirti Sawhney and Gary L. Frazier (1996), "Outcome-Based and Behavior-Based Coordination Efforts in Channel Relationships," *JMR*, 33 (May), 200–210.

SCALE ITEMS:
Directions: Please consider all your personal interactions, both formal and informal, with this supplier's sales and marketing personnel (e.g., sales representatives, sales managers, marketing managers) during the last year. Include both phone and face-to-face contacts regarding business issues. During such interactions in the past year, indicate below the extent to which the supplier's personnel focused on or emphasized each of the following areas of your business.

#555 *Coordination Efforts (Outcome-Based)*

Very little   A great deal
emphasis   of emphasis

1————2————3————4————5————6————7

1. Total sales volume.

2. Market share performance.

3. Sales growth.

4. Extent of distributor promotional efforts.

5. Distributor service capabilities.

SCALE NAME: Corporate Culture (Communication Openness)

SCALE DESCRIPTION: Kitchell (1995) used this five-item, seven-point Likert-type scale to measure the extent to which a firm's corporate culture encourages open communication among peers, subordinates, and superiors.

SCALE ORIGIN: The development of the scale is original to Kitchell (1995). Kitchell (1995) identified preliminary items through a literature review of cultural norms as they relate to the adoption of technology and exploratory interviews with vendors and technology adopters. This initial set of items was submitted to a panel of experts for assessment of content validity. The resulting measure was pretested on a sample of 80 MBA students and 30 corporate executives, whose comments allowed for additional scale refinement. Kitchell (1995) noted that multi-item scales were purified by deleting items that lowered Cronbach's alphas. Additional details were not provided.

SAMPLES: Kitchell (1995) developed a sampling frame of 219 companies in the machinery and metal works industry gathered from trade journals, equipment vendors, and academic researchers. Using stratified random sampling, 163 companies were chosen for contact. **One hundred ten** firms manufacturing equipment in 21 industries returned usable data for a response rate of 68%. Key demographics indicated that participating firms employed between 20 and 1500 people (mean = 146), had been in business between 3 and 119 years (mean = 25.2), had sales ranging from $200,000 to $22 billion (mean = $326.9 million), and experienced sales growth ranging from an unspecified negative figure to 30% annum for the past 5 years. Both the CEO and the buying center member designated by the CEO as being most involved with capital outlay purchases participated in the study for each firm.

RELIABILITY: Kitchell (1995) calculated an alpha of **.67** for this scale.

VALIDITY: Content validity was demonstrated in the pretest. Although specific details for each measure were not provided by Kitchell (1995), it appears that construct validity in the final study was assessed using measurements of internal consistency between items and by strong correlations between the measures of interest and the variables they were hypothesized to predict.

ADMINISTRATION: Kitchell (1995) stated that the scale was part of a self-administered questionnaire answered by corporate CEOs and one designated buying center member from each company. Additional qualitative data were collected by long interviews with respondents for the purpose of adding credence to the quantitative findings and interpretation and clarification of insignificant results. A higher score on the scale meant that the firm's corporate culture provided for more open communication among peers, subordinates, and superiors.

MAJOR FINDINGS: Kitchell (1995) investigated the relationship between corporate culture and innovation adoption in an industrial marketing context. No significant relationship between a **corporate culture fostering open communication** and the adoption of innovative computer-based manufacturing technologies was found.

REFERENCES:
Kitchell, Susan (1995), "Corporate Culture, Environmental Adaptation, and Innovation Adoption: A Qualitative/Quantitative Approach," *JAMS*, 23 (3), 195–205.

#556 *Corporate Culture (Communication Openness)*

SCALE ITEMS:

Strongly   Strongly
disagree   agree
　1————2————3————4————5————6————7

1. Communication between peers in this company is excellent.

2. Supervisors in this company are willing to share all relevant information with subordinates.

3. There is very little upward communication from subordinates to supervisors in this company. **(r)**

4. The direction of information flow in this company is mainly downward from bosses to subordinates. **(r)**

5. There are few opportunities for junior staff to have informal conversations with senior personnel. **(r)**

SCALE NAME: Corporate Culture (Flexibility)

SCALE DESCRIPTION: Kitchell (1995) used a four-item, seven-point Likert-type scale to measure the flexibility of the corporate culture. A flexible corporate culture was defined as one that is open to change and supportive of continuous improvements.

SCALE ORIGIN: The development of the scale is original to Kitchell (1995). Kitchell (1995) identified preliminary items through a literature review of cultural norms as they relate to the adoption of technology and exploratory interviews with vendors and technology adopters. This initial set of items was submitted to a panel of experts for assessment of content validity. The resulting measure was pretested on a sample of 80 MBA students and 30 corporate executives, whose comments allowed for additional scale refinement. Kitchell (1995) noted that multi-item scales were purified by deleting items that lowered Cronbach's alphas. Additional details were not provided.

SAMPLES: Kitchell (1995) developed a sampling frame of 219 companies in the machinery and metal works industry gathered from trade journals, equipment vendors, and academic researchers. Using stratified random sampling, 163 companies were chosen for contact. **One hundred ten** firms manufacturing equipment in 21 industries returned usable data for a response rate of 68%. Key demographics indicated that participating firms employed between 20 and 1500 people (mean = 146), had been in business between 3 and 119 years (mean = 25.2), had sales ranging from $200,000 to $22 billion (mean = $326.9 million), and experienced sales growth ranging from an unspecified negative figure to 30% annum for the past 5 years. Both the CEO and the buying center member designated by the CEO as being most involved with capital outlay purchases participated in the study for each firm.

RELIABILITY: Kitchell (1995) calculated an alpha of **.72** for this scale.

VALIDITY: Content validity was demonstrated in the pretest. Although specific details for each measure were not provided by Kitchell (1995), it appears that construct validity in the final study was assessed by measurements of internal consistency between items and by strong correlations between the measures of interest and the variables they were hypothesized to predict.

ADMINISTRATION: Kitchell (1995) stated that the scale was part of a self-administered questionnaire answered by corporate CEOs and one designated buying center member from each company. Additional qualitative data were collected through long interviews with respondents for the purpose of adding credence to the quantitative findings and interpretation and clarification of insignificant results. A high score on the flexibility measure meant that the firm was more open to change and more likely to engage in continuous improvements.

MAJOR FINDINGS: Kitchell (1995) investigated the relationship between corporate culture and innovation adoption in an industrial marketing context. The **flexibility of the corporate culture** was significantly related to the adoption of innovative computer-based manufacturing technologies, which suggests that, as computer technologies refine and enhance utility, companies must develop the ability to handle continuous change.

REFERENCES:
Kitchell, Susan (1995), "Corporate Culture, Environmental Adaptation, and Innovation Adoption: A Qualitative/Quantitative Approach," *JAMS*, 23 (3), 195–205.

#557 *Corporate Culture (Flexibility)*

SCALE ITEMS:

Strongly   Strongly
disagree   agree

1. This organization can be described as flexible and continually adapting to change.

2. New ideas are always being tried out here.

3. Top managers in this firm can be described as set in their ways. **(r)**

4. This organization is always moving toward improved ways of doing things.

SCALE NAME: Corporate Culture (Future-Oriented)

SCALE DESCRIPTION: Kitchell (1995) used this three-item, seven-point Likert-type scale to measure the extent to which a firm's corporate culture encourages planning and taking a long-term view.

SCALE ORIGIN: The development of the scale is original to Kitchell (1995). Kitchell (1995) identified preliminary items through a literature review of cultural norms as they relate to the adoption of technology and exploratory interviews with vendors and technology adopters. This initial set of items was submitted to a panel of experts for assessment of content validity. The resulting measure was pretested on a sample of 80 MBA students and 30 corporate executives, whose comments allowed for additional scale refinement. Kitchell (1995) noted that multi-item scales were purified by deleting items that lowered Cronbach's alphas. Additional details were not provided.

SAMPLES: Kitchell (1995) developed a sampling frame of 219 companies in the machinery and metal works industry gathered from trade journals, equipment vendors, and academic researchers. Using stratified random sampling, 163 companies were chosen for contact. **One hundred ten** firms manufacturing equipment in 21 industries returned usable data for a response rate of 68%. Key demographics indicated that participating firms employed between 20 and 1500 people (mean = 146), had been in business between 3 and 119 years (mean = 25.2), had sales ranging from $200,000 to $22 billion (mean = $326.9 million), and experienced sales growth ranging from an unspecified negative figure to 30% annum for the past 5 years. Both the CEO and the buying center member designated by the CEO as being most involved with capital outlay purchases participated in the study for each firm.

RELIABILITY: Kitchell (1995) calculated an alpha of **.80** for this scale.

VALIDITY: Content validity was demonstrated in the pretest. Although specific details for each measure were not provided by Kitchell (1995), it appears that construct validity in the final study was assessed by measurements of internal consistency between items and by strong correlations between the measures of interest and the variables they were hypothesized to predict.

ADMINISTRATION: Kitchell (1995) stated that the scale was part of a self-administered questionnaire answered by corporate CEOs and one designated buying center member from each company. Additional qualitative data were collected through long interviews with respondents for the purpose of adding credence to the quantitative findings and interpretation and clarification of insignificant results. A higher score on the measure meant that the firm's corporate culture was more deeply committed to planning and maintaining a long-term perspective.

MAJOR FINDINGS: Kitchell (1995) investigated the relationship between corporate culture and innovation adoption in an industrial marketing context. A positive relationship between the presence of a **future-oriented corporate culture** and the adoption of innovative computer-based manufacturing technologies was found.

REFERENCES:
Kitchell, Susan (1995), "Corporate Culture, Environmental Adaptation, and Innovation Adoption: A Qualitative/Quantitative Approach," *JAMS*, 23 (3), 195–205.

#558 *Corporate Culture (Future-Oriented)*

SCALE ITEMS:

Strongly   Strongly
disagree   agree
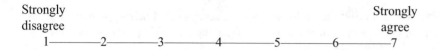
  1————2————3————4————5————6————7

1. The ability to plan ahead is highly valued here.

2. Management is constantly planning for the future of the company.

3. People here are encouraged to take a long-term view of their career with company.

SCALE NAME: Corporate Ethical Values

SCALE DESCRIPTION: Singhapakdi and colleagues (1995) used this five-item, nine-point Likert-type scale to measure a composite of the individual ethical values of managers, as well as the formal and informal policies on ethics within the firm.

SCALE ORIGIN: The corporate ethical values (CEV) scale was developed by Hunt, Wood, and Chonko (1989) to capture the extent to which employees perceived that (1) managers acted ethically in their organization, (2) managers were concerned about corporate ethical issues, and (3) ethical/unethical behavior was rewarded/punished in their organization. Hunt, Wood, and Chonko (1989) tested the measure with 1076 members of the American Marketing Association; an exploratory factor analysis found the measure to be unidimensional and reliable (coefficient alpha = .78). Although the original scale was measured in a seven-point ("strongly disagree" to "strongly agree") Likert format, Singhapakdi and colleagues (1995) adapted the scale to the nine-point format shown here.

SAMPLES: Singhapakdi and colleagues (1995) sent a mail questionnaire to a randomly drawn sample of 2000 professionals selected from the American Marketing Association mailing list. Of the 1995 that were delivered, **442** usable questionnaires were returned. Key demographics of the sample indicated that the majority of respondents were college educated (92.8%), men (51.4%), and middle mangers working in various industries.

RELIABILITY: Singhapakdi and colleagues (1995) reported a coefficient alpha of **.85** for this scale.

VALIDITY: Singhapakdi and colleagues (1995) did not specifically examine the scale's validity.

ADMINISTRATION: Singhapakdi and colleagues (1995) indicated that the measure was included as part of a self-administered mail survey. Higher scores on the CEV scale indicated that the respondent works in an organization with higher corporate ethical values.

MAJOR FINDINGS: Singhapakdi and colleagues (1995) investigated marketing practitioners' perceptions of the importance of ethics and social responsibility in achieving organizational effectiveness and how these perceptions were influenced by corporate ethical values and an individual's personal moral philosophy. An ordinary least squared regression analysis demonstrated that **corporate ethical values** positively influenced marketers' perceptions of the relative importance of ethics and social responsibility in achieving organizational effectiveness. Specifically, **corporate ethical values** positively influenced perceptions that ethical practices were (1) important to the long-term survival and profitability of the firm; (2) more important than stockholder happiness, achieving operating efficiencies, or making profits by any means possible; and (3) as important as communication and output quality to achieving corporate success.

REFERENCES:

Hunt, Shelby D., Van R. Wood, and Lawrence B. Chonko (1989), "Corporate Ethical Values and Organizational Commitment in Marketing," *JM*, 53 (July), 79–90.

Singhapakdi, Anusorn, Kenneth L. Kraft, Scott J. Vitell, and Kumar C. Rallapalli (1995), "The Perceived Importance of Ethics and Social Responsibility on Organizational Effectiveness: A Survey of Marketers," *JAMS*, 23 (1), 49–56.

#559 *Corporate Ethical Values*

SCALE ITEMS:

Completely disagree — 1—2—3—4—5—6—7—8—9 — Completely agree

1. Managers in my company often engage in behaviors that I consider to be unethical. **(r)**

2. In order to succeed in my company, it is often necessary to compromise one's ethics. **(r)**

3. Top management in my company has let it be known in no uncertain terms that unethical behaviors will not be tolerated.

4. If a manager in my company is discovered to have engaged in unethical behavior that results primarily in *personal gain* (rather than corporate gain), he or she will be promptly reprimanded.

5. If a manager in my company is discovered to have engaged in unethical behavior that results primarily in *corporate gain* (rather than personal gain), he or she will be promptly reprimanded.

SCALE NAME: Coworker Competence

SCALE DESCRIPTION: Kohli and Jaworski (1994) used this five-item, five-point Likert-type scale to measure the degree to which a salesperson perceives his or her coworkers as being knowledgeable, capable, and competent at their job and thus able to offer sales-related advice and judgment. Although one item is specific to car sales, the measure can be easily adapted for use in other industries.

SCALE ORIGIN: The scale is original to Kohli and Jaworski (1994). No additional information was provided with respect to how scale items were generated.

SAMPLES: Because the nature of the study required that salesperson behavior and output be visible to coworkers, thus enabling coworker feedback, Kohli and Jaworski (1994) chose to sample retail auto salespeople. The preliminary set of scale items was first administered to 11 auto salespeople from five dealerships; their comments enabled scale item and questionnaire revision. The final questionnaire was mailed to 303 salespeople belonging to the nationwide dealership network of a European car manufacturer. A reminder followed by a second questionnaire mailing resulted in usable responses being obtained from **150** salespeople.

RELIABILITY: Kohli and Jaworski (1994) reported a coefficient alpha of **.91** for this measure.

VALIDITY: Kohli and Jaworski (1994) used confirmatory factory analysis to test the unidimensionality of the coworker competence and satisfaction with coworker constructs. Results suggested that the measure was unidimensional. No other specific assessments of validity were discussed by the authors.

ADMINISTRATION: Kohli and Jaworski (1994) stated that the scale was part of a self-administered questionnaire that was delivered by mail. A personally addressed cover letter promising complete confidentiality accompanied the survey, as did a self-addressed reply envelope and ballpoint pen incentive. A reminder was sent one week after the initial mailing, and nonrespondents received a second reminder and questionnaire three weeks after the initial mailing. Lower scores on the scale indicated that salespeople perceived their coworkers as highly competent at their jobs and capable of offering sound advice and judgments.

MAJOR FINDINGS: Kohli and Jaworski (1994) investigated how positive output, negative output, positive behavioral, and negative behavioral forms of coworker feedback affected salespeople's output and behavioral role clarity, satisfaction with coworkers, and output and behavioral performance. **Coworker competence** was hypothesized as moderating the relationship between coworker feedback and salesperson role clarity. Hierarchical regression analysis failed to support the moderator role of **coworker competence**.

REFERENCES:
Kohli, Ajay K. and Bernard J. Jaworski (1994), "The Influence of Coworker Feedback on Salespeople," *JM*, 58 (October), 82–94.

SCALE ITEMS:

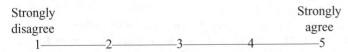

Strongly
disagree

Strongly
agree

1————2————3————4————5

1. My coworkers are knowledgeable about selling cars.

2. I trust my coworkers' judgment about business matters.

3. My coworkers can offer good advice.

4. My coworkers know a lot about selling.

5. I have high regard for my coworkers' selling capabilities.

SCALE NAME: Creativity (Marketing Program)

SCALE DESCRIPTION: This ten-item, seven-point semantic differential scale measures the extent to which the ideas developed for a product's most recent marketing program deviated in a meaningful way from industry practice. The seven-item *novelty* subscale specifically measures the degree of difference between competitive marketing programs and the product's most recent marketing program, whereas the three-item *meaningfulness* subscale addresses the extent to which the marketing initiatives are perceived to be valuable or attractive to the targeted group.

SCALE ORIGIN: Andrews and Smith (1996) noted that the adjectives for the semantic differential pairings were derived in part from the creative product scale developed by Besemer and O'Quin (1986).

SAMPLES: The American Marketing Association membership directory and a purchased mailing list provided Andrews and Smith (1996) with the sampling frame for surveying consumer goods product managers. One hundred ninety-three completed questionnaires were returned for a 33.4% response rate. No significant differences in responses to key variables existed between mailing lists or between early and late respondents. Because only respondents with a substantial impact on ideas in the marketing program were desired, 25 respondents were eliminated on the basis of a screening question, yielding a final sample size of **168**.

RELIABILITY: Andrews and Smith (1996) reported a coefficient alpha of **.91** for this measure. Reliabilities for each scale dimension were not reported because the authors argued that, though conceptually and empirically distinct, novelty and meaningfulness must be considered jointly with respect to marketing program creativity.

VALIDITY: Andrews and Smith (1996) used maximum likelihood factor analysis to confirm the two scale dimensions of novelty and meaningfulness. A second-order confirmatory factor analysis was used to support the authors' argument that the two dimensions should be combined, because both dimensions were found to load on a single higher-order factor. Convergent validity was established because the semantic differential measure correlated highly with both a single-item, seven-point global measure and a seven-point Likert-type measure of marketing program creativity. The measure was also found to correlate strongly with consumer ratings of marketing program creativity.

ADMINISTRATION: The scale was part of a self-administered mail survey in which Andrews and Smith (1996) instructed product managers to answer questions in the context of a single product with which they had been highly involved during their most recent marketing program. Higher scores on the scale indicated higher levels of the dimensions of novelty and meaningfulness and, ultimately, higher levels of marketing program creativity.

MAJOR FINDINGS: Andrews and Smith (1996) investigated the effect of individual product manager and situational/planning process characteristics on marketing program creativity. Knowledge of the operating environment and diversity of experience did not significantly influence **marketing program creativity**. However, knowledge of the macroenvironment, intrinsic motivation to plan marketing, willingness to take risks, interacting with others, and working under a moderately formal planning process were found to have a positive impact on **marketing program creativity**, whereas diversity of education and the perception of working under a time pressure negatively affected creativity. Significant interactions between variables indicated that knowledge of the macroenvironment and knowledge of the operating environment had significantly greater effects on **marketing program creativity** when risk-taking is high than when it is low. The authors also found that the effect of educational diversity on **marketing pro-**

gram creativity is greater when risk-taking is low compared with when it is high and when intrinsic motivation to plan is high rather than when it is low.

REFERENCES:

Andrews, Jonlee and Daniel C. Smith (1996), "In Search of the Marketing Imagination: Factors Affecting the Creativity of Marketing Programs for Mature Products," *JMR*, 33 (May), 174–87.

Besemer, Susan and Karen O'Quin (1986), "Analyzing Creative Products: Refinement and Test of a Judging Instrument," *Journal of Creative Behavior*, 20 (2), 115–26.

SCALE ITEMS:

The following adjectives can be used to describe marketing programs. Please rate your product's MOST RECENT marketing program on each set of adjectives.

Novelty:
Compared to what your competitors were doing last year, your product's most recent marketing program is:

1. Dull   :____:____:____:____:____:____:____: Exciting
       1   2   3   4   5   6   7

2. Fresh   :____:____:____:____:____:____:____: Routine (r)
       1   2   3   4   5   6   7

3. Conventional   :____:____:____:____:____:____:____: Unconventional
       1   2   3   4   5   6   7

4. Novel   :____:____:____:____:____:____:____: Predictable (r)
       1   2   3   4   5   6   7

5. Usual   :____:____:____:____:____:____:____: Unusual
       1   2   3   4   5   6   7

6. Unique   :____:____:____:____:____:____:____: Ordinary (r)
       1   2   3   4   5   6   7

7. Commonplace   :____:____:____:____:____:____:____: Original
       1   2   3   4   5   6   7

Meaningfulness:
The most recent marketing program for your product is:

8. Trendsetting   :____:____:____:____:____:____:____: Warmed over (r)
       1   2   3   4   5   6   7

9. Average   :____:____:____:____:____:____:____: Revolutionary
       1   2   3   4   5   6   7

10. Nothing special   :____:____:____:____:____:____:____: An industry model
       1   2   3   4   5   6   7

SCALE NAME: Cross-Functional Integration

SCALE DESCRIPTION: Song and Parry (1997b) used the full four-item, eleven-point Likert-type scale to measure the level of unity of efforts across the marketing, engineering, and manufacturing departments in developing and launching a new product. Song and Parry (1997a) reported using a reduced three-item version of the scale.

SCALE ORIGIN: The scale was adapted by Song and Parry (1997a, b) from the work of Maidique and Zirger (1984) and Zirger and Maidique (1990). Song and Parry (1997a) modified scale items on the basis of a review of the literature, pilot studies, and information obtained from 36 in-depth case study interviews conducted with both Japanese and U.S. firms. The items for all scales used by Song and Parry (1997a, b) were evaluated by an academic panel composed of both Japanese and U.S. business and engineering experts. Following revisions, the items were judged by a new panel composed of academicians and new product development (NPD) managers. Song and Parry (1997a, b) reported extensive pretesting of both the Japanese and U.S. versions of the questionnaire. Although Song and Parry (1997b) reported a four-item measure of cross-functional integration using the same sample and U.S. firms, the items listed in the scale for this study are phrased slightly differently.

SAMPLES: Song and Parry (1997a, b) randomly sampled 500 of the 611 firms trading on the Tokyo, Osaka, and Nagoya stock exchanges that had been identified as developing at least four new physical products since 1991. Usable responses pertaining to **788** NPD projects were obtained from 404 Japanese firms. Song and Parry (1997a) randomly split the resulting data into calibration (n = 394) and validation (n = 394) samples for the purpose of cross-validation. Song and Parry (1997b) used the entire Japanese data set with data provided by U.S. firms. The U.S. sampling frame used by Song and Parry (1997b) was taken from companies listed in the *High-Technology Industries Directory*. Of the 643 firms that had introduced a minimum of four new physical products since 1990, 500 firms were randomly sampled (stratified by industry to match the Japanese sample); 312 U.S. firms provided data on **612** NPD projects, of which 312 were successes and 300 were failures.

RELIABILITY: Song and Parry (1997b) reported a coefficient alpha of **.79** for this scale in the Japanese sample and **.88** in the U.S. sample. Song and Parry (1997a) used a confirmatory factor analysis of the data in the calibration sample to purify the scale. Items loading on multiple constructs or those with low item-to-scale loadings were deleted from the measure. Song and Parry (1997a) reported a coefficient alpha of **.84** for the three-item, purified measure using data from the validation sample.

VALIDITY: The extensive pretesting and evaluation of the measure with academicians and NPD managers provided strong evidence for the face validity of the measure. Song and Parry (1997a, b) did not specifically report any other examination of scale validity.

ADMINISTRATION: Song and Parry (1997a, b) indicated that the self-administered questionnaire containing the scale was originally developed in English; the Japanese version was prepared using the parallel-translation/double-translation method. The Japanese sample received a survey packet containing cover letters in both English and Japanese, two Japanese-language questionnaires, and two international postage-paid reply envelopes. Survey packets delivered to U.S. firms were similar, except no Japanese cover letter was included and the surveys were in English. Various incentives, four follow-up letters, and multiple telephone calls and faxes were used to increase the response rate with both samples. Song and Parry (1997a, b) indicated that respondents were asked to answer one questionnaire in the context of a successful new product project introduced after 1991 and one in the context of a new product project that had failed. Higher scores on the scale indicated higher levels of effort unity across the marketing, engineering, and manufacturing departments in developing and launching a new product.

MAJOR FINDINGS: Song and Parry (1997a, b) conceptualized and tested a model of NPD practices thought to influence the success of new product ventures. In both the Japanese and U.S. samples, Song and Parry (1997b) found that the level of **cross-functional integration** was positively related to all five stages of the NPD process. Song and Parry (1997a) also found that the **cross-functional integration of efforts** in Japanese firms significantly and positively influenced the relative level of new product success, as well the level of competitive and market intelligence gathered and the marketing and technical proficiencies of the firm.

REFERENCES:

Maidique, Modesto A. and Billie Jo Zierger (1984), "A Study of Success and Failure in Product Innovation: The Case of the U.S. Electronics Industry," *IEEE Transactions on Engineering Management*, 31 (4), 192–203.

Song, X. Michael and Mark E. Parry (1997a), "The Determinants of Japanese New Product Successes," *JMR*, 34 (February), 64–76.

———— and ———— (1997b), "A Cross-National Comparative Study of New Product Development Processes: Japan and the United States," *JM*, 61 (April), 1–18.

Zierger, Billie Jo and Modesto Maidique (1990), "A Model of NPD: An Empirical Test," *Management Science*, 36 (7), 867–83.

SCALE ITEMS:

Directions: Cross-functional integration is defined as the process of achieving effective unity of efforts in the accomplishment of new product development success. The degree of the integration refers to the level of cross-functional interaction and communication, level of information-sharing, degree of cross-functional coordination, and level of joint involvement in conducting specific new product development tasks.

To what extent does each statement listed below correctly describe this selected successful project? Please indicate your degree of agreement or disagreement by circling a number from zero (0) to ten (10) on the scale to the right of each statement. Here: 0 = strongly disagree, 10 = strongly agree, and numbers between 0 and 10 indicate various degrees of agreement or disagreement.

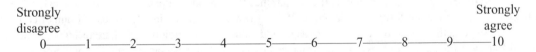

Strongly disagree 0——1——2——3——4——5——6——7——8——9——10 Strongly agree

Items used by Song and Parry (1997a):
1. The integration between R&D and manufacturing was very good for this selected project.
2. The integration between marketing and R&D was very good for this selected project.
3. The integration between marketing and manufacturing was very good for this selected project.

Items used by Song and Parry (1997b):
1. The degree of integration between R&D and manufacturing was high during the entire development process.
2. This product was developed from frequent interactions between customers and our cross-functional team effort.
3. The degree of integration between marketing and R&D was high during the entire development process.
4. The degree of integration between marketing and manufacturing was high during the entire development process.

SCALE NAME: Cultural Problems

SCALE DESCRIPTION: Three seven-point items that assess the extent to which a firm might encounter problems as a result of its ignorance of the sociocultural aspects of a foreign market. Bello and Gilliland (1997) refer to this scale as *psychic distance* in their article.

SCALE ORIGIN: Bello and Gilliland (1997) stated that the scale was adapted from Korth (1991).

SAMPLES: Bello and Gilliland's (1997) systematic random sample of 245 national manufacturers verified as exporting through foreign distributors was drawn from the 1994 edition of the *Journal of Commerce United States Importer & Exporter Directory* (1994). **One hundred sixty** usable responses were obtained from export managers employed by firms exporting a variety of industrial and consumer products to a total of 39 different countries.

RELIABILITY: A confirmatory factor analysis composite reliability of **.92** was reported by Bello and Gilliland (1997).

VALIDITY: Confirmatory factor analysis was used by Bello and Gilliland (1997) to provide evidence of discriminant and convergent validity, as well as to assess the unidimensionality of the measure. Convergent validity was deemed to be present because items loaded significantly on their posited indicators and there were low to moderate correlations between the scale and other measures. Discriminant validity was also deemed to be present because the correlation estimate between two indicators never included 1.0 (+/– two standard errors). The authors used personal interviews with export executives as part of the pretest process to verify the face validity of the measure.

ADMINISTRATION: Bello and Gilliland (1997) indicated that this scale was self-administered as part of a longer survey instrument mailed to respondents. The export manager with primary responsibility for the firm's relationship with the foreign distributor received a survey. Nonrespondents were telephoned three weeks later, and a second questionnaire followed. Instructions specified that questions were to be answered in the context of the focal distributor. The authors defined the focal distributor as the firm's fourth-largest foreign distributor in terms of unit sales volume, in order to avoid a positive evaluation bias. Higher scores on the scale indicated that a manufacturer had greater difficulties dealing with the language, culture, customers, and values of the export country.

MAJOR FINDINGS: Bello and Gilliland (1997) examined the effect of output controls, process controls, and flexibility on channel performance. Greater **cultural problems** resulted in a lower use of output controls, which suggests that, when the culture, language, and values of the foreign market are different, firms find it difficulty to obtain and process the performance documentation necessary to monitor outcomes.

REFERENCES:

Bello, Daniel C. and David I. Gilliland (1997), "The Effect of Output Controls, Process Controls, and Flexibility on Export Channel Performance," *JM*, 61 (January), 22–38.
Korth, Christopher M. (1991), "Managerial Barriers to U.S. Exports," *Business Horizons*, 34 (2), 18–26.

SCALE ITEMS: Each aspect of the foreign country presents your firm with. . .

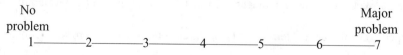

```
No                                                    Major
problem                                               problem
   1———————2———————3———————4———————5———————6———————7
```

1. Customs and values of the people.

2. Culture of the country.

3. Language of the country.

SCALE NAME: Customer Orientation (SOCO)

SCALE DESCRIPTION: Twenty-four items that measure the degree to which a salesperson engages in behaviors aimed at increasing long-term customer satisfaction versus high-pressure sales and low concern for the customer's needs. This scale was called SOCO (selling orientation–customer orientation) by its originators (Saxe and Weitz 1982). The items in the scale were modified by Michaels and Day (1985) to reflect statements of *buyers* evaluating salespeople rather than *salespeople* describing themselves.

SCALE ORIGIN: The scale was originally constructed and tested by Saxe and Weitz (1982). After a literature review and interviews with sales managers and salespeople, a pool of 104 items was generated. Seventy of those items were rated as "clearly representative" by at least half of a set of judges (sales managers and marketing academicians). Those items were administered to salespeople in 48 firms (n = 191). A final version of the scale was developed on the basis of the 12 positive and 12 negative items that had the highest corrected item–total correlations (α = .86). Scores on the scale did not show evidence of social desirability bias.

A second sample was used to further examine the psychometric properties of the scale. Four sales forces participated in the second survey (n = 95). The scale had an alpha of .83 and a six-week test–retest stability of .67 (n = 46). A factor analysis produced two factors; all items had moderate positive loadings on the first factor, and the second factor seemed to distinguish between the positive and negative items. As evidence of convergent validity, scores on this scale were found to have a negative correlation with a measure of Machiavellianism, which indicated that respondents with a strong customer orientation were less willing to engage in manipulative practices. Other evidence of the scale's nomological validity was offered in the study, but the authors characterized the results as "not strong" (Saxe and Weitz 1982, p. 351).

SAMPLES: The study by Michaels and Day (1985) was based on **1005** responses. Questionnaires were sent to a sample of 3216 persons whose names were randomly selected from the membership of the National Association of Purchasing Management. The authors reported that the respondent profile corresponded closely to the national membership profile.

Hart, Moncrief, and Parasuraman (1989) mailed questionnaires to 149 salespeople who worked for 25 independent brokers representing a major food producer. After two follow-up mailings, usable responses were received from **84** sales representatives.

Data were gathered by Siguaw, Brown, and Widing (1994) using a self-report mail questionnaire. Survey forms were distributed in a couple of different ways to salespeople in the document imaging industry. A total of 1644 questionnaires were distributed, and **278** usable responses were received. Among the characteristics of the sample were that it was predominately men (81%), college educated (71.5%), and had an average of 14.2 years of sales experience.

Swenson and Herche (1994) collected data using a national mailing list of industrial salespeople working in diverse industries, which resulted in **271** usable responses. The sample were mostly men (92%) and married (89%) and had an average age of 48 years.

RELIABILITY: Alpha values of **.84**, **.91**, **.86**, and **.88** were reported by Hart, Moncrief, and Parasuraman (1989), Michaels and Day (1985), Siguaw, Brown, and Widing (1994), and Swenson and Herche (1994), respectively.

VALIDITY: No specific examination of the scale's validity was reported in the studies. However, Michaels and Day (1985) noted that the factor structure based on their data was very similar to that reported by Saxe and Weitz (1982).

ADMINISTRATION: In each of the studies (Hart, Moncrief, and Parasuraman 1989; Michaels and Day 1985; Swenson and Herche 1994), the scale was self-administered by respondents in the form of a mail survey questionnaire. High scores on the Saxe and Weitz version of the scale indicated that a salesperson had a strong customer orientation, whereas low scores indicated a sales orientation. High scores on Michaels and Day's (1985) version of the scale suggested that a buyer viewed most salespeople as having a customer-orientation, whereas low scores meant that they thought most salespeople focus on the sale itself, not the customer's satisfaction.

MAJOR FINDINGS: Michaels and Day's (1985) study was designed as a modified replication of the Saxe and Weitz (1982) study. The difference, as mentioned previously, was that the former examined buyers' perceptions and the latter focused on sellers. To the extent that mean scores can be compared across the two studies, it was found that the mean score of customers was much lower than that of salespeople. One potential explanation for the wide gap is that sellers overestimate their **customer orientation**, whereas buyers underestimate it.

The purpose of the study by Hart, Moncrief, and Parasuraman (1989) was to investigate goal theory as it relates to sales contests. For salespeople with low self-esteem, both goal acceptance and goal acceptance/goal difficulty were related to higher **customer orientations**.

The effect of a company's market orientation on sales force attitudes and behavior was examined by Siguaw, Brown, and Widing (1994). Contrary to the hypotheses, salesperson **customer orientation** was not found to be significantly related to role ambiguity, role conflict, job satisfaction, or organizational commitment.

Swenson and Herche (1994) examined the role of social values to predict salesperson performance. Their results provided support for the incremental ability of social values to predict performance beyond the use of adaptive selling and **customer orientation** in isolation.

COMMENTS: The first 12 items are stated in the positive direction, whereas the last 12 are stated in the negative direction. Consideration should be given to intermixing the positive and negative items on a survey instrument to decrease response bias. The wisdom of that practice was questioned, however, by Herche and Engelland (1994, 1996). After testing the SOCO scale and two other scales in multiple contexts, they concluded that measures with mixed-item polarity appear to be susceptible to degradation of unidimensionality.

REFERENCES:

Hart, Sandra Hile, William C. Moncrief, and A. Parasuraman (1989), "An Empirical Investigation of Salespeople's Performance, Effort and Selling Method During a Sales Contest," *JAMS*, 17 (Winter), 29–39.

Herche, Joel and Brian Engelland (1994), "Reversed-Polarity Items, Attribution Effects and Scale Dimensionality," *Office of Scale Research Technical Report #9401,* Department of Marketing, Southern Illinois University at Carbondale.

—— and —— (1996), "Reversed-Polarity Items and Scale Unidimensionality," *JAMS*, 24 (4), 366–74.

Michaels, Ronald E. and Ralph L. Day (1985), "Measuring Customer Orientation of Salespeople: A Replication with Industrial Buyers," *JMR*, 22 (November), 443–46.

Saxe, Robert and Barton A. Weitz (1982), "The SOCO Scale: A Measure of the Customer Orientation of Salespeople," *JMR*, 19 (August), 343–51.

Siguaw, Judy A., Gene Brown, and Robert E. Widing II (1994), " The Influence of the Market Orientation of the Firm on Sales Force Behavior and Attitudes," *JMR*, 31 (February), 106–16.

Swenson, Michael J. and Joel Herche (1994), "Social Values and Salesperson Performance: An Empirical Examination," *JAMS*, 22 (3), 283–89.

SCALE ITEMS:

Directions: The statements below describe various ways a salesperson might act with customers or prospects. For each statement please indicate the proportion of your customers with whom you act as described in the statement. Do this by circling one of the numbers from 1 to 9. The meanings of your numbers are:

1 = True for NONE of your customers-NEVER
2 = True for ALMOST NONE
3 = True for A FEW
4 = True for SOMEWHAT LESS THAN HALF
5 = True for ABOUT HALF
6 = True for SOMEWHAT MORE THAN HALF
7 = True for a LARGE MAJORITY
8 = True for ALMOST ALL
9 = True for ALL of your customers-ALWAYS

1. I try to help customers achieve their goals.
2. I try to achieve my goals by satisfying customers.
3. A good salesperson has to have the customer's best interest in mind.
4. I try to get customers to discuss their needs with me.
5. I try to influence a customer by information rather than by pressure.
6. I offer the product of mine that is best suited to the customer's problem.
7. I try to find out what kind of product would be most helpful to a customer.
8. I answer a customer's questions about products as correctly as I can.
9. I try to bring a customer with a problem together with a product that helps him solve that problem.
10. I am willing to disagree with a customer in order to help him make a better decision.
11. I try to give customers an accurate expectation of what the product will do for them.
12. I try to figure out what a customer's needs are.
13. I try to sell a customer all I can convince him to buy, even if I think it is more then a wise customer would buy. **(r)**
14. I try to sell as much as I can rather than to satisfy a customer. **(r)**
15. I keep alert for weaknesses in a customer's personality so I can use them to put pressure on him to buy. **(r)**
16. If I am not sure what product is right for a customer, I will still apply pressure to get him to buy. **(r)**
17. I decide what products to offer on the basis of what I can convince customers to buy, not on the basis of what will satisfy them in the long run. **(r)**
18. I paint too rosy a picture of my products, to make them sound as good as possible. **(r)**
19. I spend more time trying to persuade a customer to buy than I do trying to discover his needs. **(r)**
20. It is necessary to stretch the truth in describing a product to a customer. **(r)**
21. I pretend to agree with customers to please them. **(r)**
22. I imply to a customer that something is beyond my control when it is not. **(r)**
23. I begin the sales talk for a product before exploring a customer's needs with him. **(r)**
24. I treat a customer as a rival. **(r)**

SCALE NAME: Decision Difficulty

SCALE DESCRIPTION: DeCarlo and Leigh (1996) used this three-item, seven-point Likert-type scale, which they called "cognitive effort," to assess the extent to which a sales manager expended thought and effort in evaluating the performance of a salesperson in the context of a hypothetical scenario. However, closer examination of the items indicates that the scale may be more appropriately used to measure the level of difficulty that is associated with making a particular decision.

SCALE ORIGIN: The scale is original to DeCarlo and Leigh (1996).

SAMPLES: DeCarlo and Leigh's (1996) sample consisted of 468 U.S. sales managers, of whom 289 were recruited from a *Fortune* 500 mailing equipment (ME) firm, 103 were recruited from an office equipment (OE) firm, and the final 79 individuals were drawn from a southeast sales and marketing executives (SME) mailing list. Usable responses were obtained from **218** sales managers, of whom 144 (49%) were ME managers, 55 (53.4%) were OE managers, and 19 (25.5%) were SME managers. Post hoc ANOVAS were performed for several firm-level effects to assess the compatibility of the three groups that composed the sample, and no significant differences were found.

RELIABILITY: DeCarlo and Leigh (1996) reported a coefficient alpha of **.77** for the scale.

VALIDITY: The scales used in DeCarlo and Leigh's (1996) study were factor analyzed; those with multiple-factor solutions were orthogonally rotated, and items with loadings of .30 or lower were eliminated. Confirmatory factor analysis using LISREL 7.16 was used to assess scale dimensionality and discriminant validity; goodness-of-fit indices and t-values associated with individual items were used to identify the final set of scale items that represented each construct.

ADMINISTRATION: DeCarlo and Leigh (1996) developed a $2 \times 2 \times 3$ full-factorial, between-groups experimentation design in which task attraction, social attraction, and information ambiguity were manipulated to observe the effect on managerial causal attributions and other dependent measures. The questionnaire containing the measure was delivered by mail; nonrespondents were sent a reminder postcard followed by a second questionnaire. A lottery incentive, promises of anonymity, letters of endorsement, and business-reply envelopes were also used to enhance response rates. Higher scores on the scale indicated that a sales manager expended more thought and effort when evaluating a salesperson's performance due to the perceived difficulty involved in making the decision.

MAJOR FINDINGS: DeCarlo and Leigh (1996) examined the relationship between a sales manager's task and social attraction to a salesperson, manager attributions for poor performance, and managerial feedback based on those attributions in an experimental context. Both task and social attraction directly influenced **perceived decision difficulty (cognitive effort)**; sales managers reported less **difficulty (effort)** in evaluating poorly performing sales representatives who were less attractive.

REFERENCES:
DeCarlo, Thomas E. and Thomas W. Leigh (1996), "Impact of Salesperson Attraction on Sales Managers' Attributions and Feedback," *JM*, 60 (April), 47–66.

SCALE ITEMS:*

Strongly disagree
Strongly agree

1———2———3———4———5———6———7

1. I would be very careful before I made conclusions in this particular situation.

2. I would make sure I had all the facts before I made a decision in this case.

3. It is difficult to make a decision without more data.

*No instructions were listed for this measure in the article; thus, the nature of the decision to be made is unclear.

SCALE NAME: Dependence (Buyer)

SCALE DESCRIPTION: A four-item, seven-point Likert-type scale describing the ability of a manufacturer to replace a supplier. Heide (1994) refers to this measure as "REPSUP" in the regression model.

SCALE ORIGIN: Although the development of the scale appears to be original to this study, Heide (1994) noted that it is based on Emerson's (1962) conceptual definition of dependence.

SAMPLES: The sample used by Heide (1994) was described fully by Heide and John (1992). A national mailing list of purchasing agents and manufacturer directors within the two-digit standard industrial classification groups of 35–37 were chosen as the sampling frame. A random sample of 1157 names was initially drawn from these groups for telephone contact and qualification. Of these, 579 purchasing agent informants meeting selection criteria were sent a mail questionnaire. Follow-up telephone calls and a second questionnaire resulted in **155** usable questionnaires being returned. Purchasing informants who agreed to participate in the study were also asked to identify key contacts in a supplier firm. A total of 96 supplier contacts were sent a mail questionnaire; follow-up telephone calls and a second questionnaire resulted in **60** usable questionnaires being returned from suppliers.

RELIABILITY: Heide (1994) calculated an alpha of **.79** for this scale.

VALIDITY: Confirmatory factor analysis was used by Heide (1994) to conclude that the scale was unidimensional and showed evidence of discriminant validity. Further evidence of discriminant validity was provided by a series of chi-square tests on the respective factor correlations. Convergent validity was demonstrated by comparing the measure with the estimated number of months required to replace the party; significant positive correlations were accepted as evidence of convergent validity.

ADMINISTRATION: Both original equipment manufacturers (buyers) and their suppliers were sampled as part of a larger study. Although not explicitly stated by Heide (1994), it appears the buyer dependence measure was incorporated in mail surveys sent to both groups, which were self-administered. It appears that a low score on the buyer dependence measure meant that the buyer was heavily dependent on the supplier and that replacing that supplier would not be easy. However, all items in the scale are listed by Heide (1994) as being reversed, and therefore, the opposite may be indicated.

MAJOR FINDINGS: Heide (1994) investigated whether parties' expected flexibility in response to changing circumstances, a form of bilateral governance, was related to the form of dependence characterizing the buyer/supplier relationship. The **buyer dependence** measure functioned as one of two key independent variables. The other was supplier dependence. Results of the ordinary least squares regression model indicated that, when dependence between buyers and suppliers is symmetric and high, greater flexibility occurs. When dependence is unilateral, indicating that one party is dependent but the other is not, flexibility is undermined.

REFERENCES:

Emerson, Richard M. (1962), "Power-Dependence Relations," *American Sociological Review*, 27 (February), 134–39.

Heide, Jan B. (1994), "Interorganizational Governance in Marketing Channels," *JM*, 58 (January), 71–85.

———— and George John (1992), "Do Norms Matter in Marketing Relationships?" *JM*, 56 (April), 32–44.

SCALE ITEMS:

Strongly   Strongly
disagree   agree

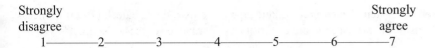

1———2———3———4———5———6———7

1. If we decided to stop purchasing from this supplier, we could easily replace their volume with purchases from other suppliers. **(r)**

2. There are many competitive suppliers for these components. **(r)**

3. Our production system can be easily adapted to using components from a new supplier. **(r)**

4. Dealing with a new supplier would only require a limited redesign and development effort on our part. **(r)**

SCALE NAME: Dependence (Distributor on Manufacturer)

SCALE DESCRIPTION: Four-item, seven-point Likert-type scale used by Andaleeb (1996) to measure respondents' perceptions of the availability and criticality of alternative sources of supply.

SCALE ORIGIN: Andaleeb (1996) apparently adapted the items representing the dependence measure from previously published studies, but he cites no specific source. The reliability of the measure and item-to-total correlations were assessed as part of the purification process and deemed acceptable.

SAMPLES: A convenience sample of **72** sales and purchasing managers with considerable negotiation experience participated in a 2 × 2 between-groups factorial design experiment. Andaleeb (1996) randomly assigned subjects to treatment conditions.

RELIABILITY: Andaleeb (1996) calculated a coefficient alpha of **.91** for the scale.

VALIDITY: Andaleeb (1996) reported conducting a factor analysis to assess the unidimensionality of the measures used in his study. A single factor with item loadings greater than .8 was extracted for each scale, which suggests that the measures were unidimensional. A confirmatory factor analysis of the measurement model provided some evidence of validity, because the standardized coefficients were significantly different from zero. However, the goodness-of-fit index of .87 was somewhat below the recommended .90 level, though the chi-square and root mean squared residual were found to be satisfactory.

ADMINISTRATION: Andaleeb (1996) provided subjects with information about a contrived manufacturer (supplier)–distributor (buyer) relationship in which the level of trust and dependence on the supplier were manipulated. After reading this information, subjects were instructed to write down their perceptions of the relationship and read a scenario that suggested that an upcoming meeting would consider methods of strengthening the company's growth through cultivation of existing suppliers. Subjects were instructed to indicate whether they thought such ties would be appropriate with the focal supplier. The satisfaction, commitment, dependence, and trust measures were then administered. Higher scores on the scale indicated a stronger willingness on the part of respondents to continue and invest in the manufacturer–distributor relationship.

MAJOR FINDINGS: Andaleeb's (1996) experiment investigated the effect of high and low levels of supplier trust and supplier dependence on satisfaction and commitment for a hypothetical dyadic exchange relationship. After confirming that the trust and **dependence** manipulation had occurred, Andaleeb (1996) found that both greater trust in a supplier and greater **dependence** on a supplier led to higher levels of buyer commitment to the supplier and satisfaction with the relationship. However, the level of commitment exhibited toward a supplier was found to be much more sensitive to different levels of trust when **dependence** was low compared with when it was high, which indicates the presence of a significant interaction effect between trust and **dependence**.

REFERENCES:
Andaleeb, Syed Saad (1996), "An Experimental Investigation of Satisfaction and Commitment in Marketing Channels: The Role of Trust and Dependence," *JR*, 72 (1), 77–93.

SCALE ITEMS:*

Strongly
disagree

Strongly
agree

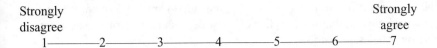

1————2————3————4————5————6————7

1. My company's alternate sources of liqueur supply are limited.

2. My company can easily switch from X to other suppliers if it wants to. **(r)**

3. Finding a replacement for X should be very difficult.

4. Maintaining liqueur in its product line is critical to my company's profitability.

*As used by Andaleeb (1996), the company name of the respondent was used in items 1, 2, and 4, and the name of the focal manufacturer was used in items 2 and 3.

SCALE NAME: Dependence (Major Supplier on Wholesaler)

SCALE DESCRIPTION: Lusch and Brown (1996) stated that this three-item, seven-point Likert-type scale was used to measure wholesale distributor perceptions of how dependent the firm's major supplier is on business generated by the wholesale distributor.

SCALE ORIGIN: Lusch and Brown (1996) adapted the scale items from previously published studies. For the first item, the authors credited Noordewier, John, and Nevin (1990) and Ganesan (1994), whereas items 2 and 3 were adapted from Kumar, Scheer, and Steenkamp's (1995) study. Lusch and Brown (1996) simplified and shortened the original items and changed the context of reference from "retailer" or "dealer" relationships to relationships with "major suppliers."

SAMPLES: A systematic random sample of 3225 firms was drawn by Lusch and Brown (1996) from a mailing list of all U.S. merchant wholesalers and agents/brokers in 16 four-digit standard industrial classification code groups. The sample was further reduced by eliminating firms with more than 20 employees. General managers were identified as the key informants for the remaining firms and were sent a mail questionnaire. Incentives and a follow-up mailing resulted in an initial response rate of 28.8%. However, this study reported usable data specific only to the **454** respondents classified as wholesale distributors and excluded data from agent and broker firms. The authors noted that the average number of suppliers reported by wholesalers in the sample was 45, with the major supplier contributing an average of 49% of the firm's annual volume.

RELIABILITY: Lusch and Brown (1996) reported a composite reliability of **.878** for this scale.

VALIDITY: Lusch and Brown (1996) reported undertaking a thorough review of the practitioner and academic literature, as well as extensive practitioner pretesting, to ensure content validity. Confirmatory factor analysis was used to establish the unidimensionality of the measure. Convergent and discriminant validity were also assessed and found to be satisfactory, which indicates that the measure possessed adequate construct validity.

ADMINISTRATION: The scale was included as part of a self-administered mail survey. A $1 incentive and the promise of shared survey results were offered as participant incentives, and a personalized cover letter accompanied the survey packet. Undeliverable questionnaires were redirected to a replacement firm. A second mailing without monetary incentive was sent one month later. Lusch and Brown (1996) instructed respondents to answer all questions pertaining to major suppliers in the context of the supplier with which the wholesale distributor did the most business. Higher scores on the measure indicated that the major supplier had a greater dependence on the wholesale distributor.

MAJOR FINDINGS: Lusch and Brown (1996) investigated how the type of dependency structure—wholesaler dependent on supplier, supplier dependent on wholesaler, or bilateral dependency—influenced whether a normative or explicit contract was used. The authors also studied whether dependency structure and the type of contract influenced the performance of wholesale distributors. Results indicated that, as **supplier dependency on the wholesale distributor** increases, the contract governing the relationship between firms becomes more explicit. No support was found linking increases in **supplier dependency** to reductions in the use of normative contracts, reduced likelihood of a long-term orientation toward the wholesale distributor, or reduced presence of relational behavior. Findings indicated that greater levels of **supplier dependency** resulted in higher levels of wholesale distributor performance.

REFERENCES:

Ganesan, Shankar (1994), "Determinants of Long-Term Orientation in Buyer-Seller Relationships," *JM*, 58 (April), 1–19.

Kumar, Nirmalya, Lisa K. Scheer, and Jan-Benedict E.M. Steenkamp (1995b), "The Effects of Perceived Interdependence on Dealer Attitudes," *JMR*, 32 (August), 348–56.

Lusch, Robert F. and James R. Brown (1996), "Interdependency, Contracting, and Relational Behavior in Marketing Channels," *JM*, 60 (October), 19–38.

Noordewier, Thomas G., George John, and John R. Nevin (1990), "Performance Outcomes of Purchasing Arrangements in Industrial Buyer-Vendor Relationships," *JM*, 54 (October), 80–93.

SCALE ITEMS:

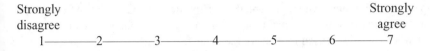

Strongly
disagree

Strongly
agree

1———2———3———4———5———6———7

1. Our supplier is dependent on us.

2. Our major supplier would find it difficult to replace us.

3. Our major supplier would find it costly to lose us.

SCALE NAME: Dependence (Retailer on Vendor)

SCALE DESCRIPTION: Ganesan (1994) developed an eight-item, seven-point Likert-type scale to measure retailer perceptions of the ease with which a vendor could be replaced and the importance of the vendor to company performance.

SCALE ORIGIN: The scale is original to Ganesan (1994), who developed separate but parallel measures of dependence for the vendor and retailer samples. Scale items were generated through interviews with retail buyers and vendors. Although some items were specific to the retailer or vendor version, the author included a core set of items with minor phrasing alterations in both scales. Item analysis and exploratory factor analysis were used to purify the measure initially, and items with low loadings and those loading on multiple factors were eliminated. A draft of the questionnaire containing this scale was also pretested with a group of 14 retail buyers who represented two department store chains. After administration to the final sample, scale items were subjected to a confirmatory factor analysis. Goodness-of-fit indices and individual item t-values were used to identify the final scale items.

SAMPLES: Five retail department store chains agreed to participate in Ganesan's (1994) study. Each firm received and distributed 30 questionnaires to senior sales representatives or sales managers who served as liaisons with vendor organizations. A total of **124** (83%) usable responses representing the *retailer* sample were obtained. Forty-eight respondents answered in the context of a long-term vendor relationship, and the remaining 76 answered in the context of a short-term vendor relationship. Contact information provided by respondents enabled the author to sample the designated 124 key vendor informants most knowledgeable about the retailer/vendor relationship with a survey similar in content to the retailer questionnaire but phrased from the vendor point-of-view. A total of **52** (42%) *vendor* representatives responded, of which 21 and 31 were in short- and long-term relationships, respectively.

RELIABILITY: Ganesan (1994) reported a coefficient alpha of **.94** for the scale.

VALIDITY: Ganesan (1994) submitted the scale to a confirmatory factor analysis using LISREL 7.16 to assess the unidimensionality, convergent validity, and discriminant validity of the measure. Although the measure was found to be unidimensional, no additional information pertaining to the outcome of the validity tests was provided.

ADMINISTRATION: Prior to being sent a survey, buyers in the retailer sample were randomly assigned to one of four cells in which the questionnaire instructions asked them to select a vendor on the basis of variations in two criteria: (1) the length of their relationship (short-term or long-term) and (2) the importance of the vendor's product to their organization (moderately important or very important). Questionnaires were distributed by a coordinator in each department store, and respondents were instructed to answer the survey in the context of this single vendor. Higher scores on the scale indicated a greater level of retailer dependence on a vendor, because the vendor was perceived as both difficult to replace and important to company performance.

MAJOR FINDINGS: Ganesan (1994) investigated a variety of factors influencing the long-term orientation of both retailers and vendors in an ongoing relationship, as well as the antecedents to long-term orientation. The **dependence of a retailer on a vendor** was positively associated with a retailer's long-term orientation, investment by the retailer in transaction specific assets, and retailer perceptions of the investments made by a vendor in transaction-specific assets. Environmental diversity was negatively associated with a **retailer's dependence on a vendor.**

REFERENCES:

Ganesan, Shankar (1994), "Determinants of Long-Term Orientation in Buyer-Seller Relationships," *JM*, 58 (April), 1–19.

SCALE ITEMS:

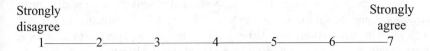

Strongly disagree — 1—2—3—4—5—6—7 — Strongly agree

1. If our relationship was discontinued with this resource, we would have difficulty in making up the sales volume in our trading area.

2. This resource is crucial to our future performance.

3. It would be difficult for us to replace this resource.

4. We are dependent on this resource.

5. We do not have a good alternative to this resource.

6. This resource is important to our business.

7. This resource's product lines are essential to round out our product offering.

8. If our relationship was discontinued, we would have difficulty replacing this resource.

SCALE NAME: Dependence (Retailer's Perception of Vendor)

SCALE DESCRIPTION: Ganesan (1994) developed a three-item, seven-point Likert-type scale to measure retailer perceptions of a vendor's dependence on the retailer in terms of the ease with which the retailer could be replaced and the importance of the retailer to vendor performance.

SCALE ORIGIN: The scale is original to Ganesan (1994), who developed separate but parallel measures of perceptions of partner dependence for the vendor and retailer samples. Scale items were generated through interviews with retail buyers and vendors. Although some items were specific to the retailer or vendor version, the author included a core set of items with minor phrasing alterations in both scales. Item analysis and exploratory factor analysis were used to initially purify the measure; items with low loadings and those loading on multiple factors were eliminated. A draft of the questionnaire containing this scale was also pretested with a group of 14 retail buyers who represented two department store chains. After administration to the final sample, scale items were subjected to a confirmatory factor analysis. Goodness-of-fit indices and individual item t-values were used to identify the final scale items.

SAMPLES: Five retail department store chains agreed to participate in Ganesan's (1994) study, and each firm received and distributed 30 questionnaires to senior sales representatives or sales managers who served as liaisons with vendor organizations. A total of **124** (83%) usable responses representing the *retailer* sample were obtained. Forty-eight respondents answered in the context of a long-term vendor relationship, and the remaining 76 answered in the context of a short-term vendor relationship. Contact information provided by respondents enabled the author to sample the designated 124 key vendor informants most knowledgeable about the retailer/vendor relationship with a survey similar in content to the retailer questionnaire but phrased from the vendor point of view. A total of **52** (42%) *vendor* representatives responded, of which 21 and 31 were in short- and long-term relationships, respectively.

RELIABILITY: Ganesan (1994) reported a coefficient alpha of **.71** for the scale.

VALIDITY: Ganesan (1994) submitted the scale to a confirmatory factor analysis using LISREL 7.16 to assess the unidimensionality, convergent validity, and discriminant validity of the measure. Although the measure was found to be unidimensional, no additional information pertaining to the outcome of the validity tests was provided.

ADMINISTRATION: Prior to being sent a survey, buyers in the retailer sample were randomly assigned to one of four cells in which the questionnaire instructions asked them to select a vendor on the basis of variations in two criteria: (1) the length of their relationship (short-term or long-term) and (2) the importance of the vendor's product to their organization (moderately important or very important). Questionnaires were distributed by a coordinator in each department store, and respondents were instructed to answer the survey in the context of this single vendor. Higher scores on the scale indicated that retailers perceived vendors as more dependent on them because of their importance to the vendor's performance and the difficulties involved in replacing them with an alternate retailer.

MAJOR FINDINGS: Ganesan (1994) investigated a variety of factors influencing the long-term orientation of both retailers and vendors in an ongoing relationship, as well as the antecedents to long-term orientation. The **retailer's perception of the dependence of a vendor on the retailer** was negatively related to a retailer's long-term orientation.

REFERENCES:
Ganesan, Shankar (1994), "Determinants of Long-Term Orientation in Buyer-Seller Relationships," *JM*, 58 (April), 1–19.

SCALE ITEMS:

Strongly   Strongly
disagree   agree

1———2———3———4———5———6———7

1. We are important to this vendor.

2. We are a major outlet for this vendor in our trading area.

3. We are not a major outlet for this resource. **(r)**

SCALE NAME: Dependence (Supplier)

SCALE DESCRIPTION: A four-item, seven-point Likert-type scale describing the ability of a supplier to replace a manufacturing customer. Heide (1994) refers to this measure as "REPBUY" in the regression model.

SCALE ORIGIN: Although the development of the scale appears to be original to this study, Heide (1994) noted that it is based on Emerson's (1962) conceptual definition of dependence.

SAMPLES: The sample used by Heide (1994) was described fully by Heide and John (1992). A national mailing list of purchasing agents and manufacturer directors within the two-digit standard industrial classification groups of 35–37 were chosen as the sampling frame. A random sample of 1157 names was initially drawn from these groups for telephone contact and qualification, and 579 purchasing agent informants meeting selection criteria were sent a mail questionnaire. Follow-up telephone calls and a second questionnaire resulted in **155** usable questionnaires being returned. Purchasing informants agreeing to participate in the study were also asked to identify key contacts in a supplier firm. A total of 96 supplier contacts were sent a mail questionnaire. Follow-up telephone calls and a second questionnaire resulted in **60** usable questionnaires being returned from suppliers.

RELIABILITY: Heide (1994) calculated an alpha of **.82** for this scale.

VALIDITY: Confirmatory factor analysis was used by Heide (1994) to conclude that the scale was unidimensional and showed evidence of discriminant validity. Further evidence of discriminant validity was provided by a series of chi-square tests on the respective factor correlations. Convergent validity was demonstrated by comparing the measure with the estimated number of months required to replace the party. Significant positive correlations were accepted as evidence of convergent validity.

ADMINISTRATION: Both original equipment manufacturers (buyers) and their suppliers were sampled with different questionnaires as part of a larger study. Although not explicitly stated, it appears that the supplier dependence measure was incorporated within mail surveys sent to both groups, which were self-administered. It appears that a low score on the supplier dependence measure meant that the supplier was perceived by respondents to be heavily dependent on the manufacturer and that replacing that manufacturer's business would not be easy. However, all items in the scale are listed by Heide (1994) as being reversed, and therefore, the opposite may be indicated.

MAJOR FINDINGS: Heide (1994) investigated whether parties' expected flexibility in response to changing circumstances, a form of bilateral governance, is related to the form of dependence characterizing the buyer/supplier relationship. The **supplier dependence** measure functioned as one of two key independent variables The other was buyer dependence. Results of the ordinary least squares regression model indicated that when dependence between buyers and suppliers is symmetric and high, greater flexibility occurs. When dependence is unilateral, indicating that one party is dependent but the other is not, flexibility is undermined.

REFERENCES:

Emerson, Richard M. (1962), "Power-Dependence Relations," *American Sociological Review*, 27 (February), 134–39.

Heide, Jan B. (1994), "Interorganizational Governance in Marketing Channels," *JM*, 58 (January), 71–85.

——— and George John (1992), "Do Norms Matter in Marketing Relationships?" *JM*, 56 (April), 32–44.

SCALE ITEMS:

Strongly   Strongly
disagree   agree

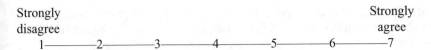

1. If we decided to stop buying from this supplier, they could easily replace our volume with sales to some other buyer. **(r)**

2. It would be relatively easy for this supplier to find another buyer for these components. **(r)**

3. Finding new buyers for these components would not have a negative impact on the price this supplier can charge. **(r)**

4. If the relationship with our company was terminated, it would not hurt this supplier's operations. **(r)**

SCALE NAME: Dependence (Vendor on Retailer)

SCALE DESCRIPTION: Ganesan (1994) developed a six-item, seven-point Likert-type scale to measure the extent to which vendors reported that they focused on long-term goals and long-term profitability in their vendor relationship, as well as a willingness to make sacrifices and share goals to develop a long-term relationship with a retailer.

SCALE ORIGIN: The scale is original to Ganesan (1994), who developed separate but parallel measures of dependence for the vendor and retailer samples. Scale items were generated through interviews with retail buyers and vendors. Although some items were specific to the retailer or vendor version, the author included a core set of items with minor phrasing alterations in both scales. Item analysis and exploratory factor analysis were used to initially purify the measure; items with low loadings and those loading on multiple factors were eliminated. A draft of the questionnaire containing this scale was also pretested with a group of 14 retail buyers who represented two department store chains. After administration to the final sample, scale items were subjected to a confirmatory factor analysis. Goodness-of-fit indices and individual item t-values were used to identify the final scale items.

SAMPLES: Five retail department store chains agreed to participate in Ganesan's (1994) study, and each firm received and distributed 30 questionnaires to senior sales representatives or sales managers who served as liaisons with vendor organizations. A total of **124** (83%) usable responses representing the *retailer* sample were obtained. Forty-eight respondents answered in the context of a long-term vendor relationship, and the remaining 76 answered in the context of a short-term vendor relationship. Contact information provided by respondents enabled the author to sample the designated 124 key vendor informants most knowledgeable about the retailer/vendor relationship with a survey similar in content to the retailer questionnaire but phrased from the vendor point-of-view. A total of **52** (42%) *vendor* representatives responded, of which 21 and 31 were in short- and long-term relationships, respectively.

RELIABILITY: Ganesan (1994) reported a coefficient alpha of **.85** for the scale.

VALIDITY: Ganesan (1994) submitted the scale to a confirmatory factor analysis using LISREL 7.16 to assess the unidimensionality, convergent validity, and discriminant validity of the measure. Although the measure was found to be unidimensional, no additional information pertaining to the outcome of the validity tests was provided.

ADMINISTRATION: Prior to being sent a survey, buyers in the retailer sample were randomly assigned to one of four cells in which the questionnaire instructions asked them to select a vendor on the basis of variations in two criteria: (1) the length of their relationship (short-term or long-term) and (2) the importance of the vendor's product to their organization (moderately important or very important). Questionnaires were distributed by a coordinator in each department store, and retailers were instructed to provide contact information for the vendor. This measure was administered as part of a mail survey sent to vendors and accompanied by a cover letter explaining the study purpose and promising confidentiality. Higher scores on the scale indicated a greater level of vendor dependence on a retailer, because the retailer was perceived as being both difficult to replace and important to company performance.

MAJOR FINDINGS: Ganesan (1994) investigated a variety of factors influencing the long-term orientation of both retailers and vendors in an ongoing relationship, as well as the antecedents to long-term orientation. The **dependence of a vendor on a retailer** was positively associated with vendor perceptions of the investments made by a retailer in transaction-specific assets, but environmental diversity was negatively associated with a **vendor's dependence on a retailer.**

REFERENCES:

Ganesan, Shankar (1994), "Determinants of Long-Term Orientation in Buyer-Seller Relationships," *JM*, 58 (April), 1–19.

SCALE ITEMS:

1. If our relationship was discontinued with this retailer, we would have difficulty in making up the sales volume in this trading area.

2. This retailer is crucial to our future performance.

3. It would be difficult for us to replace this retailer in this trading area.

4. We are dependent on this retailer for sales in this region.

5. We do not have a good alternative to this retailer.

6. This retailer generates high sales volume for us.

SCALE NAME: Dependence (Vendor's Perception of Retailer)

SCALE DESCRIPTION: Ganesan (1994) developed a three-item, seven-point Likert-type scale to measure vendor perceptions of the retailer's dependence on the vendor in terms of the ease with which the vendor could be replaced and the importance of the vendor to retailer performance.

SCALE ORIGIN: The scale is original to Ganesan (1994), who developed separate but parallel measures of perceptions of partner dependence for the vendor and retailer samples. Scale items were generated through interviews with retail buyers and vendors. Although some items were specific to the retailer or vendor version, the author included a core set of items with minor phrasing alterations in both scales. Item analysis and exploratory factor analysis were used to initially purify the measure; items with low loadings and those loading on multiple factors were eliminated. A draft of the questionnaire containing this scale was also pretested with a group of 14 retail buyers who represented two department store chains. After administration to the final sample, scale items were subjected to a confirmatory factor analysis. Goodness-of-fit indices and individual item t-values were used to identify the final scale items.

SAMPLES: Five retail department store chains agreed to participate in Ganesan's (1994) study, and each firm received and distributed 30 questionnaires to senior sales representatives or sales managers who served as liaisons with vendor organizations. A total of **124** (83%) usable responses representing the *retailer* sample were obtained. Forty-eight respondents answered in the context of a long-term vendor relationship, and the remaining 76 answered in the context of a short-term vendor relationship. Contact information provided by respondents enabled the author to sample the designated 124 key vendor informants most knowledgeable about the retailer/vendor relationship with a survey similar in content to the retailer questionnaire but phrased from the vendor point-of-view. A total of **52** (42%) *vendor* representatives responded, of which 21 and 31 were in short- and long-term relationships, respectively.

RELIABILITY: Ganesan (1994) reported a coefficient alpha of **.76** for the scale.

VALIDITY: Ganesan (1994) submitted the scale to a confirmatory factor analysis using LISREL 7.16 to assess the unidimensionality, convergent validity, and discriminant validity of the measure. Although the measure was found to be unidimensional, no additional information pertaining to the outcome of the validity tests was provided.

ADMINISTRATION: Prior to being sent a survey, buyers in the retailer sample were randomly assigned to one of four cells in which the questionnaire instructions asked them to select a vendor on the basis of variations in two criteria: (1) the length of their relationship (short-term or long-term) and (2) the importance of the vendor's product to their organization (moderately important or very important). Questionnaires were distributed by a coordinator in each department store, and retailers were instructed to provide contact information for the vendor. This measure was administered as part of a mail survey sent to vendors and accompanied by a cover letter explaining the study purpose and promising confidentiality. Higher scores on the scale indicated that vendors perceived retailers as being more dependent on them because of their importance to the retailer's performance and the difficulties involved in replacing them with an alternate vendor.

MAJOR FINDINGS: Ganesan (1994) investigated a variety of factors influencing the long-term orientation of both retailers and vendors in an ongoing relationship, as well as the antecedents to long-term orientation. The **vendor's perception of the dependence of a retailer on the vendor** was positively related to a vendor's long-term orientation, rather than negatively as was hypothesized.

REFERENCES:
Ganesan, Shankar (1994), "Determinants of Long-Term Orientation in Buyer-Seller Relationships," *JM*, 58 (April), 1–19.

SCALE ITEMS:

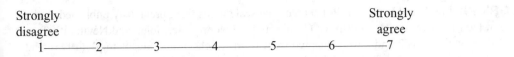

Strongly disagree — Strongly agree
1———2———3———4———5———6———7

1. We are important to this retailer.

2. We are a major supplier to this retailer in our product category.

3. If we discontinued supplying to this retailer, this retailer would have difficulty making up the sales volume in our product category.

SCALE NAME: Dependence (Wholesaler on Major Supplier)

SCALE DESCRIPTION: Lusch and Brown (1996) stated that this three-item, seven-point Likert-type scale was used to measure wholesale distributors' perceptions of their dependency on their major supplier.

SCALE ORIGIN: Lusch and Brown (1996) adapted the scale items from previously published studies. In the case of the first item, Lusch and Brown (1996) credited Noordewier, John, and Nevin (1990) and Ganesan (1994), while items 2 and 3 were adapted from Kumar, Scheer, and Steenkamp's (1995) study. Lusch and Brown simplified and shortened the original items and changed the context of reference from "retailer" or "dealer" relationships to relationships with "major suppliers."

SAMPLES: A systematic random sample of 3225 firms was drawn by Lusch and Brown (1996) from a mailing list of all U.S. merchant wholesalers and agents/brokers in 16 four-digit standard industrial classification code groups. The sample was further reduced by eliminating firms with more than 20 employees. General managers were identified as the key informants for the remaining firms and were sent mail questionnaires. Incentives and a follow-up mailing resulted in an initial response rate of 28.8%. However, this study reported usable data specific only to the **454** respondents classified as wholesale distributors and excluded data from agent and broker firms. The authors noted that the average number of suppliers reported by wholesalers in the sample was 45, with the major supplier contributing an average of 49% of the firm's annual volume.

RELIABILITY: Lusch and Brown (1996) reported a composite reliability of **.872** for this scale.

VALIDITY: Lusch and Brown (1996) reported undertaking a thorough review of the practitioner and academic literature, as well as extensive practitioner pretesting, to ensure content validity. Confirmatory factor analysis was used to establish the unidimensionality of the measure. Convergent and discriminant validity were also assessed and found to be satisfactory, which indicates that the measure possessed adequate construct validity.

ADMINISTRATION: The scale was included as part of a self-administered mail survey. A $1 incentive and the promise of shared survey results were offered as participant incentives, and a personalized cover letter accompanied the survey packet. Undeliverable questionnaires were redirected to a replacement firm. A second mailing without monetary incentive was sent one month later. Lusch and Brown (1996) instructed respondents to answer all questions pertaining to major suppliers in the context of the supplier with which the wholesale distributor did the most business. Higher scores on the measure indicated that the wholesale distributor had a greater dependence on its major supplier.

MAJOR FINDINGS: Lusch and Brown (1996) investigated how the type of dependency structure— wholesaler dependent on supplier, supplier dependent on wholesaler, or bilateral dependency—influenced whether a normative or explicit contract was used. The authors also studied whether dependency structure and the type of contract influenced the performance of wholesale distributors. Although no support was found linking **wholesale distributor dependency on a major supplier** to the use of an explicit or normative contract, the authors found that, as the **dependency on a major supplier** increased, so did the long-term orientation of the wholesale distributor. No statistically significant relationships between **dependency on a major supplier** and either the presence of relational behavior or wholesale distributor performance was found.

REFERENCES:

Ganesan, Shankar (1994), "Determinants of Long-Term Orientation in Buyer-Seller Relationships," *JM*, 58 (April), 1–19.

Kumar, Nirmalya, Lisa K. Scheer, and Jan-Benedict E.M. Steenkamp (1995b), "The Effects of Perceived Interdependence on Dealer Attitudes," *JMR*, 32 (August), 348–56.

Lusch, Robert F. and James R. Brown (1996), "Interdependency, Contracting, and Relational Behavior in Marketing Channels," *JM*, 60 (October), 19–38.

Noordewier, Thomas G., George John, and John R. Nevin (1990), "Performance Outcomes of Purchasing Arrangements in Industrial Buyer-Vendor Relationships," *JM*, 54 (October), 80–93.

SCALE ITEMS:

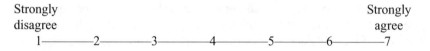

Strongly disagree — Strongly agree

1————2————3————4————5————6————7

1. We are dependent on our major supplier.

2. Our supplier would be difficult to replace.

3. Our major supplier would be costly to lose.

SCALE NAME: Dependence on the Firm (Salesperson)

SCALE DESCRIPTION: Anderson and Robertson (1995) used this nine-item, seven-point Likert-type scale to assess the level of benefits derived by a salesperson from working at a firm that would be difficult to replace.

SCALE ORIGIN: Anderson and Robertson (1995) developed the measure used in this study. A detailed construct description was built on the basis of a though review of the trade and academic literature. Multiple interviews with brokers, sales managers, and trade association officials were used to generate scale items thought to tap the construct. These items were administered to 208 brokers and factor analyzed to test for unidimensionality. Reliability assessments were also used to purify the measure.

SAMPLES: Anderson and Robertson (1995) mailed a questionnaire to the homes of 420 brokers whose names were supplied by cooperating firms, and **201** usable responses were obtained. To be evaluated, some hypotheses required the use of archival data regarding the actual sales of house brands made by salespeople. One firm, which provided **150** of the respondents in this study, agreed to supply this information. Anderson and Robertson (1995) stated that the respondent demographics closely matched those achieved in a large-scale survey of readers conducted by a nationally distributed trade magazine.

RELIABILITY: Anderson and Robertson (1995) reported a coefficient alpha of **.83** for this measure.

VALIDITY: No specific examination of scale validity was reported by Anderson and Robertson (1995).

ADMINISTRATION: Anderson and Robertson (1995) included the measure as part of a larger self-administered mail questionnaire. A summary of the results was offered in exchange for respondent cooperation. Higher scores on the scale indicated that salespeople were more dependent on the firm due to their perception that many of the benefits associated with working for that firm would be difficult to replace.

MAJOR FINDINGS: Anderson and Robertson (1995) investigated the relationship between factors thought to influence the sale of house brands by multiline salespeople. Results of analysis using the full sample indicated that salespeople who are more **dependent on the firm** rely less on external, rather than internal, sources of information. Highly **dependent** salespeople are also more successful, more experienced, and have lower levels of prior mobility. A salesperson's **dependence on the firm increases** as the firm invests in the salesperson through training and managerial attention. Finally, using the 150-member sample, analysis revealed that salespeople who are more **dependent on the firm** exhibit higher levels of house brand adoption.

REFERENCES:
Anderson, Erin and Thomas S. Robertson (1995), "Inducing Multiline Salespeople to Adopt House Brands," *JM*, 59 (April), 16–31.

SCALE ITEMS:

Strongly   Strongly
disagree   agree
1————2————3————4————5————6————7

1. This firm is a place where I can make a lot of money.

2. My firm's support makes me a much more effective broker.

3. At another firm, I'd have to work harder to make the same money as I do now.

4. Few firms would offer me the advantages I get from being with this firm.

5. I wouldn't be as effective a broker in another firm as I am here.

6. I'd be worse off if I changed jobs right now.

7. I would take a pay cut if I worked somewhere else.

8. I could get a better job tomorrow if I wanted to look. **(r)**

9. Other brokerage firms are good places to work, but here is best.

SCALE NAME: Directed Problem Solving

SCALE DESCRIPTION: Strutton and Lumpkin (1994) adapted this three-item, five-point subscale from the Ways of Coping Checklist Scale developed by Folkman and Lazarus (1980, 1985). It attempts to measure the extent to which a salesperson uses directed problem-solving tactics to cope with stressful customer sales presentations. In this study, the original items were screened for applicability to the sales setting. The remaining items were then subjected to factor analysis in a manner similar to that used by Folkman and colleagues (1986), and the subscales were identified in that manner.

SCALE ORIGIN: These items were adapted by Strutton and Lumpkin (1994) for a sales setting from the Ways of Coping Checklist (Folkman and Lazarus 1980, 1985). The original measure contained 43 items developed to measure problem-focused (24 items) and emotion-focused (19 items) tactics for handling stressful situations.

SAMPLES: Strutton and Lumpkin's (1994) sample was a nonprobability sample of **101** non-manager salespeople from three industries: communications technology (60), textiles (22), and furniture (19), predominantly in the southern United States.

RELIABILITY: Strutton and Lumpkin (1994) reported a Cronbach's alpha of **.73** for this scale.

VALIDITY: No specific validity tests were reported by Strutton and Lumpkin (1994). However, this subscale was identified as a separate subscale in Folkman's (1986) work.

ADMINISTRATION: Strutton and Lumpkin (1994) asked respondents to describe the most stressful customer-related situation they had encountered during a sales presentation during the previous two months. They were then asked to respond to the items in the scale, along with other scales and demographic questions. Higher scores on the scale indicated that directed problem-solving tactics for dealing with stress were used to a greater extent.

MAJOR FINDINGS: Strutton and Lumpkin (1994) found that the use of **directed problem solving** in coping with stress was significantly related to sales presentation effectiveness in a regression of all subscales on a self-reported measure of presentation effectiveness.

REFERENCES:

Folkman, Susan and Richard S. Lazarus (1980), "An Analysis of Coping in a Middle-Aged Community Sample," *Journal of Health and Social Behavior*, 21 (September), 219–39.

———— and ———— (1985), "If It Changes, It Must Be a Process: Study of Emotion and Coping During Three Stages of a College Examination," *Journal of Personality and Social Psychology*, 48 (January), 150–70.

————, ————, Christine Dunkel-Schetter, Anita DeLongis, and Rand J. Gruen (1986), "Dynamics of a Stressful Encounter: Cognitive Appraisal, Coping, and Encounter Outcomes," *Journal of Personality and Social Psychology*, 50 (May), 992–1003.

Strutton, David and James R. Lumpkin (1994), "Problem- and Emotion-Focused Coping Dimensions and Sales Presentation Effectiveness," *JAMS*, 22 (1), 28–37.

SCALE ITEMS:

Directions: Indicate the extent to which you used each of the following tactics to cope with a stressful sales presentation experience:

Not used at all   :____:____:____:____:____: Used a great deal
                         1   2   3   4   5

1. Drew on past experiences; I was in a similar situation before.

2. Came up with a couple of different solutions to the problem.

3. I knew what had to be done, so I redoubled my efforts to make things work.

#577 *Discretion Usage (Creative)*

SCALE NAME: Discretion Usage (Creative)

SCALE DESCRIPTION: Kelley, Longfellow, and Malehorn (1996) used this four-item scale in five- and six-point Likert formats to assess the degree to which an employee creatively develops an appropriate means for performing a task or accomplishing a goal.

SCALE ORIGIN: The scale is original to Kelley, Longfellow, and Malehorn (1996), who generated items on the basis of the literature and interviews with executives in the insurance and banking industries. The resulting items were purified during a review by a panel of banking and insurance executives, and the surviving set of items was pretested with a small sample of bank and insurance employees. One item from the pretested six-item scale, "When problems arise on the job I try to develop ways on my own to solve the problem," was eliminated from the measure in the final study because of large standardized originals in the confirmatory factor analysis. In the main study, a six-point Likert format was used with Sample 1, and a five-point Likert format was used with Sample 2.

SAMPLES: In the first sample, Kelley, Longfellow, and Malehorn (1996) surveyed all 122 customer-contact personnel employed by a bank located in the Midwest, and **113** usable responses were obtained, primarily from tellers (88) and customer service representatives (25). A stratified random sample of 381 insurance agents working in a single state of a large regional insurance company was also undertaken. In this second sample, 239 agents who represented 75 of the 77 different agencies associated with the company responded, but complete information was obtained from only **185** of these individuals.

RELIABILITY: Kelley, Longfellow, and Malehorn (1996) calculated coefficient alphas of **.729** and **.536** for this measure in Samples 1 and 2, respectively.

VALIDITY: Kelley, Longfellow, and Malehorn (1996) did not specifically discuss the validity of the measures.

ADMINISTRATION: In Sample 1, the measure was included in a questionnaire administered to customer-contact bank employees during regularly scheduled weekly meetings held in 15 branch offices. In Sample 2, Kelley, Longfellow, and Malehorn (1996) included the scale as part of a self-administered questionnaire that was delivered by mail. All responses were converted to z-scores prior to analysis because of the difference in response formats. Higher scores on the scale reflected greater usage of creative discretion in developing the appropriate means for performing a task.

MAJOR FINDINGS: Kelley, Longfellow, and Malehorn (1996) investigated the antecedents to service employees' use of routine, creative, and deviant discretion in the banking and insurance industry. **Creative discretion** was positively related to organizational support but was not significantly related to formalization or centralization.

REFERENCES:
Kelley, Scott W., Timothy Longfellow, and Jack Malehorn (1996), "Organizational Determinants of Service Employees' Exercise of Routine, Creative, and Deviant Discretion," *JR*, 72 (2), 135–57.

SCALE ITEMS:

Sample 1 response format:

Strongly   Strongly
disagree   agree
    1————————2————————3————————4————————5————————6

Sample 2 response format:

Strongly   Strongly
disagree   agree
    1————————2————————3————————4————————5

1. I use creativity to complete my job tasks when possible.

2. When necessary I make an effort to develop ways to perform my job.

3. If necessary I will go beyond what is expected of me to get the job done.

4. If there seems to be a way to perform a task that might be a little unusual I will try to find it.

SCALE NAME: Discretion Usage (Deviant)

SCALE DESCRIPTION: Kelley, Longfellow, and Malehorn (1996) used this five-item scale in five- and six-point Likert formats to assess the degree to which an employee performs behaviors that are not included in his or her job description or that are not part of management's role expectations for appropriate employee behavior.

SCALE ORIGIN: The scale is original to Kelley, Longfellow, and Malehorn (1996), who generated items on the basis of the literature and interviews with executives in the insurance and banking industries. The resulting items were purified during a review by a panel of banking and insurance executives, and the surviving set of items was pretested with a small sample of bank and insurance employees. In the main study, a six-point Likert format was used with Sample 1, and a five-point Likert format was used with Sample 2.

SAMPLES: In the first sample, Kelley, Longfellow, and Malehorn (1996) surveyed all 122 customer contact personnel employed by a bank located in the Midwest, and **113** usable responses were obtained, primarily from tellers (88) and customer service representatives (25). A stratified random sample of 381 insurance agents working in a single state of a large regional insurance company was also undertaken. In this second sample, 239 agents who represented 75 of the 77 different agencies associated with the company responded, but complete information was obtained from only **185** of these individuals.

RELIABILITY: Kelley, Longfellow, and Malehorn (1996) calculated coefficient alphas of **.833** and **.796** for this measure in Samples 1 and 2, respectively.

VALIDITY: Kelley, Longfellow, and Malehorn (1996) did not specifically discuss the validity of the measures.

ADMINISTRATION: In Sample 1, the measure was included in a questionnaire administered to customer-contact bank employees during regularly scheduled weekly meetings held in 15 branch offices. In S2, Kelley, Longfellow, and Malehorn (1996) included the scale as part of a self-administered questionnaire that was delivered by mail. All responses were converted to z-scores prior to analysis because of the difference in response formats. Higher scores on the scale reflected greater usage of deviant discretion behaviors.

MAJOR FINDINGS: Kelley, Longfellow, and Malehorn (1996) investigated the antecedents to service employees' use of routine, creative, and deviant discretion in the banking and insurance industry. **Deviant discretion** was negatively related to formalization but was not significantly related to organizational support or centralization.

REFERENCES:

Kelley, Scott W., Timothy Longfellow, and Jack Malehorn (1996), "Organizational Determinants of Service Employees' Exercise of Routine, Creative, and Deviant Discretion," *JR*, 72 (2), 135–57.

SCALE ITEMS:

Sample 1 response format:

Strongly   Strongly
disagree   agree

1————2————3————4————5————6

Sample 2 response format:

Strongly   Strongly
disagree   agree

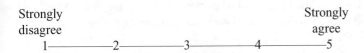

1————2————3————4————5

1. I complete my duties the way I want to even if it is viewed unfavorably by the organization.

2. If necessary I will contradict company policy in order to satisfy a customer.

3. If I think my way is better than the organization's way then I will do it my way.

4. Sometimes I perform routine tasks differently from the way the organization recommends.

5. Sometimes I take shortcuts on the job in order to get my work done more efficiently.

SCALE NAME: Discretion Usage (Routine)

SCALE DESCRIPTION: Kelley, Longfellow, and Malehorn (1996) used this five-item scale in five- and six-point Likert formats to assess the degree to which an employee selects an appropriate means for performing a task based on training, external search activities, or from a "list" provided by the organization.

SCALE ORIGIN: The scale is original to Kelley, Longfellow, and Malehorn (1996), who generated items on the basis of the literature and interviews with executives in the insurance and banking industries. The resulting items were purified during a review by a panel of banking and insurance executives, and the surviving set of items was pretested with a small sample of bank and insurance employees. One item from the pretested six-item scale, "I decide how to perform my job duties based on past experience," was eliminated from the measure in the final study because of large standardized originals in the confirmatory factor analysis. In the main study, a six-point Likert format was used with Sample 1, and a five-point Likert format was used with Sample 2.

SAMPLES: In the first sample, Kelley, Longfellow, and Malehorn (1996) surveyed all 122 customer contact personnel employed by a bank located in the Midwest, and **113** usable responses were obtained, primarily from tellers (88) and customer service representatives (25). A stratified random sample of 381 insurance agents working in a single state of a large regional insurance company was also undertaken. In this second sample, 239 agents who represented 75 of the 77 different agencies associated with the company responded, but complete information was obtained from only **185** of these individuals.

RELIABILITY: Kelley, Longfellow, and Malehorn (1996) calculated coefficient alphas of **.832** and **.745** for this measure in Samples 1 and 2, respectively.

VALIDITY: Kelley, Longfellow, and Malehorn (1996) did not specifically discuss the validity of the measures.

ADMINISTRATION: In Sample 1, the measure was included in a questionnaire administered to customer-contact bank employees during regularly scheduled weekly meetings held in 15 branch offices. In Sample 2, Kelley, Longfellow, and Malehorn (1996) included the scale as part of a self-administered questionnaire that was delivered by mail. All responses were converted to z-scores prior to analysis because of the difference in response formats. Higher scores on the scale reflected greater usage of routine discretion activities in determining the appropriate means for performing a task.

MAJOR FINDINGS: Kelley, Longfellow, and Malehorn (1996) investigated the antecedents to service employees' use of routine, creative, and deviant discretion in the banking and insurance industry. **Routine discretion** was positively related to organizational support but was not significantly related to formalization or centralization.

REFERENCES:

Kelley, Scott W., Timothy Longfellow, and Jack Malehorn (1996), "Organizational Determinants of Service Employees' Exercise of Routine, Creative, and Deviant Discretion," *JR*, 72 (2), 135–57.

SCALE ITEMS:

Sample 1 response format:

Sample 2 response format:

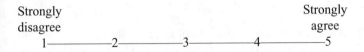

1. I use routine procedures to complete my job tasks when possible.

2. I consult other associates (agents) for ways to complete my job tasks when necessary.

3. I consult organizational manuals for the right way to complete my job tasks when necessary.

4. I decide how to perform my job duties based on training I have received.

5. I try to develop a routine for each of the typical duties involved in my job.

SCALE NAME: Distribution Intensity

SCALE DESCRIPTION: Frazier and Lassar (1996) used this four-item, five-point scale to measure the extent to which a manufacturer relies on various retailers in each trade area to carry its brand.

SCALE ORIGIN: The scale is original to Frazier and Lassar (1996), who generated items through personal interviews with manufacturers and retailers in the electronics, pet food, and hair care products industry. The authors examined intercorrelations among the items and dropped those with low correlations.

SAMPLES: Frazier and Lassar (1996) attempted to collect data related to 219 brands of stereo speakers from key informants representing 209 manufacturing firms. For manufacturers with multiple brands, only brands produced and marketed by independent divisions were treated as separate observations. A total of **85** usable questionnaires representing brands marketed by 84 manufacturers were returned. Of the 85 brands, 58 were home speakers, 22 were automotive speakers, and 5 were specialty speakers.

RELIABILITY: Frazier and Lassar (1996) reported a coefficient alpha of **.84** for this measure.

VALIDITY: Frazier and Lassar (1996) stated that an exploratory factor analysis was used to assess the unidimensionality and discriminant validity of the scale. An alternative measure of distribution intensity was constructed by visiting retail locations and counting the number of stores that carried each brand. The two measures of distribution intensity correlated at .61, which provides some evidence for the convergent validity of the measure.

ADMINISTRATION: Three versions of the questionnaire were created by Frazier and Lassar (1996): one each for home car, and specialty speakers. The only difference among questionnaires was the wording used to identify the different speakers. The measure was included in a self-administered mail survey. Nonrespondents received first a follow-up telephone call and then a second mailing. Prior notification and assurances of confidentially were provided in an attempt to increase response rate. Higher scores on the scale indicated that the manufacturer was relying on many retailers in its trade areas to carry its brand.

MAJOR FINDINGS: Frazier and Lassar (1996) investigated factors that influence the distribution intensity of brands in the electronics industry. **Distribution intensity** declined when brands were positioned on the basis of quality and when target markets were more narrowly focused. However, the inverse relationship between brand positioning and **distribution intensity** was weakened when contractual restrictiveness was high. Coordination efforts on the part of the manufacturer had a slightly negative effect on **distribution intensity** ($p < .10$), which was significantly weakened by higher levels of retailer investment. There was also some evidence to suggest that greater numbers of manufacturer support programs were related to greater **distribution intensity** ($p < .10$). This positive relationship was significantly stronger when retailer investments were high.

REFERENCES:

Frazier, Gary L. and Walfried M. Lassar (1996), "Determinants of Distribution Intensity," *JM*, 60 (October), 39–51.

SCALE ITEMS:

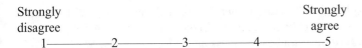

1. We are highly selective in our choice of retailers who carry our brand in each trade area. **(r)**

2. Only a select few retail outlets per trade area are allowed to carry our brand. **(r)**

3. We try to keep the number of retailers carrying our brand in each trade area to a minimum. **(r)**

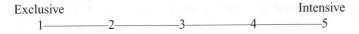

4. Compared to your competition, how would you describe your brand's distribution pattern for each trade area?

SCALE NAME: Dynamism (Market)

SCALE DESCRIPTION: Maltz and Kohli (1996) and Fisher, Maltz, and Jaworski (1997) used this four-item, five-point scale to measure how quickly customer preferences and competitor actions were perceived as changing in the market served by a strategic business unit (SBU).

SCALE ORIGIN: The scale appears to be original to Maltz and Kohli (1996), who evaluated the items in face-to-face interviews with manufacturing, finance, and R&D department managers and using a panel of academic experts. The measure and questionnaire were also pretested by Maltz and Kohli (1996) with 77 participants of an executive MBA program. Items that were found to be problematic were revised or eliminated accordingly.

Fisher, Maltz, and Jaworski (1997) pretested their scale with six marketing managers, and those items found to be unclear, ambiguous, or not applicable were dropped from the measure. Fisher, Maltz, and Jaworski (1997) administered a five-item version of market dynamism in Study 2. One item, "The price customers expect to pay," was eliminated from the scale on the basis of large modification indices in the confirmatory factor analysis.

SAMPLES: Maltz and Kohli (1996) sampled mid-level managers operating within SBUs of firms engaged in the manufacture of high-technology industrial equipment. Maltz and Kohli (1996) obtained names of 1061 nonmarketing managers in 270 SBUs from corporation presidents of participating firms. A total of **788** usable responses were returned by managers working in manufacturing (272), R&D (252), and finance (194).

In the second of two studies reported, Fisher, Maltz, and Jaworski (1997) sampled marketing managers employed by a multinational, business-to-business services firm with 36 business units in six countries outside the United States. A key informant provided a list of 100 firm members employed in a variety of marketing positions that required them to interact with engineering personnel. A total of **72** usable responses were obtained for Study 2.

RELIABILITY: Maltz and Kohli (1996) and Fisher, Maltz, and Jaworski (1997) reported alphas for this measure of **.74** and **.76**, respectively.

VALIDITY: Maltz and Kohli (1996) did not specifically examine the validity of this scale. Fisher, Maltz, and Jaworski (1997) conducted confirmatory factor analyses on the constructs used in their study in two stages to maintain an acceptable ratio of observations to variables. The first analysis included the original 17 items that composed the strategic unit dynamism, market dynamism, and the two interdependence scales. Fisher, Maltz, and Jaworski (1997) stated that, after two strategic unit dynamism items and one market dynamism item were eliminated because of large modification indices, the revised model fit the data acceptably well. Evidence of discriminant validity was provided, in that the correlation between each pair of constructs was significantly different from 1.00.

ADMINISTRATION: Although the results of two studies are reported by Fisher, Maltz, and Jaworski (1997), the market dynamism scale was only incorporated into Study 2. The measure was included by both Maltz and Kohli (1996) and Fisher, Maltz, and Jaworski (1997) as part of a self-administered questionnaire that was delivered by mail. Nonrespondents received a follow-up letter and second questionnaire mailing. Offers of anonymity and shared survey results were provided as incentives to participate in both studies. Respondents to Fisher, Maltz, and Jaworski's (1997) survey were instructed to answer questions in the context of their relationship with a single manager in the engineering function with whom they interacted regularly. Maltz and Kohli (1996) instructed respondents to focus on the intelligence they had received from the person in the marketing department with whom they had interacted the most during the previous three months. Higher scores on the measure indicated that respondents perceived customer preference and competitive strategy as occurring more quickly in the markets in which they compete.

MAJOR FINDINGS: Maltz and Kohli (1996) investigated the antecedents and consequences of the dissemination of marketing intelligence within SBUs. As expected, **market dynamism** had a negative effect on the frequency of market intelligence dissemination and on the use of market intelligence.

Fisher, Maltz, and Jaworski (1997) investigated how relative functional identification, or the strength of marketing managers' psychological connection to their functional area as compared with the firm as a whole, influences different strategies for improving communication between marketers and engineers. **Market dynamism** was included as a covariate in Study 2. The coerciveness of influence attempts was found to be negatively associated with **market dynamism**.

REFERENCES:

Fisher, Robert J., Elliot Maltz, and Bernard J. Jaworski (1997), "Enhancing Communication Between Marketing and Engineering: The Moderating Role of Relative Functional Identification," *JM*, 61 (July), 54–70.

Maltz, Elliot and Ajay K. Kohli (1996), "Market Intelligence Dissemination Across Functional Boundaries," *JMR*, 33 (February), 47–61.

SCALE ITEMS:

Very
slowly

Very
quickly

1————2————3————4————5

Maltz and Kohli (1996): Please indicate how quickly the following factors change in the market in which your SBU operates:

Fisher, Maltz, and Jaworski (1997): Please indicate how quickly the following factors *change in the market in which your Strategic Unit operates*:

1. Competitor's products and models.*

2. Customers' preferences or product features.

3. Competitor's selling strategies.

4. Competitor's promotion/advertising strategies.

*Fisher, Maltz, and Jaworski (1997) eliminated the "and models" portion of this item.

SCALE NAME: Dynamism (Marketing Program)

SCALE DESCRIPTION: Sinkula, Baker, and Noordewier (1997) used this three-item, seven-point scale to assess the frequency with which an organization changes its sales promotion/advertising strategies, sales strategies, and mix of products/brands.

SCALE ORIGIN: Sinkula, Baker, and Noordewier (1997) used Achrol and Stern's (1988) three-item, seven-point measure of marketing program dynamism. However, the origin of the scale is credited to the work of Child (1972) and Aldrich (1979).

SAMPLES: The results of preliminary interviews with business practitioners indicated that the most appropriate sample subjects for a study of organizational learning processes were those working at the high or upper organizational levels in a variety of industries. With this criterion in mind, Sinkula, Baker, and Noordewier (1997) drew a random sample of key informants from the 1994 membership list of the American Marketing Association but eliminated those whose titles suggested they were not high enough in the organizational hierarchy to provide informed responses. Of the 276 individuals who qualified for the study, **125** returned usable responses.

RELIABILITY: Sinkula, Baker, and Noordewier (1997) reported a coefficient alpha of **.77** for this measure.

VALIDITY: Sinkula, Baker, and Noordewier (1997) stated that a confirmatory factor analysis demonstrated the convergent and discriminatory validity of the measure.

ADMINISTRATION: The measure was included by Sinkula, Baker, and Noordewier (1997) as part of a self-administered questionnaire that was delivered by mail; nonrespondents received a second mailing. Higher scores on the scale reflected more frequent changes in the product mix and in sales, sales promotion, and advertising strategies.

MAJOR FINDINGS: Sinkula, Baker, and Noordewier (1997) investigated the relationship among organizational values, market information processing behaviors, and organizational actions in the context of an organizational learning framework. Results indicated that, by increasing market information generation and dissemination, a positive learning orientation affects **marketing program dynamism**, or the degree to which an organization makes changes in its marketing strategy.

REFERENCES:

Achrol, Ravi S. and Louis S. Stern (1988), "Environmental Determinants of Decision-Making Uncertainty in Marketing Channels," *JMR*, 25 (February), 36–50.
Aldrich, James C. (1987), *Organizations and Environments.* Englewood Cliffs, NJ: Prentice-Hall.
Child, John (1972), "Organizational Structure, Environment and Performance: The Role of Strategic Choice," *Sociology*, 6 (January), 2–22.
Sinkula, James M., William E. Baker, and Thomas Noordewier (1997), "A Framework for Market-Based Organizational Learning: Linking Values, Knowledge, and Behavior," *JAMS*, 25 (4), 305–18.

SCALE ITEMS:

Please respond to the degree of change as it relates to your organization with respect to the following items:

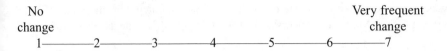

No   Very frequent
change   change

1————2————3————4————5————6————7

1. Changes in your (organization's) mix of products/brands.

2. Changes in your (organization's) sales strategies.

3. Changes in your (organization's) sales promotion/advertising strategies.

SCALE NAME: Dynamism (Strategic Unit)

SCALE DESCRIPTION: Maltz and Kohli (1996) and Fisher, Maltz, and Jaworski (1997) used all or portions of this six-item, five-point Likert-type scale to measure the degree to which procedures, supervisors, and things in general are perceived to change or fluctuate within a strategic business unit (SBU). Maltz and Kohli (1996) and Fisher, Maltz, and Jaworski (1997) referred to this scale as *structural flux* in their articles.

SCALE ORIGIN: The scale appears to be original to Maltz and Kohli (1996), who evaluated the items in face-to-face interviews with manufacturing, finance, and R&D department managers and using a panel of academic experts. The measure and questionnaire were also pretested by Maltz and Kohli (1996) with 77 participants of an executive MBA program. Items that were found to be problematic were revised or eliminated accordingly. Fisher, Maltz, and Jaworski (1997) pretested the scale items with six marketing managers, and those found to be unclear, ambiguous, or not applicable were dropped from the measure. Fisher, Maltz, and Jaworski (1997) eliminated two items, "You never know when your job is going to change in our Strategic Unit" and "I'm always evaluated based on the same criteria," from the scale on the basis of large modification indices in the confirmatory factor analysis.

SAMPLES: Maltz and Kohli (1996) sampled mid-level managers operating within SBUs of firms engaged in the manufacture of high-technology industrial equipment. Maltz and Kohli (1996) obtained names of 1061 nonmarketing managers in 270 SBUs from corporation presidents of participating firms. A total of **788** usable responses were returned by managers working in manufacturing (272), R&D (252), and finance (194).

In the second of two studies reported, Fisher, Maltz, and Jaworski (1997) sampled marketing managers employed by a multinational, business-to-business services firm with 36 business units in six countries outside the United States. A key informant provided a list of 100 firm members employed in a variety of marketing positions that required them to interact with engineering personnel. A total of **72** usable responses were obtained for Study 2.

RELIABILITY: Maltz and Kohli (1996) and Fisher, Maltz, and Jaworski (1997) reported calculating coefficient alphas for this measure of **.78** and **.83**, respectively.

VALIDITY: Maltz and Kohli (1996) did not specifically examine the validity of this scale. Fisher, Maltz, and Jaworski (1997) conducted confirmatory factor analyses on the constructs used in their study in two stages to maintain an acceptable ratio of observations to variables. The first analysis included the original 17 items that composed the strategic unit dynamism, market dynamism, and the two interdependence scales. Fisher, Maltz, and Jaworski (1997) stated that, after two strategic unit dynamism items and one market dynamism item were eliminated due to large modification indices, the revised model fit the data acceptably well. Evidence of discriminant validity was provided, in that the correlation between each pair of constructs was significantly different from 1.00.

ADMINISTRATION: Although the results of two studies are reported by Fisher, Maltz, and Jaworski (1997), the market dynamism scale was only incorporated into Study 2. The measure was included by both Maltz and Kohli (1996) and Fisher, Maltz, and Jaworski (1997) as part of a self-administered questionnaire that was delivered by mail; nonrespondents received a follow-up letter and second questionnaire mailing. Offers of anonymity and shared survey results were provided as incentives to participate in both studies. Respondents to Fisher, Maltz, and Jaworski's (1997) survey were instructed to answer questions in the context of their relationship with a single manager in the engineering function with whom they interacted regularly. Maltz and Kohli (1996) instructed respondents to focus on the intelligence they had received from the person in the marketing department with whom they had interacted the most during the previous three months. Higher scores on the measure indicated that respondents perceived higher levels of change and fluctuation as occurring throughout the SBU.

MAJOR FINDINGS: Maltz and Kohli (1996) investigated the antecedents and consequences of the dissemination of marketing intelligence within SBUs. As expected, the **dynamism of the SBU** had a negative effect on the perceived quality of the market intelligence and on the use of formal dissemination channels in the delivery of market intelligence.

Fisher, Maltz, and Jaworski (1997) investigated how relative functional identification, or the strength of marketing managers' psychological connection to their functional area as compared with the firm as a whole, influenced different strategies for improving communication between marketers and engineers. The **dynamism of the marketing unit** was included as a covariate in Study 2. The bidirectionality of communication was found to be positively associated with **dynamism**, which indicates that greater levels of change and fluctuation in an SBU are accompanied by higher levels of feedback between the marketing and engineering departments.

REFERENCES:

Fisher, Robert J., Elliot Maltz, and Bernard J. Jaworski (1997), "Enhancing Communication Between Marketing and Engineering: The Moderating Role of Relative Functional Identification," *JM*, 61 (July), 54–70.

Maltz, Elliot and Ajay K. Kohli (1996), "Market Intelligence Dissemination Across Functional Boundaries," *JMR*, 33 (February), 47–61.

SCALE ITEMS:

Strongly   Strongly
disagree   agree

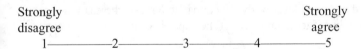

1. The way we do things at our SBU keep changing.*

2. You can never tell when you're going to have a new boss around here.

3. You never know when your job is going to change in this business unit.**

4. The only thing you can be sure of at our SBU is that something is going to change.*

5. I'm always evaluated on the same criteria. **(r)****

6. It seems like we're always reorganizing.

*Fisher, Maltz, and Jaworski (1997) substituted "strategic unit" for "SBU" in these items.
**Fisher, Maltz, and Jaworski (1997) dropped these items from the measure used in their study.

SCALE NAME: Dysfunctional Behavior (Employee)

SCALE DESCRIPTION: Six five-point items measuring the frequency with which an employee reports engaging in behaviors that, though not necessarily against the rules, help the employee at the long-range expense of the organization. Such behaviors are gaming, focusing, smoothing, and invalid reporting.

SCALE ORIGIN: The scale was apparently developed by Jaworski and MacInnis (1989). The scale and other aspects of the survey instrument were refined through a series of interviews and a pretest of marketing managers.

SAMPLES: A national sample of marketing managers was drawn randomly by Jaworski and MacInnis (1989) from the American Marketing Association's (AMA) list of members. Of the 479 managers who received questionnaires, **379** returned usable forms.

Ramaswami (1996) received usable surveys from **318** of the 1159 AMA members who were randomly selected from the AMA's membership list.

RELIABILITY: Coefficient alphas of **.75** and **.78** were reported for the scale by Jaworski and MacInnis (1989) and Ramaswami (1996), respectively.

VALIDITY: The validity of the scale was not specifically examined by either Jaworski and MacInnis (1989) or Ramaswami (1996).

ADMINISTRATION: Jaworksi and MacInnis (1989) and Ramaswami (1996) indicated that the scale was self-administered, along with many other measures, in a mail survey format. Higher scores on the scale indicated that employees engaged in a high level of dysfunctional activities, whereas lower scores suggested that they rarely did things that benefited themselves at the expense of the organization.

MAJOR FINDINGS: Among the many purposes of the study by Jaworski and MacInnis (1989) was to examine the simultaneous use of several types of managerial controls in the context of marketing management. Using structural equations, the authors found that the use of work-related self-control had a significant negative effect on **employee dysfunctional behavior**.

Ramaswami (1996) investigated both traditional and contingency theories of negative employee responses to marketing control systems. Both output and process control were positively associated with **employee dysfunctional behavior**. However, the use of a *process* control resulted in lower levels of **employee dysfunctional behavior** when procedural knowledge is high compared with when it is low, whereas higher levels of procedural knowledge combined with *output* controls resulted in lower levels of **employee dysfunctional behavior**.

REFERENCES:

Jaworski, Bernard J. and Deborah J. MacInnis (1989), "Marketing Jobs and Management Controls: Toward a Framework," *JMR*, 26 (November), 406–19.

Ramaswami, Sridhar N. (1996), "Marketing Controls and Dysfunctional Employee Behaviors: A Test of Traditional and Contingency Theory Postulates," *JM*, 60 (April), 105–20.

SCALE ITEMS:*

Never   Always
  1————————2————————3————————4————————5

1. I tend to ignore certain job related activities simply because they are not monitored by the division.

2. I work on unimportant activities simply because they are evaluated by upper management.

3. Even if my productivity is inconsistent, I still try to make it appear consistent.

4. I have adjusted marketing data to make my performance appear more in line with division goals.

5. When presenting data to upper management, I try to emphasize data that reflect favorably on me.

6. When presenting data to upper management, I try to avoid being the bearer of bad news.

*Ramaswami (1996) reported using a five-point Likert response format (1 = strongly disagree, 5 = strongly agree)

SCALE NAME: Emotions (Salesperson Negative)

SCALE DESCRIPTION: In conjunction with different directions, Brown, Cron, and Slocum (1997) used this ten-item, eleven-point scale to measure the degrees to which salespeople both anticipated experiencing a series of negative emotions should they fail to reach their stated goal *(anticipatory negative emotions)* and reported actually experiencing these negative emotions as a result of their performance relative to the goal *(outcome negative emotions)*.

SCALE ORIGIN: Brown, Cron, and Slocum (1997) indicated that the scale was taken from a working paper by Bagozzi, Baumgartner, and Pieters (1995).

SAMPLES: Sales representatives from a medical supplies distributorship that was participating in a specific promotion were sampled for this study. Brown, Cron, and Slocum (1997) attempted to sample the entire sales force at two points in time. Of the 141-member sales force, **122** returned usable responses to both questionnaires. The average sales goal reported by salespeople for the specific unit on promotion was 3.2 units, and the actual average units sold was 2.5 units. Of this group, 25% met their goal exactly, 52% did not, and 23% exceeded their sales goal.

RELIABILITY: Brown, Cron, and Slocum (1997) reported coefficient alphas of **.93** for the anticipatory negative emotion scale and **.94** for the outcome negative emotion scale.

VALIDITY: No specific examination of scale validity was reported by Brown, Cron, and Slocum (1997).

ADMINISTRATION: Brown, Cron, and Slocum (1997) distributed the first questionnaire during a sales meeting in which the focal promotion was introduced and explained. The anticipatory emotion scales were included in this questionnaire with other measures. Although it is not clear how the second questionnaire was distributed, it appears to have been self-administered also. Salespeople received this questionnaire, which contained the outcome emotions scales and other measures, following the conclusion of the promotion. Higher scores on the anticipatory and outcome scales, respectively, indicated that salespeople *anticipated* experiencing more intense negative emotions *should* they reach their goals and that they *actually experienced* more intense negative emotions as a *result* of their performance relative to their goal.

MAJOR FINDINGS: Brown, Cron, and Slocum (1997) investigated the effect of goal-directed positive and negative emotions on salesperson volition, behavior, and performance. **Negative *anticipatory* emotions** were positively related to a salesperson's anticipated planning of effort and strategies (volition), and **negative *outcome* emotions** were positively associated with the degree of goal attainment.

REFERENCES:

Bagozzi, Richard P., Hans Baumgartner, and Rik Pieters (1995), "Goal-Directed Emotions," working paper, School of Business, University of Michigan.

Brown, Steven P., William L. Cron, and John W. Slocum Jr. (1997), "Effects of Goal-Directed Emotions on Salesperson Volitions, Behavior, and Performance: A Longitudinal Study," *JM*, 61 (January), 39–50.

SCALE ITEMS:

Instructions for Anticipatory Emotions Scale:
If you *do not* succeed in achieving your goal for the [manufacturer] promotion, how intensely do you anticipate you will feel each of the following emotions?

Instructions for Outcome Emotions Scale:
As a result of your performance relative to your goal, how intensely do you feel each of the following emotions?

Not at all   Very much
1——2——3——4——5——6——7——8——9——10——11

1. Angry.
2. Frustrated.
3. Guilty.
4. Ashamed.
5. Sad.
6. Disappointed.
7. Depressed.
8. Worried.
9. Uncomfortable.
10. Fearful.

SCALE NAME: Emotions (Salesperson Positive)

SCALE DESCRIPTION: In conjunction with different directions, Brown, Cron, and Slocum (1997) used this seven-item, eleven-point scale to measure the degrees to which salespeople both anticipated experiencing a series of positive emotions should they reach their stated goal *(anticipatory positive emotions)* and reported actually experiencing these positive emotions as a result of their performance relative to the goal *(outcome positive emotions)*.

SCALE ORIGIN: Brown, Cron, and Slocum (1997) indicated that the scale was taken from the working paper by Bagozzi, Baumgartner, and Pieters (1995).

SAMPLES: Sales representatives of a medical supplies distributorship that was participating in a specific promotion were sampled for this study. Brown, Cron, and Slocum (1997) attempted to sample the entire sales force at two points in time. Of the 141-member sales force, **122** returned usable responses to both questionnaires. The average sales goal reported by salespeople for the specific unit on promotion was 3.2 units, and the actual average units sold was 2.5 units. Of this group, 25% met their goal exactly, 52% did not, and 23% exceeded their sales goal.

RELIABILITY: Brown, Cron, and Slocum (1997) reported coefficient alphas of **.94** for the anticipatory positive emotion scale and **.95** for the outcome positive emotion scale.

VALIDITY: No specific examination of scale validity was reported by Brown, Cron, and Slocum (1997).

ADMINISTRATION: Brown, Cron, and Slocum (1997) distributed the first questionnaire during a sales meeting in which the focal promotion was introduced and explained. The anticipatory emotion scales were included in this questionnaire with other measures. Although it is not clear how the second questionnaire was distributed, it appears to have been self-administered also. Salespeople received this questionnaire, which contained the outcome emotions scales and other measures, following the conclusion of the promotion. Higher scores on the anticipatory and outcome scales, respectively, indicated that salespeople *anticipated* experiencing more intense positive emotions *should* they reach their goals and that they *actually experienced* more intense positive emotions as a *result* of their performance relative to their goal.

MAJOR FINDINGS: Brown, Cron, and Slocum (1997) investigated the effect of goal-directed positive and negative emotions on salesperson volition, behavior, and performance. **Positive *anticipatory* emotions** were positively related to a salesperson's personal stake in a promotion and anticipated planning of effort and strategies (volition), and **positive *outcome* emotions** were positively associated with the degree of goal attainment.

REFERENCES:

Bagozzi, Richard P., Hans Baumgartner, and Rik Pieters (1995), "Goal-Directed Emotions," working paper, School of Business, University of Michigan.

Brown, Steven P., William L. Cron, and John W. Slocum Jr. (1997), "Effects of Goal-Directed Emotions on Salesperson Volitions, Behavior, and Performance: A Longitudinal Study," *JM*, 61 (January), 39–50.

SCALE ITEMS:

Instructions for Anticipatory Emotions Scale:
If you succeed in achieving your goal for the [manufacturer] promotion, how intensely do you anticipate you will feel each of the following emotions?

Instructions for Outcome Emotions Scale:
As a result of your performance relative to your goal, how intensely do you feel each of the following emotions?

Not at all   Very much
1———2———3———4———5———6———7———8———9———10———11

1. Excited.
2. Delighted.
3. Happy.
4. Glad.
5. Satisfied.
6. Proud.
7. Self-assured.

SCALE NAME: Empowerment (Employee)

SCALE DESCRIPTION: Hartline and Ferrell (1996) used this four-item, five-point Likert-type scale to measure the extent to which managers allow employees to use their own initiative and judgment in performing their jobs.

SCALE ORIGIN: Hartline and Ferrell (1996) indicated that the items representing this construct were taken from Cook and colleagues' (1981) eight-item tolerance-of-freedom scale. Four items, "I allow employees complete freedom in their work," "I let employees do their work the way they think best," "I assign tasks, then let employees handle them," and "I turn employees loose on a job, and let them go to it," were dropped from the measure following a confirmatory factor analysis because of nonsignificant t-values.

SAMPLES: The hotel industry was chosen as the sampling frame for this study. Hartline and Ferrell (1996) sampled the general managers, employees, and customers of 444 hotel units that represented three hotel chains. Of these, 236 different hotel units returned at least one usable questionnaire from a manager, an employee, and a customer. A total of 1769 usable questionnaires were received from **236** hotel managers, **561** customer-contact employees, and **1351** customers.

RELIABILITY: Hartline and Ferrell (1996) reported a coefficient alpha of **.71** for this measure.

VALIDITY: Hartline and Ferrell (1996) used confirmatory factor analysis to test the unidimensionality of the measures using separate analyses for managers, employees, and customers. Items with nonsignificant t-values were dropped from the measures. In investigating the discriminant validity of the scales, the authors first averaged the employee and customer responses on the scale and then matched that response with the manager responses to create a single data set in which cases represented hotel units rather individuals. Hotel units that did not provide at least three responses from both employees and customers were dropped, leaving a final sample of 97 matched responses. Confirmatory factor analysis was then used to assess the discriminant validity of the measures.

ADMINISTRATION: Each hotel manager received a survey packet containing instructions, postage-paid reply envelopes, one manager survey, five employee surveys, and forty guest surveys, which were to be self-administered. This measure was included in the manager survey. Hartline and Ferrell (1996) instructed managers to distribute employee surveys to individuals in customer-contact positions and the guest surveys during check-out. Survey packets were preceded by a letter from the corporate marketing manager endorsing the project and followed by a second wave of materials approximately two months after the first had been distributed. Higher scores on the scale indicated that the manager used a greater degree of empowerment in managing employees.

MAJOR FINDINGS: Hartline and Ferrell (1996) investigated the management of customer-contact service employees and various factors related to service quality using data generated from the customers, contact employees, and managers of hotel units. Hypotheses were tested in the context of structural equation modeling. Increased levels of management commitment to service quality resulted in increased management use of **empowerment** and behavior-based employee evaluations. **Empowerment** was found to increase both employee self-efficacy and role conflict, though the latter result was contrary to expectations. Role ambiguity was also positively, though indirectly, affected by **empowerment**. Both job satisfaction and employee adaptability were indirectly, but negatively, influenced by **empowerment**. The authors interpreted this to mean that, though **empowered** employees are more confident in their job skills, their attempts to balance role demands result in increased conflict and ambiguity. Increased commitment to service quality on the part of management was also was found to increase a manager's use of **empowerment** in managing employees.

REFERENCES:

Cook, John D., Sue J. Hepworth, Toby D. Wall, and Peter B. Wall (1981), *The Experience of Work.* New York: Academic Press.

Hartline, Michael D. and O.C. Ferrell (1996), "The Management of Customer-Contact Service Employees: An Empirical Investigation," *JM*, 60 (October), 52–70.

SCALE ITEMS:

Strongly disagree

Strongly agree

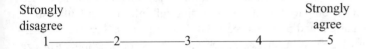

1————2————3————4————5

1. I permit employees to use their own judgment in solving problems.

2. I encourage initiative in my employees.

3. I allow employees a high degree of initiative.

4. I trust employees to exercise good judgment.

SCALE NAME: Environmental Dynamism (Technical/Market)

SCALE DESCRIPTION: Four seven-point items used to measure the degree of change in key elements of the technical and market structure experienced by a firm. Pelham and Wilson (1996) referred to this scale as "market environment dynamism" in their article.

SCALE ORIGIN: Pelham and Wilson (1996) indicated that this scale was taken from Miller and Droge's (1986) study.

SAMPLES: A longitudinal database developed by the Center for Entrepreneurship at Eastern Michigan University provided the data for the study. The Center's full panel consists of data provided by the CEOs of 370 Michigan firms and represents 71% of the firms contacted for initial participation. The data used by Pelham and Wilson (1996) were specific only to those firms providing full information with respect to all measures of interest for both the current and previous years. Of those **68** firms, 32% were classified as wholesalers, 29% as manufacturers, 26% as business services, and 13% as construction. Firm size ranged from 15 to 65 employees, with the average number of employees equaling 23.

RELIABILITY: Pelham and Wilson (1996) reported an alpha of **.72** for this scale.

VALIDITY: Pelham and Wilson (1996) stated that factor loadings and LISREL measurement model squared multiple correlations were taken as evidence of convergent/discriminant validity.

ADMINISTRATION: Pelham and Wilson (1996) did not provide details with respect to how data were collected from panel members by the Center of Entrepreneurship. Higher scores on the scale indicated a greater degree of change in the firm's market and technical structure.

MAJOR FINDINGS: Pelham and Wilson (1996) investigated the relative impact of market orientation on small business performance compared with market structure, firm structure, firm strategy, and relative product quality. Regression analysis was used to test year-to-year differences in most variables, as well as parameters based on independent and lagged variables. **Environmental dynamism** did not significantly influence any variable in either model.

REFERENCES:

Miller, Danny and Cornelia Dröge (1986), "Psychological and Traditional Determinants of Structure," *Administrative Science Quarterly*, 31 (December), 539–60.

Pelham, Alfred M. and David T. Wilson (1996), "A Longitudinal Study of the Impact of Market Structure, Firm Structure, Strategy, and Market Orientation Culture on Dimensions of Small-Firm Performance," *JAMS*, 24 (1), 27–43.

SCALE ITEMS:

Directions: Indicate the frequency of factor change in your industry.

Never change   Change very frequently

1————2————3————4————5————6————7

1. Production (or distribution) technique/process changes.

2. Changes in customers' needs.

3. Rate at which products/services become obsolete.

4. Nature of competitors's strategies and actions.

SCALE NAME: Environmental Uncertainty

SCALE DESCRIPTION: A set of semantic differential items that seek to measure the degree of market volatility and unpredictability faced by a particular group (salespeople, retailers, vendors, suppliers, etc.), often in the context of making decisions.

SCALE ORIGIN: The common origin for the various versions of this scale can typically be traced to Heide and John's (1988) market environment scale.

SAMPLES: John and Weitz (1989) mailed personalized requests to 750 sales managers or sales vice presidents of manufacturing firms that had annual sales of at least $50 million. Of the 266 people who agreed to participate, **161** returned usable questionnaires. The sample appeared to be different from the population of sales managers and vice presidents in some respects but very similar in others.

Kumar, Scheer, and Steenkamp (1995) sampled 1640 of the 2100 new car dealers listed on a commercially purchased list that covered two U.S. states. Also, 1600 new car dealers were randomly selected from a list of 4000 dealers that represented the entire Netherlands. Respectively, **417** and **289** usable responses were received from U.S. and Dutch dealers. The data were standardized separately by country to eliminate any culturally idiosyncratic patterns, then pooled for analysis.

Five retail department store chains agreed to participate in Ganesan's (1994) study, and each firm received and distributed 30 questionnaires to senior sales representatives or sales managers who served as liaisons with vendor organizations. A total of **124** (83%) usable responses representing the *retailer* sample were obtained. Contact information provided by respondents enabled Ganesan (1994) to sample the designated 124 key vendor informants most knowledgeable about the retailer/vendor relationship. A total of **52** (42%) *vendor* representatives responded.

Celly and Frazier (1996) effectively sampled 953 distributors who were randomly selected from Dun's Marketing Services' Direct Access service and who had passed a variety of screening processes. The selected distributors serviced one of four industries: machine tools and metalworking machinery, air compressors and packaging equipment, industrial tools, or abrasives and adhesives. **Two hundred seven** usable responses were obtained.

RELIABILITY: John and Weitz (1989), Kumar, Scheer, and Steenkamp (1995), and Celly and Frazier (1996) reported coefficient alphas of **.65**, **.68**, and **.85**, respectively. Coefficient alphas of **.56** (vendor perceptions) and **.72** (retailer perceptions) were reported by Ganesan (1994).

VALIDITY: Celly and Frazier (1996) examined the discriminant validity of all of the measures in their study using the results of a principal components factors analysis with orthogonal rotation. The validity of the measure was found to be satisfactory.

Ganesan (1994) submitted the scale to a confirmatory factor analysis using LISREL 7.16 to assess the unidimensionality, convergent validity, and discriminant validity of the measure. Although the measure was found to be unidimensional, no additional information pertaining to the outcome of the validity tests was provided by Ganesan (1994).

Kumar, Scheer, and Steenkamp (1995) reported that evidence of the convergent validity of the measure was obtained through a confirmatory factor analysis in which all first- and second-order constructs were found to be significant.

The validity of the scale was not specifically examined by John and Weitz (1989).

ADMINISTRATION: The scale was typically included with other measures in a self-administered survey delivered by mail (Celly and Frazier 1996; John and Weitz 1989; Kumar, Scheer, and Steenkamp 1995). Kumar, Scheer, and Steenkamp (1995) indicated that the questionnaire was originally constructed in English and then translated into Dutch. Back-translation was used to verify the accuracy of the translation. Dealers from both countries were asked to report on the automobile suppler (manufacturer or importer) whose product line accounted for the largest share of their firm's sales.

In Ganesan's (1994) study, prior to being sent a survey, buyers in the retailer sample were randomly assigned to one of four cells in which the questionnaire instructions asked them to select a vendor on the basis of variations in two criteria: (1) the length of their relationship (short-term or long-term) and (2) the importance of the vendor's product to their organization (moderately important or very important). Questionnaires were distributed by a coordinator in each department store, and respondents were instructed to answer the survey in the context of this single vendor. Higher scores on the scale indicated a more volatile, uncertain environment or market.

MAJOR FINDINGS: Celly and Frazier (1996) investigated suppliers' use of outcome- and behavior-based coordinator efforts with their distributors. Chow tests that compared information provided by exclusive dealers with that provided by nonexclusive dealers confirmed the appropriateness of analyzing the data jointly. **Environmental uncertainty** demonstrated a strong, positive effect on both outcome- and behavior-based supplier coordination efforts.

Ganesan (1994) investigated a variety of factors influencing the long-term orientation of both retailers and vendors in an ongoing relationship, as well as the antecedents to long-term orientation. Results indicated that **environmental volatility** did not have a significant impact on either the retailer's dependence on the vendor or the vendor's dependence on the retailer.

The purpose of the study by John and Weitz (1989) was to examine the role of salary in sales compensation plans by using a transaction cost analysis framework. The degree of environmental uncertainty had its most significant positive correlations with importance of employee coordination, the transaction asset specificity between the firm and the sales force, and, particularly, the complexity of the sales task.

Kumar, Scheer, and Steenkamp (1995) investigated how supplier fairness affected the development of long-term relationships between relatively smaller and vulnerable new car dealers and larger, more powerful suppliers. **Environmental uncertainty** negatively influenced relationship quality, and the importance of procedural fairness in determining relationship quality increased as **environmental uncertainty** rose.

COMMENTS: See also Dahlstrom and Nygaard (1995) and Klein, Frazier, and Roth (1990).

REFERENCES:

Celly, Kirti Sawhney and Gary L. Frazier (1996), "Outcome-Based and Behavior-Based Coordination Efforts in Channel Relationships," *JMR,* 33 (May), 200–210.

Dahlstrom, Robert and Arne Nygaard (1995), "An Exploratory Investigation of Interpersonal Trust in New and Mature Market Economies," *JR*, 71 (4), 339–61.

Ganesan, Shankar (1994), "Determinants of Long-Term Orientation in Buyer-Seller Relationships," *JM*, 58 (April), 1–19.

Heide, Jan B. and George John (1988), "The Role of Dependence Balancing in Safeguarding Transaction-Specific Assets in Conventional Channels," *JM*, 52 (January), 20–35.

John, George and Barton Weitz (1989), "Salesforce Compensation: An Empirical Investigation of Factors Related to Use of Salary Versus Incentive Compensation," *JMR*, 26 (February), 1–14.

Klein, Saul, Gary L. Frazier, and Victor J. Roth (1990), "A Transaction Cost Analysis Model of Channel Integration in International Markets," *JMR*, 27 (May), 196–208.

Kumar, Nirmalya, Lisa K. Scheer, and Jan-Benedict E. M. Steenkamp (1995b), "The Effects of Supplier Fairness on Vulnerable Resellers," *JMR*, 32 (February), 54–65.

SCALE ITEMS:*

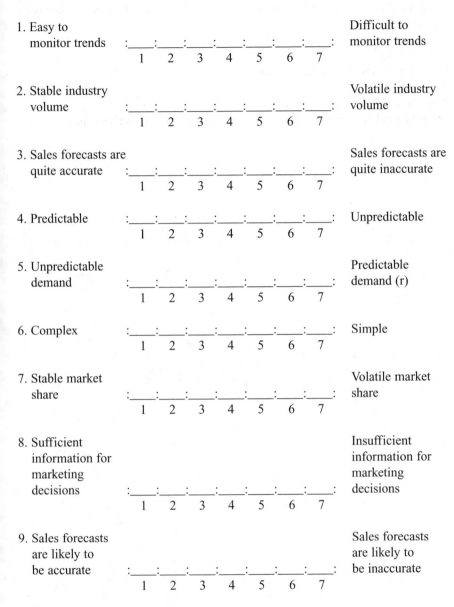

1. Easy to
   monitor trends   :___:___:___:___:___:___:___: Difficult to
                         1   2   3   4   5   6   7   monitor trends

2. Stable industry
   volume   :___:___:___:___:___:___:___: Volatile industry
                         1   2   3   4   5   6   7   volume

3. Sales forecasts are
   quite accurate   :___:___:___:___:___:___:___: Sales forecasts are
                         1   2   3   4   5   6   7   quite inaccurate

4. Predictable   :___:___:___:___:___:___:___: Unpredictable
                         1   2   3   4   5   6   7

5. Unpredictable
   demand   :___:___:___:___:___:___:___: Predictable
                         1   2   3   4   5   6   7   demand (r)

6. Complex   :___:___:___:___:___:___:___: Simple
                         1   2   3   4   5   6   7

7. Stable market
   share   :___:___:___:___:___:___:___: Volatile market
                         1   2   3   4   5   6   7   share

8. Sufficient
   information for
   marketing
   decisions   :___:___:___:___:___:___:___: Insufficient
                         1   2   3   4   5   6   7   information for
                                                          marketing
                                                          decisions

9. Sales forecasts
   are likely to
   be accurate   :___:___:___:___:___:___:___: Sales forecasts
                         1   2   3   4   5   6   7   are likely to
                                                          be inaccurate

*Scale items used in specific studies are listed here with an indication of the directions used with the scale. Some researchers reversed the polarity of items.

Celly and Frazier (1996): 1, 2, 4, 8, 9; 5-point
"For each pair of items below, please circle a number to indicate which term better describes the market for this product line."

Ganesan (1994): 1–3, 5, 6; 7-point
Retailer perceptions: "How would you describe the market for the product you buy from this vendor compared with other products in general?"

#589 *Environmental Uncertainty*

Ganesan (1994): 3, 5, 7; 7-point
Vendor perceptions: "How would you describe the market for the product you sell to this retailer compared with other products in general?"

John and Weitz (1989): 2–4; 5-point
"Describe the market for the products sold by the salesforce:"

Kumar, Scheer, and Steenkamp (1995): 1–4; 7-point
"How would you describe the market environment in your sales area for the supplier's products?"

SCALE NAME: Ethical Climate

SCALE DESCRIPTION: Schwepker, Ferrell, and Ingram (1997) used this five-item, five-point Likert-type scale to measure a salesperson's perception of the presence and enforcement of ethical codes, corporate ethical policies, and top management actions related to ethics.

SCALE ORIGIN: Schwepker, Ferrell, and Ingram (1997) indicated that the measure was based on work by Qualls and Puto (1989), who adapted their seven-item Likert-type scale from measures previously used by Ferrell and Skinner (1988) and Hunt, Chonko, and Wilcox (1984).

SAMPLES: A cross-sectional sample of southern business-to-business salespeople drawn from 33 of the 96 member firms of Sales and Marketing Executives International were sent a mail survey by Schwepker, Ferrell, and Ingram (1997). Of the 314 questionnaires distributed, a total of **152** usable responses were obtained from salespeople who represented 26 firms. The majority of respondents were men (70.4%), married (75.7%), and college educated (69.7%). Most sold products (55.9%), and the remainder sold services (35.5%) or both products and services (8.6%).

RELIABILITY: An alpha of **.892** was reported for the scale by Schwepker, Ferrell, and Ingram (1997).

VALIDITY: Schwepker, Ferrell, and Ingram (1997) found support for both the convergent and discriminant validity of the measure using intra-/interitem correlations and between-construct item correlations, respectively. Each of the ethical climate items loaded on a single factor during the exploratory factor analysis. Results of a confirmatory factor analysis using LISREL also supported the convergent and discriminant validity of the measure after two ethical climate items from the original seven-item set were eliminated.

ADMINISTRATION: Schwepker, Ferrell, and Ingram (1997) noted that the scale was part of a self-administered mail survey accompanied by a self-addressed, stamped reply envelope. Higher scores on the scale reflected a salesperson's perception of a more ethical climate in his or her organization.

MAJOR FINDINGS: Schwepker, Ferrell, and Ingram (1997) examined the relationship among ethical climate, ethical conflict, and role conflict in the sales force. Perceptions of ethical climate were negatively associated with perceived ethical conflicts; findings indicated that, the more positive the ethical climate was perceived to be, the less likely salespeople were to perceive ethical conflicts with their sales managers and top management.

REFERENCES:

Ferrell O.C. and Steven J. Skinner (1988), "Ethical Behavior and Bureaucratic Structure in Marketing Research Organizations," *JMR*, 25 (February), 103–109.

Hunt, Shelby D., Lawrence B. Chonko, and James B. Wilcox (1984), "Ethical Problems of Marketing Researchers," *JMR*, 21 (August), 309–24.

Qualls, William J. and Christopher P. Puto (1989), "Organizational Climate and Decision Framing: An Integrated Approach to Analyzing Industrial Buying Decisions," *JMR*, 26 (May), 179–92.

Schwepker, Charles H., Jr., O.C. Ferrell, and Thomas N. Ingram (1997), "The Influence of Ethical Climate and Ethical Conflict on Role Stress in the Sales Force," *JAMS*, 25 (2), 99–108.

#590 *Ethical Climate*

SCALE ITEMS:

Strongly   Strongly
disagree   agree
1————2————3————4————5

1. Enforces codes.

2. Has policies.

3. Enforces policies.

4. Unethical behavior not tolerated.

5. Reprimanded for behavior leading to corporate gain.

SCALE NAME: Ethics Position Questionnaire (Idealism)

SCALE DESCRIPTION: Singhapakdi and colleagues (1995) and Ho and colleagues (1997) used this ten-item, nine-point Likert-type scale to measure the degree to which a respondent's personal moral philosophy is rooted in an acceptance of moral absolutes based on an understanding of the inherent propriety of an action.

SCALE ORIGIN: The scale used by Singhapakdi and colleagues (1995) and Ho and colleagues (1997) is part of the EPQ (Ethics Perception Questionnaire) constructed originally by Forsyth (1980). The article by Forsyth (1980) provided information that showed the scale had high internal consistency and reasonable stability over time, as well as convergent, discriminant, and predictive validity.

SAMPLES: Both Ho and colleagues (1997) and Singhapakdi and colleagues (1995) sent a mail questionnaire to a randomly drawn sample of 2000 marketing professionals selected from the American Marketing Association mailing list. Singhapakdi and colleagues (1995) received a total of **442** usable questionnaires from the 1995 that were delivered. Key demographics of Singhapakdi and colleagues' (1995) sample indicated that the majority of respondents were college educated (92.8%), male (51.4%) middle mangers working in various industries. Ho and colleagues (1997) received a total of **415** usable questionnaires from respondents of very similar demographic make-up (55.4% men, 94.2% college educated).

RELIABILITY: Coefficient alphas of **.85** and **.805** were reported by Singhapakdi and colleagues (1995) and Ho and colleagues (1997), respectively.

VALIDITY: Singhapakdi and colleagues (1995) and Ho and colleagues (1997) did not specifically examine the scale's validity.

ADMINISTRATION: Both Singhapakdi and colleagues (1995) and Ho and colleagues (1997) indicated that the measure was included as part of a self-administered mail survey. Singhapakdi and colleagues (1995) cited Forsyth (1980) in alleging that higher scores on the idealism component of the ethics position questionnaire indicated a belief that morally "right" behavior leads to good or positive consequences. However, as used by Singhapakdi and colleagues (1995), higher scores on the measure seem instead to indicate stronger beliefs that certain behaviors are simply morally "right," regardless of the consequences.

MAJOR FINDINGS: Singhapakdi and colleagues (1995) investigated marketing practitioner's perceptions of the importance of ethics and social responsibility in achieving organizational effectiveness and how these perceptions were influenced by corporate ethical values and an individual's personal moral philosophy. An ordinary least squared regression analysis demonstrated that **idealism** positively influenced a respondent's perceptions of the relative importance of ethics and social responsibility in achieving organizational effectiveness. Specifically, **idealism** positively influenced perceptions that ethical practices were (1) important to the long-term survival and profitability of the firm and (2) as important as communication and output quality for achieving corporate success.

Ho and colleagues investigated the relationship between cognitive moral development and the personal moral philosophies of relativism, idealism, and Machiavellianism. No statistically significant relationships were found.

REFERENCES:
Forsyth, Donelson R. (1980), "A Taxonomy of Ethical Ideologies," *Journal of Personality and Social Psychology*, 39 (1), 175–84.

Ho, Foo Nin, Scott J. Vitell, James H. Barnes, and Rene Desborde (1997), "Ethical Correlates of Role Conflict and Ambiguity in Marketing: The Mediating Role of Cognitive Moral Development," *JAMS*, 25 (2), 117–26.

Singhapakdi, Anusorn, Kenneth L. Kraft, Scott J. Vitell, and Kumar C. Rallapalli (1995), "The Perceived Importance of Ethics and Social Responsibility on Organizational Effectiveness: A Survey of Marketers," *JAMS*, 23 (1), 49–56.

SCALE ITEMS:

Instructions. You will find a series of general statements listed below. Each represents a commonly held opinion and there are no right or wrong answers. You will probably disagree with some items and agree with others. We are interested in the extent to which you agree or disagree with such matters of opinion.

Please read each statement carefully. Then indicate the extent to which you agree or disagree by placing in front of the statement the number corresponding to your feelings, where:

1 = Completely disagree
2 = Largely disagree
3 = Moderately disagree
4 = Slightly disagree
5 = Neither agree nor disagree
6 = Slightly agree
7 = Moderately agree
8 = Largely agree
9 = Completely agree

1. A person should make certain that their actions never intentionally harm another even to a small degree.

2. Risks to another should never be tolerated, irrespective of how small the risks might be.

3. The existence of potential harm to others is always wrong, irrespective of the benefits to be gained.

4. One should never psychologically or physically harm another person.

5. One should not perform an action which might in any way threaten the dignity and welfare of another individual.

6. If an action could harm an innocent other, then it should not be done.

7. Deciding whether or not to perform an act by balancing the positive consequences of the act against the negative consequences of the act is immoral.

8. The dignity and welfare of people should be the most important concern of any society.

9. It is never necessary to sacrifice the welfare of others.

10. Moral actions are those which closely match ideals of the most "perfect" action.

SCALE NAME: Ethics Position Questionnaire (Relativism)

SCALE DESCRIPTION: Singhapakdi and colleagues (1995) and Ho and colleagues (1997) used this ten-item, nine-point Likert-type scale to measure the degree to which a respondent's personal moral philosophy is based on the context of time, culture, and place rather than some set of universal moral rules.

SCALE ORIGIN: The scale used by Singhapakdi and colleagues (1995) and Ho and colleagues (1997) is part of the EPQ (Ethics Perception Questionnaire) constructed originally by Forsyth (1980). The article by Forsyth (1980) provided information that showed the scale had high internal consistency and reasonable stability over time, as well as convergent, discriminant, and predictive validity.

SAMPLES: Both Ho and colleagues (1997) and Singhapakdi and colleagues (1995) sent a mail questionnaire to a randomly drawn sample of 2000 marketing professionals selected from the American Marketing Association mailing list. Singhapakdi and colleagues (1995) received a total of **442** usable questionnaires from the 1995 that were delivered. Key demographics of Singhapakdi and colleagues' (1995) sample indicated that the majority of respondents were college educated (92.8%), male (51.4%) middle mangers working in various industries. Ho and colleagues (1997) received a total of **415** usable questionnaires from respondents of very similar demographic make-up (55.4% men, 94.2% college educated).

RELIABILITY: Coefficient alphas of **.79** and **.789** were reported by Singhapakdi and colleagues (1995) and Ho and colleagues (1997), respectively.

VALIDITY: Singhapakdi and colleagues (1995) and Ho and colleagues (1997) did not specifically examine the scale's validity.

ADMINISTRATION: Both Singhapakdi and colleagues (1995) and Ho and colleagues (1997) indicated that the measure was included as part of a self-administered mail survey. Higher scores on the measure suggested that respondents viewed ethics from a relativistic point of view and thought that "proper" ethics depends on the person and situation.

MAJOR FINDINGS: Singhapakdi and colleagues (1995) investigated marketing practitioners' perceptions of the importance of ethics and social responsibility in achieving organizational effectiveness and how these perceptions were influenced by corporate ethical values and an individual's personal moral philosophy. An ordinary least squared regression analysis demonstrated that **relativism** *negatively* influenced a respondent's perceptions of the relative importance of ethics and social responsibility in achieving organizational effectiveness. Specifically, **relativism** *negatively* influenced perceptions that ethical practices were (1) important to the long-term survival and profitability of the firm; (2) more important than stockholder happiness, achieving operating efficiencies, or making profits by any means possible; and (3) as important as communication and output quality for achieving corporate success.

Ho and colleagues investigated the relationship between cognitive moral development and the personal moral philosophies of relativism, idealism, and Machiavellianism. No statistically significant relationships were found.

REFERENCES:

Forsyth, Donelson R. (1980), "A Taxonomy of Ethical Ideologies," *Journal of Personality and Social Psychology*, 39 (1), 175–84.

Ho, Foo Nin, Scott J. Vitell, James H. Barnes, and Rene Desborde (1997), "Ethical Correlates of Role Conflict and Ambiguity in Marketing: The Mediating Role of Cognitive Moral Development," *JAMS*, 25 (2), 117–26.

Singhapakdi, Anusorn, Kenneth L. Kraft, Scott J. Vitell, and Kumar C. Rallapalli (1995), "The Perceived Importance of Ethics and Social Responsibility on Organizational Effectiveness: A Survey of Marketers," *JAMS*, 23 (1), 49–56.

SCALE ITEMS:

Instructions. You will find a series of general statements listed below. Each represents a commonly held opinion and there are no right or wrong answers. You will probably disagree with some items and agree with others. We are interested in the extent to which you agree or disagree with such matters of opinion.

Please read each statement carefully. Then indicate the extent to which you agree or disagree by placing in front of the statement the number corresponding to your feelings, where:

1 = Completely disagree
2 = Largely disagree
3 = Moderately disagree
4 = Slightly disagree
5 = Neither agree nor disagree
6 = Slightly agree
7 = Moderately agree
8 = Largely agree
9 = Completely agree

1. There are no ethical principles that are so important that they should be part of any code of ethics.

2. What is ethical varies from one situation and society to another.

3. Moral standards should be seen as being individualistic; what one person considers to be moral may be judged to be immoral by another person.

4. Different types of moralities cannot be compared as to "rightness."

5. Questions of what is ethical for everyone can never be resolved since what is moral or immoral is up to the individual.

6. Moral standards are simply *personal* rules which indicate how a person should behave, and are not to be applied in making judgments of others.

7. Ethical considerations in interpersonal relations are so complex that individuals should be allowed to formulate their own individual codes.

8. Rigidly codifying an ethical position that prevents certain types of actions could stand in the way of better human relations and adjustment.

9. No rule concerning lying can be formulated; whether a lie is permissible or not permissible totally depends upon the situation.

10. Whether a lie is judged to be moral or immoral depends upon the circumstances surrounding the action.

SCALE NAME: Evaluation (Behavior-Based)

SCALE DESCRIPTION: Hartline and Ferrell (1996) used this four-item, five-point scale to measure the extent to which managers emphasized behavioral criteria in evaluating employees.

SCALE ORIGIN: Hartline and Ferrell (1996) indicated that the items representing this construct were taken from Bush and colleagues' (1990) five-item behavior-based performance scale. One item, "A track record of courteous service to customers," was dropped from the measure following a confirmatory factor analysis because of nonsignificant t-values.

SAMPLES: The hotel industry was chosen as the sampling frame for this study. Hartline and Ferrell (1996) sampled the general managers, employees, and customers of 444 hotel units that represented three hotel chains. Of these, 236 different hotel units returned at least one usable questionnaire from a manager, an employee, and a customer. A total of 1769 usable questionnaires were received from **236** hotel managers, **561** customer-contact employees, and **1351** customers.

RELIABILITY: Hartline and Ferrell (1996) reported a coefficient alpha of **.74** for this measure.

VALIDITY: Hartline and Ferrell (1996) used confirmatory factor analysis to test the unidimensionality of the measures using separate analyses for managers, employees, and customers. Items with nonsignificant t-values were dropped from the measures. In investigating the discriminant validity of the scales, the authors first averaged the employee and customer responses on the scale and then matched that response with the manager responses to create a single data set in which cases represented hotel units rather than individuals. Hotel units that did not provide at least three responses from both employees and customers were dropped, leaving a final sample of 97 matched responses. Confirmatory factor analysis was then used to assess the discriminant validity of the measures.

ADMINISTRATION: Each hotel manager received a survey packet containing instructions, postage-paid reply envelopes, one manager survey, five employee surveys, and forty guest surveys, which were to be self-administered. This measure was included in the manager survey. Hartline and Ferrell (1996) instructed managers to distribute employee surveys to individuals in customer-contact positions and the guest surveys during check-out. Survey packets were preceded by a letter from the corporate marketing manager endorsing the project and followed by a second wave of materials approximately two months after the first had been distributed. Higher scores on the scale indicated that managers emphasized behavioral criteria when conducting employee evaluations.

MAJOR FINDINGS: Hartline and Ferrell (1996) investigated the management of customer-contact service employees and various factors related to service quality using data generated from the customers, contact employees, and managers of hotel units. Hypotheses were tested in the context of structural equation modeling. **Behaviorally based evaluations** were found to increase employee adaptability and decrease employee role conflict. Job satisfaction was also positively, though indirectly, affected by **behavior-based evaluations**, whereas both employee self-efficacy and role ambiguity were indirectly, but negatively, influenced. Increased commitment to service quality on the part of management was also was found to increase a manager's use of **behavior-based evaluations**.

REFERENCES:
Bush, Robert P., Alan J. Busy, David J. Ortinau, and Joseph F. Hair Jr. (1990), "Developing a Behavior-Based Scale to Assess Retail Salesperson Performance," *JR*, 66 (Spring), 119–36.

#593 *Evaluation (Behavior-Based)*

Hartline, Michael D. and O.C. Ferrell (1996), "The Management of Customer-Contact Service Employees: An Empirical Investigation," *JM*, 60 (October), 52–70.

SCALE ITEMS:

Not at all   Extremely
important   important

1———————2———————3———————4———————5

How important is each of the following factors when you evaluate the performance of customer-contact employees?

1. The ability to resolve customer complaints or service problems in an efficient manner.

2. The ability to innovatively deal with unique situations and/or meet customer needs.

3. The employee's commitment to the organization.

4. The employee's commitment to customers.

SCALE NAME: Exit Intentions

SCALE DESCRIPTION: Ping (1994) used this six-item, five-point Likert-type scale to assess a retailer's propensity to terminate the relationship with a primary supplier.

SCALE ORIGIN: Ping (1994) noted that the scale was first published in one of his previous articles. In developing the scale, Ping (1993) generated items on the basis of presurvey interviews with hardware retailers and a review of the relevant literature. The purification process began with nine academicians evaluating how well the items fit the construct; those misclassified by more than one judge were eliminated. The resulting measure was pretested in two different phases. The first pretest sought to clarify possible misinterpretations. Responses from 63 hardware retailers in the second pretest were used in analyzing the psychometric properties of the measures using item-to-total correlations, ordered similarity coefficients, and coefficient alpha computations. The final purification of the measure was based on LISREL analysis of data provided by 288 respondents as reported by Ping (1993). Items were deleted if the internal consistency was improved without detracting from the content validity of the measure. Tests of the discriminant and convergent validity of the measure were also undertaken, and the results were found to be satisfactory.

SAMPLES: Ping (1994) used a systematic random sampling procedure of U.S. hardware retailers to generate the 600 hardware retailers sampled, and **288** usable responses were received. The sampling frame was taken from a hardware retailing trade publication's subscription list.

RELIABILITY: Ping (1994) did not report the specific reliability of the measure, though he noted that all measures in this study demonstrated latent variable reliabilities of .90 or higher. In the 1993 study, Ping reported a coefficient alpha of **.95** for this measure.

VALIDITY: Ping (1994) conducted a confirmatory factor analysis to test the unidimensionality and construct validity of the measure. The measure was judged to be unidimensional, and the average variance extracted demonstrated the scale's convergent and discriminatory validity.

ADMINISTRATION: The scale was included by Ping (1994) with other measures as part of a self-administered questionnaire that was delivered by mail. Nonrespondents received two postcard reminders. Higher scores on the scale reflected a greater intention on the part of the retailer to discontinue its relationship with the wholesaler/supplier.

MAJOR FINDINGS: In this study, Ping (1994) investigated the moderating role of satisfaction with respect to alternative supplier attractiveness and exit intentions. Using a structural equation analysis technique, Ping (1994) found that the attractiveness of alternative suppliers was positively associated with **exit intentions** for channel customers with lower levels of satisfaction. Higher levels of satisfaction negated this relationship, however, because no significant association between alternative supplier attractiveness and **exit intentions** were found.

REFERENCES:
Ping, Robert A., Jr. (1993), "The Effects of Satisfaction and Structural Constraints on Retailer Exiting, Voice, Loyalty, Opportunism, and Neglect," *JR*, 69 (Fall), 320–52.
——— (1994), "Does Satisfaction Moderate the Association Between Alternative Attractiveness and Exit Intention in a Marketing Channel?" *JAMS*, 22 (4), 364–71.

#594 *Exit Intentions*

SCALE ITEMS:

Strongly   Strongly
disagree   agree
   1————————2————————3————————4————————5

1. Occasionally, I will think about ending the business relationship with my primary wholesaler.

2. I am <u>not</u> likely to continue the business relationship with my primary wholesaler.

3. I will probably consider a replacement primary wholesaler in the near future.

4. I am looking at replacement wholesalers.

5. I will consider a replacement wholesaler soon.

6. I will probably stop doing business with my primary wholesaler in the near future.

SCALE NAME: Experience (Commissioning Consulting)

SCALE DESCRIPTION: Patterson, Johnson, and Spreng (1997) used this three-item, seven-point Likert-type scale to measure the extent to which individuals in an organization lacked experience in the purchase of similar consulting services.

SCALE ORIGIN: Patterson, Johnson, and Spreng (1997) stated that the scale was adapted from McQuiston (1989).

SAMPLES: Patterson, Johnson, and Spreng (1997) chose to survey management consulting firms' private- and public-sector client organizations. Of the 207 client organizations approached by telephone, 186 agreed to participate. Then, 142 key informants—typically senior executives or managers who were likely heavily involved in the consultant selection process—completed the Stage 1 prepurchase questionnaire. Of this group, 128 returned the second postpurchase questionnaire, which yielded a final sample size of **128** for the pre- and postpurchase measures.

RELIABILITY: Patterson, Johnson, and Spreng (1997) reported a confirmatory factor analysis construct reliability of **.88** for this measure.

VALIDITY: Patterson, Johnson, and Spreng (1997) assessed the convergent and discriminant validity of the measure by means of a confirmatory factor analysis conducted using LISREL 8. The large construct reliabilities, large and significant measurement factor loadings, and the average variance extracted provided evidence of convergent validity. Evidence of discriminant validity was also demonstrated by means of average extracted variances, which exceed the squared correlation between that construct and any other.

ADMINISTRATION: Data were collected in two stages over a twelve-month span of time. The Stage 1 questionnaire containing the novelty measure was delivered, along with a cover letter, to key informants who had indicated a willingness to participate in the study. This survey also asked respondents to indicate the expected completion date for the project. A second questionnaire assessing other variables was delivered between one and two months after the expected completion date of the project. Both questionnaires were self-administered. If responses were not received within three weeks, a follow-up telephone call was made to nonrespondents. Higher scores on the scale indicated a greater lack of purchasing experience with similar consulting assignments.

MAJOR FINDINGS: Patterson, Johnson, and Spreng (1997) examined the determinants of customers' satisfaction and dissatisfaction in the context of business consulting services. The study findings provided ample support for the application of the disconfirmation paradigm to industrial buying situations. The newness of the purchase occasion (lack of experience) was found to have a positive effect on expectations and a negative effect on performance.

REFERENCES:
McQuiston, Daniel H. (1989), "Novelty, Complexity, and Importance as Casual Determinants of Industrial Buyer Behavior," *JM*, 53 (April), 66–79.
Patterson, Paul G., Lester W. Johnson, and Richard A. Spreng (1997), "Modeling the Determinants of Customer Satisfaction for Business-to-Business Professional Services," *JAMS*, 25 (1), 4–17.

#595 *Experience (Commissioning Consulting)*

SCALE ITEMS:

Strongly   Strongly
disagree   agree
   1———————2———————3———————4———————5———————6———————7

1. Prior to this particular consulting assignment, I was experienced in commissioning this type of work. **(r)**

2. I did not have much knowledge about this type of consulting assignment prior to commissioning this one.

3. I am seldom involved in commissioning this type of consulting assignment.

SCALE NAME: Experience (Distributor)

SCALE DESCRIPTION: Celly and Frazier (1996) used this three-item, five-point scale to measure a distributor's familiarity, knowledge, and experience in marketing the focal supplier's product relative to the distributor's familiarity, knowledge, and experience in marketing other suppliers' products.

SCALE ORIGIN: There is no indication to suggest that the scale is anything other than original to Celly and Frazier (1996).

SAMPLES: Celly and Frazier (1996) effectively sampled 953 distributors who were randomly selected from Dun's Marketing Services' Direct Access service and who had passed a variety of screening processes. The selected distributors serviced one of four industries: machine tools and metalworking machinery, air compressors and packaging equipment, industrial tools, or abrasives and adhesives. **Two hundred seven** usable responses were obtained.

RELIABILITY: Celly and Frazier (1996) reported a coefficient alpha of **.86** for the scale.

VALIDITY: The discriminant validity of all of the measures used in Celly and Frazier's (1996) study were found to be satisfactory based on the results of a principal components factors analysis with orthogonal rotation.

ADMINISTRATION: Celly and Frazier (1996) included the scale with other measures as part of a self-administered survey that was delivered by mail. Prenotification and reminders, incentives, and a second survey mailing to nonrespondents were used to enhance response rates. Higher scores on the scale indicated that distributors rated their experience, knowledge, and familiarity in marketing the focal supplier's product as higher relative to their marketing experience with other suppliers' products.

MAJOR FINDINGS: Celly and Frazier (1996) investigated suppliers' use of outcome- and behavior-based coordinator efforts with their distributors. Chow tests comparing information provided by exclusive dealers with that provided by nonexclusive dealers confirmed the appropriateness of analyzing the data jointly. **Distributor experience** with the supplier's product was positively related to the use of outcome-based coordination efforts.

REFERENCES:
Celly, Kirti Sawhney and Gary L. Frazier (1996), "Outcome-Based and Behavior-Based Coordination Efforts in Channel Relationships," *JMR*, 33 (May), 200–210.

SCALE ITEMS:

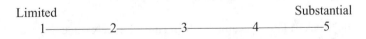

Limited   Substantial

1———————2———————3———————4———————5

Relative to our other suppliers, our

1. *Familiarity* with customers for this line is...

2. *Knowledge* of customer requirements for this supplier's line is...

3. *Overall experience* with the markets for this supplier's line is...

SCALE NAME: Experience (with New Product)

SCALE DESCRIPTION: Olson, Walker, and Ruekert (1995) used this five-item, seven-point scale to measure product managers' perceptions of the level of experience potential customers had in buying and using a product, as well the level of experience the firm itself had in engineering, manufacturing, and marketing products similar to the one being developed. Olson, Walker, and Ruekert (1995) referred to this scale as "newness of the product concept."

SCALE ORIGIN: Olson, Walker, and Ruekert (1995) stated that the scale was derived from the taxonomy of new product types proposed by Booz, Allen, and Hamilton, Inc. (1982). This taxonomy classifies new products according to whether they are new to the developing firm and new to the marketplace that uses or consumes them. The four categories of newness resulting from this classification include new-to-the-world products, me-too products, line extensions, and product modifications.

SAMPLES: Of the 24 firms solicited by Olson, Walker, and Ruekert (1995) to participate in the study, 15 divisions from 12 firms provided complete information on **45** new product development projects undertaken within a three-year time period. All firms produced tangible products and ranged in age from 12 to more than 100 years, with annual revenues between $50 million and more than $1 billion. Projects formed the unit of analysis. Of the new product projects studied, 11 represented new-to-the-world products, 9 were me-too products, 15 were line extensions, and 10 were product modifications. Data were collected first from each project manager and second from individuals identified by project managers as having key functional responsibilities related to marketing, manufacturing, R&D, and design. A total of **112** usable responses were obtained from the functional participants in addition to the information provided by the **45** product managers.

RELIABILITY: Olson, Walker, and Ruekert (1995) reported a coefficient alpha of **.81** for this scale. Scale items were also submitted to a Varimax rotated principle components factor analysis and were found to load on a single factor with an eigenvalue greater than 1.

VALIDITY: No specific examination of scale validity for this measure was reported by Olson, Walker, and Ruekert (1995).

ADMINISTRATION: Olson, Walker, and Ruekert (1995) indicated that information about each project was initially obtained from project managers through a telephone interview using a structured questionnaire. After project managers had identified the key functional personnel for their project in marketing, manufacturing, R&D, and design, self-administered mail surveys were sent to each of the functional participants of each project. Higher scores on the scale indicated greater levels of experience in buying or using the product on the part of the market and greater levels of experience on the part of the firm with engineering, manufacturing, and marketing products similar to the one being developed.

MAJOR FINDINGS: Olson, Walker, and Ruekert (1995) examined the relationship between new product coordinating structures and outcomes using a resource dependency view of the new product development process. The less **experience** members of the functional team had with a new product concept, the greater were the difficulties encountered during the development process. The more **experience** functional participants had with a new product concept, the more mechanistic and hierarchical was the structural mechanism used by the firm to coordinate interactions during the development process. When the coordination mechanism fit well with functional participants' **experience** with the concept being developed, products achieved break-even status in a shorter time and were completed within or faster than their anticipated time frame more often than did products associated with projects whose coordination structure was viewed as either too mechanistic or too organic. Higher levels of personal satisfaction among functional participants were also present on projects with good fits between **experience** and coordination mechanism, and the products themselves were judged by management as offering a more satisfactory design, being of significantly higher quality relative to other firm offerings, and being more likely to achieve management's sales objectives compared with products associated with projects whose coordination structure was viewed as either too mechanistic or too organic.

REFERENCES:

Booz, Allen & Hamilton, Inc. (1982), *New Product Management for the 1980's.* New York: Booz, Allen & Hamilton, Inc.

Olson, Eric M., Orville C. Walker Jr., and Robert W. Ruekert (1995), "Organizing for Effective New Product Development: The Moderating Role of Product Innovativeness," *JM*, 59 (January), 48–62.

SCALE ITEMS:

None   Extensive

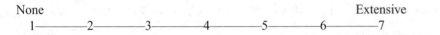

1————2————3————4————5————6————7

Prior to the development of this product, how much experience did your firm (division or business unit) have in:

1. Selling/promoting this type of product?

2. Manufacturing this type of product?

3. Engineering and designing this type of product?

4. At the time this product was initially offered for sale, how extensive was the marketplace's knowledge of the product (e.g., through advertising, sales contacts, news articles, word-of-mouth, or direct contact with similar products)?

1 = 0%
2 = 1–10%
3 = 11–30%
4 = 31–50%
5 = 51–70%
6 = 71–90%
7 = 91–100

5. At the time this product was introduced to the marketplace, what percentage of the target market had previously purchased either an earlier version of this product, or a competitor's offering?

SCALE NAME: Expertise (Salesperson)

SCALE DESCRIPTION: Doney and Cannon (1997) used this three-item, seven-point Likert-type scale to measure the degree to which a buyer perceives a salesperson as having expert knowledgeable of the product line.

SCALE ORIGIN: Doney and Cannon (1997) stated that they generated items for the scale on the basis of interviews with marketing and purchasing personnel. Exploratory factor analyses using both orthogonal and oblique rotations were used to ensure high item loadings on hypothesized constructs and low cross-loadings.

SAMPLES: Doney and Cannon (1997) sampled 657 members of the National Association of Purchasing Management who were employed by firms involved in industrial manufacturing, as classified by standard industrial classification codes 33–37. **Two hundred ten** completed questionnaires were returned from a primarily male (76%) sample with an average of 15 years of purchasing experience.

RELIABILITY: Doney and Cannon (1997) calculated a coefficient alpha of **.79** for this measure.

VALIDITY: Doney and Cannon (1997) reported using three methods to test the discriminant validity of the scales that represented the combined dimensions of trust of the salesperson and its proposed antecedents and outcomes. Each method provided strong evidence of discriminant validity. Two LISREL-based tests were also used to provide evidence for the convergent validity of the measures.

ADMINISTRATION: The scale was included with other measures as part of a self-administered survey that was delivered by mail. Nonrespondents received a postcard reminder followed by a second questionnaire a week later. Doney and Cannon (1997) instructed respondents to focus on a single, specific, recent purchase decision in which more than one supplier was seriously considered and to indicate on the survey (using initials) two of the firms considered. After answering questions pertaining to the purchase situation, half of the respondents were instructed to complete the remainder of the questionnaire in the context of the first supplier they had listed, whereas the other half was instructed to use the second supplier. Higher scores on the scale indicated that the buyer perceived the focal salesperson as having higher levels of expertise.

MAJOR FINDINGS: Doney and Cannon (1997) investigated the impact of purchasing agents' trust in the salesperson and trust in the supplier firm on a buying firm's current supplier choice and future buying intentions. The extent to which a salesperson was perceived as having **expertise** was not significantly related to the buyer's level of trust in the salesperson.

REFERENCES:
Doney, Patricia M. and Joseph P. Cannon (1997), "An Examination of the Nature of Trust in Buyer-Seller Relationships," *JM*, 61 (April), 35–51.

SCALE ITEMS:

Strongly
disagree
1———2———3———4———5———6———7
Strongly
agree

1. This salesperson is very knowledgeable.

2. This salesperson knows his/her product line very well.

3. This salesperson is not expert. **(r)**

SCALE NAME: Export Channel Performance (Economic)

SCALE DESCRIPTION: Bello and Gilliland (1997) used this four-item, seven-point scale to measure the extent to which an export distributor was effective in achieving economic, sales, profit, and growth goals for the foreign market.

SCALE ORIGIN: Bello and Gilliland (1997) stated that the scale items were adapted from Bello and Williamson's (1985) study.

SAMPLES: Bello and Gilliland's (1997) systematic random sample of 245 national manufacturers verified as exporting through foreign distributors was drawn from the 1994 edition of the *Journal of Commerce United States Importer & Exporter Directory*. **One hundred sixty** usable responses were obtained from export managers employed by firms that exported a variety of industrial and consumer products to a total of 39 different countries.

RELIABILITY: A confirmatory factor analysis composite reliability of **.93** was reported by Bello and Gilliland (1997).

VALIDITY: Confirmatory factor analysis was used by Bello and Gilliland (1997) to provide evidence of discriminant and convergent validity, as well as to assess the unidimensionality of the measure. Convergent validity was deemed to be present because items loaded significantly on their posited indicators and because of the low to moderate correlations between the scale and other measures. Discriminant validity was also deemed to be present because the correlation estimate between two indicators never included 1.0 (+/– two standard errors). The authors used personal interviews with export executives as part of the pretest process to verify the face validity of the measure.

ADMINISTRATION: Bello and Gilliland (1997) indicated that this scale was self-administered as part of a longer survey instrument mailed to respondents. The export manager with primary responsibility for the firm's relationship with the foreign distributor received a survey; nonrespondents were telephoned three weeks later, and a second questionnaire followed. Instructions specified that questions were to be answered in the context of the focal distributor. The authors defined the focal distributor as the firm's fourth-largest foreign distributor in terms of unit sales volume to avoid a positive evaluation bias. The mean score on this measure was combined with the mean scores on the strategy and economic channel performance scales to form a measure of export channel performance. Higher scores on the scale indicated that a distributor was effective in achieving economic, sales, growth, and profit goals.

MAJOR FINDINGS: Bello and Gilliland (1997) examined the effect of output controls, process controls, and flexibility on channel performance. **The economic aspect of export channel performance** was one of three factors used to assess the overall level of export channel performance. The use of output controls and flexible adjustment procedures were positively related to distributor performance, which indicates that efforts by manufacturers to monitor distributor's sales volume and other outcomes resulted in higher performance on the part of that distributor and that flexibility enhances the coordination necessary for improved channel member performance. Contrary to expectations, the use of process controls in an export situation failed to influence distributor performance.

REFERENCES:

Bello, Daniel C. and David I. Gilliland (1997), "The Effect of Output Controls, Process Controls, and Flexibility on Export Channel Performance," *JM*, 61 (January), 22–38.

——— and Nicholas C. Williamson (1985), "The American Export Trading Company: Designing a New International Marketing Institution," *JM*, 49 (Fall), 60–69.

SCALE ITEMS:*

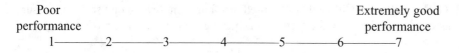

    Poor   Extremely good
performance   performance
    1————2————3————4————5————6————7

1. Economic goals for foreign market.

2. Sales goals for foreign market.

3. Growth goals for foreign market.

4. Profit goals for foreign market.

*Although the verbatim instructions were not listed in the article, Bello and Gilliland (1997) noted that when responding to the statements listed here, respondents were asked to indicate how effectively various aspects of the channel's economic goals were accomplished by the focal distributor.

SCALE NAME: Export Channel Performance (Selling)

SCALE DESCRIPTION: Bello and Gilliland (1997) used this three-item, seven-point scale to measure the extent to which an export distributor was effective in performing selling-related activities in the foreign market.

SCALE ORIGIN: Bello and Gilliland (1997) stated that the scale items were adapted from Bello and Williamson's (1985) study.

SAMPLES: Bello and Gilliland's (1997) systematic random sample of 245 national manufacturers verified as exporting through foreign distributors was drawn from the 1994 edition of the *Journal of Commerce United States Importer & Exporter Directory*. **One hundred sixty** usable responses were obtained from export managers employed by firms that exported a variety of industrial and consumer products to a total of 39 different countries.

RELIABILITY: A confirmatory factor analysis composite reliability of **.86** was reported by Bello and Gilliland (1997).

VALIDITY: Confirmatory factor analysis was used by Bello and Gilliland (1997) to provide evidence of discriminant and convergent validity, as well as to assess the unidimensionality of the measure. Convergent validity was deemed to be present because items loaded significantly on their posited indicators and because of the low to moderate correlations between the scale and other measures. Discriminant validity was also deemed to be present because the correlation estimate between two indicators never included 1.0 (+/– two standard errors). The authors used personal interviews with export executives as part of the pretest process to verify the face validity of the measure.

ADMINISTRATION: Bello and Gilliland (1997) indicated that this scale was self-administered as part of a longer survey instrument mailed to respondents. The export manager with primary responsibility for the firm's relationship with the foreign distributor received a survey; nonrespondents were telephoned three weeks later, and a second questionnaire followed. Instructions specified that questions were to be answered in the context of the focal distributor. The authors defined the focal distributor as the firm's fourth-largest foreign distributor in terms of unit sales volumeto avoid a positive evaluation bias. The mean score on this measure was combined with the mean scores on the strategy and economic channel performance scales to form a measure of export channel performance. Higher scores on the scale indicated that a distributor performed well on selling activities related to customer contact and after-sale servicing of customers.

MAJOR FINDINGS: Bello and Gilliland (1997) examined the effect of output controls, process controls, and flexibility on channel performance. **The selling aspect of export channel performance** was one of three factors used to assess the overall level of export channel performance. The use of output controls and flexible adjustment procedures was positively related to distributor performance, which indicates that efforts by manufacturers to monitor distributor's sales volume and other outcomes resulted in higher performance on the part of that distributor and that flexibility enhanced the coordination necessary for improved channel member performance. Contrary to expectations, the use of process controls in an export situation failed to influence distributor performance.

REFERENCES:
Bello, Daniel C. and David I. Gilliland (1997), "The Effect of Output Controls, Process Controls, and Flexibility on Export Channel Performance," *JM*, 61 (January), 22–38.
———— and Nicholas C. Williamson (1985), "The American Export Trading Company: Designing a New International Marketing Institution," *JM*, 49 (Fall), 60–69.

#600 *Export Channel Performance (Selling)*

SCALE ITEMS:*

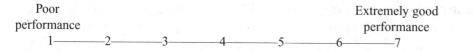

Poor
performance

Extremely good
performance

1————2————3————4————5————6————7

1. Maintaining contact with customers.

2. Calling on customers in person.

3. After-sale servicing of customers.

*Although the verbatim instructions were not listed in the article, Bello and Gilliland (1997) noted that when responding to the statements listed here, respondents were asked to indicate how effectively the export channel's selling tasks were performed by the focal distributor.

SCALE NAME: Export Channel Performance (Strategic)

SCALE DESCRIPTION: Bello and Gilliland (1997) used this four-item, seven-point scale to measure the extent to which an export distributor was effective in planning for the marketing, promotion, distribution, and pricing of goods for the foreign market.

SCALE ORIGIN: Bello and Gilliland (1997) stated that the scale items were adapted from Bello and Williamson's (1985) study.

SAMPLES: Bello and Gilliland's (1997) systematic random sample of 245 national manufacturers verified as exporting through foreign distributors was drawn from the 1994 edition of the *Journal of Commerce United States Importer & Exporter Directory*. **One hundred sixty** usable responses were obtained from export managers employed by firms that exported a variety of industrial and consumer products to a total of 39 different countries.

RELIABILITY: A confirmatory factor analysis composite reliability of **.90** was reported by Bello and Gilliland (1997).

VALIDITY: Confirmatory factor analysis was used by Bello and Gilliland (1997) to provide evidence of discriminant and convergent validity, as well as to assess the unidimensionality of the measure. Convergent validity was deemed to be present because items loaded significantly on their posited indicators and because of the low to moderate correlations between the scale and other measures. Discriminant validity was also deemed to be present because the correlation estimate between two indicators never included 1.0 (+/– two standard errors). The authors used personal interviews with export executives as part of the pretest process to verify the face validity of the measure.

ADMINISTRATION: Bello and Gilliland (1997) indicated that this scale was self-administered as part of a longer survey instrument mailed to respondents. The export manager with primary responsibility for the firm's relationship with the foreign distributor received a survey; nonrespondents were telephoned three weeks later, and a second questionnaire followed. Instructions specified that questions were to be answered in the context of the focal distributor. The authors defined the focal distributor as the firm's fourth-largest foreign distributor in terms of unit sales volumeto avoid a positive evaluation bias. The mean score on this measure was combined with the mean scores on the selling and economic channel performance scales to form a measure of export channel performance. Higher scores on the scale indicated that marketing, promotional, distribution, and pricing strategies for the foreign market were more effective.

MAJOR FINDINGS: Bello and Gilliland (1997) examined the effect of output controls, process controls, and flexibility on channel performance. The **strategic planning aspect of export channel** performance was one of three factors used to assess the overall level of export channel performance. The use of output controls and flexible adjustment procedures was positively related to distributor performance, which indicates that efforts by manufacturers to monitor the distributor's sales volume and other outcomes resulted in higher performance on the part of that distributor and that flexibility enhanced the coordination necessary for improved channel member performance. Contrary to expectations, the use of process controls in an export situation failed to influence distributor performance.

REFERENCES:

Bello, Daniel C. and David I. Gilliland (1997), "The Effect of Output Controls, Process Controls, and Flexibility on Export Channel Performance," *JM*, 61 (January), 22–38.

——— and Nicholas C. Williamson (1985), "The American Export Trading Company: Designing a New International Marketing Institution," *JM*, 49 (Fall), 60–69.

#601 *Export Channel Performance (Strategic)*

SCALE ITEMS:*

<table>
<tr><td>Poor
performance</td><td></td><td></td><td></td><td></td><td>Extremely good
performance</td></tr>
</table>

1————2————3————4————5————6————7

1. Marketing strategy for foreign market.

2. Distribution strategy for foreign market.

3. Promotion strategy for foreign market.

4. Pricing strategy for foreign market.

*Although the verbatim instructions were not listed in the article, Bello and Gilliland (1997) noted that when responding to the statements listed here, respondents were asked to indicate how effectively the export channel's operational tasks were performed by the focal distributor.

SCALE NAME: Extent of Supervision

SCALE DESCRIPTION: Oliver and Anderson (1994) used this eight-item, seven-point Likert-type scale to measure the extent to which supervisors of sales representative provided supervision, interaction, and day-to-day contact to members of the sales force.

SCALE ORIGIN: The scale is original to Oliver and Anderson (1994), who pretested the measure in a questionnaire administered to a convenience sample of sales representatives attending trade association functions. The measure was revised on the basis of the pretest and submitted to a factor analysis following administration to the final sample. The authors indicated that some items were dropped, which resulted in the purified measure shown here. The criteria for item exclusion were not indicated, though the authors noted that none of the cross-loadings among the six behavior control/outcome control measures exceeded .355.

SAMPLES: Oliver and Anderson (1994) surveyed managers and manufacturer's sales representatives employed by independently owned and operated sales agencies serving the electronics industry. Of the 350 randomly selected trade association member firms fitting this designation, 299 expressed interest in participating and, ultimately, **194** usable surveys from management and **347** surveys from manufacturer representatives were returned. The typical respondent was male (92%), a college graduate (64%), approximately 39 years of age, and had an average of 12 years sales experience with 5.5 years in the present job.

RELIABILITY: Oliver and Anderson (1994) reported a coefficient alpha of **.856** for this measure.

VALIDITY: Oliver and Anderson (1994) used the correlation matrix of the independent and classification variables in the study to provide some evidence of discriminant and convergent validity. Nomological validity was also found to be present.

ADMINISTRATION: Oliver and Anderson (1994) sent managers of the 299 firms that indicated interest in the study a packet containing a "manager's survey" and three similar self-administered surveys for salespeople, along with self-addressed, postage-paid reply envelopes. Managers were instructed to distribute one survey each to an "above-average rep," a "mid-range rep," and a "below-average rep." Each representative was promised confidentiality and the chance to win one of five $100 prizes in a random drawing. The extent of supervision was one of six scales whose scores were combined as formative indicators of the control system employed, ranging from outcome oriented to behaviorally oriented. It appears that only responses obtained from sales representatives were used in computing this measure. Higher scores on the scale indicated a greater level of supervision, interaction, and day-to-day contact between management and the sales representative.

MAJOR FINDINGS: Oliver and Anderson (1994) examined how perceptions of the presence of a behavior versus an outcome sales control system in the respondent's organizations influenced salespeople's performance outcomes and sales strategies, as well as their affective, cognitive, and behavioral states. **Extent of supervision** was significantly correlated with a salesperson's sales expertise, extrinsic motivation, motivation to the serve the agency employer, organizational commitment, and acceptance of three factors: authority, cooperation, and performance reviews. Sales presentation skills, the absence of a bottom-line orientation, infrequent use of objective outcomes, the use of subjective inputs in the evaluation process, job satisfaction, participative decision –making, and both supportive and innovative organizational cultures also influenced the extent of supervision, as did the use of pay as a control mechanism.

#602 *Extent of Supervision*

REFERENCES:

Oliver, Richard L. and Erin Anderson (1994), "An Empirical Test of the Consequences of Behavior- and Outcome-Based Sales Control Systems," *JM*, 58 (October), 53–67.

SCALE ITEMS:

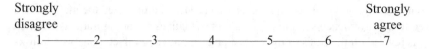

Strongly   Strongly
disagree   agree
1————2————3————4————5————6————7

1. My supervisor makes sure everyone knows what to do and how to do it.

2. My supervisor stays in close contact with me.

3. My boss rarely asks me for information on how I'm doing. **(r)**

4. I don't have much contact with my company's management. **(r)**

5. Management here stays very well informed of salespeople's activities.

6. I feel isolated from management. **(r)**

7. I don't get much day-to-day contact with management. **(r)**

8. We are subject to very little direction from our company's management. **(r)**

SCALE NAME: External Information Source Preference

SCALE DESCRIPTION: Anderson and Robertson (1995) used this five-item, seven-point Likert-type scale to assess the extent to which brokers preferred externally based sources of information to information generated internally.

SCALE ORIGIN: Anderson and Robertson (1995) developed the measure used in this study. A detailed construct description was constructed on the basis of a though review of the trade and academic literature. Multiple interviews with brokers, sales managers, and trade association officials were used to generate scale items thought to tap the construct. These items were administered to 208 brokers and factor analyzed to test for unidimensionality. Reliability assessments were also used to purify the measure.

SAMPLES: Anderson and Robertson (1995) mailed a questionnaire to the homes of 420 brokers whose names were supplied by cooperating firms, and **201** usable responses were obtained. To be evaluated, some hypotheses required the use of archival data regarding the actual sales of house brands made by salespeople. One firm, which provided **150** of the respondents in this study, agreed to provide this information. The authors stated that the respondent demographics closely matched those achieved in a large-scale survey of readers conducted by a nationally distributed trade magazine.

RELIABILITY: Anderson and Robertson (1995) reported a coefficient alpha of **.74** for this measure.

VALIDITY: No specific examination of scale validity was reported Anderson and Robertson (1995).

ADMINISTRATION: Anderson and Robertson (1995) included the measure as part of a larger self-administered mail questionnaire. A summary of the results was offered in exchange for respondent cooperation. Higher scores on the scale indicated that salespeople preferred more externally oriented sources of information.

MAJOR FINDINGS: Anderson and Robertson (1995) investigated the relationship between factors thought to influence the sale of house brands by multiline salespeople. Results of analysis using the full sample indicated that salespeople who are more dependent on the firm rely less on **external sources of information** and that perceptions of mobility hazards and customer loyalty hazards increase with higher preferences for **external information sources**. Also, using the 150-member sample, analysis revealed that salespeople who rely more on **external sources of information** are less likely to adopt house brands.

REFERENCES:
Anderson, Erin and Thomas S. Robertson (1995), "Inducing Multiline Salespeople to Adopt House Brands," *JM*, 59 (April), 16–31.

SCALE ITEMS:

Strongly   Strongly
disagree   agree

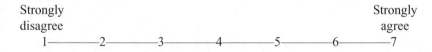

1——————2——————3——————4——————5——————6——————7

1. When it comes to economic and financial affairs, I read widely.

2. I get most of my investment information from sources within my firm. **(r)**

3. I get ideas about investments from many sources.

4. I am very attuned to outside ideas about investments.

5. I got most of investment information from outside my firm.

SCALE NAME: Fairness (Distributive)

SCALE DESCRIPTION: Kumar, Scheer, and Steenkamp (1995) used this five-item, seven-point scale to measure the extent to which a dealer evaluated the fairness of the outcomes and earnings received from carrying a supplier's line.

SCALE ORIGIN: Kumar, Scheer, and Steenkamp (1995) adapted the scale from the distributive justice index developed by Price and Mueller (1986).

SAMPLES: After deleting duplications among dealerships and dealerships for which no contact person could be identified, Kumar, Scheer, and Steenkamp (1995) sampled the remaining 1640 of 2100 new car dealers listed on a commercially purchased list covering two states in the United States. Also, 1600 new car dealers were randomly selected from a list of 4000 dealers representing the entire Netherlands. **Four hundred seventeen** and **289** usable responses were received from U.S. and Dutch dealers, respectively. The data were standardized separately by country to eliminate any culturally idiosyncratic patterns , then pooled for analysis.

RELIABILITY: Kumar, Scheer, and Steenkamp (1995) reported a coefficient alpha of **.78** for the scale.

VALIDITY: The .52 correlation between the distributive fairness scale and the single global item of distributive fairness provided some evidence of convergent validity. Additional evidence was obtained through a confirmatory factor analysis in which all first- and second-order constructs were found to be significant. Discriminant validity between the procedural and distributive fairness scales was also demonstrated using confirmatory factor analysis, because the intercorrelation of the two measures (.499) was found to be significantly below unity.

ADMINISTRATION: Kumar, Scheer, and Steenkamp (1995) indicated that the questionnaire was originally constructed in English and then translated into Dutch. Back-translation was used to verify the accuracy of the translation. Some minor changes to item and questionnaire phrasing resulted from feedback obtained during face-to-face interviews with Dutch dealership managers. The scale was included with other measures in a self-administered survey delivered by mail to both samples. Cover letters for the U.S. sample were personalized to a specific individual, and a follow-up letter was sent to nonrespondents after four weeks. The lack of a personalized cover letter and follow-up with the Dutch sample may have contributed to the lower response rate from this group. Dealers from both countries were asked to report on the automobile suppler (manufacturer or importer) whose product line accounted for the largest share of their firm's sales. Higher scores on the scale indicated that a dealer evaluated the outcomes and earnings received from carrying a supplier's line as being very fair relative to the work, effort, responsibilities, and so forth undertaken on behalf of the supplier. Lower scores indicated that dealers perceived these outcomes and earnings as being unfair.

MAJOR FINDINGS: Kumar, Scheer, and Steenkamp (1995) investigated how supplier fairness affected the development of long-term relationships between relatively smaller and vulnerable new car dealers and larger, more powerful suppliers. **Distributive fairness** was found to have a positive impact on relationship quality. Furthermore, as the positive outcomes provided by a supplier (relative to other alternatives) increased, so did the importance of **distributive fairness** in determining the quality of the relationship.

REFERENCES:

Kumar, Nirmalya, Lisa K. Scheer, and Jan-Benedict E.M. Steenkamp (1995b), "The Effects of Supplier Fairness on Vulnerable Resellers," *JMR*, 32 (February), 54–65.

Price, James L. and Charles W. Mueller (1986), *Handbook of Organizational Measurements*. Marshfield, MA: Pittman.

SCALE ITEMS:

Unfair   Fair

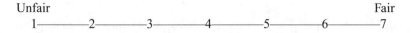

1————2————3————4————5————6————7

How fair are your firm's outcomes and earnings compared to:

1. The effort and investment that we have made to support the supplier's line.

2. The roles and responsibilities the supplier assigns to our organization.

3. What other dealers in our industry earn.

4. What the supplier earns from sales through our dealership.

5. The contributions we make to this supplier's marketing efforts.

SCALE NAME: Fairness (Procedural)

SCALE DESCRIPTION: Kumar, Scheer, and Steenkamp (1995) used this twelve-item, seven-point Likert-type scale to measure the extent to which bilateral communication, impartiality, refutability, explanation, knowledgeability, and courtesy characterized a dealer/supplier relationship.

SCALE ORIGIN: Kumar, Scheer, and Steenkamp (1995) adapted the items in this scale from measures used previously by Kim and Mauborgne (1991) and Konovsky and Cropanzano (1991).

SAMPLES: After deleting duplications among dealerships and dealerships for which no contact person could be identified, Kumar, Scheer, and Steenkamp (1995) sampled the remaining 1640 of 2100 new car dealers listed on a commercially purchased list covering two states in the United States. Also, 1600 new car dealers were randomly selected from a list of 4000 dealers representing the entire Netherlands. **Four hundred seventeen** and **289** usable responses were received from U.S. and Dutch dealers, respectively. The data were standardized separately by country to eliminate any culturally idiosyncratic patterns, then pooled for analysis.

RELIABILITY: Kumar, Scheer, and Steenkamp (1995) reported a coefficient alpha of **.88** for the scale.

VALIDITY: The .83 (United States) and .82 (Netherlands) correlations between the procedural fairness scale and the single global item of procedural fairness provided good evidence of convergent validity. Additional evidence was obtained through a confirmatory factor analysis in which all first- and second-order constructs were found to be significant. Discriminant validity between the procedural and distributive fairness scales was also demonstrated using confirmatory factor analysis, because the intercorrelation of the two measures (.499) was found to be significantly below unity.

ADMINISTRATION: Kumar, Scheer, and Steenkamp (1995) indicated that the questionnaire was originally constructed in English and then translated into Dutch. Back-translation was used to verify the accuracy of the translation. Some minor changes to item and questionnaire phrasing resulted from feedback obtained during face-to-face interviews with Dutch dealership managers. The scale was included with other measures in a self-administered survey delivered by mail to both samples. Cover letters for the U.S. sample were personalized to a specific individual, and a follow-up letter was sent to nonrespondents after four weeks. The lack of a personalized cover letter and follow-up with the Dutch sample may have contributed to the lower response rate from this group. Dealers from both countries were asked to report on the automobile suppler (manufacturer or importer) whose product line accounted for the largest share of their firm's sales. The two items measuring each of the six indicators of procedural fairness were averaged in the scoring processing. Higher scores on the scale indicated that a dealer evaluated the supplier as being more fair, from the perspective that the supplier offered high levels of bilateral communication, impartiality, refutability, explanation, knowledgeability, and courtesy.

MAJOR FINDINGS: Kumar, Scheer, and Steenkamp (1995) investigated how supplier fairness affected the development of long-term relationships between relatively smaller and vulnerable new car dealers and larger, more powerful suppliers. **Procedural fairness** was found to have a positive impact on relationship quality that was significantly stronger than the impact of distributive fairness. Furthermore, as the positive outcomes provided by a supplier (relative to other alternatives) increased, the importance of **procedural fairness** in determining relationship quality was found to decrease. **Procedural fairness** becomes more important in determining relationship quality, however, when environmental uncertainty increases.

REFERENCES:

Kim, W. Chan and Renee Mauborgne (1991), "Implementing Global Strategies: The Role of Procedural Justice," *Strategic Management Journal*, 12, 125–43.

Konovsky, Mary A. and Russell Cropanzano (1991), "Perceived Fairness of Employee Drug Testing as a Predictor of Employee Attitudes and Job Performance," *Journal of Applied Psychology*, 76 (5), 698–707.

Kumar, Nirmalya, Lisa K. Scheer, and Jan-Benedict E.M. Steenkamp (1995), "The Effects of Supplier Fairness on Vulnerable Resellers," *JMR*, 32 (February), 54–65.

SCALE ITEMS:

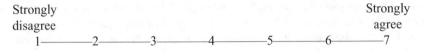

Strongly
disagree

Strongly
agree

1————2————3————4————5————6————7

In relationships with their dealers, the supplier and their personnel...

Bilateral communication
 1. Promote bilateral communication with the dealers.
 2. A high-level of two-way communication exists.

Impartiality
 3. Do not discriminate but rather treat all dealers similarly.
 4. Apply consistent policies and decision-making procedures across all dealers.

Refutability
 5. Sometimes alter their policies in response to dealer objections.
 6. Seriously consider a dealer's objections to the supplier's policies and programs.

Explanation
 7. Seldom explain their decisions to dealers. (r)
 8. Provide valid reasons for any changes in policies affecting the dealers.

Knowledgeability
 9. Are knowledgeable about the local situations faced by the dealers.
10. Take pains to learn the local conditions under which the dealers operate.

Courteous behavior
11. Treat the dealers with respect.
12. Are polite and well-mannered.

SCALE NAME: Fairness in Reward Allocation

SCALE DESCRIPTION: Netemeyer and colleagues (1997) used this four-item, five-point scale to measure the degree to which a salesperson believed that he or she had been rewarded fairly in view of his or her responsibilities, effort, and performance.

SCALE ORIGIN: Netemeyer and colleagues (1997) indicated that the items used for this measure were adapted from Price and Mueller's (1986) distributive justice index.

SAMPLES: In their first study, Netemeyer and colleagues (1997) used a convenience sample of 115 salespeople employed by a cellular telephone company in the southeastern United States, and **91** usable responses were obtained for a 79% response rate. The median age of respondents was 29 years, and their average amount of time with the organization was 1.89 years. The majority of respondents were women (56%) and college-educated (57%). In the second study, the authors sampled 700 real estate salespeople living in a large southeastern U.S. city, and **182** usable surveys were received for an effective response rate of 26%. The median age of respondents in the second study was 48 years, and their average amount of time with the organization was 8.41 years. The majority were women (78%) and college-educated (60.5%).

RELIABILITY: Netemeyer and colleagues (1997) reported coefficient alphas of **.94** for Study 1 and **.92** for Study 2.

VALIDITY: Netemeyer and colleagues (1997) examined the discriminant and construct validity of the scale using confirmatory factor analysis for both Study 1 and Study 2 data. The average variance extracted by the measure in each study was well below the .50 cut-off level suggested by Fornell and Larcker (1981), thereby providing evidence of construct validity. The square of parameter estimates between pairs of constructs was less than the average variance extracted estimates for the paired constructs across all possible construct pairings in both studies, thereby providing evidence of the discriminant validity of the measure.

ADMINISTRATION: Netemeyer and colleagues (1997) indicated that the scale was included as part of a self-administered mail survey in both studies. Study 2 participants were assured of the confidentiality and anonymity of their responses. Higher scores on the scale indicated that salespeople believed they had been rewarded fairly for their effort and performance in view of their job responsibilities.

MAJOR FINDINGS: Netemeyer and colleagues (1997) proposed and tested a model of potential predictors of organizational citizenship behavior (OCB) and job satisfaction using data from two separate studies conducted in a sales setting. Mixed results were found with respect to the role played by leadership support and **fairness in reward allocation** in predicting job satisfaction. In one study, leadership support was found to be a significant predictor, but **fairness in reward allocation** was not; in the other study, the reverse was true.

REFERENCES:

Fornell, Claes and David F. Larcker (1981), "Evaluating Structural Equation Models with Unobservable Variables and Measurement Error," *JMR*, 28 (February), 39–50.

Price, James P. and Charles W. Mueller (1986), *Handbook of Organizational Measurement.* Marshfield, MA: Pittman.

Netemeyer, Richard G., James S. Boles, Daryl O. McKee, and Robert McMurrian (1997), "An Investigation Into the Antecedents of Organizational Citizenship Behaviors in a Personal Selling Context," *JM*, 61 (July), 85–98.

SCALE ITEMS:

Very little   Very much
1————2————3————4————5

1. To what extent are you fairly rewarded considering the responsibilities you have?

2. To what extent are you fairly rewarded for the amount of effort you put forth?

3. To what extent are you fairly rewarded for the stresses and strains of your job?

4. To what extent are you fairly rewarded for the work you have done well?

SCALE NAME: Familiarity (Supplier's Product-Market)

SCALE DESCRIPTION: Celly and Frazier (1996) used this five-item, five-point semantic differential scale to measure distributor perceptions of the degree to which a supplier is familiar with and knowledgeable about the markets in which distributors sell their products.

SCALE ORIGIN: There was no information to indicate the measure was anything other than original to Celly and Frazier (1996). Multiple items were developed for the scale using the conceptual definition of the construct, prior research, and information provided during prestudy interviews with suppliers and distributors. Scale items were then purified using item analysis and an exploratory factor analysis.

SAMPLES: Celly and Frazier (1996) effectively sampled 953 distributors who were randomly selected from Dun's Marketing Services' Direct Access service and who had passed a variety of screening processes. The selected distributors serviced one of four industries: machine tools and metalworking machinery, air compressors and packaging equipment, industrial tools, or abrasives and adhesives. **Two hundred seven** usable responses were obtained.

RELIABILITY: Celly and Frazier (1996) reported a coefficient alpha of **.85** for the scale.

VALIDITY: The discriminant validity of all of the measures used in Celly and Frazier's (1996) study was found to be satisfactory based on the results of a principal components factors analysis with orthogonal rotation.

ADMINISTRATION: Celly and Frazier (1996) included the scale with other measures as part of a self-administered survey that was delivered by mail. Prenotification and reminders, incentives, and a second survey mailing to nonrespondents were used to enhance response rates. Higher scores on the scale indicated that distributors perceived their suppliers as being more familiar and knowledgeable about the markets through which their products were sold.

MAJOR FINDINGS: Celly and Frazier (1996) investigated suppliers' use of outcome- and behavior-based coordination efforts with their distributors. Chow tests comparing information provided by exclusive dealers with that provided by nonexclusive dealers confirmed the appropriateness of analyzing the data jointly. **Supplier familiarity** demonstrated a strong, positive effect on behavior-based supplier coordination efforts but did not significantly influence outcome-based coordination efforts.

REFERENCES:
Celly, Kirti Sawhney and Gary L. Frazier (1996), "Outcome-Based and Behavior-Based Coordination Efforts in Channel Relationships," *JMR*, 33 (May), 200–210.

SCALE ITEMS:
Directions: Indicate the extent to which the following terms describe this supplier's familiarity with the markets to which you sell its lines:

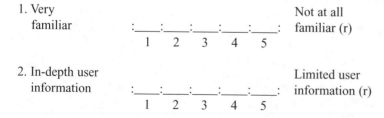

1. Very
   familiar _____ Not at all familiar (r)
   1   2   3   4   5

2. In-depth user
   information _____ Limited user information (r)
   1   2   3   4   5

3. Well-developed
   customer
   contacts   :___:___:___:___:___: Poor
                 1   2   3   4   5   customer
                                         contacts (r)

4. Excellent
   knowledge of
   buying practices   :___:___:___:___:___: Little
                 1   2   3   4   5   knowledge of
                                         buying practices (r)

5. Good
   understanding
   of customer
   requirements   :___:___:___:___:___: Poor
                1   2   3   4   5   understanding
                                         of customer
                                         requirements (r)

SCALE NAME: Fanciful Escapism

SCALE DESCRIPTION: Strutton and Lumpkin (1994) adapted this three-item, five-point subscale from the Ways of Coping Checklist Scale developed by Folkman and Lazarus (1980, 1985). It attempts to measure the extent to which a salesperson uses fanciful escapism tactics to cope with stressful customer sales presentations. In this study, the original items were screened for applicability to the sales setting. The remaining items were then subjected to factor analysis in a manner similar to Folkman and colleagues' (1986) and the subscales that matter were identified.

SCALE ORIGIN: These items were adapted by Strutton and Lumpkin (1994) for a sales setting from the Ways of Coping Checklist (Folkman and Lazarus 1980, 1985). The original measure contained 43 items developed to measure problem-focused (24 items) and emotion-focused (19 items) tactics for handling stressful situations.

SAMPLES: Strutton and Lumpkin's (1994) sample was a nonprobability sample of **101** nonmanager salespeople from three industries: communications technology (60), textiles (22), and furniture (19), all predominantly in the southern United States.

RELIABILITY: Strutton and Lumpkin (1994) reported a Cronbach's alpha of **.69** for this scale.

VALIDITY: No specific validity tests were reported by Strutton and Lumpkin (1994). However, this subscale was **not** identified as a separate subscale in Folkman's (1986) earlier work. Some caution is warranted regarding the possibility of findings idiosyncratic to this study.

ADMINISTRATION: Strutton and Lumpkin (1994) asked respondents to describe the most stressful customer-related situation they had encountered during a sales presentation during the previous two months. They were then asked to respond to the items in the scale, along with other scales and demographic questions. Higher scores on the scale indicated that fanciful escapism tactics for dealing with stress were used to a greater extent.

MAJOR FINDINGS: Strutton and Lumpkin found that **fanciful escapism** was not significantly related to sales presentation effectiveness in a regression of all subscales as measured by Behrman and Perreault's (1984) self-reported measure of presentation effectiveness.

REFERENCES:
Behrman, Douglas N. and William D. Perreault, Jr. (1984), "A Sales Role Stress Model of the Performance and Satisfaction of Industrial Salespersons," *JM*, 48 (Fall), 9–21.
Folkman, Susan and Richard S. Lazarus (1980), "An Analysis of Coping in a Middle-Aged Community Sample," *Journal of Health and Social Behavior*, 21 (September), 219–39.
———— and ———— (1985), "If It Changes, It Must Be a Process: Study of Emotion and Coping During Three Stages of a College Examination," *Journal of Personality and Social Psychology*, 48 (January), 150–70.
————, ————, Christine Dunkel-Schetter, Anita DeLongis, and Rand J. Gruen (1986), "Dynamics of a Stressful Encounter: Cognitive Appraisal, Coping, and Encounter Outcomes," *Journal of Personality and Social Psychology*, 50 (May), 992–1003.
Strutton, David and James R. Lumpkin (1994), "Problem- and Emotion-Focused Coping Dimensions and Sales Presentation Effectiveness," *JAMS*, 22 (1), 28–37.

SCALE ITEMS:

Directions: Indicate the extent to which you used each of the following tactics to cope with a stressful sales presentation experience.

Not used at all   :____:____:____:____:____: Used a great deal
                1   2   3   4   5

1. Had fantasies about how things might turn out.

2. Wished the situation would somehow go away or somehow be over with.

3. Hoped a miracle would happen.

SCALE NAME: Feedback (Coercive Actions)

SCALE DESCRIPTION: DeCarlo and Leigh (1996) used this six-item, seven-point Likert-type scale to assess the extent to which a sales manager would provide corrective feedback to a salesperson who had performed poorly by using coercive actions such as threats, transfers, salary deductions, or employment termination.

SCALE ORIGIN: DeCarlo and Leigh (1996) indicated that the scale was based on the work of McKay and colleagues (1991).

SAMPLES: DeCarlo and Leigh's (1996) sample consisted of 468 U.S. sales managers , of whom 289 were recruited from a *Fortune* 500 mailing equipment (ME) firm, 103 were recruited from an office equipment (OE) firm, and the final 79 individuals were drawn from a southeast sales and marketing executives (SME) mailing list. Usable responses were obtained from **218** sales managers, of whom 144 (49%) were ME managers, 55 (53.4%) were OE managers, and 19 (25.5%) were SME managers. Post hoc ANOVAS were performed for several firm-level effects to assess the compatibility of the three groups that composed the sample; no significant differences were found.

RELIABILITY: DeCarlo and Leigh (1996) reported a coefficient alpha of **.80** for the scale.

VALIDITY: The scales used in DeCarlo and Leigh's (1996) study were first factor analyzed. Those with multiple-factor solutions were orthogonally rotated, and items with loadings of .30 or lower were eliminated. Confirmatory factor analysis using LISREL 7.16 was used to assess scale dimensionality and discriminant validity; goodness-of-fit indices and t-values associated with individual items were used to identify the final set of scale items representing each construct.

ADMINISTRATION: DeCarlo and Leigh (1996) developed a 2 × 2 × 3 full-factorial, between-group experimentation design in which task attraction, social attraction, and information ambiguity were manipulated to observe the effect on managerial causal attributions and other dependent measures. The questionnaire containing the measure was delivered by mail. Nonrespondents were sent a reminder postcard followed by a second questionnaire. A lottery incentive, promises of anonymity, letters of endorsement, and business reply envelopes were also used to enhance response rates. Higher scores on the scale indicated that a sales manager was more likely to provide corrective feedback to the poorly performing salesperson through coercive actions such as threats, pay cuts, transfers, or job termination.

MAJOR FINDINGS: DeCarlo and Leigh (1996) examined the relationship between a sales manager's task and social attraction to a salesperson, manager attributions for poor performance, and managerial feedback based on those attributions in an experimental context. Both task and social attraction directly influenced **coercive action-based feedback**, because sales managers were less likely to use **coercive feedback** and more likely to provide nonpunitive feedback when the salesperson was highly task or socially attractive.

REFERENCES:
DeCarlo, Thomas E. and Thomas W. Leigh (1996), "Impact of Salesperson Attraction on Sales Managers' Attributions and Feedback," *JM*, 60 (April), 47–66.
McKay, Sandra, Joseph F. Hair Jr., Mark W. Johnston, and Daniel L. Sherrell (1991), "An Exploratory Investigation of Reward and Corrective Responses to Salesperson Performance: An Attributional Approach," *Journal of Personal Selling and Sales Management*, 11 (Spring), 39–48.

SCALE ITEMS:

Strongly
disagree

Strongly
agree

1————2————3———— 4 ————5————6———— 7

1. Threaten to fire this salesperson.

2. Scold this salesperson.

3. Fire this salesperson.

4. Deduct a portion of salary.

5. Threaten to deduct salary.

6. Transfer this salesperson to another territory.

SCALE NAME: Feedback (Negative)

SCALE DESCRIPTION: Sujan, Weitz, and Kumar (1994) used this eight-item, seven-point Likert-type scale to measure the level of negative feedback received by salespeople from their supervisors.

SCALE ORIGIN: Sujan, Weitz, and Kumar (1994) indicated that the measure used was adapted from the work of Jaworski and Kohli (1991), who unsuccessfully attempted to divide positive and negative feedback into evaluations of output and behavior. Sujan, Weitz, and Kumar (1994) also attempted to evaluate output and behavior separately but again found no discrimination between these dimensions for either positive or negative feedback. The authors ultimately selected eight of the ten items that represented negative output and negative behavior feedback to represent their single negative feedback measure with minor alterations to item phrasing.

SAMPLES: Sujan, Weitz, and Kumar (1994) surveyed a convenience sample of salespeople employed by eight firms representing diverse industries. Two hundred seventeen questionnaires were distributed by sales managers to members of their selling force, and **190** usable responses were obtained for an 87.5% response rate. On average, respondents were 35 years of age, had 9 years sales experience, and made 3.5 calls per day. The majority were men (78%).

RELIABILITY: Sujan, Weitz, and Kumar (1994) reported a coefficient alpha of **.89** for the measure.

VALIDITY: Sujan, Weitz, and Kumar (1994) provided extensive information on the assessment of scale validity. Measures used in their study were evaluated using confirmatory factor analysis. The authors stated that the results of this analysis supported the unidimensionality and reliability of the measure and provided evidence of convergent and discriminant validity.

ADMINISTRATION: Sujan, Weitz, and Kumar (1994) included a cover letter promising confidentiality and a self-addressed, stamped reply envelope in the survey packet distributed by sales managers to members of the sales force. Respondents were instructed to return the questionnaire directly to the researchers rather than to their superiors. Higher scores on the scale indicated that salespeople evaluated supervisors as being more likely to share negative feedback with members of the sales force.

MAJOR FINDINGS: Sujan, Weitz, and Kumar (1994) investigated the influence of goal orientations on work behavior. Results indicated that **negative feedback** increased the learning and performance orientation of the salesperson.

REFERENCES:
Jaworski, Bernard J. and Ajay K. Kohli (1991), "Supervisory Feedback: Alternative Types and Their Impact on Salespeople's Performance and Satisfaction," *JMR*, 27 (May), 190–201.
Sujan, Harish, Barton A. Weitz, and Nirmalya Kumar (1994), "Learning Orientation, Working Smart, and Effective Selling," *JM*, 58 (July), 39–52.

SCALE ITEMS:

Strongly
disagree

Strongly
agree

1———2———3———4———5———6———7

1. My supervisor lets me know when he or she is upset with my performance results.

2. When my supervisor thinks I have done something wrong, he or she lets me know about it.

3. My supervisor makes it a point to tell me he or she thinks I am not using the right selling techniques.

4. My supervisor is prompt in letting me know when my output is below his or her expectations.

5. When I deal with customers in a way which my supervisor disapproves, he or she lets me know.

6. My supervisor would let me know if I did not demonstrate a new product/service properly.

7. When I fail to meet his or her sales expectations, my supervisor indicates his or her dissatisfaction.

8. When my supervisor doesn't find me working the way he or she expects, he or she lets me know.

SCALE NAME: Feedback (Negative Behavioral)

SCALE DESCRIPTION: Kohli and Jaworski (1994) used this three-item, five-point Likert-type scale to measure the degree to which salespeople received constructive feedback from coworkers that was critical of selling approaches and behaviors used with customers.

SCALE ORIGIN: This measure was one of four scales developed by alternating the two dimensions of feedback valence (positive, negative) and locus of feedback (output, behavior). The resulting scales were used by Kohli and Jaworski (1994) to measure four distance forms of coworker feedback. No details were provided with respect to how the measure items were generated, though the authors noted that pretesting was employed to identify scale items that were not applicable, unclear, or ambiguous. One item, "If I fail to return demonstration cars to their assigned places, my coworkers criticize me," was eliminated on the basis of low interitem correlations, which resulted in the purified three-item measure.

SAMPLES: Because the nature of the study required that salesperson behavior and output be visible to coworkers, and thus allow for coworker feedback, Kohli and Jaworski (1994) chose to sample retail auto salespeople. The preliminary set of scale items was first administered to 11 auto salespeople from five dealerships, whose comments enabled scale item and questionnaire revision. The final questionnaire was mailed to 303 salespeople belonging to the nationwide dealership network of a European car manufacturer. A reminder, followed by a second questionnaire mailing, resulted in usable responses being obtained from **150** salespeople.

RELIABILITY: Kohli and Jaworski (1994) reported a coefficient alpha of **.84** for this measure.

VALIDITY: Kohli and Jaworski (1994) used confirmatory factory analysis to test the unidimensionality of the measure in conjunction with the other three coworker feedback constructs. Results suggested that the measure was unidimensional. No other specific assessments of validity were discussed by the authors.

ADMINISTRATION: Kohli and Jaworski (1994) stated that the scale was part of a self-administered questionnaire that was delivered by mail. A personally addressed cover letter promising complete confidentiality accompanied the survey, as did a self-addressed reply envelope and ballpoint pen incentive. A reminder was sent one week after the initial mailing; nonrespondents then received a second reminder and questionnaire three weeks after the initial mailing. Lower scores on the feedback (negative behavioral) scale indicated that coworkers offered higher levels of constructive feedback that criticized the various selling approaches and tactics used with customers.

MAJOR FINDINGS: Kohli and Jaworski (1994) investigated how positive output, negative output, positive behavioral, and negative behavioral forms of coworker feedback affected salespeople's output and behavioral role clarity, satisfaction with coworkers, and output and behavioral performance. **Negative behavioral–related feedback** was not significantly related to satisfaction with coworkers or behavioral role clarity but significantly influenced behavioral performance. Kohli and Jaworski (1994) suggested that **negative behavioral–related feedback** had a demoralizing influence on salespeople that deflated their desire to perform well.

REFERENCES:
Kohli, Ajay K. and Bernard J. Jaworski (1994), "The Influence of Coworker Feedback on Salespeople," *JM*, 58 (October), 82–94.

SCALE ITEMS:

Strongly   Strongly
  agree   disagree
  1————2————3————4————5

1. My coworkers let me know if I don't go about the job as is expected of me.

2. My coworkers tell me when I mess up in my selling tactics.

3. My coworkers let me know when I engage in selling tactics that they think are ineffective.

SCALE NAME: Feedback (Nonpunitive Actions)

SCALE DESCRIPTION: DeCarlo and Leigh (1996) used this three-item, seven-point Likert-type scale to assess the extent to which a sales manager would provide corrective feedback to a salesperson who had performed poorly by using nonpunitive actions such as counseling, encouragement to do better, and meeting to discuss potential problems.

SCALE ORIGIN: DeCarlo and Leigh (1996) indicated that the scale was based on the work of McKay and colleagues (1991).

SAMPLES: DeCarlo and Leigh's (1996) sample consisted of 468 U.S. sales managers, of whom 289 were recruited from a *Fortune* 500 mailing equipment (ME) firm, 103 were recruited from an office equipment (OE) firm, and the final 79 individuals were drawn from a southeast sales and marketing executives (SME) mailing list. Usable responses were obtained from **218** sales managers, of whom 144 (49%) were ME managers, 55 (53.4%) were OE managers, and 19 (25.5%) were SME managers. Post hoc ANOVAS were performed for several firm-level effects to assess the compatibility of the three groups that composed the sample; no significant differences were found.

RELIABILITY: DeCarlo and Leigh (1996) reported a coefficient alpha of **.71** for the scale.

VALIDITY: The scales used in DeCarlo and Leigh's (1996) study were first factor analyzed. Those with multiple-factor solutions were orthogonally rotated, and items with loadings of .30 or lower were eliminated. Confirmatory factor analysis using LISREL 7.16 was used to assess scale dimensionality and discriminant validity; goodness-of-fit indices and t-values associated with individual items were used to identify the final set of scale items representing each construct.

ADMINISTRATION: DeCarlo and Leigh (1996) developed a 2 × 2 × 3 full-factorial, between-group experimentation design in which task attraction, social attraction, and information ambiguity were manipulated to observe the effect on managerial causal attributions and other dependent measures. The questionnaire containing the measure was delivered by mail. Nonrespondents were sent a reminder postcard followed by a second questionnaire. A lottery incentive, promises of anonymity, letters of endorsement, and business reply envelopes were also used to enhance response rates. Higher scores on the scale indicated that a sales manager was more likely to provide corrective feedback to the poorly performing salesperson through coercive actions such as threats, pay cuts, transfers, or job termination.

MAJOR FINDINGS: DeCarlo and Leigh (1996) examined the relationship between a sales manager's task and social attraction to a salesperson, manager attributions for poor performance, and managerial feedback based on those attributions in an experimental context. Both task and social attraction directly influenced **punitive action–based feedback**, because sales managers were more less likely to use coercive feedback and more likely to provide **nonpunitive feedback** when the salesperson was highly task or socially attractive.

REFERENCES:

DeCarlo, Thomas E. and Thomas W. Leigh (1996), "Impact of Salesperson Attraction on Sales Managers' Attributions and Feedback," *JM*, 60 (April), 47–66.

McKay, Sandra, Joseph F. Hair Jr., Mark W. Johnston, and Daniel L. Sherrell (1991), "An Exploratory Investigation of Reward and Corrective Responses to Salesperson Performance: An Attributional Approach," *Journal of Personal Selling and Sales Management*, 11 (Spring), 39–48.

SCALE ITEMS:

Strongly   Strongly
disagree   agree
  1————2————3————4————5————6————7

1. Counsel this salesperson.

2. Meet with this salesperson to discuss possible problems.

3. Encourage this salesperson to improve.

SCALE NAME: Feedback (Positive)

SCALE DESCRIPTION: Sujan, Weitz, and Kumar (1994) used this eight-item, seven-point Likert-type scale to measure the level of positive feedback received by salespeople from their supervisors.

SCALE ORIGIN: Sujan, Weitz, and Kumar (1994) indicated that the measure used was adapted from the work of Jaworski and Kohli (1991), who unsuccessfully attempted to divide positive and negative feedback into evaluations of output and behavior. Sujan, Weitz, and Kumar (1994) also attempted to evaluate output and behavior separately but again found no discrimination between these dimensions for either positive or negative feedback. The authors ultimately selected eight of the ten items that represented positive output and positive behavior feedback to represent their single positive feedback measure with minor alterations to item phrasing.

SAMPLES: Sujan, Weitz, and Kumar (1994) surveyed a convenience sample of salespeople employed by eight firms representing diverse industries. Two hundred seventeen questionnaires were distributed by sales managers to members of their selling force, and **190** usable responses were obtained for an 87.5% response rate. On average, respondents were 35 years of age, had 9 years sales experience, and made 3.5 calls per day. The majority were men (78%).

RELIABILITY: Sujan, Weitz, and Kumar (1994) reported a coefficient alpha of **.94** for the measure.

VALIDITY: Sujan, Weitz, and Kumar (1994) provided extensive information on the assessment of scale validity. Measures used in their study were evaluated using confirmatory factor analysis. The authors stated that the results of this analysis supported the unidimensionality and reliability of the measure and provided evidence of convergent and discriminant validity.

ADMINISTRATION: Sujan, Weitz, and Kumar (1994) included a cover letter promising confidentiality and a self-addressed, stamped reply envelope in the survey packet distributed by sales managers to members of the sales force. Respondents were instructed to return the questionnaire directly to the researchers rather than to their superiors. Higher scores on the scale indicated that salespeople evaluated supervisors as being more likely to share positive feedback with members of the sales force.

MAJOR FINDINGS: Sujan, Weitz, and Kumar (1994) investigated the influence of goal orientations on work behavior. Results indicated that **positive feedback** increased the learning orientation of the salesperson.

REFERENCES:
Jaworski, Bernard J. and Ajay K. Kohli (1991), "Supervisory Feedback: Alternative Types and Their Impact on Salespeople's Performance and Satisfaction," *JMR*, 27 (May), 190–201.
Sujan, Harish, Barton A. Weitz, and Nirmalya Kumar (1994), "Learning Orientation, Working Smart, and Effective Selling," *JM*, 58 (July), 39–52.

SCALE ITEMS:

Strongly
disagree   Strongly
agree

1————2————3————4————5————6————7

1. When my supervisor thinks my performance is good, he or she provides me with positive feedback.

2. My supervisor makes it a point of telling me when he or she thinks I manage my time well.

3. My supervisor commends me when he or she thinks I am using the "right" selling techniques.

4. My supervisor lets me know when he or she thinks I am producing good results.

5. When I make an important sale, my supervisor makes it a point of mentioning it to me.

6. My supervisor tells me when I deal with customers appropriately.

7. My supervisor expresses his or her approval when he sees me going about my job as he or she expects.

8. When my supervisor is satisfied with my sales output, he or she comments about it.

SCALE NAME: Feedback (Positive Behavioral)

SCALE DESCRIPTION: Kohli and Jaworski (1994) used this five-item, five-point Likert-type scale to measure the degree to which salespeople received positive feedback from coworkers praising the selling approaches and behaviors used with customers.

SCALE ORIGIN: This measure was one of four scales developed by alternating the two dimensions of feedback valence (positive, negative) and locus of feedback (output, behavior). The resulting scales were used by Kohli and Jaworski (1994) to measure four distance forms of coworker feedback. No details were provided with respect to how the measure items were generated, though the authors noted that pretesting was employed to identify scale items that were not applicable, unclear, or ambiguous. No items were eliminated on the basis of low interitem correlations.

SAMPLES: Because the nature of the study required that salesperson behavior and output be visible to coworkers, and thus allow for coworker feedback, Kohli and Jaworski (1994) chose to sample retail auto salespeople. The preliminary set of scale items was first administered to 11 auto salespeople from five dealerships; their comments enabled scale item and questionnaire revision. The final questionnaire was mailed to 303 salespeople belonging to the nationwide dealership network of a European car manufacturer. A reminder, followed by a second questionnaire mailing, resulted in usable responses being obtained from **150** salespeople.

RELIABILITY: Kohli and Jaworski (1994) reported a coefficient alpha of **.92** for this measure.

VALIDITY: Kohli and Jaworski (1994) used confirmatory factory analysis to test the unidimensionality of this measure in conjunction with the other three coworker feedback constructs. Results suggested that the measure was unidimensional. No other specific assessments of validity were discussed by the authors.

ADMINISTRATION: Kohli and Jaworski (1994) stated that the scale was part of a self-administered questionnaire that was delivered by mail. A personally addressed cover letter promising complete confidentiality accompanied the survey, as did a self-addressed reply envelope and ballpoint pen incentive. A reminder was sent one week after the initial mailing; nonrespondents received a second reminder and questionnaire three weeks after the initial mailing. Lower scores on the feedback (positive behavioral) scale indicated that coworkers offered high levels of positive feedback praising the various approaches and behaviors that were used with customers.

MAJOR FINDINGS: Kohli and Jaworski (1994) investigated how positive output, negative output, positive behavioral, and negative behavioral forms of coworker feedback affected salespeople's output and behavioral role clarity, satisfaction with coworkers, and output and behavioral performance. **Positive behavioral–related feedback** was significantly related to satisfaction with coworkers, behavioral role clarity, and behavioral performance. This finding suggests that behavioral peer feedback serves an informational function when it is positive and encourages salespeople to perform at higher levels.

REFERENCES:
Kohli, Ajay K. and Bernard J. Jaworski (1994), "The Influence of Coworker Feedback on Salespeople," *JM*, 58 (October), 82–94.

SCALE ITEMS:

Strongly   Strongly
  agree   disagree
   1————2————3————4————5

1. My fellow workers tell me when I'm doing the right things on the job.

2. I receive positive encouragement from my fellow workers when I do a nice "selling job."

3. My fellow workers let me know when I engage in the right selling approach.

4. My coworkers commend me when I do things right.

5. My coworkers tell me when I do a nice selling job.

SCALE NAME: Feedback (Positive Output)

SCALE DESCRIPTION: Kohli and Jaworski (1994) used this three-item, five-point Likert-type scale to measure the degree to which salespeople received positive feedback from coworkers praising the outcome of their selling efforts, specifically with respect to the sales and gross profit generated.

SCALE ORIGIN: This measure was one of four scales developed by alternating the two dimensions of feedback valence (positive, negative) and locus of feedback (output, behavior). The resulting scales were used by Kohli and Jaworski (1994) to measure four distance forms of coworker feedback. No details were provided with respect to how the measure items were generated, though the authors noted that pretesting was employed to identify scale items that were not applicable, unclear, or ambiguous. One item, "My coworkers treat me differently when my sales performance is good," was eliminated on the basis of low interitem correlations, which left a three-item purified measure.

SAMPLES: Because the nature of the study required that salesperson behavior and output be visible to coworkers, and thus allow for coworker feedback, Kohli and Jaworski (1994) chose to sample retail auto salespeople. The preliminary set of scale items was first administered to 11 auto salespeople from five dealerships; their comments enabled scale item and questionnaire revision. The final questionnaire was mailed to 303 salespeople belonging to the nationwide dealership network of a European car manufacturer. A reminder, followed by a second questionnaire mailing, resulted in usable responses being obtained from **150** salespeople.

RELIABILITY: Kohli and Jaworski (1994) reported a coefficient alpha of **.76** for this measure.

VALIDITY: Kohli and Jaworski (1994) used confirmatory factory analysis to test the unidimensionality of this measure in conjunction with the other three coworker feedback constructs. Results suggested that the measure was unidimensional. No other specific assessments of validity were discussed by the authors.

ADMINISTRATION: Kohli and Jaworski (1994) stated that the scale was part of a self-administered questionnaire that was delivered by mail. A personally addressed cover letter promising complete confidentiality accompanied the survey, as did a self-addressed reply envelope and ballpoint pen incentive. A reminder was sent one week after the initial mailing; nonrespondents received a second reminder and questionnaire three weeks after the initial mailing. Lower scores on the feedback (positive output) scale indicated that coworkers offered high levels of positive feedback praising the salesperson's performance regarding the generation of gross profit and sales.

MAJOR FINDINGS: Kohli and Jaworski (1994) investigated how positive output, negative output, positive behavioral, and negative behavioral forms of coworker feedback affected salespeople's output and behavioral role clarity, satisfaction with coworkers, and output and behavioral performance. **Positive output–related feedback** was not significantly related to satisfaction with coworkers, role clarity, or performance, suggesting that peer feedback does not serve an informational function and is not used by salespeople in developing performance benchmarks for the output expected of them.

REFERENCES:
Kohli, Ajay K. and Bernard J. Jaworski (1994), "The Influence of Coworker Feedback on Salespeople," *JM*, 58 (October), 82–94.

SCALE ITEMS:

Strongly   Strongly
  agree   disagree

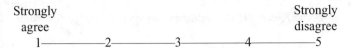

1——————2——————3——————4——————5

1. My coworkers make it a point of telling me when I make a good gross profit.

2. When I sell a large number of cars, my coworkers comment about it.

3. My coworkers tell me when my sales output is good.

SCALE NAME: Feedback (Self-Behavioral)

SCALE DESCRIPTION: Kohli and Jaworski (1994) used this four-item, five-point Likert-type scale to measure a salesperson's belief that he or she is capable of evaluating his or her own performance-related work behaviors.

SCALE ORIGIN: The scale is original to Kohli and Jaworski (1994). No additional information was provided with respect to how scale items were generated.

SAMPLES: Because the nature of the study required that salesperson behavior and output be visible to coworkers, and thus allow for coworker feedback, Kohli and Jaworski (1994) chose to sample retail auto salespeople. The preliminary set of scale items was first administered to 11 auto salespeople from five dealerships; their comments enabled scale item and questionnaire revision. The final questionnaire was mailed to 303 salespeople belonging to the nationwide dealership network of a European car manufacturer. A reminder, followed by a second questionnaire mailing, resulted in usable responses being obtained from **150** salespeople.

RELIABILITY: Kohli and Jaworski (1994) reported a coefficient alpha of **.73** for this measure.

VALIDITY: Kohli and Jaworski (1994) used confirmatory factory analysis to test the unidimensionality of the behavioral self-feedback measure in conjunction with measures of outcome self-feedback, salesperson conformity, and experience. Although details were not provided, the authors suggested that that the behavioral self-feedback measure was not unidimensional. No other specific assessments of validity were discussed by Kohli and Jaworski (1994).

ADMINISTRATION: Kohli and Jaworski (1994) stated that the scale was part of a self-administered questionnaire that was delivered by mail. A personally addressed cover letter promising complete confidentiality accompanied the survey, as did a self-addressed reply envelope and ballpoint pen incentive. A reminder was sent one week after the initial mailing; nonrespondents received a second reminder and questionnaire three weeks after the initial mailing. Lower scores on the scale indicated that salespeople believed they were capable of evaluating their own performance-related behaviors.

MAJOR FINDINGS: Kohli and Jaworski (1994) investigated how positive output, negative output, positive behavioral, and negative behavioral forms of coworker feedback affected salespeople's output and behavioral role clarity, satisfaction with coworkers, and output and behavioral performance. **Self-behavioral feedback** was hypothesized as influencing the degree to which salespeople sought out or paid attention to feedback from coworkers, thereby moderating the relationship between coworker feedback and salesperson role clarity. Hierarchical regression analysis failed to support the moderator role of **self-behavioral feedback**.

REFERENCES:

Kohli, Ajay K. and Bernard J. Jaworski (1994), "The Influence of Coworker Feedback on Salespeople," *JM*, 58 (October), 82–94.

SCALE ITEMS:

Strongly agree — 1————2————3————4————5 — Strongly disagree

1. I can tell for myself whether or not I am going about my job in the right way.

2. I can tell how effectively the sale is going on the basis of customer reactions.

3. I can tell for myself if I have been managing my time properly.

4. I know when my paperwork is not in order.

SCALE NAME: Firm Structure (Coordination)

SCALE DESCRIPTION: Pelham and Wilson (1996) used a four-item, seven-point scale to measure the extent to which cross-functional planning and decision making occurs in the firm.

SCALE ORIGIN: Pelham and Wilson (1996) indicated that this scale was taken from Miller and Dröge's (1986) study.

SAMPLES: A longitudinal database developed by the Center for Entrepreneurship at Eastern Michigan University provided the data for the study. The Center's full panel consists of data provided by the CEOs of 370 Michigan firms, which represent 71% of the firms contacted for initial participation. The data used by Pelham and Wilson (1996) were specific only to those firms providing full information with respect to all measures of interest for both the current and previous years. Of those **68** firms, 32% were classified as wholesalers, 29% as manufacturers, 26% as business services, and 13% as construction. Firm size ranged from 15 to 65 employees, with the average number of employees equaling 23.

RELIABILITY: Pelham and Wilson (1996) reported an alpha of **.71** for this scale.

VALIDITY: Pelham and Wilson (1996) did not specifically address the validity of the scale.

ADMINISTRATION: Pelham and Wilson (1996) did not provide details with respect to how data were collected from panel members by the Center of Entrepreneurship. Higher scores on the scale indicated higher levels of cross-functional planning and decision making within the firm.

MAJOR FINDINGS: Pelham and Wilson (1996) investigated the relative impact of market orientation on small business performance compared with that of market structure, firm structure, firm strategy, and relative product quality. Regression analysis was used to test year-to-year differences in most variables, as well as parameters based on independent and lagged variables. In the lagged model, a firm structure characterized by high levels of **coordination** during the previous year was found to significantly influence small-firm market orientation. No other significant relationships were found for **coordination**.

REFERENCES:
Miller, Danny and Cornelia Dröge (1986), "Psychological and Traditional Determinants of Structure," *Administrative Science Quarterly*, 31 (December), 539–60.
Pelham, Alfred M. and David T. Wilson (1996), "A Longitudinal Study of the Impact of Market Structure, Firm Structure, Strategy, and Market Orientation Culture on Dimensions of Small-Firm Performance," *JAMS*, 24 (1), 27–43.

SCALE ITEMS:
Directions: Indicate the frequency of the activity or process:

Never/rarely   Frequently
1———2———3———4———5———6———7

1. Are manager committees set up to allow joint decision making among departments/work groups?

2. Are task forces set up for collaboration on a specific project?

3. Are product or service decisions concerning production, distribution, marketing, and R&D strategies made by different departments/work groups working together?

4. Are capital budget decisions concerning the selection and financing of long-term investments made by different work groups or departments working together?

SCALE NAME: Firm Structure (Control Systems)

SCALE DESCRIPTION: Pelham and Wilson (1996) used a three-item, seven-point scale to measure the extent to which firms employed control systems as tools to evaluate the implementation of their plans.

SCALE ORIGIN: Pelham and Wilson (1996) indicated that this scale was taken from Miller and Dröge's (1986) study.

SAMPLES: A longitudinal database developed by the Center for Entrepreneurship at Eastern Michigan University provided the data for the study. The Center's full panel consists of data provided by the CEOs of 370 Michigan firms, which represent 71% of the firms contacted for initial participation. The data used by Pelham and Wilson (1996) were specific only to those firms providing full information with respect to all measures of interest for both the current and previous years. Of those **68** firms, 32% were classified as wholesalers, 29% as manufacturers, 26% as business services, and 13% as construction. Firm size ranged from 15 to 65 employees, with the average number of employees equaling 23.

RELIABILITY: Pelham and Wilson (1996) reported an alpha of **.63** for this scale.

VALIDITY: Pelham and Wilson (1996) stated that factor loadings and LISREL measurement model squared multiple correlations were taken as evidence of convergent and discriminant validity.

ADMINISTRATION: Pelham and Wilson (1996) did not provide details with respect to how data were collected from panel members by the Center of Entrepreneurship. Higher scores on the scale indicated greater use of control systems to evaluate the implementation of plans.

MAJOR FINDINGS: Pelham and Wilson (1996) investigated the relative impact of market orientation on small business performance compared with that of market structure, firm structure, firm strategy, and relative product quality. Regression analysis was used to test year-to-year differences in most variables, as well as parameters based on independent and lagged variables. Usage of **control systems** did not significantly influence any variable in either model.

REFERENCES:

Miller, Danny and Cornelia Dröge (1986), "Psychological and Traditional Determinants of Structure," *Administrative Science Quarterly*, 31 (December), 539–60.

Pelham, Alfred M. and David T. Wilson (1996), "A Longitudinal Study of the Impact of Market Structure, Firm Structure, Strategy, and Market Orientation Culture on Dimensions of Small-Firm Performance," *JAMS*, 24 (1), 27–43.

SCALE ITEMS:

Directions: Indicate the extent to which you use the following control systems:

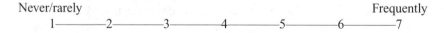

Never/rarely   Frequently

1———2———3———4———5———6———7

1. Comprehensive management control and information system.

2. Cost centers for cost control.

3. Profit centers and profit targets.

SCALE NAME: Firm Structure (Decentralization)

SCALE DESCRIPTION: Pelham and Wilson (1996) used a six-point, three-item scale to measure the extent to which work force–related decision making is undertaken at lower levels of the organization.

SCALE ORIGIN: Pelham and Wilson (1996) indicated that this scale was taken from Miller and Dröge's (1986) study.

SAMPLES: A longitudinal database developed by the Center for Entrepreneurship at Eastern Michigan University provided the data for the study. The Center's full panel consists of data provided by the CEOs of 370 Michigan firms, which represent 71% of the firms contacted for initial participation. The data used by Pelham and Wilson (1996) were specific only to those firms providing full information with respect to all measures of interest for both the current and previous years. Of those **68** firms, 32% were classified as wholesalers, 29% as manufacturers, 26% as business services, and 13% as construction. Firm size ranged from 15 to 65 employees, with the average number of employees equaling 23.

RELIABILITY: Pelham and Wilson (1996) reported an alpha of **.87** for this scale.

VALIDITY: Pelham and Wilson (1996) stated that factor loadings and LISREL measurement model squared multiple correlations were taken as evidence of convergent and discriminant validity.

ADMINISTRATION: Pelham and Wilson (1996) did not provide details with respect to how data were collected from panel members by the Center of Entrepreneurship. Low scores on the scale indicated that decision making related to the hiring and firing of workers was made at the top levels of the organization.

MAJOR FINDINGS: Pelham and Wilson (1996) investigated the relative impact of market orientation on small business performance compared with that of market structure, firm structure, firm strategy, and relative product quality. Regression analysis was used to test year-to-year differences in most variables, as well as parameters based on independent and lagged variables. The level of centralization or **decentralization** of the firm's work force–related decision making did not significantly influence any variable in either model.

REFERENCES:
Miller, Danny and Cornelia Dröge (1986), "Psychological and Traditional Determinants of Structure," *Administrative Science Quarterly*, 31 (December), 539–560.
Pelham, Alfred M. and David T. Wilson (1996), "A Longitudinal Study of the Impact of Market Structure, Firm Structure, Strategy, and Market Orientation Culture on Dimensions of Small-Firm Performance," *JAMS*, 24 (1), 27–43.

SCALE ITEMS:
Directions: Indicate the organizational level where the following decisions are made:

0 = Board of directors/owners
1 = CEO/president
2 = Upper level department manager
3 = Midlevel department manager
4 = First-line supervisor
5 = Entry level employees

1. Determines the number of workers needed.

2. Decides whether to hire entry-level worker.

3. Dismissal of a worker.

SCALE NAME: Firm Structure (Formalization)

SCALE DESCRIPTION: Pelham and Wilson (1996) used a four-item, dichotomous yes/no scale to measure the extent to which firms used written rules, policies, and procedures.

SCALE ORIGIN: It appears that the scale was first administered by the Center for Entrepreneurship at Eastern Michigan University. The extent to which Pelham and Wilson (1996) were involved with the Center and the development of the scale itself is unclear.

SAMPLES: A longitudinal database developed by the Center for Entrepreneurship at Eastern Michigan University provided the data for the study. The Center's full panel consists of data provided by the CEOs of 370 Michigan firms, which represent 71% of the firms contacted for initial participation. The data used by Pelham and Wilson (1996) were specific only to those firms providing full information with respect to all measures of interest for both the current and previous years. Of those **68** firms, 32% were classified as wholesalers, 29% as manufacturers, 26% as business services, and 13% as construction. Firm size ranged from 15 to 65 employees, with the average number of employees equaling 23.

RELIABILITY: Pelham and Wilson (1996) reported an alpha of **.73** for this scale.

VALIDITY: Pelham and Wilson (1996) stated that factor loadings and LISREL measurement model squared multiple correlations were taken as evidence of convergent and discriminant validity.

ADMINISTRATION: Pelham and Wilson (1996) did not provide details with respect to how data were collected from panel members by the Center of Entrepreneurship. Higher scores on the scale indicated a greater use of written policies, procedures, and rules by the organization.

MAJOR FINDINGS: Pelham and Wilson (1996) investigated the relative impact of market orientation on small business performance compared with that of market structure, firm structure, firm strategy, and relative product quality. Regression analysis was used to test year-to-year differences in most variables, as well as parameters based on independent and lagged variables. The level of small-firm market orientation was influenced by increased **formalization** of the firm structure. In the lagged variable regression, the previous year's level of **formalization** was found to positively influence the growth and market share of the firm, as well as new product success.

REFERENCES:
Pelham, Alfred M. and David T. Wilson (1996), "A Longitudinal Study of the Impact of Market Structure, Firm Structure, Strategy, and Market Orientation Culture on Dimensions of Small-Firm Performance," *JAMS*, 24 (1), 27–43.

SCALE ITEMS:

1 = yes   0 = no

1. Do you hand out information booklets to your employees addressing such topics as security, working conditions, and so on?

2. A written manual of procedures and fixed rules?

3. Written operating instructions to workers?

4. Written job descriptions?

SCALE NAME: Firm Structure (Product Differentiation)

SCALE DESCRIPTION: Pelham and Wilson (1996) used a three-item, seven-point scale to measure differences across product lines with respect to competition, customer buying habits, and production methods.

SCALE ORIGIN: Pelham and Wilson (1996) indicated that this scale was taken from Miller's (1988) study.

SAMPLES: A longitudinal database developed by the Center for Entrepreneurship at Eastern Michigan University provided the data for the study. The Center's full panel consists of data provided by the CEOs of 370 Michigan firms, which represent 71% of the firms contacted for initial participation. The data used by Pelham and Wilson (1996) were specific only to those firms providing full information with respect to all measures of interest for both the current and previous years. Of those **68** firms, 32% were classified as wholesalers, 29% as manufacturers, 26% as business services, and 13% as construction. Firm size ranged from 15 to 65 employees, with the average number of employees equaling 23.

RELIABILITY: Pelham and Wilson (1996) reported an alpha of **.77** for this scale.

VALIDITY: Pelham and Wilson (1996) stated that factor loadings and LISREL measurement model squared multiple correlations were taken as evidence of convergent and discriminant validity.

ADMINISTRATION: Pelham and Wilson (1996) did not provide details with respect to how data were collected from panel members by the Center of Entrepreneurship. Higher scores on the scale indicated greater differentiation in the product line with respect to the competition, customer buying habits, and production methods.

MAJOR FINDINGS: Pelham and Wilson (1996) investigated the relative impact of market orientation on small business performance compared with that of market structure, firm structure, firm strategy, and relative product quality. Regression analysis was used to test year-to-year differences in most variables, as well as parameters based on independent and lagged variables. Key findings indicated that **product differentiation** has a negative effect on the growth/market share of small firms when examining year-to-year differences and a negative effect on both the profitability and growth/share of small firms when other independent variables were lagged.

REFERENCES:
Miller, Danny (1988), "Strategic Process and Content as Mediators Between Organizational Context and Structure," *Academy of Management Journal*, 31, 544–69.
Pelham, Alfred M. and David T. Wilson (1996), "A Longitudinal Study of the Impact of Market Structure, Firm Structure, Strategy, and Market Orientation Culture on Dimensions of Small-Firm Performance," *JAMS*, 24 (1), 27–43.

SCALE ITEMS:
Directions: Indicate the extent to which there are differences across your lines with regard to the following:

No difference   Great difference

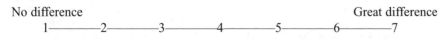
1————2————3————4————5————6————7

1. Customers' buying habits.

2. Nature of competition.

3. Required method of production or distribution of products/services.

SCALE NAME: Fixed Commitments (Receiving Firm)

SCALE DESCRIPTION: Robertson, Eliashberg, and Rymon (1995) used this three-item, six-point Likert-type scale to assess the extent to which a company receiving a new product announcement signal from a competitor has substantial investments and commitments in the corresponding product category.

SCALE ORIGIN: Robertson, Eliashberg, and Rymon (1995) developed the scale specifically for this study. The measure and questionnaire in which it was administered were initially conceptualized, tested, and purified on the basis of two pilot studies with executives participating in a management development program and a mail survey pretest. A principal components factor analysis with Varimax rotation was performed on data collected in the final study and used to determine the composition of the final measure.

SAMPLES: A total of 1554 directors of marketing in the United States (1034) and United Kingdom (520), representing a broad range of consumer and industrial product industries, were sampled for this study. Using a commercially purchased list as their sampling frame, Robertson, Eliashberg, and Rymon (1995) excluded marketing managers of wholesale, retail, and small firms prior to mailing their surveys. A total of **346** usable surveys were returned, of which 241 and 105 were from the United States and United Kingdom, respectively. No evidence of response bias was found, and Chow tests of the U.S. and U.K. data supported the pooling of data from each country.

RELIABILITY: Robertson, Eliashberg, and Rymon (1995) reported a coefficient alpha of **.76** for this measure.

VALIDITY: No specific examination of scale validity was reported by Robertson, Eliashberg, and Rymon (1995).

ADMINISTRATION: The scale was included with other measures in a self-administered survey delivered by mail. Robertson, Eliashberg, and Rymon (1995) prenotified respondents and offered a copy of the survey's tabulated results as an incentive to participate. Respondents were instructed to answer the questionnaire in the context of the last new product announcement (NPA) signal they received relative to a new product that was significantly different from existing products. Higher scores on the scale indicated that the firm receiving the NPA had made substantial levels of investment and commitment in the product category to which the NPA pertains.

MAJOR FINDINGS: Robertson, Eliashberg, and Rymon (1995) examined the relationship between NPA signals—announcements in advance of market introduction—and factors that affect the likelihood of competitive reactions to NPA signals. Firms were found to be most likely to react to an NPA signal in some fashion when they had made high levels of investment and **commitments** to the product category.

REFERENCES:
Robertson, Thomas S., Jehoshua Eliashberg, and Talia Rymon (1995), "New Product Announcement Signals and Incumbent Reactions," *JM*, 59 (July), 1–15.

SCALE ITEMS:*

Strongly   Strongly
disagree   agree
   1————2————3————4————5————6

Please tell us about your firm's position in this product category.

1. My firm has significant plant and equipment dedicated to this product category.

2. My firm has a major investment in this product category.

3. My firm has a major commitment to this product category.

*Although a six-point scale format was designated by Robertson, Eliashberg and Rymon (1995), the scale anchors were not explicitly listed. However, it is probable that the traditional Likert "strongly disagree" to "strongly agree" format was used.

SCALE NAME: Flexibility (Parties to Agreement)

SCALE DESCRIPTION: Bello and Gilliland (1997) used this three-item, seven-point Likert-type scale to measure the extent to which an export manufacturer/distributor relationship is characterized by the expectation that existing contracts or agreements can be adjusted in response to changing channel circumstances.

SCALE ORIGIN: Bello and Gilliland (1997) stated that the scale items were adapted from the relationship flexibility scale used by Heide (1994). Heide (1994) in turn noted that his scale was based on items previously developed by Kaufmann and Stern (1988). Bello and Gilliland (1997) simplified the phrasing of Heide's (1994) three-item scale and altered the second item to reflect a more specific form of adjustment (modifying a prior agreement).

SAMPLES: Bello and Gilliland's (1997) systematic random sample of 245 national manufacturers verified as exporting through foreign distributors was drawn from the 1994 edition of the *Journal of Commerce United States Importer & Exporter Directory*. **One hundred sixty** usable responses were obtained from export managers employed by firms exporting a variety of industrial and consumer products to a total of 39 different countries.

RELIABILITY: A confirmatory factor analysis composite reliability of **.70** was reported by Bello and Gilliland (1997).

VALIDITY: Confirmatory factor analysis was used by Bello and Gilliland (1997) to provide evidence of discriminant and convergent validity, as well as to assess the unidimensionality of the measure. Convergent validity was deemed to be present because items loaded significantly on their posited indicators and because of the low to moderate correlations between the scale and other measures. Discriminant validity was also deemed to be present because the correlation estimate between two indicators never included 1.0 (+/– two standard errors). The authors used personal interviews with export executives as part of the pretest process to verify the face validity of the measure.

ADMINISTRATION: Bello and Gilliland (1997) indicated that this scale was self-administered as part of a longer survey instrument mailed to respondents. The export manager with primary responsibility for the firm's relationship with the foreign distributor received a survey. Nonrespondents were telephoned three weeks later, and a second questionnaire followed. Instructions specified that questions were to be answered in the context of the focal distributor. The authors defined the focal distributor as the firm's fourth-largest foreign distributor in terms of unit sales volume, to avoid a positive evaluation bias. Higher scores on the scale indicated that channel members expected more flexibility in modifying existing agreements or contracts when market conditions changed.

MAJOR FINDINGS: Bello and Gilliland (1997) examined the effect of output controls, process controls, and flexibility on channel performance. The use of **flexible adjustment procedures** was positively related to distributor performance, which may indicate that **flexibility** enhances the coordination necessary for improved channel member performance. Higher levels of market volatility were found to decrease the use of **flexible adjustment procedures**, whereas export transactions requiring greater specialized knowledge of the product and customer resulted in greater **flexibility** between trading partners, perhaps due to the interdependence created by mutual investments in training and other nonredeployable resources.

REFERENCES:

Bello, Daniel C. and David I. Gilliland (1997), "The Effect of Output Controls, Process Controls, and Flexibility on Export Channel Performance," *JM*, 61 (January), 22–38.

Heide, Jan B. (1994), "Interorganizational Governance in Marketing Channels," *JM*, 58 (January), 71–85.

Kaufmann, Patrick J. and Louis W. Stern (1988), "Relational Exchange Norms, Perceptions of Unfairness, and Retained Hostility in Commercial Litigation," *Journal of Conflict Resolution*, 32 (September), 534–52.

SCALE ITEMS:

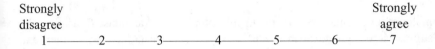

Strongly   Strongly
disagree   agree
 1———2———3———4———5———6———7

1. Flexibility in response to requests for changes is a characteristic of both parties.

2. Both parties are open to each other's request to modify a prior agreement.

3. When some unexpected situation arises, both parties would rather work out a new deal than hold each other to the original terms.

SCALE NAME: Flexibility (Supplier Relationship)

SCALE DESCRIPTION: Dahlstrom, McNeilly, and Speh (1996) used this three-item, five-point Likert-type scale to measure the ability of supply partners to react to unexpected changes in the operational situation.

SCALE ORIGIN: Dahlstrom, McNeilly, and Speh (1996) reported that the scale developed for this study was based on the work of Heide and John (1992). The questionnaire containing the scale was pretested by six members of the Warehouse Education and Research Council, who evaluated it for content, readability, and relevance to the industry.

SAMPLES: Using a sampling frame generated from the membership of the Warehouse Education and Research Council, Dahlstrom, McNeilly, and Speh (1996) surveyed 1000 manufacturer, retailer, and wholesaler members. No mention of the specific sampling technique used to generate the frame was provided. Firms that exclusively used in-house warehousing services were not part of the population of interest and were asked to return the survey without answering. Including the unanswered surveys, 383 questionnaires were returned for a 38.3% response rate. Of these, **189** contained complete data from firms using interfirm warehousing services.

RELIABILITY: Dahlstrom, McNeilly, and Speh (1996) reported a coefficient alpha of **.67** for this measure.

VALIDITY: Item-to-total correlations estimated by an exploratory factor analysis were used in the first stage of measure purification. Dahlstrom, McNeilly, and Speh (1996) submitted the remaining items to a confirmatory factor analysis, which provided evidence of construct validity. Discriminant validity was also assessed and found to be acceptable.

ADMINISTRATION: Dahlstrom, McNeilly, and Speh (1996) stated that the scale was part of a self-administered questionnaire that was returned by mail. Sampled individuals were contacted by telephone prior to survey delivery, and a postage-paid, return addressed reply envelope accompanied the questionnaire. A follow-up mailing with a second survey was sent two weeks after the first. Individuals using in-house warehousing services were asked not to complete the survey, but eligible respondents were instructed to answer in the context of the third-party warehouse service provider with whom they spent the greatest portion of their warehousing budget. Higher scores on the flexibility scale indicated that the supply relationship was characterized by the ability to adapt to unexpected changes in the operational situation.

MAJOR FINDINGS: Dahlstrom, McNeilly, and Speh (1996) investigated various antecedents to alternative forms of governance in the logistical supply market. A second topic of investigation addressed how formal controls and relational norms were employed by alternative governance forms to yield performance. Results of path analysis indicated that, in the bilateral alliance governance mode, **flexibility** was enhanced by participation and, in turn, increases performance. In the market-based exchange and short-term unilateral agreement governance modes, **flexibility** was enhanced by formalization, whereas participation increased **flexibility** in the long-term unilateral governance mode.

REFERENCES:
Dahlstrom, Robert, Kevin M. McNeilly, and Thomas W. Speh (1996), "Buyer-Seller Relationships in the Procurement of Logistical Services," *JAMS*, 24 (2), 110–24.
Heide, Jan B. and George John (1992), "Do Norms Matter in Relationships?" *JM*, 58 (January), 71–85.

SCALE ITEMS:
Please indicate your level of agreement with the following:

Strongly   Strongly
disagree   agree
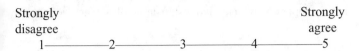

1. Flexibility in responses to requests for changes is a characteristic of this relationship.

2. The vendor and I expect to be able to make adjustments in the ongoing relationship to cope with changing circumstances.

3. When some unexpected situation arises, the vendor and I would rather work out a new deal rather than hold each other to the original terms.

SCALE NAME: Forbearance from Opportunism

SCALE DESCRIPTION: Smith and Barclay (1997) used this four-item, seven-point Likert-type scale to measure the degree to which partners acted cooperatively in a relationship and willfully avoided cheating or withholding of helpful actions.

SCALE ORIGIN: Smith and Barclay (1997) indicated that the constructs used in their study were operationalized with a mix of original and adapted scale items generated from the conceptual definition of the constructs, a review of the literature, field interviews, and pretest results. The conceptual definition of the scale as used by Smith and Barclay (1997) was consistent with John's (1984) study; some of the items may have been adapted from this source. Each of the final items representing this measure passed the extensive preliminary analysis of item reliability and validity described by the authors.

SAMPLES: Smith and Barclay (1997) collected dyadic self-reported data in two stages. The sponsor sample was composed of 338 sales representatives working for the Canadian subsidiaries of two multinational companies serving the computer industry. Forty percent of the 338 employees who were randomly selected from employee lists returned completed surveys. Using the names and contact information of relationship partners volunteered by these respondents, the authors then sampled the 135 dyadic partners. A total of **103** usable paired responses were obtained.

RELIABILITY: Smith and Barclay (1997) reported a coefficient alpha for this measure of **.70** in the sponsor model and **.72** in the partner model.

VALIDITY: Smith and Barclay (1997) reported extensive testing of the reliability, unidimensionality, and convergent and discriminant validity of the measures used in their study. LISREL and confirmatory factor analysis were used to demonstrate that the scale satisfied each of these standards, though some items from the measures as originally proposed were eliminated in the process.

ADMINISTRATION: Smith and Barclay (1997) included the scale with other measures as part of a self-administered survey that was delivered by internal company mail to sales representatives and by regular U.S. mail to the dyadic partners. E-mail follow-ups were used to increase survey response rate. Half of the sales representatives were instructed to consider a customer situation in the prior six months in which they had had some success with a selling partner, whereas the other half were to told to choose a situation in which they had had little or no success. Participants then responded to questions about the partner, their relationship, and the organization in the context of this situation. Higher scores on the scale indicated greater mutual trust between partners, in that partners act cooperatively and are less likely to cheat and withhold helpful information.

MAJOR FINDINGS: Smith and Barclay (1997) developed and tested two research models explaining selling partner relationship effectiveness. The first examined four organizational differences from the sponsor's (salesperson's) perspective, and the second examined these same differences from the partner's perspective. In both models, partners were more likely to **reduce their opportunistic behavior** the more that they perceived their partner as having trustworthy judgment, character, or motives.

REFERENCES:
John, George (1984), "An Empirical Investigation of Some Antecedents of Opportunism in a Marketing Channel," *JMR*, 21 (August), 278–89.
Smith, J. Brock and Donald W. Barclay (1997), "The Effects of Organizational Differences and Trust on the Effectiveness of Selling Partner Relationships," *JM*, 61 (January), 3–21.

SCALE ITEMS:

Strongly   Strongly
disagree   agree
  1————2————3————4————5————6————7

1. There is some cheating and deceit in our relationship. **(r)**

2. Sometimes we engage in opportunistic behavior at each other's expense. **(r)**

3. Sometimes I've had to compromise our relationship in order to look after myself. **(r)***

4. S/he has benefited from our relationship to my detriment. **(r)***

*These items were aggregated to the relationship level by taking the square root of the product of the individual responses by the sales representative and partner. All other items were conceptualized at the relationship level.

SCALE NAME: Formalization

SCALE DESCRIPTION: Heide and Weiss (1995) used this three-item, seven-point Likert-type scale to measure the emphasis buyers placed on following rules and procedures when carrying out the buying process.

SCALE ORIGIN: Heide and Weiss (1995) stated that Spekman and Stern's (1979) scale was modified and expanded for this study. Wording of existing scale items was changed to fit the context of computer workstation purchasing.

SAMPLES: Pretests of the questionnaire were conducted with two different small groups of previous workstation buyers. In the final study, Heide and Weiss (1995) drew a random sample of 900 firms from Installed Technology International's list of firms that had recently purchased workstations. Key informants were identified from this list and contacted by telephone, and 466 agreed to participate in the study and were sent a mail questionnaire. Follow-up telephone calls and a second mailing resulted in **215** usable questionnaires being returned. Industries represented by respondents included computers (31.4%), manufacturing (22.4%), medical (6.2%), services (15.2%), and other (24.8%).

RELIABILITY: Heide and Weiss (1995) reported a coefficient alpha of **.79** for this scale.

VALIDITY: Heide and Weiss (1995) initially evaluated the measure on the basis of item-to-total correlations and exploratory factor analysis. Confirmatory factor analysis was then used to establish unidimensionality. Evidence of discriminant validity was provided by a series of chi-square tests on the respective factor correlations.

ADMINISTRATION: The measure was included in a self-administered mail survey. Heide and Weiss (1995) instructed respondents to answer all questions in the context of their organization's most recent workstation purchase. Higher scores on the formalization scale indicated that buyers placed greater emphasis on rules and procedures when conducting the buying process.

MAJOR FINDINGS: Heide and Weiss (1995) investigated how buyers working in high-technology markets approached decisions in the consideration and choice stages of the purchase process. Specifically, factors influencing whether buyers included new vendors at the consideration stage and whether they ultimately switched to a new vendor at the choice stage were investigated. The authors reported that highly **formalized** buying processes limited the consideration of new vendors and reduced the likelihood that a new vendor would be selected over an existing supplier.

REFERENCES:

Heide, Jan B. and Allen M. Weiss (1995), "Vendor Consideration and Switching Behavior for Buyers in High-Technology Markets," *JM*, 59 (July), 30–43.

Spekman, Robert E. and Louis W. Stern (1979), "Environmental Uncertainty and Buying Group Structure: An Empirical Investigation," *JM*, 43 (Spring), 54–64.

SCALE ITEMS:

```
Strongly                                        Strongly
disagree                                        agree
    1———————2———————3———————4———————5———————6———————7
```

1. This process was handled to a large extent by standard procedures (either written or unwritten).

2. This workstation decision process was handled by "the rule book".

3. In deciding on this workstation, we followed standard procedures (either formal or informal).

SCALE NAME: Formalization

SCALE DESCRIPTION: The scale assesses the degree to which an organization is perceived by an employee as relying on standard operating procedures or rules to govern the action of its employees. The version used by Ferrell and Skinner (1988) had six six-point Likert-type items, whereas Kelley, Longfellow, and Malehorn (1996) used four items in five- and six-point formats.

SCALE ORIGIN: The original version of the scale was by John (1984).

SAMPLES: In Ferrell and Skinner's (1988) study, a self-administered questionnaire was mailed to a sample of 1500 researchers. The frame used was the membership list of the Marketing Research Association. The corporate classification was supplemented by the American Marketing Association membership list. From a single mailing, **550** usable questionnaires were returned. In addition, 52 questionnaires were returned by the post office, thereby resulting in a 37.9% response rate. Thirty-seven percent of the respondents were data subcontractors. More women (86%) than men (14%) represented this type of organization. Respondents employed by research firms were more balanced (54% women and 46% men). Finally, in corporate research departments, 53% of respondents were women as opposed to 47% men.

In their first sample, Kelley, Longfellow, and Malehorn (1996) surveyed all 122 customer-contact personnel employed by a bank located in the Midwest, and **113** usable responses were obtained, primarily from tellers (88) and customer service representatives (25). A stratified random sample of 381 insurance agents working in a single state of a large regional insurance company was also undertaken. In this second sample, 239 agents representing 75 of the 77 different agencies associated with the company responded, but complete information was obtained from only **185** of these individuals.

RELIABILITY: An alpha of **.75** was reported for the scale by Ferrell and Skinner (1988). Kelley, Longfellow, and Malehorn (1996) calculated coefficient alphas of **.606** and **.583** for this measure in Samples 1 and 2, respectively.

VALIDITY: Although assessment of scale validity was not the purpose of the study, Ferrell and Skinner (1988) performed a confirmatory factor analysis. According to the results of a t-test, all items in the scale were significant indicators. The factor loadings ranged between .44 to .74. Kelley, Longfellow, and Malehorn (1996) did not specifically discuss the validity of the measures.

ADMINISTRATION: In the study by Ferrell and Skinner (1988), the scale was included in a larger self-administered questionnaire. The scale was apparently scored such that lower scores reflected greater formality.

In Sample 1 of Kelley, Longfellow, and Malehorn's (1996) study, the measure was included in a questionnaire administered to customer-contact bank employees during regularly scheduled weekly meetings held in 15 branch offices. In Sample 2, the scale was included as part of a self-administered questionnaire that was delivered by mail. All responses were converted to z-scores prior to analysis because of the difference in response formats. Higher scores on the scale reflected a higher degree of formalization in the organization.

MAJOR FINDINGS: The purpose of the study by Ferrell and Skinner (1988) was to investigate the association between organizational structure and ethical behavior in firms involved with marketing research activity. **Formalization** was found to have a significant positive relationship with the ethical behavior reported by employees of each of the three different research-related organizations that were studied.

#627 *Formalization*

Kelley, Longfellow, and Malehorn (1996) investigated the antecedents to service employees' use of routine, creative, and deviant discretion in the banking and insurance industry. **Formalization** was negatively related to the performance of behaviors that were not included in the employee's formal job description (deviant discretion) but was not significantly related to either creative or routine discretion.

REFERENCES:

Ferrell, O.C., and S.J. Skinner (1988), "Ethical Behavior and Bureaucratic Structure in Marketing Research Organizations," *JMR*, 25 (February), 103–109.

John, George (1984), "An Empirical Investigation of Some Antecedents of Opportunism in a Marketing Channel," *JMR*, 21 (August), 278–89.

Kelley, Scott W., Timothy Longfellow, and Jack Malehorn (1996), "Organizational Determinants of Service Employees' Exercise of Routine, Creative, and Deviant Discretion," *JR*, 72 (2), 135–57.

SCALE ITEMS:*

Definitely agree — 1————2————3————4————5————6 — Definitely disagree

1. If a written rule does not cover some situation, we make up informal rules for doing things as we go along. **(r)**

2. There are many things in my business that are not covered by some formal procedure for doing it. **(r)**

3. Usually, my contact with my company and its representatives involves doing things "by the rule book."

4. Contact with my company and its representatives is on a formal preplanned basis.

5. I ignore the rules and reach informal agreements to handle some situations. **(r)**

6. When rules and procedures exist in my company, they are usually written agreements.

*This is the version of the scale used by Ferrell and Skinner (1988). Kelley, Longfellow, and Malehorn (1996) used items that were the same as or similar to items 1, 2, 5, and 6. Furthermore, they used a six-point response scale with Sample 1 and a five-point response format with Sample 2.

SCALE NAME: Formalization (Gasoline Station Decisions)

SCALE DESCRIPTION: Dahlstrom and Nygaard (1995) used this three-item, seven-point Likert-type scale to measure the extent to which rules and procedures were perceived as being employed by a refinery or franchiser to maintain relationships with their oil and gas retailers.

SCALE ORIGIN: Dahlstrom and Nygaard (1995) adapted the scale from the work of Dwyer and Oh (1987). Item-to-total correlations were examined using a country-by-country analysis of the data; items correlating at .25 or lower were dropped from the measure for a particular country. All three items here were retained in the measure for each country.

SAMPLES: Norwegian, German (formerly East German), and Polish oil and gas retailers were sampled by Dahlstrom and Nygaard (1995). From the 432 Norwegian service station managers, working in the retail network of a single oil refiner, who were surveyed, **216** usable responses were obtained. **Forty** of the 44 service station managers in Poland and **29** of the 50 Leipzig-area dealers in the former East Germany also provided usable data.

RELIABILITY: Dahlstrom and Nygaard (1995) reported coefficient alphas of **.65, .76** and **.73** in the Polish, German, and Norwegian samples, respectively.

VALIDITY: Dahlstrom and Nygaard (1995) did not specifically examine the validity of the measure.

ADMINISTRATION: Dahlstrom and Nygaard (1995) included the scale, with other measures, as part of a self-administered survey that was delivered by mail to the Norwegian sample. The survey was administered in person by college students to oil and gas retailers in the Polish and German samples. In each case, the questionnaire was translated into the focal language and back-translated into English, typically by university faculty in each country. Higher scores on the scale indicated that the oil and gas retailer perceived that the refinery or franchiser employed more rules and procedures to maintain relationships with oil and gas retailers.

MAJOR FINDINGS: Dahlstrom and Nygaard (1995) investigated various antecedents to and consequences of interpersonal trust in new and mature market economies using data collected in Norway, Poland, and the former East Germany. **Formalization** was not found to be a significant antecedent to interpersonal trust for Poland or Germany, but higher levels of formalized rules and procedures were significantly associated with higher levels of interpersonal trust in the Norwegian sample. In the Polish sample, **formalization** coupled with uncertainty lowered performance. No significant interaction effects between uncertainty and **formalization** were found for the German or Norwegian samples.

REFERENCES:
Dahlstrom, Robert and Arne Nygaard (1995), "An Exploratory Investigation of Interpersonal Trust in New and Mature Market Economies," *JR*, 71 (4), 339–61.
Dwyer, F. Robert and Sejo Oh (1987), "Output Sector Munificence Effects on the Internal Political Economy of Marketing Channels," *JMR*, 24 (3), 347–68.

SCALE ITEMS: To what extent would you agree with the following?

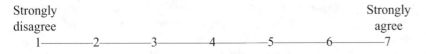

Strongly disagree — Strongly agree

1————2————3————4————5————6————7

1. There is a clear distribution of tasks between us and the *(Company)*.

2. There are no clear routines for safety training for persons employed at our station. **(r)**

3. In general, the information and routines from the *(Company)* are very unclear. **(r)**

SCALE NAME: Formalization (Manufacturer/Dealer Relationship)

SCALE DESCRIPTION: Mohr and Sohi (1995) used this four-item, five-point Likert-type scale to assess the extent to which formal mechanisms for communication existed within the manufacturer–dealer relationship.

SCALE ORIGIN: Mohr and Sohi (1995) adapted the items in this measure from the work of Anderson, Lodish, and Weitz (1987). The scale was pretested and revised on the basis of a series of personal interviews with 12 computer dealers.

SAMPLES: Mohr and Sohi (1995) sampled members of the Association of Better Computer Dealers, a national industry trade association, and supplemented this list with a random sample of outlets from a major computer franchiser. Of the 557 surveys distributed, **125** usable surveys were returned.

RELIABILITY: Mohr and Sohi (1995) reported a coefficient alpha of **.86** for this measure.

VALIDITY: Mohr and Sohi (1995) stated that a confirmatory factor analysis successfully demonstrated the unidimensionality and convergent and discriminatory validity of the measure.

ADMINISTRATION: The measure was included by Mohr and Sohi (1995) as part of a self-administered questionnaire that was delivered by mail. Nonrespondents received a reminder letter. Each dealer was asked to respond to the questionnaire with respect to a randomly assigned focal manufacturer. Lower scores on the scale reflected greater formality in the communication flow between manufacturer and dealer.

MAJOR FINDINGS: Mohr and Sohi (1995) investigated the relationship between information-sharing norms, quality and satisfaction with communication, dealers' distortion and withholding of information, and the three communication flows of frequency, bidirectionality, and formality. **Formality of communication flows** was found to have an inhibiting effect on the distortion and withholding of information by dealers but was not significantly related to perceptions of communication quality.

REFERENCES:

Anderson, Erin, Leonard Lodish and Barton Weitz (1987), "Resource Allocation Behavior in Conventional Channels," *JMR*, 22 (Fall), 77–82.

Mohr, Jakki J. and Ravipreet S. Sohi (1995), "Communication Flows in Distribution Channels: Impact on Assessments of Communication Quality and Satisfaction," *JR*, 71 (4), 393–416.

SCALE ITEMS:

Strongly   Strongly
agree   disagree

1—————2—————3—————4—————5

1. In coordinating our activities with this manufacturer, formal communication channels are followed (i.e., channels that are regularized, structured modes versus casual, informal, word-of-mouth modes).

2. The terms of our relationship have been written down in detail.

3. The manufacturer's expectations of us are communicated in detail.

4. The terms of our relationship have been explicitly verbalized and discussed.

SCALE NAME: Formalization (New Product Decisions)

SCALE DESCRIPTION: Ayers, Dahlstrom, and Skinner (1997) used this four-item, seven-point Likert-type scale to measure the extent to which management explicitly defined the role responsibilities of individuals involved in the new product development (NPD) process.

SCALE ORIGIN: Ayers, Dahlstrom, and Skinner (1997) indicated that the scale was adapted from a measure used in research by John and Martin (1984).

SAMPLES: Ayers, Dahlstrom, and Skinner (1997) collected data on 19 NPD projects undertaken by a major U.S. computer manufacturer. Seven project members from each NPD team were selected to participate in the study. Five of them were R&D, and the remaining two were from marketing. Of the 132 questionnaire booklets distributed, **115** usable surveys were returned.

RELIABILITY: Ayers, Dahlstrom, and Skinner (1997) reported a coefficient alpha of **.85** for the scale.

VALIDITY: An exploratory factor analysis on all items that composed the scales was used to verify the unidimensionality of the measures. No items were dropped on the basis of item-to-total correlations or an analysis of the factor structure. Ayers, Dahlstrom, and Skinner (1997) next subjected the measures to a confirmatory factor analysis to assess their construct validity. Again, no items were deleted on the basis of this analysis. The discriminant validity of the measures was also assessed using confirmatory factory analysis and was found to be acceptable.

ADMINISTRATION: Ayers, Dahlstrom, and Skinner (1997) included the scale with other measures as part of a self-administered questionnaire booklet that was apparently distributed to respondents at their place of employment. A cover letter explaining the study purpose and promises of anonymity accompanied the survey. The questionnaires distributed to R&D and marketing personnel were identical except that R&D personnel responded to questions about their relationship with marketing, and vice versa. Divisional managers designated the project for which responses were sought. Higher scores on the scale indicated that employees involved in the NPD process had clearly defined roles and responsibilities.

MAJOR FINDINGS: Ayers, Dahlstrom, and Skinner (1997) examined the influence of integration between marketing and R&D, managerial controls, and relational norms on new product success. Structural equation modeling was used to test the hypotheses. **Formalization** was found to enhance the level of integration between marketing and R&D but did not influence the levels of either relational norms or perceived relationship effectiveness between R&D and marketing.

REFERENCES:
Ayers, Doug, Robert Dahlstrom, and Steven J. Skinner (1997), "An Exploratory Investigation of Organizational Antecedents to New Product Success," *JMR*, 34 (February), 107–16.
John, George and John Martin (1984), "Effects of Organizational Structure of Marketing Planning on Credibility and Utilization of Plan Output," *JMR*, 21 (May), 170–83.

#630 *Formalization (New Product Decisions)*

SCALE ITEMS:
Please indicate your level of agreement with the following.

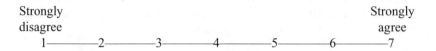

Strongly
disagree
1————2————3————4————5————6————7
Strongly
agree

1. My responsibilities were clearly defined.

2. My role in the company was clearly defined.

3. Management clearly outlined those areas for which I was responsible.

4. I did not know my role in the organization. **(r)**

SCALE NAME: Formalization (Planning Process)

SCALE DESCRIPTION: This four-item, seven-point Likert-type scale measures the degree of emphasis organizations place on rules and procedures when developing marketing plans. In their article, Andrews and Smith (1996) refer to the scale as *planning process formalization*.

SCALE ORIGIN: Andrews and Smith (1996) noted that the scale is derived from John and Martin's (1984) work on organizational structure and marketing planning.

SAMPLES: The American Marketing Association membership directory and a purchased mailing list provided Andrews and Smith (1996) with the sampling frame for surveying consumer goods product managers. One –hundred ninety-three completed questionnaires were returned for a 33.4% response rate. No significant differences in responses to key variables existed between mailing lists or between early and late respondents. Because only those respondents with a substantial impact on ideas in the marketing program were desired, 25 respondents were eliminated on the basis of a screening question, yielding a final sample size of **168**.

RELIABILITY: Andrews and Smith (1996) reported a coefficient alpha of **.78** for this measure.

VALIDITY: No specific examination of the scale's validity was reported by Andrews and Smith (1996).

ADMINISTRATION: The scale was part of a self-administered mail survey in which Andrews and Smith (1996) instructed product managers to answer questions in the context of a single product with which they had been highly involved during their most recent marketing program. Higher scores on the scale indicated higher levels of formalization in the marketing planning process through rules and established procedures.

MAJOR FINDINGS: Andrews and Smith (1996) investigated the effect of individual product manager and situational/planning process characteristics on marketing program creativity. Marketing program creativity was found to be greatest under moderate levels of **planning process formalization**.

REFERENCES:
Andrews, Jonlee and Daniel C. Smith (1996), "In Search of the Marketing Imagination: Factors Affecting the Creativity of Marketing Programs for Mature Products," *JMR*, 33 (May), 174–87.
John, George and John Martin (1984), "Effects of Organizational Structure of Marketing Planning on Credibility and Utilization of Plan Output," *JMR*, 21 (May), 170–83.

SCALE ITEMS:

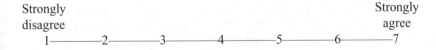

Strongly   Strongly
disagree   agree
1———2———3———4———5———6———7

1. In my company, marketing plans have a specific format that is used by everyone.

2. We have clearly defined procedures for completing each section of the marketing program.

3. We are told exactly which information sources must be used to develop the marketing plan.

4. We have a precise timetable for completing marketing plans.

SCALE NAME: Formalization (Sales Force)

SCALE DESCRIPTION: Sohi, Smith, and Ford (1996) describe this five-item, five-point Likert-type scale as measuring the degree to which selling practices and communications between the sales force and marketing department are governed by formally prescribed policies and procedures.

SCALE ORIGIN: Sohi, Smith, and Ford (1996) reported that these items were adapted from the scale used by Hage and Aiken (1969).

SAMPLES: A sample of **30** salespeople from a major midwestern corporation was used to pretest the questionnaire. In the main sample, 1650 salespeople employed by manufacturing firms in standard industrial classification codes 20–39 were randomly selected from a commercial mailing list to serve as the sampling frame. Of the 1542 questionnaires delivered to valid addresses, **230** completed surveys were returned for a response rate of 14.9%. Respondents were predominately college educated (84%), married (84%) men (89%), with a median age of 37.5 years, who had held their current sales position an average of 5.8 years. Industries represented included food products, pharmaceuticals, chemical and allied products, rubber and plastic products, electronics and computers, appliances, and audio-visual products. Sohi, Smith, and Ford (1996) reported that nonresponse bias was tested by comparing early and late responders on key variables. No significant differences were found, which suggests that nonresponse bias may not have been a problem.

RELIABILITY: Sohi, Smith, and Ford (1996) reported a coefficient alpha of **.70** for this measure.

VALIDITY: Evidence of discriminant validity was provided by a nested model confirmatory factor analysis that demonstrated that the latent–trait correlations between constructs significantly differed from 1. Sohi, Smith, and Ford (1996) stated that confirmatory factor analysis also provided satisfactory evidence of the unidimensionality of the measure.

ADMINISTRATION: Prior to data collection, the questionnaire was pretested on a small sample of salespeople. Sohi, Smith, and Ford (1996) stated that several items and the questionnaire format were revised on the basis of the pretest results. In the final study, the measure was part of a self-administered mail survey. Cover letters and postage-paid reply envelopes accompanied each questionnaire, and a copy of the survey results was offered as an incentive to participate. Reminder letters were sent three and five weeks after the initial questionnaire mailing. Higher scores on the formalization scale indicated a greater prevalence of rules, policies, and procedures governing the work activities of salespeople and communication between the sales force and marketing department.

MAJOR FINDINGS: Sohi, Smith, and Ford (1996) investigated how salespeople's role perceptions, satisfaction, and performance were affected when the sales force is shared across multiple divisions within a company. Results indicated that, as **formalization** increases, the corresponding increase in role ambiguity and role conflict, which otherwise would occur when a sales force is shared across divisions, declines. Similarly, the negative impact on work satisfaction that is experienced when sales forces are shared across divisions was lessened when **formalization** increased.

REFERENCES:

Hage, Jerald and Michael Aiken (1969), "Routine Technology, Social Structure and Organizational Goals," *Administrative Science Quarterly*, 14 (September), 366–76.

Sohi, Ravipreet S., Daniel C. Smith, and Neil M. Ford (1996), "How Does Sharing a Sales Force Between Multiple Divisions Affect Salespeople?" *JAMS*, 24 (3), 195–207.

SCALE ITEMS:

Strongly   Strongly
disagree   agree
  1—————2—————3—————4—————5

1. There are formal channels of communication between the marketing and sales departments.

2. Going though proper channels for getting the job done is constantly stressed.

3. Everyone within the organization follows strict operational procedures at all times.

4. Members of the marketing department normally go through my supervisor in case they need to tell me something.

5. Our organization operates in a very informal way when it comes to getting things done. **(r)**

SCALE NAME: Formalization (Supplier Relationship)

SCALE DESCRIPTION: Dahlstrom, McNeilly, and Speh (1996) describe this three-item, five-point Likert-type scale as measuring the extent to which a supplier follows procedures outlined by the user.

SCALE ORIGIN: Dahlstrom, McNeilly, and Speh (1996) reported that the scale was adapted from Spekman and Stern (1979) and Dwyer and Welsh (1985). The questionnaire containing the scale was pretested by six members of the Warehouse Education and Research Council, who evaluated it for content, readability, and relevance to the industry.

SAMPLES: Using a sampling frame generated from the membership of the Warehouse Education and Research Council, Dahlstrom, McNeilly, and Speh (1996) surveyed 1000 manufacturer, retailer, and wholesaler members. No mention of the specific sampling technique used to generate the frame was provided. Firms who exclusively used in-house warehousing services were not part of the population of interest and were asked to return the survey without answering. Including the unanswered surveys, 383 questionnaires were returned for a 38.3% response rate. Of these, **189** surveys contained complete data from firms using interfirm warehousing services.

RELIABILITY: Dahlstrom, McNeilly, and Speh (1996) reported a coefficient alpha of **.73** for this measure.

VALIDITY: Item-to-total correlations estimated by an exploratory factor analysis were used in the first stage of measure purification. Dahlstrom, McNeilly, and Speh (1996) submitted the remaining items to a confirmatory factor analysis. Two items were eliminated, though the resulting root mean residual of the trimmed confirmatory factor analysis model was not significant (.06). Discriminant validity was also assessed and found to be acceptable.

ADMINISTRATION: Dahlstrom, McNeilly, and Speh (1996) stated that the scale was part of a self-administered questionnaire that was returned by mail. Sampled individuals were contacted by telephone prior to survey delivery, and a postage-paid, return addressed reply envelope accompanied the questionnaire. A follow-up mailing with a second survey was sent two weeks after the first. Individuals using in-house warehousing services were asked not to complete the survey, but eligible respondents were instructed to answer in the context of the third-party warehouse service provider with whom they spent the greatest portion of their warehousing budget. Higher scores on the formalization scale indicated that suppliers more closely followed instructions and operating procedures as defined by the user.

MAJOR FINDINGS: Dahlstrom, McNeilly, and Speh (1996) investigated various antecedents to alternative forms of governance in the logistical supply market. A second topic of investigation addressed how formal controls and relational norms were employed by alternative governance forms to yield performance. Results of path analysis indicated that **formalization** increased performance, flexibility, and solidarity in the market-based exchange governance mode. **Formalization** enhanced performance, solidarity, flexibility, and information exchange in short-term unilateral agreements, whereas performance, solidarity, and information exchange were influenced in the long-term unilateral agreement governance mode. Only information exchange was enhanced by **formalization** in the bilateral alliance governance mode.

REFERENCES:
Dahlstrom, Robert, Kevin M. McNeilly, and Thomas W. Speh (1996), "Buyer-Seller Relationships in the Procurement of Logistical Services," *JAMS*, 24 (2), 110–24.

Dwyer, F. Robert and M. Ann Welsh (1985), "Environmental Relationships on the Internal Political Economy of Marketing Channels," *JMR*, 22 (November), 397–414.

Spekman, Robert E. and Louis W. Stern (1979), "Environmental Uncertainty and Buying Group Structure: An Empirical Investigation," *JM*, 43 (Spring), 56–64.

SCALE ITEMS:

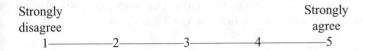

Strongly   Strongly

disagree   agree

1————2————3————4————5

Please indicate your level of agreement with the following:

The vendor:

1. Follows our previously written and verbal instructions.

2. Has responsibilities clearly specified by us.

3. Follows strict operating procedures defined by us.

SCALE NAME: Frequency of Contact with Salesperson

SCALE DESCRIPTION: Doney and Cannon (1997) used this three-item, seven-point Likert-type scale to measure the extent to which a buyer believes a salesperson maintains frequent contact for business or social purposes.

SCALE ORIGIN: Doney and Cannon (1997) stated that they generated items for the scale on the basis of interviews with marketing and purchasing personnel. Exploratory factor analyses using both orthogonal and oblique rotations were used to ensure high item loadings on hypothesized constructs and low cross-loadings.

SAMPLES: Doney and Cannon (1997) sampled 657 members of the National Association of Purchasing Management who were employed by firms involved in industrial manufacturing, as classified by standard industrial classification codes 33–37. **Two hundred ten** completed questionnaires were returned from a primarily male (76%) sample with an average of 15 years of purchasing experience.

RELIABILITY: Doney and Cannon (1997) calculated a coefficient alpha of **.85** for this measure.

VALIDITY: Doney and Cannon (1997) reported using three methods to test the discriminant validity of the scales, which represented the combined dimensions of trust of the salesperson and its proposed antecedents and outcomes. Each method provided strong evidence of discriminant validity. Two LISREL-based tests were also used to provide evidence for the convergent validity of the measures.

ADMINISTRATION: The scale was included with other measures as part of a self-administered survey that was delivered by mail. Nonrespondents received a postcard reminder followed by a second questionnaire a week later. Doney and Cannon (1997) instructed respondents to focus on a single, specific, recent purchase decision in which more than one supplier was seriously considered and to indicate on the survey (using initials) two of the firms considered. After answering questions pertaining to the purchase situation, half of the respondents were instructed to complete the remainder of the questionnaire in the context of the first supplier they had listed, whereas the other half were instructed to use the second supplier. Higher scores on the scale indicated a greater frequency of contact with the focal salesperson.

MAJOR FINDINGS: Doney and Cannon (1997) investigated the impact of purchasing agents' trust in the salesperson and the supplier firm on a buying firm's current supplier choice and future buying intentions. **Frequency of business contact** positively influenced the buying firm's trust in the salesperson.

REFERENCES:
Doney, Patricia M. and Joseph P. Cannon (1997), "An Examination of the Nature of Trust in Buyer-Seller Relationships," *JM*, 61 (April), 35–51.

SCALE ITEMS:

Strongly   Strongly
disagree   agree

1. This salesperson frequently visits our place of business.

2. This salesperson takes a lot of time learning our needs.

3. This salesperson spends considerable time getting to know our people.

SCALE NAME: Good Ethics Is Good Business

SCALE DESCRIPTION: Singhapakdi and colleagues (1995) used this seven-item, nine-point Likert-type scale to measure the importance of ethics and social responsibility in relationship to the survival of the firm, long-term profitability, and organizational competitiveness.

SCALE ORIGIN: Singhapakdi and colleagues (1995) credited Kraft and Jauch's (1992) organizational effectiveness menu with providing the foundation for the scale's development. The organizational effectiveness menu measures five categories of firm performance, including ethics and social responsibility. Sixteen items identified by Kraft and Jauch (1992) as relating ethics and social responsibility to different aspects of organizational effectiveness were adapted by Singhapakdi and colleagues (1995) for the purpose of measuring respondents' perceptions of the relative importance of ethics and social responsibility (PRESOR). An exploratory factor analysis using Varimax rotation resulted in fourteen items loading on three factors with an eigenvalue greater than 1. "Good Ethics Is Good Business" was the name given to the seven-item factor that explained 30.2% of the variance.

SAMPLES: Singhapakdi and colleagues (1995) sent a mail questionnaire to a randomly drawn sample of 2000 professionals selected from the American Marketing Association mailing list. Of the 1995 that were delivered, **442** usable questionnaires were returned. Key demographics of the sample indicated that the majority of respondents were college-educated (92.8%), male (51.4%), middle managers working in various industries.

RELIABILITY: Singhapakdi and colleagues (1995) reported a coefficient alpha of **.72** for this scale.

VALIDITY: Singhapakdi and colleagues (1995) deleted items with factor loadings of less than .40 or items loading at .40 on more than one factor. No examination of scale validity was reported.

ADMINISTRATION: Singhapakdi and colleagues (1995) indicated that the measure was included as part of a self-administered mail survey. Higher scores indicated stronger perceptions that ethical and socially responsible behavior had a positive impact on long-term profitability, organizational competitiveness, and the survival of the firm.

MAJOR FINDINGS: Singhapakdi and colleagues (1995) investigated marketing practitioners' perceptions of the importance of ethics and social responsibility in achieving organizational effectiveness and how these perceptions were influenced by corporate ethical values and an individual's personal moral philosophy. Univariate tests were employed to demonstrate that respondents perceived the **good ethics is good business** mean (7.73) to be significantly greater than a neutral value of 5, which indicated that respondents generally believed ethics and social responsibility to be at least somewhat important in achieving organizational effectiveness. An ordinary least squared regression analysis also demonstrated that the **good ethics is good business** factor of PRESOR was positively influenced by corporate ethical values and idealism and negatively influenced by relativism.

REFERENCES:

Kraft, Kenneth L. and Lawrence R. Jauch (1992), "The Organizational Effectiveness Menu: A Device for Stakeholder Assessment," *Mid-American Journal of Business*, 7-1 (Spring), 18–23.

Singhapakdi, Anusorn, Kenneth L. Kraft, Scott J. Vitell, and Kumar C. Rallapalli (1995), "The Perceived Importance of Ethics and Social Responsibility on Organizational Effectiveness: A Survey of Marketers," *JAMS*, 23 (1), 49–56.

SCALE ITEMS:

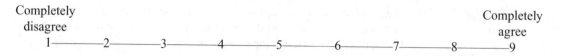

Completely disagree 1—2—3—4—5—6—7—8—9 Completely agree

1. The ethics and social responsibility of a firm is essential to its long-term profitability.

2. Business ethics and social responsibility are critical to the survival of a business enterprise.

3. The overall effectiveness of a business can be determined to a great extent by the degree to which it is ethical and socially responsible.

4. Good ethics is often good business.

5. Business has a social responsibility beyond making a profit.

6. Corporate planning and goal-setting sessions should include discussions of ethics and social responsibility.

7. Social responsibility and profitability can be compatible.

SCALE NAME: Hazard (Customer Loyalty)

SCALE DESCRIPTION: Anderson and Robertson (1995) used this five-item, seven-point Likert-type scale to measure a broker's perception that introducing customers to house brands can reduce the value of the broker's advice and the loyalty of the customer.

SCALE ORIGIN: Anderson and Robertson (1995) developed the measure used in this study. A detailed construct description was constructed on the basis of a though review of the trade and academic literature. Multiple interviews with brokers, sales managers, and trade association officials were used to generate scale items believed to tap the construct. These items were administered to 208 brokers and factor analyzed to test for unidimensionality. Reliability assessments were also used to purify the measure. The authors noted that the term "proprietary products" is standard industry terminology and therefore appropriate for this measure.

SAMPLES: Anderson and Robertson (1995) mailed a questionnaire to the homes of 420 brokers whose names were supplied by cooperating firms, and **201** usable responses were obtained. To be evaluated, some hypotheses required the use of archival data as to the actual sales of house brands made by salespeople. One firm, which provided **150** of the respondents in this study, agreed to provide this information. Anderson and Robertson (1995) stated that the respondent demographics closely matched those achieved in a large-scale survey of readers conducted by a nationally distributed trade magazine.

RELIABILITY: Anderson and Robertson (1995) reported a coefficient alpha of **.77** for this measure.

VALIDITY: No specific examination of scale validity was reported Anderson and Robertson (1995).

ADMINISTRATION: Anderson and Robertson (1995) included the measure as part of a larger self-administered mail questionnaire. A summary of the results was offered in exchange for respondent cooperation. Higher scores on the scale indicated that salespeople were more fearful that selling house brands would reduce the value of their advice and the loyalty of the customer.

MAJOR FINDINGS: Anderson and Robertson (1995) investigated the relationship between factors believed to influence the sale of house brands by multiline salespeople. Results of analysis using the full sample indicated that the perception of a **customer loyalty hazard** increased with exposure to external information sources and decreased with training, manager attention, and career success. Finally, using the 150-member sample, analysis revealed that the perception of a **customer loyalty hazard** reduced the adoption of house brands.

REFERENCES:
Anderson, Erin and Thomas S. Robertson (1995), "Inducing Multiline Salespeople to Adopt House Brands," *JM*, 59 (April), 16–31.

SCALE ITEMS:

Strongly disagree   Strongly agree

1———2———3———4———5———6———7

1. Brokers who sell proprietary products lose their customers' loyalty.

2. Customers who buy proprietary products don't care who their broker is.

3. Proprietary products keep my customers coming back to me. **(r)**

4. I like proprietary products because they make my customers think more highly of my advice.

5. The more proprietary products I sell, the better my grip on my customers.

SCALE NAME: Hazard (Job Mobility)

SCALE DESCRIPTION: Anderson and Robertson (1995) used this three-item, seven-point Likert-type scale to measure a broker's perception that selling house brands creates exit barriers that prevent the broker from switching jobs.

SCALE ORIGIN: Anderson and Robertson (1995) developed the measure used in this study. A detailed construct description was constructed on the basis of a though review of the trade and academic literature. Multiple interviews with brokers, sales managers, and trade association officials were used to generate scale items thought to tap the construct. These items were administered to 208 brokers and factor analyzed to test for unidimensionality. Reliability assessments were also used to purify the measure. Anderson and Robertson (1995) noted that the term "proprietary products" is standard industry terminology and therefore appropriate for this measure.

SAMPLES: Anderson and Robertson (1995) mailed a questionnaire to the homes of 420 brokers whose names were supplied by cooperating firms, and **201** usable responses were obtained. To be evaluated, some hypotheses required the use of archival data as to the actual sales of house brands made by salespeople. One firm, which provided **150** of the respondents in this study, agreed to provide this information. Anderson and Robertson (1995) stated that the respondent demographics closely matched those achieved in a large-scale survey of readers conducted by a nationally distributed trade magazine.

RELIABILITY: Anderson and Robertson (1995) reported a coefficient alpha of **.72** for this measure.

VALIDITY: No specific examination of scale validity was reported Anderson and Robertson (1995).

ADMINISTRATION: Anderson and Robertson (1995) included the measure as part of a larger self-administered mail questionnaire. A summary of the results was offered in exchange for respondent cooperation. Higher scores on the scale indicated stronger perceptions that selling house brands created exit barriers that may trap the broker into working for the same firm.

MAJOR FINDINGS: Anderson and Robertson (1995) investigated the relationship between factors believed to influence the sale of house brands by multiline salespeople. Results of analysis using the full sample indicated that the perception of a **mobility hazard** increased with exposure to external information sources and decreased with manager attention. Lower perceptions of **mobility hazard** were demonstrated by salespeople with greater experience and career success, contrary to predictions.

REFERENCES:
Anderson, Erin and Thomas S. Robertson (1995), "Inducing Multiline Salespeople to Adopt House Brands," *JM*, 59 (April), 16–31.

SCALE ITEMS:

Strongly   Strongly
disagree   agree

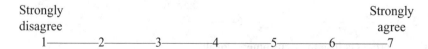

1————2————3————4————5————6————7

1. Proprietary products lock you in to your current employer.

2. Selling proprietary products is all right as long as you never want to change jobs.

3. If you have to change jobs, your clients are less likely to follow you if you sold them proprietary products.

SCALE NAME: Identification (Relative Functional)

SCALE DESCRIPTION: Fisher, Maltz, and Jaworski (1997) used this four-item, five-point scale to assess the extent to which marketing managers feel a sense of connection with their functional area compared with their feelings toward the division (strategic business unit or organization) as a whole.

SCALE ORIGIN: Fisher, Maltz, and Jaworski (1997) indicated that the scale is original to their study. Preliminary scale items were pretested with six marketing managers; those found to be unclear, ambiguous, or not applicable were dropped from the measure.

SAMPLES: In Study 1, Fisher, Maltz, and Jaworski (1997) sampled 180 marketing managers employed by a *Fortune* 100 firm serving five diverse high-technology markets. The convenience sample was composed of marketing managers attending management training sessions over a three-week period; **89** usable responses were obtained. In Study 2, the authors sampled marketing managers employed by a multinational, business-to-business services firm with 36 business units in six countries outside the United States. A key informant provided a list of 100 firm members employed in a variety of marketing positions that required them to interact with engineering personnel. A total of **72** usable responses were obtained for Study 2.

RELIABILITY: Fisher, Maltz, and Jaworski (1997) reported calculating coefficient alphas for this measure of **.78** in Study 1 and **.71** in Study 2.

VALIDITY: In Study 1, confirmatory factor analyses were conducted in two stages to maintain an acceptable ratio of observations to variables. The first analysis included the original 15 items that composed the bidirectional communication, information-sharing norms, and relative functional identification measures. Fisher, Maltz, and Jaworski (1997) stated that, after two bidirectional communication items and one information sharing norm item were eliminated due to large modification indices, the revised model fit the data acceptably well. Evidence of discriminant validity was provided in that the correlation between each pair of constructs was significantly different from 1.00.

ADMINISTRATION: The measure was included with other scales in a self-administered questionnaire. For Study 1, a survey packet containing a cover letter, reply envelope, and the survey instrument was distributed to each marketing manager participant of a company-sponsored training session. Fisher, Maltz, and Jaworski (1997) used e-mail and telephone reminders to increase response rates. In Study 2, respondents received the survey packet by mail. Offers of anonymity and shared survey results were provided as incentives to participate. Nonrespondents received a reminder letter, followed by a second mail survey packet. In both studies, respondents were instructed to answer questions in the context of their relationship with a single manager in the engineering function with whom they interacted regularly. Higher scores on the measure indicated that respondents perceived a greater sense of connection with the marketing function compared with their feelings toward the division (strategic business unit or organization) as a whole.

MAJOR FINDINGS: Fisher, Maltz, and Jaworski (1997) investigated how **relative functional identification (RFI),** or the strength of marketing managers' psychological connection to their functional area compared with the firm as a whole, influenced different strategies for improving communication between marketers and engineers. In Study 1, **RFI** positively influenced the frequency of communication between parties and negatively influenced the coerciveness of influence attempts. In Study 2, **RFI** again was found to positively influence the frequency of communication between parties but was not significantly related to the coerciveness of influence attempts. The effect of integrated goals on communication frequency, bidirectionality, and coercive influence attempts was found to be stronger for low-**RFI** managers than for high-**RFI** managers in both studies. In addition, the effect of information-sharing norms on bidirectionality was found to be stronger for low-**RFI** managers than for high-**RFI** managers in both studies.

COMMENTS: Although no instructions for this scale were provided by Fisher, Maltz, and Jaworski (1997), the unusual nature of the item phrasing and response format suggests that respondent instructions would be beneficial.

REFERENCES:

Fisher, Robert J., Elliot Maltz, and Bernard J. Jaworski (1997), "Enhancing Communication Between Marketing and Engineering: The Moderating Role of Relative Functional Identification," *JM*, 61 (July), 54–70.

SCALE ITEMS:

Division   Marketing
    1————————2————————3————————4————————5

1. First and foremost, I think of myself as a _____ person.

2. If I had to make a choice between doing what was best for the marketing function or the division, I would do what was best for _____.

3. Being a _____ person is "part of who I am."

4. It's important to me that I am part of the _____.

SCALE NAME: Indebtedness (Toward Salesperson)

SCALE DESCRIPTION: Dorsch and Kelley (1994) describe this five-item, six-point Likert-type scale as measuring purchasing executives' feelings of obligation to repay vendors who have provided them with gifts. Although used here in a purchasing context, the scale *item* phrasing is not specific to purchasing or sales and could easily be adapted to new experimental scenarios in which perceptions of indebtedness represent the dependent variable of interest. Dorsch and Kelley (1994) refer to the scale in their article as "perceived indebtedness toward salesperson."

SCALE ORIGIN: The scale is original to Dorsch and Kelley (1994), who stated that the measure was developed in accordance with procedures suggested by Churchill (1979) and Nunnally (1978). No other details of the scale development process were provided.

SAMPLES: Dorsch and Kelley (1994) sampled 1197 U.S. purchasing executives representing the ten major standard industrial classification divisions using a single questionnaire mailing. Because of mailing list restrictions, no prior notification, follow-up survey, or reminders were sent. A total of **151** usable questionnaires were received for a response rate of 12.6%. Sample respondents were predominately men (84.8%), located in the Midwest (55.2%), and employed by manufacturing firms (73.5%).

RELIABILITY: Dorsch and Kelley (1994) reported a coefficient alpha of **.90** for this measure.

VALIDITY: No specific examination of the scale's development process or validity was reported by Dorsch and Kelley (1994).

ADMINISTRATION: Dorsch and Kelley (1994) randomly assigned purchasing executives to a 3 (status of relationship) × 2 (cost of gift) × 2 (type of gift) full-factorial, between-subject research design. On the basis of their cell assignment, respondents were given a hypothetical scenario to read describing their relationship status with a vendor and the nature of the gift provided by that vendor. The scale was part of a self-administered mail survey in which questions related to the measures of interest were answered after respondents had read the scenario. Higher scores on the scale indicated stronger perceptions of indebtedness toward the salesperson in relationship to the gift received.

MAJOR FINDINGS: Dorsch and Kelley (1994) investigated the effect of buyer–vendor relationship status (no prior relationship, moderate relationship, and strong relationship), gift type (corporate versus personal), and gift cost (inexpensive versus expensive) on purchasing executives' perceptions of salesperson manipulation, feelings of indebtedness toward the sales representative, and their intention to reciprocate vendor gifts. Stronger feelings of **indebtedness toward the salesperson** were found to have a positive relationship with purchasing executives' intentions to reciprocate. Feelings of **indebtedness toward the salesperson** were stronger when gifts were expensive and of benefit to the corporation than when they were inexpensive and personally beneficial to the purchasing executive. As levels of perceived manipulation on the part of the salesperson increased, purchasing executives' feelings of **indebtedness toward the salesperson** declined.

REFERENCES:

Churchill, Gilbert A. (1979), "A Paradigm for Developing Better Measures of Marketing Constructs," *JMR*, 16 (February), 323–32.

Dorsch, Michael J. and Scott W. Kelley (1994), "An Investigation into the Intentions of Purchasing Executives to Reciprocate Vendor Gifts," *JAMS*, 22 (4), 315–27.

Nunnally, Jum C. (1978), *Psychometric Theory*, 2d. ed. New York: McGraw-Hill.

#639 *Indebtedness (Toward Salesperson)*

SCALE ITEMS:
Prior to responding to the scale items, respondents read a scenario explaining the specific gift character-istic scenario and percentage of the previous year's business that they had hypothetically conducted with the vendor. See Dorsch and Kelley (1994) for details on the experimental manipulations.

Strongly   Strongly
disagree   agree
  1———2———3———4———5———6

1. I have a strong sense of personal duty to repay the favor received from Chris. **(r)**

2. It is very important for me to repay the favor received from Chris.

3. I expect to repay the favor received from Chris.

4. I have a strong sense of professional duty to repay the favor received from Chris.

5. I have a strong sense of duty to repay the favor received from Chris.

SCALE NAME: Influence Strategy (Information Exchange)

SCALE DESCRIPTION: Venkatesh, Kohli, and Zaltman (1995) used this three-item, five-point scale to measure the extent to which purchasing agents perceived that another buying center committee member attempted to influence the group decision with a through examination of various options, an analysis of the effect of the decision on the big picture, and a nondirective discussion of the issues.

SCALE ORIGIN: Venkatesh, Kohli, and Zaltman (1995) indicated that the items representing this construct were adapted from Boyle and colleagues' (1992) and Frazier and Summers's (1984, 1986) studies.

SAMPLES: Venkatesh, Kohli, and Zaltman (1995) distributed a mail survey to an effective sample of 461 purchasing agents drawn from the membership list of the National Association of Purchasing Management. A total of **187** usable responses were obtained.

RELIABILITY: A coefficient alpha of **.47** was reported by Venkatesh, Kohli, and Zaltman (1995). Two items from the original scale, "focused on general strategies (as opposed to specific tactics) for making our business more profitable" and "appeared to underemphasize information that could have led the committee to a different decision," were dropped from the original five-item scale to improve the internal consistency of the measure.

VALIDITY: No specific examination of scale validity was reported by Venkatesh, Kohli, and Zaltman (1995).

ADMINISTRATION: The measure was included by Venkatesh, Kohli, and Zaltman (1995) as part of a self-administered questionnaire that was delivered by mail. Nonrespondents received a personalized reminder and a second copy of the questionnaire approximately 10 days after the first mailing. Respondents were asked to answer in the context of a joint purchase decision with which they were familiar and for which no purchase options were an obvious choice to members of the decision-making unit. Informants were then instructed to rate the power, influence strategies, and actual influences of a particular committee member (excluding him- or herself). Half the sample were directed to select a committee member with *less* impact than others on the decision, whereas the other half were instructed to select someone who had *more* impact. Higher scores on the scale reflected the use of a noncoercive influence strategy in which the evaluated committee member was perceived as attempting to influence the group through discussion of the issues and analysis of the decision's impact on the big picture.

MAJOR FINDINGS: Venkatesh, Kohli, and Zaltman (1995) investigated the pervasiveness, effectiveness, and antecedents to six influence strategies commonly observed in decision-making units comprised of multiple individuals. The influence strategies varied according to their coercive intensity, task orientation, and instrumentality. The recommendations, **information exchange**, and requests-based influence strategies seem to be used most commonly. The legalistic plea strategy appears to be used to a moderate extent, and the promise and threat based influence strategies seem to be used the least. A person's information power was positively related to the use of an **information exchange influence strategy**. **Information exchange influence strategies** were found to lack effectiveness; results of regression analysis indicated a nonsignficant relationship between the **information exchange influence strategy** and manifest influence.

COMMENTS: The low reliability of the scale suggests that further development and improvement is needed prior to using this measure again.

REFERENCES:

Boyle, Brett, F. Robert Dwyer, Robert A. Robicheaux, and James T. Simpson (1992), "Influence Strategies in Marketing Channels: Measures and Use in Different Relationship Structures," *JMR*, 48 (November), 462–73.

Frazier, Gary and John Summers (1984), "Interfirm Influence Strategies and Their Application Within Distribution Channels," *JMR*, 48 (Summer), 43–55.

———— and ———— (1986), "Perceptions of Interfirm Power and its Use Within a Franchise Channel of Distribution," *JMR*, 23 (May), 167–76.

Venkatesh, R., Ajay K. Kohli, and Gerald Zaltman (1995), "Influence Strategies in Buying Centers," *JM*, 59 (October), 71–82.

SCALE ITEMS:

Never   Always

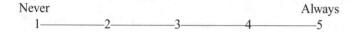

1. Discussed the issues without making specific statements about what s/he would like others to do.

2. Attempted influence the committee by presenting information related to the various options.

3. Attempted to change our perspective by looking at how our decisions affect the big picture.

SCALE NAME: Influence Strategy (Legalistic Pleas)

SCALE DESCRIPTION: Venkatesh, Kohli, and Zaltman (1995) used this six-item, five-point scale to measure the extent to which purchasing agents perceived that another buying center committee member attempted to influence the group decision by citing legalistic, contractual, or information agreements that either required or suggested the performance of a certain action, such as compliance with his or her point of view.

SCALE ORIGIN: Venkatesh, Kohli, and Zaltman (1995) indicated that the items representing this construct were adapted from Boyle and colleagues' (1992) and Frazier and Summers's (1984, 1986) studies.

SAMPLES: Venkatesh, Kohli, and Zaltman (1995) distributed a mail survey to an effective sample of 461 purchasing agents drawn from the membership list of the National Association of Purchasing Management. A total of **187** usable responses were obtained.

RELIABILITY: A coefficient alpha of **.79** was reported by Venkatesh, Kohli, and Zaltman (1995).

VALIDITY: No specific examination of scale validity was reported by Venkatesh, Kohli, and Zaltman (1995).

ADMINISTRATION: The measure was included by Venkatesh, Kohli, and Zaltman (1995) as part of a self-administered questionnaire that was delivered by mail. Nonrespondents received a personalized reminder and a second copy of the questionnaire approximately 10 days after the first mailing. Respondents were asked to answer in the context of a joint purchase decision with which they were familiar and for which no purchase options were an obvious choice to members of the decision-making unit. Informants were then instructed to rate the power, influence strategies, and actual influences of a particular committee member (excluding him- or herself). Half the sample were directed to select a committee member with *less* impact than others on the decision, whereas the other half were instructed to select someone who had *more* impact. Higher scores on the scale reflected the use of a hard coercive influence strategy in which the evaluated committee member was perceived as attempting to influence the group through citations of policies, procedures, contracts, and other agreements that suggested the performance of a certain action.

MAJOR FINDINGS: Venkatesh, Kohli, and Zaltman (1995) investigated the pervasiveness, effectiveness, and antecedents to six influence strategies commonly observed in decision-making units comprised of multiple individuals. The influence strategies varied according to their coercive intensity, task orientation, and instrumentality. The recommendations, information exchange, and requests-based influence strategies seem to be used most commonly. The **legalistic plea** strategy appears to be used to a moderate extent, and the promises and threat-based influence strategies seem to be used the least. A person's referent power was negatively related to the use of a **legalistic plea strategy**, whereas legitimate power was positively related. The greater the group's viscidity (team spirit and cohesiveness), the less likely was the usage of a **legalistic plea strategy**. However, use of a **legalistic plea influence strategy** was found to be very ineffective, because results of regression analysis indicated a significant negative relationship between the **legalistic plea influence strategy** and manifest influence.

REFERENCES:

Boyle, Brett, F. Robert Dwyer, Robert A. Robicheaux, and James T. Simpson (1992), "Influence Strategies in Marketing Channels: Measures and Use in Different Relationship Structures," *JMR*, 48 (November), 462–73.

#641 *Influence Strategy (Legalistic Pleas)*

Frazier, Gary and John Summers (1984), "Interfirm Influence Strategies and Their Application Within Distribution Channels," *JMR*, 48 (Summer), 43–55.

———— and ———— (1986), "Perceptions of Interfirm Power and its Use Within a Franchise Channel of Distribution," *JMR*, 23 (May), 167–76.

Venkatesh, R., Ajay K. Kohli, and Gerald Zaltman (1995), "Influence Strategies in Buying Centers," *JM*, 59 (October), 71–82.

SCALE ITEMS:

Never   Always

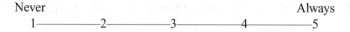

1————————2————————3————————4————————5

1. Made a point to refer to his or her legitimate right to gain our compliance on a particular issue.

2. "Reminded us" of our obligations stipulated in our company's rules and procedures.

3. Used sections of company rules and policies as a "tool" to get us to agree to his or her demand(s).

4. Made biased interpretations of company rules in order to gain our cooperation in following his or her view(s).

5. Made a point to refer to company policies when attempting to influence our actions.

6. Indicated that s/he expected others to comply with him or her because of his or her job position.

SCALE NAME: Influence Strategy (Promises)

SCALE DESCRIPTION: Venkatesh, Kohli, and Zaltman (1995) used this six-item, five-point scale to measure the extent to which purchasing agents perceived that another buying center committee member attempted to influence the group decision with promises of specific rewards that were contingent on compliance with his or her stated desires.

SCALE ORIGIN: Venkatesh, Kohli, and Zaltman (1995) indicated that the items representing this construct were adapted from Boyle and colleagues' (1992) and Frazier and Summers's (1984, 1986) studies.

SAMPLES: Venkatesh, Kohli, and Zaltman (1995) distributed a mail survey to an effective sample of 461 purchasing agents drawn from the membership list of the National Association of Purchasing Management. A total of **187** usable responses were obtained.

RELIABILITY: A coefficient alpha of **.78** was reported by Venkatesh, Kohli, and Zaltman (1995).

VALIDITY: No specific examination of scale validity was reported by Venkatesh, Kohli, and Zaltman (1995).

ADMINISTRATION: The measure was included by Venkatesh, Kohli, and Zaltman (1995) as part of a self-administered questionnaire that was delivered by mail. Nonrespondents received a personalized reminder and a second copy of the questionnaire approximately 10 days after the first mailing. Respondents were asked to answer in the context of a joint purchase decision with which they were familiar and for which no purchase options were an obvious choice to members of the decision making unit. Informants were then instructed to rate the power, influence strategies, and actual influences of a particular committee member (excluding him- or herself). Half the sample were directed to select a committee member with *less* impact than others on the decision, and the other half were instructed to select someone who had *more* impact. Higher scores on the scale reflected the use of a soft coercive influence strategy in which the evaluated committee member was perceived as attempting to influence the group by promising rewards to those who followed the proposed course of action.

MAJOR FINDINGS: Venkatesh, Kohli, and Zaltman (1995) investigated the pervasiveness, effectiveness, and antecedents to six influence strategies commonly observed in decision-making units comprised of multiple individuals. The influence strategies varied according to their coercive intensity, task orientation, and instrumentality. The recommendations, information exchange, and requests-based influence strategies seem to be used most commonly. The legalistic plea strategy appears to be used to a moderate extent, whereas the **promises** and threat-based influence strategies seem to be used the least. A person's reinforcement power was positively related to the use of a **promises influence strategy**. The **promises influence strategy** was found to lack effectiveness; results of regression analysis indicated a nonsignificant relationship between the **promises influence strategy** and manifest influence.

REFERENCES:
Boyle, Brett, F. Robert Dwyer, Robert A. Robicheaux, and James T. Simpson (1992), "Influence Strategies in Marketing Channels: Measures and Use in Different Relationship Structures," *JMR*, 48 (November), 462–73.

Frazier, Gary and John Summers (1984), "Interfirm Influence Strategies and Their Application Within Distribution Channels," *JMR*, 48 (Summer), 43–55.

——— and ——— (1986), "Perceptions of Interfirm Power and its Use Within a Franchise Channel of Distribution," *JMR*, 23 (May), 167–76.

#642 *Influence Strategy (Promises)*

Venkatesh, R., Ajay K. Kohli, and Gerald Zaltman (1995), "Influence Strategies in Buying Centers," *JM*, 59 (October), 71–82.

SCALE ITEMS:

Never   Always

1————2————3————4————5

1. Made promises to give something back in return for specific actions on our part.

2. Offered to provide incentives for agreeing to his or her suggestion(s).

3. Emphasized what s/he would offer in return for our cooperation during the decision making.

4. Offered specific incentives for us to change our positions on certain issues.

5. Offered benefits to us when we initially had been reluctant to cooperate.

6. Stated or implied that those who complied with him or her would be rewarded.

SCALE NAME: Influence Strategy (Recommendations)

SCALE DESCRIPTION: Venkatesh, Kohli, and Zaltman (1995) used this four-item, five-point Likert-type scale to measure the extent to which purchasing agents perceived that another buying center committee member attempted to influence the group decision by suggesting that following a specific course of action would likely prove beneficial for the organization.

SCALE ORIGIN: Venkatesh, Kohli, and Zaltman (1995) indicated that the items representing this construct were adapted from Boyle and colleagues' (1992) and Frazier and Summers's (1984, 1986) studies.

SAMPLES: Venkatesh, Kohli, and Zaltman (1995) distributed a mail survey to an effective sample of 461 purchasing agents drawn from the membership list of the National Association of Purchasing Management. A total of **187** usable responses were obtained.

RELIABILITY: A coefficient alpha of **.75** was reported by Venkatesh, Kohli, and Zaltman (1995). One item, "indicated that a better decision would be made by following his or her suggestions," was dropped from the original five-item scale to improve the internal consistency of the measure.

VALIDITY: No specific examination of scale validity was reported by Venkatesh, Kohli, and Zaltman (1995).

ADMINISTRATION: The measure was included by Venkatesh, Kohli, and Zaltman (1995) as part of a self-administered questionnaire that was delivered by mail. Nonrespondents received a personalized reminder and a second copy of the questionnaire approximately 10 days after the first mailing. Respondents were asked to answer in the context of a joint purchase decision with which they were familiar and for which no purchase options were an obvious choice to members of the decision-making unit. Informants were then instructed to rate the power, influence strategies, and actual influences of a particular committee member (excluding him- or herself). Half the sample were directed to select a committee member with *less* impact than others on the decision, whereas the other half were instructed to select someone who had *more* impact. Higher scores on the scale reflected the use of a soft coercive influence strategy in which the evaluated committee member was perceived as attempting to influence the group by indicating the benefits of following the proposed course of action.

MAJOR FINDINGS: Venkatesh, Kohli, and Zaltman (1995) investigated the pervasiveness, effectiveness, and antecedents to six influence strategies commonly observed in decision-making units comprised of multiple individuals. The influence strategies varied according to their coercive intensity, task orientation, and instrumentality. The **recommendations**, information exchange, and requests-based influence strategies seem to be used most commonly. The legalistic plea strategy appears to be used to a moderate extent, and the promise and threat-based influence strategies seem to be used the least. A person's expert power was positively related to the use of a **recommendations-oriented influence strategy.** However, a **recommendations influence strategy** was less likely to be used when group members were familiar with each other. The **recommendations influence strategy** was found to have the strongest positive effect on manifest influence, which indicates that a soft-coercive, task-oriented strategy was most effective in influencing group decision making.

REFERENCES:

Boyle, Brett, F. Robert Dwyer, Robert A. Robicheaux, and James T. Simpson (1992), "Influence Strategies in Marketing Channels: Measures and Use in Different Relationship Structures," *JMR*, 48 (November), 462–73.

#643 *Influence Strategy (Recommendations)*

Frazier, Gary and John Summers (1984), "Interfirm Influence Strategies and Their Application Within Distribution Channels," *JMR*, 48 (Summer), 43–55.

———— and ———— (1986), "Perceptions of Interfirm Power and its Use Within a Franchise Channel of Distribution," *JMR*, 23 (May), 167–76.

Venkatesh, R., Ajay K. Kohli, and Gerald Zaltman (1995), "Influence Strategies in Buying Centers," *JM*, 59 (October), 71–82.

SCALE ITEMS:

Never   Always

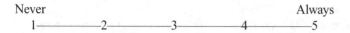

1. Made it clear that by following his or her recommendation(s), our business would benefit.

2. Made it explicit, when making a suggestion, that it was intended for the good of our operation.

3. Provided a clear picture of the anticipated positive impact on our operations his or her recommended course of action will have.

4. Outlined the logic and/or evidence for expecting success from the specific action(s) suggested by him or her.

SCALE NAME: Influence Strategy (Requests)

SCALE DESCRIPTION: Venkatesh, Kohli, and Zaltman (1995) used this four-item, five-point scale to measure the extent to which purchasing agents perceived that another buying center committee member attempted to influence the group decision by informing group members of the desired actions to be taken without mentioning or directly implying any specific consequences related to their subsequent compliance or noncompliance.

SCALE ORIGIN: Venkatesh, Kohli, and Zaltman (1995) indicated that the items representing this construct were adapted from Boyle and colleagues' (1992) and Frazier and Summers's (1984, 1986) studies.

SAMPLES: Venkatesh, Kohli, and Zaltman (1995) distributed a mail survey to an effective sample of 461 purchasing agents drawn from the membership list of the National Association of Purchasing Management. A total of **187** usable responses were obtained.

RELIABILITY: A coefficient alpha of **.50** was reported by Venkatesh, Kohli, and Zaltman (1995).

VALIDITY: Venkatesh, Kohli, and Zaltman (1995) did not specifically examine the scale's validity.

ADMINISTRATION: The measure was included by Venkatesh, Kohli, and Zaltman (1995) as part of a self-administered questionnaire that was delivered by mail. Nonrespondents received a personalized reminder and a second copy of the questionnaire approximately 10 days after the first mailing. Respondents were asked to answer in the context of a joint purchase decision with which they were familiar and for which no purchase options were an obvious choice to members of the decision-making unit. Informants were then instructed to rate the power, influence strategies, and actual influences of a particular committee member (excluding him- or herself). Half the sample were directed to select a committee member with *less* impact than others on the decision, whereas the other half were instructed to select someone who had *more* impact. Higher scores on the scale reflected the use of a noncoercive influence strategy in which the evaluated committee member was perceived as attempting to influence the group without specifically mentioning the consequences related to compliance or noncompliance with her or his ideas.

MAJOR FINDINGS: Venkatesh, Kohli, and Zaltman (1995) investigated the pervasiveness, effectiveness, and antecedents to six influence strategies commonly observed in decision-making units comprised of multiple individuals. The influence strategies varied according to their coercive intensity, task orientation, and instrumentality. The recommendations, information exchange, and **requests-based influence strategies** seem to be used most commonly. The legalistic plea strategy appears to be used to a moderate extent, and the promise and threat-based influence strategies seem to be used the least. A person's reinforcement power was positively related to the use of a **requests oriented influence strategy**. Contrary to predictions, viscidity, which refers to the cooperation and team spirit among buying center members, was negatively related to the use of a requests-oriented influence strategy. **Requests-based influence strategies** were found to lack effectiveness; results of regression analysis indicated a nonsignificant relationship between the **results-oriented influence strategy** and manifest influence.

COMMENTS: The low reliability of the scale suggests that further development and improvement is needed prior to using this measure again.

REFERENCES:

Boyle, Brett, F. Robert Dwyer, Robert A. Robicheaux, and James T. Simpson (1992), "Influence Strategies in Marketing Channels: Measures and Use in Different Relationship Structures," *JMR*, 48 (November), 462–73.

Frazier, Gary and John Summers (1984), "Interfirm Influence Strategies and Their Application Within Distribution Channels," *JMR*, 48 (Summer), 43–55.

——— and ——— (1986), "Perceptions of Interfirm Power and its Use Within a Franchise Channel of Distribution," *JMR*, 23 (May), 167–76.

Venkatesh, R., Ajay K. Kohli, and Gerald Zaltman (1995), "Influence Strategies in Buying Centers," *JM*, 59 (October), 71–82.

SCALE ITEMS:

Never   Always

1————————2————————3————————4————————5

1. Requested our compliance with his or her suggestion(s) *without* indicating any positive or negative outcome for us contingent upon our response.

2. Requested us to accept certain ideas with an explanation of what effect they would have on our firm.

3. Requested our cooperation in implementing his or her suggestion(s) *without* mentioning rewards or punishments.

4. State his or her wishes *without* implying any consequences of compliance or noncompliance.

SCALE NAME: Influence Strategy (Threats)

SCALE DESCRIPTION: Venkatesh, Kohli, and Zaltman (1995) used this seven-item, five-point scale to measure the extent to which purchasing agents perceived that another buying center committee member attempted to influence the group decision with promises of negative sanctions should group members fail to perform the desired action.

SCALE ORIGIN: Venkatesh, Kohli, and Zaltman (1995) indicated that the items representing this construct were adapted from Boyle and colleagues' (1992) and Frazier and Summers's (1984, 1986) studies.

SAMPLES: Venkatesh, Kohli, and Zaltman (1995) distributed a mail survey to an effective sample of 461 purchasing agents drawn from the membership list of the National Association of Purchasing Management. A total of **187** usable responses were obtained.

RELIABILITY: A coefficient alpha of **.91** was reported by Venkatesh, Kohli, and Zaltman (1995).

VALIDITY: No specific examination of scale validity was reported by Venkatesh, Kohli, and Zaltman (1995).

ADMINISTRATION: The measure was included by Venkatesh, Kohli, and Zaltman (1995) as part of a self-administered questionnaire that was delivered by mail. Nonrespondents received a personalized reminder and a second copy of the questionnaire approximately 10 days after the first mailing. Respondents were asked to answer in the context of a joint purchase decision with which they were familiar and for which no purchase options were an obvious choice to members of the decision-making unit. Informants were then instructed to rate the power, influence strategies, and actual influences of a particular committee member (excluding him- or herself). Half the sample were directed to select a committee member with *less* impact than others on the decision, whereas the other half were instructed to select someone who had *more* impact. Higher scores on the scale reflected the use of a hard coercive influence strategy in which the evaluated committee member was perceived as attempting to influence the group with threats of dire consequences should the desired action not be undertaken.

MAJOR FINDINGS: Venkatesh, Kohli, and Zaltman (1995) investigated the pervasiveness, effectiveness, and antecedents to six influence strategies commonly observed in decision-making units comprised of multiple individuals. The influence strategies varied according to their coercive intensity, task orientation, and instrumentality. The recommendations, information exchange, and requests-based influence strategies seem to be used most commonly. The legalistic plea strategy appears to be used to a moderate extent, and the promises and **threat**-based influence strategies seem to be used the least. A person's referent power and reinforcement power were negatively related to the use of a **threat influence strategy**. The larger the size of the group and the greater the group's viscidity (team spirit and cohesiveness), the less likely was the usage of a **threat influence strategy**. However, use of a **threat influence strategy** was found to be effective, because results of a regression analysis indicate a significant relationship between the **threat influence strategy** and manifest influence.

REFERENCES:

Boyle, Brett, F. Robert Dwyer, Robert A. Robicheaux, and James T. Simpson (1992), "Influence Strategies in Marketing Channels: Measures and Use in Different Relationship Structures," *JMR*, 48 (November), 462–73.

Frazier, Gary and John Summers (1984), "Interfirm Influence Strategies and Their Application Within Distribution Channels," *JMR*, 48 (Summer), 43–55.

———— and ———— (1986), "Perceptions of Interfirm Power and its Use Within a Franchise Channel of Distribution," *JMR*, 23 (May), 167–76.

Venkatesh, R., Ajay K. Kohli, and Gerald Zaltman (1995), "Influence Strategies in Buying Centers," *JM*, 59 (October), 71–82.

SCALE ITEMS:

Never   Always

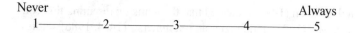

1. Made it clear that failure to comply with his or her suggestion(s) would invite his or her retaliation.

2. Threatened to become uncooperative if we failed to agree to his or her demand(s).

3. Communicated his or her ability to make "things difficult" for us if his or her specific demands were not met.

4. Stated or implied that specific benefits would be discontinued to committee members for not complying with his or her demand(s).

5. Threatened to reduce his or her support, should his or her demand(s) not be met.

6. Used threats of disrupting the decision-making process.

7. Stated or implied that those who did not comply with his or her wishes would be punished.

SCALE NAME: Information Acquisition Processes

SCALE DESCRIPTION: Moorman (1995) used this five-item, seven-point Likert-type scale to measure the extent to which an organization engaged in the collection of primary or secondary information related to various organizational stakeholders and the external environment.

SCALE ORIGIN: The scale is original to Moorman (1995). All measures used by Moorman (1995) were subjected to a purification process following data collection. The author assessed the unidimensionality of the measures in a two-factor confirmatory analysis model using LISREL VII. Items with very weak loadings and those loading on more than one factor were eliminated. The reliability of the measures was assessed by calculating coefficient alphas, and items with low item-to-total correlations were dropped if "doing so did not diminish the measure's coverage of the construct domain" (Moorman 1995, p. 325).

SAMPLES: Moorman (1995) chose to sample the vice presidents of marketing for 300 divisions of firms noted in the 1992 *Advertising Age* list of top 200 advertisers; a total of **92** usable questionnaires were received. No systematic differences were observed between early and late respondents.

RELIABILITY: Moorman (1995) reported a coefficient alpha of **.65** for this scale.

VALIDITY: Moorman (1995) performed a series of two-factor confirmatory analyses using LISREL VII to assess the discriminant validity of the measures used in her study. Chi-square difference tests were performed on constrained versus unconstrained models, and the significantly lower chi-square values observed for all of the unconstrained models tested were accepted as evidence of the discriminant validity of the measures.

ADMINISTRATION: The scale was included with other measures in a self-administered questionnaire that was delivered by mail. Moorman (1995) included a cover letter that explained the survey purpose and, in an effort to increase response rate, offered to share survey results. Nonrespondents were telephoned after three weeks and were sent a second questionnaire two weeks after the telephone reminder. All informants were instructed to answer in the context of the most recent product development project for which their division had been responsible. Focal projects were required to have been on the market for a minimum of 12 months. Higher scores on the scale indicated that an organization was heavily engaged in the collection of primary or secondary information related to various organizational stakeholders and the external environment.

MAJOR FINDINGS: Moorman (1995) examined the relationship among organizational market information processes, organizational culture, and new product outcomes. Contrary to expectations, **information acquisition** was not found to be related to new product performance or new product timeliness, and the type of organizational culture did not significantly influence **information acquisition** processes.

REFERENCES:
Moorman, Christine (1995), "Organizational Market Information Processes: Cultural Antecedents and New Product Outcomes," *JMR*, 32 (August), 318–35.

SCALE ITEMS:

Strongly   Strongly
disagree   agree
  1————2————3————4————5————6————7

During this project, my division had formal or informal processes...

1. For continuously collecting information from customers.

2. For continuously collecting information about competitor's activities.

3. For continuously collecting information about relevant publics other than customers and competitors.

4. For continuously reexamining the value of information collected in previous studies.

5. For continuously collecting information from external experts, such as consultants.

SCALE NAME: Information Exchange (Major Supplier to Wholesaler)

SCALE DESCRIPTION: Lusch and Brown (1996) stated that this three-item, seven-point Likert-type scale was used to measure wholesaler perceptions of the extent to which its major supplier kept it informed of relevant or proprietary information that could facilitate its business activities. The authors referred to this measure as *supplier keeps wholesaler informed*, or *SINFO*.

SCALE ORIGIN: Citing the work of Heide and John (1992), Lusch and Brown (1996) sought to assess the extent of relational behavior between distributors and their major suppliers by measuring the level of information exchange, flexibility, and solidarity characterizing the relationship. Whereas prior measures typically assessed the *expectations* for information exchange governing the relationship between parties in a single measure, Lusch and Brown rephrased items adapted from Heide and John (1992), Heide and Milner (1992) and Kaufmann and Dant (1992) to create two separate measures. The current scale measured wholesaler perceptions of the extent to which its suppliers *actually* kept it informed; another scale was used to assess the extent to which wholesalers *actually* kept their suppliers informed. One item adapted from the original scales, "Our major supplier will provide us any information that might be helpful," was dropped from the final analysis.

SAMPLES: A systematic random sample of 3225 firms was drawn by Lusch and Brown (1996) from a mailing list of all U.S. merchant wholesalers and agents/brokers in 16 four-digit standard industrial classification code groups. The sample was further reduced by eliminating firms with more than 20 employees. General managers were identified as the key informants for the remaining firms and were sent a mail questionnaire. Incentives and a follow-up mailing resulted in an initial response rate of 28.8%. However, this study reported usable data specific only to the **454** respondents classified as wholesale distributors and excluded data from agent and broker firms. The authors reported that the average number of suppliers reported by wholesalers in the sample was 45, with the major supplier contributing, on average, 49% of the firm's annual volume.

RELIABILITY: Lusch and Brown (1996) reported a composite reliability of **.87** for this scale.

VALIDITY: Lusch and Brown (1996) reported undertaking a thorough review of the practitioner and academic literature, as well as extensive practitioner pretesting, to ensure content validity. Confirmatory factor analysis confirmed that the measure represented one of six dimensions constituting relational behavior and demonstrated the unidimensionality of the measure. Convergent and discriminant validity were also assessed and found to be satisfactory, which indicated that the measure possessed adequate construct validity.

ADMINISTRATION: The scale was included as part of a self-administered mail survey. A $1 incentive and the promise of shared survey results were offered as participant incentives, and a personalized cover letter accompanied the survey packet. Undeliverable questionnaires were redirected to a replacement firm. A second mailing without monetary incentive was sent one month later. Lusch and Brown (1996) instructed respondents to answer all questions pertaining to major suppliers in the context of the supplier with which the wholesale distributor did the most business. Higher scores on the measure represented the perception of wholesalers that that suppliers were sharing more information with them.

MAJOR FINDINGS: Lusch and Brown (1996) investigated how the type of dependency structure—wholesaler dependent on supplier, supplier dependent on wholesaler, or bilateral dependency—influenced whether a normative or explicit contract was used. Lusch and Brown (1996) also studied whether dependency structure and the type of contract influenced the performance of wholesale distributors.

Information exchange (major supplier to wholesaler) represented one of six dimensions of relational behavior. Findings indicated that a greater degree of relational behavior between supplier and distributor was observed when more normative contracts governed the relationship or when greater levels of bilateral dependency between parties existed. When wholesalers maintained a more long-term outlook toward their relationship with the supplier, relational behavior was also enhanced. The use of explicit contracts was found to have no significant bearing on the degree of relational behavior exhibited between supplier and distributor.

REFERENCES:

Heide, Jan B. and George John (1992), "Do Norms Matter in Marketing Relationships?" *JM*, 56 (April), 32–44.

———— and Anne S. Miner (1992), "The Shadow of the Future: Effects of Anticipated Interaction and Frequency of Contact on Buyer–Seller Cooperation," *Academy of Management Journal*, 35 (June), 265–91.

Kaufmann, Patrick J. and Rajiv P. Dant (1992), "The Dimensions of Commercial Exchange" *Marketing Letters*, 3 (May), 171–85.

Lusch, Robert F. and James R. Brown (1996), "Interdependency, Contracting, and Relational Behavior in Marketing Channels," *JM*, 60 (October), 19–38.

SCALE ITEMS:

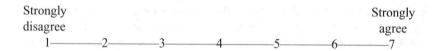

Strongly disagree — Strongly agree
1————2————3————4————5————6————7

1. Our major supplier provides us information frequently and informally, and not only according to a prespecified agreement.

2. Our major supplier will provide us with propriety information if it can help.

3. Our major supplier keeps us informed about events or changes that may affect us.

SCALE NAME: Information Exchange (Supplier Relationship)

SCALE DESCRIPTION: Dahlstrom, McNeilly, and Speh (1996) used this four-item, five-point Likert-type scale to measure the degree of openness in communication between partners in the supply relationship and the willingness to reveal proprietary information.

SCALE ORIGIN: Dahlstrom, McNeilly, and Speh (1996) reported that the scale developed for this study was based on the work of Heide and John (1992). The questionnaire containing the scale was pretested by six members of the Warehouse Education and Research Council, who evaluated it for content, readability, and relevance to the industry.

SAMPLES: Using a sampling frame generated from the membership of the Warehouse Education and Research Council, Dahlstrom, McNeilly, and Speh (1996) surveyed 1000 manufacturer, retailer, and wholesaler members. No mention of the specific sampling technique used to generate the frame was provided. Firms who exclusively used in-house warehousing services were not part of the population of interest and were asked to return the survey without answering. Including unanswered surveys, 383 questionnaires were returned for a 38.3% response rate. Of these, **189** surveys contained complete data from firms using interfirm warehousing services.

RELIABILITY: Dahlstrom, McNeilly, and Speh (1996) reported a coefficient alpha of **.72** for this measure.

VALIDITY: Item-to-total correlations estimated by an exploratory factor analysis were used in the first stage of measure purification. Dahlstrom, McNeilly, and Speh (1996) submitted the remaining items to a confirmatory factor analysis, which provided evidence of construct validity. Discriminant validity was also assessed and found to be acceptable.

ADMINISTRATION: Dahlstrom, McNeilly, and Speh (1996) stated that the scale was part of a self-administered questionnaire that was returned by mail. Sampled individuals were contacted by telephone prior to survey delivery, and a postage-paid, return addressed reply envelope accompanied the questionnaire. A follow-up mailing with a second survey was sent two weeks after the first. Individuals using in-house warehousing services were asked not to complete the survey, but eligible respondents were instructed to answer in the context of the third-party warehouse service provider with whom they spent the greatest portion of their warehousing budget. Higher scores on the information exchange scale indicated that supplier and user were open in their communication and willing to share proprietary information as required.

MAJOR FINDINGS: Dahlstrom, McNeilly, and Speh (1996) investigated various antecedents to alternative forms of governance in the logistical supply market. A second topic of investigation addressed how formal controls and relational norms were employed by alternative governance forms to yield performance. Results of path analysis indicated that **information exchange** increased performance in the long-term unilateral agreement governance mode. Formalization enhanced **information exchange** in the market-based exchange governance mode, whereas both formalization and participation increased **information exchange** in the bilateral alliance, short-term, and long-term unilateral agreement governance modes.

REFERENCES:
Dahlstrom, Robert, Kevin M. McNeilly, and Thomas W. Speh (1996), "Buyer-Seller Relationships in the Procurement of Logistical Services," *JAMS*, 24 (2), 110–24.
Heide, Jan B. and George John (1992), "Do Norms Matter in Relationships?" *JM*, 58 (January), 71–85.

#648 *Information Exchange (Supplier Relationship)*

SCALE ITEMS:
Please indicate your level of agreement with the following:

Strongly
disagree

Strongly
agree

1————2————3————4————5

1. In this relationship, it is expected that any information that might help the other party will be provided to them.

2. Exchange of information in this relationship takes place frequently and informally, and not only according to prespecified agreement.

3. It is expected that the vendor or I will provide proprietary information if it can help out the other.

4. We keep each other informed about events or changes that may affect the other.

SCALE NAME: Information Exchange (Wholesaler to Major Supplier)

SCALE DESCRIPTION: Lusch and Brown (1996) stated that this three-item, seven-point Likert-type scale was used to measure the extent to which wholesalers kept their major suppliers informed of relevant or helpful information that could facilitate their business activities. The authors referred to this measure as *wholesaler keeps supplier informed*, or *WINFO*.

SCALE ORIGIN: Citing the work of Heide and John (1992), Lusch and Brown (1996) sought to assess the extent of relational behavior between distributors and their major suppliers by measuring the level of information exchange, flexibility, and solidarity characterizing the relationship. Whereas prior measures typically assessed the *expectations* for information exchange governing the relationship between parties in a single measure, Lusch and Brown rephrased items adapted from Heide and John (1992), Heide and Milner (1992) and Kaufmann and Dant (1992) to create two separate measures. The current scale was used to assess the extent to which wholesalers *actually* kept their suppliers informed; another scale measured wholesaler perceptions of the extent to which their suppliers *actually* kept them informed. One item adapted from the original scales, "We will provide proprietary information to our major supplier if it can help," was dropped from the final analysis.

SAMPLES: A systematic random sample of 3225 firms was drawn by Lusch and Brown (1996) from a mailing list of all U.S. merchant wholesalers and agents/brokers in 16 four-digit standard industrial classification code groups. The sample was further reduced by eliminating firms with more than 20 employees. General managers were identified as the key informants for the remaining firms and were sent a mail questionnaire. Incentives and a follow-up mailing resulted in an initial response rate of 28.8%. However, this study reported usable data specific only to the **454** respondents classified as wholesale-distributors and excluded data from agent and broker firms. The authors reported that the average number of suppliers reported by wholesalers in the sample was 45, with the major supplier contributing, on average, 49% of the firm's annual volume.

RELIABILITY: Lusch and Brown (1996) reported a composite reliability of .792 for this scale.

VALIDITY: Lusch and Brown (1996) reported undertaking a thorough review of the practitioner and academic literature, as well as extensive practitioner pretesting, to ensure content validity. Confirmatory factor analysis confirmed that the measure represented one of six dimensions constituting relational behavior and demonstrated the unidimensionality of the measure. Convergent and discriminant validity were also assessed and found to be satisfactory, which indicated that the measure possessed adequate construct validity.

ADMINISTRATION: The scale was included as part of a self-administered mail survey. A $1 incentive and the promise of shared survey results were offered as participant incentives, and a personalized cover letter accompanied the survey packet. Undeliverable questionnaires were redirected to a replacement firm. A second mailing without monetary incentive was sent one month later. Lusch and Brown (1996) instructed respondents to answer all questions pertaining to major suppliers in the context of the supplier with which the wholesale distributor did the most business. Higher scores on the measure indicated that wholesalers were sharing more information exchange with their major supplier.

MAJOR FINDINGS: Lusch and Brown (1996) investigated how the type of dependency structure—wholesaler dependent on supplier, supplier dependent on wholesaler, or bilateral dependency—influenced whether a normative or explicit contract was used. The authors also studied whether dependency structure and the type of contract influenced the performance of wholesale distributors. **Information**

exchange (wholesaler to major supplier) represented one of six dimensions of relational behavior. Findings indicated that a greater degree of relational behavior between supplier and distributor was observed when more normative contracts governed the relationship or when greater levels of bilateral dependency between parties existed. When wholesalers maintained a more long-term outlook toward their relationship with the supplier, relational behavior was also enhanced. The use of explicit contracts was found to have no significant bearing on the degree of relational behavior exhibited between supplier and distributor.

REFERENCES:

Heide, Jan B. and George John (1992), "Do Norms Matter in Marketing Relationships?" *JM*, 56 (April), 32–44.

———— and Anne S. Miner (1992), "The Shadow of the Future: Effects of Anticipated Interaction and Frequency of Contact on Buyer-Seller Cooperation," *Academy of Management Journal*, 35 (June), 265–91.

Kaufmann, Patrick J. and Rajiv P. Dant (1992), "The Dimensions of Commercial Exchange" *Marketing Letters*, 3 (May), 171–85.

Lusch, Robert F. and James R. Brown (1996), "Interdependency, Contracting, and Relational Behavior in Marketing Channels," *JM*, 60 (October), 19–38.

SCALE ITEMS:

Strongly disagree   Strongly agree

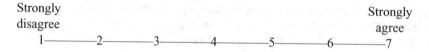

1————2————3————4————5————6————7

1. We provide any information that might help our major supplier.

2. We provide information to our major supplier frequently and informally, and not only according to a prespecified agreement.

3. We keep our major supplier informed about events or changes that may affect them.

SCALE NAME: Information Search (Purchasing)

SCALE DESCRIPTION: Bunn (1994) developed a nine-item, seven-point scale to measure the extent to which purchasing agents relied on a set of commonly used information sources in the context of a particular purchase decision. Bunn (1994) referred to this scale as "search for information."

SCALE ORIGIN: Using an iterative process, Bunn (1994) sought to develop specific measures of organizational buying behavior. An extensive review of the procurement practices and organizational buying behavior literature and personal interviews with 11 purchasing executives from a broad range of industries were used to identify several general-level organizational buying constructs. Scale items for each construct were generated using phrasing from the taped interviews with purchasing executives. A mail survey sent to purchasing executives was used to refine and confirm the constructs. Following refinement, results of a second survey of purchasing executives were used to select the final set of constructs and measures tested in this study. Bunn (1994) noted that this scale is similar to the operationalization employed by Moriarty and Spekman (1984).

SAMPLES: Bunn (1994) provided no details with respect to the two surveys conducted with samples of purchasing executives as part of the initial construct and scale development process. For the scale validation process, Bunn (1994) stated that **636** usable questionnaires were returned from a randomly selected sample of 1843 purchasing executives listed on the National Association of Purchasing Management roster. Of the respondent firms, 57% were in manufacturing industries, 16% were in service industries, and the remainder was comprised of construction, transportation, and public administration firms. The majority of responding firms were large; 59% had between 200 and 5000 employees.

RELIABILITY: Fifteen items representing various sources of information were submitted to measure purification. Three items, "purchase history records," "inquiry to vendor computer," and "catalog/directory," scored item-to-total correlations below the minimum standard of .30 and were eliminated from the measure. Three additional items were eliminated on the basis of the principal components factor analysis described subsequently. Bunn (1994) reported a coefficient alpha of **.75** for the nine-item purified measure.

VALIDITY: Bunn (1994) examined the scale for both discriminant and nomological validity. A four-dimension, promax-rotated factor solution was used to determine that items remaining after the item-to-total correlation test loaded on the proposed factor at the .40 level or greater. Two items, "other internal source" and "memo/report," loaded more heavily on a different factor, whereas the "other supplier employee" item did not load adequately on any factor. These three items were eliminated from subsequent analyses. Two additional items "your top management" (.38) and "others inside your organization" (.37) exhibited loadings below .40 but were retained because these scores represented the highest loadings for the item while relatively lower cross-loadings were observed. A confirmatory factor analysis with LISREL using nested comparisons demonstrated a superior fit for a four-factor solution, as well as statistically significant t-values for indicators. LISREL was also used to confirm the unidimensionality of the measure. Using the procedure suggested by Fornell and Larcker (1988), a second test for unidimensionality was undertaken that did not confirm unidimensionality. Nomological validity was demonstrated by significant correlations in the direction hypothesized between this measure and four theoretically related characteristics of the decision.

ADMINISTRATION: The scale was part of a self-administered mail survey in which Bunn (1994) instructed purchasing executives to answer questions in the context of the most recent purchase decision in which he or she had been involved. Higher scores on the scale indicated a greater use of multiple information sources in the purchasing decision process.

MAJOR FINDINGS: Bunn (1994) sought to develop scales for measuring four distinct constructs that he proposed as underlying organizational buying behavior. The **information search** measure underwent substantial purification, exhibited mixed results with respect to unidimensionality, and was found to explain .05 of the variance in a four-dimension, promax-rotated factor solution.

REFERENCES:

Bunn, Michele D. (1994), "Key Aspects of Organizational Buying: Conceptualization and Measurement," *JAMS*, 22 (2), 160–69.

Fornell, Claes and David F. Larcker (1981), "Evaluating Structural Equation Models with Unobservable Variables and Measurement Error," *JMR*, 18 (February), 39–53.

Moriarty, Rowland T. and Robert E. Spekman (1984), "An Empirical Investigation of the Information Sources Used During the Industrial Buying Process," *JMR*, 21 (May), 137–47.

SCALE ITEMS:*

Directions: Please indicate the extent to which each source of information was consulted for this particular purchase situation.

Not
at all

Very
much

1. Sales representative of selected vendor.

2. Sales representative of other vendor.

3. Outside business associate.

4. Your top management.

5. Users of the product.

6. Others inside your organization.

7. Trade publications.

8. Sales literature.

9. Other commercial source.

*Although the actual directions were not specifically listed in Bunn's (1994) article, they were likely to have been similar to this.

SCALE NAME: Information Sharing (Distortion and Withholding)

SCALE DESCRIPTION: Mohr and Sohi (1995) used this four-item, five-point scale to assess the extent to which dealers distorted or withheld information from a manufacturer and sales representatives.

SCALE ORIGIN: Mohr and Sohi (1995) adapted the items in this measure from the work of Roberts and O'Reilly (1974) and O'Reilly and Roberts (1974). The scale was pretested and revised on the basis of a series of personal interviews with 12 computer dealers.

SAMPLES: Mohr and Sohi (1995) sampled members of the Association of Better Computer Dealers, a national industry trade association, and supplemented this list with a random sample of outlets from a major computer franchiser. Of the 557 surveys distributed, **125** usable surveys were returned.

RELIABILITY: Mohr and Sohi (1995) reported a coefficient alpha of **.87** for this measure.

VALIDITY: Mohr and Sohi (1995) stated that a confirmatory factor analysis successfully demonstrated the unidimensionality and convergent and discriminatory validity of the measure.

ADMINISTRATION: The measure was included by Mohr and Sohi (1995) as part of a self-administered questionnaire that was delivered by mail. Nonrespondents received a reminder letter. Each dealer was asked to respond to the questionnaire with respect to a randomly assigned focal manufacturer. Lower scores on the scale indicated that dealers withheld or distorted information more frequently.

MAJOR FINDINGS: Mohr and Sohi (1995) investigated the relationship among information-sharing norms, quality and satisfaction with communication, dealers' distortion and withholding of information, and the three communication flows of frequency, bidirectionality, and formality. Formality of communication flows was found to have an inhibiting effect on the **distortion and withholding of information by dealers**.

REFERENCES:
Mohr, Jakki J. and Ravipreet S. Sohi (1995), "Communication Flows in Distribution Channels: Impact on Assessments of Communication Quality and Satisfaction," *JR*, 71 (4), 393–416.
O'Reilly, Charles and Karlene Roberts (1974), "Information Filtration in Organizations: Three Experiments," *Organizational Behavior and Human Performance*, 11 (April), 253–65.
Roberts, Karlene and Charles O'Reilly (1974), "Measuring Organizational Communication," *Journal of Applied Psychology*, 59 (3), 321–26.

SCALE ITEMS:
Directions: You may often find it necessary to either change the nature of information (for example, by using different words, shifting emphasis, simplifying, and so forth) or to not pass on information to your manufacturer or sales rep (district manager). How frequently do you:

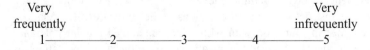

Very
frequently
1————2————3————4————5
Very
infrequently

1. Change the nature of information before passing it on to the manufacturer?

2. Change the nature of information before passing it on to the sales rep?

3. Not pass information on to the manufacturer?

4. Not pass information on to the sales rep?

SCALE NAME: Information Sharing (Functional)

SCALE DESCRIPTION: Fisher, Maltz, and Jaworski (1997) used this four-item, five-point Likert-type scale to assess marketing managers' perceptions of the extent to which organizational guidelines and expectations foster the free exchange of information between functional areas. Fisher, Maltz, and Jaworski (1997) refer to this scale as *information-sharing norms*.

SCALE ORIGIN: Fisher, Maltz, and Jaworski (1997) indicated that the scale was original to their study. Preliminary scale items were pretested with six marketing managers; those found to be unclear, ambiguous, or not applicable were dropped from the measure. A five-item version of the information-sharing norms scale was administered in Study 1, and one reversed item, "In this division no one seems to care about sharing information," was eliminated on the basis of large modification indices in the confirmatory factor analysis.

SAMPLES: In Study 1, Fisher, Maltz, and Jaworski (1997) sampled 180 marketing managers employed by a *Fortune* 100 firm serving five diverse high-technology markets. The convenience sample was composed of marketing managers attending management training sessions over a three-week period; **89** usable responses were obtained. In Study 2, the authors sampled marketing managers employed by a multinational, business-to-business services firm with 36 business units in six countries outside the United States. A key informant provided a list of 100 firm members employed in a variety of marketing positions that required them to interact with engineering personnel. A total of **72** usable responses were obtained for Study 2.

RELIABILITY: Fisher, Maltz, and Jaworski (1997) reported calculating coefficient alphas for this measure of **.79** in Study 1 and **.84** in Study 2.

VALIDITY: In Study 1, confirmatory factor analyses were conducted in two stages to maintain an acceptable ratio of observations to variables. The first analysis included the original 15 items that composed the bidirectional communication, information-sharing norms, and relative functional identification measures. Fisher, Maltz, and Jaworski (1997) stated that, after two bidirectional communication items and one information-sharing norm item were eliminated due to large modification indices, the revised model fit the data acceptably well. Evidence of discriminant validity was provided in that the correlation between each pair of constructs was significantly different from 1.00.

ADMINISTRATION: The measure was included with other scales in a self-administered questionnaire. For Study 1, a survey packet containing a cover letter, reply envelope, and the survey instrument was distributed to each marketing manager participant of a company-sponsored training session. Fisher, Maltz, and Jaworski (1997) used e-mail and telephone reminders to increase response rates. In Study 2, respondents received the survey packet by mail. Offers of anonymity and shared survey results were provided as incentives to participate. Nonrespondents received a reminder letter, followed by a second mail survey packet. In both studies, respondents were instructed to answer questions in the context of their relationship with a single manager in the engineering function with whom they interacted regularly. Higher scores on the measure indicated that respondents perceived organizational guidelines and expectations as fostering the exchange of information between marketing and engineering functions to a greater degree.

MAJOR FINDINGS: Fisher, Maltz, and Jaworski (1997) investigated how relative functional identification (RFI), or the strength of marketing managers' psychological connection to their functional area compared with the firm as a whole, influenced different strategies for improving communication between marketers and engineers. **Information-sharing** positively influenced the bidirectionality, but not the frequency, of communication between parties in Study 1. In Study 2, **information-sharing** positively influenced both the bidirectionality and frequency of communication. In addition, the effect of **information-sharing** on bidirectionality was found to be stronger for low-RFI managers than for high-RFI managers in both studies.

REFERENCES:

Fisher, Robert J., Elliot Maltz, and Bernard J. Jaworski (1997), "Enhancing Communication Between Marketing and Engineering: The Moderating Role of Relative Functional Identification," *JM*, 61 (July), 54–70.

SCALE ITEMS:

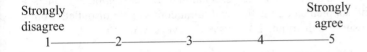

Strongly   Strongly
disagree   agree
1————————2————————3————————4————————5

1. Everyone believes that sharing information is important.

2. There is a tradition of interfunctional communication.

3. Information sharing between functions is strongly encouraged.

4. Managers of different functions are expected to share information.

SCALE NAME: Information Sharing (Norms)

SCALE DESCRIPTION: Mohr and Sohi (1995) used this four-item, five-point Likert-type scale to assess the extent to which parties in an exchange relationship kept each other fully informed about important issues, changes, and events.

SCALE ORIGIN: Mohr and Sohi (1995) originally operationalized an eight-item measure adapted from scales used by Noordeweir, John, and Nevin (1990) and Heide and John (1992). The scale was pretested and revised on the basis of a series of personal interviews with 12 computer dealers. In the initial reliability analysis based on the final study data, two items were dropped due to low item-to-total correlations. Two additional items were eliminated when they did not exhibit appropriate loadings during an exploratory factor analysis.

SAMPLES: Mohr and Sohi (1995) sampled members of the Association of Better Computer Dealers, a national industry trade association, and supplemented this list with a random sample of outlets from a major computer franchiser. Of the 557 surveys distributed, **125** usable surveys were returned.

RELIABILITY: Mohr and Sohi (1995) reported a coefficient alpha of **.68** for this measure.

VALIDITY: Mohr and Sohi (1995) stated that a confirmatory factor analysis successfully demonstrated the unidimensionality and convergent and discriminatory validity of the measure.

ADMINISTRATION: The measure was included by Mohr and Sohi (1995) as part of a self-administered questionnaire that was delivered by mail. Nonrespondents received a reminder letter. Each dealer was asked to respond to the questionnaire with respect to a randomly assigned focal manufacturer. Lower scores on the scale reflected greater information-sharing norms between exchange partners.

MAJOR FINDINGS: Mohr and Sohi (1995) investigated the relationship among information-sharing norms, quality and satisfaction with communication, dealers' distortion and withholding of information, and the three communication flows of frequency, bidirectionality, and formality. **Information-sharing norms** was positively associated with the frequency and bidirectionality of communication but was not significantly related to the formality of communication flows.

REFERENCES:

Heide, Jan B. and George John (1992), "Do Norms Matter in Marketing Relationships?" *JM*, 56 (April), 32–44.

Mohr, Jakki J. and Ravipreet S. Sohi (1995), "Communication Flows in Distribution Channels: Impact on Assessments of Communication Quality and Satisfaction," *JR*, 71 (4), 393–416.

Noordeweir, Thomas, George John, and John Nevin (1990), "Performance Outcomes of Purchasing Arrangements in Industrial Buyer-Vendor Relationships," *JM*, 54 (October), 80–93.

SCALE ITEMS:

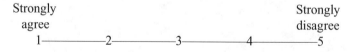

Strongly agree — Strongly disagree

1————2————3————4————5

1. We inform the manufacturer in advance of changing needs.

2. We share proprietary information with this manufacturer.

3. In this relationship, it is expected that any information which might help the other party will be provided.

4. The parties are expected to keep each other informed about events or changes that may affect the other party.

SCALE NAME: Information Transmission Processes

SCALE DESCRIPTION: Moorman (1995) used this six-item, seven-point Likert-type scale to measure the degree to which information was formally or informally diffused among members of the marketing department and other relevant users within the organization.

SCALE ORIGIN: The scale is original to Moorman (1995). All measures used by Moorman (1995) were subjected to a purification process following data collection. The author assessed the unidimensionality of the measures in a two-factor confirmatory analysis model using LISREL VII. Items with very weak loadings and those loading on more than one factor were eliminated. The reliability of the measures was assessed by calculating coefficient alphas, and items with low item-to-total correlations were dropped if "doing so did not diminish the measure's coverage of the construct domain" (Moorman 1995, p. 325).

SAMPLES: Moorman (1995) chose to sample the vice presidents of marketing for 300 divisions of firms noted in the 1992 *Advertising Age* list of top 200 advertisers; a total of **92** usable questionnaires were received. No systematic differences were observed between early and late respondents.

RELIABILITY: Moorman (1995) reported a coefficient alpha of **.70** for this scale.

VALIDITY: Moorman (1995) performed a series of two-factor confirmatory analyses using LISREL VII to assess the discriminant validity of the measures used in her study. Chi-square difference tests were performed on constrained versus unconstrained models, and the significantly lower chi-square values observed for all of the unconstrained models tested were accepted as evidence of the discriminant validity of the measures.

ADMINISTRATION: The scale was included with other measures in a self-administered questionnaire that was delivered by mail. Moorman (1995) included a cover letter that explained the survey purpose and, in an effort to increase response rate, offered to share survey results. Nonrespondents were telephoned after three weeks and sent a second questionnaire two weeks after the telephone reminder. All informants were instructed to answer in the context of the most recent product development project for which their division had been responsible. Focal projects were required to have been on the market for a minimum of 12 months. Higher scores on the scale indicated that formal and informal transmissions of information occurred to a greater extent among marketing department members and other relevant information users within the organization.

MAJOR FINDINGS: Moorman (1995) examined the relationship among organizational market information processes, organizational culture, and new product outcomes. Clan-based organizational cultures, which stress participation, teamwork, and cohesiveness, were found to have the strongest positive effect on **information transmission processes** from among the four types of organizational cultures (adhocracies, markets, hierarchies, clans) tested. However, **information transmission processes** did not influence either new product performance or new product timeliness.

REFERENCES:

Moorman, Christine (1995), "Organizational Market Information Processes: Cultural Antecedents and New Product Outcomes," *JMR*, 32 (August), 318–35.

SCALE ITEMS:

Strongly
disagree

Strongly
agree

1————2————3————4————5————6————7

During this project, my division had formal or informal processes...

1. For sharing information effectively between marketing and other departments.

2. For sharing information effectively within the marketing department.

During this project, my division...

3. Had formal information links established between all parties involved in the project.

4. Had informal networks that ensured marketing decision makers generally had the information they needed.

5. Employed people who were willing to educate others during the project.

6. Took the necessary time to properly train employees in new tasks relating to this project.

SCALE NAME: Information Use (Manager)

SCALE DESCRIPTION: Moorman (1995) used ten-item, seven-point Likert-type scale to assess the degree to which an individual manager used information in the course of project management and decision making.

SCALE ORIGIN: Moorman (1995) stated that the scale was adapted from Deshpandé and Zaltman's (1982) study. All measures used by Moorman (1995) were subjected to a purification process following data collection. The author assessed the unidimensionality of the measures in a two-factor confirmatory analysis model using LISREL VII. Items with very weak loadings and those loading on more than one factor were eliminated. The reliability of the measures was assessed by calculating coefficient alphas, and items with low item-to-total correlations were dropped if "doing so did not diminish the measure's coverage of the construct domain" (Moorman 1995, p. 325).

SAMPLES: Moorman (1995) chose to sample the vice presidents of marketing for 300 divisions of firms noted in the 1992 *Advertising Age* list of top 200 advertisers; a total of **92** usable questionnaires were received. No systematic differences were observed between early and late respondents.

RELIABILITY: Moorman (1995) reported a coefficient alpha of **.81** for this scale.

VALIDITY: Moorman (1995) performed a series of two-factor confirmatory analyses using LISREL VII to assess the discriminant validity of the measures used in her study. Chi-square difference tests were performed on constrained versus unconstrained models, and the significantly lower chi-square values observed for all of the unconstrained models tested were accepted as evidence of the discriminant validity of the measures.

ADMINISTRATION: The scale was included with other measures in a self-administered questionnaire that was delivered by mail. Moorman (1995) included a cover letter that explained the survey purpose and, in an effort to increase response rate, offered to share survey results. Nonrespondents were telephoned after three weeks and sent a second questionnaire two weeks after the telephone reminder. All informants were instructed to answer in the context of the most recent product development project for which their division had been responsible. Focal projects were required to have been on the market for a minimum of 12 months. Higher scores on the scale indicated that an individual manager was more likely to use information when managing the new product project and in making decisions.

MAJOR FINDINGS: Moorman (1995) examined the relationship among organizational market information processes, organizational culture, and new product outcomes. The **individual manager's use of information** was paired with each of the four organizational processes measures in separate two-factor confirmatory analysis models to test the discriminant validity of those measures, as described previously in the "Validity" section.

REFERENCES:

Deshpandé, Rohit and Gerald Zaltman (1982), "Factors Affecting the Use of Market Research Information: A Path Analysis," *JMR*, 19 (February), 14–31.

Moorman, Christine (1995), "Organizational Market Information Processes: Cultural Antecedents and New Product Outcomes," *JMR*, 32 (August), 318–35.

SCALE ITEMS:

Strongly   Strongly
disagree   agree
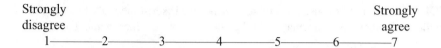

1. Market information enriched my basic understanding of the project.

2. The way I thought about this project would have been very different if research had not been conducted.

3. I thought about available market information for a long time.

4. The process of *doing* research really enlightened my understanding of the project.

5. Market information reduced my uncertainty about the project.

6. Market information helped me identify aspects of the project that would otherwise have gone unnoticed.

7. My ability to make project decisions would have been diminished without research.

8. My project decisions really did not require market information.

9. I used marketing information to make specific decisions for the project.

10. Without this market information, my decisions would have been very different.

SCALE NAME: Information Use (by Engineering)

SCALE DESCRIPTION: Fisher, Maltz, and Jaworski (1997) used this six-item, five-point Likert-type scale to measure marketing managers' perceptions of the degree to which information transmitted by marketing was used by the engineering function to understand the environment and make decisions. Although used in an engineering/marketing context here, the scale could easily be adapted to measure information use by or from any combination of functional areas.

SCALE ORIGIN: Fisher, Maltz, and Jaworski (1997) stated that the scale was adapted from the work of Anderson, Ciarlo, and Brodie (1981). Preliminary scale items were pretested with six marketing managers; those found to be unclear, ambiguous, or not applicable were dropped from the measure.

SAMPLES: In Study 2, Fisher, Maltz, and Jaworski (1997) sampled marketing managers employed by a multinational, business-to-business services firm with 36 business units in six countries outside the United States. A key informant provided a list of 100 firm members employed in a variety of marketing positions that required them to interact with engineering personnel. A total of **72** usable responses were obtained for Study 2.

RELIABILITY: Fisher, Maltz, and Jaworski (1997) reported an alpha for this measure of **.78**.

VALIDITY: Confirmatory factor analyses were conducted in two stages to maintain an acceptable ratio of observations to variables. The second analysis included the items measuring the relationship effectiveness between marketing and engineering and engineering's use of information. Fisher, Maltz, and Jaworski (1997) stated that the initial model fit the data acceptably well. Evidence of discriminant validity was provided in that the correlation between each pair of constructs was significantly different from 1.00.

ADMINISTRATION: Although the results of two studies were reported by Fisher, Maltz, and Jaworski (1997), the information usage scale was only incorporated into a self-administered questionnaire that was delivered by mail in Study 2. Offers of anonymity and shared survey results were provided as incentives to participate. Nonrespondents received a reminder letter, followed by a second mail survey packet. Respondents were instructed to answer questions in the context of their relationship with a single manager in the engineering function with whom they interacted regularly. Higher scores on the measure indicated that respondents perceived that information provided by the marketing area was being used to a greater extent by the engineering department.

MAJOR FINDINGS: Fisher, Maltz, and Jaworski (1997) investigated how relative functional identification, or the strength of marketing managers' psychological connection to their functional area compared with the firm as a whole, influences different strategies for improving communication between marketers and engineers. Marketers' perceptions of the engineering department's **use of information** was found to increase with the both the bidirectionality and frequency of communication, but **information use** declined as psychological distance increased.

REFERENCES:
Anderson, Cathy, James Ciarlo, and Susan Brodie (1981), "Measuring Evaluation-Induced Change in Mental Health Programs," in *Utilizing Evaluation Concepts and Measurement Techniques*, James Garlo, ed. Beverly Hills, CA: Sage Publications.
Fisher, Robert J., Elliot Maltz, and Bernard J. Jaworski (1997), "Enhancing Communication Between Marketing and Engineering: The Moderating Role of Relative Functional Identification," *JM,* 61 (July), 54–70.

#656 *Information Use (by Engineering)*

SCALE ITEMS:

Strongly   Strongly
disagree   agree
  1———————2———————3———————4———————5

Information I send to the Engineering contact...

1. Leads to concrete actions.

2. Shapes policies in the engineering function.

3. Affects our Strategic Unit's new product efforts.

4. Influences his/her understanding of the marketplace.

5. Affects his/her productivity.

6. Is rarely used. **(r)**

SCALE NAME: Innovativeness (New Product)

SCALE DESCRIPTION: Gatignon and Xuereb (1997) used this six-item, six-point Likert-type scale to measure perceptions of the level of innovativeness and technological change associated with a new product. Gatignon and Xuereb (1997) referred to this scale as *innovation radicalness*.

SCALE ORIGIN: Gatignon and Xuereb (1997) stated that the multiple-item scales used in their study were developed on the basis of items previously proposed and used in survey research. The measure was pretested by asking two experts in innovation research to supply names of radical and incremental innovations. Each expert then rated the innovations named by the other using the items in this survey. The new product innovation scale was found to be highly reliable (coefficient alpha of .96) across innovations and experts, and its discriminatory power was confirmed by an ANOVA analysis. A pilot test was performed on the revised questionnaire for the purpose of assessing scale validity. The resulting measures were then administered in the final questionnaire to a large sample. Gatignon and Xuereb (1997) stated that the measure was revised into its current form after a factor analysis of the items in the radicalness scale indicated the existence of separate factors when items were expressed in terms relative to the competition. Revision involved the creation of a separate scale measuring the degree of new product similarity with competitors' products. It is not clear whether this factor analysis took place during the pilot study or following the final administration.

SAMPLES: Gatignon and Xuereb (1997) mailed the final questionnaire to a list of 3000 marketing executives representing a broad cross-section of U.S. industries randomly selected from a commercially available list. Of these, 2802 were successfully delivered, and **393** usable responses were obtained for a 14% response rate. The products represented by the marketing executives surveyed included consumer durable and packaged goods, consumer services, industrial technology, and computer firms.

RELIABILITY: Gatignon and Xuereb (1997) reported a coefficient alpha of **.84** for this measure.

VALIDITY: Gatignon and Xuereb (1997) reported conducting a pilot study for the purpose of assessing scale validity, but no other details were provided.

ADMINISTRATION: The scale was part of a self-administered mail survey. Nonrespondents were sent a reminder letter with an offer of a $500 lottery award two weeks after the initial mailing. Gatignon and Xuereb (1997) instructed respondents to answer the questionnaire in the context of the last new product introduced in the market by a strategic business unit. Higher scores on the scale indicated that respondents perceived the new product as radically, versus incrementally, innovative.

MAJOR FINDINGS: Gatignon and Xuereb (1997) examined the appropriateness of a customer, competitive, and technological orientation in the context of new product development. The greater the degree of **product radicalness**, the better was the perceived performance of the product. Products with a greater degree of **radicalness** were associated with a technology orientation of the firm, whereas a customer orientation led to innovations that were less **radical**. A higher degree of **product radicalness** was also associated with a greater level of demand uncertainty and higher growth markets.

REFERENCES:
Gatignon, Hubert and Jean-Marc Xuereb (1997), "Strategic Orientation of the Firm and New Product Performance," *JMR*, 34 (February), 77–90.

#657 *Innovativeness (New Product)*

SCALE ITEMS:

Directions: Please indicate the extent to which you agree or disagree with the following statements. (Circle one number for each of the following areas)

Strongly   Strongly
disagree   agree

1————2————3————4————5————6

1. This new product is a minor improvement in a current technology. **(r)**

2. This new product has changed the market conditions.

3. This new product is one of the first applications of a technological breakthrough.

4. This new product is based on a revolutionary change in technology.

5. This new product incorporated a large new body of technological knowledge.

6. This new product has changed the nature of the competition.

SCALE NAME: Instrumental Utilization Processes

SCALE DESCRIPTION: Moorman (1995) used this thirteen-item, seven-point Likert-type scale to assess the extent to which organizations used information when making, implementing, or evaluating marketing decisions.

SCALE ORIGIN: The scale is original to Moorman (1995). All measures used by Moorman (1995) were subjected to a purification process following data collection. The author assessed the unidimensionality of the measures in a two-factor confirmatory analysis model using LISREL VII. Items with very weak loadings and those loading on more than one factor were eliminated. The reliability of the measures was assessed by calculating coefficient alphas, and items with low item-to-total correlations were dropped if "doing so did not diminish the measure's coverage of the construct domain" (Moorman 1995, p. 325).

SAMPLES: Moorman (1995) chose to sample the vice presidents of marketing for 300 divisions of firms noted in the 1992 *Advertising Age* list of top 200 advertisers; a total of **92** usable questionnaires were received. No systematic differences were observed between early and late respondents.

RELIABILITY: Moorman (1995) reported a coefficient alpha of **.91** for this scale.

VALIDITY: Moorman (1995) performed a series of two-factor confirmatory analyses using LISREL VII to assess the discriminant validity of the measures used in her study. Chi-square difference tests were performed on constrained versus unconstrained models, and the significantly lower chi-square values observed for all of the unconstrained models tested were accepted as evidence of the discriminant validity of the measures.

ADMINISTRATION: The scale was included with other measures in a self-administered questionnaire that was delivered by mail. Moorman (1995) included a cover letter that explained the survey purpose and, in an effort to increase response rate, offered to share survey results. Nonrespondents were telephoned after three weeks and sent a second questionnaire two weeks after the telephone reminder. All informants were instructed to answer in the context of the most recent product development project for which their division had been responsible. Focal projects were required to have been on the market for a minimum of 12 months. Higher scores on the scale indicated that an organization reported greater usage of information when making, implementing, or evaluating marketing decisions.

MAJOR FINDINGS: Moorman (1995) examined the relationship among organizational market information processes, organizational culture, and new product outcomes. Some evidence was found to suggest that **instrumental utilization processes** influenced new product performance and new product timeliness ($p > .10$) This indicated that organizations that value information and formally and informally process it are more likely to introduce a new product when environmental conditions are favorable to its success, thus enhancing the likelihood that profit, sales, and market share goals will be achieved.

REFERENCES:
Moorman, Christine (1995), "Organizational Market Information Processes: Cultural Antecedents and New Product Outcomes," *JMR*, 32 (August), 318–35.

SCALE ITEMS:

Strongly
disagree

Strongly
agree

1————2————3————4————5————6————7

During this project, my division had formal or informal processes...

1. For carefully evaluating various marketing strategy alternatives.

2. That relied heavily upon information to make decisions relating to the project.

3. That used information to solve specific problems encountered in the project.

4. That provided information to effectively implement the project.

5. That provided clear direction on implementation of the project.

6. That gave information to all functions regarding their role in implementation.

7. That formally evaluated the effectiveness of the project.

8. That provided informal feedback regarding the effectiveness of the project.

9. That provided feedback to decision makers regarding the outcomes of their project decisions.

10. That constructively evaluated project outcomes.

11. That encouraged managers to understand the reasons for their mistakes throughout the project.

During this project, my division...

12. Integrated information from a variety of sources when developing marketing strategies.

13. Ensured that all information sources were considered in decision making (not only those that supported the preferred action).

#SCALE NAME: Intangible Attribute Certainty

SCALE DESCRIPTION: Smith and Andrews (1995) used this four-item, seven-point scale to measure the degree to which respondents felt confident that a printing and packaging firm could meet their standards for promotional program planning, creative strategy development, copywriting, and marketing program assessment.

SCALE ORIGIN: The scale is original to Smith and Andrews (1995).

SAMPLES: Smith and Andrews (1995) sampled 2400 product/marketing managers who held primary responsibility for purchasing in-store displays and promotional materials. A total of **608** usable responses were received from individuals representing 19 industries.

RELIABILITY: Smith and Andrews (1995) reported a coefficient alpha of **.86** for the scale.

VALIDITY: Smith and Andrews (1995) conducted a series of tests to assess the validity of the measures. The structural equation measurement model provided a good fit with the data, and each relevant factor loading was large and significant at the .01 level, which provides evidence of the convergent validity of the measures. Six models, pairing each of the tangible and intangible fit and tangible and intangible certainty variables, were also estimated in which the correlations between pairs of constructs were restricted to unity. The significant chi-squares between the restricted models and the original unrestricted model provided strong evidence of the discriminant validity of the measures.

ADMINISTRATION: Smith and Andrews (1995) included the scale with other measures as part of a self-administered survey that was delivered by mail. A $1 incentive and a cover letter stating that the goal of the research was to determine the marketability of a new product that could save respondents considerable amounts of time and money were included in the survey packet. Respondents were asked to read the concept statement, then answer questions. Higher scores on the scale indicated greater confidence in the packaging and printing company's ability to meet the respondent's standards for promotional program planning, creative strategy development, copywriting, and marketing program assessment.

MAJOR FINDINGS: In an industrial context, Smith and Andrews (1995) investigated how new product evaluations were influenced by the degree to which a company's skills were perceived to fit with those required to provide a new product and the perceived certainty that a company could deliver the proposed new product. Hypotheses were evaluated using structural equation modeling. **Intangible attribute certainty** positively influenced new product evaluations. **Intangible attribute certainty** also mediated the relationship between new product evaluations and intangible attribute fit to the extent that, when the effect of customer certainty was considered, the direct effect of intangible attribute fit on new product evaluations disappeared.

REFERENCES:
Smith, Daniel C. and Jonlee Andrews (1995), "Rethinking the Effect of Perceived Fit on Customers' Evaluations of New Products," *JAMS*, 23 (1), 4–14.

SCALE ITEMS:

The Concept Statement

Below is a brief description of a new promotion service concept. After reading the description, please respond to the questions that follow.

Concept: A company that is currently in the *printing and packaging industry* and manufactures its own materials would do the following:

Promotional program planning
Creative strategy development
Copywriting
Prompt printing and manufacturing of displays, printed materials, and other promotional products
Collation of finished materials
Prepackaging of finished materials
Timely drop-shipment of finished materials
Assessment of program success

Because this company manufactures its own materials it can offer these services for 10 to 15 percent less than full-service agencies.

Not very   Very
confident   confident

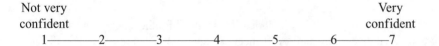

1———2———3———4———5———6———7

How confident are you that a printing and packaging company could meet your promotion service needs in the following areas (circle the number that describes how you feel)?

1. Promotional program planning.

2. Creative strategy development.

3. Copywriting.

4. Assessment.

SCALE NAME: Intangible Attribute Fit

SCALE DESCRIPTION: Smith and Andrews (1995) used this four-item, seven-point scale to measure the degree to which respondents felt that the skills possessed by a printing and packaging firm were similar to the skills needed to meet the respondent's standards for promotional program planning, creative strategy development, copywriting, and marketing program assessment.

SCALE ORIGIN: Although this scale is original to Smith and Andrews (1995), "fit" has been previously operationalized in terms of the perceived similarity between the new product and a firm's other products by Aaker and Keller (1990), Park, Milberg, and Lawson (1991), and Smith and Park (1992).

SAMPLES: Smith and Andrews (1995) sampled 2400 product/marketing managers who held primary responsibility for purchasing in-store displays and promotional materials. A total of **608** usable responses were received from individuals representing 19 industries.

RELIABILITY: Smith and Andrews (1995) reported a coefficient alpha of **.85** for the scale.

VALIDITY: Smith and Andrews (1995) conducted a series of tests to assess the validity of the measures. The structural equation measurement model provided a good fit with the data, and each relevant factor loading was large and significant at the .01 level, which provides evidence of the convergent validity of the measures. Six models, pairing each of the tangible and intangible fit and tangible and intangible certainty variables, were also estimated in which the correlations between pairs of constructs were restricted to unity. The significant chi-squares between the restricted models and the original unrestricted model provided strong evidence of the discriminant validity of the measures.

ADMINISTRATION: Smith and Andrews (1995) included the scale with other measures as part of a self-administered survey that was delivered by mail. A $1 incentive and a cover letter stating that the goal of the research was to determine the marketability of a new product that could save respondents considerable amounts of time and money were included in the survey packet. Respondents were asked to read the concept statement, then answer questions. Higher scores on the scale indicated that respondents judged the intangible services provided by the packaging and printing company to be a good fit with and very similar to their company's standards in those areas.

MAJOR FINDINGS: In an industrial context, Smith and Andrews (1995) investigated how new product evaluations were influenced by the degree to which a company's skills were perceived to fit with those required to provide a new product and the perceived certainty that a company could deliver the proposed new product. Hypotheses were evaluated using structural equation modeling. **Intangible attribute fit** positively influenced new product evaluations. However, this relationship was mediated by intangible attribute certainty to the extent that, when the effect of customer certainty was considered, the direct effect of **intangible attribute fit** on new product evaluations disappeared.

REFERENCES:
Aaker, David A. and Kevin Lane Keller (1990), "Consumer Evaluation of Brand Extensions," *JM*, 54 (January), 27–41.
Park, C. Whan, Sandra Milberg, and Robert Lawson (1991), "Evaluation of Brand Extensions: The Role of Product Feature Similarity and Brand Concept Consistency," *JCR*, 18 (September), 185–93.
Smith, Daniel C. and Jonlee Andrews (1995), "Rethinking the Effect of Perceived Fit on Customers' Evaluations of New Products," *JAMS*, 23 (1), 4–14.
——— and C. Whan Park (1992), "The Effects of Brand Extensions on Market Share and Advertising Efficiency," *JMR*, 29 (August), 296–313.

SCALE ITEMS:

The Concept Statement

Below is a brief description of a new promotion service concept. After reading the description, please respond to the questions that follow.

Concept: A company that is currently in the *printing and packaging industry* and manufactures its own materials would do the following:

Promotional program planning
Creative strategy development
Copywriting
Prompt printing and manufacturing of displays, printed materials, and other promotional products
Collation of finished materials
Prepackaging of finished materials
Timely drop-shipment of finished materials
Assessment of program success

Because this company manufactures its own materials it can offer these services for 10 to 15 percent less than full-service agencies.

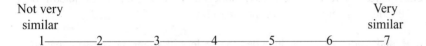

Not very   Very
  similar   similar
    1————2————3————4————5————6————7

In your opinion, how similar are the skills possessed by a printing and packaging company to the skills needed to meet your promotion needs in the following areas?

1. Promotional program planning.

2. Creative strategy development.

3. Copywriting.

4. Assessment.

SCALE NAME: Integration (Committees)

SCALE DESCRIPTION: Germain, Dröge, and Daugherty (1994) used this four-item, seven-point Likert-type scale to measure the extent to which cross-functional committees are used by an organization when formulating marketing, distribution, budgeting, and long-term strategies.

SCALE ORIGIN: Germain, Dröge, and Daugherty (1994) stated the scale was adapted from Miller and Dröge (1986).

SAMPLES: Germain, Dröge, and Daugherty (1994) randomly selected 1000 names from a sampling frame of 3280 members of the Council of Logistics Management. Of the 956 surveys delivered, **183** usable surveys were returned. The majority of respondents were directors (54.7%) or managers (27.4%) within their respective firms. The manufacturing firms represented tended to be large and covered a wide range of industries, average annual sales were $1.98 billion, and the mean number of employees across the sample firms was 9740.

RELIABILITY: Germain, Dröge, and Daugherty (1994) reported a coefficient alpha of **.81** for the scale.

VALIDITY: Germain, Dröge, and Daugherty (1994) reported that a principal components factor analysis was used to assess the unidimensionality of the measure. The items loaded on a single factor with an eigenvalue greater than 1.

ADMINISTRATION: Germain, Dröge, and Daugherty (1994) stated that the scale was included with other measures in a self-administered survey that was delivered to respondents by mail. Nonrespondents were sent a second questionnaire in two weeks and were reminded by telephone two weeks after the second mailing. Higher scores on the scale indicated that an organization used cross-functional committees to a greater extent when formulating marketing, distribution, budgeting, and long-term strategies

MAJOR FINDINGS: Germain, Dröge, and Daugherty (1994) proposed and tested a model linking environmental uncertainty, just-in-time (JIT) selling, and dimensions of organizational structure. The **integration committee** scale was one of two measures summed to form an overall measure of integration. No relationship between JIT selling practices and **integration** was found. However, increased environmental uncertainty was significantly and positively related to increased levels of **integration**.

REFERENCES:
Germain, Richard, Cornelia Dröge, and Patricia J. Daugherty (1994), "The Effect of Just-in-Time Selling on Organizational Structure: An Empirical Investigation," *JMR*, 31 (November), 471–83.
Miller, Danny and Cornelia Dröge (1986), "Psychological and Traditional Determinants of Structure," *Administrative Science Quarterly*, 31 (December), 539–60.

SCALE ITEMS:
Directions: Indicate the extent to which decision making at top levels of the firm are characterized by participative, cross-functional committees in which different departments, functions, or divisions get together to decide...

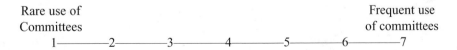

Rare use of   Frequent use
Committees   of committees
1———2———3———4———5———6———7

#661 *Integration (Committees)*

1. Distribution service strategy.

2. Marketing (or sales) strategy.

3. Capital budget decisions.

4. Long-term strategies (of growth or diversification) and decisions related to changes in the firm's operating philosophy.

SCALE NAME: Integration (Mechanisms)

SCALE DESCRIPTION: Germain, Dröge, and Daugherty (1994) used this three-item, seven-point scale to measure the extent to which cross-functional committees, temporary task forces, and liaison personnel are used by an organization to ensure the compatibility of decisions across functional areas.

SCALE ORIGIN: Germain, Dröge, and Daugherty (1994) stated the scale was adapted from Miller and Dröge (1986).

SAMPLES: Germain, Dröge, and Daugherty (1994) randomly selected 1000 names from a sampling frame of 3280 members of the Council of Logistics Management. Of the 956 surveys delivered, **183** usable surveys were returned. The majority of respondents were directors (54.7%) or managers (27.4%) within their respective firms. The manufacturing firms represented tended to be large and covered a wide range of industries, average annual sales were $1.98 billion, and the mean number of employees across the sample firms was 9740.

RELIABILITY: Germain, Dröge, and Daugherty (1994) reported a coefficient alpha of **.71** for the scale.

VALIDITY: Germain, Dröge, and Daugherty (1994) reported that a principal components factor analysis was used to assess the unidimensionality of the measure. The items loaded on a single factor with an eigenvalue greater than 1.

ADMINISTRATION: Germain, Dröge, and Daugherty (1994) stated that the scale was included with other measures in a self-administered survey that was delivered to respondents by mail. Nonrespondents were sent a second questionnaire in two weeks and were reminded by telephone two weeks after the second mailing. Higher scores on the scale indicated that an organization used cross-functional committees, task forces, and the like to a greater extent to ensure that the decisions made are compatible across functional areas.

MAJOR FINDINGS: Germain, Dröge, and Daugherty (1994) proposed and tested a model linking environmental uncertainty, just-in-time (JIT) selling, and dimensions of organizational structure. The **integration mechanisms** scale was one of two measures summed to form an overall measure of integration. No relationship between JIT selling practices and **integration** was found. However, increased environmental uncertainty was significantly and positively related to increased levels of **integration**.

REFERENCES:
Germain, Richard, Cornelia Dröge, and Patricia J. Daugherty (1994), "The Effect of Just-in-Time Selling on Organizational Structure: An Empirical Investigation," *JMR*, 31 (November), 471–83.
Miller, Danny and Cornelia Dröge (1986), "Psychological and Traditional Determinants of Structure," *Administrative Science Quarterly*, 31 (December), 539–60.

SCALE ITEMS:
Directions: Indicate the extent to which the following three devices are used in assuring the compatibility among decisions in one area (e.g., distribution) with those in other areas (e.g., marketing/sales):

#662 *Integration (Mechanisms)*

Rarely used   Frequently used

1————2————3————4————5————6————7

1. Interdepartmental committees which are set up to allow departments to engage in joint decision making.

2. Task forces which are temporary bodies set up to facilitate interdepartmental collaboration on a specific project.

3. Liaison personnel whose specific job it is to coordinate the efforts of several departments for the purposes of a project.

SCALE NAME: Intent to Leave

SCALE DESCRIPTION: This four-item, seven-point Likert-type scale measures an employee's intention to leave his or her place of employment. As used by Good, Page, and Young (1996), the measure served as a predictor of job turnover.

SCALE ORIGIN: Good, Page, and Young (1996) stated the scale was adapted from Mitchel (1981).

SAMPLES: Good, Page, and Young (1996) mailed a questionnaire to 698 retail managers employed by southern branches of a major multiunit department store. Of the **383** usable responses obtained (54.9% response rate), 280 (73.2%) were from entry-level executives, and 103 (26.9%) were from upper-level executives. The majority of respondents were women (70%).

RELIABILITY: Good, Page, and Young (1996) reported coefficient alphas of **.82** and **.80** for the entry-level and upper-level respondent samples, respectively.

VALIDITY: No specific examination of scale validity was reported by Good, Page, and Young (1996).

ADMINISTRATION: The scale was part of a self-administered mail survey. Good, Page, and Young (1996) included a cover letter promising confidentiality and anonymity, a letter from the vice president of personnel encouraging participation, and a self-addressed, stamped reply envelope. Nonrespondents were sent a second questionnaire after three weeks. Higher scores on the scale indicated a greater intention to leave the organization.

MAJOR FINDINGS: Good, Page, and Young (1996) examined the relationship of a set of antecedent constructs (role conflict and ambiguity, work–family conflict, job satisfaction, organizational commitment, and intent to leave) in explaining turnover with both entry- and upper-level retailer managers. Work–family conflict was found to increase **intentions to leave** in the entry-level management group only, and job satisfaction did not significantly influence **intentions to leave** for either sample group.

REFERENCES:
Good, Linda K., Thomas J. Page Jr., and Clifford E. Young (1996), "Assessing Hierarchical Differences in Job-Related Attitudes and Turnover Among Retail Managers," *JAMS*, 24 (2), 148–56.
Mitchel, James O. (1981), "The Effect of Intentions, Tenure, Personal, and Organizational Variables on Managerial Turnover," *Academy of Management Journal*, 24 (4), 742–51.

SCALE ITEMS:
Directions: Please circle the response to the far right of the statement indicating the degree of agreement or disagreement with respect to your own feelings about your company.

1 = Strongly disagree
2 = Disagree
3 = Slightly disagree
4 = Neutral
5 = Slightly agree
6 = Agree
7 = Strongly agree

#663 *Intent to Leave*

1. I plan to be with this company for awhile. **(r)**

2. Sometimes I get so irritated I think about changing jobs.

3. I plan to be with this company five years from now. **(r)**

4. I would turn down an offer from another retailer if it came tomorrow. **(r)**

SCALE NAME: Intention to Use Again

SCALE DESCRIPTION: Patterson, Johnson, and Spreng (1997) used this three-item, seven-point semantic differential scale to measure a client firm's repurchase intentions toward the consultancy firm previously hired to complete a project.

SCALE ORIGIN: Patterson, Johnson, and Spreng (1997) stated the scale was adapted from Oliver and Swan (1989) and noted that the scale originated with Fishbein and Ajzen (1975).

SAMPLES: Patterson, Johnson, and Spreng (1997) chose to survey management consulting firms' private- and public-sector client organizations. Of the 207 client organizations approached by telephone, 186 agreed to participate. Then, 142 key informants—typically senior executives or managers who were likely to be heavily involved in the consultant selection process—completed the Stage 1 prepurchase questionnaire. Of this group, 128 returned the postpurchase questionnaire, which yielded a final sample size of **128** for the pre- and postpurchase measures.

RELIABILITY: Patterson, Johnson, and Spreng (1997) reported a confirmatory factor analysis construct reliability of **.97** for this measure.

VALIDITY: Patterson, Johnson, and Spreng (1997) assessed the convergent and discriminant validity of the measure by means of a confirmatory factor analysis conducted using LISREL 8. The large construct reliabilities, large and significant measurement factor loadings, and the average variance extracted provided evidence of convergent validity. Evidence of discriminant validity was also demonstrated by means of average extracted variances, which exceeded the squared correlation between that construct and any other.

ADMINISTRATION: Data were collected in two stages over a 12-month span of time. The Stage 1 questionnaire was delivered, along with a cover letter, to key informants who had indicated a willingness to participate in the study. This survey also asked respondents to indicate the expected completion date for the project. The intention to use again measure was included in a second questionnaire that was delivered between one and two months after the expected completion date of the project. Both questionnaires were self-administered. If responses were not received within three weeks, a follow-up telephone call was made to nonrespondents. Higher scores on the scale indicated a greater intention to use the consultancy firms again should an appropriate situation occur.

MAJOR FINDINGS: Patterson, Johnson, and Spreng (1997) examined the determinants of customers' satisfaction and dissatisfaction in the context of business consulting services. The study findings provided ample support for the application of the disconfirmation paradigm to industrial buying situations. Disconfirmation was shown to have a stronger direct influence on satisfaction than on performance, but satisfaction was shown to be a strong predictor of **repurchase intentions**.

REFERENCES:

Fishbein, Martin and Icek Ajzen (1975), *Beliefs, Attitudes, Intention and Behavior: An Introduction to Theory and Research*. Reading, MA: Addison-Wesley.

Oliver, Richard L. and John E. Swan (1989), "Consumer Perceptions of Interpersonal Equity and Satisfaction in Transactions: A Field Survey Approach," *JM*, 53 (April), 21–35.

Patterson, Paul G., Lester W. Johnson, and Richard A. Spreng (1997), "Modeling the Determinants of Customer Satisfaction for Business-to-Business Professional Services," *JAMS*, 25 (1), 4–17.

#664 *Intention to Use Again*

SCALE ITEMS:

Directions: If your organization requires the services of a management consulting firm in the near future for a similar type of assignment, would you use the same consulting firm?

1. Very probable :____:____:____:____:____:____: ____: Not probable (r)*
                    1   2   3   4   5   6   7

2. Impossible   :____:____:____:____:____:____: ____: Very possible
                    1   2   3   4   5   6   7

3. No chance   :____:____:____:____:____:____: ____: Certain
                    1   2   3   4   5   6   7

*Item 1 is not noted as being reversed in the original article. However, examination of the scale items indicates that it is appropriate to reverse this item.

SCALE NAME: Interdependence (Engineering on Marketing)

SCALE DESCRIPTION: Fisher, Maltz, and Jaworski (1997) used this three-item, five-point scale to measure marketing managers' perceptions of the degree to which the engineering department is dependent on marketing's support, resources, and output in the accomplishment of its goals and responsibilities. Although used here in a marketing/engineering context, the scale could very easily be adapted to measure interdependence between any two functional areas.

SCALE ORIGIN: Fisher, Maltz, and Jaworski (1997) stated that the scale was adapted from the work of Ruekert and Walker (1987). Preliminary scale items were pretested with six marketing managers; those found to be unclear, ambiguous, or not applicable were dropped from the measure.

SAMPLES: In Study 2, Fisher, Maltz, and Jaworski (1997) sampled marketing managers employed by a multinational, business-to-business services firm with 36 business units in six countries outside the United States. A key informant provided a list of 100 firm members employed in a variety of marketing positions that required them to interact with engineering personnel. A total of **72** usable responses were obtained.

RELIABILITY: Fisher, Maltz, and Jaworski (1997) reported calculating a coefficient alpha for this measure of **.79**.

VALIDITY: Confirmatory factor analyses were conducted in two stages to maintain an acceptable ratio of observations to variables. The first analysis included the original seventeen-item strategic unit dynamism and market dynamism and the two interdependence scales. Fisher, Maltz, and Jaworski (1997) stated that, after two strategic unit dynamism items and one market dynamism item were eliminated due to large modification indices, the revised model fit the data acceptably well. Evidence of discriminant validity was provided in that the correlation between each pair of constructs was significantly different from 1.00.

ADMINISTRATION: Although the results of two studies were reported by Fisher, Maltz, and Jaworski (1997), interdependence measures were only incorporated into a self-administered questionnaire that was delivered by mail in Study 2. Offers of anonymity and shared survey results were provided as incentives to participate. Nonrespondents received a reminder letter, followed by a second mail survey packet. Respondents were instructed to answer questions in the context of their relationship with a single manager in the engineering function with whom they interacted regularly. Higher scores on the measure indicated that respondents perceived the resources, support, and output of the marketing area as being an important factor influencing the engineering department's ability to complete its goals and responsibilities successfully.

MAJOR FINDINGS: Fisher, Maltz, and Jaworski (1997) investigated how relative functional identification, or the strength of marketing managers' psychological connection to their functional area compared with the firm as a whole, influences different strategies for improving communication between marketers and engineers. The **interdependence of the engineering department on the marketing department** was included as a covariate in Study 2 and was combined in some fashion with a measure of the marketing department's interdependence on engineering to create a single indicator of interdependence. Both the frequency and the bidirectionality of communication were found to be positively associated with interdependence, but the coerciveness of influence attempts was negatively associated with interdependence.

#665 *Interdependence (Engineering on Marketing)*

REFERENCES:

Fisher, Robert J., Elliot Maltz, and Bernard J. Jaworski (1997), "Enhancing Communication Between Marketing and Engineering: The Moderating Role of Relative Functional Identification," *JM*, 61 (July), 54–70.

Ruekert, Robert W. and Orville C. Walker Jr. (1987c), "Marketing's Interaction with Other Functional Units: A Conceptual Model and Empirical Evidence," *JM*, 51 (January), 1–19.

SCALE ITEMS:

For Engineering to accomplish its goals and responsibilities (at your Strategic Unit), how much does it need Marketing's:

1. Resources (e.g., personnel, equipment, information)?

2. Supports (e.g., advice or technical assistance)?

3. Outputs (e.g., new product designs)?

SCALE NAME: Interdependence (Marketing on Engineering)

SCALE DESCRIPTION: Fisher, Maltz, and Jaworski (1997) used this three-item, five-point scale to measure marketing managers' perceptions of the degree to which the marketing department is dependent on engineering's support, resources, and output in the accomplishment of its goals and responsibilities. Although used here in an engineering/marketing context, the scale could very easily be adapted to measure interdependence between any two functional areas.

SCALE ORIGIN: Fisher, Maltz, and Jaworski (1997) stated that the scale was adapted from the work of Ruekert and Walker (1987). Preliminary scale items were pretested with six marketing managers; those found to be unclear, ambiguous, or not applicable were dropped from the measure.

SAMPLES: In Study 2, Fisher, Maltz, and Jaworski (1997) sampled marketing managers employed by a multinational, business-to-business services firm with 36 business units in six countries outside the United States. A key informant provided a list of 100 firm members employed in a variety of marketing positions that required them to interact with engineering personnel. A total of **72** usable responses were obtained.

RELIABILITY: Fisher, Maltz, and Jaworski (1997) reported calculating a coefficient alpha for this measure of **.84**.

VALIDITY: Confirmatory factor analyses were conducted in two stages to maintain an acceptable ratio of observations to variables. The first analysis included the original seventeen-item strategic unit dynamism and market dynamism and the two interdependence scales. Fisher, Maltz, and Jaworski (1997) stated that, after two strategic unit dynamism items and one market dynamism item were eliminated due to large modification indices, the revised model fit the data acceptably well. Evidence of discriminant validity was provided in that the correlation between each pair of constructs was significantly different from 1.00.

ADMINISTRATION: Although the results of two studies are reported by Fisher, Maltz, and Jaworski (1997), interdependence measures were only incorporated into a self-administered questionnaire that was delivered by mail in Study 2. Offers of anonymity and shared survey results were provided as incentives to participate. Nonrespondents received a reminder letter, followed by a second mail survey packet. Respondents were instructed to answer questions in the context of their relationship with a single manager in the engineering function with whom they interacted regularly. Higher scores on the measure indicated that respondents perceived the resources, support, and output of the marketing area as being an important factor influencing the engineering department's ability to complete its goals and responsibilities successfully.

MAJOR FINDINGS: Fisher, Maltz, and Jaworski (1997) investigated how relative functional identification, or the strength of marketing managers' psychological connection to their functional area compared with the firm as a whole, influences different strategies for improving communication between marketers and engineers. The **interdependence of the marketing department on the engineering department** was included as a covariate in Study 2 and was combined in some fashion with a measure of the marketing department's interdependence on engineering to create a single indicator of interdependence. Both the frequency and the bidirectionality of communication were found to be positively associated with interdependence, but the coerciveness of influence attempts was negatively associated with interdependence.

#666 *Interdependence (Marketing on Engineering)*

REFERENCES:

Fisher, Robert J., Elliot Maltz, and Bernard J. Jaworski (1997), "Enhancing Communication Between Marketing and Engineering: The Moderating Role of Relative Functional Identification," *JM*, 61 (July), 54–70.

Ruekert, Robert W. and Orville C. Walker Jr. (1987c), "Marketing's Interaction with Other Functional Units: A Conceptual Model and Empirical Evidence," *JM*, 51 (January), 1–19.

SCALE ITEMS:

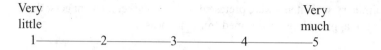

For Marketing to accomplish its goals and responsibilities (at your Strategic Unit), how much does it need Engineering's:

1. Resources (e.g., personnel, equipment, information)?

2. Supports (e.g., advice or technical assistance)?

3. Outputs (e.g., new product designs)?

SCALE NAME: Interdependency (Functional)

SCALE DESCRIPTION: Olson, Walker, and Ruekert (1995) used this six-item, seven-point scale to measure the degree of interdependency among members of functional departments working together on a new product development project. The authors referred to this scale as *functional interdependence* or *interdependency*.

SCALE ORIGIN: Olson, Walker, and Ruekert (1995) stated that the scale was adopted from Van De Ven and Ferry (1980) and previously used in a marketing context by Ruekert and Walker (1987a, b).

SAMPLES: Of the 24 firms solicited by Olson, Walker, and Ruekert (1995) to participate in the study, 15 divisions from 12 firms provided complete information on **45** new product development projects undertaken within a three-year time period. All firms produced tangible products and ranged in age from 12 to more than 100 years, with annual revenues between $50 million and more than $1 billion. Projects formed the unit of analysis. Of the new product projects studied, 11 represented new-to-the-world products, 9 were me-too products, 15 were line extensions, and 10 were product modifications. Data were collected first from each project manager and then from individuals identified by project managers as having key functional responsibilities related to marketing, manufacturing, R&D, and design. A total of **112** usable responses were obtained from the functional participants in addition to information provided by the **45** product managers.

RELIABILITY: Olson, Walker, and Ruekert (1995) reported a coefficient alpha of **.84** for this scale. Scale items were also submitted to a Varimax rotated principle components factor analysis and were found to load on a single factor with an eigenvalue greater than 1.

VALIDITY: No specific examination of scale validity for this measure was reported by Olson, Walker, and Ruekert (1995).

ADMINISTRATION: Olson, Walker, and Ruekert (1995) indicated that information about each project was initially obtained from project managers through a telephone interview using a structured questionnaire. After project managers had identified the key functional personnel for their project in marketing, manufacturing, R&D, and design, self-administered mail surveys were sent to each of the functional participants of each project. An overall project score was created for the interdependency measure by averaging responses to each scale across all the responding functional participants from a given project. Higher scores on the scale indicated that difficulties were incurred more frequently and that tasks were perceived as being more complex and difficult both during various stages of the process and overall during the project in general.

MAJOR FINDINGS: Olson, Walker, and Ruekert (1995) examined the relationship between new product coordinating structures and outcomes using a resource dependency view of the new product development process. Increased difficulties in the development process were found to result in greater levels of **perceived interdependency** among the various functional areas, whereas the flow of information and other resources was found to increase with higher levels of **interdependency**.

REFERENCES:
Olson, Eric M., Orville C. Walker Jr., and Robert W. Ruekert (1995), "Organizing for Effective New Product Development: The Moderating Role of Product Innovativeness," *JM*, 59 (January), 48–62.
Ruekert, Robert W. and Orville C. Walker Jr. (1987a), "The Organization of Marketing Activities: A Conceptual Framework and Empirical Evidence," *JM*, 51 (January), 1–19.

—— and —— (1987b), "Interactions Between Marketing and R&D Departments in Implementing Different Strategies," *Strategic Management Journal*, 8, 233–48.

Van de Ven, Andrew H. and Diane L. Ferry (1980), *Measuring and Assessing Organizations*. New York: John Wiley & Sons

SCALE ITEMS:*

Not at all   Very much

1. In order for the following groups of functions to attain their goals at stage 1, how much did they need the services, resources, or support of your department?

2. In order for the following groups of functions to attain their goals at stage 2, how much did they need the services, resources, or support of your department?

3. In order to attain your department's goals at stage 1, how much did your department need the services, resources, or support of the following groups of functions?

4. In order to attain your department's goals at stage 2, how much did your department need the services, resources, or support of the following groups of functions?

5. Overall, how important were these other units to your department in attaining the goals of your unit during stage 1 of the development process?

6. Overall, how important were these other units to your department in attaining the goals of your unit during stage 2 of the development process?

*Correspondence with the authors indicated that the instructions for these items asked respondents to evaluate their department's interaction with each of the other departments, including marketing and sales, manufacturing and production engineering, R&D and product engineering, and design.

SCALE NAME: Investment in Relationship

SCALE DESCRIPTION: Ping (1997) used this four-item, five-point Likert-type scale to assess the magnitude of investment by a retailer in building and maintaining the current relationship with a wholesaler.

SCALE ORIGIN: Ping (1997) noted that the scale was first published in one of his previous articles (Ping 1993). In developing the scale, Ping (1993) generated items on the basis of presurvey interviews with hardware retailers and a review of the relevant literature. The purification process began with nine academicians evaluating how well the items fit the construct; those misclassified by more than one judge were eliminated. The resulting measure was pretested in two different phases. The first pretest sought to clarify possible misinterpretations. Responses from 63 hardware retailers in the second pretest were used in analyzing the psychometric properties of the measures using item-to-total correlations, ordered similarity coefficients, and coefficient alpha computations. The final purification of the measure was based on LISREL analysis of data provided by 288 respondents as reported in Ping's (1993) study. Items were deleted if internal consistency was improved without detracting from the content validity of the measure. Tests of the discriminant and convergent validity of the measure were also undertaken, and the results were found to be satisfactory.

SAMPLES: Ping (1997) used a systematic random sampling procedure of U.S. hardware retailers to generate the 600 hardware retailers sampled in his study. Usable responses were received from **204** people. The sampling frame was taken from a hardware retailing trade publication's subscription list.

RELIABILITY: Ping (1997) reported a coefficient alpha of **.92** for this measure.

VALIDITY: Ping (1997) conducted a confirmatory factor analysis to test the unidimensionality and construct validity of the measure. One item, "Much of my investment with the <u>current</u> wholesaler is unique to the relationship," was dropped from the original measure during this process. The measure was judged to be unidimensional, whereas the average variance extracted demonstrated the scale's convergent and discriminatory validity. The author also stated that the measure offered content validity.

ADMINISTRATION: The scale was included with other measures as part of a self-administered questionnaire that was delivered by mail. Nonrespondents received as many as three postcard reminders. Ping (1997) used a key informant approach, in which key informants represented a single individual, typically a manager, owner, or executive of the hardware store. Higher scores on the scale reflected a greater investment on the part of the retailer with respect to building and maintaining its relationship with a supplier.

MAJOR FINDINGS: Ping (1997) proposed and empirically examined several antecedents to voice in a business-to-business context. The results of his study indicated that cost of exit was a second-order construct with first-order factor indicators of alternative supplier attractiveness, **investment in the relationship**, and switching costs. Increasing the cost of exit was found to increase the likelihood of voice.

REFERENCES:
Ping, Robert A., Jr. (1993), "The Effects of Satisfaction and Structural Constraints on Retailer Exiting, Voice, Loyalty, Opportunism, and Neglect," *JR*, 69 (Fall), 320–52.
——— (1997), "Voice in Business-to-Business Relationships: Cost-of-Exit and Demographic Antecedents," *JR*, 73 (2), 261–81.

SCALE ITEMS:

Strongly   Strongly
disagree   agree

1————2————3————4————5

1. Overall I have invested a lot in the relationship with the <u>current</u> wholesaler.

2. A lot of energy, time and effort have gone into building and maintaining the relationship with the <u>current</u> wholesaler.

3. All things considered the company has put a lot into the relationship with <u>current</u> wholesaler.

4. I have put a considerable amount of time, effort, and energy into building the relationship with the <u>current</u> wholesaler.

SCALE NAME: Investments (Buyer)

SCALE DESCRIPTION: This five-item, seven-point Likert-type scale measures the level of initial investments made by the buyer as part of the purchasing agreement with a particular supplier.

SCALE ORIGIN: Stump and Heide (1996) based the items in this measure on ones previously used by Anderson (1985) and Heide and John (1990). Extensive pretesting of the questionnaire containing the measure was reported by Stump and Heide (1996).

SAMPLES: Stump and Heide (1996) drew a random sample of 1073 names from a national mailing list of chemical manufacturing firms in standard industrial classification code 28. Of this group, 631 key informants were identified by telephone who agreed to participate in the study. A total of **164** usable surveys were returned.

RELIABILITY: Stump and Heide (1996) calculated a coefficient alpha of **.78** for this measure.

VALIDITY: Stump and Heide (1996) examined item-to-total correlations of the items composing the scale and conducted an exploratory factor analysis of the measures used in the study. A confirmatory factor analysis of all items used in each scale verified the unidimensionality of the measure. Evidence of the discriminant validity of the measure was provided by means of a series of chi-square difference tests performed on the factor correlations. The model was also evaluated and found to represent a good fit to the data.

ADMINISTRATION: The scale was included by Stump and Heide (1996) with other measures as part of a self-administered survey that was delivered by mail. Buyers were asked to identify a purchasing agreement for a particular product that had been established within the last 12 months and to answer questions in the context of that purchasing agreement. Higher scores on the scale indicated that a buyer invested significant resources in the relationship as part of the purchasing agreement.

MAJOR FINDINGS: Stump and Heide (1996) examined how chemical manufacturers used partner selection, incentive design, and monitoring approaches in the management and control of supplier relationships. When purchasing agreements called for **specific buyer investments**, buyers responded to this control problem by subjecting suppliers to more stringent qualifications of ability and motivation and by requiring reciprocal supplier specific investments.

REFERENCES:
Anderson, Erin (1985), "The Salesperson as Outside Agent or Employee: A Transaction Cost Analysis," *Marketing Science*, 4 (3), 234–54.
Heide, Jan B. and George John (1990), "Alliances in Industrial Purchasing: The Determinants of Joint Action in Buyer-Supplier Relationships," *JMR*, 27 (February), 24–36.
Stump, Rodney L. and Jan B. Heide (1996), "Controlling Supplier Opportunism in Industrial Relationships," *JMR*, 33 (November), 431–41.

#669 *Investments (Buyer)*

SCALE ITEMS:

Strongly   Strongly
disagree   agree
  1————2————3————4————5————6————7

1. Our production system that incorporates this item has been tailored to meet the requirements of dealing with this supplier.

2. We have spent significant resources to ensure that our specifications for this item fit well with this supplier's production capabilities.

3. Gearing up to deal with this supplier on this item required highly specialized tools and equipment on our part.

4. The procedures and routines we have developed to obtain this item are tailored to the particular situation of this supplier.

5. This supplier has some unusual technological norms and standards for the item, which have required extensive adaptations on our part.

SCALE NAME: Investments (Supplier)

SCALE DESCRIPTION: This six-item, seven-point Likert-type scale measures the extent to which a supplier has made investments that are dedicate to the agreement with its focal manufacturer.

SCALE ORIGIN: Stump and Heide (1996) adapted the majority of the items used in this measure from the work of Heide and John (1990). Extensive pretesting of the questionnaire containing the measure was reported by Stump and Heide (1996).

SAMPLES: Stump and Heide (1996) drew a random sample of 1073 names from a national mailing list of chemical manufacturing firms in standard industrial classification code 28. Of this group, 631 key informants were identified by telephone who agreed to participate in the study. A total of **164** usable surveys were returned.

RELIABILITY: Stump and Heide (1996) calculated a coefficient alpha of **.83** for this measure.

VALIDITY: Stump and Heide (1996) examined item-to-total correlations of the items composing the scale and conducted an exploratory factor analysis of the measures used in the study. A confirmatory factor analysis of all items used in each scale verified the unidimensionality of the measure. Evidence of the discriminant validity of the measure was provided by means of a series of chi-square difference tests performed on the factor correlations. The model was also evaluated and found to represent a good fit to the data.

ADMINISTRATION: The scale was included by Stump and Heide (1996) with other measures as part of a self-administered survey that was delivered by mail. Buyers were asked to identify a purchasing agreement for a particular product that had been established within the last 12 months and to answer questions in the context of that purchasing agreement. Higher scores on the scale indicated that a supplier invested significant resources in the relationship as part of the purchasing agreement.

MAJOR FINDINGS: Stump and Heide (1996) examined how chemical manufacturers used partner selection, incentive design, and monitoring approaches in the management and control of supplier relationships. When purchasing agreements called for specific buyer investments, buyers responded to this control problem by means of requiring reciprocal **supplier specific investments**.

REFERENCES:
Heide, Jan B. and George John (1990), "Alliances in Industrial Purchasing: The Determinants of Joint Action in Buyer-Supplier Relationships," *JMR*, 27 (February), 24–36.
Stump, Rodney L. and Jan B. Heide (1996), "Controlling Supplier Opportunism in Industrial Relationships," *JMR*, 33 (November), 431–41.

SCALE ITEMS:

Strongly disagree — Strongly agree
1————2————3————4————5————6————7

1. This supplier has spent significant resources to ensure the specifications for this item fit well with our firm's production capabilities.

2. This supplier's production system has been tailored to producing the items being sold to our firm.

3. Gearing up to deal with our firm on this item requires highly specialized tools and equipment on the part of this supplier.

4. The procedures and routines this supplier has developed for this item are tailored to the particular situation of our firm.

5. Our firm has some unusual technological norms and standards for this item, which have required extensive adaptations by this supplier.

6. Most of the training this supplier has undertaken relative to our firm's requirements for this item can not be easily adapted for use with another customer.

SCALE NAME: Involvement in Self and Surroundings (ISS)

SCALE DESCRIPTION: Strutton, Pelton, and Lumpkin (1995) described this three-item, five-point Likert-type scale as measuring a tendency to become involved, rather than alienated by, whatever circumstance or situation is encountered.

SCALE ORIGIN: Strutton, Pelton, and Lumpkin (1995) reported that these items were taken from Maddi, Kobasa, and Hoover's (1979) alienation from self and alienation from work scales and used as negative indicators of the involvement with self and surroundings (ISS) construct.

SAMPLES: Using a sampling frame generated from the telephone directories of two metropolitan statistical areas, Strutton, Pelton, and Lumpkin (1995) first identified a stratified random sample of 1000 organizations likely to have industrial salespeople. A systematic random sampling procedure was then used to identify 450 organizations for telephone contact. Of the 450 individuals contacted, 374 organizational sales managers agreed to allow one company salesperson to be randomly selected to participate in the study. Subsequently, **322** acceptable questionnaires were returned from these salespeople for an 86% response rate. Of this sample, 71% were 40 years of age or younger, 62% were men, and 76% had incomes of $35,000 or more. All levels of sales experience were adequately represented; 29% of the sample had less than four years experience, 35% has four to ten years experience, and 36% had more than ten years of sales experience.

RELIABILITY: Strutton, Pelton, and Lumpkin (1995) reported a coefficient alpha of **.742** for this measure.

VALIDITY: No specific examination of the scale's validity was reported by Strutton, Pelton, and Lumpkin (1995).

ADMINISTRATION: Strutton, Pelton, and Lumpkin (1995) stated that the scale was part of a self-administered questionnaire that was returned by mail. In addition to answering questions measuring the personality characteristics of challenge, self-determination, and involvement in self and surroundings, respondents described the most stressful job-related situation experienced during the preceding three months. The manner in which they coped with the stressful episode was assessed using Strutton and Lumpkin's (1994) sales-domain-relevant version of the Ways of Coping Checklist. With respect to the ISS measure, the mean values on the summated scale were used to determine the point at which one-third of the sample scored below or above the middle third. Strutton, Pelton, and Lumpkin (1995) then classified 88 salespeople as alienated from self and surroundings and 128 as involved with self and surroundings. High scores on the ISS scale indicated a passive attitude toward personal decision making and a lack of involvement with personal skills or values.

MAJOR FINDINGS: Strutton, Pelton, and Lumpkin (1995) investigated the relationship between how salespeople cope with job stress and the three personality characteristics of challenge, self-determination, and involvement in self and surroundings. The problem-focused coping tactics of directed problem solving and self-control were significantly positively associated with those characterized as **involved with self and situation**. Three emotional avoidance coping tactics—seeking social support, mental distancing, and emotional avoidance—were associated with those characterized as **alienated from self and situation**.

REFERENCES:

Maddi, Salvatore, Suzanne C. Kobasa, and Mark Hoover (1979), "An Alienation Test," *Journal of Humanistic Psychology*, 19 (1), 73–76.

Strutton, David and James R. Lumpkin (1994), "Problem and Emotion-Focused Coping Dimensions and Sales Presentation Effectiveness," *JAMS*, 22 (1), 28–37.

———, Lou E. Pelton, and James R. Lumpkin (1995), "Personality Characteristics and Salespeople's Choice of Coping Strategies," *JAMS*, 23 (2), 132–40.

SCALE ITEMS:

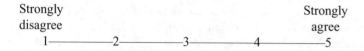

Strongly
disagree

Strongly
agree

1————2————3————4————5

1. I long for a simple life in which decisions do not have to be made. **(r)**

2. I find it difficult to imagine enthusiasm concerning work. **(r)**

3. The attempt to know yourself is a waste of time.

SCALE NAME: Job Creativity

SCALE DESCRIPTION: Ganesan and Weitz (1996) used this five-item, seven-point Likert-type scale to measure the extent to which buyers demonstrated creativity in their job. Ganesan and Weitz (1996) referred to this scale as *creative behavior* in their article.

SCALE ORIGIN: Ganesan and Weitz (1996) adapted items from the measure of innovative behavior in organizations used by Scott and Bruce (1994) to the present context. Multiple items were developed for the construct and purified using item analysis and an exploratory factor analysis. Items loading on multiple factors and those with low loadings were dropped from the scale.

SAMPLES: Ganesan and Weitz (1996) effectively sampled approximately 1500 retail buyers, divisional merchandise managers, general merchandise managers, and senior merchandise officers whose names appeared on a national list of department, specialty, and discount chain store employees. Usable responses were obtained from **207** respondents.

RELIABILITY: Ganesan and Weitz (1996) reported a coefficient alpha of **.75** for the scale.

VALIDITY: All items composing the measures used by Ganesan and Weitz (1996) were subjected to a confirmatory factor analysis to assess the unidimensionality of the measures, and items violating this principle were dropped. Scales demonstrating unidimensionality were then tested for discriminant and convergent validity using LISREL 8.10. The overall model fit was good, demonstrating a goodness-of-fit index of .96, confirmatory fit index of .99, root mean squared error of approximation of .02, and standardized root mean square residual of .06, as well as a nonsignificant chi-square.

ADMINISTRATION: Ganesan and Weitz (1996) included the scale with other measures as part of a self-administered survey that was delivered by mail. Higher scores on the scale indicated that a buyer was more creative and innovative in performing his or her job duties.

MAJOR FINDINGS: Ganesan and Weitz (1996) investigated the impact of various staffing policies on the attitudes and behavior of retail buyers. Retail buyers with higher levels of affective commitment to the organization, as well as higher levels of intrinsic motivation, were more likely to demonstrate **creativity on the job**.

REFERENCES:

Ganesan, Shankar and Barton A. Weitz (1996), "The Impact of Staffing Policies on Retail Buyer Job Attitudes and Behaviors," *JR*, 72 (1), 31–56.
Scott, Susanne G. and Reginald A. Bruce (1994), "Determinants of Innovative Behavior: A Path Model of Individual Innovation in the Workplace," *Academy of Management Journal*, 37 (3), 580–607.

SCALE ITEMS:

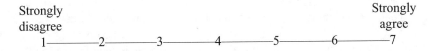

Strongly disagree — 1——2——3——4——5——6——7 — Strongly agree

1. When new trends develop, I am usually the first to get on board.

2. I experiment with new approaches to merchandising my products.

3. I am on the lookout for new ideas from my suppliers.

4. I try to be as creative as I can in my job.

5. My boss feels that I am creative in my job.

SCALE NAME: Job Description Index (JDI)

SCALE DESCRIPTION: The job description index (JDI) is a five-measure, composite scale purporting to measure job satisfaction. The five areas are type of work (18 items), opportunities for promotion (9 items), supervision (18 items), pay (9 items), and coworkers (18 items). Each job area measure consists of a list of adjectives or phrases. A summated ratings scale is used ranging from "Y" (yes) to "N" (no), with "?" (cannot decide) between for each job area. Teas (1983) modified the scale somewhat, as is discussed subsequently.

SCALE ORIGIN: The JDI scales for job satisfaction were originally developed by Smith, Kendall, and Hulin (1969). The research for these scales began in 1959 and was a result of several studies across a wide array of jobs and people. The scales were developed to measure satisfaction on the job within both an "evaluative, general, long-term framework" and a "descriptive, specific, short-term framework," as well as "to cover the important areas of satisfaction." This wide array of data was used to provide a generally applicable series of measurements of satisfaction (JDI).

Smith, Kendall, and Hulin (1969) conducted a literature review, which supported the multidimensional notion of job satisfaction. This literature review provided the basis for the original construct of the JDI and its five areas: work, pay, promotions, supervision, and coworkers. An item analysis was conducted, which included item intercorrelations and item validities. All items within each area were intercorrelated (median item intercorrelations exceeded .24). Four individual studies were conducted to evaluate the validity of the JDI using very different samples (Cornell University undergraduates, employees of a farmers' cooperative, male employees from two plants of a large electronics manufacturer, and male employees of a bank). Validity was assessed for different forms of the JDI and different scorings (graphic, interview, triadic, dyadic, and direct scoring). The analysis demonstrated that discriminate scores were "obtained from measures directed toward several aspects of the job (discriminate validity for measures and areas), and that several methods of measurement applied to the same aspect show substantial agreement (convergent validity for measures)" (Smith, Kendall, and Hulin 1969, p. 58). These analyses resulted in the final version of the JDI, which has demonstrated discriminant and convergent validity. Moreover, the JDI scales have been shown to be predictive in some situations.

SAMPLES: Apasu's (1987) data were collected from a United States-based multinational firm's sales force. **One hundred fifty-six** usable questionnaires were obtained for the analysis (the response rate was 60%). The average income of the sample was $30,000, the average sales experience was 7.5 years, and 97% of the respondents were under 40 years of age.

Busch's (1980) data were obtained from mail questionnaires sent to the sales forces of three pharmaceutical companies. The analysis was based on **477** usable questionnaires, for an overall response rate of 53.8%. The response rates of the individual companies were 51.5%, 52.5%, and 57.6%. Of the 477 respondents who provided usable questionnaires, 39 were women.

Cron and Slocum's (1986) data were obtained from six companies with national sales forces. A total of **466** usable questionnaires were obtained for a response rate of 54.5%. Seventy-two percent of the salespersons were married, 96% were men, and 51% had attended college. Income ranged from $25,000 to $50,000. The average salesperson in the sample was 39 years of age with a tenure of 8.7 years.

Good, Page, and Young (1996) mailed questionnaires to 698 retail managers employed by southern branches of a major multiunit department store. Of the **383** usable responses obtained (54.9% response rate), 280 (73.2%) were from entry-level executives and 103 (26.9%) were from upper-level executives. The majority of respondents were women (70%).

Teas's (1983) data were collected from mail questionnaires sent to two Midwest corporations' sales forces. Included with the questionnaire were cover letters from the researcher and the vice president of sales promising confidentiality and indicating company support for the survey. Usable responses were obtained from 116 salespersons, 49 and 67 salespersons from the two companies respectively (overall response rate was 55%).

RELIABILITY: Apasu (1987) reported a Cronbach's alpha of **.81** for the satisfaction with pay measure of the JDI. Busch (1980) reported a Spearman-Brown reliability coefficient of **.87** for the job satisfaction with supervision measure of the JDI. Cron and Slocum (1986) reported alpha reliability coefficients for each of the JDI measures of job satisfaction: **.76** for work; **.84** for pay; **.71** for opportunities for promotion; **.86** for supervision; and **.84** for coworkers. Good, Page, and Young (1996) reported coefficient alphas of **.95** and **.95** for the entry- and upper-level manager samples, respectively. Teas (1983) reported an alpha reliability coefficient of **.921** for the modified version of the JDI. (See "Scale Items" for a description of his modifications.)

VALIDITY: No examination of the measure's validity was reported in the reviewed articles.

ADMINISTRATION: Apasu (1987), Busch (1980), Good, Page, and Young (1996), and Teas (1983) collected data by mail, and the scale was self-administered along, with several other measures included in the questionnaire. Cron and Slocum's (1986) data were collected by two methods: Questionnaires were administered to salespersons during their national sales meeting for three of the companies used in the sample, and the other three companies of the sample were sent questionnaires by mail that were subsequently self-administered. The questionnaires used contained the JDI scales along with several other measures.

The scoring of the JDI scale was as follows:

Response	Weight
Yes to a positive item	3
No to a negative item	3
? to any item	1
Yes to a negative item	0
No to a positive item	0

A high score represented a high level of perceived job satisfaction (e.g., a maximum score of 54 for the satisfaction with work indicated high perceived job satisfaction pertaining to this area). An overall composite score can be used for overall job satisfaction by summating the five areas' summated scores.

MAJOR FINDINGS: Apasu's (1987) study used only the satisfaction with pay measure of the JDI. The results indicated that salespersons with higher achievement-oriented values, lower value congruence, and higher dissatisfaction with pay perceived pay as an important reward.

Busch (1980) used only the satisfaction with supervision portion of the JDI. The results indicated that expert and referent power were significantly related to satisfaction with supervision for all three firms. Coercive power was found to be significantly related to satisfaction with supervision for two of the three firms. Legitimate and reward were found to be significantly related to satisfaction with supervision for only one of the three firms. No significant differences were found between men and women or the power bases and job satisfaction.

Cron and Slocum (1986) found that the business strategy of a firm has a significant effect on job satisfaction. Age was found to be related to job satisfaction, with older persons being more satisfied. The results indicated that significant main effects of career stages were observed for job satisfaction.

Statistically significant differences were reported for work, supervision, and promotion satisfaction. Salespersons in the exploration stage were the least satisfied, whereas the salespersons in the established and maintenance stages were the most satisfied. The salespersons in the disengagement stage were slightly less satisfied than were salespersons in the established and maintenance stages.

Good, Page, and Young's (1996) study found that **job satisfaction** did not significantly influence intent to leave for either the entry-level retail manager or the upper-level retail manager groups.

Teas (1983) used a modified version of the JDI (see "Scale Items" for details). The results from the modified JDI measure indicated that a salesperson's perceived role conflict, consideration, participation, and selling experience were significantly related to job satisfaction. Role ambiguity was found not to be significantly related to job satisfaction.

COMMENTS: See also Teas and Horrell (1981), Michaels and Dixon (1994), Nonis, Sager, and Kumar (1996), and Siguaw, Brown and Widing (1994). It appears they used the scale or portions of it in various studies.

REFERENCES:
Apasu, Yao (1987), "The Importance of Value Structures in the Perception of Rewards by Industrial Salespersons," *JAMS*, 15 (Spring), 1–10.
Busch, Paul (1980), "The Sales Manager's Bases of Social Power and Influence Upon the Sales Force," *JM*, 44 (Summer), 91–101.
Cron, William L. and John W. Slocum Jr. (1986), "The Influence of Career Stages on Salespeople's Job Attitudes, Work Perceptions, and Performance," *JMR*, 23 (May), 119–29.
Good, Linda K., Thomas J. Page Jr., and Clifford E. Young (1996), "Assessing Hierarchical Differences in Job-Related Attitudes and Turnover Among Retail Managers," *JAMS*, 24 (2), 148–56.
Michaels, Ronald E. and Andrea L. Dixon (1994), "Sellers and Buyers on the Boundary: Potential Moderators of Role Stress-Job Outcome Relationships," *JAMS*, 22 (1), 62–73.
Nonis, Sarath A., Jeffrey K. Sager, and Kamalesh Kumar (1996), "Salespeople's Use of Upward Influence Tactics (UITs) in Coping With Role Stress," *JAMS*, 24 (1), 44–56.
Siguaw, Judy A., Gene Brown, and Robert E. Widing II (1994), "The Influence of the Market Orientation of the Firm on Sales Force Behavior and Attitudes," *JMR*, 31 (February), 106–16.
Smith, Patricia C., Lorne M. Kendall, and Charles L. Hulin (1969), *The Measurement of Satisfaction in Work and Retirement*. Chicago: Rand McNally & Company.
Teas, R. Kenneth (1983), "Supervisory Behavior, Role Stress, and the Job Satisfaction of Industrial Salespeople," *JMR*, 20 (February), 84–91.
―――― and James F. Horrell (1981), "Salespeople Satisfaction and Performance Feedback," *Industrial Marketing Management*, 10, 49–57.

SCALE ITEMS:
For each scale, subjects were instructed to put "Y" beside an item if the item described the particular aspect of his or her job (e.g., work, pay), "N" if the item did not describe that aspect, or "?" if he or she could not decide. The response beside each item is the one scored in the "satisfied" direction for each scale.

Work
Y Fascinating
N Routine
Y Satisfying
N Boring
Y Good
Y Creative
N Hot
Y Pleasant
N Tiresome
Y Challenging
Y Gives sense of accomplishment
N Endless
N Hard to meet quotas

Pay
N Frustrating
Y Satisfactory profit sharing
N Barely live on income
N Bad
Y Income provides luxuries
N Insecure
N Less than I deserve
Y Highly paid
N Underpaid
N On your feet
Y Income adequate for
   normal expenses

Coworkers
Y Stimulating
N Boring
N Slow
Y Ambitious
N Stupid
Y Responsible
Y Respected
Y Fast
Y Intelligent
Y Useful
N Easy to make enemies
N Talk too much
Y Healthful
Y Smart
N Lazy
N Unpleasant
N No privacy
N Simple
Y Active
N Narrow interests
Y Loyal

Supervision
Y Asks my advice
N Hard to please
N Impolite
Y Praises good work
Y Tactful
Y Influential
Y Up-to-date
N Doesn't supervise
N Quick tempered
Y Tells me where I stand
N Annoying
N Stubborn
Y Knows job well
N Bad
Y Intelligent
Y Leaves me on my own
N Lazy
Y Around when needed

Promotions
Y Good opportunity for advancement
N Opportunity somewhat limited
Y Promotion on ability
N Dead-end job
Y Good chance for promotion
N Unfair promotion policy
N Infrequent promotions
Y Regular promotions enough
Y Fairly good chance for promotion

In Teas's (1983) version of the JDI,* he modified the "satisfaction with supervision" measure of the JDI and added a "satisfaction with customers" measure. The coding procedure used was that a "yes" = 3, "could not decide" = 2, and "no" = 1.

*Satisfaction with supervision***	*Satisfaction with customers*
1. Asks my advice	1. Stimulating
2. Unpleasant (r)	2. Hard to please (r)
3. Impolite (r)	3. Boring (r)
4. Praises good work	4. Smart
5. Tactful	5. Impolite (r)
6. Influential	6. Stubborn (r)
7. Up-to-date	7. Intelligent
8. Doesn't supervise enough (r)	8. Talks too much (r)
9. Quick-tempered (r)	9. Narrow interests (r)
10. Tells me where I stand	10. Hard to meet (r)
11. Annoying (r)	11. Honest
12. Stubborn (r)	12. Quick-tempered (r)
13. Knows job well	13. Tactful
14. Bad (r)	14. Stupid (r)
15. Intelligent	15. Loyal
16. Leaves me on my own	16. Lazy (r)
17. Around when needed	17. Hard to please (r)
18. Lazy (r)	18. Annoying (r)

*Only the "satisfaction" portion of the JDI was included.
**Only items 2, 3, 5, 7, 9, 11, 13, 14, 15, 17, and 18 were used in the modified "satisfaction with supervision" scale.

SCALE NAME: Job Motivation (Intrinsic)

SCALE DESCRIPTION: Ganesan and Weitz (1996) used this six-item, seven-point Likert-type scale to measure the extent to which a retail buyer is motivated by the job or task itself due to the exciting, challenging, and rewarding nature of the work.

SCALE ORIGIN: Ganesan and Weitz (1996) adapted the scale from measures of intrinsic reward orientation used by Sujan (1986). Multiple items were developed for the construct and purified using item analysis and an exploratory factor analysis. Items loading on multiple factors and those with low loadings were dropped from the scale.

SAMPLES: Ganesan and Weitz (1996) effectively sampled approximately 1500 retail buyers, divisional merchandise managers, general merchandise managers, and senior merchandise officers whose names appeared on a national list of department, specialty, and discount chain store employees. Usable responses were obtained from **207** respondents.

RELIABILITY: Ganesan and Weitz (1996) reported a coefficient alpha of **.72** for the scale.

VALIDITY: All items composing the measures used by Ganesan and Weitz (1996) were subjected to a confirmatory factor analysis to assess the unidimensionality of the measures, and items violating this principle were dropped. Scales demonstrating unidimensionality were then tested for discriminant and convergent validity using LISREL 8.10. The overall model fit was good, demonstrating a goodness-of-fit index of .96, confirmatory fit index of .99, root mean squared error of approximation of .02, and standardized root mean square residual of .06, as well as a nonsignificant chi-square.

ADMINISTRATION: Ganesan and Weitz (1996) included the scale with other measures as part of a self-administered survey that was delivered by mail. Higher scores on the scale indicated that a buyer was motivated to a greater degree by intrinsic factors such as the exciting, challenging, and rewarding nature of the job itself.

MAJOR FINDINGS: Ganesan and Weitz (1996) investigated the impact of various staffing policies on the attitudes and behavior of retail buyers. Retail buyers who perceived greater promotion opportunities in the firm showed higher levels of **intrinsic motivation**, but neither salary nor incentive compensation significantly affected the **intrinsic motivation** of buyers.

REFERENCES:
Ganesan, Shankar and Barton A. Weitz (1996), "The Impact of Staffing Policies on Retail Buyer Job Attitudes and Behaviors," *JR*, 72 (1), 31–56.
Sujan, Harish (1986), "Smarter Versus Harder: An Exploratory Attributional Analysis of Salesperson's Motivation," *JMR*, 23 (February), 41–49.

#674 *Job Motivation (Intrinsic)*

SCALE ITEMS:

Strongly   Strongly
disagree   agree
 1———————2———————3———————4———————5———————6———————7

1. I really care about my job.

2. My job is exciting and challenging.

3. My job gives me an opportunity to learn something new and different.

4. If it were not for the money, I would not be in this job. **(r)**

5. My job really does not interest me. **(r)**

6. If I were wealthy, I would still be a buyer for the challenge of it.

SCALE NAME: Job Risk-Taking

SCALE DESCRIPTION: Ganesan and Weitz (1996) used this three-item, seven-point Likert-type scale to measure the extent to which retail buyers are willing to take risks in exploring and adopting new ideas in the buying of merchandise to achieve goals.

SCALE ORIGIN: Ganesan and Weitz (1996) adapted some of the consumer-oriented risk-taking items used by Raju (1980) to the present context. Multiple items were developed for the construct and purified using item analysis and an exploratory factor analysis. Items loading on multiple factors and those with low loadings were dropped from the scale.

SAMPLES: Ganesan and Weitz (1996) effectively sampled approximately 1500 retail buyers, divisional merchandise managers, general merchandise managers, and senior merchandise officers whose names appeared on a national list of department, specialty, and discount chain store employees. Usable responses were obtained from **207** respondents.

RELIABILITY: Ganesan and Weitz (1996) reported a coefficient alpha of **.63** for the scale.

VALIDITY: All items composing the measures used by Ganesan and Weitz (1996) were subjected to a confirmatory factor analysis to assess the unidimensionality of the measures, and items violating this principle were dropped. Scales demonstrating unidimensionality were then tested for discriminant and convergent validity using LISREL 8.10. The overall model fit was good, demonstrating a goodness-of-fit index of .96, confirmatory fit index of .99, root mean squared error of approximation of .02, and standardized root mean square residual of .06, as well as a nonsignificant chi-square.

ADMINISTRATION: Ganesan and Weitz (1996) included the scale with other measures as part of a self-administered survey that was delivered by mail. Higher scores on the scale indicated that a buyer was more willing to take risks when performing his or her job duties.

MAJOR FINDINGS: Ganesan and Weitz (1996) investigated the impact of various staffing policies on the attitudes and behavior of retail buyers. Retail buyers with higher levels of affective commitment to the organization, as well as higher levels of intrinsic motivation, were more likely to demonstrate **risk-taking behavior** in performing their job duties.

REFERENCES:
Ganesan, Shankar and Barton A. Weitz (1996), "The Impact of Staffing Policies on Retail Buyer Job Attitudes and Behaviors," *JR*, 72 (1), 31–56.
Raju, P.S. (1980), "Optimum Stimulation Level: Its Relationship to Personality, Demographics, and Exploratory Behavior," *JCR*, 7 (December), 272–82.

SCALE ITEMS:

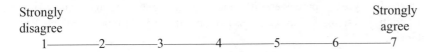

Strongly disagree 1———2———3———4———5———6———7 Strongly agree

1. I am a risk taker as far as my job is concerned.

2. I take some risk with the merchandise I buy.

3. I have achieved success by taking calculated risks at the right time.

SCALE NAME: Judgment Quality (Partner)

SCALE DESCRIPTION: Smith and Barclay (1997) used this three-item, seven-point Likert-type scale to measure perceptions of the degree to which partners perceived each other as being able to decide and act in a manner appropriate for furthering the joint interests of the partnership.

SCALE ORIGIN: Smith and Barclay (1997) indicated that the constructs used in their study were operationalized with a mix of original and adapted scale items generated from the conceptual definition of the constructs, a review of the literature, field interviews, and pretest results. Each of the final items representing this measure passed the extensive preliminary analysis of item reliability and validity described by the authors.

SAMPLES: Smith and Barclay (1997) collected dyadic self-reported data in two stages. The sponsor sample was composed of 338 sales representatives working for the Canadian subsidiaries of two multinational companies serving the computer industry. Forty percent of the 338 employees who were randomly selected from employee lists returned completed surveys. Using the names and contact information of relationship partners volunteered by these respondents, the authors then sampled the 135 dyadic partners. A total of **103** usable paired responses were obtained.

RELIABILITY: Smith and Barclay (1997) reported coefficient alphas for this measure of **.80** in both the sponsor and the partner models.

VALIDITY: Smith and Barclay (1997) reported extensive testing of the reliability, unidimensionality, and convergent and discriminant validity of the measures used in their study. LISREL and confirmatory factor analysis were used to demonstrate that the scale satisfied each of these standards, though some items from the measures as originally proposed were eliminated in the process.

ADMINISTRATION: Smith and Barclay (1997) included the scale with other measures as part of a self-administered survey that was delivered by internal company mail to sales representatives and by regular U.S. mail to the dyadic partners. E-mail follow-ups were used to increase survey response rate. Half of the sales representatives were instructed to consider a customer situation in the prior six months in which they had had some success with a selling partner, whereas the other half were to told to choose a situation in which they had had little or no success. Participants then responded to questions about the partner, their relationship, and the organization in the context of this situation. Higher scores on the scale indicated greater mutual trust between partners, in that partners perceived each other as being able to make appropriate decisions and as acting in a manner that furthered the joint interests of the relationship.

MAJOR FINDINGS: Smith and Barclay (1997) developed and tested two research models that explained selling partner relationship effectiveness. The first examined four organizational differences from the sponsor's (salesperson's) perspective, and the second examined these same differences from the partner's perspective. In both models, greater perceived differences in the reputations of partner firms, strategic horizons, and goals/control systems led to lower evaluations of the **judgment** component of mutual perceived trustworthiness.

REFERENCES:
Smith, J. Brock and Donald W. Barclay (1997), "The Effects of Organizational Differences and Trust on the Effectiveness of Selling Partner Relationships," *JM*, 61 (January), 3–21.

SCALE ITEMS:*

Strongly   Strongly
disagree   agree
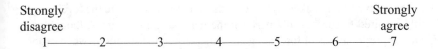

1. Sometimes his/her judgment is way off. **(r)**

2. Sometimes I have to question his/her marketing and selling skills. **(r)**

3. Sometimes I wonder about the appropriateness of decisions made by this rep. **(r)**

*All of the items in this scale were conceptualized at the individual level and then aggregated to the relationship level by taking the square root of the product of the individual responses by the sales representative and partner.

SCALE NAME: Knowledge of Product/Customer

SCALE DESCRIPTION: Three seven-point Likert-type items that attempt to measure the level of specialized knowledge and skills required to successfully perform the marketing functions. Although used in the context of evaluating the appropriateness of foreign agents versus foreign distributors when exporting products abroad, the scale items are not specific to export situations and could easily be applied to marketing in a domestic setting by changing the instructions. Bello and Lohtia (1995) referred to this scale as "human specificity."

SCALE ORIGIN: Bello and Lohtia (1995) stated that the scale was adapted from Anderson and Couglan (1987).

SAMPLES: Bello and Lohtia (1995) drew a systematic random sample of 600 manufacturers from among those listed in the 1991 edition of the *Journal of Commerce United States Importer & Exporter Directory*. From this sample, 398 firms were verified as exporting through middlemen, and one person with middleman responsibilities at each of these screened firms was sent a questionnaire. Nonrespondents were telephoned three weeks later and sent a second questionnaire. A total of **269** usable responses were obtained for a 68% response rate. Of these respondents, 60% exported through foreign distributors, whereas 40% exported using foreign agents.

RELIABILITY: A coefficient alpha of **.65** was reported by Bello and Lohtia (1995).

VALIDITY: Confirmatory factor analysis was used by Bello and Lohtia (1995) to provide evidence of discriminant and convergent validity, as well as to assess the unidimensionality of the measure. Convergent validity was deemed to be present because items loaded significantly on their posited indicators and because of the low to moderate correlations among the product specificity, human specificity, and physical specificity scales. Citing precedents set by Anderson and Gerbing (1988, p. 416), Bello and Lohtia (1995) stated that discriminant validity was also present because the correlation estimate between two indicators never included 1.0 (+/– two standard errors).

ADMINISTRATION: Bello and Lohtia (1995) indicated that this scale was self-administered as part of a longer survey instrument mailed to respondents. Instructions requested that responses be specific to a single, focal, export middleman in a foreign market. Higher scores on the scale were interpreted as indicating a greater need for training necessitated by the learning requirements of the foreign situation.

MAJOR FINDINGS: Bello and Lohtia (1995) investigated several cost indicators believed to influence the choice of foreign distributors versus foreign agents. The need for specialized **product/customer knowledge** when marketing a product abroad was of marginal difference between distributor and agent users.

COMMENTS: The low alpha level, as well as a close reading of the items, suggests that the scale is probably tapping into both product and customer dimensions. Further developmental work and validation may be called for prior to using this item set again.

REFERENCES:
Andersen, James C. and David W. Gerbing (1988), "Structural Equation Modeling in Practice: A Review and Recommended Two-Step Approach," *Psychological Bulletin*, 103 (3), 411–23.
Anderson, Erin and Anne T. Coughlan (1987), "International Market Entry and Expansion via Independent or Integrated Channels of Distribution," *JM*, 51 (January), 71–82.

Bello, Daniel C. and Ritu Lohtia (1995), "Export Channel Design: The Use of Foreign Distributors and Agents," *JAMS*, 23 (2), 83–93.

SCALE ITEMS:*

Strongly   Strongly

disagree   agree

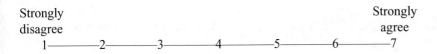

1———2———3———4———5———6———7

1. It takes a long time to learn about the product.

2. It is difficult to learn customer's needs.

3. It takes a lot of time to understand the customer.

*The specific wording of the instructions was not included in the article.

SCALE NAME: Knowledge of Product/Customer

SCALE DESCRIPTION: Bello and Gilliland (1997) used this three-item, seven-point Likert-type scale to assess the level of specialized product and customer knowledge that trading partners need to acquire for a foreign selling situation. The authors referred to this scale as *human investments*.

SCALE ORIGIN: Bello and Gilliland (1997) stated that the scale was adapted from Anderson and Couglan's (1987) study.

SAMPLES: Bello and Gilliland's (1997) systematic random sample of 245 national manufacturers verified as exporting through foreign distributors was drawn from the 1994 edition of the *Journal of Commerce United States Importer & Exporter Directory*. **One hundred sixty** usable responses were obtained from export managers employed by firms exporting a variety of industrial and consumer products to a total of 39 different countries.

RELIABILITY: A confirmatory factor analysis composite reliability of **.91** was reported by Bello and Gilliland (1997).

VALIDITY: Confirmatory factor analysis was used by Bello and Gilliland (1997) to provide evidence of discriminant and convergent validity, as well as to assess the unidimensionality of the measure. Convergent validity was deemed to be present because items loaded significantly on their posited indicators and because of the low to moderate correlations between the scale and other measures. Discriminant validity was also deemed to be present because the correlation estimate between two indicators never included 1.0 (+/– two standard errors). The authors used personal interviews with export executives as part of the pretest process to verify the face validity of the measure.

ADMINISTRATION: Bello and Gilliland (1997) indicated that this scale was self-administered as part of a longer survey instrument mailed to respondents. The export manager with primary responsibility for the firm's relationship with the foreign distributor received a survey, and nonrespondents were telephoned three weeks later, after which a second questionnaire followed. Instructions specified that questions were to be answered in the context of the focal distributor. The authors defined the focal distributor as the firm's fourth-largest foreign distributor in terms of unit sales volume to avoid a positive evaluation bias. Higher scores on the scale indicated a greater need for training and learning the customer and product requirements of the foreign selling situation.

MAJOR FINDINGS: Bello and Gilliland (1997) examined the effect of output controls, process controls, and flexibility on channel performance. Results indicated that export transactions requiring greater specialized **knowledge of the product and customer** resulted in greater flexibility between trading partners, perhaps due to the interdependence created by mutual investments in training and other nonredeployable resources.

REFERENCES:

Anderson, Erin and Anne T. Coughlan (1987), "International Market Entry and Expansion via Independent or Integrated Channels of Distribution," *JM*, 51 (January), 71–82.

Bello, Daniel C. and David I. Gilliland (1997), "The Effect of Output Controls, Process Controls, and Flexibility on Export Channel Performance," *JM*, 61 (January), 22–38.

SCALE ITEMS:

Strongly   Strongly
disagree   agree
  1————2————3————4————5————6————7

1. Special knowledge is required to sell our product effectively.

2. It takes a long time for a salesperson to learn about the product thoroughly.

3. A salesperson must put in a lot of effort to understand our customer's products needs.

SCALE NAME: Likability (Salesperson)

SCALE DESCRIPTION: Doney and Cannon (1997) used this three-item, seven-point Likert-type scale to measure the degree to which a buyer perceives a salesperson as being friendly, nice, and likable.

SCALE ORIGIN: Doney and Cannon (1997) stated that they generated items for the scale on the basis of interviews with marketing and purchasing personnel. Exploratory factor analyses using both orthogonal and oblique rotations were used to ensure high item loadings on hypothesized constructs and low cross-loadings.

SAMPLES: Doney and Cannon (1997) sampled 657 members of the National Association of Purchasing Management who were employed by firms involved in industrial manufacturing, as classified by standard industrial classification codes 33–37. **Two hundred ten** completed questionnaires were returned from a primarily male (76%) sample with an average of 15 years of purchasing experience.

RELIABILITY: Doney and Cannon (1997) calculated a coefficient alpha of **.90** for this measure.

VALIDITY: Doney and Cannon (1997) reported using three methods to test the discriminant validity of the scales representing the combined dimensions of trust of the salesperson and its proposed antecedents and outcomes. Each method provided strong evidence of discriminant validity. Two LISREL-based tests were also used to provide evidence for the convergent validity of the measures.

ADMINISTRATION: The scale was included with other measures as part of a self-administered survey that was delivered by mail. Nonrespondents received a postcard reminder followed by a second questionnaire a week later. Doney and Cannon (1997) instructed respondents to focus on a single, specific, recent purchase decision in which more than one supplier was seriously considered and to indicate on the survey (using initials) two of the firms considered. After answering questions pertaining to the purchase situation, half of the respondents were instructed to complete the remainder of the questionnaire in the context of the first supplier they had listed, whereas the other half were instructed to use the second supplier. Higher scores on the scale indicated that the buyer perceived the focal salesperson as being more likable, friendly, and nice.

MAJOR FINDINGS: Doney and Cannon (1997) investigated the impact of purchasing agents' trust in the salesperson and trust in the supplier firm on a buying firm's current supplier choice and future buying intentions. The extent to which a salesperson was perceived to be **likable** positively influenced the buyers' level of trust in the salesperson.

REFERENCES:
Doney, Patricia M. and Joseph P. Cannon (1997), "An Examination of the Nature of Trust in Buyer-Seller Relationships," *JM*, 61 (April), 35–51.

SCALE ITEMS:

| Strongly disagree | | | | | | Strongly agree |
| 1———2———3———4———5———6———7 |

1. This salesperson is friendly.

2. This salesperson is always nice to us.

3. This salesperson is someone we like to have around.

SCALE NAME: Logistical Services (Level)

SCALE DESCRIPTION: Dahlstrom, McNeilly, and Speh (1996) described this twelve-item, five-point scale as measuring the level of service provided by a logistical supplier.

SCALE ORIGIN: Dahlstrom, McNeilly, and Speh (1996) reported that the construct was designed for this study, though no specific information pertaining to scale item generation was provided. The questionnaire containing the scale was pretested by six members of the Warehouse Education and Research Council, who evaluated it for content, readability, and relevance to the industry.

SAMPLES: Using a sampling frame generated from the membership of the Warehouse Education and Research Council, Dahlstrom, McNeilly, and Speh (1996) surveyed 1000 manufacturer, retailer, and wholesaler members. No mention of the specific sampling technique used to generate the frame was provided. Firms who exclusively used in-house warehousing services were not part of the population of interest and were asked to return the survey without answering. Including unanswered surveys, 383 questionnaires were returned for a 38.3% response rate. Of these, **189** surveys contained complete data from firms using interfirm warehousing services.

RELIABILITY: Dahlstrom, McNeilly, and Speh (1996) reported a coefficient alpha of **.87** for this measure.

VALIDITY: Item-to-total correlations estimated by an exploratory factor analysis were used in the first stage of measure purification. Dahlstrom, McNeilly, and Speh (1996) submitted the remaining items to a confirmatory factor analysis. Two items, "break bulk distribution" and "assembly," were eliminated to ensure the internal consistency of the scale. Results of the trimmed model confirmatory factor analysis provided evidence of construct validity. Discriminant validity was also assessed and found to be acceptable.

ADMINISTRATION: Dahlstrom, McNeilly, and Speh (1996) stated that the scale was part of a self-administered questionnaire that was returned by mail. Sampled individuals were contacted by telephone prior to survey delivery, and a postage-paid, return addressed reply envelope accompanied the questionnaire. A follow-up mailing with a second survey was sent two weeks after the first. Individuals using in-house warehousing services were asked not to complete the survey, and eligible respondents were instructed to answer in the context of the third-party warehouse service provider with whom they spent the greatest portion of their warehousing budget. Higher scores on the logistical services scale indicated that a greater level of warehousing services were being provided by the firm's primary warehousing partner.

MAJOR FINDINGS: Dahlstrom, McNeilly, and Speh (1996) investigated various antecedents to alternative forms of governance in the logistical supply market. A second topic of investigation addressed how formal controls and relational norms were employed by alternative governance forms to yield performance. Results of discriminant analysis suggested that the bilateral alliances in logistical supply relationships are influenced by the interaction of the user's dedicated investments, warehouse-related uncertainty, and the level of **logistical services** provided by warehouse suppliers.

REFERENCES:
Dahlstrom, Robert, Kevin M. McNeilly, and Thomas W. Speh (1996), "Buyer-Seller Relationships in the Procurement of Logistical Services," *JAMS*, 24 (2), 110–24.

#680 *Logistical Services (Level)*

SCALE ITEMS:

Directions: Thinking back over the past year, how often have each of the following services been performed for you by your primary warehouse vendor?

Never   Very often

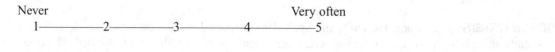

1. Order picking
2. Sorting
3. Kitting, sequencing
4. Return-goods handling
5. Product handling (pick-pack, repack, preprice, or clubstore repack)
6. Packaging
7. Inventory cycle counting
8. Customized palletizing
9. Storage and distribution of point-of-purchase displays
10. Rework of return goods
11. Labeling
12. Dedicated software

SCALE NAME: Long-Term Orientation (Retailer)

SCALE DESCRIPTION: Ganesan (1994) developed a seven-item, seven-point Likert-type scale to measure the extent to which retailers reported that they demonstrated concern for both their own and vendor outcomes and focused on long-term goals, concessions, and profitability in their relationship with vendors.

SCALE ORIGIN: The scale is original to Ganesan (1994), who developed separate but parallel measures of long-term orientation for the vendor and retailer samples. Scale items were generated through interviews with retail buyers and vendors; though some items were specific to the retailer or vendor version, the author included a core set of items with minor phrasing alterations in both scales. Item analysis and exploratory factor analysis were used to initially purify the measure, and items with low loadings and those loading on multiple factors were eliminated. A draft of the questionnaire containing this scale was also pretested with a group of 14 retail buyers representing two department store chains. After administration to the final sample, scale items were subjected to a confirmatory factor analysis. Goodness-of-fit indices and individual item t-values were used to identify the final scale items.

SAMPLES: Five retail department store chains agreed to participate in Ganesan's (1994) study, and each firm received and distributed 30 questionnaires to senior sales representatives or sales managers who served as liaisons with vendor organizations. A total of **124** (83%) usable responses representing the *retailer* sample were obtained. Of these, 48 respondents answered in the context of a long-term vendor relationship, and the remaining 76 answered in the context of a short-term vendor relationship. Contact information provided by respondents enabled the author to sample the designated 124 key vendor informants most knowledgeable about the retailer/vendor relationship with a survey similar in content to the retailer questionnaire but phrased from the vendor point of view. A total of **52** (42%) *vendor* representatives responded, of which 21 and 31 were in short- and long-term relationships, respectively.

RELIABILITY: Ganesan (1994) reported a coefficient alpha of **.94** for the scale.

VALIDITY: Ganesan (1994) submitted the scale to a confirmatory factor analysis using LISREL 7.16 to assess the unidimensionality, convergent validity, and discriminant validity of the measure. Although the measure was found to be unidimensional, no additional information pertaining to the outcome of the validity tests was provided.

ADMINISTRATION: Prior to being sent a survey, buyers in the retailer sample were randomly assigned to one of four cells in which the questionnaire instructions asked them to select a vendor on the basis of variations in two criteria: (1) the length of their relationship (short-term or long-term) and (2) the importance of the vendor's product to their organization (moderately important or very important). Questionnaires were distributed by a coordinator in each department store, and respondents were instructed to answer the survey in the context of this single vendor. Higher scores on the scale indicated that retailers focused more on long-term goals, long-term concessions, and long-term profitability in their relationship with vendors and indicated a higher concern for vendor outcomes in addition to their own.

MAJOR FINDINGS: Ganesan (1994) investigated a variety of factors influencing the long-term orientation of both retailers and vendors in an ongoing relationship, as well as the antecedents to long-term orientation. Retailer perceptions of vendor credibility, the retailer's dependence on the vendor, and the retailer's satisfaction with past outcomes were positively associated with the **retailer's long-term orientation**.

#681 *Long-Term Orientation (Retailer)*

REFERENCES:

Ganesan, Shankar (1994), "Determinants of Long-Term Orientation in Buyer-Seller Relationships," *JM*, 58 (April), 1–19.

SCALE ITEMS:

Strongly disagree
Strongly agree

1————2————3————4————5————6————7

1. We believe that over the long run our relationship with this resource will be profitable.

2. Maintaining a long-term relationship with this resource is important to us.

3. We focus on long-term goals in this relationship.

4. We are willing to make sacrifices to help this resource from time to time.

5. We are only concerned with our outcomes in this relationship. **(r)**

6. We expect this resource to be working with us for a long time.

7. Any concessions we make to help out this resource will even out in the long run.

SCALE NAME: Long-Term Orientation (Vendor)

SCALE DESCRIPTION: Ganesan (1994) developed a six-item, seven-point Likert-type scale to measure the extent to which vendors reported that they focused on long-term goals and long-term profitability in their vendor relationship, as well as a willingness to make sacrifices and share goals to develop a long-term relationship with a retailer.

SCALE ORIGIN: The scale is original to Ganesan (1994), who developed separate but parallel measures of long-term orientation for the vendor and retailer samples. Scale items were generated through interviews with retail buyers and vendors; though some items were specific to the retailer or vendor version, the author included a core set of items with minor phrasing alterations in both scales. Item analysis and exploratory factor analysis were used to initially purify the measure, and items with low loadings and those loading on multiple factors were eliminated. A draft of the questionnaire containing this scale was also pretested with a group of 14 retail buyers representing two department store chains. After administration to the final sample, scale items were subjected to a confirmatory factor analysis. Goodness-of-fit indices and individual item t-values were used to identify the final scale items.

SAMPLES: Five retail department store chains agreed to participate in Ganesan's (1994) study, and each firm received and distributed 30 questionnaires to senior sales representatives or sales managers who served as liaisons with vendor organizations. A total of **124** (83%) usable responses representing the *retailer* sample were obtained. Of these, 48 respondents answered in the context of a long-term vendor relationship, and the remaining 76 answered in the context of a short-term vendor relationship. Contact information provided by respondents enabled the author to sample the designated 124 key vendor informants most knowledgeable about the retailer/vendor relationship with a survey similar in content to the retailer questionnaire but phrased from the vendor point of view. A total of **52** (42%) *vendor* representatives responded, of which 21 and 31 were in short- and long-term relationships, respectively.

RELIABILITY: Ganesan (1994) reported a coefficient alpha of **.82** for the scale.

VALIDITY: Ganesan (1994) submitted the scale to a confirmatory factor analysis using LISREL 7.16 to assess the unidimensionality, convergent validity, and discriminant validity of the measure. Although the measure was found to be unidimensional, no additional information pertaining to the outcome of the validity tests was provided.

ADMINISTRATION: Prior to being sent a survey, buyers in the retailer sample were randomly assigned to one of four cells in which the questionnaire instructions asked them to select a vendor on the basis of variations in two criteria: (1) the length of their relationship (short-term or long-term) and (2) the importance of the vendor's product to their organization (moderately important or very important). Questionnaires were distributed by a coordinator in each department store, and retailers were instructed to identify contact information for the vendor. This measure was administered as part of a mail survey sent to vendors, which was accompanied by a cover letter explaining the study purpose and promising confidentiality. Higher scores on the scale indicated that vendors focused more on long-term goals and long-term profitability in their relationship with the retailer and indicated a greater willingness to make sacrifices and share goals with retailers to develop a long-term relationship.

MAJOR FINDINGS: Ganesan (1994) investigated a variety of factors influencing the long-term orientation of both retailers and vendors in an ongoing relationship, as well as the antecedents to long-term orientation. Vendor perceptions of retailer credibility and the vendor's satisfaction with past outcomes were found to be positively associated with the **vendor's long-term orientation**.

#682 *Long-Term Orientation (Vendor)*

REFERENCES:

Ganesan, Shankar (1994), "Determinants of Long-Term Orientation in Buyer-Seller Relationships," *JM*, 58 (April), 1–19.

SCALE ITEMS:

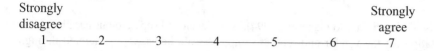

Strongly disagree

Strongly agree

1————2————3————4————5————6————7

1. We believe that over the long run our relationship with the retailer will be profitable.

2. Maintaining a long-term relationship with this retailer is important to us.

3. We focus on long-term goals in this relationship.

4. We are willing to make sacrifices to help this retailer from time to time.

5. We share our long-term goals with this retailer.

6. We would like to develop a long-term relationship with this retailer.

SCALE NAME: Machiavellianism (Mach IV)

SCALE DESCRIPTION: Twenty seven-point Likert-type statements measuring the degree to which a person expresses tendencies to control others through aggressive, manipulative, and even devious means to achieve personal or organizational objectives.

SCALE ORIGIN: The scale was constructed by Christie and Geis (1970). Initially, they drew 71 items from the writings of Machiavelli (*The Prince* and *The Discourses*). They ultimately selected the 20 items with the highest item-to-total correlations (10 stated positively and 10 stated negatively). They reported that the split-half reliability of the scale averaged approximately .79 across several samples and the average item-to-total correlation was .38. A forced choice version of the scale (MACH V) was developed when MACH IV was found to have significant social desirability bias. A version appropriate for use with children (Kiddie Mach) was also developed. See Robinson, Shaver, and Wrightsman (1991, pp. 380–85) for these other two versions of the scale.

SAMPLES: Ho and colleagues (1997) mailed surveys to a sample of 2000 practitioner marketers obtained from the American Marketing Association. Usable forms were received back from **415** respondents. The sample was a little more male (55.4%) than female, was mostly college educated (94.2%), and had an average age of 37.6 years. The majority (75%) categorized themselves as at least managers in their companies.

Hunt and Chonko (1984) mailed a questionnaire to a systematic sample of 4282 members of the American Marketing Association. Usable responses were received from **1076** respondents. Among the demographic information supplied, the typical respondent was male (70%), married (72%), and had a master's degree (53%). A little less than half of the sample worked for firms with more than 1000 employees (44%), were in marketing research jobs (41%), and were between the ages of 30 and 39 years (40%).

The study conducted by Sparks (1994) reanalyzed the data collected by Hunt and Chonko (1984). Usable responses were fewer (n = **1023**) because of a slightly different manner of handling missing values.

RELIABILITY: Alphas of **.71** and **.76** were reported for the scale by Ho and colleagues (1997) and Hunt and Chonko (1984; Sparks 1994), respectively.

VALIDITY: No examination of the scale's validity was reported by either Ho and colleagues (1997) or Hunt and Chonko (1984; Sparks 1994).

ADMINISTRATION: The scale was self-administered as part of a larger mail questionnaire in the studies by Ho and colleagues (1997) and Hunt and Chonko (1984; Sparks 1994). Per Christie and Geis (1970), the scale was scored by summing the numerical responses to all items (reverse coding 20 of the items) and adding a constant of 20. This produces a range of scores from 40 to 160 and a theoretical neutral score of 100. High scores on the scale (over 100) indicated that respondents were expressing strong Machiavellian tendencies, whereas low scores (less than 100) suggested that the respondents were low in Machiavellianism.

MAJOR FINDINGS: Ho and colleagues (1997) integrated cognitive moral development (CMD) into a model of the antecedents of role conflict and ambiguity. Unexpectedly, **Machiavellianism** was not found to be significantly related to CMD.

The purpose of the study by Hunt and Chonko (1984) was to determine whether marketers were more **Machiavellian** than other members of society. Among the findings was that **Machiavellianism** was higher for younger marketers, single marketers, and female marketers. Although no relationship was found between **Machiavellianism** and success in marketing, it was significantly related to several measures of job satisfaction, such that persons high in **Machiavellianism** were less satisfied with their jobs and marketing as a career.

Sparks (1994) reanalyzed Hunt and Chonko's (1984) data to determine if **Machiavellianism** was related to personal success in marketing when latitude for improvisation is high. The results indicated that, though **Machiavellianism** was not significantly related to success in marketing when latitude for improvisation is high, it was negatively related to success when latitude is low.

COMMENTS: See also a use of the scale by Saxe and Weitz (1982).

REFERENCES:

Christie, Richard and Florence L. Geis (1970), *Studies in Machiavellianism*. New York: Academic Press.

Ho, Foo Nin, Scott J. Vitell, James H. Barnes, and Rene Desborde (1997), "Ethical Correlates of Role Conflict and Ambiguity in Marketing: The Mediating Role of Cognitive Moral Development," *JAMS*, 25 (2), 117–26.

Hunt, Shelby D. and Lawrence B. Chonko (1984), "Marketing and Machiavellianism," *JM*, 48 (Summer), 30–42.

Robinson, John P., Phillip R. Shaver, and Lawrence S. Wrightsman (1991), *Measures of Personality and Social Psychological Attitudes*. San Diego, CA: Academic Press.

Saxe, Robert and Barton A. Weitz (1982), "The SOCO Scale: A Measure of the Customer Orientation of Salespeople," *JMR*, 19 (August), 343–51.

Sparks, John R. (1994), "Machiavellianism and Personal Success in Marketing: The Moderating Role of Latitude for Improvisation," *JAMS*, 22 (4), 393–400.

SCALE ITEMS:

Strongly disagree	Disagree	Slightly disagree	Neutral	Slightly agree	Agree	Strongly agree
1	2	3	4	5	6	7

1. The best way to handle people is to tell them what they want to hear.

2. When you ask someone to do something for you, it is best to give the real reasons for wanting it, rather than giving reasons which might carry more weight. **(r)**

3. Anyone who completely trusts anyone else is asking for trouble.

4. It is hard to get ahead without cutting corners here and there.

5. Honesty is the best policy in all cases. **(r)**

6. It is safest to assume that all people have a vicious streak, and it will come out when they are given a chance.

7. Never tell anyone the real reason you did something unless it is useful to do so.

8. One should take action only when sure it is morally right. **(r)**

9. It is wise to flatter important people.

10. All in all, it is better to be humble and honest than important and dishonest. **(r)**

11. Barnum was very wrong when he said there's a sucker born every minute. **(r)**

12. People suffering from incurable diseases should have the choice of being put painlessly to death.

13. It is possible to be good in all respects. **(r)**

14. Most people are basically good and kind. **(r)**

15. There is no excuse for lying to someone else. **(r)**

16. Most men forget more easily the death of their father than the loss of their property.

17. Most people who get ahead in the world lead clean, moral lives. **(r)**

18. Generally speaking, men won't work hard unless they're forced to do so.

19. The biggest difference between criminals and other people is that criminals are stupid enough to get caught.

20. Most men are brave. **(r)**

SCALE NAME: Manipulation (by Salesperson)

SCALE DESCRIPTION: Dorsch and Kelley (1994) described this three-item, six-point Likert-type scale as measuring purchasing executives' interpretation of a vendor's motives in offering gifts. Specifically, this scale attempts to measure the extent to which purchasing executives perceive the offer of a gift as an unfair attempt to influence their behavior. Dorsch and Kelley (1994) refer to the scale in their article as "perceived manipulation by salesperson."

SCALE ORIGIN: The scale is original to Dorsch and Kelley (1994), who stated that the measure was developed in accordance with procedures suggested by Churchill (1979) and Nunnally (1978). No other details of the scale development process were provided.

SAMPLES: Dorsch and Kelley (1994) sampled 1197 U.S. purchasing executives representing the ten major standard industrial classification divisions using a single questionnaire mailing. Due to mailing list restrictions, no prior notification, follow-up survey, or reminders were sent. A total of **151** usable questionnaires were received for a response rate of 12.6%. Sample respondents were predominately men (84.8%) located in the Midwest (55.2%) and employed by manufacturing firms (73.5%).

RELIABILITY: Dorsch and Kelley (1994) reported a coefficient alpha of **.68** for this measure.

VALIDITY: No specific examination of the scale's development process or validity was reported by Dorsch and Kelley (1994).

ADMINISTRATION: Dorsch and Kelley (1994) randomly assigned purchasing executives to a 3 (status of relationship) $\times$ 2 (cost of gift) $\times$ 2 (type of gift) full-factorial, between-subjects research design. Based on their cell assignment, respondents were given a hypothetical scenario to read describing their relationship status with a vendor and the nature of the gift provided by that vendor. The scale was part of a self-administered mail survey in which questions related to the measures of interest were answered after respondents had read the scenario. Higher scores on the scale indicated of stronger perceptions of manipulative intent on the part of the gift-giving vendor.

MAJOR FINDINGS: Dorsch and Kelley (1994) investigated the effect of buyer–vendor relationship status (no prior relationship, moderate relationship, and strong relationship), gift type (corporate versus personal), and gift cost (inexpensive versus expensive) on purchasing executives' perceptions of salesperson manipulation, feelings of indebtedness toward the sales representative, and intention to reciprocate vendor gifts. As levels of perceived **manipulation** on the part of the salesperson increased, purchasing executives' feelings of indebtedness toward the salesperson and intentions to reciprocate declined. Significant interactions between variables indicated that, when a relationship between the vendor and buyer has not been previously established, personal gifts, regardless of value, are perceived as more **manipulative** than corporate gifts. However, the level of perceived **manipulation** was not affected by the type or cost of gift under the moderate relationship condition. When the buyer–vendor relationship was strong, inexpensive personal gifts elicited the lowest levels of perceived **manipulation** overall, and expensive corporate gifts were perceived to be significantly less **manipulative** than expensive personal gifts. Inexpensive personal gifts were also judged to be significantly less **manipulative** than expensive personal gifts in the strong relationship condition.

REFERENCES:

Churchill, Gilbert A. (1979), "A Paradigm for Developing Better Measures of Marketing Constructs," *JMR*, 16 (February), 323–32.

Dorsch, Michael J. and Scott W. Kelley (1994), "An Investigation into the Intentions of Purchasing Executives to Reciprocate Vendor Gifts," *JAMS*, 22 (4), 315–27.

Nunnally, Jum C. (1978), *Psychometric Theory*, 2d ed. New York: McGraw-Hill.

SCALE ITEMS:

Prior to responding to the scale items, respondents read a scenario explaining the specific gift characteristic scenario and percentage of the previous year's business they had hypothetically conducted with the vendor. See Dorsch and Kelley (1994) for details of the experimental manipulations.

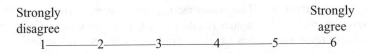

Strongly
disagree

Strongly
agree

1————2————3————4————5————6

1. I believe that Chris's favor is an attempt to influence me to buy from his company.

2. I think that Chris's favor is an act of friendship. **(r)**

3. I consider Chris's favor to be an attempt to get me to "owe him something."

SCALE NAME: Manufacturer Control

SCALE DESCRIPTION: Mohr, Fisher, and Nevin (1996) used this four-item, five-point Likert-type scale to assess the degree to which manufacturers controlled dealer decisions. This measure focuses on actual achieved control versus the ability to influence (power).

SCALE ORIGIN: The scale is original to Mohr, Fisher, and Nevin (1996), who followed the procedures for scale development outlined by Churchill (1979). The resulting scale items were pretested and revised in a series of iterative personal interviews with 12 computer dealers.

SAMPLES: Mohr, Fisher, and Nevin (1996) surveyed 557 computer retailer key informants (owners or managers), and **125** usable surveys were returned. The computer retailers selected for study were either affiliated with the microcomputer industry trade association or of 53 randomly selected outlets for a major computer franchiser. The average number of workers employed by responding retailers was 22.3, and the average monthly sales volume was $970,000.

RELIABILITY: Mohr, Fisher, and Nevin (1996) reported a coefficient alpha of **.78** for this measure.

VALIDITY: Mohr, Fisher, and Nevin (1996) reported that the measure exhibited acceptable levels of convergent and discriminatory validity according to the results of a confirmatory factor analysis.

ADMINISTRATION: The measure was included by Mohr, Fisher, and Nevin (1996) as part of a self-administered questionnaire that was delivered by mail. Nonrespondents received a reminder letter approximately one month after the initial mailing. Retailers were randomly assigned to answer questions about either their best or their worst relationship with a referent manufacturer. Higher scores on the scale indicated that the manufacturer achieved greater control over dealer decisions.

MAJOR FINDINGS: Mohr, Fisher, and Nevin (1996) investigated the relationship between collaborative communication and channel outcomes (satisfaction with the relationship, relationship commitment, relationship coordination) in the context of differing levels of dealer/manufacturer integration (independent, franchise, and company-owned). Hypotheses were tested in the context of hierarchical moderator regression analysis. With higher levels of **manufacturer control**, dealers were more satisfied and committed to the relationship and reported that their efforts were better coordinated with the manufacturer. However, significant interactions between **control** and communication indicated that higher levels of collaborative communication had stronger, more positive effects on satisfaction, commitment, and coordination under low-**manufacturer control** conditions than in situations in which **manufacturer control** was high.

REFERENCES:

Churchill, Gilbert A., Jr. (1979), "A Paradigm for Developing Better Measures of Marketing Constructs," *JMR*, 16 (February), 64–73.

Mohr, Jakki J., Robert J. Fisher, and John R. Nevin (1996), "Collaborative Communication in Interfirm Relationships: Moderating Effects of Integration and Control," *JM*, 60 (July), 103–15.

SCALE ITEMS:

Strongly disagree 1————2————3————4————5 Strongly agree

1. The manufacturer has a significant influence on our operations.

2. In the past six months, the manufacturer has changed or influenced our programs and policies.

3. This manufacturer can pretty much dictate how we sell their product.

4. We yield to recommendations of this manufacturer on general business practices.

SCALE NAME: Market Intelligence (New Product)

SCALE DESCRIPTION: Song and Parry (1997a) used this five-item, eleven-point Likert-type scale to measure the level of competitive and market intelligence efforts undertaken in preparation for the developing and launching of a new product.

SCALE ORIGIN: The origin of the scale was not stated by Song and Parry (1997a) but was likely to have been developed or modified according the procedures reported for the rest of the study measures by Song and Parry (1997b). The items for all scales used by Song and Parry (1997a, b) were evaluated by an academic panel composed of both Japanese and U.S. business and engineering experts. Following revisions, the items were judged by a new panel composed of academicians and new product development (NPD) managers. Song and Parry (1997b) reported extensive pretesting of both the Japanese and U.S. versions of the questionnaire.

SAMPLES: For this study, Song and Parry (1997a) used data provided by a random sample of 500 of the 611 firms trading on the Tokyo, Osaka, and Nagoya stock exchanges that had been identified as developing at least four new physical products since 1991. Usable responses pertaining to **788** new product development projects were obtained from 404 Japanese firms. The resulting data were randomly split into calibration (n = 394) and validation (n = 394) samples for the purpose of cross-validation.

RELIABILITY: Song and Parry (1997a) used a confirmatory factor analysis of the data in the calibration sample to purify the scale. Items loading on multiple constructs or those with low item-to-scale loadings were deleted from the measure. Song and Parry (1997a) reported a coefficient alpha of **.89** for the three-item, purified measure using data from the validation sample.

VALIDITY: The extensive pretesting and evaluation of the measure with academicians and NPD managers provided strong evidence for the face validity of the measure. Song and Parry (1997a, b) did not specifically report any other examination of scale validity.

ADMINISTRATION: The self-administered questionnaire containing the scale was originally developed in English; the Japanese version was prepared using the parallel-translation/double-translation method. Following minor revisions made on the basis of pretests with bilingual respondents and case study participants, the Japanese sample received a survey packet containing cover letters in both English and Japanese, two Japanese-language questionnaires, and two international postage-paid reply envelopes. Incentives, four follow-up letters, and multiple telephone calls and faxes were used to increase the response rate with both samples. Song and Parry (1997a, b) indicated that respondents were asked to answer one questionnaire in the context of a successful new product project introduced after 1991 and the other in the context of a new product project that had failed. Higher scores on the scale indicated greater efforts in the gathering of competitive and marketing intelligence information.

MAJOR FINDINGS: Song and Parry (1997a) conceptualized and tested a model of NPD practices believed to influence the success of new product ventures in Japan. The structural model was estimated with the calibration sample data, and the proposed model and the alternative models were tested using the validation sample. The **competitive and market intelligence efforts** in Japanese firms were found to significantly and positively influence the relative level of new product success, as well the marketing and technical proficiencies of the firm.

#686 *Market Intelligence (New Product)*

REFERENCES:

Song, X. Michael and Mark E. Parry (1997a), "The Determinants of Japanese New Product Successes,"
   JMR, 34 (February), 64–76.
—— and —— (1997b), "A Cross-National Comparative Study of New Product Development
   Processes: Japan and the United States," *JM*, 61 (April), 1–18.

SCALE ITEMS:

Directions: To what extent does each statement listed below correctly describe this selected successful project? Please indicate your degree of agreement or disagreement by circling a number from zero (0) to ten (10) on the scale to the right of each statement. Here: 0 = strongly disagree, 10 = strongly agree, and numbers between 0 and 10 indicate various degrees of agreement or disagreement.

Strongly
disagree

Strongly
agree

0———1———2———3———4———5———6———7———8———9———10

1. During the development of this product, we understood the customer's purchase decision well—the "who, what, when, where and how" of his [or her] purchase behavior for this selected product.

2. We knew how much the customer would pay for such a product—his/her price sensitivity.

3. We knew our competitors well—their products, pricing, strategies, and strengths.

4. We knew how our competitors would react to the introduction of this product.

5. We knew well the size of our potential market for this product.

SCALE NAME: Market Intelligence Quality (PIQ)

SCALE DESCRIPTION: Maltz and Kohli (1996) used this thirteen-item, five-point Likert-type scale to measure the extent to which the market intelligence received from a sender was perceived as being accurate, clear, timely, and relevant. The authors originally named this scale *perceived intelligence quality* and commonly referred to it throughout their article by the acronym *PIQ*.

SCALE ORIGIN: The scale is original to Maltz and Kohli (1996), who evaluated the items in face-to-face interviews with manufacturing, finance, and R&D department managers and with a panel of academic experts. The measure and questionnaire were also pretested with 77 participants of an executive MBA program. Items that were found to be problematic were revised or eliminated in accordance with the comments received at various stages in the pretesting process.

SAMPLES: Maltz and Kohli (1996) sampled mid-level managers operating within strategic business units (SBUs) of firms engaged in the manufacture of high-technology industrial equipment. The authors obtained names of 1061 nonmarketing managers in 270 SBUs from corporation presidents of participating firms. A total of **788** usable responses were returned by managers working in manufacturing (272), R&D (252), and finance (194).

RELIABILITY: Maltz and Kohli (1996) reported a coefficient alpha of **.86** for this measure.

VALIDITY: Maltz and Kohli (1996) stated that a confirmatory factor analysis with LISREL 7 was used to test the psychometric properties of the scale. Each of the items loaded on its conceptualized factor, and each of the four factors served as an indicator to the second-order market intelligence quality construct. The model fit was judged to be acceptable. The discriminant validity of the market intelligence quality and market intelligence use constructs were also empirically evaluated together in a LISREL model and found to be acceptable.

ADMINISTRATION: The measure was included by Maltz and Kohli (1996) as part of a self-administered questionnaire that was delivered by mail. Nonrespondents received a follow-up letter and second questionnaire mailing. When answering the survey, respondents were instructed to focus on the intelligence they had received from the person in the marketing department with whom they had interacted the most during the previous three months. A composite measure consisting of the mean of the four subscales was created and used in the evaluation of hypotheses. Higher scores on the scale reflected stronger, more positive evaluations of the accuracy, clarity, timeliness, and relevance of the marketing intelligence received.

MAJOR FINDINGS: Maltz and Kohli (1996) investigated the antecedents and consequences of the dissemination of marketing intelligence within SBUs. The frequency with which information was disseminated improved perceptions of the **quality of market intelligence** but only after a minimum threshold was reached. Perceptions of the **quality of market intelligence** suffered when that information was disseminated through either highly formal or highly informal channels but was maximized when dissemination using formal and informal channels was approximately equally split. A reciprocal relationship appeared to exist between trust and perceptions of the **quality of market intelligence,** because the results indicated that the greater the receiver's trust in the sender, the greater was the perceived **quality of the market intelligence** (and vice versa). Not surprisingly, the use of market intelligence increased with more positive perceptions of its **quality**, and dynamism, or the structural flux of the SBU, negatively affected perceptions of **market intelligence quality.**

REFERENCES:
Maltz, Elliot and Ajay K. Kohli (1996), "Market Intelligence Dissemination Across Functional Boundaries," *JMR*, 33 (February), 47–61.

SCALE ITEMS:
Directions: Please consider your work-related communication (written, oral, and electronic) with the marketing contact over the last three months, and respond to the following statements:

Strongly disagree 1————2————3————4————5 Strongly agree

Accuracy
1. The intelligence sent by the marketing contact lacked objectivity. **(r)**
2. The marketing contact provided valid estimates of the market potential for our products.
3. The information provided by the marketing contact was accurate.
4. S/he sent conflicting signals. **(r)**

Relevance
5. The marketing contact communicated important details about customer needs.
6. The marketing contact provided the data necessary to estimate the size of the market for our products.
7. S/he sent me relevant information.

Clarity
8. It was easy to follow the marketing contact's reasoning.
9. The concepts and language used by the marketing contact made sense to me.
10. S/he presented his/her ideas clearly.

Timeliness
11. The marketing contact provided information in a timely manner.
12. His/her information on changes in customer needs was too late. **(r)**
13. S/he gave me information that was "old hat." **(r)**

SCALE NAME: Market Intelligence Use

SCALE DESCRIPTION: Maltz and Kohli (1996) used this seven-item, five-point Likert-type scale to measure the extent to which the receiver used the market intelligence disseminated by the sender to understand his or her work environment and make and implement decisions.

SCALE ORIGIN: Maltz and Kohli (1996) adapted the scale from the work of Anderson, Ciarlo, and Brodie (1981). The items were evaluated in face-to-face interviews with manufacturing, finance, and R&D department managers and with a panel of academic experts. The measure and questionnaire were also pretested with 77 participants of an executive MBA program. Items that were found to be problematic were revised or eliminated in accordance with the comments received at various stages in the pretesting process.

SAMPLES: Maltz and Kohli (1996) sampled mid-level managers operating within strategic business units (SBUs) of firms engaged in the manufacture of high-technology industrial equipment. The authors obtained names of 1061 nonmarketing managers in 270 SBUs from corporation presidents of participating firms. A total of **788** usable responses were returned by managers working in manufacturing (272), R&D (252), and finance (194).

RELIABILITY: Maltz and Kohli (1996) reported a coefficient alpha of **.86** for this measure.

VALIDITY: Maltz and Kohli (1996) stated that a confirmatory factor analysis with LISREL 7 was used to test the psychometric properties of the scale. Each of the items loaded on its conceptualized factor, and each of the four factors served as an indicator to the second-order market intelligence quality construct. The model fit was judged to be acceptable. The discriminant validity of the market intelligence quality and market intelligence use constructs were also empirically evaluated together in a LISREL model and found to be acceptable.

ADMINISTRATION: The measure was included by Maltz and Kohli (1996) as part of a self-administered questionnaire that was delivered by mail. Nonrespondents received a follow-up letter and second questionnaire mailing. When answering the survey, respondents were instructed to focus on the intelligence they had received from the person in the marketing department with whom they had interacted the most during the previous three months. Higher scores on the scale reflected heavier use of market intelligence by recipients.

MAJOR FINDINGS: Maltz and Kohli (1996) investigated the antecedents and consequences of the dissemination of marketing intelligence within SBUs. The greater the formality of the channel through which information is disseminated, the greater was the **use of market intelligence**. Not surprisingly, the **use of market intelligence** also increased with more positive perceptions of its quality and greater market dynamism.

REFERENCES:

Anderson, Cathy, James Ciarlo, and Susan Brodie (1981), "Measuring Evaluation-Induced Change in Mental Health Programs," in *Utilizing Evaluation: Concepts and Measurement Techniques*, James Garlo, ed. Beverly Hills, CA: Sage Publications, 97–124.
Maltz, Elliot and Ajay K. Kohli (1996), "Market Intelligence Dissemination Across Functional Boundaries," *JMR*, 33 (February), 47–61.

SCALE ITEMS:

Strongly   Strongly
disagree   agree
   1————————2————————3————————4————————5

Over the last three months, the information I received from the marketing contact...

1. Helped shape our policies.

2. Improved implementation of new products or projects.

3. Improved my productivity.

4. Improved my understanding of the dynamics of the marketplace.

5. Was rarely used. **(r)***

6. Increased my understanding of how things work here.

7. Led to concrete actions.

*Although the appendix that lists this measure in Maltz and Kohli's (1996) article did not indicate that this item is reversed, it is probably an oversight given the nature and purpose of the scale.

SCALE NAME: Market Orientation

SCALE DESCRIPTION: A nine-item, seven-point scale measuring the degree to which an organization exhibits a corporate culture that effectively and efficiently creates value for buyers.

SCALE ORIGIN: Pelham and Wilson's (1996) scale is based on Narver and Slater's (1990) measure of market orientation.

SAMPLES: A longitudinal database developed by the Center for Entrepreneurship at Eastern Michigan University provided the data for the study. The Center's full panel consists of data provided by the CEOs of 370 Michigan firms, which represent 71% of the firms contacted for initial participation. The data used by Pelham and Wilson (1996) were specific only to those firms providing full information with respect to all measures of interest for both the current and previous years. Of those **68** firms, 32% were classified as wholesalers, 29% as manufacturers, 26% as business services, and 13% as construction. Firm size ranged from 15 to 65 employees, with the average number of employees equaling 23.

RELIABILITY: Pelham and Wilson (1996) reported an alpha of **.92** for this scale.

VALIDITY: Pelham and Wilson (1996) initially justified their selection of Narver and Slater's (1990) operationalization of market orientation on the basis of Pelham's (1993) dissertation research, which found that this measure achieved better reliability and validity when used with small firms than did Jaworski and Kohli's (1993) measure. Factor loadings and LISREL measurement model squared multiple correlations were taken as evidence of convergent and discriminant validity in this study.

ADMINISTRATION: Pelham and Wilson (1996) did not provide details with respect to how data were collected from panel members by the Center of Entrepreneurship. Higher scores on the market orientation measure reflected a corporate culture more likely to effectively and efficiently engage in behaviors that created superior value for buyers.

MAJOR FINDINGS: Pelham and Wilson (1996) investigated the relative impact of market orientation on small business performance compared with that of market structure, firm structure, firm strategy, and relative product quality. Regression analysis was used to test year-to-year differences in most variables, as well as parameters based on independent and lagged variables. Key findings indicated that **market orientation** positively influenced new product success and profitability for small firms and was also positively related to these variables in the current year when other independent variables were lagged. **Market orientation** was the only variable to significantly influence perceptions of product quality in both the yearly difference and lagged variable models, but it did not directly influence small business growth or share in either model. The level of small-firm **market orientation** was influenced by increased formalization in the firm structure. In the lagged model, competitive intensity and a firm structure characterized by high levels of coordination during the previous year influenced small-firm **market orientation**, though in the short-term, these variables did not.

REFERENCES:
Jaworski, Bernard J. and Ajay Kohli (1993), "Market Orientation: Antecedents and Consequences," *JM*, 57 (3), 53–71.
Narver, John C. and Stanley F. Slater (1990), "The Effect of a Market Orientation on Business Profitability," *JM*, 54 (October), 20–35.
Pelham, Alfred M. (1993), "Mediating and Moderating Influences on the Relationship Between Market Orientation and Performance," doctoral dissertation, Pennsylvania State University.

Pelham, Alfred M. and David T. Wilson (1996), "A Longitudinal Study of the Impact of Market Structure, Firm Structure, Strategy, and Market Orientation Culture on Dimensions of Small-Firm Performance," *JAMS*, 24 (1), 27–43.

SCALE ITEMS:

Strongly   Strongly
disagree   agree

1————2————3————4————5————6————7

1. All our functions (not just marketing and sales) are responsive to, and integrated in, serving target markets.

2. Our firm's strategy for competitive advantage is based on our thorough understanding of our customer needs.

3. All our managers understand how the entire business can contribute to creating customer value.

4. Information on customers, marketing success, and marketing failures is communicated across functions in the firm.

5. If a major competitor were to launch an intensive campaign targeted at our customers, we would implement a response immediately.

Moderate   Great

1————2————3————4————5————6————7

6. Our firm's market strategies are to a (moderate/great) extent driven by our understanding of possibilities for creating value for customers.

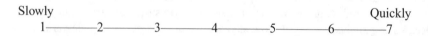

Slowly   Quickly

1————2————3————4————5————6————7

7. Our firm responds (slowly/quickly) to negative customer satisfaction information throughout the organization.

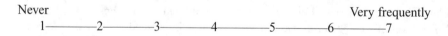

Never   Very frequently

1————2————3————4————5————6————7

8. How frequently do top managers discuss competitive strengths and weaknesses?

9. How frequently do you take advantage of targeted opportunities to take advantage of competitor's weaknesses?

SCALE NAME: Market Potential (New Product)

SCALE DESCRIPTION: Song and Parry (1997) used this four-item, eleven-point scale to measure assessments of the potential demand within the target market for the firm's new product.

SCALE ORIGIN: The scale was adapted by Song and Parry (1997) from the work of Cooper (1979a, b), Maidique and Zierger (1984), and Zierger and Maidique (1990). Song and Parry (1997) modified scale items on the basis of a review of the literature, pilot studies, and information obtained from 36 in-depth case study interviews conducted with both Japanese and U.S. firms. The items for all scales used by Song and Parry (1997) were evaluated by an academic panel composed of both Japanese and U.S. business and engineering experts. Following revisions, the items were judged by a new panel composed of academicians and new product development (NPD) managers. The authors reported extensive pretesting of both the Japanese and U.S. versions of the questionnaire.

SAMPLES: Song and Parry (1997) randomly sampled 500 of the 611 firms trading on the Tokyo, Osaka, and Nagoya stock exchanges that had been identified as developing at least four new physical products since 1991. Usable responses pertaining to **788** NPD projects were obtained from 404 Japanese firms. The U.S. sampling frame was taken from companies listed in the *High-Technology Industries Directory*. Of the 643 firms who had introduced a minimum of four new physical products since 1990, 500 firms were randomly sampled (though stratified by industry to match the Japanese sample), and 312 U.S. firms provided data on **612** NPD projects, of which 312 were successes and 300 were failures.

RELIABILITY: Song and Parry (1997) reported a coefficient alpha of **.75** for this scale in the Japanese sample and **.73** for the U.S. sample.

VALIDITY: The extensive pretesting and evaluation of the measure with academicians and NPD managers provided strong evidence for the face validity of the measure. The authors did not specifically report any other examination of scale validity.

ADMINISTRATION: The self-administered questionnaire containing the scale was originally developed in English; the Japanese version was prepared using the parallel-translation/double-translation method. Following minor revisions made on the basis of pretests with bilingual respondents and case study participants, the Japanese sample received a survey packet containing cover letters in both English and Japanese, two Japanese-language questionnaires, and two international postage-paid reply envelopes. Survey packets delivered to U.S. firms were similar, except no Japanese cover letter was included and the surveys were in English. Incentives, four follow-up letters, and multiple telephone calls and faxes were used to increase the response rate with both samples. Song and Parry (1997) indicated that respondents were asked to answer one questionnaire in the context of a successful new product project introduced after 1991 and the other in the context of a new product project that had failed. Higher scores on the scale indicated greater market potential for the new product.

MAJOR FINDINGS: Song and Parry (1997) conceptualized and tested a model of strategic, tactical, and environmental factors believed to influence new product success using data collected from both Japanese and U.S. firms. In both the Japanese and U.S. samples, the level of NPD project **market potential** was found to strengthen the relationship between product differentiation and relative product performance.

REFERENCES:
Cooper, Robert G. (1979a), "Identifying Industrial New Product Success: Project NewProd," *Industrial Marketing Management*, 8 (2), 124–35.

——— (1979b), "The Dimensions of Industrial New Product Success and Failure," *JM*, 43 (Summer), 93–103.

Maidique, Modesto A. and Billie Jo Zierger (1984), "A Study of Success and Failure in Product Innovation: The Case of the U.S. Electronics Industry," *IEEE Transactions on Engineering Management*, 31 (4), 192–203.

Song, X. Michael and Mark E. Parry (1997), "A Cross-National Comparative Study of New Product Development Processes: Japan and the United States," *JM*, 61 (April), 1–18.

Zierger, Billie Jo and Modesto Maidique (1990), "A Model of NPD: An Empirical Test," *Management Science*, 36 (7), 867–83.

SCALE ITEMS:

Directions: To what extent does each statement listed below correctly describe this selected successful project? Please indicate your degree of agreement or disagreement by circling a number from zero (0) to ten (10) on the scale to the right of each statement. Here: 0 = strongly disagree, 10 = strongly agree, and numbers between 0 and 10 indicate various degrees of agreement or disagreement.

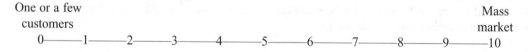

Strongly   Strongly
disagree   agree
  0———1———2———3———4———5———6———7———8———9———10

1. Potential customers had a great need for this class of product.

2. The dollar size of the market (either existing or potential) for this product was very large.

3. The market for this product was growing very quickly.

One or a few   Mass
  customers   market
  0———1———2———3———4———5———6———7———8———9———10

4. There were many potential customers for this product—a mass market, as opposed to one or a few customers.

SCALE NAME: Market Volatility

SCALE DESCRIPTION: Bello and Gilliland (1997) used three seven-point semantic differential items to assess the extent to which the environment of a foreign market changes rapidly.

SCALE ORIGIN: Bello and Gilliland (1997) stated that the scale was adapted from John and Weitz (1988).

SAMPLES: Bello and Gilliland's (1997) systematic random sample of 245 national manufacturers verified as exporting through foreign distributors was drawn from the 1994 edition of the *Journal of Commerce United States Importer & Exporter Directory*. **One hundred sixty** usable responses were obtained from export managers employed by firms exporting a variety of industrial and consumer products to a total of 39 different countries.

RELIABILITY: A confirmatory factor analysis composite reliability of **.81** was reported by Bello and Gilliland (1997).

VALIDITY: Confirmatory factor analysis was used by Bello and Gilliland (1997) to provide evidence of discriminant and convergent validity, as well as to assess the unidimensionality of the measure. Convergent validity was deemed to be present because items loaded significantly on their posited indicators and because of the low to moderate correlations between the scale and other measures. Discriminant validity was also deemed to be present because the correlation estimate between two indicators never included 1.0 (+/– two standard errors). The authors used personal interviews with export executives as part of the pretest process to verify the face validity of the measure.

ADMINISTRATION: Bello and Gilliland (1997) indicated that this scale was self-administered as part of a longer survey instrument mailed to respondents. The export manager with primary responsibility for the firm's relationship with the foreign distributor received a survey, and nonrespondents were telephoned three weeks later, after which a second questionnaire followed. Instructions specified that questions were to be answered in the context of the focal distributor. The authors defined the focal distributor as the firm's fourth-largest foreign distributor in terms of unit sales volume to avoid a positive evaluation bias. Higher scores on the scale indicated a turbulent foreign market characterized by high levels of uncertainty, volatility, and rapid change, whereas lower scores on the scale indicated a stable, fairly predictable market that changes slowly.

MAJOR FINDINGS: Bello and Gilliland (1997) examined the effect of output controls, process controls, and flexibility on channel performance. Stable rather than **volatile market** conditions were found to increase the flexibility between channel partners, in that there was a greater tendency for partners to agree to modifications of ongoing contractual obligations or agreements when the market environment was stable.

REFERENCES:
Bello, Daniel C. and David I. Gilliland (1997), "The Effect of Output Controls, Process Controls, and Flexibility on Export Channel Performance," *JM*, 61 (January), 22–38.
John, George and Barton A. Weitz (1988), "Forward Integration into Distribution: Empirical Test of Transaction Cost Analysis," *Journal of Law, Economics, and Organization*, 4 (Fall), 121–39.

#691 *Market Volatility*

SCALE ITEMS:*

1. Stable   Volatile
   environment   :____:____:____:____:____:____:____: environment
                      1   2   3   4   5   6   7

2. Certain   :____:____:____:____:____:____:____: Uncertain
                      1   2   3   4   5   6   7

3. Changes slowly :____:____:____:____:____:____:____: Changes rapidly
                      1   2   3   4   5   6   7

*Although verbatim instructions were not provided in the article, the authors indicated that respondents were instructed to rate the foreign market's environment.

SCALE NAME: Marketing Intelligence (Dissemination)

SCALE DESCRIPTION: Sinkula, Baker, and Noordewier (1997) used this three-item, five-point Likert-type scale to assess the degree to which market intelligence on current and future customer needs is disseminated and shared across an organization.

SCALE ORIGIN: The scale items used by Sinkula, Baker, and Noordewier (1997) were developed by Jaworski and Kohli (1993) as part of a larger measure. Jaworski and Kohli (1993) originally developed a 32-item scale of market orientation, of which 8 items pertained to the intelligence dissemination dimension. Items were extensively pretested, revised, and purified. Jaworski and Kohli (1993) reported a reliability of .71 for their measure of market dissemination. Following an initial assessment of internal consistency reliability, items exhibiting low item-to-total correlations were dropped. The 3 items ultimately used by Sinkula, Baker, and Noordewier (1997) are reflective of the type of market information–processing behavior essential for detecting and correcting errors.

SAMPLES: The results of preliminary interviews with business practitioners indicated that the most appropriate sample subjects for a study of organizational learning processes were those working at high or upper organizational levels in a variety of industries. With this criterion in mind, Sinkula, Baker, and Noordewier (1997) drew a random sample of key informants from the 1994 membership list of the American Marketing Association but eliminated those whose titles suggested they were not high enough in the organizational hierarchy to provide informed responses. Of the 276 individuals who qualified for the study, **125** returned usable responses.

RELIABILITY: Sinkula, Baker, and Noordewier (1997) reported a coefficient alpha of **.82** for this measure.

VALIDITY: Sinkula, Baker, and Noordewier (1997) stated that a confirmatory factor analysis demonstrated the convergent and discriminatory validity of the measure.

ADMINISTRATION: The measure was included by Sinkula, Baker, and Noordewier (1997) as part of a self-administered questionnaire that was delivered by mail. Nonrespondents received a second mailing. Higher scores on the scale reflected a higher occurrence of market intelligence sharing and dissemination within the organization.

MAJOR FINDINGS: Sinkula, Baker, and Noordewier (1997) investigated the relationship between organizational values, market information–processing behaviors, and organizational actions in the context of an organizational learning framework. Results indicated that a more positive learning orientation was directly responsible for increasing the level of **market intelligence disseminated.** Furthermore, by **increasing market information generation** and dissemination, a positive learning orientation affects marketing program dynamism, or the degree to which an organization makes changes in its marketing strategy.

REFERENCES:
Jaworski, Bernard J. and Ajay Kohli (1993), "Market Orientation: Antecedents and Consequences" *JM*, 57 (July), 53–70.
Sinkula, James M., William E. Baker, and Thomas Noordewier (1997), "A Framework for Market-Based Organizational Learning: Linking Values, Knowledge, and Behavior," *JAMS*, 25 (4), 305–18.

#692 *Marketing Intelligence (Dissemination)*

SCALE ITEMS:

Strongly   Strongly
disagree   agree
  1————————2————————3————————4————————5

1. Marketing personnel spend time discussing customers' future needs with other functional departments.

2. There is minimal communication between marketing and other departments concerning market developments. **(r)**

3. When one department finds out something important about customers, it is slow to alert other departments. **(r)**

SCALE NAME: Marketing Intelligence (Generation)

SCALE DESCRIPTION: Sinkula, Baker, and Noordewier (1997) used this three-item, five-point Likert-type scale to assess the degree to which an organization generates market intelligence on current and future customer needs.

SCALE ORIGIN: The scale items used by Sinkula, Baker, and Noordewier (1997) were developed by Jaworski and Kohli (1993) as part of a larger measure. Jaworski and Kohli (1993) originally developed a 32-item scale of market orientation, of which 10 items pertained to the market intelligence generation dimension. Items were extensively pretested, revised, and purified. Jaworski and Kohli (1993) reported a reliability of .71 for their measure of market intelligence generation. Following an initial assessment of internal consistency reliability, items exhibiting low item-to-total correlations were dropped. The 3 items ultimately used by Sinkula, Baker, and Noordewier (1997) are reflective of the type of market information–processing behavior necessary if learning is to occur.

SAMPLES: The results of preliminary interviews with business practitioners indicated that the most appropriate sample subjects for a study of organizational learning processes were those working at high or upper organizational levels in a variety of industries. With this criterion in mind, Sinkula, Baker, and Noordewier (1997) drew a random sample of key informants from the 1994 membership list of the American Marketing Association but eliminated those whose titles suggested they were not high enough in the organizational hierarchy to provide informed responses. Of the 276 individuals who qualified for the study, **125** returned usable responses.

RELIABILITY: Sinkula, Baker, and Noordewier (1997) reported a coefficient alpha of **.74** for this measure.

VALIDITY: Sinkula, Baker, and Noordewier (1997) stated that a confirmatory factor analysis demonstrated the convergent and discriminatory validity of the measure.

ADMINISTRATION: The measure was included by Sinkula, Baker, and Noordewier (1997) as part of a self-administered questionnaire that was delivered by mail. Nonrespondents received a second mailing. Higher scores on the scale reflected higher levels of market intelligence gathering related to current and future customer needs.

MAJOR FINDINGS: Sinkula, Baker, and Noordewier (1997) investigated the relationship among organizational values, market information–processing behaviors, and organizational actions in the context of an organizational learning framework. Results indicated that a more positive learning orientation was directly responsible for increasing the level of **market intelligence generated.** Furthermore, by **increasing market information generation** and dissemination, a positive learning orientation affects marketing program dynamism, or the degree to which an organization makes changes in its marketing strategy.

REFERENCES:

Jaworski, Bernard J. and Ajay Kohli (1993), "Market Orientation: Antecedents and Consequences" *JM*, 57 (July), 53–70.

Sinkula, James M., William E. Baker, and Thomas Noordewier (1997), "A Framework for Market-Based Organizational Learning: Linking Values, Knowledge, and Behavior," *JAMS*, 25 (4), 305–18.

#693 *Marketing Intelligence (Generation)*

SCALE ITEMS:

Strongly   Strongly
disagree   agree

1————2————3————4————5

1. We do a lot of in-house market research.

2. We often talk with or survey those who can influence our end users' purchases (e.g., retailers, distributors).

3. We periodically review the likely effect of changes in our business environment (e.g., regulation) on customers.

SCALE NAME: Marketing Mix Problems

SCALE DESCRIPTION: This four-item scale measures the extent to which problems were incurred in the implementation of the marketing mix. Although the scale was administered specifically to determine implementation problems in an international setting, nothing in the scale item phrasing precludes the use of this measure in a domestic context. Roth (1995) referred to the measure as *marketing implementation problems*.

SCALE ORIGIN: No indication was provided by Roth (1995) that the scale is anything other than original to his study.

SAMPLES: Roth (1995) selected brands marketed by U.S.-based manufacturers of blue jeans and athletic shoes in Argentina, Belgium, China, France, Germany, Japan, Italy, the Netherlands, Peru, and Yugoslavia for study. Of the 115 international marketing managers surveyed, 38 managers representing 11 firms returned usable questionnaires (33% response rate). Many managers directed the marketing efforts of a brand in multiple foreign markets. Collectively, respondents provided information on **209** cases of a particular brand's strategy. A sample of nonrespondents contacted by telephone indicated that nonrespondents did not significantly differ from respondents with respect to the measures of interest.

RELIABILITY: Roth (1995) reported a coefficient alpha of **.727** for this measure.

VALIDITY: Roth (1995) stated that a principal components analysis was used to demonstrate that each of the four scale items loaded on a single factor. No specific tests of scale validity were reported.

ADMINISTRATION: The scale was part of a self-administered mail survey customized for each country. Roth (1995) included a cover letter and $1 incentive. A reminder letter with a second questionnaire was sent two to three weeks later. Higher scores on the scale indicated a greater prevalence of problems in the implementation of the marketing mix.

MAJOR FINDINGS: Roth (1995) investigated the effect of various cultural and socioeconomic environmental characteristics of foreign markets on brand image and market share performance. The author found that when managers experienced **difficulties implementing their marketing mix** in foreign markets, market share suffered.

REFERENCES:
Roth, Martin S. (1995), "The Effects of Culture and Socioeconomics on the Performance of Global Brand Image Strategies," *JMR*, 32 (May), 163–75.

SCALE ITEMS:
To what extent are you experiencing marketing problems in each of the following areas?

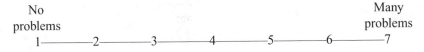

No problems 1————2————3————4————5————6————7 Many problems

1. Distribution.

2. Pricing.

3. Advertising and promotion.

4. Product characteristics

SCALE NAME: Mentoring Ability and Willingness

SCALE DESCRIPTION: Pullins, Fine, and Warren (1996) used this fifteen-item, seven-point Likert-type scale to measure salespersons' perceptions of their ability and willingness to mentor in terms of their ability to create rapport, willingness to provide support, and willingness to form new relationships.

SCALE ORIGIN: The scale appears to be original to Pullins, Fine, and Warren's (1996) study. A factor analysis of the 15-item measure indicated that the items loaded on three factors.

SAMPLES: Ten regional sales managers and a 216 salespeople employed by a national commercial food equipment manufacturer were sampled by Pullins, Fine, and Warren (1996). Regional sales managers did not complete the survey but instead were asked to provide evaluations of salesperson performance. A total of **194** usable responses were obtained from the sales force, and sales managers provided evaluations for **113** of those sales representatives.

RELIABILITY: Pullins, Fine, and Warren (1996) reported a coefficient alpha of **.84** for this measure.

VALIDITY: No specific examination of the scale's validity was reported by Pullins, Fine, and Warren (1996).

ADMINISTRATION: The scale was included with other measures as part of a self-administered survey that was delivered by mail to members of the sales force. Pullins, Fine, and Warren (1996) included a cover letter with the survey, featuring an endorsement for the project from the company's vice president of sales. Higher scores on the scale indicated greater levels of self-reported mentoring ability and willingness.

MAJOR FINDINGS: Pullins, Fine, and Warren (1996) conducted an exploratory investigation of factors influencing the willingness and ability of salespeople to act as mentors. Regression analysis was used to test hypotheses, and tests of ability were restricted to the 42 salespeople who had actually been involved in mentoring relationships. Salespeople reporting higher levels of role conflict were more **willing to mentor**, and those who scored higher with respect to their interpersonal competence, as measured by the openers scale, were both more willing and more able to mentor. Sales managers perceived salespeople with more experience and greater job satisfaction as being more likely to **choose to mentor**.

REFERENCES:
Pullins, Ellen Bolman, Leslie M. Fine, and Wendy L. Warren (1996), "Identifying Peer Mentors in the Sales Force: An Exploratory Investigation of Willingness and Ability," *JAMS*, 24 (2), 125–36.

SCALE ITEMS:

Strongly   Strongly
disagree   agree

1———————2———————3———————4———————5———————6———————7

Rapport Ability:
   1. I believe I have good interpersonal skills.
   2. I am an open communicator.
   3. I usually establish good rapport with others.
   4. I have a strong sense of purpose.
   5. I practice what I preach.
   6. I believe others have confidence in me.

Support Willingness:

7. I am willing to spend time and effort to help others out.
8. I am willing to share power.
9. I put myself in others' shoes.
10. I am willing to provide a safety net for subordinates.
11. I am nurturing.

Relational Willingness:

12. I like to establish close relationships at work.
13. I am open to establishing new relationships.
14. I am willing to enter long-term relationships.
15. I like to work with others.

SCALE NAME: Middleman Expenditures

SCALE DESCRIPTION: A three-item, seven-point Likert-type scale measuring manufacturer investments specifically dedicated to the middleman's existing infrastructure or other capital outlay items. Although used in the context of evaluating the appropriateness of foreign agents versus foreign distributors when exporting products abroad, the scale items are not specific to export situations and could easily be applied to marketing in a domestic setting by changing the instructions. Bello and Lohtia (1995) refer to this scale as "physical asset specificity" in their article.

SCALE ORIGIN: Bello and Lohtia (1995) stated that the scale was adapted from Heide and John (1990).

SAMPLES: Bello and Lohtia (1995) drew a systematic random sample of 600 manufacturers from among those listed in the 1991 edition of the *Journal of Commerce United States Importer & Exporter Directory*. From this sample, 398 firms were verified as exporting through middlemen, and one person with middleman responsibilities at each of these screened firms was sent a questionnaire. Nonrespondents were telephoned three weeks later and sent a second questionnaire. A total of **269** usable responses were obtained for a 68% response rate. Of these respondents, 60% exported through foreign distributors, and 40% exported using foreign agents.

RELIABILITY: A coefficient alpha of **.82** was reported by Bello and Lohtia (1995).

VALIDITY: Confirmatory factor analysis was used by Bello and Lohtia (1995) to provide evidence of discriminant and convergent validity, as well as to assess the unidimensionality of the measure. Convergent validity was deemed to be present because items loaded significantly on their posited indicators and because of the low to moderate correlations among the product specificity, human specificity, and physical specificity scales. Citing precedents set by Anderson and Gerbing (1988, p. 416), Bello and Lohtia stated that discriminant validity was also present because the correlation estimate between two indicators never included 1.0 (+/– two standard errors).

ADMINISTRATION: Bello and Lohtia (1995) indicated that this scale was self-administered as part of a longer survey instrument mailed to respondents. Instructions requested that responses be specific to a single, focal export middleman in a foreign market. Higher scores on the scale indicated a greater level of physical asset investment being made to support foreign middlemen.

MAJOR FINDINGS: Bello and Lohtia (1995) investigated several cost indicators believed to influence the choice of foreign distributors versus foreign agents. Differences between agent and distributor users existed with respect to **middleman expenditures**, that is, distributor users made more capital investments than did agent users.

REFERENCES:
Andersen, James C. and David W. Gerbing (1988), "Structural Equation Modeling in Practice: A Review and Recommended Two-Step Approach," *Psychological Bulletin*, 103 (3), 411–23.
Bello, Daniel C. and Ritu Lohtia (1995), "Export Channel Design: The Use of Foreign Distributors and Agents," *JAMS*, 23 (2), 83–93.
Heide, Jan B. and George John (1990), "Alliances in Industrial Purchasing: The Determinants of Joint Action in Buyer-Supplier Relationships," *JMR*, 27 (February), 24–36.

SCALE ITEMS:*

Strongly
disagree

Strongly
agree

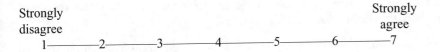

1————2————3————4————5————6————7

1. Resources are committed to physical assets.

2. Special investment in equipment is needed.

3. Capital expenditures are required.

*The specific wording of the instructions was not included in the article.

SCALE NAME: Monitoring of Supplier

SCALE DESCRIPTION: This four-item, eight-point scale measures the extent to which the buyer attempts to monitor and verify the performance of a supplier.

SCALE ORIGIN: Stump and Heide (1996) adapted the items used in this measure from the work of John (1984). Extensive pretesting of the questionnaire containing the measure was reported by Stump and Heide (1996).

SAMPLES: Stump and Heide (1996) drew a random sample of 1073 names from a national mailing list of chemical manufacturing firms in standard industrial classification code 28. Of this group, 631 key informants were identified by telephone who agreed to participate in the study. A total of **164** usable surveys were returned.

RELIABILITY: Stump and Heide (1996) calculated a coefficient alpha of **.82** for this measure.

VALIDITY: Stump and Heide (1996) examined item-to-total correlations of the items that composed the scale and conducted an exploratory factor analysis of the measures used in the study. A confirmatory factor analysis of all items used in each scale verified the unidimensionality of the measure. Evidence of the discriminant validity of the measure was provided by means of a series of chi-square difference tests performed on the factor correlations. The model was also evaluated and found to represent a good fit to the data.

ADMINISTRATION: The scale was included by Stump and Heide (1996) with other measures as part of a self-administered survey that was delivered by mail. Buyers were asked to identify a purchasing agreement for a particular product that had been established within the last 12 months and answer questions in the context of that purchasing agreement. Higher scores on the scale indicated that a buyer was strongly engaged in attempts to verify the performance of a supplier.

MAJOR FINDINGS: Stump and Heide (1996) examined how chemical manufacturers used partner selection, incentive design, and monitoring approaches in the management and control of supplier relationships. Although no significant relationships were found between buyer investments and **monitoring behavior**, performance ambiguity was negatively associated with the desirability of **monitoring efforts**, in support of Stump and Heide's (1996) contention that **monitoring** under such conditions involves unnecessary transaction costs.

REFERENCES:

John, George (1984), "An Empirical Investigation of Some Antecedents of Opportunism in a Marketing Channel," *JMR*, 21 (August), 278–89.

Stump, Rodney L. and Jan B. Heide (1996), "Controlling Supplier Opportunism in Industrial Relationships," *JMR*, 33 (November), 431–41.

SCALE ITEMS:

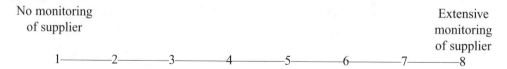

No monitoring of supplier   Extensive monitoring of supplier

1——2——3——4——5——6——7——8

1. Product quality.
2. Delivery timeliness.
3. Price competitiveness.
4. Order accuracy.

SCALE NAME: Motivation (Extrinsic)

SCALE DESCRIPTION: Oliver and Anderson (1994) used this three-item, seven-point Likert-type scale to measure a sales representative's tendency to engage in selling activities for extrinsic reasons related solely to earning money.

SCALE ORIGIN: The scale is original to Oliver and Anderson (1994), who pretested the measure in a questionnaire administered to a convenience sample of sales representatives attending trade association functions. The measure was revised on the basis of the pretest.

SAMPLES: Oliver and Anderson (1994) surveyed managers and manufacturer's sales representatives employed by independently owned and operated sales agencies serving the electronics industry. Of the 350 randomly selected trade association member firms fitting this designation, 299 firms expressed interest in participating, and ultimately **194** usable surveys from management and **347** surveys from manufacturer representatives were returned. The typical respondent was male (92%), a college graduate (64%), approximately 39 years of age, and had an average of 12 years sales experience with 5.5 years in the present job.

RELIABILITY: Oliver and Anderson (1994) reported a coefficient alpha of **.826** for this measure.

VALIDITY: Oliver and Anderson (1994) used the correlation matrix of the independent and classification variables in the study to provide some evidence of discriminant and convergent validity. Nomological validity was also found to be present.

ADMINISTRATION: Oliver and Anderson (1994) sent managers of the 299 firms indicating interest in the study a packet containing a "manager's survey" and three similar self-administered surveys for salespeople, along with self-addressed postage-paid reply envelopes. Managers were instructed to distribute one survey each to an "above-average rep," a "mid-range rep," and a "below-average rep." Each representative was promised confidentiality and the chance to win one of five $100 prizes in a random drawing. It appears that only responses obtained from sales representatives were used in computing this measure. Higher scores on the scale indicated a greater desire on the part of the sales representative to engage in selling activities for monetarily rewarding reasons.

MAJOR FINDINGS: Oliver and Anderson (1994) examined how perceptions of the presence of a behavior versus outcome sales control system in the respondents' organizations influenced salespeople's performance outcomes and sales strategies, as well as their affective, cognitive, and behavioral states. Lower levels of **extrinsic motivation** were significantly related to the use of a behavior control system.

REFERENCES:
Oliver, Richard L. and Erin Anderson (1994), "An Empirical Test of the Consequences of Behavior- and Outcome-Based Sales Control Systems," *JM*, 58 (October), 53–67.

SCALE ITEMS:

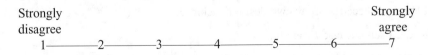

Strongly disagree — Strongly agree
1————2————3————4————5————6————7

1. If it weren't for the money, I would not be in a selling job.

2. I sell because I get paid to sell.

3. After a long hard day, I realize that if it weren't for the money, I wouldn't put up with this job.

SCALE NAME: Motivation (Intrinsic)

SCALE DESCRIPTION: Oliver and Anderson (1994) used this six-item, seven-point Likert-type scale to measure a sales representative's tendency to engage in selling activities for intrinsic reasons related to challenge, pleasure, feelings of accomplishment, and feelings of usefulness.

SCALE ORIGIN: The scale is original to Oliver and Anderson (1994), who pretested the measure in a questionnaire administered to a convenience sample of sales representatives attending trade association functions. The measure was revised on the basis of the pretest.

SAMPLES: Oliver and Anderson (1994) surveyed managers and manufacturer's sales representatives employed by independently owned and operated sales agencies serving the electronics industry. Of the 350 randomly selected trade association member firms fitting this designation, 299 firms expressed interest in participating, and ultimately **194** usable surveys from management and **347** surveys from manufacturer representatives were returned. The typical respondent was male (92%), a college graduate (64%), approximately 39 years of age, and had an average of 12 years sales experience with 5.5 years in the present job.

RELIABILITY: Oliver and Anderson (1994) reported a coefficient alpha of **.816** for this measure.

VALIDITY: Oliver and Anderson (1994) used the correlation matrix of the independent and classification variables in the study to provide some evidence of discriminant and convergent validity. Nomological validity was also found to be present.

ADMINISTRATION: Oliver and Anderson (1994) sent managers of the 299 firms indicating interest in the study a packet containing a "manager's survey" and three similar self-administered surveys for salespeople, along with self-addressed postage-paid reply envelopes. Managers were instructed to distribute one survey each to an "above-average rep," a "mid-range rep," and a "below-average rep." Each representative was promised confidentiality and the chance to win one of five $100 prizes in a random drawing. It appears that only responses obtained from sales representatives were used in computing this measure. Higher scores on the scale indicated a greater desire on the part of the sales representative to engage in selling activities for intrinsically rewarding reasons.

MAJOR FINDINGS: Oliver and Anderson (1994) examined how perceptions of the presence of a behavior versus outcome sales control system in the respondent's organizations influenced salespeople's performance outcomes and sales strategies, as well as their affective, cognitive, and behavioral states. **Intrinsic motivation** was not significantly related to the use of a behavior control system.

REFERENCES:
Oliver, Richard L. and Erin Anderson (1994), "An Empirical Test of the Consequences of Behavior- and Outcome-Based Sales Control Systems," *JM*, 58 (October), 53–67.

SCALE ITEMS:

Strongly
disagree

Strongly
agree

1————2————3————4————5————6————7

1. When I perform well, I know it's because of my own desire to achieve.

2. I don't need a reason to sell; I sell because I want to.

3. Becoming successful in sales is something that I want to do for me.

4. If I were independently wealthy, I would still sell for the challenge of it.

5. I wish I didn't have to retire someday so I could always continue selling for the pleasure of it.

6. I sell because I cherish the feeling of performing a useful service.

SCALE NAME: Motivation to Plan Marketing (Intrinsic)

SCALE DESCRIPTION: A four-item measure that combines three Likert-type items with one quasi-semantic differential and attempts to measure the extent to which respondents engage in marketing planning and ideation for intrinsically rewarding reasons. Andrews and Smith (1996) referred to the scale as *motivation to plan marketing program.*

SCALE ORIGIN: Andrews and Smith (1996) developed the scale by modifying scales by Lawler and Hall (1970) and Spiro and Weitz (1990).

SAMPLES: The American Marketing Association membership directory and a purchased mailing list provided Andrews and Smith (1996) with the sampling frame for surveying consumer goods product managers. One hundred ninety-three completed questionnaires were returned for a 33.4% response rate. No significant differences in responses to key variables existed between mailing lists or between early and late respondents. Because only respondents with a substantial impact on ideas in the marketing program were desired, 25 respondents were eliminated on the basis of a screening question, yielding a final sample size of **168**.

RELIABILITY: Andrews and Smith (1996) reported a coefficient alpha of **.60** for this measure.

VALIDITY: No specific examination of the scale's validity was reported by Andrews and Smith (1996).

ADMINISTRATION: The scale was part of a self-administered mail survey in which Andrews and Smith (1996) instructed product managers to answer questions in the context of a single product with which they had been highly involved during their most recent marketing program. Higher scores on the scale indicated higher levels of intrinsic motivation when planning marketing programs.

MAJOR FINDINGS: The effect of individual product manager and situational/planning process characteristics on marketing program creativity was investigated by Andrews and Smith (1996). They found that the greater a product manager's **intrinsic motivation to develop marketing plans**, the greater was the creativity of the resulting marketing program. When **intrinsic motivation** to plan is high, the effect of educational diversity on marketing program creativity is greater than when intrinsic motivation is low.

COMMENTS: The low coefficient alpha and closer examination of the items suggest that this scale may not adequately capture the domain of interest. Further developmental work and validation should be strongly considered prior to using this scale again.

REFERENCES:
Andrews, Jonlee and Daniel C. Smith (1996), "In Search of the Marketing Imagination: Factors Affecting the Creativity of Marketing Programs for Mature Products," *JMR*, 33 (May), 174–87.

Lawler, Edward and Douglas Hall (1970), "Relationship of Job Characteristics to Job Involvement, Satisfaction, and Intrinsic Motivation," *Journal of Applied Psychology*, 54 (4), 305–12.

Spiro, Rosann and Barton Weitz (1990), "Adaptive Selling: Conceptualization, Measurement, and Nomological Validity," *JMR*, 27 (February), 61–69.

#700 *Motivation to Plan Marketing (Intrinsic)*

SCALE ITEMS:

Strongly   Strongly
disagree   agree
   1————2————3————4————5————6————7

1. I feel a real sense of accomplishment when I come up with a good marketing program.

2. Creating marketing strategies for this product is challenging.

3. I don't especially enjoy coming up with marketing strategies for this product. **(r)**

4. Developing marketing   :____:____:____:____:____:____:____: Developing
   programs is one of   marketing
   my least favorite tasks   programs is one of
                                                                           my most favorite tasks

SCALE NAME: Motivational Orientation (Learning)

SCALE DESCRIPTION: Sujan, Weitz, and Kumar (1994) used a nine-item, seven-point Likert-type scale to measure a salesperson's motivational orientation to improve sales-related abilities and skills.

SCALE ORIGIN: Sujan, Weitz, and Kumar (1994) indicated that the scale was adapted from the work of Ames and Archer (1988). Because Ames and Archer's (1988) use of the scale was specific to an educational setting and student sample, Sujan, Weitz, and Kumar (1994) changed item phrasing to reflect selling-specific skills and abilities.

SAMPLES: Sujan, Weitz, and Kumar (1994) surveyed a convenience sample of salespeople employed by eight firms representing diverse industries. Two hundred seventeen questionnaires were distributed by sales managers to members of their selling force, and **190** usable responses were obtained for an 87.5% response rate. On average, respondents were 35 years of age, had 9 years sales experience, and made 3.5 calls per day. The majority were men (78%).

RELIABILITY: Sujan, Weitz, and Kumar (1994) reported a coefficient alpha of **.81** for the measure.

VALIDITY: Sujan, Weitz, and Kumar (1994) provided extensive information on the assessment of scale validity. Measures used in their study were evaluated using confirmatory factor analysis. The authors stated that the results of this analysis supported the unidimensionality and reliability of the measure and provided evidence of convergent and discriminant validity.

ADMINISTRATION: Sujan, Weitz, and Kumar (1994) included a cover letter promising confidentiality and a self-addressed, stamped reply envelope in the survey packet distributed by sales managers to members of the sales force. Respondents were instructed to return the questionnaire directly to the researchers rather than to their superiors. Higher scores on the scale indicated that salespeople were motivated to improve their sales-related abilities and skills.

MAJOR FINDINGS: Sujan, Weitz, and Kumar (1994) investigated the influence of goal orientations on work behavior. Results indicated that a **learning orientation** motivated salespeople to work harder and smarter and that both positive and negative feedback increased the **learning orientation** of salespeople.

REFERENCES:

Ames, Carol and Jennifer Archer (1988), "Achievement Goals in the Classroom: Students' Learning Strategies and Motivation Processes," *Journal of Educational Psychology*, 80 (3), 260–67.

Sujan, Harish, Barton A. Weitz, and Nirmalya Kumar (1994), "Learning Orientation, Working Smart, and Effective Selling," *JM*, 58 (July), 39–52.

SCALE ITEMS:

Strongly disagree 1————2————3————4————5————6————7 Strongly agree

1. Making a tough sale is very satisfying.

2. An important part of being a good salesperson is continually improving your sales skills.

3. Making mistakes when selling is just part of the learning process.

4. It is important for me to learn from each selling experience I have.

5. There really are not a lot of new things to learn about selling. **(r)**

6. I am always learning something new about my customers.

7. It is worth spending a great deal of time learning new approaches for dealing with customers.

8. Learning how to be a better salesperson is of fundamental importance to me.

9. I put in a great deal of effort sometimes in order to learn something new.

SCALE NAME: Motivational Orientation (Performance)

SCALE DESCRIPTION: Sujan, Weitz, and Kumar (1994) used a six-item, seven-point Likert-type scale to measure a salesperson's motivational orientation to demonstrate sales-related abilities and skills.

SCALE ORIGIN: Sujan, Weitz, and Kumar (1994) indicated that the scale was adapted from the work of Ames and Archer (1988). Because Ames and Archer's (1988) use of the scale was specific to an educational setting and student sample, Sujan, Weitz, and Kumar (1994) changed item phrasing to reflect selling-specific skills and abilities.

SAMPLES: Sujan, Weitz, and Kumar (1994) surveyed a convenience sample of salespeople employed by eight firms representing diverse industries. Two hundred seventeen questionnaires were distributed by sales managers to members of their selling force, and **190** usable responses were obtained for an 87.5% response rate. On average, respondents were 35 years of age, had 9 years sales experience, and made 3.5 calls per day. The majority were men (78%).

RELIABILITY: Sujan, Weitz, and Kumar (1994) reported a coefficient alpha of **.71** for the measure.

VALIDITY: Sujan, Weitz, and Kumar (1994) provided extensive information on the assessment of scale validity. Measures used in their study were evaluated using confirmatory factor analysis. The authors stated that the results of this analysis supported the unidimensionality and reliability of the measure and provided evidence of convergent and discriminant validity.

ADMINISTRATION: Sujan, Weitz, and Kumar (1994) included a cover letter promising confidentiality and a self-addressed, stamped reply envelope in the survey packet distributed by sales managers to members of the sales force. Respondents were instructed to return the questionnaire directly to the researchers rather than to their superiors. Higher scores on the scale indicated that salespeople were motivated to demonstrate their sales-related abilities and skills.

MAJOR FINDINGS: Sujan, Weitz, and Kumar (1994) investigated the influence of goal orientations on work behavior. Results indicated that a **performance orientation** motivated salespeople to work harder but not smarter. Only negative feedback was found to increase a salesperson's **performance orientation**. A **performance orientation** was also found to motivate highly self-efficacious salespeople to work harder and smarter more than did it those salespeople who were low in self-efficacy.

REFERENCES:
Ames, Carol and Jennifer Archer (1988), "Achievement Goals in the Classroom: Students' Learning Strategies and Motivation Processes," *Journal of Educational Psychology*, 80 (3), 260–67.
Sujan, Harish, Barton A. Weitz, and Nirmalya Kumar (1994), "Learning Orientation, Working Smart, and Effective Selling," *JM*, 58 (July), 39–52.

SCALE ITEMS:

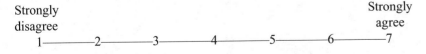

```
Strongly                                      Strongly
disagree                                       agree
  1———————2———————3———————4———————5———————6———————7
```

1. It is very important to me that my supervisor sees me as a good salesperson.

2. I very much want my coworkers to consider me to be good at selling.

3. I feel very good when I know I have outperformed other salespeople in my company.

4. I always try to communicate my accomplishments to my manager.

5. I spend a lot of time thinking about how my performance compares with other salespeople's.

6. I evaluate myself using my supervisor's criteria.

SCALE NAME: Negative Avoidance

SCALE DESCRIPTION: Strutton and Lumpkin (1994) adapted this three-item, five-point Likert-type subscale from the Ways of Coping Checklist Scale developed by Folkman and Lazarus (1980, 1985). It attempts to measure the extent to which a salesperson uses negative avoidance tactics to cope with stressful customer sales presentations. In this study, the original items were screened for applicability to the sales setting. The remaining items were then subjected to factor analysis in a manner similar to Folkman and colleagues (1986) and the subscales identified in that manner.

SCALE ORIGIN: These items were adapted by Strutton and Lumpkin (1994) for a sales setting from the Ways of Coping Checklist (Folkman and Lazarus 1980, 1985). The original measure contained 43 items developed to measure problem-focused (24 items) and emotion-focused (19 items) tactics for handling stressful situations.

SAMPLES: Strutton and Lumpkin's (1994) sample was a nonprobability sample of **101** nonmanager salespeople from three industries: communications technology (60), textiles (22), and furniture (19), predominantly in the southern United States.

RELIABILITY: Strutton and Lumpkin (1994) reported a Cronbach's alpha of **.63** for this scale.

VALIDITY: No specific validity tests were reported by Strutton and Lumpkin (1994). However, this subscale was **not** identified as a separate subscale in Folkman and colleagues' (1986) earlier work. Some caution is warranted regarding the possibility of findings idiosyncratic to this study.

ADMINISTRATION: Strutton and Lumpkin (1994) asked respondents to describe the most stressful customer-related situation they had encountered during a sales presentation during the previous two months. They were then asked to respond to the items in the scale along with other scales and demographic questions. Higher scores on the scale indicated that negative avoidance tactics for dealing with stress were used to a greater extent.

MAJOR FINDINGS: Strutton and Lumpkin (1994) found that **negative avoidance** was significantly and negatively related to sales presentation effectiveness in a regression of all subscales on a self-reported measure of presentation effectiveness.

REFERENCES:

Folkman, Susan and Richard S. Lazarus (1980), "An Analysis of Coping in a Middle-Aged Community Sample," *Journal of Health and Social Behavior*, 21 (September), 219–39.
——— and ——— (1985), "If It Changes, It Must Be a Process: Study of Emotion and Coping During Three Stages of a College Examination," *Journal of Personality and Social Psychology*, 48 (January), 150–70.
———, ———, Christine Dunkel-Schetter, Anita DeLongis, and Rand J. Gruen (1986), "Dynamics of a Stressful Encounter: Cognitive Appraisal, Coping, and Encounter Outcomes," *Journal of Personality and Social Psychology*, 50 (May), 992–1003.
Strutton, David and James R. Lumpkin (1994), "Problem- and Emotion-Focused Coping Dimensions and Sales Presentation Effectiveness," *JAMS*, 22 (1), 28–37.

#703 *Negative Avoidance*

SCALE ITEMS:

Directions: Indicate the extent to which you used each of the following tactics to cope with a stressful sales presentation experience:

Not used at all   :____:____:____:____:____: Used a great deal
                    1   2   3   4   5

1. Took it out on other people.

2. Avoided being with other people.

3. Refused to believe it had happened.

SCALE NAME: New Product Development Integration (Engineering Involvement)

SCALE DESCRIPTION: Ayers, Dahlstrom, and Skinner (1997) used this three-item, seven-point Likert-type scale to measure the extent of engineering's involvement with marketing in various activities related to the new product development (NPD) process.

SCALE ORIGIN: Ayers, Dahlstrom, and Skinner (1997) indicated that the scale was adapted from a measure used in the research of Gupta, Raj, and Wilemon (1985).

SAMPLES: Ayers, Dahlstrom, and Skinner (1997) collected data on 19 NPD projects undertaken by a major U.S. computer manufacturer. Seven project members from each NPD team were selected to participate in the study, five of whom were R&D and the remaining two from marketing. Of the 132 questionnaire booklets distributed, **115** usable surveys were returned.

RELIABILITY: Ayers, Dahlstrom, and Skinner (1997) reported a coefficient alpha of **.70** for the scale.

VALIDITY: An exploratory factor analysis on all items composing the scales was used to verify the unidimensionality of the measures. No items were dropped on the basis of item-to-total correlations or an analysis of the factor structure. Ayers, Dahlstrom, and Skinner (1997) next subjected the measures to a confirmatory factor analysis to assess their construct validity. Again, no items were deleted on the basis of this analysis. The discriminant validity of the measures was also assessed using confirmatory factory analysis and was found to be acceptable.

ADMINISTRATION: Ayers, Dahlstrom, and Skinner (1997) included the scale with other measures as part of a self-administered questionnaire booklet that was apparently distributed to respondents at their place of employment. A cover letter explaining the study purpose and promises of anonymity accompanied the survey. The questionnaires distributed to R&D and marketing personnel were identical except that R&D personnel responded to questions about their relationship with marketing, and vice versa. Divisional managers designated the project for which responses were sought. Higher scores on the scale indicated a higher degree of engineering involvement in the marketing-related aspects of the NPD process.

MAJOR FINDINGS: Ayers, Dahlstrom, and Skinner (1997) examined the influence of integration between the marketing and R&D, managerial controls, and relational norms on new product success. Structural equation modeling was used to test the hypotheses. **Engineering's involvement in the NPD task was one of three first-order factors serving as indicators of the marketing and R&D integration factor.** Both formalization and centralization were found to enhance the level of integration between marketing and R&D, and higher levels of marketing and R&D integration were significantly associated with stronger perceptions of marketing and R&D relationship effectiveness. Marketing and R&D integration was also found to influence new product success.

REFERENCES:

Ayers, Doug, Robert Dahlstrom, and Steven J. Skinner (1997), "An Exploratory Investigation of Organizational Antecedents to New Product Success," *JMR*, 34 (February), 107–16.

Gupta, Ashok K., S.P. Raj, and David Wilemon (1985), "R&D and Marketing Dialogue in High-Tech Firms," *Industrial Marketing Management*, 14 (4), 289–300.

#704 *New Product Development Integration (Engineering Involvement)*

SCALE ITEMS:
Please indicate your level of agreement with the following:

Strongly
disagree

Strongly
agree

1————2————3————4————5————6————7

Engineers were involved with product planners in:

1. Screening the new product idea.

2. Designing communication strategies for the customers of the new product.

3. Analyzing customer needs.

SCALE NAME: New Product Development Integration (Information Exchange)

SCALE DESCRIPTION: Ayers, Dahlstrom, and Skinner (1997) used this three-item, seven-point Likert-type scale to measure the extent of information provided by marketing to engineering in regard to the new product development (NPD) project.

SCALE ORIGIN: Ayers, Dahlstrom, and Skinner (1997) indicated that the scale was adapted from a measure used in the research of Gupta, Raj, and Wilemon (1985).

SAMPLES: Ayers, Dahlstrom, and Skinner (1997) collected data on 19 NPD projects undertaken by a major U.S. computer manufacturer. Seven project members from each NPD team were selected to participate in the study, five of whom were R & D and the remaining two from marketing. Of the 132 questionnaire booklets distributed, **115** usable surveys were returned.

RELIABILITY: Ayers, Dahlstrom, and Skinner (1997) reported a coefficient alpha of **.81** for the scale.

VALIDITY: An exploratory factor analysis on all items composing the scales was used to verify the unidimensionality of the measures. No items were dropped on the basis of item-to-total correlations or an analysis of the factor structure. Ayers, Dahlstrom, and Skinner (1997) next subjected the measures to a confirmatory factor analysis to assess their construct validity. Again, no items were deleted on the basis of this analysis. The discriminant validity of the measures was also assessed using confirmatory factory analysis and was found to be acceptable.

ADMINISTRATION: Ayers, Dahlstrom, and Skinner (1997) included the scale with other measures as part of a self-administered questionnaire booklet that was apparently distributed to respondents at their place of employment. A cover letter explaining the study purpose and promises of anonymity accompanied the survey. The questionnaires distributed to R&D and marketing personnel were identical except that R&D personnel responded to questions about their relationship with marketing, and vice versa. Divisional managers designated the project for which responses were sought. Higher scores on the scale indicated that marketers supplied engineers with more information pertinent to the NPD project.

MAJOR FINDINGS: Ayers, Dahlstrom, and Skinner (1997) examined the influence of integration between the marketing and R&D, managerial controls, and relational norms on new product success. Structural equation modeling was used to test the hypotheses. **Information exchange from marketing to engineering** was one of three first-order factors serving as indicators of the marketing and R&D integration factor. Both formalization and centralization were found to enhance the level of integration between marketing and R&D, and higher levels of marketing and R&D integration were significantly associated with stronger perceptions of marketing and R&D relationship effectiveness. Marketing and R&D integration was also found to influence new product success.

REFERENCES:
Ayers, Doug, Robert Dahlstrom, and Steven J. Skinner (1997), "An Exploratory Investigation of Organizational Antecedents to New Product Success," *JMR*, 34 (February), 107–16.
Gupta, Ashok K., S.P. Raj, and David Wilemon (1985), "R&D and Marketing Dialogue in High-Tech Firms," *Industrial Marketing Management*, 14 (4), 289–300.

#705 *New Product Development Integration (Information Exchange)*

SCALE ITEMS:

Please indicate your level of agreement with the following:

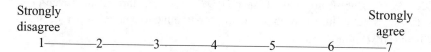

Strongly
disagree

Strongly
agree

1————2————3————4————5————6————7

Product planners provided information to engineers on:

1. Customer requirements for the new product.

2. Regulatory and legal restrictions on product performance and design.

3. Competitor actions.

SCALE NAME: New Product Development Integration (Marketing Involvement)

SCALE DESCRIPTION: Ayers, Dahlstrom, and Skinner (1997) used this four-item, seven-point Likert-type scale to measure the extent of marketing's involvement with engineering in front-end activities related to the new product development (NPD) process.

SCALE ORIGIN: Ayers, Dahlstrom, and Skinner (1997) indicated that the scale was adapted from a measure used in the research of Gupta, Raj, and Wilemon (1985).

SAMPLES: Ayers, Dahlstrom, and Skinner (1997) collected data on 19 NPD projects undertaken by a major U.S. computer manufacturer. Seven project members from each NPD team were selected to participate in the study, five of whom were R&D and the remaining two from marketing. Of the 132 questionnaire booklets distributed, **115** usable surveys were returned.

RELIABILITY: Ayers, Dahlstrom, and Skinner (1997) reported a coefficient alpha of **.86** for the scale.

VALIDITY: An exploratory factor analysis on all items comprising the scales was used to verify the unidimensionality of the measures. No items were dropped on the basis of item-to-total correlations or an analysis of the factor structure. Ayers, Dahlstrom, and Skinner (1997) next subjected the measures to a confirmatory factor analysis to assess their construct validity. Again, no items were deleted on the basis of this analysis. The discriminant validity of the measures was also assessed using confirmatory factory analysis and was found to be acceptable.

ADMINISTRATION: Ayers, Dahlstrom, and Skinner (1997) included the scale with other measures as part of a self-administered questionnaire booklet that was apparently distributed to respondents at their place of employment. A cover letter explaining the study purpose and promises of anonymity accompanied the survey. The questionnaires distributed to R&D and marketing personnel were identical except that R&D personnel responded to questions about their relationship with marketing, and vice versa. Divisional managers designated the project for which responses were sought. Higher scores on the scale indicated a higher degree of marketing involvement in engineering-related aspects of the NPD process.

MAJOR FINDINGS: Ayers, Dahlstrom, and Skinner (1997) examined the influence of integration between the marketing and R&D, managerial controls, and relational norms on new product success. Structural equation modeling was used to test the hypotheses. **Marketing's involvement in the NPD** task was one of three first-order factors serving as indicators of the marketing and R&D integration factor. Both formalization and centralization were found to enhance the level of integration between marketing and R&D, and higher levels of marketing and R&D integration were significantly associated with stronger perceptions of marketing and R&D relationship effectiveness. Marketing and R&D integration was also found to influence new product success.

REFERENCES:

Ayers, Doug, Robert Dahlstrom, and Steven J. Skinner (1997), "An Exploratory Investigation of Organizational Antecedents to New Product Success," *JMR*, 34 (February), 107–16.

Gupta, Ashok K., S.P. Raj, and David Wilemon (1985), "R&D and Marketing Dialogue in High-Tech Firms," *Industrial Marketing Management*, 14 (4), 289–300.

#706 *New Product Development Integration (Marketing Involvement)*

SCALE ITEMS:
Please indicate your level of agreement with the following:

Strongly   Strongly
disagree   agree

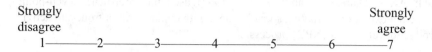

1————2————3————4————5————6————7

Product planners were involved with engineers in:

1. Setting the new product goals and priorities.

2. Establishing the new product development schedule.

3. Generating the new product idea.

4. Screening the new product idea.

SCALE NAME: New Product Development Proficiency (Commercialization)

SCALE DESCRIPTION: Song and Parry (1997) used this seven-item, eleven-point scale to measure perceptions of a firm's proficiency in the commercialization stage of the new product development (NPD) process.

SCALE ORIGIN: The scale is original to Song and Parry (1997), though item 5 is credited to Cooper (1979a, b), Maidique and Zierger (1984), and Zierger and Maidique (1990). Song and Parry (1997) generated scale items on the basis of a review of the literature, pilot studies, and information obtained from 36 in-depth case study interviews conducted with both Japanese and U.S. firms. The items for all scales used by Song and Parry (1997) were evaluated by an academic panel composed of both Japanese and U.S. business and engineering experts. Following revisions, the items were judged by a new panel composed of academicians and NPD managers. The authors reported extensive pretesting of both the Japanese and U.S. versions of the questionnaire.

SAMPLES: Song and Parry (1997) randomly sampled 500 of the 611 firms trading on the Tokyo, Osaka, and Nagoya stock exchanges that had been identified as developing at least four new physical products since 1991. Usable responses pertaining to **788** NPD projects were obtained from 404 Japanese firms. The U.S. sampling frame was taken from companies listed in the *High-Technology Industries Directory*. Of the 643 firms who had introduced a minimum of four new physical products since 1990, 500 firms were randomly sampled (though stratified by industry to match the Japanese sample), and 312 U.S. firms provided data on **612** NPD projects, of which 312 were successes and 300 were failures.

RELIABILITY: Song and Parry (1997) reported a coefficient alpha of **.86** for this scale in the Japanese sample and **.86** for the U.S. sample.

VALIDITY: The extensive pretesting and evaluation of the measure with academicians and NPD managers provides strong evidence for the face validity of the measure. The authors did not specifically report any other examination of scale validity.

ADMINISTRATION: The self-administered questionnaire containing the scale was originally developed in English; the Japanese version was prepared using the parallel-translation/double-translation method. Following minor revisions made on the basis of pretests with bilingual respondents and case study participants, the Japanese sample received a survey packet containing cover letters in both English and Japanese, two Japanese-language questionnaires, and two international postage-paid reply envelopes. Survey packets delivered to U.S. firms were similar, except no Japanese cover letter was included and the surveys were in English. Incentives, four follow-up letters, and multiple telephone calls and faxes were used to increase the response rate with both samples. Song and Parry (1997) indicated that respondents were asked to answer one questionnaire in the context of a successful new product project introduced after 1991 and the other in the context of a new product project that had failed. Higher scores on scale indicated greater proficiency in the commercialization stage of the NPD process.

MAJOR FINDINGS: Song and Parry (1997) conceptualized and tested a model of strategic, tactical, and environmental factors believed to influence new product success using data collected from both Japanese and U.S. firms. In both the Japanese and U.S. samples, **proficiency in the commercialization** phase of the NPD process was positively related to the firm's existing marketing skills and resources, the level of internal firm commitment to the project, and the level of cross-functional integration in the firm.

REFERENCES:

Cooper, Robert G. (1979a), "Identifying Industrial New Product Success: Project NewProd," *Industrial Marketing Management*, 8 (2), 124–35.

——— (1979b), "The Dimensions of Industrial New Product Success and Failure," *JM*, 43 (Summer), 93–103.

Maidique, Modesto A. and Billie Jo Zierger (1984), "A Study of Success and Failure in Product Innovation: The Case of the U.S. Electronics Industry," *IEEE Transactions on Engineering Management*, 31 (4), 192–203.

Song, X. Michael and Mark E. Parry (1997b), "A Cross-National Comparative Study of New Product Development Processes: Japan and the United States," *JM*, 61 (April), 1–18.

Zierger, Billie Jo and Modesto Maidique (1990), "A Model of NPD: An Empirical Test," *Management Science*, 36 (7), 867–83.

SCALE ITEMS:

Directions: Please circle the answer that best represents your judgment about each aspect on "how things *actually* were during the development of this project' rather than on "how things *ought* to be."

The following steps are frequently parts of a new product development process. During this project, how well was each of the following activities undertaken? Please indicate how well or adequately your firm undertook each activity in this product development process—relative to how you think it should have been done—by circling a number from 0 to 10 on the scale to the right of each statement. Here: 0 = done very poorly or mistakenly omitted altogether, 10 = done excellently, and numbers between 0 and 10 indicate various degrees of adequacy.

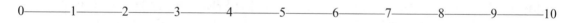

0———1———2———3———4———5———6———7———8———9———10

1. Completing the final plans for manufacturing.

2. Completing the final plans for marketing.

3. Establishing the overall direction for commercialization of this product.

4. Designating the individuals responsible for each part of the commercialization program.

5. Launching the product in the marketplace—selling, promoting and distributing.

6. Studying feedback from customers regarding this product.

7. Specifying activites and tentative plans for the product commercialization phase.

SCALE NAME: New Product Development Proficiency (Idea Generation and Screening)

SCALE DESCRIPTION: Song and Parry (1997) used this five-item, eleven-point scale to measure perceptions of a firm's proficiency in the idea-generation and screening stage of the new product development (NPD) process.

SCALE ORIGIN: The scale is original to Song and Parry (1997), though the first item is credited to Cooper (1979a, b). Song and Parry (1997) generated scale items on the basis of a review of the literature, pilot studies, and information obtained from 36 in-depth case study interviews conducted with both Japanese and U.S. firms. The items for all scales used by Song and Parry (1997) were evaluated by an academic panel composed of both Japanese and U.S. business and engineering experts. Following revisions, the items were judged by a new panel composed of academicians and NPD managers. The authors reported extensive pretesting of both the Japanese and U.S. versions of the questionnaire.

SAMPLES: Song and Parry (1997) randomly sampled 500 of the 611 firms trading on the Tokyo, Osaka, and Nagoya stock exchanges that had been identified as developing at least four new physical products since 1991. Usable responses pertaining to **788** NPD projects were obtained from 404 Japanese firms. The U.S. sampling frame was taken from companies listed in the *High-Technology Industries Directory*. Of the 643 firms who had introduced a minimum of four new physical products since 1990, 500 firms were randomly sampled (though stratified by industry to match the Japanese sample), and 312 U.S. firms provided data on **612** NPD projects, of which 312 were successes and 300 were failures.

RELIABILITY: Song and Parry (1997) reported a coefficient alpha of **.80** for this scale in the Japanese sample and **.81** for the U.S. sample.

VALIDITY: The extensive pretesting and evaluation of the measure with academicians and NPD managers provided strong evidence for the face validity of the measure. The authors did not specifically report any other examination of scale validity.

ADMINISTRATION: The self-administered questionnaire containing the scale was originally developed in English; the Japanese version was prepared using the parallel-translation/double-translation method. Following minor revisions made on the basis of pretests with bilingual respondents and case study participants, the Japanese sample received a survey packet containing cover letters in both English and Japanese, two Japanese-language questionnaires, and two international postage-paid reply envelopes. Survey packets delivered to U.S. firms were similar, except no Japanese cover letter was included and the surveys were in English. Incentives, four follow-up letters, and multiple telephone calls and faxes were used to increase the response rate with both samples. Song and Parry (1997) indicated that respondents were asked to answer one questionnaire in the context of a successful new product project introduced after 1991 and the other in the context of a new product project that had failed. Higher scores on scale indicated greater proficiency in the idea-generation and screening stage of the NPD process.

MAJOR FINDINGS: Song and Parry (1997) conceptualized and tested a model of strategic, tactical, and environmental factors believed to influence new product success using data collected from both Japanese and U.S. firms. In both the Japanese and U.S. samples, **proficiency in the idea-generation and screening** phase of the NPD process was positively related to the firm's existing marketing skills and resources, the level of internal firm commitment to the project, and the level of cross-functional integration in the firm.

REFERENCES:

Cooper, Robert G. (1979a), "Identifying Industrial New Product Success: Project NewProd," *Industrial Marketing Management*, 8 (2), 124–35.

———— (1979b), "The Dimensions of Industrial New Product Success and Failure," *JM*, 43 (Summer), 93–103.

Song, X. Michael and Mark E. Parry (1997b), "A Cross-National Comparative Study of New Product Development Processes: Japan and the United States," *JM*, 61 (April), 1–18.

SCALE ITEMS:

Directions: Please circle the answer that best represents your judgment about each aspect on "how things *actually* were during the development of this project" rather than on "how things *ought* to be."

The following steps are frequently parts of a new product development process. During this project, how well was each of the following activities undertaken? Please indicate how well or adequately your firm undertook each activity in this product development process—relative to how you think it should have been done—by circling a number from 0 to 10 on the scale to the right of each statement. Here: 0 = done very poorly or mistakenly omitted altogether, 10 = done excellently, and numbers between 0 and 10 indicate various degrees of adequacy.

0————1————2————3————4————5————6————7————8————9————10

1. Initial screening of the product idea—the first review of the venture.

2. Expanding the data into a full product concept.

3. Translating the product concept into business terms (such as market share, profitability, marketability).

4. Identifying the key business implications of the product concept and its development.

5. Preparing a written proposal of the product concept.

SCALE NAME: New Product Development Proficiency (Marketing)

SCALE DESCRIPTION: Song and Parry (1997a) used this six-item, eleven-point scale to measure perceptions of a firm's proficiency in the marketing-related aspects of new product development (NPD), such as opportunity and trend analysis, test marketing, and launching.

SCALE ORIGIN: The scale is original to Song and Parry (1997a), though some items are credited to Cooper (1979a, b), Maidique and Zierger (1984), and Zierger and Maidique (1990). Each of the items in this scale was also associated with the NPD proficiency scales related to market opportunity analysis, testing, and commercialization reported in another Song and Parry (1997b) article. Song and Parry (1997a, b) generated scale items on the basis of a review of the literature, pilot studies, and information obtained from 36 in-depth case study interviews conducted with both Japanese and U.S. firms. The items for all scales used by Song and Parry (1997a, b) were evaluated by an academic panel composed of both Japanese and U.S. business and engineering experts Following revisions, the items were judged by a new panel composed of academicians and NPD managers. Song and Parry (1997a, b) reported extensive pretesting of both the Japanese and U.S. versions of the questionnaire.

SAMPLES: For this study, Song and Parry (1997a) used data provided by a random sample of 500 of the 611 firms trading on the Tokyo, Osaka, and Nagoya stock exchanges that had been identified as developing at least four new physical products since 1991. Usable responses pertaining to **788** NPD projects were obtained from 404 Japanese firms. The resulting data were randomly split into calibration (n = 394) and validation (n = 394) samples for the purpose of cross-validation.

RELIABILITY: A confirmatory factor analysis of the data in the calibration sample was used to purify the scale. Items loading on multiple constructs or those with low item-to-scale loadings were deleted from the measure. Song and Parry (1997a) reported a coefficient alpha of **.80** for the purified measure using data from the validation sample.

VALIDITY: The extensive pretesting and evaluation of the measure with academicians and NPD managers provided strong evidence for the face validity of the measure. Song and Parry (1997a) did not specifically report any other examination of scale validity.

ADMINISTRATION: The self-administered questionnaire containing the scale was originally developed in English; the Japanese version was prepared using the parallel-translation/double-translation method. Following minor revisions made on the basis of pretests with bilingual respondents and case study participants, the Japanese sample received a survey packet containing cover letters in both English and Japanese, two Japanese-language questionnaires, and two international postage-paid reply envelopes. Incentives, four follow-up letters, and multiple telephone calls and faxes were used to increase the response rate. Song and Parry (1997a) indicated that respondents were asked to answer one questionnaire in the context of a successful new product project introduced after 1991 and the other in the context of a new product project that had failed. Higher scores on the scale indicated that a firm has greater marketing proficiency and skills related to the development and launching of new products.

MAJOR FINDINGS: Song and Parry (1997a) conceptualized and tested a model of NPD practices believed to influence the success of new product ventures in Japan. The structural model was estimated with the calibration sample data, and the proposed model and the alternative models were tested using the validation sample. The **marketing proficiency** of Japanese firms was found to significantly and positively influence the relative level of new product success.

REFERENCES:

Cooper, Robert G. (1979a), "Identifying Industrial New Product Success: Project NewProd," *Industrial Marketing Management*, 8 (2), 124–35.

——— (1979b), "The Dimensions of Industrial New Product Success and Failure," *JM*, 43 (Summer), 93–103.

Maidique, Modesto A. and Billie Jo Zierger (1984), "A Study of Success and Failure in Product Innovation: The Case of the U.S. Electronics Industry," *IEEE Transactions on Engineering Management*, 31 (4), 192–203.

Song, X. Michael and Mark E. Parry (1997a), "The Determinants of Japanese New Product Successes," *JMR*, 34 (February), 64–76.

——— and ——— (1997b), "A Cross-National Comparative Study of New Product Development Processes: Japan and the United States," *JM*, 61 (April), 1–18.

Zierger, Billie Jo and Modesto Maidique (1990), "A Model of NPD: An Empirical Test," *Management Science*, 36 (7), 867–83.

SCALE ITEMS:

Directions: Please circle the answer that best represents your judgment about each aspect on "how things *actually* were during the development of this project" rather than on "how things *ought* to be."

The following steps are frequently parts of a new product development process. During the development of this project, how well was each of the following activities undertaken? Please indicate how well or adequately your firm undertook each activity in this product development process—relative to how you think it should have been done—by circling a number from 0 to 10 on the scale to the right of each statement. Here: 0 = done very poorly or mistakenly omitted altogether, 10 = done excellently, and numbers between 0 and 10 indicate various degrees of adequacy.

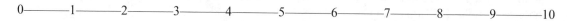

0———1———2———3———4———5———6———7———8———9———10

1. Determining market characteristics and trends.

2. Appraising competitors and their products—both existing and potential.

3. Identifying "appeal" characteristics that would differentiate and sell the product.

4. Executing test marketing programs in line with the plans for commercialization.

5. Conducting a market study or market research—a detailed study of market potential, customer preferences, purchase process, etc.

6. Launching and introducing the product in the marketplace—selling, promoting and distributing.

SCALE NAME: New Product Development Proficiency (Opportunity Analysis)

SCALE DESCRIPTION: Song and Parry (1997) used this seven-item, eleven-point scale to measure perceptions of a firm's proficiency in the business and market opportunity analysis stage of the new product development (NPD) process.

SCALE ORIGIN: The scale is original to Song and Parry (1997), though items 3 and 4 are credited to Cooper (1979a, b), Maidique and Zierger (1984), and Zierger and Maidique (1990). Song and Parry (1997) generated scale items on the basis of a review of the literature, pilot studies, and information obtained from 36 in-depth case study interviews conducted with both Japanese and U.S. firms. The items for all scales used by Song and Parry (1997) were evaluated by an academic panel composed of both Japanese and U.S. business and engineering experts. Following revisions, the items were judged by a new panel composed of academicians and NPD managers. The authors reported extensive pretesting of both the Japanese and U.S. versions of the questionnaire.

SAMPLES: Song and Parry (1997) randomly sampled 500 of the 611 firms trading on the Tokyo, Osaka, and Nagoya stock exchanges that had been identified as developing at least four new physical products since 1991. Usable responses pertaining to **788** NPD projects were obtained from 404 Japanese firms. The U.S. sampling frame was taken from companies listed in the *High-Technology Industries Directory*. Of the 643 firms who had introduced a minimum of four new physical products since 1990, 500 firms were randomly sampled (though stratified by industry to match the Japanese sample), and 312 U.S. firms provided data on **612** NPD projects, of which 312 were successes and 300 were failures.

RELIABILITY: Song and Parry (1997b) reported a coefficient alpha of **.85** for this scale in the Japanese sample and **.83** for the U.S. sample.

VALIDITY: The extensive pretesting and evaluation of the measure with academicians and NPD managers provided strong evidence for the face validity of the measure. The authors did not specifically report any other examination of scale validity.

ADMINISTRATION: The self-administered questionnaire containing the scale was originally developed in English; the Japanese version was prepared using the parallel-translation/double-translation method. Following minor revisions made on the basis of pretests with bilingual respondents and case study participants, the Japanese sample received a survey packet containing cover letters in both English and Japanese, two Japanese-language questionnaires, and two international postage-paid reply envelopes. Survey packets delivered to U.S. firms were similar, except no Japanese cover letter was included and the surveys were in English. Incentives, four follow-up letters, and multiple telephone calls and faxes were used to increase the response rate with both samples. Song and Parry (1997) indicated that respondents were asked to answer one questionnaire in the context of a successful new product project introduced after 1991 and the other in the context of a new product project that had failed. Higher scores on the scale indicated greater proficiency in the business and opportunity analysis stage of the NPD process.

MAJOR FINDINGS: Song and Parry (1997) conceptualized and tested a model of strategic, tactical, and environmental factors believed to influence new product success using data collected from both Japanese and U.S. firms. In both the Japanese and U.S. samples, **proficiency in the business and opportunity analysis** phase of the NPD process was positively related to the firm's existing marketing skills and resources, the level of internal firm commitment to the project, the level of cross-functional integration in the firm, and the level of product differentiation.

REFERENCES:

Cooper, Robert G. (1979a), "Identifying Industrial New Product Success: Project NewProd," *Industrial Marketing Management*, 8 (2), 124–35.

——— (1979b), "The Dimensions of Industrial New Product Success and Failure," *JM*, 43 (Summer), 93–103.

Maidique, Modesto A. and Billie Jo Zierger (1984), "A Study of Success and Failure in Product Innovation: The Case of the U.S. Electronics Industry," *IEEE Transactions on Engineering Management*, 31 (4), 192–203.

Song, X. Michael and Mark E. Parry (1997b), "A Cross-National Comparative Study of New Product Development Processes: Japan and the United States," *JM*, 61 (April), 1–18.

Zierger, Billie Jo and Modesto Maidique (1990), "A Model of NPD: An Empirical Test," *Management Science*, 36 (7), 867–83.

SCALE ITEMS:

Directions: Please circle the answer that best represents your judgment about each aspect on "how things *actually* were during the development of this project" rather than on "how things *ought* to be."

The following steps are frequently parts of a new product development process. During this project, how well was each of the following activities undertaken? Please indicate how well or adequately your firm undertook each activity in this product development process—relative to how you think it should have been done—by circling a number from 0 to 10 on the scale to the right of each statement. Here: 0 = done very poorly or mistakenly omitted altogether, 10 = done excellently, and numbers between 0 and 10 indicate various degrees of adequacy.

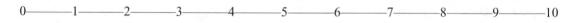

0———1———2———3———4———5———6———7———8———9———10

1. Determining the desired product features and their feasibility.

2. Determining market characteristics and trends.

3. Conducting a market study or market research—a detailed study of market potential, customer preferences, purchase process, etc.

4. Appraising competitors and their products—both existing and potential.

5. Identifying "appeal" characteristics that would differentiate and sell the product.

6. Evaluating the feasibility of developing and manufacturing a product with these features.

7. Assessing the rquired investment, time and risks of the product concept.

SCALE NAME: New Product Development Proficiency (Product Testing)

SCALE DESCRIPTION: Song and Parry (1997) used this four-item, eleven-point scale to measure perceptions of a firm's proficiency in the product testing stage of the new product development (NPD) process.

SCALE ORIGIN: The scale is original to Song and Parry (1997), though items 2 and 3 were modified from Cooper (1979a, b), Maidique and Zierger (1984), and Zierger and Maidique (1990). Song and Parry (1997) generated scale items on the basis of a review of the literature, pilot studies, and information obtained from 36 in-depth case study interviews conducted with both Japanese and U.S. firms. The items for all scales used by Song and Parry (1997) were evaluated by an academic panel composed of both Japanese and U.S. business and engineering experts. Following revisions, the items were judged by a new panel composed of academicians and NPD managers. The authors reported extensive pretesting of both the Japanese and U.S. versions of the questionnaire.

SAMPLES: Song and Parry (1997) randomly sampled 500 of the 611 firms trading on the Tokyo, Osaka, and Nagoya stock exchanges that had been identified as developing at least four new physical products since 1991. Usable responses pertaining to **788** NPD projects were obtained from 404 Japanese firms. The U.S. sampling frame was taken from companies listed in the *High-Technology Industries Directory*. Of the 643 firms who had introduced a minimum of four new physical products since 1990, 500 firms were randomly sampled (though stratified by industry to match the Japanese sample), and 312 U.S. firms provided data on **612** NPD projects, of which 312 were successes and 300 were failures.

RELIABILITY: Song and Parry (1997) reported a coefficient alpha of **.77** for this scale in the Japanese sample and **.83** for the U.S. sample.

VALIDITY: The extensive pretesting and evaluation of the measure with academicians and NPD managers provided strong evidence for the face validity of the measure. The authors did not specifically report any other examination of scale validity.

ADMINISTRATION: The self-administered questionnaire containing the scale was originally developed in English; the Japanese version was prepared using the parallel-translation/double-translation method. Following minor revisions made on the basis of pretests with bilingual respondents and case study participants, the Japanese sample received a survey packet containing cover letters in both English and Japanese, two Japanese-language questionnaires, and two international postage-paid reply envelopes. Survey packets delivered to U.S. firms were similar, except no Japanese cover letter was included and the surveys were in English. Incentives, four follow-up letters, and multiple telephone calls and faxes were used to increase the response rate with both samples. Song and Parry (1997) indicated that respondents were asked to answer one questionnaire in the context of a successful new product project introduced after 1991 and the other in the context of a new product project that had failed. Higher scores on scale indicated greater proficiency in the product testing stage of the NPD process.

MAJOR FINDINGS: Song and Parry (1997) conceptualized and tested a model of strategic, tactical, and environmental factors believed to influence new product success using data collected from both Japanese and U.S. firms. In both the Japanese and U.S. samples, **proficiency in the product testing** phase of the NPD process was positively related to the firm's existing marketing skills and resources, the level of internal firm commitment to the project, the level of cross-functional integration in the firm, and the level of product differentiation.

#711 New Product Development Proficiency (Product Testing)

REFERENCES:

Cooper, Robert G. (1979a), "Identifying Industrial New Product Success: Project NewProd," *Industrial Marketing Management*, 8 (2), 124–35.

———— (1979b), "The Dimensions of Industrial New Product Success and Failure," *JM*, 43 (Summer), 93–103.

Maidique, Modesto A. and Billie Jo Zierger (1984), "A Study of Success and Failure in Product Innovation: The Case of the U.S. Electronics Industry," *IEEE Transactions on Engineering Management*, 31 (4), 192–203.

Song, X. Michael and Mark E. Parry (1997b), "A Cross-National Comparative Study of New Product Development Processes: Japan and the United States," *JM*, 61 (April), 1–18.

Zierger, Billie Jo and Modesto Maidique (1990), "A Model of NPD: An Empirical Test," *Management Science*, 36 (7), 867–83.

SCALE ITEMS:

Directions: Please circle the answer that best represents your judgment about each aspect on "how things *actually* were during the development of this project" rather than on "how things *ought* to be."

The following steps are frequently parts of a new product development process. During this project, how well was each of the following activities undertaken? Please indicate how well or adequately your firm undertook each activity in this product development process—relative to how you think it should have been done—by circling a number from 0 to 10 on the scale to the right of each statement. Here: 0 = done very poorly or mistakenly omitted altogether, 10 = done excellently, and numbers between 0 and 10 indicate various degrees of adequacy.

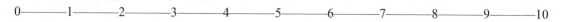

0————1————2————3————4————5————6————7————8————9————10

1. Selecting customers for testing market acceptance.

2. Submitting products to customers for in-use testing.

3. Executing test marketing programs in line with plans for commercialization.

4. Interpreting the findings from in-house and consumer trials, test markets, and trade surveys.

SCALE NAME: New Product Development Proficiency (Technical Development)

SCALE DESCRIPTION: The full nine-item, eleven-point scale was used by Song and Parry (1997b) to measure perceptions of a firm's proficiency in the technical development stage of the new product development (NPD) process. Song and Parry's (1997a) other study of new product success using the Japanese portion of the data used a six-item version of the scale to focus on the overall technical proficiency of Japanese firms.

SCALE ORIGIN: The scale is original to Song and Parry (1997a, b), though items 1 and 5 are credited to Cooper (1979a, b), Maidique and Zierger (1984), and Zierger and Maidique (1990). Song and Parry (1997a, b) generated scale items on the basis of a review of the literature, pilot studies, and information obtained from 36 in-depth case study interviews conducted with both Japanese and U.S. firms. The items for all scales used by Song and Parry (1997a, b) were evaluated by an academic panel composed of both Japanese and U.S. business and engineering experts. Following revisions, the items were judged by a new panel composed of academicians and NPD managers. The authors (1997a, b) reported extensive pretesting of both the Japanese and U.S. versions of the questionnaire.

SAMPLES: Song and Parry (1997a, b) randomly sampled 500 of the 611 firms trading on the Tokyo, Osaka, and Nagoya stock exchanges that had been identified as developing at least four new physical products since 1991. Usable responses pertaining to **788** NPD projects were obtained from 404 Japanese firms. The resulting data were randomly split by Song and Parry (1997a) into calibration (n = 394) and validation (n = 394) samples for the purpose of cross-validation. Song and Parry (1997b) said the U.S. sampling frame was from companies listed in the *High-Technology Industries Directory*. Of the 643 firms who had introduced a minimum of four new physical products since 1990, 500 firms were randomly sampled (though stratified by industry to match the Japanese sample), and 312 U.S. firms provided data on **612** NPD projects, of which 312 were successes and 300 were failures.

RELIABILITY: Song and Parry (1997b) reported a coefficient alpha of **.88** for the full version of the scale in the Japanese sample and **.87** for the U.S. sample. Song and Parry (1997a) used a confirmatory factor analysis of the data in the calibration sample to purify the scale. Items loading on multiple constructs or those with low item-to-scale loadings were deleted from the measure. Song and Parry (1997a) reported a coefficient alpha of **.91** for the six-item, purified measure using data from the validation sample.

VALIDITY: The extensive pretesting and evaluation of the measure with academicians and NPD managers provided strong evidence for the face validity of the measure. Song and Parry (1997a, b) did not specifically report any other examination of scale validity.

ADMINISTRATION: The self-administered questionnaire containing the scale was originally developed in English; the Japanese version was prepared using the parallel-translation/double-translation method. Following minor revisions made on the basis of pretests with bilingual respondents and case study participants, the Japanese sample received a survey packet containing cover letters in both English and Japanese, two Japanese-language questionnaires, and two international postage-paid reply envelopes. Survey packets delivered to U.S. firms were similar, except no Japanese cover letter was included and the surveys were in English. Incentives, four follow-up letters, and multiple telephone calls and faxes were used to increase the response rate with both samples. Song and Parry (1997a, b) indicated that respondents were asked to answer one questionnaire in the context of a successful new product project introduced after 1991 and the other in the context of a new product project that had failed. Higher scores on scale indicated greater proficiency in the technical development stage of the NPD process.

MAJOR FINDINGS: Song and Parry (1997a) conceptualized and tested a model of NPD practices believed to influence the success of new product ventures in Japan. The structural model was estimated with the calibration sample data, and the proposed model and the alternative models were tested using the validation sample. The **technical proficiency** of Japanese firms was found to significantly and positively influence the relative level of new product success.

Song and Parry (1997b) conceptualized and tested a model of strategic, tactical, and environmental factors believed to influence new product success using data collected from both Japanese and U.S. firms. In both the Japanese and U.S. samples, **proficiency in the technical development** phase of the NPD process was positively related to the firm's existing technical skills and resources, the level of internal firm commitment to the project, the level of cross-functional integration in the firm, and the level of product differentiation.

REFERENCES:

Cooper, Robert G. (1979a), "Identifying Industrial New Product Success: Project NewProd," *Industrial Marketing Management*, 8 (2), 124–35.

———— (1979b), "The Dimensions of Industrial New Product Success and Failure," *JM*, 43 (Summer), 93–103.

Maidique, Modesto A. and Billie Jo Zierger (1984), "A Study of Success and Failure in Product Innovation: The Case of the U.S. Electronics Industry," *IEEE Transactions on Engineering Management*, 31 (4), 192–203.

Song, X. Michael and Mark E. Parry (1997a), "The Determinants of Japanese New Product Successes," *JMR*, 34 (February), 64–76.

———— and ———— (1997b), "A Cross-National Comparative Study of New Product Development Processes: Japan and the United States," *JM*, 61 (April), 1–18.

Zierger, Billie Jo and Modesto Maidique (1990), "A Model of NPD: An Empirical Test," *Management Science*, 36 (7), 867–83.

SCALE ITEMS:*

Directions: Please circle the answer that best represents your judgment about each aspect on "how things *actually* were during the development of this project" rather than on "how things *ought* to be."

The following steps are frequently parts of a new product development process. During this project, how well was each of the following activities undertaken? Please indicate how well or adequately your firm undertook each activity in this product development process—relative to how you think it should have been done—by circling a number from 0 to 10 on the scale to the right of each statement. Here: 0 = done very poorly or mistakenly omitted altogether, 10 = done excellently, and numbers between 0 and 10 indicate various degrees of adequacy.

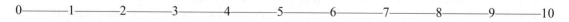

0———1———2———3———4———5———6———7———8———9———10

1. Conducting preliminary engineering, technical and manufacturing assessments.

2. Building the product to designated or revised specifications.

3. Evaluating laboratory tests to determine basic performance against specifications.

4. Establishing the standards by which product performance and market acceptance will be judged.

5. Executing prototype or "in house" sample product testing.

6. Designing and testing manufacturing facilities.

7. Determining the final product design and specifications.

8. Specifying a detailed program for full-scale manufacturing.

9. Working continuously for cost reduction and quality control.

*Items 4, 8, and 9 were eliminated from the measure in Song and Parry's (1997a) study.

SCALE NAME: New Product Success (Relative)

SCALE DESCRIPTION: Song and Parry (1997a) used this four-item, eleven-point scale to measure the degree of new product success in terms of sales volume and profitability, relative to other new products in the firm.

SCALE ORIGIN: The origin of the scale was not stated by Song and Parry (1997a) but was likely to have been developed or modified according to the procedures reported for the rest of the study measures by Song and Parry (1997b). The items for all scales used by Song and Parry (1997a, b) were evaluated by an academic panel composed of both Japanese and U.S. business and engineering experts. Following revisions, the items were judged by a new panel composed of academicians and new product development (NPD) managers. Song and Parry (1997b) reported extensive pretesting of both the Japanese and U.S. versions of the questionnaire.

SAMPLES: For this study, Song and Parry (1997a) used data provided by a random sample of 500 of the 611 firms trading on the Tokyo, Osaka, and Nagoya stock exchanges that had been identified as developing at least four new physical products since 1991. Usable responses pertaining to **788** NPD projects were obtained from 404 Japanese firms. The resulting data were randomly split into calibration (n = 394) and validation (n = 394) samples for the purpose of cross-validation.

RELIABILITY: Song and Parry (1997a) used a confirmatory factor analysis of the data in the calibration sample to purify the scale. Items loading on multiple constructs or those with low item-to-scale loadings were deleted from the measure. Song and Parry (1997b) reported a coefficient alpha of **.96** for the three-item, purified measure using data from the validation sample.

VALIDITY: The extensive pretesting and evaluation of the measure with academicians and NPD managers provided strong evidence for the face validity of the measure. Song and Parry (1997a, b) did not specifically report any other examination of scale validity.

ADMINISTRATION: The self-administered questionnaire containing the scale was originally developed in English; the Japanese version was prepared using the parallel-translation/double-translation method. Following minor revisions made on the basis of pretests with bilingual respondents and case study participants, the Japanese sample received a survey packet containing cover letters in both English and Japanese, two Japanese-language questionnaires, and two international postage-paid reply envelopes. Incentives, four follow-up letters, and multiple telephone calls and faxes were used to increase the response rate with both samples. Song and Parry (1997a, b) indicated that respondents were asked to answer one questionnaire in the context of a successful new product project introduced after 1991 and the other in the context of a new product project that had failed. Higher scores on the scale indicated that the new product experienced greater sales volume and profitability compared with other new product ventures.

MAJOR FINDINGS: Song and Parry (1997a) conceptualized and tested a model of NPD practices believed to influence the success of new product ventures in Japan. The structural model was estimated with the calibration sample data, and the proposed model and the alternative models were tested using the validation sample. The **relative level of new product success** was found to be significantly and positively influenced by cross-functional integration in Japanese firms, the level of competitive and market intelligence, the level of competitive product advantage, and the technical proficiency of the firm.

REFERENCES:
Song, X. Michael and Mark E. Parry (1997a), "The Determinants of Japanese New Product Successes," *JMR*, 34 (February), 64–76.
———— and ———— (1997b), "A Cross-National Comparative Study of New Product Development Processes: Japan and the United States," *JM*, 61 (April), 1–18.

SCALE ITEMS:
Directions: New product performance can be measured in a number of ways. Please indicate, from what you know today, how successful this selected product was or has been using the following criteria.

0————1————2————3————4————5————6————7————8————9————10

1. How successful was this product from an overall profitability standpoint?
   (*Scale anchors:* 0 = A great financial failure, i.e., far less than our minimum acceptable profitability criteria; 10 = A great financial success, i.e., far exceeded our minimum acceptable profitability criteria)

2. Relative to your firm's other new products, how successful was this from a sales volume standpoint?
   (*Scale anchors:* 0 = Far less than sales of our other new products; 10 = Far exceeded the sales of our other new products)

3. Relative to your firm's other new products, how successful was this from a profitability standpoint?
   (*Scale anchors:* 0 = Far less than our other new products; 10 = Far exceeded the our other new products)

4. Relative to your firm's objectives for this product, how successful was this product from a profitability standpoint?
   (*Scale anchors:* 0 = Far less than the objectives; 10 = Far exceeded the objectives)

SCALE NAME: Novelty (New Product)

SCALE DESCRIPTION: Moorman (1995) used this seven-item, seven-point semantic differential scale to assess the degree to which a new product is novel and its introduction changes marketing thinking and practice related to the product category. A reduced four-item version of the scale was used by Moorman and Miner (1997).

SCALE ORIGIN: The scale is original to Moorman (1995). All measures used by Moorman (1995) and Moorman and Miner (1997) were subjected to a purification process following data collection. Moorman (1995) assessed the unidimensionality of the measures in a two-factor confirmatory analysis model using LISREL VII. Items with very weak loadings and those loading on more than one factor were eliminated. The reliability of the measures was assessed by calculating coefficient alphas, and items with low item-to-total correlations were dropped if "doing so did not diminish the measure's coverage of the construct domain" (Moorman 1995, p. 325).

SAMPLES: Moorman (1995) chose to sample the vice presidents of marketing for 300 divisions of firms noted in the 1992 *Advertising Age* list of top 200 advertisers. A total of **92** usable questionnaires were received. No systematic differences were observed between early and late respondents. Moorman and Miner's (1997) study used data from the same sample.

RELIABILITY: Moorman (1995) reported a coefficient alpha of **.85** for the full seven-item version of the scale, and Moorman and Miner (1997) reported an alpha of **.78** for the reduced four-item measure.

VALIDITY: Moorman (1995) performed a series of two-factor confirmatory analyses using LISREL VII to assess the discriminant validity of the measures in her study. Chi-square difference tests were performed on constrained versus unconstrained models, and the significantly lower chi-square values observed for all of the unconstrained models tested were accepted as evidence of the discriminant validity of the measures. Moorman and Miner (1997) assessed the unidimensionality of the scale by dividing the measures used in this study into three subsets of theoretically related variables and submitting the measures to confirmatory factor analyses. The three models provided a good fit with the data. Confirmatory factor analysis was also used to assess the discriminant validity of the measure and was found to be satisfactory.

ADMINISTRATION: The scale was included with other measures in a self-administered questionnaire that was delivered by mail. Moorman (1995) included a cover letter that explained the survey purpose and, in an effort to increase response rate, offered to share survey results. Nonrespondents were telephoned after three weeks and sent a second questionnaire two weeks after the telephone reminder. All informants were instructed to answer in the context of the most recent product development project for which their division had been responsible. Focal projects were required to have been on the market for a minimum of 12 months. Higher scores on the scale indicated that an organization marketed a highly novel new product whose introduction is very likely to change existing marketing thought and practice related to the product category.

MAJOR FINDINGS: Moorman (1995) examined the relationship among organizational market information processes, organizational culture, and new product outcomes. Both conceptual utilization processes and instrumental utilization processes were found to positively influence **new product creativity**. This would indicate that organizations that value, process, and incorporate information into the marketing decision-making, implementation, and evaluation process are likely to introduce highly new novel products.

Moorman and Miner (1997) investigated the impact of organizational memory level and organizational memory dispersion on key new product development processes. Technological turbulence had a significant negative interaction with organizational memory dispersion on **new product creativity**. Specifically, the relationship was negative under highly turbulent conditions, became positive under moderately turbulent conditions, and was strongly positive when technological turbulence was low.

REFERENCES:

Moorman, Christine (1995), "Organizational Market Information Processes: Cultural Antecedents and New Product Outcomes," *JMR*, 32 (August), 318–35.

———— and Anne S. Miner (1997), "The Impact of Organizational Memory on New Product Performance and Creativity," *JMR*, 34 (February), 91–106.

SCALE ITEMS:*

1. Very novel for
   this category   :___:___:___:___:___:___:___: Very ordinary for
                           1   2   3   4   5   6   7   this category (r)

2. Challenged existing   Did not challenge
   ideas for   existing ideas
   this category   :___:___:___:___:___:___:___: this category (r)
                           1   2   3   4   5   6   7

3. Offered new   Did not offer
   ideas to   new ideas to
   the category   :___:___:___:___:___:___:___: this category (r)
                           1   2   3   4   5   6   7

4. Creative   :___:___:___:___:___:___:___: Not creative (r)
                           1   2   3   4   5   6   7

5. Interesting   :___:___:___:___:___:___:___: Uninteresting (r)
                           1   2   3   4   5   6   7

6. Spawned ideas   Did not generate
   for other   ideas for other
   products   :___:___:___:___:___:___:___: products (r)
                           1   2   3   4   5   6   7

7. Encouraged   Did not encourage
   fresh thinking   :___:___:___:___:___:___:___: fresh thinking (r)
                           1   2   3   4   5   6   7

*Moorman and Miner (1997) used items 2, 3, 4, and 6 to represent new product creativity.

SCALE NAME: Openers

SCALE DESCRIPTION: Pullins, Fine, and Warren (1996) used this ten-item, seven-point Likert-type scale to measure the degree to which salespeople are able to encourage others to "open up" and share information about themselves.

SCALE ORIGIN: Pullins, Fine, and Warren (1996) indicated that, though the scale was developed in a social-psychology context by Miller, Berg, and Archer (1983), it has been applied to dyadic sales research previously by Spiro and Weitz (1990). In developing the scale, Miller, Berg, and Archer (1983) tested the measure on a student sample of 740 undergraduates. Factor analysis with Varimax rotation confirmed that all items loaded on a single factor for the sample as a whole and for subsamples divided on the basis of gender. A test–retest reliability of .69 was computed using 134 of the 740 students originally sampled.

SAMPLES: Ten regional sales managers and 216 salespeople employed by a national commercial food equipment manufacturer were sampled by Pullins, Fine, and Warren (1996). Regional sales managers did not complete the survey but instead were asked to provide evaluations of salesperson performance. A total of **194** usable responses were obtained from the sales force, and sales managers provided evaluations for **113** of those sales representatives.

RELIABILITY: Pullins, Fine, and Warren (1996) reported a coefficient alpha of **.82** for this measure.

VALIDITY: No specific examination of the scale's validity was reported by Pullins, Fine, and Warren (1996).

ADMINISTRATION: The scale was included with other measures as part of a self-administered survey that was delivered by mail to members of the sales force. Pullins, Fine, and Warren (1996) included a cover letter with the survey, featuring an endorsement for the project from the company's vice president of sales. Higher scores on the scale indicated that a salesperson rated his or her ability to encourage others to share information about themselves as strong, indicating that this salesperson was perceived by others as responsive, warm, and a good listener.

MAJOR FINDINGS: Pullins, Fine, and Warren (1996) conducted an exploratory investigation of factors influencing the willingness and ability of salespeople to act as mentors. Regression analysis was used to test hypotheses. Tests of ability were restricted to the 42 salespeople who had actually been involved in mentoring relationships. Salespeople who scored higher with respect to their interpersonal competence, as measured by the **openers** scale, were significantly more willing and more able to mentor. Sales managers perceived salespeople with more experience and greater job satisfaction as being more likely to choose to mentor. The relationship with interpersonal competence as measured by the **openers** scale was not significant.

REFERENCES:

Miller, Lynn Carol, John A. Berg, and Richard A. Archer (1983), "Openers: Individuals Who Elicit Intimate Self-Disclosure," *Journal of Personality and Social Psychology*, 44 (6), 1234–44.

Pullins, Ellen Bolman, Leslie M. Fine, and Wendy L. Warren (1996), "Identifying Peer Mentors in the Sales Force: An Exploratory Investigation of Willingness and Ability," *JAMS*, 24 (2), 125–36.

Spiro, Rosann L. and Barton A. Weitz (1990), "Adaptive Selling; Conceptualization, Measurement and Nomological Validity," *JMR*, 27 (February), 61–69.

SCALE ITEMS:

Strongly disagree

Strongly agree

1————2————3————4————5————6————7

1. People frequently tell me about themselves.

2. I've been told that I'm a good listener.

3. I'm very accepting of others.

4. People trust me with their secrets.

5. I easily get people to "open up."

6. People feel relaxed around me.

7. I enjoy listening to people.

8. I'm sympathetic to people's problems.

9. I encourage people to tell me how they are feeling.

10. I can keep people talking about themselves.

SCALE NAME: Organizational Bureaucratization

SCALE DESCRIPTION: Moorman and Miner (1997) used this eight-item, seven-point Likert-type scale to measure the degree to which an organization was managed through formalized relationships and centralized authority.

SCALE ORIGIN: Moorman and Miner (1997) adapted Deshpandé's (1982) scale to measure this construct. The data and methodology (though not the scales) reported in this study were previously reported by Moorman (1995). All measures used by Moorman and Miner (1997) were subjected to a purification process following data collection.

SAMPLES: Moorman and Miner (1997) chose to sample the vice presidents of marketing for 300 divisions of firms noted in the 1992 *Advertising Age* list of top 200 advertisers. A total of **92** usable questionnaires were received. No systematic differences were observed between early and late respondents.

RELIABILITY: Moorman and Miner (1997) reported a coefficient alpha of **.85** for the scale.

VALIDITY: Moorman and Miner (1997) assessed the unidimensionality of the scale by dividing the measures used in this study into three subsets of theoretically related variables and submitting the measures to confirmatory factor analyses. The three models provided a good fit with the data. Confirmatory factor analysis was also used to assess the discriminant validity of the measure and was found to be satisfactory.

ADMINISTRATION: The scale was included with other measures in a self-administered questionnaire that was delivered by mail. Moorman and Miner's (1997) cover letter explained the survey purpose and, in an effort to increase response rate, offered to share survey results. Nonrespondents were telephoned after three weeks and sent a second questionnaire two weeks after the telephone reminder. All informants were instructed to answer in the context of the most recent product development project for which their division had been responsible. Focal projects were required to have been on the market for a minimum of 12 months. Higher scores on the scale indicated that the organization was highly bureaucratic and managed through formalized processes relationships and centralized authority.

MAJOR FINDINGS: Moorman and Miner (1997) investigated the impact of organizational memory level and organizational memory dispersion on key new product development processes. **Organizational bureaucratization** was included the model as control variable.

REFERENCES:
Deshpandé, Rohit (1982), "The Organizational Context of Market Research Use," *JM*, 46 (Fall), 91–101.
Moorman, Christine (1995), "Organizational Market Information Processes: Cultural Antecedents and New Product Outcomes," *JMR*, 32 (August), 318–35.
———— and Anne S. Miner (1997), "The Impact of Organizational Memory on New Product Performance and Creativity," *JMR*, 34 (February), 91–106.

SCALE ITEMS:

Strongly   Strongly
disagree   agree
  1————2————3————4————5————6————7

1. Whenever employees have a problem, they are supposed to go to the same person for an answer.

2. There is little action taken until a superior approves the decision.

3. If employees wished to make their own decisions, they would be quickly discouraged.

4. Going through the proper channels in getting a job done is constantly stressed.

5. Employees have to ask their boss before they do almost anything.

6. Any decision employees make has to have their boss' approval.

7. There is no specific rule manual detailing what employees should do. **(r)**

8. In this organization, everyone has a specific job to do.

SCALE NAME: Organizational Citizenship Behavior (Civic Virtue)

SCALE DESCRIPTION: Posdakoff and MacKenzie (1994) used this three-item, seven-point scale to measure the degree to which sales managers perceived agents as responsibly participating in and being concerned about matters related to the company (attending meetings, functions, etc.).

SCALE ORIGIN: Organizational citizenship behaviors (OCBs) represent forms of behavior not explicitly rewarded by the formal organizational reward system. Civic virtue is one form of citizenship behavior originally conceptualized by Organ (1988, 1990a, b). Posdakoff and MacKenzie (1994) developed the specific items used in this measure by following typical scale development procedures. Items were generated to tap into each construct, revised on the basis of expert opinion, discussed with sales representatives to determine face validity and applicability to the sales context, and pretested with a sample of insurance sales managers. The final items used to represent the measure were selected on the basis of confirmatory factor analyses and item reliability analyses.

SAMPLES: In their first study, Posdakoff and MacKenzie (1994) used a national sample of sales managers, who provided ratings of **987** full-time agents employed by a major insurance company. The salespeople who were rated were predominately men (79.8%) and college educated (91% had some college, 68.1% had at least a bachelor's degree). In the second study, the authors aggregated the individual agent OCB data used in Study 1 to create unit-level scores to represent the average amount of OCB exhibited by agents in each sales unit. Matching sales performance data were obtained from the company for a total of **116** sales (containing 839 of the 987 agent ratings used in Study 1). The average size of a unit was 7.2 and ranged from 2 to 21 employees.

RELIABILITY: Posdakoff and MacKenzie (1994) reported coefficient alphas of **.82** for Study 1 and **.80** for Study 2.

VALIDITY: Posdakoff and MacKenzie (1994) examined the discriminant and convergent validity of the scale using confirmatory factor analysis for both Study 1 and Study 2 data. Strong evidence for both types of validity was present in Study 1. However, the confirmatory factor analysis results of the second study suggest that discriminant validity was lacking between the OCB (helping) and OCB (civic virtue) scales.

ADMINISTRATION: Posdakoff and MacKenzie (1994) indicated that sales managers' ratings of their agents' OCBs and job performance were obtained through a self-administered mail survey distributed to sales managers. A preaddressed, stamped reply envelope was included with the survey. Higher scores on the scale indicated that managers perceived their agents as exhibiting more voluntary actions to help the company, such as attending nonmandatory meetings or functions.

MAJOR FINDINGS: Posdakoff and MacKenzie (1994) investigated the impact of OCBs on objective unit performance and compared this effect with the impact of OCBs on managerial evaluations of agents. The results of Study 1 indicated that **OCB civic virtue behavior** significantly and positively influenced managers' overall performance rating of their agents. In Study 2, **OCB civic virtue behavior** was also found to have a significant positive effect on unit performance.

REFERENCES:

Organ, Dennis W. (1988), *Organizational Citizenship Behavior: The Good Soldier Syndrome.* Lexington, MA: Lexington Books.

———— (1990a), "The Motivational Basis of Organizational Citizenship Behavior," in *Research in Organizational Behavior*, Vol. 12, Barry M. Staw and Lawrence L. Cummings, eds. Greenwich, CT: JAI Press, 43–72.

——— (1990b), "The Subtle Significance of Job Satisfaction," *Clinical Laboratory Management Review*, 4, 94–98.

Podsakoff, Philip M. and Scott B. MacKenzie (1994), "Organizational Citizenship Behaviors and Sales Unit Effectiveness," *JMR*, 31 (August), 351–63.

SCALE ITEMS:

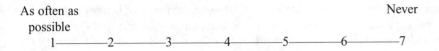

As often as possible   Never

1————2————3————4————5————6————7

1. Attends functions that are not required but help the agency/company image.

2. Attends training/information sessions that agents are encouraged but not required to attend.

3. Attends and actively participates in agency meetings.

SCALE NAME: Organizational Citizenship Behavior (Global)

SCALE DESCRIPTION: Netemeyer and colleagues (1997) used this twelve-item, seven-point scale to measure employee self-reports of the level to which they engage in discretionary behaviors that directly promote the effective functioning of the organization, without necessarily influencing their objective sales productivity.

SCALE ORIGIN: Organizational citizenship behaviors (OCB) represent forms of behavior not explicitly rewarded by the formal organizational reward system. Netemeyer and colleagues (1997) stated that the items used in this measure were adapted from the work of MacKenzie, Podsakoff, and Fetter (1993), who based their scale on the conceptual work of Organ (1988, 1990a, b). The various forms of OCB include sportsmanship, civic virtue, altruism, courtesy, conscientiousness, helping behavior, peacemaking, and cheerleading. Netemeyer and colleagues (1997) used three items each to assess the sportsmanship, civic virtue, conscientiousness, and altruism dimensions of a respondent's self-reported OCB. The summed item scores for each dimension were then used as four indicators of a "global" OCB construct.

SAMPLES: In their first study, Netemeyer and colleagues (1997) used a convenience sample of 115 salespeople employed by a cellular telephone company in the Southeastern United States. From this, **91** usable responses were obtained for a 79% response rate. The median age of respondents was 29 years, and their average amount of time with the organization was 1.89 years. The majority of respondents were women (56%) and college-educated (57%). In the second study, the authors sampled 700 real estate salespeople living in a large southeastern city, and **182** usable surveys were received for an effective response rate of 26%. The median age of respondents in the second study was 48 years, and their average amount of time with the organization was 8.41 years. The majority were women (78%) and college-educated (60.5%).

RELIABILITY: Netemeyer and colleagues (1997) reported coefficient alphas of **.69** for Study 1 and **.54** for Study 2.

VALIDITY: Netemeyer and colleagues (1997) examined the discriminant and construct validity of the scale using confirmatory factor analysis for both Study 1 and Study 2 data. Although evidence was provided of the measure's discriminant validity in both Studies 1 and 2, the OCB global measure did *not* demonstrate construct validity because the .39 and .25 average variance extracted figures for Study 1 and Study 2, respectively, were well below the .50 cut-off level indicated by Fornell and Larcker (1981). The coefficient alpha (.69, .54) and composite reliabilities (.69, .55) of the measures were also quite low.

ADMINISTRATION: Netemeyer and colleagues (1997) indicated that the scale was included as part of a self-administered mail survey in both studies. Study 2 participants were assured of the confidentiality and anonymity of their responses. Higher scores on the scale indicated greater self-reported efforts on the part of a salesperson to engage in discretionary behaviors that directly promoted the effective functioning of the organization without necessarily influencing their objective sales productivity.

MAJOR FINDINGS: Netemeyer and colleagues (1997) proposed and tested a model of potential predictors of **OCB** using data from two separate studies conducted in a sales setting. Both samples demonstrated support for the role of job satisfaction as a predictor of **OCB** in the original models, which were tested using LISREL VII. However, person–organization fit was found to be a predictor of job satisfaction in both studies, and when this variable was added to the model, the job satisfaction to **OCB** path became nonsignificant in Study 1.

COMMENTS: The low reliabilities reported for the measure, taken in conjunction with its apparent lack of construct validity, indicate that further work on the conceptualization and measurement of the OCB scale is needed.

REFERENCES:
Fornell, Claes and David F. Larcker (1981), "Evaluating Structural Equation Models with Unobservable Variables and Measurement Error," *JMR*, 28 (February), 39–50.
MacKenzie, Scott B., Philip M. Podsakoff, and Richard Fetter (1993), "The Impact of Organizational Citizenship Behavior on Evaluations of Salesperson Performance," *JM*, 57 (January), 70–80.
Netemeyer, Richard G., James S. Boles, Daryl O. McKee, and Robert McMurrian (1997), "An Investigation into the Antecedents of Organizational Citizenship Behaviors in a Personal Selling Context," *JM*, 61 (July), 85–98.
Organ, Dennis W. (1988), *Organizational Citizenship Behavior: The Good Soldier Syndrome.* Lexington, MA: Lexington Books.
———— (1990a), "The Motivational Basis of Organizational Citizenship Behavior," in *Research in Organizational Behavior*, Vol. 12, Barry M. Staw and Lawrence L. Cummings, eds. Greenwich, CT: JAI Press, 43–72.
———— (1990b), "The Subtle Significance of Job Satisfaction," *Clinical Laboratory Management Review*, 4, 94–98.

SCALE ITEMS:

As often as possible						Never
1————	2————	3————	4————	5————	6————	7

*Sportsmanship:**
 1. Consume a lot of time complaining about trivial matters. **(r)**
 2. Tend to make "mountains out molehills" (make problems bigger than they are). **(r)**
 3. Always focus on what's wrong with my situation, rather than the positive side of it. **(r)**

Civic Virtue:
 4. "Keep up" with developments in the company.
 5. Attend functions that are not required, but that help the company image.
 6. Risk disapproval in order to express my beliefs about what's best for the company.

Conscientiousness:
 7. Conscientiously follow company regulations and procedures.
 8. Turn in budgets, sales projections, expense reports, etc. earlier than is required.
 9. Return phone calls and respond to other messages and requests for information promptly.

Altruism:
10. Help orient new agents even though it is not required.
11. Always ready to help or lend a helping hand to those around me.
12. Willingly give of my time to others.

*Although the items composing the sportsmanship subscale were not designated as reversed in Netemeyer and colleagues' (1997) article, it is appropriate to do so in light of the conceptual definition of sportsmanship and the nature of the OCB scale.

SCALE NAME: Organizational Citizenship Behavior (Helping)

SCALE DESCRIPTION: Posdakoff and MacKenzie (1994) used this four-indicator, seven-item, seven-point scale to measure the degree to which sales managers perceived that agents exhibited voluntary actions that helped coworkers solve or avoid work-related problems.

SCALE ORIGIN: Organizational citizenship behaviors (OCBs) represent forms of behavior not explicitly rewarded by the formal organizational reward system. The helping scale is actually a composite of several types of citizenship behavior originally conceptualized by Organ (1988, 1990a, b), including altruism, courtesy, peacekeeping, and cheerleading. Posdakoff and MacKenzie (1994) developed the specific items used in this measure by following typical scale development procedures. Items were generated to tap into each construct, revised on the basis of expert opinion, discussed with sales representatives to determine face validity and applicability to the sales context, and pretested with a sample of insurance sales managers. The final items used to represent the measure were selected on the basis of confirmatory factor analyses and item reliability analyses.

SAMPLES: In their first study, Posdakoff and MacKenzie (1994) used a national sample of sales managers who provided ratings of **987** full-time agents employed by a major insurance company. The salespeople who were rated were predominately men (79.8%) and college educated (91% had some college, 68.1% had at least a bachelor's degree). In the second study, the authors aggregated the individual agent OCB data used in Study 1 to create unit-level scores demonstrating the average amount of OCB exhibited by agents in each sales unit. Matching sales performance data were obtained from the company for a total of **116** sales (related to 839 of the 987 agent ratings used in Study 1). The average size of a unit was 7.2 and ranged from 2 to 21 employees.

RELIABILITY: Posdakoff and MacKenzie (1994) reported coefficient alphas of **.89** for Study 1 and **.90** for Study 2.

VALIDITY: Posdakoff and MacKenzie (1994) examined the discriminant and convergent validity of the scale using confirmatory factor analysis for both Study 1 and Study 2 data. Strong evidence for both types of validity was present in Study 1. However, the confirmatory factor analysis results of the second study suggested that discriminant validity was lacking between the OCB (helping) and OCB (civic virtue) scales.

ADMINISTRATION: Posdakoff and MacKenzie (1994) indicated that sales managers' ratings of their agents' OCBs and job performance were obtained through a self-administered mail survey distributed to sales managers. A preaddressed, stamped reply envelope was included with the survey. Higher scores on the scale indicated that managers perceived that their agents exhibited more voluntary actions to help their coworkers solve or avoid work-related problems.

MAJOR FINDINGS: Posdakoff and MacKenzie (1994) investigated the impact of OCBs on objective unit performance and compared this effect with the impact of OCBs on managerial evaluations of agents. The results of Study 1 indicated that **OCB helping behavior** significantly and positively influenced managers' overall performance rating of their agents. In fact, the results indicated that **helping behavior** had five times as great an impact on managerial evaluations than any other individual OCB. Contrary to expectations in Study 2, **OCB helping behavior** was found to have a significant *negative* effect on unit performance.

REFERENCES:

Organ, Dennis W. (1988), *Organizational Citizenship Behavior: The Good Soldier Syndrome.* Lexington, MA: Lexington Books.

———— (1990a), "The Motivational Basis of Organizational Citizenship Behavior," in *Research in Organizational Behavior*, Vol. 12, Barry M. Staw and Lawrence L. Cummings, eds. Greenwich, CT: JAI Press, 43–72.

———— (1990b), "The Subtle Significance of Job Satisfaction," *Clinical Laboratory Management Review*, 4, 94–98.

Podsakoff, Philip M. and Scott B. MacKenzie (1994), "Organizational Citizenship Behaviors and Sales Unit Effectiveness," *JMR*, 31 (August), 351–63.

SCALE ITEMS:

As often as
  possible   Never

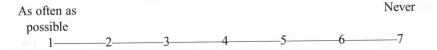

Altruism Scale: *
1a. Willingly gives of his or her time to help other agents who have work-related problems.
1b. Is willing to take time out of his or her own busy schedule to help with recruiting or training new agents.

Courtesy Scale: *
2a. "Touches base" with others before initiating actions that might affect them.
2b. Takes steps to try to prevent problems with other agents and/or other personnel in the agency.

Cheerleading Scale:
3. Encourages other agents when they are down.

Peacemaking Scale: *
4a. Acts as a "peacemaker" when others in the agency have disagreements.
4b. Is a stabilizing influence in the agency when dissension occurs.

*It appears that when multiple items were used to represent a particular subscale, the scores on those items were summed and possibly averaged to provide a single indicator of the score for that scale. The scores for each of the four subscales were then summated to represent the OCB (helping) construct.

SCALE NAME: Organizational Citizenship Behavior (Sportsmanship)

SCALE DESCRIPTION: Posdakoff and MacKenzie (1994) used this four-item, seven-point scale to measure the degree to which sales managers perceived agents as willing to tolerate less-than-ideal circumstances without complaining.

SCALE ORIGIN: Organizational citizenship behaviors (OCBs) represent forms of behavior not explicitly rewarded by the formal organizational reward system. Sportsmanship is one form citizenship behavior originally conceptualized by Organ (1988, 1990a, b). Posdakoff and MacKenzie (1994) developed the specific items used in this measure by following typical scale development procedures. Items were generated to tap into each construct, revised on the basis of expert opinion, discussed with sales representatives to determine face validity and applicability to the sales context, and pretested with a sample of insurance sales managers. The final items used to represent the measure were selected on the basis of confirmatory factor analyses and item reliability analyses.

SAMPLES: In their first study, Posdakoff and MacKenzie (1994) used a national sample of sales managers who provided ratings of **987** full-time agents employed by a major insurance company. The salespeople who were rated were predominately men (79.8%) and college educated (91% had some college, 68.1% had at least a bachelor's degree). In the second study, the authors aggregated the individual agent OCB data used in Study 1 to create unit-level scores demonstrating the average amount of OCB exhibited by agents in each sales unit. Matching sales performance data were obtained from the company for a total of **116** sales (relating to 839 of the 987 agent ratings used in Study 1). The average size of a unit was 7.2 and ranged from 2 to 21 employees.

RELIABILITY: Posdakoff and MacKenzie (1994) reported coefficient alphas of **.84** for Study 1 and **.83** for Study 2.

VALIDITY: Posdakoff and MacKenzie (1994) examined the discriminant and convergent validity of the scale using confirmatory factor analysis for both Study 1 and Study 2 data. Strong evidence for both types of validity was present in Study 1 and Study 2.

ADMINISTRATION: Posdakoff and MacKenzie (1994) indicated that sales managers' ratings of their agents' OCBs and job performance were obtained through a self-administered mail survey distributed to sales managers. A preaddressed, stamped reply envelope was included with the survey. Higher scores on the scale indicated that managers perceived their agents as more tolerant of less-than-ideal conditions and as less likely to make complaints or exaggerations about these working conditions.

MAJOR FINDINGS: Posdakoff and MacKenzie (1994) investigated the impact of OCBs on objective unit performance and compared this effect with the impact of OCBs on managerial evaluations of agents. The results of Study 1 indicated that **OCB sportsmanship behavior** significantly and positively influenced managers' overall performance rating of their agents. In Study 2, **OCB sportsmanship behavior** was also found to have a significant positive effect on unit performance.

REFERENCES:
Organ, Dennis W. (1988), *Organizational Citizenship Behavior: The Good Soldier Syndrome.* Lexington, MA: Lexington Books.

——— (1990a), "The Motivational Basis of Organizational Citizenship Behavior," in *Research in Organizational Behavior*, Vol. 12, Barry M. Staw and Lawrence L. Cummings, eds. Greenwich, CT: JAI Press, 43–72.

——— (1990b), "The Subtle Significance of Job Satisfaction," *Clinical Laboratory Management Review*, 4, 94–98.

Podsakoff, Philip M. and Scott B. MacKenzie (1994), "Organizational Citizenship Behaviors and Sales Unit Effectiveness," *JMR*, 31 (August), 351–63.

SCALE ITEMS:

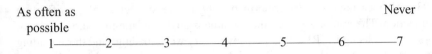

As often as possible   Never

1————2————3————4————5————6————7

1. Consumes a lot of time complaining about trivial matters. **(r)**

2. Always finds fault with what the agency/company is doing. **(r)**

3. Tends to make "mountains out of molehills" (makes problems bigger than they are). **(r)**

4. Always focuses on what is wrong with his or her situation rather than the positive side of it. **(r)**

SCALE NAME: Organizational Culture (Adhocracy)

SCALE DESCRIPTION: Moorman (1995) used this four-item, seven-point Likert-type scale to assess the extent to which an organization's culture emphasizes entrepreneurship, creativity, adaptability, and risk-taking.

SCALE ORIGIN: Moorman (1995) indicates that the scale was taken from the work of Deshpandé, Farley, and Webster (1993). All measures used by Moorman (1995) were subjected to a purification process following data collection. The author assessed the unidimensionality of the measures in a two-factor confirmatory analysis model using LISREL VII. Items with very weak loadings and those loading on more than one factor were eliminated. The reliability of the measures was assessed by calculating coefficient alphas, and items with low item-to-total correlations were dropped if "doing so did not diminish the measure's coverage of the construct domain" (Moorman 1995, p. 325). It would appear from the reliability of this measure that Moorman (1995) decided to retain all four items from Deshpandé, Farley, and Webster's (1993) original scale rather than removing the item(s) with low item-to-total correlations.

SAMPLES: Moorman (1995) chose to sample the vice presidents of marketing for 300 divisions of firms noted in the 1992 *Advertising Age* list of top 200 advertisers; a total of **92** usable questionnaires were received. No systematic differences were observed between early and late respondents.

RELIABILITY: Moorman (1995) reported a coefficient alpha of **.57** for this scale.

VALIDITY: Moorman (1995) performed a series of two-factor confirmatory analyses using LISREL VII to assess the discriminant validity of the measures used in her study. Chi-square difference tests were performed on constrained versus unconstrained models, and the significantly lower chi-square values observed for all of the unconstrained models tested were accepted as evidence of the discriminant validity of the measures.

ADMINISTRATION: The scale was included with other measures in a self-administered questionnaire that was delivered by mail. Moorman (1995) included a cover letter that explained the survey purpose and, in an effort to increase response rate, offered to share survey results. Nonrespondents were telephoned after three weeks and sent a second questionnaire two weeks after the telephone reminder. All informants were instructed to answer in the context of the most recent product development project for which their division had been responsible. Focal projects were required to have been on the market for a minimum of 12 months. Higher scores on the scale indicated that an organization's culture strongly stressed entrepreneurship, creativity, and adaptability.

MAJOR FINDINGS: Moorman (1995) examined the relationship among organizational market information processes, organizational culture, and new product outcomes. No significant relationships were found between an **adhocracy-based organizational culture** and informational acquisition processes, information transmission processes, conceptual utilization processes, or instrumental utilization processes.

COMMENTS: The low reliability of the measure suggests that further development and refinement may be necessary prior to using this scale again.

REFERENCES:
Deshpandé, Rohit, John U. Farley, and Frederick E. Webster Jr. (1993), "Corporate Culture, Customer Orientation, and Innovativeness in Japanese Firms: A Quadrad Analysis," *JM*, 52 (January), 3–15.

Moorman, Christine (1995), "Organizational Market Information Processes: Cultural Antecedents and New Product Outcomes," *JMR*, 32 (August), 318–35.

SCALE ITEMS:*

Directions: Most businesses will be some mixture of the various descriptions noted below. Indicate the degree to which these qualities reflect your division.

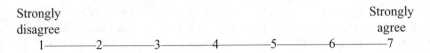

Strongly
disagree
1————2————3————4————5————6————7

Strongly
agree

My division is very:

1. Dynamic and entrepreneurial. People are willing to stick their necks out and take risks.

The head of my division is generally considered to be:

2. An entrepreneur, an innovator, or a risk taker.

The glue that holds my division together is:

3. A commitment to innovation and development. There is an emphasis on being first.

My division emphasizes:

4. Growth and acquiring new resources. Readiness to meet new challenges is important.

*Sixteen items representing four distinct organizational cultures (adhocracy, clan, market, and hierarchy) were administered together in the same section of the questionnaire. The items here pertain only to the adhocracy organizational culture.

SCALE NAME: Organizational Culture (Clan)

SCALE DESCRIPTION: Moorman (1995) used this four-item, seven-point Likert-type scale to assess the extent to which an organization's culture emphasizes teamwork, participation, and cohesiveness.

SCALE ORIGIN: Moorman (1995) indicated that the scale was taken from the work of Deshpandé, Farley, and Webster (1993). All measures used by Moorman (1995) were subjected to a purification process following data collection. The author assessed the unidimensionality of the measures in a two-factor confirmatory analysis model using LISREL VII. Items with very weak loadings and those loading on more than one factor were eliminated. The reliability of the measures was assessed by calculating coefficient alphas, and items with low item-to-total correlations were dropped if "doing so did not diminish the measure's coverage of the construct domain" (Moorman 1995, p. 325).

SAMPLES: Moorman (1995) chose to sample the vice presidents of marketing for 300 divisions of firms noted in the 1992 *Advertising Age* list of top 200 advertisers; a total of **92** usable questionnaires were received. No systematic differences were observed between early and late respondents.

RELIABILITY: Moorman (1995) reported a coefficient alpha of **.85** for this scale.

VALIDITY: Moorman (1995) performed a series of two-factor confirmatory analyses using LISREL VII to assess the discriminant validity of the measures used in her study. Chi-square difference tests were performed on constrained versus unconstrained models, and the significantly lower chi-square values observed for all of the unconstrained models tested were accepted as evidence of the discriminant validity of the measures.

ADMINISTRATION: The scale was included with other measures in a self-administered questionnaire that was delivered by mail. Moorman (1995) included a cover letter that explained the survey purpose and, in an effort to increase response rate, offered to share survey results. Nonrespondents were telephoned after three weeks and sent a second questionnaire two weeks after the telephone reminder. All informants were instructed to answer in the context of the most recent product development project for which their division had been responsible. Focal projects were required to have been on the market for a minimum of 12 months. Higher scores on the scale indicated that an organization's culture strongly stressed teamwork, participation, and cohesiveness.

MAJOR FINDINGS: Moorman (1995) examined the relationship among organizational market information processes, organizational culture, and new product outcomes. **Clan-based organizational cultures** were found to have significantly stronger organizational conceptual utilization processes than hierarchy-based organizational cultures. No significant relationship was found between **clan-based organizational cultures** and the use of informational acquisition processes, but some evidence was found to suggest that clan-based organizational cultures make greater use of information transmission and instrumental utilization processes.

REFERENCES:

Deshpandé, Rohit, John U. Farley, and Frederick E. Webster Jr. (1993), "Corporate Culture, Customer Orientation, and Innovativeness in Japanese Firms: A Quadrad Analysis," *JM*, 52 (January), 3–15.

Moorman, Christine (1995), "Organizational Market Information Processes: Cultural Antecedents and New Product Outcomes," *JMR*, 32 (August), 318–35.

SCALE ITEMS:*

Directions: Most businesses will be some mixture of the various descriptions noted below. Indicate the degree to which these qualities reflect your division.

Strongly
disagree

Strongly
agree

1———2———3———4———5———6———7

My division is very:

1. Personal. It's like an extended family. People seem to share a lot of themselves.

The head of my division is generally considered to be:

2. A mentor, sage, or father or mother figure.

The glue that holds my division together is:

3. Loyalty and tradition. Commitment to this firm runs high.

My division emphasizes:

4. Human resources. High cohesion and morale in the firm are important.

*Sixteen items representing four distinct organizational cultures (adhocracy, clan, market, and hierarchy) were administered together in the same section of the questionnaire. The items here pertain only to the clan organizational culture.

SCALE NAME: Organizational Culture (Hierarchy)

SCALE DESCRIPTION: Moorman (1995) used this three-item, seven-point Likert-type scale to assess the extent to which an organization's culture emphasizes order, uniformity, stability, control, and certainty.

SCALE ORIGIN: Moorman (1995) indicated that the scale was taken from the work of Deshpandé, Farley, and Webster (1993). All measures used by Moorman (1995) were subjected to a purification process following data collection. The author assessed the unidimensionality of the measures in a two-factor confirmatory analysis model using LISREL VII. Items with very weak loadings and those loading on more than one factor were eliminated. The reliability of the measures was assessed by calculating coefficient alphas, and items with low item-to-total correlations were dropped if "doing so did not diminish the measure's coverage of the construct domain" (Moorman 1995, p. 325). One of the items from the original Deshpandé, Farley, and Webster (1993) four-item measure was dropped during the purification process.

SAMPLES: Moorman (1995) chose to sample the vice presidents of marketing for 300 divisions of firms noted in the 1992 *Advertising Age* list of top 200 advertisers; a total of **92** usable questionnaires were received. No systematic differences were observed between early and late respondents.

RELIABILITY: Moorman (1995) reported a coefficient alpha of **.57** for this scale.

VALIDITY: Moorman (1995) performed a series of two-factor confirmatory analyses using LISREL VII to assess the discriminant validity of the measures used in her study. Chi-square difference tests were performed on constrained versus unconstrained models, and the significantly lower chi-square values observed for all of the unconstrained models tested were accepted as evidence of the discriminant validity of the measures.

ADMINISTRATION: The scale was included with other measures in a self-administered questionnaire that was delivered by mail. Moorman (1995) included a cover letter that explained the survey purpose and, in an effort to increase response rate, offered to share survey results. Nonrespondents were telephoned after three weeks and sent a second questionnaire two weeks after the telephone reminder. All informants were instructed to answer in the context of the most recent product development project for which their division had been responsible. Focal projects were required to have been on the market for a minimum of 12 months. Higher scores on the scale indicated that an organization's culture strongly stressed order, stability, control, certainty, and uniformity.

MAJOR FINDINGS: Moorman (1995) examined the relationship among organizational market information processes, organizational culture, and new product outcomes. Clan-based organizational cultures, which stress participation, teamwork, and cohesiveness, were found to have significantly stronger organizational conceptual utilization processes than **hierarchy-based organizational cultures**. No significant relationships were found between a **hierarchy-based organizational culture** and informational acquisition processes, information transmission processes, or instrumental utilization processes.

COMMENTS: The low reliability of the measure suggests that further development and refinement may be necessary prior to using this scale again.

REFERENCES:

Deshpandé, Rohit, John U. Farley, and Frederick E. Webster Jr. (1993), "Corporate Culture, Customer Orientation, and Innovativeness in Japanese Firms: A Quadrad Analysis," *JM*, 52 (January), 3–15.

Moorman, Christine (1995), "Organizational Market Information Processes: Cultural Antecedents and New Product Outcomes," *JMR*, 32 (August), 318–35.

SCALE ITEMS:*

Directions: Most businesses will be some mixture of the various descriptions noted below. Indicate the degree to which these qualities reflect your division.

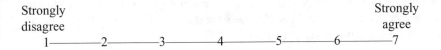

Strongly disagree 1————2————3————4————5————6————7 Strongly agree

The head of my division is generally considered to be:

1. A coordinator, an organizer, or an administrator.

The glue that holds my division together is:

2. Formal rules and policies. Maintaining a smooth-running institution is important here.

My division emphasizes:

3. Permanence and stability. Efficient, smooth operations are important.

*Sixteen items representing four distinct organizational cultures (adhocracy, clan, market, and hierarchy) were administered together in the same section of the questionnaire. The items here pertain only to the hierarchy organizational culture.

SCALE NAME: Organizational Culture (Market)

SCALE DESCRIPTION: Moorman (1995) used this four-item, seven-point Likert-type scale to assess the extent to which an organization's culture stresses goal achievement, productivity, and efficiency.

SCALE ORIGIN: Moorman (1995) indicated that the scale was taken from the work of Deshpandé, Farley, and Webster (1993). All measures used by Moorman (1995) were subjected to a purification process following data collection. The author assessed the unidimensionality of the measures in a two-factor confirmatory analysis model using LISREL VII. Items with very weak loadings and those loading on more than one factor were eliminated. The reliability of the measures was assessed by calculating coefficient alphas, and items with low item-to-total correlations were dropped if "doing so did not diminish the measure's coverage of the construct domain" (Moorman 1995, p. 325).

SAMPLES: Moorman (1995) chose to sample the vice presidents of marketing for 300 divisions of firms noted in the 1992 *Advertising Age* list of top 200 advertisers; a total of **92** usable questionnaires were received. No systematic differences were observed between early and late respondents.

RELIABILITY: Moorman (1995) reported a coefficient alpha of **.81** for this scale.

VALIDITY: Moorman (1995) performed a series of two-factor confirmatory analyses using LISREL VII to assess the discriminant validity of the measures used in her study. Chi-square difference tests were performed on constrained versus unconstrained models, and the significantly lower chi-square values observed for all of the unconstrained models tested were accepted as evidence of the discriminant validity of the measures.

ADMINISTRATION: The scale was included with other measures in a self-administered questionnaire that was delivered by mail. Moorman (1995) included a cover letter that explained the survey purpose and, in an effort to increase response rate, offered to share survey results. Nonrespondents were telephoned after three weeks and sent a second questionnaire two weeks after the telephone reminder. All informants were instructed to answer in the context of the most recent product development project for which their division had been responsible. Focal projects were required to have been on the market for a minimum of 12 months. Higher scores on the scale indicated that an organization's culture strongly stressed goal achievement, productivity, and efficiency.

MAJOR FINDINGS: Moorman (1995) examined the relationship among organizational market information processes, organizational culture, and new product outcomes. No significant relationships were found between a **market-based organizational culture** and informational acquisition processes, information transmission processes, conceptual utilization processes, or instrumental utilization processes.

REFERENCES:

Deshpandé, Rohit, John U. Farley, and Frederick E. Webster Jr. (1993), "Corporate Culture, Customer Orientation, and Innovativeness in Japanese Firms: A Quadrad Analysis," *JM*, 52 (January), 3–15.

Moorman, Christine (1995), "Organizational Market Information Processes: Cultural Antecedents and New Product Outcomes," *JMR*, 32 (August), 318–35.

SCALE ITEMS:*

Directions: Most businesses will be some mixture of the various descriptions noted below. Indicate the degree to which these qualities reflect your division.

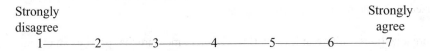

Strongly disagree — 1—————2—————3—————4—————5—————6—————7 — Strongly agree

My division is very:

1. Production oriented. The major concern is with getting the job done. People aren't very personally involved.

The head of my division is generally considered to be:

2. A producer, a technician, or a hard-driver.

The glue that holds my division together is:

3. An emphasis on tasks and goal accomplishment. A production orientation is shared.

My division emphasizes:

4. Competitive actions and achievement. Measurable goals are important.

*Sixteen items representing four distinct organizational cultures (adhocracy, clan, market, and hierarchy) were administered together in the same section of the questionnaire. The items here pertain only to the market organizational culture.

SCALE NAME: Organizational Culture Index (Bureaucratic)

SCALE DESCRIPTION: Oliver and Anderson (1994) used this eight-item, four-point scale to measure the degree to which an organization reflects a bureaucratic culture that delineates in hierarchical fashion where work is organized and systematic.

SCALE ORIGIN: The organizational culture index (OCI) is a 24-item measure that profiles an organization's culture on bureaucratic, innovative, and supportive dimensions. Oliver and Anderson (1994) used the 8 items listed by Wallach (1983) as tapping into the bureaucratic component of the OCI to represent this scale. However, it appears that the scale was developed by Litwin and Stringer (1968). Oliver and Anderson (1994) pretested the measure in a questionnaire administered to a convenience sample of sales representatives attending trade association functions.

SAMPLES: Oliver and Anderson (1994) surveyed managers and manufacturer's sales representatives employed by independently owned and operated sales agencies serving the electronics industry. Of the 350 randomly selected trade association member firms fitting this designation, 299 expressed interest in participating, and ultimately, **194** usable surveys from management and **347** surveys from manufacturer representatives were returned. The typical respondent was a male (92%), college graduate (64%), approximately 39 years of age, and had an average of 12 years sales experience with 5.5 years in the present job.

RELIABILITY: Oliver and Anderson (1994) reported a coefficient alpha of **.739** for this measure.

VALIDITY: Oliver and Anderson (1994) used the correlation matrix of the independent and classification variables used in the study to provide some evidence of discriminant and convergent validity. Nomological validity was also found to be present.

ADMINISTRATION: Oliver and Anderson (1994) sent managers of the 299 firms indicating interest in the study a packet containing a "manager's survey" and three similar self-administered surveys for salespeople, along with self-addressed, postage-paid reply envelopes. Managers were instructed to distribute one survey each to an "above-average rep," a "mid-range rep," and a "below-average rep." Each representative was promised confidentiality and the chance to win one of five $100 prizes in a random drawing. It appears that only responses obtained from sales representatives were used in computing this measure. Higher scores on the scale reflected a more bureaucratic, hierarchical culture where work is organized and systematic.

MAJOR FINDINGS: Oliver and Anderson (1994) examined how perceptions of the presence of a behavior versus outcome sales control system in the respondents' organizations influenced salespeople's performance outcomes and sales strategies as well as their affective, cognitive, and behavioral states. The use of a behavior control system was not related to a **bureaucratic organizational culture**.

REFERENCES:

Litwin, G.H. and R.A. Stringer (1968), *Motivation and Organizational Climate*. Cambridge, MA: Harvard University Press.

Oliver, Richard L. and Erin Anderson (1994), "An Empirical Test of the Consequences of Behavior- and Outcome-Based Sales Control Systems," *JM*, 58 (October), 53–67.

Wallach, Ellen J. (1983), "Individuals and Organizations: The Cultural March," *Training and Development Journal*, 37 (February), 29–36.

SCALE ITEMS:

Please circle a score from the scale below which most closely corresponds with how you see your organization.

Does not describe my organization	Describes my organization a little	Describes my organization a fair amount	Describes my organization most of the time
0	1	2	3

1. Hierarchical.

2. Procedural.

3. Structured.

4. Ordered.

5. Regulated.

6. Established, solid.

7. Cautious.

8. Power-oriented.

SCALE NAME: Organizational Culture Index (Innovative)

SCALE DESCRIPTION: Oliver and Anderson (1994) used this eight-item, four-point scale to measure the degree to which an organization reflects an innovative culture that encourages risk-taking and is a stimulating but stressful environment in which to work.

SCALE ORIGIN: The organizational culture index (OCI) is a 24-item measure that profiles an organization's culture on bureaucratic, innovative, and supportive dimensions. Oliver and Anderson (1994) used the 8 items listed by Wallach (1983) as tapping into the innovative component of the OCI to represent this scale. However, it appears that the scale was developed by Litwin and Stringer (1968). Oliver and Anderson (1994) pretested the measure in a questionnaire administered to a convenience sample of sales representatives attending trade association functions.

SAMPLES: Oliver and Anderson (1994) surveyed managers and manufacturer's sales representatives employed by independently owned and operated sales agencies serving the electronics industry. Of the 350 randomly selected trade association member firms fitting this designation, 299 expressed interest in participating, and ultimately, **194** usable surveys from management and **347** surveys from manufacturer representatives were returned. The typical respondent was a male (92%), college graduate (64%), approximately 39 years of age, and had an average of 12 years sales experience with 5.5 years in the present job.

RELIABILITY: Oliver and Anderson (1994) reported a coefficient alpha of **.829** for this measure.

VALIDITY: Oliver and Anderson (1994) used the correlation matrix of the independent and classification variables used in the study to provide some evidence of discriminant and convergent validity. Nomological validity was also found to be present.

ADMINISTRATION: Oliver and Anderson (1994) sent managers of the 299 firms indicating interest in the study a packet containing a "manager's survey" and three similar self-administered surveys for salespeople, along with self-addressed, postage-paid reply envelopes. Managers were instructed to distribute one survey each to an "above-average rep," a "mid-range rep," and a "below-average rep." Each representative was promised confidentiality and the chance to win one of five $100 prizes in a random drawing. It appears that only responses obtained from sales representatives were used in computing this measure. Higher scores on the scale reflected a more innovative, risk-taking culture.

MAJOR FINDINGS: Oliver and Anderson (1994) examined how perceptions of the presence of a behavior versus outcome sales control system in the respondents' organizations influenced salespeople's performance outcomes and sales strategies, as well as their affective, cognitive, and behavioral states. The use of a behavior control system was significantly related to organizations having more **innovative organizational cultures**.

REFERENCES:

Litwin, G.H. and R.A. Stringer (1968), *Motivation and Organizational Climate*. Cambridge, MA: Harvard University Press.

Oliver, Richard L. and Erin Anderson (1994), "An Empirical Test of the Consequences of Behavior- and Outcome-Based Sales Control Systems," *JM*, 58 (October), 53–67.

Wallach, Ellen J. (1983), "Individuals and Organizations: The Cultural March," *Training and Development Journal*, 37 (February), 29–36.

SCALE ITEMS:

Please circle a score from the scale below which most closely corresponds with how you see your organization.

Does not describe my organization	Describes my organization a little	Describes my organization a fair amount	Describes my organization most of the time
0—————————	—1—————————	—2—————————	—3

1. Risk taking.

2. Results-oriented.

3. Creative.

4. Pressurized.

5. Stimulating.

6. Challenging.

7. Enterprising.

8. Driving.

SCALE NAME: Organizational Culture Index (Supportive)

SCALE DESCRIPTION: Oliver and Anderson (1994) used this eight-item, four-point scale to measure the degree to which an organization reflects a supportive culture that is harmonious and humanistic.

SCALE ORIGIN: The organizational culture index (OCI) is a 24-item measure that profiles an organization's culture on bureaucratic, innovative, and supportive dimensions. Oliver and Anderson (1994) used the 8 items listed by Wallach (1983) as tapping into the supportive component of the OCI to represent this scale. However, it appears that the scale was developed by Litwin and Stringer (1968). Oliver and Anderson (1994) pretested the measure in a questionnaire administered to a convenience sample of sales representatives attending trade association functions.

SAMPLES: Oliver and Anderson (1994) surveyed managers and manufacturer's sales representatives employed by independently owned and operated sales agencies serving the electronics industry. Of the 350 randomly selected trade association member firms fitting this designation, 299 expressed interest in participating, and ultimately, **194** usable surveys from management and **347** surveys from manufacturer representatives were returned. The typical respondent was a male (92%), college graduate (64%), approximately 39 years of age, and had an average of 12 years sales experience with 5.5 years in the present job.

RELIABILITY: Oliver and Anderson (1994) reported a coefficient alpha of **.782** for this measure.

VALIDITY: Oliver and Anderson (1994) used the correlation matrix of the independent and classification variables used in the study to provide some evidence of discriminant and convergent validity. Nomological validity was also found to be present.

ADMINISTRATION: Oliver and Anderson (1994) sent managers of the 299 firms indicating interest in the study a packet containing a "manager's survey" and three similar self-administered surveys for salespeople, along with self-addressed, postage-paid reply envelopes. Managers were instructed to distribute one survey each to an "above-average rep," a "mid-range rep," and a "below-average rep." Each representative was promised confidentiality and the chance to win one of five $100 prizes in a random drawing. It appears that only responses obtained from sales representatives were used in computing this measure. Higher scores on the scale reflected a more supportive, harmonious organizational culture.

MAJOR FINDINGS: Oliver and Anderson (1994) examined how perceptions of the presence of a behavior versus outcome sales control system in the respondents' organizations influenced salespeople's performance outcomes and sales strategies, as well as their affective, cognitive, and behavioral states. The use of a behavior control system was significantly related to organizations having more **supportive organizational cultures**.

REFERENCES:

Litwin, G.H. and R.A. Stringer (1968), *Motivation and Organizational Climate.* Cambridge, MA: Harvard University Press.

Oliver, Richard L. and Erin Anderson (1994), "An Empirical Test of the Consequences of Behavior- and Outcome-Based Sales Control Systems," *JM*, 58 (October), 53–67.

Wallach, Ellen J. (1983), "Individuals and Organizations: The Cultural March," *Training and Development Journal*, 37 (February), 29–36.

SCALE ITEMS:
Please circle a score from the scale below which most closely corresponds with how you see your organization.

Does not describe my organization	Describes my organization a little	Describes my organization a fair amount	Describes my organization most of the time
0	1	2	3

1. Collaborative.

2. Relationships-oriented.

3. Encouraging.

4. Sociable.

5. Personal freedom.

6. Equitable.

7. Safe.

8. Trusting.

SCALE NAME: Organizational Memory Dispersion

SCALE DESCRIPTION: Moorman and Miner (1997) used this five-item, seven-point scale to measure the degree of consensus or shared knowledge among new product participants.

SCALE ORIGIN: The scale is original to Moorman and Miner (1997). However, the data and methodology (though not the scales) reported in this study have been previously been reported by Moorman (1995). All measures used by Moorman and Miner (1997) were subjected to a purification process following data collection that assessed the unidimensionality of the measures in a confirmatory analysis model using LISREL VII. Items with very weak loadings and those loading on more than one factor were eliminated.

SAMPLES: Moorman and Miner (1997) chose to sample the vice presidents of marketing for 300 divisions of firms noted in the 1992 *Advertising Age* list of top 200 advertisers; a total of **92** usable questionnaires were received. No systematic differences were observed between early and late respondents.

RELIABILITY: Moorman and Miner (1997) reported a coefficient alpha of **.62** for the scale.

VALIDITY: Moorman and Miner (1997) assessed the unidimensionality of the scale by dividing the measures used in this study into three subsets of theoretically related variables and submitting the measures to confirmatory factor analyses. The three models provided a good fit with the data. Confirmatory factor analysis was also used to assess the discriminant validity of the measure. The organizational memory measures possessed discriminant validity from one another, from measures of both manager and organizational use of information, and from the different forms of organizational culture.

ADMINISTRATION: The scale was included with other measures in a self-administered questionnaire that was delivered by mail. Moorman and Miner's (1997) cover letter explained the survey purpose and, in an effort to increase response rate, offered to share survey results. Nonrespondents were telephoned after three weeks and sent a second questionnaire two weeks after the telephone reminder. All informants were instructed to answer in the context of the most recent product development project for which their division had been responsible. Focal projects were required to have been on the market for a minimum of 12 months. Higher scores on the scale indicated that an organization had a greater degree of consensus or shared knowledge among new product participants.

MAJOR FINDINGS: Moorman and Miner (1997) investigated the impact of organizational memory level and organizational memory dispersion on key new product development processes. **Organizational memory dispersion** positively influenced the short-term financial performance of the new product and new product creativity. However, the relationship between short-term financial performance and **organizational memory dispersion** was weakened with increasing levels of market turbulence. Technological turbulence, in contrast, had a significant negative interaction with **memory dispersion** on new product creativity. Specifically, the relationship was negative under highly turbulent conditions, became positive under moderately turbulent conditions, and became strongly positive when technological turbulence was low.

REFERENCES:

Moorman, Christine (1995), "Organizational Market Information Processes: Cultural Antecedents and New Product Outcomes," *JMR*, 32 (August), 318–35.

———— and Anne S. Miner (1997), "The Impact of Organizational Memory on New Product Performance and Creativity," *JMR*, 34 (February), 91–106.

SCALE ITEMS:

Low   High
 1———————2———————3———————4———————5———————6———————7

Rate the degree of consensus among the people working on the project for the following new product areas:

1. Product design.

2. Brand name.

3. Packaging.

4. Promotional content.

5. Product quality level.

SCALE NAME: Organizational Memory Level

SCALE DESCRIPTION: Moorman and Miner (1997) used this four-item, seven-point Likert-type scale to measure the extent of knowledge, experience, and familiarity that an organization has with a particular product category.

SCALE ORIGIN: The scale is original to Moorman and Miner (1997). However, the data and methodology (though not all of the scales) reported in this study were previously reported by Moorman (1995). All measures used by Moorman and Miner (1997) were subjected to a purification process following the data collection process that assessed the unidimensionality of the measures in a confirmatory analysis model using LISREL VII. Items with very weak loadings and those loading on more than one factor were eliminated.

SAMPLES: Moorman and Miner (1997) chose to sample the vice presidents of marketing for 300 divisions of firms noted in the 1992 *Advertising Age* list of top 200 advertisers; a total of **92** usable questionnaires were received. No systematic differences were observed between early and late respondents.

RELIABILITY: Moorman and Miner (1997) reported a coefficient alpha of **.96** for the scale.

VALIDITY: Moorman and Miner (1997) assessed the unidimensionality of the scale by dividing the measures used in this study into three subsets of theoretically related variables and submitting the measures to confirmatory factor analyses. The three models provided a good fit with the data. Confirmatory factor analysis was also used to assess the discriminant validity of the measure. The organizational memory measures possessed discriminant validity from one another, from measures of both manager and organizational use of information, and from the different forms of organizational culture.

ADMINISTRATION: The scale was included with other measures in a self-administered questionnaire that was delivered by mail. Moorman and Miner's (1997) cover letter explained the survey purpose and, in an effort to increase response rate, offered to share survey results. Nonrespondents were telephoned after three weeks and sent a second questionnaire two weeks after the telephone reminder. All informants were instructed to answer in the context of the most recent product development project for which their division had been responsible. Focal projects were required to have been on the market for a minimum of 12 months. Higher scores on the scale indicated that an organization had greater knowledge, experience, and familiarity with a particular product category.

MAJOR FINDINGS: Moorman and Miner (1997) investigated the impact of organizational memory level and organizational memory dispersion on key new product development processes. **Organizational memory level** positively influenced the short-term financial performance of the new product but failed to significantly reduce new product creativity. The hypothesized interaction effects in which **organizational memory level** was expected to have a role also failed to materialize.

REFERENCES:
Moorman, Christine (1995), "Organizational Market Information Processes: Cultural Antecedents and New Product Outcomes," *JMR*, 32 (August), 318–35.
——— and Anne S. Miner (1997), "The Impact of Organizational Memory on New Product Performance and Creativity," *JMR*, 34 (February), 91–106.

SCALE ITEMS:

Strongly   Strongly
disagree   agree
  1———2———3———4———5———6———7

Prior to the project, compared to firms in our industry, my division had:

1. A great deal of knowledge about this category.

2. A great deal of experience in this category.

3. A great deal of familiarity in this category.

4. Invested a great deal of R&D in this category.

SCALE NAME: Organization's Commitment to Learning

SCALE DESCRIPTION: Sinkula, Baker, and Noordewier (1997) used this four-item, five-point Likert-type scale to assess the degree to which an organization valued learning as instrumental to improvement, maintaining competitive advantage, and guaranteeing organizational survival.

SCALE ORIGIN: Sinkula, Baker, and Noordewier (1997) indicated that the items representing this construct were adapted from Galer and van der Heijden (1992), Garratt (1987), and Tobin (1993).

SAMPLES: The results of preliminary interviews with business practitioners indicated that the most appropriate sample subjects for a study of organizational learning processes were those working at high or upper organizational levels in a variety of industries. With this criterion in mind, Sinkula, Baker, and Noordewier (1997) drew a random sample of key informants from the 1994 membership list of the American Marketing Association but eliminated those whose titles suggested they were not high enough in the organizational hierarchy to provide informed responses. Of the 276 individuals who qualified for the study, **125** returned usable responses.

RELIABILITY: Sinkula, Baker, and Noordewier (1997) reported a coefficient alpha of **.87** for this measure.

VALIDITY: Sinkula, Baker, and Noordewier (1997) stated that a confirmatory factor analysis demonstrated the convergent and discriminatory validity of the measure.

ADMINISTRATION: The measure was included by Sinkula, Baker, and Noordewier (1997) as part of a self-administered questionnaire that was delivered by mail. Nonrespondents received a second mailing. Higher scores on the scale reflected a higher commitment to the learning process on the part of the organization.

MAJOR FINDINGS: Sinkula, Baker, and Noordewier (1997) investigated the relationship among organizational values, market information-processing behaviors, and organizational actions in the context of an organizational learning framework. An **organization's commitment to learning** was one of three first-order factors used to represent the higher construct of learning orientation. Results indicated that a more positive learning orientation was directly responsible for increasing the generation and dissemination of market information. Furthermore, by increasing market information generation and dissemination, a positive learning orientation affected marketing program dynamism, or the degree to which an organization makes changes in its marketing strategy.

REFERENCES:

Galer, Graham and Dees van der Heijden (1992), "The Learning Organization: How Planners Create Organizational Learning," *Marketing Intelligence and Planning*, 10 (6), 5–12.

Garratt, Robert (1987), "Learning is the Core of Organizational Survival: Action Learning Is the Key Integrating Process," *Journal of Management Development*, 6 (2), 38–44.

Sinkula, James M., William E. Baker, and Thomas Noordewier (1997), "A Framework for Market-Based Organizational Learning: Linking Values, Knowledge, and Behavior," *JAMS*, 25 (4), 305–18.

Tobin, Daniel R. (1993), *Re-Educating the Corporation: Foundations for the Learning Organization*. Essex Junction, VT: Oliver Wright.

SCALE ITEMS:

Strongly   Strongly
disagree   agree
  1————2————3————4————5

1. Managers basically agree that our organization's ability to learn is the key to our competitive advantage.

2. The basic values of this organization include learning as key to improvement.

3. The sense around here is that employee learning is an investment, not an expense.

4. Learning in my organization is seen as a key commodity necessary to guarantee organizational survival.

SCALE NAME: Organization's Open-Mindedness

SCALE DESCRIPTION: Sinkula, Baker, and Noordewier (1997) used this three-item, five-point Likert-type scale to assess the degree to which an organization displays an open mind, in that it questions assumptions and perceptions held about customers and markets on a regular basis.

SCALE ORIGIN: Although the scale is original to Sinkula, Baker, and Noordewier (1997), their crafting of scale items was influenced by the writings of Senge (1990, 1992), and Slater and Narver (1994). Items were reworded, added, and dropped on the basis of the recommendations of a panel of academics and business practitioners.

SAMPLES: The results of preliminary interviews with business practitioners indicated that the most appropriate sample subjects for a study of organizational learning processes were those working at high or upper organizational levels in a variety of industries. With this criterion in mind, Sinkula, Baker, and Noordewier (1997) drew a random sample of key informants from the 1994 membership list of the American Marketing Association but eliminated those whose titles suggested they were not high enough in the organizational hierarchy to provide informed responses. Of the 276 individuals who qualified for the study, **125** returned usable responses.

RELIABILITY: Sinkula, Baker, and Noordewier (1997) reported a coefficient alpha of **.80** for this measure.

VALIDITY: Sinkula, Baker, and Noordewier (1997) stated that a confirmatory factor analysis demonstrated the convergent and discriminatory validity of the measure.

ADMINISTRATION: The measure was included by Sinkula, Baker, and Noordewier (1997) as part of a self-administered questionnaire that was delivered by mail. Nonrespondents received a second mailing. Higher scores on the scale reflected higher levels of open-mindedness in the organization.

MAJOR FINDINGS: Sinkula, Baker, and Noordewier (1997) investigated the relationship among organizational values, market information-processing behaviors, and organizational actions in the context of an organizational learning framework. An **organization's open-mindedness** was one of three first-order factors used to represent the higher construct of learning orientation. Results indicated that a more positive learning orientation was directly responsible for increasing the generation and dissemination of market information. Furthermore, by increasing market information generation and dissemination, a positive learning orientation affected marketing program dynamism, or the degree to which an organization makes changes in its marketing strategy.

REFERENCES:
Senge, Peter M. (1990), *The Fifth Discipline: The Art and Practice of the Learning Organization.* New York: Doubleday.
———— (1992), "Mental Models," *Planning Review*, 20 (March-April), 4–10, 44.
Sinkula, James M., William E. Baker, and Thomas Noordewier (1997), "A Framework for Market-Based Organizational Learning: Linking Values, Knowledge, and Behavior," *JAMS*, 25 (4), 305–18.
Slater, Stanley F. and John C. Narver (1994), *Market Oriented Isn't Enough: Build a Learning Organization.* Report No. 94-103, Cambridge, MA: Marketing Science Institute.

SCALE ITEMS:

Strongly   Strongly
disagree   agree
   1————————2————————3————————4————————5

1. We are not afraid to reflect critically on the shared assumptions we have made about our customers.

2. Personnel in this enterprise realize that the very way they perceive the marketplace must be continually questioned.

3. We rarely collectively question our own biases about the way we interpret customer information. **(r)**

SCALE NAME: Organization's Shared Vision/Purpose

SCALE DESCRIPTION: Sinkula, Baker, and Noordewier (1997) used this four-item, five-point Likert-type scale to assess the degree to which a sense of shared vision, goals, and purpose exists within an organization.

SCALE ORIGIN: Sinkula, Baker, and Noordewier (1997) stated that the items representing this construct were based on the writings of Senge (1992) and Tobin (1993).

SAMPLES: The results of preliminary interviews with business practitioners indicated that the most appropriate sample subjects for a study of organizational learning processes were those working at high or upper organizational levels in a variety of industries. With this criterion in mind, Sinkula, Baker, and Noordewier (1997) drew a random sample of key informants from the 1994 membership list of the American Marketing Association but eliminated those whose titles suggested they were not high enough in the organizational hierarchy to provide informed responses. Of the 276 individuals who qualified for the study, **125** returned usable responses.

RELIABILITY: Sinkula, Baker, and Noordewier (1997) reported a coefficient alpha of **.86** for this measure.

VALIDITY: Sinkula, Baker, and Noordewier (1997) stated that a confirmatory factor analysis demonstrated the convergent and discriminatory validity of the measure.

ADMINISTRATION: The measure was included by Sinkula, Baker, and Noordewier (1997) as part of a self-administered questionnaire that was delivered by mail. Nonrespondents received a second mailing. Higher scores on the scale reflected higher levels of shared vision and purpose throughout the organization.

MAJOR FINDINGS: Sinkula, Baker, and Noordewier (1997) investigated the relationship among organizational values, market information-processing behaviors, and organizational actions in the context of an organizational learning framework. An **organization's shared vision and purpose** was one of three first-order factors used to represent the higher construct of learning orientation. Results indicated that a more positive learning orientation was directly responsible for increasing the generation and dissemination of market information. Furthermore, by increasing market information generation and dissemination, a positive learning orientation affected marketing program dynamism, or the degree to which an organization makes changes in its marketing strategy.

REFERENCES:

Senge, Peter M. (1992), "Mental Models," *Planning Review*, 20 (March-April), 4–10, 44.
Sinkula, James M., William E. Baker, and Thomas Noordewier (1997), "A Framework for Market-Based Organizational Learning: Linking Values, Knowledge, and Behavior," *JAMS*, 25 (4), 305–18.
Tobin, Daniel R. (1993), *Re-Educating the Corporation: Foundations for the Learning Organization.* Essex Junction, VT: Oliver Wright.

SCALE ITEMS:

Strongly disagree — 1 — 2 — 3 — 4 — 5 — Strongly agree

1. There is a commonality of purpose in my organization.

2. There is a total agreement on our organizational vision across all levels, functions, and divisions.

3. All employees are committed to the goals of this organization.

4. Employees view themselves as partners in charting the direction of the organization.

SCALE NAME: Orientation (Technology)

SCALE DESCRIPTION: Gatignon and Xuereb (1997) used this twelve-item, six-point Likert-type scale to measure the extent to which the strategic orientation of a firm stresses the use, development, and rapid integration of sophisticated technologies in the new product development process. The authors referred to this scale as *technology orientation*.

SCALE ORIGIN: Gatignon and Xuereb (1997) stated that the multiple-item scales used in their study were developed on the basis of items previously proposed and used in survey research. Items were adapted from Van de Ven (1986), Kanter (1988), Burgelman and Sayles (1986), and Garud and Van de Ven (1989). The measure was pretested with others on the questionnaire, and some phrasing was revised. A pilot test was performed on the revised questionnaire for the purpose of assessing scale validity. The resulting measures were then administered in the final questionnaire to a large sample. When submitted to a factor analysis, the items that composed the measure loaded on two highly correlated factors (correlation = .62) according to whether the items were competitively framed or not. All items were retained in a single scale because the split in loadings was attributed to the wording of items rather than conceptual differences. It is not clear whether this factor analysis took place during the pilot study or following the final administration.

SAMPLES: Gatignon and Xuereb (1997) mailed the final questionnaire to a list of 3000 marketing executives representing a broad cross-section of U.S. industries randomly selected from a commercially available list, and 2802 were successfully delivered. Of this number, **393** usable responses were obtained for a 14% response rate. The products represented by the marketing executives surveyed included consumer durable and packaged goods, consumer services, industrial technology, and computer firms.

RELIABILITY: Gatignon and Xuereb (1997) reported a coefficient alpha of **.89** for this measure.

VALIDITY: Gatignon and Xuereb (1997) reported conducting a pilot study for the purpose of assessing scale validity; no other details were provided.

ADMINISTRATION: The scale was part of a self-administered mail survey. Nonrespondents were sent a reminder letter with an offer of a $500 lottery award two weeks after the initial mailing. Gatignon and Xuereb (1997) instructed respondents to answer the questionnaire in the context of the last new product introduced in the market by a strategic business unit. Higher scores on the scale indicated a strong technological orientation in the firm, as evidenced by the use, development, and rapid integration of sophisticated technologies in the new product development process

MAJOR FINDINGS: Gatignon and Xuereb (1997) examined the appropriateness of a customer, competitive, and technological orientation in the context of new product development. In uncertain markets, a technological orientation was found to improve the performance of the new product. Greater levels of product radicalness, product relative advantage, and product costs relative to the competition were associated with firms characterized by **technological strategic orientations**, as were lower levels of similarity between the product and its competition.

REFERENCES:

Burgelman, Robert A. and Leonard R. Sayles (1986), *Inside Corporate Innovation: Strategy, Structure and Managerial Skills.* New York: The Free Press.

Garud, Raghu and Andrew H. Van de Ven (1989), "Technological Innovation and Industry Emergence: The Case of Cochlear implants," in *Research on Management of Innovation,* A.H. Van de Ven, H.L. Angle, and M.S. Poole, eds. New York: Harper and Row, 489–532.

Gatignon, Hubert and Jean-Marc Xuereb (1997), "Strategic Orientation of the Firm and New Product Performance," *JMR,* 34 (February), 77–90.

Kanter, Rosabeth M. (1988), "When a Thousand Flowers Bloom: Structural, Collective, and Social Conditions for Innovation in Organization," *in Research in Organizational Behavior*, Vol. 10, B.M. Staw and L.L. Cummings, eds. Greenwich, CT: JAI Press, 169–211.

Van de Ven, Andrew H. (1986), "Central Problems in the Management of Innovation," *Management Science*, 32 (5), 590–608.

SCALE ITEMS:

Directions: We would like to know about the main objectives and the philosophy of the Strategic Business Unit (SBU) which was in charge of the development of this new product.

Rate the extent to which the following activities or objectives are carried out by the SBU which is in charge of this new product. (Circle one number of each of the following sentences).

```
Strongly                                      Strongly
disagree                                       agree
    1———————2———————3———————4———————5———————6
```

1. Our SBU uses sophisticated technologies in its new product development.

2. Our new products are always at the state of the art of the technology.

3. Our SBU is very proactive in the development of new technologies.

4. Our SBU has the will and the capacity to build and to market a technological breakthrough.

5. Our SBU has built a large and strong network of relationships with suppliers of technological equipment.

6. Our SBU has an aggressive technological patent strategy.

7. Our SBU has better industrial methods than the competition.

8. We have a better technological knowledge than our competitors.

9. Relative to our competitors, our new products are more ambitious.

10. Relative to our competitors, our R&D programs are more ambitious.

11. Our SBU is very proactive in the construction of new technical solutions to answer users' needs.

12. Our firm is always the first one to use a new technology for its new product development.

SCALE NAME: Output Control (Information)

SCALE DESCRIPTION: Challagalla and Shervani (1996) used this four-item, five-point Likert-type summated ratings scale to measure employee perceptions of the degree to which supervisors set market share and sales volume goals, monitored and evaluated performance, and provided feedback related to sales and market share goal achievement. This measure focuses on outcomes of the selling process (market share, sales volume) rather than on the selling activities themselves (call rate, number of demos, reports turned in, customers contacted) or a person's selling skills.

SCALE ORIGIN: Challagalla and Shervani (1996) indicated that some of the items used in this measure were adapted from Jaworski and MacInnis's (1989) study. In modifying the measure, the authors undertook extensive pretesting and purification procedures in four sequential stages involving both academic experts and industrial salespeople.

SAMPLES: Challagalla and Shervani (1996) surveyed 302 field salespeople employed in the industrial products divisions of two *Fortune* 500 companies. Usable responses were received from **270** salespeople, the majority of whom were men and college educated.

RELIABILITY: Challagalla and Shervani (1996) reported a coefficient alpha of **.87** for the scale.

VALIDITY: The nine dimensions of control measured in the study were evaluated by Challagalla and Shervani (1996) using confirmatory factor analysis. This scale demonstrated acceptable levels of convergent and discriminant validity and was found to be unidimensional.

ADMINISTRATION: Challagalla and Shervani (1996) indicated that the scale was self-administered, along with many other measures, in a questionnaire delivered directly to the homes of salespeople. Prior to administration, each salesperson received a note from a senior sales executive in his or her organization alerting him or her to the study. Business reply envelopes, cover letters promising confidentiality, and two follow-up attempts were used to increase response rate. Higher scores on the scale indicated that sales managers were perceived as being highly likely to set market share and sales volume goals, monitor and evaluate salesperson performance, and provide feedback related to goal achievement to salespeople.

MAJOR FINDINGS: Challagalla and Shervani (1996) extended existing conceptual work related to marketing control systems by (1) investigating the effect of information and reinforcement on salesperson job outcomes, (2) separating the global behavior control construct into activity control and capability control, and (3) examining the casual mechanisms through which controls operate. **Output information** was negatively related to supervisory role ambiguity, which indicated that supervisors who provide goal information and feedback were more likely to convey their expectations effectively to salespeople. Contrary to expectations, a supervisor's sharing of **output information** had no direct influence on salesperson performance and was not shown to reduce customer role ambiguity. However, a supervisor's provision of **output information** to the salesperson was positively related to that salesperson's satisfaction with the supervisor.

REFERENCES:
Challagalla, Goutam N. and Tasadduq A. Shervani (1996), "Dimensions and Types of Supervisory Control: Effects on Salesperson Performance and Satisfaction," *JM*, 60 (January), 89–105.
Jaworski, Bernard J. and Deborah J. MacInnis (1989), "Marketing Jobs and Management Controls: Toward a Framework," *JMR*, 26 (November), 406–19.

SCALE ITEMS:

Instructions to respondents: In answering the following questions, please focus ONLY on *sales volume or market share* targets.

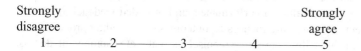

Strongly disagree 1—————2—————3—————4—————5 Strongly agree

1. My manager tells me about the level of achievement expected on sales volume or market share targets.

2. I receive feedback on whether I am meeting expectations on sales volume or market share targets.

3. My manager monitors my progress on achieving sales volume or market share targets.

4. My manager ensures I am aware of the extent to which I attain sales volume or market share goals.

SCALE NAME: Output Control (Punishments)

SCALE DESCRIPTION: Challagalla and Shervani (1996) used this four-item, five-point Likert-type summated ratings scale to measure employee perceptions of the degree to which supervisors punished salespeople who failed to achieve output goals such as market share and sales volume. This measure does not assess perceptions of punishment due to inferior selling skills or inability to achieve activity-related goals (call rate, number of demos, customer contacts, etc.).

SCALE ORIGIN: Challagalla and Shervani (1996) indicated that some of the items used in this measure were adapted from Podsakoff and colleagues' (1984) study. In modifying the measure, Challagalla and Shervani (1996) undertook extensive pretesting and purification procedures in four sequential stages involving both academic experts and industrial salespeople.

SAMPLES: Challagalla and Shervani (1996) surveyed 302 field salespeople employed in the industrial products divisions of two *Fortune* 500 companies. Usable responses were received from **270** salespeople, the majority of whom were men and college educated.

RELIABILITY: Challagalla and Shervani (1996) reported a coefficient alpha of **.72** for the scale.

VALIDITY: The nine dimensions of control measured in the study were evaluated by Challagalla and Shervani (1996) using confirmatory factor analysis. This scale demonstrated acceptable levels of convergent and discriminant validity and was found to be unidimensional.

ADMINISTRATION: Challagalla and Shervani (1996) indicated that the scale was self-administered, along with many other measures, in a questionnaire delivered directly to the homes of salespeople. Prior to administration, each salesperson received a note from a senior sales executive in his or her organization alerting him or her to the study. Business reply envelopes, cover letters promising confidentiality, and two follow-up attempts were used to increase response rate. Higher scores on the scale indicated that sales managers were perceived as highly likely to punish salespeople who failed to meet their assigned market share or sales volume goals.

MAJOR FINDINGS: Challagalla and Shervani (1996) extended existing conceptual work related to marketing control systems by (1) investigating the effect of information and reinforcement on salesperson job outcomes, (2) separating the global behavior control construct into activity control and capability control, and (3) examining the casual mechanisms through which controls operate. Contrary to expectations, no relationship was found between **output punishments** and performance, customer role ambiguity, supervisory role ambiguity, or satisfaction with a supervisor.

REFERENCES:

Challagalla, Goutam N. and Tasadduq A. Shervani (1996), "Dimensions and Types of Supervisory Control: Effects on Salesperson Performance and Satisfaction," *JM*, 60 (January), 89-105.

Podsakoff, Philip M., William D. Todor, Richard A. Grover, and Vandra L. Huber (1984), "Situational Moderators of Leader Reward and Punishment Behaviors: Fact or Fiction?" *Organizational Behavior and Human Performance,* 34 (1), 21-63.

#735 *Output Control (Punishments)*

SCALE ITEMS:

Instructions to respondents: In answering the following questions, please focus ONLY on *sales activities* (e.g., call rate, number of demos, customers to be contacted, reports to turn in, etc.)

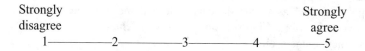

1. I would receive an informal warning if sales or volume market share targets are not achieved.

2. I would receive a formal warning if sales volume or market share targets are not achieved.

3. I would be put on probation if sales volume or market share targets are not achieved with some consistency.

4. My pay increases would suffer if sales volume or market share targets are not met.

SCALE NAME: Output Control (Rewards)

SCALE DESCRIPTION: Challagalla and Shervani (1996) used this four-item, five-point Likert-type summated ratings scale to measure employee perceptions of the degree to which supervisors rewarded salespeople for achieving output goals such as market share and sales volume. This measure does not assess perceptions of rewards given for superior selling skills or the achievement of activity-related goals (call rate, number of demos, customer contacts, etc.).

SCALE ORIGIN: Challagalla and Shervani (1996) indicated that some of the items used in this measure were adapted from Podsakoff and colleagues (1984) study. In modifying the measure, Challagalla and Shervani (1996) undertook extensive pretesting and purification procedures in four sequential stages involving both academic experts and industrial salespeople.

SAMPLES: Challagalla and Shervani (1996) surveyed 302 field salespeople employed in the industrial products divisions of two *Fortune* 500 companies. Usable responses were received from **270** salespeople, the majority of whom were men and college educated.

RELIABILITY: Challagalla and Shervani (1996) reported a coefficient alpha of **.77** for the scale.

VALIDITY: The nine dimensions of control measured in the study were evaluated by Challagalla and Shervani (1996) using confirmatory factor analysis. This scale demonstrated acceptable levels of convergent and discriminant validity and was found to be unidimensional.

ADMINISTRATION: Challagalla and Shervani (1996) indicated that the scale was self-administered, along with many other measures, in a questionnaire delivered directly to the homes of salespeople. Prior to administration, each salesperson received a note from a senior sales executive in his or her organization alerting him or her to the study. Business reply envelopes, cover letters promising confidentiality, and two follow-up attempts were used to increase response rate. Higher scores on the scale indicated that sales managers were perceived as highly likely to reward salespeople who met their assigned market share or sales volume goals.

MAJOR FINDINGS: Challagalla and Shervani (1996) extended existing conceptual work related to marketing control systems by (1) investigating the effect of information and reinforcement on salesperson job outcomes, (2) separating the global behavior control construct into activity control and capability control, and (3) examining the casual mechanisms through which controls operate. Contrary to expectations, **output rewards** were unrelated to salesperson performance and customer role ambiguity and resulted in lower rather than higher levels of satisfaction with the supervisor. Surprisingly, **output rewards** also were negatively related to performance.

REFERENCES:

Challagalla, Goutam N. and Tasadduq A. Shervani (1996), "Dimensions and Types of Supervisory Control: Effects on Salesperson Performance and Satisfaction," *JM,* 60 (January), 89–105.

Podsakoff, Philip M., William D. Todor, Richard A. Grover, and Vandra L. Huber (1984), "Situational Moderators of Leader Reward and Punishment Behaviors: Fact or Fiction?" *Organizational Behavior and Human Performance,* 34 (1), 21–63.

#736 *Output Control (Rewards)*

SCALE ITEMS:

Instructions to respondents: In answering the following questions, please focus ONLY on *sales activities* (e.g., call rate, number of demos, customers to be contacted, reports to turn in, etc.)

Strongly disagree				Strongly agree

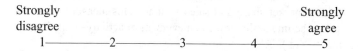

1————2————3————4————5

1. I would get bonuses if I exceed my sales or volume market share targets.

2. Promotion opportunities depend on how well I perform on sales volume or market share targets.

3. I would be recognized by my company if I perform well on sales volume and market share targets.

4. There are pay increases if I do well on sales volume or market share targets.

SCALE NAME: Output Controls

SCALE DESCRIPTION: Bello and Gilliland (1997) used this three-item, seven-point scale to measure the extent to which a manufacturer attempts to monitor the distributor outcomes related to new product market penetration, sales volume, and increasing the customer base.

SCALE ORIGIN: Bello and Gilliland (1997) stated that the scale items were adapted from the work of Ouchi and Maguire (1975) and Jaworski and MacInnis (1989).

SAMPLES: Bello and Gilliland's (1997) systematic random sample of 245 national manufacturers verified as exporting through foreign distributors was drawn from the 1994 edition of the *Journal of Commerce United States Importer & Exporter Directory*. **One hundred sixty** usable responses were obtained from export managers employed by firms exporting a variety of industrial and consumer products to a total of 39 different countries.

RELIABILITY: A confirmatory factor analysis composite reliability of **.76** was reported by Bello and Gilliland (1997).

VALIDITY: Confirmatory factor analysis was used by Bello and Gilliland (1997) to provide evidence of discriminant and convergent validity, as well as to assess the unidimensionality of the measure. Convergent validity was deemed to be present because items loaded significantly on their posited indicators and because of the low to moderate correlations between the scale and other measures. Discriminant validity was also deemed to be present because the correlation estimate between two indicators never included 1.0 (+/– two standard errors). The authors used personal interviews with export executives as part of the pretest process to verify the face validity of the measure.

ADMINISTRATION: Bello and Gilliland (1997) indicated that this scale was self-administered as part of a longer survey instrument mailed to respondents. The export manager with primary responsibility for the firm's relationship with the foreign distributor received a survey. Nonrespondents were telephoned three weeks later, and a second questionnaire followed. Instructions specified that questions were to be answered in the context of the focal distributor. The authors defined the focal distributor as the firm's fourth-largest foreign distributor in terms of unit sales volume to avoid a positive evaluation bias. Higher scores on the scale indicated stronger monitoring efforts of distributor results by the manufacturer.

MAJOR FINDINGS: Bello and Gilliland (1997) examined the effect of output controls, process controls, and flexibility on channel performance. The use of **output controls** was positively related to distributor performance, which indicates that efforts by manufacturers to monitor distributor's sales volume and other outcomes resulted in higher performance on the part of that distributor. Higher levels of technical product complexity were found to result in greater **output controls**, whereas cultural problems marked by stronger differences in the language, culture, and values of the foreign market reduced the use of **output controls**, perhaps because such conditions made it difficult for the manufacturer to obtain and process the performance documentation necessary to monitor distributor outcomes.

REFERENCES:

Bello, Daniel C. and David I. Gilliland (1997), "The Effect of Output Controls, Process Controls, and Flexibility on Export Channel Performance," *JM*, 61 (January), 22–38.

Jaworski, Bernard J. and Deborah J. MacInnis (1989), "Marketing Jobs and Management Controls: Toward A Framework," *JMR*, 26 (November), 406–19.

#737 *Output Controls*

Ouchi, William G. and Mary Ann Maguire (1975), "Organizational Control: Two Functions," *Administrative Science Quarterly*, 20 (December), 559–69.

SCALE ITEMS:

Do not   Monitor a
monitor   great deal
1————2————3————4————5————6————7

Our efforts to monitor the distributor's results on each factor can be described as...

1. Market penetration of new products.

2. Increasing the customer base in their market.

3. Sales volume of our products.

SCALE NAME: Participation in Decision Making (Supplier Relationship)

SCALE DESCRIPTION: Dahlstrom, McNeilly, and Speh (1996) describe this three-item, five-point Likert-type scale as measuring the extent to which a supplier is involved with the user in warehousing-related decision making. Dahlstrom, McNeilly, and Speh (1996) refer to this scale as *participation* in their article.

SCALE ORIGIN: Dahlstrom, McNeilly, and Speh (1996) reported that the scale was adapted from Spekman and Stern (1979) and Dwyer and Welsh (1985). The questionnaire containing the scale was pretested by six members of the Warehouse Education and Research Council, who evaluated it for content, readability, and relevance to the industry.

SAMPLES: Using a sampling frame generated from the membership of the Warehouse Education and Research Council, Dahlstrom, McNeilly, and Speh (1996) surveyed 1000 manufacturer, retailer, and wholesaler members. No mention of the specific sampling technique used to generate the frame was provided. Firms that exclusively used in-house warehousing services were not part of the population of interest and were asked to return the survey without answering. Including unanswered surveys, 383 questionnaires were returned for a 38.3% response rate. Of these, **189** surveys contained complete data from firms using interfirm warehousing services.

RELIABILITY: Dahlstrom, McNeilly, and Speh (1996) reported a coefficient alpha of **.74** for this measure.

VALIDITY: Item-to-total correlations estimated by an exploratory factor analysis were used in the first stage of measure purification. Dahlstrom, McNeilly, and Speh (1996) submitted the remaining items to a confirmatory factor analysis. Two items were eliminated, though the resulting root mean residual of the trimmed confirmatory factor analysis model was not significant (.06). Discriminant validity was also assessed and found to be acceptable.

ADMINISTRATION: Dahlstrom, McNeilly, and Speh (1996) stated that the scale was part of a self-administered questionnaire that was returned by mail. Sampled individuals were contacted by telephone prior to survey delivery, and a postage-paid, return addressed reply envelope accompanied the questionnaire. A follow-up mailing with a second survey was sent two weeks after the first. Individuals using in-house warehousing services were asked not to complete the survey, but eligible respondents were instructed to answer in the context of the third-party warehouse service provider with whom they spent the greatest portion of their warehousing budget. Higher scores on the participation scale indicated that suppliers were more closely involved with users in warehousing-related decision making.

MAJOR FINDINGS: Dahlstrom, McNeilly, and Speh (1996) investigated various antecedents to alternative forms of governance in the logistical supply market. A second topic of investigation addressed how formal controls and relational norms were employed by alternative governance forms to yield performance. Results of path analysis indicated that **participation in decision making** increased performance, flexibility, information exchange, and solidarity in both the bilateral alliance and the long-term unilateral agreement governance modes, but only solidarity and information exchange were enhanced in short-term unilateral agreements.

REFERENCES:
Dahlstrom, Robert, Kevin M. McNeilly, and Thomas W. Speh (1996), "Buyer–Seller Relationships in the Procurement of Logistical Services," *JAMS*, 24 (2), 110–24.

#738 *Participation in Decision Making (Supplier Relationship)*

Dwyer, F. Robert and M. Ann Welsh (1985), "Environmental Relationships on the Internal Political Economy of Marketing Channels," *JMR*, 22 (November), 397–414.

Spekman, Robert E. and Louis W. Stern (1979), "Environmental Uncertainty and Buying Group Structure: An Empirical Investigation," *JM*, 43 (Spring), 56–64.

SCALE ITEMS:

Please indicate your level of agreement with the following:

The vendor:

1. Plays an active part in decisions made concerning warehousing.

2. Is consulted concerning inventory storage decisions.

3. Is involved in warehousing decisions concerning servicing customers.

SCALE NAME: Participation (Leadership Style)

SCALE DESCRIPTION: Netemeyer and colleagues (1997) used this five-item, seven-point scale to measure the degree to which a salesperson perceives that his or her immediate supervisor gives serious consideration to the salesperson's opinions before making decisions.

SCALE ORIGIN: Netemeyer and colleagues (1997) indicated that the items measuring leadership support were adapted from the measures of leadership support and consideration developed by House and Dessler (1974).

SAMPLES: In their first study, Netemeyer and colleagues (1997) used a convenience sample of 115 salespeople employed by a cellular telephone company in the southeastern United States, and **91** usable responses were obtained for a 79% response rate. The median age of respondents was 29 years, and their average amount of time with the organization was 1.89 years. The majority of respondents were women (56%) and college educated (57%). In the second study, the authors sampled 700 real estate salespeople living in a large southeastern city, and **182** usable surveys were received for an effective response rate of 26%. The median age of respondents in the second study was 48 years, and their average amount of time with the organization was 8.41 years. The majority were women (78%) and college educated (60.5%).

RELIABILITY: Netemeyer and colleagues (1997) reported coefficient alphas of **.87** for Study 1 and **.89** for Study 2.

VALIDITY: Netemeyer and colleagues (1997) examined the discriminant and construct validity of the scale using confirmatory factor analysis for both Study 1 and Study 2 data. The average variance extracted by the measure in each study was well below the .50 cut-off level suggested by Fornell and Larcker (1981), which provided evidence of construct validity. The square of parameter estimates between pairs of constructs was less than the average variance extracted estimates for the paired constructs across all possible construct pairings in both studies, which provided evidence of the discriminant validity of the measure.

ADMINISTRATION: Netemeyer and colleagues (1997) indicated that the scale was included as part of a self-administered mail survey in both studies. Study 2 participants were assured of the confidentiality and anonymity of their responses. Higher scores on the scale indicated that salespeople perceived their immediate supervisor as giving serious consideration to their opinions when making decisions.

MAJOR FINDINGS: Netemeyer and colleagues (1997) proposed and tested a model of potential predictors of organizational citizenship behavior and job satisfaction using data from two separate studies conducted in a sales setting. Mixed results were found with respect to the role played by **leadership support** and fairness in reward allocation in predicting job satisfaction. In one study, **leadership support** was found to be a significant predictor while fairness in reward allocation was not; in the other study, the reverse was true.

REFERENCES:
Fornell, Claes and David F. Larcker (1981), "Evaluating Structural Equation Models with Unobservable Variables and Measurement Error," *JMR*, 28 (February), 39–50.
House, Robert J. and Gary Dessler (1974), "The Path-Goal Theory of Leadership: Some PostHoc and A Priori Tests," in *Contingency Approaches to Leadership*, J. Hunt and L. Arson, eds. Carbondale, IL: Southern Illinois University Press.

#739 *Participation (Leadership Style)*

Netemeyer, Richard G., James S. Boles, Daryl O. McKee, and Robert McMurrian (1997), "An Investigation into the Antecedents of Organizational Citizenship Behaviors in a Personal Selling Context," *JM,* 61 (July), 85–98.

SCALE ITEMS:

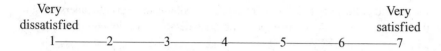

Very
dissatisfied

Very
satisfied

1———2———3———4———5———6———7

1. My supervisor asks salespeople for their suggestions on what assignments should be made.

2. My supervisor gives advance notice of changes.

3. My supervisor treats all the salespeople s/he supervises as his/her equal.

4. My supervisor is friendly and approachable.

5. My supervisor asks salespeople for their suggestions concerning how to carry out assignments.

SCALE NAME: Participative Decision Making

SCALE DESCRIPTION: Oliver and Anderson (1994) used this four-item, seven-point Likert-type scale to measure the degree to which management considers input from sales representatives when making decisions that affect them.

SCALE ORIGIN: The scale is original to Oliver and Anderson (1994), who pretested the measure in a questionnaire administered to a convenience sample of sales representatives attending trade association functions. The measure was revised on the basis of the pretest.

SAMPLES: Oliver and Anderson (1994) surveyed managers and manufacturer's sales representatives employed by independently owned and operated sales agencies serving the electronics industry. Of the 350 randomly selected trade association member firms fitting this designation, 299 expressed interest in participating, and ultimately, **194** usable surveys from management and **347** surveys from manufacturer representatives were returned. The typical respondent was a male (92%), college graduate (64%), approximately 39 years of age, and had an average of 12 years sales experience with 5.5 years in the present job.

RELIABILITY: Oliver and Anderson (1994) reported a coefficient alpha of **.754** for this measure.

VALIDITY: Oliver and Anderson (1994) used the correlation matrix of the independent and classification variables used in the study to provide some evidence of discriminant and convergent validity. Nomological validity was also found to be present.

ADMINISTRATION: Oliver and Anderson (1994) sent managers of the 299 firms indicating interest in the study a packet containing a "manager's survey" and three similar self-administered surveys for salespeople, along with self-addressed, postage-paid reply envelopes. Managers were instructed to distribute one survey each to an "above-average rep," a "mid-range rep," and a "below-average rep." Each representative was promised confidentiality and the chance to win one of five $100 prizes in a random drawing. It appears that only responses obtained from sales representatives were used in computing this measure. Higher scores on the scale indicated that managers considered sales representatives' input when making decisions that affected them.

MAJOR FINDINGS: Oliver and Anderson (1994) examined how perceptions of the presence of a behavior versus outcome sales control system in the respondents' organizations influenced salespeople's performance outcomes and sales strategies, as well as their affective, cognitive, and behavioral states. Higher levels of **participative decision making** were found to be significantly related to the use of a behavior control system.

REFERENCES:
Oliver, Richard L. and Erin Anderson (1994), "An Empirical Test of the Consequences of Behavior- and Outcome-Based Sales Control Systems," *JM*, 58 (October), 53–67.

SCALE ITEMS:

Strongly
disagree

1———2———3———4———5———6———7

Strongly
agree

1. Decisions are made at the top around here. **(r)**

2. Salespeople and management tend to hammer out issues together in this organization.

3. My boss actively seeks my ideas all the time.

4. Management makes decisions without much regard for what salespeople think. **(r)**

SCALE NAME: Patent Protection

SCALE DESCRIPTION: Robertson, Eliashberg, and Rymon (1995) used this three-item, six-point Likert-type scale to assess the degree to which a product category is characterized by patent protection.

SCALE ORIGIN: Robertson, Eliashberg, and Rymon (1995) developed the scale specifically for this study. The measure and the questionnaire in which it was administered were initially conceptualized, tested, and purified on the basis of two pilot studies with executives participating in a management development program and a mail survey pretest. A principal components factor analysis with Varimax rotation was performed on data collected in the final study and used to determine the composition of the final measure.

SAMPLES: A total of 1554 directors of marketing in the United States (1,034) and United Kingdom (520), representing a broad range of consumer and industrial product industries, were sampled for this study. Using a commercially purchased list as their sampling frame, Robertson, Eliashberg, and Rymon (1995) excluded marketing managers of wholesale, retail, and small firms prior to mailing their surveys. A total of **346** usable surveys were returned, of which 241, and 105 were from the United States and United Kingdom, respectively. No evidence of response basis was found, and Chow tests of the U.S. and U.K. data supported the pooling together of data from each country.

RELIABILITY: Robertson, Eliashberg, and Rymon (1995) reported a coefficient alpha of **.85** for this measure.

VALIDITY: No specific examination of scale validity was reported by Robertson, Eliashberg, and Rymon (1995).

ADMINISTRATION: The scale was included with other measures in a self-administered survey delivered by mail. Robertson, Eliashberg, and Rymon (1995) prenotified respondents and offered a copy of the survey's tabulated results as an incentive to participate. Respondents were instructed to answer the questionnaire in the context of the last new product announcement (NPA) signal received relative to a new product that was significantly different from existing products. Higher scores on the scale indicated a high degree of patent protection in the product category targeted by the NPA.

MAJOR FINDINGS: Robertson, Eliashberg, and Rymon (1995) examined the relationship between NPA signals—announcements in advance of market introduction—and factors affecting the likelihood of competitive reactions to NPA signals. Firms were found to be most likely to react to an NPA signal in some fashion when the product category was characterized by a high degree of **patent protection**. Furthermore, a firm's aggressiveness in responding to an NPA signal was also positively associated with high degrees of **patent protection**.

REFERENCES:

Robertson, Thomas S., Jehoshua Eliashberg, and Talia Rymon (1995), "New Product Announcement Signals and Incumbent Reactions," *JM*, 59 (July), 1–15.

SCALE ITEMS:*

Strongly
disagree

Strongly
agree

1———2———3———4———5———6

Please tell us about this product category by indicating how much you agree or disagree with the following statements.

1. There is opportunity for patent advantage in this product category.

2. Patents are irrelevant in the product category. **(r)** **

3. Very few patents exist in this product category.

*Although a six-point scale format was designated by Robertson, Eliashberg and Rymon (1995), the scale anchors were not explicitly listed. However, it is probable that the traditional Likert "strongly disagree" to "strongly agree" format was used.

**The appendix listing the measures used by Robertson, Eliashberg and Rymon (1995) does not indicate that this item was reversed. However, this is very likely to be necessary and should be considered when calculating scale scores.

SCALE NAME: Pay as a Control Mechanism

SCALE DESCRIPTION: Oliver and Anderson (1994) used this four-item, seven-point Likert-type scale to measure the degree to which sales representatives perceive that pay is used as the sole mechanism for reward and punishment.

SCALE ORIGIN: The scale is original to Oliver and Anderson (1994), who pretested the measure in a questionnaire administered to a convenience sample of sales representatives attending trade association functions. The measure was revised on the basis of the pretest.

SAMPLES: Oliver and Anderson (1994) surveyed managers and manufacturer's sales representatives employed by independently owned and operated sales agencies serving the electronics industry. Of the 350 randomly selected trade association member firms fitting this designation, 299 expressed interest in participating, and ultimately, **194** usable surveys from management and **347** surveys from manufacturer representatives were returned. The typical respondent was a male (92%), college graduate (64%), approximately 39 years of age, and had an average of 12 years sales experience with 5.5 years in the present job.

RELIABILITY: Oliver and Anderson (1994) reported a coefficient alpha of **.645** for this measure.

VALIDITY: Oliver and Anderson (1994) used the correlation matrix of the independent and classification variables used in the study to provide some evidence of discriminant and convergent validity. Nomological validity was also found to be present.

ADMINISTRATION: Oliver and Anderson (1994) sent managers of the 299 firms indicating interest in the study a packet containing a "manager's survey" and three similar self-administered surveys for salespeople, along with self-addressed, postage-paid reply envelopes. Managers were instructed to distribute one survey each to an "above-average rep," a "mid-range rep," and a "below-average rep." Each representative was promised confidentiality and the chance to win one of five $100 prizes in a random drawing. It appears that only responses obtained from sales representatives were used in computing this measure. Higher scores on the scale indicated that sales representatives perceived that management used pay for reward and punishment purposes in an effort to control their behavior.

MAJOR FINDINGS: Oliver and Anderson (1994) examined how perceptions of the presence of a behavior versus outcome sales control system in the respondents' organizations influenced salespeople's performance outcomes and sales strategies, as well as their affective, cognitive, and behavioral states. The use of a behavior control system was significantly but inversely related to sales representatives' perceptions that managers **used pay as a control mechanism** solely for reward and punishment purposes.

REFERENCES:

Oliver, Richard L. and Erin Anderson (1994), "An Empirical Test of the Consequences of Behavior- and Outcome-Based Sales Control Systems," *JM*, 58 (October), 53–67.

SCALE ITEMS:

Strongly   Strongly
disagree   agree
  1———————2———————3———————4———————5———————6———————7

1. The main reason for pay in this organization is to get me to do what supervisors and managers want me to do.

2. I feel that the company uses pay to try and control everything I do.

3. The compensation system really influences what I do on my job.

4. The main reason for pay in this organization is to give me concrete feedback on what I do here.

SCALE NAME: Performance (Behavioral)

SCALE DESCRIPTION: Kohli and Jaworski (1994) used this five-item, five-point scale to measure salespersons' self-reports of how well they performed typical sales-related job tasks such as delivering customer presentations and negotiating prices.

SCALE ORIGIN: To measure salespeople's self-reports of the behavioral dimension of their performance, Kohli and Jaworski (1994) selected and adapted five of the nine performance items originally developed by Behrman and Perreault (1982).

SAMPLES: Because the nature of the study required that salesperson behavior and output be visible to coworkers, and thus allow for coworker feedback, Kohli and Jaworski (1994) chose to sample retail auto salespeople. The preliminary set of scale items was first administered to 11 auto salespeople from five dealerships. Their comments enabled scale item and questionnaire revision. The final questionnaire was mailed to 303 salespeople belonging to the nationwide dealership network of a European car manufacturer. A reminder, followed by a second questionnaire mailing, resulted in usable responses being obtained from **150** salespeople.

RELIABILITY: Kohli and Jaworski (1994) reported a coefficient alpha of **.76** for this measure.

VALIDITY: Kohli and Jaworski (1994) used confirmatory factory analysis to test the unidimensionality of the measure in conjunction with the role clarity and performance constructs. Results suggested that the measure was unidimensional. No other specific assessments of validity were discussed by the authors.

ADMINISTRATION: Kohli and Jaworski (1994) stated that the scale was part of a self-administered questionnaire that was delivered by mail. A personally addressed cover letter promising complete confidentiality accompanied the survey, as did a self-addressed reply envelope and ballpoint pen incentive. A reminder was sent one week after the initial mailing. Nonrespondents received a second reminder and questionnaire three weeks after the initial mailing. Lower scores on the behaviorally oriented performance scale indicated that salespeople reported higher assessments of their time management, paperwork accuracy, negotiation, presentation, and selling performance.

MAJOR FINDINGS: Kohli and Jaworski (1994) investigated how positive output, negative output, positive behavioral, and negative behavioral forms of coworker feedback affected salespeople's output and behavioral role clarity, satisfaction with coworkers, and output and behavioral performance. Behavioral role clarity and both positive and negative behavioral feedback significantly influenced salespeople's assessments of their **behavioral-oriented performance.** Specifically, whereas the positive form of feedback seemed to encourage higher levels of performance, negative feedback seemed to result in a demoralizing effect that depressed salespeople's desire to perform.

REFERENCES:

Behrman, Douglas N. and William D. Perreault Jr. (1982), "Measuring the Performance of Industrial Salespersons," *Journal of Business Research*, 10 (3), 355–70.

Kohli, Ajay K. and Bernard J. Jaworski (1994), "The Influence of Coworker Feedback on Salespeople," *JM*, 58 (October), 82–94.

SCALE ITEMS:

Excellent   Poor
1———————2———————3———————4———————5

1. Accuracy of paperwork.

2. Time management.

3. Customer presentations.

4. Price negotiations.

5. Selling tactics.

SCALE NAME: Performance (Company)

SCALE DESCRIPTION: Three seven-point items that measure the level of success achieved by retailers with respect to marketing, training, and management activities. Dahlstrom and Nygaard (1995) used the scale with oil and gas retailers.

SCALE ORIGIN: Dahlstrom and Nygaard (1995) adapted the scale from the work of Nygaard (1992), noting that it had also been previously employed by Hyvonen (1983) in a study of Finnish channels. Item-to-total correlations were examined using a country-by-country analysis of the data; items correlating at .25 or lower were dropped from the measure for a particular country. All items were retained for the measure in each country.

SAMPLES: Norwegian, German (formerly East German), and Polish oil and gas retailers were sampled by Dahlstrom and Nygaard (1995). Of the 432 Norwegian service station managers working in the retail network of a single oil refiner who were surveyed, **216** usable responses were obtained. **Forty** of the 44 service station managers in Poland and **29** of the 50 Leipzig-area dealers in the former East Germany also provided usable data.

RELIABILITY: Dahlstrom and Nygaard (1995) reported coefficient alphas of **.50**, **.80**, and **.78** in the Polish, German, and Norwegian samples, respectively.

VALIDITY: Dahlstrom and Nygaard (1995) did not specifically examine the validity of the measure.

ADMINISTRATION: Dahlstrom and Nygaard (1995) included the scale with other measures as part of a self-administered survey that was delivered by mail to the Norwegian sample. The survey was administered in person by college students to oil and gas retailers in the Polish and German samples. In each case, the questionnaire was translated into the focal language and back-translated into English, typically by university faculty in each country. Higher scores on the scale indicated that the oil and gas retailers judged their marketing, training, and management activities as highly successful.

MAJOR FINDINGS: Dahlstrom and Nygaard (1995) investigated various antecedents to and consequences of interpersonal trust in new and mature market economies using data collected in Norway, Poland, and the former East Germany. Interpersonal trust raised performance in both the Polish and Norwegian samples, though contrary to expectations, interpersonal trust negatively influenced performance in the German sample. In the Polish sample, centralized decision making, coupled with uncertainty, raised **performance**, whereas formalization, coupled with uncertainty, lowered **performance**. In the Norwegian sample, the interaction between uncertainty and centralized decision making damaged **performance**. No significant interaction effects between uncertainty and either centralized decision making or formalization were found for the German sample or between uncertainty and formalization in the Norwegian sample.

REFERENCES:

Dahlstrom, Robert and Arne Nygaard (1995), "An Exploratory Investigation of Interpersonal Trust in New and Mature Market Economies," *JR*, 71 (4), 339–61.

Hyvonen, S. (1983), "Coordination and Cooperation in Vertical Marketing Systems: A Model of Verification," license degree report, Helsinki School of Economics, Finland.

Nygaard, Arne (1992), "An Empirical Analysis of Performance in Principal-Agent Relationships," doctoral dissertation, Norwegian School of Economics and Business Administration, Bergen, Norway.

SCALE ITEMS:

Directions: Characterize how successful the *(Brand Name Company)* has been in these fields of activities.

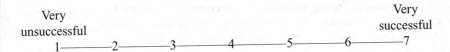

Very
unsuccessful

Very
successful

1———2———3———4———5———6———7

1. Marketing activities.

2. Training and courses.

3. Management and control.

SCALE NAME: Performance (Departmental)

SCALE DESCRIPTION: Olson, Walker, and Ruekert (1995) used this four-item, seven-point scale to measure the departmental performance of unit a during the new product development process on the basis of work quality, work quantity, the efficiency of unit operations, and the achievement of departmental objectives. The authors refer to this measure as *attainment of departmental goals*.

SCALE ORIGIN: Olson, Walker, and Ruekert (1995) stated the scale was adopted from Van de Ven and Ferry (1980) and previously used in a marketing context by Ruekert and Walker (1987a, b).

SAMPLES: Of the 24 firms solicited by Olson, Walker, and Ruekert (1995) to participate in the study, 15 divisions from 12 firms provided complete information on **45** new product development projects undertaken within a three-year time period. All firms produced tangible products and ranged in age from 12 to more than 100 years, with annual revenues between $50 million and more than $1 billion. Projects formed the unit of analysis. Of the new product projects studied, 11 represented new-to-the-world products, 9 were me-too products, 15 were line extensions, and 10 were product modifications. Data were collected first from each project manager and then from individuals identified by project managers as having key functional responsibilities related to marketing, manufacturing, R&D, and design. A total of **112** usable responses were obtained from the functional participants in addition to the information provided by the **45** product managers.

RELIABILITY: Olson, Walker, and Ruekert (1995) reported a coefficient alpha of **.82** for this scale. Scale items were also submitted to a Varimax-rotated principle components factor analysis and were found to load on a single factor with an eigenvalue greater than 1.

VALIDITY: No specific examination of scale validity for this measure was reported by Olson, Walker, and Ruekert (1995).

ADMINISTRATION: Olson, Walker, and Ruekert (1995) indicated that information about each project was initially obtained from project managers through a telephone interview using a structured questionnaire. After project managers had identified the key functional personnel for their project in marketing, manufacturing, R&D, and design, self-administered mail surveys were sent to each of the functional participants of each project. An overall project score was created for the departmental performance measure by averaging responses to each scale across all the responding functional participants from a given project. Higher scores on the scale indicated greater departmental performance in terms of the quantity and quality of work produced, the efficiency of unit operations, and the achievement of departmental objectives.

MAJOR FINDINGS: Olson, Walker, and Ruekert (1995) examined the relationship between new product coordinating structures and outcomes using a resource dependency view of the new product development process. When the project's coordination structure fit participants' experience with the product, functional participants rated their **department's performance** on obligations and objectives as higher than when the coordination mechanisms was too organic or too mechanistic.

REFERENCES:

Olson, Eric M., Orville C. Walker Jr., and Robert W. Ruekert (1995), "Organizing for Effective New Product Development: The Moderating Role of Product Innovativeness," *JM*, 59 (January), 48–62.

Ruekert, Robert W. and Orville C. Walker, Jr. (1987a), "Marketing's Interaction with other Functional Units: A Conceptual Framework and Empirical Evidence," *JM*, 51 (January), 1–19.

———— and ———— (1987b), "Interactions Between Marketing and R&D Departments in Implementing Different Strategies," *Strategic Management Journal*, 8, 233–48.

Van de Ven, Andrew H. and Diane L. Ferry (1980), *Measuring and Assessing Organizations*. New York: John Wiley & Sons.

SCALE ITEMS:

Far below   Far above
expectations   expectations

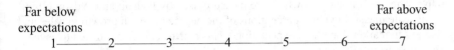

1——————2——————3——————4——————5——————6——————7

How did your department rate on each of the following factors for this project?

1. The quantity or amount of work produced?

2. The quality or accuracy of the work produced?

3. Attainment of department's objectives?

4. Efficiency of unit operations?

SCALE NAME: Performance (Growth/Share)

SCALE DESCRIPTION: The performance growth/share measure used by Pelham and Wilson (1996) is a three-item, seven-point scale measuring CEO perceptions of the degree to which growth in sales and employees, as well as changes in market share, met expectations. This construct is also referred to as *business position* by Pelham and Wilson (1996).

SCALE ORIGIN: It appears that the scale was first administered by the Center for Entrepreneurship at Eastern Michigan University. The extent to which Pelham and Wilson (1996) were involved with the Center and the development of the scale itself is unclear.

SAMPLES: A longitudinal database developed by the Center for Entrepreneurship at Eastern Michigan University provided the data for the study. The Center's full panel consists of data provided by the CEOs of 370 Michigan firms, which represent 71% of the firms contacted for initial participation. The data used by Pelham and Wilson (1996) were specific only to those firms providing full information with respect to all measures of interest for both the current and previous years. Of those **68** firms, 32% were classified as wholesalers, 29% as manufacturers, 26% as business services, and 13% as construction. Firm size ranged from 15 to 65 employees, with the average number of employees equaling 23.

RELIABILITY: Pelham and Wilson (1996) reported an alpha of **.75** for this scale.

VALIDITY: Pelham and Wilson (1996) stated that factor loadings and LISREL measurement model squared multiple correlations were taken as evidence of convergent and discriminant validity.

ADMINISTRATION: Pelham and Wilson (1996) did not provide details with respect to how data were collected from panel members by the Center of Entrepreneurship. High scores on the scale indicated that sales growth, employment growth, and market share exceeded expectations.

MAJOR FINDINGS: Pelham and Wilson (1996) investigated the relative impact of market orientation on small business performance compared with that of market structure, firm structure, firm strategy, and relative product quality. Regression analysis was used to test year-to-year differences in most variables, as well as parameters based on independent and lagged variables. Key findings indicated that product differentiation had a negative effect on the **growth/market share** of small firms. Increased usage of low-cost strategies and higher levels of new product success positively influenced **growth/share** in the short-term but not when other independent variables were lagged. However, the previous year's level of formalization positively influenced **growth/market share** in the lagged regression model. Whereas increases in **growth/market share** positively influenced profitability, the lagged variable regression model results indicated that high levels of **growth/share** in the previous year *negatively* influenced profitability in the current year.

REFERENCES:
Pelham, Alfred M. and David T. Wilson (1996), "A Longitudinal Study of the Impact of Market Structure, Firm Structure, Strategy, and Market Orientation Culture on Dimensions of Small-Firm Performance," *JAMS*, 24 (1), 27–43.

SCALE ITEMS:

Much below
expectations

Much above
expectations

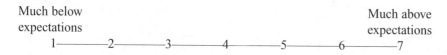

1. Sales growth rate.

2. Employment growth rate.

3. Market share.

SCALE NAME: Performance (Information Gathering)

SCALE DESCRIPTION: Oliver and Anderson (1994) used this five-item, seven-point scale to tap the dimension of performance related to gathering information and completing paperwork accurately and on time. The scale asks salespeople to evaluate their own performance relative to other salespeople in similar selling situations and should be viewed as performance input, which does not represent a result in and of itself but rather is expected to contribute to other outcome results.

SCALE ORIGIN: The scale used by Oliver and Anderson (1994) represents one of five factors composing a job performance scale developed by Behrman and Perreault (1982). The latter proposed a seven-factor self-reported measure of job performance for use with salespeople. Items were generated on the basis of information found in the literature, sales text books, sales job descriptions, and performance evaluation forms. Items limited to particular industrial selling situations were eliminated, as were redundant items and those judged to be deficient or ambiguous by a panel of judges. The resulting 65-item measure hypothesized as tapping seven performance dimensions was administered to a sample of 200 salespeople and 42 sales managers. Item purification procedures yielded a 31-item measure representing five aspects of industrial sales performance. When reliabilities were calculated using the hold-out sample, each factor achieved a reliability in excess of .80. Both the concurrent and predictive validity of the measure were assessed by Behrman and Perreault (1982) and found to be satisfactory.

SAMPLES: Oliver and Anderson (1994) surveyed managers and manufacturer's sales representatives employed by independently owned and operated sales agencies serving the electronics industry. Of the 350 randomly selected trade association member firms fitting this designation, 299 expressed interest in participating, and ultimately, **194** usable surveys from management and **347** surveys from manufacturer representatives were returned. The typical respondent was a male (92%), college graduate (64%), approximately 39 years of age, and had an average of 12 years sales experience with 5.5 years in the present job.

RELIABILITY: Oliver and Anderson (1994) reported a coefficient alpha of **.821** for this measure.

VALIDITY: Oliver and Anderson (1994) used the correlation matrix of the independent and classification variables used in the study to provide some evidence of discriminant and convergent validity. Nomological validity was also found to be present.

ADMINISTRATION: Oliver and Anderson (1994) sent managers of the 299 firms indicating interest in the study a packet containing a "manager's survey" and three similar self-administered surveys for salespeople, along with self-addressed, postage-paid reply envelopes. Managers were instructed to distribute one survey each to an "above-average rep," a "mid-range rep," and a "below-average rep." Each representative was promised confidentiality and the chance to win one of five $100 prizes in a random drawing. It appears that only responses obtained from sales representatives were used in computing this measure. Higher scores on this self-reported measure indicated that salespeople rated their performance in completing paperwork and gathering information as superior to the performance of salespeople in similar selling situations.

MAJOR FINDINGS: Oliver and Anderson (1994) examined how perceptions of the presence of a behavior versus outcome sales control system in the respondents' organizations influenced salespeople's performance outcomes and sales strategies, as well as their affective, cognitive, and behavioral states. Salespeople's self-evaluation of their ability to **gather information** and complete paperwork was not significantly related to the use of a behavior control system.

REFERENCES:

Behrman, Douglas N. and William D. Perreault Jr. (1982), "Measuring the Performance of Industrial Salespersons," *Journal of Business Research*, 10 (September), 355–70.

Oliver, Richard L. and Erin Anderson (1994), "An Empirical Test of the Consequences of Behavior- and Outcome-Based Sales Control Systems," *JM*, 58 (October), 53–67.

SCALE ITEMS:*

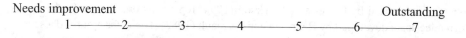

Needs improvement   Outstanding
1————2————3————4————5————6————7

1. Carrying out our company policies, procedures, and programs for providing information.

2. Providing accurate and complete paperwork related to orders, expenses, and other routine reports.

3. Recommending on you own initiative how company operations and procedures can be improved.

4. Submitting required reports on time.

5. Maintaining company-specified records that are accurate, complete, and up to date.

*Although the verbatim instructions for this scale were not indicated, Behrman and Perreault (1982) stated that salespeople were instructed to rate their "own current level of performance" by evaluating how well they performed on each item "compared with an average salesperson in similar selling situations."

SCALE NAME: Performance (Market Share)

SCALE DESCRIPTION: Song and Parry (1997) used this three-item, eleven-point scale to assess the market share performance of a new product both with respect to established performance goals and relative to other new products marketed by the firm and competition.

SCALE ORIGIN: The scale is original to Song and Parry (1997), though it is very similar in content to those used by Cooper (1979a, b) in measuring other types of performance. Scale items were modified on the basis of a review of the literature, pilot studies, and information obtained from 36 in-depth case study interviews conducted with both Japanese and U.S. firms. The items for all scales used by Song and Parry (1997) were evaluated by an academic panel composed of both Japanese and U.S. business and engineering experts; following revisions, the items were judged by a new panel composed of academicians and new product development (NPD) managers. The authors reported extensive pretesting of both the Japanese and U.S. versions of the questionnaire.

SAMPLES: Song and Parry (1997) randomly sampled 500 of the 611 firms trading on the Tokyo, Osaka, and Nagoya stock exchanges that had been identified as developing at least four new physical products since 1991. Usable responses pertaining to **788** NPD projects were obtained from 404 Japanese firms. The U.S. sampling frame was taken from companies listed in the *High-Technology Industries Directory*. Of the 643 firms that had introduced a minimum of four new physical products since 1990, 500 firms were randomly sampled (though stratified by industry to match the Japanese sample); 312 U.S. firms provided data on **612** NPD projects, of which 312 were successes and 300 were failures.

RELIABILITY: Song and Parry (1997) reported a coefficient alpha of **.96** for this scale in the Japanese sample and **.94** for the U.S. sample.

VALIDITY: The extensive pretesting and evaluation of the measure with academicians and NPD managers provided strong evidence for the face validity of the measure. Song and Parry (1997) did not specifically report any other examination of scale validity.

ADMINISTRATION: The self-administered questionnaire containing the scale was originally developed in English; the Japanese version was prepared using the parallel-translation/double-translation method. Following minor revisions made on the basis of pretests with bilingual respondents and case study participants, the Japanese sample received a survey packet containing cover letters in both English and Japanese, two Japanese-language questionnaires, and two international postage-paid reply envelopes. Survey packets delivered to U.S. firms were similar, except no Japanese cover letter was included and the surveys were in English. Incentives, four follow-up letters, and multiple telephone calls and faxes were used to increase the response rate with both samples. Song and Parry (1997) indicated that respondents were asked to answer one questionnaire in the context of a successful new product project introduced after 1991 and the other in the context of a new product project that had failed. Higher scores on the scale indicated higher evaluations of the performance of the new product with respect to market share.

MAJOR FINDINGS: Song and Parry (1997) conceptualized and tested a model of strategic, tactical, and environmental factors believed to influence new product success using data collected from both Japanese and U.S. firms. The market share performance of the new product was one of three factors used to assess relative product performance. In both the Japanese and U.S. NPD samples, the relationship between product differentiation and **relative product performance** was strengthened by high levels of (1) project fit with the firm's marketing skills and resources, (2) internal firm commitment to the project, and (3) NPD project market potential. However, higher levels of competitive intensity were also found to weaken the relationship between product differentiation and **relative product performance**.

#748 *Performance (Market Share)*

REFERENCES:

Cooper, Robert G. (1979a), "Identifying Industrial New Product Success: Project NewProd," *Industrial Marketing Management*, 8 (2), 124–35.

——— (1979b), "The Dimensions of Industrial New Product Success and Failure," *JM*, 43 (Summer), 93–103.

Song, X. Michael and Mark E. Parry (1997b), "A Cross-National Comparative Study of New Product Development Processes: Japan and the United States," *JM*, 61 (April), 1–18.

SCALE ITEMS:

Directions: New product performance can be measured in a number of ways. Please indicate, from what you know today, how successful this selected product was or has been using the following criteria.

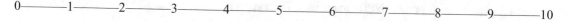

0————1————2————3————4————5————6————7————8————9————10

1. Relative to your firm's other new products, how successful was this product in terms of market share? (*Scale anchors:* 0 = Far less than our other new products; 10 = Far exceeded our other new products)

2. Relative to competing products, how successful was this product in terms of market share? (*Scale anchors:* 0 = Far less than the competing products; 10 = Far exceeded the competing products)

3. Relative to your firm's objectives for this product, how successful was this product in terms of market share? (*Scale anchors:* 0 = Far less than the objectives; 10 = Far exceeded the objectives)

SCALE NAME: Performance (Meeting Sales Objectives)

SCALE DESCRIPTION: Seven eleven-point items intended to measure self-reported assessments of a salesperson's performance in meeting sales and profit objectives relative to other salespeople working for a company.

SCALE ORIGIN: The scale used by Sujan, Weitz, and Kumar (1994) was adapted from one of five factors that composed a job performance scale developed by Behrman and Perreault (1982). Sujan, Weitz, and Kumar (1994) added items on identifying prospects and assisting the sales supervisor in meeting his or her goals, changed the scale anchors from "needs improvement"/"outstanding" to "much worse"/"much better," and increased the number of scale points to eleven. Behrman and Perreault (1982) originally proposed a seven-factor self-reported measure of job performance for use with salespeople. Items were generated on the basis of information found in the literature, sales text books, sales job descriptions, and performance evaluation forms. Items limited to particular industrial selling situations were eliminated, as were redundant items and those judged to be deficient or ambiguous by a panel of judges. The resulting 65-item measure hypothesized as tapping seven performance dimensions was administered to a sample of 200 salespeople and 42 sales managers. Item purification procedures yielded a 31-item measure representing five aspects of industrial sales performance. When reliabilities were calculated using the hold-out sample, each factor achieved a reliability in excess of .80. Both the concurrent and predictive validity of the measure were assessed by Behrman and Perreault (1982) and found to be satisfactory.

SAMPLES: Sujan, Weitz, and Kumar (1994) surveyed a convenience sample of salespeople employed by eight firms representing diverse industries. Two hundred seventeen questionnaires were distributed by sales managers to members of their selling force, and **190** usable responses were obtained for an 87.5% response rate. On average, respondents were 35 years of age, had 9 years sales experience, and made 3.5 calls per day. The majority were men (78%).

Challagalla and Shervani (1996) surveyed 302 field salespeople employed in the industrial products divisions of two *Fortune* 500 companies. Usable responses were received from **270** salespeople, the majority of whom were male and college educated.

RELIABILITY: Sujan, Weitz, and Kumar (1994) and Challagalla and Shervani (1996) reported coefficient alphas of **.91** and **.86** for the measure, respectively.

VALIDITY: Sujan, Weitz, and Kumar (1994) provided extensive information on the assessment of scale validity. Both Challagalla and Shervani (1996) and Sujan, Weitz, and Kumar (1994) stated that the results of confirmatory factor analysis supported the unidimensionality and reliability of the measure and provided evidence of convergent and discriminant validity.

ADMINISTRATION: Sujan, Weitz, and Kumar (1994) included a cover letter promising confidentiality and a self-addressed, stamped reply envelope in the survey packet distributed by sales managers to members of the sales force. Respondents were instructed to return the questionnaire directly to the researchers rather than to their superiors.

Challagalla and Shervani (1996) indicated that the scale was self-administered, along with many other measures, in a questionnaire delivered directly to the homes of salespeople. Prior to administration, each salesperson received a note from a senior sales executive in his or her organization alerting him or her to the study. Business reply envelopes, cover letters promising confidentiality, and two follow-up attempts were used to increase response rate. Higher scores on the scale indicated that salespeople judged themselves as being better at meeting sales and profit objectives than other salespeople working for the company.

MAJOR FINDINGS: Sujan, Weitz, and Kumar (1994) investigated the influence of goal orientations on work behavior. Results indicated that working harder and working smarter both increase **performance**.

Challagalla and Shervani (1996) extended existing conceptual work related to marketing control systems by (1) investigating the effect of information and reinforcement on salesperson job outcomes, (2) separating the global behavior control construct into activity control and capability control, and (3) examining the casual mechanisms through which controls operate. Only output rewards and capability punishments were directly related to **performance**; a negative relationship was observed in both cases.

REFERENCES:

Behrman, Douglas N. and William D. Perreault (1982), "Measuring the Performance of Industrial Salespersons," *Journal of Business Research*, 10, 355–70.

Challagalla, Goutam N. and Tasadduq A. Shervani (1996), "Dimensions and Types of Supervisory Control: Effects on Salesperson Performance and Satisfaction," *JM*, 60 (January), 89–105.

Sujan, Harish, Barton A. Weitz, and Nirmalya Kumar (1994), "Learning Orientation, Working Smart, and Effective Selling," *JM*, 58 (July), 39–52.

SCALE ITEMS:*

Much worse					Average				Much better	
-5	-4	-3	-2	-1	0	+1	+2	+3	+4	+5

1. Contributing to your company's acquiring a good market share.

2. Selling high profit-margin products.

3. Generating a high level of dollar sales

4. Quickly generating sales of new company products.

5. Identifying major accounts in your territory and selling to them.

6. Exceeding sales targets.

7. Assisting your sales supervisor meet his or her goals.

*Although the verbatim instructions were not provided, the authors noted that salespeople were asked to evaluate themselves relative to other salespeople working for their company.

SCALE NAME: Performance (Meeting Sales Objectives)

SCALE DESCRIPTION: Oliver and Anderson (1994) used this seven-item, seven-point scale to tap the dimension of outcome performance related to meeting sales and profit objectives. The scale asks salespeople to evaluate their own performance relative to other salespeople in similar selling situations.

SCALE ORIGIN: The scale used by Oliver and Anderson (1994) represents one of five factors that composed a job performance scale developed by Behrman and Perreault (1982). The latter originally proposed a seven-factor self-reported measure of job performance for use with salespeople. Items were generated on the basis of information found in the literature, sales text books, sales job descriptions, and performance evaluation forms. Items limited to particular industrial selling situations were eliminated, as were redundant items and those judged to be deficient or ambiguous by a panel of judges. The resulting 65-item measure hypothesized as tapping seven performance dimensions was administered to a sample of 200 salespeople and 42 sales managers. Item purification procedures yielded a 31-item measure representing five aspects of industrial sales performance. When reliabilities were calculated using the holdout sample, each factor achieved a reliability in excess of .80. Both the concurrent and predictive validity of the measure were assessed by Behrman and Perreault (1982) and found to be satisfactory.

SAMPLES: Oliver and Anderson (1994) surveyed managers and manufacturer's sales representatives employed by independently owned and operated sales agencies serving the electronics industry. Of the 350 randomly selected trade association member firms fitting this designation, 299 expressed interest in participating, and ultimately, **194** usable surveys from management and **347** surveys from manufacturer representatives were returned. The typical respondent was a male (92%), college graduate (64%), approximately 39 years of age, and had an average of 12 years sales experience with 5.5 years in the present job.

RELIABILITY: Oliver and Anderson (1994) reported a coefficient alpha of **.872** for this measure.

VALIDITY: Oliver and Anderson (1994) used the correlation matrix of the independent and classification variables used in the study to provide some evidence of discriminant and convergent validity. Nomological validity was also found to be present.

ADMINISTRATION: Oliver and Anderson (1994) sent managers of the 299 firms indicating interest in the study a packet containing a "manager's survey" and three similar self-administered surveys for salespeople, along with self-addressed, postage-paid reply envelopes. Managers were instructed to distribute one survey each to an "above-average rep," a "mid-range rep," and a "below-average rep." Each representative was promised confidentiality and the chance to win one of five $100 prizes in a random drawing. It appears that only responses obtained from sales representatives were used in computing this measure. Higher scores on this self-reported measure indicated that salespeople rated their performance in meeting sales and profit objectives as being superior to the performance of other salespeople in similar selling situations.

MAJOR FINDINGS: Oliver and Anderson (1994) examined how perceptions of the presence of a behavior versus outcome sales control system in the respondents' organizations influenced salespeople's performance outcomes and sales strategies, as well as their affective, cognitive, and behavioral states. Salesperson's self-evaluation of their ability to **meet sales and profit goals** was not significantly related to the use of a behavior control system.

#750 *Performance (Meeting Sales Objectives)*

REFERENCES:

Behrman, Douglas N. and William D. Perreault Jr. (1982), "Measuring the Performance of Industrial Salespersons," *Journal of Business Research*, 10 (September), 355–70.

Oliver, Richard L. and Erin Anderson (1994), "An Empirical Test of the Consequences of Behavior- and Outcome-Based Sales Control Systems," *JM*, 58 (October), 53–67.

SCALE ITEMS:*

Needs improvement   Outstanding

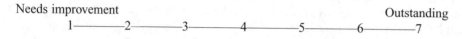

1. Producing a high market share for your company in your territory.

2. Making sales of those products with the highest profit margin.

3. Generating a high level of dollar sales.

4. Quickly generating sales of new company products.

5. Identifying and selling to major accounts in your territory.

6. Producing sales or blanket contracts with long-term profitability.

7. Exceeding all sales targets and objectives for your territory during the year.

*Although the verbatim instructions for this scale were not indicated, Behrman and Perreault (1982) stated that salespeople were instructed to rate their "own current level of performance" by evaluating how well they performed on each item "compared with an average salesperson in similar selling situations."

SCALE NAME: Performance (New Product)

SCALE DESCRIPTION: Gatignon and Xuereb (1997) used this six-item, six-point Likert-type scale to measure the degree to which respondents perceived that the objectives set for a new product had been achieved. The authors referred to this scale as *innovation success*.

SCALE ORIGIN: Gatignon and Xuereb (1997) stated that the multiple-item scales used in their study were developed on the basis of items previously proposed and used in survey research. The new product performance measure was based on the conceptual work of Moenaert and colleagues (1994) and Deshpandé, Farley, and Webster (1993). The measure was pretested with others on the questionnaire, and some phrasing was revised. A pilot test was performed on the revised questionnaire for the purpose of assessing scale validity. The resulting measures were then administered in the final questionnaire to a large sample.

SAMPLES: Gatignon and Xuereb (1997) mailed the final questionnaire to a list of 3000 marketing executives representing a broad cross-section of U.S. industries randomly selected from a commercially available list. Of these, 2802 were successfully delivered, and **393** usable responses were obtained for a 14% response rate. The products represented by the marketing executives surveyed included consumer durable and packaged goods, consumer services, industrial technology, and computer firms.

RELIABILITY: Gatignon and Xuereb (1997) reported a coefficient alpha of **.82** for this measure.

VALIDITY: Gatignon and Xuereb (1997) reported conducting a pilot study for the purpose of assessing scale validity; no other details were provided.

ADMINISTRATION: The scale was part of a self-administered mail survey. Nonrespondents were sent a reminder letter with an offer of a $500 lottery award two weeks after the initial mailing. Gatignon and Xuereb (1997) instructed respondents to answer the questionnaire in the context of the last new product introduced in the market by a strategic business unit. Higher scores on the scale indicated stronger perceptions of new product performance, in that the product was perceived as successfully achieving its objectives.

MAJOR FINDINGS: Gatignon and Xuereb (1997) examined the appropriateness of a customer, competitive, and technological orientation in the context of new product development. The perceived **performance of the new product** was positively influenced by a greater degree of product radicalness and product advantage, a smaller degree of product similarity with competitors, and lower product costs. **Performance of the new product** was positively influenced by a high customer or technological orientation when demand uncertainty is high and negatively influenced by both a competitive and technological orientation when demand is easy to forecast and predict. Conversely, when demand is easy to forecast, a high competitive orientation was beneficial to **new product performance**, whereas a competitive orientation negatively influenced **performance** when demand uncertainty is high.

REFERENCES:

Deshpandé, Rohit, John U. Farley, and Frederick E. Webster (1993), "Corporate Culture, Customer Orientation, and Innovativeness in Japanese Firms: A Quadrad Analysis," *JM*, 57 (January), 23–37.

Gatignon, Hubert and Jean-Marc Xuereb (1997), "Strategic Orientation of the Firm and New Product Performance," *JMR*, 34 (February), 77–90.

Moenaert, Ridy K., William E. Souder, Arnoud De Meyer, and Dirk Deschoolmeester (1994), "R&D-Marketing Integration Mechanisms, Communication Flows, and Innovation Success," *Journal of Product Innovation Management*, 11 (1), 31–45.

SCALE ITEMS:

Directions: Please circle the number following each sentence that best approximates the actual performance your new product.

Strongly
disagree

Strongly
agree

1————2————3————4————5————6

1. The growth of this new product's market share is superior to the market share growth of its main competitors.

2. With this new product we have increased our market share in this category.

3. Relative to other products of our firm, this one has a better return on investment.

4. Relative to our competitor's products, this one has a better return on investment.

5. This new product has succeeded in achieving its main objectives.

6. Overall, this new product is a commercial success.

SCALE NAME: Performance (New Product)

SCALE DESCRIPTION: Moorman (1995) used this five-item, seven-point scale to assess the extent to which organizational profit, sales, share, return on investment (ROI), and return on assets (ROA) goals have been reached. In a later study, Moorman and Miner (1997) used four of the original five items for their assessment of new product performance.

SCALE ORIGIN: The scale is original to Moorman (1995). All measures used by Moorman (1995) and Moorman and Miner (1997) were subjected to a purification process following data collection. Moorman (1995) assessed the unidimensionality of the measures in a two-factor confirmatory analysis model using LISREL VII. Items with very weak loadings and those loading on more than one factor were eliminated. The reliability of the measures was assessed by calculating coefficient alphas, and items with low item-to-total correlations were dropped if "doing so did not diminish the measure's coverage of the construct domain" (Moorman 1995, p. 325).

SAMPLES: Moorman (1995) chose to sample the vice presidents of marketing for 300 divisions of firms noted in the 1992 *Advertising Age* list of top 200 advertisers; a total of **92** usable questionnaires were received. No systematic differences were observed between early and late respondents. Moorman and Miner's (1997) study used data from the same sample.

RELIABILITY: Moorman (1995) reported a coefficient alpha of **.95** for the full five-item version of the scale, and Moorman and Miner (1997) also reported an alpha of **.95** for the reduced four-item measure.

VALIDITY: Moorman (1995) performed a series of two-factor confirmatory analyses using LISREL VII to assess the discriminant validity of the measures used in her study. Chi-square difference tests were performed on constrained versus unconstrained models, and the significantly lower chi-square values observed for all of the unconstrained models tested were accepted as evidence of the discriminant validity of the measures.

Moorman and Miner (1997) assessed the unidimensionality of the scale by dividing the measures used in this study into three subsets of theoretically related variables and submitting the measures to confirmatory factor analyses. The three models provided a good fit with the data. Confirmatory factor analysis was also used to assess the discriminant validity of the measure, which was found to be satisfactory.

ADMINISTRATION: The scale was included with other measures in a self-administered questionnaire that was delivered by mail. Moorman (1995) included a cover letter that explained the survey purpose and, in an effort to increase response rate, offered to share survey results. Nonrespondents were telephoned after three weeks and sent a second questionnaire two weeks after the telephone reminder. All informants were instructed to answer in the context of the most recent product development project for which their division had been responsible. Focal projects were required to have been on the market for a minimum of 12 months. Higher scores on the scale indicated that an organization has been more successful in achieving the goals set for the new product.

MAJOR FINDINGS: Moorman (1995) examined the relationship between organizational market information processes, organizational culture, and new product outcomes. Some evidence was found to suggest that conceptual utilization processes and instrumental utilization processes positively influenced **new product performance**. This would indicate that when information is valued, processed, and incorporated by an organization into the marketing decision making, implementation, and evaluation process, new products are more likely to meet profit, sales, share, ROI, and ROA goals.

Moorman and Miner (1997) investigated the impact of organizational memory level and organizational memory dispersion on key new product development processes. Both organizational memory level and organizational memory dispersion positively influenced the **performance of the new product**. However, the positive impact of organizational memory dispersion on the **performance of a new product** was significantly weakened by high levels of market turbulence.

REFERENCES:

Moorman, Christine (1995), "Organizational Market Information Processes: Cultural Antecedents and New Product Outcomes," *JMR*, 32 (August), 318–35.

——— and Anne S. Miner (1997), "The Impact of Organizational Memory on New Product Performance and Creativity," *JMR*, 34 (February), 91–106.

SCALE ITEMS:*

Directions: Rate the extent to which the product has achieved the following outcomes during the first 12 months of its life in the marketplace.

Low   High

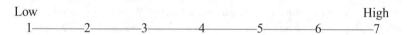

1——————2——————3——————4——————5——————6——————7

1. Market share relative to its stated objective.

2. Sales relative to its stated objective.

3. Return on assets relative to its stated objective.

4. Profit margin relative to its stated objective.

5. Return on investment relative to its stated objective.

*Moorman and Miner (1997) used items 2–5 in computing their measure of new product performance.

SCALE NAME: Performance (New Product Profitability)

SCALE DESCRIPTION: Song and Parry (1997) used this four-item, eleven-point scale to assess the profitability of a new product both with respect to established performance goals and relative to other new products marketed by the firm and competition.

SCALE ORIGIN: The development of the scale is attributed to the work of Cooper (1979a, b). The items for all scales used by the authors were evaluated by an academic panel composed of both Japanese and U.S. business and engineering experts. Following revisions, the items were judged by a new panel composed of academicians and new product development (NPD) managers. The authors reported extensive pretesting of both the Japanese and U.S. versions of the questionnaire.

SAMPLES: Song and Parry (1997) randomly sampled 500 of the 611 firms trading on the Tokyo, Osaka, and Nagoya stock exchanges that had been identified as developing at least four new physical products since 1991. Usable responses pertaining to **788** NPD projects were obtained from 404 Japanese firms. The U.S. sampling frame was taken from companies listed in the *High-Technology Industries Directory.* Of the 643 firms that had introduced a minimum of four new physical products since 1990, 500 firms were randomly sampled (though stratified by industry to match the Japanese sample); 312 U.S. firms provided data on **612** NPD projects, of which 312 were successes and 300 were failures.

RELIABILITY: Song and Parry (1997) reported a coefficient alpha of **.97** for this scale in the Japanese sample and **.96** for the U.S. sample.

VALIDITY: The extensive pretesting and evaluation of the measure with academicians and NPD managers provides strong evidence for the face validity of the measure. The authors did not specifically report any other examination of scale validity.

ADMINISTRATION: The self-administered questionnaire containing the scale was originally developed in English; the Japanese version was prepared using the parallel-translation/double-translation method. Following minor revisions made on the basis of pretests with bilingual respondents and case study participants, the Japanese sample received a survey packet containing cover letters in both English and Japanese, two Japanese-language questionnaires, and two international postage-paid reply envelopes. Survey packets delivered to U.S. firms were similar, except no Japanese cover letter was included and the surveys were in English. Incentives, four follow-up letters, and multiple telephone calls and faxes were used to increase the response rate with both samples. Song and Parry (1997) indicated that respondents were asked to answer one questionnaire in the context of a successful new product project introduced after 1991 and the other in the context of a new product project that had failed. Higher scores on the scale indicated higher evaluations of the performance of the new product with respect to its profitability.

MAJOR FINDINGS: Song and Parry (1997) conceptualized and tested a model of strategic, tactical, and environmental factors believed to influence new product success using data collected from both Japanese and U.S. firms. The profitability of the new product was one of three factors used to assess relative product performance. In both the Japanese and U.S. NPD samples, the relationship between product differentiation and **relative product performance** was strengthened by high levels of (1) project fit with the firm's marketing skills and resources, (2) internal firm commitment to the project, and (3) NPD project market potential. However, higher levels of competitive intensity were also found to weaken the relationship between product differentiation and **relative product performance**.

REFERENCES:
Cooper, Robert G. (1979a), "Identifying Industrial New Product Success: Project NewProd," *Industrial Marketing Management*, 8 (2), 124–35.
———— (1979b), "The Dimensions of Industrial New Product Success and Failure," *JM*, 43 (Summer), 93–103.
Song, X. Michael and Mark E. Parry (1997b), "A Cross-National Comparative Study of New Product Development Processes: Japan and the United States," *JM*, 61 (April), 1–18.

SCALE ITEMS:
Directions: New product performance can be measured in a number of ways. Please indicate, from what you know today, how successful this selected product was or has been using the following criteria.

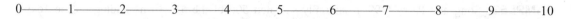

0————1————2————3————4————5————6————7————8————9————10

1. How successful was this product from an overall profitability standpoint?
   (*Scale anchors:* 0 = A great financial failure, i.e., far less than our minimum acceptable profitability criteria; 10 = A great financial success, i.e., far exceeded our minimum acceptable profitability criteria)

2. Relative to your firm's other new products, how successful was this product in terms of profits?
   (*Scale anchors:* 0 = Far less than our other new products; 10 = Far exceeded our other new products)

3. Relative to competing products, how successful was this product in terms of profits?
   (*Scale anchors:* 0 = Far less than the competing products; 10 = Far exceeded the competing products)

4. Relative to your firm's objectives for this product, how successful was this product in terms of profits?
   (*Scale anchors:* 0 = Far less than the objectives; 10 = Far exceeded the objectives)

SCALE NAME: Performance (New Product Sales)

SCALE DESCRIPTION: Song and Parry (1997) used this three-item, eleven-point scale to assess the sales performance of a new product both with respect to established performance goals and relative to other new products marketed by the firm and competition.

SCALE ORIGIN: The scale is original to Song and Parry (1997), though items 1 and 3 were adapted from Cooper (1979a, b). Song and Parry (1997) generated scale items on the basis of a review of the literature, pilot studies, and information obtained from 36 in-depth case study interviews conducted with both Japanese and U.S. firms. The items for all scales used by Song and Parry (1997) were evaluated by an academic panel composed of both Japanese and U.S. business and engineering experts. Following revisions, the items were judged by a new panel composed of academicians and new product development (NPD) managers. The authors reported extensive pretesting of both the Japanese and U.S. versions of the questionnaire.

SAMPLES: Song and Parry (1997) randomly sampled 500 of the 611 firms trading on the Tokyo, Osaka, and Nagoya stock exchanges that had been identified as developing at least four new physical products since 1991. Usable responses pertaining to **788** NPD projects were obtained from 404 Japanese firms. The U.S. sampling frame was taken from companies listed in the *High-Technology Industries Directory*. Of the 643 firms that had introduced a minimum of four new physical products since 1990, 500 firms were randomly sampled (though stratified by industry to match the Japanese sample); 312 U.S. firms provided data on **612** NPD projects, of which 312 were successes and 300 were failures.

RELIABILITY: Song and Parry (1997) reported a coefficient alpha of **.93** for this scale in the Japanese sample and **.92** for the U.S. sample.

VALIDITY: The extensive pretesting and evaluation of the measure with academicians and NPD managers provides strong evidence for the face validity of the measure. The authors did not specifically report any other examination of scale validity.

ADMINISTRATION: The self-administered questionnaire containing the scale was originally developed in English; the Japanese version was prepared using the parallel-translation/double-translation method. Following minor revisions made on the basis of pretests with bilingual respondents and case study participants, the Japanese sample received a survey packet containing cover letters in both English and Japanese, two Japanese-language questionnaires, and two international postage paid reply envelopes. Survey packets delivered to U.S. firms were similar, except no Japanese cover letter was included and the surveys were in English. Incentives, four follow-up letters, and multiple telephone calls and faxes were used to increase the response rate with both samples. Song and Parry (1997) indicated that respondents were asked to answer one questionnaire in the context of a successful new product project introduced after 1991 and the other in the context of a new product project that had failed. Higher scores on the scale indicated higher evaluations of the performance of the new product with respect to its sales.

MAJOR FINDINGS: Song and Parry (1997) conceptualized and tested a model of strategic, tactical, and environmental factors believed to influence new product success using data collected from both Japanese and U.S. firms. The sales performance of the new product was one of three factors used to assess relative product performance. In both the Japanese and U.S. NPD samples, the relationship between product differentiation and **relative product performance** was strengthened by high levels of (1) project fit with the firm's marketing skills and resources, (2) internal firm commitment to the project, and (3) NPD project market potential. However, higher levels of competitive intensity were also found to weaken the relationship between product differentiation and **relative product performance**.

#754 *Performance (New Product Sales)*

REFERENCES:

Cooper, Robert G. (1979a), "Identifying Industrial New Product Success: Project NewProd," *Industrial Marketing Management*, 8 (2), 124–35.

——— (1979b), "The Dimensions of Industrial New Product Success and Failure," *JM*, 43 (Summer), 93–103.

Song, X. Michael and Mark E. Parry (1997), "A Cross-National Comparative Study of New Product Development Processes: Japan and the United States," *JM*, 61 (April), 1–18.

SCALE ITEMS:

Directions: New product performance can be measured in a number of ways. Please indicate, from what you know today, how successful this selected product was or has been using the following criteria.

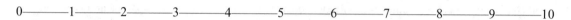

0———1———2———3———4———5———6———7———8———9———10

1. Relative to your firm's other new products, how successful was this product in terms of sales?
   (*Scale anchors:* 0 = Far less than our other new products; 10 = Far exceeded our other new products)

2. Relative to competing products, how successful was this product in terms of sales?
   (*Scale anchors:* 0 = Far less than the competing products; 10 = Far exceeded the competing products)

3. Relative to your firm's objectives for this product, how successful was this product in terms of sales?
   (*Scale anchors:* 0 = Far less than the objectives; 10 = Far exceeded the objectives)

SCALE NAME: Performance (Profitability)

SCALE DESCRIPTION: The performance profitability measure used by Pelham and Wilson (1996) is a five-item, seven-point scale measuring CEO perceptions of the degree to which the profitability of the firm met expectations.

SCALE ORIGIN: It appears that the scale was first administered by the Center for Entrepreneurship at Eastern Michigan University. The extent to which Pelham and Wilson (1996) were involved with the Center and the development of the scale itself is unclear.

SAMPLES: A longitudinal database developed by the Center for Entrepreneurship at Eastern Michigan University provided the data for the study. The Center's full panel consists of data provided by the CEOs of 370 Michigan firms, which represent 71% of the firms contacted for initial participation. The data used by Pelham and Wilson (1996) were specific only to those firms providing full information with respect to all measures of interest for both the current and previous years. Of those **68** firms, 32% were classified as wholesalers, 29% as manufacturers, 26% as business services, and 13% as construction. Firm size ranged from 15 to 65 employees, with the average number of employees equaling 23.

RELIABILITY: Pelham and Wilson (1996) reported an alpha of **.88** for this scale.

VALIDITY: Pelham and Wilson (1996) stated that factor loadings and LISREL measurement model squared multiple correlations were taken as evidence of convergent and discriminant validity.

ADMINISTRATION: Pelham and Wilson (1996) did not provide details with respect to how data were collected from panel members by the Center of Entrepreneurship. High scores on the scale indicated that the firm's profitability exceeded expectations.

MAJOR FINDINGS: Pelham and Wilson (1996) investigated the relative impact of market orientation on small business performancecompared with that of market structure, firm structure, firm strategy, and relative product quality. Regression analysis was used to test year-to-year differences in most variables, as well as parameters based on independent and lagged variables. Key findings indicated that product differentiation had a negative effect on the **profitability** of small firms when other independent variables were lagged. Market orientation positively influenced **profitability** for small firms and was also positively related to **profitability** in the current year in the lagged regression model. Whereas increases in growth/market share positively influenced **profitability**, the lagged variable regression model results indicated that high levels of growth/share in the previous year *negatively* influenced **profitability** in the current year.

REFERENCES:
Pelham, Alfred M. and David T. Wilson (1996), "A Longitudinal Study of the Impact of Market Structure, Firm Structure, Strategy, and Market Orientation Culture on Dimensions of Small-Firm Performance," *JAMS*, 24 (1), 27–43.

SCALE ITEMS:

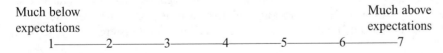

Much below expectations — Much above expectations

1————2————3————4————5————6————7

1. Operating profits.

2. Profit to sales ratio.

3. Cash flow from operations.

4. Return on investment.

5. Return on assets.

SCALE NAME: Performance (Relative)

SCALE DESCRIPTION: Oliver and Anderson (1994) used this three-item, nine-point scale to measure sales representatives' self-reports of their performance on achieving agency goals, effort, and overall performance compared with other representatives in the agency.

SCALE ORIGIN: The scale is original to Oliver and Anderson (1994), who pretested the measure in a questionnaire administered to a convenience sample of sales representatives attending trade association functions. The measure was revised on the basis of the pretest.

SAMPLES: Oliver and Anderson (1994) surveyed managers and manufacturer's sales representatives employed by independently owned and operated sales agencies serving the electronics industry. Of the 350 randomly selected trade association member firms fitting this designation, 299 expressed interest in participating, and ultimately, **194** usable surveys from management and **347** surveys from manufacturer representatives were returned. The typical respondent was a male (92%), college graduate (64%), approximately 39 years of age, and had an average of 12 years sales experience with 5.5 years in the present job.

RELIABILITY: Oliver and Anderson (1994) reported a coefficient alpha of **.862** for this measure.

VALIDITY: Oliver and Anderson (1994) cross-validated the measure against the managerial performance designation collected in the managerial survey, which classified the representative as above average, average, or below average, as well as against percentile rankings of the scale of annual sales. Grouped comparisons were used to demonstrate convergent validity of the self-reported measure. The authors also used the correlation matrix of the independent and classification variables used in the study to provide some evidence of discriminant and convergent validity. Nomological validity was also found to be present.

ADMINISTRATION: Oliver and Anderson (1994) sent managers of the 299 firms indicating interest in the study a packet containing a "manager's survey" and three similar self-administered surveys for salespeople, along with self-addressed, postage-paid reply envelopes. Managers were instructed to distribute one survey each to an "above-average rep," a "mid-range rep," and a "below-average rep." Each representative was promised confidentiality and the chance to win one of five $100 prizes in a random drawing. It appears that only responses obtained from sales representatives were used in computing this measure. Higher scores on the scale indicated that salespeople evaluated their own performance as better than that of other representatives employed by the agency.

MAJOR FINDINGS: Oliver and Anderson (1994) examined how perceptions of the presence of a behavior versus outcome sales control system in the respondents' organizations influenced salespeople's performance outcomes and sales strategies, as well as their affective, cognitive, and behavioral states. Self-reported measures of a **salesperson's performance relative to others employed by the same agency** was not found to be significantly related to the use of a behavior control system.

REFERENCES:
Oliver, Richard L. and Erin Anderson (1994), "An Empirical Test of the Consequences of Behavior- and Outcome-Based Sales Control Systems," *JM*, 58 (October), 53–67.

SCALE ITEMS:

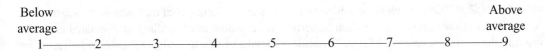

Below   Above
average   average
 1———2———3———4———5———6———7———8———9

1. How would you evaluate your performance on your agency's sales goals?

2. Compared with other salespeople working for your company, how would you evaluate your effort?

3. Compared with other salespeople working for your company, how would you evaluate your overall performance?

SCALE NAME: Performance (Sales Expense Control)

SCALE DESCRIPTION: Oliver and Anderson (1994) used six items from the seven-item, seven-point scale shown here to tap into the dimension of performance related to controlling sales-related expenses incurred in the course of doing business. The scale asks salespeople to evaluate their own performance relative to other salespeople in similar selling situations and should be viewed as performance input, which does not represent a result in and of itself but rather is expected to contribute to other outcome results.

SCALE ORIGIN: The scale used by Oliver and Anderson (1994) represents one of five factors that compose a job performance scale developed by Behrman and Perreault (1982). The latter originally proposed a seven-factor self-reported measure of job performance for use with salespeople. Items were generated on the basis of information found in the literature, sales text books, sales job descriptions, and performance evaluation forms. Items limited to particular industrial selling situations were eliminated, as were redundant items and those judged to be deficient or ambiguous by a panel of judges. The resulting 65-item measure hypothesized as tapping seven performance dimensions was administered to a sample of 200 salespeople and 42 sales managers. Item purification procedures yielded a 31-item measure representing five aspects of industrial sales performance. When reliabilities were calculated using the hold-out sample, each factor achieved a reliability in excess of .80. Both the concurrent and predictive validity of the measure were assessed by Behrman and Perreault (1982) and found to be satisfactory.

SAMPLES: Oliver and Anderson (1994) surveyed managers and manufacturer's sales representatives employed by independently owned and operated sales agencies serving the electronics industry. Of the 350 randomly selected trade association member firms fitting this designation, 299 expressed interest in participating, and ultimately, **194** usable surveys from management and **347** surveys from manufacturer representatives were returned. The typical respondent was a male (92%), college graduate (64%), approximately 39 years of age, and had an average of 12 years sales experience with 5.5 years in the present job.

RELIABILITY: Oliver and Anderson (1994) reported a coefficient alpha of **.853** for this measure.

VALIDITY: Oliver and Anderson (1994) used the correlation matrix of the independent and classification variables used in the study to provide some evidence of discriminant and convergent validity. Nomological validity was also found to be present.

ADMINISTRATION: Oliver and Anderson (1994) sent managers of the 299 firms indicating interest in the study a packet containing a "manager's survey" and three similar self-administered surveys for salespeople, along with self-addressed postage paid reply envelopes. Managers were instructed to distribute one survey each to an "above-average rep," a "mid-range rep," and a "below-average rep." Each representative was promised confidentiality and the chance to win one of five $100 prizes in a random drawing. It appears that only responses obtained from sales representatives were used in computing this measure. Higher scores on this self-reported measure indicated that salespeople rated their performance in controlling sales-related expenses as being superior to the performance of other salespeople in similar selling situations.

MAJOR FINDINGS: Oliver and Anderson (1994) examined how perceptions of the presence of a behavior versus outcome sales control system in the respondents' organizations influenced salespeople's performance outcomes and sales strategies, as well as their affective, cognitive, and behavioral states. Higher self-evaluations of salespeople's ability to **control expenses** was significantly related to the use of a behavior control system.

REFERENCES:

Behrman, Douglas N. and William D. Perreault Jr. (1982), "Measuring the Performance of Industrial Salespersons," *Journal of Business Research*, 10 (September), 355–70.

Oliver, Richard L. and Erin Anderson (1994), "An Empirical Test of the Consequences of Behavior- and Outcome-Based Sales Control Systems," *JM*, 58 (October), 53–67.

SCALE ITEMS:*

Needs improvement   Outstanding

1————2————3————4————5————6————7

1. Operating within the budgets set by the company.

2. Using expense accounts with integrity.

3. Using business gift and promotional allowances responsibly.

4. Spending travel and lodging money carefully.

5. Arranging sales call patterns and frequency to cover your territory economically.

6. Entertaining only when it is clearly in the best interest of the company to do so.

7. Controlling costs in other areas of the company (order processing and preparation, delivery, etc.) when taking sales orders.

*Although the verbatim instructions for this scale were not indicated, Behrman and Perreault (1982) stated that salespeople were instructed to rate their "own current level of performance" by evaluating how well they performed on each item "compared with an average salesperson in similar selling situations."

*Oliver and Anderson (1994) indicated that only six of the seven items comprising this scale were used in their study. However, no information was provided to determine which of the seven items was dropped.

SCALE NAME: Performance (Sales Force Financial)

SCALE DESCRIPTION: Sohi, Smith, and Ford (1996) used this three-item, five-point scale to assess how salespeople had performed during the previous year with respect to sales, profit, and market share objectives.

SCALE ORIGIN: Sohi, Smith, and Ford (1996) reported that the scale was original to their study but provided no details.

SAMPLES: A sample of **30** salespeople from a major Midwestern corporation were used to pretest the questionnaire. Then, 1650 salespeople employed by manufacturing firms in standard industrial classification codes 20–39 were randomly selected from a commercial mailing list to serve as the sampling frame. Of the 1542 questionnaires delivered to valid addresses, **230** completed surveys were returned for a response rate of 14.9%. Respondents were predominately college-educated (84%), married (84%) men (89%), with a median age of 37.5 years and who had held their current sales position an average of 5.8 years. Industries represented included food products, pharmaceuticals, chemical and allied products, rubber and plastic products, electronics and computers, appliances, and audio-visual products. Nonresponse bias was tested by comparing early and late responders on key variables. No significant differences were found, which suggests that nonresponse bias may not have been a problem.

RELIABILITY: Sohi, Smith, and Ford (1996) reported a coefficient alpha of **.80** for this measure.

VALIDITY: Evidence of discriminant validity was provided by a nested model confirmatory factor analysis that demonstrated that the latent-trait correlations between constructs significantly differed from 1. Confirmatory factor analysis also provided satisfactory evidence of the unidimensionality of the measure.

ADMINISTRATION: Prior to data collection, the questionnaire was pretested on a small sample of salespeople. Sohi, Smith, and Ford (1996) stated that several items and the questionnaire format were revised on the basis of the pretest results. In the final study, the measure was part of a self-administered mail survey. Cover letters and postage-paid reply envelopes accompanied each questionnaire, and a copy of the survey results was offered as an incentive to participate. Reminder letters were sent three and five weeks after the initial questionnaire mailing. With the scale anchors employed, lower scores on the performance scale indicated that the sales representative exceeded financial objectives in the previous year.

MAJOR FINDINGS: Sohi, Smith, and Ford (1996) investigated how salespeople's role perceptions, satisfaction, and performance were affected when the sales force is shared across multiple divisions within a company. Sharing of the sales force did not significantly influence a salesperson's **performance with respect to financial objectives**, nor was this relationship influenced significantly by formalization or centralization.

COMMENTS: Because the scale was administered to members of the sales force rather than management, the self-reported nature of the data may reflect an upward bias. However, research by Churchill and colleagues (1985) has found that self-reports of salesperson performance are equivalent to data provided by managers and peers.

REFERENCES:

Churchill, Gilbert A., Jr., Neil M. Ford, Steven W. Hartley, and Orville C. Walker Jr. (1985), "Determinants of Salesperson Performance: A Meta-Analysis," *JMR,* 22 (May), 103–18.
Sohi, Ravipreet S., Daniel C. Smith, and Neil M. Ford (1996), "How Does Sharing a Sales Force Between Multiple Divisions Affect Salespeople?" *JAMS,* 24 (3), 195–207.

SCALE ITEMS:
Performance on the following objectives during the previous year:

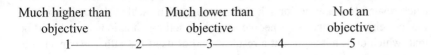

Much higher than objective — Much lower than objective — Not an objective

1————2————3————4————5

1. Sales.

2. Profitability.

3. Market share.

SCALE NAME: Performance (Sales Presentation Planning)

SCALE DESCRIPTION: Oliver and Anderson (1994) used this six-item, seven-point scale to tap into the dimension of performance related to planning for sales presentations. The scale asks salespeople to evaluate their own performance relative to other salespeople in similar selling situations and should be viewed as performance input, which does not represent a result in and of itself but rather is expected to contribute to other outcome results.

SCALE ORIGIN: The scale used by Oliver and Anderson (1994) represents one of five factors that compose a job performance scale developed by Behrman and Perreault (1982). The latter originally proposed a seven-factor self-reported measure of job performance for use with salespeople. Items were generated on the basis of information found in the literature, sales text books, sales job descriptions, and performance evaluation forms. Items limited to particular industrial selling situations were eliminated, as were redundant items and those judged to be deficient or ambiguous by a panel of judges. The resulting 65-item measure hypothesized as tapping seven performance dimensions was administered to a sample of 200 salespeople and 42 sales managers. Item purification procedures yielded a 31-item measure representing five aspects of industrial sales performance. When reliabilities were calculated using the hold-out sample, each factor achieved a reliability in excess of .80. Both the concurrent and predictive validity of the measure were assessed by Behrman and Perreault (1982) and found to be satisfactory.

SAMPLES: Oliver and Anderson (1994) surveyed managers and manufacturer's sales representatives employed by independently owned and operated sales agencies serving the electronics industry. Of the 350 randomly selected trade association member firms fitting this designation, 299 expressed interest in participating, and ultimately, **194** usable surveys from management and **347** surveys from manufacturer representatives were returned. The typical respondent was a male (92%), college graduate (64%), approximately 39 years of age, and had an average of 12 years sales experience with 5.5 years in the present job.

RELIABILITY: Oliver and Anderson (1994) reported a coefficient alpha of **.836** for this measure.

VALIDITY: Oliver and Anderson (1994) used the correlation matrix of the independent and classification variables used in the study to provide some evidence of discriminant and convergent validity. Nomological validity was also found to be present.

ADMINISTRATION: Oliver and Anderson (1994) sent managers of the 299 firms indicating interest in the study a packet containing a "manager's survey" and three similar self-administered surveys for salespeople, along with self-addressed postage paid reply envelopes. Managers were instructed to distribute one survey each to an "above-average rep," a "mid-range rep," and a "below-average rep." Each representative was promised confidentiality and the chance to win one of five $100 prizes in a random drawing. It appears that only responses obtained from sales representatives were used in computing this measure. Higher scores on this self-reported measure indicated that salespeople rated their performance in planning their sales presentations as being superior to the performance of other salespeople in similar selling situations.

MAJOR FINDINGS: Oliver and Anderson (1994) examined how perceptions of the presence of a behavior versus outcome sales control system in the respondents' organizations influenced salespeople's performance outcomes and sales strategies, as well as their affective, cognitive, and behavioral states. Higher self-evaluations of salespeople's ability to **plan for sales presentations** was significantly related to the use of a behavior control system.

REFERENCES:

Behrman, Douglas N. and William D. Perreault Jr. (1982), "Measuring the Performance of Industrial Salespersons," *Journal of Business Research*, 10 (September), 355–70.

Oliver, Richard L. and Erin Anderson (1994), "An Empirical Test of the Consequences of Behavior- and Outcome-Based Sales Control Systems," *JM*, 58 (October), 53–67.

SCALE ITEMS:*

Needs improvement   Outstanding

1————2————3————4————5————6————7

1. Listening attentively to identify and understand the real concerns of your customer.

2. Convincing customers that you understand their unique problems and concerns.

3. Using established contacts to develop new customers.

4. Communicating your sales presentation clearly and concisely.

5. Making effective use of audiovisual aids (charts, tables, and the like) to improve your sales presentation.

6. Working out solutions to a customer's questions or objections.

*Although the verbatim instructions for this scale were not indicated, Behrman and Perreault (1982) stated that salespeople were instructed to rate their "own current level of performance" by evaluating how well they performed on each item "compared with an average salesperson in similar selling situations."

SCALE NAME: Performance (Salesperson)

SCALE DESCRIPTION: Rich (1997) used this three-item, seven-point Likert-type scale to measure a manager's perception of a salesperson's overall level of performance.

SCALE ORIGIN: Rich (1997) stated that the scale was adapted from Cammann and colleagues (1983) and was revised into its final form on the basis of the results of a confirmatory factor analysis.

SAMPLES: Salespeople and their immediate supervisors from 10 different U.S.-based business-to-business sales organizations representing different industries formed the sample for this study. Two hundred forty-four salesperson–manager dyads received questionnaires, and usable responses were obtained from 193 salespeople and 218 managers, resulting in complete responses from a total of **183** matched salesperson–manager dyads.

RELIABILITY: Rich (1997) reported a coefficient alpha of **.90** for the measure.

VALIDITY: Results of the confirmatory factor analysis reported by Rich (1997) provided strong evidence for the discriminant and convergent validity of the measures, and the extensive pretesting provided evidence of content validity.

ADMINISTRATION: Rich (1997) indicated that the scale was part of a self-administered mail survey sent directly to each member of the salesperson–manager dyads. Follow-up telephone calls made by research assistants, the promise to share survey results, and encouragement from the management of participating firms enhanced respondent participation. It appears that the measure was only administered to the sales manager sample. Higher scores on the scale indicated that a sales manager was more satisfied with the salesperson's overall performance.

MAJOR FINDINGS: Rich (1997) examined the relationship between the role-modeling behavior of sales managers and a set of key outcome variables, including trust in the manager, job satisfaction, and salesperson performance. Through its relationship with trust, sales manager role-modeling behavior was found to indirectly influence both job satisfaction and **salesperson performance**.

REFERENCES:

Cammann, Cortlandt, Mark Fichman, G. Douglas Jenkins, and John R. Klesh (1983), "Assessing the Attitudes and Perceptions of Organizational Members," in *Assessing Organizational Change: A Guide to Methods, Measures, and Practices*, Stanley E. Seashore, Edward E. Lawler, Philip H. Mervis, and Cortlandt Cammann, eds. New York: John Wiley & Sons, 71–138.

Rich, Gregory A. (1997), "The Sales Manager as a Role Model: Effects on Trust, Job Satisfaction, and Performance of Salespeople," *JAMS*, 25 (4), 319–28.

SCALE ITEMS:

1 = Strongly disagree
2 = Moderately disagree
3 = Slightly disagree
4 = Neither agree nor disagree
5 = Slightly agree
6 = Moderately agree
7 = Strongly agree

1. Performs his or her job the way I like to see it performed.

2. Is one of the company's most valuable salespeople.

3. All things considered, this salesperson is outstanding.

SCALE NAME: Performance (Salesperson)

SCALE DESCRIPTION: Podsakoff and MacKenzie (1994) used this three-item, seven-point scale to measure a sales manager's rating of an individual sales agent's performance.

SCALE ORIGIN: There is nothing in the article to indicate that the measure is anything but original to Podsakoff and MacKenzie (1994). If original to this study, it would appear that Podsakoff and MacKenzie (1994) developed the specific items used in this measure by following typical scale development procedures. Items were generated to tap into each construct, revised on the basis of expert opinion, discussed with sales representatives to determine face validity and applicability to the sales context, and pretested with a sample of insurance sales managers. The final items used to represent the measure were selected on the basis of confirmatory factor analyses and item reliability analyses.

SAMPLES: In their first study, Podsakoff and MacKenzie (1994) used a national sample of sales managers, who provided ratings of **987** full-time agents employed by a major insurance company. The salespeople who were rated were predominately men (79.8%) and college educated (91% had some college, 68.1% had at least a bachelor's degree). In the second study, the authors aggregated the individual agent organizational citizenship behavior (OCB) data used in Study 1 to create unit-level scores demonstrating the average amount of OCB exhibited by agents in each sales unit. Matching sales performance data were obtained from the company for a total of **116** sales (relating to 839 of the 987 agent ratings used in Study 1). The average size of a unit was 7.2 and ranged from 2 to 21 employees.

RELIABILITY: Podsakoff and MacKenzie (1994) reported coefficient alphas of **.92** for this measure in Study 1.

VALIDITY: Podsakoff and MacKenzie (1994) examined the discriminant and convergent validity of the scale using confirmatory factor analysis and found strong evidence for both types of validity for this measure.

ADMINISTRATION: Podsakoff and MacKenzie (1994) indicated that sales managers' ratings of their agents' OCBs and job performance were obtained through a self-administered mail survey distributed to sales managers. A preaddressed, stamped reply envelope was included with the survey. Higher scores on the scale indicated that managers perceived an agent as being better at performing his or her job.

MAJOR FINDINGS: Podsakoff and MacKenzie (1994) investigated the impact of OCBs on objective unit performance and compared this effect with the impact of OCBs on managerial evaluations of agents. In Study 1, OCB sportsmanship behavior, OCB civic virtue behavior, and OCB helping behavior were all found to positively influence managers' evaluations of **salesperson performance**, though helping behavior had five times the impact on performance evaluations than any other form OCB.

REFERENCES:
Podsakoff, Philip M. and Scott B. MacKenzie (1994), "Organizational Citizenship Behaviors and Sales Unit Effectiveness," *JMR*, 31 (August), 351–63.

#761 *Performance (Salesperson)*

SCALE ITEMS:

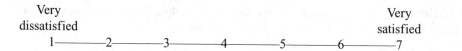

Very
dissatisfied

Very
satisfied

1————2————3————4————5————6————7

1. All things considered, this agent is outstanding.

2. This agent performs his or her job the way I like to see it performed.

3. This agent is one of the agency's most valuable assets.

SCALE NAME: Performance (Salesperson Objective Outcomes)

SCALE DESCRIPTION: Oliver and Anderson (1994) used this three-item, seven-point scale to measure the degree to which sales representatives reported that management *infrequently* used objective performance measures such as sales, market penetration, and quota achievement when evaluating sales representative performance.

SCALE ORIGIN: Oliver and Anderson (1994) indicated that the scale items were abbreviated from the extensive list provided by Jackson, Keith, and Schlacter (1983). The measure was pretested in a questionnaire administered to a convenience sample of sales representatives attending trade association functions and revised on the basis of this pretest. Oliver and Anderson (1994) indicated that, after being submitted to a factor analysis following administration to the final sample, some items were dropped, resulting in the purified measure shown here. The criterion for item exclusion was not indicated, though it was noted by the authors that none of the cross-loadings between the six behavior-control/outcome-control measures exceeded the .355 level.

SAMPLES: Oliver and Anderson (1994) surveyed managers and manufacturer's sales representatives employed by independently owned and operated sales agencies serving the electronics industry. Of the 350 randomly selected trade association member firms fitting this designation, 299 expressed interest in participating, and ultimately, **194** usable surveys from management and **347** surveys from manufacturer representatives were returned. The typical respondent was a male (92%), college graduate (64%), approximately 39 years of age, and had an average of 12 years sales experience with 5.5 years in the present job.

RELIABILITY: Oliver and Anderson (1994) reported a coefficient alpha of **.618** for this measure.

VALIDITY: Oliver and Anderson (1994) used the correlation matrix of the independent and classification variables used in the study to provide some evidence of discriminant and convergent validity. Nomological validity was also found to be present.

ADMINISTRATION: Oliver and Anderson (1994) sent managers of the 299 firms indicating interest in the study a packet containing a "manager's survey" and three similar self-administered surveys for salespeople, along with self-addressed postage paid reply envelopes. Managers were instructed to distribute one survey each to an "above-average rep," a "mid-range rep," and a "below-average rep." Each representative was promised confidentiality and the chance to win one of five $100 prizes in a random drawing. The measure was one of six scales whose scores were combined as formative indicators of the control system employed, ranging from outcome-oriented to behaviorally oriented. It appears that only responses obtained from sales representatives were used in computing this measure. Due to the reversed nature of the items, higher scores on the scale indicated that salespeople perceived management as rarely using objective outcome measures such as sales volume, market penetration, and quota achievement to evaluate their performance.

MAJOR FINDINGS: Oliver and Anderson (1994) examined how perceptions of the presence of a behavior versus outcome sales control system in the respondents' organizations influenced salespeople's performance outcomes and sales strategies, as well as their affective, cognitive, and behavioral states. The **infrequent use of objective outcomes** was significantly related to a salesperson's knowledge of the company and product, motivation to the serve the agency employer, intrinsic motivation level, organizational commitment, and acceptance of cooperation/teamwork. A salesperson's amount of planning, relative performance, performance percentile, performance on sales and profit objectives, sales presentation skills, and job satisfaction were also related to the **infrequent use of objective outcomes,** as were the use of pay as a control mechanism, the use of subjective inputs in the evaluation process, the extent of supervision, the absence of a bottom-line orientation, and supportive, bureaucratic, and innovative organizational cultures.

REFERENCES:

Jackson, Donald W., Jr., Janet E. Keith, and John L. Schlacter (1983), "Evaluation of Selling Performance: A Study of Current Practices," *Journal of Personal Selling and Sales Management*, 3 (November), 43–51.

Oliver, Richard L. and Erin Anderson (1994), "An Empirical Test of the Consequences of Behavior- and Outcome-Based Sales Control Systems," *JM*, 58 (October), 53–67.

SCALE ITEMS:*

Not at all   Quite a bit

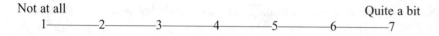

1———2———3———4———5———6———7

How heavily do you think your manager relies on these kinds of measures in evaluating your performance?

1. Sales volume. **(r)**

2. Market penetration. **(r)**

3. Achievement of quota. **(r)**

*The anchors for the response scale were not descibed in the article by Oliver and Anderson (1994) but appear to have been some sort of frequency measure similar to this.

SCALE NAME: Performance (Salesperson Paper Inputs)

SCALE DESCRIPTION: Oliver and Anderson (1994) used this three-item, seven-point scale to measure the degree to which sales representatives reported that management used paper or call-related performance measures such as sales expenses, the number of calls made, and the quality and completeness of call reports when evaluating sales representative performance.

SCALE ORIGIN: Oliver and Anderson (1994) indicated that the scale items were abbreviated from the extensive list provided by Jackson, Keith, and Schlacter (1983). The measure was pretested in a questionnaire administered to a convenience sample of sales representatives attending trade association functions and revised on the basis of this pretest. Oliver and Anderson (1994) indicated that, after being submitted to a factor analysis following administration to the final sample, some items were dropped, resulting in the purified measure shown here. The criterion for item exclusion was not indicated, though it was noted by the authors that none of the cross-loadings between the six behavior-control/outcome-control measures exceeded the .355 level.

SAMPLES: Oliver and Anderson (1994) surveyed managers and manufacturer's sales representatives employed by independently owned and operated sales agencies serving the electronics industry. Of the 350 randomly selected trade association member firms fitting this designation, 299 expressed interest in participating, and ultimately, **194** usable surveys from management and **347** surveys from manufacturer representatives were returned. The typical respondent was a male (92%), college graduate (64%), approximately 39 years of age, and had an average of 12 years sales experience with 5.5 years in the present job.

RELIABILITY: Oliver and Anderson (1994) reported a coefficient alpha of **.595** for this measure.

VALIDITY: Oliver and Anderson (1994) used the correlation matrix of the independent and classification variables used in the study to provide some evidence of discriminant and convergent validity. Nomological validity was also found to be present.

ADMINISTRATION: Oliver and Anderson (1994) sent managers of the 299 firms indicating interest in the study a packet containing a "manager's survey" and three similar self-administered surveys for salespeople, along with self-addressed postage paid reply envelopes. Managers were instructed to distribute one survey each to an "above-average rep," a "mid-range rep," and a "below-average rep." Each representative was promised confidentiality and the chance to win one of five $100 prizes in a random drawing. The measure was one of six scales whose scores were combined as formative indicators of the control system employed, ranging from outcome-oriented to behaviorally oriented. It appears that only responses obtained from sales representatives were used in computing this measure. Higher scores on the scale indicated that salespeople perceived management as using paper input measures such as the quality and completeness of the call report, sales expenses, and the number of calls made when evaluating the performance of sales representatives.

MAJOR FINDINGS: Oliver and Anderson (1994) examined how perceptions of the presence of a behavior versus outcome sales control system in the respondents' organizations influenced salespeople's performance outcomes and sales strategies, as well as their affective, cognitive, and behavioral states. The **use of paper inputs in evaluating salesperson performance** was significantly related to a salesperson's knowledge of the company and product, motivation to work harder, ability to control expenses, acceptance of performance reviews, and a bureaucratic organizational culture. A salesperson's relative performance, performance percentile, performance on sales and profit objectives, and sales presentation skills were also related to **use of paper inputs in evaluating salesperson performance,** as was the infrequent use of objective outcomes when measuring salesperson performance.

#763 *Performance (Salesperson Paper Inputs)*

COMMENTS: The low reliability of the scale suggests that further development may be necessary prior to using this measure again.

REFERENCES:

Jackson, Donald W., Jr., Janet E. Keith, and John L. Schlacter (1983), "Evaluation of Selling Performance: A Study of Current Practices," *Journal of Personal Selling and Sales Management*, 3 (November), 43–51.

Oliver, Richard L. and Erin Anderson (1994), "An Empirical Test of the Consequences of Behavior- and Outcome-Based Sales Control Systems," *JM*, 58 (October), 53–67.

SCALE ITEMS:*

Not at all   Quite a bit

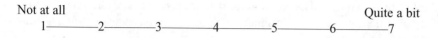

1———2———3———4———5———6———7

How heavily do you think your manager relies on these kinds of measures in evaluating your performance?

1. Number of calls. **(r)**

2. Sales expense. **(r)**

3. Quality and completeness of call reports. **(r)**

*The anchors for the response scale were not described in the article by Oliver and Anderson (1994) but appear to have been some sort of frequency measure similar to this.

SCALE NAME: Performance (Salesperson Self-Report)

SCALE DESCRIPTION: Swenson and Herche (1994) used this 31-item, seven-point scale to measure self-reports of the level of salesperson performance relative to the average salesperson in similar situations. Salesperson performance is evaluated on six dimensions related to meeting sales objectives, processing technical knowledge, providing information, controlling expenses, and delivering sales presentations.

SCALE ORIGIN: Swenson and Herche (1994) used the 31-item salesperson performance measure developed by Behrman and Perreault (1982). Behrman and Perreault (1982) originally proposed a seven-factor self-reported measure of job performance for use with salespeople. Items were generated on the basis of information found in the literature, sales text books, sales job descriptions, and performance evaluation forms. Items limited to particular industrial selling situations were eliminated, as were redundant items and those judged to be deficient or ambiguous by a panel of judges. The resulting 65-item measure hypothesized as tapping seven performance dimensions was administered to a sample of 200 salespeople and 42 sales managers. Item purification procedures yielded a 31-item measure representing five aspects of industrial sales performance. When reliabilities were calculated using the hold-out sample, each factor achieved a reliability in excess of .80.

SAMPLES: A national sample of 1800 industrial salespeople was undertaken by Swenson and Herche (1994), and **271** usable responses were obtained. The majority of respondents were married (79%) men (92%), primarily associated with the general manufacturing (25%), services (17%), transportation (14%), food processing (10%), and electronics (7%) industries.

RELIABILITY: Swenson and Herche (1994) calculated a coefficient alpha of **.89** for the measure.

VALIDITY: No specific examination of scale validity was reported Swenson and Herche (1994). However, both the concurrent and predictive validity of the measure were assessed by Behrman and Perreault (1982) and found to be satisfactory.

ADMINISTRATION: The scale was included by Swenson and Herche (1994) among other measures in a self-administered survey delivered by mail. An overall salesperson performance score was computed by summing the scores across all performance dimensions. Higher scores on the scale indicated that salespeople judged themselves as performing better, relatively speaking, when compared with the average salesperson working in similar situations.

MAJOR FINDINGS: Swenson and Herche (1994) investigated the ability of the achievement and hedonism dimensions of the list of values (LOV), a social values scale, to predict **salesperson performance**. A statistically significant positive relationship was found between the LOV achievement dimension and **salesperson performance**, which indicated that achievement dimension values were associated with higher levels of **salesperson performance**. No support was found for the hypothesized inverse relationship between the LOV hedonism dimension and **salesperson performance**. Both adaptive selling (ADAPTS) and customer orientation (SOCO) were significantly related to **salesperson performance**. Finally, the LOV social values scale was found to explain significantly more variation in **salesperson performance** than the ADAPT and SOCO measures when used alone.

REFERENCES:
Behrman, Douglas N. and William D. Perreault Jr. (1982), "Measuring the Performance of Industrial Salespersons," *Journal of Business Research*, 10 (September), 355–70.

#764 *Performance (Salesperson Self-Report)*

Swenson, Michael J. and Joel Herche (1994), "Social Values and Salesperson Performance: An Empirical Examination," *JAMS*, 22 (3), 283–89.

SCALE ITEMS:*

Needs improvement   Outstanding

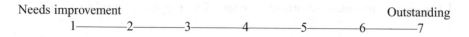

1————2————3————4————5————6————7

Sales Objectives:

1. Producing a high market share for your company in your territory.
2. Making sales of those products with the highest profit margins.
3. Generating a high level of dollar sales.
4. Quickly generating sales of new company products.
5. Identifying and selling to major accounts in your territory.
6. Producing sales or blanket contracts with long-term profitability.
7. Exceeding all sales targets and objectives for your territory during the year.

Technical Knowledge:

8. Knowing the design and specifications of company products.
9. Knowing the applications and functions of company products.
10. Being able to detect causes of operating failure of company products.
11. Acting as a special resource to other departments that need your assistance.
12. Keeping abreast of your company's production and technological developments.
13. When possible, troubleshooting system problems and conducting minor field service to correct product misapplications and/or product failures.

Providing Information:

14. Carrying out company policies, procedures, and programs for providing information.
15. Providing accurate and complete paperwork related to orders, expenses, and other routine reports.
16. Recommending on your own initiative how company operations and procedures can be improved.
17. Submitting required reports on time.
18. Maintaining company specified records that are accurate, complete, and up to date.

Controlling Expenses:

19. Operating within the budgets set by the company.
20. Using expense accounts with integrity.
21. Using business gift and promotional allowances responsibly.
22. Spending travel and lodging money carefully.
23. Arranging sales call patterns and frequency to cover your territory economically.
24. Entertaining only when it is clearly in the best interest of the company to do so.
25. Controlling costs in other areas of the company (order-processing and preparation, delivery, etc.) when taking sales orders.

Sales Presentations:

26. Listening attentively to identify and understand the real concerns of your customer.
27. Convincing customers that you understand their unique problems and concerns.
28. Using established contacts to develop new customers.
29. Communicating your sales presentation clearly and concisely.
30. Making effective use of audiovisual aids (charts, tables, and the like) to improve your sales presentation.
31. Working out solutions to a customer's questions or objections.

*Although the verbatim instructions were not provided by Swenson and Herche (1994) or Behrman and Perreault (1982), the latter indicated that respondents were asked to rate their own "current level of performance" on the previously indicated items by evaluating how well they "perform(ed) in that area compared with an average salesperson in similar selling situations."

SCALE NAME: Performance (Salesperson Self-Report)

SCALE DESCRIPTION: Babin and Boles (1996) used this seven-item, five-point Likert-type scale to assess the respondent's evaluation of his or her own work performance relative to coworkers.

SCALE ORIGIN: It appears that the scale is original to Babin and Boles (1996).

SAMPLES: Babin and Boles (1996) surveyed a convenience sample of 390 food service workers employed by full-service restaurants located in a major southern U.S. metropolitan area. A total of **261** usable responses were returned. The majority of respondents were high school graduates (99%), of whom 80% had some college education, which indicated that the majority of respondents were students.

RELIABILITY: Babin and Boles (1996) calculated a coefficient alpha of **.88** for this measure.

VALIDITY: Babin and Boles (1996) tested the measurement model using confirmatory factor analysis. Although the goodness-of-fit index of .861 was somewhat low, the observed loading estimates and construct reliabilities provided evidence of the convergent validity of the measure. An examination of the proportion of variance extracted in each construct compared with the square of the phi (ϕ) suggested that the scale possessed discriminant validity.

ADMINISTRATION: The scale was included by Babin and Boles (1996) with other measures as part of a self-administered questionnaire distributed to employees at their place of work and returned by self-addressed, postage-paid reply envelopes. Higher scores on the scale indicated that respondents perceived their performance on the job as being superior to that of their coworkers.

MAJOR FINDINGS: The influence of supervisor support and coworker involvement on the role stress, performance, and job satisfaction of food service workers was investigated by Babin and Boles (1996). Higher self-evaluations of **job performance** relative to other employees were associated with higher levels of role conflict, whereas increased levels of role ambiguity resulted in lower self-reported **performance** evaluations.

REFERENCES:
Babin, Barry J. and James S. Boles (1996), "The Effects of Perceived Co-Worker Involvement and Supervisor Support on Service Provider Role Stress, Performance and Job Satisfaction," *JR*, 72 (1), 57–75.

SCALE ITEMS:

Strongly
disagree

Strongly
agree

1————2————3————4————5

Relative to other servers here...

1. I average higher sales per check than most.

2. I am in the top 10% of the servers here.

3. I manage my work time better than most.

4. I know more about the menu items.

5. I know what my customers expect.

6. I am good at my job.

7. I get better tips than most of the others.

SCALE NAME: Performance (Salesperson Subjective Inputs)

SCALE DESCRIPTION: Oliver and Anderson (1994) used this three-item, seven-point scale to measure the degree to which sales representatives reported that management used subjective "effort-" or "attitude-"related inputs when evaluating sales representative performance.

SCALE ORIGIN: Oliver and Anderson (1994) indicated that the scale items were abbreviated from the extensive list provided by Jackson, Keith, and Schlacter (1983). The measure was pretested in a questionnaire administered to a convenience sample of sales representatives attending trade association functions and revised on the basis of this pretest. Oliver and Anderson (1994) indicated that, after being submitted to a factor analysis following administration to the final sample, some items were dropped, resulting in the purified measure shown here. The criterion for item exclusion was not indicated, though it was noted by the authors that none of the cross-loadings between the six behavior-control/outcome-control measures exceeded the .355 level.

SAMPLES: Oliver and Anderson (1994) surveyed managers and manufacturer's sales representatives employed by independently owned and operated sales agencies serving the electronics industry. Of the 350 randomly selected trade association member firms fitting this designation, 299 expressed interest in participating, and ultimately, **194** usable surveys from management and **347** surveys from manufacturer representatives were returned. The typical respondent was a male (92%), college graduate (64%), approximately 39 years of age, and had an average of 12 years sales experience with 5.5 years in the present job.

RELIABILITY: Oliver and Anderson (1994) reported a coefficient alpha of **.843** for this measure.

VALIDITY: Oliver and Anderson (1994) used the correlation matrix of the independent and classification variables used in the study to provide some evidence of discriminant and convergent validity. Nomological validity was also found to be present.

ADMINISTRATION: Oliver and Anderson (1994) sent managers of the 299 firms indicating interest in the study a packet containing a "manager's survey" and three similar self-administered surveys for salespeople, along with self-addressed postage paid reply envelopes. Managers were instructed to distribute one survey each to an "above-average rep," a "mid-range rep," and a "below-average rep." Each representative was promised confidentiality and the chance to win one of five $100 prizes in a random drawing. The measure was one of six scales whose scores were combined as formative indicators of the control system employed, ranging from outcome-oriented to behaviorally oriented. It appears that only responses obtained from sales representatives were used in computing this measure. Higher scores on the scale indicated that salespeople perceived management as making use of subjective inputs related to the salesperson's effort or attitude when evaluating sales representative performance.

MAJOR FINDINGS: Oliver and Anderson (1994) examined how perceptions of the presence of a behavior versus outcome sales control system in the respondents' organizations influenced salespeople's performance outcomes and sales strategies, as well as their affective, cognitive, and behavioral states. The **use of subjective inputs when evaluating salesperson performance** was significantly related to a salesperson's expertise, motivation to the serve the agency employer, motivation to work smarter, intrinsic and extrinsic motivation level, organizational commitment, and acceptance of three factors: cooperation/teamwork, authority/direction, and performance reviews. A salesperson's amount of planning, performance on sales and profit objectives, ability to control expenses and gather information, sales presentation skills, and job satisfaction were also related to the **use of subjective inputs when evaluating salesperson performance**. Other factors related to the **use of subjective inputs when evaluating**

salesperson performance included participative decision making, the extent of supervision, the percentage of salary in the compensation plan, the use of paper inputs in the evaluation of salespeople, the absence of a bottom-line orientation, infrequent use of objective outcomes in salesperson evaluation, and both supportive and innovative organizational cultures.

REFERENCES:

Jackson, Donald W., Jr., Janet E. Keith, and John L. Schlacter (1983), "Evaluation of Selling Performance: A Study of Current Practices," *Journal of Personal Selling and Sales Management*, 3 (November), 43–51.

Oliver, Richard L. and Erin Anderson (1994), "An Empirical Test of the Consequences of Behavior- and Outcome-Based Sales Control Systems," *JM*, 58 (October), 53–67.

SCALE ITEMS:*

Not at all   Quite a bit

How heavily do you think your manager relies on these kinds of measures in evaluating your performance?

1. Attitude.

2. Ability.

3. Effort.

*The anchors for the response scale were not described in the article by Oliver and Anderson (1994) but appear to have been some sort of frequency measure similar to this.

SCALE NAME: Performance (Supplier Demand Stimulation)

SCALE DESCRIPTION: Brown, Lusch, and Nicholson (1995) used this seven-item, seven-point scale to measure dealers' perceptions of manufacturer performance with respect to seven marketing-related services provided to dealers.

SCALE ORIGIN: It is unclear whether the scale is original to Brown, Lusch, and Nicholson (1995) was adapted from measures used in prior studies.

SAMPLES: Brown, Lusch, and Nicholson (1995) mailed a questionnaire to 1052 farm equipment dealers located in the states of Iowa, Nebraska, and Kansas. Usable responses were received from a single key informant, typically an owner or manager, for **203** of the dealerships. The sample differed from the population in general in that dealers in this sample reported having significantly higher sales of their primary brand, as well as a significantly smaller workforce.

RELIABILITY: Brown, Lusch, and Nicholson (1995) reported a coefficient alpha of **.872** for this measure.

VALIDITY: The construct validity of the scale was examined using a confirmatory factor analysis. Brown, Lusch, and Nicholson (1995) reported that the model achieved an acceptable goodness of fit and reliability only after one item, "New equipment inventory financing programs for dealers," was dropped from the measure. Examination of the standardized residuals in the final model provided evidence for the construct validity of the measure. A confirmatory factor analysis of all measures used in the study was also undertaken to assess the overall construct validity of the measures. The measurement model's goodness of fit was acceptable, and all construct reliabilities exceeded .70, with the exception of instrumental commitment (.674).

ADMINISTRATION: The scale was included with other measures as part of a self-administered survey that was delivered by mail. Brown, Lusch, and Nicholson (1995) instructed respondents to focus on their relationship with the supplier of the one brand of new farm equipment that accounted for the highest dollar sales in their dealership. Higher scores on the scale indicated that manufacturers provided greater marketing support to encourage demand stimulation for their products relative to other manufacturers in the industry.

MAJOR FINDINGS: Brown, Lusch, and Nicholson (1995) examined the impact of a supplier's use of various types of power on manufacturer and dealer performance and on the dealer's commitment to the channel relationship. Structural equation modeling was used to test the study's hypotheses. The **demand stimulation component of manufacturer performance** was one of two first-order indicators of the second-order construct of manufacturer performance. Results indicated that, when manufacturers had more power in the channel relationship, higher levels of instrumental commitment resulted in lower dealer evaluations of manufacturer performance. The negative influence of mediated power on evaluations of manufacturer performance was strongest when dealers had more power in the relationship and when power was balanced. The use of nonmediated power resulted in higher performance evaluations of manufacturers when manufacturers had more power in the relationship, and high levels of instrumental commitment negatively influenced performance evaluations. Finally, high levels of dealer performance were associated with high levels of manufacturer performance.

REFERENCES:

Brown, James R., Robert F. Lusch, and Carolyn Y. Nicholson (1995), "Power and Relationship Commitment: Their Impact on Marketing Channel Member Performance," *JR*, 71 (4), 363–92.

#767 *Performance (Supplier Demand Stimulation)*

SCALE ITEMS:*

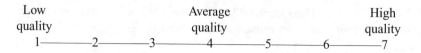

| Low quality | | Average quality | | High quality |
| 1————2————3————4————5————6————7 |

1. Product availability.

2. National advertising.

3. Dealer incentive programs, such as bonuses, contests, trips, and so forth.

4. Sales promotion materials and point-of-sale displays.

5. Customer financing programs for new equipment purchases.

6. Local and cooperative advertising.

7. Product quality.

*Although the verbatim instructions were not provided, Brown, Lusch, and Nicholson (1995) indicated that the scale anchoring implies a comparative measure between the focal manufacturer and other manufacturers in the industry.

SCALE NAME: Performance (Supplier Relationship)

SCALE DESCRIPTION: Dahlstrom, McNeilly, and Speh (1996) used this six-item, five-point scale to provide a global rating of a vendor's performance of multiple logistical duties.

SCALE ORIGIN: There is nothing to indicate that scale is anything other than original to the research reported by Dahlstrom, McNeilly, and Speh (1996). The questionnaire containing the scale was pretested by six members of the Warehouse Education and Research Council, who evaluated it for content, readability, and relevance to the industry.

SAMPLES: Using a sampling frame generated from the membership of the Warehouse Education and Research Council, Dahlstrom, McNeilly, and Speh (1996) surveyed 1000 manufacturer, retailer, and wholesaler members. No mention of the specific sampling technique used to generate the frame was provided. Firms that exclusively used in-house warehousing services were not part of the population of interest and were asked to return the survey without answering. Including unanswered surveys, 383 questionnaires were returned for a 38.3% response rate. Of these, **189** surveys contained complete data from firms using interfirm warehousing services.

RELIABILITY: Dahlstrom, McNeilly, and Speh (1996) reported a coefficient alpha of **.83** for this measure.

VALIDITY: Item-to-total correlations estimated by an exploratory factor analysis were used in the first stage of measure purification. Dahlstrom, McNeilly, and Speh (1996) submitted the remaining items to a confirmatory factor analysis. Two items, "meets agreed upon costs per unit" and "inventory accuracy," were eliminated to ensure the internal consistency of the scale. Results of the trimmed model confirmatory factor analysis provided evidence of construct validity. Discriminant validity was also assessed and found to be acceptable.

ADMINISTRATION: Dahlstrom, McNeilly, and Speh (1996) stated that the scale was part of a self-administered questionnaire that was returned by mail. Sampled individuals were contacted by telephone prior to survey delivery, and a postage-paid, return addressed reply envelope accompanied the questionnaire. A follow-up mailing with a second survey was sent two weeks after the first. Individuals using in-house warehousing services were asked not to complete the survey, but eligible respondents were instructed to answer in the context of the third-party warehouse service provider with whom they spent the greatest portion of their warehousing budget. Higher scores on the performance scale indicated a greater level of satisfaction with the services provided by the vendor.

MAJOR FINDINGS: Dahlstrom, McNeilly, and Speh (1996) investigated various antecedents to alternative forms of governance in the logistical supply market. A second topic of investigation addressed how formal controls and relational norms were employed by alternative governance forms to yield performance. Results of path analysis indicated that **performance** was enhanced by formalization and participation in both the market-based exchange and short-term unilateral agreement governance modes. Participation and flexibility increased **performance** in the bilateral alliance governance mode, whereas formalization, participation, and information exchange influenced **performance** in the long-term unilateral governance mode.

REFERENCES:
Dahlstrom, Robert, Kevin M. McNeilly, and Thomas W. Speh (1996), "Buyer–Seller Relationships in the Procurement of Logistical Services," *JAMS*, 24 (2), 110–24.

SCALE ITEMS:

A = Excellent
B = Good
C = Average
D = Poor
F = Unsatisfactory

How would you rate your current warehouse vendor on these performance issues?

1. Order processing accuracy.

2. Percentage of orders damaged.

3. Meets productivity standards.

4. Meets on-time delivery standards.

5. Responds to our customers' requests

6. Provides order status information.

SCALE NAME: Performance (Supplier Support)

SCALE DESCRIPTION: Brown, Lusch, and Nicholson (1995) used this four-item, seven-point scale to measure dealers' perceptions of manufacturer support with respect to payment for warranty work, record keeping, service representative, and sales representatives.

SCALE ORIGIN: It is unclear whether the scale is original to Brown, Lusch, and Nicholson (1995) or has been adapted from measures used in prior studies.

SAMPLES: Brown, Lusch, and Nicholson (1995) mailed a questionnaire to 1052 farm equipment dealers located in the states of Iowa, Nebraska, and Kansas. Usable responses were received from a single key informant, typically an owner or manager, for **203** of the dealerships. The sample differed from the population in general in that dealers in this sample reported having significantly higher sales of their primary brand, as well as a significantly smaller workforce.

RELIABILITY: Brown, Lusch, and Nicholson (1995) reported a coefficient alpha of **.764** for this measure.

VALIDITY: The construct validity of the scale was examined using a confirmatory factor analysis. Brown, Lusch, and Nicholson (1995) reported that the model achieved an acceptable goodness of fit and reliability only after four items were dropped from the measure. Examination of the standardized residuals in the final model provided evidence for the construct validity of the measure. A confirmatory factor analysis of all measures used in the study was also undertaken to assess the overall construct validity of the measures. The measurement model's goodness of fit was acceptable, and all construct reliabilities exceeded .70, with the exception of instrumental commitment (.674).

ADMINISTRATION: The scale was included with other measures as part of a self-administered survey that was delivered by mail. Brown, Lusch, and Nicholson (1995) instructed respondents to focus on their relationship with the supplier of the one brand of new farm equipment that accounted for the highest dollar sales in their dealership. Higher scores on the scale indicated that manufacturers were perceived as providing better support to the dealership relative to other manufacturers in the industry.

MAJOR FINDINGS: Brown, Lusch, and Nicholson (1995) examined the impact of a supplier's use of various types of power on manufacturer and dealer performance and on the dealer's commitment to the channel relationship. Structural equation modeling was used to test the study's hypotheses. The **support component of manufacturer performance** was one of two first-order indicators of the second-order construct of manufacturer performance. Results indicated that, when manufacturers had more power in the channel relationship, higher levels of instrumental commitment resulted in lower dealer evaluations of manufacturer performance. The negative influence of mediated power on evaluations of manufacturer performance was strongest when dealers had more power in the relationship and when power was balanced. The use of nonmediated power resulted in higher performance evaluations of manufacturers when manufacturers had more power in the relationship, and high levels of instrumental commitment negatively influenced performance evaluations. Finally, high levels of dealer performance were associated with high levels of manufacturer performance.

REFERENCES:
Brown, James R., Robert F. Lusch, and Carolyn Y. Nicholson (1995), "Power and Relationship Commitment: Their Impact on Marketing Channel Member Performance," *JR*, 71 (4), 363–92.

#769 *Performance (Supplier Support)*

SCALE ITEMS:*

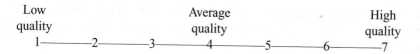

Low   Average   High
quality   quality   quality
1———2———3———4———5———6———7

1. Service representatives.

2. Office record keeping systems.

3. Prompt payment for warranty work.

4. Sales representatives.

*Although the verbatim instructions were not provided, Brown, Lusch, and Nicholson (1995) indicated that the scale anchoring implies a comparative measure between the focal manufacturer and other manufacturers in the industry.

SCALE NAME: Performance (Supplier's Logistical Services)

SCALE DESCRIPTION: Gassenheimer and Ramsey (1994) used this four-item, seven-point scale to measure dealer evaluations of the excellence of logistical support provided by a supplier with respect to such factors as meeting delivery dates and offering favorable cycle times and fill rates.

SCALE ORIGIN: The scale is original to Gassenheimer and Ramsey (1994), who generated items on the basis of a review of the literature and in-depth interviews with dealers. Details of the scale purification process were not discussed by the authors.

SAMPLES: Gassenheimer and Ramsey (1994) sampled key informants of 939 office furniture/systems dealers. The specific individual surveyed was identified as being responsible for the evaluation and selection of office furniture/systems suppliers. Of those contacted, **324** key informants returned usable responses.

RELIABILITY: Gassenheimer and Ramsey (1994) calculated separate reliabilities for data pertaining to each of three suppliers evaluated by respondents, as well as an overall reliability for the measure using the pooled data. The alphas for suppliers A, B, and C were **.85, .84,** and **.83**, respectively. A coefficient alpha of **.80** was calculated for the combined data.

VALIDITY: The items composing the logistics, sales, and product support service scales were subjected to factor analysis first using the combined data and then using data provided by each individual supplier. In each case, a three-factor solution was found in which the same items loaded consistently on their posited factor. This provided some support for the unidimensionality of the measure. Gassenheimer and Ramsey (1994) did not otherwise examine the validity of the measure.

ADMINISTRATION: Gassenheimer and Ramsey (1994) included the scale with other measures as part of a self-administered survey that was delivered by mail. Nonrespondents received a postcard reminder as well as a second survey mailing. Each dealer was asked to specify its primary (A), secondary (B), and tertiary (C) suppliers and to answer questions for each of these suppliers on an individual basis. Higher scores on the scale indicated that a dealer rated the quality of logistical service support provided by a particular supplier highly.

MAJOR FINDINGS: Gassenheimer and Ramsey (1994) examined the influence of mutual dependence and power-dependence imbalances on primary, secondary, and tertiary supplier–dealer relationships in the office systems/furniture industry. Stronger evaluations of a supplier's performance with respect to **logistical support services** strengthened dealer's satisfaction with all three types of suppliers. Evaluations of the **logistical support services** provided by primary suppliers were also found to be significantly more favorable than those of secondary and tertiary suppliers.

REFERENCES:
Gassenheimer, Jule B. and Rosemary Ramsey (1994), "The Impact of Dependence on Dealer Satisfaction: A Comparison of Reseller-Supplier Relationships," *JR*, 70 (3), 253–66.

SCALE ITEMS:* Please rate the performance of your three main office systems/furniture suppliers regarding the following on a scale of 1 (poor) to 7 (excellent):

Poor   Excellent

1———2———3———4———5———6———7

1. Manufacturer's performance in meeting promised delivery dates.

2. Length of promised order cycle (lead) times (from order submission to delivery).

3. Accuracy of manufacturer in committing to estimated shipping dates.

4. Fill rate on base/line in stock items (% of order included in initial shipment).

*Although Gassenheimer and Ramsey (1994) did not provide the verbatim instructions for this scale, their discussion indicated that they were similar to those listed here.

SCALE NAME: Performance (Supplier's Product Support)

SCALE DESCRIPTION: Gassenheimer and Ramsey (1994) used this four-item, seven-point scale to measure dealer evaluations of the excellence of product support provided by a supplier with respect to such factors as product design, breadth and continuity of line, and provision of current and updated product information.

SCALE ORIGIN: The scale is original to Gassenheimer and Ramsey (1994), who generated items on the basis of a review of the literature and in-depth interviews with dealers. Details of the scale purification process were not discussed by the authors.

SAMPLES: Gassenheimer and Ramsey (1994) sampled key informants of 939 office furniture/systems dealers. The specific individual surveyed was identified as being responsible for the evaluation and selection of office furniture/systems suppliers. Of those contacted, **324** key informants returned usable responses.

RELIABILITY: Gassenheimer and Ramsey (1994) calculated separate reliabilities for data pertaining to each of three suppliers evaluated by respondents, as well as an overall reliability for the measure using the pooled data. The alphas for suppliers A, B, and C were **.67, .62,** and **.69,** respectively. A coefficient alpha of **.70** was calculated for the combined data.

VALIDITY: The items composing the logistics, sales, and product support service scales were subjected to factor analysis first using the combined data and then using data provided by each individual supplier. In each case, a three-factor solution was found in which the same items loaded consistently on their posited factor. This provided some support for the unidimensionality of the measure. Gassenheimer and Ramsey (1994) did not otherwise examine the validity of the measure.

ADMINISTRATION: Gassenheimer and Ramsey (1994) included the scale with other measures as part of a self-administered survey that was delivered by mail. Nonrespondents received a postcard reminder as well as a second survey mailing. Each dealer was asked to specify its primary (A), secondary (B), and tertiary (C) suppliers and to answer questions for each of these suppliers on an individual basis. Higher scores on the scale indicated that a dealer rated the quality of product support services provided by a particular supplier highly.

MAJOR FINDINGS: Gassenheimer and Ramsey (1994) examined the influence of mutual dependence and power-dependence imbalances on primary, secondary, and tertiary supplier–dealer relationships in the office systems/furniture industry. Stronger evaluations of a supplier's performance with respect to **product support services** strengthened dealer's satisfaction with all three types of suppliers. Evaluations of the **product support services** provided by primary suppliers were also found to be significantly more favorable than those of secondary and tertiary suppliers, and the performance evaluations of the secondary supplier were also found to be significantly better than those of the tertiary supplier.

REFERENCES:

Gassenheimer, Jule B. and Rosemary Ramsey (1994), "The Impact of Dependence on Dealer Satisfaction: A Comparison of Reseller-Supplier Relationships," *JR*, 70 (3), 253–66.

SCALE ITEMS:*

Directions: Please rate the performance of your three main office systems/furniture suppliers regarding the following on a scale of 1 (poor) to 7 (excellent):

Poor   Excellent

1————2————3————4————5————6————7

1. Overall aesthetics and design of the product.

2. The breadth of the product offering.

3. Updated and current price data, specifications and promotion materials provided.

4. Continuity (non-obsolescence) of system products/product lines over time.

*Although Gassenheimer and Ramsey (1994) did not provide the verbatim instructions for this scale, their discussion indicated that they were similar to those listed here.

SCALE NAME: Performance (Supplier's Sales Support)

SCALE DESCRIPTION: Gassenheimer and Ramsey (1994) used this three-item, seven-point scale to measure dealer evaluations of the excellence of sales support provided by a supplier's representative with respect to such factors as availability, timeliness of response, and follow-up activities.

SCALE ORIGIN: The scale is original to Gassenheimer and Ramsey (1994), who generated items on the basis of a review of the literature and in-depth interviews with dealers. Details of the scale purification process were not discussed by the authors.

SAMPLES: Gassenheimer and Ramsey (1994) sampled key informants of 939 office furniture/systems dealers. The specific individual surveyed was identified as being responsible for the evaluation and selection of office furniture/systems suppliers. Of those contacted, **324** key informants returned usable responses.

RELIABILITY: Gassenheimer and Ramsey (1994) calculated separate reliabilities for data pertaining to each of three suppliers evaluated by respondents, as well as an overall reliability for the measure using the pooled data. The alphas for suppliers A, B, and C were **.84, .79,** and **.83**, respectively. A coefficient alpha of **.80** was calculated for the combined data.

VALIDITY: The items composing the logistics, sales, and product support service scales were subjected to factor analysis first using the combined data and then using data provided by each individual supplier. In each case, a three-factor solution was found in which the same items loaded consistently on their posited factor. This provided some support for the unidimensionality of the measure. Gassenheimer and Ramsey (1994) did not otherwise examine the validity of the measure.

ADMINISTRATION: Gassenheimer and Ramsey (1994) included the scale with other measures as part of a self-administered survey that was delivered by mail. Nonrespondents received a postcard reminder as well as a second survey mailing. Each dealer was asked to specify its primary (A), secondary (B), and tertiary (C) suppliers and to answer questions for each of these suppliers on an individual basis. Higher scores on the scale indicated that a dealer rated the quality of sales support services provided by a particular supplier highly.

MAJOR FINDINGS: Gassenheimer and Ramsey (1994) examined the influence of mutual dependence and power-dependence imbalances on primary, secondary, and tertiary supplier–dealer relationships in the office systems/furniture industry. Stronger evaluations of a supplier's performance with respect to **sales support services** strengthened dealer's satisfaction with all three types of suppliers. Evaluations of the **sales support services** provided by primary suppliers were also found to be significantly more favorable than those of secondary and tertiary suppliers, and the performance evaluations of the secondary supplier were also found to be significantly better than those of the tertiary supplier.

REFERENCES:
Gassenheimer, Jule B. and Rosemary Ramsey (1994), "The Impact of Dependence on Dealer Satisfaction: A Comparison of Reseller-Supplier Relationships," *JR*, 70 (3), 253–66.

SCALE ITEMS:*

Directions: Please rate the performance of your three main office systems/furniture suppliers regarding the following on a scale of 1 (poor) to 7 (excellent):

Poor   Excellent

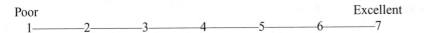

1. Availability of manufacturer sales rep to participate in customer sales calls.

2. Timely response to requests for assistance from manufacturer's sales rep.

3. After the sale follow-up by sales rep.

*Although Gassenheimer and Ramsey (1994) did not provide the verbatim instructions for this scale, their discussion indicated that they were similar to those listed here.

SCALE NAME: Performance (Wholesaler)

SCALE DESCRIPTION: Lusch and Brown (1996) used this five-item, seven-point scale to measure a wholesaler distributor's business performance with respect to efficiency and productivity. The authors referred to this as *wholesaler business performance*.

SCALE ORIGIN: There is no information to indicate that the scale is anything but original to Lusch and Brown (1996).

SAMPLES: A systematic random sample of 3225 firms was drawn by Lusch and Brown (1996) from a mailing list of all U.S. merchant wholesalers and agents/brokers in 16 four-digit standard industrial classification code groups. The sample was further reduced by eliminating firms with more than 20 employees. General managers were identified as the key informants for the remaining firms and were sent a mail questionnaire. Incentives and a follow-up mailing resulted in an initial response rate of 28.8%. However, this study reported usable data specific only to the **454** respondents classified as wholesale distributors and excluded data from agent and broker firms. Lusch and Brown (1996) indicated that the average number of suppliers reported by wholesalers in the sample was 45, with the major supplier contributing an average of 49% of the firm's annual volume.

RELIABILITY: Lusch and Brown (1996) reported a composite reliability of **.916** for this scale.

VALIDITY: Lusch and Brown (1996) reported undertaking a thorough review of the practitioner and academic literature, as well as extensive practitioner pretesting, to ensure content validity. Confirmatory factor analysis confirmed that the measure was unidimensional after one item, "liquidity," was dropped from the analysis. Convergent and discriminant validity were also assessed and found to be satisfactory, which indicated that the measure possessed adequate construct validity.

ADMINISTRATION: The scale was included as part of a self-administered mail survey. A $1 incentive and the promise of shared survey results were offered as participant incentives, and a personalized cover letter accompanied the survey packet. Undeliverable questionnaires were redirected to a replacement firm. A second mailing without monetary incentive was sent one month later. Lusch and Brown (1996) instructed respondents to answer all questions pertaining to major suppliers in the context of the supplier with which the wholesale distributor did the most business. All items were reverse scored so that higher scores on the measure indicated greater efficiency and productivity by the wholesale distributor.

MAJOR FINDINGS: Lusch and Brown (1996) investigated how the type of dependency structure—wholesaler dependent on supplier, supplier dependent on wholesaler, or bilateral dependency—influenced whether a normative or explicit contract was used. The authors also studied whether dependency structure and the type of contract influenced the performance of wholesale distributors. Findings related to the **wholesaler's performance** indicated that higher performance occurred when the supplier was dependent on the wholesale distributor. Additional findings indicated that, as the use of normative contracts to govern the wholesaler distributor and supplier relationship increased, so did the **performance** of the wholesale distributor.

REFERENCES:
Lusch, Robert F. and James R. Brown (1996), "Interdependency, Contracting, and Relational Behavior in Marketing Channels," *JM*, 60 (October), 19–38.

SCALE ITEMS:

Significantly better performance that others in the industry — Significantly worse performance

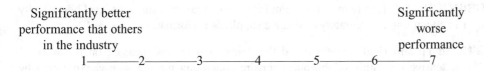

1———2———3———4———5———6———7

In regard to other distributors or agents/brokers in our industry, how would you rate your firm's performance over the last year in terms of:

1. Sales growth. **(r)**

2. Profit growth. **(r)**

3. Overall profitability. **(r)**

4. Labor productivity. **(r)**

5. Cash flow. **(r)**

SCALE NAME: Performance Ambiguity

SCALE DESCRIPTION: This four-item, seven-point Likert-type scale measures the level of difficulty faced by the buyer in attempting to accurately evaluate a supplier's performance.

SCALE ORIGIN: Stump and Heide (1996) based the items used in this measure on the work of Anderson (1985). Extensive pretesting of the questionnaire containing the measure was reported by Stump and Heide (1996).

SAMPLES: Stump and Heide (1996) drew a random sample of 1073 names from a national mailing list of chemical manufacturing firms in standard industrial classification code 28. Of this group, 631 key informants were identified by telephone who agreed to participate in the study. A total of **164** usable surveys were returned.

RELIABILITY: Stump and Heide (1996) calculated a coefficient alpha of **.67** for this measure.

VALIDITY: Stump and Heide (1996) examined item-to-total correlations of the items composing the scale and conducted an exploratory factor analysis of the measures used in the study. A confirmatory factor analysis of all items used in each scale verified the unidimensionality of the measure. Evidence of the discriminant validity of the measure was provided by means of a series of chi-square difference tests performed on the factor correlations. The model was also evaluated and found to represent a good fit to the data.

ADMINISTRATION: The scale was included by Stump and Heide (1996), with other measures, as part of a self-administered survey that was delivered by mail. Buyers were asked to identify a purchasing agreement for a particular product that had been established within the last 12 months and answer questions in the context of that purchasing agreement. Higher scores on the scale indicated that a buyer faced a greater degree of difficulty when attempting to evaluate the performance of the supplier.

MAJOR FINDINGS: Stump and Heide (1996) examined how chemical manufacturers used partner selection, incentive design, and monitoring approaches in the management and control of supplier relationships. **Performance ambiguity** was negatively associated with the desirability of both monitoring efforts and the qualification of supplier ability, in support of Stump and Heide's (1996) contention that attempting these actions under such conditions involves unnecessary transaction costs.

REFERENCES:

Anderson, Erin (1985), "The Salesperson as Outside Agent or Employee: A Transaction Cost Analysis," *Marketing Science*, 4 (3), 234–54.

Stump, Rodney L. and Jan B. Heide (1996), "Controlling Supplier Opportunism in Industrial Relationships," *JMR*, 33 (November), 431–41.

SCALE ITEMS:

Strongly   Strongly
disagree   agree

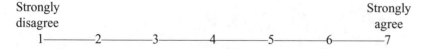

1————2————3————4————5————6————7

1. Precise standards by which to assess this supplier's performance are not readily available.

2. Evaluating this supplier's performance is a highly subjective process.

3. This supplier is performing so many different tasks that it is difficult to ascertain whether a good job is being done.

4. It is difficult to determine whether agreed upon quality standards and specifications are adhered to.

SCALE NAME: Performance Control (External)

SCALE DESCRIPTION: Germain, Dröge, and Daugherty (1994) used this four-item, seven-point scale to measure the extent to which firm performance is compared with industry leaders or against industry standards. The authors referred to this scale as *competitive performance control.*

SCALE ORIGIN: Germain, Dröge, and Daugherty (1994) stated that the scale was adapted with slight modifications from Khandwalla's (1974) study.

SAMPLES: Germain, Dröge, and Daugherty (1994) randomly selected 1000 names from a sampling frame of 3280 members of the Council of Logistics Management. Of the 956 surveys delivered, **183** usable surveys were returned. The majority of respondents were directors (54.7%) or managers (27.4%) within their respective firms. The manufacturing firms represented tended to be large and covered a wide range of industries; average annual sales were $1.98 billion, and the mean number of employees across the sample firms was 9740.

RELIABILITY: Germain, Dröge, and Daugherty (1994) reported a coefficient alpha of **.86** for the scale.

VALIDITY: Germain, Dröge, and Daugherty (1994) reported that a principal components factor analysis was used to assess the unidimensionality of the measure. The items loaded on a single factor with an eigenvalue greater than 1.

ADMINISTRATION: Germain, Dröge, and Daugherty (1994) stated that the scale was included with other measures in a self-administered survey that was delivered to respondents by mail. Nonrespondents were sent a second questionnaire in two weeks and were reminded by telephone two weeks after the second mailing. Higher scores on the scale indicated that an organization was more likely to benchmark its performance against industry leaders or other industry standards.

MAJOR FINDINGS: Germain, Dröge, and Daugherty (1994) proposed and tested a model linking environmental uncertainty, just-in-time (JIT) selling, and dimensions of organizational structure. The **external (competitive) performance control** scale was one of two measures summed to form an overall measure of **performance control**. Both environmental uncertainty and JIT selling practices were found to positively predict **performance controls**.

REFERENCES:
Germain, Richard, Cornelia Dröge, and Patricia J. Daugherty (1994), "The Effect of Just-in-Time Selling on Organizational Structure: An Empirical Investigation," *JMR*, 31 (November), 471–83.
Khandwalla, Pradip (1974), "Mass Output Orientation of Operations Technology and Organizational Structure," *Administrative Science Quarterly*, 19 (March), 74–97.

SCALE ITEMS:
Indicate the extent to which performance is compared with industry standards or competitors on:

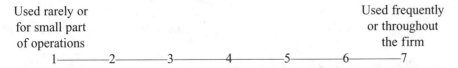

Used rarely or   Used frequently
for small part   or throughout
of operations   the firm
1————2————3————4————5————6————7

1. Functional costs (e.g., transportation, manufacturing, selling).

2. Customer service (e.g., fill rate, cycle time, on-time delivery).

3. Productivity levels.

4. Operations (e.g., warehousing, manufacturing, transportation).

SCALE NAME: Performance Control (Internal)

SCALE DESCRIPTION: Germain, Dröge, and Daugherty (1994) used this five-item, seven-point scale to measure the extent to which firm performance was measured internally using functional cost, variance analysis, customer satisfaction, customer service, and productivity analysis.

SCALE ORIGIN: Germain, Dröge, and Daugherty (1994) stated the scale was adapted with slight modifications from Khandwalla's (1974) study.

SAMPLES: Germain, Dröge, and Daugherty (1994) randomly selected 1000 names from a sampling frame of 3280 members of the Council of Logistics Management. Of the 956 surveys delivered, **183** usable surveys were returned. The majority of respondents were directors (54.7%) or managers (27.4%) within their respective firms. The manufacturing firms represented tended to be large and covered a wide range of industries; average annual sales were $1.98 billion, and the mean number of employees across the sample firms was 9740.

RELIABILITY: Germain, Dröge, and Daugherty (1994) reported a coefficient alpha of **.78** for the scale.

VALIDITY: Germain, Dröge, and Daugherty (1994) reported that a principal components factor analysis was used to assess the unidimensionality of the measure. The items loaded on a single factor with an eigenvalue greater than 1.

ADMINISTRATION: Germain, Dröge, and Daugherty (1994) stated that the scale was included with other measures in a self-administered survey that was delivered to respondents by mail. Nonrespondents were sent a second questionnaire in two weeks and were reminded by telephone two weeks after the second mailing. Higher scores on the scale indicated that an organization was more likely to benchmark its performance against industry leaders or other standards.

MAJOR FINDINGS: Germain, Dröge, and Daugherty (1994) proposed and tested a model linking environmental uncertainty, just-in-time (JIT) selling, and dimensions of organizational structure. The **internal performance control** scale was one of two measures summed to form an overall measure of **performance control**. Both environmental uncertainty and JIT selling practices were found to positively predict **performance controls**.

REFERENCES:

Germain, Richard, Cornelia Dröge, and Patricia J. Daugherty (1994), "The Effect of Just-in-Time Selling on Organizational Structure: An Empirical Investigation," *JMR*, 31 (November), 471–83.

Khandwalla, Pradip (1974), "Mass Output Orientation of Operations Technology and Organizational Structure," *Administrative Science Quarterly*, 19 (March), 74–97.

SCALE ITEMS:

Indicate the extent to which performance is monitored on:

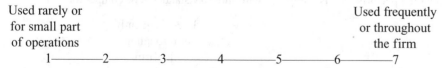

| Used rarely or for small part of operations | | | | | | Used frequently or throughout the firm |
| 1 | 2 | 3 | 4 | 5 | 6 | 7 |

1. Functional costs (e.g., selling, transportation, manufacturing).

2. Customer service (e.g., fill rate, cycle time).

3. Cost controls by fixing standard costs and analyzing variation.

4. Productivity analysis.

5. Customer satisfaction and follow-up.

SCALE NAME: Performance Documentation

SCALE DESCRIPTION: Four five-point Likert-type items measuring the degree to which an employee perceives that available forms of assessment in an organization can document his or her performance.

SCALE ORIGIN: Ramaswami (1996) cited Jaworski and MacInnis (1989) as the source of the scale.

SAMPLES: A national sample of marketing managers was drawn randomly by Jaworski and MacInnis (1989) from the American Marketing Association's (AMA) list of members. Of the 479 managers who were to have received questionnaires, **379** returned usable forms.

Ramaswami (1996) received usable surveys from **318** of the 1159 AMA members who were randomly selected from the AMA's membership list.

RELIABILITY: Coefficient alphas of **.76** on the two-item version and **.85** for the four-item version were reported for the scale by Jaworski and MacInnis (1989) and Ramaswami (1996), respectively.

VALIDITY: The validity of the scale was not specifically examined by Jaworski and MacInnis (1989). Ramaswami (1996) used confirmatory factor analysis to assess the unidimensionality of the measure in conjunction with the procedural knowledge and found that each scale tapped distinct dimensions of the task context.

ADMINISTRATION: Jaworski and MacInnis (1989) and Ramaswami (1996) indicated that the scale was self-administered, along with many other measures, in a mail survey format. Higher scores on the scale indicated that employees strongly believed that present documentation could be used to evaluate their work, whereas lower scores suggested that they thought their work could not be adequately assessed with present documentation.

MAJOR FINDINGS: Among the many purposes of the study by Jaworski and MacInnis (1989) was to examine the simultaneous use of several types of managerial controls in the context of marketing management. Using structural equations, the authors found that **performance documentation** had a significant positive impact on the use of output, professional, and control.

Ramaswami (1996) investigated both traditional and contingency theories of negative employee responses to marketing control systems. In his study, **performance documentation** was not found to alter the relationship between dysfunctional employee behavior and either output or process control.

REFERENCES:
Jaworski, Bernard J. and Deborah J. MacInnis (1989), "Marketing Jobs and Management Controls: Toward a Framework," *JMR*, 26 (November), 406–19.
Ramaswami, Sridhar N. (1996), "Marketing Controls and Dysfunctional Employee Behaviors: A Test of Traditional and Contingency Theory Postulates," *JM*, 60 (April), 105–20.

SCALE ITEMS:*

Strongly disagree	Disagree	Neutral	Agree	Strongly agree
1	2	3	4	5

1. Documents exist to measure my performance after activities are complete.

2. My performance can be adequately assessed using existing documents.

3. Documents exist to assess my performance on most of my activities.

4. Information about how my performance will be evaluated has been directly communicated to me.

*Ramaswami (1996) altered item 2 slightly to read, "The documents that exist can adequately assess my performance."

SCALE NAME: Person–Organization Fit

SCALE DESCRIPTION: Netemeyer and colleagues (1997) used this four-item, five-point Likert-type scale to measure employee self-reports of the level of fit between their personal values and their organization's values.

SCALE ORIGIN: The scale is original to Netemeyer and colleagues (1997). Details of the scale development process were not reported.

SAMPLES: In their first study, Netemeyer and colleagues (1997) used a convenience sample of 115 salespeople employed by a cellular telephone company in the southeastern United States, and **91** usable responses were obtained for a 79% response rate. The median age of respondents was 29 years, and their average amount of time with the organization was 1.89 years. The majority of respondents were women (56%) and college educated (57%). In the second study, the authors sampled 700 real estate salespeople living in a large southeastern city, and **182** usable surveys were received for an effective response rate of 26%. The median age of respondents in the second study was 48 years, and their average amount of time with the organization was 8.41 years. The majority were women (78%) and college educated (60.5%).

RELIABILITY: Netemeyer and colleagues (1997) reported coefficient alphas of **.88** for Study 1 and **.85** for Study 2.

VALIDITY: Netemeyer and colleagues (1997) examined the discriminant and construct validity of the scale using confirmatory factor analysis for both Study 1 and Study 2 data. The average variance extracted by the measure in each study was well below the .50 cut-off level suggested by Fornell and Larcker (1981), thereby providing evidence of construct validity. The square of parameter estimates between pairs of constructs was less than the average variance extracted estimates for the paired constructs across all possible construct pairings in both studies, thereby providing evidence of the discriminant validity of the measure.

ADMINISTRATION: Netemeyer and colleagues (1997) indicated that the scale was included as part of a self-administered mail survey in both studies. Study 2 participants were assured of the confidentiality and anonymity of their responses. Higher scores on the scale indicated that salespeople reported a better fit between their personal values regarding honesty, concern for others, and fairness and the values held by the organization.

MAJOR FINDINGS: Netemeyer and colleagues (1997) proposed and tested a model of potential predictors of organizational citizenship behavior (OCB) and job satisfaction using data from two separate studies conducted in a sales setting. Both samples demonstrated support for the role of job satisfaction as a predictor of OCB in the original models, which were tested using LISREL VII. However, **person–organization fit** was found to be a predictor of job satisfaction in both studies, and when this variable was added to the model, the job satisfaction to OCB path became nonsignificant in Study 1.

REFERENCES:
Fornell, Claes and David F. Larcker (1981), "Evaluating Structural Equation Models with Unobservable Variables and Measurement Error," *JMR*, 28 (February), 39–50.

Netemeyer, Richard G., James S. Boles, Daryl O. McKee, and Robert McMurrian (1997), "An Investigation Into the Antecedents of Organizational Citizenship Behaviors in a Personal Selling Context," *JM,* 61 (July), 85–98.

SCALE ITEMS:

Strongly   Strongly
disagree   agree
  1————————2————————3————————4————————5

1. I feel that my personal values are a good fit with this organization.

2. This organization has the same values as I do with regard to concern for others.

3. This organization has the same values as I do with regard to honesty.

4. This organization has the same values as I do with regard to fairness.

SCALE NAME: Physical Distribution Service Quality (Availability)

SCALE DESCRIPTION: This five-item, seven-point Likert-type scale focuses on the availability dimension of physical distribution service quality (PDSQ) and seeks to assess the degree to which a purchasing manager believes that suppliers *should* generally maintain adequate levels of product inventory nearby. With different instructions, the slightly modified items can be used to assess the *actual* performance of a particular supplier with respect to this distribution service quality dimension.

SCALE ORIGIN: The availability subscale is one of three measures composing the overall PDSQ instrument that was developed by Bienstock, Mentzer, and Bird (1997) for use with industrial customers. Items for the PDSQ instrument were initially generated through a review of the literature and interviews with purchasing managers. The resulting 45 items were rephrased on the basis of input received from a panel of five academic researchers, then pretested with 33 purchasing managers. An analysis of item-to-total correlations was combined with a qualitative assessment of item face and content validity in purifying the measure. The purified 35-item instrument was administered to the final sample and further refined on the basis of both an examination of item-to-total correlations and an exploratory factor analysis. The three PDSQ subscales were then evaluated for unidimensionality using LISREL 8.12. The authors reported that three items were deleted on the basis of the magnitude of standardized residuals, modification indices, and improvements in the model fit indexes. The final 15-item PDSQ instrument is comprised of a 6-item timeliness subscale, a 5-item availability subscale, and a 4-item condition subscale.

SAMPLES: A random sample of 797 members of the National Association of Purchasing Managers was undertaken by Bienstock, Mentzer, and Bird (1997). Four hundred forty-six usable responses were obtained, which were split into two separate groups. Group 1 contained data from **201** respondents and was used to further refine the PDSQ subscales. The **245** responses in the second group were used to verify the unidimensionality and reliability of the PDSQ measures and to test for the convergent, discriminant, and predictive validity of the PDSQ instrument.

RELIABILITY: Bienstock, Mentzer, and Bird (1997) reported a coefficient alpha of **.83** for the final measure when used to assess purchasing managers' expectations of PDSQ and **.89** when used to evaluate a supplier's actual PDSQ performance.

VALIDITY: Bienstock, Mentzer, and Bird (1997) verified the unidimensionality of the PDSQ subscales, as well as their predictive validity, by estimating a LISREL model using data from Group 2. The model fit was satisfactory. The convergent and discriminant validity of the PDSQ subscales was also successfully demonstrated through confirmatory factor analyses.

ADMINISTRATION: The scale was included with other measures as part of a self-administered survey that was delivered by mail. One follow-up mailing containing a second questionnaire was delivered to nonrespondents. The authors created three versions of the questionnaire that alternately instructed respondents to focus on the primary, secondary, or tertiary most often used supplier of their most often purchased product in answering the questionnaire. Higher scores on the expectation scale indicated that respondents strongly believed that a supplier should maintain adequate levels of product inventory nearby. Higher scores on the performance scale indicated that a particular supplier's performance had been evaluated favorably with respect to these same factors.

MAJOR FINDINGS: The purpose of Bienstock, Mentzer, and Bird's (1997) study was to develop a valid and reliable scale for measuring industrial customer's perceptions of the PDSQ they received from suppliers. Scale development followed standard psychometric procedures, and extensive pretesting and item purification procedures were undertaken throughout the scale development process. The resulting 15-item PDSQ instrument contained subscales measuring the timeliness, **availability**, and condition dimensions of PDSQ. Each subscale exhibited acceptable reliability and unidimensionality, and strong evidence of the predictive, convergent, and discriminant validity for the instrument as a whole was also found.

REFERENCES:

Bienstock, Carol C., John T. Mentzer, and Monroe Murphy Bird (1997), "Measuring Physical Distribution Service Quality," *JAMS*, 25 (1), 31–44.

SCALE ITEMS:

Strongly disagree

Strongly agree

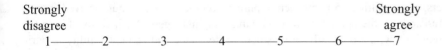

1————2————3————4————5————6————7

Expectations:
Directions: Circle a number to the right of each feature of physical distribution service, indicating whether you think suppliers in general should offer the feature; that is, whether you feel it is reasonable to expect a supplier to offer the feature.

1. Orders should be available in inventory when ordered.

2. Suppliers should have inventory available near my facility.

3. If suppliers are notified of possible increases in upcoming orders, they should maintain extra inventory.

4. Products ordered should be available in inventory.

5. Products should consistently be available in inventory.

*Perceived Performance:**
Directions: This question concerns the physical distribution service performance of a specific supplier. For this question, please think about your [primary, secondary, and third] most often used supplier for the product you most often purchase and indicate the extent to which you agree of disagree that the performance you receive from this supplier possess each feature below.

1. Orders are available in inventory when ordered.

2. This supplier has inventory available near my facility.

3. If this supplier is notified of possible increases in upcoming orders, extra inventory is maintained.

4. Products ordered are available in inventory.

5. Products are consistently available in inventory.

*Three versions of the survey instructed respondents to choose their primary, secondary, or tertiary most often used supplier in answering the questionnaire. The bracketed text was modified to reflect the correct designation for that survey version.

SCALE NAME: Physical Distribution Service Quality (Condition)

SCALE DESCRIPTION: This four-item, seven-point Likert-type scale focuses on the availability dimension of physical distribution service quality (PDSQ) and seeks to assess the degree to which a purchasing manager believes that suppliers *should* generally deliver products that are undamaged and conveniently packaged. With different instructions, the slightly modified items can be used to assess the *actual* performance of a particular supplier with respect to this distribution service quality dimension.

SCALE ORIGIN: The availability subscale is one of three measures composing the overall PDSQ instrument that was developed by Bienstock, Mentzer, and Bird (1997) for use with industrial customers. Items for the PDSQ instrument were initially generated through a review of the literature and interviews with purchasing managers. The resulting 45 items were rephrased on the basis of input received from a panel of five academic researchers, then pretested with 33 purchasing managers. An analysis of item-to-total correlations was combined with a qualitative assessment of item face and content validity in purifying the measure. The purified 35-item instrument was administered to the final sample and further refined on the basis of both an examination of item-to-total correlations and an exploratory factor analysis. The three PDSQ subscales were then evaluated for unidimensionality using LISREL 8.12. The authors reported that three items were deleted on the basis of the magnitude of standardized residuals, modification indices, and improvements in the model fit indexes. The final 15-item PDSQ instrument is comprised of a 6-item timeliness subscale, a 5-item availability subscale, and a 4-item condition subscale.

SAMPLES: A random sample of 797 members of the National Association of Purchasing Managers was undertaken by Bienstock, Mentzer, and Bird (1997). Four hundred forty-six usable responses were obtained, which were split into two separate groups. Group 1 contained data from **201** respondents and was used to further refine the PDSQ subscales. The **245** responses in the second group were used to verify the unidimensionality and reliability of the PDSQ measures and to test for the convergent, discriminant, and predictive validity of the PDSQ instrument.

RELIABILITY: Bienstock, Mentzer, and Bird (1997) reported a coefficient alpha of **.83** for the final measure when used to assess purchasing manager's expectations of PDSQ and **.87** when used to evaluate a supplier's actual PDSQ performance.

VALIDITY: Bienstock, Mentzer, and Bird (1997) verified the unidimensionality of the PDSQ subscales, as well as their predictive validity, by estimating a LISREL model using data from Group 2. The model fit was satisfactory. The convergent and discriminant validity of the PDSQ subscales was also successfully demonstrated through confirmatory factor analyses.

ADMINISTRATION: The scale was included with other measures as part of a self-administered survey that was delivered by mail. One follow-up mailing containing a second questionnaire was delivered to nonrespondents. The authors created three versions of the questionnaire that alternately instructed respondents to focus on the primary, secondary, or tertiary most often used supplier of their most often purchased product in answering the questionnaire. Higher scores on the expectation scale indicated that respondents strongly believed that a supplier should conveniently package orders and deliver them undamaged. Higher scores on the performance scale indicated that a particular supplier's performance had been evaluated favorably with respect to these same factors.

MAJOR FINDINGS: The purpose of Bienstock, Mentzer, and Bird's (1997) study was to develop a valid and reliable scale for measuring industrial customers' perceptions of the PDSQ they received from suppliers. Scale development followed standard psychometric procedures, and extensive pretesting and item purification procedures were undertaken throughout the scale development process. The resulting 15-item PDSQ instrument contained subscales measuring the timeliness, availability, and **condition** dimensions of PDSQ. Each subscale exhibited acceptable reliability and unidimensionality, and strong evidence of the predictive, convergent, and discriminant validity for the instrument as a whole was also found.

REFERENCES:

Bienstock, Carol C., John T. Mentzer, and Monroe Murphy Bird (1997), "Measuring Physical Distribution Service Quality," *JAMS*, 25 (1), 31–44.

SCALE ITEMS:

Expectations:
Directions: Circle a number to the right of each feature of physical distribution service, indicating whether you think suppliers in general should offer the feature; that is, whether you feel it is reasonable to expect a supplier to offer the feature.

1. All orders should be delivered undamaged.

2. All orders should be accurate (i.e., items ordered should arrive, not unordered items).

3. All products should be delivered undamaged.

4. Orders should be packaged conveniently.

*Perceived Performance:**
Directions: This question concerns the physical distribution service performance of a specific supplier. For this question, please think about your [primary, secondary, and third] most often used supplier for the product you most often purchase and indicate the extent to which you agree of disagree that the performance you receive from this supplier possess each feature below.

1. All orders are delivered undamaged.

2. All orders are accurate (i.e., items ordered arrive, not unordered items).

3. All products are delivered undamaged.

4. Orders are packaged conveniently.

*Three versions of the survey instructed respondents to choose their primary, secondary, or tertiary most often used supplier in answering the questionnaire. The bracketed text was modified to reflect the correct designation for that survey version.

SCALE NAME: Physical Distribution Service Quality (Timeliness)

SCALE DESCRIPTION: This six-item, seven-point Likert-type scale focuses on the timeliness dimension of physical distribution service quality (PDSQ) and seeks to assess the degree to which a purchasing manager believes that suppliers *should* generally offer short, consistent times between order placement, fulfillment, and delivery. With different instructions, slightly modified items can be used to assess the *actual* performance of a particular supplier with respect to this distribution service quality dimension.

SCALE ORIGIN: The timeliness subscale is one of three measures composing the overall PDSQ instrument that was developed by Bienstock, Mentzer, and Bird (1997) for use with industrial customers. Items for the PDSQ instrument were initially generated through a review of the literature and interviews with purchasing managers. The resulting 45 items were rephrased on the basis of input received from a panel of five academic researchers, then pretested with 33 purchasing managers. An analysis of item-to-total correlations was combined with a qualitative assessment of item face and content validity in purifying the measure. The purified 35-item instrument was administered to the final sample and further refined on the basis of both an examination of item-to-total correlations and an exploratory factor analysis. The three PDSQ subscales were then evaluated for unidimensionality using LISREL 8.12. The authors reported that three items were deleted on the basis of the magnitude of standardized residuals, modification indices, and improvements in the model fit indexes. The final 15-item PDSQ instrument is comprised of a 6-item timeliness subscale, a 5-item availability subscale, and a 4-item condition subscale.

SAMPLES: A random sample of 797 members of the National Association of Purchasing Managers was undertaken by Bienstock, Mentzer, and Bird (1997). Four hundred forty-six usable responses were obtained, which were split into two separate groups. Group 1 contained data from **201** respondents and was used to further refine the PDSQ subscales. The **245** responses in the second group were used to verify the unidimensionality and reliability of the PDSQ measures and to test for the convergent, discriminant, and predictive validity of the PDSQ instrument.

RELIABILITY: Bienstock, Mentzer, and Bird (1997) report a coefficient alpha of **.88** for the final measure when used to assess purchasing manager's expectations of PDSQ and **.93** when used to evaluate a supplier's actual PDSQ performance.

VALIDITY: Bienstock, Mentzer, and Bird (1997) verified the unidimensionality of the PDSQ subscales, as well as their predictive validity, by estimating a LISREL model using data from Group 2 The model fit was satisfactory. The convergent and discriminant validity of the PDSQ subscales was also successfully demonstrated through confirmatory factor analyses.

ADMINISTRATION: The scale was included with other measures as part of a self-administered survey that was delivered by mail. One follow-up mailing containing a second questionnaire was delivered to nonrespondents. The authors created three versions of the questionnaire that alternately instructed respondents to focus on the primary, secondary, or tertiary most often used supplier of their most often purchased product in answering the questionnaire. Higher scores on the expectation scale indicated that respondents strongly believed that a supplier should offer short, consistent times between order placement, fulfillment, and delivery. Higher scores on the performance scale indicated that a particular supplier's performance had been evaluated favorably with respect to these same factors.

MAJOR FINDINGS: The purpose of Bienstock, Mentzer, and Bird's (1997) study was to develop a valid and reliable scale for measuring industrial customers' perceptions of the PDSQ they received from suppliers. Scale development followed standard psychometric procedures, and extensive pretesting and item purification procedures were undertaken throughout the scale development process. The resulting 15-item PDSQ instrument contained subscales measuring the **timeliness**, availability, and condition dimensions of

PDSQ. Each subscale exhibited acceptable reliability and unidimensionality, and strong evidence of the predictive, convergent, and discriminant validity for the instrument as a whole was also found.

REFERENCES:

Bienstock, Carol C., John T. Mentzer, and Monroe Murphy Bird (1997), "Measuring Physical Distribution Service Quality," *JAMS*, 25 (1), 31–44.

SCALE ITEMS:

Strongly   Strongly
disagree   agree

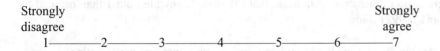

1———2———3———4———5———6———7

Expectations:
Directions: Circle a number to the right of each feature of physical distribution service, indicating whether you think suppliers in general should offer the feature; that is, whether you feel it is reasonable to expect a supplier to offer the feature.

1. The time between placing and receiving an order should be short.

2. Delivery should be rapid.

3. The time between placing and receiving an order should be consistent.

4. The time it takes my supplier to put my order together should be consistent.

5. The time between my supplier receiving and shipping my order should be short.

6. The time it takes my supplier to put my order together should be short.

Perceived Performance: *
Directions: This question concerns the physical distribution service performance of a specific supplier. For this question, please think about your [primary, secondary, and third] most often used supplier for the product you most often purchase and indicate the extent to which you agree of disagree that the performance you receive from this supplier possess each feature below.

1. The time between placing and receiving an order is short.

2. Delivery is rapid.

3. The time between placing and receiving an order is consistent.

4. The time it takes my supplier to put my order together is consistent.

5. The time between my supplier receiving and shipping my order is short.

6. The time it takes my supplier to put my order together is short.

*Three versions of the survey instructed respondents to choose their primary, secondary, or tertiary most often used supplier in answering the questionnaire. The bracketed text was modified to reflect the correct designation for that survey version.

SCALE NAME: Planning (Account)

SCALE DESCRIPTION: In a longitudinal study, Brown, Cron, and Slocum (1997) used this three-item, five-point Likert-type scale to measure both the degree to which salespeople anticipated planning account management activities related to the promotion *(anticipated account planning)* and the degree to which salespeople reported actually planning promotion-related account management activities *(actual account planning)*.

SCALE ORIGIN: There is no information to indicate that the scale is anything other than original to Brown, Cron, and Slocum's (1997) study.

SAMPLES: Sales representatives of a medical supplies distributorship that was participating in a specific promotion were sampled for this study. Brown, Cron, and Slocum (1997) attempted to sample the entire sales force at two points in time, and **122** of the 141-member sales force returned usable responses to both questionnaires. The average sales goal reported by salespeople for the specific unit on promotion was 3.2 units, though the actual average units sold was 2.5 units. Of the salespeople, 25% met their goal exactly, 52% did not, and 23% exceeded their sales goal.

RELIABILITY: Brown, Cron, and Slocum (1997) reported a coefficient alpha of **.77** for the anticipatory territory planning scale and **.84** for the actual territory planning scale.

VALIDITY: No specific examination of scale validity was reported by Brown, Cron, and Slocum (1997).

ADMINISTRATION: Brown, Cron, and Slocum (1997) distributed the first questionnaire during a sales meeting in which the focal promotion was introduced and explained. The anticipatory planning scales were included in this questionnaire with other measures. Although it is not clear how the second questionnaire was distributed, it appears to have been self-administered also. Salespeople received this questionnaire, containing the actual planning scales and other measures, following the conclusion of the promotion. Higher scores on the anticipatory and actual scales, respectively, indicated that salespeople *anticipated* engaging in more account planning activities related to the promotion and that they *actually engaged* in more account planning activities related to the promotion.

MAJOR FINDINGS: Brown, Cron, and Slocum (1997) investigated the effect of goal-directed positive and negative emotions on salesperson volition, behavior, and performance. **Anticipated account planning** was one of three first-order factors representing the higher-order volition construct in the model tested. Similarly, goal-directed behaviors was a higher-order construct represented by actual account territory planning activities and two other constructs. Both positive and negative anticipatory emotions were positively related to a salesperson's anticipated planning of effort and strategies (volition), and volitions were in turn strongly and positively related to goal-directed behaviors. Finally, goal-directed behaviors were positively associated with the degree of goal attainment.

REFERENCES:
Brown, Steven P., William L. Cron, and John W. Slocum Jr. (1997), "Effects of Goal-Directed Emotions on Salesperson Volitions, Behavior, and Performance: A Longitudinal Study," *JM*, 61 (January), 39–50.

SCALE ITEMS: *

Strongly   Strongly
disagree   agree
  1————————2————————3————————4————————5

1. I will target specific accounts for this promotion.

2. I am careful to work my highest priority accounts first.

3. I will target particular customers for this promotion.

*Brown, Cron, and Slocum (1997) stated that the same items were used to measure both volitions and actual goal-directed behaviors. It is possible, however, that these items were slightly rephrased into the past tense when used to measure actual behaviors.

SCALE NAME: Planning (Territory)

SCALE DESCRIPTION: In a longitudinal study, Brown, Cron, and Slocum (1997) used this five-item, five-point Likert-type scale to measure both the degree to which salespeople anticipated planning territory management activities related to the promotion *(anticipated territory planning)* and the degree to which salespeople reported actually planning promotion-related territory management activities *(actual territory planning)*.

SCALE ORIGIN: There is no information to indicate that the scale is anything other than original to Brown, Cron, and Slocum's (1997) study.

SAMPLES: Sales representatives of a medical supplies distributorship that was participating in a specific promotion were sampled for this study. Brown, Cron, and Slocum (1997) attempted to sample the entire sales force at two points in time, and **122** of the 141-member sales force returned usable responses to both questionnaires. The average sales goal reported by salespeople for the specific unit on promotion was 3.2 units, though the actual average units sold was 2.5 units. Of the salespeople, 25% met their goal exactly, 52% did not, and 23% exceeded their sales goal.

RELIABILITY: Brown, Cron, and Slocum (1997) reported a coefficient alpha of **.80** for the anticipatory territory planning scale and **.93** for the actual territory planning scale.

VALIDITY: No specific examination of scale validity was reported by Brown, Cron, and Slocum (1997).

ADMINISTRATION: Brown, Cron, and Slocum (1997) distributed the first questionnaire during a sales meeting in which the focal promotion was introduced and explained. The anticipatory planning scales were included in this questionnaire with other measures. Although it is not clear how the second questionnaire was distributed, it appears to have been self-administered also. Salespeople received this questionnaire, containing the actual planning scales and other measures, following the conclusion of the promotion. Higher scores on the anticipatory and actual scales, respectively, indicated that salespeople *anticipated* engaging in more territory planning activities related to the promotion and that they *actually engaged* in more territory planning activities related to the promotion.

MAJOR FINDINGS: Brown, Cron, and Slocum (1997) investigated the effect of goal-directed positive and negative emotions on salesperson volition, behavior, and performance. **Anticipated territory planning** was one of three first-order factors representing the higher-order volition construct in the model tested. Similarly, goal-directed behaviors was a higher-order construct represented by **actual account territory planning** activities and two other constructs. Both positive and negative anticipatory emotions were positively related to a salesperson's anticipated planning of effort and strategies (volition), and volitions were in turn strongly and positively related to goal-directed behaviors. Finally, goal-directed behaviors were positively associated with the degree of goal attainment.

REFERENCES:

Brown, Steven P., William L. Cron, and John W. Slocum Jr. (1997), "Effects of Goal-Directed Emotions on Salesperson Volitions, Behavior, and Performance: A Longitudinal Study," *JM*, 61 (January), 39–50.

SCALE ITEMS:*

Strongly   Strongly
disagree   agree

1————2————3————4————5

1. I will spend a good deal of time thinking about my selling strategy for this promotion.

2. I will develop a plan for how much time to spend on this promotion.

3. I will list the steps necessary for reaching my goal.

4. I will think about strategies I can fall back on if problems arise during this promotion.

5. Each week I will make a plan for what I need to accomplish regarding this promotion.

*Brown, Cron, and Slocum (1997) stated that the same items were used to measure both volitions and actual goal-directed behaviors. It is possible, however, that these items were slightly rephrased into the past tense when used to measure actual behaviors.

SCALE NAME: Planning for the Sale

SCALE DESCRIPTION: Sujan, Weitz, and Kumar (1994) used this twelve-item, seven-point scale to measure the importance placed by salespeople on planning, the extent to which salespeople developed plans, and the energy devoted to the planning process.

SCALE ORIGIN: Sujan, Weitz, and Kumar (1994) stated that the scale was adapted from Earley, Wojnaroski, and Prest (1987) and expanded to 12 items.

SAMPLES: Sujan, Weitz, and Kumar (1994) surveyed a convenience sample of salespeople employed by eight firms representing diverse industries. Two hundred seventeen questionnaires were distributed by sales managers to members of their selling force, and **190** usable responses were obtained for an 87.5% response rate. On average, respondents were 35 years of age, had 9 years sales experience, and made 3.5 calls per day. The majority were men (78%).

RELIABILITY: Sujan, Weitz, and Kumar (1994) reported a coefficient alpha of **.82** for the measure.

VALIDITY: Sujan, Weitz, and Kumar (1994) provided extensive information on the assessment of scale validity. Measures used in their study were evaluated using confirmatory factor analysis. The authors stated that the results of this analysis supported the unidimensionality and reliability of the measure and provided evidence of convergent and discriminant validity.

ADMINISTRATION: Sujan, Weitz, and Kumar (1994) included a cover letter promising confidentiality and a self-addressed, stamped reply envelope in the survey packet distributed by sales managers to members of the sales force. Respondents were instructed to return the questionnaire directly to the researchers rather than to their superiors. Higher scores on the scale indicated that salespeople placed greater importance on planning, developed plans to a greater extent, and devoted more energy to the planning process.

MAJOR FINDINGS: Sujan, Weitz, and Kumar (1994) investigated the influence of goal orientations on work behavior. **Planning the sale** was one of three dimensions used to represent the broader "working smart" construct. Results indicated that a learning orientation motivated salespeople to work smart and that working smart increased salespeople's performance. A performance orientation motivated working smart behaviors more when salespeople were high in self-efficacy than when they were low in it.

REFERENCES:

Earley, P. Christopher, Pauline Wojnaroski, and William Prest (1987), "Task Planning and Energy Expended: Exploration of How Goals Influence Performance," *Journal of Applied Psychology*, 72 (1), 107–14.

Sujan, Harish, Barton A. Weitz, and Nirmalya Kumar (1994), "Learning Orientation, Working Smart, and Effective Selling," *JM*, 58 (July), 39–52.

SCALE ITEMS:

Describes my style not at all / Describes my style perfectly

1————2————3————4————5————6————7

1. I get to my work without spending too much time on planning. **(r)**

2. I list the steps necessary for getting an order.

3. I think about strategies I will fall back on if problems in a sales interaction arise.

4. Because too many aspects of my job are unpredictable, planning is not useful. **(r)**

5. I keep good records about my accounts.

6. I set personal goals for each sales call.

7. Each week I make a plan for what I need to do.

8. I do not waste time thinking about what I should do. **(r)**

9. I am careful to work on the highest priority tasks first.

10. Planning is a waste of time. **(r)**

11. Planning is an excuse for not working. **(r)**

12. I don't need to develop a strategy for a customers to get the order. **(r)**

SCALE NAME: Positive Reinterpretation

SCALE DESCRIPTION: Strutton and Lumpkin (1994) adapted this three-item, five-point subscale from the Ways of Coping Checklist Scale developed by Folkman and Lazarus (1980, 1985). It attempts to measure the extent to which a salesperson uses positive reinterpretation problem-solving tactics to cope with stressful customer sales presentations. In this study, the original items were screened for applicability to the sales setting. The remaining items were then subjected to factor analysis in a manner similar to Folkman and colleagues' (1986) and the subscales identified in that manner.

SCALE ORIGIN: These items were adapted by Strutton and Lumpkin (1994) for a sales setting from the Ways of Coping Checklist (Folkman and Lazarus 1980, 1985). The original measure contained 43 items developed to measure problem-focused (24 items) and emotion-focused (19 items) tactics for handling stressful situations.

SAMPLES: Strutton and Lumpkin's (1994) sample was a nonprobability sample of **101** nonmanager salespeople from three industries: communications technology (60), textiles (22), and furniture (19), predominantly in the southern United States.

RELIABILITY: Strutton and Lumpkin (1994) reported a Cronbach's alpha of **.72** for this scale.

VALIDITY: No specific validity tests were reported by Strutton and Lumpkin (1994). However, this subscale was identified as a separate subscale in Folkman and colleagues' (1986) earlier work.

ADMINISTRATION: Strutton and Lumpkin (1994) asked respondents to describe the most stressful customer-related situation they had encountered during a sales presentation during the previous two months. They were then asked to respond to the items in the scale along with other scales and demographic questions. Higher scores on the scale indicated that positive reinterpretation tactics for dealing with stress were used to a greater extent.

MAJOR FINDINGS: Strutton and Lumpkin (1994) found **positive reinterpretation** to be significantly related to sales presentation effectiveness in a regression of all subscales on a self-reported measure of presentation effectiveness.

REFERENCES:

Folkman, Susan and Richard S. Lazarus (1980), "An Analysis of Coping in a Middle-Aged Community Sample," *Journal of Health and Social Behavior*, 21 (September), 219–39.

———— and ———— (1985), "If It Changes, It Must Be a Process: Study of Emotion and Coping During Three Stages of a College Examination," *Journal of Personality and Social Psychology*, 48 (January), 150–70.

————, ————, Christine Dunkel-Schetter, Anita DeLongis, and Rand J. Gruen (1986), "Dynamics of a Stressful Encounter: Cognitive Appraisal, Coping, and Encounter Outcomes," *Journal of Personality and Social Psychology*, 50 (May), 992–1003.

Strutton, David and James R. Lumpkin (1994), "Problem- and Emotion-Focused Coping Dimensions and Sales Presentation Effectiveness," *JAMS*, 22 (1), 28–37.

SCALE ITEMS:

Directions: Indicate the extent to which you used each of the following tactics to cope with a stressful sales presentation experience.

Not used at all   :____:____:____:____:____: Used a great deal
                    1   2   3   4   5

1. Grew as a person in a good way.

2. Came out of the experience better than I went in.

3. Changed something about myself.

SCALE NAME: Power (Coercive)

SCALE DESCRIPTION: Brown, Lusch, and Nicholson (1995) used this four-item, seven-point Likert-type scale to measure the degree to which a manufacturer relied on coercive power in attempting to influence dealers to accept its recommendations. Coercive power in this context refers to the ability of the manufacturer to punish dealers in some fashion for failing to accept its recommendations.

SCALE ORIGIN: Brown, Lusch, and Nicholson (1995) said the scale was adapted from John (1981) and Gaski (1986). The measure was refined on the basis of pretest interviews with farm equipment dealers.

SAMPLES: Brown, Lusch, and Nicholson (1995) mailed a questionnaire to 1052 farm equipment dealers located in the states of Iowa, Nebraska, and Kansas. Usable responses were received from a single key informant, typically an owner or manager, for **203** of the dealerships. The sample differed from the population in general in that dealers in this sample reported having significantly higher sales of their primary brand, as well as a significantly smaller workforce.

RELIABILITY: Brown, Lusch, and Nicholson (1995) reported a coefficient alpha of **.84** for this measure.

VALIDITY: The construct validity of the scale was examined using a confirmatory factor analysis. Brown, Lusch, and Nicholson (1995) reported that one item, "The manufacturer threatened to cancel, or refused to renew, our contract," was eliminated from the scale because of large standardized residuals. The model was reestimated and achieved an acceptable goodness of fit and reliability coefficient. A confirmatory factor analysis of all measures used in the study was also undertaken to assess the overall construct validity of the measures. The measurement model's goodness of fit was acceptable, and all construct reliabilities exceeded .70, with the exception of instrumental commitment (.674). Multiple tests of the power constructs provided substantial evidence for the discriminant validity of the constructs.

ADMINISTRATION: The scale was included with other measures as part of a self-administered survey that was delivered by mail. Brown, Lusch, and Nicholson (1995) instructed respondents to focus on their relationship with the supplier of the one brand of new farm equipment that accounted for the highest dollar sales in their dealership. Higher scores on the scale indicated that the manufacturer's ability to punish dealers was a stronger factor in influencing dealers to comply with manufacturer recommendations.

MAJOR FINDINGS: Brown, Lusch, and Nicholson (1995) examined the impact of a supplier's use of various types of power on manufacturer and dealer performance and on the dealer's commitment to the channel relationship. **Coercive power** was one of three first-order indicators of the mediated power construct. Structural equation modeling was used to test the study's hypotheses. Results indicated that greater use of mediated power by a manufacturer resulted in greater dealer instrumental commitment and lower dealer normative commitment to the channel relationship. The negative relationship between mediated power and normative commitment was stronger when the dealer had more power in the relationship or when power was balanced. Higher usage of mediated power resulted in lower dealer evaluations of manufacturer performance, particularly when dealers had more power in the relationship.

REFERENCES:
Brown, James R., Robert F. Lusch, and Carolyn Y. Nicholson (1995), "Power and Relationship Commitment: Their Impact on Marketing Channel Member Performance," *JR*, 71 (4), 363–92.

Gaski, John F. (1986), "Interrelations Among a Channel Entity's Power Sources: Impact on the Exercise of Reward and Coercion on Expert, Referent, and Legitimate Power Sources," *JMR*, 23 (February), 62–77.

John, George (1981), "Interorganizational Coordination in Marketing Channels: An Investigation of Opportunism and Involvement Orientation as Mediators of the Process," doctoral dissertation, Northwestern University.

SCALE ITEMS:

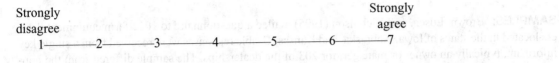

1. The manufacturer's personnel would somehow get back at us if we didn't do as they asked and they would've found out.

2. The manufacturer often hinted that they would take certain actions that would reduce our profits if we didn't go along with their requests.

3. The manufacturer might have withdrawn certain needed services from us if we didn't go along with them.

4. If we didn't agree to their suggestions, the manufacturer could have made things difficult for us.

SCALE NAME: Power (Dealer–Supplier Symmetry)

SCALE DESCRIPTION: Brown, Lusch, and Nicholson (1995) used this ten-item, seven-point scale to measure the balance of power between dealers and manufacturers with respect to ten dealership operations. Brown, Lusch, and Nicholson (1995) referred to this measure as *balance of dealer–supplier power*.

SCALE ORIGIN: It appears that Brown, Lusch, and Nicholson (1995) adapted the measure from existing research by Lusch (1976) and Etgar (1977). The measure was refined on the basis of pretest interviews with farm equipment dealers.

SAMPLES: Brown, Lusch, and Nicholson (1995) mailed a questionnaire to 1052 farm equipment dealers located in the states of Iowa, Nebraska, and Kansas. Usable responses were received from a single key informant, typically an owner or manager, for **203** of the dealerships. The sample differed from the population in general in that dealers in this sample reported having significantly higher sales of their primary brand, as well as a significantly smaller workforce.

RELIABILITY: Brown, Lusch, and Nicholson (1995) reported a coefficient alpha of **.77** for this measure.

VALIDITY: The construct validity of the scale was examined using a confirmatory factor analysis. Brown, Lusch, and Nicholson (1995) reported that the model achieved an acceptable goodness of fit and reliability only after four items were dropped from the measure. Examination of the standardized residuals in the final model provided evidence for the construct validity of the measure. A confirmatory factor analysis of all measures used in the study was also undertaken to assess the overall construct validity of the measures. The measurement model's goodness of fit was acceptable, and all construct reliabilities exceeded .70, with the exception of instrumental commitment (.674).

ADMINISTRATION: The scale was included with other measures as part of a self-administered survey that was delivered by mail. Brown, Lusch, and Nicholson (1995) instructed respondents to focus on their relationship with the supplier of the one brand of new farm equipment that accounted for the highest dollar sales in their dealership. Higher scores on the scale indicated that manufacturers had more power in the relationship, lower scores indicated that dealers had more power, and scores in the midrange indicated that power was balanced between channel members.

MAJOR FINDINGS: Brown, Lusch, and Nicholson (1995) examined the impact of a supplier's use of various types of power on manufacturer and dealer performance and on the dealer's commitment to the channel relationship. Structural equation modeling was used to test the study's hypotheses. Prior to analysis, scores on this measure were sorted from high to low and divided into three categories representing the most powerful dealers (low), the most powerful manufacturers (high), and balanced power (middle). Results indicated that when **manufacturers had more power** in the channel relationship, higher levels of instrumental commitment resulted in lower dealer evaluations of manufacturer performance, whereas the use of nonmediated power resulted in greater normative commitment to and higher performance evaluations of manufacturers. The negative influence of mediated power on normative commitment was strongest when **dealers had more power** in the relationship and **when power was balanced**.

REFERENCES:

Brown, James R., Robert F. Lusch, and Carolyn Y. Nicholson (1995), "Power and Relationship Commitment: Their Impact on Marketing Channel Member Performance," *JR*, 71 (4), 363–92.

Etgar, Michael (1977), "Channel Environment and Channel Leadership," *JMR*, 13 (February), 69–76.

Lusch, Robert F. (1976), "Sources of Power: Their Impact on Intrachannel Conflict," *JMR*, 13 (November), 382–90.

SCALE ITEMS:

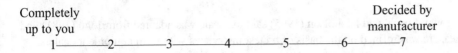

Completely up to you   Decided by manufacturer

1————2————3————4————5————6————7

1. Your dealership's physical layout.

2. Your dealership's local media advertising.

3. The amount of training your employees got.

4. Number of employees in your dealership.

5. Your dealership's parts inventory levels.

6. Your dealership's policies for financing used equipment sales.

7. Your dealership's office record keeping system, including computers.

8. Employee relations within your dealership.

9. Your dealership's parts and service credit policies.

10. Your dealership's new equipment inventory levels.

SCALE NAME: Power (Expert)

SCALE DESCRIPTION: Brown, Lusch, and Nicholson (1995) used this four-item, seven-point Likert-type scale to measure the degree to which a manufacturer relied on expert power in attempting to influence dealers to accept its recommendations. Expert power in this context refers to the manufacturer's expertise, special knowledge, or training.

SCALE ORIGIN: Brown, Lusch, and Nicholson (1995) said the scale was adapted from John (1981) and Gaski (1986). The measure was refined on the basis of pretest interviews with farm equipment dealers.

SAMPLES: Brown, Lusch, and Nicholson (1995) mailed a questionnaire to 1052 farm equipment dealers located in the states of Iowa, Nebraska, and Kansas. Usable responses were received from a single key informant, typically an owner or manager, for **203** of the dealerships. The sample differed from the population in general in that dealers in this sample reported having significantly higher sales of their primary brand, as well as a significantly smaller workforce.

RELIABILITY: Brown, Lusch, and Nicholson (1995) reported a coefficient alpha of **.82** for this measure.

VALIDITY: The construct validity of the scale was examined using a confirmatory factor analysis. Brown, Lusch, and Nicholson (1995) reported that one item, "We trusted the manufacturer's judgment," was eliminated from the scale because of large standardized residuals. The model was reestimated and achieved an acceptable goodness of fit and reliability coefficient. A confirmatory factor analysis of all measures used in the study was also undertaken to assess the overall construct validity of the measures. The measurement model's goodness of fit was acceptable, and all construct reliabilities exceeded .70, with the exception of instrumental commitment (.674). Multiple tests of the power constructs provided substantial evidence for the discriminant validity of the constructs.

ADMINISTRATION: The scale was included with other measures as part of a self-administered survey that was delivered by mail. Brown, Lusch, and Nicholson (1995) instructed respondents to focus on their relationship with the supplier of the one brand of new farm equipment that accounted for the highest dollar sales in their dealership. Higher scores on the scale indicated that the manufacturer's expertise and specialized knowledge made dealers more likely to accept manufacturer recommendations.

MAJOR FINDINGS: Brown, Lusch, and Nicholson (1995) examined the impact of a supplier's use of various types of power on manufacturer and dealer performance and on the dealer's commitment to the channel relationship. **Expert power** was one of four first-order constructs serving as an indicator of the second-order construct of nonmediated power usage. Structural equation modeling was used to test the study's hypotheses. Results indicated that greater use of nonmediated power by a manufacturer increased the dealer's normative commitment to the channel relationship and increased the dealer's evaluations of manufacturer performance, particularly when manufacturers had more power in the relationship.

REFERENCES:

Brown, James R., Robert F. Lusch, and Carolyn Y. Nicholson (1995), "Power and Relationship Commitment: Their Impact on Marketing Channel Member Performance," *JR*, 71 (4), 363–92.

Gaski, John F. (1986), "Interrelations Among a Channel Entity's Power Sources: Impact on the Exercise of Reward and Coercion on Expert, Referent, and Legitimate Power Sources," *JMR*, 23 (February), 62–77.

John, George (1981), "Interorganizational Coordination in Marketing Channels: An Investigation of Opportunism and Involvement Orientation as Mediators of the Process," doctoral dissertation, Northwestern University.

SCALE ITEMS:

Strongly   Strongly
disagree   agree

1————2————3————4————5————6————7

1. The manufacturer's business expertise made them likely to suggest the proper thing to do.

2. The people in the manufacturer's organization knew what they were doing.

3. We usually got good advice from the manufacturer.

4. The manufacturer had specially trained people who really knew what had to be done.

SCALE NAME: Power (Functional Unit)

SCALE DESCRIPTION: Fisher, Maltz, and Jaworski (1997) used this four-item, five-point Likert-type scale to measure marketing managers' perceptions of the degree of power, contribution, resources, and respect that were attributed to the marketing functional area. Although used here in a marketing context, the scale could very easily be adapted to measure the power of any functional area. Fisher, Maltz, and Jaworski (1997) referred to this scale as *functional power* in their article.

SCALE ORIGIN: Fisher, Maltz, and Jaworski (1997) indicated that the items developed for this construct were based on the work of Salancik and Pfeffer (1977). Preliminary scale items were pretested with six marketing managers; those found to be unclear, ambiguous, or not applicable were dropped from the measure.

SAMPLES: In Study 1, Fisher, Maltz, and Jaworski (1997) sampled 180 marketing managers employed by a *Fortune* 100 firm serving five diverse high-technology markets. The convenience sample was composed of marketing managers attending management training sessions over a three-week period, from which **89** usable responses were obtained. In Study 2, Fisher, Maltz, and Jaworski (1997) sampled marketing managers employed by a multinational, business-to-business services firm with 36 business units in six countries outside the United States. A key informant provided a list of 100 firm members employed in a variety of marketing positions that required them to interact with engineering personnel. A total of **72** usable responses were obtained for Study 2.

RELIABILITY: Fisher, Maltz, and Jaworski (1997) reported calculating coefficient alphas for this measure of **.78** in Study 1 and **.75** in Study 2.

VALIDITY: In Study 1, confirmatory factor analyses were conducted in two stages to maintain an acceptable ratio of observations to variables. The second analysis included the original ten items composing the psychological distance and marketing functional power measures. Fisher, Maltz, and Jaworski (1997) stated that, after the two psychological distance items were eliminated because of large modification indices, the revised model fit the data acceptably well. Evidence of discriminant validity was provided in that the correlation between each pair of constructs was significantly different from 1.00.

ADMINISTRATION: The measure was included with other scales in a self-administered questionnaire. For Study 1, a survey packet containing a cover letter, reply envelope, and the survey instrument was distributed to each marketing manager participant of a company-sponsored training session. Fisher, Maltz, and Jaworski (1997) used e-mail and telephone reminders to increase response rates. In Study 2, respondents received the survey packet by mail. Offers of anonymity and shared survey results were provided as incentives to participate. Nonrespondents received a reminder letter, followed by a second mail survey packet. In both studies, respondents were instructed to answer questions in the context of their relationship with a single manager in the engineering function with whom they interacted regularly. Higher scores on the measure indicated that respondents perceived the marketing function as commanding greater power, resources, and respect in the organization and as being a key element to corporate success.

MAJOR FINDINGS: Fisher, Maltz, and Jaworski (1997) investigated how relative functional identification, or the strength of marketing managers' psychological connection to their functional area compared with the firm as a whole, influenced different strategies for improving communication between marketers and engineers. The **functional power of the marketing unit** was included as a covariate in the study and was not significantly related to any communication behaviors in Study 1. In Study 2, the coerciveness of influence attempts was negatively associated with **marketing's functional power**.

REFERENCES:

Fisher, Robert J., Elliot Maltz, and Bernard J. Jaworski (1997), "Enhancing Communication Between Marketing and Engineering: The Moderating Role of Relative Functional Identification," *JM*, 61 (July), 54–70.

Salancik, Gerald R. and Jeffrey Pfeffer (1977), "Who Gets Power and How They Hold on to It: A Strategic Contingency Model of Power," *Organizational Dynamics*, 5 (Winter), 3–21.

SCALE ITEMS:

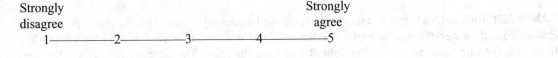

Strongly
disagree

Strongly
agree

1————————2————————3————————4————————5

1. Most people in my division have respect for Marketing.

In my division, Marketing...

2. Is one of the most powerful functions.

3. Is a significant contributor to our success.

4. Receives more resources than other functions.

SCALE NAME: Power (Information)

SCALE DESCRIPTION: Brown, Lusch, and Nicholson (1995) used this four-item, seven-point Likert-type scale to measure the degree to which a manufacturer relied on information power in attempting to influence dealers to accept its recommendations. Information power in this context refers to the provision of persuasive, useful, and helpful information.

SCALE ORIGIN: Brown, Lusch, and Nicholson (1995) said the scale was adapted from John (1981) and Gaski (1986). The measure was refined on the basis of pretest interviews with farm equipment dealers.

SAMPLES: Brown, Lusch, and Nicholson (1995) mailed a questionnaire to 1052 farm equipment dealers located in the states of Iowa, Nebraska, and Kansas. Usable responses were received from a single key informant, typically an owner or manager, for **203** of the dealerships. The sample differed from the population in general in that dealers in this sample reported having significantly higher sales of their primary brand, as well as a significantly smaller workforce.

RELIABILITY: Brown, Lusch, and Nicholson (1995) reported a coefficient alpha of **.62** for this measure.

VALIDITY: The construct validity of the scale was examined using a confirmatory factor analysis. Brown, Lusch, and Nicholson (1995) reported that one item, "We went along with what the manufacturer wanted last year because the information they provided was very convincing," was eliminated from the scale because of large standardized residuals. The model was reestimated and achieved an acceptable goodness of fit, though the reliability coefficient of .622 was slightly below the .70 standard. A confirmatory factor analysis of all measures used in the study was also undertaken to assess the overall construct validity of the measures. The measurement model's goodness of fit was acceptable, and all construct reliabilities exceeded .70, with the exception of instrumental commitment (.674). Multiple tests of the power constructs provided substantial evidence for the discriminant validity of the constructs.

ADMINISTRATION: The scale was included with other measures as part of a self-administered survey that was delivered by mail. Brown, Lusch, and Nicholson (1995) instructed respondents to focus on their relationship with the supplier of the one brand of new farm equipment that accounted for the highest dollar sales in their dealership. Higher scores on the scale indicated that dealers were more likely to follow the recommendations of manufacturers because of the persuasiveness of the information provided.

MAJOR FINDINGS: Brown, Lusch, and Nicholson (1995) examined the impact of a supplier's use of various types of power on manufacturer and dealer performance and on the dealer's commitment to the channel relationship. **Information power** was one of four first-order constructs serving as an indicator of the second-order construct of nonmediated power usage. Structural equation modeling was used to test the study's hypotheses. Results indicated that greater use of nonmediated power by a manufacturer increased the dealer's normative commitment to the channel relationship and evaluations of manufacturer performance, particularly when manufacturers had more power in the relationship.

REFERENCES:

Brown, James R., Robert F. Lusch, and Carolyn Y. Nicholson (1995), "Power and Relationship Commitment: Their Impact on Marketing Channel Member Performance," *JR*, 71 (4), 363–92.

Gaski, John F. (1986), "Interrelations Among a Channel Entity's Power Sources: Impact on the Exercise of Reward and Coercion on Expert, Referent, and Legitimate Power Sources," *JMR*, 23 (February), 62–77.

John, George (1981), "Interorganizational Coordination in Marketing Channels: An Investigation of Opportunism and Involvement Orientation as Mediators of the Process," doctoral dissertation, Northwestern University.

SCALE ITEMS:

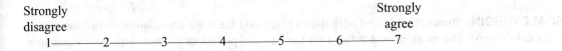

Strongly disagree
1——2——3——4——5——6——7
Strongly agree

1. The information the manufacturer provided us made sense.

2. The manufacturer often had more information than we did.

3. The manufacturer convinced us that it made sense to follow their suggestions.

4. The manufacturer knew more than we did about what needed to be done.

SCALE NAME: Power (Legitimate)

SCALE DESCRIPTION: Brown, Lusch, and Nicholson (1995) used this four-item, seven-point Likert-type scale to measure the degree to which a manufacturer relied on legitimate power in attempting to influence dealers to accept its recommendations. Legitimate power in this context refers to the duty and obligation owed the manufacturer by right of its formal position.

SCALE ORIGIN: Brown, Lusch, and Nicholson (1995) said the scale was adapted from John (1981) and Gaski (1986). The measure was refined on the basis of pretest interviews with farm equipment dealers.

SAMPLES: Brown, Lusch, and Nicholson (1995) mailed a questionnaire to 1052 farm equipment dealers located in the states of Iowa, Nebraska, and Kansas. Usable responses were received from a single key informant, typically an owner or manager, for **203** of the dealerships. The sample differed from the population in general in that dealers in this sample reported having significantly higher sales of their primary brand, as well as a significantly smaller workforce.

RELIABILITY: Brown, Lusch, and Nicholson (1995) reported a coefficient alpha of **.73** for this measure.

VALIDITY: The construct validity of the scale was examined using a confirmatory factor analysis. Brown, Lusch, and Nicholson (1995) reported that one item, "The manufacturer often pointed out a contract clause that made us feel obligated to do as asked," was eliminated from the scale because of large standardized residuals. The model was reestimated and achieved an acceptable goodness of fit and reliability coefficient. A confirmatory factor analysis of all measures used in the study was also undertaken to assess the overall construct validity of the measures. Legitimate power loaded on both the mediated and nonmediated power second-order constructs with standardized loadings of .548 and .596, respectively. The measurement model's goodness of fit was acceptable, and all construct reliabilities exceeded .70, with the exception of instrumental commitment (.674). Multiple tests of the power constructs provided substantial evidence for the discriminant validity of the constructs.

ADMINISTRATION: The scale was included with other measures as part of a self-administered survey that was delivered by mail. Brown, Lusch, and Nicholson (1995) instructed respondents to focus on their relationship with the supplier of the one brand of new farm equipment that accounted for the highest dollar sales in their dealership. Higher scores on the scale indicated that the dealer was more likely to follow manufacturer recommendations because of contractual or duty obligations owed to that manufacturer.

MAJOR FINDINGS: Brown, Lusch, and Nicholson (1995) examined the impact of a supplier's use of various types of power on manufacturer and dealer performance and on the dealer's commitment to the channel relationship. **Legitimate power** was one of three first-order indicators of the mediated power construct and one of four first-order indicators of the nonmediated power construct. This result was as expected, because the measure contains both a mediated component (legitimacy based on legal contracts) and a nonmediated component (legitimacy based on shared norms and values). Structural equation modeling was used to test the study's hypotheses. Results indicated that greater use of nonmediated power by a manufacturer increased the dealer's normative commitment to the channel relationship and the dealer's evaluations of manufacturer performance, particularly when manufacturers had more power in the relationship. Greater use of mediated power by a manufacturer resulted in greater dealer instrumental commitment and lower dealer normative commitment to the channel relationship. The negative relationship between mediated power and normative commitment was stronger when the dealer had more power in the relationship or when power was balanced. Higher usage of mediated power resulted in lower dealer evaluations of manufacturer performance, particularly when dealers had more power in the relationship.

REFERENCES:

Brown, James R., Robert F. Lusch, and Carolyn Y. Nicholson (1995), "Power and Relationship Commitment: Their Impact on Marketing Channel Member Performance," *JR*, 71 (4), 363–92.

Gaski, John F. (1986), "Interrelations Among a Channel Entity's Power Sources: Impact on the Exercise of Reward and Coercion on Expert, Referent, and Legitimate Power Sources," *JMR*, 23 (February), 62–77.

John, George (1981), "Interorganizational Coordination in Marketing Channels: An Investigation of Opportunism and Involvement Orientation as Mediators of the Process," doctoral dissertation, Northwestern University.

SCALE ITEMS:

Strongly disagree — Strongly agree

1————2————3————4————5————6————7

1. It was our duty to do as the manufacturer requested.

2. We had an obligation to do what the manufacturer wanted, even though it wasn't a part of the contract.

3. Since they were the manufacturer, we accepted their recommendations.

4. The manufacturer had a right to expect us to go along with their requests.

SCALE NAME: Power (Referent)

SCALE DESCRIPTION: Brown, Lusch, and Nicholson (1995) used this four-item, seven-point Likert-type scale to measure the degree to which a manufacturer relied on referent power in attempting to influence dealers to accept its recommendations. Referent power in this context refers to the dealers' regard for and identification with the manufacturer.

SCALE ORIGIN: Brown, Lusch, and Nicholson (1995) said the scale was adapted from John (1981) and Gaski (1986). The measure was refined on the basis of pretest interviews with farm equipment dealers.

SAMPLES: Brown, Lusch, and Nicholson (1995) mailed a questionnaire to 1052 farm equipment dealers located in the states of Iowa, Nebraska, and Kansas. Usable responses were received from a single key informant, typically an owner or manager, for **203** of the dealerships. The sample differed from the population in general in that dealers in this sample reported having significantly higher sales of their primary brand, as well as a significantly smaller workforce.

RELIABILITY: Brown, Lusch, and Nicholson (1995) reported a coefficient alpha of **.68** for this measure.

VALIDITY: The construct validity of the scale was examined using a confirmatory factor analysis. Brown, Lusch, and Nicholson (1995) reported that one item, "We went along with the manufacturer's requests because we wanted to earn the respect of the manufacturer's personnel," was eliminated from the scale because of large standardized residuals. The model was reestimated and achieved an acceptable goodness of fit, though the reliability coefficient of .683 was slightly below the .70 standard. A confirmatory factor analysis of all measures used in the study was also undertaken to assess the overall construct validity of the measures. The measurement model's goodness of fit was acceptable, and all construct reliabilities exceeded .70, with the exception of instrumental commitment (.674). Multiple tests of the power constructs provided substantial evidence for the discriminant validity of the constructs.

ADMINISTRATION: The scale was included with other measures as part of a self-administered survey that was delivered by mail. Brown, Lusch, and Nicholson (1995) instructed respondents to focus on their relationship with the supplier of the one brand of new farm equipment that accounted for the highest dollar sales in their dealership. Higher scores on the scale indicated that dealers' admiration for and identification with the manufacturer influenced their acceptance of manufacturer recommendations to a higher degree.

MAJOR FINDINGS: Brown, Lusch, and Nicholson (1995) examined the impact of a supplier's use of various types of power on manufacturer and dealer performance and on the dealer's commitment to the channel relationship. **Referent power** was one of four first-order constructs serving as an indicator of the second-order construct of nonmediated power usage. Structural equation modeling was used to test the study's hypotheses. Results indicated that greater use of nonmediated power by a manufacturer increased the dealer's normative commitment to the channel relationship and evaluations of manufacturer performance, particularly when manufacturers had more power in the relationship.

REFERENCES:
Brown, James R., Robert F. Lusch, and Carolyn Y. Nicholson (1995), "Power and Relationship Commitment: Their Impact on Marketing Channel Member Performance," *JR*, 71 (4), 363–92.

Gaski, John F. (1986), "Interrelations Among a Channel Entity's Power Sources: Impact on the Exercise of Reward and Coercion on Expert, Referent, and Legitimate Power Sources," *JMR*, 23 (February), 62–77.

John, George (1981), "Interorganizational Coordination in Marketing Channels: An Investigation of Opportunism and Involvement Orientation as Mediators of the Process," doctoral dissertation, Northwestern University.

SCALE ITEMS:

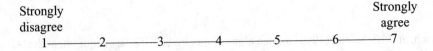

Strongly disagree

Strongly agree

1————2————3————4————5————6————7

1. We really admire the way the manufacturer runs their business, so we tried to follow their lead.

2. We generally wanted to operate our dealership very similar to the way we thought the manufacturer would.

3. Our dealership did what the manufacturer wanted because we have similar feelings about the way a business should be run.

4. Because our dealership is proud to be affiliated with the manufacturer, we often did what they asked last year.

SCALE NAME: Power (Reward)

SCALE DESCRIPTION: Brown, Lusch, and Nicholson (1995) used this four-item, seven-point Likert-type scale to measure the degree to which a manufacturer relied on reward power in attempting to influence dealers to accept its recommendations. Reward power in this context refers to the ability of the manufacturer to grant rewards or favorable treatment to the dealer.

SCALE ORIGIN: Brown, Lusch, and Nicholson (1995) said the scale was adapted from John (1981) and Gaski (1986). The measure was refined on the basis of pretest interviews with farm equipment dealers.

SAMPLES: Brown, Lusch, and Nicholson (1995) mailed a questionnaire to 1052 farm equipment dealers located in the states of Iowa, Nebraska, and Kansas. Usable responses were received from a single key informant, typically an owner or manager, for **203** of the dealerships. The sample differed from the population in general in that dealers in this sample reported having significantly higher sales of their primary brand, as well as a significantly smaller workforce.

RELIABILITY: Brown, Lusch, and Nicholson (1995) reported a coefficient alpha of **.74** for this measure.

VALIDITY: The construct validity of the scale was examined using a confirmatory factor analysis. Brown, Lusch, and Nicholson (1995) reported that one item, "We believed that we could get some needed help from the manufacturer by agreeing to their requests," was eliminated from the scale because of large standardized residuals. The model was reestimated and achieved an acceptable goodness of fit and reliability coefficient. A confirmatory factor analysis of all measures used in the study was also undertaken to assess the overall construct validity of the measures. The measurement model's goodness of fit was acceptable, and all construct reliabilities exceeded .70, with the exception of instrumental commitment (.674). Multiple tests of the power constructs provided substantial evidence for the discriminant validity of the constructs.

ADMINISTRATION: The scale was included with other measures as part of a self-administered survey that was delivered by mail. Brown, Lusch, and Nicholson (1995) instructed respondents to focus on their relationship with the supplier of the one brand of new farm equipment that accounted for the highest dollar sales in their dealership. Higher scores on the scale indicated that the manufacturer's ability to reward dealers was a stronger factor in influencing dealers to concur with manufacturer recommendations.

MAJOR FINDINGS: Brown, Lusch, and Nicholson (1995) examined the impact of a supplier's use of various types of power on manufacturer and dealer performance and on the dealer's commitment to the channel relationship. **Reward power** was one of three first-order indicators of the mediated power construct. Structural equation modeling was used to test the study's hypotheses. Results indicated that greater use of mediated power by a manufacturer resulted in greater dealer instrumental commitment and lower dealer normative commitment to the channel relationship. The negative relationship between mediated power and normative commitment was stronger when the dealer had more power in the relationship or when power was balanced. Higher usage of mediated power resulted in lower dealer evaluations of manufacturer performance, particularly when dealers had more power in the relationship.

REFERENCES:
Brown, James R., Robert F. Lusch, and Carolyn Y. Nicholson (1995), "Power and Relationship Commitment: Their Impact on Marketing Channel Member Performance," *JR*, 71 (4), 363–92.

Gaski, John F. (1986), "Interrelations Among a Channel Entity's Power Sources: Impact on the Exercise of Reward and Coercion on Expert, Referent, and Legitimate Power Sources," *JMR*, 23 (February), 62–77.

John, George (1981), "Interorganizational Coordination in Marketing Channels: An Investigation of Opportunism and Involvement Orientation as Mediators of the Process," doctoral dissertation, Northwestern University.

SCALE ITEMS:

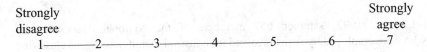

1. If we didn't do as the manufacturer asked, we wouldn't have received very good treatment from them.

2. We felt that by going along with the manufacturer, we would have been favored on some other occasions.

3. By going along with the manufacturer's requests, we avoided some of the problems other dealers face.

4. The manufacturer often rewarded us last year to get our dealership to go along with their wishes.

SCALE NAME: Power (Salesperson)

SCALE DESCRIPTION: Doney and Cannon (1997) used this three-item, seven-point Likert-type scale to measure the degree to which a buyer perceives a salesperson as capable of providing outcomes that match what the salesperson says or promises due to that individual's power in the supplier firm.

SCALE ORIGIN: Doney and Cannon (1997) stated that they generated items for the scale on the basis of interviews with marketing and purchasing personnel. Exploratory factor analyses using both orthogonal and oblique rotations were used to ensure high item loadings on hypothesized constructs and low cross-loadings.

SAMPLES: Doney and Cannon (1997) sampled 657 members of the National Association of Purchasing Management who were employed by firms involved in industrial manufacturing, as classified by standard industrial classification codes 33–37. **Two hundred ten** completed questionnaires were returned from a primarily male (76%) sample with an average of 15 years of purchasing experience.

RELIABILITY: Doney and Cannon (1997) calculated a coefficient alpha of **.90** for this measure.

VALIDITY: Doney and Cannon (1997) reported using three methods to test the discriminant validity of the scales representing the combined dimensions of trust of the salesperson and its proposed antecedents and outcomes. Each method provided strong evidence of discriminant validity. Two LISREL-based tests were also used to provide evidence for the convergent validity of the measures.

ADMINISTRATION: The scale was included with other measures as part of a self-administered survey that was delivered by mail. Nonrespondents received a postcard reminder followed by a second questionnaire a week later. Doney and Cannon (1997) instructed respondents to focus on a single, specific, recent purchase decision in which more than one supplier was seriously considered and to indicate on the survey (using initials) two of the firms considered. After answering questions pertaining to the purchase situation, half of the respondents were instructed to complete the remainder of the questionnaire in the context of the first supplier they had listed, and the other half were instructed to use the second supplier. Higher scores on the scale indicated that the buyer perceived the focal salesperson as having the power to fulfill promises and obligations.

MAJOR FINDINGS: Doney and Cannon (1997) investigated the impact of purchasing agents' trust in the salesperson and the supplier firm on a buying firm's current supplier choice and future buying intentions. The extent to which a salesperson was perceived as having the **power** to fulfill promises was not significantly related to the buyers' level of trust in the salesperson.

REFERENCES:

Doney, Patricia M. and Joseph P. Cannon (1997), "An Examination of the Nature of Trust in Buyer-Seller Relationships," *JM*, 61 (April), 35–51.

SCALE ITEMS:

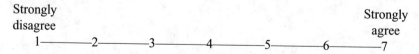

Strongly disagree						Strongly agree
1	2	3	4	5	6	7

1. This salesperson has the clout to get his/her way with the supplier.

2. This salesperson is one of this supplier's most important salespeople.

3. This salesperson has power in his/her firm.

SCALE NAME: Prior Experience (Purchase)

SCALE DESCRIPTION: Heide and Weiss (1995) used this three-item, seven-point Likert-type scale to measure a buying firm's lack of experience in purchasing computer workstations.

SCALE ORIGIN: Heide and Weiss (1995) adapted items from Anderson, Chu, and Weitz (1987) by altering the original items to fit the context of computer workstation purchasing.

SAMPLES: Pretests of the questionnaire were conducted with two different small groups of previous workstation buyers. In the final study, Heide and Weiss (1995) drew a random sample of 900 firms from Installed Technology International's list of firms that had recently purchased workstations. Key informants were identified from this list and contacted by telephone, of which 466 agreed to participate in the study and were sent a mail questionnaire. Follow-up telephone calls and a second mailing resulted in **215** usable questionnaires being returned. Industries represented by respondents included computers (31.4%), manufacturing (22.4%), medical (6.2%), services (15.2%), and other (24.8%).

RELIABILITY: Heide and Weiss (1995) reported a coefficient alpha of **.81** for this scale.

VALIDITY: Heide and Weiss (1995) initially evaluated the measure on the basis of item-to-total correlations and exploratory factor analysis. Confirmatory factor analysis was then used to establish unidimensionality. Evidence of discriminant validity was provided by a series of chi-square tests on the respective factor correlations.

ADMINISTRATION: The measure was included in a self-administered mail survey. Heide and Weiss (1995) instructed respondents to answer all questions in the context of their organization's most recent workstation purchase. Higher scores on the prior experience scale indicated a lack of experience in purchasing computer workstations.

MAJOR FINDINGS: Heide and Weiss (1995) investigated how buyers working in high-technology markets approached decisions in the consideration and choice stages of the purchase process. Specifically, factors influencing whether buyers included new vendors at the consideration stage and whether they ultimately switched to a new vendor at the choice stage were investigated. Although Heide and Weiss (1995) were surprised to find that **prior experience** had no effect on the firm's consideration set, they found that, when the consideration set was opened to new vendors, limited **prior experience** with the purchase decreased the likelihood that an existing vendor would be chosen.

REFERENCES:

Anderson, Erin, Wujin Chu, and Barton A. Weitz (1987), "Industrial Purchasing: An Empirical Exploration of the Buyclass Framework," *JM*, 51 (July), 71–86.

Heide, Jan B. and Allen M. Weiss (1995), "Vendor Consideration and Switching Behavior for Buyers in High-Technology Markets," *JM*, 59 (July), 30–43.

SCALE ITEMS:

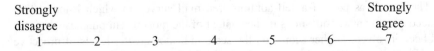

| Strongly disagree | | | | | | Strongly agree |
| 1 | 2 | 3 | 4 | 5 | 6 | 7 |

1. Overall, our firm had limited technical knowledge about workstations before we considered purchasing one.

2. We had limited information from past purchases when we were defining the specifications for a workstation purchase.

3. This was a rather new type of purchase for us.

SCALE NAME: Proactive Focus (Purchasing)

SCALE DESCRIPTION: Bunn (1994) developed a nine-item, seven-point Likert-type scale to measure the extent to which purchasing objectives, contingency planning, and supplier relationships had been proactively determined prior to confronting a specific purchasing situation.

SCALE ORIGIN: The scale is original to Bunn (1994). Using an iterative process, Bunn (1994) sought to develop specific measures of organizational buying behavior. An extensive review of the procurement practices and organizational buying behavior literature and personal interviews with 11 purchasing executives from a broad range of industries were used to identify several general-level organizational buying constructs. Scale items for each construct were generated using phrasing from the taped interviews with purchasing executives. A mail survey sent to purchasing executives was used to refine and confirm the constructs. Following refinement, results of a second survey of purchasing executives was used to select the final set of constructs and measures tested in this study.

SAMPLES: Bunn (1994) provided no details with respect to the two surveys conducted with samples of purchasing executives as part of the initial construct and scale development process. For the scale validation process, Bunn (1994) stated that **636** usable questionnaires were returned from a randomly selected sample of 1843 purchasing executives listed on the National Association of Purchasing Management roster. Of the respondent firms, 57% were in manufacturing industries, 16% were in service industries, and the remainder was comprised of construction, transportation, and public administration firms. The majority of responding firms were large; 59% had between 200 and 5000 employees.

RELIABILITY: All of the items in the proactive focus scale scored item-to-total correlations greater than the minimum standard of .30 and were retained as part of the measure. Bunn (1994) reported a coefficient alpha of **.82** for the scale.

VALIDITY: Bunn (1994) examined the scale for both discriminant and nomological validity. A four-dimension, promax-rotated factor solution was used to determine that items loaded on the proposed factor at the .40 level or above. One item, "procedure was straightforward," failed to meet this standard. It was retained, however, because this loading represented the highest factor loading and corresponding cross-loadings were relatively low. A confirmatory factor analysis with LISREL using nested comparisons demonstrated a superior fit for a four-factor solution, as well as statistically significant t-values for indicators. LISREL was also used to confirm the unidimensionality of the measure. Using the procedure suggested by Fornell and Larcker (1988), a second test for unidimensionality was undertaken that did not confirm unidimensionality. Nomological validity was demonstrated through significant correlations in the direction hypothesized between this measure and four theoretically related characteristics of the decision.

ADMINISTRATION: The scale was part of a self-administered mail survey in which Bunn (1994) instructed purchasing executives to answer questions in the context of the most recent purchase decision in which he or she had been involved. Higher scores on the scale indicates greater levels of proactive planning with respect to objective setting, contingency planning, and supplier relationship management.

MAJOR FINDINGS: Bunn (1994) sought to develop scales for measuring four distinct constructs that he proposed as underlying organizational buying behavior. The **proactive focus** measure exhibited mixed results with respect to unidimensionality and was found to explain .10 of the variance in a four-dimension, promax-rotated factor solution.

REFERENCES:

Bunn, Michele D. (1994), "Key Aspects of Organizational Buying: Conceptualization and Measurement," *JAMS*, 22 (2), 160–69.

Fornell, Claes and David F. Larcker (1981), "Evaluating Structural Equation Models with Unobservable Variables and Measurement Error," *JMR*, 18 (February), 39–53.

SCALE ITEMS:

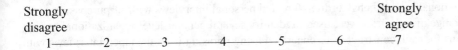

Strongly disagree

Strongly agree

1————2————3————4————5————6————7

1. It was not necessary to consider long-range purchasing objectives when making this purchase. **(r)**

2. Contingency plans were considered for problems that might be related to this purchase.

3. We had to make certain that this purchase fit with our forecasts.

4. We didn't give any thought to our long-range supply of this product. **(r)**

5. Consideration was given to the long-range supply of this product.

6. Future plans were not an important issue in purchasing this product. **(r)**

7. We considered how this purchase would impact the organization's long-range profitability.

8. Input from the corporate planning process was an essential prerequisite for this purchase.

9. We didn't need to devlop plans for possible supply disruptions. **(r)**

SCALE NAME: Procedural Control

SCALE DESCRIPTION: Bunn (1994) developed a ten-item, seven-point Likert-type scale to measure the extent to which buyers rely on procedures, policies, or rules of thumb when confronted with a specific purchasing situation.

SCALE ORIGIN: The scale is original to Bunn (1994). Using an iterative process, Bunn (1994) sought to develop specific measures of organizational buying behavior. An extensive review of the procurement practices and organizational buying behavior literature and personal interviews with 11 purchasing executives from a broad range of industries were used to identify several general-level organizational buying constructs. Scale items for each construct were generated using phrasing from the taped interviews with purchasing executives. A mail survey sent to purchasing executives was used to refine and confirm the constructs. Following refinement, results of a second survey of purchasing executives were used to select the final set of constructs and measures tested in this study.

SAMPLES: Bunn (1994) provided no details with respect to the two surveys conducted with samples of purchasing executives as part of the initial construct and scale development process. For the scale validation process, Bunn (1994) stated that **636** usable questionnaires were returned from a randomly selected sample of 1843 purchasing executives listed on the National Association of Purchasing Management roster. Of the respondent firms, 57% were in manufacturing industries, 16% were in service industries, and the remainder was comprised of construction, transportation, and public administration firms. The majority of responding firms were large; 59% had between 200 and 5000 employees.

RELIABILITY: All of the items in the procedural control scale scored item-to-total correlations greater than the minimum standard of .30 and were retained as part of the measure. Bunn (1994) reported a coefficient alpha of **.87** for the scale.

VALIDITY: Bunn (1994) examined the scale for both discriminant and nomological validity. A four-dimension, promax-rotated factor solution was used to determine that items loaded on the proposed factor at the .40 level or above. One item, "procedure was straightforward," loaded on its primary factor at .52 but exhibited a relatively high cross-loading (−.30). A confirmatory factor analysis with LISREL using nested comparisons demonstrated a superior fit for a four-factor solution, as well as statistically significant t-values for indicators. LISREL was also used to confirm the unidimensionality of the measure. Using the procedure suggested by Fornell and Larcker (1988), a second test for unidimensionality was undertaken and confirmed for the procedural control measure. Nomological validity was demonstrated through significant correlations in the direction hypothesized between this measure and four theoretically related characteristics of the decision.

ADMINISTRATION: The scale was part of a self-administered mail survey in which Bunn (1994) instructed purchasing executives to answer questions in the context of the most recent purchase decision in which he or she had been involved. Higher scores on the scale indicated a greater reliance on procedures, policies, or rules of thumb during the purchasing process.

MAJOR FINDINGS: Bunn (1994) sought to develop scales for measuring four distinct constructs that he proposed as underlying organizational buying behavior. The **procedural control** measure exhibited unidimensionality and was found to explain .21 of the variance in a four-dimension, promax-rotated factor solution.

REFERENCES:
Bunn, Michele D. (1994), "Key Aspects of Organizational Buying: Conceptualization and Measurement," *JAMS*, 22 (2), 160–69.
Fornell, Claes and David F. Larcker (1981), "Evaluating Structural Equation Models with Unobservable Variables and Measurement Error," *JMR*, 18 (February), 39–53.

SCALE ITEMS:

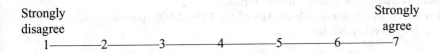

Strongly
disagree

Strongly
agree

1————2————3————4————5————6————7

1. The procedure for buying this product was straightforward.

2. The terms and conditions for this purchase order were standard.

3. The standard operating procedures did not tell us what to do for this purchase. **(r)**

4. Each step in the purchase process required new decisions. **(r)**

5. We didn't have clear-cut rules about how to make this purchase. **(r)**

6. When the need arose, there were no existing guidelines about how to fill it. **(r)**

7. The purchase is made the same way each time.

8. The organization didn't have an established way of doing things for this purchase situation. **(r)**

9. Responsibility was not clearly defined for the accomplishment of each step of the purchase procedure in this situation. **(r)**

10. All the conditions that arose in this purchase situation were covered by established procedure.

SCALE NAME: Procedural Knowledge

SCALE DESCRIPTION: Four five-point Likert-type items measuring the degree to which an employee can clearly specify the activities that must be performed to achieve desired outcomes.

SCALE ORIGIN: Ramaswami (1996) cited Jaworski and MacInnis (1989) as the source of the scale.

SAMPLES: A national sample of marketing managers was drawn randomly by Jaworski and MacInnis (1989) from the American Marketing Association's (AMA) list of members. Of the 479 managers who were to have received questionnaires, **379** returned usable forms.

Ramaswami (1996) received usable surveys from **318** of the 1159 AMA members who were randomly selected from the AMA's membership list.

RELIABILITY: Coefficient alphas of **.50** on the two-item version and **.77** for the four-item version were reported for the scale by Jaworski and MacInnis (1989) and Ramaswami (1996), respectively.

VALIDITY: The validity of the scale was not specifically examined by Jaworski and MacInnis (1989). Ramaswami (1996) used confirmatory factor analysis to assess the unidimensionality of the measure in conjunction with the performance documentation and found that each scale tapped distinct dimensions of the task context.

ADMINISTRATION: Jaworski and MacInnis (1989) and Ramaswami (1996) indicated that the scale was self-administered, along with many other measures, in a mail survey format. Higher scores on the scale indicated that employees strongly believed that information and rules were available to guide their work, whereas lower scores suggested that they had few formal procedures to help them in approaching work.

MAJOR FINDINGS: Among the many purposes of the study by Jaworski and MacInnis (1989) was to examine the simultaneous use of several types of managerial controls in the context of marketing management. Using structural equations, the authors found that **procedural knowledge** had a significant positive impact on the extent of reliance on process controls but was not significantly related to the use of professional or self-control.

Ramaswami (1996) investigated both traditional and contingency theories of negative employee responses to marketing control systems. In his study, higher levels of **procedural knowledge** were found to lower dysfunctional behavior by employees when both output and process controls were used.

REFERENCES:

Jaworski, Bernard J. and Deborah J. MacInnis (1989), "Marketing Jobs and Management Controls: Toward a Framework," *JMR*, 26 (November), 406–19.

Ramaswami, Sridhar N. (1996), "Marketing Controls and Dysfunctional Employee Behaviors: A Test of Traditional and Contingency Theory Postulates," *JM*, 60 (April), 105–20.

SCALE ITEMS: *

Strongly disagree	Disagree	Neutral	Agree	Strongly agree
1—————	—2—————	—3—————	—4—————	—5

1. There exists a clearly defined body of knowledge or subject matter that can guide me in doing my work.

2. It is possible to rely upon existing procedures and practices to do my work.

3. On my job, there exist objective procedures that tell me exactly how to respond in all situations.

4. On my job, I have to actively search for solutions beyond normal procedures many times.

*Ramaswami (1996) modified item 1 slightly to read, "There exists a clearly defined body of knowledge or subject matter that can guide me during my work."

SCALE NAME: Process Control

SCALE DESCRIPTION: Bello and Gilliland (1997) used this three-item, seven-point scale to measure the extent to which a manufacturer attempts to influence a distributor's marketing procedures and activities.

SCALE ORIGIN: Bello and Gilliland (1997) stated that the scale items were adapted from the work of Ouchi and Maguire (1975) and Jaworski and MacInnis (1989).

SAMPLES: Bello and Gilliland's (1997) systematic random sample of 245 national manufacturers verified as exporting through foreign distributors was drawn from the 1994 edition of the *Journal of Commerce United States Importer & Exporter Directory*. **One hundred sixty** usable responses were obtained from export managers employed by firms exporting a variety of industrial and consumer products to a total of 39 different countries.

RELIABILITY: A confirmatory factor analysis composite reliability of **.87** was reported by Bello and Gilliland (1997).

VALIDITY: Confirmatory factor analysis was used by Bello and Gilliland (1997) to provide evidence of discriminant and convergent validity, as well as to assess the unidimensionality of the measure. Convergent validity was deemed to be present because items loaded significantly on their posited indicators and because of the low to moderate correlations between the scale and other measures. Discriminant validity was also deemed to be present because the correlation estimate between two indicators never included 1.0 (+/− two standard errors). The authors used personal interviews with export executives as part of the pretest process to verify the face validity of the measure.

ADMINISTRATION: Bello and Gilliland (1997) indicated that this scale was self-administered as part of a longer survey instrument mailed to respondents. The export manager with primary responsibility for the firm's relationship with the foreign distributor received a survey. Nonrespondents were telephoned three weeks later, and a second questionnaire followed. Instructions specified that questions were to be answered in the context of the focal distributor. The authors defined the focal distributor as the firm's fourth-largest foreign distributor in terms of unit sales volume to avoid a positive evaluation bias. Higher scores on the scale indicated greater effort on the part of the manufacturer to influence the distributor's marketing procedures and activities.

MAJOR FINDINGS: Bello and Gilliland (1997) examined the effect of output controls, process controls, and flexibility on channel performance. Contrary to expectations, the use of **process controls** in an export situation failed to influence distributor performance. As hypothesized, manufacturer resources and the use of **process controls** were significantly related, because firms with inadequate managerial and financial resources were less able to influence their distributor's marketing activities and procedures. The use of **process controls** was also related to the sophistication or technical complexity of the product. The more technically complex the product, the more prevalent was the use of **process controls.**

REFERENCES:
Bello, Daniel C. and David I. Gilliland (1997), "The Effect of Output Controls, Process Controls, and Flexibility on Export Channel Performance," *JM*, 61 (January), 22–38.
Jaworski, Bernard J. and Deborah J. MacInnis (1989), "Marketing Jobs and Management Controls: Toward A Framework," *JMR*, 26 (November), 406–19.
Ouchi, William G. and Mary Ann Maguire (1975), "Organizational Control: Two Functions," *Administrative Science Quarterly*, 20 (December), 559–69.

#799 *Process Control*

SCALE ITEMS:
Our efforts to influence the way distributor performs activities can be described as...

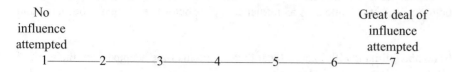

No
influence
attempted

Great deal of
influence
attempted

1————2————3————4————5————6————7

1. Distributor's promotional activities for our product.

2. The way distributor introduces new products.

3. Distributor's selling policy and procedures for new products.

SCALE NAME: Product Development (Customer Involvement)

SCALE DESCRIPTION: A four-item, five-point scale was reported by Ittner and Larcker (1997) as assessing the frequency with which an organization involved customers in the product development process.

SCALE ORIGIN: Ittner and Larcker (1997) indicated that the scale was developed by a consulting company as part of a multinational study of the automobile and computer industries. The items were reportedly developed on the basis of a review of the literature, focus groups with industry individuals from four countries, and interviews with international experts in the fields covered by the survey. The instrument containing the measure was pilot tested in each industry and country and modified as necessary. Back-translation of the modified items was used to verify that the original intent of the question had been preserved through the translating and modification process.

SAMPLES: Ittner and Larcker (1997) analyzed data from a 1991 survey of Canadian, Japanese, German, and U.S. automobile and computer manufacturers, assemblers, and suppliers that was originally conducted by a consulting company. Typically, every assembler or manufacturer within the respective industries was invited to participate, and random samples were taken of suppliers. Of the 249 organizations who agreed to participate in the consulting firm's study, a total of **184** firms returned usable data (**95** were from the auto industry, and **89** were from the computer industry). The distribution of automobile and computer industry firms by country is as follows: Canada, 14 and 23; Germany, 22 and 14; Japan, 21 and 23; and the United States, 38 and 30. The data were apparently pooled across countries, though separate regression models were estimated by industry when investigating certain hypotheses.

RELIABILITY: Ittner and Larcker (1997) reported a coefficient alpha of **.74** for this measure.

VALIDITY: Ittner and Larcker (1997) did not specifically examine the validity of the measure.

ADMINISTRATION: Ittner and Larcker (1997) stated that the survey containing the measure was administered to participants by a member of either the consulting company or one of the cosponsoring organizations. The score for the construct was computed by first standardizing the items to a zero mean and unit variance and then computing the equally weighted average of the standardized item scores associated with the construct. The resulting construct scores were then rescaled from 0 to 1, where higher scores on the scale reflected a higher degree of customer involvement in the product development process.

MAJOR FINDINGS: Ittner and Larcker (1997) investigated the relationship between product development cycle time and organizational performance. **Customer involvement in the product development** process was not significantly associated with performance. However, an analysis of interaction effects indicated that higher levels of **customer involvement** negatively influenced performance when cycle times were higher.

REFERENCES:
Ittner, Christopher D. and David F. Larcker (1997), "Product Development Cycle Time and Organizational Performance," *JMR*, 34 (February), 13–23.

#800 *Product Development (Customer Involvement)*

SCALE ITEMS:*

Directions: Please indicate the frequency with which the following practices are used to verify that the design meets customer requirements.

1 = Never—0% of the time
2 = Seldom—1–20% of the time
3 = Occasionally—21–50% of the time
4 = Usually—51–90% of the time
5 = Always or almost always—91–100% of the time

1. Cross-functional teams with customers.

2. Design review by customers.

3. Design review with customer representatives.

4. Customer pilot runs.

*Although the verbatim instructions were not listed by Ittner and Larcker (1997), they were likely to have been similar to those shown here.

SCALE NAME: Product Development (Use of Supplier)

SCALE DESCRIPTION: This four-item scale mixes four- and five-point formats to assess the importance of an organization's use of suppliers and engineering firms in the product development process, as well as the frequency of subsequent design reviews.

SCALE ORIGIN: Ittner and Larcker (1997) indicated that the scale was developed by a consulting company as part of a multinational study of the automobile and computer industry. The items were reportedly developed on the basis of a review of the literature, focus groups with industry individuals from four countries, and interviews with international experts in the fields covered by the survey. The instrument containing the measure was pilot tested in each industry and country and modified as necessary. Back-translation of the modified items was used to verify that the original intent of the question had been preserved through the translating and modification process.

SAMPLES: Ittner and Larcker (1997) analyzed data from a 1991 survey of Canadian, Japanese, German, and U.S. automobile and computer manufacturers, assemblers, and suppliers that which was originally conducted by a consulting company. Typically, every assembler or manufacturer within the respective industries was invited to participate, and random samples were taken of suppliers. Of the 249 organizations who agreed to participate in the consulting firm's study, a total of **184** firms returned usable data (**95** were from the auto industry, and **89** were from the computer industry). The distribution of automobile and computer industry firms by country is as follows: Canada, 14 and 23; Germany, 22 and 14; Japan, 21 and 23; and the United States, 38 and 30. The data were apparently pooled across countries, though separate regression models were estimated by industry when investigating certain hypotheses.

RELIABILITY: Ittner and Larcker (1997) reported a coefficient alpha of **.62** for this measure.

VALIDITY: Ittner and Larcker (1997) did not specifically examine the validity of the measure.

ADMINISTRATION: Ittner and Larcker (1997) stated that the survey containing the measure was administered to participants by a member of either the consulting company or one of the cosponsoring organizations. The score for the construct was computed by first standardizing the items to a zero mean and unit variance and then computing the equally weighted average of the standardized item scores associated with the construct. The resulting construct scores were then rescaled from 0 to 1, where higher scores on the scale reflected a higher use of engineering firms and suppliers in the product development process, as well as a greater frequency of design reviews.

MAJOR FINDINGS: Ittner and Larcker (1997) investigated the relationship between product development cycle time and organizational performance. An organization's **use of suppliers and engineering firms in the product development** process was not significantly associated with performance. However, when the data were analyzed separately by industry, an organization's **use of suppliers and engineering firms in the product development** process negatively affected return on assets and return on sales in the computer industry.

REFERENCES:
Ittner, Christopher D. and David F. Larcker (1997), "Product Development Cycle Time and Organizational Performance," *JMR*, 34 (February), 13–23.

#801 *Product Development (Use of Supplier)*

SCALE ITEMS:*

Please indicate the frequency with which the following practices are used to verify that the design meets customer requirements.

1 = Never—0% of the time
2 = Seldom—1–20% of the time
3 = Occasionally—21–50% of the time
4 = Usually—51–90% of the time
5 = Always or almost always—91–100% of the time

1. Design reviews by multidisciplinary teams.

2. Design reviews by technical teams.

Please indicate the importance of the following practices in speeding up product development.

1 = Slight or not at all—trivial or of no importance
2 = Secondary—less important, but not trivial
3 = Major—important, together with others
4 = Primary—this is the dominant practice

3. Supplier involvement in the design process.

4. Contract out of engineering work.

*Although the verbatim instructions were not listed by Ittner and Larcker (1997), they were likely to have been similar to those shown here.

SCALE NAME: Product Differentiation

SCALE DESCRIPTION: Song and Parry (1997b) used this ten-item, eleven-point Likert-type scale to assess the level of perceived new product superiority relative to competing products. In a separate article, Song and Parry (1997a) used a stripped-down, five-item version of the scale to measure competitive advantage of the product.

SCALE ORIGIN: The scale is original to Song and Parry (1997a, b), though many of the items are attributed to the work of Cooper (1979) and Zierger and Maidique (1990). Song and Parry (1997a, b) generated some scale items on the basis of a review of the literature, pilot studies, and information obtained from 36 in-depth case study interviews conducted with both Japanese and U.S. firms. The items for all scales used by Song and Parry (1997a, b) were evaluated by an academic panel composed of both Japanese and U.S. business and engineering experts. Following revisions, the items were judged by a new panel composed of academicians and new product development (NPD) managers. Song and Parry (1997a, b) reported extensive pretesting of both the Japanese and U.S. versions of the questionnaire.

SAMPLES: Song and Parry (1997a, b) randomly sampled 500 of the 611 firms trading on the Tokyo, Osaka, and Nagoya stock exchanges that had been identified as developing at least four new physical products since 1991. Usable responses pertaining to **788** NPD projects were obtained from 404 Japanese firms. The resulting data were randomly split by Song and Parry (1997a) into calibration (n = 394) and validation (n = 394) samples for the purpose of cross-validation. Song and Parry (1997b) said the U.S. sampling frame was from companies listed in the *High-Technology Industries Directory*. Of the 643 firms that had introduced a minimum of four new physical products since 1990, 500 were randomly sampled (though stratified by industry to match the Japanese sample), and 312 U.S. firms provided data on **612** NPD projects, of which 312 were successes and 300 were failures.

RELIABILITY: Song and Parry (1997b) reported a coefficient alpha of **.90** for this scale in the Japanese sample and **.89** for the U.S. sample. Song and Parry (1997a) used a confirmatory factor analysis of the data in the calibration sample to purify the scale. Items loading on multiple constructs or those with low item-to-scale loadings were deleted from the measure. Song and Parry (1997a) reported a coefficient alpha of **.89** for the five-item, purified measure using data from the validation sample.

VALIDITY: The extensive pretesting and evaluation of the measure with academicians and NPD managers provided strong evidence for the face validity of the measure. Song and Parry (1997a, b) did not specifically report any other examination of scale validity.

ADMINISTRATION: The self-administered questionnaire containing the scale was originally developed in English; the Japanese version was prepared using the parallel-translation/double-translation method. Following minor revisions made on the basis of pretests with bilingual respondents and case study participants, the Japanese sample received a survey packet containing cover letters in both English and Japanese, two Japanese-language questionnaires, and two international postage-paid reply envelopes. Survey packets delivered to U.S. firms were similar, except no Japanese cover letter was included and the surveys were in English. Incentives, four follow-up letters, and multiple telephone calls and faxes were used to increase the response rate with both samples. Song and Parry (1997a, b) indicated that respondents were asked to answer one questionnaire in the context of a successful new product project introduced after 1991 and the other in the context of a new product project that had failed. Higher scores on the scale indicated greater perceived new product superiority relative to the competition.

MAJOR FINDINGS: Song and Parry (1997a) conceptualized and tested a model of NPD practices believed to influence the success of new product ventures in Japan. The structural model was estimated with the calibration sample data, and the proposed model and the alternative models were tested using the validation sample. The **competitive advantage** of the product was found to significantly and positively influence the relative level of new product success for Japanese firms.

Song and Parry (1997b) conceptualized and tested a model of strategic, tactical, and environmental factors believed to influence new product success using data collected from both Japanese and U.S. firms. In both the Japanese and U.S. NPD samples, the relationship between **product differentiation** and relative product performance was strengthened by high levels of (1) project fit with the firm's marketing skills and resources, (2) internal firm commitment to the project, and (3) NPD project market potential. However, higher levels of competitive intensity were also found to weaken the relationship between **product differentiation** and relative product performance.

REFERENCES:

Cooper, Robert G. (1979b), "The Dimensions of Industrial New Product Success and Failure," *JM*, 43 (Summer), 93–103.

Song, X. Michael and Mark E. Parry (1997a), "The Determinants of Japanese New Product Successes," *JMR*, 34 (February), 64–76.

———— and ———— (1997b), "A Cross-National Comparative Study of New Product Development Processes: Japan and the United States," *JM*, 61 (April), 1–18.

Zierger, Billie Jo and Modesto Maidique (1990), "A Model of NPD: An Empirical Test," *Management Science*, 36 (7), 867–83.

SCALE ITEMS:*

Directions: To what extent does each statement listed below correctly describe this selected successful project? Please indicate your degree of agreement or disagreement by circling a number from zero (0) to ten (10) on the scale to the right of each statement. Here: 0 = strongly disagree, 10 = strongly agree, and numbers between 0 and 10 indicate various degrees of agreement or disagreement.

Strongly disagree 0———1———2———3———4———5———6———7———8———9———10 Strongly agree

1. This product relied on technology never used in the industry before.

2. This product caused significant changes in the whole industry.

3. This product was one of the first of its kind introduced into the market.

4. This product was highly innovative—totally new to the market.

5. Compared to competitive products, this product offered some unique features or attributes to the customer.

6. This product was clearly superior to competing products in terms of meeting customers' needs.

7. This product permitted the customer to do a job or do something he [or she] could not presently do with what was available.

8. This product was higher quality than competing products—tighter specifications, stronger, lasted longer, or more reliable.

9. This product had superior technical performance relative to competing products.

10. We were the first into the market with this type of product.

*Items 5–9 were used by Song and Parry (1997a) as a measure of competitive advantage.

SCALE NAME: Product Line Sophistication

SCALE DESCRIPTION: Five seven-point semantic differential items measuring the technical complexity of the product. Although used in the context of evaluating the appropriateness of foreign agents versus foreign distributors when exporting products abroad, the scale is not specific to export situations and could easily be applied to marketing in a domestic setting by changing the instructions. Bello and Lohtia (1995) referred to the scale as *product specificity*, but Bello and Gilliland (1997) called a three-item reduced version of the scale *product complexity*.

SCALE ORIGIN: Bello and Lohtia (1995) and Bello and Gilliland (1997) stated that the scale was adapted from Anderson (1985).

SAMPLES: Bello and Lohtia (1995) drew a systematic random sample of 398 firms that were verified as exporting through middlemen from among those listed in the 1991 edition of the *Journal of Commerce United States Importer & Exporter Directory*. A total of **269** usable responses were obtained for a 68% response rate. Of the respondents, 60% exported through foreign distributors, and 40% exported using foreign agents. Bello and Gilliland's (1997) systematic random sample of 245 national manufacturers was drawn from the 1994 edition of the same source, and **160** usable responses were obtained from export managers working for firms exporting a variety of industrial and consumer products to a total of 39 different countries.

RELIABILITY: A coefficient alpha of **.77** and a confirmatory factor analysis composite reliability of **.86** were reported by Bello and Lohtia (1995) and Bello and Gilliland (1997), respectively.

VALIDITY: Confirmatory factor analysis was used by both Bello and Lohtia (1995) and Bello and Gilliland (1997) to provide evidence of discriminant and convergent validity, as well as to assess the unidimensionality of the measure. Convergent validity was deemed to be present because items loaded significantly on their posited indicators and because of the low to moderate correlations between the scale and other measures. Discriminant validity was also deemed to be present in both studies because the correlation estimate between two indicators never included 1.0 (+/– two standard errors). Bello and Gilliland (1997) used personal interviews with export executives to verify the face validity of the measure.

ADMINISTRATION: Both Bello and Lohtia (1995) and Bello and Gilliland (1997) indicated that this scale was self-administered as part of a longer survey instrument mailed to respondents. One individual with middleman responsibilities at each of these screened firms was sent a questionnaire by Bello and Lohtia (1995). Nonrespondents were telephoned three weeks later and sent a second questionnaire. Instructions requested that responses be specific to a single, focal export middleman in a foreign market. Bello and Gilliland (1997) used similar follow-up procedures but specified that the focal distributor should be the firm's fourth-largest foreign distributor in terms of unit sales volume to avoid a positive evaluation bias. Higher scores on the scale indicated greater product technical complexity in a more highly engineered product.

MAJOR FINDINGS: Bello and Lohtia (1995) investigated several cost indicators believed to influence the choice of foreign distributors versus foreign agents. Differences between agent and distributor users existed with respect to **product line sophistication**, because users with more technically complex and sophisticated products were likely to use agents for middlemen. Bello and Gilliland (1997) examined the effect of output controls, process controls, and flexibility on channel performance and found that greater **product line complexity (sophistication)** increased the use of both process controls and output controls over foreign distributors.

#803 *Product Line Sophistication*

REFERENCES:
Anderson, Erin (1985), "The Salesperson as Outside Agent or Employee: A Transaction Cost Analysis," *Marketing Science*, 4 (3), 234–54.
Bello, Daniel C. and David I. Gilliland (1997), "The Effect of Output Controls, Process Controls, and Flexibility on Export Channel Performance," *JM*, 61 (January), 22–38.
———— and Ritu Lohtia (1995), "Export Channel Design: The Use of Foreign Distributors and Agents," *JAMS*, 23 (2), 83–93.

SCALE ITEMS:*
Directions: Describe the product you sell through middlemen to the focal foreign country.**

1. Unsophisticated   :___:___:___:___:___:___:___: Sophisticated
                 1   2   3   4   5   6   7

2. Nontechnical   :___:___:___:___:___:___:___: Technical
             1   2   3   4   5   6   7

3. Simple   :___:___:___:___:___:___:___: Complex
          1   2   3   4   5   6   7

4. Low engineering content   :___:___:___:___:___:___:___: High engineering content
                 1   2   3   4   5   6   7

5. Commodity   :___:___:___:___:___:___:___: Customized
           1   2   3   4   5   6   7

*Items 1, 2, and 4 were used by Bello and Gilliland (1997) as a measure of product complexity.

**The actual directions for filling out the scale were not provided but were likely to have been similar to those shown here.

SCALE NAME: Product Quality

SCALE DESCRIPTION: A three-item, five-point scale measuring the overall quality of the respondent's products and services with respect to customer perceptions and competitive comparisons.

SCALE ORIGIN: Menon, Jaworski, and Kohli (1997) provided no information to indicate that the scale was anything other than original to their study.

SAMPLES: Using the *Dun and Bradstreet Million Dollar Directory* as the sampling frame, Menon, Jaworski, and Kohli (1997) selected for initial contact every other company name from among the top 1000 companies by sales revenues. Participation from multiple strategic business units (SBUs) within an organization was requested. A total of 102 companies agreed to participate, and ultimately, responses representing **222** SBUs were obtained from marketing and nonmarketing executives.

RELIABILITY: Menon, Jaworski, and Kohli (1997) reported a **.79** alpha reliability coefficient.

VALIDITY: No specific examination of scale validity was presented by Menon, Jaworski, and Kohli (1997) in this article or by Jaworski and Kohli (1993).

ADMINISTRATION: The 206 marketing and 187 nonmarketing executives identified by participating corporations were directly contacted by Menon, Jaworski, and Kohli (1997). Initial contact was followed by a self-administered mail questionnaire, and a follow-up questionnaire was sent three weeks later to nonrespondents. Most (79.6%) of the marketing executives and 70% of the nonmarketing executives contacted provided data for the study. When both nonmarketing and marketing executives from a single SBU responded, their scores were averaged to provide a single score for the construct. A higher score on the market turbulence scale indicated a more volatile market characterized by a higher degree of customer composition and preference changes.

MAJOR FINDINGS: Menon, Jaworski, and Kohli (1997) investigated the role of organizational factors affecting interdepartmental interactions and the resulting impact on product quality. Findings indicated that **product quality** was affected by both interdepartmental conflict and connectedness. Whereas interdepartmental connectedness was found to be more important for **product quality** when technological and market turbulence was high, the relationship between interdepartmental conflict and **product quality** was robust across various levels of market and technological turbulence.

REFERENCES:
Jaworski, Bernard and Ajay K. Kohli (1993), "Market Orientation: Antecedents and Consequences," *JM*, 57 (July), 53–70.
Menon, Ajay, Bernard J. Jaworski, and Ajay K. Kohli (1997), "Product Quality: Impact of Interdepartmental Interactions," *JAMS*, 25 (3), 187–200.

SCALE ITEMS:*

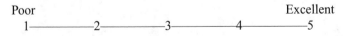

Poor   Excellent
1————————2————————3————————4————————5

1. Our customers often praise our product quality.

2. The quality of our products and services is better than that of our major competitors.

3. Our customers are firmly convinced that we offer very good quality products.

* Although Menon, Jaworski, and Kohli (1997) specified the scale anchors as ranging from "poor" to "excellent", the phrasing of the items suggests that they may also be used in a traditional Likert "strongly disagree" to "strongly agree" format.

SCALE NAME: Product Relative Advantage

SCALE DESCRIPTION: Gatignon and Xuereb (1997) used this eleven-item, six-point scale to measure the various sources of a product's relative advantage over the competition with respect to factors such as economies of scale, product image, product design, product quality, product cost, and various other marketing characteristics. The authors referred to this scale as *innovation relative advantage.*

SCALE ORIGIN: Gatignon and Xuereb (1997) stated that the multiple-item scales used in their study were developed on the basis of items previously proposed and used in survey research. The measure was pretested with others on the questionnaire, and some phrasing was revised. A pilot test was performed on the revised questionnaire for the purpose of assessing scale validity. The resulting measures were then administered in the final questionnaire to a large sample.

SAMPLES: Gatignon and Xuereb (1997) mailed the final questionnaire to a list of 3000 marketing executives representing a broad cross-section of U.S. industries randomly selected from a commercially available list, and 2802 were successfully delivered. Of this number, **393** usable responses were obtained for a 14% response rate. The products represented by the marketing executives surveyed included consumer durable and packaged goods, consumer services, industrial technology, and computer firms.

RELIABILITY: Gatignon and Xuereb (1997) reported a coefficient alpha of **.74** for this measure.

VALIDITY: Gatignon and Xuereb (1997) reported conducting a pilot study for the purpose of assessing scale validity, but no other details were provided.

ADMINISTRATION: The scale was part of a self-administered mail survey. Nonrespondents were sent a reminder letter with an offer of a $500 lottery award two weeks after the initial mailing. Gatignon and Xuereb (1997) instructed respondents to answer the questionnaire in the context of the last new product introduced in the market by a strategic business unit. Higher scores on the scale indicated that respondents perceived the new product as having stronger relative product advantages over the competition.

MAJOR FINDINGS: Gatignon and Xuereb (1997) examined the appropriateness of a customer, competitive, and technological orientation in the context of new product development. The greater the **relative product advantage**, the higher was the perceived performance of the product. Products with a greater degree of **relative advantage** were associated with a technology orientation, greater levels of firm resources, and products thought to be dissimilar to the competition.

REFERENCES:

Gatignon, Hubert and Jean-Marc Xuereb (1997), "Strategic Orientation of the Firm and New Product Performance," *JMR*, 34 (February), 77–90.

SCALE ITEMS:

Directions: Please tell us about your firm's level of competitive advantage or disadvantage in this category for this new product. (Circle one number for each of the following areas)

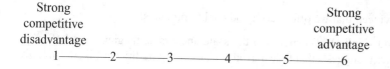

Strong competitive disadvantage   Strong competitive advantage

1———2———3———4———5———6

1. Overall advantage.

2. Product performance.

3. Economies of scale.

4. Product design (functionality, features).

5. Product positioning (product image).

6. Distribution channels.

7. Sales force.

8. Reputation.

9. Product technology.

10. Product quality.

11. Cost.

SCALE NAME: Product Relative Costs

SCALE DESCRIPTION: Gatignon and Xuereb (1997) used this four-item, six-point scale to measure the costs associated with the marketing, manufacturing and operations, and research and development of a new product relative to the competition. The authors referred to this scale as *relative cost.*

SCALE ORIGIN: Gatignon and Xuereb (1997) stated that the multiple-item scales used in their study were developed on the basis of items previously proposed and used in survey research. The measure was pretested with others on the questionnaire, and some phrasing was revised. A pilot test was performed on the revised questionnaire for the purpose of assessing scale validity. The resulting measures were then administered in the final questionnaire to a large sample.

SAMPLES: Gatignon and Xuereb (1997) mailed the final questionnaire to a list of 3000 marketing executives representing a broad cross-section of U.S. industries randomly selected from a commercially available list, and 2802 were successfully delivered. Of this number, **393** usable responses were obtained for a 14% response rate. The products represented by the marketing executives surveyed included consumer durable and packaged goods, consumer services, industrial technology, and computer firms.

RELIABILITY: Gatignon and Xuereb (1997) reported a coefficient alpha of **.73** for this measure.

VALIDITY: Gatignon and Xuereb (1997) reported conducting a pilot study for the purpose of assessing scale validity, but no other details were provided.

ADMINISTRATION: The scale was part of a self-administered mail survey. Nonrespondents were sent a reminder letter with an offer of a $500 lottery award two weeks after the initial mailing. Gatignon and Xuereb (1997) instructed respondents to answer the questionnaire in the context of the last new product introduced in the market by a strategic business unit. Higher scores on the scale indicated that respondents perceived the new product as having higher marketing, manufacturing and operations, and research and development costs relative to the competition.

MAJOR FINDINGS: Gatignon and Xuereb (1997) examined the appropriateness of a customer, competitive, and technological orientation in the context of new product development. Firms that have a technological orientation were found to have higher **relative product costs** than their competitors, whereas in high-growth markets, a competitive orientation decreased the **relative cost** of the new products. New **product relative costs** were also higher in markets characterized by higher levels of demand uncertainty.

REFERENCES:
Gatignon, Hubert and Jean-Marc Xuereb (1997), "Strategic Orientation of the Firm and New Product Performance," *JMR*, 34 (February), 77–90.

SCALE ITEMS:
Directions: Please tell us about the relative cost of the new product which you introduced compared to your main competitors. (Circle one number for each of the following sentences)

Our costs are much lower ————— Our costs are much higher

1————2————3————4————5————6

1. Marketing costs.

2. Manufacturing/operations.

3. Research and development.

4. Overall costs.

SCALE NAME: Product Similarity (to Competition)

SCALE DESCRIPTION: Gatignon and Xuereb (1997) used this five-item, six-point Likert-type scale to measure the level of similarity between a new product and competitors' products with respect to its technology and how the product is positioned, used, and perceived by consumers.

SCALE ORIGIN: Gatignon and Xuereb (1997) stated that the multiple-item scales used in their study were developed on the basis of items previously proposed and used in survey research. The measure was pretested with others on the questionnaire, and some phrasing was revised. A pilot test was performed on the revised questionnaire for the purpose of assessing scale validity. The resulting measures were then administered in the final questionnaire to a large sample. The authors stated that the measure was developed after a factor analysis of the items in the radicalness scale indicated the existence of separate factors when items were expressed in terms relative to the competition. It is not clear whether this factor analysis took place during the pilot study or following the final administration.

SAMPLES: Gatignon and Xuereb (1997) mailed the final questionnaire to a list of 3000 marketing executives representing a broad cross-section of U.S. industries randomly selected from a commercially available list, and 2802 were successfully delivered. Of this number, **393** usable responses were obtained for a 14% response rate. The products represented by the marketing executives surveyed included consumer durable and packaged goods, consumer services, industrial technology, and computer firms.

RELIABILITY: Gatignon and Xuereb (1997) reported a coefficient alpha of **.78** for this measure.

VALIDITY: Gatignon and Xuereb (1997) reported conducting a pilot study for the purpose of assessing scale validity, but no other details were provided.

ADMINISTRATION: The scale was part of a self-administered mail survey. Nonrespondents were sent a reminder letter with an offer of a $500 lottery award two weeks after the initial mailing. Gatignon and Xuereb (1997) instructed respondents to answer the questionnaire in the context of the last new product introduced in the market by a strategic business unit. Higher scores on the scale indicated that respondents perceived the new product as being similar to competitors' products with respect to its positioning, application, and use of technology.

MAJOR FINDINGS: Gatignon and Xuereb (1997) examined the appropriateness of a customer, competitive, and technological orientation in the context of new product development. The smaller the degree of **similarity with competitors' products**, the higher was the perceived performance of the product and the greater that product's relative advantage. A customer orientation in the firm, high growth-market conditions, and competitively intense markets led to greater **similarity** between new products and the competition, whereas a technological orientation resulted in new products that were **less** similar to the competition. Greater degrees of both demand uncertainty and interfunctional coordination resulted in new products that were **less similar** to the competition.

REFERENCES:
Gatignon, Hubert and Jean-Marc Xuereb (1997), "Strategic Orientation of the Firm and New Product Performance," *JMR*, 34 (February), 77–90.

#807 *Product Similarity (to Competition)*

SCALE ITEMS:

Directions: Can you tell us a little about the degree of similarity of this new product with your main competitor's products. (Circle one number for each of the following sequences)

1. Overall, this new product is very similar to our main competitors' products.

2. The technology of this new product is very similar to the technology of our main competitor's products.

3. The positioning of this new product is very similar to the positioning of our main competitors' products.

4. The applications of this new product are totally different from applications of our main competitors' products. **(r)**

5. From the point of view of the user, this new product is totally different from our main competitor's products. **(r)**

SCALE NAME: Profits Are Not Paramount

SCALE DESCRIPTION: Singhapakdi and colleagues (1995) used this five-item, nine-point scale to measure the importance of ethics and social responsibility compared with achieving operating efficiencies, stockholder happiness, and profit.

SCALE ORIGIN: Singhapakdi and colleagues (1995) credited Kraft and Jauch's (1992) organizational effectiveness menu as providing the foundation for the scale's development. The organizational effectiveness menu measures five categories of firm performance, including ethics and social responsibility. Sixteen items identified by Kraft and Jauch (1992) as relating ethics and social responsibility to different aspects of organizational effectiveness were adapted by Singhapakdi and colleagues (1995) for the purpose of measuring respondents' perceptions of the relative importance of ethics and social responsibility (PRESOR). An exploratory factor analysis using Varimax rotation resulted in fourteen items loading on three factors with an eigenvalue greater than 1; "Profits Are Not Paramount" was the name given to the five-item factor explaining 9.3% of the variance.

SAMPLES: Singhapakdi and colleagues (1995) sent a mail questionnaire to a randomly drawn sample of 2000 professionals selected from the American Marketing Association mailing list. Of the 1995 that were delivered, **442** usable questionnaires were returned. Key demographics of the sample indicated that the majority of respondents were college-educated (92.8%), male (51.4%), middle mangers working in various industries.

RELIABILITY: Singhapakdi and colleagues (1995) reported a coefficient alpha of **.69** for this scale.

VALIDITY: Singhapakdi and colleagues (1995) deleted items with factor loadings of less than .40 or items loading at .40 on more than one factor. No examination of scale validity was reported.

ADMINISTRATION: Singhapakdi and colleagues (1995) indicated that the measure was included as part of a self-administered mail survey. As all items were reverse scored, and higher scores indicated stronger perceptions that acting in an ethical and socially responsible manner was more important than achieving profit, organizational efficiencies, and stakeholder happiness.

MAJOR FINDINGS: Singhapakdi and colleagues (1995) investigated marketing practitioners' perceptions of the importance of ethics and social responsibility in achieving organizational effectiveness and how these perceptions were influenced by corporate ethical values and an individual's personal moral philosophy. Univariate tests were employed to demonstrate that respondents perceived the **profits are not paramount** mean (7.34) to be significantly greater than a neutral value of 5, which indicated that respondents generally believed ethical and socially responsible behavior to be at least somewhat more important than achieving profits, stakeholder happiness, and organizational efficiencies. An ordinary least squared regression analysis also demonstrated that the **profits are not paramount** factor of PRESOR was positively influenced by corporate ethical values and negatively influenced by relativism. The influence of idealism on the **profits are not paramount** factor was insignificant at the .05 level.

REFERENCES:
Kraft, Kenneth L. and Lawrence R. Jauch (1992), "The Organizational Effectiveness Menu: A Device for Stakeholder Assessment," *Mid-American Journal of Business*, 7-1 (Spring), 18–23.
Singhapakdi, Anusorn, Kenneth L. Kraft, Scott J. Vitell, and Kumar C. Rallapalli (1995), "The Perceived Importance of Ethics and Social Responsibility on Organizational Effectiveness: A Survey of Marketers," *JAMS*, 23 (1), 49–56.

#808 *Profits Are Not Paramount*

SCALE ITEMS:

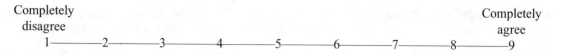

Completely
  disagree
    1————2————3————4————5————6————7————8————9

Completely
agree

1. If stockholders are unhappy, nothing else matters. **(r)**

2. If the survival of a business enterprise is at stake, then you must forget about ethics and social responsibility. **(r)**

3. The most important concern for a firm is making a profit, even if it means bending or breaking the rules. **(r)**

4. To remain competitive in a global environment, business firms will have to disregard ethics and social responsibility. **(r)**

5. Efficiency is much more important to a firm than whether or not the firm is seen as ethical or socially responsible. **(r)**

SCALE NAME: Promotion from Within

SCALE DESCRIPTION: Ganesan and Weitz (1996) used this four-item, seven-point Likert-type scale to measure the extent to which a retail organization is perceived as practicing a policy of promoting buyers from within the firm as opposed to hiring outside the firm.

SCALE ORIGIN: Ganesan and Weitz (1996) stated that the scale was taken from the work of Landau and Hammer (1986).

SAMPLES: Ganesan and Weitz (1996) effectively sampled approximately 1500 retail buyers, divisional merchandise managers, general merchandise managers, and senior merchandise officers whose names appeared on a national list of department, specialty, and discount chain store employees. Usable responses were obtained from **207** respondents.

RELIABILITY: Ganesan and Weitz (1996) reported a coefficient alpha of **.70** for the scale.

VALIDITY: All items composing the measures used by Ganesan and Weitz (1996) were subjected to a confirmatory factor analysis to assess the unidimensionality of the measures, and items violating this principle were dropped. Scales demonstrating unidimensionality were then tested for discriminant and convergent validity using LISREL 8.10. The overall model fit was good, demonstrating a goodness-of-fit index of .96, confirmatory fit index of .99, root mean squared error of approximation of .02, and standardized root mean square residual of .06, as well as a nonsignificant chi-square.

ADMINISTRATION: Ganesan and Weitz (1996) included the scale with other measures as part of a self-administered survey that was delivered by mail. Higher scores on the scale indicated that a retail organization was more likely to promote from within the firm when filling a job vacancy, whereas lower scores on the scale indicated that the firm preferred to hire from outside the company.

MAJOR FINDINGS: Ganesan and Weitz (1996) investigated the impact of various staffing policies on the attitudes and behavior of retail buyers. A retail firm's policy of **promoting from within** the firm had a significant positive effect on buyer's perceptions of promotion opportunities and a significant negative effect on the buyer's salary.

REFERENCES:

Ganesan, Shankar and Barton A. Weitz (1996), "The Impact of Staffing Policies on Retail Buyer Job Attitudes and Behaviors," *JR*, 72 (1), 31–56.

Landau, Jacqueline and Tove Helland Hammer (1986), "Clerical Employee's Perceptions of Intraorganizational Opportunities," *Academy of Management Journal*, 29 (2), 385–404.

SCALE ITEMS:

Strongly disagree / Strongly agree
1————2————3————4————5————6————7

1. Our organization has a policy of promotion from within the organization.

2. Our organization rarely hires people for senior management positions from outside the organization.

3. Job vacancies in our buying department are usually filled by people from outside the department. **(r)**

4. An employee in the buying department who applies for a job in the store has a better chance of getting that job than someone outside the organization applying for the same job.

SCALE NAME: Promotion Opportunity

SCALE DESCRIPTION: Ganesan and Weitz (1996) used this three-item, seven-point Likert-type scale to measure the extent to which a buyer perceived promotion opportunities within the retail organization.

SCALE ORIGIN: The scale is original to Ganesan and Weitz (1996). Multiple items were developed for the construct and purified using item analysis and an exploratory factor analysis. Items loading on multiple factors and those with low loadings were dropped from the scale.

SAMPLES: Ganesan and Weitz (1996) effectively sampled approximately 1500 retail buyers, divisional merchandise managers, general merchandise managers, and senior merchandise officers whose names appeared on a national list of department, specialty, and discount chain store employees. Usable responses were obtained from **207** respondents.

RELIABILITY: Ganesan and Weitz (1996) reported a coefficient alpha of **.85** for the scale.

VALIDITY: All items composing the measures used by Ganesan and Weitz (1996) were subjected to a confirmatory factor analysis to assess the unidimensionality of the measures, and items violating this principle were dropped. Scales demonstrating unidimensionality were then tested for discriminant and convergent validity using LISREL 8.10. The overall model fit was good, demonstrating a goodness-of-fit index of .96, confirmatory fit index of .99, root mean squared error of approximation of .02, and standardized root mean square residual of .06, as well as a nonsignificant chi-square.

ADMINISTRATION:

Ganesan and Weitz (1996) included the scale with other measures as part of a self-administered survey that was delivered by mail. Higher scores on the scale indicated that a buyer perceived greater promotion opportunities as existing within the retail organization.

MAJOR FINDINGS: Ganesan and Weitz (1996) investigated the impact of various staffing policies on the attitudes and behavior of retail buyers. A retail firm's policy of promoting from within the firm and perceptions of intraorganizational mobility both had a significantly positive effect on buyer's perceptions of **promotion opportunities**, whereas a staffing policy of promoting employees through seniority negatively influenced buyers' perceptions of **promotion opportunities**.

REFERENCES:

Ganesan, Shankar and Barton A. Weitz (1996), "The Impact of Staffing Policies on Retail Buyer Job Attitudes and Behaviors," *JR*, 72 (1), 31–56.

SCALE ITEMS:

Strongly   Strongly
disagree   agree

1————2————3————4————5————6————7

1. My opportunities for promotion in this organization are excellent.

2. I am very satisfied with the promotion opportunities in this organization.

3. This organization has a lot of promotion opportunities for me.

SCALE NAME: Psychological Distance

SCALE DESCRIPTION: Fisher, Maltz, and Jaworski (1997) used this four-item, five-point Likert-type scale to assess marketing managers' perceptions of the degree of dissimilarity between themselves and engineers with respect to attitudes toward risk tolerance, customer understanding, time needed to make decisions, and technology focus.

SCALE ORIGIN: Fisher, Maltz, and Jaworski (1997) indicated that the items developed for this construct were based on the work of Gupta, Raj, and Wilemon (1986). Preliminary scale items were pretested with six marketing managers; those found to be unclear, ambiguous, or not applicable were dropped from the measure. A six-item version of psychological distance was administered in Study 1, and two reversed items, "our decision-making style" and "our belief that there is always a 'right' answer," were eliminated on the basis of large modification indices in the confirmatory factor analysis.

SAMPLES: In Study 1, Fisher, Maltz, and Jaworski (1997) sampled 180 marketing managers employed by a *Fortune* 100 firm serving five diverse high-technology markets. The convenience sample was composed of marketing managers attending management training sessions over a three-week period, from which **89** usable responses were obtained. In Study 2, the authors sampled marketing managers employed by a multinational, business-to-business services firm with 36 business units in six countries outside the United States. A key informant provided a list of 100 firm members employed in a variety of marketing positions that required them to interact with engineering personnel. A total of **72** usable responses were obtained for Study 2.

RELIABILITY: Fisher, Maltz, and Jaworski (1997) reported calculating coefficient alphas for this measure of **.82** in Study 1 and **.69** in Study 2.

VALIDITY: In Study 1, confirmatory factor analyses were conducted in two stages to maintain an acceptable ratio of observations to variables. The second analysis included the original ten items composing the psychological distance and functional power measures. Fisher, Maltz, and Jaworski (1997) stated that, after the two psychological distance items were eliminated because of large modification indices, the revised model fit the data acceptably well. Evidence of discriminant validity was provided in that the correlation between each pair of constructs was significantly different from 1.00.

ADMINISTRATION: The measure was included with other scales in a self-administered questionnaire. For Study 1, a survey packet containing a cover letter, reply envelope, and the survey instrument was distributed to each marketing manager participant of a company-sponsored training session. Fisher, Maltz, and Jaworski (1997) used e-mail and telephone reminders to increase response rates. In Study 2, respondents received the survey packet by mail. Offers of anonymity and shared survey results were provided as incentives to participate. Nonrespondents received a reminder letter, followed by a second mail survey packet. In both studies, respondents were instructed to answer questions in the context of their relationship with a single manager in the engineering function with whom they interacted regularly. All items in this scale were reversed; as such, higher scores on the measure indicated that respondents perceived their attitudes as being highly dissimilar or psychologically distant from those held by engineers.

MAJOR FINDINGS: Fisher, Maltz, and Jaworski (1997) investigated how relative functional identification, or the strength of marketing managers' psychological connection to their functional area compared with the firm as a whole, influenced different strategies for improving communication between marketers and engineers. **Psychological distance** was included as a covariate in the study and was found to negatively influence both the frequency and bidirectionality of communication between parties in

#811 *Psychological Distance*

Study 1. This results indicated that, as the perceived **psychological distance** between engineers and marketers increases, both the number of communications and the amount of feedback provided by each party declines. In Study 2, only the negative relationship between **psychological distance** and bidirectionality was supported. However, **psychological distance** was found to have a strong negative association with both the use of information by engineering and the degree of relationship effectiveness perceived by marketers, two new dependent variables specific to Study 2.

REFERENCES:

Fisher, Robert J., Elliot Maltz, and Bernard J. Jaworski (1997), "Enhancing Communication Between Marketing and Engineering: The Moderating Role of Relative Functional Identification," *JM*, 61 (July), 54–70.

Gupta, Ashok, K., S.P. Raj, and David Wilemon (1985), "The R&D-Marketing Interface in High-Tech Firms," *Journal of Product Innovation Management*, 2 (March), 12–24.

SCALE ITEMS:

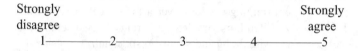

The engineering contact and I are similar in terms of...

1. The time it takes to make a decision. **(r)**

2. Our tolerance for risk. **(r)**

3. How much we focus on technology. **(r)**

4. Our understanding of customers. **(r)**

SCALE NAME: Purchase Importance

SCALE DESCRIPTION: This three-item, seven-point semantic differential-type scale measures the importance of the purchase to the buyer in terms of the purchased item's potential impact on the buyer's end product.

SCALE ORIGIN: Stump and Heide (1996) appear to have based the items used in this measure on the work of Spekman (1988). Extensive pretesting of the questionnaire containing the measure was reported by Stump and Heide (1996).

SAMPLES: Stump and Heide (1996) drew a random sample of 1073 names from a national mailing list of chemical manufacturing firms in standard industrial classification code 28. Of this group, 631 key informants were identified by telephone who agreed to participate in the study. A total of **164** usable surveys were returned.

RELIABILITY: Stump and Heide (1996) calculated a coefficient alpha of **.63** for this measure.

VALIDITY: Stump and Heide (1996) examined item-to-total correlations of the items composing the scale and conducted an exploratory factor analysis of the measures used in the study. A confirmatory factor analysis of all items used in each scale verified the unidimensionality of the measure. Evidence of the discriminant validity of the measure was provided by means of a series of chi-square difference tests performed on the factor correlations. The model was also evaluated and found to represent a good fit to the data.

ADMINISTRATION: The scale was included by Stump and Heide (1996) with other measures as part of a self-administered survey that was delivered by mail. Buyers were asked to identify a purchasing agreement for a particular product that had been established within the last twelve months and to answer questions in the context of that purchasing agreement. Higher scores on the scale indicated that a buyer evaluated a purchase as being of greater importance to the end product produced.

MAJOR FINDINGS: Stump and Heide (1996) examined how chemical manufacturers used partner selection, incentive design, and monitoring approaches in the management and control of supplier relationships. Slight evidence was provided linking **purchase importance** to the qualification of supplier ability, though this relationship was only significant at the $p < .10$ level.

REFERENCES:
Spekman, Robert E. (1988), "Strategic Supplier Selection: Understanding Long-Term Buyer Relationships," *Business Horizons*, 31 (4), 75–81.
Stump, Rodney L. and Jan B. Heide (1996), "Controlling Supplier Opportunism in Industrial Relationships," *JMR*, 33 (November), 431–41.

#812 *Purchase Importance*

SCALE ITEMS:

1. Item represents a minor (major) portion of the end product's value.

Minor :___:___:___:___:___:___:___: Major

               1   2   3   4   5   6   7

2. Item is very unimportant (important) element of the end product.

Unimportant :___:___:___:___:___:___:___: Important

                    1   2   3   4   5   6   7

3. Item specification and quality have little (a high) impact on the performance of the end product.

Little :___:___:___:___:___:___:___: High

              1   2   3   4   5   6   7

SCALE NAME: Purchase Importance

SCALE DESCRIPTION: Heide and Weiss (1995) used this four-item, seven-point Likert-type scale to measure the perceived impact of the purchase decision on an organization's productivity and profitability.

SCALE ORIGIN: Heide and Weiss (1995) stated that the scale items were adapted from McQuiston (1989).

SAMPLES: Pretests of the questionnaire where conducted with two different small groups of previous workstation buyers. In the final study, Heide and Weiss (1995) drew a random sample of 900 firms from Installed Technology International's list of firms that had recently purchased workstations. Key informants were identified from this list and contacted by telephone, of which 466 agreed to participate in the study and were sent a mail questionnaire. Follow-up telephone calls and a second mailing resulted in **215** usable questionnaires being returned. Industries represented by respondents included computers (31.4%), manufacturing (22.4%), medical (6.2%), services (15.2%), and other (24.8%).

RELIABILITY: Heide and Weiss (1995) reported a coefficient alpha of **.85** for this scale.

VALIDITY: Heide and Weiss (1995) initially evaluated the measure on the basis of item-to-total correlations and exploratory factor analysis. Confirmatory factor analysis was then used to establish unidimensionality. Evidence of discriminant validity was provided by a series of chi-square tests on the respective factor correlations.

ADMINISTRATION: The measure was included in a self-administered mail survey. Heide and Weiss (1995) instructed respondents to answer all questions in the context of their organization's most recent workstation purchase. Higher scores on the scale indicated that buyers perceived the purchase as having a significant influence on firm profitability and productivity.

MAJOR FINDINGS: Heide and Weiss (1995) investigated how buyers working in high-technology markets approached decisions in the consideration and choice stages of the purchase process. Specifically, factors influencing whether buyers included new vendors at the consideration stage and whether they ultimately switched to a new vendor at the choice stage were investigated. Heide and Weiss (1995) reported that, as perceptions of **purchase importance** rose, buyers became less likely to exclude new vendors from the consideration set. **Purchase importance** had no influence on whether a new or existing vendor was chosen.

REFERENCES:
Heide, Jan B. and Allen M. Weiss (1995), "Vendor Consideration and Switching Behavior for Buyers in High-Technology Markets," *JM*, 59 (July), 30–43.
McQuiston, Daniel H. (1989), "Novelty, Complexity, and Importance as Casual Determinants of Industrial Buyer Behavior," *JM*, 53 (April), 66–79.

SCALE ITEMS:

Strongly   Strongly
disagree   agree

1———2———3———4———5———6———7

1. We anticipated this purchase would make a significant improvement in our operations.

2. We felt that this purchase was important to our overall profitability.

3. It was expected that this purchase would enhance our ability to compete.

4. We expected this purchase to impact our "bottom line."

SCALE NAME: Qualification of Supplier (Ability)

SCALE DESCRIPTION: This eight-item, eight-point scale measures the level of effort put forth by buyers to verify a supplier's present skills and ability necessary to support the purchasing agreement.

SCALE ORIGIN: Stump and Heide (1996) developed the items on the basis of the work of Leenders and Fearon (1993). Extensive pretesting of the questionnaire containing the measure was reported, and the items for this scale were modified as a result of feedback obtained during field interviews.

SAMPLES: Stump and Heide (1996) drew a random sample of 1073 names from a national mailing list of chemical manufacturing firms in standard industrial classification code 28. Of this group, 631 key informants were identified by telephone who agreed to participate in the study. A total of **164** usable surveys were returned.

RELIABILITY: Stump and Heide (1996) calculated a coefficient alpha of **.88** for this measure.

VALIDITY: Stump and Heide (1996) examined item-to-total correlations of the items that composed the scale and conducted an exploratory factor analysis of the measures used in the study. A confirmatory factor analysis of all items used in each scale verified the unidimensionality of the measure. Evidence of the discriminant validity of the measure was provided by means of a series of chi-square difference tests performed on the factor correlations. The model was also evaluated and found to represent a good fit to the data.

ADMINISTRATION: The scale was included by Stump and Heide (1996) with other measures as part of a self-administered survey that was delivered by mail. Buyers were asked to identify a purchasing agreement for a particular product that had been established within the last 12 months and to answer questions in the context of that purchasing agreement. Higher scores on the scale indicated that a buyer invested more effort ex ante in attempting to assess the ability of the manufacturer in several key areas.

MAJOR FINDINGS: Stump and Heide (1996) examined how chemical manufacturers used partner selection, incentive design, and monitoring approaches in the management and control of supplier relationships. When purchasing agreements called for specific buyer investments, buyers responded to this control problem by subjecting suppliers to more **stringent qualifications of ability** and motivation. Higher levels of performance ambiguity were found to negatively influence attempts to **qualify a supplier's ability**.

REFERENCES:

Leenders, Michiel R. and Harold E. Fearon (1993), *Purchasing and Material Management*, 10th ed. Homewood, IL: Richard D. Irwin.

Stump, Rodney L. and Jan B. Heide (1996), "Controlling Supplier Opportunism in Industrial Relationships," *JMR*, 33 (November), 431–41.

SCALE ITEMS:

No qualification
of supplier

Extensive
qualification
effort

1————2————3————4————5————6————7————8

1. Product quality.

2. Technical capability.

3. Manufacturing capability.

4. Financial strength.

5. Personnel/management resources.

6. Customer services provided.

7. Delivery capability.

8. Compatibility of production processes.

SCALE NAME: Qualification of Supplier (Motivation)

SCALE DESCRIPTION: This five-item, eight-point scale measures the extent to which buyers attempt to verify a supplier's motivation to support the purchasing agreement by gathering evidence of the supplier's willingness to make investments in the relationship and benevolence in customer practices and general business philosophy.

SCALE ORIGIN: The scale appears to be original to Stump and Heide (1996), who reported extensive pretesting of the questionnaire containing the measure.

SAMPLES: Stump and Heide (1996) drew a random sample of 1073 names from a national mailing list of chemical manufacturing firms in standard industrial classification code 28. Of this group, 631 key informants were identified by telephone who agreed to participate in the study. A total of **164** usable surveys were returned.

RELIABILITY: Stump and Heide (1996) calculated a coefficient alpha of **.76** for this measure.

VALIDITY: Stump and Heide (1996) examined item-to-total correlations of the items that composed the scale and conducted an exploratory factor analysis of the measures used in the study. A confirmatory factor analysis of all items used in each scale verified the unidimensionality of the measure. Evidence of the discriminant validity of the measure was provided by means of a series of chi-square difference tests performed on the factor correlations. The model was also evaluated and found to represent a good fit to the data.

ADMINISTRATION: The scale was included by Stump and Heide (1996) with other measures as part of a self-administered survey that was delivered by mail. Buyers were asked to identify a purchasing agreement for a particular product that had been established within the last 12 months and to answer questions in the context of that purchasing agreement. Higher scores on the scale indicated that a buyer invested more effort ex ante in attempting to assess the motivation of the manufacturer to support the purchasing agreement.

MAJOR FINDINGS: Stump and Heide (1996) examined how chemical manufacturers used partner selection, incentive design, and monitoring approaches in the management and control of supplier relationships. When purchasing agreements called for specific buyer investments, buyers responded to this control problem by subjecting suppliers to more **stringent qualifications of motivation** and ability.

REFERENCES:
Stump, Rodney L. and Jan B. Heide (1996), "Controlling Supplier Opportunism in Industrial Relationships," *JMR*, 33 (November), 431–41.

SCALE ITEMS:

No qualification
  of supplier

Extensive
qualification
effort

1————2————3————4————5————6————7————8

1. Supplier's general business philosophy.

2. Supplier's practices toward dealing with customers.

3. Restrictions on marketing rights.

4. Ownership of technical rights related to the identified item.

5. Supplier's willingness to (re)locate production facilities to support your firm's procurement of the identified item.

#816 *Quality (Relationship)*

SCALE NAME: Quality (Relationship)

SCALE DESCRIPTION: Kumar, Scheer, and Steenkamp (1995) used this 25-item scale to measure the overall quality of the dealer–supplier relationship, as reflected by the level of conflict, trust, commitment, continuity, and willingness to invest. Most of the dimensions were measured on a seven-point format with the exception of affective conflict, which was measured on a five-point scale.

SCALE ORIGIN: With the exceptions of affective conflict and willingness to invest, each of the dimensions that served as indicators to relationship quality were represented by items taken from scales that have been used in prior research. Kumar, Scheer, and Steenkamp (1995) made slight modifications to some of these items on the basis of interviews with Dutch dealers, but the affective conflict and willingness to invest subscales were developed specifically for this study. The measures for the other dimensions were taken from the following sources: manifest conflict from Frazier, Gill, and Kale (1989); trust in partner's honesty and trust in partner's benevolence, not reported; affective commitment from Meyer, Allen, and Smith (1993); and expectation of continuity from Noordeweir, John, and Nevin (1990) and Anderson and Weitz (1989).

SAMPLES: After deleting duplications among dealerships and dealerships for which no contact person could be identified, Kumar, Scheer, and Steenkamp (1995) sampled the remaining 1640 of the 2100 new car dealers listed on a commercially purchased list covering two states in the United States. Also, 1600 new car dealers were randomly selected from a list of 4000 dealers representing the entire Netherlands. **Four hundred seventeen** and **289** usable responses were received from U.S. and Dutch dealers, respectively. The data were standardized separately by country to eliminate any culturally idiosyncratic patterns from the data, then pooled for analysis.

RELIABILITY: Kumar, Scheer, and Steenkamp (1995) reported a coefficient alpha of **.94** for the scale.

VALIDITY: The correlations between manifest and affective conflict and trust in partner's honesty and benevolence were found to be significantly below unity, which provided some evidence of the discriminant validity of the measure. Additional evidence was obtained through a confirmatory factor analysis in which each of the items loaded appropriately on the correct first-order factor. Furthermore, all first- and second-order constructs were found to be significant, which provides evidence of convergent validity.

ADMINISTRATION: Kumar, Scheer, and Steenkamp (1995) indicated that the questionnaire was originally constructed in English and then translated into Dutch. Back-translation was used to verify the accuracy of the translation. Some minor changes to item and questionnaire phrasing resulted from feedback obtained during face-to-face interviews with Dutch dealership managers. The scale was included with other measures in a self-administered survey delivered by mail to both samples. Cover letters to the U.S. sample were personalized to a specific individual, and a follow-up letter was sent to nonrespondents after four weeks. The lack of a personalized cover letter and follow-up with the Dutch sample may have contributed to the lower response rate from this group. Dealers from both countries were asked to report on the automobile suppler (manufacturer or importer) whose product line accounted for the largest share of their firm's sales. The two items measuring each of the six indicators of procedural fairness were averaged in the scoring processing. Higher scores on the scale indicated that a dealer believed the relationship with a supplier was of higher quality, as evidenced by lower evaluations of relationship conflict and higher evaluations of supplier trust, commitment, continuity, and willingness to invest.

MAJOR FINDINGS: Kumar, Scheer, and Steenkamp (1995) investigated how supplier fairness affected the development of long-term relationships between relatively smaller and vulnerable new car dealers and larger, more powerful suppliers. Both procedural and distributive fairness positively influenced **relationship quality**, though the impact of procedural fairness was significantly stronger. However, as the outcomes derived from the relationship became more positive, the importance of procedural fairness in determining **relationship quality** declined, whereas the importance of distributive fairness grew. Environmental uncertainty negatively influenced **relationship quality**, and the importance of procedural fairness in determining **relationship quality** increased as environmental uncertainty rose.

REFERENCES:

Anderson, Erin and Barton A. Weitz (1989), "Determinants of Continuity in Conventional Industrial Channel Dyads," *Marketing Science*, 8 (Fall), 310–23.

Frazier, Gary L. (1983), "Interorganizational Exchange Behavior in Marketing Channels: A Broadened Perspective," *JM*, 47 (Fall), 68–78.

Kumar, Nirmalya, Lisa K. Scheer, and Jan-Benedict E.M. Steenkamp (1995), "The Effects of Supplier Fairness on Vulnerable Resellers," *JMR*, 32 (February), 54–65.

Meyer, John P., Natalie J. Allen, and Catherine A. Smith (1993), "Commitment to Organizations and Occupations: Extension and Test of a Three-Component Conceptualization," *Journal of Applied Psychology*, 78 (4), 538–51.

Noordeweir, Thomas G., George John, and John R. Nevin (1990), "Performance Outcomes of Purchasing Agents in Industrial Buyer-Vendor Relationships," *JM*, 54 (October), 80–93.

SCALE ITEMS:

Affective conflict
When your firm reflects on the relationship with the supplier, does your firm feel:

1. Anger.
2. Frustration.
3. Resentment.
4. Hostility.

Manifest conflict
5. A high degree of conflict exists between the supplier and our firm.
6. The supplier and our firm have major disagreements on certain key issues.

Trust in partner's honesty
7. Even when the supplier gives us a rather unlikely explanation, we are confident that they are telling the truth.
8. The supplier has often provided us information which has later proven to be inaccurate. **(r)**
9. The supplier usually keeps the promises they make to our firm.
10. Whenever the supplier gives us advice on our business operations, we know they are sharing their best judgment.
11. Our organization can count on the supplier to be sincere.

Trust in partner's benevolence

12. Though circumstances change, we believe that the supplier will be ready and willing to offer us assistance and support.
13. When making important decisions, the supplier is concerned about our welfare.
14. When we share our problems with the supplier, we know that they will respond with understanding.
15. In the future we can count on the supplier to consider how its decisions and actions will affect us.
16. When it comes to things which are important to us, we can depend on the supplier's support.

Commitment

17. Even if we could, we would not drop the supplier because we like being associated with them.
18. We want to remain a member of the supplier's network, because we genuinely enjoy our relationship with them.
19. Our positive feelings towards the supplier are a major reason we continue working with them.

Expectation of continuity

20. We expect our relationship with the supplier to continue for a long time.
21. Renewal of relationship with supplier is virtually automatic.
22. It is unlikely that our firm will still be doing business with this supplier in 2 years. **(r)**

Willingness to invest

23. If the supplier requested it, we would be willing to make further investment in supporting the supplier's line.
24. We are willing to put more effort and investment in building our business in the supplier's product.
25. In the future, we will work to link our firm with the supplier's in the customer's mind.

SCALE NAME: Quantitative Analysis (Purchasing)

SCALE DESCRIPTION: Bunn (1994) developed a ten-item, seven-point scale to measure the extent to which quantitative analysis and structured tools or techniques were used to analyze specific purchasing situations. Bunn (1994) referred to this scale as *use of analysis techniques.*

SCALE ORIGIN: The scale is original to Bunn (1994). Using an iterative process, Bunn (1994) sought to develop specific measures of organizational buying behavior. An extensive review of the procurement practices and organizational buying behavior literature and personal interviews with 11 purchasing executives from a broad range of industries were used to identify several general-level organizational buying constructs. Scale items for each construct were generated using phrasing from the taped interviews with purchasing executives. A mail survey sent to purchasing executives was used to refine and confirm the constructs. Following refinement, the results of a second survey of purchasing executives were used to select the final set of constructs and measures tested in this study.

SAMPLES: Bunn (1994) provided no details with respect to the two surveys conducted with samples of purchasing executives as part of the initial construct and scale development process. For the scale validation process, Bunn (1994) stated that **636** usable questionnaires were returned from a randomly selected sample of 1843 purchasing executives listed on the National Association of Purchasing Management roster. Of the respondent firms, 57% were in manufacturing industries, 16% were in service industries, and the remainder was comprised of construction, transportation, and public administration firms. The majority of responding firms were large; 59% had between 200 and 5000 employees.

RELIABILITY: Ten of the eleven items submitted to measure purification scored item-to-total correlations above the minimum standard of .30 and were retained as part of the measure. One item, "quantitative models," did not meet this standard and was eliminated. Bunn (1994) reported a coefficient alpha of **.80** for the purified measure.

VALIDITY: Bunn (1994) examined the scale for both discriminant and nomological validity. A four-dimension, promax-rotated factor solution was used to determine that items loaded on the proposed factor at the .40 level or above. Bunn (1994) also reported that all cross loadings were relatively low. A confirmatory factor analysis with LISREL using nested comparisons demonstrated a superior fit for a four-factor solution, as well as statistically significant t-values for indicators. LISREL was also used to confirm the unidimensionality of the measure. Using the procedure suggested by Fornell and Larcker (1988), a second test for unidimensionality was undertaken that did not confirm unidimensionality. Nomological validity was demonstrated by significant correlations in the direction hypothesized between this measure and four theoretically related characteristics of the decision.

ADMINISTRATION: The scale was part of a self-administered mail survey in which Bunn (1994) instructed purchasing executives to answer questions in the context of the most recent purchase decision in which he or she had been involved. Higher scores on the scale indicated a greater use of quantitative analysis techniques in the purchasing decision process.

MAJOR FINDINGS: Bunn (1994) sought to develop scales for measuring four distinct constructs that he proposed as underlying organizational buying behavior. The **quantitative analysis** measure exhibited mixed results with respect to unidimensionality and was found to explain .06 of the variance in a four-dimension, promax-rotated factor solution.

REFERENCES:

Bunn, Michele D. (1994), "Key Aspects of Organizational Buying: Conceptualization and Measurement," *JAMS*, 22 (2), 160–69.

Fornell, Claes and David F. Larcker (1981), "Evaluating Structural Equation Models with Unobservable Variables and Measurement Error," *JMR*, 18 (February), 39–53.

SCALE ITEMS:*

Directions: Please indicate the extent to which each of the following tools was used for the focal purchase.

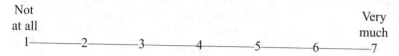

Not at all
Very much

1————2————3————4————5————6————7

1. Price analysis.

2. Cost analysis.

3. Extrapolation of historic trends.

4. Comparison of alternative methods of contract pricing.

5. Make or buy analysis.

6. Spread sheet analysis.

7. Value analysis.

8. Economic analysis.

9. Computer modeling or simulation.

10. Other mathematical analysis.

*Although the actual directions were not specifically listed in Bunn's (1994) article, they are likely to have been similar to those shown here.

SCALE NAME: Reaction Aggressiveness

SCALE DESCRIPTION: Robertson, Eliashberg, and Rymon (1995) used this five-item, six-point Likert-type scale to assess the extent to which a company responded aggressively in some fashion to a new product announcement (NPA) signal released by the competition.

SCALE ORIGIN: Robertson, Eliashberg, and Rymon (1995) developed the scale specifically for this study. The measure and questionnaire in which it was administered were initially conceptualized, tested, and purified on the basis of two pilot studies with executives participating in a management development program and a mail survey pretest. A principal components factor analysis with Varimax rotation was performed on data collected in the final study and used to determine the composition of the final measure.

SAMPLES: A total of 1554 directors of marketing in the United States (1034) and United Kingdom (520), who represented a broad range of consumer and industrial product industries, were sampled for this study. Using a commercially purchased list as their sampling frame, Robertson, Eliashberg, and Rymon (1995) excluded marketing managers of wholesale, retail, and small firms prior to mailing their surveys. A total of **346** usable surveys were returned, of which 241 and 105 were from the United States and United Kingdom, respectively. No evidence of response basis was found, and Chow tests of the U.S. and U.K. data supported the pooling together of data from each country.

RELIABILITY: Robertson, Eliashberg, and Rymon (1995) reported a coefficient alpha of **.69** for this measure.

VALIDITY: No specific examination of scale validity was reported by Robertson, Eliashberg, and Rymon (1995).

ADMINISTRATION: The scale was included with other measures in a self-administered survey delivered by mail. Robertson, Eliashberg, and Rymon (1995) prenotified respondents and offered a copy of the survey's tabulated results as an incentive to participate. Respondents were instructed to answer the questionnaire in the context of the last NPA signal received relative to a new product that was significantly different from existing products. Higher scores on the scale indicated stronger, more aggressive levels of company reaction to a competitor's NPA, whereas lower scores indicated that the company had very little reaction in response to the NPA.

MAJOR FINDINGS: Robertson, Eliashberg, and Rymon (1995) examined the relationship between NPA signals—announcements in advance of market introduction—and factors affecting the likelihood of competitive reactions to NPA signals. Firms were found to be most likely to **react aggressively** to NPA signals issued by competitors when the signal was perceived to be credible and when the industry was characterized by a high degree of patent protection.

REFERENCES:
Robertson, Thomas S., Jehoshua Eliashberg, and Talia Rymon (1995), "New Product Announcement Signals and Incumbent Reactions," *JM*, 59 (July), 1–15.

#818 *Reaction Aggressiveness*

SCALE ITEMS:*

Strongly   Strongly
disagree   agree
  1————2————3————4————5————6

Please tell us how you would characterize your company's response.

1. A cooperative reaction toward our competitor.

2. A reaction to try and take advantage of our competitor.

3. An aggressive reaction.

4. An accomodative reaction.

5. A matching reaction.

*Although a six-point scale format was designated by Robertson, Eliashberg, and Rymon (1995), the scale anchors were not explicitly listed. However, it is probable that the traditional Likert "strongly disagree" to "strongly agree" format was used.

SCALE NAME: Relational Norms (Conflict Harmonization)

SCALE DESCRIPTION: Ayers, Dahlstrom, and Skinner (1997) used this three-item, seven-point Likert-type scale to measure the extent to which the marketing–engineering relationship was characterized by a willingness to resolve conflicts in a good faith manner without involving higher level managers.

SCALE ORIGIN: Ayers, Dahlstrom, and Skinner (1997) indicated that the scale was adapted from a measure developed by Heide and John (1992).

SAMPLES: Ayers, Dahlstrom, and Skinner (1997) collected data on 19 new product development (NPD) projects undertaken by a major U.S. computer manufacturer. Seven project members from each NPD team were selected to participate in the study, five of whom were R&D and the remaining two from marketing. Of the 132 questionnaire booklets distributed, **115** usable surveys were returned.

RELIABILITY: Ayers, Dahlstrom, and Skinner (1997) reported a coefficient alpha of **.75** for the scale.

VALIDITY: An exploratory factor analysis on all items composing the scales was used to verify the uni-dimensionality of the measures. No items were dropped on the basis of item-to-total correlations or an analysis of the factor structure. Ayers, Dahlstrom, and Skinner (1997) next subjected the measures to a confirmatory factor analysis to assess their construct validity. Again, no items were deleted on the basis of this analysis. The discriminant validity of the measures was also assessed by confirmatory factory analysis and was found to be acceptable.

ADMINISTRATION: Ayers, Dahlstrom, and Skinner (1997) included the scale with other measures as part of a self-administered questionnaire booklet that was apparently distributed to respondents at their place of employment. A cover letter explaining the study purpose and promises of anonymity accompanied the survey. The questionnaires distributed to R&D and marketing personnel were identical except that R&D personnel responded to questions about their relationship with marketing, and vice versa. Divisional managers designated the project for which responses were sought. Higher scores on the scale indicated that conflicts were more likely to be resolved harmoniously without involving higher level managers in the process.

MAJOR FINDINGS: Ayers, Dahlstrom, and Skinner (1997) examined the influence of integration between marketing and R&D, managerial controls, and relational norms on new product success. Structural equation modeling was used to test the hypotheses. **Conflict harmonization** was one of three first-order factors serving as an indicator of the relational construct, which was used to represent the extent to which the R&D and marketing NPD team members attempted to maintain and enhance their interpersonal relationships. Relational **norms** positively influenced new product success and were in turn positively influenced by the level of integration between marketing and R&D and negatively influenced by centralization.

REFERENCES:

Ayers, Doug, Robert Dahlstrom, and Steven J. Skinner (1997), "An Exploratory Investigation of Organizational Antecedents to New Product Success," *JMR*, 34 (February), 107–16.

Heide, Jan B. and George John (1992), "Do Norms Matter in Marketing Relationships?" *JM*, 56 (April), 32–44.

#819 *Relational Norms (Conflict Harmonization)*

SCALE ITEMS:
Please indicate your level of agreement with the following:

Strongly
disagree

Strongly
agree

1———2———3———4———5———6———7

1. When conflicts arose in the relationship, it was expected that a higher level manager was needed to resolve the dispute. **(r)**

2. It was expected that the parties would act in good faith manner when resolving disputes.

3. When conflicts arose in the relationship, it was expected that the parties directly involved would resolve the dispute.

SCALE NAME: Relational Norms (Flexibility)

SCALE DESCRIPTION: Ayers, Dahlstrom, and Skinner (1997) used this three-item, seven-point Likert-type scale to measure the extent to which the marketing—engineering relationship was characterized by the ability to accommodate unexpected changes in the new product development (NPD) situation.

SCALE ORIGIN: Ayers, Dahlstrom, and Skinner (1997) indicated that the scale was adapted from a measure developed by Heide and John (1992).

SAMPLES: Ayers, Dahlstrom, and Skinner (1997) collected data on 19 NPD projects undertaken by a major U.S. computer manufacturer. Seven project members from each NPD team were selected to participate in the study, five of whom were R&D and the remaining two from marketing. Of the 132 questionnaire booklets distributed, **115** usable surveys were returned.

RELIABILITY: Ayers, Dahlstrom, and Skinner (1997) reported a coefficient alpha of **.76** for the scale.

VALIDITY: An exploratory factor analysis on all items composing the scales was used to verify the unidimensionality of the measures. No items were dropped on the basis of item-to-total correlations or an analysis of the factor structure. Ayers, Dahlstrom, and Skinner (1997) next subjected the measures to a confirmatory factor analysis to assess their construct validity. Again, no items were deleted on the basis of this analysis. The discriminant validity of the measures was also assessed by confirmatory factory analysis and was found to be acceptable.

ADMINISTRATION: Ayers, Dahlstrom, and Skinner (1997) included the scale with other measures as part of a self-administered questionnaire booklet that was apparently distributed to respondents at their place of employment. A cover letter explaining the study purpose and promises of anonymity accompanied the survey. The questionnaires distributed to R&D and marketing personnel were identical except that R&D personnel responded to questions about their relationship with marketing, and vice versa. Divisional managers designated the project for which responses were sought. Higher scores on the scale indicated that the marketing–engineering relationship was characterized by greater flexibility toward unexpected changes.

MAJOR FINDINGS: Ayers, Dahlstrom, and Skinner (1997) examined the influence of integration between marketing and R&D, managerial controls, and relational norms on new product success. Structural equation modeling was used to test the hypotheses. **Flexibility** was one of three first-order factors serving as an indicator of the relational construct, which was used to represent the extent to which the R&D and marketing NPD team members attempted to maintain and enhance their interpersonal relationships. Relational norms positively influenced new product success and were in turn positively influenced by the level of integration between marketing and R&D and negatively influenced by centralization.

REFERENCES:

Ayers, Doug, Robert Dahlstrom, and Steven J. Skinner (1997), "An Exploratory Investigation of Organizational Antecedents to New Product Success," *JMR*, 34 (February), 107–16.

Heide, Jan B. and George John (1992), "Do Norms Matter in Marketing Relationships?" *JM*, 56 (April), 32–44.

#820 *Relational Norms (Flexibility)*

SCALE ITEMS:

Please indicate your level of agreement with the following:

Strongly
disagree
$$\text{Strongly agree}$$

1————2————3————4————5————6————7

1. Flexibility in response to requests for change was a characteristic of this relationship.

2. The parties expected to be able to make adjustments in the ongoing relationship to cope with changing circumstances.

3. When some unexpected situation arose, the parties preferred to work out a new deal rather than hold each other to the original terms.

SCALE NAME: Relational Norms (Solidarity)

SCALE DESCRIPTION: Ayers, Dahlstrom, and Skinner (1997) used this three-item, seven-point Likert-type scale to measure the extent to which the marketing–engineering relationship was characterized by dependency between parties and commitment to the relationship as a whole.

SCALE ORIGIN: Ayers, Dahlstrom, and Skinner (1997) indicated that the scale was adapted from a measure developed by Heide and John (1992).

SAMPLES: Ayers, Dahlstrom, and Skinner (1997) collected data on 19 new product development (NPD) projects undertaken by a major U.S. computer manufacturer. Seven project members from each NPD team were selected to participate in the study, five of whom were R&D and the remaining two from marketing. Of the 132 questionnaire booklets distributed, **115** usable surveys were returned.

RELIABILITY: Ayers, Dahlstrom, and Skinner (1997) reported a coefficient alpha of **.76** for the scale.

VALIDITY: An exploratory factor analysis on all items composing the scales was used to verify the unidimensionality of the measures. No items were dropped on the basis of item-to-total correlations or an analysis of the factor structure. Ayers, Dahlstrom, and Skinner (1997) next subjected the measures to a confirmatory factor analysis to assess their construct validity. Again, no items were deleted on the basis of this analysis. The discriminant validity of the measures was also assessed by confirmatory factory analysis and was found to be acceptable.

ADMINISTRATION: Ayers, Dahlstrom, and Skinner (1997) included the scale with other measures as part of a self-administered questionnaire booklet that was apparently distributed to respondents at their place of employment. A cover letter explaining the study purpose and promises of anonymity accompanied the survey. The questionnaires distributed to R&D and marketing personnel were identical except that R&D personnel responded to questions about their relationship with marketing, and vice versa. Divisional managers designated the project for which responses were sought. Higher scores on the scale indicated that the marketing–engineering relationship was characterized by greater dependency and commitment between parties.

MAJOR FINDINGS: Ayers, Dahlstrom, and Skinner (1997) examined the influence of integration between marketing and R&D, managerial controls, and relational norms on new product success. Structural equation modeling was used to test the hypotheses. **Solidarity** was one of three first-order factors serving as an indicator of the relational construct, which was used to represent the extent to which the R&D and marketing NPD team members attempted to maintain and enhance their interpersonal relationships. Relational norms positively influenced new product success and were in turn positively influenced by the level of integration between marketing and R&D and negatively influenced by centralization.

REFERENCES:

Ayers, Doug, Robert Dahlstrom, and Steven J. Skinner (1997), "An Exploratory Investigation of Organizational Antecedents to New Product Success," *JMR*, 34 (February), 107–16.

Heide, Jan B. and George John (1992), "Do Norms Matter in Marketing Relationships?" *JM*, 56 (April), 32–44.

#821 *Relational Norms (Solidarity)*

SCALE ITEMS:
Please indicate your level of agreement with the following:

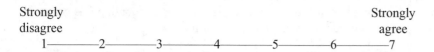

Strongly   Strongly
disagree   agree

1————2————3————4————5————6————7

1. Problems that arose in the course of the relationship were treated by the parties as joint rather than individual responsibilities.

2. The parties were committed to improvements that benefited the relationship as a whole and not only the individual parties.

3. The parties did not mind owing each other favors.

SCALE NAME: Relationalism (Mutuality)

SCALE DESCRIPTION: Li and Dant (1997) described this four-item, five-point Likert-type scale as measuring the extent to which parties in an exchange relationship fairly and evenly shared gains and losses.

SCALE ORIGIN: Li and Dant (1997) reported that the items used in this scale were adapted from Boyle and colleagues (1992). Mutuality, solidarity, and role integrity represented three relational norms commonly employed in the channel literature as second-order constructs when operationalizing the level of relationalism between channel parties.

SAMPLES: Li and Dant (1997) used a cross-sectional survey approach to sample 2553 office machine dealership key informants (owners/presidents) from the membership list of the National Office Machine Dealers Association. Questionnaires were returned from 573 dealerships; incomplete surveys and those completed by individuals not fitting the key informant status were eliminated from the study. The final sample was composed of **461** distributors, of which 286 were classified as having exclusive dealing (ED) arrangements with the photocopier manufacturer for which they sold the most units, whereas the remaining 175 maintained nonexclusive dealing (NED) arrangements.

RELIABILITY: Li and Dant (1997) reported a reliability coefficient of **.82** for this measure.

VALIDITY: Li and Dant (1997) stated that the five measures used in the study were subjected to confirmatory factor analysis using LISREL. After one of the original five solidarity items, "our relationship with them is best described as a 'cooperative effort'," was dropped, support was found for measure unidimensionality. Convergent and discriminant validity were also found to be satisfactory, thereby providing evidence of construct validity.

ADMINISTRATION: Li and Dant (1997) stated that the scale was part of a self-administered mail questionnaire that was completed by respondents, along with other measures, using a paper-and-pencil format. A cover letter from the National Office Machine Dealers Association endorsing the study accompanied the survey packet. Respondents were instructed to answer their questionnaires in the context of the copier manufacturer for which they sold the most copy machines. In response to a question that directly asked whether distributors exclusively sold this focal manufacturer's copiers, respondents were classified as ED or NED. Higher scores on the scale indicated higher levels of relational behavior, in that both parties were perceived as sharing evenly and fairly in gains and losses over time.

MAJOR FINDINGS: Li and Dant (1997) investigated how ED arrangements between manufacturers and dealers affected dealers' perceptions of relationalism, communication, and perceived performance. **Mutuality** was one of three second-order constructs used to model relationalism. Results indicated that ED arrangements between manufacturers and dealers resulted in a higher level of relationalism compared with NED arrangements.

REFERENCES:
Boyle, Brett F., Robert Dwyer, Robert A. Robicheaux, and James T. Simpson (1992), "Influence Strategies in Marketing Channels: Measures and Uses in Different Relationship Structures," *JMR*, 29 (November), 462–73.

Li, Zhan G. and Rajiv P. Dant (1997), "An Exploratory Study of Exclusive Dealing in Channel Relationships," *JAMS*, 25 (3), 201–13.

#822 *Relationalism (Mutuality)*

SCALE ITEMS:

Strongly   Strongly
disagree   agree
  1————————2————————3————————4————————5

1. In our relationship, one of us benefits more than one deserves. **(r)**

2. We each benefit in proportion to the efforts we put in. **(r)**

3. We do more to help them than they do to help us.

4. Even if costs and benefits are not evenly shared between us in a given time period, they balance out over time.

SCALE NAME: Relationalism (Role Integrity)

SCALE DESCRIPTION: Li and Dant (1997) described this four-item, five-point Likert-type scale as measuring the extent to which the roles played by relationship parties are seen as complex and covering both business and nonbusiness issues.

SCALE ORIGIN: Li and Dant (1997) reported that the items used in this scale were adapted from Kaufmann and Dant (1992). Mutuality, solidarity, and role integrity represented three relational norms commonly employed in the channel literature as second-order constructs when operationalizing the level of relationalism between channel parties.

SAMPLES: Li and Dant (1997) used a cross-sectional survey approach to sample 2553 office machine dealership key informants (owners/presidents) from the membership list of the National Office Machine Dealers Association. Questionnaires were returned from 573 dealerships; incomplete surveys and those completed by individuals not fitting the key informant status were eliminated from the study. The final sample was composed of **461** distributors, of which 286 were classified as having exclusive dealing (ED) arrangements with the photocopier manufacturer for which they sold the most units, whereas the remaining 175 maintained nonexclusive dealing (NED) arrangements.

RELIABILITY: Li and Dant (1997) reported a reliability coefficient of **.66** for this measure.

VALIDITY: Li and Dant (1997) stated that the five measures used in the study were subjected to confirmatory factor analysis using LISREL. After one of the original five solidarity items, "our relationship with them is best described as a 'cooperative effort'," was dropped, support was found for measure unidimensionality. Convergent and discriminant validity were also found to be satisfactory, thereby providing evidence of construct validity.

ADMINISTRATION: Li and Dant (1997) stated that the scale was part of a self-administered mail questionnaire that was completed by respondents, along with other measures, using a paper-and-pencil format. A cover letter from the National Office Machine Dealers Association endorsing the study accompanied the survey packet. Respondents were instructed to answer their questionnaires in the context of the copier manufacturer for which they sold the most copy machines. In response to a question that directly asked whether distributors exclusively sold this focal manufacturer's copiers, respondents were classified as ED or NED. Higher scores on the scale indicated higher levels of relational behavior, in that parties routinely discussed both nonbusiness- and business-related issues.

MAJOR FINDINGS: Li and Dant (1997) investigated how ED arrangements between manufacturers and dealers affected dealers' perceptions of relationalism, communication, and perceived performance. **Role integrity** was one of three second-order constructs used to model relationalism. Results indicated that ED arrangements between manufacturers and dealers resulted in a higher level of relationalism compared with NED arrangements.

REFERENCES:
Kaufmann, Patrick J. and Rajiv P. Dant (1992), "The Dimensions of Commercial Exchange," *Marketing Letters*, 3 (2), 171–85.
Li, Zhan G. and Rajiv P. Dant (1997), "An Exploratory Study of Exclusive Dealing in Channel Relationships," *JAMS*, 25 (3), 201–13.

#823 *Relationalism (Role Integrity)*

SCALE ITEMS:

Strongly   Strongly
disagree   agree
   1————————2————————3————————4————————5

1. They routinely discuss issues with us which go beyond just buying and selling.

2. What we expect from each other is quite complex, since it covers both business and nonbusiness issues.

3. Our roles are simple: we are the buyer, and they are the supplier. **(r)**

4. All we are concerned with is that they meet our requirements of quantity, quality, delivery schedules, and price. **(r)**

SCALE NAME: Relationalism (Solidarity)

SCALE DESCRIPTION: Li and Dant (1997) described this four-item, five-point Likert-type scale as measuring the extent to which a relationship is viewed as a long-term venture rather than an "arm's-length" encounter.

SCALE ORIGIN: Li and Dant (1997) reported that the items used in this scale were adapted from Kaufmann and Dant (1992). Mutuality, solidarity, and role integrity represented three relational norms commonly employed in the channel literature as second-order constructs when operationalizing the level of relationalism between channel parties.

SAMPLES: Li and Dant (1997) used a cross-sectional survey approach to sample 2553 office machine dealership key informants (owners/presidents) from the membership list of the National Office Machine Dealers Association. Questionnaires were returned from 573 dealerships; incomplete surveys and those completed by individuals not fitting the key informant status were eliminated from the study. The final sample was composed of **461** distributors, of which 286 were classified as having exclusive dealing (ED) arrangements with the photocopier manufacturer for which they sold the most units, whereas the remaining 175 maintained nonexclusive dealing (NED) arrangements.

RELIABILITY: Li and Dant (1997) reported a reliability coefficient of **.74** for this measure.

VALIDITY: Li and Dant (1997) stated that the five measures used in the study were subjected to confirmatory factor analysis using LISREL. After one of the original five solidarity items, "our relationship with them is best described as a 'cooperative effort'," was dropped, support was found for measure unidimensionality. Convergent and discriminant validity were also found to be satisfactory, thereby providing evidence of construct validity.

ADMINISTRATION: Li and Dant (1997) stated that the scale was part of a self-administered mail questionnaire that was completed by respondents, along with other measures, using a paper-and-pencil format. A cover letter from the National Office Machine Dealers Association endorsing the study accompanied the survey packet. Respondents were instructed to answer their questionnaires in the context of the copier manufacturer for which they sold the most copy machines. In response to a question that directly asked whether distributors exclusively sold this focal manufacturer's copiers, respondents were classified as ED or NED. Higher scores on the scale indicated higher levels of relational behavior, in that parties viewed their relationship as a long-term venture rather than an "arm's-length" encounter.

MAJOR FINDINGS: Li and Dant (1997) investigated how ED arrangements between manufacturers and dealers affected dealers' perceptions of relationalism, communication, and perceived performance. **Solidarity** was one of three second-order constructs used to model relationalism. Results indicated that ED arrangements between manufacturers and dealers resulted in a higher level of relationalism compared with NED arrangements.

REFERENCES:

Kaufmann, Patrick J. and Rajiv P. Dant (1992), "The Dimensions of Commercial Exchange," *Marketing Letters*, 3 (2), 171–85.

Li, Zhan G. and Rajiv P. Dant (1997), "An Exploratory Study of Exclusive Dealing in Channel Relationships," *JAMS*, 25 (3), 201–13.

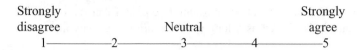

#824 *Relationalism (Solidarity)*

SCALE ITEMS:

Strongly   Strongly
disagree   Neutral   agree
   1————2————3————4————5

1. We consider them as just another supplier. **(r)**

2. Our relationship with them is best described as "arm's-length negotiations." **(r)**

3. Our relationship with them is a long-term venture.

4. Our relationship with them is a series of one-shot dealings. **(r)**

SCALE NAME: Relationship Continuity Expectation

SCALE DESCRIPTION: Lusch and Brown (1996) used this four-item, seven-point Likert-type scale to measure the wholesale distributor's expectation that its relationship with its major supplier will continue into the future. The authors referred to this measure as *long-term orientation toward the relationship*, or LTO.

SCALE ORIGIN: Lusch and Brown (1996) adapted items 1 and 2 from scales previously reported by Noordewier, John, and Nevin (1990) and Heide and Miner (1992) by changing the context of reference from "parties" in the relationship to that of the "major supplier." Items 3 and 4 appear to be original to Lusch and Brown (1996).

SAMPLES: A systematic random sample of 3225 firms was drawn by Lusch and Brown (1996) from a mailing list of all U.S. merchant wholesalers and agents/brokers in 16 four-digit standard industrial classification code groups. The sample was further reduced by eliminating firms with more than 20 employees. General managers were identified as the key informants for the remaining firms and were sent a mail questionnaire. Incentives and a follow-up mailing resulted in an initial response rate of 28.8%. However, this study reported usable data specific only to the **454** respondents classified as wholesale distributors and excluded data from agent and broker firms. The authors reported that the average number of suppliers reported by wholesalers in the sample was 45, with the major supplier contributing an average of 49% of the firm's annual volume.

RELIABILITY: Lusch and Brown (1996) reported a composite reliability of **.889** for this scale.

VALIDITY: Lusch and Brown (1996) reported undertaking a thorough review of the practitioner and academic literature, as well as extensive practitioner pretesting, to ensure content validity. Convergent and discriminant validity were also assessed and found to be satisfactory, which indicates the measure possessed adequate construct validity.

ADMINISTRATION: The scale was included as part of a self-administered mail survey. A $1 incentive and the promise of shared survey results were offered as participant incentives, and a personalized cover letter accompanied the survey packet. Undeliverable questionnaires were redirected to a replacement firm. A second mailing without monetary incentive was sent one month later. Lusch and Brown (1996) instructed respondents to answer all questions pertaining to major suppliers in the context of the supplier with which the wholesale distributor did the most business. Higher scores on the measure indicated a greater expectation on the part of the wholesaler that it will maintain a long-term relationship with its major supplier.

MAJOR FINDINGS: Lusch and Brown (1996) investigated how the type of dependency structure—wholesaler dependent on supplier, supplier dependent on wholesaler, or bilateral dependency—influenced whether a normative or explicit contract was used. The authors also studied whether dependency structure and the type of contract influenced the performance of wholesale distributors. Findings related to **relationship continuity expectations** indicated that a greater long-term orientation was related to the degree to which the wholesale distributor is dependent on the supplier and that more relational behavior should develop as a result of a long-term orientation. Wholesale distributors with longer **relationship continuity expectations** were found to rely more on explicit and nominal contracts than did those wholesale distributors that maintained short-term orientations toward the relationship with their major supplier.

REFERENCES:

Heide, Jan B. and Anne S. Miner (1992), "The Shadow of the Future: Effects of Anticipated Interaction and Frequency of Contact on Buyer-Seller Cooperation," *Academy of Management Journal*, 35 (June), 265–91.

Lusch, Robert F. and James R. Brown (1996), "Interdependency, Contracting, and Relational Behavior in Marketing Channels," *JM*, 60 (October), 19–38.

Noordewier, Thomas G., George John, and John R. Nevin (1990), "Performance Outcomes of Purchasing Arrangements in Industrial Buyer-Vendor Relationships," *JM*, 54 (October), 80–93.

SCALE ITEMS:

Strongly
disagree

Strongly
agree

1————2————3————4————5————6————7

1. We expect our relationship with our major supplier to continue a long time.

2. Renewal of the relationship with our major supplier is virtually automatic.

3. Our relationship with our major supplier is enduring.

4. Our relationship with our major supplier is a long-term alliance.

SCALE NAME: Relationship Effectiveness (Marketing with Engineering)

SCALE DESCRIPTION: Fisher, Maltz, and Jaworski (1997) used this five-item, five-point scale to measure marketing managers' evaluations of the productivity of their interactions with their engineering contacts.

SCALE ORIGIN: Fisher, Maltz, and Jaworski (1997) stated that the scale was adapted from the work of Ruekert and Walker (1987). Preliminary scale items were pretested with six marketing managers; those found to be unclear, ambiguous, or not applicable were dropped from the measure.

SAMPLES: In Study 2, Fisher, Maltz, and Jaworski (1997) sampled marketing managers employed by a multinational, business-to-business services firm with 36 business units in six countries outside the United States. A key informant provided a list of 100 firm members employed in a variety of marketing positions that required them to interact with engineering personnel. A total of **72** usable responses were obtained.

RELIABILITY: Fisher, Maltz, and Jaworski (1997) reported calculating a coefficient alpha for this measure of **.94**.

VALIDITY: Confirmatory factor analyses were conducted in two stages to maintain an acceptable ratio of observations to variables. The second analysis included the items measuring the relationship effectiveness between marketing and engineering and engineering's use of information. Fisher, Maltz, and Jaworski (1997) stated that the initial model fit the data acceptably well. Evidence of discriminant validity was provided in that the correlation between each pair of constructs was significantly different from 1.00.

ADMINISTRATION: Although the results of two studies were reported by Fisher, Maltz, and Jaworski (1997), the relationship effectiveness scale was only incorporated into a self-administered questionnaire that was delivered by mail in Study 2. Offers of anonymity and shared survey results were provided as incentives to participate. Nonrespondents received a reminder letter, followed by a second mail survey packet. Respondents were instructed to answer questions in the context of their relationship with a single manager in the engineering function with whom they interacted regularly. Higher scores on the measure indicated that respondents perceived that greater productivity resulted from interactions with their engineering contact.

MAJOR FINDINGS: Fisher, Maltz, and Jaworski (1997) investigated how relative functional identification, or the strength of marketing managers' psychological connection to their functional area compared with the firm as a whole, influenced different strategies for improving communication between marketers and engineers. Marketers' perceptions of the **effectiveness of their relationship** with engineering was found to increase with the both the bidirectionality and frequency of communication, whereas perceptions of **relationship effectiveness** declined as psychological distance increased.

REFERENCES:

Fisher, Robert J., Elliot Maltz, and Bernard J. Jaworski (1997), "Enhancing Communication Between Marketing and Engineering: The Moderating Role of Relative Functional Identification," *JM*, 61 (July), 54–70.

Ruekert, Robert W. and Orville C. Walker Jr. (1987a), "Marketing's Interaction with Other Functional Units: A Conceptual Model and Empirical Evidence," *JM*, 51 (January), 1–19.

#826 *Relationship Effectiveness (Marketing with Engineering)*

SCALE ITEMS:

```
   No                                          Great
 extent                                        extent
   1————————2————————3————————4————————5
```

To what extent...

1. Have you had an effective working relationship with the engineering contact?

2. Has the engineering contact carried out his/her responsibilities and commitments to you?

3. Do you feel your relationship with the engineering contact is productive?

4. Is the time and effort spent developing and maintaining this relationship worthwhile?

5. Are you satisfied with your relationship?

SCALE NAME: Relationship Flexibility

SCALE DESCRIPTION: The relationship flexibility measure is a three-item, seven-point scale describing the flexibility an exchange partner displays in response to changing circumstances. Heide (1994) refers to this measure as *flexible adjustment processes* in the article and *FLEX* in the regression model.

SCALE ORIGIN: Heide (1994) stated that the scale was based on items previously developed by Kaufmann and Stern (1988).

SAMPLES: The sample used by Heide (1994) was described fully in Heide and John (1992). A national mailing list of purchasing agents and manufacturer directors within the two-digit standard industrial classification groups 35–37 was chosen as the sampling frame. A random sample of 1157 names was initially drawn from these groups for telephone contact and qualification, and 579 purchasing agent informants meeting selection criteria were sent a mail questionnaire. Follow-up telephone calls and a second questionnaire resulted in **155** usable questionnaires being returned. Purchasing informants agreeing to participate in the study were also asked to identify key contacts in a supplier firm. A total of 96 supplier contacts were sent a mail questionnaire; follow-up telephone calls and a second questionnaire resulted in **60** usable questionnaires being returned from suppliers.

RELIABILITY: Heide (1994) calculated an alpha of **.73** for this scale.

VALIDITY: Confirmatory factor analysis was used by Heide (1994) to conclude that the scale was unidimensional and showed evidence of discriminant validity. Further evidence of discriminant validity was provided by a series of chi-square tests on the respective factor correlations.

ADMINISTRATION: Both original equipment manufacturers (buyers) and their suppliers were sampled as part of a larger study. Although not explicitly stated, it is believed that the relationship flexibility measure was incorporated within mail surveys sent to both groups, which were self-administered. It appears that a higher score on the relationship flexibility measure meant that the exchange relationship was characterized by greater flexibility in response to changing circumstances.

MAJOR FINDINGS: Heide (1994) investigated whether parties' expected flexibility in response to changing circumstances, a form of bilateral governance, was related to the form of dependence characterizing the buyer–supplier relationship. Results of the ordinary least squares regression model indicated that, when dependence between buyers and suppliers was symmetric and high, greater **flexibility** occurred. When dependence was unilateral, indicating that one party is dependent while the other is not, **flexibility** was undermined. **Flexibility** was also positively influenced when large purchase volumes characterized the **relationship** and the product in question was customized. As automation of the manufacturing operation increased, **relationship flexibility** tended to decrease.

REFERENCES:
Heide, Jan B. (1994), "Interorganizational Governance in Marketing Channels," *JM*, 58 (January), 71–85.
———— and George John (1992), "Do Norms Matter in Marketing Relationships?" *JM*, 56 (April), 32–44.
Kaufmann, Patrick J. and Louis W. Stern (1988), "Relational Exchange Norms, Perceptions of Unfairness, and Retained Hostility in Commercial Litigation," *Journal of Conflict Resolution*, 32 (September), 534–52.

#827 *Relationship Flexibility*

SCALE ITEMS:

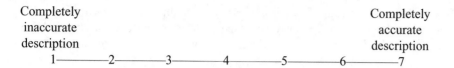

Completely   Completely
inaccurate   accurate
description   description
  1————2————3————4————5————6————7

1. Flexibility in response to requests for changes is a characteristic of this relationship.

2. The parties expect to be able to make adjustments in the ongoing relationship to cope with changing circumstances.

3. When some unexpected situation arises, the parties would rather work out a new deal than hold each other to the original terms.

SCALE NAME: Relationship Investment and Communication Openness (RICOMM)

SCALE DESCRIPTION: The five Likert-type items in this scale were used by Smith and Barclay (1997) both as separate three- and two-item measures of the extent of relationship investment and communication openness, respectively, and as a combined measure of the two (RICOMM). The relationship investment dimension refers to the degree of resource, effort, and attention devoted to a relationship, and communication openness assesses the extent of formal and informal sharing of timely information between partners.

SCALE ORIGIN: Smith and Barclay (1997) indicated that the constructs used in their study were operationalized with a mix of original and adapted scale items generated from the conceptual definition of the constructs, a review of the literature, field interviews, and pretest results. The conceptual definition of relationship investment as used by Smith and Barclay is consistent with Wilson and Mummulaneni's (1988) study; some of the items may have been adapted from this source. Communication openness items were probably based on the work of Anderson and Narus (1984) and Anderson and Weitz (1989). Several of the items originally proposed for each measure failed the extensive preliminary analysis of item reliability and validity described by Smith and Barclay (1997). Although the measures were used separately in the sponsor model, Smith and Barclay (1997) chose to combine the five items into a single measure in the partner model, because the cross-loadings and factor coefficients based on this data suggested that the items tapped a single construct. Each of the final items representing this measure passed the extensive preliminary analysis of item reliability and validity described by the authors.

SAMPLES: Smith and Barclay (1997) collected dyadic self-report data in two stages. The sponsor sample was composed of 338 sales representatives working for the Canadian subsidiaries of two multinational companies serving the computer industry. Forty percent of the 338 employees who were randomly selected from employee lists returned completed surveys. Using the names and contact information of relationship partners volunteered by these respondents, the authors then sampled the 135 dyadic partners. A total of **103** usable paired responses were obtained.

RELIABILITY: Smith and Barclay (1997) reported coefficient alphas of **.75** and **.64** for the separate relationship investment and communication openness scales in the sponsor model and **.84** for the combined RICOMM measure in the partner model.

VALIDITY: Smith and Barclay (1997) reported extensive testing of the reliability, unidimensionality, and convergent and discriminant validity of the measures used in their study. LISREL and confirmatory factor analysis were used to demonstrate that the scale satisfied each of these standards, though some items from the measures as originally proposed were eliminated in the process.

ADMINISTRATION: Smith and Barclay (1997) included the scale with other measures as part of a self-administered survey that was delivered by internal company mail to sales representatives and by regular U.S. mail to the dyadic partners. E-mail follow-ups were used to increase survey response rate. Half of the sales representatives were instructed to consider a customer situation in the prior six months in which they had had some success with a selling partner, whereas the other half were told to choose a situation in which they had had little or no success. Participants then responded to questions about the partner, their relationship, and the organization in the context of this situation. Higher scores on the relationship investment dimension indicated that the dyadic partners invested a greater degree of resources, effort, and attention in the relationship. Higher scores on the communication openness scale indicated a greater formal and informal sharing of timely information.

MAJOR FINDINGS: Smith and Barclay (1997) developed and tested two research models explaining selling partner relationship effectiveness. The first examined four organizational differences from the sponsor's (salesperson's) perspective, and the second examined these same differences from the partner's perspective. In the sponsor model, only **communication openness** was found to be a significant predictor of mutual satisfaction with the relationship. However, the degree of **relationship investment** and **communication openness** were positively associated with perceived task performance in both the sponsor and partner models (though in the partner model, relationship investment and communication openness were combined into a single measure called **RICOMM**).

REFERENCES:

Anderson, Erin and Barton Weitz (1989), "Determinants of Continuity in Conventional Industrial Channel Dyads," *Marketing Science*, 8 (4), 310–23.

Anderson, James C. and James A. Narus (1984), "A Model of the Distributor's Perspective of Distributor-Manufacturer Working Relationships," *JM*, 48 (Fall), 62–74.

Smith, J. Brock and Donald W. Barclay (1997), "The Effects of Organizational Differences and Trust on the Effectiveness of Selling Partner Relationships," *JM*, 61 (January), 3–21.

Wilson, David T. and Venkatapparao Mummulaneni (1988), "Modelling and Measuring Buyer-Seller Relationships," working paper, Institute for the Study of Business Markets, #3-1988, Pennsylvania State University.

SCALE ITEMS:

Strongly   Strongly
disagree   agree

1———2———3———4———5———6———7

Relationship Investment:
1. This rep and I have devoted a lot of time and energy to making our relationship work.
2. We have made an effort to increase the amount of time we spend together.
3. I've made an effort to demonstrate my interest in our relationship. *

Communication Openness:
4. We tell each other things we wouldn't want others to know.
5. We provide each other with timely information.

*This item was aggregated to the relationship level by taking the square root of the product of the individual responses by the sales representative and partner. All other items were conceptualized at the relationship level.

SCALE NAME: Relationship with Product Planners (Effectiveness)

SCALE DESCRIPTION: Ayers, Dahlstrom, and Skinner (1997) used this six-item, seven-point Likert-type scale to measure the extent to which marketers and engineers perceived that interactions with the other functional area were worthwhile, productive, and satisfying.

SCALE ORIGIN: Ayers, Dahlstrom, and Skinner (1997) indicated that the scale was adapted from the work of Ruekert and Walker (1987).

SAMPLES: Ayers, Dahlstrom, and Skinner (1997) collected data on 19 new product development (NPD) projects undertaken by a major U.S. computer manufacturer. Seven project members from each NPD team were selected to participate in the study, five of whom were R&D and the remaining two from marketing. Of the 132 questionnaire booklets distributed, **115** usable surveys were returned.

RELIABILITY: Ayers, Dahlstrom, and Skinner (1997) reported a coefficient alpha of **.93** for the scale.

VALIDITY: An exploratory factor analysis on all items composing the scales was used to verify the unidimensionality of the measures. No items were dropped on the basis of item-to-total correlations or an analysis of the factor structure. Ayers, Dahlstrom, and Skinner (1997) next subjected the measures to a confirmatory factor analysis to assess their construct validity. Again, no items were deleted on the basis of this analysis. The discriminant validity of the measures was also assessed by confirmatory factory analysis and was found to be acceptable.

ADMINISTRATION: Ayers, Dahlstrom, and Skinner (1997) included the scale with other measures as part of a self-administered questionnaire booklet that was apparently distributed to respondents at their place of employment. A cover letter explaining the study purpose and promises of anonymity accompanied the survey. The questionnaires distributed to R&D and marketing personnel were identical except that R&D personnel responded to questions about their relationship with marketing, and vice versa. Divisional managers designated the project for which responses were sought. Higher scores on the scale indicated stronger perceptions on the part of marketing and engineering that interactions with the other functional area were worthwhile, productive, and satisfying.

MAJOR FINDINGS: Ayers, Dahlstrom, and Skinner (1997) examined the influence of integration between marketing and R&D, managerial controls, and relational norms on new product success. Structural equation modeling was used to test the hypotheses. Higher levels of relational norms, integration between marketing and engineering, and centralization were all found to increase **perceptions of relationship effectiveness**. However, the **perceived effectiveness of the relationship** was not significantly related to new product success.

REFERENCES:
Ayers, Doug, Robert Dahlstrom, and Steven J. Skinner (1997), "An Exploratory Investigation of Organizational Antecedents to New Product Success," *JMR*, 34 (February), 107–16.
Ruekert, Robert W. and Orville C. Walker Jr. (1987a), "Marketing's Interaction With Other Functional Units: A Conceptual Framework and Empirical Evidence," *JM*, 51 (January), 1–19.

#829 *Relationship with Product Planners (Effectiveness)*

SCALE ITEMS:
Please indicate your level of agreement with the following:

Strongly
disagree
1————2————3————4————5————6————7

Strongly
agree

1. To what extent did you have an effective working relationship with product planners?

2. To what extent did product planners carry out responsibilities and commitments to you?

3. To what extent did you carry out responsibilities and commitments to the product planners?

4. To what extent did you feel that the relationship between yourself and product planners was productive?

5. To what extent was the time and effort spent in developing and maintaining the relationship with product planners worthwhile?

6. Overall, to what extent were you satisfied with the relationship between yourself and the product planners?

SCALE NAME: Replaceability (Supplier)

SCALE DESCRIPTION: Celly and Frazier (1996) used this three-item, seven-point Likert-type scale to measure the degree of difficulty associated with replacing a supplier, switching to a new supplier, and making up income lost from switching between suppliers.

SCALE ORIGIN: Celly and Frazier (1996) adapted the scale from the work of Heide and John (1988).

SAMPLES: Celly and Frazier (1996) effectively sampled 953 distributors randomly selected from Dun's Marketing Services' Direct Access service who had passed a variety of screening processes. The selected distributors serviced one of four industries: machine tools and metalworking machinery, air compressors and packaging equipment, industrial tools, or abrasives and adhesives. **Two hundred seven** usable responses were obtained.

RELIABILITY: Celly and Frazier (1996) reported a coefficient alpha of **.88** for the scale.

VALIDITY: The discriminant validity of all of the measures used in Celly and Frazier's (1996) study were found to be satisfactory on the basis of the results of a principal components factors analysis with orthogonal rotation.

ADMINISTRATION: Celly and Frazier (1996) included the scale with other measures as part of a self-administered survey that was delivered by mail. Prenotification and reminders, incentives, and a second survey mailing to nonrespondents were used to enhance response rates. Higher scores on the scale indicated that distributors perceived little difficulty in replacing or switching suppliers.

MAJOR FINDINGS: Celly and Frazier (1996) investigated suppliers' use of outcome- and behavior-based coordinator efforts with their distributors. Chow tests comparing information provided by exclusive dealers with that provided by nonexclusive dealers confirmed the appropriateness of analyzing the data jointly. The use of both outcome- and behavior-based coordination efforts were negatively related to distributors' perceptions of **supplier replaceability**.

REFERENCES:
Celly, Kirti Sawhney and Gary L. Frazier (1996), "Outcome-Based and Behavior-Based Coordination Efforts in Channel Relationships," *JMR*, 33 (May), 200–210.
Heide, Jan B. and George John (1988), "The Role of Dependence Balancing in Safeguarding Transaction-Specific Assets in Conventional Channels," *JM*, 52 (January), 20–35.

SCALE ITEMS:

Strongly   Strongly
disagree   agree

1—————2—————3—————4—————5—————6—————7

1. If we no longer represented this supplier, we could easily compensate for the loss of income by switching to other suppliers.

2. It would be quite easy for my distributorship to find an adequate replacement for this supplier.

3. If we wanted to, we could switch to another supplier's line quite easily.

SCALE NAME: Reputation (Company)

SCALE DESCRIPTION: Anderson and Robertson (1995) used this nine-item, seven-point semantic differential scale to measure the extent to which brokers believe clients view the company as being reputable.

SCALE ORIGIN: Anderson and Robertson (1995) developed the measure used in this study. A detailed construct description was constructed on the basis of a though review of the trade and academic literature. Multiple interviews with brokers, sales managers, and trade association officials were used to generate scale items believed to tap the construct. These items were administered to 208 brokers and factor analyzed to test for unidimensionality. Reliability assessments were also used to purify the measure.

SAMPLES: Anderson and Robertson (1995) mailed a questionnaire to the homes of 420 brokers whose names were supplied by cooperating firms, and **201** usable responses were obtained. To be evaluated, some hypotheses required the use of archival data as to the actual sales of house brands made by salespeople. One firm, providing **150** of the respondents in this study, agreed to provide this information. The authors stated that the respondent demographics closely matched those achieved in a large-scale survey of readers conducted by a nationally distributed trade magazine.

RELIABILITY: Anderson and Robertson (1995) reported a coefficient alpha of **.91** for this measure.

VALIDITY: No specific examination of scale validity was reported Anderson and Robertson (1995).

ADMINISTRATION: Anderson and Robertson (1995) included the measure as part of a larger self-administered mail questionnaire. A summary of the results was offered in exchange for respondent cooperation. Higher scores on the scale indicated that salespeople perceived clients as more likely to regard the firm as being reputable and trustworthy.

MAJOR FINDINGS: Anderson and Robertson (1995) investigated the relationship between factors believed to influence the sale of house brands by multiline salespeople. The **company's reputation among customers** was not significantly related to the adoption of house products by the sales force.

REFERENCES:
Anderson, Erin and Thomas S. Robertson (1995), "Inducing Multiline Salespeople to Adopt House Brands," *JM*, 59 (April), 16–31.

SCALE ITEMS:
My customers think my firm is: (Please give use your opinion on each.)

1. Not reputable   :___:___:___:___:___:___:___: Highly reputable
                     1   2   3   4   5   6   7

2. Trustworthy   :___:___:___:___:___:___:___: Not trustworthy (r)
                     1   2   3   4   5   6   7

3. Usually correct :___:___:___:___:___:___:___: Usually wrong (r)
                     1   2   3   4   5   6   7

4. A leader   :___:___:___:___:___:___:___: A follower (r)
                    1   2   3   4   5   6   7

5. Uninformed   :___:___:___:___:___:___:___: Well informed
                    1   2   3   4   5   6   7

6. First with   Last with
   new products   :___:___:___:___:___:___:___: new products (r)
                    1   2   3   4   5   6   7

7. Knowledgeable   :___:___:___:___:___:___:___: Ignorant (r)
                    1   2   3   4   5   6   7

8. Reputable   :___:___:___:___:___:___:___: Not reputable
                    1   2   3   4   5   6   7

9. Reliable   :___:___:___:___:___:___:___: Unreliable (r)
                    1   2   3   4   5   6   7

SCALE NAME: Reputation (Company)

SCALE DESCRIPTION: Brown (1995) defined this construct as buyers' perceptions of the extent to which a particular supplier is well known, good or bad, reliable, trustworthy, reputable, and believable. Company reputation was measured using a six-item, seven-point semantic differential scale.

SCALE ORIGIN: The development of the scale appears to be original to Brown (1995).

SAMPLES: Brown (1995) administered a pretest questionnaire to assess the reliability and validity of the measures to a sample of 100 buyers, and **39** surveys were returned. Following minor modifications to the questionnaire, the final questionnaire was sent to a regional probability sample of 932 organizational buyers located in 20 Eastern U.S. states. Individuals with the job title of "buyer" or "purchasing agent" on the National Association of Purchasing Managers mailing list served as the sampling frame. For this survey, **379** usable questionnaires were returned for a response rate of 40.67%. Comparisons between early and late respondents suggested that nonresponse bias was not an issue. Of the respondents, 64% worked in manufacturing, 18% in services, 12% in government or nonprofit, and the remaining 6% worked in retail (4%) and agriculture (2%). In addition, 68% of respondents were men, with an average age of 40 years and 8.9 average years of work experience in purchasing.

RELIABILITY: Brown (1995) calculated a Cronbach's alpha of **.92** for this scale in the final study. No reliability information with respect to the pretest was reported.

VALIDITY: Brown (1995) noted that the purpose of the pretest was to assess the reliability and validity of the measures but provided very little information pertaining to this process. Buyers interviewed during the pretest study indicated that the items tapped into the fundamental facets of how they perceived vendor company reputation.

ADMINISTRATION: A cover letter, with a self-addressed, stamped reply envelope, accompanied the mail questionnaire containing the measures of interest. Respondents were instructed to recall the last sales presentation made by either an insupplier or outsupplier sales representative. Each respondent was assigned to either the insupplier or the outsupplier condition but not both, to minimize respondent fatigue. Higher scores on the company reputation measure indicated a more favorable perception of the company's reputation.

MAJOR FINDINGS: Brown (1995) investigated the interrelationships among buyer perceptions of and attitudes toward vendor companies, products, and salespeople, as well as insupplier/outsupplier status (company currently has or does not have an ongoing relationship with the buyer's firm). Although the relationship was significantly stronger for insuppliers, perceived **company reputation** was significantly related to salesperson attitude for both insupplier and outsupplier groups. However, perceived **company reputation** was significantly related to product attitude for the insupplier group only.

REFERENCES:
Brown, Steven P. (1995), "The Moderating Effects of Insupplier/Outsupplier Status on Organizational Buyer Attitudes," *JAMS*, 23 (3), 170–81.

SCALE ITEMS:
Instructions: We are investigating the effectiveness of interactions between salespeople and organizational buyers. We would like to ask your help in evaluating salespeople who have called on you within the last two weeks. Specifically, we would like to ask you to recall in detail the last sales presentation made to you by a salesperson whose company you current buy from/do not currently buy from.

The following questions ask for your impressions, evaluations, and thoughts about this salesperson, his or her company, and the products and/or services that the salesperson discussed with you. Your time and help are gratefully appreciated.

Compared to all companies in this salesperson's industry, how would you rate this salesperson's company?

1. The very best   :____:____:____:____:____:____:____: The very worst (r)
                      1   2   3   4   5   6   7

2. The least reliable   :____:____:____:____:____:____:____: The most reliable
                          1   2   3   4   5   6   7

3. The least reputable   :____:____:____:____:____:____:____: The most reputable
                           1   2   3   4   5   6   7

4. The least
   believable   :____:____:____:____:____:____:____: The most
                  1   2   3   4   5   6   7   believable

5. Not at all known   :____:____:____:____:____:____:____: The best known
                        1   2   3   4   5   6   7

6. The least
   trustworthy   :____:____:____:____:____:____:____: The most
                   1   2   3   4   5   6   7   trustworthy

SCALE NAME: Reputation (Partner)

SCALE DESCRIPTION: Smith and Barclay (1997) used this three-item, seven-point scale to measure perceptions of the degree to which selling partners perceive the other firm as having a better or worse reputation for professional conduct, ethics, and standards.

SCALE ORIGIN: Smith and Barclay (1997) indicated that the constructs used in their study were operationalized with a mix of original and adapted scale items generated from the conceptual definition of the constructs, a review of the literature, field interviews, and pretest results. Each of the final items representing this measure passed the extensive preliminary analysis of item reliability and validity described by the authors.

SAMPLES: Smith and Barclay (1997) collected dyadic self-report data in two stages. The sponsor sample was composed of 338 sales representatives working for the Canadian subsidiaries of two multinational companies serving the computer industry. Forty percent of the 338 employees who were randomly selected from employee lists returned completed surveys. Using the names and contact information of relationship partners volunteered by these respondents, the authors then sampled the 135 dyadic partners. A total of **103** usable paired responses were obtained.

RELIABILITY: Smith and Barclay (1997) reported a coefficient alpha of **.71** for this measure in the sponsor model.

VALIDITY: Smith and Barclay (1997) reported extensive testing of the reliability, unidimensionality, and convergent and discriminant validity of the measures used in their study. LISREL and confirmatory factor analysis were used to demonstrate that the scale satisfied each of these standards, though some items from the measures as originally proposed were eliminated in the process.

ADMINISTRATION: Smith and Barclay (1997) included the scale with other measures as part of a self-administered survey that was delivered by internal company mail to sales representatives and by regular U.S. mail to the dyadic partners. E-mail follow-ups were used to increase survey response rate. Half of the sales representatives were instructed to consider a customer situation in the prior six months in which they had had some success with a selling partner, whereas the other half were told to choose a situation in which they had had little or no success. Participants then responded to questions about the partner, their relationship, and the organization in the context of this situation. Higher scores on the scale indicated that a partner's firm was perceived as having higher standards, ethics, and levels of professional conduct than the firm of the individual completing the rating.

MAJOR FINDINGS: Smith and Barclay (1997) developed and tested two research models explaining selling partner relationship effectiveness. The first examined four organizational differences from the sponsor's (salesperson's) perspective, and the second examined these same differences from the partner's perspective. In the sponsor model, greater perceived differences in the **reputations of partner firms** led to lower evaluations of the judgment, role competence, and character/motive components of mutual perceived trustworthiness.

REFERENCES:

Smith, J. Brock and Donald W. Barclay (1997), "The Effects of Organizational Differences and Trust on the Effectiveness of Selling Partner Relationships," *JM*, 61 (January), 3–21.

SCALE ITEMS:*

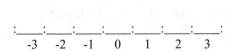

My partner's firm is much less/lower than my firm	:___:___:___:___:___:___:___:	My partner's firm is much greater/more than my firm
	-3 -2 -1 0 1 2 3	

1. Reputation for professionalism.

2. Ethical standards.

3. Customer orientation.

*All of the items in this scale were conceptualized at the organizational level.

SCALE NAME: Reputation (Retailer)

SCALE DESCRIPTION: Ganesan (1994) used this four-item, seven-point Likert-type scale to measure the extent to which a retailer was perceived by vendors as having a reputation for fairness, honesty, and concern for vendor partners' needs.

SCALE ORIGIN: Ganesan (1994) reported developing separate but parallel measures of retailer and vendor reputation on the basis of scale items adapted from Anderson and Weitz's (1992) measures of distributor/supplier reputation for fairness in dealing suppliers/distributors. Anderson and Weitz (1992) followed Nunally's (1978) procedure for scale development in generating item measures and purifying their scales for use with distributor and manufacturer samples. Ganesan (1994) used item analysis and exploratory factor analysis to initially purify his measure; items with low loadings and those loading on multiple factors were eliminated. A draft of the questionnaire containing this scale was also pretested with a group of 14 retail buyers representing two department store chains. After administration to the final sample, scale items were subjected to a confirmatory factor analysis. Goodness-of-fit indices and individual item t-values were used to identify the final scale items.

SAMPLES: Five retail department store chains agreed to participate in Ganesan's (1994) study, and each firm received and distributed 30 questionnaires to senior sales representatives or sales managers who served as liaisons with vendor organizations. A total of **124** (83%) usable responses representing the *retailer* sample were obtained. Of these, 48 respondents answered in the context of a long-term vendor relationship, and the remaining 76 answered in the context of a short-term vendor relationship. Contact information provided by respondents enabled the author to sample the designated 124 key vendor informants most knowledgeable about the retailer/vendor relationship with a survey similar in content to the retailer questionnaire but phrased from the vendor point of view. A total of **52** (42%) *vendor* representatives responded, of which 21 and 31 were in short- and long-term relationships, respectively.

RELIABILITY: Ganesan (1994) reported a coefficient alpha of **.75** for the scale.

VALIDITY: Ganesan (1994) submitted the scale to a confirmatory factor analysis using LISREL 7.16 to assess the unidimensionality, convergent validity, and discriminant validity of the measure. The measure was found to be unidimensional, but no additional information pertaining to the outcome of the validity tests was provided.

ADMINISTRATION: Prior to being sent a survey, buyers in the retailer sample were randomly assigned to one of four cells in which the questionnaire instructions asked them to select a vendor on the basis of variations in two criteria: (1) the length of their relationship (short-term or long-term) and (2) the importance of the vendor's product to their organization (moderately important or very important). Questionnaires were distributed by a coordinator in each department store, and respondents were instructed to answer the survey in the context of this single vendor. Higher scores on the scale indicated that vendors perceived retailers as more honest, fair, and concerned for their welfare.

MAJOR FINDINGS: Ganesan (1994) investigated a variety of factors influencing the long-term orientation of both retailers and vendors in an ongoing relationship, as well as the antecedents to long-term orientation. Results indicated that **retailer reputation** was not significantly related to either retailer credibility or retailer benevolence.

REFERENCES:

Anderson, Erin and Barton A. Weitz (1992), "The Use of Pledges to Build and Sustain Commitment in Distribution Channels," *JMR*, 29 (February), 18–34.

Ganesan, Shankar (1994), "Determinants of Long-Term Orientation in Buyer-Seller Relationships," *JM*, 58 (April), 1–19.

Nunnally, Jum C. (1978), *Psychometric Theory*. New York: McGraw-Hill.

SCALE ITEMS:

Strongly disagree — 1————2————3————4————5————6————7 — Strongly agree

1. This retailer has a reputation for being honest.

2. This retailer has a reputation for being concerned about their suppliers.

3. This retailer has a bad reputation in the market. **(r)**

4. Most suppliers would like to deal with this retailer.

SCALE NAME: Reputation (Supplier)

SCALE DESCRIPTION: Doney and Cannon (1997) used this three-item, seven-point Likert-type scale to measure the extent to which a supplier was perceived as being honest and concerned about its customers.

SCALE ORIGIN: Although Doney and Cannon (1997) did not specifically state the origin of this scale, similar scales have been used by Anderson and Weitz (1992) and Ganesan (1994) in measuring the reputation of manufacturers, distributors, retailers, and vendors.

SAMPLES: Doney and Cannon (1997) sampled 657 members of the National Association of Purchasing Management who were employed by firms involved in industrial manufacturing, as classified by standard industrial classification codes 33–37. **Two hundred ten** completed questionnaires were returned from a primarily male (76%) sample with an average of 15 years of purchasing experience.

RELIABILITY: Doney and Cannon (1997) reported a coefficient alpha of **.78** for this measure.

VALIDITY: Doney and Cannon (1997) reported using three methods to test the discriminant validity of the scale. The supplier reputation scale failed to exhibit discriminant validity and was eliminated from subsequent analysis.

ADMINISTRATION: The scale was included with other measures as part of a self-administered survey that was delivered by mail. Nonrespondents received a postcard reminder, followed by a second questionnaire. Doney and Cannon (1997) instructed respondents to focus on a single, specific, recent purchase decision in which more than one supplier was seriously considered and to indicate on the survey (using initials) two of the firms considered. After answering questions pertaining to the purchase situation, half of the respondents were instructed to complete the remainder of the questionnaire in the context of the first supplier they had listed, whereas the other half were instructed to use the second supplier. Higher scores on the scale indicated that respondents perceived the focal supplier as exhibiting high levels of honesty and customer concern.

MAJOR FINDINGS: Doney and Cannon (1997) investigated the impact of purchasing agents' trust in the salesperson and trust in the supplier firm on a buying firm's current supplier choice and future buying intentions. **Supplier reputation** was proposed as an antecedent to supplier trust; however, this measure was eliminated from the model and data analysis because of its lack of discriminant validity.

REFERENCES:

Anderson, Erin and Barton A. Weitz (1992), "The Use of Pledges to Build and Sustain Commitment in Distribution Channels," *JMR*, 29 (February), 18–34.

Doney, Patricia M. and Joseph P. Cannon (1997), "An Examination of the Nature of Trust in Buyer-Seller Relationships," *JM*, 61 (April), 35–51.

Ganesan, Shankar (1994), "Determinants of Long-Term Orientation in Buyer-Seller Relationships," *JM*, 58 (April), 1–19.

SCALE ITEMS:

Strongly disagree / Strongly agree

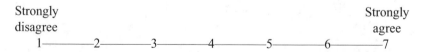

1. This supplier has a reputation for being honest.

2. This supplier is known to be concerned about customers.

3. This supplier had a bad reputation in the market. (r)

SCALE NAME: Reputation (Vendor)

SCALE DESCRIPTION: Ganesan (1994) used this four-item, seven-point Likert-type scale to measure the extent to which a vendor was perceived by retailers as having a reputation for fairness, honesty, and concern for retailer partners' needs.

SCALE ORIGIN: Ganesan (1994) reported developing separate but parallel measures of retailer and vendor reputation on the basis of scale items adapted from Anderson and Weitz's (1992) measures of distributor/supplier reputation for fairness in dealing suppliers/distributors. Anderson and Weitz (1992) followed Nunnally's (1978) procedure for scale development in generating item measures and purifying their scales for use with distributor and manufacturer samples. The author used item analysis and exploratory factor analysis to initially purify his measure; items with low loadings and those loading on multiple factors were eliminated. A draft of the questionnaire containing this scale was also pretested with a group of 14 retail buyers representing two department store chains. After administration to the final sample, scale items were subjected to a confirmatory factor analysis. Goodness-of-fit indices and individual item t-values were used to identify the final scale items.

SAMPLES: Five retail department store chains agreed to participate in Ganesan's (1994) study, and each firm received and distributed 30 questionnaires to senior sales representatives or sales managers who served as liaisons with vendor organizations. A total of **124** (83%) usable responses representing the *retailer* sample were obtained. Of these, 48 respondents answered in the context of a long-term vendor relationship, and the remaining 76 answered in the context of a short-term vendor relationship. Contact information provided by respondents enabled the author to sample the designated 124 key vendor informants most knowledgeable about the retailer/vendor relationship with a survey similar in content to the retailer questionnaire but phrased from the vendor point of view. A total of **52** (42%) *vendor* representatives responded, of which 21 and 31 were in short- and long-term relationships, respectively.

RELIABILITY: Ganesan (1994) reported a coefficient alpha of **.82** for the scale.

VALIDITY: Ganesan (1994) submitted the scale to a confirmatory factor analysis using LISREL 7.16 to assess the unidimensionality, convergent validity, and discriminant validity of the measure. Although the measure was found to be unidimensional, no additional information pertaining to the outcome of the validity tests was provided.

ADMINISTRATION: Prior to being sent a survey, buyers in the retailer sample were randomly assigned to one of four cells in which the questionnaire instructions asked them to select a vendor on the basis of variations in two criteria: (1) the length of their relationship (short-term or long-term) and (2) the importance of the vendor's product to their organization (moderately important or very important). Questionnaires were distributed by a coordinator in each department store, and respondents were instructed to answer the survey in the context of this single vendor. Higher scores on the scale indicated that retailers perceived vendors as more honest, fair, and concerned for their welfare.

MAJOR FINDINGS: Ganesan (1994) investigated a variety of factors influencing the long-term orientation of both retailers and vendors in an ongoing relationship, as well as the antecedents to long-term orientation. Results indicated that **vendor reputation** had a significant positive impact on a vendor credibility.

#836 *Reputation (Vendor)*

REFERENCES:

Anderson, Erin and Barton A. Weitz (1992), "The Use of Pledges to Build and Sustain Commitment in Distribution Channels," *JMR*, 29 (February), 18–34.

Ganesan, Shankar (1994), "Determinants of Long-Term Orientation in Buyer-Seller Relationships," *JM*, 58 (April), 1–19.

Nunnally, Jum C. (1978), *Psychometric Theory*. New York: McGraw-Hill.

SCALE ITEMS:

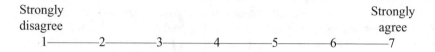

Strongly disagree — Strongly agree

1————2————3————4————5————6————7

1. This resource has a reputation for being honest.

2. This resource has a reputation for being concerned about the retailers.

3. This resource has a bad reputation in the market. **(r)**

4. Most retailers think that this resource has a reputation for being fair.

SCALE NAME: Resource Constraints (Supplier)

SCALE DESCRIPTION: Celly and Frazier (1996) used this five-item, seven-point Likert-type scale to measure distributor perceptions of the extent to which suppliers had insufficient personnel available to coordinate the channel relationship.

SCALE ORIGIN: There is no indication to suggest that the scale is anything other than original to Celly and Frazier (1996).

SAMPLES: Celly and Frazier (1996) effectively sampled 953 distributors randomly selected from Dun's Marketing Services' Direct Access service who had passed a variety of screening processes. The selected distributors serviced one of four industries: machine tools and metalworking machinery, air compressors and packaging equipment, industrial tools, or abrasives and adhesives. **Two hundred seven** usable responses were obtained.

RELIABILITY: Celly and Frazier (1996) reported a coefficient alpha of **.79** for the scale.

VALIDITY: The discriminant validity of all of the measures used in Celly and Frazier's (1996) study were found to be satisfactory on the basis of the results of a principal components factors analysis with orthogonal rotation.

ADMINISTRATION: Celly and Frazier (1996) included the scale with other measures as part of a self-administered survey that was delivered by mail. Prenotification and reminders, incentives, and a second survey mailing to nonrespondents were used to enhance response rates. Higher scores on the scale indicated that distributors perceived greater supplier constraints, in that insufficient personnel were available to help manage the channel relationship.

MAJOR FINDINGS: Celly and Frazier (1996) investigated suppliers' use of outcome- and behavior-based coordinator efforts with their distributors. Chow tests comparing information provided by exclusive dealers with that provided by nonexclusive dealers confirmed the appropriateness of analyzing the data jointly. The use of both outcome- and behavior-based coordination efforts were significantly and negatively related to distributors' perceptions of **supplier resource constraints**.

REFERENCES:
Celly, Kirti Sawhney and Gary L. Frazier (1996), "Outcome-Based and Behavior-Based Coordination Efforts in Channel Relationships," *JMR*, 33 (May), 200–210.

SCALE ITEMS:

Strongly   Strongly
disagree   agree

1———2———3———4———5———6———7

1. This supplier pays enough attention to managing its distribution in this trade area. **(r)**

2. The number of supplier salespeople assigned to this channel is insufficient.

3. This supplier has assigned enough personnel to coordinate its relationship with its distributors in this trade area. **(r)**

4. Supplier sales representatives are thinly stretched over several territories of accounts.

5. Supplier sales personnel are unable to devote the time necessary to manage this channel.

SCALE NAME: Resource Inadequacy

SCALE DESCRIPTION: Bello and Gilliland (1997) used this three-item, seven-point Likert-type scale to describe the extent of a firm's deficiencies in its capacity to engage in export activities.

SCALE ORIGIN: Bello and Gilliland (1997) stated that the scale was adapted from Welch and Luostarinen's (1988) study.

SAMPLES: Bello and Gilliland's (1997) systematic random sample of 245 national manufacturers verified as exporting through foreign distributors was drawn from the 1994 edition of the *Journal of Commerce United States Importer & Exporter Directory*. **One hundred sixty** usable responses were obtained from export managers employed by firms exporting a variety of industrial and consumer products to a total of 39 different countries.

RELIABILITY: A confirmatory factor analysis composite reliability of **.81** was reported by Bello and Gilliland (1997).

VALIDITY: Confirmatory factor analysis was used by Bello and Gilliland (1997) to provide evidence of discriminant and convergent validity, as well as to assess the unidimensionality of the measure. Convergent validity was deemed to be present because items loaded significantly on their posited indicators and because of the low to moderate correlations between the scale and other measures. Discriminant validity was also deemed to be present because the correlation estimate between two indicators never included 1.0 (+/– two standard errors). The authors used personal interviews with export executives as part of the pretest process to verify the face validity of the measure.

ADMINISTRATION: Bello and Gilliland (1997) indicated that this scale was self-administered as part of a longer survey instrument mailed to respondents. The export manager with primary responsibility for the firm's relationship with the foreign distributor received a survey. Nonrespondents were telephoned three weeks later, and a second questionnaire followed. Instructions specified that questions were to be answered in the context of the focal distributor. The authors defined the focal distributor as the firm's fourth-largest foreign distributor in terms of unit sales volume to avoid a positive evaluation bias. Higher scores on the scale indicated that a manufacturer lacked the management time and effort, personnel, and resources necessary for exporting.

MAJOR FINDINGS: Bello and Gilliland (1997) examined the effect of output controls, process controls, and flexibility on channel performance. Firms with **inadequate resources** were less likely to process controls over foreign distributors, which indicated that firms with **inadequate managerial and financial resources** were less capable of influencing their distributor's marketing methods and procedures.

REFERENCES:

Bello, Daniel C. and David I. Gilliland (1997), "The Effect of Output Controls, Process Controls, and Flexibility on Export Channel Performance," *JM*, 61 (January), 22–38.

Welch, Lawrence S. and Reijo Luostarinen (1988), "Internationalization: Evolution of a Concept," *Journal of General Management*, 14 (Winter), 34–55.

SCALE ITEMS:

Strongly   Strongly
disagree   agree
   1————2————3————4————5————6————7

1. Our export expansion is limited by the time and effort that senior management can devote to exporting.

2. Human resources limit our firm's ability to increase export activities.

3. Our firm lacks the financial resources needed to expand our export efforts.

SCALE NAME: Reward System (Market-Based)

SCALE DESCRIPTION: A five-item, five-point Likert-type scale measuring the extent to which market intelligence gathering activities and customer satisfaction/customer relations-oriented behaviors influence employee evaluations and rewards within an organization. Menon, Jaworski, and Kohli (1997) referred to this scale as *market-based reward systems*.

SCALE ORIGIN: Menon, Jaworski, and Kohli (1997) indicated that the scale was developed and first reported by Jaworski and Kohli (1993). Closer examination of the source article revealed that the sample and data used to develop the scale were identical to those reported in Menon, Jaworski, and Kohli (1997).

SAMPLES: Using the *Dun and Bradstreet Million Dollar Directory* as the sampling frame, Menon, Jaworski, and Kohli (1997) selected for initial contact every other company name from among the top 1000 companies by sales revenues. Participation from multiple strategic business units (SBUs) within an organization was requested. A total of 102 companies agreed to participate, and ultimately, responses representing **222** SBUs were obtained from marketing and nonmarketing executives.

RELIABILITY: Menon, Jaworski, and Kohli (1997) reported a **.73** alpha reliability coefficient. One item with low interitem correlations was eliminated from the original six-item scale set to yield the final five-item measure listed here.

VALIDITY: No specific examination of scale validity was presented by Menon, Jaworski, and Kohli (1997) or by Jaworski and Kohli (1993).

ADMINISTRATION: The 206 marketing and 187 nonmarketing executives identified by participating corporations were directly contacted by Menon, Jaworski, and Kohli (1997). Initial contact was followed by a self-administered mail questionnaire, and a follow-up questionnaire was sent three weeks later to nonrespondents. Most (79.6%) of the marketing executives and 70% of the nonmarketing executives contacted provided data for the study. When both nonmarketing and marketing executives from a single SBU responded, their scores were averaged to provide a single score for the construct. A low score on the reward system scale indicated that customer satisfaction and market intelligence gathering activities did not influence employee evaluations or rewards.

MAJOR FINDINGS: Menon, Jaworski, and Kohli (1997) investigated the role of organizational factors affecting interdepartmental interactions and the resulting impact on product quality. A **market-based reward system** was investigated as a potential antecedent of interdepartmental interactions using regression analysis. Use of a **market-based reward system** appeared to increase interdepartmental connectedness while lessening conflict between departments.

REFERENCES:

Jaworski, Bernard and Ajay K. Kohli (1993), "Market Orientation: Antecedents and Consequences," *JM*, 57 (July), 53–70.

Menon, Ajay, Bernard J. Jaworski, and Ajay K. Kohli (1997), "Product Quality: Impact of Interdepartmental Interactions," *JAMS*, 25 (3), 187–200.

SCALE ITEMS:

Strongly   Strongly
disagree   agree

1————2————3————4————5

1. No matter which department they are in, people in this business unit get recognized for being sensitive to competitive moves.

2. Customer satisfaction assessments influence senior managers' pay in this business unit.

3. Formal rewards (i.e., pay raise, promotion) are forthcoming to anyone who consistently provides good market intelligence.

4. Salespeople's performance in this business unit is measured by the strength of relationships they build with customers.

5. We use customer polls for evaluating our salespeople.

SCALE NAME: Risk Aversion (Top Manager's)

SCALE DESCRIPTION: A five-item, five-point Likert-type scale measuring the unwillingness of top managers to accept occasional failure as a normal business occurrence.

SCALE ORIGIN: Menon, Jaworski, and Kohli (1997) indicated that the scale was developed and first reported in Jaworski and Kohli (1993). Closer examination of the source article revealed that the sample and data used to develop the scale were identical to those reported in Menon, Jaworski, and Kohli (1997).

SAMPLES: Using the *Dun and Bradstreet Million Dollar Directory* as the sampling frame, Menon, Jaworski, and Kohli (1997) selected for initial contact every other company name from among the top 1000 companies by sales revenues. Participation from multiple strategic business units (SBUs) within an organization was requested. A total of 102 companies agreed to participate, and ultimately, responses representing **222** SBUs were obtained from marketing and nonmarketing executives.

RELIABILITY: Menon, Jaworski, and Kohli (1997) reported a **.85** alpha reliability coefficient. One item with low interitem correlations was eliminated from the original six-item scale set to yield the final five-item measure listed here.

VALIDITY: No specific examination of scale validity was presented by Menon, Jaworski, and Kohli (1997) or Jaworski and Kohli (1993).

ADMINISTRATION: The 206 marketing and 187 nonmarketing executives identified by participating corporations were directly contacted by Menon, Jaworski, and Kohli (1997). Initial contact was followed by a self-administered mail questionnaire, and a follow-up questionnaire was sent three weeks later to nonrespondents. Most (79.6%) of the marketing executives and 70% of the nonmarketing executives contacted provided data for the study. When both nonmarketing and marketing executives from a single SBU responded, their scores were averaged to provide a single score for the construct. A higher score on the risk aversion scale indicated that top management was more risk adverse.

MAJOR FINDINGS: Menon, Jaworski, and Kohli (1997) investigated the role of organizational factors affecting interdepartmental interactions and the resulting impact on product quality. **Risk aversion** of top management was investigated as a potential antecedent of interdepartmental interactions using regression analysis. Top managers' **risk aversion** was found to increase interdepartmental conflict while lowering interdepartmental connectedness.

REFERENCES:

Jaworski, Bernard and Ajay K. Kohli (1993), "Market Orientation: Antecedents and Consequences," *JM*, 57 (July), 53–70.

Menon, Ajay, Bernard J. Jaworski, and Ajay K. Kohli (1997), "Product Quality: Impact of Interdepartmental Interactions," *JAMS*, 25 (3), 187–200.

SCALE ITEMS:

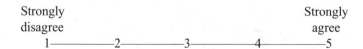

Strongly disagree — 1 — 2 — 3 — 4 — 5 — Strongly agree

1. Top managers in this business unit believe that higher financial risks are worth taking for higher rewards. **(r)**

2. Top managers in this business unit like to take big financial risks. **(r)**

3. Top managers here encourage the development of innovative marketing strategies, knowing well that some will fail. **(r)**

4. Top managers in this business unit like to "play it safe."

5. Top managers around here like to implement plans only if they are very certain that they will work.

SCALE NAME: Risk-Taking (Marketing Program Development)

SCALE DESCRIPTION: Andrews and Smith (1996) described this three-item, seven-point Likert-type scale as measuring the extent to which respondents were willing to engage in the development of new ideas despite outcome uncertainty and the potential for failure. In their article, Andrews and Smith (1996) referred to the scale as *willingness to take risks*, or *risk-taking*.

SCALE ORIGIN: Andrews and Smith (1996) stated that the measure was developed through discussions with product managers but provided no additional details or citations.

SAMPLES: The American Marketing Association membership directory and a purchased mailing list provided Andrews and Smith (1996) with the sampling frame for surveying consumer goods product managers. One hundred ninety-three completed questionnaires were returned for a 33.4% response rate. No significant differences in responses to key variables existed between mailing lists or between early and late respondents. Because only respondents with a substantial impact on ideas in the marketing program were desired, 25 respondents were eliminated on the basis of a screening question, yielding a final sample size of **168**.

RELIABILITY: Andrews and Smith (1996) reported a coefficient alpha of **.69** for this measure.

VALIDITY: No specific examination of the scale's development process or validity in the context of the current study was reported by Andrews and Smith (1996).

ADMINISTRATION: The scale was part of a self-administered mail survey in which Andrews and Smith (1996) instructed product managers to answer questions in the context of a single product with which they had been highly involved during their most recent marketing program. Higher scores on the scale indicated higher levels of risk-taking in the marketing planning process.

MAJOR FINDINGS: Andrews and Smith (1996) investigated the effect of individual product manager and situational/planning process characteristics on marketing program creativity. **Willingness to take risks** was found to have a positive impact on marketing program creativity. Significant interactions between variables indicated that knowledge of the macroenvironment and the operating environment had significantly greater effects on marketing program creativity when **risk-taking** was high than when it was low. Andrews and Smith (1996) also found that when **risk-taking** is low, the effect of educational diversity on marketing program creativity is greater.

REFERENCES:
Andrews, Jonlee and Daniel C. Smith (1996), "In Search of the Marketing Imagination: Factors Affecting the Creativity of Marketing Programs for Mature Products," *JMR*, 33 (May), 174–87.

SCALE ITEMS:

Strongly
disagree
1———2———3———4———5———6———7
Strongly
agree

1. I like to play it safe when I'm developing ideas to market this product. **(r)**

2. I am a risk-taker when it comes to proposing ideas to market this product.

3. I prefer to think conservatively when I develop ideas for this product's marketing program. **(r)**

SCALE NAME: Rivalry (Interfunctional)

SCALE DESCRIPTION: Maltz and Kohli (1996) used this seven-item, five-point Likert-type scale to measure the extent to which members of different functional areas see themselves as competitors. Although in the current usage, the scale specifically assesses intrafirm rivalry with the marketing function, it could easily be adapted to measure rivalry with other areas.

SCALE ORIGIN: Maltz and Kohli (1996) adapted the scale from the work of Van De Ven and Ferry (1980). The items were evaluated in face-to-face interviews with manufacturing, finance, and R&D department managers and by a panel of academic experts. The measure and questionnaire were also pretested with 77 participants of an executive MBA program. Items that were found to be problematic were revised or eliminated in accordance with the comments received at various stages in the pretesting process.

SAMPLES: Maltz and Kohli (1996) sampled mid-level managers operating within strategic business units (SBUs) of firms engaged in the manufacture of high-technology industrial equipment. The authors obtained names of 1061 nonmarketing managers in 270 SBUs from corporation presidents of participating firms. A total of **788** usable responses were returned by managers working in manufacturing (272), R&D (252), and finance (194).

RELIABILITY: Maltz and Kohli (1996) reported a coefficient alpha of **.82** for this measure.

VALIDITY: Maltz and Kohli (1996) evaluated the discriminant validity of trust in source and interfunctional rivalry constructs together in a LISREL model. The results provided evidence of the discriminant validity of the measures.

ADMINISTRATION: The measure was included by Maltz and Kohli (1996) as part of a self-administered questionnaire that was delivered by mail. Nonrespondents received a follow-up letter and second questionnaire mailing. When answering the survey, respondents were instructed to focus on the intelligence they had received from the person in the marketing department with whom they had interacted the most during the previous three months. Higher scores on the scale indicated that respondents felt greater rivalry with the marketing function.

MAJOR FINDINGS: Maltz and Kohli (1996) investigated the antecedents and consequences of the dissemination of marketing intelligence within SBUs. As expected, **interfunctional rivalry** had a negative effect on respondent's trust of the marketing intelligence provider.

REFERENCES:

Maltz, Elliot and Ajay K. Kohli (1996), "Market Intelligence Dissemination Across Functional Boundaries," *JMR*, 33 (February), 47–61.
Van De Ven, Andrew H. and Diane L. Ferry (1980), *Measuring and Assessing Organizations.* New York: John Wiley & Sons.

#842 *Rivalry (Interfunctional)*

SCALE ITEMS:
Please focus on the marketing/sales group to which the marketing contact belongs.

Strongly   Strongly
disagree   agree
  1————————2————————3————————4————————5

Over the last three months our functional group and the marketing group...

1. Experienced problems coordinating work activities.

2. Had compatible goals and objectives. **(r)**

3. Agreed on the priorities of each department. **(r)**

4. Had senior managers who were "at odds".

5. Hindered each other's performance.

6. Competed for the same resources.

7. Cooperated with each other. **(r)**

SCALE NAME: Role Ambiguity

SCALE DESCRIPTION: The scale is intended to capture the certainty (or lack thereof) a person has in a variety of job-related activities such as duties, authority, allocation of time, and the clarity of guidelines and policies. Several users of the scale in marketing have modified it to some extent by adjusting the wording of items to better apply to certain employee groups, dropping less relevant items, or using slightly different response formats.

SCALE ORIGIN: The scale was originally developed by Rizzo, House, and Lirtzman (1970; henceforth RHL). Their study discussed the rationale for the scale and the initial developmental and purification process. Data were gathered from a variety of employees of a firm and then divided into two samples, one representative of the firm in general (Sample A) and the other focused on the research and engineering division (Sample B). Development of a role conflict scale occurred at the same time (see #848). It began with 15 items, but the factor analysis, examination of internal consistency, and judgement led to a final version of the role ambiguity scale with 6 items. The reliability of the scale was reported to be .78 with Sample A and .81 with Sample B.

Subsequent analyses have provided further support for the scale (Schuler, Aldag, and Brief 1977; Shepherd and Fine 1994), though other work has cast doubt on its validity (McGee, Ferguson, and Seers 1989).

SELECTED SAMPLES: Ho and colleagues (1997) mailed surveys to a sample of 2000 practitioner marketers obtained from the American Marketing Association. Usable forms were received back from **415** respondents. The sample was a little more male (55.4%) than female, was mostly college educated (94.2%), and had an average age of 37.6 years. The majority (75%) categorized themselves as at least managers in their companies.

Data were gathered by Michaels and colleagues (1988) from two groups. Questionnaires were distributed to full-line salespeople of an industrial building materials manufacturer, with usable questionnaires being returned by **215** salespeople (response rate of 84.3%). The second sample was of industrial buyers randomly selected from the National Association of Purchasing Management. Usable surveys were returned by **330** buyers (59.6% response rate).

The study conducted by Singh, Goolsby, and Rhoads (1994) gathered data from customer service representatives who worked at large telemarketing service centers throughout the United States and who were specifically selected because of the high stress experienced in such positions. Usable survey forms were received from **351** respondents. The majority (69%) of the sample were women, and almost half (47%) had been with their respective firms for two years or less.

Teas (1980) collected data through a mail questionnaire from a Midwestern U.S. corporation's industrial sales force. Usable responses were obtained from **127** out of 184 salesmen surveyed (response rate of 69%).

SELECTED RELIABILITIES: The internal consistencies of the scale have ranged widely from .71 (Singh, Verbeke, and Rhoads 1996) to .90 (Fry et al. 1986; Ramaswami 1996). (Those versions with low reliabilities are typically abbreviated sets of items.) Specific reliabilities are provided for the studies described in the "Selected Samples" and "Major Findings" sections:

.84 by Ho and colleagues (1997)
.85 by Michaels and colleagues (1988);
.73 by Singh, Goolsby, and Rhoads (1994); and
.80 by Teas (1980).

VALIDITY: Beyond the work mentioned in the "Scale Origin" section, evidence in support of the scale's unidimensionality and convergent and discriminant validities can be found in Babin and Boles (1996) and Sohi, Smith, and Ford (1996).

ADMINISTRATION: The scale was self-administered in most of the studies, along with several other measures, in a mail questionnaire format. The approach used by RHL (1970) was to reverse code the responses before final scoring. Therefore, a higher score would imply that a person had a <u>high</u> degree of role ambiguity.

MAJOR FINDINGS: Ho and colleagues (1997) integrated cognitive moral development (CMD) into a model of the antecedents of **role ambiguity** and conflict. Support was found for the hypothesis that marketers with higher levels of CMD would also experience higher **role ambiguity**.

Findings by Michaels and colleagues (1988) indicated that higher levels of organizational formalization were associated with lower levels of **role ambiguity** among salespeople and buyers. Higher levels of role conflict and **ambiguity** were associated with lower levels of organizational commitment. Also, higher levels of **role ambiguity** were associated with higher levels of work alienation.

"Burnout" experienced by marketing boundary spanners (customer service reps) was the focus of the study by Singh, Goolsby, and Rhoads (1994). As expected, greater perceived role stress (e.g., **role ambiguity**) was found to have a positive impact on burnout tendencies.

The study by Teas (1980) indicated that participation and closeness of supervision were significantly related to **role ambiguity**. However, the hypothesis that experience was negatively related to **role ambiguity** was not supported by the results. **Role ambiguity** was found to be related to job satisfaction.

COMMENTS: See Futrell (1980) for an early use of the scale with male and female salespeople. See also Spriggs (1994) for a variation on the measurement of this construct.

REFERENCES:

Babin, Barry J. and James S. Boles (1996), "The Effects of Perceived Co-Worker Involvement and Supervisor Support on Service Provider Role Stress, Performance and Job Satisfaction," *JR*, 72 (1), 57–75.

Brown, Steven P. and Robert A. Peterson (1994), "The Effect of Effort on Sales Performance and Job Satisfaction," *JM*, 58 (April), 70–80.

Cummings, W. Theodore, Donald W. Jackson, and Lonnie L. Ostrom Jr. (1989), "Examining Product Managers' Job Satisfaction and Performance Using Selected Organizational Behavior Variables," *JAMS*, 17 (2), 147–56.

Dubinsky, Alan J. and Steven W. Hartley (1986), "A Path-Analytic Study of a Model of Salesperson Performance," *JAMS*, 14 (Spring), 36–46.

Fry, Louis W., Charles M. Futrell, A. Parasuraman, and Margaret A. Chmielewski (1986), "An Analysis of Alternative Causal Models of Salesperson Role Perceptions and Work-Related Attitudes," *JM*, 23 (May), 153–63.

Futrell, Charles M. (1980), "Salesmen and Saleswomen Job Satisfaction," *Industrial Marketing Management*, 9, 27–30.

Good, Linda K., Thomas J. Page Jr., and Clifford E. Young (1996), "Assessing Hierarchical Differences in Job-Related Attitudes and Turnover Among Retail Managers," *JAMS*, 24 (2), 148–56.

Hampton, Ron, Alan J. Dubinsky, and Steven J. Skinner (1986), "A Model of Sales Supervisor Leadership Behavior and Retail Salespeople's Job-Related Outcomes," *JAMS*, 14 (Fall), 33–43.

Ho, Foo Nin, Scott J. Vitell, James H. Barnes, and Rene Desborde (1997), "Ethical Correlates of Role Conflict and Ambiguity in Marketing: The Mediating Role of Cognitive Moral Development," *JAMS*, 25 (2), 117–26.

Lysonski, Steven (1985), "A Boundary Theory Investigation of the Product Manager's Role," *JM*, 49 (Winter), 26–40.

McGee, Gail W., Carl E. Ferguson Jr., and Anson Seers (1989), "Role Conflict and Role Ambiguity: Do the Scales Measure These Two Constructs?" *Journal of Applied Psychology*, 74 (October), 815–18.

Michaels, Ronald E., William L. Cron, Alan J. Dubinsky, and Erich A. Joachimsthaler (1988), "Influence of Formalization on the Organizational Commitment and Work Alienation of Salespeople and Industrial Buyers," *JMR*, 25 (November), 376–83.

——— and Andrea L. Dixon (1994), "Sellers and Buyers on the Boundary: Potential Moderators of Role Stress-Job Outcome Relationships," *JAMS*, 22 (1), 62–73.

Nonis, Sarath A., Jeffrey K. Sager, and Kamalesh Kumar (1996), "Salespeople's Use of Upward Influence Tactics (UITs) in Coping With Role Stress," *JAMS*, 24 (1), 44–56.

Pullins, Ellen Bolman, Leslie M. Fine, and Wendy L. Warren (1996), "Identifying Peer Mentors in the Sales Force: An Exploratory Investigation of Willingness and Ability," *JAMS*, 24 (2), 125–36.

Ramaswami, Sridhar N. (1996), "Marketing Controls and Dysfunctional Employee Behaviors: A Test of Traditional and Contingency Theory Postulates," *JM*, 60 (April), 105–20.

Rizzo, John R., Robert J. House, and Sidney I. Lirtzman (1970), "Role Conflict and Ambiguity in Complex Organizations," *Administration Science Quarterly*, 15 (June), 150–63.

Sager, Jeffrey K. (1994b), "A Structural Model Depicting Salespeople's Job Stress," *JAMS*, 22 (1), 74–84.

Schuler, R.S., R.J. Aldag, and A.P. Brief (1977), "Role Conflict and Ambiguity: A Scale Analysis," *Organizational Behavior and Human Performance*, 20 (October), 111–28.

Shepherd, C. David and Leslie M. Fine (1994), "Role Conflict and Role Ambiguity Reconsidered," *Journal of Personal Selling & Sales Management*, 14 (Spring), 57–65.

Siguaw, Judy A., Gene Brown, and Robert E. Widing II (1994), "The Influence of the Market Orientation of the Firm on Sales Force Behavior and Attitudes," *JMR*, 31 (February), 106–16.

Singh, Jagdip, Jerry R. Goolsby, and Gary K. Rhoads (1994), "Behavioral and Psychological Consequences of Boundary Spanning Burnout for Customer Service Representatives," *JMR*, 31 (November), 558–69.

———, Willem Verbeke, and Gary K. Rhoads (1996), "Do Organizational Practices Matter in Role Stress Processes? A Study of Direct and Moderating Effects for Marketing-Oriented Boundary Spanners," *JM*, 60 (July), 69–86.

Sohi, Ravipreet S., Daniel C. Smith, and Neil M. Ford (1996), "How Does Sharing a Sales Force Between Multiple Divisions Affect Salespeople?" *JAMS*, 24 (3), 195–207.

Spriggs, Mark T. (1994), "A Framework for More Valid Measures of Channel Member Performance," *JR*, 70 (4), 327–43.

Teas, R. Kenneth (1980), "An Empirical Test of Linkages Proposed in the Walker, Churchill, and Ford Model of Salesforce Motivation and Performance," *JAMS*, 8 (Winter), 58–72.

——— (1983), "Supervisory Behavior, Role Stress, and the Job Satisfaction of Industrial Salespeople," *JMR*, 20 (February), 84–91.

SCALE ITEMS:

Items used in most of the studies were not specified, but all authors indicated in some way that they used the RHL (1970) version. Enough information was available in some cases to note with greater certainty that the items used were very similar if not identical to those in the original by RHL (1970) version. The first six items are designated as the RHL (1970) items.

#843 *Role Ambiguity*

Very false   Very true
1————2————3————4————5————6————7

1. I feel certain about how much authority I have. **(r)**

2. I have clear, planned goals and objectives for my job. **(r)**

3. I know that I have divided my time properly. **(r)**

4. I know what my responsibilities are. **(r)**

5. I know exactly what is expected of me. **(r)**

6. Explanation is clear of what has to be done. **(r)**

7. I know the scope of my job. **(r)**

8. I am certain about how frequently I should call on my customers. **(r)**

9. I know how my performance is going to be evaluated. **(r)**

Babin and Boles (1996): items similar to 2, 4, 5, and 6; 5-point format
Brown and Peterson (1994): six items
Cummings, Jackson, and Ostrom (1989): four-item subset; 5-point format
Dubinsky, and Hartley (1986): RHL items and format
Fry and colleagues (1986): eight items*
Good, Page, and Young (1996): appear to have used the RHL items and format
Hampton, Dubinsky, and Skinner (1986): RHL items and format
Ho and colleagues (1997): appear to have used the RHL items and format
Lysonski (1985): appears to have used the RHL items
Michaels and colleagues (1988): nine items; 7-point format*
Michaels and Dixon (1994): six (purchasing sample) and ten (sales sample) items*
Nonis, Sager, and Kumar (1996): appear to have used the RHL items and format
Pullins, Fine, and Warren (1996): appear to have used the RHL items and format
Sager (1994): RHL items; 5-point response scale
Ramaswami (1996): items 1, 4, 5, and 7; 5-point format
Siguaw, Brown, and Widing (1994): appear to have used the RHL items
Singh, Goolsby, and Rhoads (1994): three-item subset; 5-point format
Singh, Verbeke, and Rhoads (1996): used 2, 5, and 9 and 5-point format.
Sohi, Smith, and Ford (1996): items 4, 5, 8 and items similar to 1 and 2; 5-point format
Teas (1980): slightly modified versions of the RHL items; 5-point format
Teas (1983): appears to have used the RHL items; 5-point format

*The extra items used in these studies were not identified. They could have been items from the original set of 15 created in the original study by RHL (1970) that did not make it into the final six-item version of the scale.

SCALE NAME: Role Ambiguity (Customer Facet)

SCALE DESCRIPTION: Eight five-point items that are intended to measure the extent of certainty that a marketing-oriented boundary spanner (e.g., salesperson, customer service employee) experiences with regard to his or her roles with customers.

SCALE ORIGIN: The scale was constructed by Singh and Rhoads (1991). Their purpose was to develop an instrument that would be superior to the more popular scale (#843) by Rizzo, House, and Lirtzman (1970). The latter had been criticized in the literature for having several serious shortcomings (e.g., King and King 1990). The full version of the instrument was referred to as MULTIRAM because it was a multidimensional, multifaceted measure. The scale represented here (customer) was just one of the seven dimensions assessed in the full 45-item instrument. A considerable amount of validation work was conducted by Singh and Rhoads (1991), some of which is mentioned here.

SAMPLES: Challagalla and Shervani (1996) collected data using a mail survey from salespeople who worked for the industrial product divisions of two *Fortune* 500 companies. Usable responses were received from **270** salespeople. No demographics were provided except for the general observation that the population from which the sample was drawn was predominantly male and mostly college educated.

Three phases of scale testing and refinement were used by Singh and Rhoads (1991), but only the final one is described here. In that step, data were gathered from two divisions of a U.S.-based *Fortune* 500 industrial manufacturer apparently using a mail questionnaire. The population was described as composed of salespeople and customer service employees. Usable responses were received from **216** people.

RELIABILITY: An alpha of **.89** was reported for this scale by Challagalla and Shervani (1996). In their third study, Singh and Rhoads (1991) reported the scale's construct reliability and variance extracted to be **.81** and **.59**, respectively.

VALIDITY: Examination of the scale's validity was not specifically addressed by Challagalla and Shervani (1996), probably because of the considerable evidence supplied by Singh and Rhoads (1991). The latter's three studies addressed and found evidence in support of the scale's content validity, dimensionality, convergent and discriminant validity, and nomological validity.

ADMINISTRATION: Both studies appear to have administered the scale as part of much larger mail questionnaires (Challagalla and Shervani 1996; Singh and Rhoads 1991). Higher scores on the scale indicated that respondents were expressing greater role ambiguity as it specifically relates to their interactions with customers.

MAJOR FINDINGS: The purpose of the study by Challagalla and Shervani (1996) was to extend previous work on supervisory control. Among the many findings was that activity rewards were the only control awards found to have a significant effect (negative) on customer **role ambiguity**.

As mentioned, the research of Singh and Rhoads (1991) involved three studies to develop and test a new multidimensional measure of role ambiguity (MULTIRAM). Among their findings was that customer **role ambiguity** was more strongly related to job performance than the other dimensions of **role ambiguity**.

REFERENCES:

Challagalla, Goutam N. and Tasadduq A. Shervani (1996), "Dimensions and Types of Supervisory Control: Effects on Salesperson Performance and Satisfaction," *JM*, 60 (January), 89–105.

#844 *Role Ambiguity (Customer Facet)*

King, L.A. and D.W. King (1990), "Role Conflict and Role Ambiguity: A Critical Assessment of Construct Validity," *Psychological Bulletin*, 107 (1), 48–64.

Rizzo, John R., Robert J. House, and Sidney I. Lirtzman (1970), "Role Conflict and Ambiguity in Complex Organizations," *Administration Science Quarterly*, 15 (June), 150–63.

Singh, Jagdip and Gary K. Rhoads (1991), "Boundary Role Ambiguity in Marketing-Oriented Positions: A Multidimensional, Multifaceted Operationalization," *JMR*, 28 (August), 328–38.

SCALE ITEMS:

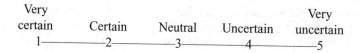

Very certain	Certain	Neutral	Uncertain	Very uncertain
1	2	3	4	5

1. How I am expected to interact with my customers.

2. How much service I should provide my customers.

3. How I should behave (with customers) while on the job.

4. How I am expected to handle my customers' objections.

5. How I am expected to handle unusual problems and situations.

6. How I am expected to deal with customers' criticism.

7. Which specific company strengths I should present to customers.

8. Which specific product benefits I am expected to highlight for customers.

SCALE NAME: Role Clarity (Behavioral)

SCALE DESCRIPTION: Kohli and Jaworski (1994) used this four-item, five-point Likert-type scale to measure the degree to which salespeople understand the manner in which they are expected to go about their jobs.

SCALE ORIGIN: Kohli and Jaworski (1994) adapted a six-item role clarity scale originally developed by Rizzo, House, and Lirtzman (1970) by creating two separate scales that measured the output and behavioral aspects of role clarity. The original scale items were essentially rephrased into two separate statements, the first of which reflected an output-focused role clarity item and the second of which was behaviorally focused. For example, the original item "I know exactly what is expected of me" was adapted as "I know exactly what output is expected of me" and "I know exactly what is expected to do my job." A second modification resulted in the elimination of items tapping into the comfort dimension in addition to role clarity. The resulting five-item measures were pretested as described subsequently. One item, "I know that I divide my time properly," was eliminated from the final role clarity (behavioral) measure on the basis of low interitem correlations.

SAMPLES: Because the nature of the study required that salesperson behavior and output be visible to coworkers, and thus allow for coworker feedback, Kohli and Jaworski (1994) chose to sample retail auto salespeople. The preliminary set of scale items was first administered to 11 auto salespeople from five dealerships, and their comments enabled scale item and questionnaire revision. The final questionnaire was mailed to 303 salespeople belonging to the nationwide dealership network of a European car manufacturer. A reminder, followed by a second questionnaire mailing, resulted in usable responses being obtained from **150** salespeople.

RELIABILITY: Kohli and Jaworski (1994) reported a coefficient alpha of **.52** for this measure.

VALIDITY: Kohli and Jaworski (1994) used confirmatory factory analysis to test the unidimensionality of the measure in conjunction with the other role clarity and performance constructs. Results suggested that the measure was unidimensional. No other specific assessments of validity were discussed by the authors.

ADMINISTRATION: Kohli and Jaworski (1994) stated that the scale was part of a self-administered questionnaire that was delivered by mail. A personally addressed cover letter promising complete confidentiality accompanied the survey, as did a self-addressed reply envelope and ballpoint pen incentive. A reminder was sent one week after the initial mailing, and nonrespondents received a second reminder and questionnaire three weeks after the initial mailing. Lower scores on the role clarity (behavioral) scale indicated that salespeople understood the manner in which they were expected to go about their jobs.

MAJOR FINDINGS: Kohli and Jaworski (1994) investigated how positive output, negative output, positive behavioral, and negative behavioral forms of coworker feedback affected salespeople's output and behavioral role clarity, satisfaction with coworkers, and output and behavioral performance. **Behavior-related role clarity** was influenced by positive behavioral feedback but not by negative behavior feedback, which suggests that salespeople are unwilling to redefine their work roles on the basis of coworker criticism. **Behavior-related role clarity** was also found to positively influence behavior performance.

COMMENTS: The low coefficient alpha suggests that further development and testing may be required prior to administering this measure in the future.

#845 *Role Clarity (Behavioral)*

REFERENCES:

Kohli, Ajay K. and Bernard J. Jaworski (1994), "The Influence of Coworker Feedback on Salespeople," *JM*, 58 (October), 82–94.

Rizzo, John R., Robert J. House, and Sidney I. Lirtzman (1970), "Role Conflict and Ambiguity in Complex Organizations," *Administrative Science Quarterly*, 15 (June), 150–63.

SCALE ITEMS:

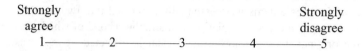

Strongly
  agree

Strongly
  disagree

1————2————3————4————5

1. I am unclear about the "right" way of doing my job. **(r)**

2. I lack information to carry out my job. **(r)**

3. There are few guidelines or policies to help me. **(r)**

4. I know exactly how I am expected to do my job.

SCALE NAME: Role Clarity (Output)

SCALE DESCRIPTION: Kohli and Jaworski (1994) used this four-item, five-point Likert-type scale to measure the degree to which salespeople are aware of the results they are expected to attain.

SCALE ORIGIN: Kohli and Jaworski (1994) adapted a six-item role clarity scale originally developed by Rizzo, House, and Lirtzman (1970) by creating two separate scales that measured the output and behavioral aspects of role clarity. The original scale items were essentially rephrased into two separate statements, the first of which reflected an output-focused role clarity item and the second of which was behaviorally focused. For example, the original item "I know exactly what is expected of me" was adapted as "I know exactly what output is expected of me" and "I know exactly what is expected to do my job." A second modification resulted in the elimination of items tapping into the comfort dimension in addition to role clarity. The resulting five-item measures were pretested as described subsequently. One reversed item, "I am unclear of the performance levels expected of me," was eliminated from the final role clarity (output) measure on the basis of low interitem correlations.

SAMPLES: Because the nature of the study required that salesperson behavior and output be visible to coworkers, and thus allow for coworker feedback, Kohli and Jaworski (1994) chose to sample retail auto salespeople. The preliminary set of scale items was first administered to 11 auto salespeople from five dealerships, and their comments enabled scale item and questionnaire revision. The final questionnaire was mailed to 303 salespeople belonging to the nationwide dealership network of a European car manufacturer. A reminder, followed by a second questionnaire mailing, resulted in usable responses being obtained from **150** salespeople.

RELIABILITY: Kohli and Jaworski (1994) reported a coefficient alpha of **.81** for this measure.

VALIDITY: Kohli and Jaworski (1994) used confirmatory factory analysis to test the unidimensionality of the measure in conjunction with the other role clarity and performance constructs. Results suggested that the measure was unidimensional. No other specific assessments of validity were discussed by the authors.

ADMINISTRATION: Kohli and Jaworski (1994) stated that the scale was part of a self-administered questionnaire that was delivered by mail. A personally addressed cover letter promising complete confidentiality accompanied the survey, as did a self-addressed reply envelope and ballpoint pen incentive. A reminder was sent one week after the initial mailing, and nonrespondents received a second reminder and questionnaire three weeks after the initial mailing. Lower scores on the role clarity (output) scale indicated that salespeople were aware of the results expected of them.

MAJOR FINDINGS: Kohli and Jaworski (1994) investigated how positive output, negative output, positive behavioral, and negative behavioral forms of coworker feedback affected salespeople's output and behavioral role clarity, satisfaction with coworkers, and output and behavioral performance. **Output-related role clarity** was unrelated to whether salespeople received negative or positive output-related feedback from coworkers; however, **output-related role clarity** was found to positively influence output performance.

REFERENCES:

Kohli, Ajay K. and Bernard J. Jaworski (1994), "The Influence of Coworker Feedback on Salespeople," *JM*, 58 (October), 82–94.

Rizzo, John R., Robert J. House, and Sidney I. Lirtzman (1970), "Role Conflict and Ambiguity in Complex Organizations," *Administrative Science Quarterly*, 15 (June), 150–63.

#846 *Role Clarity (Output)*

SCALE ITEMS:

Strongly   Strongly
  agree   disagree

1————————2————————3————————4————————5

1. My performance targets are clear and unambiguous.

2. I know exactly what output is expected of me.

3. Clear, planned goals and objectives exist for my job.

4. I know what I am expected to achieve on this job.

SCALE NAME: Role Competence (Partner)

SCALE DESCRIPTION: Smith and Barclay (1997) used this four-item, seven-point Likert-type scale to measure perceptions of the degree to which partners perceived each other as having the skills, abilities, and knowledge necessary for effective task performance.

SCALE ORIGIN: Smith and Barclay (1997) indicated that the constructs used in their study were operationalized with a mix of original and adapted scale items generated from the conceptual definition of the constructs, a review of the literature, field interviews, and pretest results. Each of the final items representing this measure passed the extensive preliminary analysis of item reliability and validity described by the authors.

SAMPLES: Smith and Barclay (1997) collected dyadic self-report data in two stages. The sponsor sample was composed of 338 sales representatives working for the Canadian subsidiaries of two multinational companies serving the computer industry. Forty percent of the 338 employees who were randomly selected from employee lists returned completed surveys. Using the names and contact information of relationship partners volunteered by these respondents, the authors then sampled the 135 dyadic partners. A total of **103** usable paired responses were obtained.

RELIABILITY: Smith and Barclay (1997) reported coefficient alphas of **.86** for this measure in the sponsor model and **.86** in the partner model as well.

VALIDITY: Smith and Barclay (1997) reported extensive testing of the reliability, unidimensionality, and convergent and discriminant validity of the measures used in their study. LISREL and confirmatory factor analysis were used to demonstrate that the scale satisfied each of these standards, though some items from the measures as originally proposed were eliminated in the process.

ADMINISTRATION: Smith and Barclay (1997) included the scale with other measures as part of a self-administered survey that was delivered by internal company mail to sales representatives and by regular U.S. mail to the dyadic partners. E-mail follow-ups were used to increase survey response rate. Half of the sales representatives were instructed to consider a customer situation in the prior six months in which they had had some success with a selling partner, whereas the other half were told to choose a situation in which they had had little or no success. Participants then responded to questions about the partner, their relationship, and the organization in the context of this situation. Higher scores on the scale indicated greater mutual trust between partners, in that partners perceived each other as having the skills, abilities, and knowledge necessary for effective task performance.

MAJOR FINDINGS: Smith and Barclay (1997) developed and tested two research models explaining selling partner relationship effectiveness. The first examined four organizational differences from the sponsor's (salesperson's) perspective, and the second examined these same differences from the partner's perspective. In both models, greater perceived differences in the reputations of partner firms and partner job stability led to lower evaluations of the **role competence** component of mutual perceived trustworthiness.

REFERENCES:

Smith, J. Brock and Donald W. Barclay (1997), "The Effects of Organizational Differences and Trust on the Effectiveness of Selling Partner Relationships," *JM*, 61 (January), 3–21.

#847 *Role Competence (Partner)*

SCALE ITEMS:*

Strongly   Strongly
disagree   agree

1————2————3————4————5————6————7

1. When it comes to hardware, this rep knows enough to be effective.

2. S/he understands the customer's business.

3. I can count on this rep's ability to adapt to specific customer situations.

4. This rep really knows the industry.

*All of the items in this scale were conceptualized at the individual level and then aggregated to the relationship level by taking the square root of the product of the individual responses by the sales representative and partner.

SCALE NAME: Role Conflict

SCALE DESCRIPTION: The scale is intended to measure the compatibility (or lack thereof) a person experiences in the requirements of a job-related role. Incompatibility may be the result of such things as person–role conflict, role overload, and conflicting organizational demands and standards. Several users of the scale in marketing have modified it to some extent by adjusting the wording of items to better apply to certain employee groups, dropping less relevant items, or using slightly different response formats.

SCALE ORIGIN: The scale was originally developed by Rizzo, House, and Lirtzman (1970; hereafter RHL). Their study discussed the rationale for the scale and the initial developmental and purification process. Data were gathered from a variety of employees of a firm and then divided into two samples, one representative of the firm in general (Sample A) and the other focused on the research and engineering division (Sample B). Development of a role ambiguity scale occurred at the same time (see #843). It began with 15 items, but the factor analysis, examination of internal consistency, and judgement led to the final version of the role conflict scale with 8 items. The reliability of the scale was reported to be .82 with both samples.

Subsequent analyses have provided further support for the scale (Schuler, Aldag, and Brief 1977; Shepherd and Fine 1994), though other work has cast doubt on its validity (McGee, Ferguson, and Seers 1989).

SELECTED SAMPLES: Data were gathered by Fry and colleagues (1986) through a mail survey of a national pharmaceutical manufacturer's sales force. Questionnaires were returned by **216** of 347 salespeople surveyed (response rate of 62%). The data analyzed were from men only, and demographics were not specified.

Ho and colleagues (1997) mailed surveys to a sample of 2000 practitioner marketers obtained from the American Marketing Association. Usable forms were received back from **415** respondents. The sample was a little more male (55.4%) than female, was mostly college educated (94.2%), and had an average age of 37.6 years. The majority (75%) categorized themselves as at least managers in their companies.

The study conducted by Singh, Goolsby, and Rhoads (1994) gathered data from customer service representatives who worked at large telemarketing service centers throughout the United States and who were specifically selected because of the high stress experienced in such positions. Usable survey forms were received from **351** respondents. The majority (69%) of the sample were women, and almost half (47%) had been with their respective firms for two years or less.

Skinner, Dubinsky, and Donnelly (1984) collected data from retail salespeople employed by a small departmental store chain. All salespeople employed by the firm participated in the study. Questionnaires were administered to participants at their workplace, and a total of **157** usable questionnaires were received.

SELECTED RELIABILITIES: The internal consistencies for those versions with three or more items have ranged from .68 (Singh, Goolsby, and Rhoads 1994) to .88 (Teas 1983). Specific reliabilities are provided for the studies described in the "Selected Samples" and "Major Findings" sections:

.86 by Fry and colleagues (1986);
.82 by Ho and colleagues (1997);
.68 by Singh, Goolsby, and Rhoads (1994); and
.79 by Skinner, Dubinsky, and Donnelly (1984).

VALIDITY: Beyond the work mentioned in the "Scale Origin" section, evidence in support of the scale's unidimensionality and convergent and discriminant validities can be found in Babin and Boles (1996), Sager (1994), and Sohi, Smith, and Ford (1996).

ADMINISTRATION: The scale was self-administered in most of the studies, along with several other measures, in a mail questionnaire format. As shown subsequently, a higher score implied that a person had a <u>high</u> degree of role conflict.

SELECTED FINDINGS: Fry and colleagues' (1986) results indicated that **role conflict** had a negative effect on all job satisfaction dimensions (e.g., job, fellow workers, supervisor, pay promotion and development, company policy and support) except satisfaction with customer.

Ho and colleagues (1997) integrated cognitive moral development (CMD) into a model of the antecedents of **role conflict** and ambiguity. Support was found for the hypothesis that marketers with higher levels of CMD would also experience higher **role conflict**.

"Burnout" experienced by marketing boundary spanners (customer service reps) was the focus of the study by Singh, Goolsby, and Rhoads (1994). As expected, greater perceived role stress (e.g., **role conflict**) was found to have a positive impact on burnout tendencies.

Skinner, Dubinsky, and Donnelly (1984) studied the relationship between retail sales managers' social bases of power and retail salespeople's job-related outcomes. They found that legitimate and expert power were inversely related to **role conflict**.

COMMENTS: See Futrell (1980) for an early use of the scale with male and female salespeople. See also a two-item variation of the scale used by Ramaswami (1996).

REFERENCES:

Babin, Barry J. and James S. Boles (1996), "The Effects of Perceived Co-Worker Involvement and Supervisor Support on Service Provider Role Stress, Performance and Job Satisfaction," *JR*, 72 (1), 57–75.

Brown, Steven P. and Robert A. Peterson (1994), "The Effect of Effort on Sales Performance and Job Satisfaction," *JM*, 58 (April), 70–80.

Cummings, W. Theodore, Donald W. Jackson, and Lonnie L. Ostrom Jr. (1989), "Examining Product Managers' Job Satisfaction and Performance Using Selected Organizational Behavior Variables," *JAMS*, 17 (2), 147–56.

Dubinsky, Alan J. and Steven W. Hartley (1986), "A Path-Analytic Study of a Model of Salesperson Performance," *JAMS*, 14 (Spring), 36–46.

Fry, Louis W., Charles M. Futrell, A. Parasuraman, and Margaret A. Chmielewski (1986), "An Analysis of Alternative Causal Models of Salesperson Role Perceptions and Work-Related Attitudes," *JMR*, 23 (May), 153–63.

Futrell, Charles M. (1980), "Salesmen and Saleswomen Job Satisfaction," *Industrial Marketing Management*, 9, 27–30.

Good, Linda K., Thomas J. Page Jr., and Clifford E. Young (1996), "Assessing Hierarchical Differences in Job-Related Attitudes and Turnover Among Retail Managers," *JAMS*, 24 (2), 148–56.

Hampton, Ron, Alan J. Dubinsky, and Steven J. Skinner (1986), "A Model of Sales Supervisor Leadership Behavior and Retail Salespeople's Job-Related Outcomes," *JAMS*, 14 (Fall), 33–43.

Ho, Foo Nin, Scott J. Vitell, James H. Barnes, and Rene Desborde (1997), "Ethical Correlates of Role Conflict and Ambiguity in Marketing: The Mediating Role of Cognitive Moral Development," *JAMS*, 25 (2), 117–26.

Lysonski, Steven (1985), "A Boundary Theory Investigation of the Product Manager's Role," *JM*, 49 (Winter), 26–40.

Michaels, Ronald E., William L. Cron, Alan J. Dubinsky, and Erich A. Joachimsthaler (1988), "Influence of Formalization on the Organizational Commitment and Work Alienation of Salespeople and Industrial Buyers," *JMR*, 25 (November), 376–83.

———— and Andrea L. Dixon (1994), "Sellers and Buyers on the Boundary: Potential Moderators of Role Stress-Job Outcome Relationships," *JAMS*, 22 (1), 62–73.

Nonis, Sarath A., Jeffrey K. Sager, and Kamalesh Kumar (1996), "Salespeople's Use of Upward Influence Tactics (UITs) in Coping With Role Stress," *JAMS*, 24 (1), 44–56.

Pullins, Ellen Bolman, Leslie M. Fine, and Wendy L. Warren (1996), "Identifying Peer Mentors in the Sales Force: An Exploratory Investigation of Willingness and Ability," *JAMS*, 24 (2), 125–36.

Ramaswami, Sridhar N. (1996), "Marketing Controls and Dysfunctional Employee Behaviors: A Test of Traditional and Contingency Theory Postulates," *JM*, 60 (April), 105–20.

Rizzo, J., R.J. House, and S.I. Lirtzman (1970), "Role Conflict and Ambiguity in Complex Organizations," *Administrative Science Quarterly*, 15 (June), 150–63.

Sager, Jeffrey K. (1994), "A Structural Model Depicting Salespeople's Job Stress," *JAMS*, 22 (1), 74–84.

Siguaw, Judy A., Gene Brown, and Robert E. Widing II (1994), " The Influence of the Market Orientation of the Firm on Sales Force Behavior and Attitudes," *JMR*, 31 (February), 106–16.

Singh, Jagdip, Jerry R. Goolsby, and Gary K. Rhoads (1994), "Behavioral and Psychological Consequences of Boundary Spanning Burnout for Customer Service Representatives," *JMR*, 31 (November), 558–69.

————, Willem Verbeke, and Gary K. Rhoads (1996), "Do Organizational Practices Matter in Role Stress Processes? A Study of Direct and Moderating Effects for Marketing-Oriented Boundary Spanners," *JM*, 60 (July), 69–86.

Schuler, Randall S., Ramon J. Aldag, and Arthur P. Brief (1977), "Role Conflict and Ambiguity: A Scale Analysis," *Organizational Behavior and Human Performance*, 16, 111–28.

Skinner S.J., A. Dubinsky, and J.H. Donnelly (1984), "The Use of Social Bases of Power in Retail Sales," *Journal of Personal Selling & Sales Management*, 4 (November), 49–56.

Sohi, Ravipreet S., Daniel C. Smith, and Neil M. Ford (1996), "How Does Sharing a Sales Force Between Multiple Divisions Affect Salespeople?" *JAMS*, 24 (3), 195–207.

Teas, R. Kenneth (1983), "Supervisory Behavior, Role Stress, and the Job Satisfaction of Industrial Salespeople," *JMR*, 20 (February), 84–91.

SCALE ITEMS:

Items used in most of the studies were not specified but all authors indicated in some way that they used the RHL (1970) version. Enough information is available in some cases to say with greater certainty that the items used were very similar if not identical to those in the original by RHL (1970) version. The first eight items shown are designated the RHL items.

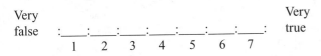

Very false :____:____:____:____:____:____:____: Very true
      1   2   3   4   5   6   7

1. I have to do things that should be done differently.

2. I receive an assignment without the manpower to complete it.

3. I have to buck a rule or policy in order to carry out an assignment.

4. I work with two or more groups who operate quite differently.

5. I receive incompatible requests from two or more people.

6. I do things that are apt to be accepted by one person and not accepted by others.

7. I receive an assignment without adequate resources and materials to execute it.

8. I work on unnecessary things.

9. I work under incompatible policies and guidelines.

10. I have to work under vague directives and orders.

Babin and Boles (1996): items 3, 5, 6, and 7; 5-point format
Brown and Peterson (1994): six-item subset
Cummings, Jackson, and Ostrom (1989): six-item subset; 5-point format
Dubinsky and Hartley (1986): RHL items and format
Fry and colleagues (1986): seven items
Good, Page, and Young (1996): appear to have used the RHL items and format
Hampton, Dubinsky, and Skinner (1986): RHL items and format
Ho and colleagues (1997): appear to have used the RHL items
Lysonski (1985): ten items*
Michaels and colleagues (1988): eleven items; 7-point format*
Michaels and Dixon (1994): eight (purchasing sample) and thirteen (sales sample) items*
Nonis, Sager, and Kumar (1996): appear to have used the RHL items and format
Pullins, Fine, and Warren (1996): appear to have used the RHL items and format
Sager (1994): six-item subset; 5-point response scale
Siguaw, Brown, and Widing (1994): appear to have used the RHL items
Singh, Goolsby, and Rhoads (1994): three-item subset; 5-point format
Singh, Verbeke, and Rhoads (1996): items 2, 4, and 5; 5-point format
Sohi, Smith, and Ford (1996): items 1, 5, 8, 9, and 10; 5-point format
Teas (1983): appears to have used the RHL items; 5-point format

*The extra items used in these studies were not identified. They could have been items from the original set of fifteen created in the original study by RHL (1970) that did not make it into the final eight-item version of the scale.

SCALE NAME: Role Conflict

SCALE DESCRIPTION: The full version of the scale measures the job-related incompatibilities experienced by customer-contact employees between them and their supervisors, their job expectations and the actual job, them and their customers, them and their families, and their personal principles and various sales activities.

SCALE ORIGIN: Chonko and Burnett (1983) developed the scale as part of a larger study of industrial sales force behavior. Potential scale items were pretested using 6 sales managers and 30 salespeople. Data for the main study were gathered from sales-related employees of a *Fortune* 500 firm. Out of 260 questionnaires mailed, **215** useful responses were received (122 sales representatives, 19 area managers, and 74 sales support staff personnel). Cronbach's alpha coefficients for the salesperson portion of the sample, broken down for each subscale, were **.89** for supervisor, **.90** for job, **.81** for customer relations, **.85** for family, and **.86** for ethics. Factor analyses were run twice (one on the sample of salespeople and one on the sample of sales managers and support personnel) on the full set of 31 items. For both groups, four role conflict factors were obtained: job, family, ethics, and customer relations (a combined supervisor and customer factor). Therefore, the instrument was treated as composed of four subscales with a total of 27 items.

Chonko, Howell, and Bellenger (1986) was based on just the salesperson portion of this sample. Furthermore, for unexplained reasons, five subscales with a total of 30 of the items were utilized.

SAMPLES: Data were gathered by Hartline and Ferrell (1996) from hotel managers, employees, and customers representing three chains and 279 different hotel units. Usable survey forms were returned by 236 hotel managers, 743 hotel employees, and 1351 customers. This scale was only filled out by the employee group. Data from some employees were eliminated before analysis when it became clear that their jobs did not involve customer contact. This left **561** completed questionnaires from employees. The majority were women (68%) between 20 and 30 years of age (63.8%), were not college graduates (74%), held positions at the front desk or with customer service (53.7%), and had 10 or more years of industry experience (54.5%).

Schwepker, Ferrell, and Ingram (1997) sent questionnaires to industry salespeople of 33 firms and received usable forms from **152** respondents. The majority of the sample were men (70.4%), married (75.7%), college educated (69.7%), less than 40 years of age (51.4%), and sold goods verses services (55.9%).

RELIABILITY: An alpha of **.83** was reported by Hartline and Ferrell (1996) for the 12-item version they used. The 23-item version used by Schwepker, Ferrell, and Ingram (1997) was reported to have an alpha of **.87**.

VALIDITY: As with the other measures used in their studies, Hartline and Ferrell (1996) and Schwepker, Ferrell, and Ingram (1997) employed confirmatory factor analysis to assess the psychometric qualities of their respective versions of the **role conflict** scale. In both studies, evidence was found in support of their scales' convergent and discriminant validities.

ADMINISTRATION: In each of the studies, the scale was self-administered by respondents in a mail survey design. A higher score represented greater perceived role conflict.

MAJOR FINDINGS: The purpose of the study by Hartline and Ferrell (1996) was to develop a model of service employee management and simultaneously examine the manager–employee, employee–role, and employee–customer interfaces. Among the findings was that employees' **role conflict** appeared to increase their self-efficacy.

Schwepker, Ferrell, and Ingram (1997) examined the relationship of an organization's ethical climate with salespeople's ethical conflict. Among the findings was that perceived ethical differences between salespeople and their managers increased **role conflict**.

COMMENTS: The evidence presented by both Chonko and Burnett (1983) and Chonko, Howell, and Bellenger (1986) shows clearly that the full instrument is <u>not</u> unidimensional. Although it is possible that subsets of items, such as used by Hartline and Ferrell (1996) and Schwepker, Ferrell, and Ingram (1997), could be unidimensional, strong consideration should be given to treating the different sources of role conflict as separate scales.

REFERENCES:

Chonko, Lawrence B. and John J. Burnett (1983), "Measuring the Importance of Ethical Situations as a Source of Role Conflict: A Survey of Salespeople, Sales Managers, and Sales Support Personnel," *Journal of Personal Selling & Sales Management*, 3 (May), 41–47.

————, Roy D. Howell, and Danny N. Bellenger (1986), "Congruence in Sales Force Evaluations: Relation to Sales Force Perceptions of Conflict and Ambiguity," *Journal of Personal Selling & Sales Management*, 6 (May), 35–48.

Hartline, Michael D. and O.C. Ferrell (1996), "The Management of Customer-Contact Service Employees: An Empirical Investigation," *JM*, 60 (October), 52–70.

Schwepker, Charles H., Jr., O.C. Ferrell, and Thomas N. Ingram (1997), "The Influence of Ethical Climate and Ethical Conflict on Role Stress in the Sales Force," *JAMS*, 25 (2), 99–108.

SCALE ITEMS:

Directions: As an industrial sale representative you often must satisfy a number of people in the performance of your job. Your sales supervisor, your family, your customers, and you, yourself, have expectations about the activities you should perform in your job, and how you should perform these activities. Please circle the number code that best expresses your feeling about the degree of agreement between you and various people with whom you must work. Please use the following scale:

Complete agreement	Very much agreement	Moderate agreement	Some agreement	No agreement
1	2	3	4	5

FACTOR 1: Customer Orientation

How much agreement would you say there is between you and your supervisor on...

1. How much maintenance service you should provide for your customers.
2. How much authority you should have regarding delivery adjustments for your customers.
3. How much authority you should have regarding price negotiations with customers.
4. How much training you should provide your customers.

How much agreement would you say there is between you and your customer on...

5. Your performance of field tests for customers.
6. How much training you should provide customers.
7. When you should be available to your customers.
8. The extent to which you should develop personal relations with your customers.
9. How you should handle competition in your sales presentations.
10. How you should present the benefits of your firm's products to your customers.
11. How much maintenance service you should provide for your customers.

FACTOR 2: Job

How much agreement would you say there is between...

12. The amount of sales territory I expect to cover and the territory I actually cover.
13. The number of customers I expect to have and the number of customers I actually have.
14. The non-selling tasks I expected to perform and the non-selling tasks I actually perform.
15. The amount of leisure time I expected to have and the leisure time I actually have.

How much agreement would you say there is between you and your supervisor on...

16. How much customer research I should provide.
17. How much troubleshooting I should do for my customers.
18. Your role in setting sales goals.
19. How often you should report to your supervisor.
20. What acceptable performance is for you.
21. How you can best help to achieve the organization's objectives.

FACTOR 3: Family

How much agreement would you say there is between you and your family on...

22. The time you spend working.
23. The time you spend socializing with customers.
24. The time you spend socializing with other salespeople.
25. How much you travel on your job.

FACTOR 4: Ethics

How much agreement would you say there is between you and your personal principles and...

26. How far I should stretch the truth to make a sale.
27. How often your customers offer you favors to bend the rules of your company.
28. How often your customers offer you favors to bend government laws and regulations.
29. How often you try to sell a product to a customer even if you feel the product has little or no value to that customer.
30. How often you feel pressure to stretch the truth in order to make a sale.
31. How often you feel pressure to apply the "hard sale" in order to make a sale.

Chonko and Burnett (1983): all items except 18–21; 5-point Likert-type format
Chonko, Howell, and Bellenger (1986): all items except 7; 5-point Likert-type format
Hartline and Ferrell (1996): 12 items similar to some of these
Schwepker, Ferrell, and Ingram (1997): all items except 5, 7, and 22–27; 5-point items

SCALE NAME: Role Modeling

SCALE DESCRIPTION: Rich (1997) used this five-item, seven-point Likert-type scale to measure the degree to which behavior on the part of the sales manager is perceived as being consistent with both the values espoused by the sales manager and the goals of the organization.

SCALE ORIGIN: Although the scale is original to Rich (1997), some items were adapted from leadership scales by Bass (1985) and Podsakoff and colleagues (1990). In developing the scale, Rich (1997) mixed 10 items believed to tap the role modeling domain with 40 leadership items taken from a variety of scales. Colleagues were asked to assess the extent to which each of the 50 items reflected the construct definition of role modeling on a 10-point scale ranging from "not at all appropriate" to "entirely appropriate." The most appropriate items were retained and analyzed by sales practitioners for relevance. The scale was then pretested and purified using results obtained from a sample of 98 insurance agents. The measure was revised into its final form on the basis of the results of a confirmatory factor analysis.

SAMPLES: Salespeople and their immediate supervisors from 10 different U.S.-based business-to-business sales organizations representing different industries formed the sample for this study. Of the 244 salesperson–manager dyads that received questionnaires, usable responses were obtained from 193 salespeople and 218 managers, resulting in complete responses from a total of **183** matched salesperson–manager dyads.

RELIABILITY: Rich (1997) reported a coefficient alpha of **.96** for the measure.

VALIDITY: Results of the confirmatory factor analysis reported by Rich (1997) provided strong evidence for the discriminant and convergent validity of the measures, and the extensive pretesting provided evidence of content validity.

ADMINISTRATION: Rich (1997) indicated that the scale was part of a self-administered mail survey sent directly to each member of the salesperson–manager dyad. Follow-up telephone calls made by research assistants, the promise to share survey results, and encouragement from the management of participating firms enhanced respondent participation. It appears that the measure was only administered to the salesperson sample. Higher scores on the scale indicated that the behavior on the part of the sales manager was perceived as highly consistent with both the values espoused by that sales manager and the goals of the organization.

MAJOR FINDINGS: Rich (1997) examined the relationship between the role modeling behavior of sales managers and a set of key outcome variables, including trust in the manager, job satisfaction, and salesperson performance. Salespeople's perceptions of their **managers' role modeling behavior** were positively related to their trust in the sales manager. Through its relationship with trust, **sales manager role modeling behavior** was found to indirectly influence both job satisfaction and salesperson performance.

REFERENCES:

Bass, Bernard M. (1985), *Leadership and Beyond Expectations*. New York: The Free Press.
Podsakoff, Philip M., Scott B. MacKenzie, R.H. Moorman, and Richard Fetter (1990), "Transformational Leader Behaviors and Their Effects on Followers' Trust in Leader, Satisfaction, and Organizational Citizenship Behaviors," *Leadership Quarterly*, 1 (Summer), 102–42.
Rich, Gregory A. (1997), "The Sales Manager as a Role Model: Effects on Trust, Job Satisfaction, and Performance of Salespeople," *JAMS*, 25 (4), 319–28.

SCALE ITEMS:

1 = Strongly disagree
2 = Moderately disagree
3 = Slightly disagree
4 = Neither agree nor disagree
5 = Slightly agree
6 = Moderately agree
7 = Strongly agree

My manager:

1. Provides a good model for me to follow.

2. Leads by example.

3. Sets a positive example for others to follow.

4. Exhibits the kind of work ethic and behavior that I try to imitate.

5. Acts as a role model for me.

#851 *Salesperson Adaptability (ADAPTS)*

SCALE NAME: Salesperson Adaptability (ADAPTS)

SCALE DESCRIPTION: The full version of the scale is composed of sixteen statements designed to capture the extent to which a salesperson attempts to adjust his or her selling behaviors during an interaction with a customer using information about the nature of sales situation. Because the scale assesses the *practice* of salespeople, it is not appropriate to use it as a screening or selection tool for people who do not have sales experience.

SCALE ORIGIN: The scale is original to Spiro and Weitz (1990). Forty-two items were generated and tested for measuring six facets of adaptive selling. Factor analysis indicated that items representing five of the six facets loaded high on the first component. A final sixteen-item scale was developed with several objectives in mind (e.g., highly interrelated items, minimum number of items, high standard deviation). More information about the scale's psychometric characteristics is provided subsequently.

SAMPLES: Data were gathered by Hartline and Ferrell (1996) from hotel managers, employees, and customers representing three chains and 279 different hotel units. Usable survey forms were returned by 236 hotel managers, 743 hotel employees, and 1351 customers. **ADAPTS** was only filled out by the employee group. Data from some employees were eliminated before analysis when it became clear that their jobs did not involve customer contact. This left **561** completed questionnaires from employees. The majority were women (68%) between 20 and 30 years of age (63.8%), were not college graduates (74%), held positions at the front desk or with customer service (53.7%), and had 10 or more years of industry experience (54.5%).

Spiro and Weitz (1990) gathered data from salespeople in ten divisions of a major national manufacturing company. The company handled the distribution of the questionnaires, but the forms were returned directly to the researchers. Usable responses were received from **268** salespeople.

The study conducted by Sujan, Weitz, and Kumar (1994) collected data from salespeople at eight firms in diverse industries. Survey forms were distributed by sales managers but were returned by mail to the researchers. Usable responses were apparently received from **190** salespeople. The sample was mostly men (78%) who had an average age of 35 years and 9 years of sales experience.

Swenson and Herche (1994) collected data using a national mailing list of industrial salespeople working in diverse industries resulting in **271** usable responses. The sample was mostly married (89%) men (92%) with an average of 48 years.

RELIABILITY: Alphas (or construct reliabilities) of **.85**, **.88**, and **.87** were reported for the full version of the scale used by Spiro and Weitz (1990), Sujan, Weitz, and Kumar (1994), and Swenson and Herche (1994), respectively. An alpha of **.77** was reported by Hartline and Ferrell (1996) for the 10-item version they used.

VALIDITY: As with the other measures used in their study, Hartline and Ferrell (1996) employed confirmatory factor analysis to assess the psychometric quality of the **adaptive selling** scale. Evidence was found in support of the scale's convergent and discriminant validities.

Spiro and Weitz (1990) provided some evidence in support of the scale's nomological validity. However, their principal component factor analysis indicated the presence of two factors with eigenvalues greater than 1, and the authors admitted that the scale was not unidimensional.

ADMINISTRATION: In each of the studies, the scale was administered, along with several other measures, as part of a larger questionnaire. Higher scores on the scale indicated that respondents were expressing the ability to be flexible in their sales approaches used with customers.

MAJOR FINDINGS: The purpose of the study by Hartline and Ferrell (1996) was to develop a model of service employee management and simultaneously examine the manager–employee, employee–role, and employee–customer interfaces. Despite expectations to the contrary, employee **adaptability** was not found to have a significant effect on customers' perceived service quality.

Spiro and Weitz (1990) constructed and tested a scale of **adaptive selling (ADAPTS)**. Among the findings was that **ADAPTS** was significantly correlated with eight measures of interpersonal flexibility and one hypothesized antecedent (intrinsic motivation).

Sujan, Weitz, and Kumar (1994) examined the relationships between learning and performance goals with working smart and hard. **ADAPTS** was one of three measures used to capture the *working smart* construct. The results indicated that a learning orientation had a positive impact on working smart, which in turn had a positive impact on performance.

The study by Swenson and Herche (1994) examined the role of social values to predict salesperson performance. Their results provided support for the incremental ability of social values to predict performance beyond the use of **adaptive selling** and customer orientation in isolation.

COMMENTS: Spiro and Weitz (1990) noted that the mean score on the scale was 5.51 with an standard deviation of .66.

Note that the unidimensionality of this scale, as well as the wisdom of using reverse-coded items, has been questioned by Herche and Engelland (1994, 1996). After testing the **ADAPTS** scale and two other scales in multiple contexts, they concluded that measures with mixed-item polarity appear to be susceptible to degradation of unidimensionality.

See also Sharma and Levy (1995) for another use of the scale.

REFERENCES:

Hartline, Michael D. and O.C. Ferrell (1996), "The Management of Customer-Contact Service Employees: An Empirical Investigation," *JM*, 60 (October), 52–70.

Herche, Joel and Brian Engelland (1994), "Reversed-Polarity Items, Attribution Effects and Scale Dimensionality," *Office of Scale Research Technical Report #9401,* Department of Marketing, Southern Illinois University at Carbondale.

——— and ——— (1996) "Reversed-Polarity Items and Scale Unidimensionality," *JAMS*, 24 (4), 366–74.

Sharma, Arun and Michael Levy (1995), "Categorization of Customers by Retail Salespeople," *JR*, 71 (1), 71–81.

Spiro, Rosann L. and Barton A. Weitz (1990), "Adaptive Selling: Conceptualization, Measurement, and Nomological Validity," *JMR*, 27 (February), 61–19.

Sujan, Harish, Barton A. Weitz, and Nirmalya Kumar (1994), "Learning Orientation, Working Smart, and Effective Selling," *JM*, 58 (July), 39–52.

Swenson, Michael J. and Joel Herche (1994), "Social Values and Salesperson Performance: An Empirical Examination," *JAMS*, 22 (3), 283–89.

SCALE ITEMS:*

Strongly disagree / Strongly agree

1 2 3 4 5 6 7

1. Each customer requires a unique approach.

2. When I feel that my sales approach is not working, I can easily change to another approach.

3. I like to experiment with different sales approaches.

4. I am very flexible in the selling approach I use.

5. I feel that most buyers can be dealt with in pretty much the same manner. **(r)**

6. I don't change my approach from one customer to another. **(r)**

7. I can easily use a wide variety of selling approaches.

8. I use a set sales approach. **(r)**

9. It is easy for me to modify my sales presentation if the situation calls for it.

10. Basically I use the same approach with most customers. **(r)**

11. I am very sensitive to the needs of my customers.

12. I find it difficult to adapt my presentation style to certain buyers. **(r)**

13. I vary my sales style from situation to situation.

14. I try to understand how one customer differs from another.

15. I feel confident that I can effectively change my planned presentation when necessary.

16. I treat all of my buyers pretty much the same. **(r)**

*The response format used by Spiro and Weitz (1990) was not explicitly described but appears to have been a seven-point Likert-type scale. Hartline and Ferrell (1996) used ten items similar to or the same as 1–3, 6, and 11–16.

SCALE NAME: Sales Presentation Effectiveness

SCALE DESCRIPTION: Strutton and Lumpkin (1994) used this six-item, five-point Likert-type scale purporting to measure salespeople's self-evaluation of the effectiveness of a sales presentation.

SCALE ORIGIN: Strutton and Lumpkin (1994) indicated that this scale was developed by Behrman and Perreault (1984).

SAMPLES: Strutton and Lumpkin's (1994) sample was a nonprobability sample of **101** nonmanager salespeople from three industries: communications technology (60), textiles (22), and furniture (19), predominantly in the southern United States.

RELIABILITY: Strutton and Lumpkin (1994) reported a Cronbach's alpha of **.80** for this scale.

VALIDITY: Behrman and Perreault (1984) reported evidence of both discriminant and convergent validity. Strutton and Lumpkin (1994) subjected their data to a maximum likelihood confirmatory factor analysis to test for unidimensionality of the underlying construct. The analysis yielded one underlying factor.

ADMINISTRATION: Strutton and Lumpkin (1994) stated that this was a self-administered, paper-and-pencil measure in which subjects were asked to rate themselves with respect to their sales presentation effectiveness. Higher scores on the scale indicated higher self-evaluations of sales presentation effectiveness.

MAJOR FINDINGS: Strutton and Lumpkin (1994) regressed factors from a modified version of the Ways of Coping Checklist (Folkman and Lazarus 1980, 1985; Folkman et al. 1986) on this measure of **sales presentation effectiveness**. The authors claimed no problems with multicollinearity but reported significant positive correlations (betas) with pure problem focus, positive reinterpretation, and directed problem solving and significantly negative betas for self-indulgent escapism, seeking avoidance, and negative avoidance tactics for reducing stress in a sales presentation circumstance.

REFERENCES:

Behrman, Douglas N. and William D. Perreault Jr. (1984), "A Sales Role Stress Model of the Performance and Satisfaction of Industrial Salespersons," *JM*, 48 (Fall), 9–21.

Folkman, Susan and Richard S. Lazarus (1980), "An Analysis of Coping in a Middle-Aged Community Sample," *Journal of Health and Social Behavior*, 21 (September), 219–39.

—— and —— (1985), "If It Changes, It Must Be a Process: Study of Emotion and Coping During Three Stages of a College Examination," *Journal of Personality and Social Psychology*, 48 (January), 150–70.

——, ——, Christine Dunkel-Schetter, Anita DeLongis, and Rand J. Gruen (1986), "Dynamics of a Stressful Encounter: Cognitive Appraisal, Coping, and Encounter Outcomes," *Journal of Personality and Social Psychology*, 50 (May), 992–1003.

Strutton, David and James R. Lumpkin (1994), "Problem- and Emotion-Focused Coping Dimensions and Sales Presentation Effectiveness," *JAMS*, 22 (1), 28–37.

#852 *Sales Presentation Effectiveness*

SCALE ITEMS:

Strongly   Strongly
disagree   agree

1————2————3————4————5

1. I am able to convince customers that I understand their unique problems and concerns.

2. I am able to work out solutions to customers' questions or objections.

3. I communicate my sales presentations clearly and concisely.

4. I make effective use of sales aids (charts, audiovisuals) to improve my sales presentations.

5. I listen attentively to identify and understand the real concerns of my customers and prospects.

6. I am able to establish contacts to develop new customers.

SCALE NAME: Satisfaction (Dealer)

SCALE DESCRIPTION: Gassenheimer and Ramsey (1994) used this seven-item, seven-point scale to measure the degree to which a dealer was satisfied with the outcomes associated with a particular supplier or manufacturer relationship.

SCALE ORIGIN: The scale is original to Gassenheimer and Ramsey (1994), who generated items on the basis of a review of the literature and in-depth interviews with dealers. Details of the scale purification process were not discussed by the authors.

SAMPLES: Gassenheimer and Ramsey (1994) sampled key informants of 939 office furniture/systems dealers. The specific individual surveyed was identified as being responsible for the evaluation and selection of office furniture/systems suppliers. Of those contacted, **324** key informants returned usable responses.

RELIABILITY: Gassenheimer and Ramsey (1994) calculated separate reliabilities for data pertaining to each of three suppliers evaluated by respondents, as well as an overall reliability for the measure using the pooled data. The alphas for suppliers A, B, and C were **.89, .83,** and **.83**, respectively. A coefficient alpha of **.86** was calculated for the combined data.

VALIDITY: Gassenheimer and Ramsey (1994) did not report an examination of the scale's validity.

ADMINISTRATION: Gassenheimer and Ramsey (1994) included the scale with other measures as part of a self-administered survey that was delivered by mail. Nonrespondents received a postcard reminder, as well as a second survey mailing. Each dealer was asked to specify its primary (A), secondary (B), and tertiary (C) suppliers and to answer questions for each of those suppliers on an individual basis. Higher scores on the scale indicated that a dealer was more satisfied with the outcomes associated with a particular supplier or manufacturer relationship.

MAJOR FINDINGS: Gassenheimer and Ramsey (1994) examined the influence of mutual dependence and power-dependence imbalances on primary, secondary, and tertiary supplier–dealer relationships in the office systems/furniture industry. Dealers were significantly more **satisfied** with their primary suppliers than with either their secondary or tertiary suppliers. Each of the three support services—logistics, sales, and product—strengthened dealers' **satisfaction** with each type of supplier, though sales support had the largest positive influence on **satisfaction** for all three suppliers. Coercive influence attempts exerted by primary suppliers negatively affected dealers' **satisfaction** with that supplier but did not significantly influence **satisfaction** with secondary and tertiary suppliers.

REFERENCES:
Gassenheimer, Jule B. and Rosemary Ramsey (1994), "The Impact of Dependence on Dealer Satisfaction: A Comparison of Reseller-Supplier Relationships," *JR*, 70 (3), 253–66.

#853 *Satisfaction (Dealer)*

SCALE ITEMS:

Directions: Indicate your level of satisfaction with the following "global" outcomes resulting from the relationship with each manufacturer (supplier).

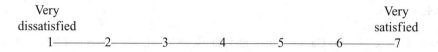

Very
dissatisfied

Very
satisfied

1————2————3————4————5————6————7

1. Sales growth potential from carrying manufacturer's product lines.

2. New product market opportunities manufacturer provided you.

3. Profits generated from manufacturer's product lines.

4. Interest and concern manufacturer has displayed in helping you accomplish goals and objectives.

5. Overall manner you were treated by manufacturer's regional office or headquarters.

6. Overall "sales support"/relationship with the manufacturer's local sales representative.

7. Overall fairness and honesty of manufacturer.

SCALE NAME: Satisfaction (Job)

SCALE DESCRIPTION: Hartline and Ferrell (1996) used this five-item, five-point scale to measure overall employee satisfaction with their jobs.

SCALE ORIGIN: Hartline and Ferrell (1996) indicated that the items representing this construct were adapted from Brown and Peterson (1993) and Churchill, Ford, and Walker (1974). Three items, "Your fellow workers," "Your salary or wages," and "Your organization's customers," were dropped from the measure following a confirmatory factor analysis because of nonsignificant t-values.

SAMPLES: The hotel industry was chosen as the sampling frame for this study. Hartline and Ferrell (1996) sampled the general managers, employees, and customers of 444 hotel units representing three hotel chains. Of these, 236 different hotel units returned at least one usable questionnaire from a manager, an employee, and a customer. A total of 1769 usable questionnaires were received from **236** hotel managers, **561** customer contact employees, and **1351** customers.

RELIABILITY: Hartline and Ferrell (1996) reported a coefficient alpha of **.82** for this measure.

VALIDITY: Hartline and Ferrell (1996) used confirmatory factor analysis to test the unidimensionality of the measures with separate analyses for managers, employees, and customers. Items with nonsignificant t-values were dropped from the measures. In investigating the discriminant validity of the scales, the authors first averaged the employee and customer responses on the scale and then matched that response with the manager responses to create a single data set in which cases represented hotel units rather than individuals. Hotel units that did not provide at least three responses from employees and customers were dropped, leaving a final sample of **97** matched responses. Confirmatory factor analysis was then used to assess the discriminant validity of the measures.

ADMINISTRATION: Each hotel manager received a survey packet containing instructions, postage-paid reply envelopes, one manager survey, five employee surveys, and forty guest surveys, which were to be self-administered. This measure was included in the employee survey. Hartline and Ferrell (1996) instructed managers to distribute employee surveys to individuals in customer-contact positions and the guest surveys during check-out. Survey packets were preceded by a letter from the corporate marketing manager endorsing the project and followed by a second wave of materials approximately two months after the first had been distributed. Higher scores on the scale indicated higher levels of overall job satisfaction.

MAJOR FINDINGS: Hartline and Ferrell (1996) investigated the management of customer-contact service employees and various factors related to service quality using data generated from the customers, contact employees, and managers of hotel units. Hypotheses were tested in the context of structural equation modeling. Although both **job satisfaction** and employee self-efficacy were found to have a positive effect on customers' perceptions of service quality, the effect of self-efficacy was strongest. Employee self-efficacy was also significantly and negatively related to **job satisfaction**, which indicated that highly efficacious customer-contact employees tended to be less **satisfied** with their jobs. Role ambiguity negatively influenced **job satisfaction**; however, contrary to expectations, role conflict had no effect. Employee empowerment had an indirect, negative effect on employee's **job satisfaction**, and the use of behavior-based evaluations had an indirect, positive effect on **job satisfaction**. Although not hypothesized, management's commitment to service quality was found to increase employee **job satisfaction**.

#854 *Satisfaction (Job)*

REFERENCES:

Brown, Steven P. and Robert A. Peterson (1993), "Antecedents and Consequences of Salesperson Job
    Satisfaction: Meta-Analysis and Assessment of Causal Effects," *JMR*, 30 (February), 63–77.
Churchill, Gilbert A., Jr., Neil M. Ford, and Orville Walker Jr. (1974), "Measuring the Job Satisfaction of
    Industrial Salesmen," *JMR*, 11 (August), 254–60.
Hartline, Michael D. and O.C. Ferrell (1996), "The Management of Customer-Contact Service
    Employees: An Empirical Investigation," *JM*, 60 (October), 52–70.

SCALE ITEMS:

Extremely   Extremely
satisfied   dissatisfied

1. Your overall job.

2. Your supervisor(s).

3. Your organization's policies.

4. The support provided by your organization.

5. Your opportunities for advancement with this organization.

SCALE NAME: Satisfaction (Job)

SCALE DESCRIPTION: Fourteen seven-point Likert-type items measuring the degree to which respondents are satisfied with the information and feedback received from supervisors, the variety of activities and freedoms associated with the job, the opportunities for closure and completion of tasks, and the pay and security offered by the job. Although the scale taps various dimensions, all items are combined to form a single measure of total job satisfaction.

SCALE ORIGIN:
The scale used by Sparks (1994) was developed by Hunt and Chonko (1984), who generated seven of the items on the basis of pretests. The remaining seven items were selected from the job characteristics inventory by Sims, Szilagyi, and Keller (1976).

SAMPLES:
The data used by Sparks (1994) were collected and reported in Hunt and Chonko's (1984) study. Hunt and Chonko (1984) mailed a questionnaire to a systematic sample of 4282 marketing practitioners drawn from the American Marketing Association membership list. Educators and students were excluded from the sample. A total of **1076** usable responses were returned for a 25.1% response rate.

RELIABILITY:
A coefficient alpha of **.89** was reported by Hunt and Chonko (1984).

VALIDITY:
No specific examination of scale validity was reported by Sparks (1994) or Hunt and Chonko (1984). An exploratory factor analysis of the items indicated that the 14 items loaded on four factors, labeled "satisfaction with information," "satisfaction with variety and freedom," "satisfaction with complete tasks," and "satisfaction with pay and security."

ADMINISTRATION:
Hunt and Chonko (1984) indicated that the scale was part of a self-administered mail survey. Higher scores on the scale indicated greater levels of total job satisfaction.

MAJOR FINDINGS:
Hunt and Chonko (1984) examined the relationship between Machiavellianism and job satisfaction using a variety of job satisfaction measures. Their results indicated that marketers who are more Machiavellian are less **satisfied** with their jobs in general and that this relationship holds true even when income, age, sex, and education are entered into the regression equation as control variables. Using Hunt and Chonko's (1984) data set, Sparks (1994) reanalyzed their data using a measure of latitude for improvisation as a moderating variable and success in the job as a dependent variable. Machiavellianism was positively related to personal success in marketing when latitude for improvement was high but negatively related to success when the moderating variable was low.

REFERENCES:
Hunt, Shelby D. and Lawrence B. Chonko (1984), "Marketing and Machiavellianism," *JM*, 48 (Summer), 30–42.

Sims, Henry P., Jr., Andrew D. Szilagyi, and Robert T. Keller (1976), "The Measurement of Job Characteristics," *Academy of Management Journal*, 19 (June), 195–212.

Sparks, John R. (1994), "Machiavellianism and Personal Success in Marketing: The Moderating Role of Latitude for Improvisation," *JAMS*, 22 (4), 393–400.

#855 *Satisfaction (Job)*

SCALE ITEMS:

Strongly   Strongly
disagree   agree
1————2————3————4————5————6————7

Satisfaction with information
1. I am satisfied with the information I receive from my superior about my job performance.
2. I receive enough information from my supervisor about my job performance.
3. I receive enough feedback from my supervisor on how well I'm doing.
4. There is enough opportunity in my job to find out how I'm doing.

Satisfaction with variety
5. I am satisfied with the variety of activities my job offers.
6. I am satisfied with the freedom I have to do what I want on my job.
7. I am satisfied with the opportunities my job provides me to interact with others.
8. There is enough variety in my job.
9. I have enough freedom to do what I want in my job.
10. My job has enough opportunity for independent thought and action.

Satisfaction with closure
11. I am satisfied with the opportunities my job gives me to complete tasks from beginning to end.
12. My job has enough opportunity to complete the work I start.

Satisfaction with pay
13. I am satisfied with the pay I receive for my job.
14. I am satisfied with the security my job provides me.

SCALE NAME: Satisfaction (Job)

SCALE DESCRIPTION: Rich (1997) used this three-item, seven-point Likert-type scale to measure a salesperson's overall level of general satisfaction with his or her job.

SCALE ORIGIN: Rich (1997) stated that the scale was adapted from Cammann and colleagues (1983) and was revised into its final form on the basis of the results of a confirmatory factor analysis.

SAMPLES: Salespeople and their immediate supervisors from 10 different U.S.-based business-to-business sales organizations representing different industries formed the sample for this study. Of the 244 salesperson–manager dyads that received questionnaires, usable responses were obtained from 193 salespeople and 218 managers, resulting in complete responses from a total of **183** matched salesperson–manager dyads.

RELIABILITY: Rich (1997) reported a coefficient alpha of **.82** for the measure.

VALIDITY: Results of the confirmatory factor analysis reported by Rich (1997) provided strong evidence for the discriminant and convergent validity of the measures, and the extensive pretesting provided evidence of content validity.

ADMINISTRATION: Rich (1997) indicated that the scale was part of a self-administered mail survey sent directly to each member of the salesperson–manager dyad. Follow-up telephone calls made by research assistants, the promise to share survey results, and encouragement from the management of participating firms enhanced respondent participation. It appears that the measure was only administered to the salesperson sample. Higher scores on the scale indicated that a salesperson was more satisfied with his or her job.

MAJOR FINDINGS: Rich (1997) examined the relationship between the role modeling behavior of sales managers and a set of key outcome variables, including trust in the manager, job satisfaction, and salesperson performance. Through its relationship with trust, sales manager role modeling behavior was found to indirectly influence both **job satisfaction** and salesperson performance.

REFERENCES:

Cammann, Cortlandt, Mark Fichman, G. Douglas Jenkins, and John R. Klesh (1983), "Assessing the Attitudes and Perceptions of Organizational Members," in *Assessing Organizational Change: A Guide to Methods, Measures, and Practices*, Stanley E. Seashore, Edward E. Lawler, Philip H. Mirvis, and Cortlandt Cammann, eds. New York: John Wiley & Sons, 71–138.

Rich, Gregory A. (1997), "The Sales Manager as a Role Model: Effects on Trust, Job Satisfaction, and Performance of Salespeople," *JAMS*, 25 (4), 319–28.

SCALE ITEMS:

1 = Strongly disagree
2 = Moderately disagree
3 = Slightly disagree
4 = Neither agree nor disagree
5 = Slightly agree
6 = Moderately agree
7 = Strongly agree

1. All in all, I'm satisfied with my job.

2. In general, I like working at my company.

3. In general, I don't like my job. **(r)**

SCALE NAME: Satisfaction (Job)

SCALE DESCRIPTION: Netemeyer and colleagues (1997) used this three-item, seven-point scale to measure employee self-reports of their overall level of job satisfaction.

SCALE ORIGIN: Netemeyer and colleagues (1997) stated that the scale was adapted from several sources, citing Price and Mueller (1986) specifically.

SAMPLES: In their first study, Netemeyer and colleagues (1997) used a convenience sample of 115 salespeople employed by a cellular telephone company in the southeastern United States, and **91** usable responses were obtained for a 79% response rate. The median age of respondents was 29 years, and their average amount of time with the organization was 1.89 years. The majority of respondents were women (56%) and college educated (57%). In the second study, the authors sampled 700 real estate salespeople living in a large southeastern U.S. city, and **182** usable surveys were received for an effective response rate of 26%. The median age of respondents in the second study was 48 years, and their average amount of time with the organization was 8.41 years. The majority were women (78%) and college educated (60.5%).

RELIABILITY: Netemeyer and colleagues (1997) reported coefficient alphas of **.90** for Study 1 and **.94** for Study 2.

VALIDITY: Netemeyer and colleagues (1997) examined the discriminant and construct validity of the scale using confirmatory factor analysis for both Study 1 and Study 2 data. The average variance extracted by the measure in each study was well below the .50 cut-off level suggested by Fornell and Larcker (1981), providing evidence of construct validity. The square of parameter estimates between pairs of constructs was less than the average variance extracted estimates for the paired constructs across all possible construct pairings in both studies, thus providing evidence of the discriminant validity of the measure.

ADMINISTRATION: Netemeyer and colleagues (1997) indicated that the scale was included as part of a self-administered mail survey in both studies. Study 2 participants were assured of the confidentiality and anonymity of their responses. Higher scores on the scale indicated that salespeople reported greater levels of overall satisfaction with their job.

MAJOR FINDINGS: Netemeyer and colleagues (1997) proposed and tested a model of potential predictors of organizational citizenship behavior (OCB) and **job satisfaction** using data from two separate studies conducted in sales settings. Both samples demonstrated support for the role of **job satisfaction** as a predictor of OCB in the original models, which were tested using LISREL VII. However, person–organization fit was found to be a predictor of **job satisfaction** in both studies, and when this variable was added to the model, the **job satisfaction** to OCB path became nonsignificant in Study 1. Mixed results were found with respect to the role played by leadership support and fairness in reward allocation in predicting **job satisfaction**. In one study, leadership support was found to be a significant predictor but fairness in reward allocation was not; in the other study, the reverse was true.

REFERENCES:

Fornell, Claes and David F. Larcker (1981), "Evaluating Structural Equation Models with Unobservable Variables and Measurement Error," *JMR*, 28 (February), 39–50.

Netemeyer, Richard G., James S. Boles, Daryl O. McKee, and Robert McMurrian (1997), "An Investigation into the Antecedents of Organizational Citizenship Behaviors in a Personal Selling Context," *JM*, **61** (July), 85–98.

Price, James P. and Charles W. Mueller (1986), *Handbook of Organizational Measurement*. Marshfield, MA: Pittman.

SCALE ITEMS:

Strongly   Strongly
disagree   agree

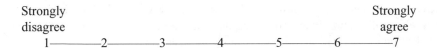

1. I feel fairly well satisfied with my present line of work.

2. I feel a great sense of satisfaction from my line of work.

Very   Very
dissatisfied   satisfied

3. All things considered (i.e., pay, promotion, supervisors, co-workers, etc.), how satisfied are you with your present line of work?

#858 *Satisfaction (Manufacturer–Distributor Relationship)*

SCALE NAME: Satisfaction (Manufacturer–Distributor Relationship)

SCALE DESCRIPTION: This three-item, seven-point Likert-type scale was used by Andaleeb (1996) to measure the overall level of satisfaction indicated by respondents based on exposure to a contrived manufacturer (supplier)–distributor (buyer) experimental relationship scenario.

SCALE ORIGIN: Andaleeb (1996) apparently adapted his satisfaction operationalization from studies previously conducted by Crosby, Evans, and Cowles (1990) and Schurr and Ozanne (1985). The reliability of the measure and item-to-total correlations were assessed as part of the purification process and deemed to be acceptable.

SAMPLES: A convenience sample of **72** sales and purchasing managers with considerable negotiation experience participated in a 2 × 2 between-groups factorial design experiment. Andaleeb (1996) randomly assigned subjects to treatment conditions.

RELIABILITY: Andaleeb (1996) calculated a coefficient alpha of **.95** for the scale.

VALIDITY: Andaleeb (1996) reported conducting a factor analysis to assess the unidimensionality of the measures used in his study. A single factor with item loadings greater than .8 was extracted for each scale, which suggested that the measures were unidimensional. A confirmatory factor analysis of the measurement model provided some evidence of validity, because the standardized coefficients were significantly different from 0. However, the goodness-of-fit index of .87 was somewhat below the recommended .90 level, though the chi-square and root mean square residual were found to be satisfactory.

ADMINISTRATION: Andaleeb (1996) provided subjects with information about a contrived manufacturer (supplier)–distributor (buyer) relationship in which the level of trust and dependence on the supplier were manipulated. After reading this information, subjects were instructed to write down their perceptions of the relationship and read a scenario suggesting that an upcoming meeting would consider methods of strengthening the company's growth through cultivation of existing suppliers. Subjects were instructed to indicate whether they thought such ties would be appropriate with the focal supplier. The satisfaction, commitment, dependence, and trust measures were then administered. Higher scores on the scale indicated stronger evaluations of respondent's overall satisfaction with the manufacturer–distributor relationship.

MAJOR FINDINGS: Andaleeb's (1996) experiment investigated the effect of high and low levels of supplier trust and supplier dependence on satisfaction and commitment for a hypothetical dyadic exchange relationship. After confirming that the trust and dependence manipulation had occurred, Andaleeb (1996) found that greater trust in a supplier led to higher levels of buyer **satisfaction**.

REFERENCES:

Andaleeb, Syed Saad (1996), "An Experimental Investigation of Satisfaction and Commitment in Marketing Channels: The Role of Trust and Dependence," *JR*, 72 (1), 77–93.

Crosby, Lawrence A., Kenneth R. Evans, and Deborah Cowles (1990), "Relationship Quality in Services Selling: An Interpersonal Influence Perspective," *JM*, 54 (July), 68–81.

Schurr, Paul H. and Julie L. Ozanne (1985), "Influences on Exchange Processes: Buyers' Preconceptions of a Seller's Trustworthiness and Bargaining Toughness," *JCR*, 11, 939–53.

SCALE ITEMS:*

Strongly   Strongly
disagree   agree

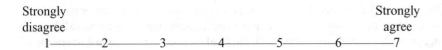

1——————2——————3——————4——————5——————6——————7

1. The relationship between my company and X does not seem to reflect a happy situation.

2. The relationship between the two companies is very positive.

3. My company should be very satisfied with X.

*As used by Andaleeb (1996), the company name of the respondent and the name of the focal manufacturer were used in items 1 and 3.

SCALE NAME: Satisfaction (Participant)

SCALE DESCRIPTION: Olson, Walker, and Ruekert (1995) used this four-item, seven-point scale to measure the degree to which individuals involved in the new product development process exhibited a sense of accomplishment, camaraderie, and satisfaction with the final product and the contributions made by their departments in developing the product.

SCALE ORIGIN: Olson, Walker, and Ruekert (1995) stated that the scale was adopted from Van De Ven and Ferry (1980) and previously used in a marketing context by Ruekert and Walker (1987a, b).

SAMPLES: Of the 24 firms solicited by Olson, Walker, and Ruekert (1995) to participate in the study, 15 divisions from 12 firms provided complete information on **45** new product development projects undertaken within a three-year time period. All firms produced tangible products and ranged in age from 12 to more than 100 years, with annual revenues between $50 million and more than $1 billion. Projects formed the unit of analysis. Of the new product projects studied, 11 represented new-to-the-world products, 9 were me-too products, 15 were line extensions, and 10 were product modifications. Data were collected first from each project manager and then from individuals identified by project managers as having key functional responsibilities related to marketing, manufacturing, R&D, and design. A total of **112** usable responses were obtained from the functional participants in addition to information provided by the **45** product managers.

RELIABILITY: Olson, Walker, and Ruekert (1995) reported a coefficient alpha of **.83** for this scale. Scale items were also submitted to a Varimax rotated principle components factor analysis and found to load on a single factor with an eigenvalue greater than 1.

VALIDITY: No specific examination of scale validity for this measure was reported by Olson, Walker, and Ruekert (1995).

ADMINISTRATION: Olson, Walker, and Ruekert (1995) indicated that information about each project was initially obtained from project managers through a telephone interview using a structured questionnaire. After project managers had identified the key functional personnel for their project in marketing, manufacturing, R&D, and design, self-administered mail surveys were sent to each of the functional participants of each project. An overall project score was created for the participant satisfaction measure by averaging responses to each scale across all the responding functional participants from a given project. Lower scores on the scale indicated greater feelings of achievement, camaraderie, and satisfaction on the part of project participants.

MAJOR FINDINGS: Olson, Walker, and Ruekert (1995) examined the relationship between new product coordinating structures and outcomes using a resource dependency view of the new product development process. When the project's coordination structure fit participants' experience with the product, functional participants exhibited higher levels of **satisfaction** than when the coordination mechanism was too organic or mechanistic.

REFERENCES:

Olson, Eric M., Orville C. Walker Jr., and Robert W. Ruekert (1995), "Organizing for Effective New Product Development: The Moderating Role of Product Innovativeness," *JM*, 59 (January), 48–62.
Ruekert, Robert W. and Orville C. Walker Jr. (1987a), "The Organization of Marketing Activities: A Conceptual Framework and Empirical Evidence," *JM,* 51 (January), 1–19.

————— and ————— (1987b), "Interactions Between Marketing and R&D Departments in Implementing Different Strategies," *Strategic Management Journal*, 8, 233–48.

Van de Ven, Andrew H. and Diane L. Ferry (1980), *Measuring and Assessing Organizations*. New York: John Wiley & Sons.

SCALE ITEMS:

Euphoric   Depressed
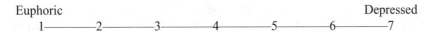

1. How would you rate the sense of accomplishment experienced by your department with the development of this project at the time of its introduction to the marketplace?

Great team spirit   Great animosity
among members   among members
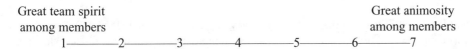

2. At the time it was introduced to the marketplace, what level of comradeship existed among members of your department?

Very satisfied   Very dissatisfied
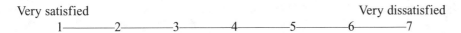

3. At the time this product was introduced to the marketplace, how satisfied with their contributions to the development of this product were the members of your department overall?

4. Overall, how satisfied were you with this product's development?

#860 *Satisfaction (Relationship)*

SCALE NAME: Satisfaction (Relationship)

SCALE DESCRIPTION: Li and Dant (1997) described this three-item, five-point Likert-type scale as how satisfactory, worthwhile, and productive a trade party's relationship with a channel member is perceived to be.

SCALE ORIGIN: Li and Dant (1997) adapted three of the five items used by Bucklin and Sengupta (1993) to measure the perceived effectiveness of a channel relationship. Bucklin and Sengupta (1993) in turn credited Ruekert and Walker (1987) and Van de Ven and Ferry (1980) as the "motivating forces" behind the use of this measure in an interorganizational dyad context. The true origin of the scale can be traced back to its development in an organizational theory context by Van de Ven (1976). In adapting the scale for their use, Li and Dant (1997) changed the scale anchor points from "to no extent"/"to a great extent" to the "disagree"/"agree" format shown here.

SAMPLES: Li and Dant (1997) used a cross-sectional survey approach to sample 2553 office machine dealership key informants (owners/presidents) from the membership list of the National Office Machine Dealers Association. Questionnaires were returned from 573 dealerships; incomplete surveys and those completed by individuals not fitting the key informant status were eliminated from the study. The final sample was composed of **461** distributors, of which 286 were classified as having exclusive dealing (ED) arrangements with the photocopier manufacturer for which they sold the most units and the remaining 175 maintained nonexclusive dealing (NED) arrangements.

RELIABILITY: Li and Dant (1997) reported a reliability coefficient of **.90** for this measure.

VALIDITY: Li and Dant (1997) stated that the five measures used in the study were subjected to confirmatory factor analysis using LISREL. After one of the original five solidarity items, "our relationship with them is best described as a 'cooperative effort'," was dropped, support was found for measure unidimensionality. Convergent and discriminant validity were also found to be satisfactory, thereby providing evidence of construct validity.

ADMINISTRATION: Li and Dant (1997) stated that the scale was part of a self-administered mail questionnaire that was completed by respondents, along with other measures, using a paper-and-pencil format. A cover letter from the National Office Machine Dealers Association endorsing the study accompanied the survey packet. Respondents were instructed to answer their questionnaires in the context of the copier manufacturer for which they sold the most copy machines. In response to a question that directly asked whether distributors exclusively sold this focal manufacturer's copiers, respondents were classified as ED or NED. Higher scores on the scale indicated that respondents perceived their relationship with manufacturers as more productive, satisfactory, and worthwhile.

MAJOR FINDINGS: Li and Dant (1997) investigated how ED arrangements between manufacturers and dealers affected dealers' perceptions of relationalism, communication, and perceived performance. Results indicated that ED between manufacturers and dealers resulted in a higher level of **perceived performance** between channel partners compared with that achieved under NED arrangements.

REFERENCES:
Bucklin, Louis P. and Sanjit Sengupta (1993), "Organizing Successful Co-Marketing Alliances," *JM*, 57 (April), 32–46.
Li, Zhan G. and Rajiv P. Dant (1997), "An Exploratory Study of Exclusive Dealing in Channel Relationships," *JAMS*, 25 (3), 201–13.

Ruekert, Robert W. and Orville C. Walker Jr. (1987c), "Marketing's Interaction with Other Functional Units: A Conceptual Framework and Empirical Evidence," *JM*, 51 (January), 1–19.

Van de Ven, Andrew H. (1976), "On the Nature, Formation, and Maintenance of Relations Among Organizations," *Academy of Management Review*, 1 (October), 24–36.

———— and Diane L. Ferry (1980), *Measuring and Assessing Organizations*. New York: John Wiley & Sons.

SCALE ITEMS:

Strongly disagree		Neutral		Strongly agree
1————	—2————	—3————	—4————	—5

1. Our relationship with them has been productive.

2. The time and effort we spent in the relationship with them has been worthwhile.

3. The relationship with them has been satisfactory.

SCALE NAME: Satisfaction (Relationship with Manufacturer)

SCALE DESCRIPTION: Mohr, Fisher, and Nevin (1996) used this four-item, five-point Likert-type scale to assess the degree of dealer satisfaction with specific aspects of its relationship with a manufacturer, including the manufacturer's promotional program and dealings with the manufacturer sales representative.

SCALE ORIGIN: It appears that scale was either adapted from or based on the work of Ruekert and Churchill (1984). The measure was pretested and revised in a series of iterative personal interviews with 12 computer dealers. Two items, "Assistance in managing inventory" and "Profit on sales of manufacturer's product", were eliminated during item purification.

SAMPLES: Mohr, Fisher, and Nevin (1996) surveyed 557 computer retailer key informants (owners or managers), and **125** usable surveys were returned. The computer retailers selected for study were either affiliated with the microcomputer industry trade association or one of 53 randomly selected outlets for a major computer franchiser. The average number of workers employed by responding retailers was 22.3, and the average monthly sales volume was $970,000.

RELIABILITY: Mohr, Fisher, and Nevin (1996) reported a coefficient alpha of **.85** for this measure.

VALIDITY: Mohr, Fisher, and Nevin (1996) stated that the measure exhibited acceptable levels of convergent and discriminatory validity according to the results of a confirmatory factor analysis.

ADMINISTRATION: The measure was included by Mohr, Fisher, and Nevin (1996) as part of a self-administered questionnaire that was delivered by mail. Nonrespondents received a reminder letter approximately one month after the initial mailing. Retailers were randomly assigned to answer questions about either their best or their worst relationship with a manufacturer. Higher scores on the scale indicated that retailers were satisfied with the promotional offerings of a manufacturer and their dealings with the manufacturer's sales representative.

MAJOR FINDINGS: Mohr, Fisher, and Nevin (1996) investigated the relationship between collaborative communication and channel outcomes (satisfaction with the relationship, relationship commitment, relationship coordination) in the context of differing levels of dealer/manufacturer integration (franchise versus company-owned). Hypotheses were tested by hierarchical moderator regression analysis. The results indicated that with higher levels of manufacturer control, dealers were more **satisfied** and committed to the relationship and reported that their efforts were better coordinated with the manufacturer. However, significant interactions between control and communication demonstrated that higher levels of collaborative communication have stronger, more positive effects on **satisfaction**, commitment, and coordination under low manufacturer control conditions than in situations in which manufacturer control is high, as well as under less integrated relationship conditions (e.g., franchise versus company-owned).

REFERENCES:

Mohr, Jakki J., Robert J. Fisher, and John R. Nevin (1996), "Collaborative Communication in Interfirm Relationships: Moderating Effects of Integration and Control," *JM*, 60 (July), 103–15.

Ruekert, Robert and Gilbert A. Churchill Jr. (1984), "Reliability and Validity of Alternative Measures of Channel Member Satisfaction" *JMR*, 21 (May), 226–32.

SCALE ITEMS:

Very
dissatisfied

Very
satisfied

1————2————3————4————5

How satisfied are you with the following aspects of the relationship with this manufacturer?

1. Personal dealings with manufacturer's sales representatives?

2. Cooperative advertising?

3. Promotional support (coupons, rebates, displays)?

4. Off-invoice promotional allowances?

SCALE NAME: Satisfaction (Wholesaler)

SCALE DESCRIPTION: A five-item, five-point Likert-type scale to assess a retailer's beliefs that its relationship with a wholesaler is satisfactory.

SCALE ORIGIN: Ping (1997) stated that the satisfaction measure was modified version of Dwyer and Oh's (1987) satisfaction scale, which was inspired by Gaski and Nevin (1985), and that he modified for use in earlier studies (Ping 1993, 1994). The modified measure was pretested in two different phases. The first pretest sought to clarify possible misinterpretations. Responses from 63 hardware retailers in the second pretest were used in analyzing the psychometric properties of the measures using item-to-total correlations, ordered similarity coefficients, and coefficient alpha computations. The final purification of the measure was based on LISREL analysis of data provided by 288 respondents, as reported in the Ping (1993) study. Items were deleted if internal consistency was improved without detracting from the content validity of the measure. Tests of the discriminant and convergent validity of the measure were also undertaken, and the results were found to be satisfactory.

SAMPLES: Ping (1994, 1997) used a systematic random sampling procedure of U.S. hardware retailers to generate the 600 hardware retailers sampled in the studies reported in both 1994 and 1997. **Two hundred eighty-eight** and **204** usable responses were received in 1994 and 1997, respectively. The sampling frame in both instances was taken from a hardware retailing trade publication's subscription list.

RELIABILITY: Ping (1994) did not report the specific reliability of the measure, though he noted that all measures in this study demonstrated latent variable reliabilities of .90 or higher. In the 1997 study, Ping reported a coefficient alpha of **.94**.

VALIDITY: Ping (1994, 1997) conducted a confirmatory factor analysis to test the unidimensionality and construct validity of the measure. The measure was judged to be unidimensional, and the average variance extracted demonstrated the scale's convergent and discriminatory validity. Ping (1997) also stated that the measure had content validity.

ADMINISTRATION: The scale was included with other measures as part of a self-administered questionnaire that was delivered by mail in both Ping (1994, 1997) studies. Nonrespondents received as multiple postcard reminders. Ping (1997) used a key informant approach in which key informants represented a single individual, typically a manager, owner, or executive of the hardware store. Higher scores on the scale reflected greater retailer satisfaction with the wholesaler relationship.

MAJOR FINDINGS: In the study described in his 1994 article, Ping investigated the moderating role of satisfaction with respect to alternative supplier attractiveness and exit intentions. Using a structural equation analysis technique, Ping (1994) found that the attractiveness of alternative suppliers was positively associated with exit intentions for channel customers with lower levels of **satisfaction**. Higher levels of **satisfaction** negated this relationship, however, because no significant association between alternative supplier attractiveness and exit intentions were found. Ping (1997) proposed and empirically examined several antecedents to voice in a business-to-business context. The results of his study indicated that the use of voice was more likely when a retailer's **satisfaction** with its relationship with a wholesaler is higher.

REFERENCES:

Dwyer, F.R., and S. Oh (1987), "Output Sector Munificence Effects on the Internal Political Economy of Marketing Channels," *JMR*, 24 (November), 347–58.

Gaski, John and J.R. Nevin (1985), "The Theory of Power and Conflict in Channels of Distribution," *JM*, 47 (Fall), 68–78.

Ping, Robert A., Jr. (1993), "The Effects of Satisfaction and Structural Constraints on Retailer Exiting, Voice, Loyalty, Opportunism, and Neglect," *JR*, 69 (Fall), 320–52.

——— (1994), "Does Satisfaction Moderate the Association Between Alternative Attractiveness and Exit Intention in a Marketing Channel?" *JAMS*, 22 (4), 364–71.

——— (1997), "Voice in Business-to-Business Relationships: Cost-of-Exit and Demographic Antecedents," *JR*, 73 (2), 261–81.

SCALE ITEMS:

Strongly disagree   Strongly agree

1————2————3————4————5

1. All in all, my primary wholesaler is very fair with me.

2. Overall, my primary wholesaler is a good company to do business with.

3. In general I am pretty satisfied with my relationship with my primary wholesaler.

4. Overall, my primary wholesaler treats me fairly.

5. All in all, my relationship with my primary wholesaler is very satisfactory.

SCALE NAME: Satisfaction (with Consulting Firm)

SCALE DESCRIPTION: Patterson, Johnson, and Spreng (1997) used this three-item, seven-point scale combining Likert- and semantic differential–type items to measure the extent of satisfaction that a client firm expressed relative to its choice of a consultancy firm.

SCALE ORIGIN: Patterson, Johnson, and Spreng (1997) stated the scale was adapted from Oliver and Swan (1989).

SAMPLES: Patterson, Johnson, and Spreng (1997) chose to survey management consulting firms' private- and public-sector client organizations. Of the 207 client organizations approached by telephone, 186 agreed to participate. Then, 142 key informants—typically senior executives or managers who were likely to be heavily involved in the consultant selection process—completed the Stage 1 prepurchase questionnaire. Of this group, 128 returned the second postpurchase questionnaire, yielding a final sample size of **128** for the pre- and postpurchase measures.

RELIABILITY: Patterson, Johnson, and Spreng (1997) reported a confirmatory factor analysis construct reliability of **.95** for this measure.

VALIDITY: Patterson, Johnson, and Spreng (1997) assessed the convergent and discriminant validity of the measure by means of a confirmatory factor analysis conducted using LISREL 8. The large construct reliabilities, large and significant measurement factor loadings, and the average variance extracted provided evidence of convergent validity. Evidence of discriminant validity was also demonstrated by means of average extracted variances that exceeded the squared correlation between that construct and any other.

ADMINISTRATION: Data were collected in two stages over a 12-month span. The Stage 1 questionnaire containing several measures was delivered along with a cover letter to key informants who had indicated a willingness to participate in the study. This survey also asked respondents to indicate the expected completion date for the project. The satisfaction measure was included in a second questionnaire that was delivered between one and two months after the expected completion date of the project. Both questionnaires were self-administered. If responses were not received within three weeks, a follow-up telephone call was made to nonrespondents. Higher scores on the scale indicated a greater level of satisfaction relative to the choice of consultancy firms.

MAJOR FINDINGS: Patterson, Johnson, and Spreng (1997) examined the determinants of customers' satisfaction and dissatisfaction in the context of business consulting services. The study findings provided ample support for the application of the disconfirmation paradigm to industrial buying situations. Disconfirmation was shown to have a stronger direct influence on **satisfaction** than on performance, and **satisfaction** was shown to be a strong predictor of repurchase intentions.

REFERENCES:

Oliver, Richard L. and John E. Swan (1989), "Consumer Perceptions of Interpersonal Equity and Satisfaction in Transactions: A Field Survey Approach," *JM*, 53 (April), 21–35.
Patterson, Paul G., Lester W. Johnson, and Richard A. Spreng (1997), "Modeling the Determinants of Customer Satisfaction for Business-to-Business Professional Services," *JAMS*, 25 (1), 4–17.

SCALE ITEMS:

Strongly   Strongly
disagree   agree
   1————2————3————4————5————6————7

1. I am very satisfied with our decision to commission this consultancy firm.

Taking everything into consideration, how do you feel about what you have received from the consultancy firm during the course of the assignment?

2. Very dissatisfied   :____:____:____:____:____:____:____: Very satisfied
                          1   2   3   4   5   6   7

3. Very pleased   :____:____:____:____:____:____:____: Very displeased* (r)
                          1   2   3   4   5   6   7

*Item 2 was noted as being reversed in the original article. However, in all probability, that designation is a mistake because both items 1 and 2 must be reversed to maintain scale item consistency. Also, reversal of items 1 and 2 would seem to yield a measure of dissatisfaction as opposed to satisfaction. For that reason, we chose to reverse item 3 instead, as shown.

SCALE NAME: Satisfaction (with Coworker)

SCALE DESCRIPTION: Kohli and Jaworski (1994) used this six-item, five-point Likert-type scale to measure a salesperson's satisfaction with his or her coworkers.

SCALE ORIGIN: In constructing this scale, Kohli and Jaworski (1994) combined new items specifically developed for this study with those adapted from a subset of the scale items developed by Churchill, Ford, and Walker (1974) to measure coworker satisfaction. No additional information was provided with respect to how new scale items were generated.

SAMPLES: Because the nature of the study required that salesperson behavior and output be visible to coworkers, and thus allow for coworker feedback, Kohli and Jaworski (1994) chose to sample retail auto salespeople. The preliminary set of scale items was first administered to 11 auto salespeople from five dealerships, and their comments enabled scale item and questionnaire revision. The final questionnaire was mailed to 303 salespeople belonging to the nationwide dealership network of a European car manufacturer. A reminder, followed by a second questionnaire mailing, resulted in usable responses being obtained from **150** salespeople.

RELIABILITY: Kohli and Jaworski (1994) reported a coefficient alpha of **.81** for this measure.

VALIDITY: Kohli and Jaworski (1994) used confirmatory factory analysis to test the unidimensionality of the satisfaction with coworker measure in conjunction with the coworker competence construct. Results suggested that both measures were unidimensional. No other specific assessments of validity were discussed by the authors.

ADMINISTRATION: Kohli and Jaworski (1994) stated that the scale was part of a self-administered questionnaire that was delivered by mail. A personally addressed cover letter promising complete confidentiality accompanied the survey, as did a self-addressed reply envelope and ballpoint pen incentive. A reminder was sent one week after the initial mailing. Nonrespondents received a second reminder and questionnaire three weeks after the initial mailing. Lower scores on the scale indicated that salespeople were more satisfied with their coworkers.

MAJOR FINDINGS: Kohli and Jaworski (1994) investigated how positive output, negative output, positive behavioral, and negative behavioral forms of coworker feedback affected salespeople's output and behavioral role clarity, satisfaction with coworkers, and output and behavioral performance. Output feedback, both positive and negative, was unrelated to salespeople's **satisfaction with their coworkers**. Conversely, it appears that behavioral feedback functions in an informational capacity, in that it was related to salespeople's **satisfaction with coworkers** when behavioral feedback was positive but not when behavioral feedback was negative.

REFERENCES:
Churchill, Gilbert A., Neil M. Ford, and Orville C. Walker Jr. (1974), "Measuring the Job Satisfaction of Industrial Salesperson Performance: A Meta-Analysis," *JMR*, 11 (August), 254–60.
Kohli, Ajay K. and Bernard J. Jaworski (1994), "The Influence of Coworker Feedback on Salespeople," *JM*, 58 (October), 82–94.

SCALE ITEMS:

Strongly
agree

Strongly
disagree

1———————2————————3————————4————————5

1. My fellow workers are the kind I would like to have around.

2. Overall, I am dissatisfied with my coworkers. **(r)**

3. I get along well with my coworkers.

4. I am happy with my relationship with my fellow salespersons.

5. My fellow workers are boring. **(r)**

6. My fellow workers are stimulating.

SCALE NAME: Satisfaction (with Past Outcomes)

SCALE DESCRIPTION: Ganesan (1994) used this four-item, seven-point semantic differential–type scale to measure retailers' and vendors' positive affective evaluation of their channel partner based on the outcomes resulting from their relationship during the past year.

SCALE ORIGIN: Ganesan (1994) reported developing separate but parallel measures of satisfaction with past outcomes for the retailer and vendor samples. Item analysis and exploratory factor analysis were used to initially purify the measure; items with low loadings and those loading on multiple factors were eliminated. A draft of the questionnaire containing this scale was also pretested with a group of 14 retail buyers representing two department store chains. After administration to the final sample, scale items were subjected to a confirmatory factor analysis. Goodness-of-fit indices and individual item t-values were used to identify the final scale items.

SAMPLES: Five retail department store chains agreed to participate in Ganesan's (1994) study, and each firm received and distributed 30 questionnaires to senior sales representatives or sales managers who served as liaisons with vendor organizations. A total of **124** (83%) usable responses representing the *retailer* sample were obtained. Of these, 48 respondents answered in the context of a long-term vendor relationship, and the remaining 76 answered in the context of a short-term vendor relationship. Contact information provided by respondents enabled the author to sample the designated 124 key vendor informants most knowledgeable about the retailer/vendor relationship with a survey similar in content to the retailer questionnaire but phrased from the vendor point of view. A total of **52** (42%) *vendor* representatives responded, of which 21 and 31 were in short- and long-term relationships, respectively.

RELIABILITY: Ganesan (1994) reported a coefficient alpha of **.94** for the scale in both the retailer and vendor samples.

VALIDITY: Ganesan (1994) submitted the scale to a confirmatory factor analysis using LISREL 7.16 to assess the unidimensionality, convergent validity, and discriminant validity of the measure. Although the measure was found to be unidimensional, no additional information pertaining to the outcome of the validity tests was provided.

ADMINISTRATION: Prior to being sent a survey, buyers in the retailer sample were randomly assigned to one of four cells in which the questionnaire instructions asked them to select a vendor on the basis of variations in two criteria: (1) the length of their relationship (short-term or long-term) and (2) the importance of the vendor's product to their organization (moderately important or very important). Questionnaires were distributed by a coordinator in each department store, and respondents were instructed to answer the survey in the context of this single vendor. Higher scores on the scale indicated more positive affective evaluations of the channel partner based on outcomes experienced in the relationship during the prior year.

MAJOR FINDINGS: Ganesan (1994) investigated a variety of factors influencing the long-term orientation of both retailers and vendors in an ongoing relationship, as well as the antecedents to long-term orientation. Results indicated that a **retailer's satisfaction with past outcomes** was significantly related to the retailer's long-term orientation, and the **vendor's satisfaction with past outcomes** was likewise significantly related to the vendor's long-term orientation.

REFERENCES:

Ganesan, Shankar (1994), "Determinants of Long-Term Orientation in Buyer-Seller Relationships," *JM*, 58 (April), 1–19.

SCALE ITEMS:

Describe your feelings with respect to the outcomes with this (resource/retailer) in the past one year:*

1. Pleased   :____:____:____:____:____:____:____: Displeased (r)
              1   2   3   4   5   6   7

2. Sad   :____:____:____:____:____:____:____: Happy
              1   2   3   4   5   6   7

3. Contented   :____:____:____:____:____:____:____: Disgusted (r)
              1   2   3   4   5   6   7

4. Dissatisfied :____:____:____:____:____:____:____: Satisfied
               1   2   3   4   5   6   7

*Retailer instructions used the term "resource"; vendore instructions used the term "retailer."

SCALE NAME: Satisfaction with Job (General)

SCALE DESCRIPTION: Five seven-point Likert-type items assessing the degree to which an employee is generally satisfied with the kind of work he or she does. The scale is "general" in the sense that the items do not get into specific issues such as pay, supervision, coworkers, and so on. The short form of the scale with three items was used by Dubinsky and colleagues (1986).

SCALE ORIGIN: The scale used by Dubinsky and colleagues (1986) was apparently the short version of the job satisfaction scale developed by Hackman and Oldham (1974, 1975). No specific psychometric information was provided regarding the three-item version, but the five-item version was indicated to be reasonably reliable and valid. Specifically, the internal consistency of the scale was reported to be .76. Evidence of convergent validity was that the scale had high positive correlations with several other related but conceptually different measures, such as social satisfaction, supervisory satisfaction, growth satisfaction, and work meaningfulness.

SAMPLES: Analysis in Dubinsky and colleagues (1986) was based on data collected from **189** salespeople. Letters were sent to a national sample of 2000 senior-level executives asking them to have their least experienced salesperson complete the questionnaire. The respondents represented 189 different companies marketing 50 different product categories. The sample had a median age of 30.5 years, had spent 1.4 years (median) in their present positions, and were mostly men (86%).

Dubinsky and Hartley (1986) based their analysis on completed questionnaires returned by **120** respondents. Questionnaires were sent to 467 agents who sold lines of a large, multi-insurance company. No nonresponse bias was apparent. The sample had a mean age of 39.1 years, had spent 6.6 years (mean) in their present positions, were mostly men (91%), and more than half were college graduates (56%).

The sample used by Hampton, Dubinsky, and Skinner (1986) was based on **116** usable responses from a census of 121 retail salespeople who worked in one of five outlets of a department store chain. The sample had a median age of 23.2 years, had spent 1.4 years (median) in their present positions and 1.1 years (median) with their current supervisors, were mostly women (78%), and 66% had some college education.

Ten regional sales managers and a 216 salespeople employed by a national commercial food equipment manufacturer were sampled by Pullins, Fine, and Warren (1996). Regional sales managers did not complete the survey but instead were asked to provide evaluations of salesperson performance. A total of **194** usable responses were obtained from the sales force, and sales managers provided evaluations for **113** of those sales representatives.

Skinner, Dubinsky, and Donnelly (1984) collected data from retail salespeople employed by a small departmental store chain. All salespeople employed by the firm participated in the study. Questionnaires were administered to participants at their workplace, and a total of **157** usable questionnaires were received.

RELIABILITY: A LISREL estimate of reliability was **.83** (Dubinsky et al 1986), and alphas of **.73, .81,** and **.74** were reported by Dubinsky and Hartley (1986), Hampton, Dubinsky, and Skinner (1986), and Pullins, Fine, and Warren (1996). Skinner, Dubinsky, and Donnelly (1984) reported an alpha of **.82**.

VALIDITY: No examination of scale validity was reported in any of the studies.

ADMINISTRATION: The scale was self-administered by respondents in the studies by Dubinsky (Dubinsky and Hartley 1986; Dubinsky et al. 1986), along with many other measures, in a mail survey format. Hampton, Dubinsky, and Skinner (1986) distributed the survey instrument to respondents in a conference room in each store, where they were self-administered. In the study by Skinner, Dubinsky, and

Donnelly (1984), the scale was self-administered by respondents. The scale was included with other measures as part of a self-administered survey that was delivered by mail to members of the sales force in the Pullins, Fine, and Warren (1996) study. High scores on the scale indicated that respondents had a high level of general satisfaction with the work they perform in their jobs, whereas low scores indicated respondents were very dissatisfied with their jobs.

MAJOR FINDINGS: Dubinsky and colleagues (1986) examined a model of sales force assimilation. Job suitability and dealing with conflicts at work were both found to have significant positive impacts on general **job satisfaction**.

The purpose of Dubinsky and Hartley's (1986) study was to investigate several predictors of salesperson performance and the relationships among those predictors. A path analysis indicated that, though **job satisfaction** had some effect on job involvement, it had a stronger (positive) effect on organizational commitment. In turn, it was most significantly affected (negatively) by role ambiguity.

A causal model of retail sales supervisor leadership behavior was studied by Hampton, Dubinsky, and Skinner (1986). The results indicated that **job satisfaction** had strong positive effects on organizational commitment and "work motivation." In turn, role conflict had a strong negative impact on **job satisfaction**.

Pullins, Fine, and Warren (1996) conducted an exploratory investigation of factors influencing the willingness and ability of salespeople to act as mentors. Regression analysis was used to test hypotheses. Tests of ability were restricted to the 42 salespeople who had actually been involved in mentoring relationships. Salespeople who scored higher with respect to their **job satisfaction** were neither significantly more willing nor more able to mentor. Sales managers perceived salespeople with more experience and greater **job satisfaction** as being more likely to choose to mentor.

Skinner, Dubinsky, and Donnelly (1984) studied the relationship between retail sales managers' social bases of power and retail salespeople's job-related outcomes. They found that sales managers' legitimate and expert power bases were positively related to retail salespeople's overall **job satisfaction**.

REFERENCES:

Dubinsky, Alan J. and Steven W. Hartley (1986), "A Path-Analytic Study of a Model of Salesperson Performance," *JAMS*, 14 (Spring), 36–46.

———, Roy D. Howell, Thomas N. Ingram, and Danny Bellenger (1986), "Salesforce Socialization," *JM*, 50 (October), 192–207.

Hackman, J. Richard and Greg R. Oldham (1974), "The Job Diagnostic Survey: An Instrument for the Diagnosis of Jobs and the Evaluation of Job Redesign Projects," *Technical Report #4*. New Haven, CT: Department of Administrative Sciences, Yale University.

——— and ——— (1975), "Development of the Job Diagnostic Survey," *Journal of Applied Psychology*, 60 (2), 159–70.

Hampton, Ron, Alan J. Dubinsky, and Steven J. Skinner (1986), "A Model of Sales Supervisor Leadership Behavior and Retail Salespeople's Job-Related Outcomes," *JAMS*, 14 (Fall), 33–43.

Pullins, Ellen Bolman, Leslie M. Fine, and Wendy L. Warren (1996), "Identifying Peer Mentors in the Sales Force: An Exploratory Investigation of Willingness and Ability," *JAMS*, 24 (2), 125–36.

Skinner Steven J., Alan Dubinsky, and J.H. Donnelly (1984), "The Use of Social Bases of Power in Retail Sales," *Journal of Personal Selling and Sales Management*, 4 (November), 49–56.

#866 *Satisfaction with Job (General)*

SCALE ITEMS:*

Strongly disagree	Disagree	Slightly disagree	Neutral	Slightly agree	Agree	Strongly agree
1	2	3	4	5	6	7

1. Generally speaking, I am very satisfied with this job.

2. I frequently think of quitting this job. **(r)**

3. I am generally satisfied with the kind of work I do in this job.

4. Most people on this job are very satisfied with the job.

5. People on this job often think of quitting. **(r)**

*Items 1–3 constitute the short form of the scale and are the ones used by Dubinsky and colleagues (1986).

SCALE NAME: Satisfaction with Job (Sales Force)

SCALE DESCRIPTION: The five-item, five-point Likert-type scale assesses the degree to which a salesperson is satisfied with the work he or she does. Although used in a selling context, this measure is not specific to salespeople and could be administered to other samples with little or no adaptation. In their article, Sohi, Smith, and Ford (1996) referred to this scale as *work satisfaction*.

SCALE ORIGIN: Sohi, Smith, and Ford (1996) reported that they drew a subset of items dealing with a salesperson's satisfaction with the job itself from Churchill, Ford, and Walker's (1974) INDSALES scale and adapted them for this study.

SAMPLES: A sample of **30** salespeople from a major Midwestern U.S. corporation was used by Sohi, Smith, and Ford (1996) to pretest the questionnaire. Salespeople employed by manufacturing firms in standard industrial classification codes 20–39 were randomly selected from a commercial mailing list to serve as the sampling frame. Of the 1542 questionnaires delivered to valid addresses, **230** completed surveys were returned for a response rate of 14.9%. Respondents were predominately college educated (84%), married (84%) men (89%) with a median age of 37.5 years, who had held their current sales position an average of 5.8 years. Industries represented included food products, pharmaceuticals, chemical and allied products, rubber and plastic products, electronics and computers, appliances, and audiovisual products. Nonresponse bias was tested by comparing early and late responders on key variables, and no significant differences were found, which suggests that nonresponse bias may not have been a problem.

RELIABILITY: Sohi, Smith, and Ford (1996) reported a coefficient alpha of **.91** for this measure.

VALIDITY: Evidence of discriminant validity was provided by Sohi, Smith, and Ford (1996) through a nested model confirmatory factor analysis that demonstrated that the latent trait correlations between constructs significantly differed from 1. Confirmatory factor analysis also provided satisfactory evidence of the unidimensionality of the measure.

ADMINISTRATION: Prior to data collection, the questionnaire was pretested by Sohi, Smith, and Ford (1996) on a small sample of salespeople. Several items and the questionnaire format were revised on the basis of the pretest results. In the final study, the measure was part of a self-administered mail survey. Cover letters and postage-paid reply envelopes accompanied each questionnaire, and a copy of the survey results was offered as an incentive to participate. Reminder letters were sent three and five weeks after the initial questionnaire mailing. According to the scale anchors, lower scores on the work satisfaction scale indicated that salespeople were more satisfied with the job itself.

MAJOR FINDINGS: Sohi, Smith, and Ford (1996) investigated how salespeople's role perceptions, satisfaction, and performance are affected when the sales force is shared across multiple divisions within a company. Results indicated that an inverse relationship exists between **job satisfaction** and sharing; when a sales force is shared across divisions, salespeople's **satisfaction** with the job declines. This relationship is moderated by the level of formalization and centralization in the organization. As both formalization and centralization increase, the negative impact of sales force sharing on **job satisfaction** decreases.

REFERENCES:

Churchill, Gilbert A., Jr., Neil M. Ford, and Orville C. Walker Jr. (1974), "Measuring the Job Satisfaction of Industrial Salesmen," *JMR*, 11 (August), 254–60.

Sohi, Ravipreet S., Daniel C. Smith, and Neil M. Ford (1996), "How Does Sharing a Sales Force Between Multiple Divisions Affect Salespeople?" *JAMS*, 24 (3), 195–207.

SCALE ITEMS:

Strongly   Strongly
agree   disagree
1————————2————————3————————4————————5

1. I find my work very satisfying.

2. I feel that I am really doing something worthwhile in my job.

3. My work is challenging.

4. My job is very interesting.

5. My work gives me a sense of accomplishment.

SCALE NAME: Seeking Distance

SCALE DESCRIPTION: Strutton and Lumpkin (1994) adapted this five-item, five-point subscale from the Ways of Coping Checklist Scale developed by Folkman and Lazarus (1980, 1985). It attempts to measure the extent to which a salesperson uses seeking distance tactics to cope with stressful customer sales presentations. In this study, the original items were screened for applicability to the sales setting. The remaining items were then subjected to factor analysis in a manner similar to Folkman and colleagues' (1986) and the subscales identified in that manner.

SCALE ORIGIN: These items were adapted by Strutton and Lumpkin (1994) for a sales setting from the Ways of Coping Checklist (Folkman and Lazarus 1980, 1985). The original measure contained 43 items developed to measure problem-focused (24 items) and emotion-focused (19 items) tactics for handling stressful situations.

SAMPLES: Strutton and Lumpkin's (1994) sample was a nonprobability sample of **101** nonmanager salespeople from three industries: communications technology (60), textiles (22), and furniture (19), predominantly in the southern United States.

RELIABILITY: Strutton and Lumpkin (1994) reported a Cronbach's alpha of **.72** for this scale.

VALIDITY: No specific validity tests were reported by Strutton and Lumpkin (1994). However, this subscale was identified as a separate subscale in Folkman and colleagues' (1986) earlier work.

ADMINISTRATION: Strutton and Lumpkin (1994) asked respondents to describe the most stressful customer-related situation they had encountered during a sales presentation during the previous two months. They were then asked to respond to the items in the scale along with other scales and demographic questions. Higher scores on the scale indicated that seeking distance tactics for dealing with stress were used to a greater extent.

MAJOR FINDINGS: Strutton and Lumpkin found that **seeking distance** was significantly and negatively related to sales presentation effectiveness in a regression of all subscales on a self-reported measure of presentation effectiveness.

REFERENCES:
Folkman, Susan and Richard S. Lazarus (1980), "An Analysis of Coping in a Middle-Aged Community Sample," *Journal of Health and Social Behavior*, 21 (September), 219–39.
————— and ————— (1985), "If It Changes, It Must Be a Process: Study of Emotion and Coping During Three Stages of a College Examination," *Journal of Personality and Social Psychology*, 48 (January), 150–70.
—————, —————, Christine Dunkel-Schetter, Anita DeLongis, and Rand J. Gruen (1986), "Dynamics of a Stressful Encounter: Cognitive Appraisal, Coping, and Encounter Outcomes," *Journal of Personality and Social Psychology*, 50 (May), 992–1003.
Strutton, David and James R. Lumpkin (1994), "Problem- and Emotion-Focused Coping Dimensions and Sales Presentation Effectiveness," *JAMS*, 22 (1), 28–37.

#868 *Seeking Distance*

SCALE ITEMS:
Directions: Indicate the extent to which you used each of the following tactics to cope with a stressful sales presentation experience:

Not used at all   Used a great deal

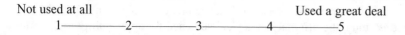

1———————2———————3———————4———————5

1. Went along with fate; sometimes I just have bad luck.

2. Didn't let it get to me; refused to think about it too much.

3. Tried to forget the whole thing.

4. Went on as if nothing happened.

5. Made light of the situation; refused to get too serious about it.

SCALE NAME: Seeking Social Support

SCALE DESCRIPTION: Strutton and Lumpkin (1994) adapted this three-item, five-point subscale from the Ways of Coping Checklist Scale developed by Folkman and Lazarus (1980, 1985). It attempts to measure the extent to which a salesperson uses social support tactics to cope with stressful customer sales presentations. In this study, the original items were screened for applicability to the sales setting. The remaining items were then subjected to factor analysis in a manner similar to Folkman and colleagues' (1986) and the subscales identified in that manner.

SCALE ORIGIN: These items were adapted by Strutton and Lumpkin (1994) for a sales setting from the Ways of Coping Checklist (Folkman and Lazarus 1980, 1985). The original measure contained 43 items developed to measure problem-focused (24 items) and emotion-focused (19 items) tactics for handling stressful situations.

SAMPLES: Strutton and Lumpkin's (1994) sample was a nonprobability sample of **101** nonmanager salespeople from three industries: communications technology (60), textiles (22), and furniture (19), predominantly in the southern United States.

RELIABILITY: Strutton and Lumpkin (1994) reported a Cronbach's alpha of **.66** for this scale.

VALIDITY: No specific validity tests were reported by Strutton and Lumpkin (1994). However, this subscale was identified as a separate subscale in previous work (Folkman et al. 1986). On the face, two items in this scale may be a rank-ordered subset in which the response to item 3 necessarily indicates a response to item 2. To the extent that the items are correlated, some item redundancy may be a factor in both inflating the reliability indicator and increasing measurement error.

ADMINISTRATION: Strutton and Lumpkin (1994) asked respondents to describe the most stressful customer-related situation they had encountered during a sales presentation during the previous two months. They were then asked to respond to the items in the scale along with other scales and demographic questions. Higher scores on the scale indicated that seeking social support tactics for dealing with stress were used to a greater extent.

MAJOR FINDINGS: Strutton and Lumpkin found that **seeking social support** was **not** significantly related to sales presentation effectiveness in a regression of all subscales on a self-reported measure of presentation effectiveness.

REFERENCES:

Folkman, Susan and Richard S. Lazarus (1980), "An Analysis of Coping in a Middle-Aged Community Sample," *Journal of Health and Social Behavior*, 21 (September), 219–39.

——— and ——— (1985), "If It Changes, It Must Be a Process: Study of Emotion and Coping During Three Stages of a College Examination," *Journal of Personality and Social Psychology*, 48 (January), 150–70.

———, ———, Christine Dunkel-Schetter, Anita DeLongis, and Rand J. Gruen (1986), "Dynamics of a Stressful Encounter: Cognitive Appraisal, Coping, and Encounter Outcomes," *Journal of Personality and Social Psychology*, 50 (May), 992–1003.

Strutton, David and James R. Lumpkin (1994), "Problem- and Emotion-Focused Coping Dimensions and Sales Presentation Effectiveness," *JAMS*, 22 (1), 28–37.

#869 *Seeking Social Support*

SCALE ITEMS:

Indicate the extent to which you used each of the following tactics to cope with a stressful sales presentation experience:

Not used at all   Used a great deal

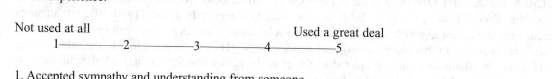

1. Accepted sympathy and understanding from someone.

2. Talked to someone about how I was feeling.

3. Asked a colleague I respected for advice.

SCALE NAME: Selectivity (Brand)

SCALE DESCRIPTION: Fein and Anderson (1997) used this four-item, seven-point Likert-type scale to assess the degree to which a distributor refrains from carrying brands of competing manufacturers/suppliers in a particular product category.

SCALE ORIGIN: Fein and Anderson (1997) indicated that the scale is similar to a measure previously used by Anderson and Weitz (1992). An initial factor analysis was used to check the unidimensionality of the measure, and the items were purified on the basis of an examination of item means, intercorrelations, and standard deviations. A principal components factor analysis was then conducted on the remaining scale items, and those loading on the hypothesized factor at or above the .40 level were retained.

SAMPLES: Fein and Anderson (1997) mailed questionnaires to 518 matched dyads of distributors and suppliers of a wide range of products sold to business-to-business markets. Eleven divisions of five major supply companies located in the United States participated in the project. The branch-level employee and distributor firm employee most knowledgeable about a supplier/distributor relationship represented the matched dyad for a particular relationship; **362** matched pairs provided completely usable data for this study.

RELIABILITY: Fein and Anderson (1997) reported a coefficient alpha of **.81** for this measure.

VALIDITY: No specific examination of scale validity was reported by Fein and Anderson (1997).

ADMINISTRATION: The scale was included with other measures as part of a self-administered survey that was delivered by mail to the supplier portion of the sample. Fein and Anderson (1997) included a cover letter from both the researchers and the supplier that explained the purpose of the study and promised confidentiality. The surveys were coded to permit matching responses. Postage-paid reply envelopes were also included in the mailing, and one follow-up attempt was made to nonrespondents. Higher scores on the scale indicated that suppliers perceived their focal distributors as providing them with a greater degree of brand selectivity.

MAJOR FINDINGS: Fein and Anderson (1997) investigated credible commitments—interrelated exchanges of pledges between suppliers and distributors—in the context of their effect on the territory and brand selectivity decisions made by suppliers and distributors in industrial distribution relationships. The results of their analysis indicated that reciprocity was a major factor influencing pledges of territory and **brand selectivity**. The more that distributors refrained from selling competing brands, the more likely suppliers were to grant greater territory selectivity. Conversely, distributors gave a greater degree of **brand selectivity** to suppliers who provided greater territory selectivity. A supplier's transaction-specific investments in a distributor and its perceptions of the distributor's influence over customers were also positively associated with the degree of **brand selectivity** granted to suppliers. Distributors were more likely to grant **brand selectivity** when the supplier's product category was relatively unimportant but less likely to limit the number of brands when the product category was highly competitive.

REFERENCES:
Anderson, Erin and Barton Weitz (1992), "The Use of Pledges to Build and Sustain Commitment in Distribution Channels," *JMR*, 29 (February), 18–34.

Fein, Adam J. and Erin Anderson (1997), "Patterns of Credible Commitments: Territory and Brand Selectivity in Industrial Distribution Channels," *JM*, 61 (April), 19–34.

#870 *Selectivity (Brand)*

SCALE ITEMS:

Strongly   Strongly
disagree   agree
  1———2———3———4———5———6———7

1. This distributor carries only our brand for the type of product we make.

2. This distributor voluntarily refrains from adding suppliers that would compete with us.

3. This distributor has so many suppliers that its suppliers are bound to compete with each other. **(r)**

4. How many companies that make products competitive with your line does this distributor carry? _____ suppliers **(r)**

SCALE NAME: Selectivity (Territory)

SCALE DESCRIPTION: Fein and Anderson (1997) used this four-item, seven-point Likert-type scale to assess the degree to which a supplier limits the number of intermediaries operating in a particular geographic market.

SCALE ORIGIN: Fein and Anderson (1997) indicated that the scale is similar to a measure previously used by Anderson and Weitz (1992). An initial factor analysis was used to check the unidimensionality of the measure, and the items were purified on the basis of an examination of item means, intercorrelations, and standard deviations. A principal components factor analysis was then conducted on the remaining scale items, and those loading on the hypothesized factor at or above the .40 level were retained.

SAMPLES: Fein and Anderson (1997) mailed questionnaires to 518 matched dyads of distributors and suppliers of a wide range of products sold to business-to-business markets. Eleven divisions of five major supply companies located in the United States participated in the project. The branch-level employee and distributor firm employee most knowledgeable about a supplier/distributor relationship represented the matched dyad for a particular relationship; **362** matched pairs provided completely usable data for this study.

RELIABILITY: Fein and Anderson (1997) reported a coefficient alpha of **.69** for this measure.

VALIDITY: No specific examination of scale validity was reported by Fein and Anderson (1997).

ADMINISTRATION: The scale was included with other measures as part of a self-administered survey that was delivered by mail to the distributor portion of the sample. Fein and Anderson (1997) included a cover letter from both the researchers and the supplier that explained the purpose of the study and promised confidentiality. The surveys were coded to permit matching responses. Postage-paid reply envelopes were also included in the mailing, and one follow-up attempt was made to nonrespondents. Higher scores on the scale indicated that distributors perceived their focal suppliers as providing them with a greater degree of territory selectivity.

MAJOR FINDINGS: Fein and Anderson (1997) investigated credible commitments—interrelated exchanges of pledges between suppliers and distributors—in the context of their effect on the territory and brand selectivity decisions made by suppliers and distributors in industrial distribution relationships. The results of their analysis indicated that reciprocity was a major factor influencing pledges of brand and **territory selectivity**. The more that distributors refrained from selling competing brands, the more likely suppliers were to grant greater **territory selectivity**. Conversely, distributors gave a greater degree of brand selectivity to suppliers who provided greater **territory selectivity**. A distributor's transaction-specific investments in a supplier, its perceptions of the strength of the supplier's brand name, and the level of direct sales made by a distributor were also positively associated with the degree of **territory selectivity** granted by suppliers. Suppliers were more likely to grant **territory selectivity** when the territory was relatively unimportant but refused to limit the number of distributors when the product category was highly competitive.

REFERENCES:

Anderson, Erin and Barton Weitz (1992), "The Use of Pledges to Build and Sustain Commitment in Distribution Channels," *JMR*, 29 (February), 18–34.

Fein, Adam J. and Erin Anderson (1997), "Patterns of Credible Commitments: Territory and Brand Selectivity in Industrial Distribution Channels," *JM*, 61 (April), 19–34.

#871 *Selectivity (Territory)*

SCALE ITEMS:

Strongly disagree 1———2———3———4———5———6———7 Strongly agree

1. This supplier has given us an exclusive territory for their products.

2. This supplier voluntarily refrains from adding distributors that would compete with us.

3. This supplier has so many distributors that its distributors are bound to compete with each other when selling this supplier's products. **(r)**

4. Of distributors in your territory capable of carrying this supplier's line, how many carry this supplier's line? _____ distributors. **(r)**

SCALE NAME: Self-Control

SCALE DESCRIPTION: Strutton and Lumpkin (1994) adapted this four-item, five-point subscale from the Ways of Coping Checklist Scale developed by Folkman and Lazarus (1980, 1985). It attempts to measure the extent to which a salesperson uses self-control–based tactics to cope with stressful customer sales presentations. In this study, the original items were screened for applicability to the sales setting. The remaining items were then subjected to factor analysis in a manner similar to Folkman and colleagues' (1986) and the subscales identified in that manner.

SCALE ORIGIN: These items were adapted by Strutton and Lumpkin (1994) for a sales setting from the Ways of Coping Checklist (Folkman and Lazarus 1980, 1985). The original measure contained 43 items developed to measure problem-focused (24 items) and emotion-focused (19 items) tactics for handling stressful situations.

SAMPLES: Strutton and Lumpkin's (1994) sample was a nonprobability sample of **101** nonmanager salespeople from three industries: communications technology (60), textiles (22), and furniture (19), predominantly in the southern United States.

RELIABILITY: Strutton and Lumpkin (1994) reported a Cronbach's alpha of **.78** for this scale.

VALIDITY: No specific validity tests were reported by Strutton and Lumpkin (1994). This subscale was identified as a separate subscale in Folkman and colleagues' (1986) earlier work and reidentified in this study using exploratory factor analysis.

ADMINISTRATION: Strutton and Lumpkin (1994) asked respondents to describe the most stressful customer-related situation they had encountered during a sales presentation during the previous two months. They were then asked to respond to the items in the scale along with other scales and demographic questions. Higher scores on the scale indicated that self-control tactics for coping with stress were used to a greater extent.

MAJOR FINDINGS: Strutton and Lumpkin (1994) found that the use of **self-control** as a stress coping tactic was not significantly related to sales presentation effectiveness.

REFERENCES:
Folkman, Susan and Richard S. Lazarus (1980), "An Analysis of Coping in a Middle-Aged Community Sample," *Journal of Health and Social Behavior*, 21 (September), 219–39.
———— and ———— (1985), "If It Changes, It Must Be a Process: Study of Emotion and Coping During Three Stages of a College Examination," *Journal of Personality and Social Psychology*, 48 (January), 150–70.
————, ————, Christine Dunkel-Schetter, Anita DeLongis, and Rand J. Gruen (1986), "Dynamics of a Stressful Encounter: Cognitive Appraisal, Coping, and Encounter Outcomes," *Journal of Personality and Social Psychology*, 50 (May), 992–1003.
Strutton, David and James R. Lumpkin (1994), "Problem- and Emotion-Focused Coping Dimensions and Sales Presentation Effectiveness," *JAMS*, 22 (1), 28–37.

#872 *Self-Control*

SCALE ITEMS:

Indicate the extent to which you used each of the following tactics to cope with a stressful sales presentation experience:

Not used at all   :___:___:___:___:___: Used a great deal
                    1   2   3   4   5

1. Tried to keep my feelings to myself.

2. Kept others from knowing how bad things were.

3. Tried not to burn my bridges but leave things somewhat open.

4. Tried not to act too hastily to follow my first hunch.

SCALE NAME: Self-Determination

SCALE DESCRIPTION: Strutton, Pelton, and Lumpkin (1995) described this three-item, five-point Likert-type scale as a person's tendency to perceive and behave as if he or she is influential, rather than helpless, when faced with life's contingencies.

SCALE ORIGIN: Strutton, Pelton, and Lumpkin (1995) reported that these items were adapted from the external locus of control scale by Rotter, Seeman, and Liverant (1962). The external locus of control scale was developed to measure the extent to which a person believes he or she is controlled by external forces.

SAMPLES: Using a sampling frame generated from the telephone directories of two metropolitan statistical areas, Strutton, Pelton, and Lumpkin (1995) first identified a stratified random sample of 1000 organizations likely to have industrial salespeople. A systematic random sampling procedure was then used to identify 450 organizations for telephone contact. Of the 450 individuals contacted, 374 organizational sales managers agreed to allow one company salesperson to be randomly selected to participate in the study. Of these salespeople, **322** acceptable questionnaires were returned for an 86% response rate. The sample demographics were as follows: 71% was 40 years of age or younger, 62% were men, and 76% had incomes of $35,000 or more. All levels of sales experience were adequately represented; 29% of the sample had less than four years experience, 35% has four to ten years experience, and 36% had more than ten years of sales experience.

RELIABILITY: Strutton, Pelton, and Lumpkin (1995) reported a coefficient alpha of .763 for this measure.

VALIDITY: No specific examination of the scale's validity was reported by Strutton, Pelton, and Lumpkin (1995).

ADMINISTRATION: Strutton, Pelton, and Lumpkin (1995) stated that the scale was part of a self-administered questionnaire that was returned by mail. In addition to answering questions measuring the personality characteristics of challenge, self-determination, and involvement in self and surroundings, respondents described the most stressful job-related situation they experienced during the preceding three months. The manner in which they coped with the stressful episode was assessed using Strutton and Lumpkin's (1994) sales-domain-relevant version of the Ways of Coping Checklist. With respect to the self-determination measure, the mean values on the summated scale were used to determine the point at which one-third of the sample scored below or above the middle third. Strutton, Pelton, and Lumpkin (1995) then classified 76 salespeople as other-determination and 126 as self-determination. Lower scores on the self-determination scale indicated that a person had a greater belief that he or she was controlled by external forces rather than his or her own actions.

MAJOR FINDINGS: Strutton, Pelton, and Lumpkin (1995) investigated the relationship between how salespeople cope with job stress and the three personality characteristics of challenge, self-determination, and involvement in self and surroundings. Four problem-focused coping tactics, directed problem solving, self-control, confrontive coping, and taking responsibility demonstrated significantly positive associations with the degree to which salespeople believed in **self-determination**, whereas only the emotional avoidance coping tactic was negatively associated with **self-determination**.

REFERENCES:
Rotter, Jerome B., Michael Seeman, and Stephen Liverant (1962), "Internal Versus External Locus of Control in Behavior Theory," in *Decisions, Values and Groups*, Norman Foster Washburne, ed. New York: Pergamon.

Strutton, David, and James R. Lumpkin (1994), "Problem and Emotion-Focused Coping Dimensions and Sales Presentation Effectiveness," *JAMS*, 22 (1), 28–37.

———, Lou E. Pelton, and James R. Lumpkin (1995), "Personality Characteristics and Salespeople's Choice of Coping Strategies," *JAMS*, 23 (2), 132–40.

SCALE ITEMS:

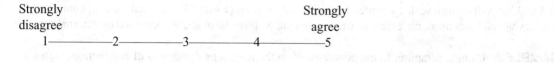

1. What happens is my own doing.

2. Capable people who fail to become leaders have not taken advantage of their opportunities.

3. People's misfortunes often result from the mistakes they make.

SCALE NAME: Self-Efficacy

SCALE DESCRIPTION: Sujan, Weitz, and Kumar (1994) used this seven-item, seven-point Likert-type scale to measure the degree to which salespeople judged themselves to be capable of organizing and executing courses of action required to successfully perform their jobs.

SCALE ORIGIN: Sujan, Weitz, and Kumar (1994) indicated that the scale items used in this measure were adapted from the 20-item measure of self-efficacy in negotiations originally developed by Chowdhury (1993). The authors reduced the number of items in the scale to seven and changed item phrasing from the context of negotiation to sales.

SAMPLES: Sujan, Weitz, and Kumar (1994) surveyed a convenience sample of salespeople employed by eight firms representing diverse industries. Two hundred seventeen questionnaires were distributed by sales managers to members of their selling force, and **190** usable responses were obtained for an 87.5% response rate. On average, respondents were 35 years of age, had 9 years sales experience, and made 3.5 calls per day. The majority were men (78%).

RELIABILITY: Sujan, Weitz, and Kumar (1994) reported a coefficient alpha of **.77** for the measure.

VALIDITY: Sujan, Weitz, and Kumar (1994) provided extensive information on the assessment of scale validity. Measures used in their study were evaluated using confirmatory factor analysis. The authors stated that the results of this analysis supported the unidimensionality and reliability of the measure and provided evidence of convergent and discriminant validity.

ADMINISTRATION: Sujan, Weitz, and Kumar (1994) included a cover letter promising confidentiality and a self-addressed, stamped reply envelope in the survey packet distributed by sales managers to members of the sales force. Respondents were instructed to return the questionnaire directly to the researchers rather than to their superiors. Higher scores on the scale indicated that salespeople judged themselves as being highly capable of organizing and executing those courses of action required to successfully perform their jobs.

MAJOR FINDINGS: Sujan, Weitz, and Kumar (1994) investigated the influence of goal orientations on work behavior. Results indicated that a performance orientation motivates salespeople high in **self-efficacy** to work harder and smarter than those who are low in **self-efficacy**.

REFERENCES:
Chowdhury, Jhinuk (1993), "The Motivational Impact of Sales Quotas," *JMR*, 30 (February), 28–41.
Sujan, Harish, Barton A. Weitz, and Nirmalya Kumar (1994), "Learning Orientation, Working Smart, and Effective Selling," *JM*, 58 (July), 39–52.

#874 *Self-Efficacy*

SCALE ITEMS:

Strongly   Strongly
disagree   agree
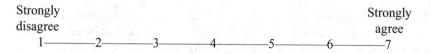

1. I am good at selling.

2. It is difficult for me to put pressure on a customer. **(r)**

3. I know the right thing to do in selling situations.

4. I find it difficult to convince a customer that has a different viewpoint from mine. **(r)**

5. My temperament is not well-suited for selling. **(r)**

6. I am good at finding out what customers want.

7. It is easy for me to get customers to see my point of view.

SCALE NAME: Self-Efficacy (Employee)

SCALE DESCRIPTION: Hartline and Ferrell (1996) used this four-item, seven-point Likert-type scale to measure the extent to which employees felt confident about their job skills and abilities. However, the four items retained in this measure seem to focus more on the extent to which the employees feel that their qualifications and skills exceed those required for the job.

SCALE ORIGIN: Hartline and Ferrell (1996) indicated that the items representing this construct were taken from Jones's (1986) eight-item measure of self-efficacy. Four items, "My job is well within the scope of my abilities," "I did not experience any problems in adjusting to work at this organization," "I have all the technical knowledge I need to deal with my job, all I need now is practical experience," and "My past experiences and accomplishments increase my confidence that I will be able to perform successfully in this organization," were dropped from the measure following a confirmatory factor analysis because of nonsignificant t-values.

SAMPLES: The hotel industry was chosen as the sampling frame for this study. Hartline and Ferrell (1996) sampled the general managers, employees, and customers of 444 hotel units representing three hotel chains. Of these, 236 different hotel units returned at least one usable questionnaire from a manager, an employee, and a customer. A total of 1769 usable questionnaires were received from **236** hotel managers, **561** customer-contact employees, and **1351** customers.

RELIABILITY: Hartline and Ferrell (1996) reported a coefficient alpha of **.67** for this measure.

VALIDITY: Hartline and Ferrell (1996) used confirmatory factor analysis to test the unidimensionality of the measures using separate analyses for managers, employees, and customers. Items with nonsignificant t-values were dropped from the measures. In investigating the discriminant validity of the scales, the authors first averaged the employee and customer responses on the scale and then matched that response with the manager responses to create a single data set in which cases represented hotel units rather than individuals. Hotel units that did not provide at least three responses from both employees and customers were dropped, leaving a final sample of 97 matched responses. Confirmatory factor analysis was then used to assess the discriminant validity of the measures.

ADMINISTRATION: Each hotel manager received a survey packet containing instructions, postage-paid reply envelopes, one manager survey, five employee surveys, and forty guest surveys, which were to be self-administered. This measure was included in the employee survey. Hartline and Ferrell (1996) instructed managers to distribute employee surveys to individuals in customer-contact positions and the guest surveys during check-out. Survey packets were preceded by a letter from the corporate marketing manager endorsing the project and followed by a second wave of materials approximately two months after the first had been distributed. Higher scores on the scale indicated higher perceptions of self-efficacy.

MAJOR FINDINGS: Hartline and Ferrell (1996) investigated the management of customer-contact service employees and various factors related to service quality using data generated from the customers, contact employees, and managers of hotel units. Hypotheses were tested in the context of structural equation modeling. Although both job satisfaction and employee **self-efficacy** were found to have a positive effect on customers' perceptions of service quality, the effect of **self-efficacy** was strongest. Employee **self-efficacy** was also significantly and negatively related to job satisfaction, which indicated that highly **efficacious** customer-contact employees tend to be less satisfied with their jobs. Role ambiguity negatively influenced **self-efficacy**, whereas, contrary to expectations, role conflict had no effect. When management empowered employees, **self-efficacy** was enhanced.

#875   *Self-Efficacy (Employee)*

REFERENCES:

Hartline, Michael D. and O.C. Ferrell (1996), "The Management of Customer-Contact Service Employees: An Empirical Investigation," *JM*, 60 (October), 52–70.

Jones, Gareth R. (1986), "Socialization Tactics, Self-Efficacy, and Newcomers' Adjustments to Organizations," *Academy of Management Journal*, 29 (June), 262–79.

SCALE ITEMS:

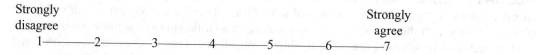

Strongly
disagree

1———————2———————3———————4———————5———————6———————7

Strongly
agree

1. I feel that I am overqualified for the job I am doing.

2. I feel confident that my skills and abilities equal or exceed those of my colleagues.

3. I could have handled a more challenging job that the one I am doing.

4. Professionally speaking, my job exactly satisfies my expectations of myself. **(r)**

SCALE NAME: Signal Credibility

SCALE DESCRIPTION: Robertson, Eliashberg, and Rymon (1995) used this five-item, six-point Likert-type scale to assess the extent to which a company perceived a new product announcement (NPA) signal as informative, credible, and believable.

SCALE ORIGIN: Robertson, Eliashberg, and Rymon (1995) developed the scale specifically for this study. The measure and questionnaire in which it was administered were initially conceptualized, tested, and purified on the basis of two pilot studies with executives participating in a management development program and a mail survey pretest. A principal components factor analysis with Varimax rotation was performed on data collected in the final study and used to determine the composition of the final measure.

SAMPLES: A total of 1554 directors of marketing in the United States (1034) and United Kingdom (520), representing a broad range of consumer and industrial product industries, were sampled for this study. Using a commercially purchased list as their sampling frame, Robertson, Eliashberg, and Rymon (1995) excluded marketing managers of wholesale, retail, and small firms prior to mailing their surveys. A total of **346** usable surveys were returned, of which 241 and 105 were from the United States and United Kingdom, respectively. No evidence of response basis was found, and Chow tests of the U.S. and U.K. data supported the pooling together of data from each country.

RELIABILITY: Robertson, Eliashberg, and Rymon (1995) reported a coefficient alpha of **.83** for this measure.

VALIDITY: No specific examination of scale validity was reported by Robertson, Eliashberg, and Rymon (1995).

ADMINISTRATION: The scale was included with other measures in a self-administered survey delivered by mail. Robertson, Eliashberg, and Rymon (1995) prenotified respondents and offered a copy of the survey's tabulated results as an incentive to participate. Respondents were instructed to answer the questionnaire in the context of the last NPA signal received relative to a new product that was significantly different from existing products. Higher scores on the scale indicated that a competitor's NPA was perceived as being highly informative, believable, and credible by the receiving firm.

MAJOR FINDINGS: Robertson, Eliashberg, and Rymon (1995) examined the relationship between NPA signals—announcements in advance of market introduction—and factors affecting the likelihood of competitive reactions to NPA signals. Firms were found to be most likely to react aggressively to NPA signals when the **signal was perceived to be credible** by the receiving firm.

REFERENCES:
Robertson, Thomas S., Jehoshua Eliashberg, and Talia Rymon (1995), "New Product Announcement Signals and Incumbent Reactions," *JM*, 59 (July), 1–15.

SCALE ITEMS:*

Strongly   Strongly
disagree   agree

1————2————3————4————5————6

Please describe for us the new product preannouncement signal that your firm received from its competitor:

1. The competitor's product preannouncement signal was very informative.

2. It was not very believable. **(r)****

3. It was very unclear. **(r)****

4. It was somehow deceptive. **(r)****

5. It was a credible signal.

*Although a six-point scale format was designated by Robertson, Eliashberg, and Rymon (1995), the scale anchors were not explicitly listed. However, it is probable that the traditional Likert "strongly disagree" to "strongly agree" format was used.

**The appendix listing the measures used by Robertson, Eliashberg, and Rymon (1995) does not indicate that these items were reversed. However, this is very likely to be necessary and should be considered when calculating scale scores.

SCALE NAME: Signal Hostility

SCALE DESCRIPTION: Robertson, Eliashberg, and Rymon (1995) used this three-item, six-point Likert-type scale to assess the extent to which a company perceived a new product announcement (NPA) signal as a threat to their firm's livelihood.

SCALE ORIGIN: Robertson, Eliashberg, and Rymon (1995) developed the scale specifically for this study. The measure and questionnaire in which it was administered were initially conceptualized, tested, and purified on the basis of two pilot studies with executives participating in a management development program and a mail survey pretest. A principal components factor analysis with Varimax rotation was performed on data collected in the final study and used to determine the composition of the final measure.

SAMPLES: A total of 1554 directors of marketing in the United States (1034) and United Kingdom (520), representing a broad range of consumer and industrial product industries, were sampled for this study. Using a commercially purchased list as their sampling frame, Robertson, Eliashberg, and Rymon (1995) excluded marketing managers of wholesale, retail, and small firms prior to mailing their surveys. A total of **346** usable surveys were returned, of which 241 and 105 were from the United States and United Kingdom, respectively. No evidence of response basis was found, and Chow tests of the U.S. and U.K. data supported the pooling together of data from each country.

RELIABILITY: Robertson, Eliashberg, and Rymon (1995) reported a coefficient alpha of **.63** for this measure.

VALIDITY: No specific examination of scale validity was reported by Robertson, Eliashberg, and Rymon (1995).

ADMINISTRATION: The scale was included with other measures in a self-administered survey delivered by mail. Robertson, Eliashberg, and Rymon (1995) prenotified respondents and offered a copy of the survey's tabulated results as an incentive to participate. Respondents were instructed to answer the questionnaire in the context of the last NPA signal received relative to a new product that was significantly different from existing products. Higher scores on the scale indicated that a competitor's NPA was perceived as a greater threat to the livelihood of the receiving firm.

MAJOR FINDINGS: Robertson, Eliashberg, and Rymon (1995) examined the relationship between NPA signals—announcements in advance of market introduction—and factors affecting the likelihood of competitive reactions to NPA signals. Firms were found to be most likely to react in some fashion to NPA signals when the **signal was perceived to be hostile**, though the use of **hostile signals** by a competitor did not significantly influence aggressive reactions on the part of the receiving firm.

REFERENCES:
Robertson, Thomas S., Jehoshua Eliashberg, and Talia Rymon (1995), "New Product Announcement Signals and Incumbent Reactions," *JM*, 59 (July), 1–15.

#877 *Signal Hostility*

SCALE ITEMS:*

Strongly   Strongly
disagree   agree

  1————2————3————4————5————6

Please describe for us the new product preannouncement signal that your firm received from its competitor:

1. It would have resulted in a harmful outcome for my firm.

2. My company perceived it as a threat.

3. It was an aggressive signal.

*Although a six-point scale format was designated by Robertson, Eliashberg, and Rymon (1995), the scale anchors were not explicitly listed. However, it is probable that the traditional Likert "strongly disagree" to "strongly agree" format was used.

SCALE NAME: Similarity to Others in Firm (Salesperson)

SCALE DESCRIPTION: Doney and Cannon (1997) used this three-item, seven-point Likert-type scale to measure the degree to which a buyer perceives a salesperson as having similar interests and values to others employed by the buying firm.

SCALE ORIGIN: Doney and Cannon (1997) stated that they generated items for the scale on the basis of interviews with marketing and purchasing personnel. Exploratory factor analyses using both orthogonal and oblique rotations were used to ensure high item loadings on hypothesized constructs and low cross-loadings.

SAMPLES: Doney and Cannon (1997) sampled 657 members of the National Association of Purchasing Management who were employed by firms involved in industrial manufacturing, as classified by standard industrial classification codes 33–37. **Two hundred ten** completed questionnaires were returned from a primarily male (76%) sample with an average of 15 years of purchasing experience.

RELIABILITY: Doney and Cannon (1997) calculated a coefficient alpha of **.90** for this measure.

VALIDITY: Doney and Cannon (1997) reported using three methods to test the discriminant validity of the scales representing the combined dimensions of trust of the salesperson and its proposed antecedents and outcomes. Each method provided strong evidence of discriminant validity. Two LISREL-based tests were also used to provide evidence for the convergent validity of the measures.

ADMINISTRATION: The scale was included with other measures as part of a self-administered survey that was delivered by mail. Nonrespondents received a postcard reminder followed by a second questionnaire a week later. Doney and Cannon (1997) instructed respondents to focus on a single, specific, recent purchase decision in which more than one supplier was seriously considered and indicate on the survey (using initials) two of the firms considered. After answering questions pertaining to the purchase situation, half of the respondents were instructed to complete the remainder of the questionnaire in the context of the first supplier they had listed, whereas the other half were instructed to use the second supplier. Higher scores on the scale indicated a higher level of perceived similarity between the focal salesperson and members of the buying firm.

MAJOR FINDINGS: Doney and Cannon (1997) investigated the impact of purchasing agents' trust in the salesperson and the supplier firm on a buying firm's current supplier choice and future buying intentions. The extent to which a salesperson was perceived to be **similar to members of the buying firm** positively influenced the level of trust in the salesperson.

REFERENCES:
Doney, Patricia M. and Joseph P. Cannon (1997), "An Examination of the Nature of Trust in Buyer-Seller Relationships," *JM*, 61 (April), 35–51.

SCALE ITEMS:

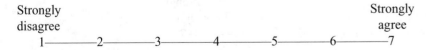

Strongly   Strongly
disagree   agree

1————2————3————4————5————6————7

1. This salesperson shares similar interests with people in our firm.

2. This salesperson has values similar to people in our firm.

3. This salesperson is very similar to people in our firm.

SCALE NAME: Size (Supplier)

SCALE DESCRIPTION: Doney and Cannon (1997) used this three-item, seven-point Likert-type scale to assess the size of a firm in terms of its overall size and market share position.

SCALE ORIGIN: Doney and Cannon (1997) generated items for the scale on the basis of interviews with marketing and purchasing personnel. Exploratory factor analyses using both orthogonal and oblique rotations were used to ensure high item loadings on hypothesized constructs and low cross-loadings.

SAMPLES: Doney and Cannon (1997) sampled 657 members of the National Association of Purchasing Management who were employed by firms involved in industrial manufacturing, as classified by standard industrial classification codes 33–37. **Two hundred ten** completed questionnaires were returned from a primarily male (76%) sample with an average of 15 years of purchasing experience.

RELIABILITY: Doney and Cannon (1997) calculated a coefficient alpha of **.83** for this measure.

VALIDITY: Doney and Cannon (1997) reported using three methods to test the discriminant validity of the scales representing trust of the supplier firm and its proposed antecedents and outcomes. Each method provided strong evidence of discriminant validity. Two LISREL-based tests were also used to provide evidence for the convergent validity of the measure.

ADMINISTRATION: The scale was included with other measures as part of a self-administered survey that was delivered by mail. Nonrespondents received a postcard reminder followed by a second questionnaire a week later. Doney and Cannon (1997) instructed respondents to focus on a single, specific, recent purchase decision in which more than one supplier was seriously considered and indicate on the survey (using initials) two of the firms considered. After answering questions pertaining to the purchase situation, half of the respondents were instructed to complete the remainder of the questionnaire in the context of the first supplier they had listed, whereas the other half were instructed to use the second supplier. Higher scores on the scale indicated that respondents perceived the focal supplier as being a larger, more dominant firm in the industry.

MAJOR FINDINGS: Doney and Cannon (1997) investigated the impact of purchasing agents' trust in the salesperson and the supplier firm on a buying firm's current supplier choice and future buying intentions. The buying firm's trust in the supplying firm was found to be positively related to the **supplier's size**.

REFERENCES:
Doney, Patricia M. and Joseph P. Cannon (1997), "An Examination of the Nature of Trust in Buyer-Seller Relationships," *JM*, 61 (April), 35–51.

SCALE ITEMS:

Strongly   Strongly
disagree   agree

1. This supplier is a very large company.

2. This supplier is the industry's biggest supplier of this product.

3. This supplier is a small player in the market. **(r)**

SCALE NAME: Skepticism of Salesperson Advice (Business Customer)

SCALE DESCRIPTION: Anderson and Robertson (1995) used this nine-item, seven-point Likert-type scale to measure broker perceptions of the extent to which clients make their own judgments and disregard broker advice.

SCALE ORIGIN: Anderson and Robertson (1995) developed the measure used in this study. A detailed construct description was constructed on the basis of a though review of the trade and academic literature. Multiple interviews with brokers, sales managers, and trade association officials were used to generate scale items believed to tap the construct. These items were administered to 208 brokers and factor analyzed to test for unidimensionality. Reliability assessments were also used to purify the measure.

SAMPLES: Anderson and Robertson (1995) mailed a questionnaire to the homes of 420 brokers whose names were supplied by cooperating firms, and **201** usable responses were obtained. To be evaluated, some hypotheses required the use of archival data as to the actual sales of house brands made by salespeople. One firm, providing **150** of the respondents in this study, agreed to provide this information. The authors stated that the respondent demographics closely matched those achieved in a large-scale survey of readers conducted by a nationally distributed trade magazine.

RELIABILITY: Anderson and Robertson (1995) reported a coefficient alpha of **.74** for this measure.

VALIDITY: No specific examination of scale validity was reported Anderson and Robertson (1995).

ADMINISTRATION: Anderson and Robertson (1995) included the measure as part of a larger self-administered mail questionnaire. A summary of the results was offered in exchange for respondent cooperation. Higher scores on the scale indicated that salespeople perceived clients as more likely to disregard a broker's advice when making decisions.

MAJOR FINDINGS: Anderson and Robertson (1995) investigated the relationship between factors believed to influence the sale of house brands by multiline salespeople. **Customer skepticism of a salesperson's advice** was not significantly related to the adoption of house products by the sales force.

REFERENCES:
Anderson, Erin and Thomas S. Robertson (1995), "Inducing Multiline Salespeople to Adopt House Brands," *JM*, 59 (April), 16–31.

SCALE ITEMS:

Strongly   Strongly
disagree   agree

1————2————3————4————5————6————7

1. My customers decide what they want, then tell me.

2. My customers actively direct their financial affairs.

#880 *Skepticism of Salesperson Advice (Business Customer)*

3. My customers tend to seek and use my advice. **(r)**

4. My customers get their investment ideas from many sources.

5. My customers spend a lot of time selecting and following their portfolios.

6. My customers treat my ideas as just another opinion.

7. My customers tend to view my opinions with some skepticism.

8. I have a lot of influence over my client's investment decisions. **(r)**

9. My clients are rather cynical about a broker's opinions on financial matters.

SCALE NAME: Skills and Resources (Marketing)

SCALE DESCRIPTION: Song and Parry (1997b) used this eight-item, eleven-point Likert-type scale to measure the degree to which a new product development (NPD) project fit with the firm's existing marketing capabilities. Song and Parry (1997a) referred to a four-item version of this scale as *marketing synergy*.

SCALE ORIGIN: The scale was adapted by Song and Parry (1997a, b) from the work of Cooper (1979a, b). Song and Parry (1997a, b) modified scale items on the basis of a review of the literature, pilot studies, and information obtained from 36 in-depth case study interviews conducted with both Japanese and U.S. firms. The items for all scales used by Song and Parry (1997a, b) were evaluated by an academic panel composed of both Japanese and U.S. business and engineering experts. Following revisions, the items were judged by a new panel composed of academicians and NPD managers. Song and Parry (1997a, b) reported extensive pretesting of both the Japanese and U.S. versions of the questionnaire.

SAMPLES: Song and Parry (1997a, b) randomly sampled 500 of the 611 firms trading on the Tokyo, Osaka, and Nagoya stock exchanges that had been identified as developing at least four new physical products since 1991. Usable responses pertaining to **788** NPD projects were obtained from 404 Japanese firms. The resulting data were randomly split by Song and Parry (1997a) into calibration (n = 394) and validation (n = 394) samples for the purpose of cross-validation. Song and Parry (1997b) said the U.S. sampling frame was from companies listed in the *High-Technology Industries Directory*. Of the 643 firms that had introduced a minimum of four new physical products since 1990, 500 firms were randomly sampled (though stratified by industry to match the Japanese sample), and 312 U.S. firms provided data on **612** NPD projects, of which 312 were successes and 300 were failures.

RELIABILITY: Song and Parry (1997b) reported a coefficient alpha of **.97** for this scale in the Japanese sample and **.89** for the U.S. sample. In their other study using only the Japanese data, Song and Parry (1997a) conducted a confirmatory factor analysis of the data on the calibration sample to purify the scale. Items loading on multiple constructs or those with low item-to-scale loadings were deleted from the measure. Song and Parry (1997a) reported a coefficient alpha of **.91** for the three-item, purified measure using data from the validation sample.

VALIDITY: The extensive pretesting and evaluation of the measure with academicians and NPD managers provided strong evidence for the face validity of the measure. Song and Parry (1997a, b) did not specifically report any other examination of scale validity.

ADMINISTRATION: The self-administered questionnaire containing the scale was originally developed in English; the Japanese version was prepared using the parallel-translation/double-translation method. Following minor revisions made on the basis of pretests with bilingual respondents and case study participants, the Japanese sample received a survey packet containing cover letters in both English and Japanese, two Japanese-language questionnaires, and two international postage-paid reply envelopes. Survey packets delivered to U.S. firms were similar, except no Japanese cover letter was included and the surveys were in English. Incentives, four follow-up letters, and multiple telephone calls and faxes were used to increase the response rate with both samples. Song and Parry (1997a, b) indicated that respondents were asked to answer one questionnaire in the context of a successful new product project introduced after 1991 and the other in the context of a new product project that had failed. Higher scores on the scale indicated a good NPD project fit with the firm's marketing capabilities, in that marketing skills and resources were judged as being more than adequate for the project's needs.

MAJOR FINDINGS: Song and Parry (1997a) conceptualized and tested a model of NPD practices believed to influence the success of new product ventures in Japan. The structural model was estimated with the calibration sample data, and the proposed model and the alternative models were tested using the validation sample. The **marketing skills and resources (synergy)** of Japanese firms was found to significantly and positively influence the level of competitive and marketing intelligence gathering and the marketing proficiency of the firm.

Song and Parry (1997b) conceptualized and tested a model of strategic, tactical, and environmental factors believed to influence new product success using data collected from both Japanese and U.S. firms. In both the Japanese and U.S. samples, a high level of project fit with the firm's **marketing skills and resources** was found to strengthen the relationship between product differentiation and relative product performance. The project fit with the firm's **marketing skills and resources** was also found to be positively related to the (1) idea development and screening, (2) market opportunity analysis, (3) product testing, and (4) commercialization stages of the NPD process.

REFERENCES:

Cooper, Robert G. (1979a), "Identifying Industrial New Product Success: Project NewProd," *Industrial Marketing Management*, 8 (2), 124–35.

——— (1979b), "The Dimensions of Industrial New Product Success and Failure," *JM*, 43 (Summer), 93–103.

Song, X. Michael and Mark E. Parry (1997a), "The Determinants of Japanese New Product Successes," *JMR*, 34 (February), 64–76.

——— and ——— (1997b), "A Cross-National Comparative Study of New Product Development Processes: Japan and the United States," *JM*, 61 (April), 1–18.

SCALE ITEMS:*

Directions: To what extent does each statement listed below correctly describe this selected successful project? Please indicate your degree of agreement or disagreement by circling a number from zero (0) to ten (10) on the scale to the right of each statement. Here: 0 = strongly disagree, 10 = strongly agree, and numbers between 0 and 10 indicate various degrees of agreement or disagreement.

Strongly disagree 0———1———2———3———4———5———6———7———8———9———10 Strongly agree

1. Our company's marketing research skills were more than adequate for this project.

2. Our company's salesforce skills were more than adequate for this project.

3. Our company's distribution skills were more than adequate for this project.

4. Our company's advertising/promotion skills were more than adequate for this project.

5. Our company's marketing research resources were more than adequate for this project.

6. Our company's salesforce resources were more than adequate for this project.

7. Our company's distribution resources were more than adequate for this project.

8. Our company's advertising/promotion resources were more than adequate for this project.

*Items 2, 6, 7, and 8 were used as a measure of marketing synergy by Song and Parry (1997a).

SCALE NAME: Skills and Resources (Technical)

SCALE DESCRIPTION: The full six-item, eleven-point Likert-type scale was used by Song and Parry (1997b) to measure the degree to which a new product development (NPD) project fit with the firm's existing technical capabilities. Song and Parry (1997a) referred to the four-item reduced version of the scale as *technical synergy*.

SCALE ORIGIN: The scale was adapted by Song and Parry (1997a, b) from the work of Cooper (1979a, b). Song and Parry (1997a, b) modified scale items on the basis of a review of the literature, pilot studies, and information obtained from 36 in-depth case study interviews conducted with both Japanese and U.S. firms. The items for all scales used by Song and Parry (1997a, b) were evaluated by an academic panel composed of both Japanese and U.S. business and engineering experts. Following revisions, the items were judged by a new panel composed of academicians and NPD managers. Song and Parry (1997a, b) reported extensive pretesting of both the Japanese and U.S. versions of the questionnaire.

SAMPLES: Song and Parry (1997a, b) randomly sampled 500 of the 611 firms trading on the Tokyo, Osaka, and Nagoya stock exchanges that had been identified as developing at least four new physical products since 1991. Usable responses pertaining to **788** NPD projects were obtained from 404 Japanese firms. The resulting data were randomly split by Song and Parry (1997a) into calibration (n = 394) and validation (n = 394) samples for the purpose of cross-validation. Song and Parry (1997b) said the U.S. sampling frame was from companies listed in the *High-Technology Industries Directory*. Of the 643 firms that had introduced a minimum of four new physical products since 1990, 500 firms were randomly sampled (though stratified by industry to match the Japanese sample), and 312 U.S. firms provided data on **612** NPD projects, of which 312 were successes and 300 were failures.

RELIABILITY: Song and Parry (1997b) reported a coefficient alpha of **.95** for this scale in the Japanese sample and **.84** for the U.S. sample. Song and Parry (1997a) used a confirmatory factor analysis of the data in the calibration sample to purify the scale. Items loading on multiple constructs or those with low item-to-scale loadings were deleted from the measure. Song and Parry (1997a) reported a coefficient alpha of **.81** for the six-item, purified measure using data from the validation sample.

VALIDITY: The extensive pretesting and evaluation of the measure with academicians and NPD managers provided strong evidence for the face validity of the measure. Song and Parry (1997a, b) did not specifically report any other examination of scale validity.

ADMINISTRATION: The self-administered questionnaire containing the scale was originally developed in English; the Japanese version was prepared using the parallel-translation/double-translation method. Following minor revisions made on the basis of pretests with bilingual respondents and case study participants, the Japanese sample received a survey packet containing cover letters in both English and Japanese, two Japanese-language questionnaires, and two international postage-paid reply envelopes. Survey packets delivered to U.S. firms were similar, except no Japanese cover letter was included and the surveys were in English. Incentives, four follow-up letters, and multiple telephone calls and faxes were used to increase the response rate with both samples. Song and Parry (1997a, b) indicated that respondents were asked to answer one questionnaire in the context of a successful new product project introduced after 1991 and the other in the context of a new product project that had failed. Higher scores on the scale indicated a good NPD project fit with the firm's technical capabilities, in that technical skills and resources were judged as being more than adequate for the project's needs.

MAJOR FINDINGS: Song and Parry (1997a) conceptualized and tested a model of NPD practices believed to influence the success of new product ventures in Japan. The structural model was estimated with the calibration sample data, and the proposed model and the alternative models were tested using the validation sample. The **technical skills and resources (synergy)** of Japanese firms were found to significantly and positively influence the gathering of competitive and market intelligence, the firm's technical proficiency, and product competitive advantage.

Song and Parry (1997b) conceptualized and tested a model of strategic, tactical, and environmental factors believed to influence new product success using data collected from both Japanese and U.S. firms. In both the Japanese and U.S. samples, the level of project fit with the firm's **technical skills and resources** was found to be positively related to proficiency in the technical development stage of the NPD process.

REFERENCES:

Cooper, Robert G. (1979a), "Identifying Industrial New Product Success: Project NewProd," *Industrial Marketing Management*, 8 (2), 124–35.

——— (1979b), "The Dimensions of Industrial New Product Success and Failure," *JM*, 43 (Summer), 93–103.

Song, X. Michael and Mark E. Parry (1997a), "The Determinants of Japanese New Product Successes," *JMR*, 34 (February), 64–76.

——— and ——— (1997b), "A Cross-National Comparative Study of New Product Development Processes: Japan and the United States," *JM*, 61 (April), 1–18.

SCALE ITEMS: *

Directions: To what extent does each statement listed below correctly describe this selected successful project? Please indicate your degree of agreement or disagreement by circling a number from zero (0) to ten (10) on the scale to the right of each statement. Here: 0 = strongly disagree, 10 = strongly agree, and numbers between 0 and 10 indicate various degrees of agreement or disagreement.

Strongly disagree
Strongly agree

0———1———2———3———4———5———6———7———8———9———10

1. Our company's R&D skills were more than adequate for this project.

2. Our company's engineering skills were more than adequate for this project.

3. Our company's manufacturing skills were more than adequate for this project.

4. Our company's R&D resources were more than adequate for this project.

5. Our company's engineering resources were more than adequate for this project.

6. Our company's manufacturing resources were more than adequate for this project.

*Items 1, 2, 3, and 4 were used by Song and Parry (1997a) as a measure of technical synergy.

SCALE NAME: Solidarity (Major Supplier with Wholesaler)

SCALE DESCRIPTION: Lusch and Brown (1996) used this three-item, seven-point Likert-type scale to measure the efforts undertaken by a supplier toward preserving its relationship with the wholesale distributor. The authors referred to this measure as *supplier solidarity with wholesaler*, or SSOLID.

SCALE ORIGIN: Citing the work of Heide and John (1992), Lusch and Brown (1996) sought to assess the extent of relational behavior between distributors and their major suppliers by measuring the level of information exchange, flexibility, and solidarity characterizing the relationship. Whereas prior measures typically assessed the *expected* efforts of the parties toward preserving the relationship in a single measure, Lusch and Brown rephrased items adapted from Heide and John (1992), Heide and Milner (1992) and Kaufmann and Dant (1992) to create two separate measures. The current scale measured wholesaler perceptions of the extent to which their suppliers *actually* worked toward preserving the relationship with them; the second scale was used to assess the extent to which wholesalers *actually* engaged in solidarity efforts on behalf of the supplier. One item adapted from the original scales, "Our major supplier does not mind owing us favors," was dropped from the final analysis.

SAMPLES: A systematic random sample of 3225 firms was drawn by Lusch and Brown (1996) from a mailing list of all U.S. merchant wholesalers and agents/brokers in 16 four-digit standard industrial classification code groups. The sample was further reduced by eliminating firms with more than 20 employees. General managers were identified as the key informants for the remaining firms and were sent a mail questionnaire. Incentives and a follow-up mailing resulted in an initial response rate of 28.8%. However, this study reported usable data specific only to the **454** respondents classified as wholesale distributors and excluded data from agent and broker firms. The authors reported that the average number of suppliers reported by wholesalers in the sample was 45, with the major supplier contributing an average of 49% of the firm's annual volume.

RELIABILITY: Lusch and Brown (1996) reported a construct reliability of **.914** for this scale.

VALIDITY: Lusch and Brown (1996) reported undertaking a thorough review of the practitioner and academic literature, as well as extensive practitioner pretesting, to ensure content validity. Confirmatory factor analysis confirmed that the measure represented one of six dimensions that composed relational behavior and demonstrated the unidimensionality of the measure. Convergent and discriminant validity were also assessed and found to be satisfactory, thereby indicating the measure possessed adequate construct validity.

ADMINISTRATION: The scale was included as part of a self-administered mail survey. A $1 incentive and the promise of shared survey results were offered as participant incentives, and a personalized cover letter accompanied the survey packet. Undeliverable questionnaires were redirected to a replacement firm. A second mailing without monetary incentive was sent one month later. Lusch and Brown (1996) instructed respondents to answer all questions pertaining to major suppliers in the context of the supplier with which the wholesale distributor did the most business. Higher scores on the measure indicated that wholesalers perceived suppliers as expending more effort to preserve the relationship with them.

MAJOR FINDINGS: Lusch and Brown (1996) investigated how the type of dependency structure—wholesaler dependent on supplier, supplier dependent on wholesaler, or bilateral dependency—influenced whether a normative or explicit contract was used. The authors also studied whether dependency structure and the type of contract influenced the performance of wholesale-distributors. **Solidarity (major supplier with wholesaler)** represented one of six dimensions of relational behavior. Findings indicated that a greater degree of relational behavior between a supplier and distributor was observed when more normative contracts governed the relationship or greater levels of bilateral dependency between parties existed. When wholesalers maintained a more long-term outlook toward their relationship with the supplier, relational behavior was also enhanced. The use of explicit contracts was found to have no significant bearing on the degree of relational behavior exhibited between supplier and distributor.

REFERENCES:

Heide, Jan B. and Anne S. Miner (1992), "The Shadow of the Future: Effects of Anticipated Interaction and Frequency of Contact on Buyer-Seller Cooperation," *Academy of Management Journal*, 35 (June), 265–291.

———— and George John (1992), "Do Norms Matter in Marketing Relationships?" *JM*, 56 (April), 32–44.

Kaufmann, Patrick J. and Rajiv P. Dant (1992), "The Dimensions of Commercial Exchange," *Marketing Letters*, 3 (May), 171–185.

Lusch, Robert F. and James R. Brown (1996), "Interdependency, Contracting, and Relational Behavior in Marketing Channels," *JM*, 60 (October), 19–38.

SCALE ITEMS:

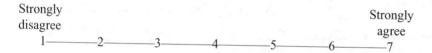

Strongly
disagree

Strongly
agree

1————2————3————4————5————6————7

1. When we incur problems, our major supplier tries to help.

2. Our major supplier shares in the problems that arise in the course of our dealings.

3. Our major supplier is committed to improvements tht may benefit our relationship as a whole and not only themselves.

SCALE NAME: Solidarity (Supplier Relationship)

SCALE DESCRIPTION: Dahlstrom, McNeilly, and Speh (1996) used this three-item, five-point Likert-type scale to measure the degree of dependency and commitment in the supplier relationship.

SCALE ORIGIN: Dahlstrom, McNeilly, and Speh (1996) reported that the scale developed for this study was based on the work of Heide and John (1992). The questionnaire containing the scale was pretested by six members of the Warehouse Education and Research Council, who evaluated it for content, readability, and relevance to the industry.

SAMPLES: Using a sampling frame generated from the membership of the Warehouse Education and Research Council, Dahlstrom, McNeilly, and Speh (1996) surveyed 1000 manufacturer, retailer, and wholesaler members. No mention of the specific sampling technique used to generate the frame was provided. Firms that exclusively used in-house warehousing services were not part of the population of interest and were asked to return the survey without answering. Including unanswered surveys, 383 questionnaires were returned for a 38.3% response rate. Of these, **189** surveys contained complete data from firms using interfirm warehousing services.

RELIABILITY: Dahlstrom, McNeilly, and Speh (1996) reported a coefficient alpha of **.63** for this measure.

VALIDITY: Item-to-total correlations estimated by an exploratory factor analysis were used in the first stage of measure purification. Dahlstrom, McNeilly, and Speh (1996) submitted the remaining items to a confirmatory factor, which provided evidence of construct validity. Discriminant validity was also assessed and found to be acceptable.

ADMINISTRATION: Dahlstrom, McNeilly, and Speh (1996) stated that the scale was part of a self-administered questionnaire that was returned by mail. Sampled individuals were contacted by telephone prior to survey delivery, and a postage-paid, return addressed reply envelope accompanied the questionnaire. A follow-up mailing with a second survey was sent two weeks after the first. Individuals using in-house warehousing services were asked not to complete the survey, but eligible respondents were instructed to answer in the context of the third-party warehouse service provider with whom they spent the greatest portion of their warehousing budget. Higher scores on the solidarity scale indicated that suppliers and users were more committed to maintaining the relationship.

MAJOR FINDINGS: Dahlstrom, McNeilly, and Speh (1996) investigated various antecedents to alternative forms of governance in the logistical supply market. A second topic of investigation addressed how formal controls and relational norms were employed by alternative governance forms to yield performance. Results of path analysis indicated that **solidarity** increased performance in both the market-based exchange and the short-term unilateral agreement governance modes. Formalization enhanced **solidarity** in the market-based exchange mode, whereas both formalization and participation increased **solidarity** in the short- and long-term unilateral agreement governance modes. Only participation enhanced **solidarity** in the bilateral alliance governance mode.

REFERENCES:

Dahlstrom, Robert, Kevin M. McNeilly, and Thomas W. Speh (1996), "Buyer-Seller Relationships in the Procurement of Logistical Services," *JAMS*, 24 (2), 110–24.

Heide, Jan B. and George John (1992), "Do Norms Matter in Relationships?" *JM*, 58 (January), 71–85.

#884 *Solidarity (Supplier Relationship)*

SCALE ITEMS:

Please indicate your level of agreement with the following:

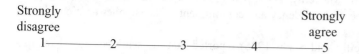

Strongly
disagree

Strongly
agree

1————2————3————4————5

1. Problems that arise in the course of this relationship are treated as joint rather than individual responsibilities.

2. The vendor and I are committed to improvements that may help the relationship as a whole, and not only the individual parties.

3. The vendor and I do not mind owing each other favors.

SCALE NAME: Solidarity (Wholesaler with Major Supplier)

SCALE DESCRIPTION: Lusch and Brown (1996) used this three-item, seven-point Likert-type scale to measure the efforts undertaken by a wholesaler toward preserving its relationship with the supplier. The authors referred to this measure as *wholesaler solidarity with supplier*, or WSOLID.

SCALE ORIGIN: Citing the work of Heide and John (1992), Lusch and Brown (1996) sought to assess the extent of relational behavior between distributors and their major suppliers by measuring the level of information exchange, flexibility, and solidarity characterizing the relationship. Whereas prior measures typically assessed the *expected* efforts of the parties toward preserving the relationship in a single measure, Lusch and Brown rephrased items adapted from Heide and John (1992), Heide and Milner (1992) and Kaufmann and Dant (1992) to create two separate measures. The current scale was used to assess the extent to which wholesalers *actually* engaged in solidarity efforts on behalf of the supplier; the second scale measured wholesaler perceptions of the extent to which their suppliers *actually* worked toward preserving the relationship with them. One item adapted from the original scales, "We do not mind owing our major supplier favors," was dropped from the final analysis.

SAMPLES: A systematic random sample of 3225 firms was drawn by Lusch and Brown (1996) from a mailing list of all U.S. merchant wholesalers and agents/brokers in 16 four-digit standard industrial classification code groups. The sample was further reduced by eliminating firms with more than 20 employees. General managers were identified as the key informants for the remaining firms and were sent a mail questionnaire. Incentives and a follow-up mailing resulted in an initial response rate of 28.8%. However, this study reported usable data specific only to the **454** respondents classified as wholesale distributors and excluded data from agent and broker firms. The authors reported that the average number of suppliers reported by wholesalers in the sample was 45, with the major supplier contributing an average of 49% of the firm's annual volume.

RELIABILITY: Lusch and Brown (1996) reported a reliability coefficient of **.829** for this scale.

VALIDITY: Lusch and Brown (1996) reported undertaking a thorough review of the practitioner and academic literature, as well as extensive practitioner pretesting, to ensure content validity. Confirmatory factor analysis confirmed that the measure represented one of six dimensions that composed relational behavior and demonstrated the unidimensionality of the measure. Convergent and discriminant validity were also assessed and found to be satisfactory, which indicated that the measure possessed adequate construct validity.

ADMINISTRATION: The scale was included as part of a self-administered mail survey. A $1 incentive and the promise of shared survey results were offered as participant incentives, and a personalized cover letter accompanied the survey packet. Undeliverable questionnaires were redirected to a replacement firm. A second mailing without monetary incentive was sent one month later. Lusch and Brown (1996) instructed respondents to answer all questions pertaining to major suppliers in the context of the supplier with which the wholesale distributor did the most business. Higher scores on the measure indicated that wholesalers expended more effort to preserve the relationship with its major supplier.

MAJOR FINDINGS: Lusch and Brown (1996) investigated how the type of dependency structure—wholesaler dependent on supplier, supplier dependent on wholesaler, or bilateral dependency—influenced whether a normative or explicit contract was used. Lusch and Brown (1996) also studied whether dependency structure and the type of contract influenced the performance of wholesale distributors. **Solidarity (wholesaler with major supplier)** represented one of six dimensions of relational behavior.

#885 *Solidarity (Wholesaler with Major Supplier)*

Findings indicated that a greater degree of relational behavior between the supplier and distributor was observed when more normative contracts governed the relationship or when greater levels of bilateral dependency between parties existed. When wholesalers maintained a more long-term outlook toward their relationship with the supplier, relational behavior was also enhanced. The use of explicit contracts was found to have no significant bearing on the degree of relational behavior exhibited between supplier and distributor.

REFERENCES:

Heide, Jan B. and Anne S. Miner (1992), "The Shadow of the Future: Effects of Anticipated Interaction and Frequency of Contact on Buyer-Seller Cooperation," *Academy of Management Journal*, 35 (June), 265–291.

———— and George John (1992), "Do Norms Matter in Marketing Relationships?" *JM*, 56 (April), 32–44.

Kaufmann, Patrick J. and Rajiv P. Dant (1992), "The Dimensions of Commercial Exchange," *Marketing Letters*, 3 (May), 171–185.

Lusch, Robert F. and James R. Brown (1996), "Interdependency, Contracting, and Relational Behavior in Marketing Channels," *JM*, 60 (October), 19–38.

SCALE ITEMS:

Strongly disagree — Strongly agree

1————2————3————4————5————6————7

1. When our major supplier incurs problems, we try to help.

2. We share in the problems that arise in the course of dealing with our major supplier.

3. We are committed to improvements that may benefit relationshiops with our major suppliler as a whole and not only ourselves.

SCALE NAME: Specialization

SCALE DESCRIPTION: Germain, Dröge, and Daugherty (1994) used ten dichotomous (yes/no) scale items to measure the number of specialized responsibilities from a list of ten for which at least one full-time specialist was employed.

SCALE ORIGIN: Germain, Dröge, and Daugherty (1994) stated the scale was a modified version of that used by Inkson, Pugh, and Hickson (1970).

SAMPLES: Germain, Dröge, and Daugherty (1994) randomly selected 1000 names from a sampling frame of 3280 members of the Council of Logistics Management. Forty-four mail questionnaires were returned undeliverable, and of the 956 surveys delivered, **183** usable surveys were returned. The majority of respondents were directors (54.7%) or managers (27.4%) within their respective firms. The manufacturing firms represented tended to be large and covered a wide range of industries; average annual sales were $1.98 billion, and the mean number of employees across the sample firms was 9740.

RELIABILITY: Germain, Dröge, and Daugherty (1994) reported a coefficient alpha of **.76** for the scale.

VALIDITY: Germain, Dröge, and Daugherty (1994) reported that a principal components factor analysis was used to assess the unidimensionality of the measure. The items loaded on a single factor with an eigenvalue greater than 1.

ADMINISTRATION: Germain, Dröge, and Daugherty (1994) stated that the scale was included with other measures in a self-administered survey that was delivered to respondents by mail. Nonrespondents were sent a second questionnaire in two weeks and reminded by telephone two weeks after the second mailing. Higher scores on the scale indicated a greater degree of specialization throughout the firm.

MAJOR FINDINGS: Germain, Dröge, and Daugherty (1994) proposed and tested a model linking environmental uncertainty, just-in-time (JIT) selling, and dimensions of organizational structure. The JIT selling practices were found to positively predict **specialization,** whereas, contrary to predictions, environmental uncertainty was unrelated to **specialization**.

REFERENCES:

Germain, Richard, Cornelia Dröge, and Patricia J. Daugherty (1994), "The Effect of Just-in-Time Selling on Organizational Structure: An Empirical Investigation," *JMR*, 31 (November), 471–83.

Inkson, J.H., Derek Pugh, and David Hickson (1970), "Organization, Context and Structure: An Abbreviated Replication," *Administrative Science Quarterly*, 15 (September), 318–29.

SCALE ITEMS:*

At least one full-time specialist deals with...

Yes = 1
No = 0

1. Warehouse facilities design.

2. Plant facilities design.

#886 *Specialization*

3. Material handling.

4. Market research.

5. Sales forecasting.

6. Distribution equipment procurement.

7. Plant or warehouse facility location.

8. Production scheduling.

9. Transportation scheduling.

10. Manufacturing quality control.

*Verbatim instructions were not provided; however, they were likely similar to the instructions shown here.

SCALE NAME: Spiritually Based Coping Tactics

SCALE DESCRIPTION: Strutton and Lumpkin (1994) adapted this three-item, five-point subscale from the Ways of Coping Checklist Scale developed by Folkman and Lazarus (1980, 1985). It attempts to measure the extent to which a salesperson uses spiritually based self-improvement tactics to cope with stressful customer sales presentations. In this study, the original items were screened for applicability to the sales setting. The remaining items were then subjected to factor analysis in a manner similar to Folkman and colleagues' (1986) and the subscales identified in that manner.

SCALE ORIGIN: These items were adapted by Strutton and Lumpkin (1994) for a sales setting from the Ways of Coping Checklist (Folkman and Lazarus 1980, 1985). The original measure contained 43 items developed to measure problem-focused (24 items) and emotion-focused (19 items) tactics for handling stressful situations.

SAMPLES: Strutton and Lumpkin's (1994) sample was a nonprobability sample of **101** nonmanager salespeople from three industries: communications technology (60), textiles (22), and furniture (19), predominantly in the southern United States.

RELIABILITY: Strutton and Lumpkin (1994) reported a Cronbach's alpha of **.79** for this scale.

VALIDITY: No specific validity tests were reported by Strutton and Lumpkin (1994). This subscale was not identified as a separate subscale in Folkman and colleagues' (1986) earlier work. In Folkman and colleagues' (1986) work, the items that constitute this scale were subsumed in the original "directed problem solving" and "positive reinterpretation" subscales of the problem-focused coping factors measure.

ADMINISTRATION: Strutton and Lumpkin (1994) asked respondents to describe the most stressful customer-related situation they had encountered during a sales presentation during the previous two months. They were then asked to respond to the items in the scale along with other scales and demographic questions. Higher scores on the scale indicated that spiritually based coping tactics for dealing with stress were used to a greater extent.

MAJOR FINDINGS: In Strutton and Lumpkin's (1994) study, the **spiritually based coping tactics** measure was not found to be significantly related to sales presentation effectiveness of all subscales on a self-reported measure of presentation effectiveness.

REFERENCES:
Folkman, Susan and Richard S. Lazarus (1980), "An Analysis of Coping in a Middle-Aged Community Sample," *Journal of Health and Social Behavior*, 21 (September), 219–39.

———— and ———— (1985), "If It Changes, It Must Be a Process: Study of Emotion and Coping During Three Stages of a College Examination," *Journal of Personality and Social Psychology*, 48 (January), 150–70.

————, ————, Christine Dunkel-Schetter, Anita DeLongis, and Rand J. Gruen (1986), "Dynamics of a Stressful Encounter: Cognitive Appraisal, Coping, and Encounter Outcomes," *Journal of Personality and Social Psychology*, 50 (May), 992–1003.

Strutton, David and James R. Lumpkin (1994), "Problem- and Emotion-Focused Coping Dimensions and Sales Presentation Effectiveness," *JAMS*, 22 (1), 28–37.

#887 *Spiritually Based Coping Tactics*

SCALE ITEMS:

Directions: Indicate the extent to which you used each of the following tactics to cope with a stressful sales presentation experience:

Not used at all   Used a great deal

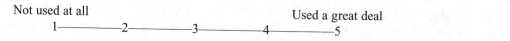

1. Rediscovered what is important in life.

2. I prayed.

3. Found new faith.

SCALE NAME: Strategy (Innovation)

SCALE DESCRIPTION: Pelham and Wilson (1996) used a five-item, seven-point scale to measure the degree to which a firm innovates or differentiates through product refinement and new product development, quality control, manufacturing innovation, and appealing to higher-priced market segments. Pelham and Wilson (1996) referred to this scale as *innovation/differentiation strategy* in their article.

SCALE ORIGIN: It appears that the scale was first administered by the Center for Entrepreneurship at Eastern Michigan University. The extent to which Pelham and Wilson (1996) were involved with the Center and the development of the scale itself is unclear.

SAMPLES: A longitudinal database developed by the Center for Entrepreneurship at Eastern Michigan University provided the data for the study. The Center's full panel consists of data provided by the CEOs of 370 Michigan firms, representing 71% of the firms contacted for initial participation. The data used by Pelham and Wilson (1996) were specific only to those firms providing full information with respect to all measures of interest for both the current and previous years. Of those **68** firms, 32% were classified as wholesalers, 29% as manufacturers, 26% as business services, and 13% as construction. Firm size ranged from 15 to 65 employees, with the average number of employees equaling 23.

RELIABILITY: Pelham and Wilson (1996) reported an alpha of **.70** for this scale.

VALIDITY: Pelham and Wilson (1996) stated that factor loadings and LISREL measurement model squared multiple correlations were taken as evidence of convergent and discriminant validity.

ADMINISTRATION: Pelham and Wilson (1996) did not provide details with respect to how data were collected from panel members by the Center of Entrepreneurship. Higher scores on the scale indicated a greater tendency to innovate or differentiate through manufacturing processes, quality control, target marketing, and product development and refinement.

MAJOR FINDINGS: Pelham and Wilson (1996) investigated the relative impact of market orientation on small business performance compared with that of market structure, firm structure, firm strategy, and relative product quality. Regression analysis was used to test year-to-year differences in most variables, as well as parameters based on independent and lagged variables. Changes in the **innovation/differentiation strategy** of the firm had no significant influence on any performance variable tested. However, lagged regression results indicated that previously high levels of **innovative strategy** positively influenced the growth/share of small firms, perhaps indicating that the results of such a strategy required time to affect performance.

REFERENCES:
Pelham, Alfred M. and David T. Wilson (1996), "A Longitudinal Study of the Impact of Market Structure, Firm Structure, Strategy, and Market Orientation Culture on Dimensions of Small-Firm Performance," *JAMS*, 24 (1), 27–43.

#888 *Strategy (Innovation)*

SCALE ITEMS:

Directions: Indicate the degree to which your firm emphasized each competitive method over the past five years.

Not   Major constant
considered   emphasis

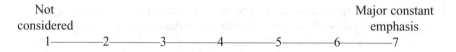

1———2———3———4———5———6———7

1. New product development.

2. Extremely strict product quality control procedures.

3. Developing and refining existing products.

4. Innovation in manufacturing process.

5. Products in higher priced market segments.

SCALE NAME: Strategy (Low Cost)

SCALE DESCRIPTION: Pelham and Wilson (1996) used a three-item, seven-point scale to measure the degree to which a firm employed a lost-cost strategy in production, pricing, and market targeting.

SCALE ORIGIN: It appears that the scale was first administered by the Center for Entrepreneurship at Eastern Michigan University. The extent to which Pelham and Wilson (1996) were involved with the Center and the development of the scale itself is unclear.

SAMPLES: A longitudinal database developed by the Center for Entrepreneurship at Eastern Michigan University provided the data for the study. The Center's full panel consists of data provided by the CEOs of 370 Michigan firms, representing 71% of the firms contacted for initial participation. The data used by Pelham and Wilson (1996) were specific only to those firms providing full information with respect to all measures of interest for both the current and previous years. Of those **68** firms, 32% were classified as wholesalers, 29% as manufacturers, 26% as business services, and 13% as construction. Firm size ranged from 15 to 65 employees, with the average number of employees equaling 23.

RELIABILITY: Pelham and Wilson (1996) reported an alpha of **.72** for this scale.

VALIDITY: Pelham and Wilson (1996) stated that factor loadings and LISREL measurement model squared multiple correlations were taken as evidence of convergent and discriminant validity.

ADMINISTRATION: Pelham and Wilson (1996) did not provide details with respect to how data were collected from panel members by the Center of Entrepreneurship. Higher scores on the scale indicated a greater tendency to use a low-cost strategy with respect to production, pricing, and target marketing.

MAJOR FINDINGS: Pelham and Wilson (1996) investigated the relative impact of market orientation on small business performance compared with that of market structure, firm structure, firm strategy, and relative product quality. Regression analysis was used to test year-to-year differences in most variables, as well as parameters based on independent and lagged variables. Key findings indicated that increasing use of a **low-cost strategy** negatively influenced the change in new product success but positively influenced changes in the growth/market share of the firm. The authors cautioned, however, that the lack of significant lagged regression parameters for **low-cost strategy** in any model suggests that the **low-cost strategy** provides only a short-term influence on small firm performance.

REFERENCES:

Pelham, Alfred M. and David T. Wilson (1996), "A Longitudinal Study of the Impact of Market Structure, Firm Structure, Strategy, and Market Orientation Culture on Dimensions of Small-Firm Performance," *JAMS*, 24 (1), 27–43.

SCALE ITEMS:

Directions: Indicate the degree to which your firm emphasized each competitive method over the past five years.

```
    Not                                          Major constant
 considered                                        emphasis
    1————2————3————4————5————6————7
```

1. Pricing below competitors.

2. Continuing, overriding concern for lowest cost per unit.

3. Product in lower priced market segments.

SCALE NAME: Supervisory Consideration

SCALE DESCRIPTION: Ramaswami (1996) used this five-item, five-point Likert-type summated ratings scale to measure employee perceptions of the degree to which their supervisors developed a work climate of psychological support, helpfulness, friendliness, and mutual trust and respect.

SCALE ORIGIN: The scale appears to be original to Ramaswami (1996).

SAMPLES: Ramaswami (1996) received usable surveys from **318** of the 1159 American Marketing Association (AMA) members who were randomly selected from the AMA's membership list.

RELIABILITY: Ramaswami (1996) reported a coefficient alpha of **.89** for the scale.

VALIDITY: Ramaswami (1996) used a confirmatory factor analysis to assess the unidimensionality of the measure in conjunction with measures of supervisory knowledge and participation and found that each scale tapped distinct dimensions of the supervisory context.

ADMINISTRATION: Ramaswami (1996) indicated that the scale was self-administered, along with many other measures, in a mail survey format. Higher scores on the scale indicated that employees strongly believed their supervisors developed a supportive, helpful, friendly, and trusting work environment.

MAJOR FINDINGS: Ramaswami (1996) investigated both traditional and contingency theories of negative employee responses to marketing control systems. Contrary to expectations, **supervisory consideration,** participation, and knowledge had no effect on employee dysfunctional behavior, regardless of whether output or process controls were used.

REFERENCES:

Ramaswami, Sridhar N. (1996), "Marketing Controls and Dysfunctional Employee Behaviors: A Test of Traditional and Contingency Theory Postulates," *JM*, 60 (April), 105–20.

SCALE ITEMS:

Strongly agree 1————2————3————4————5 Strongly disagree

My supervisor...

1. Is friendly and approachable.

2. Helps make my job more pleasant.

3. Does little things to make it pleasant to be a member of the work unit.

4. Treats all people (s)he supervises equally.

5. Looks out for the personal welfare of group members.

SCALE NAME: Supervisory Knowledge

SCALE DESCRIPTION: A six-item, five-point Likert-type summated ratings scale measuring the degree to which an employee perceives that his or her supervisors are knowledgeable and familiar with their job and thus can specify performance objectives and assess performance.

SCALE ORIGIN: The scale appears to be original to Ramaswami (1996).

SAMPLES: Ramaswami (1996) received usable surveys from **318** of the 1159 American Marketing Association (AMA) members who were randomly selected from the AMA's membership list.

RELIABILITY: Ramaswami (1996) reported a coefficient alpha of **.93** for the scale.

VALIDITY: Ramaswami (1996) used a confirmatory factor analysis to assess the unidimensionality of the measure in conjunction with measures of supervisory participation and consideration and found that each scale tapped distinct dimensions of the supervisory context.

ADMINISTRATION: Ramaswami (1996) indicated that the scale was self-administered, along with many other measures, in a mail survey format. Higher scores on the scale indicated that employees strongly believed their supervisor's knowledge and familiarity with their jobs enabled them to specify performance objectives and evaluate their performance.

MAJOR FINDINGS: Ramaswami (1996) investigated both traditional and contingency theories of negative employee responses to marketing control systems. Contrary to expectations, **supervisory knowledge**, consideration, and participation had no effect on employee dysfunctional behavior, regardless of whether output or process controls were used.

REFERENCES:
Ramaswami, Sridhar N. (1996), "Marketing Controls and Dysfunctional Employee Behaviors: A Test of Traditional and Contingency Theory Postulates," *JM*, 60 (April), 105–20.

SCALE ITEMS:

Strongly disagree 1————2————3————4————5 Strongly agree

1. My supervisor knows how to accomplish the work I normally encounter.

2. My supervisor is intimately familiar with the day-to-day decisions related to my work.

3. My supervisor has developed an excellent working knowledge of my job.

4. I am confident that my supervisor can assess my job performance.

5. My supervisor can specify the most important variables to monitor in my work.

6. My supervisor can specify performance objectives to cover the range of activities I perform.

SCALE NAME: Supervisory Participation

SCALE DESCRIPTION: Ramaswami (1996) used this four-item, five-point Likert-type summated ratings scale to measure employee perceptions of the extent of influence that they have on their supervisors regarding matters related to their job.

SCALE ORIGIN: The scale appears to be original to Ramaswami (1996).

SAMPLES: Ramaswami (1996) received usable surveys from **318** of the 1159 American Marketing Association (AMA) members who were randomly selected from the AMA's membership list.

RELIABILITY: Ramaswami (1996) reported a coefficient alpha of **.85** for the scale.

VALIDITY: Ramaswami (1996) used a confirmatory factor analysis to assess the unidimensionality of the measure in conjunction with measures of supervisory knowledge and consideration and found that each scale tapped distinct dimensions of the supervisory context.

ADMINISTRATION: Ramaswami (1996) indicated that the scale was self-administered, along with many other measures, in a mail survey format. Higher scores on the scale indicated that employees strongly believed that they were influential with their supervisors in matters related to their work.

MAJOR FINDINGS: Ramaswami (1996) investigated both traditional and contingency theories of negative employee responses to marketing control systems. Contrary to expectations, **supervisory participation,** consideration, and knowledge had no effect on employee dysfunctional behavior, regardless of whether output or process controls were used.

REFERENCES:

Ramaswami, Sridhar N. (1996), "Marketing Controls and Dysfunctional Employee Behaviors: A Test of Traditional and Contingency Theory Postulates," *JM*, 60 (April), 105–20.

SCALE ITEMS:

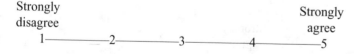

Strongly
disagree
1————2————3————4————5

Strongly
agree

1. I generally feel I have a lot of influence on what goes on in my work unit.

2. I feel that I can influence the decisions of my supervisor regarding things of concern to me.

3. My supervisor usually asks for my opinion on issues related to my work.

4. It is easy to get my ideas across to my supervisor on issues relating to improving my job or changing the set-up in some way.

SCALE NAME: Supervisory Support

SCALE DESCRIPTION: Babin and Boles (1996) used this five-item, five-point Likert-type scale to assess the degree to which supervisors supported and demonstrated concern for employees.

SCALE ORIGIN: Babin and Boles (1996) indicated that the items representing this construct were adapted from a subscale of Moos's (1981) working environment scale. The authors stated that a preliminary analysis of all measures used in their study led to the preclusion of several items from further analysis, but they did not provide specific details.

SAMPLES: Babin and Boles (1996) surveyed a convenience sample of 390 food service workers employed by full-service restaurants located in a major southern U.S. metropolitan area. A total of **261** usable responses were returned. The majority of respondents were high school graduates (99%), of whom 80% had some college education, which indicated that the majority of respondents were students.

RELIABILITY: Babin and Boles (1996) calculated a coefficient alpha of **.71** for this measure.

VALIDITY: Babin and Boles (1996) tested the measurement model using confirmatory factor analysis. Although the goodness-of-fit index of .861 was somewhat low, the observed loading estimates and construct reliabilities provided evidence of the convergent validity of the measure. An examination of the proportion of variance extracted in each construct compared with the square of the phi (ϕ) suggested that the scale possessed discriminant validity.

ADMINISTRATION: The scale was included by Babin and Boles (1996) with other measures as part of a self-administered questionnaire distributed to employees at their place of work and returned by self-addressed, postage-paid reply envelopes. Higher scores on the scale reflected a greater level of supervisor support and concern for the employee.

MAJOR FINDINGS: The influence of supervisor support and coworker involvement on the role stress, performance, and job satisfaction of food service workers was investigated by Babin and Boles (1996). Increased perceptions of a **supportive and concerned management team** reduced employee role conflict and role ambiguity and increased job satisfaction.

REFERENCES:

Babin, Barry J. and James S. Boles (1996), "The Effects of Perceived Co-Worker Involvement and Supervisor Support on Service Provider Role Stress, Performance and Job Satisfaction," *JR*, 72 (1), 57–75.

Moos, Rudolph H. (1981), *Work Environment Scale Manual*. Palo Alto, CA: Consulting Psychologists Press.

#893 *Supervisory Support*

SCALE ITEMS:

Strongly   Strongly
disagree   agree

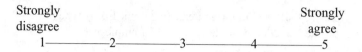

1————————2————————3————————4————————5

1. Supervisors tend to talk down to employees. **(r)***

2. Supervisors usually give full credit to ideas contributed by employees.

3. Supervisors often criticize employees over minor things. **(r)***

4. Supervisors expect far too much from employees. **(r)***

5. Supervisors really stand up for people.

*Although the appendix listing the scales used by Babin and Boles (1996) did not indicate that these items were reversed, this was probably an oversight given the nature and purpose of the measure.

SCALE NAME: Support (Organizational)

SCALE DESCRIPTION: Kelley, Longfellow, and Malehorn (1996) used this 16-item scale in five- and six-point Likert formats to assess the degree to which an employee perceives that the organization values his or her contributions and cares about his or her well-being.

SCALE ORIGIN: Kelley, Longfellow, and Malehorn (1996) indicated that the organizational support construct was measured using the survey of perceived organizational support (SPOS) originally developed by Eisenberger and colleagues (1986). A six-point Likert format was used with Sample 1, and a five-point Likert format was used with Sample 2.

SAMPLES: In the first sample, Kelley, Longfellow, and Malehorn (1996) surveyed all 122 customer-contact personnel employed by a bank located in the Midwest United States, and **113** usable responses were obtained, primarily from tellers (88) and customer service representatives (25). A stratified random sample of 381 insurance agents working in a single state of a large regional insurance company was also undertaken. In this second sample, 239 agents representing 75 of the 77 different agencies associated with the company responded, but complete information was obtained from only **185** of these individuals.

RELIABILITY: Kelley, Longfellow, and Malehorn (1996) calculated coefficient alphas of **.948** and **.953** for this measure in Samples 1 and 2, respectively.

VALIDITY: Kelley, Longfellow, and Malehorn (1996) did not specifically discuss the validity of the measures.

ADMINISTRATION: In Sample 1, the measure was included in a questionnaire administered to customer-contact bank employees during regularly scheduled weekly meetings held in 15 branch offices. In Sample 2, Kelley, Longfellow, and Malehorn (1996) included the scale as part of a self-administered questionnaire that was delivered by mail. All responses were converted to z-scores prior to analysis because of the difference in response formats. Higher scores on the scale reflected stronger perceptions on the part of the employee that the organization cared for his or her well-being and valued his or her contributions.

MAJOR FINDINGS: Kelley, Longfellow, and Malehorn (1996) investigated the antecedents to service employees' use of routine, creative, and deviant discretion in the banking and insurance industries. **Organizational support** was positively related to creative discretion and routine discretion, but the relationship between organizational support and deviant discretion was not significant.

REFERENCES:

Eisenberger, Robert, Robin Huntington, Steven Hutchison and Debra Sowa (1986), "Perceived Organizational Support," *Journal of Applied Psychology*, 71 (3), 500–507.

Kelley, Scott W., Timothy Longfellow, and Jack Malehorn (1996), "Organizational Determinants of Service Employees' Exercise of Routine, Creative, and Deviant Discretion," *JR*, 72 (2), 135–57.

#894 *Support (Organizational)*

SCALE ITEMS:

Sample 1 response format:

Sample 2 response format:

1. The organization values my contribution to its well-being.

2. If the organization could hire (contract) someone to replace me at a lower salary (commission) it would do so. **(r)**

3. The organization fails to appreciate any extra effort from me. **(r)**

4. The organization strongly considers my goals and values.

5. The organization would ignore any complaint from me. **(r)**

6. The organizational disregards my best interests when it makes decisions that affect me. **(r)**

7. Help is available from the organization when I have a problem.

8. The organization really cares about my well-being.

9. Even if I did the best job possible, the organization would fail to notice. **(r)**

10. The organization is willing to help me when I need a special favor.

11. The organization cares about my general satisfaction.

12. If given the opportunity, the organization would take advantage of me. **(r)**

13. The organization shows very little concern for me. **(r)**

14. The organization cares about my opinions.

15. The organization takes pride in my accomplishments.

16. The organization tries to make my job as interesting as possible.

SCALE NAME: Support to Foreign Distributor/Subsidiary

SCALE DESCRIPTION: Cavusgil and Zou (1994) used this three-item, five-point scale to assess the level of promotional, sales force training, and overall support offered by an exporter to a foreign distributor or subsidiary.

SCALE ORIGIN: The scale is original to Cavusgil and Zou (1994), who adopted a parsimonious multiphase research design to operationalize and test measures within their proposed conceptual framework. Preliminary interviews with export marketing managers were used to verify and improve scale items suggested by the literature. Data were collected using the resulting measures and split into two groups. An exploratory factor analysis performed on the analysis subsample using Varimax rotation resulted in 17 factors. Only items whose meanings were consistent with the conceptualization of the measure were retained.

SAMPLES: Export marketing managers directly involved with export ventures from 79 firms in 16 industries provided Cavusgil and Zou (1994) with information pertinent to **202** export venture cases. Of the 202 venture cases analyzed, 47.5% were related to consumer goods, 42.6% related to industrial goods, and the remainder could not be classified clearly. All respondents were from manufacturing firms with average annual sales in excess of $200 million. The sample was split into analysis and hold-out subsamples, each of which contained **101** export venture cases.

RELIABILITY: Cavusgil and Zou (1994) reported a coefficient alpha of **.853** for this measure.

VALIDITY: Cavusgil and Zou (1994) stated that the content validity of the measure was established during the preliminary interviews. Confirmatory factor analysis performed on the hold-out sample demonstrated patterns of item-to-item correlations and item-factor correlations suggestive of measure unidimensionality.

ADMINISTRATION: Cavusgil and Zou (1994) developed a semistructured instrument that outlined a list of variables and intended scales but contained no specific questions. This allowed the researchers to tailor questions to the specific context of the export venture being discussed or probed during the personal interview. During each in-depth interview, two experienced international marketing researchers independently assigned a score to each of the variables. Scoring was based on the researcher's judgment about the executive's answer to the questions pertinent to the variable, as well as the words given by the executive when expressing an answer. Following the interview, the researchers met to discuss their ratings, resolved differences of opinion, and finalized the scores assigned to each variable. Interrater reliability averaged approximately 80% prior to resolving these differences. Higher scores on the scale indicated that exporters were perceived as offering greater levels of promotional, sales force training, and overall support to a foreign distributor or subsidiary.

MAJOR FINDINGS: Cavusgil and Zou (1994) investigated the relationship between marketing strategy and performance in the context of export ventures. **Support to foreign distributor/subsidiary** was one of five factors found to represent the export marketing strategy in an exploratory factor analysis. This structure was confirmed through confirmatory factor analysis with the hold-out sample. Tests of the overall model indicated the level of **support to foreign distributor/subsidiaries** was related strongly and positively to the technology orientation of the industry and the commitment to the export venture and moderately and positively to export market competitiveness.

#895 *Support to Foreign Distributor/Subsidiary*

REFERENCES:

Cavusgil, S. Tamer and Shaoming Zou (1994), "Marketing Strategy-Performance Relationship: An Investigation of the Empirical Link in Export Market Ventures," *JM*, 58 (January), 1–21.

SCALE ITEMS:

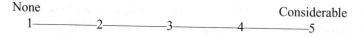

None
Considerable
1————2————3————4————5

1. Overall support to foreign distributor/subsidiary.

2. Amount of training to sales force of foreign distributor/subsidiary.

3. Extent of promotion support provided to foreign distributor/subsidiary.

SCALE NAME: Supportive Actions (Wholesaler)

SCALE DESCRIPTION: This 17-item, 11-point scale was used by Chatterjee, Hyvönen, and Anderson (1995) to measure retailer perceptions of how well the wholesaler's actions on each dimension supported them in the management of their store. Chatterjee, Hyvönen, and Anderson (1995) refer to this scale as the *role performance of the focal wholesaler*.

SCALE ORIGIN: The scale appears to be original to Chatterjee, Hyvönen, and Anderson (1995), who assessed the unidimensionality of the measure using factor analysis and the reliability of the scale using calculations of coefficient alpha. No items were deleted from the measure.

SAMPLES: Chatterjee, Hyvönen, and Anderson (1995) sampled a cross-section of 305 food and grocery retailers whose names had been submitted by two major wholesalers working in the Finnish market. A total of **236** usable questionnaires were received for an effective response rate of 77.4%. The sample was described as being well distributed across regions of the country, store categories, and store size.

RELIABILITY: Chatterjee, Hyvönen, and Anderson (1995) reported a coefficient alpha of **.90** for this measure.

VALIDITY: Chatterjee, Hyvönen, and Anderson (1995) examined the correlation matrix of the measures used in their study and stated that the low intercorrelations exhibited suggested that the measures offered discriminant validity.

ADMINISTRATION: Although the study was clearly identified to potential respondents as academic in orientation, the questionnaire was administered in Finnish by members of the Finnish Office of Free Trade to a key informant, typically the top manager or owner of the retail store. The questions were close-ended and had been previously translated and pretested. It was not clear whether the survey was administered at the retailer's place of business or if retailers came to the Finnish Office of Free Trade. Chatterjee, Hyvönen, and Anderson (1995) indicated that retailers were asked to answer the survey in the context of the focal wholesaler that had provided their name for the study. Higher scores on the scale indicated that a retailer perceived the wholesalers' actions as being highly supportive.

MAJOR FINDINGS: Chatterjee, Hyvönen, and Anderson (1995) investigated purchasing decisions in closed markets with respect to the choice of a concentrated versus balanced sourcing strategy. The better the **wholesaler's support and role performance** in the judgment of the retailer, the more likely retailers were to increase their concentration of purchases from that wholesaler.

REFERENCES:
Chatterjee, Sharmila C., Saara Hyvönen, and Erin Anderson (1995), "Concentrated vs. Balanced Sourcing: An Examination of Retailer Purchasing Decisions in Closed Markets," *JR*, 71 (1), 23–46.

SCALE ITEMS:
Directions: Please indicate how well various cooperative actions with this wholesaler support the management of your store.

Not
at all

Supports
extremely well

0———1———2———3———4———5———6———7———8———9———10

#896 *Supportive Actions (Wholesaler)*

1. Product varieties and number of sizes in this wholesaler's inventory from which to choose our supplies.

2. Product selection in joint campaigns.

3. Marketing support provided by this wholesaler.

4. The wholesale management's cooperativeness.

5. Discount policy and terms of payment of this wholesaler.

6. Favorable margins of supplies.

7. Purchasing from this wholesaler in general.

8. "Invoice via wholesaler"—principle in connection with direct industry purchases.

9. Wholesaler organized local marketing programs.

10. Wholesaler organized national marketing programs.

11. Promptness of deliveries.

12. Training programs and methods.

13. Establishment of retail outlets policy.

14. Planning of store facilities and equipment services.

15. Sharing of promotional expenses with this wholesaler.

16. The business premises franchised by this wholesaler.

Please indicate how useful you find the wholesaler support services and other incentives as related to the *costs* that you have to pay as a contribution to the wholesaler. If your payment is 50, what return have you got on your money?

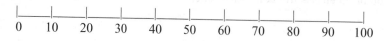

|___|___|___|___|___|___|___|___|___|___|
0   10   20   30   40   50   60   70   80   90   100

SCALE NAME: Switching Costs

SCALE DESCRIPTION: Ping (1997) used this four-item, five-point Likert-type scale to assess the magnitude of perceived cost and additional effort required to switch suppliers.

SCALE ORIGIN: Ping (1997) noted that the scale was first published in one of his earlier articles (Ping 1993). In developing the scale, Ping (1993) generated items on the basis of presurvey interviews with hardware retailers and a review of the relevant literature. The purification process began with nine academicians evaluating how well the items fit the construct; those misclassified by more than one judge were eliminated. The resulting measure was pretested in two different phases. The first pretest sought to clarify possible misinterpretations. Responses from 63 hardware retailers in the second pretest were used in analyzing the psychometric properties of the measures using item-to-total correlations, ordered similarity coefficients, and coefficient alpha computations. The final purification of the measure was based on LISREL analysis of data provided by 288 respondents as reported in Ping's (1993) study. Items were deleted if internal consistency was improved without detracting from the content validity of the measure. Tests of the discriminant and convergent validity of the measure were also undertaken, and the results were found to be satisfactory.

SAMPLES: Ping (1997) used a systematic random sampling procedure of U.S. hardware retailers to generate the 600 hardware retailers sampled in his study. Usable responses were received from **204** people. The sampling frame was taken from a hardware retailing trade publication's subscription list.

RELIABILITY: Ping (1997) reported a coefficient alpha of **.94** for this measure.

VALIDITY: Ping (1997) conducted a confirmatory factor analysis to test the unidimensionality and construct validity of the measure. The measure was judged to be unidimensional, and the average variance extracted demonstrated the scale's convergent and discriminatory validity. Ping (1997) also stated that the measure offered content validity.

ADMINISTRATION: The scale was included with other measures as part of a self-administered questionnaire that was delivered by mail. Nonrespondents received as many as three postcard reminders. Ping (1997) used a key informant approach, in which key informants represented a single individual, typically a manager, owner, or executive of the hardware store. Higher scores on the scale reflected greater perceived costs being associated with switching from the current wholesaler to another supplier.

MAJOR FINDINGS: Ping (1997) proposed and empirically examined several antecedents to voice in a business-to-business context. The results of his study indicated that cost-of-exit was a second-order construct with first-order factor indicators of alternative supplier attractiveness, investment in the relationship, and **switching costs**. Increasing the cost-of-exit was found to increase the likelihood of voice.

REFERENCES:
Ping, Robert A., Jr. (1993), "The Effects of Satisfaction and Structural Constraints on Retailer Exiting, Voice, Loyalty, Opportunism, and Neglect," *JR*, 69 (Fall), 320–52.
———— (1997), "Voice in Business-to-Business Relationships: Cost-of-Exit and Demographic Antecedents," *JR*, 73 (2), 261–81.

#897 *Switching Costs*

SCALE ITEMS:

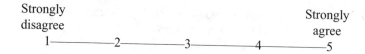

1. All things considered, the company would lose a lot in changing primary wholesalers.

2. Generally speaking, the costs in time, money, effort, and grief to switch primary wholesalers would be high.

3. Overall, I would spend a lot and lose a lot if I changed primary wholesalers.

4. Considering everything, the costs to stop doing business with the <u>current</u> wholesaler and start up with the <u>alternative</u> wholesaler would be high.

SCALE NAME: Switching Costs (Vendor-Related)

SCALE DESCRIPTION: Heide and Weiss (1995) used this three-item, seven-point Likert-type scale to measure a buyer's anticipated time investment and training costs related to developing a relationship with new vendor.

SCALE ORIGIN: The scale is original to Heide and Weiss (1995). Items were initially developed in accordance with the conceptual definition of the construct, then modified on the basis of field interviews, discussions with industry observers, and trade journal information. The scale was pretested, revised, and then pretested again before final administration.

SAMPLES: Pretests of the questionnaire were conducted with two different small groups of previous workstation buyers. In the final study, Heide and Weiss (1995) drew a random sample of 900 firms from Installed Technology International's list of firms that had recently purchased workstations. Key inform- ants were identified from this list and contacted by telephone, and 466 of them agreed to participate in the study and were sent a mail questionnaire. Follow-up telephone calls and a second mailing resulted in **215** usable questionnaires being returned. Industries represented by respondents included computers (31.4%), manufacturing (22.4%), medical (6.2%), services (15.2%), and other (24.8%).

RELIABILITY: Heide and Weiss (1995) reported a coefficient alpha of **.79** for this scale.

VALIDITY: Heide and Weiss (1995) initially evaluated the measure on the basis of item-to-total corre- lations and exploratory factor analysis. Confirmatory factor analysis was then used to establish unidi- mensionality. Evidence of discriminant validity was provided by a series of chi-square tests on the respec- tive factor correlations.

ADMINISTRATION: The measure was included in a self-administered mail survey. Heide and Weiss (1995) indicated that respondents were instructed to answer all questions in the context of their organi- zation's most recent workstation purchase. Higher scores on the switching cost measure indicated a greater anticipated time commitment and a greater need for employee retraining to develop a relationship with a new vendor.

MAJOR FINDINGS: Heide and Weiss (1995) investigated how buyers working in high-technology markets approached decisions in the consideration and choice stages of the purchase process. Specifically, factors influencing whether buyers included new vendors at the consideration stage and whether they ultimately switched to a new vendor at the choice stage were investigated. When **switching costs** were perceived to be high, there was a reduced tendency to both consider additional vendors and switch from an existing supplier to a new vendor.

REFERENCES:
Heide, Jan B. and Allen M. Weiss (1995), "Vendor Consideration and Switching Behavior for Buyers in High-Technology Markets," *JM*, 59 (July), 30–43.

SCALE ITEMS:

Strongly disagree 1———2———3———4———5———6———7 Strongly agree

1. We thought that purchasing from a new supplier would require retraining for a number of our employees.

2. Our belief was that developing procedures to deal effectively with a new supplier would take a lot of time and effort.

3. We thought that developing working relationships with new suppliers would be a time-consuming process.

SCALE NAME: Taking Responsibility

SCALE DESCRIPTION: Strutton and Lumpkin (1994) adapted this three-item, five-point subscale from the Ways of Coping Checklist Scale developed by Folkman and Lazarus (1980, 1985). It attempts to measure the extent to which a salesperson uses taking responsibility for the situation as a tactic to cope with stressful customer sales presentations. In this study, the original items were screened for applicability to the sales setting. The remaining items were then subjected to factor analysis in a manner similar to Folkman and colleagues' (1986) and the subscales identified in that manner.

SCALE ORIGIN: These items were adapted by Strutton and Lumpkin (1994) for a sales setting from the Ways of Coping Checklist (Folkman and Lazarus 1980, 1985). The original measure contained 43 items developed to measure problem-focused (24 items) and emotion-focused (19 items) tactics for handling stressful situations.

SAMPLES: Strutton and Lumpkin's (1994) sample was a nonprobability sample of **101** nonmanager sale's people from three industries: communications technology (60), textiles (22), and furniture (19), predominantly in the southern United States.

RELIABILITY: Strutton and Lumpkin (1994) reported a Cronbach's alpha of **.61** for this scale.

VALIDITY: No specific validity tests were reported by Strutton and Lumpkin (1994). However, this subscale was identified as a separate subscale in Folkman and colleagues' (1986) earlier work.

ADMINISTRATION: Strutton and Lumpkin (1994) asked respondents to describe the most stressful customer-related situation they had encountered during a sales presentation during the previous two months. They were then asked to respond to the items in the scale along with other scales and demographic questions. Higher scores on the scale indicated that taking responsibility tactics for dealing with stress were used to a greater extent.

MAJOR FINDINGS: Strutton and Lumpkin (1994) found that **taking responsibility** was not significantly related to sales presentation effectiveness in a regression of all subscales on a self-reported measure of presentation effectiveness.

REFERENCES:

Folkman, Susan and Richard S. Lazarus (1980), "An Analysis of Coping in a Middle-Aged Community Sample," *Journal of Health and Social Behavior*, 21 (September), 219–39.

——— and ——— (1985), "If It Changes, It Must Be a Process: Study of Emotion and Coping During Three Stages of a College Examination," *Journal of Personality and Social Psychology*, 48 (January), 150–70.

———, ———, Christine Dunkel-Schetter, Anita DeLongis, and Rand J. Gruen (1986), "Dynamics of a Stressful Encounter: Cognitive Appraisal, Coping, and Encounter Outcomes," *Journal of Personality and Social Psychology*, 50 (May), 992–1003.

Strutton, David and James R. Lumpkin (1994), "Problem- and Emotion-Focused Coping Dimensions and Sales Presentation Effectiveness," *JAMS*, 22 (1), 28–37.

SCALE ITEMS:
Directions: Indicate the extent to which you used each of the following tactics to cope with a stressful sales presentation experience:

Not used at all   :____:____:____:____:____: Used a great deal
                    1   2   3   4   5

1. Criticized or lectured myself.

2. Made a promise to myself that next time things would be different.

3. Apologized or did something to make it up.

SCALE NAME: Tangible Attribute Certainty

SCALE DESCRIPTION: Smith and Andrews (1995) used this four-item, seven-point scale to measure the degree to which respondents felt confident that a printing and packaging firm could meet their standards for printing, collating, prepackaging, and drop-shipping services.

SCALE ORIGIN: The scale is original to Smith and Andrews (1995).

SAMPLES: Smith and Andrews (1995) sampled 2400 product/marketing managers who held primary responsibility for purchasing in-store displays and promotional materials. A total of **608** usable responses were received from individuals representing 19 industries.

RELIABILITY: Smith and Andrews (1995) reported a coefficient alpha of **.95** for the scale.

VALIDITY: Smith and Andrews (1995) conducted a series of tests to assess the validity of the measures. The structural equation measurement model provided a good fit with the data, and each relevant factor loading was large and significant at the .01 level, thereby providing evidence of the convergent validity of the measures. Six models, pairing each of the tangible and intangible fit and tangible and intangible certainty variables, were also estimated in which the correlations between pairs of constructs were restricted to unity. The significant chi-squares between the restricted models and the original unrestricted model provided strong evidence of the discriminant validity of the measures.

ADMINISTRATION: Smith and Andrews (1995) included the scale with other measures as part of a self-administered survey that was delivered by mail. A $1 incentive and a cover letter stating that the goal of the research was to determine the marketability of a new product that could save respondents considerable amounts of time and money were included in the survey packet. Respondents were asked to read the concept statement then answer questions. Higher scores on the scale indicated greater confidence in the packaging and printing company's ability to meet the respondent's standards for printing, collating, prepackaging, and drop-shipping services.

MAJOR FINDINGS: In an industrial context, Smith and Andrews (1995) investigated how new product evaluations were influenced by the degree to which a company's skills were perceived to fit with those required to provide a new product and the perceived certainty that a company can deliver the proposed new product. Hypotheses were evaluated using structural equation modeling. **Tangible attribute certainty** positively influenced new product evaluations. **Tangible attribute certainty** also mediated the relationship between new product evaluations and tangible attribute fit to the extent that, when the effect of customer certainty was considered, the direct effect of tangible attribute fit on new product evaluations disappeared.

REFERENCES:
Smith, Daniel C. and Jonlee Andrews (1995), "Rethinking the Effect of Perceived Fit on Customers' Evaluations of New Products," *JAMS*, 23 (1), 4–14.

SCALE ITEMS:
Below is a brief description of a new promotion service concept. After reading the description, please respond to the questions that follow.

Concept: A company that is currently in the *printing and packaging industry* and manufactures its own materials would do the following:

Promotional program planning
Creative strategy development
Copywriting
Prompt printing and manufacturing of displays, printed materials, and other promotional products
Collation of finished materials
Prepackaging of finished materials
Timely drop-shipment of finished materials
Assessment of program success

Because this company manufactures its own materials it can offer these services for 10 to 15 percent less than full-service agencies.

How confident are you that a printing and packaging company could meet your promotion service needs in the following areas (circle the number that describes how you feel)?

1. Printing.

2. Collating.

3. Prepackaging.

4. Drop-shipping.

SCALE NAME: Tangible Attribute Fit

SCALE DESCRIPTION: Smith and Andrews (1995) used this four-item, seven-point scale to measure the degree to which respondents felt that the skills possessed by a printing and packaging firm were similar to the skills needed to meet the respondent's standards for printing, collating, prepackaging, and drop-shipping services.

SCALE ORIGIN: Although this scale is original to Smith and Andrews (1995), "fit" has been previously operationalized in terms of the perceived similarity between the new product and a firm's other products by Aaker and Keller (1990), Park, Milberg, and Lawson (1991), and Smith and Park (1992).

SAMPLES: Smith and Andrews (1995) sampled 2400 product/marketing managers who held primary responsibility for purchasing in-store displays and promotional materials. A total of **608** usable responses were received from individuals representing 19 industries.

RELIABILITY: Smith and Andrews (1995) reported a coefficient alpha of **.93** for the scale.

VALIDITY: Smith and Andrews (1995) conducted a series of tests to assess the validity of the measures. The structural equation measurement model provided a good fit with the data, and each relevant factor loading was large and significant at the .01 level, thereby providing evidence of the convergent validity of the measures. Six models, pairing each of the tangible and intangible fit and tangible and intangible certainty variables, were also estimated in which the correlations between pairs of constructs were restricted to unity. The significant chi-squares between the restricted models and the original unrestricted model provided strong evidence of the discriminant validity of the measures.

ADMINISTRATION: Smith and Andrews (1995) included the scale with other measures as part of a self-administered survey that was delivered by mail. A $1 incentive and a cover letter stating that the goal of the research was to determine the marketability of a new product that could save respondents considerable amounts of time and money were included in the survey packet. Respondents were asked to read the concept statement then answer questions. Higher scores on the scale indicated that respondents judged the tangible services provided by the packaging and printing company to be a good fit with and very similar to their company's standards in those areas.

MAJOR FINDINGS: In an industrial context, Smith and Andrews (1995) investigated how new product evaluations were influenced by the degree to which a company's skills were perceived to fit with those required to provide a new product and the perceived certainty that a company can deliver the proposed new product. Hypotheses were evaluated using structural equation modeling. **Tangible attribute fit** positively influenced new product evaluations. However, this relationship was mediated by tangible attribute certainty to the extent that, when the effect of customer certainty was considered, the direct effect of **tangible attribute fit** on new product evaluations disappeared.

REFERENCES:

Aaker, David A. and Kevin Lane Keller (1990), "Consumer Evaluation of Brand Extensions," *JM*, 54 (January), 27–41.

Park, C. Whan, Sandra Milberg, and Robert Lawson (1991), "Evaluation of Brand Extensions: The Role of Product Feature Similarity and Brand Concept Consistency," *JCR*, 18 (September), 185–93.

Smith, Daniel C. and Jonlee Andrews (1995), "Rethinking the Effect of Perceived Fit on Customers' Evaluations of New Products," *JAMS*, 23 (1), 4–14.

——— and C. Whan Park (1992), "The Effects of Brand Extensions on Market Share and Advertising Efficiency," *JMR*, 29 (August), 296–313.

SCALE ITEMS:
Below is a brief description of a new promotion service concept. After reading the description, please respond to the questions that follow.

Concept: A company that is currently in the *printing and packaging industry* and manufactures its own materials would do the following:

Promotional program planning
Creative strategy development
Copywriting
Prompt printing and manufacturing of displays, printed materials, and other promotional products
Collation of finished materials
Prepackaging of finished materials
Timely drop-shipment of finished materials
Assessment of program success

Because this company manufactures its own materials it can offer these services for 10 to 15 percent less than full-service agencies.

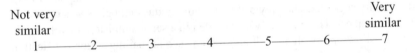

Not very
similar

Very
similar

1———2———3———4———5———6———7

In your opinion, how similar are the skills possessed by a printing and packaging company to the skills needed to meet your promotion needs in the following areas?

1. Printing.

2. Collating.

3. Prepackaging.

4. Drop-shipping.

SCALE NAME: Target Market Focus

SCALE DESCRIPTION: Frazier and Lassar (1996) used this three-item, five-point Likert-type scale to measure the extent to which a manufacturer concentrates on a narrow spectrum of the general market.

SCALE ORIGIN: The scale is original to Frazier and Lassar (1996), who generated items through personal interviews with manufacturers and retailers in the electronics, pet food, and hair care products industries. The authors examined intercorrelations among the items and dropped those exhibiting low correlations.

SAMPLES: Frazier and Lassar (1996) attempted to collect data related to 219 brands of stereo speakers from key informants representing 209 manufacturing firms. For manufacturers with multiple brands, only brands produced and marketed by independent divisions were treated as separate observations. A total of **85** usable questionnaires representing brands marketed by 84 manufacturers were returned. Of the 85 brands, 58 were home speakers, 22 were automotive speakers, and 5 were specialty speakers.

RELIABILITY: Frazier and Lassar (1996) reported a coefficient alpha of **.74** for this measure.

VALIDITY: Frazier and Lassar (1996) stated that an exploratory factor analysis was used to assess the unidimensionality and discriminant validity of the scale.

ADMINISTRATION: Three versions of the questionnaire were created by Frazier and Lassar (1996), one each for home, car, and specialty speakers. The only difference among questionnaires was the wording used to identify the different speakers. The measure was included in a self-administered mail survey. Nonrespondents received first a follow-up telephone call and then a second mailing. Prior notification and assurances of confidentially were provided in an attempt to increase response rate. Higher scores on the scale indicated that the manufacturer targeted the brand to a narrow niche of the overall market.

MAJOR FINDINGS: Frazier and Lassar (1996) investigated factors influencing the distribution intensity of brands in the electronics industry. Distribution intensity declined when **target markets** were more narrowly focused.

REFERENCES:

Frazier, Gary L. and Walfried M. Lassar (1996), "Determinants of Distribution Intensity," *JM*, 60 (October), 39–51.

SCALE ITEMS:

1. By design, our brand has a small number of potential customers.

2. By design, our speaker brand appeals to a narrow spectrum of consumers only.

3. We use a niche strategy for marketing our brand.

SCALE NAME: Task Difficulty

SCALE DESCRIPTION: Olson, Walker, and Ruekert (1995) used this six-item, seven-point scale to measure the level of task complexity and difficulty at various stages of the product development process, as well as the frequency with which difficult tasks were encountered.

SCALE ORIGIN: Olson, Walker, and Ruekert (1995) stated that the scale was adopted from Van de Ven and Ferry (1980) and previously used in a marketing context by Ruekert and Walker (1987a, b).

SAMPLES: Of the 24 firms solicited by Olson, Walker, and Ruekert (1995) to participate in the study, 15 divisions from 12 firms provided complete information on **45** new product development projects undertaken within a three-year time period. All firms produced tangible products and ranged in age from 12 to more than 100 years, with annual revenues between $50 million and more than $1 billion. Projects formed the unit of analysis. Of the new product projects studied, 11 represented new-to-the-world products, 9 were me-too products, 15 were line extensions, and 10 were product modifications. Data were collected first from each project manager and then from individuals identified by project managers as having key functional responsibilities related to marketing, manufacturing, R&D, and design. A total of **112** usable responses were obtained from the functional participants in addition to information provided by the **45** product managers.

RELIABILITY: Olson, Walker, and Ruekert (1995) reported a coefficient alpha of .72 for this scale. Scale items were also submitted to a Varimax rotated principle components factor analysis and found to load on two factors with an eigenvalue greater than 1. However, because analysis of scale items indicated no obvious reason to separate this measure into two separate scales, all six items were retained in a single measure.

VALIDITY: No specific examination of scale validity for this measure was reported by Olson, Walker, and Ruekert (1995).

ADMINISTRATION: Olson, Walker, and Ruekert (1995) indicated that information about each project was initially obtained from project managers through a telephone interview using a structured questionnaire. After project managers had identified the key functional personnel for their project in marketing, manufacturing, R&D, and design, self-administered mail surveys were sent to each of the functional participants of each project. An overall project score was created for the task difficulty measure by averaging responses to each scale across all the responding functional participants from a given project. Higher scores on the scale indicated that difficulties were incurred more frequently and that tasks were perceived as being more complex and difficult during both various stages of the process and the project in general.

MAJOR FINDINGS: Olson, Walker, and Ruekert (1995) examined the relationship between new product coordinating structures and outcomes using a resource dependency view of the new product development process. Increased **task difficulties** in the development process were found to result in greater levels of perceived interdependency among the various functional areas.

REFERENCES:

Olson, Eric M., Orville C. Walker Jr., and Robert W. Ruekert (1995), "Organizing for Effective New Product Development: The Moderating Role of Product Innovativeness," *JM*, 59 (January), 48–62.

Ruekert, Robert W. and Orville C. Walker Jr. (1987a), "The Organization of Marketing Activities: A Conceptual Framework and Empirical Evidence," *JM,* 51 (January), 1–19.

———— and ———— (1987b), "Interactions Between Marketing and R&D Departments in Implementing Different Strategies," *Strategic Management Journal*, 8, 233–48.

Van de Ven, Andrew H. and Diane L. Ferry (1980), *Measuring and Assessing Organizations*. New York: John Wiley & Sons.

SCALE ITEMS:

Very easy   Very difficult

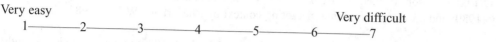
1————2————3————4————5————6————7

Overall, how difficult was it for members of your department to complete the tasks they were responsible for at this stage of the development process?

1. Stage 1 (product concept formation: opportunity identification, product design)

2. Stage 2: (product commercialization: product/market testing, production, distribution, promotion, and sales)

3. During this project, how easy was it for members of your department to know whether they did their work correctly?

1 = 0–15%
2 = 16–30%
3 = 31–45%
4 = 46–60%
5 = 61–75%
6 = 76–90%
7 = 91–100%

4. What percentage of time were you generally sure of what the outcome of the work efforts would be?

1 = Under once a week
2 = Once a week
3 = About 2–3 times a week
4 = About 4–5 times a week
5 = About 2–3 times a day
6 = About 4–5 times a day
7 = More than 5 times a day

5. How often did difficult problems arise in your work for which there were no immediate or apparent solutions?

Very easy   Very difficult

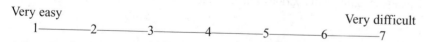
1————2————3————4————5————6————7

6. Overall, how much difficulty did your department encounter completing the tasks in the development of this product?

SCALE NAME: Task Performance (Partner Relationship)

SCALE DESCRIPTION: Smith and Barclay (1997) used this three-item, seven-point Likert-type scale to measure the extent to which both selling partners perceived that their relationship had been effective in realizing performance objectives.

SCALE ORIGIN: Smith and Barclay (1997) indicated that the constructs used in their study were operationalized with a mix of original and adapted scale items generated from the conceptual definition of the constructs, a review of the literature, field interviews, and pretest results. The conceptual definition of task performance is consistent with Bucklin and Sengupta's (1993) study; some of the items may have been adapted from this source. Each of the three items proposed for this measure passed the extensive preliminary analysis of item reliability and validity described by Smith and Barclay (1997).

SAMPLES: Smith and Barclay (1997) collected dyadic self-report data in two stages. The sponsor sample was composed of 338 sales representatives working for the Canadian subsidiaries of two multinational companies serving the computer industry. Forty percent of the 338 employees who were randomly selected from employee lists returned completed surveys. Using the names and contact information of relationship partners volunteered by these respondents, the authors then sampled the 135 dyadic partners. A total of **103** usable paired responses were obtained.

RELIABILITY: Smith and Barclay (1997) reported coefficient alphas of **.75** for the scale in the sponsor model and **.71** in the partner model.

VALIDITY: Smith and Barclay (1997) reported extensive testing of the reliability, unidimensionality, and convergent and discriminant validity of the measures used in their study. LISREL and confirmatory factor analysis were used to demonstrate that the measure satisfied each of these standards.

ADMINISTRATION: Smith and Barclay (1997) included the scale with other measures as part of a self-administered survey that was delivered by internal company mail to sales representatives and by regular U.S. mail to the dyadic partners. E-mail follow-ups were used to increase survey response rate. Half of the sales representatives were instructed to consider a customer situation in the prior six months in which they had had some success with a selling partner, whereas the other half were to told to choose a situation in which they had had little or no success. Participants then responded to questions about the partner, their relationship, and the organization in the context of this situation. Higher scores on the scale indicated that the dyadic partners perceived their relationship as being highly effective in accomplishing performance objectives.

MAJOR FINDINGS: Smith and Barclay (1997) developed and tested two research models explaining selling partner relationship effectiveness. The first examined four organizational differences from the sponsor's (salesperson's) perspective, and the second examined these same differences from the partner's perspective. In both the sponsor and partner models, perceived **task performance** was found to be a strong predictor of mutual satisfaction with the relationship. The degree of relationship investment and communication openness was in turn positively associated with perceived **task performance** (though in the partner model, relationship investment and communication openness were combined into a single measure called "RICOMM"). Only in the partner model was perceived **task performance** significantly enhanced by reduced levels of opportunistic behavior.

REFERENCES:
Bucklin, Louis P. and Anjit Sengupta (1993), "Organizing Successful Co-Marketing Alliances," *JM*, 57 (April) 32–46.

#904 *Task Performance (Partner Relationship)*

Smith, J. Brock and Donald W. Barclay (1997), "The Effects of Organizational Differences and Trust on the Effectiveness of Selling Partner Relationships," *JM*, 61 (January), 3–21.

SCALE ITEMS:

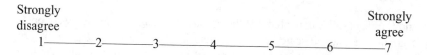

Strongly disagree

Strongly agree

1————2————3————4————5————6————7

1. The customers we've dealt with together have been pleased with our work.

2. We have closed a lot of business together.

3. From a performance perspective, our working relationship has been effective.

SCALE NAME: Technological Change

SCALE DESCRIPTION: Heide and Weiss (1995) indicate that this four-item, seven-point scale measures buyer perceptions of the extent of change in workstation hardware, software, and operating systems. They referred to this measure as *pace of technological change*.

SCALE ORIGIN: The scale is original to Heide and Weiss (1995). Items were initially developed in accordance with the conceptual definition of the construct, then modified on the basis of field interviews, discussions with industry observers, and trade journal information. The scale was pretested, revised, and then pretested again before final administration.

SAMPLES: Pretests of the questionnaire were conducted with two different small groups of previous workstation buyers. In the final study, Heide and Weiss (1995) drew a random sample of 900 firms from Installed Technology International's list of firms that had recently purchased workstations. Key informants were identified from this list and contacted by telephone, and 466 agreed to participate in the study and were sent a mail questionnaire. Follow-up telephone calls and a second mailing resulted in **215** usable questionnaires being returned. Industries represented by respondents included computers (31.4%), manufacturing (22.4%), medical (6.2%), services (15.2%), and other (24.8%).

RELIABILITY: Heide and Weiss (1995) reported a coefficient alpha of **.74** for this scale.

VALIDITY: Heide and Weiss (1995) initially evaluated the measure on the basis of item-to-total correlations and exploratory factor analysis. Confirmatory factor analysis was then used to establish unidimensionality. Evidence of discriminant validity was provided by a series of chi-square tests on the respective factor correlations.

ADMINISTRATION: The measure was included in a self-administered mail survey. Heide and Weiss (1995) instructed respondents to answer all questions in the context of their organization's most recent workstation purchase. Higher scores on the technological change measure indicated more frequent changes with respect to an organization's workstation technology, hardware, software, and operating systems.

MAJOR FINDINGS: Heide and Weiss (1995) investigated how buyers working in high-technology markets approached decisions in the consideration and choice stages of the purchase process. Specifically, factors influencing whether buyers included new vendors at the consideration stage and whether they ultimately switched to a new vendor at the choice stage were investigated. Buyer perceptions of **rapid technological change** resulted in a greater tendency to consider additional vendors but also decreased the likelihood of switching away from the existing supplier.

REFERENCES:
Heide, Jan B. and Allen M. Weiss (1995), "Vendor Consideration and Switching Behavior for Buyers in High-Technology Markets," *JM*, 59 (July), 30–43.

SCALE ITEMS:

No changes   Frequent changes
taking place   taking place

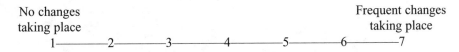

1———2———3———4———5———6———7

1. Nature of the workstation hardware.

2. Nature of workstation operating systems.

3. Nature of workstation applications software.

4. Nature of workstation technology overall.

SCALE NAME: Technological Compatibility

SCALE DESCRIPTION: Heide and Weiss (1995) used this three-item, seven-point Likert-type scale to measure the extent to which a new workstation's compatibility with existing equipment was a concern to buyers.

SCALE ORIGIN: The scale is original to Heide and Weiss (1995). Items were initially developed in accordance with the conceptual definition of the construct, then modified on the basis of field interviews, discussions with industry observers, and trade journal information. The scale was pretested, revised, and then pretested again before final administration.

SAMPLES: Pretests of the questionnaire were conducted with two different small groups of previous workstation buyers. In the final study, Heide and Weiss (1995) drew a random sample of 900 firms from Installed Technology International's list of firms that had recently purchased workstations. Key informants were identified from this list and contacted by telephone, and 466 agreed to participate in the study and were sent a mail questionnaire. Follow-up telephone calls and a second mailing resulted in **215** usable questionnaires being returned. Industries represented by respondents included computers (31.4%), manufacturing (22.4%), medical (6.2%), services (15.2%), and other (24.8%).

RELIABILITY: Heide and Weiss (1995) reported a coefficient alpha of .75 for this scale.

VALIDITY: Heide and Weiss (1995) initially evaluated the measure on the basis of item-to-total correlations and exploratory factor analysis. Confirmatory factor analysis was then used to establish unidimensionality. Evidence of discriminant validity was provided by a series of chi-square tests on the respective factor correlations.

ADMINISTRATION: The measure was included in a self-administered mail survey. Heide and Weiss (1995) instructed respondents to answer all questions in the context of their organization's most recent workstation purchase. Higher scores on the technological compatibility measure indicated a greater level of concern that new workstation purchases be compatible with existing equipment.

MAJOR FINDINGS: Heide and Weiss (1995) investigated how buyers working in high-technology markets approached decisions in the consideration and choice stages of the purchase process. Specifically, factors influencing whether buyers included new vendors at the consideration stage and whether they ultimately switched to a new vendor at the choice stage were investigated. When **technological compatibility** concerns were high, there was a reduced tendency to consider additional vendors. However, **technological compatibility** concerns had no effect on switching behavior.

REFERENCES:
Heide, Jan B. and Allen M. Weiss (1995), "Vendor Consideration and Switching Behavior for Buyers in High-Technology Markets," *JM*, 59 (July), 30–43.

SCALE ITEMS:

Strongly
disagree

Strongly
agree

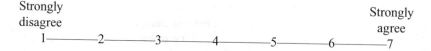

1——————2——————3——————4——————5——————6——————7

1. When we were considering which workstations to purchase, compatibility with our existing systems was not an issue. **(r)**

2. Technically speaking, we were concerned about how compatible these workstations were with the other computer-based systems.

3. System compatibility was not an issue when we were considering adopting workstations. **(r)**

SCALE NAME: Technological Heterogeneity

SCALE DESCRIPTION: Heide and Weiss (1995) used this four-item, seven-point semantic differential scale to measure the diversity and heterogeneity of computer workstations and their software, operating systems, and system components.

SCALE ORIGIN: Heide and Weiss (1995) adapted items from Achrol and Stern's (1988) study to fit the context of computer workstation purchasing.

SAMPLES: Pretests of the questionnaire were conducted with two different small groups of previous workstation buyers. In the final study, Heide and Weiss (1995) drew a random sample of 900 firms from Installed Technology International's list of firms that had recently purchased workstations. Key informants were identified from this list and contacted by telephone, and 466 agreed to participate in the study and were sent a mail questionnaire. Follow-up telephone calls and a second mailing resulted in **215** usable questionnaires being returned. Industries represented by respondents included computers (31.4%), manufacturing (22.4%), medical (6.2%), services (15.2%), and other (24.8%).

RELIABILITY: Heide and Weiss (1995) reported a coefficient alpha of **.70** for this scale.

VALIDITY: Heide and Weiss (1995) initially evaluated the measure on the basis of item-to-total correlations and exploratory factor analysis. Confirmatory factor analysis was then used to establish unidimensionality. Evidence of discriminant validity was provided by a series of chi-square tests on the respective factor correlations.

ADMINISTRATION: The measure was included in a self-administered mail survey. Heide and Weiss (1995) instructed respondents to answer all questions in the context of their organization's most recent workstation purchase. Higher scores on the technological heterogeneity scale appeared to indicate greater levels of diversity in the different dimensions of the computer workstation market.

MAJOR FINDINGS: Heide and Weiss (1995) investigated how buyers working in high-technology markets approached decisions in the consideration and choice stages of the purchase process. Specifically, factors influencing whether buyers included new vendors at the consideration stage and whether they ultimately switched to a new vendor at the choice stage were investigated. Heide and Weiss (1995) found that **technological heterogeneity** had no significant effect on either the composition of the consideration set or the specific choice of vendor.

REFERENCES:
Achrol, Ravi and Louis W. Stern (1988), "Environmental Determinants of Decision-Making Uncertainty in Marketing Channels," *JMR*, 25 (February), 36–50.
Heide, Jan B. and Allen M. Weiss (1995), "Vendor Consideration and Switching Behavior for Buyers in High-Technology Markets," *JM*, 59 (July), 30–43.

SCALE ITEMS:

1. Existing workstations were very:

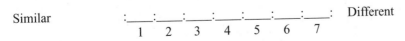

Similar : ___ : ___ : ___ : ___ : ___ : ___ : ___ : Different
      1   2   3   4   5   6   7

2. Operating systems were very:

Similar :___:___:___:___:___:___:___: Different
          1   2   3   4   5   6   7

3. Software alternatives were very:

Similar :___:___:___:___:___:___:___: Different
          1   2   3   4   5   6   7

4. Widely accepted standards for systems components (e.g. networks, windows, applications, graphics):

No industry standards for systems components

:___:___:___:___:___:___:___:
  1   2   3   4   5   6   7

SCALE NAME: Technological Unpredictability

SCALE DESCRIPTION: This four-item, seven-point scale measures the extent to which the buyer is unable to accurately predict the technological changes in the product purchased and its underlying manufacturing process.

SCALE ORIGIN: Stump and Heide (1996) adapted the items used in this measure from the work of Heide and John (1990). Extensive pretesting of the questionnaire containing the measure was reported by Stump and Heide (1996).

SAMPLES: Stump and Heide (1996) drew a random sample of 1073 names from a national mailing list of chemical manufacturing firms in standard industrial classification code 28. Of this group, 631 key informants were identified by telephone who agreed to participate in the study. A total of **164** usable surveys were returned.

RELIABILITY: Stump and Heide (1996) calculated a coefficient alpha of **.69** for this measure.

VALIDITY: Stump and Heide (1996) examined item-to-total correlations of the items composing the scale and conducted an exploratory factor analysis of the measures used in the study. A confirmatory factor analysis of all items used in each scale verified the unidimensionality of the measure. Evidence of the discriminant validity of the measure was provided by means of a series of chi-square difference tests performed on the factor correlations. The model was also evaluated and found to represent a good fit to the data.

ADMINISTRATION: The scale was included by Stump and Heide (1996) with other measures as part of a self-administered survey that was delivered by mail. Buyers were asked to identify a purchasing agreement for a particular product which had been established within the last 12 months and answer questions in the context of that purchasing agreement. Higher scores on the scale indicated that a buyer was less able to predict accurately the technological changes in the product purchased and its underlying manufacturing process.

MAJOR FINDINGS: Stump and Heide (1996) examined how chemical manufacturers used partner selection, incentive design, and monitoring approaches in the management and control of supplier relationships. No significant relationship was found between supplier investments and the level of **technological unpredictability**.

REFERENCES:

Heide, Jan B. and George John (1990), "Alliances in Industrial Purchasing: The Determinants of Joint Action in Buyer-Supplier Relationships," *JMR*, 27 (February), 24–36.

Stump, Rodney L. and Jan B. Heide (1996), "Controlling Supplier Opportunism in Industrial Relationships," *JMR*, 33 (November), 431–41.

SCALE ITEMS:

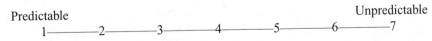

Predictable   Unpredictable
1———2———3———4———5———6———7

1. Technological changes in the end product.

2. General technological developments in the supply market for the identified item.

3. Your firm's changes in specifications for the identified item.

4. This supplier's changes in specifications for the identified item.

SCALE NAME: Time Pressure (Work)

SCALE DESCRIPTION: This six-item Likert-type scale was used by Andrews and Smith (1996) to measure the degree to which respondents believed themselves to be under time pressures to complete their tasks in a work-related environment.

SCALE ORIGIN: Andrews and Smith (1996) stated that the measure was based on the role overload scale originally developed by Reilly (1982) for use with female consumers and refined for the business setting through discussions with product managers. Two of the six items composing the scale appear to have been adapted from Reilly's (1982) work (for Reilly's scale see Vol. 1 #224 or Vol. 2 #217).

SAMPLES: The American Marketing Association membership directory and a purchased mailing list provided Andrews and Smith (1996) with the sampling frame for surveying consumer goods product managers. One hundred ninety-three completed questionnaires were returned for a 33.4% response rate. No significant differences in responses to key variables existed between mailing lists or between early and late respondents. Because only respondents with a substantial impact on ideas in the marketing program were desired, 25 respondents were eliminated on the basis of a screening question, yielding a final sample size of **168**.

RELIABILITY: Andrews and Smith (1996) reported a coefficient alpha of **.81** for this measure.

VALIDITY: No specific examination of the scale's validity was reported by Andrews and Smith (1996).

ADMINISTRATION: The scale was part of a self-administered mail survey in which Andrews and Smith (1996) instructed product managers to answer questions in the context of a single product with which they had been highly involved during their most recent marketing program. Higher scores on the scale indicated stronger perceptions of time limitations for work-related task completion.

MAJOR FINDINGS: Andrews and Smith (1996) investigated the effect of individual product manager and situational/planning process characteristics on marketing program creativity. When respondents perceived themselves to be working under a **time pressure**, marketing program creativity was negatively affected.

REFERENCES:

Andrews, Jonlee and Daniel C. Smith (1996), "In Search of the Marketing Imagination: Factors Affecting the Creativity of Marketing Programs for Mature Products," *JMR*, 33 (May), 174–87.

Reilly, Michael D. (1982), "Working Wives and Convenience Consumption," *JCR*, 8 (March), 407–18.

SCALE ITEMS:

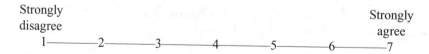

Strongly
disagree

1———2———3———4———5———6———7

Strongly
agree

1. I need more hours in the day to get my work done.

2. I *don't* have to overextend myself to find the time to get my work done. **(r)**

3. I feel like I'm always "fighting fires."

4. I seldom have to take shortcuts to get my work done on time. **(r)**

5. I never have enough time to think ahead.

6. I feel like I
  have a lot of
  time on my hands

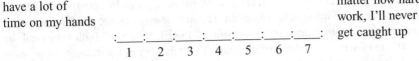

I feel like no
matter how hard I
work, I'll never
get caught up

:___:___:___:___:___:___:___:
  1   2   3   4   5   6   7

SCALE NAME: Timeliness (New Product)

SCALE DESCRIPTION: Moorman (1995) used this three-item, seven-point semantic differential scale to assess the extent to which new products are introduced during environmental conditions that promote their success.

SCALE ORIGIN: The scale is original to Moorman (1995). All measures used by Moorman (1995) were subjected to a purification process following data collection. The author assessed the unidimensionality of the measures in a two-factor confirmatory analysis model using LISREL VII. Items with very weak loadings and those loading on more than one factor were eliminated. The reliability of the measures was assessed by calculating coefficient alphas, and items with low item-to-total correlations were dropped if "doing so did not diminish the measure's coverage of the construct domain" (Moorman 1995, p. 325).

SAMPLES: Moorman (1995) chose to sample the vice presidents of marketing for 300 divisions of firms noted in the 1992 *Advertising Age* list of top 200 advertisers, and a total of **92** usable questionnaires were received. No systematic differences were observed between early and late respondents.

RELIABILITY: Moorman (1995) reported a coefficient alpha of **.92** for this scale.

VALIDITY: Moorman (1995) performed a series of two-factor confirmatory analyses using LISREL VII to assess the discriminant validity of the measures used in her study. Chi-square difference tests were performed on constrained versus unconstrained models, and the significantly lower chi-square values observed for all of the unconstrained models tested were accepted as evidence of the discriminant validity of the measures.

ADMINISTRATION: The scale was included with other measures in a self-administered questionnaire that was delivered by mail. Moorman's (1995) cover letter explained the survey purpose and, in an effort to increase response rate, offered to share survey results. Nonrespondents were telephoned after three weeks and sent a second questionnaire two weeks after the telephone reminder. All informants were instructed to answer in the context of the most recent product development project for which their division had been responsible. Focal projects were required to have been on the market for a minimum of 12 months. Higher scores on the scale indicated that an organization was more successful in introducing new products at times when environmental factors were favorable to the introduction of the product.

MAJOR FINDINGS: Moorman (1995) examined the relationship among organizational market information processes, organizational culture, and new product outcomes. Some evidence was found to suggest that conceptual utilization processes and instrumental utilization processes positively influenced **new product timeliness**. This would indicate that when information is valued, processed, and incorporated by an organization into the marketing decision making, implementation, and evaluation process, new products are more likely to be introduced to the marketplace when environmental conditions favor their ultimate success.

REFERENCES:

Moorman, Christine (1995), "Organizational Market Information Processes: Cultural Antecedents and New Product Outcomes," *JMR*, 32 (August), 318–35.

SCALE ITEMS:

1. Timely   :___:___:___:___:___:___:___: Untimely (r)
              1   2   3   4   5   6   7

2. Opportune :___:___:___:___:___:___:___: Inopportune (r)
              1   2   3   4   5   6   7

3. Well-timed :___:___:___:___:___:___:___: Poorly timed (r)
              1   2   3   4   5   6   7

SCALE NAME: Transaction Flows

SCALE DESCRIPTION: Olson, Walker, and Ruekert (1995) used this four-item, seven-point scale to measure the degree to which information, technical assistance, raw materials, work objects, people, money, and equipment were transferred between functional departments over the course of the new product development project.

SCALE ORIGIN: Olson, Walker, and Ruekert (1995) stated that the scale was adopted from Van de Ven and Ferry (1980) and previously used in a marketing context by Ruekert and Walker (1987a, b).

SAMPLES: Of the 24 firms solicited by Olson, Walker, and Ruekert (1995) to participate in the study, 15 divisions from 12 firms provided complete information on **45** new product development projects undertaken within a three-year time period. All firms produced tangible products and ranged in age from 12 to more than 100 years, with annual revenues between $50 million and more than $1 billion. Projects formed the unit of analysis. Of the new product projects studied, 11 represented new-to-the-world products, 9 were me-too products, 15 were line extensions, and 10 were product modifications. Data were collected first from each project manager and then from individuals identified by project managers as having key functional responsibilities related to marketing, manufacturing, R&D, and design. A total of **112** usable responses were obtained from the functional participants in addition to information provided by the **45** product managers.

RELIABILITY: Olson, Walker, and Ruekert (1995) reported a coefficient alpha of **.82** for this scale. Scale items were also submitted to a Varimax rotated principle components factor analysis and found to load on a single factor with an eigenvalue greater than 1.

VALIDITY: No specific examination of scale validity for this measure was reported by Olson, Walker, and Ruekert (1995).

ADMINISTRATION: Olson, Walker, and Ruekert (1995) indicated that information about each project was initially obtained from project managers through a telephone interview using a structured questionnaire. After project managers had identified the key functional personnel for their project in marketing, manufacturing, R&D, and design, self-administered mail surveys were sent to each of the functional participants of each project. An overall project score was created for the transaction flows measure by averaging responses to each scale across all the responding functional participants from a given project. Higher scores on the scale indicated greater resource transfers between functional areas over the course of the new product development project.

MAJOR FINDINGS: Olson, Walker, and Ruekert (1995) examined the relationship between new product coordinating structures and outcomes using a resource dependency view of the new product development process. The **flow of information and other resources** was found to increase with higher levels of interdependency, and greater reliance on less formal coordination structures corresponded with higher levels of **information and resource flow** between functional areas.

REFERENCES:

Olson, Eric M., Orville C. Walker Jr., and Robert W. Ruekert (1995), "Organizing for Effective New Product Development: The Moderating Role of Product Innovativeness," *JM*, 59 (January), 48–62.

Ruekert, Robert W. and Orville C. Walker Jr. (1987a), "The Organization of Marketing Activities: A Conceptual Framework and Empirical Evidence," *JM*, 51 (January), 1–19.

———— and ———— (1987b), "Interactions Between Marketing and R&D Departments in Implementing Different Strategies," *Strategic Management Journal*, 8, 233–48.

SCALE ITEMS:*

Not at all   Very much
1———2———3———4———5———6———7

How much was your department involved in transferring work (e.g., raw materials or work objects) or resources (e.g. money, personnel, equipment) to or from the following departments during:

1. Stage 1 (product concept formation: opportunity identification, product design)

2. Stage 2 (product commercialization: product/market testing, production, distribution, promotion, and sales)

How much was your department involved in transferring information, technical assistance to or from the following departments during:

3. Stage 1 (product concept formation: opportunity identification, product design)

4. Stage 2 (product commercialization: product/market testing, production, distribution, promotion, and sales)

*Correspondence with the authors indicated that the instructions for these items asked respondents to evaluate their department's interaction with each of the other departments, including marketing and sales, manufacturing and production engineering, R&D and product engineering, and design.

SCALE NAME: Transaction-Specific Investments (Retailer)

SCALE DESCRIPTION: Ganesan (1994) used this four-item, seven-point Likert-type scale to measure the extent to which retailers dedicated resources to a vendor relationship by making specific investments in assets that could not be redeployed to other relationships, such as specialized displays for the vendor's products or vendor-specialized sales training.

SCALE ORIGIN: Ganesan (1994) reported developing separate but parallel measures of transaction-specific investments for both the retailer and vendor samples based on scale items adapted from Anderson and Weitz's (1992) measures of distributor and supplier idiosyncratic investment. Anderson and Weitz (1992) followed Nunnally's (1978) procedure for scale development in generating item measures and purifying their scales for use with distributor and manufacturer samples. The author used item analysis and exploratory factor analysis to initially purify his measure; items with low loadings and those loading on multiple factors were eliminated. A draft of the questionnaire containing this scale was also pretested with a group of 14 retail buyers representing two department store chains. After administration to the final sample, scale items were subjected to a confirmatory factor analysis. Goodness-of-fit indices and individual item t-values were used to identify the final scale items.

SAMPLES: Five retail department store chains agreed to participate in Ganesan's (1994) study, and each firm received and distributed 30 questionnaires to senior sales representatives or sales managers who served as liaisons with vendor organizations. A total of **124** (83%) usable responses representing the *retailer* sample were obtained. Of these, 48 respondents answered in the context of a long-term vendor relationship, and the remaining 76 answered in the context of a short-term vendor relationship. Contact information provided by respondents enabled the author to sample the designated 124 key vendor informants most knowledgeable about the retailer/vendor relationship with a survey similar in content to the retailer questionnaire but phrased from the vendor point of view. A total of **52** (42%) *vendor* representatives responded, of which 21 and 31 were in short- and long-term relationships, respectively.

RELIABILITY: Ganesan (1994) reported a coefficient alpha of **.76** for the scale.

VALIDITY: Ganesan (1994) submitted the scale to a confirmatory factor analysis using LISREL 7.16 to assess the unidimensionality, convergent validity, and discriminant validity of the measure. Although the measure was found to be unidimensional, no additional information pertaining to the outcome of the validity tests was provided.

ADMINISTRATION: Prior to being sent a survey, buyers in the retailer sample were randomly assigned to one of four cells in which the questionnaire instructions asked them to select a vendor on the basis of variations in two criteria: (1) the length of their relationship (short-term or long-term) and (2) the importance of the vendor's product to their organization (moderately important or very important). Questionnaires were distributed by a coordinator in each department store, and respondents were instructed to answer the survey in the context of this single vendor. Higher scores on the scale indicated a greater level of retailer investment in resources dedicated to a specific vendor that could not be easily redeployed to other relationships.

MAJOR FINDINGS: Ganesan (1994) investigated a variety of factors influencing the long-term orientation of both retailers and vendors in an ongoing relationship, as well as the antecedents to long-term orientation. Results indicated that **transaction-specific investments made by a retailer** had a significant positive impact on a retailer's dependence on the vendor and a retailer's perception of the vendor's dependence on it.

#912 *Transaction-Specific Investments (Retailer)*

REFERENCES:

Anderson, Erin and Barton A. Weitz (1992), "The Use of Pledges to Build and Sustain Commitment in Distribution Channels," *JMR*, 29 (February), 18–34.

Ganesan, Shankar (1994), "Determinants of Long-Term Orientation in Buyer-Seller Relationships," *JM*, 58 (April), 1–19.

Nunnally, Jum C. (1978), *Psychometric Theory*. New York: McGraw-Hill.

SCALE ITEMS:

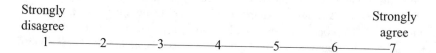

1. We have made significant investments in displays, trained salespeople, etc., dedicated our relationship with this vendor.

2. If we switched to a competing resource, we would lose a lot of the investment we have made in this resource.

3. We have invested substantially in personnel dedicated to this resource.

4. If we decided to stop working with this resource, we would be wasting a lot of knowledge regarding their method of operation.

SCALE NAME: Transaction-Specific Investments (Retailer's Perception of Vendor)

SCALE DESCRIPTION: Ganesan (1994) used this three-item, seven-point Likert-type scale to measure the extent to which retailers perceived that vendors had dedicated resources to their relationship by making specific investments in assets that could not be redeployed to other relationships.

SCALE ORIGIN: Ganesan (1994) reported developing separate but parallel measures of perceived retailer and vendor transaction-specific investments based on scale items adapted from Anderson and Weitz's (1992) measures of perceived distributor and supplier idiosyncratic investment. Anderson and Weitz (1992) followed Nunnally's (1978) procedure for scale development in generating item measures and purifying their scales for use with distributor and manufacturer samples. The author used item analysis and exploratory factor analysis to initially purify his measure; items with low loadings and those loading on multiple factors were eliminated. A draft of the questionnaire containing this scale was also pretested with a group of 14 retail buyers representing two department store chains. After administration to the final sample, scale items were subjected to a confirmatory factor analysis. Goodness-of-fit indices and individual item t-values were used to identify the final scale items.

SAMPLES: Five retail department store chains agreed to participate in Ganesan's (1994) study, and each firm received and distributed 30 questionnaires to senior sales representatives or sales managers who served as liaisons with vendor organizations. A total of **124** (83%) usable responses representing the *retailer* sample were obtained. Of these, 48 respondents answered in the context of a long-term vendor relationship, and the remaining 76 answered in the context of a short-term vendor relationship. Contact information provided by respondents enabled the author to sample the designated 124 key vendor informants most knowledgeable about the retailer/vendor relationship with a survey similar in content to the retailer questionnaire but phrased from the vendor point of view. A total of **52** (42%) *vendor* representatives responded, of which 21 and 31 were in short- and long-term relationships, respectively.

RELIABILITY: Ganesan (1994) reported a coefficient alpha of **.67** for the scale.

VALIDITY: Ganesan (1994) submitted the scale to a confirmatory factor analysis using LISREL 7.16 to assess the unidimensionality, convergent validity, and discriminant validity of the measure. Although the measure was found to be unidimensional, no additional information pertaining to the outcome of the validity tests was provided.

ADMINISTRATION: Prior to being sent a survey, buyers in the retailer sample were randomly assigned to one of four cells in which the questionnaire instructions asked them to select a vendor on the basis of variations in two criteria: (1) the length of their relationship (short-term or long-term) and (2) the importance of the vendor's product to their organization (moderately important or very important). Questionnaires were distributed by a coordinator in each department store, and respondents were instructed to answer the survey in the context of this single vendor. Higher scores on the scale indicated that retailers perceived vendors as directing more dedicated resources to their relationship.

MAJOR FINDINGS: Ganesan (1994) investigated a variety of factors influencing the long-term orientation of both retailers and vendors in an ongoing relationship, as well as the antecedents to long-term orientation. Results indicated that **retailer perceptions of the transaction-specific investments made by vendors** had a significant positive impact on a retailer's dependence on the vendor.

REFERENCES:
Anderson, Erin and Barton A. Weitz (1992), "The Use of Pledges to Build and Sustain Commitment in Distribution Channels," *JMR*, 29 (February), 18–34.

#913 *Transaction-Specific Investments (Retailer's Perception of Vendor)*

Ganesan, Shankar (1994), "Determinants of Long-Term Orientation in Buyer-Seller Relationships," *JM*, 58 (April), 1–19.

Nunnally, Jum C. (1978), *Psychometric Theory*. New York: McGraw-Hill.

SCALE ITEMS:

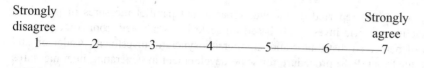

1. This resource has gone out of their way to link us with their business.

2. This vendor has tailored its merchandise and procedures to meet the specific needs of our company.

3. It would be difficult for this resource to recoup its investment in us if they switched to another retailer as an outlet for their products.

SCALE NAME: Transaction-Specific Investments (Vendor)

SCALE DESCRIPTION: Ganesan (1994) used this four-item, seven-point Likert-type scale to measure the extent to which vendors dedicated resources to a retailer relationship by making specific investments in assets that could not be redeployed to other relationships, such as displays, training programs, and products exclusive to a particular retailer.

SCALE ORIGIN: Ganesan (1994) reported developing separate but parallel measures of transaction-specific investments for both the retailer and vendor samples based on scale items adapted from Anderson and Weitz's (1992) measures of distributor and supplier idiosyncratic investment. Anderson and Weitz (1992) followed Nunnally's (1978) procedure for scale development in generating item measures and purifying their scales for use with distributor and manufacturer samples. The author used item analysis and exploratory factor analysis to initially purify his measure; items with low loadings and those loading on multiple factors were eliminated. A draft of the questionnaire containing this scale was also pretested with a group of 14 retail buyers representing two department store chains. After administration to the final sample, scale items were subjected to a confirmatory factor analysis. Goodness-of-fit indices and individual item t-values were used to identify the final scale items.

SAMPLES: Five retail department store chains agreed to participate in Ganesan's (1994) study, and each firm received and distributed 30 questionnaires to senior sales representatives or sales managers who served as liaisons with vendor organizations. A total of **124** (83%) usable responses representing the *retailer* sample were obtained. Of these, 48 respondents answered in the context of a long-term vendor relationship, and the remaining 76 answered in the context of a short-term vendor relationship. Contact information provided by respondents enabled the author to sample the designated 124 key vendor informants most knowledgeable about the retailer/vendor relationship with a survey similar in content to the retailer questionnaire but phrased from the vendor point of view. A total of **52** (42%) *vendor* representatives responded, of which 21 and 31 were in short- and long-term relationships, respectively.

RELIABILITY: Ganesan (1994) reported a coefficient alpha of **.71** for the scale.

VALIDITY: Ganesan (1994) submitted the scale to a confirmatory factor analysis using LISREL 7.16 to assess the unidimensionality, convergent validity, and discriminant validity of the measure. Although the measure was found to be unidimensional, no additional information pertaining to the outcome of the validity tests was provided.

ADMINISTRATION: Prior to being sent a survey, buyers in the retailer sample were randomly assigned to one of four cells in which the questionnaire instructions asked them to select a vendor on the basis of variations in two criteria: (1) the length of their relationship (short-term or long-term) and (2) the importance of the vendor's product to their organization (moderately important or very important). Questionnaires were distributed by a coordinator in each department store, and respondents were instructed to answer the survey in the context of this single vendor. Higher scores on the scale indicated a greater level of vendor investment in resources dedicated to a specific retailer that could not be easily redeployed to other relationships.

MAJOR FINDINGS: Ganesan (1994) investigated a variety of factors influencing the long-term orientation of both retailers and vendors in an ongoing relationship, as well as the antecedents to long-term orientation. Results indicated that **transaction-specific investments made by a vendor** did not have a significant positive impact on a vendor's dependence on the retailer or on a vendor's perception of the retailer's dependence on them.

#914 *Transaction-Specific Investments (Vendor)*

REFERENCES:

Anderson, Erin and Barton A. Weitz (1992), "The Use of Pledges to Build and Sustain Commitment in Distribution Channels," *JMR*, 29 (February), 18–34.

Ganesan, Shankar (1994), "Determinants of Long-Term Orientation in Buyer-Seller Relationships," *JM*, 58 (April), 1–19.

Nunnally, Jum C. (1978), *Psychometric Theory*. New York: McGraw-Hill.

SCALE ITEMS:

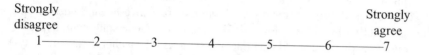

1. We have made significant investments in displays, training salespeople, etc., dedicated our relationship with this retailer.

2. If we switched to a competing retailer, we would lose a lot of the investment we have made in this retailer.

3. We have invested substantially in personnel dedicated to this retailer.

4. If we decided to stop working with this retailer, we would be wasting a lot of knowledge regarding their method of operation.

SCALE NAME: Transaction-Specific Investments (Vendor's Perception of Retailer)

SCALE DESCRIPTION: Ganesan (1994) used this three-item, seven-point Likert-type scale to measure the extent to which vendors perceived that retailers had dedicated resources to their relationship by making specific investments in assets that could not be redeployed to other relationships.

SCALE ORIGIN: Ganesan (1994) reported developing separate but parallel measures of transaction-specific investments for both the retailer and vendor samples based on scale items adapted from Anderson and Weitz's (1992) measures of distributor and supplier idiosyncratic investment. Anderson and Weitz (1992) followed Nunnally's (1978) procedure for scale development in generating item measures and purifying their scales for use with distributor and manufacturer samples. The author used item analysis and exploratory factor analysis to initially purify his measure; items with low loadings and those loading on multiple factors were eliminated. A draft of the questionnaire containing this scale was also pretested with a group of 14 retail buyers representing two department store chains. After administration to the final sample, scale items were subjected to a confirmatory factor analysis. Goodness-of-fit indices and individual item t-values were used to identify the final scale items.

SAMPLES: Ganesan (1994) generated his sample of retailers and vendors in two stages. Five retail department store chains agreed to participate in the study, and each firm received and distributed 30 questionnaires to senior sales representatives or sales managers who served as liaisons with vendor organizations. A total of **124** (83%) usable responses representing the *retailer* sample were obtained. Of these, 48 respondents answered in the context of a long-term vendor relationship, and the remaining 76 answered in the context of a short-term vendor relationship. Each of the retailer respondents provided contact information for the key vendor informant most knowledgeable about their relationship, and Ganesan (1994) sent the 124 vendors identified by retailers a survey similar in content to the retailer questionnaire but phrased from the vendor point of view. A total of **52** (42%) *vendor* representatives responded, of which 21 and 31 were in short- and long-term relationships, respectively.

RELIABILITY: Ganesan (1994) reported a coefficient alpha of **.66** for the scale.

VALIDITY: Ganesan (1994) submitted the scale to a confirmatory factor analysis using LISREL 7.16 to assess the unidimensionality, convergent validity, and discriminant validity of the measure. Although the measure was found to be unidimensional, no additional information pertaining to the outcome of the validity tests was provided.

ADMINISTRATION: Prior to being sent a survey, buyers in the retailer sample were randomly assigned to one of four cells in which the questionnaire instructions asked them to select a vendor on the basis of variations in two criteria: (1) the length of their relationship (short-term or long-term) and (2) the importance of the vendor's product to their organization (moderately important or very important). Questionnaires were distributed by a coordinator in each department store, and respondents were instructed to answer the survey in the context of this single vendor. Higher scores on the scale indicated that vendors perceived retailers as directing more dedicated resources to their relationship.

MAJOR FINDINGS: Ganesan (1994) investigated a variety of factors influencing the long-term orientation of both retailers and vendors in an ongoing relationship, as well as the antecedents to long-term orientation. Results indicated that **vendor perceptions of the transaction-specific investments made by retailers** had a significant positive impact on vendor's perception of the retailer's dependence on them.

#915 *Transaction-Specific Investments (Vendor's Perception of Retailer)*

REFERENCES:

Anderson, Erin and Barton A. Weitz (1992), "The Use of Pledges to Build and Sustain Commitment in Distribution Channels," *JMR*, 29 (February), 18–34.

Ganesan, Shankar (1994), "Determinants of Long-Term Orientation in Buyer-Seller Relationships," *JM*, 58 (April), 1–19.

Nunnally, Jum C. (1978), *Psychometric Theory*. New York, NY: McGraw-Hill Publications.

SCALE ITEMS:

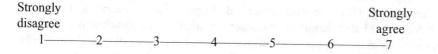

Strongly
disagree

Strongly
agree

1————2————3————4————5————6————7

1. This retailer has gone out of their way to link us with their business.

2. This retailer has changed their floor displays to meet the specific needs of our products.

3. This retailer has made significant investments in training their sales staff to handle questions about out products.

SCALE NAME: Trust (Distributor in Manufacturer)

SCALE DESCRIPTION: This four-item, seven-point Likert-type scale was used by Andaleeb (1996) to measure the level of trust respondents felt toward the focal manufacturer.

SCALE ORIGIN: Andaleeb (1996) apparently adapted his trust operationalization from studies previously conducted by Crosby, Evans, and Cowles (1990) and Schurr and Ozanne (1985). The reliability of the measure and item-to-total correlations were assessed as part of the purification process and deemed to be acceptable.

SAMPLES: A convenience sample of **72** sales and purchasing managers with considerable negotiation experience participated in a 2×2 between-groups factorial design experiment. Andaleeb (1996) randomly assigned subjects to treatment conditions.

RELIABILITY: Andaleeb (1996) calculated a coefficient alpha of **.95** for the scale.

VALIDITY: Andaleeb (1996) reported conducting a factor analysis to assess the unidimensionality of the measures used in his study. A single factor with item loadings greater than .8 was extracted for each scale, which suggested that the measures were unidimensional. A confirmatory factor analysis of the measurement model provided some evidence of validity, because the standardized coefficients were significantly different from 0. However, the goodness-of-fit index of .87 was somewhat below the recommended .90 level, though the chi-square and root mean squared residual were found to be satisfactory.

ADMINISTRATION: Andaleeb (1996) provided subjects with information about a contrived manufacturer (supplier)–distributor (buyer) relationship in which the level of trust and dependence on the supplier were manipulated. After reading this information, subjects were instructed to write down their perceptions of the relationship and read a scenario suggesting that an upcoming meeting would consider methods of strengthening the company's growth through cultivation of existing suppliers. Subjects were instructed to indicate whether they thought such ties would be appropriate with the focal supplier. The satisfaction, commitment, dependence, and trust measures were then administered. Higher scores on the scale indicated a stronger trust in the manufacturer on the part of respondents.

MAJOR FINDINGS: Andaleeb's (1996) experiment investigated the effect of high and low levels of supplier trust and supplier dependence on satisfaction and commitment for a hypothetical dyadic exchange relationship. After confirming that the **trust** and dependence manipulation had occurred, Andaleeb (1996) found that both greater **trust** in a supplier and greater dependence on a supplier led to higher levels of buyer commitment to the supplier and satisfaction with the relationship. However, the level of commitment exhibited toward a supplier was found to be much more sensitive to different levels of **trust** when dependence was low compared with when it was high, which indicated the presence of a significant interaction effect between **trust** and dependence.

REFERENCES:

Andaleeb, Syed Saad (1996), "An Experimental Investigation of Satisfaction and Commitment in Marketing Channels: The Role of Trust and Dependence," *JR*, 72 (1), 77–93.

Crosby, Lawrence A., Kenneth R. Evans, and Deborah Cowles (1990), "Relationship Quality in Services Selling: An Interpersonal Influence Perspective," *JM*, 54 (July), 68–81.

Schurr, Paul H. and Julie L. Ozanne (1985), "Influences on Exchange Processes: Buyers' Preconceptions of a Seller's Trustworthiness and Bargaining Toughness," *JCR*, 11, 939–53.

#916 *Trust (Distributor in Manufacturer)*

SCALE ITEMS:*

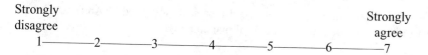

Strongly
disagree

Strongly
agree

1————2————3————4————5————6————7

1. Company X is very dependable.

2. Company X is not sincere about keeping its commitments. **(r)**

3. Company X can not be counted on to be helpful. **(r)**

4. Company X is not very reliable. **(r)**

*The name of the focal manufacturer should begin each item. Also, even though the appendix listing the scales used by Andaleep (1996) does not indicate that three of these items were reversed, it appears to be necessary.

SCALE NAME: Trust in Manager

SCALE DESCRIPTION: Rich (1997) used this five-item, seven-point Likert-type scale to measure the extent to which a salesperson has confidence in the manager's reliability and integrity.

SCALE ORIGIN: Rich (1997) stated that the scale was adapted from Podsakoff and colleagues (1990), and was revised into its final form on the basis of the results of a confirmatory factor analysis.

SAMPLES: Salespeople and their immediate supervisors from 10 different U.S.-based business-to-business sales organizations representing different industries formed the sample for this study. Questionnaires were received by 244 salesperson–manager dyads; usable responses were obtained from 193 salespeople and 218 managers, resulting in complete responses from a total of **183** matched salesperson–manager dyads.

RELIABILITY: Rich (1997) reported a coefficient alpha of **.94** for the measure.

VALIDITY: Results of the confirmatory factor analysis reported by Rich (1997) provided strong evidence for the discriminant and convergent validity of the measures, and the extensive pretesting provided evidence of content validity.

ADMINISTRATION: Rich (1997) indicated that the scale was part of a self-administered mail survey sent directly to each member of the salesperson–manager dyad. Follow-up telephone calls made by research assistants, the promise to share survey results, and encouragement from the management of participating firms enhanced respondent participation. It appears that the measure was only administered to the salesperson sample. Higher scores on the scale indicated that a salesperson had more confidence in his or her manager's reliability and integrity.

MAJOR FINDINGS: Rich (1997) examined the relationship between the role modeling behavior of sales managers and a set of key outcome variables, including trust in the manager, job satisfaction, and salesperson performance. Salespeople's perceptions of their managers' role modeling behavior were positively related to their **trust in the sales manager**. Through its relationship with **trust**, sales manager role modeling behavior was found to indirectly influence both job satisfaction and salesperson performance.

REFERENCES:

Podsakoff, Philip M., Scott B. MacKenzie, R.H. Moorman, and Richard Fetter (1990), "Transformational Leader Behaviors and Their Effects on Followers' Trust in Leader, Satisfaction, and Organizational Citizenship Behaviors," *Leadership Quarterly*, 1 (Summer), 102–42.

Rich, Gregory A. (1997), "The Sales Manager as a Role Model: Effects on Trust, Job Satisfaction, and Performance of Salespeople," *JAMS*, 25 (4), 319–28.

SCALE ITEMS:

1 = Strongly disagree
2 = Moderately disagree
3 = Slightly disagree
4 = Neither agree nor disagree
5 = Slightly agree
6 = Moderately agree
7 = Strongly agree

#917 *Trust in Manager*

1. My manager would never try to gain an advantage by deceiving workers.

2. I feel a strong loyalty to my manager.

3. I have complete faith in the integrity of my manager.

4. I feel quite confident that my manager will always try to treat me fairly.

5. I have strong sense of loyalty toward my manager.

SCALE NAME: Trust in Retailer (Benevolence)

SCALE DESCRIPTION: Ganesan (1994) developed a three-item, seven-point Likert-type scale to measure the benevolence dimension of a vendor's trust in a retailer. Although Ganesan (1994) defines benevolence as focusing on the qualities, intentions, and characteristics of the exchange partner rather than its specific behavior, the scale items selected also seem to measure the extent to which a retailer acts in ways helpful or otherwise beneficial to the vendor.

SCALE ORIGIN: The scale is original to Ganesan (1994), who developed separate but parallel benevolence measures for the vendor and retailer samples. Scale items were generated through interviews with retail buyers and vendors, and though some items were specific to the retailer or vendor version, the author included a core set of items with minor phrasing alterations in both scales. Item analysis and exploratory factor analysis were used to initially purify the measure; items with low loadings and those loading on multiple factors were eliminated. A draft of the questionnaire containing this scale was also pretested with a group of 14 retail buyers representing two department store chains.

SAMPLES: Five retail department store chains agreed to participate in Ganesan's (1994) study, and each firm received and distributed 30 questionnaires to senior sales representatives or sales managers who served as liaisons with vendor organizations. A total of **124** (83%) usable responses representing the *retailer* sample were obtained. Of these, 48 respondents answered in the context of a long-term vendor relationship, and the remaining 76 answered in the context of a short-term vendor relationship. Contact information provided by respondents enabled the author to sample the designated 124 key vendor informants most knowledgeable about the retailer/vendor relationship with a survey similar in content to the retailer questionnaire but phrased from the vendor point of view. A total of **52** (42%) *vendor* representatives responded, of which 21 and 31 were in short- and long-term relationships, respectively.

RELIABILITY: Ganesan (1994) reported a coefficient alpha of **.76** for the scale.

VALIDITY: Ganesan (1994) performed an exploratory factor analysis using an oblimin rotation on all items representing trust in the retailer representative, as measured by the vendor's trust in the retailer (credibility) and the vendor's trust in the retailer (benevolence) scales. Items loading above .40 were submitted to a confirmatory factor analysis with LISREL VII. Unidimensional two- and three-factor models were tested, and despite a significant chi-square test result, the root mean square residual suggested the acceptance of the two-factor model. It also appeared that the convergent validity and discriminant validity of the measure were assessed with confirmatory factor analysis using LISREL 7.16, though no information pertaining to the outcome of the validity tests was provided.

ADMINISTRATION: Prior to being sent a survey, buyers in the retailer sample were randomly assigned to one of four cells in which the questionnaire instructions asked them to select a vendor on the basis of variations in two criteria: (1) the length of their relationship (short-term or long-term) and (2) the importance of the vendor's product to their organization (moderately important or very important). Questionnaires were distributed by a coordinator in each department store, and respondents were instructed to answer the survey in the context of this single vendor. Higher scores on the scale indicated that vendors perceived retailers as being more benevolent; retailers were perceived as taking actions beneficial to the vendor in a variety of contexts.

MAJOR FINDINGS: Ganesan (1994) investigated a variety of factors influencing the long-term orientation of both retailers and vendors in an ongoing relationship, as well as the antecedents to long-term orientation. The **vendor's perception of the retailer's benevolence** was positively related to a vendor's satisfaction with past relationship outcomes.

#918 *Trust in Retailer (Benevolence)*

REFERENCES:

Ganesan, Shankar (1994), "Determinants of Long-Term Orientation in Buyer-Seller Relationships," *JM*, 58 (April), 1–19.

SCALE ITEMS:

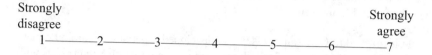

Strongly disagree 1————2————3————4————5————6————7 Strongly agree

1. The buyer representing this retailer has made sacrifices for us in the past.

2. The buyer representing this retailer cares for my welfare.

3. In times of delivery problems, the buyer representing this retailer has been very understanding.

SCALE NAME: Trust in Retailer (Credibility)

SCALE DESCRIPTION: Ganesan (1994) developed a four-item, seven-point Likert-type scale to measure the benevolence dimension of a vendor's trust in a retailer. The scale assesses the extent to which a retailer is reliable, has the required expertise to perform its duties in the relationship effectively, and is true to its word.

SCALE ORIGIN: The scale is original to Ganesan (1994), who developed separate but parallel credibility measures for the vendor and retailer samples. Scale items were generated through interviews with retail buyers and vendors, and though some items were specific to the retailer or vendor version, the author included a core set of items with minor phrasing alterations in both scales. Item analysis and exploratory factor analysis were used to initially purify the measure; items with low loadings and those loading on multiple factors were eliminated. A draft of the questionnaire containing this scale was also pretested with a group of 14 retail buyers representing two department store chains.

SAMPLES: Five retail department store chains agreed to participate in Ganesan's (1994) study, and each firm received and distributed 30 questionnaires to senior sales representatives or sales managers who served as liaisons with vendor organizations. A total of **124** (83%) usable responses representing the *retailer* sample were obtained. Of these, 48 respondents answered in the context of a long-term vendor relationship, and the remaining 76 answered in the context of a short-term vendor relationship. Contact information provided by respondents enabled the author to sample the designated 124 key vendor informants most knowledgeable about the retailer/vendor relationship with a survey similar in content to the retailer questionnaire but phrased from the vendor point of view. A total of **52** (42%) *vendor* representatives responded, of which 21 and 31 were in short- and long-term relationships, respectively.

RELIABILITY: Ganesan (1994) reported a coefficient alpha of **.80** for the scale.

VALIDITY: Ganesan (1994) performed an exploratory factor analysis using an oblimin rotation on all items representing trust in the retailer representative, as measured by the vendor's trust in the retailer (credibility) and the vendor's trust in the retailer (benevolence) scales. Items loading above .40 were submitted to a confirmatory factor analysis with LISREL VII. Unidimensional two- and three-factor models were tested, and despite a significant chi-square test result, the root mean square residual suggested the acceptance of the two-factor model. It also appeared that the convergent validity and discriminant validity of the measure were assessed by confirmatory factor analysis using LISREL 7.16, though no information pertaining to the outcome of the validity tests was provided.

ADMINISTRATION: Prior to being sent a survey, buyers in the retailer sample were randomly assigned to one of four cells in which the questionnaire instructions asked them to select a vendor on the basis of variations in two criteria: (1) the length of their relationship (short-term or long-term) and (2) the importance of the vendor's product to their organization (moderately important or very important). Questionnaires were distributed by a coordinator in each department store, and respondents were instructed to answer the survey in the context of this single vendor. Higher scores on the scale indicated that vendors perceived retailers as being more credible; retailers were perceived as being reliable, true to their word, and having the expertise necessary to perform their job effectively.

MAJOR FINDINGS: Ganesan (1994) investigated a variety of factors influencing the long-term orientation of both retailers and vendors in an ongoing relationship, as well as the antecedents to long-term orientation. The **vendor's perception of the retailer's credibility** was positively related to a vendor's long-term orientation, perceptions of investments made by the retailer in transaction specific assets, and satisfaction with past relationship outcomes.

#919 *Trust in Retailer (Credibility)*

REFERENCES:

Ganesan, Shankar (1994), "Determinants of Long-Term Orientation in Buyer-Seller Relationships," *JM*, 58 (April), 1–19.

SCALE ITEMS:

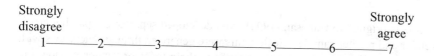

Strongly disagree 1——2——3——4——5——6——7 Strongly agree

1. The buyer representing this retailer has been frank in dealing with me.

2. Promises made by the buyer representing this retailer are reliable.

3. The buyer representing this retailer is knowledgeable about the product.

4. The buyer representing this retailer has problems understanding our position. **(r)**

SCALE NAME: Trust in Salesperson

SCALE DESCRIPTION: Doney and Cannon (1997) used this seven-item, seven-point Likert-type scale to measure the extent to which a buyer believes a salesperson is able to perform effectively and reliably (credibility) and is interested in the customer's best interests (benevolence).

SCALE ORIGIN: Doney and Cannon (1997) stated that they generated items for the scale on the basis of interviews with marketing and purchasing personnel; however, several items appear to have been adapted from Anderson and Weitz (1992) and Ganesan (1994). Exploratory factor analyses using both orthogonal and oblique rotations were used to ensure high item loadings on hypothesized constructs and low cross-loadings.

SAMPLES: Doney and Cannon (1997) sampled 657 members of the National Association of Purchasing Management who were employed by firms involved in industrial manufacturing, as classified by standard industrial classification codes 33–37. **Two hundred ten** completed questionnaires were returned from a primarily male (76%) sample with an average of 15 years of purchasing experience.

RELIABILITY: Doney and Cannon (1997) calculated a coefficient alpha of **.90** for this measure.

VALIDITY: Doney and Cannon (1997) reported using three methods to test the discriminant validity of the scales representing the combined dimensions of trust of the salesperson and its proposed antecedents and outcomes. Each method provided strong evidence of discriminant validity. Two LISREL-based tests were also used to provide evidence for the convergent validity of the measures. Finally, two additional tests of discriminant validity were performed using the measures of trust of a salesperson and trust of the firm through a nested models confirmatory factory analysis. The results provided evidence that these two latent constructs were discriminant.

ADMINISTRATION: The scale was included with other measures as part of a self-administered survey that was delivered by mail. Nonrespondents received a postcard reminder followed by a second questionnaire a week later. Doney and Cannon (1997) instructed respondents to focus on a single, specific, recent purchase decision in which more than one supplier was seriously considered and indicate on the survey (using initials) two of the firms considered. After answering questions pertaining to the purchase situation, half of the respondents were instructed to complete the remainder of the questionnaire in the context of the first supplier they had listed, whereas the other half were instructed to use the second supplier. Higher scores on the scale indicated that respondents perceived the focal salesperson as being more credible and benevolent.

MAJOR FINDINGS: Doney and Cannon (1997) investigated the impact of purchasing agents' trust in the salesperson and the supplier firm on a buying firm's current supplier choice and future buying intentions. The extent to which a salesperson was perceived to be likable and similar to members of the buying firm positively influenced their level of **trust in the salesperson**. Frequency of business contact and trust of the supplier also positively influenced the buying firm's **trust in the salesperson**. Although salespeople representing the selected suppliers were more trusted than those representing suppliers who were not chosen, **trust in the salesperson** did not explain any additional variance in purchase choice after controlling for previous supplier experience and supplier performance.

REFERENCES:
Anderson, Erin and Barton A. Weitz (1992), "The Use of Pledges to Build and Sustain Commitment in Distribution Channels," *JMR*, 29 (February), 18–34.

#920 *Trust in Salesperson*

Doney, Patricia M. and Joseph P. Cannon (1997), "An Examination of the Nature of Trust in Buyer-Seller Relationships," *JM*, 61 (April), 35–51.

Ganesan, Shankar (1994), "Determinants of Long-Term Orientation in Buyer-Seller Relationships," *JM*, 58 (April), 1–19.

SCALE ITEMS:

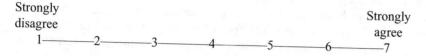

Strongly disagree 1—2—3—4—5—6—7 Strongly agree

1. This salesperson has been frank in dealing with us.

2. This salesperson does not make false claims.

3. We do not think this salesperson is completely open in dealing with us. **(r)**

4. This salesperson is only concerned about himself/herself. **(r)**

5. This salesperson does not seem to be concerned with our needs. **(r)**

6. The people at my firm do not trust this salesperson. **(r)**

7. This salesperson is not trustworthy. **(r)**

SCALE NAME: Trust in Sales Manager (Interpersonal)

SCALE DESCRIPTION: Five seven-point Likert-type items measuring the extent to which a retailer is willing to rely on its sales manager to make decisions affecting its business. Dahlstrom and Nygaard (1995) used the scale with oil and gas retailers.

SCALE ORIGIN: Dahlstrom and Nygaard (1995) adapted the scale from the work of Moorman, Zaltman, and Deshpandé (1992). Item-to-total correlations were examined using a country-by-country analysis of the data; items correlating at .25 or lower were dropped from the measure for a particular country. Item 1 cross-loaded on the centralization factor in the German sample but was retained on the basis of face validity and a desire to use a consistent set of items for each country.

SAMPLES: Norwegian, German (formerly East German), and Polish oil and gas retailers were sampled by Dahlstrom and Nygaard (1995). Of the 432 Norwegian service station managers working in the retail network of a single oil refiner who were surveyed, **216** usable responses were obtained. **Forty** of the 44 service station managers in Poland and **29** of the 50 Leipzig-area dealers in the former East Germany also provided usable data.

RELIABILITY: Dahlstrom and Nygaard (1995) reported coefficient alphas of **.80, .62**, and **.87** in the Polish, German, and Norwegian samples, respectively.

VALIDITY: Dahlstrom and Nygaard (1995) did not specifically examine the validity of the measure.

ADMINISTRATION: Dahlstrom and Nygaard (1995) included the scale with other measures as part of a self-administered survey that was delivered by mail to the Norwegian sample. The survey was administered in person by college students to oil and gas retailers in the Polish and German samples. In each case, the questionnaire was translated into the focal language and back-translated into English, typically by university faculty in each country. Higher scores on the scale indicated that the oil and gas retailer felt a greater trust for the sales manager, as demonstrated by a greater willingness to allow the sales manager to make decisions that would affect the retailer's business.

MAJOR FINDINGS: Dahlstrom and Nygaard (1995) investigated various antecedents to and consequences of interpersonal trust in new and mature market economies using data collected in Norway, Poland, and the former East Germany. Retailers' perceptions of **interpersonal trust** in their sales managers was influenced by their country of origin. Specifically, Norwegian retailers were less trustful than either German or Polish retailers. **Interpersonal trust** was not significantly affected by centralization in any country, and higher levels of formalized rules and procedures were significantly associated with higher levels of **interpersonal trust** in the Norwegian sample only. **Interpersonal trust** raised performance in both the Polish and Norwegian samples, whereas, contrary to expectations, **interpersonal trust** negatively influenced performance in the German sample.

REFERENCES:
Dahlstrom, Robert and Arne Nygaard (1995), "An Exploratory Investigation of Interpersonal Trust in New and Mature Market Economies," *JR*, 71 (4), 339–61.
Moorman, Christine, Gerald Zaltman and Rohit Deshpandé (1992), "Relationships Between Providers and Users of Market Research: The Dynamics of Trust Within and Between Organizations," *JMR*, 29 (3), 314–28.

#921 *Trust in Sales Manager (Interpersonal)*

SCALE ITEMS:

To what extent would you agree with the following?

Strongly
disagree   Strongly
                                                agree
1———2———3———4———5———6———7

1. If my sales manager cannot reach me and has to make a decision affecting my station, I am willing to let him make the decision without me.

2. I fully trust my sales manager and think he is doing the best for me and the other *(Brand name)* dealers.

3. I fully trust that the area sales manager is important to the distribution system.

4. I trust the sales manager to do things I can't do myself.

5. I generally do not trust the sales manager. **(r)**

SCALE NAME: Trust in Source of Market Intelligence

SCALE DESCRIPTION: Maltz and Kohli (1996) used this six-item, five-point Likert-type scale to measure the extent to which the receiver perceived the information provider as having the ability and motivation to provide good intelligence.

SCALE ORIGIN: The scale is apparently original to Maltz and Kohli (1996). The items were evaluated in face-to-face interviews with manufacturing, finance, and R&D department managers and by a panel of academic experts. The measure and questionnaire were also pretested with 77 participants of an executive MBA program. Items that were found to be problematic were revised or eliminated in accordance with the comments received at various stages in the pretesting process.

SAMPLES: Maltz and Kohli (1996) sampled mid-level managers operating within strategic business units (SBUs) of firms engaged in the manufacture of high-technology industrial equipment. The authors obtained names of 1061 nonmarketing managers in 270 SBUs from corporation presidents of participating firms. A total of **788** usable responses were returned by managers working in manufacturing (272), R&D (252), and finance (194).

RELIABILITY: Maltz and Kohli (1996) reported a coefficient alpha of .77 for this measure.

VALIDITY: Maltz and Kohli (1996) evaluated the discriminant validity of the trust in source and interfunctional rivalry constructs together in a LISREL model. The results provided evidence of the discriminant validity of the measures.

ADMINISTRATION: The measure was included by Maltz and Kohli (1996) as part of a self-administered questionnaire that was delivered by mail. Nonrespondents received a follow-up letter and second questionnaire mailing. When answering the survey, respondents were instructed to focus on the intelligence they had received from the person in the marketing department with whom they had interacted the most during the previous three months. Higher scores on the scale reflected greater trust in the marketing information provider's ability and motivation to provide good intelligence.

MAJOR FINDINGS: Maltz and Kohli (1996) investigated the antecedents and consequences of the dissemination of marketing intelligence within SBUs. The results indicated that higher levels of **trust in the source of marketing intelligence** were significantly associated with more frequent information dissemination, the use of less formal information channels, and more positive evaluations of the quality of the market intelligence. As expected, interfunctional rivalry had a negative effect on respondent's **trust of the marketing intelligence provider**.

REFERENCES:
Maltz, Elliot and Ajay K. Kohli (1996), "Market Intelligence Dissemination Across Functional Boundaries," *JMR*, 33 (February), 47–61.

SCALE ITEMS: *

Strongly
disagree

Strongly
agree

1————2————3————4————5

The marketing contact...

1. Can be depended on to provide a good view of the marketplace.

2. Keeps his/her commitments to me.

3. Has a good understanding of customers and competitors.

4. Is competent.

5. Tries to get me to make decisions that are not in my best interest. **(r)**

6. And I see our relationship as kind of a partnership.

* Although Maltz and Kohli (1996) do not designate item 5 as reversed in the appendix listing their scale items, further examination of the scale indicates that this is necessary.

SCALE NAME: Trust in Supplier

SCALE DESCRIPTION: Kumar, Scheer, and Steenkamp (1995) used this ten-item, seven-point Likert-type scale to measure a firm's trust in the honesty and benevolence of its partner. Perceptions of honesty reflect the degree to which a firm believes that the partner is honest, truthful, and reliable, and benevolence refers to the extent to which a firm believes that the partner is interested in the welfare of the dealer firm.

SCALE ORIGIN: It is unclear whether the items were developed by Kumar, Scheer, and Steenkamp (1995) or adapted from existing scales. Regardless, the origin of the measure can be traced through several articles detailing the conceptualization of trust (Anderson and Narus 1990; Detusch 1958; Dwyer and Oh 1987; Lazelere and Huston 1980; Rempel, Holmes, and Zanna 1985; Scheer and Stern 1992).

SAMPLES: Kumar, Scheer, and Steenkamp (1995) mailed surveys to 1640 new car dealers obtained from a commercial list covering two states, and **417** usable responses were returned. No significant differences between early and late respondents was present, which suggested that nonresponse bias was not a problem.

RELIABILITY: Kumar, Scheer, and Steenkamp (1995) calculated a coefficient alpha of **.91** for the scale.

VALIDITY: Confirmatory factor analysis was used to assess the validity of the measures. Kumar, Scheer, and Steenkamp (1995) specified honesty and benevolence as two first-order factors for the second-order factor of trust. Significant factor loadings on all items were accepted as evidence of convergent validity. Although trust, conflict, and commitment were significantly correlated as expected, the intercorrelations were significantly below unity, thereby providing evidence for the discriminant validity of the measure.

ADMINISTRATION: Kumar, Scheer, and Steenkamp (1995) stated that the scale was part of a self-administered mail survey that was accompanied by a personalized cover letter. Dealers that did not respond in four weeks received a reminder letter. Higher scores on the scale indicated that dealers reported stronger beliefs in the honesty and benevolence of their partners.

MAJOR FINDINGS: Kumar, Scheer, and Steenkamp (1995) investigated how interdependence asymmetry (the difference between the dealer's dependence on the supplier and the supplier's dependence on the dealer) and total interdependence (the sum of both firm's dependency) affected the development of interfirm **trust**, commitment, and conflict. The results of the regression analysis indicated that **trust** is greater both when total interdependence is higher and when asymmetry interdependence between firms is lower.

REFERENCES:
Anderson, James C. and James A. Narus (1990), "A Model of Distributor Firm and Manufacturer Firm Working Relationships," *JM*, 54 (January), 42–58.
Deutsch, Morton (1958), "Trust and Suspicion," *Journal of Conflict Resolution*, 2 (4), 265–79.
Dwyer, F. Robert and Sejo Oh (1987), "Output Sector Munificence Effects on the Internal Political Economy of Marketing Channels," *JMR*, 24 (November), 347–58.
Kumar, Nirmalya, Lisa K. Scheer, and Jan-Benedict E.M. Steenkamp (1995a), "The Effects of Perceived Interdependence on Dealer Attitudes," *JMR*, 32 (August), 348–56.
Lazelere, Robert E. and Ted L. Huston (1980), "The Dyadic Trust Scale: Toward Understanding Interpersonal Trust in Close Relationships," *Journal of Marriage and the Family*, 42 (August), 595–604.

Rempel, John K., John G. Holmes, and Mark P. Zanna (1985), "Trust in Close Relationships," *Journal of Personality and Social Psychology*, 49 (1), 95–112.

Scheer, Lisa K. and Louis W. Stern (1992), "The Effect of Influence Type and Performance Outcomes on Attitude Toward the Influencer," *JMR*, 29 (February), 128–42.

SCALE ITEMS:

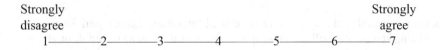

| Strongly disagree | | | | | | Strongly agree |
| 1————2————3————4————5————6————7 |

Trust in partner's honesty

1. Even when the supplier gives us a rather unlikely explanation, we are confident that it is telling the truth.
2. The supplier has often provided us information that has later proven to be inaccurate. **(r)**
3. The supplier usually keeps the promises that it makes to our firm.
4. Whenever the supplier gives us advice on our business operations, we know that it is sharing its best judgment.
5. Our organization can count on the supplier to be sincere.

Trust in partner's benevolence:

6. Though circumstances change, we believe that the supplier will be ready and willing to offer us assistance and support.
7. When making important decisions, the supplier is concerned about our welfare.
8. When we share our problems with the supplier, we know that it will respond with understanding.
9. In the future, we can count on the supplier to consider how its decisions and actions will affect us.
10. When it comes to things that are important to us, we can depend on the supplier's support.

SCALE NAME: Trust in Supplier Firm

SCALE DESCRIPTION: Doney and Cannon (1997) used this eight-item, seven-point Likert-type scale to measure the extent to which a buyer believes a supplier is able to perform effectively and reliably (credibility) and is interested in the customer's best interests (benevolence).

SCALE ORIGIN: Doney and Cannon (1997) stated that they generated items for the scale on the basis of interviews with marketing and purchasing personnel; however, several items appear to have been adapted from Anderson and Weitz (1992) and Ganesan (1994). Although Ganesan (1994) used separate measures for the credibility and benevolence components of trust, Doney and Cannon's (1997) analysis found these two trust dimensions to be highly correlated and, on the basis of a lack of discriminatory validity between the measures, combined all items to form a single unidimensional measure of trust.

SAMPLES: Doney and Cannon (1997) sampled 657 members of the National Association of Purchasing Management who were employed by firms involved in industrial manufacturing, as classified by standard industrial classification codes 33–37. **Two hundred ten** completed questionnaires were returned from a primarily male (76%) sample with an average of 15 years of purchasing experience.

RELIABILITY: Doney and Cannon (1997) calculated a coefficient alpha of **.94** for this measure.

VALIDITY: Doney and Cannon (1997) reported using three methods to test the discriminant validity of the scales representing the combined dimensions of trust of the supplier firm and its proposed antecedents and outcomes. Each method provided strong evidence of discriminant validity. Two LISREL-based tests were also used to provide evidence for the convergent validity of the measure. Finally, two additional tests of discriminant validity were performed using the measures of trust of a salesperson and trust of the firm through a nested models confirmatory factory analysis. The results provided evidence that these two latent constructs were discriminant.

ADMINISTRATION: The scale was included with other measures as part of a self-administered survey that was delivered by mail. Nonrespondents received a postcard reminder followed by a second questionnaire a week later. Doney and Cannon (1997) instructed respondents to focus on a single, specific, recent purchase decision in which more than one supplier was seriously considered and indicate on the survey (using initials) two of the firms considered. After answering questions pertaining to the purchase situation, half of the respondents were instructed to complete the remainder of the questionnaire in the context of the first supplier they had listed, whereas the other half were instructed to use the second supplier. Higher scores on the scale indicated that respondents perceived the focal supplier as being more credible and benevolent.

MAJOR FINDINGS: Doney and Cannon (1997) investigated the impact of purchasing agents' trust in the salesperson and the supplier firm on a buying firm's current supplier choice and future buying intentions. The buying firm's **trust in the supplying firm** was found to be positively associated with the supplier's size and the supplier's willingness to customize. Although selected suppliers were more trusted than those not chosen, **trust in the supplying firm** did not explain any additional variance in purchase choice after controlling for previous supplier experience and supplier performance. However, when performance, past purchase experience, and current purchase choice were controlled for, **trust in the supplying firm** was significantly and positively related to anticipated future interaction with the supplier.

REFERENCES:
Anderson, Erin and Barton A. Weitz (1992), "The Use of Pledges to Build and Sustain Commitment in Distribution Channels," *JMR*, 29 (February), 18–34.

#924 *Trust in Supplier Firm*

Doney, Patricia M. and Joseph P. Cannon (1997), "An Examination of the Nature of Trust in Buyer-Seller Relationships," *JM*, 61 (April), 35–51.

Ganesan, Shankar (1994), "Determinants of Long-Term Orientation in Buyer-Seller Relationships," *JM*, 58 (April), 1–19.

SCALE ITEMS:

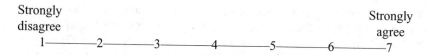

Strongly disagree 1————2————3————4————5————6————7 Strongly agree

1. This supplier keeps promises it makes to our firm.

2. This supplier is not always honest with us. **(r)**

3. We believe the information that this vendor provides us.

4. This supplier is genuinely concerned that our business succeeds.

5. When making important decisions, this supplier considers our welfare as well as its own.

6. We trust this vendor keeps our best interests in mind.

7. This supplier is trustworthy.

8. We find it necessary to be cautious with this supplier. **(r)**

SCALE NAME: Trust in Vendor (Benevolence)

SCALE DESCRIPTION: Ganesan (1994) developed a five-item, seven-point Likert-type scale to measure the benevolence dimension of a retailer's trust in a vendor. Although Ganesan (1994) defines benevolence as focusing on the qualities, intentions, and characteristics of the exchange partner rather than its specific behavior, the scale items selected also seem to measure the extent to which a vendor acts in ways helpful or otherwise beneficial to the retailer.

SCALE ORIGIN: The scale is original to Ganesan (1994), who developed separate but parallel benevolence measures for the vendor and retailer samples. Scale items were generated through interviews with retail buyers and vendors, and though some items were specific to the retailer or vendor version, the author included a core set of items with minor phrasing alterations in both scales. Item analysis and exploratory factor analysis were used to initially purify the measure; items with low loadings and those loading on multiple factors were eliminated. A draft of the questionnaire containing this scale was also pretested with a group of 14 retail buyers representing two department store chains.

SAMPLES: Five retail department store chains agreed to participate in Ganesan's (1994) study, and each firm received and distributed 30 questionnaires to senior sales representatives or sales managers who served as liaisons with vendor organizations. A total of **124** (83%) usable responses representing the *retailer* sample were obtained. Of these, 48 respondents answered in the context of a long-term vendor relationship, and the remaining 76 answered in the context of a short-term vendor relationship. Contact information provided by respondents enabled the author to sample the designated 124 key vendor informants most knowledgeable about the retailer/vendor relationship with a survey similar in content to the retailer questionnaire but phrased from the vendor point of view. A total of **52** (42%) *vendor* representatives responded, of which 21 and 31 were in short- and long-term relationships, respectively.

RELIABILITY: Ganesan (1994) reported a coefficient alpha of **.88** for the scale.

VALIDITY: Ganesan (1994) performed an exploratory factor analysis using an oblimin rotation on all items representing trust in the vendor representative as measured by the retailer's trust in the vendor (credibility) and the retailer's trust in the vendor (benevolence) scales. Items loading above .40 were submitted to a confirmatory factor analysis with LISREL VII. Unidimensional two- and three-factor models were tested, and despite a significant chi-square test result, the root mean square residual suggested the acceptance of the two-factor model. It also appeared that the convergent validity and discriminant validity of the measure were assessed by confirmatory factor analysis using LISREL 7.16, though no information pertaining to the outcome of the validity tests was provided.

ADMINISTRATION: Prior to being sent a survey, buyers in the retailer sample were randomly assigned to one of four cells in which the questionnaire instructions asked them to select a vendor on the basis of variations in two criteria: (1) the length of their relationship (short-term or long-term) and (2) the importance of the vendor's product to their organization (moderately important or very important). Questionnaires were distributed by a coordinator in each department store, and respondents were instructed to answer the survey in the context of this single vendor. Higher scores on the scale indicated that retailers perceived vendors as being more benevolent; vendors were perceived as taking actions beneficial to the retailer in a variety of contexts.

MAJOR FINDINGS: Ganesan (1994) investigated a variety of factors influencing the long-term orientation of both retailers and vendors in an ongoing relationship, as well as the antecedents to long-term orientation. The **retailer's perception of the vendor's benevolence** was positively related to a retailer's perceptions of investments made by the vendor in transaction-specific assets.

#925 *Trust in Vendor (Benevolence)*

REFERENCES:

Ganesan, Shankar (1994), "Determinants of Long-Term Orientation in Buyer-Seller Relationships," *JM*, 58 (April), 1–19.

SCALE ITEMS:

Strongly disagree / Strongly agree

1———2———3———4———5———6———7

1, This resource's representative has made sacrifices for us in the past.

2. This resource's representative cares for us.

3. In times of shortages, this resource's representative has gone out on a limb for us.

4. This resource's representative is like a friend.

5. We feel the resource's representative has been on our side.

SCALE NAME: Trust in Vendor (Credibility)

SCALE DESCRIPTION: Ganesan (1994) developed a seven-item, seven-point Likert-type scale to measure the benevolence dimension of a retailer's trust in a vendor. The scale assesses the extent to which a vendor is reliable, has the required expertise to perform its duties in the relationship effectively, and is true to its word.

SCALE ORIGIN: The scale is original to Ganesan (1994), who developed separate but parallel credibility measures for the vendor and retailer samples. Scale items were generated through interviews with retail buyers and vendors, and though some items were specific to the retailer or vendor version, the author included a core set of items with minor phrasing alterations in both scales. Item analysis and exploratory factor analysis were used to initially purify the measure; items with low loadings and those loading on multiple factors were eliminated. A draft of the questionnaire containing this scale was also pretested with a group of 14 retail buyers representing two department store chains.

SAMPLES: Five retail department store chains agreed to participate in Ganesan's (1994) study, and each firm received and distributed 30 questionnaires to senior sales representatives or sales managers who served as liaisons with vendor organizations. A total of **124** (83%) usable responses representing the *retailer* sample were obtained. Of these, 48 respondents answered in the context of a long-term vendor relationship, and the remaining 76 answered in the context of a short-term vendor relationship. Contact information provided by respondents enabled the author to sample the designated 124 key vendor informants most knowledgeable about the retailer/vendor relationship with a survey similar in content to the retailer questionnaire but phrased from the vendor point of view. A total of **52** (42%) *vendor* representatives responded, of which 21 and 31 were in short- and long-term relationships, respectively.

RELIABILITY: Ganesan (1994) reported a coefficient alpha of **.90** for the scale.

VALIDITY: Ganesan (1994) performed an exploratory factor analysis using an oblimin rotation on all items representing trust in the vendor representative as measured by the retailer's trust in the vendor (credibility) and the retailer's trust in the vendor (benevolence) scales. Items loading above .40 were submitted to a confirmatory factor analysis with LISREL VII. Unidimensional two- and three-factor models were tested, and despite a significant chi-square test result, the root mean square residual suggested the acceptance of the two-factor model. It also appeared that the convergent validity and discriminant validity of the measure were assessed by confirmatory factor analysis using LISREL 7.16, though no information pertaining to the outcome of the validity tests was provided.

ADMINISTRATION: Prior to being sent a survey, buyers in the retailer sample were randomly assigned to one of four cells in which the questionnaire instructions asked them to select a vendor on the basis of variations in two criteria: (1) the length of their relationship (short-term or long-term) and (2) the importance of the vendor's product to their organization (moderately important or very important). Questionnaires were distributed by a coordinator in each department store, and respondents were instructed to answer the survey in the context of this single vendor. Higher scores on the scale indicated that retailers perceived vendors as being more credible; vendors were perceived as being reliable, true to their word, and having the expertise necessary to perform their job effectively.

MAJOR FINDINGS: Ganesan (1994) investigated a variety of factors influencing the long-term orientation of both retailers and vendors in an ongoing relationship, as well as the antecedents to long-term orientation. The **retailer's perception of the vendor's credibility** was positively related to a retailer's long-term orientation, a vendor's reputation for fairness, and perceptions of investments made by the vendor in transaction-specific assets.

#926 *Trust in Vendor (Credibility)*

REFERENCES:

Ganesan, Shankar (1994), "Determinants of Long-Term Orientation in Buyer-Seller Relationships," *JM*, 58 (April), 1–19.

SCALE ITEMS:

Strongly   Strongly
disagree   agree
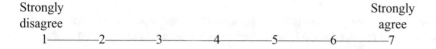

1. This resource's representative has been frank in dealing with us.

2. Promises made by this resource's representative are reliable.

3. This resource's representative is knowledgeable regarding his/her products.

4. This resource's representative does not make false claims.

5. This resource's representative is not open in dealing with us. **(r)**

6. If problems such as shipment delays arise, the resource's representative is honest about the problems.

7. This resource's representative has problems answering our questions. **(r)**

SCALE NAME: Turbulence (Competitive Intensity)

SCALE DESCRIPTION: Moorman (1995) used this six-item, seven-point Likert-type scale to assess the level of competitiveness in an industry as indicated by the ability of competitors to differentiate themselves from one another on the basis of price, promotion, and other factors.

SCALE ORIGIN: Moorman (1995) stated that the scale was adapted from Jaworski and Kohli's (1993) study. All measures used by Moorman (1995) were subjected to a purification process following data collection. The author assessed the unidimensionality of the measures in a two-factor confirmatory analysis model using LISREL VII. Items with very weak loadings and those loading on more than one factor were eliminated. The reliability of the measures was assessed by calculating coefficient alphas, and items with low item-to-total correlations were dropped if "doing so did not diminish the measure's coverage of the construct domain" (Moorman 1995, p. 325).

SAMPLES: Moorman (1995) chose to sample the vice presidents of marketing for 300 divisions of firms noted in the 1992 *Advertising Age* list of top 200 advertisers, and a total of **92** usable questionnaires were received. No systematic differences were observed between early and late respondents.

RELIABILITY: Moorman (1995) reported a coefficient alpha of **.84** for this scale.

VALIDITY: Moorman (1995) performed a series of two-factor confirmatory analyses using LISREL VII to assess the discriminant validity of the measures used in her study. Chi-square difference tests were performed on constrained versus unconstrained models. The significantly lower chi-square values observed for all of the unconstrained models tested were accepted as evidence of the discriminant validity of the measures.

ADMINISTRATION: The scale was included with other measures in a self-administered questionnaire that was delivered by mail. Moorman's (1995) cover letter explained the survey purpose and, in an effort to increase response rate, offered to share survey results. Nonrespondents were telephoned after three weeks and sent a second questionnaire two weeks after the telephone reminder. All informants were instructed to answer in the context of the most recent product development project for which their division had been responsible. Focal projects were required to have been on the market for a minimum of 12 months. Higher scores on the scale indicated that the competitive intensity was high, making it difficult for competitors to differentiate themselves from one another.

MAJOR FINDINGS: Moorman (1995) examined the relationship among organizational market information processes, organizational culture, and new product outcomes. The **competitive intensity aspect of environmental turbulence** was treated as a control variable in the model and was found to have a significant, negative relationship with new product creativity.

REFERENCES:
Jaworski, Bernard J. and Ajay K. Kohli (1993), "Market Orientation: Antecedents and Consequences," *JM*, 57 (July), 53–71.
Moorman, Christine (1995), "Organizational Market Information Processes: Cultural Antecedents and New Product Outcomes," *JMR*, 32 (August), 318–35.

#927 *Turbulence (Competitive Intensity)*

SCALE ITEMS:

Strongly   Strongly
disagree   agree

1. Competition in this product area is cutthroat.

2. There are many promotion wars in this product area.

3. Anything that one competitor can offer in this product area, others can match readily.

4. Price competition is a hallmark in this area.

5. One hears of a new competitive move in this product area almost everyday.

6. Our competitors in this product area are relatively weak. **(r)**

SCALE NAME: Turbulence (Market)

SCALE DESCRIPTION: A five-item Likert-type scale measuring the degree of changes in the composition of customers and preferences of an organization's customers.

SCALE ORIGIN: The scale was developed by Jaworski and Kohli (1993). Close examination of Menon, Jaworski, and Kohli's (1997) work indicates that the sample and data used to develop the scale are identical to those reported in Jaworski and Kohli (1993). Likewise, the data and methodology (though not the scales) reported in Moorman and Miner (1997) were previously reported by Moorman (1995). All measures used by Moorman and Miner (1997) were subjected to a purification process following data collection.

SAMPLES: Using the *Dun and Bradstreet Million Dollar Directory* as the sampling frame, Menon, Jaworski, and Kohli (1997; Jaworski and Kohli 1993) selected for initial contact every other company name from among the top 1000 companies by sales revenues. Participation from multiple strategic business units (SBUs) within an organization was requested. A total of 102 companies agreed to participate, and ultimately, responses representing **222** SBUs were obtained from marketing and nonmarketing executives.

Moorman (1995; Moorman and Miner 1997) chose to sample the vice presidents of marketing for 300 divisions of firms noted in the 1992 *Advertising Age* list of top 200 advertisers, and a total of **92** usable questionnaires were received. No systematic differences were observed between early and late respondents.

RELIABILITY: Menon, Jaworski, and Kohli (1997) reported a **.68** alpha reliability coefficient. One item with low interitem correlations was eliminated from the original six-item scale set to yield the final five-item measure listed here. Moorman and Miner (1997) reported an alpha of **.70** for the scale.

VALIDITY: No specific examination of scale validity was presented by Menon, Jaworski, and Kohli (1997) or Jaworski and Kohli (1993). Moorman and Miner (1997) assessed the unidimensionality of the scale by dividing the measures used in this study into three subsets of theoretically related variables and submitting the measures to confirmatory factor analyses. The three models provided a good fit with the data. Confirmatory factor analysis was also used to assess the discriminant validity of the measure and was found to be satisfactory.

ADMINISTRATION: The 206 marketing and 187 nonmarketing executives identified by participating corporations were directly contacted by Menon, Jaworski, and Kohli (1997). Initial contact was followed by a self-administered mail questionnaire, and a follow-up questionnaire was sent three weeks later to nonrespondents. When both nonmarketing and marketing executives from a single SBU responded, their scores were averaged to provide a single score for the construct.

The scale was included in the study by Moorman and Miner (1997) with other measures in a self-administered questionnaire that was delivered by mail. All informants were instructed to answer in the context of the most recent product development project for which their division had been responsible. Focal projects were required to have been on the market for a minimum of 12 months.

A higher score on the market turbulence scale indicated a more volatile market characterized by a higher degree of customer composition and preference changes.

MAJOR FINDINGS: Menon, Jaworski, and Kohli (1997) investigated the role of organizational factors affecting interdepartmental interactions and the resulting impact on product quality. Although the relationship between product quality and interdepartmental conflict was found to be robust across various levels of **market turbulence**, interdepartmental connectedness was more important for product quality when **market turbulence** conditions were high.

Moorman and Miner (1997) investigated the impact of organizational memory level and organizational memory dispersion on key new product development processes. The positive impact of organizational memory dispersion on the short-term financial performance of a new product was significantly weakened by high levels of **market turbulence.**

REFERENCES:

Jaworski, Bernard and Ajay K. Kohli (1993), "Market Orientation: Antecedents and Consequences," *JM*, 57 (July), 53–70.

Menon, Ajay, Bernard J. Jaworski, and Ajay K. Kohli (1997), "Product Quality: Impact of Interdepartmental Interactions," *JAMS*, 25 (3), 187–200.

Moorman, Christine (1995), "Organizational Market Information Processes: Cultural Antecedents and New Product Outcomes," *JMR*, 32 (August), 318–35.

——— and Anne S. Miner (1997), "The Impact of Organizational Memory on New Product Performance and Creativity," *JMR*, 34 (February), 91–106.

SCALE ITEMS: *

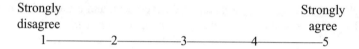

Strongly disagree — Strongly agree
1————2————3————4————5

1. In our kind of business, customers' product preferences change quite a bit over time.

2. Our customers tend to look for new products all the time.

3. We are witnessing demand for our products and services from customers who never bought them before.

4. New customers tend to have product-related needs that are different from those of our existing customers.

5. We cater to much the same customers that we used to in the past. **(r)**

*This is the version of the scale used by Menon, Jaworski, and Kohli (1997; Jaworski and Kohli 1993). Moorman (1995; Moorman and Miner 1997) used a seven-point response format.

SCALE NAME: Turbulence (Technological)

SCALE DESCRIPTION: This scale measures the perceived degree of technological change within an industry. The version used by Menon, Jaworski, and Kohli (1997) had four five-point items, whereas the version used by Moorman and Miner (1997) had five seven-point items.

SCALE ORIGIN: The scale was developed by Jaworski and Kohli (1993). Close examination of Menon, Jaworski, and Kohli's (1997) work indicates that the sample and data used to develop the scale are identical to those reported by Jaworski and Kohli (1993). Likewise, the data and methodology (though not the scales) reported in Moorman and Miner (1997) were previously reported by Moorman (1995). All measures used by Moorman and Miner (1997) were subjected to a purification process following data collection.

SAMPLES: Using the *Dun and Bradstreet Million Dollar Directory* as the sampling frame, Menon, Jaworski, and Kohli (1997; Jaworski and Kohli 1993) selected for initial contact every other company name from among the top 1000 companies by sales revenues. Participation from multiple strategic business units (SBUs) within an organization was requested. A total of 102 companies agreed to participate, and ultimately, responses representing **222** SBUs were obtained from marketing and nonmarketing executives.

Moorman (1995; Moorman and Miner 1997) chose to sample the vice presidents of marketing for 300 divisions of firms noted in the 1992 *Advertising Age* list of top 200 advertisers, and a total of **92** usable questionnaires were received. No systematic differences were observed between early and late respondents.

RELIABILITY: Menon, Jaworski, and Kohli (1997) reported a **.88** alpha coefficient. One item with low interitem correlations was eliminated from the original five-item scale set to yield the final four-item measure listed here. Moorman and Miner (1997) reported an alpha of **.84** for the version of the scale they used.

VALIDITY: No specific examination of scale validity was presented by Menon, Jaworski, and Kohli (1997). Moorman and Miner (1997) assessed the unidimensionality of the scale by dividing the measures used in this study into three subsets of theoretically related variables and submitting the measures to confirmatory factor analyses. The three models provided a good fit with the data. Confirmatory factor analysis was also used to assess the discriminant validity of the measure and was found to be satisfactory.

ADMINISTRATION: The 206 marketing and 187 nonmarketing executives identified by participating corporations were directly contacted by Menon, Jaworski, and Kohli (1997). Initial contact was followed by a self-administered mail questionnaire, and a follow-up questionnaire was sent three weeks later to nonrespondents. When both nonmarketing and marketing executives from a single SBU responded, their scores were averaged to provide a single score for the construct.

The scale was included in the study by Moorman and Miner (1997) with other measures in a self-administered questionnaire that was delivered by mail. All informants were instructed to answer in the context of the most recent product development project for which their division had been responsible. Focal projects were required to have been on the market for a minimum of 12 months.

Higher scores on the scale indicated that the rate of technological change in a particular product category was very high.

MAJOR FINDINGS: Menon, Jaworski, and Kohli (1997) investigated the role of organizational factors affecting interdepartmental interactions and the resulting impact on product quality. The relationship between product quality and interdepartmental conflict was found to be robust across various levels of **technological turbulence.** Findings also indicated that the greater the level of **technological turbulence,** the stronger was the relationship between product quality and interdepartmental connectedness. Specifically, timely communication between departments was essential in improving product quality when technology within the industry changes rapidly.

Moorman and Miner (1997) investigated the impact of organizational memory level and organizational memory dispersion on key new product development processes. **Technological turbulence** had a significant negative interaction with organizational memory dispersion on new product creativity. Specifically, the relationship was negative under **highly turbulent** conditions, became positive under **moderately turbulent** conditions, and was strongly positive when **technological turbulence** was low.

REFERENCES:

Jaworski, Bernard and Ajay K. Kohli (1993), "Market Orientation: Antecedents and Consequences, *JM*, 57 (July), 53–70.

Menon, Ajay, Bernard J. Jaworski, and Ajay K. Kohli (1997), "Product Quality: Impact of Interdepartmental Interactions," *JAMS*, 25 (3), 187–200.

Moorman, Christine (1995), "Organizational Market Information Processes: Cultural Antecedents and New Product Outcomes," *JMR*, 32 (August), 318–35.

——— and Anne S. Miner (1997), "The Impact of Organizational Memory on New Product Performance and Creativity," *JMR*, 34 (February), 91–106.

SCALE ITEMS: *

Strongly   Strongly
agree   disagree
1————2————3————4————5

1. The technology in our industry is changing rapidly.

2. Technological changes provide big opportunities in our industry.

3. A large number of new product ideas have been made possible through technological breakthroughs in our industry.

4. Technological developments in our industry are rather minor. **(r)**

5. It is very difficult to forecast where the technology in this product area will be in the next five years.

*Except for item 5, this is the version of the scale used by Menon, Jaworski, and Kohli (1997; Jaworski and Kohli 1993). Moorman and Miner (1997) used all five items and a seven-point response format.

SCALE NAME: Turnover Intentions

SCALE DESCRIPTION: Ganesan and Weitz (1996) used this five-item, seven-point Likert-type scale to measure the extent to which buyers believe that they will be leaving an organization within a short period of time.

SCALE ORIGIN: Ganesan and Weitz (1996) adapted the scale from measures used by Good, Sisler, and Gentry (1992) and Keaveney (1992). Multiple items were developed for the construct and purified using item analysis and an exploratory factor analysis. Items loading on multiple factors and those with low loadings were dropped from the scale.

SAMPLES: Ganesan and Weitz (1996) effectively sampled approximately 1500 retail buyers, divisional merchandise managers, general merchandise managers, and senior merchandise officers whose names appeared on a national list of department, specialty, and discount chain store employees. Usable responses were obtained from **207** respondents.

RELIABILITY: Ganesan and Weitz (1996) reported a coefficient alpha of **.83** for the scale.

VALIDITY: All items composing the measures used by Ganesan and Weitz (1996) were subjected to a confirmatory factor analysis to assess the unidimensionality of the measures, and items violating this principle were dropped. Scales demonstrating unidimensionality were then tested for discriminant and convergent validity using LISREL 8.10. The overall model fit was good, demonstrating a goodness-of-fit index of .96, confirmatory fit index of .99, root mean square error of approximation of .02, and standardized root mean square residual of .06, as well as a nonsignificant chi-square.

ADMINISTRATION: Ganesan and Weitz (1996) included the scale with other measures as part of a self-administered survey that was delivered by mail. Higher scores on the scale indicated that a buyer was more likely to leave the job in the near future.

MAJOR FINDINGS: Ganesan and Weitz (1996) investigated the impact of various staffing policies on the attitudes and behavior of retail buyers. Retail buyers with lower levels of affective commitment to the organization were more likely to **leave the firm** in the near future. No relationship was found between **turnover intentions** and the buyer's intrinsic motivation.

REFERENCES:

Ganesan, Shankar and Barton A. Weitz (1996), "The Impact of Staffing Policies on Retail Buyer Job Attitudes and Behaviors," *JR*, 72 (1), 31–56.

Good, Linda K., Grovalynn F. Sisler, and James W. Gentry (1988), "Antecedents of Turnover Intentions Among Retail Management Personnel," *JR*, 64 (3), 295–310.

Keaveney, Ususan M. (1992), "An Empirical Investigation of Dysfunctional Organizational Turnover Among Chain and Non-Chain Retail Store Buyers," *JR*, 68 (2), 145–73.

SCALE ITEMS:

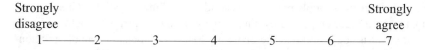

Strongly disagree 1————2————3————4————5————6————7 Strongly agree

1. I do not think I will spend all my career with this organization.

2. I intend to leave this organization within a short period of time.

3. I have decided to quit this organization.

4. I am looking at some other jobs now.

5. If I do not get promoted soon, I will look for a job elsewhere.

SCALE NAME: User Investment (Supplier)

SCALE DESCRIPTION: Dahlstrom, McNeilly, and Speh (1996) described this seven-item, five-point Likert-type scale as measuring the extent to which a service user has dedicated assets such as personnel, facilities, information systems, and operating procedures to a relationship with a logistical supplier.

SCALE ORIGIN: Dahlstrom, McNeilly, and Speh (1996) reported that the scale was adapted from Anderson (1982). The questionnaire containing the scale was pretested by six members of the Warehouse Education and Research Council, who evaluated it for content, readability, and relevance to the industry.

SAMPLES: Using a sampling frame generated from the membership of the Warehouse Education and Research Council, Dahlstrom, McNeilly, and Speh (1996) surveyed 1000 manufacturer, retailer, and wholesaler members. No mention of the specific sampling technique used to generate the frame was provided. Firms that exclusively used in-house warehousing services were not part of the population of interest and were asked to return the survey without answering. Including unanswered surveys, 383 questionnaires were returned for a 38.3% response rate. Of these, **189** surveys contained complete data from firms using interfirm warehousing services.

RELIABILITY: Dahlstrom, McNeilly, and Speh (1996) reported a coefficient alpha of **.82** for this measure.

VALIDITY: Item-to-total correlations estimated by an exploratory factor analysis were used in the first stage of measure purification. Dahlstrom, McNeilly, and Speh (1996) submitted the remaining items to a confirmatory factor analysis. One item was eliminated to ensure the internal consistency of the scale. Results of the trimmed model confirmatory factor analysis provided evidence of construct validity. Discriminant validity was also assessed and found to be acceptable.

ADMINISTRATION: Dahlstrom, McNeilly, and Speh (1996) stated that the scale was part of a self-administered questionnaire that was returned by mail. Sampled individuals were contacted by telephone prior to survey delivery; a postage-paid, return addressed reply envelope accompanied the questionnaire. A follow-up mailing with a second survey was sent two weeks after the first. Individuals using in-house warehousing services were asked not to complete the survey, but eligible respondents were instructed to answer in the context of the third-party warehouse service provider with whom they spent the greatest portion of their warehousing budget. Higher scores on the user investment scale indicated that service users made a greater commitment of assets such as personnel, procedures, facilities, and information systems to the logistical partner.

MAJOR FINDINGS: Dahlstrom, McNeilly, and Speh (1996) investigated various antecedents to alternative forms of governance in the logistical supply market. A second topic of investigation addressed how formal controls and relational norms were employed by alternative governance forms to yield performance. Results of discriminant analysis suggested that the bilateral alliances in logistical supply relationships were influenced by the interaction of the **user's dedicated investments**, warehouse-related uncertainty, and the level of logistical services provided by warehouse suppliers.

REFERENCES:
Anderson, Erin (1982), "Contracting the Selling Function: The Salesperson as Outside Agent or Employee," doctoral dissertation, University of California, Los Angeles.
Dahlstrom, Robert, Kevin M. McNeilly, and Thomas W. Speh (1996), "Buyer-Seller Relationships in the Procurement of Logistical Services," *JAMS*, 24 (2), 110–24.

SCALE ITEMS:

Directions: The questions in this section address the level and type of investment you have made with the warehouse vendor. Indicate your level of agreement with the following.

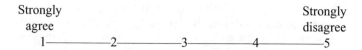

Strongly agree 1————2————3————4————5 Strongly disagree

1. If we switched to another warehouse vendor, we would lose a lot of the investment made with our current warehouse vendor in systems and procedures.

2. It would be difficult for us to recoup investments made with this warehouse vendor if we switched to a competitor.

3. It we decided to stop using this warehouse vendor, we would have a lot of trouble redeploying our people and facilities presently assigned to this warehouse vendor.

4. If we decided to stop working with this warehouse vendor, we would be wasting a lot of knowledge that is tailored to their operation.

5. We have made a substantial investment in personnel dedicated this warehouse vendor.

6. If we decided to stop working with this warehouse vendor, we would lose investments made to cover the fixed costs of their operations.

7. We have invested in computers designed to interact with this vendor's information systems.

#932 *Voice*

SCALE NAME: Voice

SCALE DESCRIPTION: Ping (1997) used this four-item, five-point Likert-type scale to assess the degree to which a retailer intended to work constructively with a wholesaler in solving relationship problems.

SCALE ORIGIN: Ping (1997) noted that the scale was first published in one of his earlier articles (Ping 1993). In developing the scale, Ping (1993) generated items on the basis of presurvey interviews with hardware retailers and a review of the relevant literature. The purification process began with nine academicians evaluating how well the items fit the construct; those misclassified by more than one judge were eliminated. The resulting measure was pretested in two different phases. The first pretest sought to clarify possible misinterpretations. Responses from 63 hardware retailers in the second pretest were used in analyzing the psychometric properties of the measures using item-to-total correlations, ordered similarity coefficients, and coefficient alpha computations. The final purification of the measure was based on LISREL analysis of data provided by 288 respondents, as reported in Ping's (1993) study. Items were deleted if internal consistency was improved without detracting from the content validity of the measure. Tests of the discriminant and convergent validity of the measure were also undertaken, and the results were found to be satisfactory.

SAMPLES: Ping (1997) used a systematic random sampling procedure of U.S. hardware retailers to generate the 600 hardware retailers sampled in his study. Usable responses were received from **204** people. The sampling frame was taken from a hardware retailing trade publication's subscription list.

RELIABILITY: Ping (1997) reported a coefficient alpha of **.93** for this measure.

VALIDITY: Ping (1997) conducted a confirmatory factor analysis to test the unidimensionality and construct validity of the measure. The measure was judged to be unidimensional, and the average variance extracted demonstrated the scale's convergent and discriminatory validity. The author also stated that the measure offered content validity.

ADMINISTRATION: The scale was included with other measures as part of a self-administered questionnaire that was delivered by mail. Nonrespondents received as many as three postcard reminders. Ping (1997) used a key informant approach, in which key informants represented a single individual, typically a manager, owner, or executive of the hardware store. Higher scores on the scale reflected a greater intention on the part of the retailer to work constructively with a wholesaler in solving relationship problems.

MAJOR FINDINGS: Ping (1997) proposed and empirically examined several antecedents to voice in a business-to-business context. The results of his study indicated that higher levels of **voice** were more likely when revenue was lower and exit costs, satisfaction, and the number of retailer employees were higher.

REFERENCES:

Ping, Robert A., Jr. (1993), "The Effects of Satisfaction and Structural Constraints on Retailer Exiting, Voice, Loyalty, Opportunism, and Neglect," *JR*, 69 (Fall), 320–52.

———— (1997), "Voice in Business-to-Business Relationships: Cost-of-Exit and Demographic Antecedents," *JR*, 73 (2), 261–81.

SCALE ITEMS:

Strongly disagree — Strongly agree

1————2————3————4————5

1. If there are any problems with my primary wholesaler I will work jointly with them to improve the situation.

2. I will work with my primary wholesaler to correct any mutual problems.

3. I will try to discuss any primary wholesaler-related problems with them.

4. I will cooperatively discuss mutual problems with my primary wholesaler.

SCALE NAME: Warehousing Uncertainty

SCALE DESCRIPTION: Dahlstrom, McNeilly, and Speh (1996) described this twelve-item, seven-point semantic differential–type scale as measuring the complexity associated with warehousing real estate management, hourly labor markets, and vendor competition.

SCALE ORIGIN: Dahlstrom, McNeilly, and Speh (1996) reported that the scale was adapted from Anderson (1982). The questionnaire containing the scale was pretested by six members of the Warehouse Education and Research Council, who evaluated it for content, readability, and relevance to the industry.

SAMPLES: Using a sampling frame generated from the membership of the Warehouse Education and Research Council, Dahlstrom, McNeilly, and Speh (1996) surveyed 1000 manufacturer, retailer, and wholesaler members. No mention of the specific sampling technique used to generate the frame was provided. Firms that exclusively used in-house warehousing services were not part of the population of interest and were asked to return the survey without answering. Including unanswered surveys, 383 questionnaires were returned for a 38.3% response rate. Of these, **189** surveys contained complete data from firms using interfirm warehousing services.

RELIABILITY: Dahlstrom, McNeilly, and Speh (1996) reported a coefficient alpha of **.70** for this measure and reliabilities of **.74, .74,** and **.82** for the property-based, competition-based, and labor-based uncertainty subscales.

VALIDITY: Item-to-total correlations estimated by an exploratory factor analysis were used in the first stage of measure purification. Dahlstrom, McNeilly, and Speh (1996) submitted the remaining items to a confirmatory factor analysis, which provided evidence of construct validity. Discriminant validity was also assessed and found to be acceptable.

ADMINISTRATION: Dahlstrom, McNeilly, and Speh (1996) stated that the scale was part of a self-administered questionnaire that was returned by mail. Sampled individuals were contacted by telephone prior to survey delivery; a postage-paid, return addressed reply envelope accompanied the questionnaire. A follow-up mailing with a second survey was sent two weeks after the first. Individuals using in-house warehousing services were asked not to complete the survey, but eligible respondents were instructed to answer in the context of the third-party warehouse service provider with whom they spent the greatest portion of their warehousing budget. Higher scores on the uncertainty scale indicated greater levels of uncertainty related to the competitive situation, labor market, and property management aspects of warehousing.

MAJOR FINDINGS: Dahlstrom, McNeilly, and Speh (1996) investigated various antecedents to alternative forms of governance in the logistical supply market. A second topic of investigation addressed how formal controls and relational norms were employed by alternative governance forms to yield performance. Results of discriminant analysis suggested the bilateral alliances in logistical supply relationships were influenced by the interaction of the user's dedicated investments, **warehouse-related uncertainty**, and the level of logistical services provided by warehouse suppliers.

REFERENCES:
Anderson, Erin (1982), "Contracting the Selling Function: The Salesperson as Outside Agent or Employee," doctoral dissertation, University of California, Los Angeles.
Dahlstrom, Robert, Kevin M. McNeilly, and Thomas W. Speh (1996), "Buyer-Seller Relationships in the Procurement of Logistical Services," *JAMS*, 24 (2), 110–24.

SCALE ITEMS:

Property-based uncertainty
How would you describe the real estate market for warehouse property?

1. Complex :____:____:____:____:____:____:____: Simple (r)
            1   2   3   4   5   6   7

2. Stable :____:____:____:____:____:____:____: Volatile
           1   2   3   4   5   6   7

3. Easy to monitor :____:____:____:____:____:____:____: Difficult to monitor
           1   2   3   4   5   6   7

4. Uncertain :____:____:____:____:____:____:____: Certain
           1   2   3   4   5   6   7

Competition-based uncertainty
How would you describe the competition among warehouse vendors?

1. Complex :____:____:____:____:____:____:____: Simple (r)
           1   2   3   4   5   6   7

2. Stable :____:____:____:____:____:____:____: Volatile
           1   2   3   4   5   6   7

3. Easy to monitor :____:____:____:____:____:____:____: Difficult to monitor
           1   2   3   4   5   6   7

4. Uncertain :____:____:____:____:____:____:____: Certain
           1   2   3   4   5   6   7

Labor-based uncertainty
How would you describe the market for hourly warehousing labor?

1. Complex :____:____:____:____:____:____:____: Simple (r)
           1   2   3   4   5   6   7

2. Stable :____:____:____:____:____:____:____: Volatile
           1   2   3   4   5   6   7

3. Easy to monitor :____:____:____:____:____:____:____: Difficult to monitor
           1   2   3   4   5   6   7

4. Uncertain :____:____:____:____:____:____:____: Certain
           1   2   3   4   5   6   7

SCALE NAME: Work Controls (Output)

SCALE DESCRIPTION: Five five-point items measuring the frequency with which an employee perceives that he or she is given work goals, performance is assessed, feedback is provided, and rewards are affected. The emphasis in this measure is on evaluating the output of the work rather than procedures used to product the results.

SCALE ORIGIN: The scale was apparently developed by Jaworski and MacInnis (1989). The scale and other aspects of the survey instrument were refined through a series of interviews and a pretest of marketing managers.

SAMPLES: A national sample of marketing managers was drawn randomly by Jaworski and MacInnis (1989) from the American Marketing Association's (AMA) list of members. Of the 479 managers who were to have received questionnaires, **379** returned usable forms.

Ramaswami (1996) received usable surveys from **318** of the 1159 AMA members who were randomly selected from the AMA's membership list.

RELIABILITY: Coefficient alphas of **.88** and **.85** were reported for the scale by Jaworski and MacInnis (1989) and Ramaswami (1996), respectively.

VALIDITY: The validity of the scale was not specifically examined by Jaworski and MacInnis (1989); Ramaswami (1996) used confirmatory factor analysis to assess the unidimensionality of the measure in conjunction with other work control measures and found that each scale tapped distinct dimensions.

ADMINISTRATION: Jaworski and MacInnis (1989) and Ramaswami (1996) indicated that the scale was self-administered, along with many other measures, in a mail survey format. Higher scores on the scale indicated that employees strongly believed their performance was monitored and their rewards were affected, whereas lower scores suggested that they thought goals were not set for their work and performance did not affect rewards.

MAJOR FINDINGS: Among the many purposes of the study by Jaworski and MacInnis (1989) was to examine the simultaneous use of several types of managerial controls in the context of marketing management. Using structural equations, the authors found that performance documentation had a significant positive impact on **output controls**, which in turn had a significant negative effect on a subordinate's greater knowledge of a job (relative to superiors).

Ramaswami (1996) investigated both traditional and contingency theories of negative employee responses to marketing control systems. The use of **output controls** was positively related to dysfunctional behavior. Tests for interaction effects indicated that though the availability of performance documentation did not alter the relationship between **output control** and dysfunctional behavior, higher levels of procedural knowledge decreased dysfunctional behavior when **output controls** were used.

REFERENCES:

Jaworski, Bernard J. and Deborah J. MacInnis (1989), "Marketing Jobs and Management Controls: Toward a Framework," *JMR*, 26 (November), 406–19.

Ramaswami, Sridhar N. (1996), "Marketing Controls and Dysfunctional Employee Behaviors: A Test of Traditional and Contingency Theory Postulates," *JM*, 60 (April), 105–20.

#934 *Work Controls (Output)*

SCALE ITEMS:*

Never   Always

1. Specific goals are established for my job.

2. My immediate boss monitors the extent to which I attain my performance goals.

3. If my performance goals were not met, I would be required to explain why.

4. I receive feedback from my immediate superior concerning the extent to which I achieve my goals.

5. My pay increases are based upon how much my performance compares with my goals.

*Ramaswami (1996) reported using a five-point Likert response format (1 = strongly disagree, 5 = strongly agree) and altered item 1 slightly to read, "specific performance goals are established for my job."

SCALE NAME: Work Controls (Process)

SCALE DESCRIPTION: Four five-point items measuring the frequency with which an employee perceives that the procedures used to accomplish his or her assigned work are assessed by an immediate supervisor. The emphasis in this measure is on the process used to produce the work rather than the results of the work.

SCALE ORIGIN: The scale was apparently developed by Jaworski and MacInnis (1989). The scale and other aspects of the survey instrument were refined through a series of interviews and a pretest of marketing managers.

SAMPLES: A national sample of marketing managers was drawn randomly by Jaworski and MacInnis (1989) from the American Marketing Association's (AMA) list of members. Of the 479 managers who were to have received questionnaires, **379** returned usable forms.

Ramaswami (1996) received usable surveys from **318** of the 1159 AMA members who were randomly selected from the AMA's membership list.

RELIABILITY: Coefficient alphas of **.82** and **.85** were reported for the scale by Jaworski and MacInnis (1989) and Ramaswami (1996), respectively.

VALIDITY: The validity of the scale was not specifically examined by Jaworski and MacInnis (1989). Ramaswami (1996) used confirmatory factor analysis to assess the unidimensionality of the measure in conjunction with other work control measures and found that each scale tapped distinct dimensions.

ADMINISTRATION: Jaworski and MacInnis (1989) and Ramaswami (1996) indicated that the scale was self-administered, along with many other measures, in a mail survey format. Higher scores on the scale indicated that employees strongly believed the procedures they used were monitored, whereas lower scores suggested they thought their immediate bosses did not closely watch how tasks were accomplished.

MAJOR FINDINGS: Among the many purposes of the study by Jaworski and MacInnis (1989) was to examine the simultaneous use of several types of managerial controls in the context of marketing management. Using structural equations, the authors found that procedural knowledge had a significant positive impact on **process controls**, which in turn had a significant negative effect on a subordinate's greater knowledge of a job (relative to superiors).

Ramaswami (1996) investigated both traditional and contingency theories of negative employee responses to marketing control systems. The use of **process controls** was positively related to dysfunctional behavior. Tests for interaction effects indicated that higher levels of procedural knowledge decreased dysfunctional behavior when **process controls** were used.

REFERENCES:

Jaworski, Bernard J. and Deborah J. MacInnis (1989), "Marketing Jobs and Management Controls: Toward a Framework," *JMR*, 26 (November), 406–19.

Ramaswami, Sridhar N. (1996), "Marketing Controls and Dysfunctional Employee Behaviors: A Test of Traditional and Contingency Theory Postulates," *JM*, 60 (April), 105–20.

#935 *Work Controls (Process)*

SCALE ITEMS:*

Never   Always

1————2————3————4————5

1. My immediate boss monitors the extent to which I follow established procedures.

2. My immediate boss evaluates the procedures I use to accomplish a given task.

3. My immediate boss modifies my procedures when desired results are not obtained.

4. I receive feedback on *how* I accomplish my performance goals.

*Ramaswami (1996) reported using a five-point Likert response format (1 = strongly disagree, 5 = strongly agree).

SCALE NAME: Work Controls (Professional)

SCALE DESCRIPTION: Five five-point Likert-type items measuring the degree to which an employee reports that the division he or she works for encourages interaction and cooperation among marketing professionals on their work activities. The scale focuses on the professional colleagues' positive influence on performance rather than the negative effect they may also have.

SCALE ORIGIN: The scale was apparently developed by Jaworski and MacInnis (1989). The scale and other aspects of the survey instrument were refined through a series of interviews and a pretest of marketing managers. Ramaswami (1996) made minor modifications to the scale, substituting the words "department" for "division" and "members" for "marketing professionals."

SAMPLES: A national sample of marketing managers was drawn randomly by Jaworski and MacInnis (1989) from the American Marketing Association's (AMA) list of members. Of the 479 managers who were to have received questionnaires from Jaworski and MacInnis (1989), **379** returned usable forms.

Ramaswami (1996) received usable surveys from **318** of the 1159 AMA members who were randomly selected from the AMA's membership list.

RELIABILITY: Coefficient alphas of **.89** and **.85** were reported for the scale by Jaworski and MacInnis (1989) and Ramaswami (1996), respectively.

VALIDITY: The validity of the scale was not specifically examined by Jaworski and MacInnis (1989). Ramaswami (1996) used confirmatory factor analysis to assess the unidimensionality of the measure in conjunction with other work control measures and found that each scale tapped distinct dimensions.

ADMINISTRATION: Jaworski and MacInnis (1989) and Ramaswami (1996) indicated that the scale was self-administered, along with many other measures, in a mail survey format. Higher scores on the scale indicated that employees strongly believed that the areas they work for encouraged cooperation among members in their work, whereas lower scores suggested that employees were discouraged from interacting with peers in their area of the workplace.

MAJOR FINDINGS: Among the many purposes of the study by Jaworski and MacInnis (1989) was to examine the simultaneous use of several types of managerial controls in the context of marketing management. Using structural equations, the authors found that performance control had a significant positive impact on the use of **professional work controls**.

Ramaswami (1996) investigated both traditional and contingency theories of negative employee responses to marketing control systems. In the model tested, **professional work controls** was not found to be a significant covariate on dysfunctional behavior.

REFERENCES:

Jaworski, Bernard J. and Deborah J. MacInnis (1989), "Marketing Jobs and Management Controls: Toward a Framework," *JMR*, 26 (November), 406–19.

Ramaswami, Sridhar N. (1996), "Marketing Controls and Dysfunctional Employee Behaviors: A Test of Traditional and Contingency Theory Postulates," *JM*, 60 (April), 105–20.

#936 *Work Controls (Professional)*

SCALE ITEMS:*

Strongly disagree	Disagree	Neutral	Agree	Strongly agree
1———————	—2———————	—3———————	—4———————	—5

1. The division encourages cooperation between marketing professionals.

2. Most of the marketing professionals in my division are familiar with each other's productivity.

3. The division fosters an environment where marketing professional respect each other's work.

4. The division encourages job-related discussions between marketing professionals.

5. Most marketing professionals in my division are able to provide accurate appraisals of each other's work.

*Ramaswami (1996) altered items 1 through 5 slightly, substituting "department" for "division" and "members" for "marketing professionals."

SCALE NAME: Work Controls (Self)

SCALE DESCRIPTION: A four-item, five-point Likert-type summated ratings scale measuring the degree to which an employee reports a commitment to his or her work and a willingness to take responsibility for his or her performance.

SCALE ORIGIN: Items 1–3 of the scale were apparently developed by Jaworski and MacInnis (1989). The scale and other aspects of the survey instrument were refined through a series of interviews and a pretest of marketing managers. Ramaswami (1996) tested a five-item version of the scale that included Jaworski and MacInnis's (1989) original three items plus two items apparently developed by Ramaswami (1996). Only one of the new items was retained following measure purification.

SAMPLES: A national sample of marketing managers was drawn randomly by Jaworski and MacInnis (1989) from the American Marketing Association's (AMA) list of members. Of the 479 managers who were to have received questionnaires from Jaworski and MacInnis (1989), **379** returned usable forms.

Ramaswami (1996) received usable surveys from **318** of the 1159 AMA members who were randomly selected from the AMA's membership list.

RELIABILITY: Coefficient alphas of **.60** on the three-item version and **.70** on the four-item version were reported for the scale by Jaworski and MacInnis (1989) and Ramaswami (1996), respectively.

VALIDITY: The validity of the scale was not specifically examined by Jaworski and MacInnis (1989). Ramaswami (1996) used confirmatory factor analysis to assess the unidimensionality of the measure in conjunction with other work control measures and found that each scale tapped distinct dimensions.

ADMINISTRATION: Jaworski and MacInnis (1989) and Ramaswami (1996) indicated that the scale was self-administered, along with many other measures, in a mail survey format. Higher scores on the scale indicated that employees were strongly committed to their work, whereas lower scores suggested that they had a low amount of interest in their work and did not want to take responsibility for their performance.

MAJOR FINDINGS: Among the many purposes of the study by Jaworski and MacInnis (1989) was to examine the simultaneous use of several types of managerial controls in the context of marketing management. Using structural equations, the authors found that performance documentation had a significant positive impact on the use of **work-related self-control,** which in turn had a significant negative effect on employee dysfunctional behavior.

Ramaswami (1996) investigated both traditional and contingency theories of negative employee responses to marketing control systems. In the model tested, **work-related self-controls** was retained as a significant covariate for dysfunctional behavior.

REFERENCES:

Jaworski, Bernard J. and Deborah J. MacInnis (1989), "Marketing Jobs and Management Controls: Toward a Framework," *JMR,* 26 (November), 406–19.

Ramaswami, Sridhar N. (1996), "Marketing Controls and Dysfunctional Employee Behaviors: A Test of Traditional and Contingency Theory Postulates," *JM,* 60 (April), 105–20.

SCALE ITEMS:

Strongly disagree	Disagree	Neutral	Agree	Strongly agree
1—————	2—————	3—————	4—————	5

1. The major satisfactions in my life come from my job.

2. The work I do on this job is very meaningful to me.

3. I feel that I should take credit or blame for the results of my work.

4. I like to do more than my share of the work at my job.

SCALE NAME: Work Involvement

SCALE DESCRIPTION: Babin and Boles (1996) used this five-item, five-point Likert-type scale to assess the general level of job involvement exhibited by coworkers.

SCALE ORIGIN: Babin and Boles (1996) indicated that the items representing this construct were adapted from a subscale of Moos's (1981) working environment scale. The authors stated that a preliminary analysis of all measures used in their study led to the preclusion of several items from further analysis, but they did not provide specific details.

SAMPLES: Babin and Boles (1996) surveyed a convenience sample of 390 food service workers employed by full-service restaurants located in a major southern U.S. metropolitan area. A total of **261** usable responses were returned. The majority of respondents were high school graduates (99%), of whom 80% had some college education, which indicated that the majority of respondents were students.

RELIABILITY: Babin and Boles (1996) calculated a coefficient alpha of **.76** for this measure.

VALIDITY: Babin and Boles (1996) tested the measurement model using confirmatory factor analysis. Although the goodness-of-fit index of .861 was somewhat low, the observed loading estimates and construct reliabilities provided evidence of the convergent validity of the measure. An examination of the proportion of variance extracted in each construct compared with the square of the phi (ϕ) suggested that the scale possessed discriminant validity.

ADMINISTRATION: The scale was included by Babin and Boles (1996) with other measures as part of a self-administered questionnaire distributed to employees at their place of work and returned by self-addressed, postage-paid reply envelopes. Higher scores on the scale reflected a greater perception of coworkers' involvement with their jobs.

MAJOR FINDINGS: The influence of supervisor support and coworker involvement on the role stress, performance, and job satisfaction of food service workers was investigated by Babin and Boles (1996). Increased perceptions of **coworker job involvement** were significantly related to lower levels of respondent role conflict and higher levels of job satisfaction.

REFERENCES:

Babin, Barry J. and James S. Boles (1996), "The Effects of Perceived Co-Worker Involvement and Supervisor Support on Service Provider Role Stress, Performance and Job Satisfaction," *JR*, 72 (1), 57–75.

Moos, Rudolph H. (1981), *Work Environment Scale Manual*. Palo Alto, CA: Consulting Psychologists Press.

SCALE ITEMS:

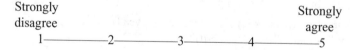

Strongly disagree — 1————2————3————4————5 — Strongly agree

1. People seem to take pride in the organization.

2. People put quite a lot of effort into what they do.

3. A lot of people here seem to be just putting in their time. **(r)***

4. It's hard to get people to do any extra work. **(r)***

5. Few people ever volunteer. **(r)***

*Although the appendix listing the scales used by Babin and Boles (1996) did not indicate that these items were reversed, this was probably an oversight given the nature and purpose of the measure.

SCALE NAME: Work/Family Conflict

SCALE DESCRIPTION: Good, Page, and Young (1996) used this 13-item, five-point Likert-type scale to measure the family life and employment stressors that create conflict between the work and family domains.

SCALE ORIGIN: Good, Page, and Young (1996) stated that the scale was adapted from Fournier (1981).

SAMPLES: Good, Page, and Young (1996) mailed a questionnaire to 698 retail managers employed by southern branches of a major multiunit department store. Of the **383** usable responses obtained (54.9% response rate), 280 (73.2%) were from entry-level executives and 103 (26.9%) were from upper-level executives. The majority of respondents were women (70%).

RELIABILITY: Good, Page, and Young (1996) reported coefficient alphas of **.85** and **.86** for the entry- and upper-level respondent samples, respectively.

VALIDITY: No specific examination of scale validity was reported by Good, Page, and Young (1996).

ADMINISTRATION: The scale was part of a self-administered mail survey. Good, Page, and Young (1996) included a cover letter promising confidentiality and anonymity, a letter from the vice president of personnel encouraging participation, and a self-addressed, stamped reply envelope. Nonrespondents were sent a second questionnaire in three weeks. Higher scores on the scale indicated greater amounts of work and family conflict due to increased family life and employment stressors.

MAJOR FINDINGS: Good, Page, and Young (1996) examined the relationship of a set of antecedent constructs (role conflict and ambiguity, work–family conflict, job satisfaction, organizational commitment, and intent to leave) in explaining turnover with both entry- and upper-level retailer managers. **Work–family conflict** was found to increase intentions to leave in the entry-level management group only.

REFERENCES:
Fournier, David G. (1981), *PROFILES—Personal Reflections on Family Life and Employment Stressors.* Stillwater, OK: Oklahoma State University.
Good, Linda K., Thomas J. Page Jr., and Clifford E. Young (1996), "Assessing Hierarchical Differences in Job-Related Attitudes and Turnover Among Retail Managers," *JAMS*, 24 (2), 148–56.

SCALE ITEMS:
Directions: Please circle the response to the far right of the statement that best describes your answer.

1 = Strongly disagree
2 = Disagree
3 = Agree
4 = Agree strongly
5 = Not applicable

1. I am able to do things as well as most other people.

2. Personal concerns reduce my productivity at work.

3. My family has the resources to meet our desired lifestyle. **(r)**

4. My spouse's job or career conflicts with mine.

5. I certainly feel useless at times. **(r)**

6. Family problems cause loss of time at work for me.

7. All in all, I am inclined to feel that I am a failure. **(r)**

8. I am nervous, tense, or frustrated when I get home from work.

9. I take a positive attitude toward myself.

10. On the whole, I am satisfied with myself.

11. My spouse is content with his/her work status. **(r)**

12. I am content with my spouse's work status. **(r)**

13. I am content with the city in which I live.

SCALE NAME: Working Hard

SCALE DESCRIPTION: Sujan, Weitz, and Kumar (1994) used a four-item, seven-point scale to measure a salesperson's persistence in performing job-related activities, plus an open-ended question assessing how many hours a week, on average, the salesperson worked.

SCALE ORIGIN: There is nothing to indicate that scale is anything but original to Sujan, Weitz, and Kumar (1994). However, work with this construct and other attempts to measure it date back to at least Sujan (1986).

SAMPLES: Sujan, Weitz, and Kumar (1994) surveyed a convenience sample of salespeople employed by eight firms representing diverse industries. Two hundred seventeen questionnaires were distributed by sales managers to members of their selling force, and **190** usable responses were obtained for an 87.5% response rate. On average, respondents were 35 years of age, had 9 years sales experience, and made 3.5 calls per day. The majority were men (78%).

RELIABILITY: Sujan, Weitz, and Kumar (1994) reported a coefficient alpha of **.68** for the measure.

VALIDITY: Sujan, Weitz, and Kumar (1994) provided extensive information on the assessment of scale validity. Measures used in their study were evaluated using confirmatory factor analysis. The authors stated that the results of this analysis supported the unidimensionality and reliability of the measure and provided evidence of convergent and discriminant validity.

ADMINISTRATION: Sujan, Weitz, and Kumar (1994) included a cover letter promising confidentiality and a self-addressed, stamped reply envelope in the survey packet distributed by sales managers to members of the sales force. Respondents were instructed to return the questionnaire directly to the researchers rather than to their superiors. Higher scores on the scale indicated that salespeople were more persistent in fulfilling their work duties and that they worked longer hours.

MAJOR FINDINGS: Sujan, Weitz, and Kumar (1994) investigated the influence of goal orientations on work behavior. Results indicated that a performance orientation motivated salespeople to work hard and that working hard increased salespeople's performance. A performance orientation motivated **hard work** more when salespeople were high in self-efficacy than when they were low in it.

REFERENCES:

Sujan, Harish (1986), "Smarter Versus Harder: An Exploratory Attributional Analysis of Salespeople's Motivation," *JMR*, 23 (February), 41–49.

————, Barton A. Weitz, and Nirmalya Kumar (1994), "Learning Orientation, Working Smart, and Effective Selling," *JM*, 58 (July), 39–52.

SCALE ITEMS:

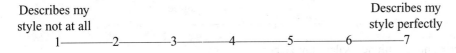

Describes my
style not at all

Describes my
style perfectly

1————2————3————4————5————6————7

1. I work long hours to meet my sales objectives.

2. I do not give up easily when I encounter a customer who is difficult to sell.

3. I work untiringly at selling a customer until I get an order.

4. On average, how many hours a week do you currently work? _____

SCALE NAME: Working Smart

SCALE DESCRIPTION: Oliver and Anderson (1994) used this five-item, seven-point Likert-type scale to purportedly measure a sales representative's motivation to engage in "smarter" selling activities such as planning, lost account analysis, and experimentation with new selling techniques.

SCALE ORIGIN: The scale is original to Oliver and Anderson (1994), who pretested the measure in a questionnaire administered to a convenience sample of sales representatives attending trade association functions. The measure was revised on the basis of the pretest.

SAMPLES: Oliver and Anderson (1994) surveyed managers and manufacturer's sales representatives employed by independently owned and operated sales agencies serving the electronics industry. Of the 350 randomly selected trade association member firms fitting this designation, 299 firms expressed interest in participating, and ultimately, **194** usable surveys from management and **347** surveys from manufacturer representatives were returned. The typical respondent was a male (92%), college graduate (64%), approximately 39 years of age, with an average of 12 years sales experience and 5.5 years in the present job.

RELIABILITY: Oliver and Anderson (1994) reported a coefficient alpha of **.461** for this measure.

VALIDITY: Oliver and Anderson (1994) used the correlation matrix of the independent and classification variables used in the study to provide some evidence of discriminant and convergent validity. Nomological validity was also found to be present.

ADMINISTRATION: Oliver and Anderson (1994) sent managers of the 299 firms indicating interest in the study a packet containing a "manager's survey" and three similar self-administered surveys for salespeople, along with self-addressed, postage-paid reply envelopes. Managers were instructed to distribute one survey each to an "above-average rep," a "mid-range rep," and a "below-average rep." Each representative was promised confidentiality and the chance to win one of five $100 prizes in a random drawing. It appears that only responses obtained from sales representatives were used in computing this measure. Higher scores on the scale indicated a greater motivation on the part of the sales representative to engage in "smarter" selling activities.

MAJOR FINDINGS: Oliver and Anderson (1994) examined how perceptions of the presence of a behavior versus outcome sales control system in the respondent's organizations influenced salespeople's performance outcomes and sales strategies, as well as their affective, cognitive, and behavioral states. A sales representative's motivation to **"work smarter"** was significantly related to the use of a behavior-control system.

COMMENTS: The low scale reliability suggests that further developmental work and testing is necessary prior to using this measure in future research.

REFERENCES:
Oliver, Richard L. and Erin Anderson (1994), "An Empirical Test of the Consequences of Behavior- and Outcome-Based Sales Control Systems," *JM*, 58 (October), 53–67.

SCALE ITEMS:

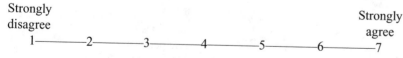

Strongly
disagree

Strongly
agree

1————2————3————4————5————6————7

1. I am always experimenting with new sales approaches.

2. There really isn't much to learn about selling. **(r)**

3. Selling requires that I put more thought into how I sell rather than more time.

4. I believe that the best salespeople are those who know how to sell, not those who put in long hours.

5. Every time I lose an order, I analyze what went wrong in great detail.

Reading List for
Scale Development and Use
....

The following is a list of articles and books readers could peruse to better understand psychometrics and related issues. In this limited list, the emphasis is on literature focusing on the field of marketing, but a few important publications from other fields are mentioned as well. Some of the articles are dated but are listed either because they are classics or because familiarity with their contents is still valuable. Several readings have been added since the last volume, especially those touching on item response theory, that give some indication of the future of psychological measurement.

American Educational Research Association (AERA), American Psychological Association (APA), and National Council on Measurement in Education (NCME) (1999), *Standards for Educational and Psychological Testing*. Washington, DC: American Educational Research Association.

Anderson, James C. and David W. Gerbing (1988), "Structural Equation Modeling in Practice: A Review and Recommended Two-Step Approach," *Psychological Bulletin*, 103 (3), 411–23.

Bagozzi, Richard P. and Youjae Yi (1991), "Multitrait-Multimethod Matrices in Consumer Research," *JCR*, 17 (March), 426–39.

Ballard, Rebecca, Michael D. Crino, and Stephen Rubenfeld (1988), "Social Desirability Response Bias and the Marlowe-Crowne Social Desirability Scale," *Psychological Reports*, 63, 227–37.

Bocker, Franz (1988), "Scale Forms and Their Impact on Ratings' Reliability and Validity," *Journal of Business Research*, 17 (August), 15–26.

Boyle, Gregory J. (1991), "Does Item Homogeneity Indicate Internal Consistency or Item Redundancy in Psychometric Scales?" *Personality & Individual Differences*, 12 (3), 291–94.

Bruner, Gordon C., II (1998), "Standardization & Justification: Do Aad Scales Measure Up?" *Journal of Current Issues & Research in Advertising,* 20 (Spring), 1–18.

Campbell, Donald T. and Donald W. Fiske (1959), "Convergent Validity and Discriminant Validity by the Multitrait-Multimethod Matrix," *Psychological Bulletin*, 56 (March), 81–105.

Churchill, Gilbert A., Jr. (1979), "A Paradigm for Developing Better Measures of Marketing Constructs," *JMR*, 16 (February), 64–73.

——— and J. Paul Peter (1984), "Research Design Effects on the Reliability of Rating Scales: A Meta-Analysis," *JMR*, 21 (November), 360–75.

Comrey, Andrew L. (1988), "Factor Analytic Methods of Scale Development in Personality and Clinical Psychology," *Journal of Consulting and Clinical Psychology*, 56 (October), 754–61.

Cortina, Jose M. (1993), "What Is Coefficient Alpha? An Examination of Theory and Applications," *Journal of Applied Psychology*, 78 (1), 98–104.

Cox, Eli P., III (1980), "The Optimal Number of Response Alternatives for a Scale: A Review," *JMR*, 17 (November), 407–22.

Cronbach, Lee J. (1951), "Coefficient Alpha and the Internal Structure of Tests," *Psychometrika*, 16 (September), 297–334.

———— (1955), "Construct Validity in Psychological Tests," *Psychological Bulletin*, 52 (July), 281–302.

Crowne, Douglas P. and David Marlowe (1960), "A New Scale of Social Desirability Independent of Psychopathology," *Journal of Consulting Psychology*, 24 (August), 349–54.

DeVellis, Robert F. (1991), *Scale Development: Theory and Applications*. Newbury Park, CA: Sage Publications.

Embretson, Susan E. (1996), "The New Rules of Measurement," *Psychological Assessment*, 8 (4), 341–49.

Finn, Adam and Ujwal Kawande (1997), "Reliability Assessment and Optimization of Marketing Measurement," *JMR*, 34 (May), 262–75.

Gerbing, David W. and James C. Anderson (1988), "An Updated Paradigm for Scale Development Incorporating Uni-dimensionality and Its Assessment," *JMR*, 25 (May), 186–92.

Givon, Moshe M. and Zur Shapira (1984), "Response to Rating Scales: A Theoretical Model and Its Application to the Number of Categories Problem," *JMR*, 21 (November), 410–19.

Green, Paul E. and Vithala R. Rao (1970), "Rating Scales and Information Recovery: How Many Scales and Response Categories to Use?" *JM*, 34 (July), 33–39.

Hambleton, Ronald K., H. Swaminathan, and H. Jane Rogers (1991), *Fundamentals of Item Response Theory*. Newbury Park, CA: Sage Publications.

Herche, Joel and Brian Engelland (1996), "Reversed-Polarity Items and Scale Unidimensionality," *JAMS*, 24 (4), 366–74.

Jacoby, Jacob (1978), "Consumer Research: A State of the Art Review," *JM*, 42 (April), 87–96.

Komorita, S.S. (1963), "Attitude Content, Intensity, and the Neutral Point on a Likert Scale," *Journal of Social Psychology*, 61 (December), 327–34.

Little, Todd D., Ulman Lindenberger, and John R. Nesselroade (1999), "On Selecting Indicators for Multivariate Measurement and Modeling with Latent Variables: When 'Good' Indicators Are Bad and 'Bad' Indicators Are Good," *Psychological Methods*, 4 (2), 192–211.

Martin, Warren S. (1973), "The Effects of Scaling on the Correlation Coefficient: A Test of Validity," *JMR*, 10 (August), 316–18.

———— (1978), "Effects of Scaling on the Correlation Coefficient: Additional Considerations." *JMR*, 15 (May), 304–308.

Nunnally, Jum C. and Ira H. Bernstein (1994), *Psychometric Theory*. New York: McGraw-Hill.

Peter, J. Paul (1979), "Reliability: A Review of Psychometric Basics and Recent Marketing Practices," *JMR*, 16 (February), 6–17.

———— (1981), "Construct Validity: A Review of Basic Issues and Marketing Practices," *JMR*, 18 (May), 133–45.

———— and Gilbert A. Churchill Jr. (1986), "Relationships Among Research Design Choices and Psychometric Properties of Rating Scales: A Meta-Analysis," *JMR*, 23 (February), 1–10.

Peterson, Robert A. (1994), "A Meta-Analysis of Cronbach's Coefficient Alpha," *JCR*, 21 (September), 381–91.

Reise, Steven P., Keith F. Widaman, and Robin H. Pugh (1993), "Confirmatory Factor Analysis and Item Response Theory: Two Approaches for Exploring Measurement Invariance," *Psychological Bulletin*, 114 (3), 552–66.

Rentz, Joseph O. (1988), "An Exploratory Study of the Generalizability of Selected Marketing Measures," *JAMS*, 16 (Spring), 141–50.

Santor, Darcy A. and J.O. Ramsay (1998), "Progress in the Technology of Measurement: Applications of Item Response Models," *Psychological Assessment*, 10 (4), 345–59.

Schuman, Howard and Stanley Presser (1996), *Questions and Answers in Attitude Surveys: Experiments on Question Form, Wording, and Context*. Thousand Oaks, CA: Sage Publications.

Singh, Jagdip, Roy D. Howell, and Gary K. Rhoads (1990), "Adaptive Designs for Likert-Type Data: An Approach for Implementing Marketing Surveys," *JMR*, 27 (August), 304–21.

Spector, Paul E. (1992), *Summated Ratings Scale Construction*. Newbury Park, CA: Sage Publications.

Author Index

....

The numbers following authors' names refer to the *scale number* located at the top of each page.

Author Index

Subject Index

∙∙∙∙∙∙∙∙∙∙∙∙∙∙∙∙∙∙∙∙∙∙

The numbers following the key word refer to the *scale number* located at the top of a page, not the page numbers.